HUMAN BEHAVIOUR IN ORGANIZATIONS

A Canadian Perspective

Richard H.G. Field
University of Alberta

Robert J. House
The University of Pennsylvania

PRENTICE HALL CANADA INC., SCARBOROUGH, ONTARIO

Canadian Cataloguing in Publication Data

Field, R. H. George, 1951–
    Human behaviour in organizations

Includes index.
ISBN 0-13-328089-6

1. Organizational behavior. I. House, Robert J.
II. Title.

HD58.7.F54 1995   302.3'5   C94-931670-9

Prentice-Hall, Inc., Englewood Cliffs, New Jersey
Prentice-Hall International (UK) Limited, London
Prentice-Hall of Australia, Pty. Limited, Sydney
Prentice-Hall Hispanoamericana, S.A., Mexico City
Prentice-Hall of India Private Limited, New Delhi
Prentice-Hall of Japan, Inc., Tokyo
Simon & Schuster Asia Private Limited, Singapore
Editora Prentice-Hall do Brasil, Ltda., Rio de Janeiro

ISBN 0-13-328089-6

Acquisitions Editor: Patrick Ferrier
Developmental Editor: Maurice Esses
Copy Editor: Chelsea Donaldson
Production Editor: Valerie Adams
Production Coordinator: Sharon Houston
Permissions/Photo Research: Karen Taylor
Cover and Interior Design: Olena Serbyn
Cover Image: Gérard
Page Layout: Arlene Edgar

2 3 4 5   99 98 97 96

Printed and bound in the U.S.A.

Every reasonable effort has been made to obtain permissions for all articles and data
used in this edition. If errors or omissions have occurred, they will be corrected in future
editions provided written notification has been received by the publisher.

This book has been printed on recycled paper.

To my teachers of organizational behaviour:
Jim Erskine, Ian Meadows, Hugh Arnold, Martin Evans,
Robert House and Harvey Kolodny.
To my teachers about life:
Nancy, Finlay, Daniel, and Caitlyn.

– R.H.G.F.

To Tessa

– R.J.H.

Richard Field was born in Hamilton, Ontario, and raised in Hamilton, Winnipeg, and West Hill, Ontario. He is a Full Professor in the Organizational Analysis department of the University of Alberta's Faculty of Business. After receiving his undergraduate degree in 1973 in Mathematics (co-op program) from the University of Waterloo, he worked for a year and then obtained his Master of Business from McMaster University in 1976. He then attended the University of Toronto where he received a Ph.D. in Organizational Behaviour in 1981. Dr. Field has

Richard Field

worked as a computer programmer, at Simon Fraser University in Burnaby, B.C., and in retail sales in the travel industry. His teaching interests are in organizational behaviour and leadership at the undergraduate, M.B.A., and Ph.D. levels. In 1994 Dr. Field was awarded the University of Alberta's Labatt Faculty of Business Teaching Award for 1993/94. He has published numerous articles in academic and practitioner journals on the topics of decision making and leadership. Dr. Field is a married father of two young children, and his hobby is raising Belgian sheepdogs.

Dr. Robert J. House is the Joseph Frank Bernstein Professor of Organizational Studies in the Department of Management at the Wharton School of the University of Pennsylvania, a post he has held for over five years. Raised in Toledo, Ohio, he received his doctorate in the principles of management from Ohio State University just as the study of organizations underwent its 1960 paradigm shift from management principles to the scientific study of organizations. He has joked that his Ph.D. and his obsolescence finished in dead heat. However, he successfully retrained himself and worked in private industry, at Ohio State University, at the Baruch College in New

Robert House

York, and then at the University of Toronto. He was the Shell Professor of Organizational Behaviour at the University of Toronto's Faculty of Management Studies for over fifteen years, and made an outstanding contribution to the development of many doctoral students. Dr. House has published numerous articles in top organizational journals and is internationally known for his work on the Path-Goal theory of leadership and Charismatic Leadership. His latest work involves a major cross-cultural study of leadership in over 60 nations. Dr. House is the father of three grown children. He enjoys travelling the world and listening to jazz music in his spare time.

BRIEF TABLE OF CONTENTS

Preface xv

PART I **YOUR ARRIVAL IN THE ORGANIZATION 2**
Chapter 1 Introduction to Organizational Analysis 5
Chapter 2 Organizational Structure and Design 43
Chapter 3 Organizational Culture and Socialization 85
Chapter 4 The Nature of Work and Job Design 125
Part I Case - *Mrs. Fields' Secret Ingredient* 160

PART II **WORKING WITH PEOPLE 166**
Chapter 5 Individual Differences: Biological and Psychological 169
Chapter 6 Perception and Performance Evaluation 209
Chapter 7 Communication 247
Chapter 8 Managership and Motivation 287
Chapter 9 Groups and Intergroup Behaviour 327
Chapter 10 Leadership 369
Chapter 11 Decision Making 413
Chapter 12 Power, Politics, and Conflict 455
Part II Case - *Mutual Life Assurance Company of Canada:
The Knowledge Engineering Group* 494

PART III **WHAT THE FUTURE HOLDS 500**
Chapter 13 Stress 503
Chapter 14 Careers 541
Chapter 15 Change 585
Part III Case - *Whitbread Merseyside* 626

PART IV **EPILOGUE 634**
Chapter 16 Organizational Behaviour in the Future 637
Part IV Case 1 - *Grass Fragrances SA* 676
Part IV Case 2 - *A & W Canada* 685
Part IV Case 3 - *Federal Express Quality Improvement
Program* 693

LONG TABLE OF CONTENTS

PART I

YOUR ARRIVAL IN THE ORGANIZATION   2

Chapter 1
Introduction to Organizational Analysis   5

The Watson Siding Case   7

Types of Organizations   10
  Forms of Ownership   10
  Breadth of Ownership   11
  Organization Purpose   12
  Principals and Agents   13
  Organizational Products   13
  Organization Size   14

Organizations around the World   14

Systems Theory of Organizations   16

Organizational Effectiveness   19

Organizational Life Cycle   22

The Study of Organizations   24
  Founding Disciplines of Organizational
    Thought   24
  The Evolution of Organizational Analysis   26
  Sources of Organizational Thought   29
  Looking Ahead   31

Chapter Summary   32

Questions for Review   33

Self-Diagnostic Exercise 1.1   33

Experiential Exercise 1.1   36

Self-Guided Learning Activity   36

CASE 1.1:   *Manager's Case File:*
        The Bonus Check   37

CASE 1.2:   *Remarks of Akio Morita,*
        Chair of the Sony Corporation   38

References   40
Further Reading   41

Chapter 2
Organizational Structure and Design   43

Organization Structure   44
  Creating a Structure   46
  Departmentation   49
  Measures of Structure   51
  Types of Structure   54
  Coordination   58

Factors Effecting Structure   59
  Age and Size   60
  Technology   60
  Environment   62

Strategy and Structure   64
  Types of Organizational Strategies   65
  Strategy, Structure, and the Environment   66

Conclusion   69

Chapter Summary   69

Questions for Review   70

Self-Diagnostic Exercise 2.1   71

Experiential Exercise 2.1   73

Self-Guided Learning Activity   75

CASE 2.1:   *Manager's Case File:*
        Passing the Torch   76

CASE 2.2:   *Chemco International Inc.*   77

References   81

Further Reading   82

Chapter 3
Organizational Culture and Socialization 85

Societal Culture 87
  Cultural Dimensions and Clusters 90
  Work Cultures By Country 92

Organizational Culture 93
  Creating an Organizational Culture 94
  Manifestations of Culture 98
  Culture Profiles 101
  Subcultures 102
  Merge of Two Cultures 105
  Culture Strength 106
  Culture of Multinational Corporations 107

Organizational Socialization 108
  Socialization Phases 108
  Socialization Strategies 109

Conclusion 113

Chapter Summary 113

Questions for Review 114

Self-Diagnostic Exercise 3.1 114

Self-Diagnostic Exercise 3.2 115

Experiential Exercise 3.1 116

Experiential Exercise 3.2 117

Self-Guided Learning Activity 118

CASE 3.1: *Manager's Case File: Don't Bet on It* 119

CASE 3.2: *Kyocera America Inc.* 120

References 122

Further Reading 124

Chapter 4
The Nature of Work and Job Design 125

Three Revolutions in the Nature of Work 126

The Context of Work 128
  Places of Work 128
  Hours of Work 130

Job Design 133
  Engineering 134
  Ergonomics 134
  Biological 135
  Psychological 137
  Integrative Views 144

Conclusion 149

Chapter Summary 149

Questions for Review 151

Self-Diagnostic Exercise 4.1 151

Experiential Exercise 4.1 153

Self-Guided Learning Activity 153

CASE 4.1: *Manager's Case File: The Case of the Missing Staffer* 154

CASE 4.2: *B & B Containers* 155

References 158

Further Reading 159

PART 1 CASE *Mrs. Fields' Secret Ingredient* 160

PART II

WORKING WITH PEOPLE 166

Chapter 5
Individual Differences: Biological and Psychological 169

Biological Individual Differences 170

Sex 171
Physical Characteristics 172
Age 174
Intelligence 175
Psychological Individual Differences 179
  Gender 179
  Personality 179
  Attitudes 188

Conclusion   193

Chapter Summary   193

Questions for Review   194

Self-Diagnostic Exercise 5.1   194

Experiential Exercise 5.1   198

Experiential Exercise 5.2   199

Self-Guided Learning Activity   199

CASE 5.1:   *Manager's Case File:*
          A Woman in the House   200

CASE 5.2:   *Unholy Toledo*   201

References   205

Further Reading   208

Chapter 6

Perception and Performance Evaluation   209

The Perception Process   210
   Environmental Stimuli and
      Observation   210
   Perceptual Selection   213
   Perceptual Organization   215
   Perception   216
   Interpretation   216
   Response   222

Performance Evaluation   223
   Methods of Performance Evaluation   223
   Errors in Performance Evaluation   228

Conclusion   233

Chapter Summary   234

Questions for Review   234

Self-Diagnostic Exercise 6.1   235

Experiential Exercise 6.1   236

Self-Guided Learning Activity   237

CASE 6.1:   *Manager's Case File:*
          "I Deserve a Bigger Raise"   238

CASE 6.2:   *The Tenerife Airport Disaster*   239

References   243

Further Reading   245

Chapter 7

Communication   247

Verbal and Non-Verbal Communication   250

Influences on Communication   255
   Physical Aspect of
      Communication   255
   Personal Factors Influencing the
      Communication Process   263

Improving Communication   264
   The Resume and Job Interview   265
   Listening and Responding   269

Conclusion   273

Chapter Summary   273

Questions for Review   273

Self-Diagnostic Exercise 7.1   274

Experiential Exercise 7.1   275

Experiential Exercise 7.2   276

Experiential Exercise 7.3   277

Self-Guided Learning Activity   278

CASE 7.1:   *Manager's Case File:*
          I Heard a Rumour   279

CASE 7.2:   *Words: Say What You Mean,*
          Mean What You Say   281

References   284

Further Reading   286

Chapter 8

Managership and Motivation   287

Managerial Roles   288

The Nature of Managerial Work   291

Motivation   292
   Needs/Personality/Interests   294
   Motives   297
   Cognitive Choice   298
   Intentions   300
   Goals   301
   Self-Regulation   303

Reward Systems   309

Conclusion   313

Chapter Summary   314

Questions for Review   315

Self-Diagnostic Exercise 8.1   316

Experiential Exercise 8.1   317

Self-Guided Learning Activity   320

CASE 8.1:   *Manager's Case File:*
The Long Weekends   321

CASE 8.2:   *Moosajees, Limited   322*

References   324

Further Reading   326

Chapter 9
Groups and Intergroup Behaviour   327

Types of Groups   328

Work Group Effectiveness   329
   Organizational Context   329
   Work Group Design   331
   Internal Group Processes   335
   Strategies for External Integration
      and Boundary Maintenance   346

The Management of Groups in
   Organizations   347

Conclusion   351

Chapter Summary   351

Questions for Review   351

Self-Diagnostic Exercise 9.1   352

Self-Diagnostic Exercise 9.2   353

Experiential Exercise 9.1   355

Self-Guided Learning Activity   357

CASE 9.1:   *Manager's Case File:*
Short Shift   358

CASE 9.2:   *Fab Sweets Limited   360*

References   364

Further Reading   367

Chapter 10
Leadership   369

The History of Leadership Thought   370

How Leadership Operates   374
   Leadership By Who the Leader Is   374

Perceptions of Leaders   388

Leadership Considerations   392
   Ethical Leadership   392
   Leadership of Ethics   393
   Leading People from Diverse Cultures   395
   Leader Succession   395
   Leadership of Self-Managed Groups   395

Conclusion   395

Chapter Summary   396

Questions for Review   397

Self-Diagnostic Exercise 10.1   397

Experiential Exercise 10.1   400

Self-Guided Learning Activity   401

CASE 10.1:   *Manager's Case File:*
A Question of Loyalty   402

CASE 10.2:   *The Art of War   404*

References   406

Further Reading   410

Chapter 11
Decision Making   413

Rational and Expert Models of Information
   Processing   414
   At the Individual Level   414
   At the Group Level   421
   At the Organizational Level   425

Ethics in Decision Making   427
   At the Individual Level   430
   At the Group Level   433
   At the Organizational Level   433

Improving Decision Making   434
   At the Individual Level   434
   At the Group Level   438
   At the Organizational Level   440

Conclusion   440

Chapter Summary   440

Questions for Review   441

Self-Diagnostic Exercise 11.1   441

Experiential Exercise 11.1   443

Experiential Exercise 11.2   443

Self-Guided Learning Activity   446

CASE 11.1:   *Manager's Case File:*
            The Letter of Recommendation   447

CASE 11.2:   *Cradle Toys, Inc.   448*

References   449

Further Reading   452

Chapter 12

Power, Politics, and Conflict   455

Power   456
   Individual Power   456
   Group and Department Power   459

Organizational Power   462

Organizational Politics   463

Conflict   469
   The Creation and Management of
      Conflict   472

Conclusion   478

Chapter Summary   478

Questions for Review   479

Self-Diagnostic Exercise 12.1   479

Experiential Exercise 12.1   480

Experiential Exercise 12.2   480

Self-Guided Learning Activity   482

CASE 12.1:   *Manager's Case File:*
            The Memo   483

CASE 12.2:   *Squaring Off à la Forestiére   484*

References   490

Further Reading   492

PART II CASE   *Mutual Life Assurance Company*
            of Canada: The Knowledge
            Engineering Group   494

PART III

WHAT THE FUTURE HOLDS   500

Chapter 13

Stress   503

Stressors   505
   Stressors Outside the Organization   506
   Stressors Produced by the Organizational
      Structure and Systems   506
   Stressors in the Physical Environment   509
   Group Factors Affecting Stress   509
   Individual Factors Affecting Stress   511

Perceived Stress   512

Responses to Stress   514

Consequences of Stress   518

Managing Stress   519
   Altering the Stressors Themselves   519

Altering the Stress Moderators   520
   Lessening Responses to Stress   520
   Alleviating the Consequences of Stress   520

Conclusion   521

Chapter Summary   524

Questions For Review   525

Self-Diagnostic Exercise 13.1   525

Self-Diagnostic Exercise 13.2   527

Experiential Exercise 13.1   532

Self-Guided Learning Activity   534

CASE 13.1:   *Manager's Case File:*
            In the Fast Lane   535

CASE 13.2:   *Frank Pepper   536*

References   537

Further Reading   539

Chapter 14
Careers 541

Life Stages 542

Careers in Organizations 544
  Career Stages and Career Movement 544
  Career Systems 545
  Organizational Approaches to the
    International Assignment 546
  Discrimination 548

Managing Your Career 549
  The Career Edge 550
  Choosing a Career 552
  Selecting a First Job 555
  Goals For Success 557
  Breaking the Glass Ceiling 558
  Mentors 559
  The Dual-Career Couple 559
  The International Assignment 561
Conclusion 564
Chapter Summary 565
Questions for Review 566
Self-Diagnostic Exercise 14.1 566
Experiential Exercise 14.1 570
Experiential Exercise 14.2 572
Experiential Exercise 14.3 573
Self-Guided Learning Activity 573
CASE 14.1: *Manager's Case File:*
  Mailroom Mayhem 574
CASE 14.2: *The Carpenter Case 575*
References 579
Further Reading 581

Chapter 15
Change 585

Organization Development 588
  How OD has Changed 588
  Five Factors of Change: The Organizational
    Work Setting 595
  Two Types of Change 597
  Three Levels of Change 598
  OD Methods and Techniques 598

Putting it All Together: A Model of
  Organizational Performance and
  Change 611
Conclusion 612
Chapter Summary 615
Questions for Review 616
Self-Diagnostic Exercise 15.1 616
Experiential Exercise 15.1 617
Self-Guided Learning Activity 617
CASE 15.1: *Manager's Case File:*
  Changes for Better or Worse 618
CASE 15.2: *The Limora Community*
  Health Centre and the Limora
  Hospital 620
References 622
Further Reading 624
PART III CASE *Whitbread Merseyside 626*

PART IV

EPILOGUE 634

Chapter 16
Organizational Behaviour in the Future 637

Organizations in the Future: Towards
  the Year 2000 638

The Work Force 638
The Nature of Organizations 640

The Methods of Organizational Science 643
  Theory 643
  Boundary Conditions 646
  Theory Testing 647

Other Approaches to Organizational
      Science   658
   Modernism and Postmodernism   658
   Critical Theory   660
   Poststructuralism   661
   Feminist Research   661
Conclusion   665
Chapter Summary   665
Questions for Review   666
Self-Diagnostic Exercise 16.1   666
Experiential Exercise 16.1   667
Self-Guided Learning Activity   667

CASE 16.1:   *Manager's Case File:*
              Divided They Stand   668

CASE 16.2:   *Paradigms for the Emperical*
              Validation of Common Proverbs   669
References   671
Further Reading   674
PART IV CASE 1   *Grass Fragrances SA*   676
PART IV CASE 2   *A & W Canada*   685
PART IV CASE 3   *Federal Express Quality*
                  Improvement
                  Program   693

Manager's Dictionary (Glossary)   *d - 1*
Name and Organization Index   *i - 2*
Subject Index   *i - 13*
Photo Credits   *i - 20*

The purpose of this text is to provide the instructors and students of organizational behaviour with a comprehensive and readable guide to human behaviour in organizations. We have made a particular effort that the book be easy to read. We have tried to avoid any jargon that would make the understanding of our points more difficult.

While we have aimed for readability and ease of understanding, we have not sacrificed breadth and depth of the material presented. Discussion is presented of some classic articles and theories as well as up-to-date research findings and ideas. At the end of each chapter, notes for further information are presented to encourage a student's self-exploration of each topic area.

This text has been designed to have a logical chapter structure that intuitively "makes sense." Text chapters examine, in order, what a person entering a particular organization for the first time would confront. There are four parts to this book. Part I, "Your Arrival in the Organization," looks at organizations in general, how they are structured, their cultures and socialization practices, and how jobs are designed. Part II, "Working with People," is concerned with individuals and groups in organizations and how the work gets done. This part covers individual differences between people, perceptual processes and how performance is evaluated, communication, managership, group behaviour, leadership, decision making, and the processes of power, politics and conflict. Part III, "What the Future Holds," examines stresses that an organizational member will face, issues of careers and career planning, and the processes of personal and organizational change. Part IV, the epilogue to this text, examines what organizations and organizational behaviour will be like in the future. It also considers what the student of organizations needs to know about theories and theory testing in order to understand research about organizations.

Text chapters are designed to stand alone. Each instructor using this book can therefore choose the order of chapters that makes most sense for a particular course design. A few references between chapters have been made to show the linkages between topics. But these references are not so extensive that the reader will feel that the topics must be covered in the order presented by the text. One important example of this chapter independence is Part IV of this text, "Organizational Behaviour in the Future," which stands alone as one chapter. This allows it to be used at the start of a course, at the end, or not at all.

A particular strength of this text is its focus on the Canadian experience. Many examples of Canadian businesses are used and Canadian research is presented in the body of the text. Adding to this are a number of cases that present Canadian business experience and features in several chapters that profile the work or organizational researchers in Canadian universities.

But the international business world is not ignored. A number of examples and cases come from the United States, Great Britain and France. A number of other international examples of research and theory are provided so that the student of organizations is aware of the global nature of business in the 1990s. Several chapter features come from magazines and journals from around the world.

Another important feature of this text is its balanced approach when dealing with men and women in organizations. The work of both male and female academics is featured. Given names of researchers are used whenever possible in the text to help make it clear to every student that males and females have both contributed to the growing literature on organizations. Evidence and discussion of male/female issues at work is also incorporated in the text.

There are a number of features and supporting elements that are included in this text to aid the learning of the student of organizations, and to aid the teacher in the presentation of the theories and concepts.

First, as already mentioned, the text has a number of cases that present organizational situations. These cases present a good opportunity for individual students, small groups, and whole classes to discuss and consider the issues. Each chapter has a short case that can be discussed fairly quickly and a case of medium length that may be examined in more depth. As well, there are six longer cases found at the end of the four parts of this text. These cases may be used as the basis for in-depth class discussion. They might also be used for examinations or group assignments.

Second, the text has several different kinds of featured inserts that add interest and depth to the chapters. The "A Rose By Any Other Name" feature describes cross-cultural aspects of organizations. "A Word to the Wise" presents useful information to the student of organizations. The "A Little Knowledge" feature presents a review of an organizational research study that can serve as the starting point for the student's own reading on a subject. "Seeing is Believing" contains an actual organizational example to illustrate a chapter concept. The "On the One Hand" chapter feature presents two points of view about how best to understand a particular organizational concept.

Third, each chapter has experiential and self-diagnostic exercises. These provide the student with the chance to learn by doing, either individually or in a group.

Fourth, at the end of each chapter we have provided a summary of the main chapter points and questions that may be reviewed in order to think further about the topics covered.

Finally, the humorous side of organizations is illustrated in each chapter by an Overboard cartoon.

This text has been the product of a long developmental process and we hope that it helps students of organizations to learn and grow. Many people contributed their time and effort to the development of the text. We would like to recognize these people.

First and foremost are all the academics and practicing managers from around the world whose writings have been summarized, excerpted, quoted and reproduced here in this book. Without their work there would be no field of organization behaviour to summarize.

We would also like to thank all the people at Prentice Hall Canada Inc. who have spent countless hours working on this text. The initial idea for the book was developed with Acquisitions Editor Yolanda de Rooy. It was her friendship that made this project possible. Jackie Wood has been the senior editor for the project for the last two years. Her constant and continuing input and support have been and are most appreciated! Thank you Jackie. We look forward to working with you in the future. Prentice Hall sales representative Victoria Martin-Iverson played an important role in getting this project started and most recently in helping to make others aware of the text and its goals. We value her friendship and her continuing support.

Several developmental editors have worked to shape the chapters as they were written, to contact outside reviewers and interpret their guidance to us. David Jolliffe worked hard on the early chapters of the book and provided useful advice when that was most needed. Marta Tomins took over from David and worked on the middle parts of the book. Linda Gorman helped guide the book's later chapters, and Maurice Esses has supported us in the late stages by working on the book as a whole and thinking of the "big picture." Thank you all for your help. It was a team effort! Copy editing of the text's manuscript and proofreading of its finished pages was capably done by Chelsea Donaldson. Her comments and suggestions helped a great deal to improve the text. Permissions editors Karen Taylor and Robin Craig have helped to organize the permissions needed for reprinted material, to obtain permissions, and to pay fees as required. Theirs is a big job and their help, as that of their staff, is appreciated. Valerie Adams has worked tirelessly as production editor to get the manuscript into book form and to make sure that no detail is overlooked. We appreciate her support in a role of tight deadlines and high complexity. Behind the scenes are graphic artists, market analysts, computer support personnel, layout designers, the cover design artist, and all the support staff at Prentice Hall Canada who worked to make this text what it is. We hold their efforts in high regard.

Another group of people that deserve our thanks are the academic reviewers of the manuscript from which this text was created. Their job was to read chapters in draft form and then to provide helpful advice and commentary designed to help improve the overall quality of the book. Their advice was often heeded and was always appreciated. Some reviewers read blocks of chapters while others reviewed the final manuscript as a whole. We would like to thank:

Ann Armstrong, *University of Guelph*
Pennie Carr-Harris, *St. Lawrence College*
Deborah F. Crown, *University of Alabama*
Martin Evans, *University of Toronto*
Brian Harrocks, *Algonquin College*
Jack K. Ito, *University of Regina*
Stephen Jackson, *Sir Sandford Fleming College*
Paul Keaton, *University of Wisconsin*
Eli Levanoni, *Brock University*
Ariel Levi, *Wayne State University*
Charles W. Luckenbill, *Indiana University*
M. L. Newell, *Fanshawe College*
Nelson Phillips, *McGill University*
Barbara Pitts, *McMaster University*
Yaghoub Shafai, *Dalhousie University*

We also thank the students who read and worked with the text manuscript as part of their course in organizational behaviour. Their comments helped to make the book more readable and usable.

As you can see, this book is the product of many people, each bringing her or his own expertise and point of view to the whole. We are interested in making the book even better. We would be happy to hear from any instructor or student using the book about your comments or suggestions for its improvement. Please write either of us. For faster communication, contact Richard Field at 403-492-5921 (office telephone and answering machine), 403-492-3325 (fax), and E-mail address rfield@gpu.srv.ualberta.ca. Contact Robert House at 215-898-2278 (office telephone), 215-573-5613 (fax), and E-mail address house@wmgt-mail.wharton.upenn.edu.

We hope that you enjoy your course in organizations and that using this text proves enjoyable and valuable. Good luck in your studies about organizations!

Richard H.G. Field
Robert J. House
1995

PART

1

YOUR ARRIVAL IN THE ORGANIZATION

This text examines the aspects of organizations that a person would confront on entering a particular organization for the first time. Part I, "Your Arrival in the Organization," looks at organizations in general, how they are structured, their cultures and socialization practices, and how jobs are designed. Part II, "Working with People," is concerned with individuals and groups in organizations and how the work gets done. This part covers individual differences between people, perceptual processes and how performance is evaluated, communication, managership, group behaviour, leadership, decision making, and the processes of power, politics, and conflict. Part III, "What the Future Holds," examines stresses that an organizational member will face, issues of careers and career planning, and the processes of personal and organizational change. Part IV, the "Epilogue" to this text, deals with the topics of what organizations and organizational behaviour will be like in the future. It also considers what the student of organizations needs to know about theories and theory testing in order to understand research about organizations.

As stated above, in Part I we will examine the basics of organizations, in the order in which they might be encountered by a new employee. Chapter 1 discusses background issues that a new organizational entrant would need to address before any others: what organizations are, why they exist, how they are formed, grow, and die.

Next, the new organizational member needs to find out the structure of his tasks and responsibilities. Who reports to whom? How are departments set up to divide the organization's work?

Once he has constructed the overall picture of the organization, the new member will want to know where he "fits in," where his place is on the organization chart. These questions of structure are described in Chapter 2.

Having established a place in the broader context of the organization as a whole, the next questions that a new employee might ask when joining an organization would be "What is it like to work here?" and "What are the organization's goals and values?" The concepts of organizational culture and socialization are discussed in Chapter 3.

Finally, the new employee would ask about his own job, what tasks he will perform and under what conditions. Chapter 4 on job design examines these issues.

CHAPTER 1

INTRODUCTION TO ORGANIZATIONAL ANALYSIS

CHAPTER OUTLINE

Types of Organizations

    Ownership Forms

    Breadth of Ownership

    Organization Purpose

    Principals and Agents

    Organizational Products

    Organization Size

Organizations Around the World

Systems Theory of Organizations

Organizational Effectiveness

Organizational Life Cycle

The Study of Organizations

    Founding Disciplines of Organizational Thought

    The Evolution of Organizational Analysis

    Sources of Organizational Thought

Looking Ahead

QUESTIONS TO CONSIDER

- *What is an organization?*
- *What types of organization are there and how do they differ?*
- *Does everyone interact with organizations?*
- *How are organizations in other countries different?*
- *How do organizations function?*
- *How does an organization fit into a larger society?*
- *What outcomes do organizations care about and how do they measure them?*
- *Who studies organizations?*

It is impossible not to be constantly and deeply affected by organizations. We are born into a family, which itself is an organization. Most people are educated in a school system. Social and community activities are often conducted by clubs, community leagues, or religious organizations. Some people even live in a condominium or cooperative. These are organizations created to provide the benefits of common ownership. Our jobs as providers of services or goods to others are usually performed within the context of an organization. What we buy is usually provided by an organization. Understanding organizations, then, is critical in both our work and our lives outside work.

This is a book about organizations, particularly about people in organizations. It has two aims. The first is to help the reader to understand how people work in organizations and how the organization affects the people in it. The second is to help the reader to learn to be effective in organizations. Our overall approach taken in this text is to examine the questions and issues faced by a person about to join a work organization.

Theory A set of statements that link organizational factors of importance.

Each chapter of this text will review what organizational scientists now know about organizations and the people in them. This knowledge comes in the form of facts, and is often also presented in the form of theories. A **theory** links organizational factors of importance that can vary, called **independent variables**, with other factors that are proposed to be affected by those independent variables. These are called **dependent variables**. **Hypotheses** are the theorist's best guesses of the relationship that might exist between the variables. Theories therefore summarize the variables that are considered important in explaining an organizational phenomenon and how these variables are expected to interact.

Independent variables
The factors in a theory that are proposed to vary.

Our purpose in presenting these facts and theories is to help guide the new organizational member through the complex and fascinating world of the work organization. A thorough discussion of theories and theory testing is left to the end of this text, Chapter 16, to help prepare the student of organizations for further study beyond this text and the course of which it is a part.

Dependent variables
The factors in a theory that are proposed to be affected by variation in independent variables.

In order to look at certain important issues in detail each chapter contains up to seven featured inserts.

"A Little Knowledge"   It may be, as Alexander Pope said, that a little knowledge can be a dangerous thing. He therefore encouraged his readers to "drink deep" from the spring of learning. This feature presents a review of an organizational research study that can serve as the starting point for the student's own reading on a subject.

Hypotheses Best guesses of the relationship that might exist between the independent and dependent variables of a theory.

Seeing is Believing   This feature contains an actual organizational example to illustrate a chapter concept.

A Rose by Any Other Name   Shakespeare wrote "A rose by any other name would smell as sweet." This feature offers a cross-cultural or multi-cultural view of how organizational behaviour principles operate in different cultures.

A Word to the Wise   These features contain tips related to the chapter's subject about how to be more personally effective in organizations.

If You Can't Ride Two Horses at Once, You Shouldn't Be in the Circus   Just as circus performers have to be flexible and skilled, the point is made in this feature that managers need to consider how organizational behaviour concepts apply (and can differ) in organizations with different structures. Looking at how particular chapter concepts apply in these different structures will help future managers to be more flexible and adaptive.

On the One Hand   This chapter feature presents two points of view about how best to understand a particular organizational concept. It is meant to show that there are still many differences of opinion and unanswered questions in the study of organizations.

Experience is the Best Teacher   These features offer personal insights by leading organizational scholars about their own interests, careers, and study of organizations.

Besides these features, the humorous side of organizations is illustrated in each chapter by an *Overboard* cartoon by Chip Dunham. In our first cartoon, the question is asked, "What's ahead?" for the pirate ship "Revenge." What's ahead in this text? As the Captain said: "Danger and excitement, impossible odds, incredible risks, thrills and chills."

At the end of each chapter we have provided a summary of the main chapter points and questions to help you review the material. *Experiential Exercises* are an excellent way to learn in class by doing. *Self-Diagnostic Exercises* may be completed either inside or outside class. They can be used as a first step to examining and thinking about traits, abilities, and skills as they relate to life in organizations. It is important to note that these self-diagnostic exercises are provided in this text as tools to be used for educational purposes only. For accurate psychological assessments and interpretations it is necessary to consult a professionally trained tester.

The *Self-Guided Learning Activities, References* and *Further Reading* sections are provided to help the scholar of organizations explore a topic in even more depth outside of the classroom. *Cases* are located at the end of each chapter and part. These are useful for stimulating thought and discussion in or outside class.

The Watson Siding Case[1]

As a first example of organizational life, consider the Watson Siding case that follows, and ask yourself "What is the problem here?"

> A train has run over an open switch, causing it to go off the rails. Mr. Baxter is in charge of the area where the train has crashed and is calling Mr. Jackson, the subdivision superintendent of another area.

A train derailment in January 1988. There were no serious injuries reported.

---

[1] SOURCE: Professor Richard N. Farmer, Graduate School of Business, Indiana University. Reprinted and adapted by permission. A wrecking crane in this case is a large crane mounted on a rail car that is capable of moving heavy loads.

Bob Jackson picked up the phone.

– Yes?

– Mr. Jackson, there's been a derailment at Watson Siding. The ten o'clock freight hit a split switch and jumped the track. It skidded over to the second main line, and the whole railroad's blocked!

– Who is this?

– I'm Baxter, the Yardmaster at Daggett.

– Baxter, you know that Watson Siding is in the Westport subdivision. The responsibility for the wreck belongs to Atkins at Westport. I handle only the road up to Juniper—and that's four miles this side of Watson Siding.

– Yes sir, but the wrecking crane for the Westport subdivision is tied up in the shops. Yours is out at Juniper, and it would only take a few minutes to run it down and clear the main line.

– Baxter, have you ever read the delegations of authorities to subdivision superintendents? It says very clearly that they will not, under any circumstances, move their assigned equipment to another subdivision without written authorization from the division superintendent.

– But sir, Mr. Bagley is out of town!

– Well, wait 'till he gets back in town! If you think I'm going to lose my job just because someone made a mistake in the Watson subdivision, you're crazy.

Baxter drew a deep breath.

– Mr. Jackson, we have the whole railroad tied up. You have at least two trains waiting now for clearance because of the wreck. We have our crack passenger train tied up at Watson Siding now, and all the passengers are having a good look at a bunch of boxcars scattered all over the right of way. I'm sure that many of them ship by our railroad. Can you please send over your wrecking crane for a few minutes, so we can clear one track at least?

– Confound it, Baxter, no!

Bob slammed down the phone. He remembered once in 1980 when he tried to help those people over in the Westport subdivision. He had sent them a wheel car [a small handpowered rail car], and as a result he had been suspended for a month. This time, he was not about to get in trouble. He sighed. The trouble with these young kids trying to run the show these days was that they just didn't realize how important it was to maintain proper channels. He picked up the phone.

– Jim, check on how many trains we'll delay if the line stays closed for a couple of days. It looks like we'll be sitting here for some time. Those Westport subdivision people are not very efficient.[1]

Is the problem Bob Jackson, who has a wrecking crane but will not send it? Is the problem that the rules and regulations of the train company are too restrictive of personal initiative? Is it that Baxter is not asking the right person for authorization to send the crane? Or is Baxter right, that the problem is the train wreck and the solution is clearing the track? These are all valid ways of seeing the problem. There are likely others as well.

Another question to ask is who has ownership of this problem; that is, whose problem is it? Baxter, the Daggett yardmaster? Atkins, the subdivision superintendent for the Westport area? Jackson, the subdivision superintendent for the Juniper area? Mr. Bagley, the division superintendent? Or the railroad as a whole? While the case as described here may suggest that Baxter has the problem and Jackson has the solution, the decision of who has the problem can change depending on whose perspective is taken in the case.

Our next question is, why did Bob Jackson refuse to send his wrecking crane across subdivision lines? Was he being stubborn, mean, or fearful? Was he just following the rules, afraid of possible punishment for breaking them? Was Jackson asked by the wrong person, someone below him in the organization's hierarchy who did not report to him directly? Because there is not enough information given in the case, the true answer could be any or all of these.

Our last question is: what should Baxter do now? Again, there are many options. He could call Bob Jackson back and negotiate for the crane. He could pass the problem up the hierarchy to his boss, Mr. Atkins. He could find out where Mr. Bagley is and call him so that he could fax an authorization to Mr. Jackson. Or Baxter could act on his own initiative and hire a crane to clear the track.

What at first look seems a simple problem with a straightforward solution is in fact complicated. In this book we will examine organizations and the people who work in them in a way that helps us unravel such complexities. At the end of this book the student will be better able to answer the kinds of questions posed by the Watson Siding situation.

It should be remembered that there are generally several ways of looking at any problem and that a simple solution will not always emerge. Since there are no ready-made solutions, each organizational problem must be examined on its own in order to arrive at an effective solution.

In the remainder of this chapter we will define what an organization is and look at different kinds of organizations. Then we will examine how organizations form part of a larger social and economic environment. Next we will investigate how organizations

EXPERIENCE IS THE BEST TEACHER

Organizations have an enormous impact on our lives. Global competitiveness, economic growth, social prosperity, and the quality of human experience—these are all built on a foundation of coordinated human effort. The coordination of that effort is the job of organizations.

As someone devoting her life to the study of organizations, I can think of nothing more exciting and important than the process of mobilizing human potential. I was inspired to work in the field of organizational behaviour by a belief that organizations, as fundamental building blocks of nations and societies, can enrich both individuals and economies, and that collective objectives, such as organizational effectiveness and return on investment, need not be incompatible with the needs and aspirations of individual employees. In places where I worked prior to formal study I was repeatedly struck by the tendency of managers to underestimate the talents and potential of their

Christine Oliver is an Associate Professor in the Faculty of Administrative Studies at York University in Toronto.

employees. In these turbulent times an organization might have the most innovative technology, the most sophisticated budgeting procedure, or the most advanced strategic planning process, but without the full involvement and commitment of its employees to make these systems work, the organization is destined for mediocrity or failure.

I believe that today's organizations can only succeed by harnessing the full complement of the employees' skills and insights. When employees are treated with dignity and given the opportunity to demonstrate their full potential—through equitable reward systems, meaningful job design, inspiring leadership, and invigorating group relations—the productivity and effectiveness of an organization is potentially limitless. And that, after all, is the real economic challenge: to increase the value and usefulness of what our citizens, as employees, can contribute to the national and global economy.

are created, grow, and sometimes die. We will also discuss how organizations *have been* studied and are *now* studied and how organizational knowledge has developed over the years. Finally, a review of the Watson Siding case will give us a look ahead to other topics covered in this textbook.

TYPES OF ORGANIZATIONS

Organization Two or more people working together to achieve a goal or a set of goals that they cannot achieve alone.

An **organization** involves two or more people working together to achieve a goal or a set of goals that they cannot achieve alone. There are certainly businesses or corporations that consist of one person, the owner, who does all the work (for example a person who washes cars for a fee). However, these enterprises have no organization in the sense that we will use the term.

A vast number of types of organization are possible. They may vary in terms of who owns them, why they were created, who runs or manages them, what their products are, and how many members they have.

Forms of Ownership

Corporation

Corporations issue shares of ownership in themselves. A particular corporation may be wholly owned by one person, by one family, or by one other corporation. Or, ownership may be spread over many shareholders. One benefit of share ownership is that owners risk only the funds they have invested, not other personal assets. Another benefit is that dividends, usually a share in the profits, are paid by the corporation to share owners. A third benefit is the possible increase in value of the shares.

An organization that is incorporated at the federal or provincial level has the rights, privileges and responsibilities of a person. However, unlike people, the corporation may live forever. It has the status of a person in the eyes of the law, except that it cannot vote. The corporation can borrow money; own assets such as machines, buildings, and land; employ people; and be sued or charged in the courts for its activities. However, because a corporation is not actually a person, an officer or director of the corporation would have to go to jail for crimes committed by the organization. In Canada and the United States, the word Incorporated (Inc.) or Limited (Ltd.) in the corporation's name indicates its legal status as a person and that liability for the corporation's debts is limited to the assets owned by the corporation. Recently, however, some corporate directors have been held responsible for both its actions and its debts.

Partnership

Organizations may also be owned through an agreement between principals or partners, as is the case in many legal and accounting practices. Unlike corporate owners, partners are personally responsible for the organization's actions and outcomes, be they profits or losses. The famous insurer Lloyd's of London operates as a partnership. A group of individuals forms a pool of funds to back a certain insurance policy or group of policies. However, if losses are very high those individuals will have to dip into their bank accounts or sell their assets to pay policy claims.

Sole Proprietorship

Many organizations are owned by only one person, often an entrepreneur who manages a small business and carries out the day-to-day work. This person performs the work of the organization and takes the risks and the returns of the organization's activity. For example, the owner-manager of a small local restaurant may purchase the food, hire staff, greet guests, help serve the food, and operate the cash register.

Co-operative

In this form of organization individuals join together to jointly own and operate an enterprise that each needs but none can manage alone. Farmers have joined together to form grain co-operatives that store and sell grain. There are co-op stores that buy food in bulk to resell to members. Housing can also be jointly owned.

Breadth of Ownership

Family

There are many family businesses, ranging from small "Mom and Pop" operations that are owned and run by a few members of one family to large corporations such as Eaton's. One estimate (Kets de Vries, 1993) is that 80% of all businesses are family controlled and one-third of U.S. *Fortune 500* companies are family-controlled. Family businesses may have goals somewhat different from a publicly owned corporation in that the hiring, development, and promotion of family members is usually of great importance. This aspect of the family firm has been noted as of potential benefit to women in their careers (see Frishkoff & Brown, 1993), helping them achieve equity in promotions and pay. Family businesses may be corporations, partnerships, or proprietorships. This chapter's *Seeing is Believing* feature lists several advantages and disadvantages of family controlled firms.

Privately Held Organizations

Not necessarily owned by one family, privately held organizations are usually owned by a small group of people. They may have a partnership agreement or corporate shares, but the shares would not be openly traded on a stock market. As a result, public financial reporting of income, assets, and the production of an annual report is not required by government agencies, such as Consumer and Corporate Affairs in Canada and the U.S. Securities and Exchange Commission (SEC). Even though privately held organizations are a widespread and important part of the Canadian economy, they are only rarely studied by management scholars. One reason for this is the lack of publicly available information about the organization's activities and results.

Publicly Held Organizations

A corporation is publicly held if its ownership shares are traded freely on a stock market and are owned by a large number of individuals. Newspaper stock market pages list the names of many publicly held organizations and the details of stock price and changes in price. Besides corporations whose stock is traded in a market, governments are excellent examples of publicly held organizations because they are owned by their citizens. Governments exist as publicly held organizations at different levels—typically the federal, regional and local.

SEEING IS BELIEVING

ADVANTAGES AND DISADVANTAGES OF FAMILY-CONTROLLED FIRMS

ADVANTAGES	DISADVANTAGES
• Long-term orientation	• Less access to capital markets may curtail growth
• Greater independence of action	• Confusing organization
– less (or no) pressure from stock market	– messy structure
– less (or no) takeover risk	– no clear division of tasks
• Family culture as a source of pride	• Nepotism
– stability	– tolerance of inept family members as managers
– strong identification/commitment/motivation	– inequitable reward systems
– continuity in leadership	– greater difficulties in attracting professional management
• Greater resilience in hard times	• Spoiled kid syndrome
– willing to plow back profits	• Internecine strife
• Less bureaucratic and impersonal	– family disputes overflow into business
– greater flexibility	• Paternalistic/autocratic rule
– quicker decision making	– resistance to change
• Financial benefits	– secrecy
– possibility of great success	– attraction of dependent personalities
• Knowing the business	• Financial strain
– early training for family members	– family members milking the business
	– disequilibrium between contribution and compensation
	• Succession dramas

SOURCE: Reprinted from Manfred F.R. Kets de Vries (1993), "The dynamics of family controlled firms: The good and the bad news," *Organizational Dynamics* 21(3): 59-71. Excerpted and reprinted, by permission of publisher, from *ORGANIZATIONAL DYNAMICS*, Winter 1993. ©1993 American Management Association, New York. All rights reserved.

They maintain departments which are also organizations in their own right, such as the Department of Lands and Forests, or the Department of Defence. Governments also own or create organizations to accomplish certain tasks. These include public schools, universities, and community colleges to provide education; and public utilities to supply water, gas, and electricity. In Canada, Crown corporations are created to fulfill public policy in specific economic areas. Two examples are Canada Post Corporation and the Canadian Broadcasting Corporation. There are also hybrids like Petro-Canada, which are partially owned by the government and partially owned by the public.

Organization Purpose

Organizations can also be classified into those that are run primarily for profit and those not-for-profit (NFP) organizations that exist for another reason. Examples in the NFP category are governments, religious organizations, charities, and most museums and public art galleries.

The **bottom line** in for-profit organizations is the summary line of a profit-and-loss statement, how much money was made or lost. The bottom line of a not-for-profit organization is not money but something else. A museum, for example, might be most concerned with the total number of visitors to its exhibits and obtaining artifacts to add to its collection.

Bottom line In for-profit organizations, the summary line of a profit-and-loss statement.

We will examine the different ways of looking at organizational effectiveness in more detail later in this chapter. It is important to note that profit and assets are different measures: NFP organizations may hold significant assets in the form of land, buildings, and material goods while not showing a monetary profit.

Principals and Agents

The owners of an organization are its principals. These people may run the organization themselves or they may hire agents to act on their behalf. If agents are hired the principals must decide what level of influence they wish to maintain over the activities of the corporation. Managers and employees who own shares in the corporation that employs them are both principals and agents—and may at times find these two roles in conflict.

With the corporate form of ownership, the influence of the principals (the organization's shareholders) is carried out through a board of directors. The board members direct the organization's agents (the managers) on how to conduct the business of the corporation. Board members are either appointed or elected by the corporation's owners. They usually remain on the board for a fixed period—for example, three years. Board members may be asked to serve on the board because of their ownership of a significant amount of corporate stock; because of their expertise in the law, manufacturing, banking, etc.; or because of their knowledge and personal contacts in the corporation's industry. Therefore, board members, who are paid for their efforts, are often an important determinant of the success of the organization.

Board members are responsible to the organization's principals for their decisions and actions. They may be held personally responsible for their actions by the courts.

When boards are elected, shareholders are allocated one vote for each share of the corporation they own. If shareholders so wish, they may assign their voting rights to someone else by giving them a voting proxy. A conflict over who will be elected to the board, and therefore who will control the corporation, may turn into a battle for these votes. This is called a **proxy fight**.

Many not-for-profit organizations also have boards of directors. Public hospitals, colleges, universities, and charities often have a board composed of well-known and influential community members who direct the organization's paid managers. For example, the chair of the board of directors of a charity is usually a volunteer who heads the board and directs the charity's salaried chief executive officer (CEO).

In a partnership the principals are those who have been admitted into the partnership. Sometimes there is a buy-in fee to pay for their new part-ownership of the business. The agents in the partnership are the managers and employees who are hired to conduct work on behalf of the partnership. Partners share in the profits made by the organization. Partnerships, instead of calling a board meeting to discuss the organization's business, would call a council of partners.

Proxy fight A battle for the right to exercise the voting rights of a share owner in an election of a board of directors.

Organizational Products

Organizations can be grouped into four major classes according to their products. The first (and oldest) class *produces* food and *extracts* resources. It includes family and corporate farms, and mining and forestry companies. The second class *manufactures* a physical item. Examples of organizational activities that belong in this category are brick making, printing, oil refining, and automobile manufacturing. The third class of organizations provides a *service*. Examples are hair cutting, automobile repair, and air transportation. The fourth organizational class *supplies information.* Examples of organizations in this group are those that provide market research, legal opinions, or news broadcasts.

In Canada and the United States the class of organization employing the most people prior to 1800 was food production and resource extraction. Then, as a result of the Industrial Revolution (1800s on), it became the manufacturing of physical items.

In the 1960s and 1970s more people came to be employed in the provision of services. This has been called the **post-industrial society**. Case 1.2 is a speech given by Sony Chair Akio Morita about the post-industrial society. His position is that societies need to reemphasize their commitment to manufacturing.

Post-industrial society
A society whose economy is not dependent on primary industry and the manufacture of goods.

Today we are entering the information age (Naisbitt, 1982). In this latest age information is itself the product. Examples of such products are stock market prices, interest rates, and knowledge of technical processes. More and more people, especially professionals, are coming to be employed in the information organization.

Organization Size

Organizations range in size from the very large to the very small. We are all familiar with very large organizations such as governments, IBM, and Sony. Smaller organizations are the independent grocer down the street, a three-store chain of travel agencies, and a growing chain of cookie stores (see the Part I ending case about Mrs. Fields' cookies). While large organizations are more familiar to us, smaller organizations also have important effects on the people who work in them and deal with them.

Though large organizations are more often in the news, small and medium sized organizations (defined as firms with less that 500 employees) make up a large part of the Canadian economy. Moreover, the proportion of people they employ has been growing: these small and medium-sized organizations increased their share of total Canadian employment from 56% to 63% between 1978 and 1989 (Baldwin and others, 1994).

ORGANIZATIONS AROUND THE WORLD

Organizations vary in terms of ownership, purpose, management, product, and size. They can also vary culturally, from country to country and even within themselves. However, the recent movement toward globalization has meant that ways of organizing and operating are under pressure for standardization. Products are now developed for global markets (see *A Rose by Any Other Name*) instead of many regional or single-country markets. For example, when one country uses low-cost labour and high-technology robots to produce automobiles, others assume they must do the same to compete on quality and price.

A ROSE BY ANY OTHER NAME

REBORN IN RIMOUSKI

Wearing a white lab coat, gloves, and slippers, Marcel Rouleau sits watching a fibre-optic strand silently coil out of a sophisticated screening device.

Every few seconds, the 23-year veteran machine operator turns from the spinning spool to a nearby monitor to check for optical faults in the delicate hair-sized fibre.

Upstairs, Yukikatsu Aida, a Japanese optical engineer, has just returned from his daily French class. Mr. Aida moved to Rimouski with his family last year and may stay until 1997 to help Mr. Rouleau and nearly 30 French-speaking co-workers transform this once-outdated Phillips Cables Ltd. factory into a world leader in the production of fibre-optic ground wire.

Mr. Rouleau, 46, and Mr. Aida, 29, are part of a bold manufacturing experiment for Toronto-based Phillips and its joint venture partner, Furukawa Electric Co. Ltd. of Japan.

It is a story, so far successful, of saving manufacturing jobs in an isolated community by introducing Japanese technology, equipment, and work methods into a very traditional Canadian workplace.

Phillips executives hope the plant, which was set to close permanently in 1991 because of dwindling markets for its copper wire products, will become an export success story within two years. Production of fibre-optic ground wire—a highly specialized cable used mainly by power utilities and telephone companies—is slowly being shifted to Rimouski from Japan.

"This is high technology," Mr. Rouleau says enthusiastically. "It's like night and day, compared with what we were doing here before."

The arrangement also suits Furukawa, which saw an opportunity to crack the North American market with the help of Phillips' sales power and Rimouski's relatively low-cost labour.

The joint venture, Phillips-Fitel Inc., invested nearly $13 million to convert the plant in Rimouski, 300 kilometres northeast of Quebec City on the south shore of the St. Lawrence River. Reopened in January with half its former work force, it buys U.S.-made fibre-optic cables, and coats and strands them before sealing them in aluminum tubing.

But it is not just the imported technology that has Mr. Rouleau and the company excited.

When the old machines were scrapped, the old ways of doing things went out the door, too. The union, eager to save as many jobs as it could, agreed to revamp the collective agreement. The company was allowed to rehire laid-off workers based on education and dexterity

The plant, which used to make more than 100 different wire products, now produces just one: a cable for high-speed data and voice transmission that offers protection from blackouts and lightning.

The work force has been completely retrained—some at Furukawa's Japanese factory. Today, every worker can handle any process in the plant. Shifts have been increased from 8 to 12 hours, which allows an entire batch to be completed by a single shift.

The reporting structure has been flattened [there are fewer layers between the head of the organization and its production workers]. The foreman's job has been eliminated and vital information—product destination, shipment schedules, and market data—goes directly to the workers.

"The only boss we have is the plant manager," says Mr. Rouleau, who has been president of the union local for 15 years. "We don't have incompetents telling us what to do when we know better. Now they consult us.... The operators know their machines better than anyone; we feel a lot more creative and it's rewarding."

Japanese touches are apparent throughout the plant. Slogans on the walls proclaim "Quality Today. Jobs Tomorrow." And every employee from the plant manager to the shop floor worker now wears the same uniform—blue pants and a striped blue-and-white shirt.

The biggest change has been in the "attitude of the work force," says Malcolm Stagg, president and chief executive of Phillips Cables. The company, once wary of the local work force, is "watching Rimouski very carefully" and could eventually apply some of what it has learned at its other Canadian plants. But Phillips is taking a go-slow approach, and introducing Japanese methods gradually, he adds, for fear of making the same mistakes as many other North American manufacturers.

Phillips chose Rimouski for the experiment because of the lure of a $70-million, five-year contract to supply fibre-optic cable to Hydro-Québec. It won the job last year. The electrical utility is installing fibre-optic cable on up to 7000 kilometres of its vast transmission network and has insisted on substantial Quebec content.

In spite of its relatively old work force—an average employee age of 45—and its remoteness from key markets, Rimouski had other advantages. The location helped secure $2.5-million in federal grants, its labour is 30 per cent cheaper than Japan's and it offered a nearby supply of aluminum for coating the optical fibres.

While the Hydro-Québec contract was the motive for starting the company, says Phillips-Fitel president Jim Barney, the ultimate objective is selling to the rest of the world. "This is an export facility. It was set up because we felt it could compete in the international market."

The North American market alone for fibre-optic ground wire is worth up to $70-million a year and Phillips-Fitel intends to capture 20 to 30 per cent of that.

Phillips offers marketing clout to Furukawa, which has had trouble beating its key rival, Alcoa-Fujikura, in the United States. At the same time, Phillips, which through its British parent, BICC PLC, holds the world rights to the unique product, gets Furukawa's technological lead and know-how.

The marriage has been a learning experience for both sides. "We have learned from the Japanese to be more disciplined and vigorous, and to communicate with our employees," says plant manager Michel Huot, who has twice visited Furukawa plants in Japan.

The Phillips-Fitel Inc. cable factory located in Rimouski, Quebec.

It has taken considerable ingenuity to overcome major language and cultural barriers. Most of the plant's employees speak almost no English, let alone Japanese. Mr. Aida and other Furukawa employees speak no French, despite the lessons. The two groups communicate using common industrial hand signals, halting English and a lot of finger pointing, Mr. Huot says.

Phillips executives complain about the slowness of the Japanese to make key decisions. Japanese tradition is to reach a consensus before acting. The Japanese found Canadians slow in other ways. "The biggest difference I felt in Rimouski is that people are slow to move and walk, but their work is very accurate," says Koji Yoshida, vice-president of technology for Phillips-Fitel, who is now based in Toronto. "The operators are not as quick as Japanese operators."

The idea of training older workers to handle new machinery was also foreign to the Japanese. Workers at Furukawa's optical fibre plant in Japan range in age from 20 to 40, with the youngest ones normally trained on any new machines.

For machine operator Mr. Rouleau, some Japanese ways are just not applicable. But on balance, he says, Phillips-Fitel is a better company thanks to the Japanese.

"With a new technology like this, it's like getting your second wind. We can see the future and we don't see any black clouds. We see lots of opportunity."

Source: Barrie McKenna (1993), "Reborn in Rimouski," The *Globe and Mail*, July 20, 1993, p. B20. Reprinted with permission.

Maquiladora A U.S. factory in Mexico, usually near the Mexican/U.S. border, that is allowed to produce goods and send them back to the U.S. while paying duty only on the value added of Mexican labour.

To obtain low-cost labour many manufacturing organizations build or relocate factories where labour is cheaper. For example, some United States companies have located their manufacturing or assembly plants in Mexico, usually just inside the U.S.-Mexican border. These border factories are called **maquiladoras**. With the creation of regional free trade agreements such as NAFTA and the lowering of import tariffs, we should see more relocation of manufacturing plants to areas of low-cost labour. Often products are designed in one country but manufactured in another where labour is relatively cheap. The People's Republic of China, for example, is now exporting a vast array of products into Canada.

This movement toward globalization presumes that the basic principles of how people think, act and are organized are the same everywhere, even though there are some differences in the ways people around the world may work. In this text we will approach the study of organizations from the Canadian and Western perspectives while discussing some of the cultural differences to be expected in organizations around the world.

SYSTEMS THEORY OF ORGANIZATIONS

Organizations were once thought of as closed systems. They were thought to operate independently, free from outside environmental influences. The failure to reach an organizational goal was therefore seen as due to some shortcoming within the organization rather than some development outside the organization. Internal adjustments to the organization's operating system were made when goals were not being met. According to this way of looking at organizations, when a charity's fund raising campaign is falling short of its target it responds by increasing advertising or asking volunteers to call on more potential donors. It looks only to its *own activities* for improvement.

Open systems theory Organizations are part of their environment and the success of the organization depends on how well it interacts with its environment.

This closed-systems perspective has given way to the open systems view (Katz & Kahn, 1978: see Exhibit 1.1). **Open systems theory** states that organizations are part of their environment and that the success of the organization depends on how well it interacts with its environment. According to this viewpoint, organizations receive inputs from their environment, transform them, and strive to produce outputs acceptable to their environment.

EXHIBIT 1.1

Systems Theory of Organizations

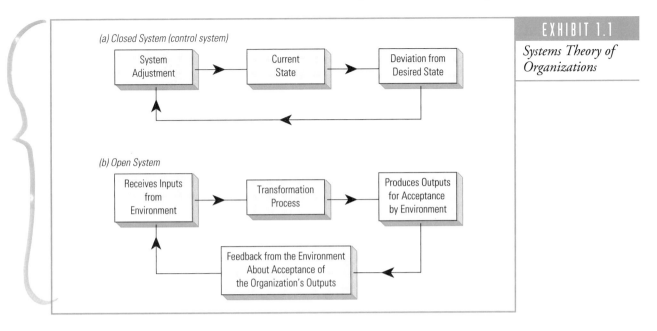

(a) Closed System (control system)

System Adjustment → Current State → Deviation from Desired State

(b) Open System

Receives Inputs from Environment → Transformation Process → Produces Outputs for Acceptance by Environment

Feedback from the Environment About Acceptance of the Organization's Outputs

Feedback from the environment about acceptance of the organization's outputs then influences future inputs and actions. It is the open systems view which is used in this text.

An organization operates within its environment at the local, national, and global levels (see Exhibit 1.2). Locally, individuals and other organizations provide the inputs the organization requires and they receive the organization's outputs as well. People are the organization's work force and also its customers. They make up the social context within which the organization operates.

Other organizations are also part of the local environment. Examples are local governments, unions, suppliers, competitors, and organizations that are customers for the products of other organizations. Unions are an important component of the local environment because they exist both within and outside of the organization. A union is an organization itself with a structure, hierarchy, and systems of operation. It provides resources, financial and informational, for its members in their interactions with employers. But part of a union's structure exists within the boundaries of the organization that employs the union's members. Union stewards represent other union members both to the employer and to the union itself.

Unions have been a steady and important part of the Canadian work environment. In 1990 the total number of union members in Canada was just over 4 million. Since 1955 the percentage of non-agricultural workers who were unionized has held fairly steady at about 36%. In the United States, however, trade unionism has been in decline since 1955. There the percentage of non-agricultural workers who were unionized dropped from 31.8% in 1955 to 16.1% in 1990 (Arrowsmith, 1992).

The national and global environments can be divided into six components:

1. *Demographic* —including characteristics of the population such as age distribution;

2. *Governmental* —which includes the system of government, number of levels, approaches to subsidies and social supports;

3. *Economic* —for instance the unemployment rate, money supply and interest rates, or the amount of disposable income in the population;

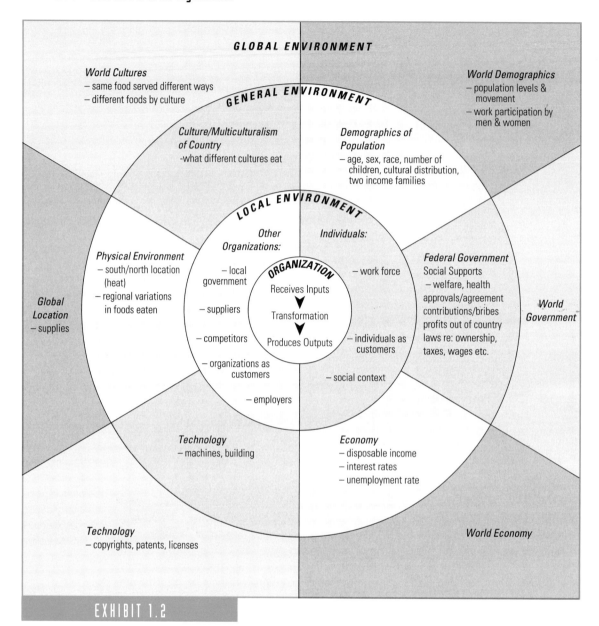

GLOBAL ENVIRONMENT

GENERAL ENVIRONMENT

LOCAL ENVIRONMENT

World Cultures
— same food served different ways
— different foods by culture

Culture/Multiculturalism of Country
-what different cultures eat

Physical Environment
— south/north location (heat)
— regional variations in foods eaten

Global Location
— supplies

World Demographics
— population levels & movement
— work participation by men & women

Demographics of Population
— age, sex, race, number of children, cultural distribution, two income families

Other Organizations:
— local government
— suppliers
— competitors
— organizations as customers
— employers

Individuals:
— work force
— individuals as customers
— social context

ORGANIZATION
Receives Inputs
▼
Transformation
▼
Produces Outputs

Federal Government
Social Supports
— welfare, health approvals/agreement contributions/bribes profits out of country laws re: ownership, taxes, wages etc.

World Government

Technology
— machines, building

Economy
— disposable income
— interest rates
— unemployment rate

Technology
— copyrights, patents, licenses

World Economy

EXHIBIT 1.2

Environment of a Fast-Food Restaurant

4. *Technological* —including how many inventions are created and patents awarded, the technical sophistication of machines and their impact on the organization;
5. *Physical* —which can include where a country is located on the globe, altitude, proximity to oceans and transportation systems, general climate; and
6. *Cultural* —for example the cultures existing in the country, their values and ways of living.

The trend to a global economy means that the organization's environment is no longer confined to the local and national levels. Organizations are now influenced by global developments. Examples are the rates of pay in other countries, technological breakthroughs occurring around the world, and world markets and demands for commodities.

In a fast-food restaurant such as that illustrated in Exhibit 1.2, the *inputs* include human effort, food supplies, machines, and utilities. The *transformation* process is the creation and provision of meals. The *outputs* are meals, an experienced work force, and garbage. If consumers choose not to accept the organization's outputs the organization must change its outputs or risk customer dissatisfaction. This happened when McDonald's customers became reluctant to accept meals packaged in styrofoam clamshell containers, forcing McDonald's to adopt a paper wrap (*The Economist*, 1992).

Using the open systems way of looking at organizations, the concept of **equifinality** is important. This means that the same end result can be reached by various methods or internal organizational systems. The implication is that there is not necessarily one best way for an organization to do its work. Different systems can produce the same results. Therefore, the Sears and K-Mart department stores can take different approaches to customer sales and service and yet both be successful.

Equifinality A concept in systems theory that the same end result can be reached by various means or directions.

ORGANIZATIONAL EFFECTIVENESS

To be effective and achieve its goals, an organization must successfully respond to environmental factors. The question then arises of how to tell whether an organization is responding well and achieving its goals. How can the effectiveness of an organization be measured? What measures can be used? Various models of determining organizational effectiveness have been proposed. These are shown in Exhibit 1.3. Different models exist because organizations face different environments, they produce different products, their organizational members are made up of different kinds of people, and the organizations are at different stages of development. Each model is most useful to an organization having a particular combination of these environmental and organizational attributes.

According to the **rational goal model of effectiveness**, an organization is effective to the extent that it accomplishes its stated goals. For example, the formal goals of the Toronto Blue Jays are to win their division, the American League pennant, and the World Series.

Rational goal model of effectiveness

With an **open system model** an organization is effective to the degree that it acquires inputs from its environment and has outputs accepted by its environment. Queen's University follows this model when it is concerned about the quality and number of students applying for admission and what jobs they receive on graduation.

Open system model of effectiveness

The **internal process model** focuses on the effectiveness of the internal transformation process. When Stelco examines its steel-making methods to determine price and quality competitiveness, it is focusing on its internal processes.

Internal process model of effectiveness

The **human relations model** focuses on the development of the organization's personnel. Thomas Cooke Travel sends its agents on familiarization trips (called "fams" in the industry) to expand their knowledge of specific hotels, cruises, and destinations.

Human relations model of effectiveness

The **competing values model** (also see Exhibit 8.1) requires that an organization scrutinize the balance among the above four effectiveness models. In this model there are three sets of competing values. The first is the tension between *internal versus external* focus. The more the organization focuses on one, the less it can concentrate on the other. For example Apple Computer has been focused externally on its customers and making computers that are intuitive and easy to use. The computer chip maker Intel has had a more internal focus on how to make faster and more powerful central processing units at a low price. The second set of values in competition is *flexibility versus control*. Flexibility allows quick response to changing conditions and values innovation. Control values the opposite. Stability and predictability mean that routine activities are performed well but change is more

Competing values model of effectiveness

EXHIBIT 1.3 MODELS OF ORGANIZATIONAL EFFECTIVENESS

MODEL	AN ORGANIZATION IS EFFECTIVE TO THE EXTENT THAT:	MEANS	ENDS	THE MODEL IS MOST USEFUL TO AN ORGANIZATION WHEN:
Rational Goal	It accomplishes its stated goals	Planning; Goal Setting; Evaluation	Productivity; Efficiency	Goals are clear, agreed on, time bound, and measurable
Open System	It acquires needed resources	Flexibility; Readiness	Resource acquisition; External support; Growth	A clear connection exists between inputs and performance
Internal Process	It has an absence of internal strain with smooth internal functioning	Information management; Communication	Stability; Control	A clear connection exists between organizational processes and performance
Human Relations	It develops the capacities of its personnel	Cohesion; Morale	Value of human resources	A capable and cohesive staff is required to meet changing environmental conditions
Competing Values	It achieves appropriate balance in internal vs external focus; in flexibility vs control orientation; and in emphasis on people vs organization	All of the above	All of the above	The organization is unclear about its own criteria or change in criteria over time are of interest
Strategic Constituencies	All individuals and organizations of importance are at least minimally satisfied	Adapt to find at least a minimal fit with required ends	Resource acquisition; External support	Constituencies have powerful influences on the organization, and it has to respond to their demands
Legitimacy	It survives by acting in a manner seen by other organizations as following accepted organizational practices	Acquire the systems and structures used by other legitimate organizations	Survival; External support	The organization's survival is at stake, goals and accomplishments are difficult to measure, and other organizations can provide or withhold the resources needed for survival
Fault-Driven	It has an absence of faults or traits of ineffectiveness	Measurement; Quality management	Efficiency; Error reduction	Criteria of effectiveness are unclear, or strategies for organizational improvement are needed
High Performing System	It is judged excellent relative to other similar organizations	Adaptability; Innovation; Comparison to others in and outside industry	Resource acquisition; External support; Internal productivity and efficiency	Favourable comparisons with other similar organizations are important

SOURCES: Seven models adapted from Kim S. Cameron (1984), "The effectiveness of ineffectiveness," in Barry M. Staw and Larry L. Cummings (eds.), *Research in Organizational Behavior*, 6: 276. ©1984 by JAI Press, Greenwich, CT. Reprinted by permission of JAI Press. High performing systems model reprinted by permission of Kim S. Cameron from "Effectiveness as paradox: Consensus and conflict in conceptions of organizational effectiveness," *Management Science 32(5)*, May 1986. Copyright 1986, The Institute of Management Sciences, 290 Westminster St., Providence, RI 02903. Human relations model reprinted by permission of Robert E. Quinn and Kim Cameron from "Organizational life cycles and some shifting criteria of effectiveness: Some preliminary evidence," *Management Science 2(1)*, January 1983. Copyright 1983, The Institute of Management Sciences, 290 Westminster St., Providence, RI 02903. Means/end data for the first four models reprinted by permission of Robert E. Quinn and John Rohrbaugh from "A spatial model of effectiveness criteria: Towards a competing values approach to organizational analysis," *Management Science 29(3)*, March 1983. Copyright 1983, The Institute of Management Sciences, 290 Westminster Street, Providence, RI 02903.

difficult. The third set of competing values is the relative concern with the feelings, needs, and development of the *people* making up the organization *versus the organization* and its requirement to accomplish its tasks.

A private hospital, for example, is concerned with how patients are treated and the success rate of surgeries (the rational goal model). It is also interested in how hospital procedures are performed (the internal process model) and with the skills and abilities of hospital staff (the human relations model). Finally, because it is a private hospital and must make a profit to survive, it needs to take into account how many and what kinds of patients are admitted (the open system model). The hospital must balance the three sets of competing values in order to be effective.

With the **strategic constituencies model** an organization would aim to at least minimally satisfy the most important constituents (or stakeholders) in its environment. The owner of an A&W franchise must satisfy the customers and A&W head office management. Customers care about the quality and price of the food as well as the speed and friendliness of service. Head office cares about these issues along with, among others, financial reporting, product promotions, and the store's relationship with its community.

An organization seeking **legitimacy** survives by acting in a manner seen by other organizations as legitimate. An example would be producing a business plan and projected income statement in order to obtain a bank loan. This chapter's *A Little Knowledge* feature describes research into the survival of voluntary social service organizations in Toronto during 1970-1982. The researchers found that having an externally legitimate form significantly lowered the chance of dying for a voluntary organization. Their conclusion was that if an agency must keep obtaining grants from governments and foundations in order to survive, the legitimacy model is a useful model of effectiveness. In this case organizational members must focus on acquiring the systems and structures used by other legitimate organizations in order to maintain the external support of their environment.

Strategic constituencies model of effectiveness An organization aims to satisfy the most important constituents in its environment.

Legitimacy Being in agreement with the standard type of organizational form and procedures.

A LITTLE KNOWLEDGE

Jitendra Singh and Robert House, then of the University of Toronto, and David Tucker of McMaster University in Hamilton studied the liability of newness on organizational death by examining all the voluntary social service organizations that came into existence in Metropolitan Toronto during 1970-1980. These 389 organizations were all non-profit and had boards of directors. Their missions were to change, constrain, or support the actions of individuals. Many, like a neighbourhood centre for newly arrived immigrants, offered information and referral services. These authors defined an organizational birth as a formal incorporation, while death was said to occur when the organization ceased to exist as a distinct legal entity. Out of 389 organizations, 107 died (28%) during the 1970-

1982 period. Their findings showed that *external legitimacy* (see the legitimacy model of organizational effectiveness of Exhibit 1.3) *significantly lowered organizational death rates*. Legitimacy was achieved by acquiring a listing in the Community Directory of Services (other providers of services would refer clients), the acquisition of a Charitable Registration Number (which allowed donations to be tax deductible), and a large board of directors at birth (which provided influential contacts in the community). The message for the creators of new social service organizations is clear: to survive it is necessary to be seen as a legitimate provider of services by individuals and organizations in the environment.

Source: Jitendra V. Singh, David J. Tucker, and Robert J. House (1986), "Organizational legitimacy and the liability of newness," *Administrative Science Quarterly* 31: 171-193; Jitendra V. Singh, Robert J. House, and David J. Tucker (1986), "Organizational change and organizational mortality," *Administrative Science Quarterly* 31: 587-611.

Fault-driven model of effectiveness The organization seeks to eliminate traces of ineffectiveness in its internal functioning.

The organization adopting the **fault-driven model** of effectiveness seeks to eliminate traces of ineffectiveness in its internal functioning. The National Aeronautics and Space Administration (NASA) in the United States is a good example. Its systems are designed with backups to be reliable even if some components fail.

Finally, the organization as a **high performing system** compares itself to other similar organizations. The Vancouver Symphony Orchestra can measure ticket sales and customer satisfaction with performances. But to determine the quality of the orchestra itself comparison is made to other orchestras in the world. Effectiveness is seen as the degree to which that comparison is positive. One method used by high performers to make such comparisons is to examine industry rankings. Such rankings are available for industrial organizations—the *Fortune 500* for example—and for some public organizations—for example the *Maclean's* magazine ratings of Canadian universities.

High performing system model of effectiveness The organization determines how well it is doing by comparing itself to other similar organizations.

ORGANIZATIONAL LIFE CYCLE

What makes an organization effective varies with its stage of development. Organizations pass through common stages during their life. It should be remembered, however, that organizations may not grow continuously but may remain at one stage of development for long periods. Though organizations do not have to die, most do. In fact, most live significantly fewer years than the average human life span. We know that failure or death is very common with new organizations. Restaurants, for example, are notorious for their high birth and death rates. This tendency is called the **liability of newness**. Older organizations die, too, though we often feel a sense of shock when we read of a well-established airline or bank that closes its doors.

Liability of newness New organizations are more likely to die than are older organizations.

The first stage of an organization's development is its birth (see Exhibit 1.4). Here growth is through creativity, the goal is survival, and the structure is non-bureaucratic. The organization's founder is often ruling the organization and does not rely on formalized rules and relationships. Predictable crises are encountered by growing organizations. The first crisis is that of leadership—will the transition be made from being managed by the organization's founder to being managed by professional managers? The next stage of development is the organization's youth. Growth now is by direction, as professional managers brought into the company start to impose organizational rules and bureaucracy. The goal is growth and management aims to provide a sense of mission to members of the organization. The crisis faced at this stage is that senior managers may not wish to relinquish control to more junior managers by delegating tasks and authority to them.

At the organization's midlife, growth is through delegation and coordination, the goal is efficiency, and the structure becomes more bureaucratic and departmentalized. To be able to change from a red-tape bureaucracy to a collaborative team-oriented organization is the crisis that will eventually arise. At maturity this collaboration will be achieved. The crisis at this stage is to avoid becoming stagnant and enduring a slow decline and eventual death. Instead, the organization must continually renew itself. In the final stage of decline and death some organizations cannot change because their management becomes a roadblock to change. Also, the organization's current structure can become a constraint on necessary change.

Population ecology A theoretical approach aimed at understanding birth, death, and change in populations of organizations.

The death of organizations has also been proposed to be a function of environmental change. The **population ecology** approach (Hannan & Freeman, 1977) is derived from biological theories of populations and evolution in those populations.

The biological theory of population ecology is that individual organisms produce genetic variation at random and that if a particular variation is selected by the environment it will be retained in future generations. The implication for organizational survival is that

EXHIBIT 1.4   STAGES IN THE ORGANIZATIONAL LIFE CYCLE

STAGE OF DEVELOPMENT	GROWTH THROUGH	STRUCTURE	GOAL	MANAGEMENT	CRISIS FACED
Birth	Creativity	Non-bureaucratic: the organization's founder makes most decisions	Survival	Entrepreneurial, open, task-oriented	Leadership—replacing founder rule with professional managers
Youth	Direction	Beginnings of bureaucracy: rules, splitting into different departments, procedures and policies are introduced	Growth	Providing a sense of mission	Autonomy and control
Midlife	Delegation and coordination	Bureaucratic: more departments are formed, decision making is allowed lower in the organization's hierarchy, more project groups are created, task forces are used along with mechanisms to make sure that activities between groups are coordinated	Efficiency	Delegation with control	Red tape
Maturity	Collaboration	Bureaucratic with emphasis on rules: decision making is dispersed through the organization, there are multiple departments both to do the work (line) and to support the work (staff)	Renewal	Collaboration and team approach	Turnaround, rebirth, or decline and death
Decline and Death	Negative growth	Constraining	Survival	A roadblock to change	Change

SOURCES: Based on ideas in Larry E. Greiner (1972), "Evolution and revolution as organizations grow," *Harvard Business Review* 50(4): 37-46; Figure 1 from Robert E. Quinn and Kim Cameron, "Organizational life cycles and some shifting criteria of effectiveness: Some preliminary evidence," *Management Science* 29(1), January 1983, Copyright 1983, The Institute of Management Sciences, 290 Westminster St., Providence, RI 02903; and from Exhibit 8.6 of *Organizations: A Micro/Macro Approach* by Richard L. Daft and Richard M. Steers. Copyright © 1986 by Scott, Foresman and Company. Reprinted by permission of HarperCollins Publishers.

organizations that are born in large numbers, varying slightly from each other in their characteristics, will also vary in how well they fit with the environment. Those with good fit will survive. This is theorized to be especially true for small organizations that have little impact on their environment.

In resource-rich environments, survival is easier. These environments are called **munificent** because there is an abundance of the resources organizations need to survive. In munificent environments even organizations with a poorer environmental fit than others will be able to survive.

Munificent environment

Possessed of an abundance of the resources organizations need to survive.

For instance, small family-run grocery stores used to be very common in cities when customers did not have automobiles and purchased food in their neighbourhood. But the environment changed as customers began to own cars and were willing to drive longer distances to shop. Then large supermarkets were established that could offer lower prices and greater selection. These supermarkets drove most of the smaller grocery stores out of business.

The main point we are making is that organizations change throughout their life cycle—their structure changes, their basis of growth changes, and their goals change.

THE STUDY OF ORGANIZATIONS

People have long been interested in creating organizations and making them effective instruments to attain their goals. For example, in the fifth century B.C. the citizens of the Greek city-states of Athens and Sparta set up the differing systems of democratic and kingship government. The effects of these different systems of government are still felt today. In the first century B.C. the Roman army developed a system of organization, training, and fighting that allowed expansion of their empire. About the same time the Catholic church established an organization that is still operating today. Another organization that has operated continuously for centuries is the University of Paris, established in 1211 as a centre of learning and scholarship. In Canada the Hudson's Bay Company was formed by Royal Charter in 1670 to exploit and sell the natural resources of the land surrounding Hudson Bay. The owners and managers of these and other organizations worked to make them effective, but little scientific study of organizations was collected in written form until the 1800s.

At that time the rapid industrialization of Canada and the U.S. started people thinking about work efficiency (Taylor, 1911, 1947; Gilbreth & Gilbreth, 1919: see Exhibit 1.5), the operation of groups at work (Roethlisberger & Dickson, 1939), and how to manage (Barnard, 1938). After the Second World War the amount of inquiry into organizations skyrocketed. Universities and colleges dramatically expanded to first absorb returning veterans and then later on the "baby boomers," born from 1946-1960. More and more scholars interested in organizations were recruited. They began to produce a large body of thought about the structure and functioning of organizations.

Founding Disciplines of Organizational Thought

These organizational scholars came primarily from the disciplines of psychology, sociology, anthropology, economics, political science, and engineering. Psychologists have contributed knowledge about how individuals learn, think, act, and how we differ from each other. Social psychologists brought knowledge of how groups form, how individuals act within a group, and how groups interact. Sociologists have studied the structures, technologies, and environments of organizations, as well as the actions of groups. Knowledge of social and organizational culture has been one contribution to management thought from anthropologists. Studies of the nature of employment, the principal-agent relationship, and the model of human decision making based on rationality have been contributions of economists. Political scientists have examined the nature of leadership and influence. Engineers have imparted their knowledge of systems and the design of jobs.

Individual scholars from these basic disciplines have been grouped together into departments of management or organizational analysis within faculties of commerce,

EXHIBIT 1.5   FRANK GILBRETH: TIME AND MOTION STUDIES

All Gilbreth's work had one objective—to discover the best method of doing a job. Once at an exhibition in London he gave a devastating display of his ability to do this. This example was quoted by Henry L. Gantt in his introduction to Gilbreth's book Motion Study:

While in London with the American Society of Mechanical Engineers, Mr. Gilbreth cornered an old friend of his and explained to him the wonderful results that could be accompanied by motion study. He declared that he did not care what the work was, he would be able to shorten the time usually required, provided that nobody had previously applied the principles of motion study to the work.

A few days before, this friend had been at the Japanese-British Exposition and had seen there a girl putting papers on boxes of shoe polish at a wonderful speed. Without saying what he had in mind, Mr. Gilbreth's friend invited him to visit the Exposition, and in a most casual way led him to the stand where the girl was doing this remarkable work, with the feeling that here at least was an operation which could not be improved upon.

No sooner had Mr. Gilbreth spied this phenomenal work than out came his stop watch and he timed accurately how long it took the girl to do twenty-four boxes. The time was forty seconds. When he had obtained this information he told the girl that she was not working right. She, of course, was greatly incensed that a man from the audience should presume to criticize what she was doing, when she was acknowledged to be the most skilled girl that had ever done that work. He had observed that while all her motions were made with great rapidity about half of them would be unnecessary if she arranged her work a little differently. He had a very persuasive way, and although the girl was quite irritated by his remark, she consented to listen to his suggestion that he could show her how to do the work more rapidly. Inasmuch as she was on piece work the prospect of larger earnings induced her to try his suggestion. The first time she tried to do as he directed she did twenty-four boxes in twenty-six seconds; the second time she tried she did it in twenty seconds. She was not working any harder, only making fewer motions.

This account the writer heard in Manchester, England, from the man himself who had put up the job on Mr. Gilbreth, and it is safe to say that this man is now about as firm a believer in motion study as Mr. Gilbreth.

SOURCE: Anthony D. Tillett, Thomas Kempner, and Gordon Wills (eds.), (1970), *Management Thinkers,* pp. 102-103. Penguin Books: Harmondsworth. The excerpt from the book *Motion Study* by Frank Gilbreth (1911/1972) is reproduced by permission of Hive Publications.

administration, or business. Within those departments, specialists study Organizational Behaviour (OB: the focus of this text), Organization Theory (OT), Industrial Relations (IR), Human Resource Management (HRM), Business Policy and International Business, among others.

Organization Theory examines in detail how organizations are put together, their different forms, relationships between organizations and their environments, and inter-organizational relations. Industrial Relations focuses on the union-management relationship in the public and private sectors of the economy, laws relating to unions, conflict, bargaining, and dispute resolution. Human Resource Management takes a managerial and applied look at organizational behaviour, investigating in depth such issues as staffing the organization, compensating its members, planning for promotion, and the training of organizational members. It also considers in detail the legal environment that affects managerial activity. The legal environment includes the Canadian Human Rights Act, Workers Compensation, The Freedom of Information Act, and laws relating to union formation and labour relations. Business Policy concentrates on the practical side of business planning, while International Business accentuates doing business globally.

Because organizations have been studied from a number of different perspectives, to understand organizations requires an interdisciplinary approach. Throughout this text we will draw on the most fundamental and useful contributions from each of the above areas of academic thought in order to present an integrated understanding of organizations.

The Evolution of Organizational Analysis

Exhibit 1.6 shows key events in the evolution of organizational analysis from the late 1800s to the present. As the men and women studying organizations have found new perspectives and conducted research, they have understood more and more about organizations and the people in them. To put their new understandings into a concise form, theories have been constructed.

Of course, there has been and always will be disagreement over how best to understand particular pieces of organizational research. For example, this chapter's *On the One Hand* feature presents different viewpoints on the famous Hawthorne experiments. These disagreements are discussed in the academic and practical management journals and at conferences as organizational researchers publish their findings and evaluate the findings of others. Some findings contradict each other. Further research is conducted to resolve the differences and come to a conclusion of how best to understand the organizational behaviour being studied.

EXHIBIT 1.6   THE EVOLUTION OF ORGANIZATIONAL ANALYSIS

AREA OF STUDY AND MAJOR INVESTIGATORS	DATE	FINDINGS
Scientific Management Frederick Taylor Frank Gilbreth and Lillian Gilbreth	1911	Aimed to discover the most efficient way to perform a job through the use of time and motion studies, tools used, and the selection, training, and development of workers. The benefits of efficiencies were to be divided between management and workers.
Principles of Management Henri Fayol	1916	Developed a set of management principles to guide the organization and management of work.
Bureaucracy Theory Max Weber	1924	Outlined the principles of an "ideal" bureaucracy.
Human Relations Elton Mayo	1933	Discovered in the Hawthorne studies that paying attention to the worker as a person had an impact on that person's productivity and work satisfaction.
Social Factors Fritz Roethlisberger and Bill Dickson	1939	Uncovered at the Hawthorne bank wiring room that groups affect the individuals in them.
Leadership of Groups Kurt Lewin, Ronald Lippitt, and Ralph White	1939	Compared the effects of autocratic and democratic group leadership on group members.
Ohio State Leadership Studies Ralph Stogdill	1948	Identified that two key leader behaviours were the leader's consideration of employees and the leader's structuring of work tasks.
Socio-Technical Systems Eric Trist and Ken Bamforth	1951	Examined the interrelationship of the social group at work and the technology used by the group.
Decision Making James March and Herbert Simon	1958	Proposed that people in organizations make decisions that are not always completely rational, but that decisions are bounded in their rationality.
Job Design Frederick Herzberg	1959	Identified that some elements of a task can give workers satisfaction but that other elements help to motivate workers to perform better.

Area of Study and Major Investigators	Date	Findings
Human Resources Douglas McGregor	1961	Introduced the concept that managers have internal theories about why individuals work—these then influence managerial actions.
Organization Structure and Environment Fit Tom Burns and George Stalker	1961	Developed the idea that organizations have different structures that are appropriate for different environments.
Strategic Management Alfred Chandler	1962	Proposed that organization members can first choose a strategy and then an organizational structure to match the strategy chosen in order to attain greater organizational effectiveness.
Aston Studies Derek Pugh	1963	Examined multiple factors of organizations, finding that structure must match the external environment for the organization to be effective.
Motivation Victor Vroom	1964	Theorized in the book *Work and Motivation* that individual worker decisions about how much effort to exert towards attaining work outcomes can be explained by Expectancy Theory.
Technological Imperative Joan Woodward	1965	Described the effect an organization's technology has on its structure.
Equity Theory J. Stacey Adams	1965	Developed a motivation theory that people compare their inputs and outcomes to those of others and act when there is a perceived imbalance.
Organizations as Open Systems Daniel Katz and Robert Kahn	1966	Considered the organization as a part of its environment.
Goal Setting Ed Locke	1968	Proposed that in order to be motivational, goals should be specific and challenging.
Effective Leader Behaviour is Contingent on the Situation Fred Fiedler, Robert House, Victor Vroom and Philip Yetton	1967 to 1973	Prescribed that leader behaviour must match the requirements of the situation faced by a leader and the work group.
Environment's Effect on Organizations Michael Hannan and John Freeman	1977	Proposed that the environment of organizations exerts a selection effect—only those organizations that match their environment will survive.
Resource Dependence Jeffrey Pfeffer and Gerald Salancik	1978	Considered that organizations are dependent on the environment for resources that enable the organization to survive.
Excellent Organizations Tom Peters and Robert Waterman	1982	Directed management to consider how organizations could provide higher quality products and services in their book "In Search of Excellence."
Organizational Culture Edgar Schein	1985	Developed the idea that organizations have cultures that affect organizational actions.
Competitive Advantage Michael Porter	1985	Instructed organizations to seek a competitive advantage in order to be successful.
Total Quality Management W. Edwards Deming Joseph Juran Kaoru Ishikawa	1988	Changed thinking on quality. The corporate culture as a whole became quality oriented. Quality seen as an organization's competitive advantage.

ON THE ONE HAND . . .

The Hawthorne effect probably owes its existence to the Relay Assembly Test Room Study. Five female employees who spent each work day assembling [telephone switch] relays were separated from their large department and placed into a special test room where all relevant variables could be better controlled or evaluated. The study was designed to explore the optimal cycle of rest and work periods. During the experiment the investigators controlled the length and timing of rest periods, the length of the work week, the length of the work day, and whether or not the company provided lunch and/or beverage. Considerable interest and attention was expressed toward the worker. Productivity seemed to increase regardless of the changes introduced by the researchers. Finally, well into the second year the investigators decided to discontinue all [experimental] treatments and to return the workers to full work days and weeks without breaks or lunches. Unexpectedly, rather than dropping to pre-experiment levels, productivity was maintained. Obviously the workers' behaviour was influenced by the effects of some other variable [or factor] that the investigators had unintentionally varied. It was these unintentional changes, researchers were forced to conclude, that had caused the subjects to improve their overall productivity and that had given birth to the Hawthorne effect.

SOURCE: Excerpted from John G. Adair (1984), "The Hawthorne effect: A reconsideration of the methodological artifact," *Journal of Applied Psychology* 69: 336-337. Adair's article goes on to examine whether in fact these unintentional changes—Hawthorne effects—can make a difference.

ON THE OTHER HAND . . .

Was the unintentional change the attention paid to these assembly workers? Gary Yunker of Jacksonville State University has examined the Hawthorne Studies, and offers these insights.

The Hawthorne Studies were conducted at the Western Electric Company's Hawthorne Works in Chicago and Cicero, Illinois, which supplied telephone equipment to the Bell Telephone system. The five main phases of the Hawthorne Studies were the Illumination Experiments (1924-1927), the Relay Assembly Test Room (1927-1933), the Mass Interviewing Program (1928-1931), the Bank Wiring Observation Room (1931-1932), and the Personnel Counseling Program (1936-1956). In the Relay Assembly Test Room workers assembled a telephone relay that was a little smaller than a human fist by putting together about 35 small parts with four screws. Their regular work week was 48 hours long spread over the week and Saturday morning. The six operators selected for the test were not selected at random; the foreman of the Relay Assembly department, Frank Platenka, picked an experienced relay assembler, Wanda Blazejak, and instructed her to pick five other women for the test. Part way into the series of test periods, two operators, Adeline Bogotowicz and Irene Rybacki, were replaced by Mary Volango and Jeannie Sirchio. The two new operators produced many more relays than their predecessors, and group output increased by nearly 11% in their first period of work. Also, Jeannie Sirchio, who was the most productive operator, became the informal leader of the group and used her position to try to increase the group's production.

Besides these two important factors, there were other differences in the way the work was done in the test room that made the increases in productivity noted as the "Hawthorne effect" more likely attributable to other causes than the attention paid to workers by the Hawthorne experimenters.

SOURCE: Based on information in Gary W. Yunker (1990), "The Hawthorne studies: Facts and myths," Chapter 8 in *Issues in the Management of Human Behavior: Analyses, Explorations, and Insights.* To further explore the Hawthorne experiments, see Fritz J. Roethlisberger and William J. Dickson's 1939 classic book *Management and the Worker,* where they are described in detail. A reexamination of the Hawthorne Studies is presented by Alex Carey (1967), "The Hawthorne studies: A radical criticism," *American Sociological Review* 32: 403-416. The more human side of the Hawthorne experiment is described in an interesting article about the actual participants in the Hawthorne Works Relay Assembly Test Room. See Ronald G. Greenwood, Alfred A. Bolton, and Regina A. Greenwood's 1983 article "Hawthorne a half century later: Relay assembly participants remember," *Journal of Management,* 9: 217-231.

It seems clear that how we study and understand organizations is affected by the major social issues of the time. Since business schools were formed in the 1950s, the general approach to teaching OB has shifted several times. Generally speaking, a person who studied OB in the 1950s would have studied principles of management (for example the division of work, unity of command and direction, and line of authority: Fayol, 1949). In the 1960s the focus was on the value of people in organizations. This value was the foundation of the human resources perspective. In the 1970s models of manager action that "fit" the situation were dominant. This was the time when many contingency theories were constructed. In the 1980s the interrelationship between people, the organization, and the environment came to the fore. Effective management was seen to be dependent on the fit between the manager's actions and the situation. In the 1990s, in addition to these previous approaches we are investigating how organizations function internationally. Issues of the social responsibilities of individuals and organizations are also important.

Today's social trends—for instance environmentalism, the breakup of countries, and the rise of global information technology—will undoubtedly have their effects on the current operation and understanding of organizations. The world is changing at a pace that seems to quicken every year. To be effective in organizations an individual will therefore need to take our current knowledge about human behaviour in organizations as a base upon which to build.

Sources of Organizational Thought

The primary source of new theories, tests of theories, and new thinking about organizations is the scientific journals (see Exhibit 1.7). Scholars of organizations, mostly professors at universities and colleges, write papers describing their thoughts and findings and then submit these papers to journals. Then the editor, usually an academic as well, sends the paper out to reviewers who read and write comments on the validity and usefulness of the article. Most papers are rejected, at least at first. The authors revise a paper based on the comments of the editor and the reviewers, sometimes over several cycles of review, before the paper is finally published.

There are also quite a few journals aimed at the practising manager. These summarize knowledge, present actual business cases and organizational examples, and aim to be of immediate practical use.

Falling in between these two sources are yearly books of chapters summarizing or reviewing specific areas of research. There are also many management books written by academics and/or practitioners. These are summaries of theories, and sometimes research, aimed at providing advice to the manager or organizational participant.

A bookstore's business section usually has a large selection of "how to" management books. These spotlight current trends in management and how managers and organizations could take advantage of new ideas.

The business sections of newspapers and business magazines attempt to keep pace with the fast-changing business world. They publish articles about current practices, events and thinking. These are normally produced by professional writers either on staff or writing freelance for a fee. For a humourous yet useful summary of business knowledge from one such magazine, see this chapter's *A Word to the Wise* feature.

Finally, textbooks such as this one attempt to integrate management thought and practice from these diverse sources. The objective of a textbook is to present a picture of our current knowledge about human behaviour in organizations.

EXHIBIT 1.7   SOURCES OF KNOWLEDGE ABOUT ORGANIZATIONS

1. SELECTED ACADEMIC/SCHOLARLY JOURNALS

Academy of Management Journal. Data-based studies of organizational analysis.

Academy of Management Review. Review articles and theory development. A main source of new theory.

Administrative Science Quarterly. A top-ranked journal focusing on organization theory.

American Psychologist. A monthly journal for members of the American Psychological Association. Good review articles.

British Journal of Management. Journal of the British Academy of Management.

Canadian Journal of Administrative Sciences. Journal of the Administrative Sciences Association of Canada. Contains a mix of marketing, finance, and organizational articles.

Human Relations. English journal reporting data-based studies, reviews, and essays.

Journal of Applied Behavioral Science. Mainly data-based. Focuses on applications.

Journal of Applied Psychology. A scholarly journal with an emphasis on application.

Journal of Management. A mix of data-based articles and review articles.

Journal of Management Inquiry. A relatively new journal with interesting articles and sections.

Journal of Management Studies. An English journal of review and data-based articles. Often an interesting set of articles.

Journal of Organizational Behavior. A blend of European and North American approaches.

Journal of Personality and Social Psychology. An American Psychological Association journal with useful sections on individual differences and group processes.

Leadership Quarterly. A newer journal focusing on leadership.

Management Science. A good source of more quantitative organizational articles.

Organization. A new journal.

Organizational Behavior and Human Decision Processes. Focuses on decision making. Has a strong quantitative emphasis.

Organization Science. A relatively new journal that seeks to publish innovative articles.

Organization Studies. A European focus. Good source of postmodern articles and articles with an unusual (for North America) approach.

Psychological Bulletin. Review articles and statistical notes.

2. YEARLY BOOKS CONTAINING SCHOLARLY CHAPTERS

All of the following are excellent sources of general reviews

Annual Review of Psychology

Annual Review of Sociology

International Review of Industrial and Organizational Psychology

Research in Organizational Behavior

Research in Organizational Change and Development

3. SELECTED PRACTICAL MANAGEMENT JOURNALS

Academy of Management Executive. From the Academy of Management. Many interesting data-based articles and book reviews.

Business Horizons. From Indiana University. Interesting shorter articles with a practical bent.

Business Quarterly. From the University of Western Ontario. A mix of scholarly and practical articles with a Canadian focus.

California Management Review. From the University of California at Berkeley. Well-written and easy to read review articles on current topics of interest.

Harvard Business Review. From Harvard University's business school. Well-known and widely read. Articles, cases, book reviews and comments.

Journal of General Management. From the Henley management school in England. Interesting articles for managers with a European flavour.

Organizational Dynamics. Published by the American Management Association. Up-to-date articles by well-known academics summarizing their findings and theories for the practising manager.

Sloan Management Review. From the Massachusetts Institute of Technology's Sloan School. Current reviews of interest by academics.

4. BUSINESS MAGAZINES AND NEWSPAPERS

Business Week. For up-to-date business news.

Business Month. Business news and summaries.

Canadian Business. Business news with a focus on Canada.

Forbes. American business magazine.

Fortune. American magazine with many in-depth and interesting business articles.

Inc. A magazine about business.

The Financial Post. A well-known business newspaper.

The Globe and Mail. A must-read for managers and employees in Canadian business.

The Wall Street Journal. Many in-depth articles of interest.

A WORD TO THE WISE

EVERYTHING I KNOW ABOUT BUSINESS I COULD HAVE LEARNED FROM STAR TREK

1. Always obey the Prime Directive—except of course when it gets in the way.
2. Logic is never enough.
3. Very few conflicts can be settled with a phaser.
4. Anyone can do Warp 14. But they can't keep it up very long.
5. No matter how advanced we think we are, there's always someone who's faster, stronger, or smarter.
6. The unidentified crewman always gets killed.
7. Engineering can always get things done sooner than they say they can.
8. Never judge anyone by their ears.
9. "Boldly" is the only way to go.
10. Being captain is the best job there is.

SOURCE: Excerpted from "Everything I know about business I could have learned from Star Trek," *Profit,* March 1994, p. 9.

LOOKING AHEAD

Let's look back at the Watson Siding case as a means of looking ahead into this text. What issues did the case raise? Were the railroad's rules and regulations and the strict ordering of superior-subordinate relationships a problem? Questions of organizational design, structure, bureaucracy, and hierarchy are examined in Chapter 2, along with the effects of an organization's environment and technology. Did the railroad have a culture of risk aversion? Did Bob Jackson refuse to act because he was well socialized into that culture? Organizational culture and socialization are examined in Chapter 3. Was Mr. Jackson's way of looking at the problem affected by the nature of his work? To help us better understand the kinds of jobs people have and how jobs affect the people who hold them, job design is discussed in Chapter 4.

You may have decided that the problem was not the organization, but one or more of the specific individuals in it. Was Bob Jackson just plain stubborn? Was he too old? Had he become organizational "dead wood?" How people at work are similar and different and the impact of these individual differences on the organization's functioning are discussed in Chapter 5.

Jackson and Baxter clearly had different perceptions of who had ownership of the problem. How individuals perceive the organizational world and how they evaluate the actions of others is discussed in Chapter 6. Baxter communicated his problem and proposed solution to Jackson over the telephone. Was this an effective communication medium? Alternative communication methods and problems that are likely to be encountered are detailed in Chapter 7. What about how Jackson could be encouraged to help Baxter or could be made to help? These questions of motivation and management are covered in Chapter 8.

In the Watson Siding case, the train company divided the physical world into geographic areas and assigned a group to each area. Baxter attempted, with poor results, to cross these group boundaries. The characteristics of groups and inter-group behaviour are the subjects of Chapter 9.

What could Baxter have done to alter the relationship between himself and Jackson? How could Jackson have been persuaded so that he would *want* to help Baxter? The question of leadership is the topic of Chapter 10. In the case, Baxter assumed the solution to the problem was to obtain Jackson's crane and then to clear the track. Assumptions and decision making are examined in Chapter 11. Baxter and Jackson were in conflict, they had different sources and amounts of organizational power, and organizational politics may have been required to solve this problem. Power, politics, and conflict are the topics of Chapter 12.

Was Baxter frustrated by Jackson's flat-out refusal to help? Did this obstacle to his plans and the mounting pressure of delayed trains add to the stress he felt in his job? Almost certainly the answer is yes. Stress and organizational careers are examined in Chapters 13 and 14. What could the train company do to deal with train wrecks in the future? Should Baxter or Jackson be trained in what to do? Should more rules be created to cover this situation or contingency plans created? The issue of change at the individual, group, and organizational levels is the focus of Chapter 15. Finally, Chapter 16 examines how knowledge about organizations develops. The purpose of this final chapter is to help individuals in organizations, like those in our case, to better understand ideas about organizations and the people in them.

Now that you have a sense of what organizations are and how they have been studied, we will turn to the design of organizations. The focus of Chapter 2 will be on how organizations are divided into parts and how the parts are coordinated in order to get the work done. This is an important topic for consideration because in order to understand how any one organization operates it is necessary to know how its parts are meant to work together. Also, the effectiveness of an organization is likely affected by how it is structured and how well its structure fits with its environment.

CHAPTER SUMMARY

The main theme of Chapter 1 is that organizations are everywhere in Canadian society. We live our lives in organizations and are surrounded by them. We work in them and ask them to work for us. It is therefore important for the student of business to learn as much as possible about organizations, how they operate, and how the people in organizations both affect and are affected by them.

An organization was defined as involving two or more people working together to achieve a goal or a set of goals that they cannot achieve alone. This definition shows the importance of the concepts of working together in groups and of the organization's purpose, or goals. Organizations are created for a reason, to accomplish a task, an activity, or an objective. We should never lose sight of this most fundamental point.

There are a variety of organizational forms, types of ownership, and products. Here it is important to realize that there is no one best way to create an organization that can work effectively in different markets, countries, and with different members. Organizational forms are often selected, changed, and can be expected to change in the future as the members of the organization attempt to make their organization better able to compete and survive in its environment. This environmental connection is known as open systems theory.

Chapter 1 also made clear that organizational effectiveness cannot be described by only one model. What it means for an organization to be effective differs depending on the type of organization and its environment.

Stages of organizational life were then examined. Knowing the commonly experienced pangs of growth, the stability of maturity, and the crises that can be expected along the way can help the student of organizations to understand the forces operating in a particular organization.

Finally, we described some sources of information about organizational theory and practice. It is important that every student of organizations look for organizational knowledge beyond this text. An active search of business journals and magazines can provide alternative viewpoints, new information and trends, and in-depth coverage of specific issues.

QUESTIONS FOR REVIEW

1. What is an organization? What is organized activity? What do people do that is not done in the context of an organization?

2. If effectiveness can be defined many different ways, which one is best? How does an organization determine which model of effectiveness should be used?

3. What is closed systems theory? To what would it apply? Why is it less applicable to organizations? Are there organizations for which closed systems theory would apply?

4. Why do organizations tend to live only a short time? How do some organizations manage to live for hundreds of years?

5. Is it a valid organizational goal to simply make money? Must the organization's focus be on the product or service provided to customers? Could an organization focus on the amount of money made instead of the activity required to make that money?

SELF-DIAGNOSTIC EXERCISE 1.1

OB as Common Sense

Is organizational behaviour just common sense? After all, we all have had experience with organizations and have learned how to act in organizations in order to attain our goals. But what is common about common sense? To find out, choose (a) or (b) for each pair of statements that follow.

1. (a) Supervisors are well advised to treat, as much as possible, all members of their groups exactly the same way.
   (b) Supervisors are well advised to adjust their behaviour according to the unique characteristics of the members of a group.

2. (a) Generally speaking, individual motivation is greatest when someone sets personal goals that are difficult to achieve.
   (b) Generally speaking, individual motivation is greatest when someone sets personal goals that are easy to achieve.

3. (a) A major reason organizations are not as productive as they could be these days is that managers are too concerned with managing the work group rather than the individual.

   (b) A major reason organizations are not as productive as they could be these days is that managers are too concerned with managing the individual rather than the work group.

4. (a) Supervisors who, sometime prior to becoming a supervisor, have performed the job of the people they are currently supervising are apt to be more effective supervisors than those who have never performed that particular job.

   (b) Supervisors who, sometime prior to becoming a supervisor, have performed the job of the people they are currently supervising are apt to be less effective supervisors than those who have never performed that particular job.

5. (a) On almost every matter relevant to the work, managers are well advised to be completely honest and open with their subordinates.

   (b) There are very few matters in the workplace where managers are well advised to be completely honest and open with their subordinates.

6. (a) On almost every matter relevant to the work, managers are well advised to be completely honest and open with their superiors.

   (b) There are very few matters in the workplace where managers are well advised to be completely honest and open with their superiors.

7. (a) One's need for power is a better predictor of managerial advancement than one's motivation to do the work well.

   (b) One's motivation to do the work well is a better predictor of managerial advancement than one's need for power.

8. (a) When people fail at something, they try harder the next time.

   (b) When people fail at something, they quit trying.

9. (a) Performing well as a manager depends most on how much education you have.

   (b) Performing well as a manager depends most on how much experience you have.

10. (a) The most effective leaders are those who give more emphasis to getting the work done than they do to relating to people.

   (b) The most effective leaders are those who give more emphasis to relating to people than they do to getting the work done.

11. (a) It is very important for leaders to "stick to their guns."

   (b) It is not very important for leaders to "stick to their guns."

12. (a) Pay is the most important factor in determining how hard people work.

   (b) The nature of the task people are doing is the most important factor in determining how hard people work.

13. (a) Pay is the most important factor in determining how satisfied people are at work.

   (b) The nature of the task people are doing is the most important factor in determining how satisfied people are at work.

14. (a) Generally speaking, the top level executives of major corporations can be expected to make decisions which maximize the best interests of the organization as a whole.

   (b) Generally speaking, the top level executives of major corporations can be expected to make decisions which make them look good (or at least not look bad) even if the interests of the organization as a whole are not maximized.

15. (a) Generally speaking, it is correct to say that a person's attitudes cause his behaviour.
    (b) Generally speaking, it is correct to say that a person's attitudes are primarily rationalizations for his behaviour.

16. (a) Satisfied workers produce more than workers who are not satisfied.
    (b) Satisfied workers produce no more than workers who are not satisfied.

17. (a) Generally speaking, the structure of an organization determines the technology it uses.
    (b) Generally speaking, the technology of an organization determines its structure.

18. (a) The statement, "A manager's authority needs to correspond to her responsibility" is, practically speaking, a very meaningful statement.
    (b) The statement, "A manager's authority needs to correspond to her responsibility" is, practically speaking, a meaningless statement.

19. (a) A major reason for the relative decline in North American productivity is that the division of labour and job specialization have gone too far.
    (b) A major reason for the relative decline in North American productivity is that the division of labour and job specialization have not been carried far enough.

20. (a) The notion that most semi-skilled workers desire work that is interesting and meaningful is most likely incorrect.
    (b) The notion that most semi-skilled workers desire work that is interesting and meaningful is most likely correct.

21. (a) People welcome change for the better.
    (b) Even if change is for the better, people will resist it.

22. (a) Leaders are born, not made.
    (b) Leaders are made, not born.

23. (a) Groups make better decisions than individuals.
    (b) Individuals make better decisions than groups.

24. (a) Generally speaking, the largest corporations would be more efficient if they were larger.
    (b) Generally speaking, the largest corporations would be more efficient if they were smaller.

Scoring:

Find a partner and compare your answers. Was your common sense the same as your classmate's? Now poll the entire class for their answers and find out how many people answered (a) or (b) for each of the 24 questions. Did everyone agree that (a) or (b) was the correct answer for any of the questions? For which of the 24 questions was there a strong consensus of opinion and for which was there just about a 50/50 split of opinion? Now ask your instructor for her or his opinion of the "correct" answers to some of the questions. Will you be discussing in your course how to evaluate these questions and when one answer or the other could be correct?

SOURCE: Adapted from Robert Weinberg and Walter Nord (1982), "Coping with 'It's All Common Sense,'" *Exchange: The Organizational Behavior Teaching Journal*, 7(2): 29-32. Reprinted by permission of the authors and the Organizational Behavior Teaching Society.

EXPERIENTIAL EXERCISE 1.1

Forming Groups of Dissimilar Individuals

The object of this exercise is to form a group composed of members as different as possible. These differences could be along the lines of sex, age, marital status, national origin, culture, and employment background.

Step 1: *(15 minutes)* All students in the class are to briefly introduce themselves by telling the others where they are from and what they are considering as their major area of study. Then walk around the classroom and introduce yourself to people who are very different from yourself. Discuss your backgrounds and past experiences, and your present attitudes towards school and work. Meeting new people often takes some effort, but the results can be interesting. Meet as many people as possible in the time available.

Step 2: *(5 minutes)* Now find a partner from the people spoken to who is dissimilar to yourself.

Step 3: *(15 minutes)* With your partner, introduce yourselves to other pairs; again, try to find pairs that are very different from yourselves.

Step 4: *(5 minutes)* When your instructor tells you, form groups of four, six, or eight by combining with one, two, or three other pairs. Try to maximize the diversity in your group.

Step 5: *(10 minutes)* Discuss in your group how each member is different, and whether those differences would make it easier or harder to work together in the future.

SELF-GUIDED LEARNING ACTIVITY

A good way to get started in learning about organizations is to explore your university or college library. Each library (if there is more than one) has on hand a fascinating array of information about organizations. Most offer tours that will get the student acquainted with the facilities. The library reference area has an interesting set of archival material that lists books that have been published (*Books in Print*), journals from all disciplines (*Ulrich's Periodicals Directory*), corporate directories that list the addresses of the world's corporations, and much more. Many libraries now have computerized databases listing journal articles by subject, title, and author, and that include a short abstract of the article's contents. Business libraries usually have financial data on major corporations and a selection of corporate annual reports—these make interesting reading and are a good place to start for the person interested in finding out about a particular company.

CASE 1.1

MANAGER'S CASE FILE: THE BONUS CHECK

Karen Moskowitz had been employed as an assembly line worker at Rocky Toy Manufacturing for a year and a half when she submitted a detailed plan to improve production and cut down on defective finished products to her supervisor, Ralph Johnson. Although the plan involved several major changes, Ralph believed that Karen had included all the necessary functions and felt that it could work.

"Karen, I'm impressed with the care and effort you obviously put into this proposal," Ralph commended her. "I wouldn't be surprised if you got a check for this. You know, a couple of those new v-ps are anxious to see what ideas the people who really do the work can come up with. This is right up their alley." Karen left Ralph's office feeling pleased and hopeful. He was also pleased and immediately forwarded the proposal with a covering memo to his boss.

Neither Karen nor Ralph heard anything about the plan for six weeks. Then a general staff meeting was called, and Ralph received a memo telling him to stop production early to let his subordinates attend it. At the meeting, a vice-president spoke for several minutes about the future of Rocky Toy and commended the production workers for their contributions. Then he asked Ralph Johnson to come forward. While the VP stood shaking Ralph's hand, he briefly described the "fine plan Johnson submitted," congratulated him, and gave him a $500 bonus check for his idea. Ralph was so dumbfounded that he merely mumbled a thank you and returned to his seat.

By the time the meeting had ended, Ralph had regained his senses, and he immediately looked for Karen.

"Karen, let me explain."

"Never mind. It's not necessary. And congratulations," she replied.

"No, Karen, listen. There's some mistake. You should get credit for your idea, and I'll make it right," Ralph asserted.

"Don't give me that. Why didn't you say something at the meeting? Management will rip off workers every time," Karen added and hurried toward the door.

The next morning, Ralph explained to his boss what had happened and returned the check. The manager was surprised, but he promised to look into it. He told Ralph that his memo attached to the report gave the impression that it was his proposal.

In the meantime, Karen still assumed that Ralph had stolen her idea and proceeded to share the story with her friends on the line. Morale throughout the plant began to decline as the story spread. Ralph knew the grapevine was active by the looks workers and managers alike were giving him.

Two days after the workers' meeting, Ralph overheard two employees, one a recent recruit who to date had shown a genius for spotting ways to get the work done more efficiently. "Why waste your ideas on Ralph?" his co-worker was saying. "Save your ideas for a manager who will give employees the recognition they deserve."

Ralph was hurt. He had been waiting for management to rectify the Karen situation and had not tried to speak to her about it. But he wondered, would management's answer come too late to save department production or his professional credibility?

SOURCE: Reprinted, by permission of publisher, from SUPERVISORY MANAGEMENT, January 1986. © 1986 American Management Association, New York. All rights reserved.

Questions

1. What could Ralph have done to prevent this misunderstanding during the employee meeting?

2. What should management do to rectify the situation and deal with its repercussions?

3. What could Ralph have said to Karen after the meeting?

CASE 1.2

REMARKS OF AKIO MORITA,
CHAIR OF THE SONY CORPORATION

I am not a believer in the idea of the Post-Industrial Society. For me, the very essence of business—the very foundation of the economy—is manufacturing. Why? Because manufacturing creates real goods by applying technology and creativity to resources and materials.

The value-added results of manufacturing are products that provide utility, convenience and enjoyment to all people. This, in turn, enriches people's lives, which must be the mission of any industry.

To succeed in this mission, a supportive corporate culture must be established: an environment in which creativity is encouraged, group dynamics are fostered, and individuals can find meaning and satisfaction in seeing their efforts blossom into tangible results. This environment is found in companies where management and labour have developed a relationship based on mutual benefits, respect and cooperation — what I like to call a *family* or *fate-sharing* approach to business.

Through this system, the long-term goals of the company reflect the workers' long-term goals as well. This means that during hard times, the FAMILY must stick together to see it through. If there is a recession or collapse, management and employees have to be flexible enough to adapt and survive. In this way a company creates a deep sense of sharing and common purpose, which in turn promotes corporate harmony.

To ensure the long-term success of this management-labour relationship, it is vital that companies continually breed and nurture new talent. Educating promising young managers in the values and culture of the company, and then providing them with opportunities, real responsibilities and decision-making authority is the only way to secure the company's future. As the co-founder of Sony, more than 40 years ago, I long ago learned that we must prepare young people today to be the leaders of tomorrow.

Long-term, co-operative relationships must also be forged between companies and their customers, suppliers, local communities and shareholders. This multi-level relationship has become known as the stakeholder concept, underlining the fact that there are many people who have a strong, interrelated interest, or stake, in the company's well-being.

Another basic key to health in manufacturing is a strong commitment to quality, reliability, service and over-all attractiveness of product. This ensures fundamental competitiveness in the market, not only domestically but globally.

In meeting these goals, the role of the engineer is of key importance. Unfortunately today, in many companies and countries, engineers do not enjoy the high esteem they deserve. Such an attitude is shortsighted and dangerous. Society needs to value engineers, because they are the driving force that sustains the development of industrial strength.

Very often it is engineers who are uniquely qualified to rise to the top management level in successful, high-technology-oriented companies. This is natural, because only with an understanding of technology, together with business, can top management maintain a vision that keeps long-term emphasis on developing new technologies. Such a vision also places a high corporate priority on research, product creativity and investments in factory automation and manufacturing capacity.

Once again, I cannot stress enough the importance of manufacturing. Nothing is more fundamental to any nation or economy than the ability to produce real goods. I cannot help but marvel at the amount of money, talent and energy that is being used up in the financial world. Many of the sharpest young business minds are being swept up into this frantic "buy-sell" fever. The securities and banking industry, which used to play a supporting role to manufacturing and other production businesses, has become an end unto itself—making money by moving it around; buying companies and then breaking them apart.

This worrisome trend has developed over the past 30 years, especially in the West, as more and more ways have been invented for making money without creating new and tangible results. This is sapping the strength and blurring the focus of the economy.

Capital should be invested to support needed research and development costs for the future creation of new products. Money should not be traded as just another commodity. The true future of a nation will be shaped by its ability to produce planes, cars, electronics, high technology, and so forth, not by how slickly its financial markets can shuffle and exploit paper assets.

While manufacturing must be the core of the economy, it is becoming more and more expensive to support this core, because the R&D for today's and tomorrow's high technology requires an incredible amount of investment money. This is why I believe companies should co-operate more.

Many new and promising technologies cannot be realized by one company alone—not at today's costs. So there should be a willingness to pursue co-operation with other companies, while at the same time remaining strong competitors.

For example, Sony and Philips, two of the world's largest electronics makers, are tough rivals in the market. But these two companies were also the co-operative, co-developers of the world's first digital recording technology.

This was possible because both firms quickly recognized the great potential for a digital recording system. So they agreed to work together to see this new audio storage system through the R&D and planning stages all the way up to standardization. But it was agreed at that point that collaborators would return to being competitors—and may the best product win!

On a broader scale, there is the European Community/Japan Consumer Electronics Roundtable, established in 1982, where members of industry can discuss long-range outlooks for business and technology. We hope that by discussing each other's perspectives of how a new market or technology may develop, we can better foresee general trends so that each company can independently plan investment and R&D commitments for the future.

The roundtable concept should be initiated and shared among a wider range of industries and nations worldwide. This could offer a forum for addressing the key economic issues of not just a few nations, but all countries. This approach should involve not only the European Community, Japan and the United States; it must also invite participation from new and rapidly developing economies. We can build a roundtable big enough to seat us all.

The challenges we all face—now and through the turn of the century—can be met with renewed commitment. Now more than ever, we need to return to the basic philosophies, concepts and ideals of business. We have to re-emphasize the fundamental roles each business sector should play, whether manufacturing, service, retailing or finance.

By getting back to basics, at all levels, we can get ahead to meet the future.

SOURCE: Mr. Morita is Chair of Sony Corporation. His remarks are taken from the Ninth Tun Ismail Annual Lecture, delivered in Kuala Lumpur, Malaysia. Reprinted in the *Globe and Mail*, November 24, 1990. Reprinted here with the permission of Mr. Morita. Mr. Morita's autobiography, titled *Made in Japan*, was published in 1987 in London by Collins.

Questions

1. Is Mr. Morita's emphasis on manufacturing appropriate in the information world of today or in the Canadian free trade economy of the 1990s?

2. Is a corporate culture that integrates the individual and the organization into a family atmosphere an appropriate approach to business in Canada and the United States?

3. Are engineers the group that should rise to the top of a manufacturing organization? What about the other functions of accounting, marketing and sales, and human resources?

4. Should companies seek to cooperate in the area of research and development or should they retain their independence and compete in the open market?

5. What is the role of government in promoting the success of industries within the country and internationally?

REFERENCES

Adair, John G. (1984). The Hawthorne effect: A reconsideration of the methodological artifact. *Journal of Applied Psychology* 69: 334-345.

Arrowsmith, J. David (1992). *Canada's trade unions: An information manual.* Kingston, Ontario: Industrial Relations Centre, Queen's University.

Baldwin, J., M. Rafiquzzaman, & W. Chandler (1994). "A profile of growing small firms." *Canadian Economic Observer,* February 1994, pp. 3.1-3.16.

Barnard, Chester I. (1938). *The Functions of the Executive.* Cambridge, MA: Harvard University Press. Barnard was a manager and executive at New Jersey Bell Telephone Company for over 30 years, eventually becoming its president. This book summarizes his practical wisdom and is still good reading today.

Cameron, Kim S. (1984). "The effectiveness of ineffectiveness." In Barry M. Staw & Larry L. Cummings (eds.), *Research in Organizational Behavior.* Greenwich, CT: JAI Press, pp.235-285.

Cameron, Kim S. (1986). "Effectiveness as paradox: Consensus and conflict in conceptions of organizational effectiveness." *Management Science* 32: 539-553.

Daft, Richard L., & Richard M. Steers (1986). *Organizations: A Micro-Macro Approach.* Glenview, Illinois: Scott, Foresman and Company.

The Economist (1992). "Management brief: Food for thought." August 29, 1992, pp. 64, 66.

Fayol, Henri (1949). *General and Industrial Management.* Translated from the French by Constance Storrs. London: Pitman Publishing Corporation. Revised edition 1984, revised by Irwin Gray, New York: IEEE Press.

Frishkoff, Patricia A., & Bonnie M. Brown (1993). "Women on the move in family business." *Business Horizons,* March-April 1993, pp. 66-70.

Gilbreth, Frank B. (1911/1972). *Motion Study.* Easton, PA: Hive Publications.

Gilbreth, Frank B., & Lillian M. Gilbreth (1919). *Fatigue Study.* New York: Macmillan.

Greiner, Larry E. (1972). "Evolution and revolution as organizations grow." *Harvard Business Review* 50(4): 37-46.

Hannan, Michael T., & John Freeman (1977). "The population ecology of organizations." *American Journal of Sociology* 82: 929-964.

Katz, Daniel, & Robert L. Kahn (1978). *The Social Psychology of Organizations* (2nd ed.). New York: John Wiley & Sons, Inc.

Kets de Vries, Manfred F.R. (1993). "The dynamics of family controlled firms: The good and the bad news." *Organizational Dynamics* 21(3): 59-71.

McKenna, Barrie (1993). "Reborn in Rimouski." The *Globe and Mail.* July 20, 1993, p. B20.

Naisbitt, John (1982). *Megatrends: Ten New Directions Transforming our Lives.* New York: Warner Books.

Profit (1994). "Everything I know about business I could have learned from Star Trek." March 1994, p. 9.

Quinn, Robert E. & Kim Cameron (1983). "Organizational life cycles and some shifting criteria of effectiveness: Some preliminary evidence." *Management Science* 29: 33-51.

Quinn, Robert E. & John Rohrbaugh (1983). "A spatial model of effectiveness criteria: Towards a competing values approach to organizational analysis." *Management Science* 29: 363-377.

Roethlisberger, Fritz J., & William J. Dickson (1939). *Management and the Worker.* Cambridge, MA: Harvard University Press. This book is a fascinating account of the work done at Western Electric's Hawthorne works in Chicago. Look in the library under the call number HD31R71.

Singh, Jitendra V., Robert J. House, & David J. Tucker (1986). "Organizational change and organizational mortality." *Administrative Science Quarterly* 31: 587-611.

Singh, Jitendra V., David J. Tucker, & Robert J. House (1986). "Organizational legitimacy and the liability of newness." *Administrative Science Quarterly* 31: 171-193.

Taylor, Frederick W. (1911). *The Principles of Scientific Management.* New York: Harper.

Taylor, Frederick W. (1947). *Scientific Management.* New York: Harper and Row. Taylor's ideas about scientific management didn't sit too well with many people of his time. This book includes his testimony in front of a U.S. House of Representatives Committee in 1912 and makes interesting reading.

Tillett, Anthony D., Thomas Kempner, & Gordon Wills (eds.), (1970). *Management Thinkers.* Penguin Books: Harmondsworth.

Weinberg, Robert & Walter Nord (1982). "Coping with 'It's All Common Sense.'" *Exchange: The Organizational Behavior Teaching Journal* 7(2): 29-32.

Yunker, Gary W. (1990). *Issues in the Management of Human Behavior: Analyses, Explorations, and Insights.* Greenwich, CT: JAI Press.

FURTHER READING

A discussion of quality and the move of manufacturing to Mexico can be found in Stephen Baker (1991), "If you're lucky, your next car will be made in Mexico," *Business Week* (Special Issue on Quality), pp. 72-73. The 25-year-old U.S. maquiladora program is now considered moot because of the North American Free Trade Agreement (NAFTA). An article dealing with maquiladora issues and how Mexican workers and management interact with Western North Americans, see Mariah E. de Forest's 1994 article "Thinking of a plant in Mexico?", *Academy of Management Executive*, 8(1): 33-40.

An important book that examines the resource dependence perspective is Jeffrey Pfeffer and Gerry Salancik (1978), *The External Control of Organizations,* New York: Harper & Row.

For a good biography of Frederick Taylor, read Charles D. Wrege and Ronald G. Greenwood (1991), *Frederick W. Taylor: The Father of Scientific Management: Myth and Reality,* Homewood, Ill.: Irwin.

The book *Beyond Rational Management: Mastering the Paradoxes and Competing Demands of High Performance,* by Robert E. Quinn (1991), published by Jossey-Bass, explores in more depth the competing values model and how managers can think about the process of managing in organizations.

An article on the knowledge society by the famous management author Peter F. Drucker is titled "The new society of organizations," to be found in the September/October 1992 edition of the *Harvard Business Review*, pp. 95-104. Drucker based the article on his book, *Post-Capitalist Society,* published in 1993 by HarperBusiness, a division of HarperCollins. For an interview with Peter Drucker about this book and his ideas read T. George Harris (1993), "The post-capitalist executive: An interview with Peter F. Drucker," in the May/June 1993 issue of the *Harvard Business Review*, pp. 115-122.

CHAPTER 2

ORGANIZATIONAL STRUCTURE AND DESIGN

CHAPTER OUTLINE

Organization Structure

   Creating a Structure

   Departmentation

   Measures of Structure

   Types of Structure

   Coordination

Factors Affecting Structure

   Age and Size

   Technology

   Environment

Strategy and Structure

   Types of Organizational Strategies

   Strategy, Structure, and the Environment

Conclusion

QUESTIONS TO CONSIDER

- *Why are organizations structured?*
- *How do organizational structures grow and change?*
- *What types of structures are there?*
- *What affects the nature of an organizational structure?*
- *How is structure measured and why is structure measured?*
- *How are organizational structures designed?*
- *What are the effects of the design of the organization on its members?*

ORGANIZATION STRUCTURE

We saw in Chapter 1 that organizations are created to perform tasks and to pursue goals that one person, acting alone, cannot achieve. One of the first questions that arises in groups is how to divide the work to be done. Another question that commonly emerges is who will be the leader of the group. This division of work, or labour, also occurs in formal organizations. **Organizational structure** is defined as how the organization is divided into parts and the parts coordinated in order to get the organization's work done. The work is divided horizontally into different activities that need to be done and vertically into who will be in charge of each related group of activities.

Organizational structure
How the organization is divided into parts and the parts coordinated in order to get the organization's work done.

For example, in a student group whose mission (or goal) is to perform a case analysis of the local fire department, the horizontal divisions might be interviewing fire department members, studying published reports about fire departments, analyzing and summarizing the results, and presenting the findings to the class. While each group member could work on each part of the assignment, typically each person works on only one or two parts. A vertical division of labour would occur if one group member were given the job of coordinating the others and reporting to higher authority, here the teacher. The structure of a formal organization is essentially the same.

Organization chart
Shows the structure of the organization. A set of boxes (often with names of individuals in the boxes) indicate positions in the organization. The relationships between these positions are shown by lines that connect the boxes.

On an **organization chart** the parts are normally illustrated as boxes and the coordination shown by lines that connect the boxes. This system is used in the sample organization charts that follow. For a humorous look at how organizations are seen to be structured in different countries, see this chapter's cross-cultural feature, *A Rose by Any Other Name*. Another look at "connectedness" in organizations is illustrated in this chapter's *Overboard* cartoon.

SOURCE: OVERBOARD © Universal Press Syndicate. Reprinted with permission. All rights reserved.

A ROSE BY ANY OTHER NAME

These organization charts illustrate in a humorous way the experience of some executives in the way organizations are structured around the world. Of course not all organizations are the same in any one country or area, but these broad categorizations help to show that organizations do not always operate as bureaucracies and hierarchies with authority flowing from the top to the bottom.

In the American example, an individualist orientation is evident. American workers believe that workers should be able to talk directly, freely, and with familiarity to the boss, and in fact do so. In other countries, Mexico for example, such familiarity between manager and worker is not considered acceptable (see de Forest, 1994). The Italian example illustrates how departments can be run as separate units from the rest of the organization. Loyalty runs between the manager and his workers, and is perhaps less evident for the organization as a whole. In contrast, the British example shows how lateral communication between peers at the same level is good, but upward communication is more problematic. This could be because class differences between managers and line workers are difficult to cross.

American: In United States organizations everyone thinks they have a direct pipeline to the boss.

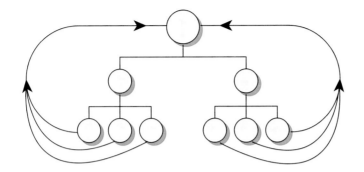

Italian: Italian organizations have bad lateral communication.

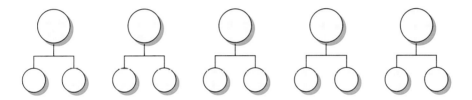

British: British organizations have good lateral communication but precious little upward communication

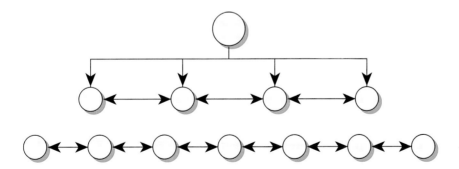

SOURCE: From "Executive epigrams," *International Management*, January 1981, 36(1): 6. Reprinted by permission of International Management © Reed Business Publishing 1981.

Creating a Structure

The founder of an organization has to make a series of decisions about what business to be in, what the organization's goals and objectives are, what work has to be performed to attain those goals, how the work will be divided and coordinated, and who will do the work. These decisions may be interdependent if the organization is small. That is, making one decision will affect other later decisions. For example, the skills and abilities of the particular people hired into the organization will then affect decisions about what the organization can do and how to do it. At this stage of the organization's life there may be more job titles than people, as one person may be in charge of marketing and accounting, another of sales and shipping/receiving.

A small organization, for example a shoe store, would have a **simple structure**, such as that shown in the diagram below. Here everyone, including the managers, is involved in selling. Some specialized functions, such as accounting and advertising, may be contracted out to a bookkeeper and an advertising agency.

Simple structure
Composed of a few direct relationships between organizational positions. Has little specialization, a low degree of formalization, and a high degree of centralization.

A small travel agency would also have a simple structure. It could consist of only two divisions, one with two sales agents working exclusively with corporate clients and the other with two agents selling personal holidays to the general public. The manager (who may also be the owner) would sell travel to corporate and holiday clients, hire and train staff, pay the bills, and try to build agency sales by finding new corporate and holiday clients.

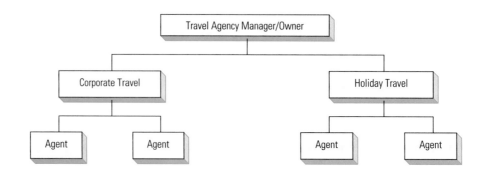

Another simple form of organization would be a restaurant whose manager has divided the staff into three groups: the bar, the food, and the service.

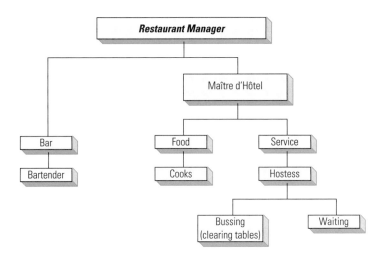

These simple forms could be much enlarged by adding more people to the basic structure. But as more people work in an organization, coordination becomes more difficult. There often isn't enough time for the manager to deal with every person on every issue individually. To solve this problem more vertical division of labour would occur. In the travel agency example an assistant manager could be hired to manage the Corporate Travel department. Those ten agents (let's say) would report to the assistant manager, whose job would be to help them sell, deal with problems, and manage their work life (holidays, pay, training, etc.). In other words, some coordination would be handled by this new assistant. The agency manager would then, in this example, manage the holiday travel agents as well as the assistant manager of corporate travel.

As a business grows more people are hired to do the basic work of the organization. It often then creates new departments to perform specialized services that used to be contracted or hired out to other organizations or individuals. For example, a growing corporation that contracts its accounting to a public accounting partnership might set up its own accounting department and hire an accounting manager as its head. Such specialized services are known as **staff** functions.

The word staff refers to a person, group, or department that provides a service to the rest of the organization. For example, a cost accountant who studies the cost of making steel at Dofasco is on the staff. The opposite of staff is the line. People, groups and departments that are engaged in making or selling the organization's product, or managing those who do, are in the **line**. In our travel agency example the travel agents are line personnel.

Besides accounting, other staff services might include public relations, advertising, finance, and legal services. However, whether these activities are staff or line services depends on the basic work of the organization. For example, accountants working for a public accounting firm are line personnel, not staff.

Staff   Refers to a person, group, or department that provides a service to the rest of the organization.

Line   People, groups and departments engaged in making or selling the organization's product or managing those who do.

Specialization Occurs when organizational members focus their efforts on a particular skill, ability, customer or geographic area. The specialist learns one thing well but is not a generalist who knows many things.

As an organization grows it may become inefficient to have employees who each deal with many different products and/or a variety of clients. It begins to make sense for the organization to increase the amount of **specialization** of its personnel. The travel agency may assign its corporate travel agents to different teams. Each team might deal with only a certain group of corporate clients or one large client such as a federal government department (see the sample organization chart below). The teams are therefore specialized by customer and would all be managed by an assistant manager in charge of all corporate travel. Holiday travel agents may be divided by their specialty knowledge of a particular geographic region or type of travel (for example cruises, adventure travel). These agents would have their own assistant manager.

Also shown in the sample organization chart for this travel agency is a three-person accounting group. This group consists of a corporate accountant, a holiday travel accountant, and an accounting manager. There is one person in advertising and promotion whose sole job is to increase agency sales by soliciting holiday and corporate travellers. As this example indicates, organizational growth leads to reorganizations and restructuring. This occurs both horizontally in who does the work and in what work is done, and vertically in who coordinates and manages the work.

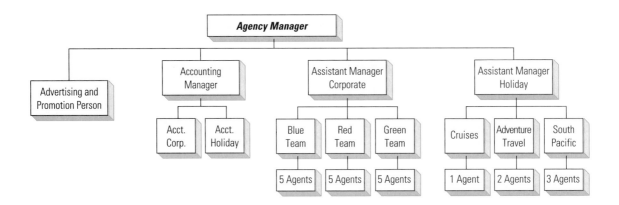

In the travel agency example we have presented an organization that is growing. Sometimes organizations are created large at the outset, usually because size is an advantage or a necessity. For example, the owner of an independent supermarket does not open a small store in a newly built subdivision and then grow larger as demand warrants. Instead, a large store is designed and built that has the capacity to deal with the expected number of customers in the neighborhood. A small grocery store could not compete effectively in price and selection with other nearby supermarkets.

A large structure such as this is carefully thought out before the organization begins operating. Decisions are made about what the organization will do and how the work will be done. Generally, the founders of a large new organization examine the structures of similar organizations as possible models before finalizing their own structure. As a result, supermarkets, for instance, often have similar structures, typically one similar to that shown in the organization chart on the following page.

However, not all large structures stay large and organizations do not always grow. Sometimes organizations restructure by subtracting departments and people. Our example travel agency may decide to get out of the adventure travel market by letting go or reassigning those agents. The loss of large corporate clients may necessitate laying off an entire corporate travel team. Similarly, a vertical simplification of structure would occur if one assistant manager were to quit the travel agency and the other was put in charge of both corporate and holiday travel.

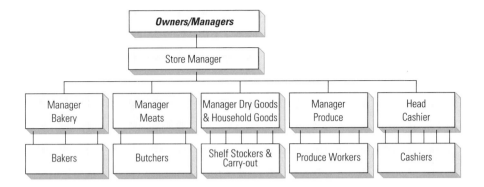

Departmentation

Departmentation is the horizontal division of work into logical groupings. Departmentation can be done on the basis of customer, product, geographic location, function performed or special knowledge, project, or a mixture of these components.

Customer   The division of the travel agency into corporate and holiday travel is a division by type of customer. This separation assumes that there are two distinct kinds of travellers, with different perspectives and needs. Work with each group may be both more efficient and more effective if agents specialize and train to understand either corporate or holiday travellers, but not both.

Product   A division by product is illustrated in the supermarket example. There work is split into bakery, meats, dry goods, and produce, the four classes of product provided. Employees would specialize in working with and knowing one type of product.

Geographic Location   An organization can divide the work it does into geographic areas. This arrangement is employed when each unit operates relatively independently, as is the case with outlets of a nation-wide chain of travel agencies. Geographic departmentation is also used when a large territory needs to be divided into parts (or regions) of manageable size.

Function   In a manufacturing firm, for example the shoe factory shown below, the functions would include production, marketing and sales, and research and development. Production makes the shoes; marketing and sales is responsible for advertising, distribution, and pricing; and R&D studies new designs and materials for shoes.

Departmentation
The horizontal division of work into logical groupings.

Project   Organizations may divide their work into separate groups or teams. This form of departmentation is especially useful when the work comes in discrete pieces with a beginning and an end. For example, a software house that contracts with other companies to design and build programs could set up a separate project team of designers, systems analysts, and programmers to produce each system required. This structure is illustrated below. When the software is delivered to the customer, installed and debugged, the team would disband. The team's members would then be immediately reassigned to another project team or would go into a pool of employees without project assignment. When new contracts were won these personnel would be assigned to the new project.

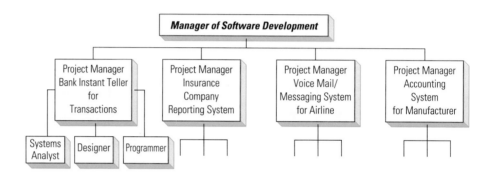

Mixture   Organizations often create a mixture, or hybrid, of the above-mentioned ways to departmentalize. In the following example of a national chain of travel agencies, four vice-presidents (VPs) are located at the head office, each with her own staff. Reporting to the vice-president for sales are four regional managers. Because this organization has a number of travel agencies in each geographic area they have been grouped by area into regions. If a number of new agencies were to be opened in one region their coordination might overwhelm their regional manager. In that case a new region could be added. For instance, the Eastern region in the example shown below could be divided into two areas: North-Eastern and South-Eastern.

Below the regional managers are agency managers organized by customer and product. These women and men run agencies dealing only with larger corporations, the government, last-minute travel, and the travel of individuals and smaller corporations.

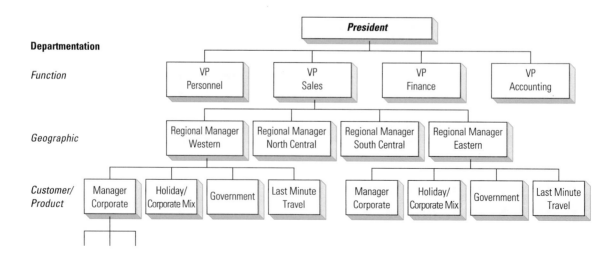

Measures of Structure

Structure concerns more than the division of labour or the boxes on the organization chart. It is also about the *reporting relationships* between organizational members—the lines connecting the boxes, rules and regulations about how the work is performed, and whether organizational decisions are made at the top of the organization or lower down. In order to compare one organization's structure with that of another or to study the effects of structure on organizational performance, we need to have consistent ways to measure structure. Three important structure measures are complexity, formalization, and centralization.

Complexity

Complexity refers to the number of separate parts in an organization's structure. The more tasks are divided among individuals and specialized, the more the organization is **horizontally complex**. As the vertical chain of command lengthens more organizational layers are inserted between top management and production workers. The organization becomes more **vertically complex** in such circumstances. Vertical complexity is often also called the "tallness" of the organization, as shown below. Organizations today are tending to move towards flatter organizations by eliminating whole levels of middle management (see this chapter's *A Word to the Wise*). This **downsizing** (see Cascio, 1993) increases the number of people supervised. Therefore the **span of control** increases for the managers that remain.

Horizontally complex
When an organization's tasks are divided among many individuals and specialized.

Vertically complex
When organizational layers are inserted between top management and production workers.

Downsizing The reduction of the number of people who work for an organization. Also called rightsizing.

Span of control The number of workers directly reporting to a manager.

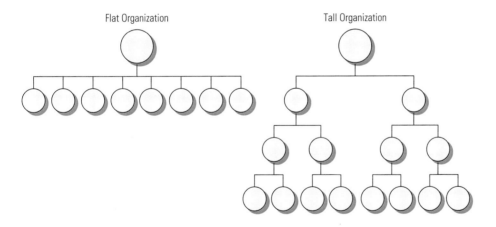

Flat Organization   Tall Organization

A WORD TO THE WISE

From the dawn of organizational time the pyramid structure of management has dominated business. But as the century draws to a close the edifice is beginning to crumble under the weight of technological change.

Until now, regardless of country or industry, the average worker's aim has been to try to climb the pyramid, assuming greater power as he or she ascends towards the top. The key to power is information, and information has been passed down only to those of sufficient seniority and importance.

But the increasing integration into business of innovative information technology (IT) is undermining the pyramid by paving the way for flatter management structures. Eventually it will demolish it.

There is little doubt that by the time the next millennium arrives most commercial organizations will be equipped with much more sophisticated IT systems than they use now. Powerful personal computers, for example, will probably be available to every employee in most companies, and will no longer be regarded just as a tool for writing letters or storing data. They will be a conduit for information to flow around the company, giving employees the freedom to see, manage, and pass it on as and when they wish to do so.

Such a development in the use of computers will have important consequences for company culture: with information at their fingertips, employees will be in a position to take more and more decisions for themselves. At that point, each company will have to weigh up how much authority it is prepared to allow staff— whether it wants so many employees to be decision-makers. If it comes down on the side of granting greater freedom then it will, to use a buzzword, have empowered its people.

Empowering staff will mean, essentially, that they no longer have to wait for approval from higher management before they can make decisions, and that they will be licensed to work more closely with customers. The benefits could be significant: with quicker decisions and a more motivated work force which recognizes its own value, companies will be able to respond more rapidly to customers' needs and offer them better service. The result will be happier customers, more than willing to do business in the future.

Clearly, though, empowerment must be tempered with practicality. What will happen to middle managers when responsibility for many decisions is passed down to their juniors? Will it mean the death of management as we know it?

The answer is that the manager's role need not become redundant — though some managers may be — but it will have to be adapted. As staff lower down the hierarchy gain more control over their own actions, their managers will have to learn to play a coaching role. This will require them to pass on their experience and ensure their teams work to a common goal. The manager will have to be facilitator, counsellor, problem-solver, coach, and developer of staff.

Some managers might find it difficult to accept this. They might ask why management techniques that seem to have worked perfectly well have to be changed. The answer lies in getting, and keeping, a competitive edge. Simply, those organizations in which decision-making power is divested to employees who are closer to the action than managers will react more swiftly to customers' wishes. Managers will have to accept that they must learn to open up their companies and not be afraid of surrendering the precious power to which they have clung so long; perhaps too long. The carrot will be the satisfaction of stealing a march on competitors and pleasing customers.

But even these benefits may not be enough to force some managers to adopt a different approach. Evidence suggests that the British, French, and Germans in particular are naturally averse to change and traditionally resent any upheaval or diminution of managerial power. Yet they will have to overcome their reluctance if organizations are to develop management structures and cultures capable of quick response to change. The key to the future success of business lies in harnessing the dynamism that empowerment can bring.

The message to the manager is unavoidable: forget past prejudices, adapt to new management techniques, and embrace the advantages of a brave new age of technology.

SOURCE: Reprinted from "Pyramid felling" by George McNeil, *International Management,* October 1993, p. 68. George McNeil is president and chief executive of Bull Europe. Reprinted by permission, International Management (October, 1993).

Formalization

Formalization refers to the extent to which job activity is defined and controlled by rules. The more rules there are about how to do the work and how decisions are made, the more an organization is formalized. Police departments are often very formalized as the activities of officers are strictly controlled by rules that cover almost every situation that may arise. A campus radio station, on the other hand, may be much less formal, having only a few rules governing the broadcasting behaviour of station members.

Centralization

Centralization concerns where in the organization decisions are made. When decision making is reserved for top management, **vertical centralization** is high. Vertical centralization is low when lower level employees in the hierarchy are given decision making authority. **Horizontal decentralization** occurs when workers in many different organizational units are allowed to make decisions without referring them to a more central authority. For example, travel agencies in a national chain might be expected to make their own hiring decisions. Agent hiring would be horizontally decentralized. Advertising decisions might be made by head office and would therefore be horizontally centralized.

These structural measures of complexity, centralization, and formalization may be combined into two broad and descriptive categories: *mechanistic*, having a structure appropriate for an unchanging environment; and *organic*, having a structure appropriate for a changing environment. These labels were created by Tom Burns and George Stalker (1961). They studied 20 industrial organizations in the United Kingdom in order to determine what happens to an organization's structure when product innovation is required and the environment is constantly changing.

Vertical centralization
When decisions are made higher up in the organization's hierarchy.

Horizontal decentralization
When workers in many different organizational units are allowed to make decisions without referring them to a more central authority.

Mechanistic Organizations

Mechanistic organizations were so named because they can be seen to operate as machines. They are characterized by highly specialized tasks that tend to be rigidly defined, hierarchical authority and control, and communications that primarily take the form of instructions and decisions issued by superiors to subordinates. Communication is mostly vertical from the top down. Further, loyalty to the organization and obedience to superiors is a condition of membership. Mechanistic organizations tend to be complex, formalized, and centralized. An automobile factory that uses a production line technology is a good example of an organization with a mechanistic structure.

Organic Organizations

Organic organizations act more as living things. They have tasks that are more interdependent and that are continually adjusted and redefined through interaction with organizational members. An advertising agency, for instance, needs to be flexible in dealing with customers and in creating concepts for television commercials and print advertisements.

In an organic organization, control depends less on formal job position and more on expertise relevant to the particular problem being considered. Communication is both vertical (up and down the hierarchy) and horizontal (across different departments of the organization) depending on where the needed information resides. These communications primarily take the form of information and advice. Commitment in the organic organization is to the organization's tasks and goals. Members accept general responsibility for task accomplishment beyond their individual role definition. That is, they do not stick to a job description as a definition of the work they will do. Organic organizations tend to be simple, low in formalization, and decentralized. They adapt to and create change in their environments.

To this point we have considered structure as a *description* of the organization. The measures we have discussed can be used to measure and describe the current state of the organization. The descriptive viewpoint does not attempt to comment upon the likely costs and benefits of a particular structure or form of organizing. It is content to establish what an organization is doing.

But structure may also be considered as *prescription*. The prescriptive point of view may also be called "normative," in that norms or rules are created to explain what an organization should do. With this viewpoint the question changes from what the structure or form of organizing is to what it should be. The next section examines different types of structure and the conditions under which each is likely to be effective.

Types of Structure

Generally speaking, an organization can be thought of as having five different parts of varying size and importance (Mintzberg, 1983). Three line roles are top management, middle management, and the production core. The production core consists of the people who do the work of the organization—making its product or serving its clients. Two staff roles are those of clerical support staff and technical support staff. Exhibit 2.1 shows these five parts for a manufacturing firm.

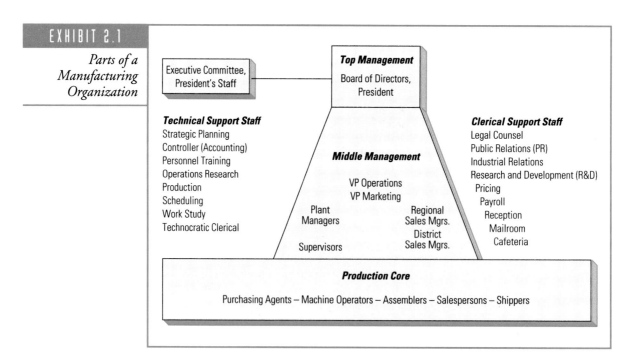

EXHIBIT 2.1

Parts of a Manufacturing Organization

Source: Henry Mintzberg, STRUCTURE IN FIVES: Designing effective organizations, ©1983, p. 18. Adapted/reprinted by permission of Prentice Hall Inc., Englewood Cliffs, NJ.

Given these different organizational parts, organizations adopt a wide variety of structures. Henry Mintzberg (1979), of Montreal's McGill University, summarized these into five basic types. They are: simple structure, machine bureaucracy, professional bureaucracy, divisionalized form, and adhocracy. Exhibit 2.2 summarizes how these five types of structure vary and which parts of the organization they emphasize.

Simple Structure   Small organizations, especially those that are young, often adopt a simple structure. They have little specialization, a low degree of formalization, and a high degree of centralization.

EXHIBIT 2.2   FIVE ORGANIZATIONAL TYPES OF STRUCTURE

	SIMPLE STRUCTURE	MACHINE BUREAUCRACY	PROFESSIONAL BUREAUCRACY	DIVISIONALIZED FORM	ADHOCRACY / MATRIX
STRUCTURE MEASURES					
Complexity	Little specialization	Much horizontal & vertical specialization	Much horizontal specialization	Some horizontal & vertical specialization between divisions and head office	Much horizontal specialization
Formalization	Low	High	Low	Within divisions	Low
Centralization	Vertical & horizontal	Limited horizontal decentralization	Vertical & horizontal decentralization	Limited vertical decentralization	Selective decentralization
Mechanistic/Organic	Organic	Mechanistic	Mechanistic	Mechanistic	Organic
PARTS OF THE ORGANIZATION					
Production core	Informal work with little discretion	Routine, formalized work with little discretion	Skilled, standardized work with much individual autonomy	Tendency to formalize due to divisionalization	Merged with administration to do project work
Technical support staff	None	Many to formalize work	Few	Many at head office for performance control	Few and role status blurred when part of a project team
Clerical support staff	Small	Often elaborated to reduce uncertainty	Elaborated to support professionals	Split between head office & divisions	Many but role status blurred when part of a project team
Key part	Top Management	Technical support staff	Production core	Middle Management	Support staff and technical core

SOURCE: Henry Mintzberg, THE STRUCTURING OF ORGANIZATIONS, ©1979, pp. 466-467. Adapted/reprinted by permission of Prentice Hall, Inc., Englewood Cliffs, NJ.

Machine bureaucracy
An organization that is specialized, formalized, and bureaucratic.

Bureaucratic red tape
Usually seen in a negative light, referring to a complicated set of rules, regulations and forms required by a bureaucratic organization.

Ideal type bureaucracy
The most perfect example of the bureaucracy type of organizing.

Machine Bureaucracy   Those organizations that survive the dangerous first few years often grow, becoming specialized, formalized, and therefore more bureaucratic. They acquire the characteristics of a **machine bureaucracy**. Bureaucracies are often large, impersonal organizations. They can be so specialized that it often seems impossible to find the person who can make a decision or give a specific piece of information. Both customers and staff can chafe under the organization's set of bureaucratic rules and curse it's so-called **bureaucratic red tape**. However, red tape is just one side of the bureaucratic coin. Most people in Canada would be upset, for example, if a motor vehicle registrations clerk refused to give someone a license plate because the customer did not pay a bribe.

Bureaucratic theory (see this chapter's *A Little Knowledge* feature) makes the assumption that people are rational and can work within the bureaucracy's rules. The rules would guide behaviour, meaning that conflict would be avoided. This is the **ideal type bureaucracy**— bureaucracy as it *should* work. In the ideal type bureaucracy, non-rational behaviour and conflict between individuals are not anticipated. However, we now know that non-rationality and conflict are present in bureaucratic structures.

A LITTLE KNOWLEDGE

Max Weber (1864-1920), was a German sociologist who studied organizations in the early 1900s. He was a first-hand observer of industrialization and a trend in society towards organizations that were run less on the authority of one person and more on a set of formalized rules and relationships. This form of organization can be called a bureaucracy, which means a set of related offices. Weber described his "ideal type" of bureaucracy, the most perfect example of this type of organizing. This list is shown below. Note in his list how important the concept of "office" or bureau is.

- **Formalization**
  - "A continuous organization of official functions bound by rules"

- **Records**
  - "Administrative acts, decisions and rules are formulated and recorded in writing"

- **Office**
  - "The combination of written documents and a continuous organization of official functions constitutes the 'office' which is the central focus of all types of modern corporate action."

- **Specialization**
  - "Each office has a clearly defined sphere of competence."

- **Hierarchy**
  - "Each lower office is under the control and supervision of a higher one."

- **Officials**
  - "Candidates are selected on the basis of technical qualifications. They are appointed, not elected."
  - "The office is treated as the sole, or at least the primary, occupation of the incumbent."
  - The job "constitutes a career. There is a system of 'promotion' according to seniority or to achievement, or both."
  - "There is a complete absence of appropriation of official position by the incumbent."

- **Ownership**
  - "There exists … complete separation of the property belonging to the organization, which is controlled within the sphere of office, and the personal property of the official"
  - "Members of the administrative staff should be completely separated from ownership of the means of production or administration"

- **Impersonality**
  - "The dominance of a spirit of formalistic impersonality, without hatred or passion, and hence without affection or enthusiasm … Everyone is subject to formal equality of treatment … This is the spirit in which the ideal official conducts (the) office"

SOURCE: Adapted with the permission of The Free Press, a Division of Macmillan, Inc. from THE THEORY OF SOCIAL AND ECONOMIC ORGANIZATION by Max Weber, Translated by A.M. Henderson and Talcott Parsons. Edited by Talcott Parsons. Copyright ©1947, copyright renewed 1975 by Talcott Parsons.

Also little considered were the unintended consequences of bureaucratic methods and rules. An example of such unforeseen consequences was uncovered by Peter Blau (1956), who studied employment counsellors in an unemployment office. He found that rules created to ensure fairness among counsellors were bent to personal advantage. Although new job openings were supposed to be posted so that all counsellors could tell their clients about them, Blau found that counsellors would keep news of particularly good or easy-to-fill jobs for their particular clients only.

Professional Bureaucracy   This type of bureaucracy relies on the professionalism of its production workers to work on their own and make decisions. Production workers are highly trained specialists. In this it differs from a machine bureaucracy. One example is that of a public accounting firm. Each accountant on an audit uses Generally Accepted Accounting Principles (GAAP) to guide the work and the decisions that are made. Staff accountants report to a supervisor but remain professionals responsible for their own judgments and decisions.

Divisionalized Form   Very large organizations often divide their operations into product or market groups. These are called "divisions" or "strategic business units" (SBUs). Each is run as an almost independent machine bureaucracy. The function of the divisions is to make a profit for the firm. The head office provides overall planning, research, and specialized services such as the negotiation of technology licenses, patenting of inventions, and acquisition of new and related businesses. This arrangement is termed a **divisionalized form**, and is shown in the diagram below.

Divisionalized form
Organizations that divide their operations into product or market groups.

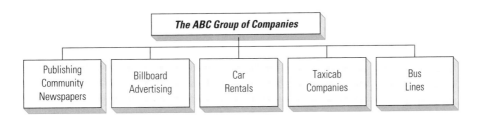

Adhocracy   An adhocracy is usually structured in a matrix. The organization chart of a matrix organization has functions shown as rows and products or programs shown as columns. In the adhocracy or matrix organization some members identify their work as part of both a product and a functional area. These members report to two bosses. One boss is the person in charge of the product, the other is the person in charge of a specific function.

For example, in an organization that manufactures hospital diagnostic imaging equipment, the functions might be Marketing, Research and Development, and Manufacturing. The products could be machines that monitor body functions, that perform body scans, and that analyze tissue and blood samples. In the example shown on the following page there are three types of scanners built. They are ultrasound, computerized tomography (CT), and X-ray. The manager of CT scanner production in this example reports to two bosses—the Vice-President Manufacturing and the Product Manager for Scanners. Note in this example organization chart that only a part of the total organization is shown.

The dual-authority structure of the matrix is usually found only at the top of the organization (Davis & Lawrence, 1977). All employees who report to the manager of CT scanners would find themselves in a bureaucracy. They would not be part of the matrix or have two bosses. Therefore, an adhocracy has both matrix-like dual-authority elements and more common bureaucratic elements. Most employees report to only one boss.

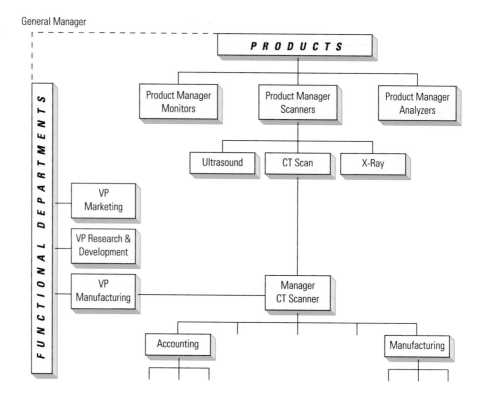

Coordination

Once the organization has been divided into parts, the parts must be coordinated. The organization's components are usually seen as stable. Coordination, however, is a process. According to Mintzberg (1979), coordination depends on five factors. They are:

1. How authority is distributed through the organization and how it "flows," or moves, from one part of the organization to another.
2. The flow of informal communication throughout the organization.
3. Who has power in the organization.
4. Who makes decisions in the organization.
5. What is the most important or "key" coordinating mechanism.

Mintzberg theorized that methods of coordination would be different for the five kinds of organizational structure.

In the simple structure power is in the hands of the chief executive, often the owner/manager, who makes the decisions and communicates them down the hierarchy. Authority, therefore, flows down from the owner/manager at the top of the organization. Informal communication is common because of the organization's small size and frequent face-to-face interactions among the organization's members. The key day-to-day coordinating mechanism is direct supervision of employees by the owner/manager.

Decisions in the machine bureaucracy flow from the top of the organization down and are communicated officially, in writing, instead of being communicated informally. Authority is distributed throughout the organization. The work is separated into offices occupied by a trained professional staff, who make and carry out decisions at their level. Here the key coordinating mechanism is the standardization of the work. The work is routine and predictable.

In the professional bureaucracy decisions are made from the bottom of the organization up. The highly trained professionals doing the work are in touch with problems and issues as they happen. Professionals hold the power and authority in this type of organization because it is their professional standards that form the basis of decisions that are made. There is significant informal communication in the administration of the organization, but less so in the work of the professionals. Those higher up in the organization achieve coordination of the organization's work by training and standardization of the professional's skills.

Day-to-day operating decisions in the divisionalized form are made by each division. The head office makes more long-term decisions about budgets and lines of business. Division managers have significant power and authority for their divisions. Head office exerts control by requiring operating reports from divisions, though there is some informal communication as well between head office and the divisions. Any coordination between divisions focuses on the products themselves — for example, how products from one division can be used with the products of other divisions.

In an adhocracy, coordination is a continuous process of mutual adjustment between people in the technical core and those in the support staffs. Relationships rely more on collegiality and an attitude of professionalism rather than on authority and rules. Therefore, informal communication is important. Because coordination is by mutual adjustment and not by authority, conflict is common. Conflict resolution skills and the time to resolve conflicts are therefore required.

FACTORS AFFECTING STRUCTURE

Three main aspects of an organization affect its structure. They are age and size; technology; and environment. Exhibit 2.3 shows how these three factors vary for different structural types.

EXHIBIT 2.3   HOW THE FACTORS AFFECTING STRUCTURE VARY BY ORGANIZATIONAL TYPE

EFFECT	SIMPLE STRUCTURE	MACHINE BUREAUCRACY	PROFESSIONAL BUREAUCRACY	DIVISIONALIZED FORM	ADHOCRACY/ MATRIX
Age and size	Typically young and small	Typically old and large	Varies	Typically old and very large	Typically young
Technology	Simple	Machines but not automated, not very sophisticated	Not machine or sophisticated	Divisible, otherwise like machine bureaucracy	Very sophisticated, often automated
Appropriate for environment	Simple and dynamic	Simple and stable	Complex and stable	Relatively simple and stable; diversified markets	Complex and dynamic

SOURCE: Henry Mintzberg. THE STRUCTURING OF ORGANIZATIONS, ©1979, pp. 466-467. Adapted/reprinted by permission of Prentice Hall, Inc., Englewood Cliffs, NJ.

Age and Size

Although some organizations are created large, most start small and grow over time. They gradually add people to perform more work and different kinds of work. As an organization becomes older and larger its structure changes. A program of inquiry by Derek Pugh and his colleagues at the University of Aston in Birmingham, England, later called the **Aston Studies**, investigated the relationship between age, structure, and size. They found that larger organizations tended to be more specialized, standardized, and formalized but *less* centralized than smaller organizations (Pugh and others, 1969). They observed (p. 112) that:

> An increased scale of operation increases the frequency of recurrent events and the repetition of decisions, which are then standardized and formalized. Once the number of positions and people grows beyond control by personal interaction, the organization must be more explicitly structured.

Technology

Technology is defined as the sequence of physical techniques, knowledge, and equipment used to turn organizational inputs into outputs. Joan Woodward (1965) conducted research into the connection between technology and structure by studying 100 manufacturing firms in the southern part of England. She identified three types of technology.

The first was **small batch**. This is the production of one or a few custom items by one person or a small team working closely together. An example of small batch technology would be custom cabinet making. Here the cabinet maker produces a unique product or a few similar products. A second example is the individual fitting and making of a fine suit of clothes.

Woodward's second technology type was **large batch/mass production**. This is the production of many units of an identical product. A common example of mass production is an automobile assembly line. When in operation, many units of the same product are made. An example of large batch production is the making of beer, which in a brewery is made in large fermentation kettles that may each hold many thousands of litres. Each kettle holds one batch of beer.

Woodward's third technology type was **continuous process**. This is the production of a standard product without pause. An example of continuous process technology is a nuclear power plant. Once started, electricity is generated without pause for a long period of time. The nuclear reaction is monitored by a few highly skilled technicians. Expended uranium fuel rods may even be replaced while the reactor is in operation. A second example of this type of technology is an oil refinery. Crude oil is continually input into the refinery's cracking and distilling apparatus and refined products such as gasoline are continually extracted.

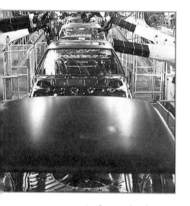

Industrial robots welding car bodies on a mass production assembly line.

Woodward and her colleagues found that organizations were more effective when their technology matched, or "fit" with the organization's structure. Specifically, for small batch production, an organic structure was best because the production of custom items requires a good deal of informal communication and adaptation. Organizations using a mass production technology were more effective when using a mechanistic structure. The reason was that control over a complex and repetitive process could be effectively exerted by rules and regulations. When a continuous process technology was used, Woodward found that an organic structure was more effective. In this case highly trained technicians monitored machines producing the organization's output and needed to communicate freely about the production process and any irregularities that were noticed. The concept that technology determines the best organizational structure was termed the **technological imperative**.

James Thompson (1967) thought of technology in a somewhat different way. He considered the way organizational members were interdependent while the inputs of the organization were transformed into its outputs (see Exhibit 2.4).

Thompson's first technology type is **mediating**. Here each organizational member processes inputs into outputs on his own. There is only pooled interdependence between individual workers. Workers are interdependent only in terms of the total work of the organization, not in each product made or service rendered. The organization is effective to the extent that each person performs her job effectively. An example of a mediating technology is a bank where tellers may work beside each other but deal with client requests individually.

Mediating technology

Each organizational member processes inputs into outputs independently with only pooled interdependence between members.

EXHIBIT 2.4   TECHNOLOGY AND WORK UNIT INTERDEPENDENCE

TECHNOLOGY	INTERDEPENDENCE TYPE	EXAMPLE	COORDINATION BETWEEN WORK UNITS IS ACHIEVED BY:	COMMUNICATION REQUIRED BETWEEN WORK UNITS
Mediating	Pooled	clients / A B C / bank	Standardization Rules Supervision	Low—vertical
Long-linked	Sequential	input / A→B→C / output / production line in a factory	Standardization Rules Supervision Planning & scheduling	Medium—scheduled meetings, feedback
Intensive	Reciprocal	A→B→C / A←B←C / client / hospital	Standardization Rules Supervision Planning & scheduling Cooperation Mutual adjustments	High—unscheduled meetings, horizontal
Intensive	Team	A / B client C / hospital trauma team	Standardization Rules Supervision Planning & scheduling Cooperation Mutual adjustments Teamwork	Highest—mutual adjustments are made as required in "real time"

SOURCE: Adapted from James D. Thompson (1967), *Organizations in Action*, New York: McGraw-Hill, Inc., ©1967, pp. 51-65, reproduced with permission of McGraw-Hill, Inc.; Andrew H. Van de Ven, Andre L. Delbecq, and Richard Koenig, Jr. (1976), "Determinants of coordination modes within organizations," *American Sociological Review* 41: 322-338; Exhibit 9.10 of *ORGANIZATIONS: A Micro/Macro Approach* by Richard L. Daft and Richard M. Steers, Copyright © 1986 by Scott, Foresman and Company, reprinted by permission of HarperCollins Publishers; and Figure 6-5 on page 164 from Daniel Robey (1991), *Designing organizations*, 3rd edition, Homewood, Illinois: Irwin, by permission of Richard D.Irwin, Inc.

Long-linked technology

Inputs are transformed step by step into outputs as they move from worker to worker. There is sequential interdependence between individual workers.

Long-linked technology is Thompson's second technology type. It is noted for its sequential interdependence between individual workers. Inputs are transformed step by step into outputs as they move from worker to worker. Each adds to the work of all those who have gone before. In an engine manufacturing factory, for instance, an error by a worker installing pistons in the engine block will affect workers that have to install other engine parts later in the production process.

Thompson's third technology type is that of **intensive technology**, marked by reciprocal interdependence between organizational members who work on the product. In a hospital, for example, a patient may be admitted complaining of abdominal pain. Staff members rely on one another to accurately complete diagnostic tests and perform treatments so that the patient may be cured. There is no set order of tests and treatments (it is not a sequential process). The particular staff members involved in the patient's treatment will depend on how the patient's condition improves or worsens.

Intensive technology

Inputs are processed by organizational members as is required by the product. There is reciprocal interdependence between organizational members.

Intensive technology may also involve team interdependence (Van de Ven and others, 1976). In this case team members from multiple disciplines interact and adjust to each other in "real time" as required in order to obtain an effective outcome. A hospital trauma team, for example, is trained to work together to save a patient's life by doing what is necessary as it becomes necessary. Time is "real" because each specialist required to save the patient must be present and ready to perform his function as needed. Again, it is the patient's condition that will dictate what treatment is required.

Thompson's view of technology is particularly useful for understanding how technology affects the interdependence of work units. For example, a shoe factory might be organized so that one unit makes cowboy boots, one shoes, and one winter boots. Here the interdependence between units is pooled and coordination can be achieved through the use of production standards, operating rules, and supervision.

Alternatively, one unit might make all the soles, which are then passed along to the next unit for the addition of the upper part of the shoe or boot. The next unit in line could then add the lacing guides and the laces, and package the product. Here, interdependence is sequential.

Beyond the pooled coordination methods of production standards, operating rules, and supervision, planning and scheduling are also required to achieve coordination between the different work units. When an intensive technology is employed, more coordination between work units is required. Cooperation, mutual adjustment, and possibly teamwork are then added to the list of necessary coordinating mechanisms.

Environment

Simple environment

Inputs come from relatively few environmental components (or factors) and outputs are sent to relatively few environmental components.

As we saw in Chapter 1, organizations receive inputs from their environment and send outputs into the environment. The environment may be characterized as simple or complex, and static or dynamic.

The organization has a **simple environment** when the inputs received come from relatively few components (or factors) of the environment and the organization's outputs are sent to relatively few environmental components. The organization's environment is **complex** when the organization must deal with many environmental components on the input or output side.

Complex environment

The organization must deal with many environmental components on the input or output side.

For example, a shoe factory may obtain all its leather from one supplier, its machines from another, and sell its completed product to a shoe wholesaler. It has a relatively simple environment. If the factory deals with multiple suppliers of leather and machines, and sells to multiple wholesalers as well as directly to the public, the environment is more complex.

EXPERIENCE IS THE BEST TEACHER

The study of organization structure has been a central topic in organization theory right from its origins in the work of Max Weber. This is because it is primarily through the design of structure that managers try to ensure that work is performed and acceptable outcomes achieved. The emphases throughout the 1980s and into the 1990s on such topics as empowerment, transformational leadership, total quality management (TQM), and teams are all part of "restructuring", attempts to change the way organizations are structured.

Structure will remain important as a topic because these ideas about organizational process come to fruition through structures. TQM, for example, demands that the division of work between units is examined, that procedures are reviewed, that the distribution of authority is altered, and so on. Similarly, changing the structure of an organi-

Professor C.R. Hinings is the Thornton A. Graham Professor of Business in the Department of Organizational Analysis, University of Alberta. [1]

zation is often the starting point for trying to revitalize the way a company is managed. Managers will decide to divisionalize, to redraw the relationships between headquarters and local branches, to emphasize marketing more, etc. All of these mean that we have to examine the basics of organization structure.

Structure, then, is central, and interconnected with all aspects of organizational functioning. We are living in an era of constant restructuring and there does not seem to be any end of this in sight. Through restructuring managers try to change the behaviours and attitudes of people in organizations. And when a manager starts organizational change by trying to deal with motivation or leadership, there are always consequences for structure. So, structure has been, is, and will continue to be important in understanding organizations.

When the environment remains basically the same it is **static**. In a static environment there is little change in the components of the environment and the input/output transactions of the organization with the environment.

An environment that undergoes continual change is **dynamic.** Sources of input may vary, the suppliers of inputs may be replaced, and outputs may have to go to different receiving organizations. For instance, the micro-computer industry faces a dynamic environment with constantly changing types of integrated circuit chips, suppliers of those chips, new suppliers of "add-on" equipment and replacement parts, and new software that may be bundled with a new computer.

When considering the nature of the environment, it is also important to consider how similar environmental factors are to one another and the predictability of environmental changes. Dealing with many similar factors in the environment is not likely to be difficult for the shoe factory in our example, and so its environment would still be simple. If changes in the environment are very predictable, such as a changing demand for different types of shoes and boots depending on the season, then the environment is more static than dynamic.

Static environment

The environment remains basically the same over time.

Dynamic environment

An environment that undergoes continual change.

---

[1] For a sample of Professor Hinings' work, with Professor Royston Greenwood of the University of Alberta, see "Understanding strategic change: The contribution of archetypes," in the October 1993 issue of the *Academy of Management Journal*, 6:1052-1081.

Analyzability   Whether or not the factors and change in the environment can be seen and understood by members of an organization.

Another environmental dimension of importance is **analyzability**: that is, whether or not the factors and change in the environment can be seen and understood by members of an organization. The same objective environment may be analyzable by the members of one organization but not by the members of others. Organizational members may be trained and experienced in looking for and seeing the condition of the environment. For example, stock brokers, investment bankers, and economists attempt to make environments more analyzable so that future conditions are more predictable.

Subenvironments

Definable parts of the environment dealt with by parts of the organization. In Lawrence and Lorsch's terms, subenvironments are scientific, technical, and market.

Paul Lawrence and Jay Lorsch (1969) thought of the organizational environment as composed of three **subenvironments**. These are the scientific, technical, and market subenvironments. In direct and corresponding contact with these are the three organizational subunits of research and development (R&D), production, and marketing. The marketing department deals with the market. The production department deals with technical developments in machinery and production methods. The R&D department is in contact with scientific advances in theory and methods.

Lawrence and Lorsch studied six organizations in different industries. They found that organizations were more effective when the structure of the R&D, production, and marketing subunits matched the uncertainty in the scientific, technical, and market subenvironments. For example, if the scientific subenvironment was complex and dynamic the organization's R&D unit was best structured organically. If the technical subenvironment was simple and stable the production core needed to be structured mechanistically. And a complex and dynamic market should have as its counterpart an organically structured marketing department.

Differentiation   The more an organization's three subunits of Production, Research & Development, and Marketing differ in structure, time orientation and goals the greater is the differentiation of the organization's structure.

The more an organization's three subunits differ in structure, time orientation, and goals, the greater is the organization's level of **differentiation**. If marketing, production, and R&D are all structured organically the organization is low on differentiation. Similarly, if all three subunits are mechanistic, the organization is low on differentiation. However, if one or two subunits are mechanistic and the other one or two are organic, then the organization is high on structural differentiation.

There may be differences in time orientation and goals between marketing, production, and R&D. Scientists in R&D, for instance, tend to think about the long-term results of their work. Their goals are far out into the future. Production people are oriented towards this week's and this month's results. These are more medium-term goals. Those in marketing tend to think about the short term—today's results and tomorrow's objectives.

Integration   The coordination required between organizational units.

Lawrence and Lorsch found that greater differentiation required more **integration**. The more distinct the three subunits were from one another the more coordination and communication were required between the different units. Coordination required more face-to-face meetings and permanent teams of integrators to help resolve differences between subunits.

Organizational structure is also affected by how dependent the organization is on parts of its environment. For instance, the Aston studies (Pugh and others, 1969) found that organizations that were dependent on other organizations had higher centralization and less autonomy in decision making. In one case, pressure for public accountability in public organizations caused authority to be concentrated at the top management level and required the approval of central committees for many decisions.

STRATEGY AND STRUCTURE

Strategy   The organization's plan of how to become more effective.

To this point we have examined the five types of organizational structure and the effects on structure of size and age, technology, and the environment. The assumption has been that over time, as organizations attempt to become more effective in their own environmental context, structures grow and evolve. But organizations also adopt a **strategy**, a plan of how to interact with their market—the parts of the environment that accept organizational outputs. Organizational design is concerned with the organization's choice of strategy and structure to be effective in its environment.

Types of Organizational Strategies

Ray Miles and Chuck Snow (1978; see also Miles and others, 1978) divided organizational strategies into four types: reactor, defender, analyzer, and prospector.

Reactor

The **reactor strategy** is simply to react to what comes. The environment is seen to have little effect on the organization. Such an organization is passive in its relationship with the environment and does not look at the environment in any formal or directed way. An example of a reactor would be a small corner grocery store that attempts to change when required. This reactor strategy tends to be less effective than others because it cannot reliably anticipate large-scale changes in the environment, and therefore cannot react effectively when they occur. The creation of supermarkets with low prices and a wide selection of goods caused many small grocery stores to close because they could not react in time to this environmental change.

> **Reactor strategy** The organization reacts to what occurs in its environment.

Defender

A **defender strategy** is to protect an existing share of the market. The defender assumes the environment can be analyzed, but still interacts with it passively. It has been conditioned by past experience to view the environment in one way. It is liable, therefore, to ignore environmental changes. A defender would be, for instance, a manufacturer of mechanical watches that has been conditioned to see efficiency and lower manufacturing costs as the way to keep market share. It might be unable to see how a revolutionary new approach to watch design and manufacture, such as battery-powered microchip technology, might be important. This kind of outlook can have disastrous results (see the feature *Seeing is Believing*).

> **Defender strategy** The organization aims to protect its share of the market.

SEEING IS BELIEVING

The Swiss watchmaking industry has long been renowned for the quality of its mechanical watches. The many Swiss firms involved in watch production had well-trained personnel. They had fine-tuned their systems to produce fine watches for the world market. The invention of the transistor was not considered to be important by the industry; after all, of what concern was an electronic invention to watchmakers?

It seems that using the defender approach to looking at the environment did not allow the Swiss watch industry to see what was coming. What happened, of course, is that transistors led to electronic timing mechanisms that could be built into watches, providing cheap and accurate timepieces. Also, microchips allowed stopwatch timing, date calendars, alarms and the like to be part of even the most inexpensive watch. Though there are still fine Swiss watchmakers (Rolex for example), the introduction of electronics led to a shake-up of the Swiss watch industry. As a group they lost market share to companies in other countries that were more aggressive in moving to the new technology.

But in 1983 there began a turnaround. Two large Swiss watch manufacturers merged to form the Swiss Corporation for Microelectronics and Watchmaking (SMH). It's Swatch watch has been a huge worldwide success, recapturing Swiss market share in the sale of low-cost watches.

Swatch watches helped SMH to fight back and regain worldwide market share of low cost watch sales.

SOURCE: Partially based on information in William Taylor (1993), "Message and muscle: An interview with Swatch titan Nicolas Hayek," *Harvard Business Review*, March/April 1993, pp. 99-110.

Analyzer

The **analyzer strategy**, by contrast, is a more active approach to environmental interaction. The analyzer believes the environment is understandable. This strategy seeks to discover moderately large changes in the environment, such as changes in customer preferences or technology, and then to gain some advantage from the changes. While protecting its current market position, it tries to add small changes that will make its product more attractive to the customer. An example of an analyzer would be a bank which, while wanting to keep its services and prices in line with those of other banks, tries to anticipate market demand for new services and products. These are then carefully added so that the bank is competitive with other banks but not too different from them.

Prospector

The **prospector** strategy also involves active interaction with the environment, but does not assume that environmental change can be analyzed. This organizational type scans the environment and actually creates its own environment—or enacts it, as it looks around and learns what it can do by what it has done. **Enactment** means that in the process of dealing with the environment the company creates its own environment. For example, Apple Computer learned about customer needs and how computers could work by selling computers to these customers and then listening to their reactions. A prospector organization's perceived environment is therefore created by its own actions and then affects future actions. A prospector sees a dynamic and changing environment and is willing to take risks to find and exploit or to create opportunities.

Strategy, Structure, and the Environment

Michael Porter (1980) distinguished three generic organizational strategies. These are differentiation, cost leadership, and focus. (For a discussion of Porter's more recent work, see this chapter's *On the One Hand*.) The **strategy of differentiation** attempts to create a product or service that customers in the organization's market will see as different from those of competitors. The **cost leadership strategy** may be followed by organizations that aim to become the lowest-cost producers in an industry. The **focus strategy** involves targeting a particular customer, product, or geographic area, and attempting to serve the target market better than other more broadly based competitors.

A study by Danny Miller (1988) of 89 firms in Quebec investigated the relationships of Porter's three strategies to organizational structure and environment. He found that "strategy, structure, and environment should be closely aligned; otherwise performance may suffer" (p. 304). For example, a high-technology firm would have a strategy of innovation, an organic structure, and an environment of change. A low-technology mass-production manufacturer would have a strategy of routine, low-cost production, a mechanistic structure, and a stable environment. How these variables affect each other can be seen in several ways. The environment and organizational structure can affect strategy. The organization's strategy and its environment can affect its structure. Or the organization's strategy and structure can affect its environment. We will look at each of these configurations in turn.

ON THE ONE HAND...

THE COMPETITIVE ADVANTAGE OF NATIONS

Michael Porter is the superstar of the management policy profession. Porter's early work, *Competitive Strategy* (1980), codified the industrial organization literature. A later book, *Competitive Advantage* (1985), attempted to integrate some basic organizational concepts with his prior work on strategy. *The Competitive Advantage of Nations* (1990) deals with large questions of political economy: What factors determine the economic success of nations? Are there identifiable stages of economic development? What is government's role in promoting development? Porter believes that the answers to these questions are to be found in the types of strategies followed by a nation's leading firms and industries.

The essence of the argument is that nations will be competitive when their firms and industries are leading exporters of high value-added goods (taking a raw material or product and processing it in a way to make it more valuable for sale to others) or significant investors in the industry of other countries (when the investment is in relatively low-productivity tasks like basic fabrication or final assembly). The best parts of the book concern the idea of "industrial clustering," where a nation's strong industries find themselves part of a dense network of vertical and horizontal relationships with other strong industries in the country. They both support and compete against each other.

Porter writes that strong industries are everywhere characterized by the favorable interaction of four elements in the national environment. These create what Porter calls a self-generating force field, or "diamond," that requires participating firms to pursue a strategy of continuous improvement. The first element in the diamond is the presence of sophisticated domestic demand, the second is the existence of strong related and supporting industries, the third is the intensity of domestic competition, and the final element in the diamond is a nation's factor-creating mechanisms—a nation's firms must create the institutions to provide for the continuous upgrading of its technical ability, scientific knowledge, and human capital.

Yet Porter ignores the lessons of his own case studies, which show that it is often not the general national environment, but the local environment which is responsible for the dynamism of many firms and industries. The success of the Italian wood furniture industry, for instance, is due less to the quality of education in Italian schools than to the existence of unique institutions such as the Cabiate cabinetmakers school, which is jointly funded by local unions, the Cabiate municipal government, and local employers. Porter points out the weaknesses of the Milan stock exchange but he ignores the active role played in Italy by municipal savings institutions and localized credit markets, which are entirely suited to the size of Italian industry.

Porter, blinkered by an ideology which sees no role for national governments in promoting strong industries, is blind to the importance of regional governments, too. Moreover, in his insistence that intense competitive rivalry is the key to the development of successful strategies, Porter also underestimates the importance of cooperation between firms (for example Japan, Italy) and among labour, government, and employers (for example Sweden, Germany).

QUESTIONS

1. How does Canada "stack up" using Porter's diamond model of the national environment?
2. What could the Canadian government do to increase the competitive position of Canadian organizations?
3. What systems, structures, and decision making bodies does the Japanese government use to foster their international competitiveness?
4. Should Canada follow the Japanese example? Is it possible to follow the Japanese example given the Canadian context?

Source: Excerpted and adapted with permission from a book review of Michael E. Porter (1990), The Competitive Advantage of Nations, New York: The Free Press, by Mick Carney of Concordia University, published in 1991 in the Canadian Journal of Administrative Sciences 8: 288-293. For further information on Porter's work see David Knights (1992), "Changing spaces: The disruptive impact of a new epistemological location for the study of management," Academy of Management Review 17: 524-529. A shorter article based on Porter's book is "The competitive advantage of nations," Harvard Business Review, March/April 1990, pp. 73-93.

Institutional theory

Organizations structure to be like other organizations or structure in the way required for organizations in their environment.

Environment and Structure Lead to Strategy   One way of thinking about strategy is as a result of a given structure and perceived environment. **Institutional theory** (Meyer & Rowan, 1977) takes the point of view that organizations structure to be like other organizations or structure in the way required by organizations in their environment. Their strategy, therefore, is to be the same as other successful organizations in their particular environment.

One type of institutionalization is that of an organization choosing to model (or mimic) the structure and systems of another successful organization in the hope of becoming successful itself (Galaskiewicz & Wasserman, 1989). For instance a restaurant might take the theme, decor, and approach to staff selection and training of another restaurant.

A second type of institutionalization is normative. To be successful an organization must follow norms, or rules, of how to structure its activity. Professional systems and structures are a good example. An accounting firm opening for business will tend to follow the professional model of what an accounting firm *should* look like and how it should operate.

The third type of institutionalization is coercive. In this case, for the organization to survive, it *must* follow the structure prescribed by others, whether rational or not. A new travel agency, for example, has to sign agreements with suppliers that specify minimum training of staff and some operating procedures that deal with banking and ticket security.

Strategy and Environment Lead to Structure   From this perspective, structure is seen as deriving from an organization's perception of the environment and the strategy it chooses to deal with the environment. In other words, structure is made to suit a strategy created for a particular environment. It is important to note that different organizations in the same industry, whose environments are the same except for each other, can see the environment in very different ways. Therefore, how the organization divides and coordinates its work and how it operates is an outcome of that perception and the strategy devised to succeed in the perceived environment. An example of an organization structuring itself so that its strategy fits its environment is Mrs. Fields Cookies of Park City, Utah (see Integrative Case I.1 at the end of Chapter 4).

Strategy and Structure Lead to Environment   An organization's design affects its perceived environment. An organization that chooses an active prospector strategy and structures organically may interact with and enact its own environment. Alternatively, when strategy and structure is unchanging the organization is in a poor position to notice or affect environmental changes. A relatively rigid system will not be able to sense changes which are beyond the original design. The organization will therefore not detect trends which threaten the organization.

This sort of organization regards the environment as simple and stable, whether or not that is actually the case. For example, North American auto makers were unprepared for the consumer's willingness to purchase smaller, more fuel efficient cars after the oil crisis of 1973. Their definition of the environment was that consumers would accept the cars that they built. They were surprised when small cars imported from Japan started to sell well. When the new automobile environment favouring smaller cars was accepted and North American auto makers attempted to change their strategy, they found that they were constrained by their large size and bureaucratic structures. They were also constrained by their employees whose lifetime of experience led them to see the automotive environment as favouring large cars.

CONCLUSION

The interaction of strategy, structure, and environment forms a design for the organization that affects how the organization's work is done. These three variables interact; they influence each other. The organization's design helps shape the meaning work gives to people's lives. It affects how they work, why they work, what they care about, and how they see the world. An organization's design is therefore important for a person considering joining a particular company (see *If You Can't Ride Two Horses At Once, You Shouldn't Be in the Circus*).

In Chapter 3 we will examine how values are made part of an organization and its design in the process of creating an organizational culture. Then we will look at the effects of organizational culture and how organizations transfer their values to members through the process of socialization. We will also examine the culture of whole societies and how they differ from each other. We investigate societal culture for two reasons. The first is that organizations are embedded in societies and are therefore affected by them. The second is that members of organizations are strongly influenced by their own societal culture. Organizational members bring their home culture with them to their company.

CHAPTER SUMMARY

In this chapter we have seen that organizations structure themselves by dividing vertically and horizontally into parts. The vertical division of labour forms the traditional organization hierarchy. Horizontal division of labour, or departmentation, can be done several different ways. They are by customer; product; geographic location; function performed or special knowledge; project; or a mixture of these components.

Once structured, organizations and those that study them can find it useful to apply measurements to the structures created. Three important structure measures are complexity, formalization, and centralization. Organizations can also be broadly considered to be mechanistic, operating like machines, or organic, operating more as living things. Three factors that are known to affect an organization's structure are age and size; technology; and the environment.

IF YOU CAN'T RIDE TWO HORSES AT ONCE, YOU SHOULDN'T BE IN THE CIRCUS

Asking about an organization's design when looking for work in an organization can be important. Is the organization more mechanistic or organic? Is the position one of line or staff? Where does the position fit in the hierarchy? What is the organization's dominant strategy? Answers to these questions will help to give you insight into organizational relationships, the amount of bureaucracy in the organization, your task in the organization, how the job is seen (and therefore how you will be seen) by the other members of the organization, and the kind of reporting relationship to expect. There are no right or wrong answers to these questions, just as there is no "one best way" for an organization to structure. The answers will, however, help you to analyze the organization and judge how well the job and organization fit your needs and aptitudes.

Organizations that are older and larger tend to be more bureaucratic. Successful organizations with large batch or mass production technologies tend to be structured more mechanistically. Successful organizations with either a unit/small batch technology or continuous process technology tend to have more organic structures. We also discussed how organizations have to pay attention to their environments. Organizational environments can be characterized as simple/complex and static/dynamic. Organizations in simple/static environments are more effective when they are mechanistic. Those in complex/dynamic environments need an organic structure.

There is not just one kind of environment and way of dealing with it. Organizations may take four different strategies when dealing with their environment. These strategic types are to be a reactor, defender, analyzer, or prospector. It makes a difference how the people of an organization see and react to their organization's environment because that affects how they will guide the organization in the future. Reactors take a passive approach, defenders attempt to hold on to what they have by fighting off others. Analyzers try to determine where the environment is headed so that they can plan a beneficial strategy. Prospectors take a proactive approach and attempt to shape their own environment so that it wants what the organization can provide.

QUESTIONS FOR REVIEW

1. What is Max Weber's "ideal type" of bureaucracy? Why is it important to the study of organizational forms?

2. How can the environment not be the same for every organization in a given industry? Is it true or not that environments are real and therefore the same for every organization?

3. What are the effects on structure of an organization growing older and larger, adding more specialists and staff personnel?

4. Compare and contrast a mechanistic and an organic organization. What is it like to manage in these two types, to make decisions? What behaviours are likely to be rewarded? What type of environment is each best suited to?

5. What reasons are there that explain why there is no "one best way" to organize?

SELF-DIAGNOSTIC EXERCISE 2.1

Attitudes Towards Computer Usage

We are in the information age, information technology is having a profound impact on the way organizations operate, and the "information superhighway" is under construction. But individual attitudes towards these changes and receptiveness to computers will vary. Answer the following questions to gauge your own receptiveness to the use of computers.

Use this scale for your answers:

1	2	3	4	5	6	7
Strongly Agree	Agree	Slightly Agree	Neutral	Slightly Disagree	Disagree	Strongly Disagree

1. I would prefer to type a paper on a word processor than on a typewriter.

2. Whenever I use something that is computerized, I am afraid I will break it.

3. I like to keep up with technological advances.

4. I know that I will *not* understand how to use computers.

5. Using a computer is too time consuming.

6. I feel that having a computer at work would help me with my job.

7. I prefer *not* to learn how to use a computer.

8. I would like to own, or do own, a computer.

9. I like to play video games.

10. I feel that the use of computers in schools will help children to learn mathematics.

11. I prefer to use an automatic teller machine for most of my banking.

12. If I had children, I would *not* buy them computerized toys.

13. I have had bad experiences with computers.

14. I would prefer to order items in a store through a computer than wait for a store clerk.

15. I feel that the use of computers in schools will negatively affect children's reading and writing abilities.

16. I do *not* like using computers because I cannot see how the work is being done.

17. I would prefer to go to a store that uses computerized price-scanners than go where the clerks enter each price into the cash register.

18. I do *not* feel I have control over what I do when I use a computer.

19. I think that computers and other technological advances have helped to improve our lives.

20. I do *not* like to program computerized items such as VCRs and microwave ovens.

Scoring:

Item	Score
1.	_____
3.	_____
6.	_____
8.	_____
9.	_____
10.	_____
11.	_____
14.	_____
17.	_____
19.	_____

Item	Score
2.	_____
4.	_____
5.	_____
7.	_____
12.	_____
13.	_____
15.	_____
16.	_____
18.	_____
20.	_____

Reverse scored items: Subtract your item score from 8 for the following items. For example if your score for item 2 were "5," the revised score would be 8 - 5 = 3) Use these new item scores in the subscale calculations below.

Subscale 1: Negative reactions to computers.
Add your scores for items 2, 4, 5, 13, 16, 18, 20.

Subscale 2: Positive reactions to computers.
Add your scores for items 1, 6, 7, 8, 9.

Subscale 3: Computers and children/education.
Add your scores for items 3, 10, 12, 15, 19.

Subscale 4: Reactions to familiar computer-related mechanisms.
Add your scores for items 11, 14, 17.

Your overall score is the total of the four subscales. A higher score means less favorable reactions to computers and computerized technology. A lower total score means that you have more positive attitudes towards computers.

SOURCE: Paula M. Popovich, Karen R. Hyde, Todd Zakrajsek, and Catherine Blumer (1987), "The development of the attitudes toward computer usage scale," *Educational & Psychological Measurement* 47: 261-269. Reprinted with permission.

EXPERIENTIAL EXERCISE 2.1

Measuring the Dimensions of Organizational Structure

Outside of class, find a person currently working in an organization and ask them for a 20-minute interview. Ask the following questions about measures of organizational structure.

1. **Complexity**

   Check which of the following activities in the firm are dealt with *exclusively* by at least one full-time person who:

   ❏ a. Is responsible for public relations, advertising, or promotion.

   ❏ b. Disposes of, distributes, or services the firm's output.

   ❏ c. Carries outputs, resources, and other material from one place to another.

   ❏ d. Acquires and allocates human resources.

   ❏ e. Develops and trains personnel.

   ❏ f. Takes care of employee welfare, security, or social services.

   ❏ g. Obtains and controls materials and equipment (buying and stock control).

   ❏ h. Maintains and erects buildings and equipment.

   ❏ i. Records and controls financial resources (accounting).

   ❏ j. Controls work flow (planning, scheduling).

   ❏ k. Takes care of quality control (inspection).

   ❏ l. Assesses and devises ways of producing output (work-study methods, operations study, etc.).

   ❏ m. Devises new outputs, equipment, and processes (design and development).

   ❏ n. Develops and carries out administrative procedures (statistics, information systems, filing, etc.).

   ❏ o. Deals with legal and insurance requirements.

   ❏ p. Acquires information on the market of the firm.

   The greater the number of check marks to the above questions, the more complex is the organization.

2. **Centralization**

   Which level in the organization has the authority to make the following decisions? Record a score of:

   5   if the decision is made by employees at the operating or shop level
   4   if the decision is made by a first-level supervisor
   3   if the decision is made by a subdepartment head
   2   if the decision is made by a divisional or functional manager
   1   if the decision is made by the chief executive
   0   if the decision is made by the board of directors or owner

a.	The number of workers required	0	1	2	3	4	5
b.	Whether to employ a worker	0	1	2	3	4	5
c.	Internal labour disputes	0	1	2	3	4	5
d.	Overtime to be worked at the shop level	0	1	2	3	4	5
e.	Delivery dates and and priority of orders	0	1	2	3	4	5
f.	Production plans	0	1	2	3	4	5
g.	Dismissal of a worker	0	1	2	3	4	5
h.	Methods of personnel selection	0	1	2	3	4	5
i.	Method of work to be used	0	1	2	3	4	5
j.	Machinery or equipment to be used	0	1	2	3	4	5
k.	Allocation of work among employees	0	1	2	3	4	5

Add up the points. The higher the number the higher is the organization's decentralization.

3. ***Formalization***

Check which of the following applies to the documents used in the organization.

a. Written contract of employment? ☐ Yes ☐ No

b. Information booklets treating, for example, security, working conditions, etc. are given to:

☐ 0 No one

☐ 1 Only a few persons

☐ 2 Many

☐ 3 All

c. An organization chart is given to:

☐ 1 The chief executive only

☐ 2 A few top executives only

☐ 3 The chief executive and most managers

☐ 4 All managers and supervisors

d. Written job descriptions are available for:

☐ Yes ☐ No Direct production workers

☐ Yes ☐ No Clerical workers

☐ Yes ☐ No Supervisors

☐ Yes ☐ No Specialists

☐ Yes ☐ No Chief executive

e.g. In this organization, is there:

☐ Yes ☐ No A written business policy?

☐ Yes ☐ No A written manual of procedures and rules?

☐ Yes ☐ No Written operating instructions for employees?

Score 1 point for each YES answer, then add up the total points. The higher the number the higher is the organization's formalization.

Bring your results to class for discussion and comparison with others.

Source: Adapted from Danny Miller and Cornelia Droge (1986), "Psychological and traditional determinants of structure," *Administrative Science Quarterly* 31: 558-559, who in turn adapted the scales from J.H. Kerr Inkson, Derek S. Pugh, and David J. Hickson (1970), "Organizational context and structure: An abbreviated replication," *Administrative Science Quarterly* 15: 327-329. Reprinted/adapted with permission.

SELF-GUIDED LEARNING ACTIVITY

Individual Task

Go to your college or university library and read the article titled "Toward a model of organizations as interpretation systems" by Richard L. Daft and Karl E. Weick. It can be found in the *Academy of Management Review*, 1984, Volume 9, pages 284-295. Then find an organizational example for each strategic type and relationship with the environment. Choose one of these companies for an interview, call the company on the telephone, and ask the general manager for a half-hour appointment to discuss the organization. At the interview, ask about the organization's strategy and how people in the organization interact with the environment. The manager being interviewed will likely be interested in seeing Daft and Weick's model and discussing how the organization fits or does not fit into one of the four cells.

Group Task

Choose a Canadian organization and analyze it according to the factors described in this chapter. In your group's view, at what stage of growth would you determine this organization to be? On what do you base this conclusion? In your group's view, is this organization appropriately structured for the future?

MANAGER'S CASE FILE: PASSING THE TORCH

Sonny Messini was the supervisor of the electronics division of Gilman Industries and was responsible for consolidating the budgets for his department. This year's budgets were proving to be no less difficult than last year's, and with all the interruptions, Sonny was unable to make much headway with the figures. He called Hector Cruz, his senior engineer, into his office to ask for his help.

"Hector," Sonny said, "I'm not getting these budgets done with all the interruptions—phone calls, visitors, problems, questions. You're my senior staffer, and you know this business backwards and forwards. Do you think that you would be able to handle the administrative duties for me until I can finish this project? I should be finished by Monday, so you only would have to take over for a few days or so."

"You mean you want me to make decisions?" Hector asked, wanting to be sure he understood what was being asked of him.

"Well, don't give away the company, but I think you can handle anything that comes up," Sonny said with confidence. "Just keep people away from my door until I'm finished."

"Okay," Hector said. "You can count on me."

"Great," Sonny said as he closed his door and went to work.

For the rest of the week Hector answered questions, handled problems, made decisions, and posted a "do not disturb" sign on Sonny's door. All in all, he felt very good about the way he took control of the business. He was satisfied that the work was going smoothly, no complaint had gone unresolved, and no major problems had occurred. He even typed up a report of activities to bring Sonny up to date on the happenings during his seclusion.

On Monday, when Sonny had finished his work and handed it to his boss, he checked Hector's report and gasped.

"You hired someone for the position of engineer without checking with me first?" Sonny asked.

"You said I was in charge," Hector said. "We had management's approval for the hire and I didn't want to let the work pile up. I interviewed the applicants who were sent by personnel, called back two of them after checking their references, and made a decision. I think you'll be pleased with her. She comes highly recommended."

"But I have two people coming in later this week I promised to interview," Sonny lamented.

"You didn't tell me that," Hector said. "You said I was to make decisions so I did. I questioned you about that before I agreed to take over for you."

"I didn't think that you'd take on so much responsibility," Sonny said. He got even more excited when he discovered that Hector had authorized some overtime.

"We had a job that had to go out on time. Before I hired the new person, we just couldn't keep up with the orders, so I asked four people to work late a few nights. It cost a few dollars, but we got the order out on time and the customer was satisfied," Hector explained.

"And nobody questioned you?" Sonny asked.

"I told everybody that I had your permission so nobody questioned me."

"You should have checked with me before you did any of these things," Sonny said.

"If you had wanted me to check with you, you should have told me so," Hector countered.

Questions

1. Should Hector have made such important decisions?

2. How could the situation have been avoided?

3. What should Sonny do to avoid these problems in the future?

CHEMCO INTERNATIONAL INC.

As the New York commuter flight halted at Toronto's International Airport, Alan Richardson, President of Chemco Inc. closed his briefcase and fished his sportsbag containing the week's laundry from under his seat. Chemco's Vice-President, Bill Ross, mechanically repeated the exercise. For the past year Richardson and Ross had shared the company's New York apartment as they put in 15-hour days managing Mundt Inc., an American company acquired by Chemco a year previously. Most weekends the two men caught a Friday evening flight home to Toronto. Over the past year flights to Mundt's European operation in Brussels, as well as to its joint ventures in South America and the Far East, had become routine. Richardson broke the tired silence. "See you tomorrow Bill, among all of us we ought to work out something to get us off this grindstone." Richardson would spend Saturday discussing restructuring alternatives in the executive committee meeting at Chemco's Toronto head office and on Sunday evening catch a flight back to New York.

Chemco was founded in 1927 as Ontario Chemical Company, an amalgamation of several small firms supplying industrial chemicals to the agricultural, mining, and pulp and paper industries. Originally the firm was highly centralized, with all orders coming down from the President. The Selling Department had sold mostly to wholesalers. In the 1950s the sales department had been enlarged and organized into product divisions.

In 1972 Chemco gradually began decentralizing management into four product divisions based on its major product lines—pulp and paper chemicals, agricultural products, mining explosives and consumer products, a branded line of chemicals for swimming pools and water purification (see Exhibit 2.5). At the same time the corporate name was shortened to Chemco Inc. to reflect its sales to industrial and consumer clients across Canada. The divisionalized structure allowed senior executives time to examine long range plans, freeing them from being constantly con-

cerned with day-to-day operating decisions. Each of the divisions was responsible for its own accounting, marketing, and human resource functions. All divisions operated out of the company's Toronto headquarters. Until the acquisition of Mundt Inc., the senior vice-presidents had been in day-to-day contact with the divisional vice-presidents.

The firm's three primary manufacturing plants producing basic material were located in Welland, Cornwall, and Montreal. Because the products of the four divisions required similar raw materials, and the waste products of one process could sometimes be used in other processes, an MIS[1] system kept track of each division's costs. The secondary manufacturing plants in Toronto, Montreal, and Hamilton also served more than one product division.

A subsidiary, Polymir, acquired in 1979, producing polyethylene resins with moulding applications for insulating wire and cable, was still managed by Paul Balardo, its entrepreneurial founder. Balardo successfully resisted any attempt to apply Chemco's MIS system to his operation. He reported directly to Richardson and in the past year had operated virtually independently. In view of Balardo's record-keeping, Chemco could not easily determine whether this operation was profitable or not.

The industrial chemical industry in Canada stagnated in the recession of the early 1980s. Chemco continued to increase its sales by gaining market share from several Canadian competitors who failed in the face of tough financial markets. Chemco executives felt this growth would soon reach its limits. The executives could not accept this prospect of stagnation and began looking for acquisitions outside Canada in order to sustain growth.

In early 1986 it was known through the industry grapevine that Mundt Inc., New York, a firm which seemed to fit Chemco's shopping list of a firm half its size in the industrial chemical industry, was near bankruptcy. Potential U.S. purchasers, waiting for Mundt to go bankrupt before they moved in on the

---

[1] MIS stands for Management Information System—a system for gathering information about the organization's operations and making that information available as input into decisions.

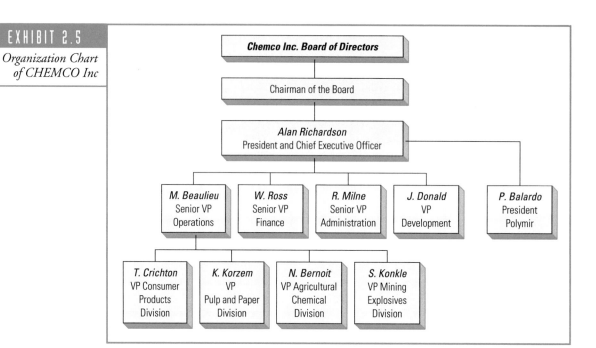

EXHIBIT 2.5

Organization Chart of CHEMCO Inc

assets, were caught off guard when the Canadian un-known, Chemco, announced it had acquired Mundt. Chemco's Senior Vice-President Bill Ross was able to get Mundt as a going concern by promising its debtors it would continue debt payments, thus in fact acquiring the company for its long term debt.

While a public company, the shares of Mundt Inc. were closely held by two Mundt brothers, Jerry and Larry, and their cousins Shelly Mundt and Scott Merzon. The cousins had formed the company in 1949 to manufacture chemicals for the leather and textile industries. The manufacturing plants in Newark, New Jersey, Fall River, Massachusetts, and Providence, Rhode Island were now old and inefficient. The family preferred to live well rather than keep the plants up to date. Jerry Mundt also had developed a European business with headquarters in Brussels which marketed American-produced, patented industrial chemical products for which the demand was too small to justify European plants. This moderately profitable business was operated as an International Division from New York. Jerry Mundt also set up joint ventures manufacturing leather and textile chemicals, based on friendships made in the industry, with partners in Hong Kong, Mexico City, Rio de Janeiro, Barcelona, Cape Town, Milan, and Paris.

In 1982 Mundt Inc. financed, through short-term bank loans, the acquisition of Hammond Chemicals Co. Ltd., a company with a modern profitable plant in Syracuse, New York, producing polyethylene resins for insulating cable wire. Ed Dunlop, Hammond's President, reported directly to Jerry Mundt. While Hammond was the most profitable part of Mundt, the debt charges on the bank loans had brought Mundt virtually to bankruptcy before its acquisition.

Executive positions at Mundt Inc. were filled by the family: Jerry Mundt was President; brother Larry, Vice-President; cousin Shelly Mundt, Vice-President, Sales; and cousin Scott Merzon, Vice-President, Finance. Scott's wife Edie, the sister of the Mundt brothers, was company Secretary (see Exhibit 2.6). Overhead at head office was unusually high. Among the employees on staff was the family's golf pro. The Mundt Inc. Lear jet was used to shuttle family members between homes on Long Island and Florida.

Chemco assumed on taking over Mundt that the senior executives would continue to work for them, at least during the transition period, to help them understand the personal arrangements on which much of the company's business was based. Instead, all the family members immediately resigned, along with

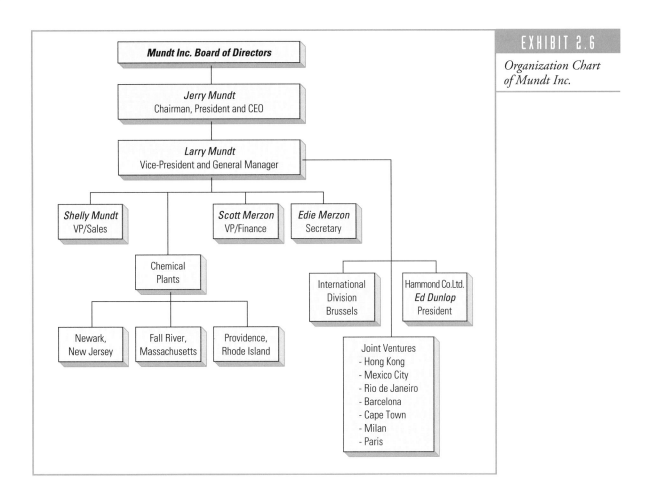

EXHIBIT 2.6

*Organization Chart
of Mundt Inc.*

their golf pro, leaving no one with inside information in the company. All management functions had to be taken over by Canadian executives from the Toronto head office. Fortunately the Canadian firm's divisionalized structure allowed it to send top men down to New York to manage Mundt without seriously damaging the Canadian operations, at least in the short run.

For the first six months the Canadian managers, operating from Mundt's New York offices, managed crisis by crisis keeping the three parts of the company afloat. Now, by the end of the second six months Mundt is no longer in critical condition. Hammond Co. Ltd., under its own President, Ed Dunlop, continues to perform well. The European marketing business held steady, but the basic business of leather and textile chemicals continues to lose money. Shortly after the acquisition the New Jersey plant was ordered closed

by the U.S. government because it exceeded pollution standards. Establishing a working relationship with the seven joint ventures proved difficult because the agreements hinged on personal deals made by Jerry Mundt. The problems in dealing with different national business cultures had strained the adaptability of the Toronto executives.

Now, a year later, the initial shock caused by the acquisition has been overcome. It is time for Chemco to adjust its structure to include the enlarged international operations. Until now Canadian managers have been used as expatriate managers, but the company hopes to develop local managers in the countries where new operations are located.

The Canadian executives are uncertain whether or not to have all operations directed from the Toronto headquarters or locally, and how best to manage the joint ventures. The Canadian executives know that in the U.S., firms with international operations are usually handled by an International Division administered by the U.S. parent at head office. Yet already the international operations comprise 40% of the firm's sales. Hammond Co. Ltd. and the Brussels sales operation are growing faster than the Canadian business.

The executives wonder whether they can respond to different national conditions from their Toronto headquarters. The situation cannot remain the way it is much longer because the New York office is taking the full attention of several key Canadian executives whose talents are needed in Toronto. The subsidiary Polymir, under Paul Balardo, needs close attention. The change in capital markets in the mid-1980s means the company can consider building a new plant and perhaps reorganize its manufacturing facilities. Richardson hopes that the meeting of the senior vice-presidents tomorrow will generate possible ways of restructuring Chemco to reflect the international operation it has become.

SOURCE: Used with permission of Dr. Barbara J. Austin of Brock University, St. Catharines, Ontario. This case was prepared as a basis for class discussion rather than to illustrate either effective or ineffective handling of an administrative situation. Copyright ©1987 by Professor B.J. Austin.

Questions

1. How should Chemco be restructured? How will Polymir, Hammond Co., Chemco's four divisions, Mundt's three chemical plants, international division, and joint ventures be integrated?

2. What should be done about Polymir's refusal to provide data for the company-wide MIS system on costs?

3. Where should the parent company be located? Should Mundt Inc. become the parent and Chemco the Canadian subsidiary?

4. How should Mundt's joint ventures around the world be managed?

5. Describe Chemco and Mundt's current type of departmentation and the departmentation once restructured.

REFERENCES

Blau, Peter. (1956). *Bureaucracy in Modern Society.* New York: Random House.

Burns, Tom & George M. Stalker (1961). *The Management of Innovation.* London: Tavistock Publications, Ltd.

Carney, Mick. (1991) "Book review of Porter: The Competitive Advantage of Nations." *Canadian Journal of Administrative Sciences* 8: 288-293.

Cascio, Wayne F. (1993). "Downsizing: what do we know? What have we learned?" *Academy of Management Executive* 7(1): 95-104.

Daft, Richard L., & Richard M. Steers (1986). *Organizations: A Micro/macro Approach.* 2nd edition. Glenview, Illinois: Scott-Foresman & Co.

Daft, Richard L., & Karl E. Weick (1984). "Toward a model of organizations as interpretation systems." *Academy of Management Review* 9: 284-295.

Davis, Stanley M., & Paul R. Lawrence. (1977). *Matrix. Reading.* Massachusetts: Addison-Wesley.

de Forest, Mariah E. (1994). "Thinking of a plant in Mexico?" *Academy of Management Executive* 8(1): 33-40.

Executive Epigrams. (1981). *International Management* 36(1): 6.

Galaskiewicz, Joseph, & Stanley Wasserman (1989). "Mimetic and normative processes within an interorganizational field: An empirical test." *Administrative Science Quarterly* 34: 454-479.

Greenwood, Royston, & C.R. (Bob) Hinings (1993). "Understanding strategic change: The contribution of archetypes." *Academy of Management Journal* 36: 1052-1081.

Inkson, J.H. Kerr, Derek S. Pugh, & David J. Hickson (1970). "Organizational context and structure: An abbreviated replication." *Administrative Science Quarterly* 15: 318-329.

Knights, David (1992). "Changing spaces: The disruptive impact of a new epistemological location for the study of management." *Academy of Management Review* 17: 514-536.

Lawrence, Paul R., & Jay W. Lorsch (1969). *Organization and Environment: Managing Differentiation and Integration.* Homewood, IL: Richard D. Irwin.

Meyer, John W., & Brian Rowan (1977). "Institutionalized organizations: Formal structure as myth and ceremony." *American Journal of Sociology* 83: 340-363.

Miles, Raymond E. & Charles C. Snow. (1978). *Organizational Strategy, Structure, and Process.* New York: McGraw-Hill.

Miles, Raymond E., Charles C. Snow, Alan D. Meyer, & Henry J. Coleman, Jr. (1978). "Organizational strategy, structure, and process." *Academy of Management Review* 3: 546-562.

Miller, Danny. (1988). "Relating Porter's business strategies to environment and structure: Analysis and performance implications." *Academy of Management Journal* 31: 280-308.

Miller, Danny & Cornelia Droge (1986). "Psychological and traditional determinants of structure." *Administrative Science Quarterly* 31: 539-560.

Mintzberg, Henry. (1979). *The Structuring of Organizations: A Synthesis of the Research.* Englewood Cliffs, NJ: Prentice Hall, Inc.

Mintzberg, Henry. (1983). *Structure in Fives: Designing Effective Organizations.* Englewood Cliffs, NJ: Prentice Hall, Inc.

Popovich, Paula M., Karen R. Hyde, Todd Zakrajsek, & Catherine Blumer. (1987). "The development of the attitudes toward computer usage scale." *Educational & Psychological Measurement* 47: 261-269.

Porter, Michael E. (1980). *Competitive Strategy.* New York: The Free Press.

Porter, Michael E. (1985). *Competitive Advantage.* New York: The Free Press.

Porter, Michael E. (1990). *The Competitive Advantage of Nations.* New York: The Free Press.

Porter, Michael E. (1990). "The competitive advantage of nations." *Harvard Business Review,* March/April 1990, pp. 73-93.

Pugh, Derek S., David J. Hickson, C.R. (Bob) Hinings, & Christopher Turner (1969). "The context of organization structures." *Administrative Science Quarterly* 14: 91-114.

Robey, Daniel. (1991). *Designing Organizations.* 3rd edition. Homewood, Illinois: Irwin.

Taylor, William (1993). "Message and muscle: An interview with Swatch titan Nicolas Hayek." *Harvard Business Review,* March/April 1993, pp. 99-110.

Thompson, James D. (1967). *Organizations in Action.* New York: McGraw-Hill.

Van de Ven, Andrew H., Andre L. Delbecq, & Richard Koenig, Jr. (1976). "Determinants of coordination modes within organizations." *American Sociological Review* 41: 322-338.

Weber, Max (1947). *The Theory of Social and Economic Organization.* Translated and edited by A.M. Henderson and Talcott Parsons. Glencoe, Ill.: Free Press.

Woodward, Joan (1965). *Industrial Organisation: Theory and Practice.* London: Oxford University Press.

FURTHER READING

A classic and interesting book about the contingent fit between the organization and its environment is by Alvin Gouldner (1954), titled *Patterns of Industrial Bureaucracy,* Glencoe, Illinois: The Free Press.

Management Laureates: A Collection of Autobiographical Essays, edited by Arthur Bedeian and published in 1992/93 by JAI Press, is a book full of fascinating chapters written by management scholars about themselves. Henry Mintzberg's chapter is titled "The illusive strategy ... 25 years later."

An area of organizational thought that critiques many of the assumptions people have about organizations is Critical Theory. For an introduction, see the article by Robert Cooper and Gibson Burrell (1988), titled "Modernism, postmodernism, and organizational analysis," to be found in *Organization Studies* 9: 91-112. A related article that uses four different theoretical approaches of understanding organizations is by John Hassard (1991), titled "Multiple paradigms and organizational analysis: A case study". This paper analyzes the operation of a British fire department, and is found in *Organization Studies,* Volume 12, pages 275-299.

A very good read with respect to mechanistic organizations and all their problems is a book entitled *Rude Awakening: The Rise, Fall, and Struggle for Recovery of General Motors,* by Maryann Keller (New York: HarperCollins, 1990). It reads like a novel and illustrates all of the dysfunctions of mechanistic organizations and highly institutionalized and isolated cultures.

Measures of organic and mechanistic structures are to be found in Christopher Gresov (1989), "Exploring fit and misfit with multiple contingencies," *Administrative Science Quarterly* 34: 431-453; and in Alberto Zanzi (1987), "How organic is your organization? — Determinants of organic/mechanistic tendencies in a public accounting firm," *Journal of Management Studies* 24: 125-142.

For a measure of the Miles and Snow typology of organizational strategies (reactor, defender, analyzer, and prospector), see Jeffrey S. Conant, Michael P. Mokwa, P. Rajan Varadarajan (1990), "Strategic types, distinctive marketing competencies and organizational performance: A multiple measures-based study," *Strategic Management Journal* 11: 365-383. A test that found businesses could successfully use a combination of strategies is that of John A. Parnell and Peter Wright (1993), "Generic strategy and performance: an empirical test of the Miles and Snow typology," *British Journal of Management* 4: 29-36.

Well worth reading is a fantastic article in the January-February 1994 *Harvard Business Review* by Ricardo Semler, majority owner of a Brazilian manufacturing company, Semco S/A. He describes a radically new organizational form and way of functioning that is different from mechanistic, organic, and everything in-between. For example, read the first paragraph of his article. "I own a manufacturing company in Brazil called Semco, about which I can report the following curious fact: no one in the company really knows how many people we employ. When we walk through our manufacturing plants, we rarely even know who works for us. Some of the people in the factory are full-time Semco employees; some work for us part-time; some work for themselves and supply Semco with components or services; some work for themselves under contract to outside companies (even Semco's competitors); and some of them work for each other." (p. 64). The article is titled "Why my former employees still work for me" and is on pages 64 to 74.

CHAPTER 3

ORGANIZATIONAL CULTURE AND SOCIALIZATION

CHAPTER OUTLINE

Societal Culture

    Cultural Dimensions and Clusters

    Work Cultures By Country

Organizational Culture

    Creating an Organizational Culture

    Manifestations of Culture

    Culture Profiles

    Subcultures

    Merging of Two Cultures

    Culture Strength

    Culture of Multinational Corporations

Organizational Socialization

    Socialization Phases

    Socialization Strategies

Conclusion

QUESTIONS TO CONSIDER

- *What is culture?*

- *What influence does the culture of a society have on organizational cultures in that society?*

- *How is one organization's culture different from that of others?*

- *How is culture created, and measured, and what are its functions and problems?*

- *From an organization's point of view, how are people hired into the organization and how do they fit in?*

Organizations are part of their environments. The culture of the society that surrounds an institution will affect in very basic ways how the members of the organization live and work. Societal culture affects how people in the organization see their relationship to the environment; how they perceive reality, time, and space; and the assumptions they make about the essence of human nature, activity, and relationships. We cannot understand how individuals conduct themselves at work without comprehending the culture they are from and the cultural environment in which the organization is embedded.

Culture can now be defined as (a) a pattern of basic assumptions, (b) invented, discovered, or developed by a given group, (c) as it learns to cope with its problems of external adaptation and internal integration, (d) that has worked well enough to be considered valid and therefore (e) is to be taught to new members as the (f) correct way to perceive, think, and feel in relation to those problems. (Schein, 1990, p. 111).

Societal culture and corporate culture are different (Hofstede, 1993). Corporate culture may be created or managed. A single corporate culture may be created for all employees even though they, as individuals, have different national cultures.

A basic definition of organizational culture is that it is a summary of the beliefs and values of the members of an organization and the observable objects with which they surround themselves. This conception of organizational culture includes the meanings that these people assign to events and to their life in the organization. Culture affects how they talk about the organization, act within it and feel about it, and the physical items they share. Just as we each have an individual identity that summarizes how we feel, think, and act, so organizational culture encapsulates an organization's identity.

An organization's culture is created as its members develop a strategy, a structure, and a consensus on how to deal with their common problem of how to adapt to the external environment while being internally integrated.

Within the organization, the basic assumptions/beliefs of its members are taken for granted. They are invisible to organization members because they exist below the level of consciousness. These basic assumptions about the world and how it works form the base from which the organization's members build their values of how the world *should* be. Assumptions and values then influence the behaviours of company members and the physical things with which they surround themselves.

These three levels of culture (assumptions, values, and artifacts/behaviours: from Schein, 1992) are shown in Exhibit 3.1 as an iceberg of which only the tip is visible — here artifacts and creations. Values and assumptions are not exposed. The outside observer can easily see a company's building, its offices, pictures hung on its walls, and how its members act. These are part of the organization's culture but are not the whole story. Less easy to see are the values that underlie these things and behaviours. Values might be discovered by talking to company members. Assumptions are even harder to view. An organizational outsider may, by being objective, be able to determine the assumptions made by members. Those inside the organization hold the assumptions and are less able to see them.

All people are affected by the culture of their society. Even a hermit living on top of a mountain is defined by his distance from the society he has left. We will now examine the basic assumptions learned by people in societies. Then we will return to a more detailed examination of organizational culture.

Culture A pattern of basic assumptions, invented, discovered, or developed by a given group as it learns to cope with its problems of external adaptation and internal integration, that has worked well enough to be considered valid and, therefore is to be taught to new members as the correct way to perceive, think, and feel in relation to those problems.

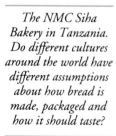

The NMC Siha Bakery in Tanzania. Do different cultures around the world have different assumptions about how bread is made, packaged and how it should taste?

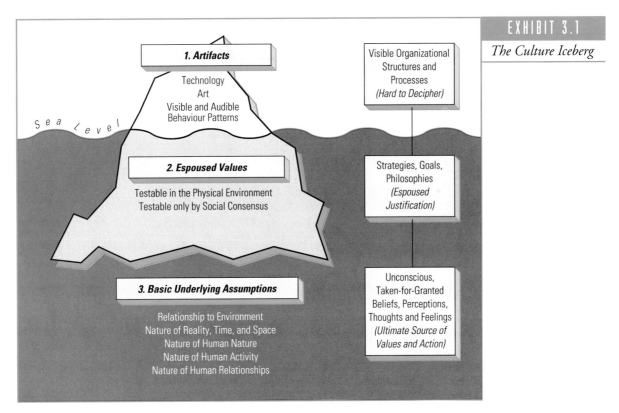

SOURCE: From Edgar H. Schein (1992), Organizational Culture and Leadership, Second edition. San Francisco: Jossey-Bass Inc., p. 17. Adapted with permission.

SOCIETAL CULTURE

People, in the course of living, confront five basic questions about their lives (Adler, 1991). These questions are:

1. How do I see the world?
2. How do I use time and space?
3. Who am I?
4. What do I do? and
5. How do I relate to other people?[1]

Answers to these questions vary among societies, and in a broad sense determine how people in a given society experience life. Though disparate cultures determine different answers to these five questions, there are commonalities shared by all cultures. A set of cultural universals is shown in Exhibit 3.2.

How Do I See the World?   This question deals with the person's relationship to the environment. Reflecting even more basic assumptions about the relationship of humanity to nature, one can assess whether people view the relationship as one of dominance, submission, harmony, or finding an appropriate niche. For example, in Canada and the United

EXHIBIT 3.2   CULTURAL UNIVERSALS

age grading	etiquette	joking	population policy
athletic sports	faith healing	kin groups	postnatal care
bodily adornment	family	kinship nomenclature	property rights
calendar	feasting	language	propitiation of super-
cleanliness training	fire making	law	natural beings
community organiza- tion	folklore	luck superstitions	puberty customs
	food taboos	magic	religious ritual
cooking	funeral rites	marriage	residence rules
cooperative labor	games	mealtimes	sexual restrictions
cosmology	gestures	medicine	soul concepts
courtship	gift giving	modesty concerning	status differentiation
dancing	government	natural functions	surgery
decorative art	greetings	mourning	tool making
divination	hair styles	music	trade
division of labor	hospitality	mythology	visiting
dream interpretation	housing	numerals	weaning
education	hygiene	obstetrics	weather control
ethics	incest taboos	penal sanctions	
ethnobotany	inheritance rules	personal names	

SOURCE: Excerpted from George P. Murdock (1945), "The common denominator of cultures," in *The Science of Man in the World Crisis*, Ralph Linton editor, New York: Columbia University Press, p. 124.

NOTE: On commonalities in cross-cultural values, see Shalom Schwartz (1992), "Universals in the content and structure of values: Theoretical advances and empirical tests in 20 countries." In Mark Zanna (Ed.), *Advances in Experimental Social Psychology* (pp. 1-65), New York: Academic Press.

States the dominant culture has seen the natural environment as something to conquer and exploit. This outlook is beginning to change, however, as exemplified by the "Green" movement. North American Indigenous peoples have traditionally viewed nature as something humans have to live with in harmony.

How Do I Use Time and Space?   The focus here is on the nature of reality, time, and space. Here are the linguistic and behavioural rules that define what is real and what is not, what is a "fact," how truth is ultimately to be determined, and whether truth is revealed or discovered; basic concepts of time as linear or cyclical, space as limited or infinite, and property as communal or individual.

---

[1] Question descriptions are from Edgar H. Schein (1983), "The role of the founder in creating organizational culture." Adapted/excerpted and reprinted, by permission of publisher, from ORGANIZATIONAL DYNAMICS, Summer 1983. © 1983 American Management Association, New York. All rights reserved. More complete descriptions of these basic cultural questions are provided in Schein (1992).

Time is typically experienced in Western societies as linear. The past, present, and future are assumed to be all on one time line. People are seen as moving in one direction along that line, from the past through the present to the future. People in Western societies measure time with great precision. It is counted, and valued as a resource. People say "Time is money" or "I don't want to waste my time" because they believe that once past, the present time is gone forever.

Other societies and cultures experience time differently. The present may be thought of as just the current one of many cycles or loops of time. Time repeats in a series of endless cycles. Therefore, what one does this minute, today, or tomorrow is not seen as having great urgency.

Concepts of space also differ by culture. Many people in Canada "own" their home and land. They have a sense that the land and buildings belong to them for their own personal use. In other cultures this concept makes no sense. The Australian aboriginal believes that the land cannot be owned; it is for all to live with.

What a house looks like and how people live in it also differ by culture. This is important because house design and living space affect how people see themselves and think about themselves. This chapter's *A Rose by any other Name* feature describes the traditional Japanese house and its effects on the occupants.

A ROSE BY ANY OTHER NAME

The following excerpt is from the book Pictures from the Water Trade: An Englishman in Japan *by John David Morley. In it he speaks of how the structure of the traditional Japanese house affects how its members experience their world and learn to think about insiders and outsiders.*

The most striking feature of the Japanese house was the lack of privacy; the lack of individual, inviolable space. In winter, when the *fusuma* [movable screens] were kept closed, any sound above a whisper was clearly audible on the other side, and of course in summer they were usually removed altogether. It is impossible to live under such conditions for very long without a common household identity emerging which naturally takes precedence over individual wishes. This enforced family unity was still held up to Boon [the Englishman in Japan] as an ideal, but in practice it was ambivalent, as much a yoke as a bond. There was no such thing as the individual's private room, no bedroom, dining- or sitting-room as such, since in the traditional Japanese house there was no furniture determining that a room should be reserved for any particular function. A person slept in a room, for example, without thinking of it as a bedroom or as his room. In the morning his bedding would be rolled up and stored away in a cupboard; a small table known as the *kotatsu*, which could also be plugged into the mains to provide heating, was moved back into the centre of the room and here the family ate, drank, worked and relaxed for the rest of the day. Although it was becoming stan-

dard practice in modern Japan for children to have their own rooms, many middle-aged and nearly all older Japanese still lived in this way. They regarded themselves as "one flesh," their property as common to all; the *uchi* (household, home) was constituted according to a principle of indivisibility. The system of moveable screens meant that the rooms could be used by all the family and for all purposes: walls were built round the *uchi*, not inside it.

Boon later discovered analogies between this concept of house and the Japanese concept of self. The Japanese carried his house around in his mouth and produced it in everyday conversation, using the word uchi, to mean "I," the representative of my house in the world outside. The common Japanese term for outsider was tanin (literally, another person) or occasionally yoso no hito/mono (person from another place). The neutral meaning, therefore, corresponded to the English word "stranger," a person of different blood or who comes from different parts, but the unmistakable hostility with which the use of tanin was infused in the Japanese language made the factual description (stranger) indistinguishable from the moral judgement (outsider). He was the person outside the uchi (loosely, household), a social unit originally constituted by relationships of blood or a common locality, but also covering any group of persons brought together physically and spiritually in a common cause, typically their work. All Japanese were members of various uchi, ranging from their own immediate family to the firm in which they were employed. In very simple terms, members of one's own uchi were familiar, trustworthy and above question; inversely, those who did not belong to the same uchi were unfamiliar, their trust untried, and therefore faintly suspect. In short, it was not the outsider as a possible Tokugawa spy who was suspect; it was the outsider per se. This seam of thought ran through the entire structure of Japanese society.

SOURCE: Excerpted with permission of the publisher from John David Morley (1985), *Pictures from the Water Trade: An Englishman in Japan.* London: André Deutsch Limited, pp. 37-38, 72.

Who am I?   This fundamental question deals with the nature of human nature. What does it mean to be "human," and what attributes are considered intrinsic or ultimate? Is human nature good, evil, or neutral? Are human beings perfectible or not?

In some cultures life and death are seen as determined and preordained—people are not in control of their own destiny. For example, the caste system in India, although outlawed, ranks members of society, fixes one's destiny, and defines what occupation one must enter.

What Do I Do?   What is the "right" thing for human beings to do, on the basis of the above assumptions about reality, the environment, and human nature? To be active, passive, self-developmental, fatalistic, or what? What is work and what is play? Western culture makes the general assumptions that people should be active, responsible for their own actions, that it is right to work, and that work and play are different. These assumptions are not universally held by other cultures of the world.

How Do I Relate to Other People?   The key here is the nature of human relationships. What is considered to be the "right" way for people to relate to each other, to distribute power and love? Is life cooperative or competitive; individualistic, collaborative, or communal? Is it based on traditional lineal authority, law, or charisma?

Many cultures give status partly as a function of age ("respect your elders") whereas others award status for skills (e.g., a surgeon), actions (e.g., scoring goals in the NHL) or possessions (e.g., the car a person drives). The traditional Haida culture of Northwestern British Columbia awarded status not for the amount of household goods owned but for how much was given away to others at a potlach.

Cultural Dimensions and Clusters

To help us understand how societal cultures differ from one another, we will look at five cultural dimensions identified by Geert Hofstede (1980, 1993). They are:

1. Power distance;
2. Individualism/collectivism;
3. Masculinity/femininity;
4. Uncertainty avoidance; and
5. Long-term versus short-term orientation.

In Hofstede's research countries are represented by their dominant culture. It must be remembered, however, that many countries, including Canada and the United States, are multicultural.

Power Distance

Power distance is the extent to which the less powerful members of society accept that power is distributed unequally and accept the orders of those in power. China would be high in power distance, Canada and the United States, low.

Individualism/Collectivism

In individualistic cultures people tend to look out for themselves and their family, they prefer to act as individuals. In collectivistic cultures people look out for each other, they prefer to act as members of groups. Canada is more individualistic, China and Japan are more collectivistic. However, Canada may be seen as more collectivistic than the United States, as evidenced by Canada's relatively greater emphasis on commonly available medical care and the predominance of public institutions of higher learning (rather than a mix of public and private). Also, Canada has a greater proportion of unionized workers than is the case in the United States and has more government workers when size disparities are taken into account. These both point to a more collectivist orientation in Canada.

Masculinity/Femininity

Masculine cultures value success, money and material possessions, assertiveness and competition. Feminine cultures value caring for others, maintaining warm personal relationships, solidarity with others, and the quality of how life is lived. The United States and Canada are high on masculinity, whereas Iceland is more feminine.

Uncertainty Avoidance

Uncertainty avoidance is the extent to which people in the society want to avoid situations where it is not clear what to do. People in high uncertainty avoidance cultures prefer structured over unstructured situations. Cultures high in uncertainty avoidance tend to have strict laws and punishments and a feeling of "What is different is dangerous." Saudi Arabia and Singapore have high uncertainty avoidance, Canada and the U.S. are moderate, and Denmark is low on this variable.

Long-Term versus Short-Term Orientation

Cultures with a long-term orientation value future-oriented behaviours such as persistence and saving money. Short-term orientation cultures have values oriented more towards the past and the present such as respect for tradition and the fulfilling of social obligations. Japan has been noted to have a long-term outlook. China seems to have more of a short-term orientation.

Groups of countries may be characterized as sharing similar cultural characteristics (Ronen & Shenkar, 1985). Exhibit 3.3 shows eight cultural clusters of countries and four countries that did not fit into one of the cultural groupings. Because organizational cultures are affected by the culture in their environment, the culture of organizations in one country should tend to be similar to the culture of organizations from other countries in the same cluster. Work culture should differ in dissimilar countries.

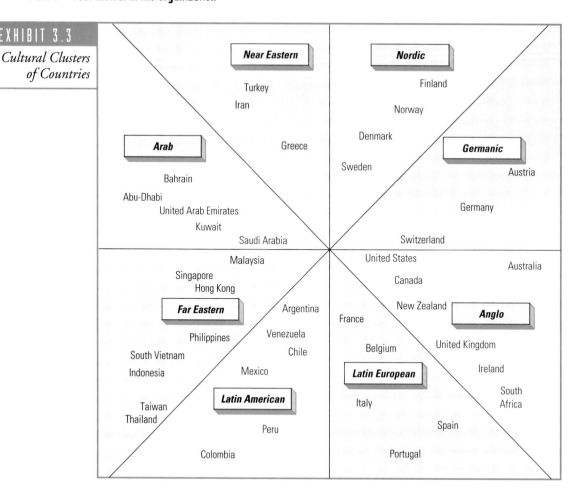

NOTE: A smallest space analysis was used to form the most parsimonious clustering of countries. Four countries which did not fit into the eight clusters noted above are Brazil, Japan, India, and Israel.

SOURCE: Simcha Ronen and Oded Shenkar (1985), "Clustering countries on attitudinal dimensions: A review and synthesis," *Academy of Management Review* 10: 449. Reprinted by permission of the Academy of Management. Also see Simcha Ronen (1986), *Comparative and Multinational Management*. New York: Wiley.

Work Cultures By Country

Societal culture has been used as an explanation of organizational culture and its effects. In the early 1950s Japan was recovering from the effects of World War II, with significant help from the United States and the head of its occupation army, General Douglas MacArthur. Its products exported to North America were typically poorly made and very inexpensive. In the 1960s, when a made-in-Japan six-transistor portable radio appeared on the market, it was a revelation to North Americans that a radio could be made that small. In the 1970s the turnaround was complete. Japanese products came to be recognized as being of the highest quality.

Many business analysts attempted to understand this dramatic change. Bill Ouchi examined the American and Japanese societal cultures as a basis for understanding organizations within those cultures (Ouchi & Jaeger, 1978; Ouchi, 1981). His purpose was to understand how Japanese quality had become so high. Ouchi created three categories: the Type A, Type J, and Type Z organization.

EXPERIENCE IS THE BEST TEACHER

The last few decades have made it eminently clear that organizations will increasingly have to operate in an unpredictable, global, and complex environment. As we try to analyze what this will mean for organizations, we come to realize increasingly how important the human factor will be in the capacity of organizations to survive, adapt, and innovate. We are finally discovering that organizations are indeed made up of people who work together in groups and who

in that process create cultures. It is only as we begin to take cultural behaviour, group, and individual behaviour more seriously that we will have a chance to better understand how to live in organizations and how to make them more effective.

Edgar Schein is a Professor of Management at the Massachusetts Institute of Technology.

The **Type A** (American) **organization** was characterized as having short-term employment; individual decision making; individual responsibility; rapid evaluation and promotion; explicit, formalized control; a specialized career path; and concern for the worker doing the job (Ouchi & Jaeger, 1978).

The **Type J** (Japanese) **organization** had lifetime employment; a long-term business plan; consensual decision making; collective responsibility; slow evaluation and promotion; implicit informal control; a nonspecialized career path; and holistic concern for the worker's job and life situation.

The **Type Z** (Modified American) **organization** was proposed as a blend of Types A and J in order to meet the Japanese on quality and price. This organization type would have: long-term employment; consensual decision making; individual responsibility; slow evaluation and promotion; implicit informal control with explicit formal measures; a moderately specialized career path; and holistic concern for the worker's job and family.

The Type Z organization can be thought of as a cultural model that North American organizations could use, along with structure and strategy, to create an organizational identity that might be effective in a given environmental context. It is an ideal type that managers could use as a model when creating or developing an organization's culture. A summary of Types A, J, Z and other organizational forms is shown in Exhibit 3.4.

Type A Organization
Typical American organization.

Type J Organization
Typical Japanese organization.

Type Z Organization
Modified American organization proposed as a blend of Types A and J.

ORGANIZATIONAL CULTURE

Organizational cultures vary, and can have important effects on their members. These effects can include job satisfaction and tenure. In one study of entry-level auditors (Chatman, 1991), recruits whose values most closely matched those of the firm reported feeling most satisfied and intended to remain with their firm for a longer period of time. In another study of 904 tax and audit entry level accounting professionals (Sheridan, 1992), there were two main findings. The first was that cultural values did vary across six public accounting firms in the same city. The second was that the people hired by firms that had stronger interpersonal relationship values stayed with the firms 14 months longer on average than the people hired by firms emphasizing work task values.

EXHIBIT 3.4 STYLIZED ORGANIZATIONAL FORMS

ORGANIZATIONAL FORMS	CHARACTERISTICS
Japanese-style (Type J)	High recruitment selectivity Intensive socialization by management Long-term employment High growth rate
American manufacturing (Type A)	Low recruitment selectivity Weak socialization by management High turnover High growth rate
Governmental-bureaucratic	Moderate recruitment selectivity Weak socialization by management Low turnover Low growth rate
Professional	Very high recruitment selectivity Weak socialization by management Moderate turnover Low growth rate
Entrepreneurial	Moderate recruitment selectivity Moderate socialization by management Moderate turnover Very high growth rate
Z-type	Moderate recruitment selectivity Moderate socialization by management Low turnover High growth rate
Collectivist-democratic	High recruitment selectivity Intensive socialization by coworkers Low turnover No growth

SOURCE: Adapted/reprinted from J. Richard Harrison and Glenn R. Carroll (1991), "Keeping the faith: A model of cultural transmission in formal organizations," *Administrative Science Quarterly* 36: 564.

NOTE: There is some evidence that the foundations of the Type J form in Japan is crumbling. See Kilburn (1994).

Creating an Organizational Culture

Founders and leaders of organizations can develop an organization's culture. Evidence of how this was done in 50 Australian business and government organizations is presented in this chapter's *A Little Knowledge* feature. However, not all organizational scholars believe that culture can be created. This chapter's *On the One Hand* feature describes two points of view on this issue.

To develop organizational culture (Gross & Shichman, 1987) leaders need to:

- Develop a sense of the history of the organization;
- Create a sense of oneness among organizational members;
- Promote a sense of membership in the organization; and
- Increase exchange among members.

A LITTLE KNOWLEDGE

The infusion of meaning into an organization and the management of the organization's identity is a prime concern of the top officer of any company. David Limerick of Griffith University in Brisbane and his colleagues looked at the linkages among strategy, structure, and culture in 50 Australian business and government organizations. Here, in his own words, are their findings.

Our study provides abundant data on the continuing and almost obsessive attempts of CEOs to come to grips with and mold the field of meaning within the organization—to manage its culture.

Many of those attempts were related to crises that had demanded not only radical structural change but also massive cultural change for the organization. For most CEOs we interviewed, the strategies and variables they used to manage culture included language and slogans, legends and models, systems and sanctions, as well as self-modeling.

Language and Slogans. The CEOs used a variety of images couched in rich, expressive language to approximate the values they sought. Many of those images recurred a number of times during a CEO's interview. It became clear that the images had assumed the status of slogans and in all probability were used frequently in everyday contact with others in the organization. For example, when Brian Loton, CEO of Australia's largest company, BHP, said "Big is out. Good is in," I noted that he had an almost visceral identification with the phrase. The executives around him, too, nodded intensely.

Legends and Models. Many organizations in the study had key figures in their history who had assumed legendary status and who were held up to others as models for action. The CEOs we interviewed were intimately aware of those legends and eager to tell us about them. A mining company's deeply held values of care for people in the

organization were neatly wrapped up in the following legend told during our interview with its CEO: "There is the story that George Fisher, in the half an hour it took him to get to the gate of his factory from his car, would get to know absolutely everything that was happening simply by talking to various people."

Systems and Sanctions. In our study, organizations that had retained some staff strength at corporate headquarters used such human resources systems as orientation and training programs and performance appraisal to back up their values. Most CEOs, however, ultimately had to back up core values by resorting to the strongest sanctions of all: promoting, demoting or firing.

Self-Modeling. Most of the CEOs preferred not to resort to such sanctions and attempted to use positive modeling whenever possible. Since the systems available to them were so scarce, most of them in the end relied on personal example. They networked extensively within their organizations, asserting their values and attempting to represent core values and meanings personally. One CEO reflected, "The influence of the top person in the organization is quite frightening, really." Yet our data also suggest that this influence is not exerted from an isolated position. Most of the CEOs we spoke to had built around them a tight cohort of senior executives aimed at creating a culture with its own momentum. Ideally it would "get to a point that even if the leader is not there, the culture will go on," as one CEO noted.

The creation and management of organizational culture is therefore a prime concern of the leaders of organizations. But does it matter that these CEOs and their organizations are from Australia? Would a sample of 50 CEOs from Canada or the United States have a wholly different point of view? This is a question that is worth considering.

SOURCE: David C. Limerick (1990), "Managers of meaning: From Bob Geldof's band aid to Australian CEOs," *Organizational Dynamics* 18(4): 22-33. Excerpted and reprinted, by permission of publisher, from ORGANIZATIONAL DYNAMICS, Spring 1990. ©1990 American Management Association, New York. All rights reserved.

The study of organizational culture—the proposition that organizations create myths and legends, engage in rites and rituals, and are governed through shared symbols and customs—is much in vogue. There has been a tendency for some researchers to treat organizational culture as a 'variable' that can be controlled and manipulated like any other organizational variable. Culture *as a whole* cannot be manipulated, turned on and off, although it needs to be recognized that some are in a better position than others to attempt to intentionally influence aspects of it. The tendency to assume otherwise results, at least in part, from the selective way in which the concept of culture has been borrowed from anthropology and sociology. Culture should be regarded as something that an organization 'is', not as something that an organization 'has': it is not an independent variable, nor can it be created, discovered or destroyed by the whims of management.

SOURCE: Excerpted from V. Lynn Meek (1988), "Organizational culture: Origins and weaknesses," *Organization Studies* 9: 453-473.

One can observe leaders doing a number of different things, usually in combination, to produce the desired cultural changes: 1) Leaders may unfreeze the present system by highlighting the threats to the organization if no change occurs, and, at the same time, encourage the organization to believe that change is possible and desirable; 2) They may articulate a new direction and a new set of assumptions, thus providing a clear and new role model; 3) Key positions in the organization may be filled with new incumbents who hold the new assumptions because they are either hybrids, mutants, or brought in from the outside; 4) Leaders systematically may reward the adoption of new directions and punish adherence to the old direction; 5) Organization members may be seduced or coerced into adopting new behaviours that are more consistent with new assumptions; 6) Visible scandals may be created to discredit sacred cows, to explode myths that preserve traditions that do not help the organization to be effective, and to destroy symbolically the artifacts associated with those traditions; and 7) Leaders may create new emotionally charged rituals and develop new symbols and artifacts around the new assumptions to be embraced.

SOURCE: Excerpted from Edgar H. Schein (1990), "Organizational culture," *American Psychologist* 45(2): p. 117. Copyright 1990 by the American Psychological Association. See also Edgar H. Schein (1992), *Organizational Culture and Leadership,* Second edition. San Francisco: Jossey-Bass Inc.

History

History The story of the organization's past.

Here the function of the founder and/or leaders is to talk about the **history** of the organization. The aims are to promote a sense of the past and the continuity of the organization and its members. It is important for the leader to interpret events and give them meaning for organizational members. The leader must either talk about organizational heroes and their actions or have key people in the organization's history speak directly to current organizational members.

For example, many sports teams set aside a special room in their arena for their "old-timers" to gather before a game. They often sponsor an old-timer or alumni team and encourage retired stars of the team to come and talk to current team members. The Montreal Canadiens in ice hockey are well known for their sense of history. Players often report a special feeling of being part of that heritage upon joining the team.

Oneness

The job of the leader in promoting **oneness** is to summarize the organization's dominant value into a simple phrase that can be accepted and repeated by others. This simple statement of the organization's key value can help to promote a sense of oneness and togetherness from the top of the organization to the bottom. An example of this phrase at Dofasco in Hamilton, Ontario (formerly named Dominion Foundaries and Steel Company) is "Our product is steel, our strength is people."

It is also crucial for the leader intent on creating a cohesive organizational culture to communicate organizational norms and values. It is important that everyone in the organization knows its mission. It can be equally important that people *outside* the organization, such as suppliers and customers, know what the organization stands for, what it values, and how it intends to operate. Then deviations from the culture as communicated will be noticed and corrected.

For example, to communicate a Total Quality Management culture, two key actions have been proposed (Klassen, 1993). The first is to "give your employees a picture of how customers perceive your company and where performance does not meet customer needs or expectations" (p. 15). The second is to "build interpersonal communication skills in your management team that support the problem solving required to achieve the desired improvements" (p. 18). Skill is required both to paint the picture of where the company is and then to work with others to make corrections.

A related and important part of the leader's job is to model important behaviours. The creator of culture must spend time on an important activity. Nothing makes a greater impact on organizational members than what its top leaders spend their time on and pay attention to. If a CEO monitored product quality every day and personally dealt with customers having problems with the company's product, the message of the organization's key value would become clear. At Black & Decker Canada Inc. senior managers obtained feedback on how well their behaviour was seen to match the organization's values relating to Total Quality Management (Klassen, 1993). The feedback they received helped to focus their attention on their own role modeling, when it was effective and when it was less effective.

> **Oneness** A feeling that organizational members have of all being in the same boat.

Membership

To promote a sense of **cultural membership** in the organization, people joining the organization need to have a feeling of importance and belonging. The socialization of new staff members into the organization's culture is critical. Socialization will be covered in more detail later in this chapter. Reward systems need to emphasize continuity of membership and the importance of the worker's group as well as the organization as a whole. A focus on training and developing organizational members will help to promote a sense of the value of each person. Providing long-term careers in the organization is one way to emphasize that each member is valuable as a part of the larger whole.

Managers may also use status as a reward instead of creating large differences in salaries for members of the organization at different hierarchical levels. Japan as a society is one that emphasizes membership. Type J organizations are very effective in promoting the sense of membership through the use of socialization, long-term careers and lifetime employment, and low differentials in pay between organizational levels.

> **Cultural membership** A feeling of belonging among organizational members.

Exchange

To increase **cultural exchange** among members and thereby foster a sense of oneness and membership, the creator of culture can promote contact between members, encourage members to participate in decisions, increase interaction and coordination between organizational groups, and be personally involved with the people of the organization.

> **Cultural exchange** The interactions among organizational members.

People who interact with one another come to share similar understandings of organizational events; members of different groups come to understand the meaning of similar events differently (Rentsch, 1990). So, for example, if more openness and contact between employees were desired, a new and attractive lounge could be opened, with places to work in groups, to eat, and to chat. Similarly, members of a product team could be assigned their own team room to decorate and use as they wished in the course of getting their job done.

Manifestations of Culture

To this point we have discussed how to create organizational culture. Now we will turn our attention to how organizational culture is expressed. The four main ways of expressing culture are through shared things, shared talk, shared behaviour, and shared feelings (Sathe, 1983).

Shared Things: Physical Setting, Artifacts, Symbols

The physical space and setting for work and the organization's building are manifestations of that organization's culture. For example, if the organization's senior executives are housed in opulent offices on the top floor of a skyscraper, the cultural message is that hierarchy and power are highly valued by the organization.

Artifacts are material objects such as art and technology that people use to exhibit or express their culture. Paintings and sculptures, pictures of organizational founders, pictures and plaques recognizing employees of the month, and a framed copy of the organization's culture or mission statement are all artifacts. One example of a corporate culture statement is that of Cray Research, Inc., presented as this chapter's *Seeing is Believing* feature.

SEEING IS BELIEVING

THE CRAY STYLE

The Cray culture statement is a printed summary of what is important at Cray Research and can serve as a guide to action by Cray personnel.

At Cray Research, we take what we do very seriously, but we don't take ourselves too seriously.

There is a sense of pride at Cray Research. Professionalism is important. People are treated like and act like professionals. But people are professional without being stuffy.

Cray Research people trust each other to do their jobs well and with the highest ethical standards. We take each other very seriously.

We have a strong sense of quality—quality in our products and services, of course—but also quality in our financial results, our working environment, in the people we work with, in the tools that we use to do our work, and in the components we choose to make what we make.

Economy comes from high value, not from low cost. Aesthetics are part of quality.

The effort to create quality extends to our shareholders who invest in us to see a significant return and to the communities in which we work and live.

The Cray Research approach is informal and non-bureaucratic but thorough. People are accessible at all levels.

Communication is key. We stop by or call if we can. Keeping people informed is part of everyone's job.

People also have fun working at Cray Research. There is laughing in the halls, as well as serious discussion. More than anything else, the organization is personable and approachable, but still dedicated to getting the job done.

With informality, however, there is also a sense of confidence. Cray people feel like they are on the winning side. They feel successful, and they are. It is this sense of confidence that generates the attitude, "go ahead and try it, we'll make it work."

Cray Research people like taking responsibility for what they do and thinking for themselves. At the same time, we work together and are proud to share a single mission—to create the most powerful and highest quality computational tools to solve the world's most challenging scientific and industrial problems.

Because the individual is key at Cray, there is a real diversity in the view of what we really are. In fact, Cray Research is many things to many people. Consistency comes in providing those diverse people with the opportunity to fulfill themselves and experience achievement individually and as part of the Cray Research team.

The creativity, then, that emerges from the company comes from the many ideas of the individuals who are here and from teams of Cray Research people who make these ideas into quality products for our customers. And that is the real strength of Cray Research.

SOURCE: Courtesy of Cray Research, Inc., a manufacturer of supercomputers.

A shared thing can also convey symbolic meaning by representing something else. An example is the mace used at a university or college convocation ceremony. The mace was originally a weapon, then became the symbol of a warlord's physical power, and now has become the symbol of authority passed on by higher powers of the institution to grant diplomas or degrees.

Shared Talk

Members of a culture share language and talk about how problems of external adaptation and internal integration were handled in the past. Shared talk serves to produce a common ground of understanding of how problems were handled by the organization in the past. Shared talk also helps to define who members of the organization are and how they will deal with similar problems in the future.

Janice Beyer and Harrison Trice (1987) differentiated six different kinds of shared talk that occur in organizations. They are language, myth, saga, legend, folktale, and story.[2]

- **Language** is "a particular manner in which members of a group use vocal sounds and written signs to convey meanings to each other."   **Language**
- A **myth** is "a dramatic narrative of imagined events, usually used to explain origins or transformations of something. Also, an unquestioned belief about the practical benefits of certain techniques and behaviours that is not supported by demonstrated facts."   **Myth**
- A **saga** is "a historical narrative describing (usually in heroic terms) the unique accomplishments of a group and its leaders."   **Saga**
- A **legend** is "a handed-down narrative of some wonderful event that has a historical basis but has been embellished with fictional details."   **Legend**
- A **folktale** is "a completely fictional narrative."   **Folktale**
- A **story** is "a narrative based on true events—often a combination of truth and fiction."   **Story**

Joanne Martin and her colleagues (1983) identified seven types of common organizational stories. Here is a list of the seven types of stories told in organizations along with examples of what these stories might be about.

---

2   List excerpted and reprinted, by permission of publisher, from ORGANIZATIONAL DYNAMICS, Spring 1987. © 1987 American Management Association, New York. All rights reserved.

1. *How important is status when rules are broken?*   "Do you remember Joe? He worked on the loading dock. One day he received a shipment of lamps and one was badly broken. No way we could sell it in the store. He took it home and fixed it up. When the boss found out, Joe was fired for theft. But when the accounting department found out that the store manager was buying store merchandise for relatives but using his employee discount, which is also against the rules, nothing happened."

2. *Is the boss human?*   "At our annual company picnic the boss really let her hair down. She made sure everyone was involved in the games, helped to cook the burgers, and even created the 'dunk-the-boss' event. When I hit the target with the baseball and she dropped into the water I wasn't sure how she would take it, but she was a really good sport."

3. *Can a little person rise to the top?*   "There's no way I'll ever get to the top around here. You have to be related to the boss. That's the way it always has been and always will be."

4. *What is it like getting fired in this organization?*   "When Cindy got to work and tried to sign on to the computer, her password had been changed. Then the boss came down and told her in front of all of us that she was fired. She had to turn in her keys and was escorted out of the building by a security guard."

5. *Will the company help an employee who has to move?*   "When head office was moved to Regina we were given air tickets to go and look the city over before we made our decision on whether to move or not. When we did decide to go, they paid for our moving expenses and even for shipping our dog out on the airplane."

6. *How will the boss react to mistakes?*   "I really messed up on that deal. I figured it cost the company $100 000. When I went in, expecting to be fired, the boss said 'Why should I fire you when I've just invested $100 000 in your training?'"

7. *How does the organization deal with obstacles?*   "Around here we never give up. For the longest time we couldn't find the mix of ingredients that would make our new outdoor plastic sign stand up to heat, cold, impact, and ultraviolet radiation. But R&D kept looking and testing until we found the right blend. Now we've got a quality product that the competition can't match."

A person with work experience should be able, upon reflection, to recall examples of most of these seven types of stories.

Shared Behaviour: Ceremonies, Rites, Rituals, Gestures

Actions in organizations often have meaning for the particular organization's culture. These actions are more than day-to-day task accomplishment. They serve to define what the organization is and what it cares about. For example, the convocation ceremony for graduates of a university, college, high school, public school, and even a kindergarten is a rite of passage marking a person's transition from one status to another.

Other organizational rites (Beyer & Trice, 1987) are those of degradation (e.g., firing a high level manager to emphasize a split with the past), of enhancement (e.g., a salesperson of the year award), of renewal (e.g., executive development programs), of conflict reduction (e.g., collective bargaining), and of integration (e.g., the office Christmas party).

Rituals are engaged in by organizational members, often without knowing exactly why, except that it is part of "the way we do things around here." For example, employees of the T. Eaton Company in Toronto touch the toe of Timothy Eaton's statue as they walk by.

Ritualistic behaviour follows a set pattern and may not produce consequences of any importance. However, rituals may also be used to intimidate, and to block change by potential reformers. A four-tier hierarchy of intimidation rituals is: 1) nullifying the validity of the reformer's suggestions; 2) isolating the reformer; 3) defaming a persistent reformer; and finally 4) expulsion of the reformer from the organization (O'Day, 1974).

In addition to rites and rituals, some gestures may become accepted by culture members as having specific meanings. An example of a specific gesture would be a secret handshake that identifies members of a group to each other without words being spoken or non-members knowing that this identification was taking place.

Shared Feelings

This group of culture manifestations includes standards of expected behaviour of culture members (called norms), beliefs about the world and how it works, and what the organization values. Vijay Sathe (1983, p. 11) described different types of shared feelings.

- "**Cultural beliefs** are the basic assumptions of the organization concerning the world and how it works."   **Cultural beliefs**
- "**Cultural values** are also basic assumptions, but they have an 'ought to' implicit in them."   **Cultural values**
- "**Cultural identity** includes the understandings that members share concerning who they are and what they stand for as a community."   **Cultural identity**
- "**Cultural attitudes** are the set of understandings that members of a community share about a specific object or situation."   **Cultural attitudes**
- "**Cultural ideology** is the dominant set of interrelated ideas that explain to members of a community why the important understandings they share make sense. An ideology gives meaning to the content of a culture."[3]   **Cultural ideology**

To understand corporate culture, managers may conduct a culture audit (Wilkins, 1983; Schein, 1984). The organization's culture can be analyzed by examining the methods used to create culture and the manifestations of the culture. Exhibit 3.5 presents a model that combines these four methods of creating organizational culture and shows the ways the culture is then manifested.

Culture Profiles

Terrence Deal and Allen Kennedy (1982) examined numerous companies and determined four cultural profiles (or types) of corporate cultures. The two critical factors they identified that shaped the corporate culture were "the degree of risk associated with the company's activities, and the speed at which companies—and the employees—get feedback on whether decisions or strategies are successful" (Deal & Kennedy, 1982, p. 107). The four culture types they identified were the Tough-Guy/Macho culture, the Work Hard/Play Hard culture, the Bet-Your-Company culture, and the Process culture. A summary of these four profiles is shown in Exhibit 3.6.

The Tough-Guy/Macho culture is one of high risk and fast feedback. Heroes of these organizations are tough and individualistic. Examples are police, fire fighting, and construction. The Bet-Your-Company culture is also high risk but slow in receiving feedback from the environment. Examples of this type are the military and oil exploration companies. Their heroes have character and confidence.

In the Work Hard/Play Hard culture risk is low but feedback is fast. Their heroes are super salespeople. Example organizations of this type are real estate companies, car dealerships,

---

[3]   Quotes are reprinted, by permission of publisher, from ORGANIZATIONAL DYNAMICS, Autumn 1983 ©1983. American Management Association, New York. All rights reserved.

EXHIBIT 3.5   DEVELOPMENT OF AN ORGANIZATION'S CULTURE

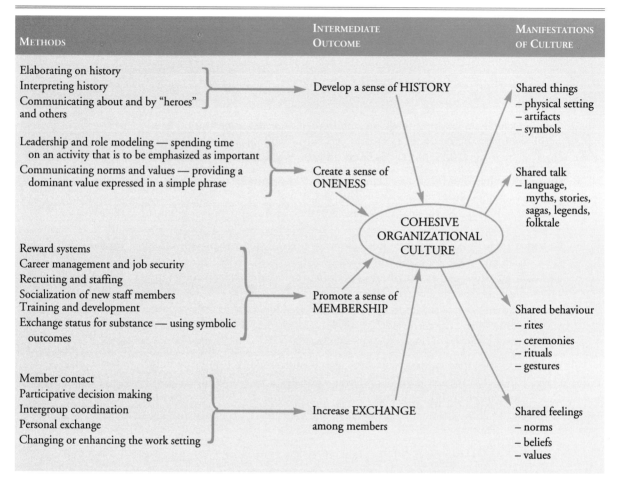

SOURCES: From Warren Gross and Shula Shichman (1987), "How to grow an organizational culture." Excerpted/adapted and reprinted, by permission of publisher, from PERSONNEL, September 1987. © 1987 American Management Association, New York, all rights reserved; and from Vijay Sathe (1983), "Implications of corporate culture: A manager's guide to action." Excerpted/adapted and reprinted, by permission of publisher, from ORGANIZATIONAL DYNAMICS, Autumn 1983. © 1983 American Management Association, New York, all rights reserved. Methods detail based on information in Jeffrey Pfeffer (1981), "Management as symbolic action: The creation and maintenance of organizational paradigms." In Larry L. Cummings and Barry M. Staw (Editors), *Research in Organizational Behavior* 3: 1-52.

and Mary Kay Cosmetics. The Process culture has low risk and little feedback from the environment on the organization's success. Examples are governments, insurance companies, and banks. Their heroes are cautious, orderly, attend to detail, and follow procedure.

Subcultures

While a company may most closely fit one of the four cultural profiles, a large organization will likely have a mix of cultures. For example, the marketing department may best fit the Tough-Guy/Macho culture, the sales department the Work Hard/Play Hard culture, the R&D group the Bet-Your-Company culture, and the accounting department the Process culture. These are subcultures based on function. Subcultures may also exist in an organization based on the operating unit, on hierarchical level, or around social activities (Caudron, 1992).

Exhibit 3.6   Organizational Culture Profiles

Culture Profile	Tough-Guy/Macho	Work Hard/Play Hard	Bet-Your-Company	Process
Degree of risk associated with the company's activities	High	Low	High	Low
Speed at which feedback is received on whether decisions or strategies are successful	Fast	Fast	Slow	Little or none
Typical kinds of organizations that use this culture	Police, construction, surgical departments in hospitals, cosmetics, management consulting, television, radio, venture capital	Real estate, computer firms, auto distributors, door-to-door sales operations, retail stores, mass consumer sales	Oil, aerospace, heavy equipment manufacturers, architectural firms, investment banks, mining and smelting companies, the military	Banks, insurance companies, financial service organizations, the government, utilities, pharmaceuticals, accounting
The ways survivors and/or heroes in this culture behave	They have a tough attitude. They are individualistic. They can tolerate all-or-nothing risks. They need constant feedback. Their goal is to become a star. They are superstitious.	They are super sales-people. They are friendly, hail-fellow-well-met kinds of people. They aren't worried or superstitious. They take small risks and get quick feedback. They revel in intensive games.	They have character and confidence. They can endure long-term ambiguity. They take time to make a decision, then double check it. They respect authority and technical competence. Decision making comes from the top down.	They are very cautious and have a "cover yourself" mentality. They are orderly, punctual, and attend to detail. They carry out procedures whether they make sense or not.
Strengths of the personnel/culture	They can do what needs to be done in short order	They get a lot done. They have good customer service.	They can make high-quality inventions and major scientific breakthroughs.	They provide order and system.
Weaknesses of the personnel/culture	It is short-term in orientation. No value is placed on long term persistence. The virtues of cooperation are forgotten.	They often look for quick-fix solutions and have a short-term perspective. Sales forces can become disillusioned and cynical.	They move with awesome slowness. They are vulnerable to short-term fluctuations in the economy and cash-flow problems while they wait for major ventures to pay off.	There is lots of red tape. How the work is done is often more important than what work is done.

Source: Adapted with permission from Terrence E. Deal and Allen A. Kennedy (1982), *Corporate Cultures: The Rites and Rituals of Corporate Life.* © 1982, by Addison-Wesley Publishing Company, Inc. Chapter 6. Reprinted with permission of the publisher.

It can be difficult for a large organization, if the values and systems of its subcultures are very different, to move all its existing subcultures towards one dominant, central organization culture. This is one reason why culture change is so difficult for larger, older organizations and relatively easier for younger, smaller, and more entrepreneurial organizations. A statement about how to create an organizational vision is found in this chapter's *A Word to the Wise.*

A WORD TO THE WISE

'Vision' is probably the most romantic and starry-eyed of all the control systems company leaders are employing to guide their organisations. Why then, especially if their owners are in love with them, do so many visions fail? One answer is that they weren't visions at all, merely missions, or desires, or random convictions, or wistful irrelevancies, or power-crazed hallucinations. They were merely masquerading as visions.

Another answer is that they were old-fashioned or were based on secondary issues such as quality, just-in-time, excellence, and so on, rather than on fundamental strategic needs like the needs for new growth strategies, exploitable R&D, new products and new markets.

But assuming our heroic leaders have exactly the right visions to fit the strategic situations that they are trapped in, and wish to escape from, how can they then ensure that their visions come to fruition and are not wrecked by ill-conceived and badly planned implementation programmes?

The first point to consider is the idea and ownership of a vision. It is wishful thinking to assume, either that my vision is like yours, and therefore equally inspiring to you, or that having a vision guarantees success. What some company leaders fail to recognise is that people at every level of the organisation are driven by their own very personal "visions" and that these subordinate "visions" are usually about how they see their present and future roles within the firm's culture, their need for security and how their bosses can, do or will affect their futures.

Indeed, subordinates will be much more concerned with their own "visions" of their positions, jobs and prospects than with the strange, intrusive and seemingly out of this world desire of a boss to realise his or her dreams, in spite of theirs.

The leader's problem, therefore, is how to get staff to follow his or her vision, especially when it is right. The solution involves two management techniques: one to validate the strategic promise implicit in the vision, and to communicate it clearly; and the other to ensure its promise can be delivered by the people at the leader's disposal.

I call the whole approach "visaction" consisting of both an ability to develop competitive visions that people can become committed to and a vision management process that ensures the leader's vision is so well implemented that it becomes the whole organisation's operational reality.

First we must have a way of binding each individual to his or her department or subgroup, and then we must bind each sectional interest to the whole, thereby creating a shared vision of precisely what we are and what we might, together, wish to achieve. Such a process of integration is essential if people are to have the confidence to act on their own initiative, within the context of the new vision, and make mid-course corrections when the need arises. The technique of generating the binding commitment's shared sense of purpose and related values that company leaders wish to spread throughout their organisations is called "ethos management."

The second task in the Visaction process is to ensure everyone understands the vision, its meaning, its benefits for them, what it expects of them and the re-definition of their responsibilities as required by the new vision. To guarantee employee involvement, a monitoring and measuring process must be installed at the start.

Later on, once the driving ethos is operating and the shared vision is controlling daily work, freedom of maneuver can be enlarged in a planned transition phase, designed to maximise autonomy and initiative. This is real, constitutional, empowerment, not just lip-service. Once goals are created and advanced across a whole society they may be justly called constitutional. When this ideal state has been reached, the self-sustaining "ethos reflex" can be left to run the show until it is necessary to start the constitutional reform and organisational renewal again.

The leader's primary role is to offer strategic guidance, whilst allowing talented staff to exercise vision-guided initiatives. The Visaction process is the best tool for the job, irrespective of whether the leaders need to maintain control in the present or to reposition their organisations so that they are prepared for the opportunities of a new era.

Source: By Norman Strauss, "Make your visions valid & viable," *Management Today*, February 1993, p. 92. Mr. Strauss is the Managing Director of Corporate Positioning Services in the United Kingdom. Note: Visaction™ is a registered trademark in the United Kingdom.

Organizational culture can be expected to serve different functions depending on the growth stage of the organization (Exhibit 3.7). At the birth and early growth stage culture is the "glue" that holds the organization together and a source of the organization's distinctive competence. At organizational midlife new subcultures emerge. This results in the weakening of the cultural integration of the organization. When the organization reaches maturity, culture can become a constraint on change and innovation. The organization may transform itself by holding on to crucial elements of its culture but changing other elements. Alternatively, the organization's culture may change fundamentally when it goes bankrupt, is taken over by another organization, or is merged with and assimilated into a second organization.

Merging Two Cultures

The merger of two healthy organizations is an interesting case of potential culture conflict. A successful merger requires more than the combination of assets, debts, and physical

---

EXHIBIT 3.7   FUNCTIONS OF CULTURE AT DIFFERENT ORGANIZATIONAL GROWTH STAGES

GROWTH STAGE	FUNCTION OF CULTURE/ISSUE
I. *Birth and Early Growth* • Founder domination, possible family domination	• Culture is a distinctive competence and source of identity. • Culture is the "glue" that holds organization together. • Organization strives toward more integration and clarity. • Heavy emphasis on socialization as evidence of commitment.
Succession Phase	• Culture becomes battleground between conservatives and liberals. • Potential successors are judged on whether they will preserve or change cultural elements.
II. *Organizational Midlife* • Expansion of products/markets • Vertical integration • Geographical expansion • Acquisitions, mergers	• Cultural integration declines as new subcultures are spawned. • Loss of key goals, values, and assumptions creates crisis of identity. • Opportunity to manage direction of cultural change is provided.
III. *Organizational Maturity* • Maturity or decline of markets • Increasing internal stability and/or stagnation • Lack of motivation to change	• Culture becomes a constraint on innovation. • Culture preserves the glories of the past, hence is valued as a source of self-esteem, defense.
Transformation Option	• Culture change is necessary and inevitable, but not all elements of culture can or must change. • Essential elements of culture must be identified, preserved. • Culture change can be managed or simply allowed to evolve.
Destruction Option • Bankruptcy and reorganization • Takeover and reorganization • Merger and assimilation	• Culture changes at fundamental paradigm levels. • Culture changes through massive replacement of key people.

SOURCE: Edgar H. Schein (1985), *Organizational Culture and Leadership*. San Francisco: Jossey-Bass Inc., pp. 271-272. Adapted/reprinted with permission.

structures. It also requires the integration of two often different corporate cultures (Cartwright & Cooper, 1993). For example, Anthony Buono and his colleagues (1985) studied the merger of two state banks in the U.S. In their words:

> Bank A was the fourth largest savings bank in the state, with approximately $600 million in assets and 325 full-time employees. The institution served a largely blue-collar clientele, which was a function of its urban setting and the location of its branches. It operated with a divisional structure, and was rather bureaucratic in nature, with clearly defined and bounded jobs at all levels. Bank B was the fifth largest ($500 million in assets) mutual savings bank in the state, with approximately 275 employees. In contrast to Bank A, the merger partner had both its headquarters and all branches in suburban areas and served largely white-collar and professional customers. The institution operated with a centrally controlled functional organization, but with individual jobs more loosely defined, particularly at the professional and managerial levels (pp. 484-485).

The researchers found that what was to be a "merger of equals" did not turn out that way. There was significant discomfort among bank personnel over what the post-merger culture would be, and a "culture shock" was experienced during the merger. The resultant culture of the merged bank was more like that of Bank B than A, resulting in significantly lower feelings of satisfaction and commitment by Bank A members.

A merger can even be difficult between two organizations that are initially quite similar in structures, decision processes, and overall cultures. This chapter's *If You Can't Ride Two Horses At Once, You Shouldn't Be in the Circus* feature describes such a merger between two Canadian accounting firms. Senior staff in the newly merged firm needed to be able to absorb the other culture and to adapt to the newly integrated culture.

Culture Strength

Organizations may seek to create a strong (or intensive) organizational culture as a source of competitive advantage. A shared organizational culture will help the members to know where the organization is going and how they fit in. Uncertainty in what to do can then be dealt with by falling back on the organization's overall mission and goals. An example of this is Nelson's memo to the English fleet off Cadiz before the Battle of Trafalgar on October 9, 1805. Nelson wrote "No captain can do very wrong if he places his ship alongside that of the enemy" (John Bartlett, 1980).

But a strong culture can be a liability to required change. An example from Geoffrey Lewis of the University of Melbourne illustrates this point.

> A manager ... took over a transportation company that had grown up with a royal charter one hundred years earlier and had developed strong traditions around its blue trucks with the royal coat of arms painted on their sides. The company was losing money because it was not aggressively seeking new concepts of how to sell transportation. After observing the company for a few months, the new chief executive officer abruptly and without giving reasons ordered that the entire fleet of trucks be painted solid white. Needless to say, there was consternation. Delegations urging the president to reconsider, protestations about loss of identity, predictions of total economic disaster, and other forms of resistance arose. The CEO listened patiently to all these but simply reiterated that he wanted the painting done, and soon. He eroded the resistance by making the request nonnegotiable. After the trucks were painted white, the drivers suddenly noticed that people were curious about what they had done and inquired what they would now put on the trucks in the way of a new logo. This got the employees at all levels thinking about what business they were in and initiated the market-oriented focus that the president had been trying to establish (Schein, 1992, p. 320).

IF YOU CAN'T RIDE TWO HORSES AT ONCE, YOU SHOULDN'T BE IN THE CIRCUS

Royston Greenwood, Bob Hinings, and John Brown at the University of Alberta in Edmonton conducted a longitudinal case study of the merger of two large accounting firms in Canada. These two firms were fairly similar in their structures, decision processes, and overall cultures. They were both professional partnerships, used a common technology to perform audits and other accountancy work, and shared common beliefs and values about organizational purpose. Furthermore, the merger was overwhelmingly agreed to by the senior personnel of both firms, who likely took into account the problems of merging two firms. They decided to merge at the physical, procedural, and managerial/sociocultural levels. That is, they would share one office, share a common way of operating and making decisions, and have a single shared culture.

The expectation was that their initial similarities would help pave the way for a smooth integration. But difficulties were created by differences in detail between the two firms. Specifically, they differed on their openness of information and degree of entrepreneurial aggressiveness. These differences were noticed by the two firms before the merger. But it was not until the two firms were integrated and began to practise together that problems cropped up.

Greenwood, Hinings, and Brown write:

However, as the merger unfolded members of the two firms were recognising that an integrated culture required not merely the adoption of new values (e.g., greater entrepreneurialism) but the diminution of existing values (e.g., high professional standards). Such a trade-off began to "mean something" when it had to be practised. Each firm was beginning to see the other's approach as unnecessary and inappropriate.

These perceptions existed even though financially the merger was seen to be successful. Clearly, even organizational cultures that appear similar can have underlying differences in values that cause the organizations to not merge so much as collide. Managers have to be able to absorb and adapt, to balance two styles of operating. In this new merged organization such a skill would seem to be especially useful. Forty-two months after this merger, as the merged organization was settling down, a second merger was announced as imminent.

SOURCE: Based on information in Royston Greenwood, C.R. (Bob) Hinings, and John Brown (1994), "Merging professional service firms," *Organization Science* 5: 239-257.

The development of a strong organizational culture can encourage conflict between subcultures, as organizational members fight to maintain the assumptions and values of their own subculture that do not fit with those proposed for the overall organizational culture. A weaker organizational culture will encounter fewer subculture conflicts as subcultures can exist independently within the larger framework of the organization. Coordination may be more difficult in this case, though, as strong cultural mechanisms providing coordination are missing.

Culture of Multinational Corporations

Multinational corporations (MNC's) operate in different countries, and therefore have to consider how the organizational culture fits in with the culture of local employees. For example, many Japanese organizations have been able to transplant their cultural characteristics and methods to their American and Canadian subsidiaries, though some have had difficulty (see Case 3.2 at the end of this chapter).

Domestic phase

Attention is focused on the home market.

International phase

Operations are opened in one or several other cultures and managed by an expatriate manager.

Multinational phase

The organization deals with many nations. Managers from the other countries come to the organization's national headquarters.

Transnational phase

Networks of firms and divisions are created with multiple headquarters and cultural synergy.

Nancy Adler and Susan Bartholomew (1992) described four phases a firm might go through as it becomes more internationally oriented. First is the **domestic phase** when attention is focused on the home market. Next, in the **international phase**, operations are opened in one or several other cultures. The operation in each country is managed by an expatriate manager on an international assignment. With the British style of overseas operation a home-country national manages the entire foreign operation with high autonomy. The American style places a professional manager of whatever nationality overseas, but monitors the operation closely from the home office. The Japanese style fills most senior management posts by home-country nationals and tightly controls foreign operations (Fukuda, 1992).

The next phase is **multinational**. Here many nations have to be dealt with and by more "inpatriate" managers—those from the other countries who have come to the national headquarters. At this stage "international and cross-cultural skills become needed for managers throughout the firm, not just for those few imminently leaving for foreign postings" (Adler & Bartholomew, 1992, p. 55).

Finally, at the **transnational phase** it is thought that power may not need to be centralized in the "home" culture. Also, networks of firms and divisions can be created with multiple headquarters and cultural synergy. Adler and Bartholomew found, however, that even firms doing business transnationally did not have multi-cultural senior leadership or even a majority of executives with international experience.

ORGANIZATIONAL SOCIALIZATION

An organization has a culture but its individual members will be replaced over time. Therefore, for the organization's culture to endure it must be transmitted from current organizational members to new members. This process is called organizational socialization. It is especially important in organizations with strong cultures. Organizations with weak cultures have less to transmit and will tend to experience culture change as members come and go with their own particular cultures.

Socialization Phases

Socialization has been described as having three phases: anticipatory socialization, encounter, and change and acquisition (Feldman, 1981).

Anticipatory Socialization

A certain degree of socialization occurs even before the new member joins the organization. For example, what a person has heard about working for a local fast-food chain gives her an idea of what to expect if hired. Individuals who do not believe they would fit in may not even apply to join. The socialization of those who do join is therefore easier. At A&W, employees are required to read a handbook about what to do and how to serve customers before they begin work.

Realistic job preview

An attempt is made by the organizational interviewer to paint a realistic picture of what to expect from the job and the organization.

Organizations use the interviewing process to begin the socialization of new members. A **realistic job preview** attempts to paint a realistic picture of what to expect from the job and the organization. The idea is that upon entry the recruit is not shocked by unanticipated problems. For example, a recently graduated business student interviewing for an articling job in auditing in a public accounting firm could be told about the extensive travel that is required in going to client's offices, the proportion of time spent working alone and as part of an auditing team, and the many unpaid overtime hours required during the busy season of January to April.

Interviewing is also used to determine the degree of match between the values of potential recruits and the values of the organization. New recruits with personal values matching those of the firm have been found to adjust to the organization's culture more quickly than recruits with non-matching values (Chatman, 1991).

Organizations also send cultural messages to potential new members during interviews. When there are several rounds of interviews with progressively senior members of the organization, the message sent is of the importance of finding the best person for the position. In contrast, hiring for a part-time job at the lowest level of the organization is often accomplished quickly, with a person having minimally acceptable qualifications hired on the spot. The cultural message in this case is that such employees are easily let into and out of the organization.

Interviewing A face-to-face meeting often used to determine the degree of match between the values of potential recruits and the values of the organization.

Encounter

The first day on a new job is one of encounter. The new recruit is told what to do and how to do it. Most people can recall being shown around an organization and meeting many new people but not remembering their names. A common feeling in the encounter phase is of being lost, confused, and overwhelmed with information. Since many new employees do not get a very good first impression of the organization, a practical way to help the new member become socialized is to provide a newcomer's welcome package that contains useful information about the organization and how it works (Kliem, 1987). Such a package could easily pay for itself through reduced turnover.

The assumption to this point has been that the new employee is being hired for and socialized into a particular job. But some organizations bring in new members based on general criteria (for example, educational achievement). After being hired, the company may subject the recruit to extensive testing of abilities, interests, and attitudes before deciding where to place him. One example is that of a bank that has management trainees work a predetermined series of jobs over the first two years of their employment. The bank may then allow the individual some choice in her next assignment, either on the line in a branch or on the staff at the bank's head office. A second example is the armed forces. Recruits undergo a common basic training and testing before assignment to different units and jobs.

Change and Acquisition

At this stage the newcomer begins to acquire and internalize the culture of the organization. This results in some change in his beliefs and values. When a member of an organization is considered an "old hand" and is asked to show new organizational members the ropes, she may be considered to have successfully acquired the organization's culture.

Culture acquisition is normally accompanied by a sense of pride in organizational membership and superiority over new members. In this chapter's *Overboard* cartoon Nate the pirate is an old hand trying to socialize the new pirates, but he isn't getting much help from his Captain!

Socialization Strategies

Exhibit 3.8 details a set of seven organizational socialization strategies developed by John Van Maanen (1978). These strategies are useful descriptions of the socialization practices that a new organizational entrant may face.

EXHIBIT 3.8 SOCIALIZATION STRATEGIES

STRATEGY	DEFINITION	EXAMPLE
Formal versus	Segregates newcomers from regular organizational members	Basic training for the military
Informal	Treats newcomers as undifferentiated from other members	Transferred employees
Collective versus	Puts newcomer through a common set of experiences as part of a group	First year college/university freshman orientation
Individual	Processes recruits singly and in isolation from each other	On-the-job training, Apprenticeship
Sequential Steps versus	Requires entrant to move through a series of discrete and identifiable steps to achieve a defined role	Specialized training in banking, medicine
Nonsequential Steps	Accomplishes achievement of a defined role in one transitional stage	Promotion
Fixed versus	Gives the recruit complete knowledge of time required to complete passage	Most schooling
Variable	Does not give recruits any advance notice of their transition timetable	PhD studies
Tournament versus	Separates clusters of recruits into different programs on the basis of presumed differences in ability, ambition, or background	Academic tracked programs
Contest	Avoids sharp distinctions between clusters of recruits	MBA school
Serial versus	Experienced members groom newcomers about to assume similar roles in the organization	Apprenticeship program
Disjunctive	Newcomer does not have role models available	First holder of newly defined job
Investiture versus	Ratifies and establishes the usefulness of the characteristics the person already possesses	High level management
Divestiture	Seeks to deny and strip away certain characteristics of an entering recruit	Professional athletics

1. *Formal versus informal.*   The Canadian army, like other armed forces around the world, requires recruits to go through a period of basic training. This is a time of formal socialization into the practices of the army. The recruit is kept away from regular organization members and from other societal influences. An informal strategy may be used by the owner of a small corner restaurant who, upon hiring a new waiter, simply says "There's your area, get to work."

2. *Collective versus individual.*   A collective socialization puts all newcomers into a group and socializes them together. In Japan there is one day in the year when all new graduates join large organizations. At Toyota these beginners are taught about the company in one large room. A salesperson joining a car dealership in Canada, on the other hand, would usually be trained as an individual and on-the-job.

Canadian soldiers on parade.

3. *Sequential steps versus nonsequential steps.*   An example of socialization by sequential steps is the making of a doctor. On the first day at medical school, student doctor status is awarded along with a picture ID name tag and a white lab coat. After taking courses and passing exams the status of intern is achieved. The internship provides training and experience after which provincial medical exams are written. If passed the status of doctor is achieved. In contrast, socialization by nonsequential steps is marked by one transitional stage. The coach of the Winnipeg Jets of the National Hockey League may be plucked out of the ranks of college or junior coaches. Promotion is immediate. The role of coach is achieved all at once.

4. *Fixed versus variable timing.*   A program of fixed socialization provides the recruit complete knowledge of how long it will take to complete the journey from newcomer to seasoned member. Basic training in a police academy is of fixed duration. An example of variable timing is that of a backup quarterback on a professional football team. When he becomes the first string starter depends on how quickly he learns, his skills, and on the health of the current starting quarterback.

5. *Tournament versus contest.*   In a contest there are no initial distinctions made between recruits. They are all pooled together and the best are allowed to emerge. Staff accountants joining a professional accounting firm find themselves in a contest. A tournament model of socialization pays attention to differences between recruits. Military recruits are streamed into general training or officer's candidate school.

6. *Serial versus disjunctive.*   Serial socialization relies on experienced organizational members to teach newcomers about their roles. When a job is newly created there is no experienced person to act as a role model. Socialization in this case is disjunctive.

7. *Investiture versus divestiture.*   Socialization that seeks to strip away certain characteristics from the recruit is that of divestiture. The United States Marine Corps is famous for its brush cuts, military clothes, and name tags. The message in this kind of socialization is that what the recruit *was* is not that important. What he or she *is now* is what matters. Investiture, on the other hand, makes it clear that the skills brought by the person are important. The specialist hired by the hospital to treat juvenile diabetes patients is commended for her skills.

Organizations can combine these seven strategies into many different possible forms of socialization, depending on the kinds of employees entering the organization and the kind of culture desired. For example, a collective socialization can be expected to build more of a sense of group, a formal socialization will emphasize the experience and knowledge of those already in the organization, and a contest form of socialization will promote conflict by emphasizing that there can only be a few winners.

A model of intense socialization is shown in Exhibit 3.9. In this process the organization is seeking to build a strong culture by first putting candidates through a rigorous selection procedure. For example, top ranked universities have, without exception, very rigorous selection. This allows the organization to admit only highly qualified candidates. Most candidates are "deselected," that is, not chosen. The candidates who are admitted know that they are special, different, and valued by the organization.

Then, in order to make these newcomers open to change, they are exposed to a humility inducing experience. Often they are asked to do more work than one person could possibly do alone. This experience can also teach the recruit the necessity of teamwork. In-the-trenches training is the day-to-day work, learning, and skill acquisition that builds up the individual's sense of being capable. Rewards and control systems reinforce desired behaviour and cultural values.

Personal sacrifice is often demanded in order for the person being socialized to fully acquire the organization's values. Those who cannot or will not make the required sacrifices will often leave the organization (or the part of it with these strong values). In the Canadian military, for example, refusal to accept a job transfer usually means leaving the organization. Finally, folklore and role models are provided to explain values and sacrifices and give examples of other members who have successfully entered into the culture and are enjoying its benefits.

How robust are organizational cultures in the face of membership turnover and growth? Researchers Richard Harrison and Glenn Carroll (1991) built a model of cultural transmission. They included variables for the entry and exit rates of workers, the organization's

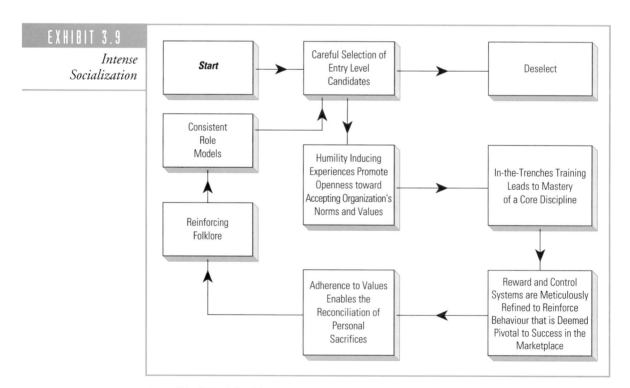

EXHIBIT 3.9

Intense Socialization

SOURCE: Richard T. Pascale (1985). Copyright ©1985 by the Regents of the University of California. Reprinted from the *California Management Review*, Vol 27, No.2. By permission of The Regents.

growth rate, selectiveness of organizational recruiting, intensity of socialization, and the rate at which such socialization decays if not reinforced. Their simulation showed that organizational cultures are very sturdy. Even with high turnover and rapid growth, cultures reached a state of equilibrium.

CONCLUSION

In this chapter we have examined organizational culture and how it is part of the strategy-structure-culture mix. Culture is important in giving meaning to the organization's structure. We have also seen how an individual can be socialized into an organization's culture. But the new organizational member has a particular job to do. Therefore, after understanding organizational structure and culture, the student of organizations needs to examine how the organization's work is divided into specific jobs. It is also important to understand what it is like to perform different jobs. This is the nature of work. Job design and the nature of work are therefore the topics of Chapter 4.

CHAPTER SUMMARY

In this chapter we have examined societal and organizational culture. Societal culture is important for understanding how people in a given society experience life. People from different countries and cultures will have dissimilar ways of understanding basic ideas about life. For example, time may be seen as linear in one culture but as cyclical in another. Nature may be seen as something to be dominated and exploited by the people of one culture but as something to be lived with in another. When these individuals create and join organizations they can be expected to bring cultural understandings with them. Therefore, the kind of organizations that are formed can be expected to differ across world cultures and societies.

An organization can also been seen to have its own culture. Organizational culture is a summary of the beliefs and values of the members of an organization and the observable objects with which they surround themselves. An organization's culture is created as its members develop a strategy, a structure, and a consensus on how to deal with their common problem of how to adapt to the external environment while being internally integrated.

Some managers believe that organizational culture can be actively developed and managed. To accomplish this the manager needs to do four things. First, develop a sense of history of the organization. Second, create a sense of oneness among organizational members. Third, promote a sense of membership in the organization. Fourth, increase exchange among organizational members.

Once created, culture shows itself through shared things, shared talk, shared behaviour, and the shared feelings of organizational members.

When organizations merge, it is important to consider how their separate cultures will fit together.

The last topic of this chapter was organizational socialization. This is the process of acquiring the organization's culture. Organizations use many different strategies for socializing their new members. The stronger the organization's culture, the more intense should be the new recruit's socialization into it.

QUESTIONS FOR REVIEW

1. How would you describe the socialization process at your college or university? Does it vary across faculties? How does the socialization process you are most familiar with compare to those you have heard of at other universities, colleges, or faculties?

2. Describe how people of the culture with which you are most familiar would answer the five culture questions presented in this chapter. How are these answers the same or different from other cultures with which you are familiar?

3. Present the case that supports the argument that organizational cultures can be created and actively managed. What are the arguments that this is not true?

4. Which is more powerful—an organization's culture or the societal culture which surrounds the organization?

5. How useful are cultural profiles of organizations? How easily can we place organizations into the profiles of the Tough-Guy/Macho culture, the Work Hard/Play Hard culture, the Bet-Your-Company culture, and the Process culture?

SELF-DIAGNOSTIC EXERCISE 3.1

Polychronic Attitude Index

Consider how you feel about the following statements. Circle your choice on the scale provided: strongly agree, agree, neutral, disagree, or strongly disagree.

	Strongly Disagree	Disagree	Neutral	Agree	Strongly Agree
I do not like to juggle several activites at once.	5pt.	4pts.	3pts.	2pts.	1pts.
People should not try to do many things at once.	5pt.	4pts.	3pts.	2pts.	1pts.
When I sit down at my desk job, I work on one project at a time.	5pt.	4pts.	3pts.	2pts.	1pts.
I am comfortable doing several things at one time.	1pt.	2pts.	3pts.	4pts.	5pts.

Add up your points, and divide the total by 4. The lower your score (below 3.0) the more monochronic your orientation; and the higher your score (above 3.0) the more polychronic you are.

Source: Allen C. Bluedorn, Carol Felker Kaufman, and Paul M. Lane (1992), "How many things do you like to do at once? An introduction to monochronic and polychronic time," *Academy of Management Executive* 6(4): 20.

SELF-DIAGNOSTIC EXERCISE 3.2

Socialization Intensity Scale

These questions allow the interested student of organizations to rate the intensity of a company's socialization processes. To complete the scale, respond to the items below as they apply to the handling of professional employees. Upon completion, compute your total score. For comparison, scores for a number of strong, intermediate, and weak culture firms are to be found below.

	Not true of this company			*Very true of this company*	
1. Recruiters receive at least one week of intensive training.	1	2	3	4	5
2. Recruitment firms identify several key traits deemed crucial to the firm's success, traits are defined in concrete terms, and interviewer records specific evidence of each trait.	1	2	3	4	5
3. Recruits are subjected to at least four in-depth interviews	1	2	3	4	5
4. Company actively facilitates de-selection during the recruiting process by revealing minuses as well as pluses.	1	2	3	4	5
5. New hires work long hours, are exposed to intensive training of considerable difficulty and/or perform relatively menial tasks in the first months.	1	2	3	4	5
6. The intensity of entry level experience builds cohesiveness among peers in each entering class.	1	2	3	4	5
7. All professional employees in a particular discipline begin in entry level positions regardless of prior experience or advanced degrees.	1	2	3	4	5
8. Reward systems and promotion criteria require mastery of a core discipline as a precondition for advancement.	1	2	3	4	5
9. The career path for professional employees is relatively consistent over the first six to ten years with the company.	1	2	3	4	5
10. Reward systems, performance incentives, promotion criteria and other primary measures of success reflect a high degree of congruence.	1	2	3	4	5
11. Virtually all professional employees can identify and articulate the firm's shared values (i.e., the purpose or mission that ties the firm to society, the customer, or its employees).	1	2	3	4	5

		Not true of this company				Very true of this company
12.	There are very few instances when actions of management appear to violate the firm's espoused values.	1	2	3	4	5
13.	Employees frequently make personal sacrifices for the firm out of commitment to the firm's shared values.	1	2	3	4	5
14.	When confronted with trade-offs between systems measuring short-term results and doing what's best for the company in the long term, the firm usually decides in favour of the long-term.	1	2	3	4	5
15.	This organization fosters mentor-protégé relationships.	1	2	3	4	5
16.	There is considerable similarity among high potential candidates in each particular discipline.	1	2	3	4	5

Compute your score: _____

For comparative purposes:

Scores:

Strongly Socialized Firms: 65-80 . . . . IBM, Procter & Gamble
55-64 . . . . AT&T, Morgan Stanley, Delta Airlines
45-54 . . . . United Airlines, Coca Cola
35-44 . . . . General Foods, Pepsi Co.
25-34 . . . . United Technologies, ITT

Weakly Socialized Firms: Below 25 . . . . . . Atari

SOURCE: Excerpted from Richard Pascale (1985). Copyright ©1985 by the Regents of the University of California. Reprinted from the *California Management Review*, Vol 27, No.2. By permission of The Regents.

EXPERIENTIAL EXERCISE 3.1

Reading an Organization's Culture

Method: Each student will be assigned to a team and instructed to visit an organization by the instructor.

1. Visit the site assigned as a team.
2. Take detailed notes on the cultural forms that are observed.
3. Prepare a presentation for class that describes these forms and draw inferences about the nature of the culture of the organization—its ideologies, values, and norms of behaviour.
4. Be sure to explain the basis of your inferences in terms of the cultural forms observed.

Each group will have twenty minutes in class to report its findings, so plan the presentation carefully. Use visual aids to help the rest of the class to understand what you found.

Instructions: You are to pretend that you have just arrived on Earth in the first spaceship from a distant planet. You have been ordered to learn as much about one Earthling organization as you can without doing anything to make them aware that you are from outer space. The crash course in Earth languages taught by the Bureau of Interplanetary Intelligence has enabled you to read their language, but beyond simple greeting phrases, you *cannot* talk to the "natives."

These instructions limit your data collection to observation only. There are two reasons for this. First, your objective is to learn what the organization does when it is simply going about its normal business and not responding to a group of students asking questions. Second, you are likely to be surprised at how much you can learn by simply observing if you put your mind to it. Many skilled managers employ this ability in sensing what is going on as they walk through their plant or office area. Since you cannot talk to people, some of the cultural forms (legends, sagas, etc.) will be difficult to spot unless you are able to pick up copies of the organization's promotional literature (brochures, company reports, advertisements) during your visit. Do not be discouraged, because the visible forms such as artifacts, setting, symbols, and (sometimes) rituals can convey a great deal about the culture. Just keep your eyes, ears, and antennae open!

Source: Adapted from Donald D. Bowen (1988), "Alien invasion: An organizational culture assignment," In *Experiences in Management and Organizational Behavior*, 3rd edition, edited by Roy J. Lewicki, Donald D. Bowen, Douglas T. Hall, and Francine S. Hall. New York: John Wiley & Sons, Inc. Copyright © 1988 by John Wiley & Sons, Inc. Reprinted by permission of John Wiley & Sons, Inc.

EXPERIENTIAL EXERCISE 3.2

Promoting Cross-Cultural Awareness Among Management Students

Goals:
  1. To heighten awareness of the need for people to be well-prepared to work with people from other cultures.
  2. To demonstrate specific problems that can occur when people attempt to establish cross-cultural working relationships without familiarizing themselves with the other culture first.

Time Required: 1 1/2 hours.

Materials: A copy of the International Management Role Play for each student.

A Canadian Vice-president for Denim Unlimited, Inc., a maker of fashionable denim clothes (jeans, jackets, skirts, etc.), has set up a meeting with a representative of the most prominent retail distributor in a particular foreign country. At the meeting, they will discuss the possibility of the distributor distributing Denim Unlimited clothes in that country, or manufacturing and distributing Denim Unlimited clothes in that country. The Canadian VP initiated the contact and has asked for a face-to-face meeting and a tour of the distributor's facilities. Each person wants to get a feel for whether he/she will be able to work well with the other person—that is the major purpose of the meeting." Note: If the meeting is in a country in which the government controls the production of goods, you may assume that the government has granted permission for the meeting to take place and is interested in its outcome.

Procedure:

Two or more classes before the role play is to be held, the instructor solicits three volunteers, two with experience in working with people from the same foreign country and one without such experience. The inexperienced volunteer is asked to play the role of the Canadian Vice-President and to act as a stereotypical businessperson who is ignorant of other cultures. The two experienced volunteers make a plan, with the instructor's help, and build into the role play as many elements as possible of the culture with which they are familiar. One will play the role of the representative of the foreign retail distributor, and the other will play whatever role(s) the two decide. All class members read the role play scenario. The role play is then held in class, taking whatever time is necessary up to 30 minutes.

The instructor then leads a discussion that examines the role play from the perspective of:

a) The experienced volunteers—their intentions in designing the role play, and what they incorporated into it.

b) The inexperienced volunteer—how it felt to be in the situation, what he/she would have done differently if not required to act in a way ignorant of the other culture.

c) The observers—what they saw happening in the role play, questions they have of the volunteers, what they would have done differently.

Source: Adapted from an exercise by Gary N. Powell, University of Connecticut. Originally published in the *Proceedings of the Third Biennial International Management Conference of the Eastern Academy of Management*, Hong Kong, June 1989. Adapted/reprinted by permission.

SELF-GUIDED LEARNING ACTIVITY

The Organizational Culture Inventory has been created as a tool for measuring the cultural styles of organizations. A useful exercise to learn about organizational culture is to study the inventory and then apply it to an actual organization. Two articles that describe the Organizational Culture Inventory and its use are: Robert A. Cooke and Denise M. Rousseau (1988), "Behavioral norms and expectations: A quantitative approach to the assessment of organizational culture," in *Group & Organization Studies* 13: 245-273; and Robert A. Cooke and J.C. Lafferty (1986), "Level V: Organizational Culture Inventory—Form III," Plymouth, MI: Human Synergistics.

CASE 3.1

MANAGER'S CASE FILE: DON'T BET ON IT

Bob Adler walked back to his office with a smile on his face. Everything seemed to be going his way. Bob had joined Harrison Services six months ago, and yesterday he'd had his first performance appraisal—a favorable one. And today, after the staff meeting, he'd been invited by the other supervisors to join them for drinks after work. They had been standoffish at first, but his dedication to the job and his determination to generate the best materials possible seemed to be winning their trust and acceptance. As he got closer to his office, he was roused from his reverie by all the commotion surrounding his secretary's desk.

He waited until the other workers had gone back to their desks, then he called Linda into his office.

"I see you're the center of attraction this morning. Did you get engaged or something? I know you've been seeing someone for a couple of years," he said.

"No, nothing like that, Mr. Adler. But I did win $100."

"Terrific. Did you hit the lottery?"

"Oh, didn't you know? I won the pool."

"What pool?"

"The baseball pool," Linda said. "Everyone was in it, but I picked the World Series winner, the game number, and the score."

Suddenly Linda became quiet, realizing that she'd said too much.

"Do I understand you correctly, Linda? Are you telling me that there is gambling on company premises?"

"Well, it's not hard gambling exactly, Mr. Adler. It's more like the lottery. Everything over the $100 pot goes to a good cause. Because I won, I get to pick the charity that will get the rest of the money."

"Don't you know there's a company rule against gambling?" he asked.

"Well, no. I ..."

"Just last week Mr. Ashford gave a speech to a business group on gambling. He made it a point to note that gambling has been outlawed in this company for years and that there were severe consequences for anyone who was caught in the act."

"But Mr. Adler," Linda said, "this pool has been going on for years. And it helps a good cause, too."

"But it's against the rules."

"I'm sorry that I said anything, Mr. Adler. Remember we were having a personal conversation. Not that it's much of a secret. Everybody must know except you and Mr. Ashford. Mr. Gavin was happy enough when he won last year, and Mr. Sanders the year before."

Mr. Gavin and Mr. Sanders were fellow supervisors—the same supervisors whom Bob had slowly been making friends with. Bob and Linda just looked at each other until she turned and left his office.

Bob looked in his desk for the company rule book that had been given him six months before. There it was printed, just as he'd remembered it: "DISMISSALS FOR CAUSE: Any employee making a bet on company time, or on the premises of the company, is subject to suspension for the first offense, and to dismissal should the offense be repeated. Any employee soliciting bets on company time, or on the premises of the company, is subject to immediate dismissal."

Bob wondered what, if anything, he should do.

Source: Reprinted, by permission of publisher, from MANAGEMENT SOLUTIONS, November 1986. © 1986 American Management Association, New York. All rights reserved.

Questions

1. Could Bob consider the rule a dead issue since it apparently is not enforced?

2. Is Bob honour bound to keep Linda's information to him confidential?

3. What, if anything, should Bob do?

CASE 3.2

KYOCERA AMERICA INC.

It was exactly 7 o'clock on a foggy morning in San Diego. In the parking lot just a few feet away from Kiyohide Shirai's very American Oldsmobile 98, 700 employees of Kyocera America Inc. (KAI) were participating in a very Japanese ritual. Lined up on white dots and dressed in identical baby blue jackets, they politely applauded a series of motivational speeches made by their colleagues. Then they started gyrating and jumping up and down in unison, exercising as if they were a single organism. Most of the employees were Americans. "This," said Shirai, KAI's president, "is the Kyocera way."

The "Kyocera way" may have seemed odd to the American employees, but it has proved very good for business. With $2.7 billion in sales worldwide last year, the 31-year-old Kyoto-based company (the name combines *Kyoto* and *ceramics*) is the most successful producer of industrial ceramics in the world. No mere pottery kiln, Kyocera makes everything from satellite parts to false teeth out of complex synthetic materials with tonsil-twisting names. The company also owns the Yashica camera company and makes laser printers for Unisys and laptops for Tandy. It has recently purchased two American companies—Elco Corp., which makes electrical connectors, and AVX Corp., the largest U.S. producer of multilayer ceramic capacitors—that give it additional products and plants in Western Europe and Southeast Asia. Its future plans include the application of ceramic technologies to semiconductivity, automobile engines, even paper products.

At Kyocera there is a virtual personality cult surrounding its maverick founder and chairman, Dr. Kazuo Inamori. As Sony is made in the image of Akio Morita, so is Kyocera the expression of Inamori's passion and ambition. To motivate his minions, he produces a stream of philosophical tracts, known as Inamori-isms. He once compared the broadcasting of his wisdom throughout the company's plants around the world to "the way Christ's disciples spread his teachings to the lands he couldn't visit." Beneath this New Age-ish veneer, however, is a company built on traditional values. "Work is life," Inamori likes to say.

Shirai, 49, is a ceramics engineer trained in Nagoya, Japan. He joined Kyocera in 1964 and was named president of KAI in April 1988. He is an affable character given to long technical descriptions of the company's products. His U.S. operation—which he insisted is largely autonomous from Kyoto—has a lock on 67 percent of the U.S. market for ceramic semiconductor-chip packages and is renowned for its quality and service. "Inamori-*san* set my destiny after college," Shirai said, nodding deferentially to a photograph of his mentor on the wall of what serves as Inamori's office when he's in town and the conference room when he isn't. "I am like his apprentice. This is my first job and my final job." But, he continued, "I wear two caps. I have the responsibility for selling products made in Kyoto at the same time that I am selling [some of the same] products made here. Although there is a strong bond at the bottom of our hearts, we are in competition with headquarters. Dr. Inamori likes to keep the entrepreneurial spirit alive. It's a dilemma."

Shirai learned of Inamori's faith in the entrepreneurial spirit firsthand when the revered founder decided to expand to the U.S. in 1971. Kyocera bought the struggling Fairchild Semiconductor plant in San Diego (which had been one of its best customers) so the factory would be near the nascent computer industry. Inamori then gave Shirai and four other Japanese engineers one-way tickets to California and said, "Unless you create a successful company, I never want to see you again. To reach our goal of being number one, you have to work harder than anyone else." Unfortunately, the five disciples arrived along with the recession of the early 1970s. "Frankly, we really struggled to survive," said Shirai, who regularly worked 15-hour days, seven days a week. "Inamori-*san* insisted we sacrifice our life to lead."

Source: Prud'homme, Alex (1990). "Cult of personality." Reprinted with permission, BUSINESS MONTH magazine, August 1990. Copyright © 1990 by Goldhirsh Group, Inc., 38 Commercial Wharf, Boston, MA 02110.

These days, KAI has no major American competitors, which is ironic, since most of the technology it uses was pioneered by the American Lava Company in the 1950s. KAI improved on the technology in the 1970s, when it began producing custom-designed ceramic housings for semiconductor chips at a lower price than the standard-sized products offered by 3M, Coors Porcelain, and Owens-Illinois. "Some Americans claim that the Japanese stole their technology," said Shirai. "In my opinion, the Japanese are more humble. They are willing to learn from the Americans."

Shirai is unimpressed by the quality of American-made goods. "It's a common problem of the manufacturing industries in the U.S.," he said. "I don't like to admit it, but the yield at this plant is not as good as it should be. If you compare an American operator with a Japanese operator, there is no difference. But when we work as a team, I see a difference. It takes 70 or 80 steps to make each part. If just one person is sloppy, we lose out. The key is the mind of the people. When mistakes are made, I feel like we haven't convinced the workers of our way."

There is a note of arrogance in the company's boasting of the Kyocera way, as if it were infallible. That inflexibility may explain why KAI has had a dismal track record in keeping qualified Americans on staff. Not that management hasn't tried. There have been three American plant managers: Two quit, and one was fired. "Unfortunately," said Shirai, "many capable people have left. In most cases, they were frustrated. They felt they were not utilized 100 percent, or they did not agree with our way of thinking. Being number one means being able to work with us. My impression is that the most capable Americans still don't want to join a Japanese company."

An engineer who recently left KAI concurs. "It was a difficult, high-pressure place to work," he says. "Their attitude is that they have a good system and it's not going to change. If you can work in it, fine; if not, too bad. It was discouraging. Of the 12 Americans who came in with me, only two are left."

Shirai seemed genuinely troubled by this. "I do not have an answer," he said. "I'm still reaching."

Questions

1. Is there an answer for this problem of keeping qualified Americans on staff in a Japanese-culture company?

2. Should a Japanese company be allowed to set up a subsidiary in Canada and run it using Japanese cultural methods?

3. What evidence is there in this case that Kyocera is a Type A, J, or Z company?

REFERENCES

Adler, Nancy J. (1991). *International Dimensions of Organizational Behavior*, Second edition. Boston: PWS-KENT. This is a fascinating book about the international applications of organizational behaviour.

Adler, Nancy J., & Susan Bartholomew (1992). "Managing globally competent people." *Academy of Management Executive* 6(3): 52-65.

Bartlett, John. (1980). *Familiar Quotations*, 15th edition. Boston: Little, Brown and Company.

Beyer, Janice M., & Harrison M. Trice (1987). "How an organization's rites reveal its culture." 15(4): 4-24.

Bluedorn, Allen C., Carol Felker Kaufman, & Paul M. Lane (1992). "How many things do you like to do at once? An introduction to monochronic and polychronic time." *Academy of Management Executive* 6(4): 17-26.

Bowen, Donald D. (1988). "Alien invasion: An organizational culture assignment." In Roy J. Lewicki, Donald D. Bowen, Douglas T. Hall, & Francine S. Hall (Eds.), *Experiences in Management and Organizational Behavior*, 3rd edition. New York: John Wiley & Sons, Inc, pp. 180-186.

Buono, Anthony F., James L. Bowditch, & John W. Lewis, III (1985). "When cultures collide: The anatomy of a merger." *Human Relations* 38: 477-500.

Cartwright, Susan, & Carl L. Cooper (1993). "The role of culture compatibility in successful organizational marriage." *Academy of Management Executive* 7(2): 57-70.

Caudron, Shari (1992). "Subculture strife hinders productivity." *Personnel Journal*, December 1992, pp. 60-64.

Chatman, Jennifer A. (1991). "Matching people and organizations: Selection and socialization in public accounting firms." *Administrative Science Quarterly* 36: 459-484.

Cooke, Robert A., & Denise M. Rousseau (1988). "Behavioral norms and expectations: A quantitative approach to the assessment of organizational culture." *Group & Organization Studies* 13: 245-273.

Cooke, Robert A., & J. Clayton Lafferty (1986). *Level V: Organizational Culture Inventory - Form III*. Plymouth, MI: Human Synergistics.

Deal, Terrence E., & Allen A. Kennedy (1982). *Corporate Cultures: The Rites and Rituals of Corporate Life*. Reading, MA: Addison-Wesley Publishing Co., Chapter 6.

Feldman, Daniel C. (1981). "The multiple socialization of organizational members." *Academy of Management Review* 6: 309-318.

Fukuda, K. John (1992). "The internationalization of Japanese business: Different approaches, similar problems." *The International Executive* 34(1): 27-41.

Greenwood, Royston, C.R. (Bob) Hinings, & John L. Brown (1994). "Merging professional service firms." *Organization Science* 5: 239-257.

Gross, Warren, & Shula Shichman (1987). "How to grow an organizational culture." *Personnel* 64(9): 52-56.

Harrison, J. Richard, & Glenn R. Carroll (1991). "Keeping the faith: A model of cultural transmission in formal organizations." *Administrative Science Quarterly* 36: 552-582.

Hofstede, Geert (1980). *Culture's Consequences: International Differences in Work-related Values*. Beverly Hills, CA: Sage Publications.

Hofstede, Geert (1993). "Cultural constraints in management theories." *Academy of Management Executive* 7(1): 81-94.

Kilburn, David (1994). "Life-time employment, promotion through seniority and single-company unions — are the foundations of Japanese management crumbling?" *Management Today*, January 1994, pp. 46-47.

Klassen, Cathryn (1993). "Improving quality means improving communication." *Canadian Business Review*, Summer 1993, pp. 15-18.

Kliem, Ralph L. (1987). "Welcoming new employees the right way." *Administrative Management*, 48(7): 14-15.

Limerick, David C. (1990). "Managers of meaning: From Bob Geldof's band aid to Australian CEOs." *Organizational Dynamics*, 18(4): 22-33.

Martin, Joanne, Martha S. Feldman, Mary Jo Hatch, & Sim B. Sitkin (1983). "The uniqueness paradox in organizational stories." *Administrative Science Quarterly* 28: 438-453. This article gives examples of stories, sagas, and myths.

Meek, V. Lynn (1988). "Organizational culture: Origins and weaknesses." *Organization Studies* 9: 453-473.

Morley, John David (1985). *Pictures from the Water Trade: An Englishman in Japan*. London: André Deutsch Limited.

Murdock, George P. (1945). "The common denominator of cultures." In Ralph Linton (Ed.), *The Science of Man in the World Crisis* (pp. 123-142). New York: Columbia University Press.

O'Day, R. (1974). "Intimidation rituals: Reactions to reform." *Journal of Applied Behavioral Science* 10: 373-386.

Ouchi, William G. (1981). *Theory Z: How American Business can Meet the Japanese Challenge*. Reading, MA: Addison-Wesley.

Ouchi, William G., & Alfred M. Jaeger (1978). "Type Z organization: Stability in the midst of mobility." *Academy of Management Review* 3: 305-314.

Pascale, Richard (1985). "The paradox of 'corporate culture': Reconciling ourselves to socialization." *California Management Review* 27(2): 26-41.

Pfeffer, Jeffrey (1981). "Management as symbolic action: The creation and maintenance of organizational paradigms." In Larry L. Cummings & Barry M. Staw (Eds.), *Research in Organizational Behavior* (pp. 1-52). Greenwich, CT: JAI Press.

Powell, Gary N. (1989). *Promoting Cross-cultural Awareness Among Management Students*. Proceedings of the Third Biennial International Management Conference of the Eastern Academy of Management, Hong Kong, June 1989.

Prud'homme, Alex (1990). "Cult of Personality." *Business Month*, August 1990: pp. 42-44.

Rentsch, Joan R. (1990). "Climate and culture: Interaction and qualitative differences in organizational meanings." *Journal of Applied Psychology* 75: 668-681.

Ronen, Simcha (1986). *Comparative and Multinational Management*. New York: Wiley.

Ronen, Simcha, & Oded Shenkar (1985). "Clustering countries on attitudinal dimensions: A review and synthesis." *Academy of Management Review* 10: 435-454.

Sathe, Vijay (1983). "Implications of corporate culture: A manager's guide to action." *Organizational Dynamics* 12(2): 4-23.

Schein, Edgar H. (1983). "The role of the founder in creating organizational culture." *Organizational Dynamics* 12(1): 13-28.

Schein, Edgar H. (1984). "Coming to a new awareness of organizational culture." *Sloan Management Review*, 25(2): 3-16.

Schein, Edgar H. (1985). *Organizational Culture and Leadership*. San Francisco: Jossey-Bass Inc.

Schein, Edgar H. (1990). "Organizational culture." *American Psychologist* 45(2): 109-119.

Schein, Edgar H. (1992). *Organizational Culture and Leadership.* Second edition. San Francisco: Jossey-Bass Inc.

Schwartz, Shalom (1992). "Universals in the content and structure of values: Theoretical advances and empirical tests in 20 countries." In Mark Zanna (Ed.), *Advances in Experimental Social Psychology* (pp. 1-65). New York: Academic Press.

Sheridan, John E. (1992). "Organizational culture and employee retention." *Academy of Management Journal* 35: 1036-1056.

Strauss, Norman (1993). "Make your visions valid & viable." *Management Today*, February 1993, p. 92.

Van Maanen, John (1978). "People processing: Strategies of organizational socialization." *Organizational Dynamics* 7(1): 19-36.

Wilkins, A.L. (1983). "The culture audit: A tool for understanding organizations." *Organizational Dynamics* 12(2): 24-38.

FURTHER READING

For an in-depth look at research and theory on corporate culture, as well as the practical use of the concept of culture, see the book by Mats Alvesson and Per Olof Berg (1992), *Corporate Culture and Organizational Symbolism: An Overview,* Hawthorne, NY: Walter de Gruyter, Inc. Also see the 1985 book by Vijay Sathe titled *Managerial Action and Corporate Culture,* published by Irwin. The book by John P. Kotter and James L. Heskett (1992), *Corporate Culture and Performance,* examines a series of cases of major culture change in corporations. Another case-based book on culture is by Joanne Martin (1992), *Cultures in Organizations: Three Perspectives.*

A short article that examines the practical side of organizational culture is by W. Jack Duncan (1989), "Organizational culture: 'Getting a fix' on an elusive concept," *Academy of Management Executive* 3: 229-238.

A look at how a leader would affect an organization's culture is that of Linda Smircich and Gareth Morgan (1982), "Leadership: The management of meaning," *The Journal of Applied Behavioral Science* 18: 257-273. Also see Linda Smircich (1983), "Concepts of culture and organizational analysis," *Administrative Science Quarterly* 28: 339-358; Ralph H. Kilmann, Mary J. Saxton, and R. Serpa (1986), "Issues in understanding and changing culture," *California Management Review* 28(2): 87-94; and P. Gagliardi (1986), "The creation and change of organizational cultures," *Organization Studies* 7: 117-134.

On subcultures and counter-cultures, see the article by Joanne Martin and Caren Siehl (1983) titled "Organizational culture and counter culture: An uneasy symbiosis" in the Autumn 1983 issue of *Organizational Dynamics*, pages 52 to 64.

A 1991 book that contains a number of articles about organizational culture is edited by the University of British Columbia's Peter J. Frost and Larry F. Moore, Meryl Reis Louis, Craig C. Lundberg, and Joanne Martin. It is titled *Reframing Organizational Culture,* published in Thousand Oaks, CA by Sage Publications.

An examination of the specific advantages that are likely to accrue to organizations that have members from cultures either very high or very low on Hofstede's culture dimensions is found in Geert Hofstede's 1991 book *Cultures and Organizations: Software of the Mind,* published in New York by McGraw-Hill. An article dealing with the measurement of organizational culture is by Geert Hofstede, Bram Neuijen, Denise Daval Ohayv, and Geert Sanders (1990), "Measuring organizational cultures: A qualitative and quantitative study across twenty cases," in *Administrative Science Quarterly* 35: 286-316. "A conversation with Geert Hofstede" by Richard Hodgetts is to be found in *Organizational Dynamics*, 1993, 21(4): 53-61.

THE NATURE OF WORK
AND JOB DESIGN

CHAPTER OUTLINE

Three Revolutions in the Nature of Work

The Context of Work

    Places of Work

    Hours of Work

Job Design

    Engineering

    Ergonomics

    Biological

    Psychological

    Integrative Views

Conclusion

QUESTIONS TO CONSIDER

- *How do people work and where do they work?*

- *How is the work day structured for different people and jobs?*

- *What is it like to work in different jobs?*

- *How are jobs designed and analyzed?*

Organizations divide their work to be done into tasks, then combine tasks together into jobs that can each be held by an individual. The way jobs are designed affects the individual job holder's internal state and external behaviours—how he feels and acts. Organizations are therefore interested in job design as a means of increasing worker satisfaction, motivation, and performance. Job design is the essence of this chapter.

Before we examine theories of job design, it is important to consider the nature of work generally, first by surveying how work has changed over the years and then by discussing the context of work.

THREE REVOLUTIONS IN THE NATURE OF WORK

The nature of work and how work is done has been changing over thousands of years. It is still changing, and the rate of change has quickened significantly in the last twenty years. An examination of the history of work will help us to better understand the nature of work as it is today.

The modern form of humans has lived on Earth for over 30 000 years (Beazley, 1979). For most of this time their work was providing food and shelter for themselves. At the beginning, people's "jobs" were determined by their sex and role in the group, the season of the year, and the group's geographic location. Women had primary responsibility for child care, the gathering of wild plants, and food preparation. Men hunted and fished, usually cooperatively. Some people still live this way in the world today.

Agricultural Revolution

Began with the purposeful planting of crops, which allowed people to live in one place and eventually develop towns and cities.

About 10 000 years ago people living in the area that is now Iran, Iraq, Syria, and Southern Turkey began to domesticate wild plants and animals. This change, though gradual, was nothing short of revolutionary, and is known today as the **agricultural revolution**. The planting of crops allowed people to live in one place, a place with abundant water, fertile soil, and a warm climate. They could grow much more plant food than could previously be gathered. The shepherding of animals allowed a secure source of milk, meat, and wool. As a result, the number of people that could be supported grew dramatically. Thus were born the first towns.

The nature of jobs changed with the agricultural revolution. Food producers had work that continued to follow the seasons, much like that of the earlier hunter-gatherers. But another type of job was created, that of the specialist. Since the people who produced food could grow much more than they themselves needed to survive, the excess could be used to feed other people who did not engage in any food production. These others could then specialize in the making of tools and household objects and sell or barter their production for food. These were the manufacturers of 8000 years ago. Their products might be made in the home, in a public place like a market, or in a small factory.

Industrial Revolution

A series of inventions that made machines faster, more powerful and more efficient, and that allowed more physical goods to be made more inexpensively than before.

Merchants acquired goods from manufacturers and engaged in trade over wide areas. A growing town also needed the infrastructure of roads, housing, a safe water supply, and sewage disposal. The coordination of these activities was undertaken by a first government—a city leader, group of elders, or chieftain. The job of working for the government was created. Other specialist jobs followed, such as teacher, soldier, and priest. These new jobs were often restricted to males. Females worked in the market, produced goods in the home, and raised the children. The world's population grew slowly over the next millenia. New areas were settled and new towns formed, but the basic form of life and jobs remained the same. The jobs of food producer, government worker, small manufacturer, and specialist are still with us, of course.

Then, starting about the year 1779 came the **industrial revolution**. With the industrial revolution the nature of work changed dramatically for a large number of people. A series of inventions made machines faster, more powerful, and more efficient, allowing more physical goods to be made more inexpensively than before. The factory job was created as production was moved from the less efficient home producers to the large centralized factory full of efficient water or steam-powered machines. People began to move from the countryside to the towns in order to take these new factory jobs. In Canada and the U.S. the movement of people from farms and smaller towns to the larger cities is still in progress today. Some parts of the world are just now starting their industrial revolution. Some are firmly in the industrial era, producing primary goods such as steel and secondary manufactured products. Some are, however, entering the post-industrial era.

This latest and most recent revolution has been called the **information revolution**. Jobs are changing from making things or providing a service (for example, fire fighting) to the manipulation and production of information. Whereas work at the agricultural and industrial levels depends on strength and physical skill, information jobs require more mental skills and abilities. Stock market analysts, management consultants, scientists, auditors, teachers, librarians—all these can be considered as having this new type of job. The invention of computers and their recent explosive growth in availability and power, coupled with steep price declines has allowed information to be captured, manipulated, and sent to others around the world with increasing ease. More scientists are producing more knowledge. Information jobs are revolutionizing how and where work is done. People no longer have to be physically in the same place to work together. Information work can be done in a remote corner of the world and sent by satellite to a user anywhere in the world.

We have seen that over thousands of years how people do their work has changed. But one reason why people work has remained the same—to provide food and shelter for themselves and their families. An examination of why people and organizations work, not how they work, is found in this chapter's *A Word to the Wise.*

Women workers in an early factory rolling the steel for pens in Birmingham, England.

Information revolution

With the advent of microcomputers and telecommunications technology, work is increasingly involved with the manipulation and production of information.

A WORD TO THE WISE

The recession has precipitated a discussion that has not yet extended beyond crisis management in politics and industry. Management literature and seminars of all kinds are in great demand, but they are usually concerned with one question alone: how? How can we solve problems as quickly as possible? How can commercial enterprises increase productivity and optimize costs? How do we decide our priorities?

Such questions are justified, but they show that a company is divided into separate parts in order to find individual answers. The whole is worth more than the sum of its parts, however.

Managing is no longer a question of setting priorities between, for example, shareholders, customers or social responsibility to employees. This approach does no justice to the future tasks of commercial enterprises. If we are concerned with the entire company and its environment, we cannot be satisfied with the question of "how?" because the answers are at best temporary.

Instead we must be able to ask "why?" As a manager of a car company I must be able to ask why we build

cars. Only if I accept the meaning of this product for our society can I be convincing as a manager.

With the answers we can develop concepts which take into account the company's and employees' requirements. Because when we ask "why?" of a company we examine both the purpose and the permanence of each individual, as well as the tasks they perform and their dependence on the company.

A time of economic crisis reveals whether a company has developed an all-embracing philosophy and a feasible corporate culture. Only if each individual in the corporate body understands the tasks and objectives of the whole and adjusts accordingly can survival be guaranteed.

Like most other companies, Volkswagen is undergoing this acid test. But it has created a solid basis from which to emerge with redoubled strength. A key element is labour relations, which have been based on the principle of partnership since 1945. It means that Volkswagen's strategy in the current economic crisis is broadly accepted: every employee who is aware of what he can achieve strengthens the company internally and externally.

Partnership also characterizes the increasingly co-operative style of management and group work at Volkswagen. Hierarchies are being removed. External relationships—with the car components industry, for example—are also becoming more partnership-based.

The catalysts for these developments are managers and entrepreneurs. They must proceed according to a notion freely adapted from Goethe: tell someone why and they will always find out how.

That is what the management philosophy of the future must be based upon. Executive functions will change as a result. Tomorrow's manager will bear wider responsibility; he will have to build bridges between employees and trade unions, management and shareholders, and customers and the general public. He must make each individual understand his company's objectives, and that will involve values which go well beyond traditional commercial priorities.

To meet this demand, we need managers who are innovative and, above all, who think comprehensively. They will possess high potential for solving problems, reflected in creative thinking and readiness to make decisions. And they will have a "helicopter" ability to view a problem from an elevated position and still be able to swoop to tackle its individual aspects.

Volkswagen's management trainees increasingly conform to this image of what we term the "one-world manager." Tomorrow's managers will speak several languages and feel at home in other cultures. They give reason to hope that ideas will spread on a more international scale.

Volkswagen has been the leader of Europe's car market for several years and has steadily increased its share of the sector to 17% from 10%. But just to maintain our leadership requires management to have a plausible philosophy. The Japanese car industry has shown us how a collective idea can be successfully implemented in all areas of a company. Only if we develop a distinct concept embedded in our European culture will we, as managers, be able to motivate our employees and demand that they work together.

- -

SOURCE: By Daniel Goeudevert "Age of reasons," Reprinted with permission, *International Management* (May, 1993), p. 68. Mr. Goeudevert is Deputy Chair of Volkswagen AG and Chair of the Volkswagen division.

THE CONTEXT OF WORK

The series of revolutions have brought about changes in the context of work. The context of work includes the place where the work is performed and the hours of work. These elements vary from job to job.

Places of Work

Where people work varies. We often think of the workplace as a factory or office building, but many jobs are not tied to a particular building. These jobs are performed by people who are commonly said to work "in the field." Bus and truck drivers, couriers, police and fire personnel, salespeople who call on individuals and corporations to sell or service products, construction workers, and many others spend much of their time moving from place to place. They may spend time in a home office but are not restricted to it. (The jobs of fire fighter and salt miner are described in this chapter's *Seeing is Believing* feature.) In addition, some people work at home.

Communications technology allows regular and easy contact between people in the course of doing their work. The information revolution, some analysts believe, will promote a return to the dispersed work sites of the past. This may be termed **flexiplace**. Individuals could work from their homes to produce an information product while being linked to the rest of the world physically by couriers and electronically by fax and phone lines. This **telecommuting** usually does not replace working from an office building but allows work to be spread over two or more sites. While these may be primarily the office and the home, work could take place on the road, in a hotel room, or on the beach (Caudron, 1992).

Flexiplace Work not tied to a particular work site.

Telecommuting Work that is spread over two or more sites, typically the office and the home.

SEEING IS BELIEVING

A NIGHT IN THE LIFE OF NO. 5

It is seven minutes to three on a Saturday morning. In the watch room of No. 5 fire station in downtown Toronto, the dispatch monitors are silent. Lewandowski does not complain. In a year when merely having a job has become a status symbol, he has one he loves. Eight years ago, he took a cut in pay when he gave up a career as a surveyor to "get on" with the fire department. It was, he says, "the best move I ever made." Acting district Chief Jim Bonner, on duty at No. 5 station, says that is typical. "All the guys love their job," he said, sitting in the kitchen earlier that night after a communal meal of pea soup and ham, pie and ice cream. There is not much not to like on this 14-hour night shift, which consists almost entirely of waiting for emergency calls that do not come. No. 5 station is well equipped for waiting, with exercise equipment, a lounge, a large kitchen and dining room and sleeping quarters for 15 or so firefighters.

During the day, firefighters train, do fire-prevention inspections, maintain their equipment and clean the fire hall in between calls. Everything gleams. Even the brass poles from the sleeping quarters are regularly shined when the station gets "stoked" once a week.

On this quiet night, the third and last call comes in just before 2 a.m. The station awakes; the boots get filled and the trucks roll. Four minutes and 35 seconds later, Pumper No. 5 arrives at a waterfront hotel. It is a false alarm. If it had been the real thing, a relaxing night at the fire hall would have been transformed into a dangerous, dirty job. In 1990, 166 firefighters were injured. The work can be tough but it is almost always extremely satisfying, firefighters say. "We're always showing up as a friend," Chief Bonner says.

SOURCE: Excerpted from Craig McInnes (1992), "A night in the life of No. 5," The *Globe and Mail*, February 15, 1992, p. D3. Reprinted with permission.

I HEARD IT IN THE SALT MINE

When Ken McKenzie says, "Good afternoon," the "Good" is perfunctory and the "afternoon" theoretical. Here, 295 metres beneath the Detroit River, we are in the salt mines under Windsor, Ont., and Ken McKenzie, salt miner, grade II, a "greaser" who has worked the mines for 23 years, is on his afternoon shift, the 4 p.m. to midnight. As a greaser, it is his job to make underground rounds in an unesthetic grease truck offering a smorgasbord of goo to the functional and fearsome-looking array of specialized machinery that blasts rock salt from under Windsor.

Because salt is soft it allows for spacious "room-and-pillar" mining. Parallel shafts about 12 by 8 metres extend out and are intersected by crosscuts, creating huge intersections called "rooms" supported by pillars of salt 20 metres square. In this mine, you don't duck. Wearing a helmet anyway, greaser Ken McKenzie and his fellow miners—muckers, drillers, cuttermen, and loader/blasters—go "down the hole" (the mine-service shaft) at the start of a shift. At the bottom of the shaft the atmosphere is cool, dry, well-ventilated, and dimly lit. The foreman drives each man to his post, some at spots widely separated. He may see them again only twice in an eight-hour shift, when he ferries them back to the lunchroom for breaks or a meal. The work is solitary, specialized, and screamingly noisy.

Up on the surfaces, his shift over, Ken McKenzie takes off his helmet, wipes sweat from his brow and allows as how he likes it underground. "It is a job, a unique environment, that's about it." But he could not work above ground now. He tried once, quitting the mine for a few years for a factory job, only to return. Not for him a workplace with a window. In a place so isolated, so highly mechanized, it is surprising that he cites the people he works with as the main attraction. "Here they leave you alone. We know our work. I do my job. In a factory you can work 10 feet away from somebody and never get to know him. The foreman is always on you. You can't blow your nose. It is just work. Here," he says, "we're miners."

Mining Salt

SOURCE: Excerpted from Anthony Jenkins (1992), "I heard it in the salt mine," The *Globe and Mail*, January 18, 1992, p. D3. Reprinted with permission.

Hours of Work

During the Industrial Revolution, factory hours were long and work was carried out six days a week (see Exhibit 4.1 for an example). More recently in Canada and the U.S. the total number of hours worked on average in a year has been declining. The workday has shortened to 7.5 or 8 hours; holidays have lengthened from one or two weeks to two weeks or more per year; and people work on average only five days a week. This decline in total hours worked from about 2000 hours per year (40 hours per week times 50 weeks) is likely to continue as people continue to expect more free time from their regular job.

EXHIBIT 4.1   RULES & REGULATIONS TO BE OBSERVED BY ALL PERSONS EMPLOYED IN THE FACTORY OF AMASA WHITNEY

RULE 1: The Mill will be put into operation 10 minutes before sunrise at all seasons of the year. The gate will be shut 10 minutes past sunset from the 20th of March to the 20th of September; at 30 minutes past 8, from the 20th of September to the 20th of March. Saturdays at sunset.

SECOND: It will be required of every person employed, that they be in the room in which they are employed, at the time mentioned above for the mill to be in operation.

THIRD: Hands are not allowed to leave the factory in working hours, without the consent of their Overseer; if they do, they will be liable to have their time set off.

FOURTH: Anyone who by negligence or misconduct causes damage to the machinery, or impedes the progress of the work, will be liable to make good the damage for the same.

FIFTH: Anyone employed for a certain length of time, will be expected to make up their lost time, if required, before they will be entitled to their pay.

SIXTH: Any person employed for no certain length of time, will be required to give at least 4 weeks notice of their intention to leave, (sickness excepted) or forfeit 4 weeks' pay, unless by particular agreement.

SEVENTH: Anyone wishing to be absent any length of time, must get permission of the Overseer.

EIGHTH: All who have leave of absence for any length of time, will be expected to return in that time; and in case they do not return in that time, and do not give satisfactory reason, they will be liable to forfeit one week's work or less if they commence work again. If they do not, they will be considered as one who leaves without giving any notice.

NINTH: Anything tending to impede the progress of manufacturing in working hours, such as unnecessary conversation, reading, eating fruit, &c.&c., must be avoided.

TENTH: While I shall endeavor to employ a judicious Overseer, the help will follow his direction in all cases.

ELEVENTH: No smoking will be allowed in the Factory, as it is considered very unsafe, and particularly specified in the Insurance.

TWELFTH: In order to forward the work, job hands will follow the above regulations as well as those otherwise employed.

THIRTEENTH: It is intended that the bell be rung 5 minutes before the gate is hoisted, so that all persons may be ready to start their machines precisely at the time mentioned.

FOURTEENTH: All persons who cause damage to the machinery, break glass out of the windows, &c., will immediately inform the overseer of the same.

FIFTEENTH: The hands will take breakfast, from the 1st of November till the 1st of March, before going to work—they will take supper from the 1st of May till the last of August, 30 minutes past 5 o'clock, P.M.—from the 20th of September till the 20th of March, between sundown and dark—25 minutes will be allowed for breakfast, 30 minutes for dinner, and 25 minutes for supper, and no more, from the time the gate is shut till started again.

SIXTEENTH: The hands will leave the Factory so that the doors may be fastened within 10 minutes from the time of leaving off work.

AMASA WHITNEY. Winchendon, July 5, 1830.

NOTE: The gate referred to in this notice is the watergate. When raised, water would turn the waterwheel which would supply the power to the machines in the factory.

There are, however, other reasons for this decline in total hours worked. One is the recent increased emphasis on part-time work. The organization's work is divided into pieces that are small enough that each employee only works a part of the "regular" 40-hour week. Part-time jobs are often low-paying, offer limited employment benefits, and allow the employee to work only 20 to 24 hours per week. This approach creates more jobs in total, but each job provides less pay and benefits. Breaking the organization's tasks into pieces of part-time employment is a strategy that some companies are using to lower the cost of labour and benefits.

A second reason for the decline in total hours worked per person is job sharing. Though not common, **job sharing** involves splitting one full-time job between two people, so that each does part of the job. For example, an organization may have one full-time job for an advertising copywriter. This one job may be shared between two people, one who works mornings (for example) and the other who works the afternoons. Parents who have some time available for work but who cannot meet a full-time work commitment are good candidates for job sharing, especially for more highly skilled professional jobs. Pay and benefits are shared by agreement between the two job sharers.

Job sharing Splitting one full-time job between two people.

There are, of course, some exceptions to this average decline. Because of organizational downsizing, middle managers who have kept their jobs are working longer hours. In one study of 1344 middle managers, 33% reported working 40 to 45 hours per week, 57% said they worked 46 to 60 hours per week, and 6% worked 61 or more hours per week (Fisher, 1992). Professionals (for example lawyers, doctors, and accountants) work long hours, often 50 to 60 hours per week. Their work is often conducted at the office, at home, and while travelling on business. Entrepreneurs can expect to work very long hours, sometimes twelve hours a day six days a week. They decide what work to do and how to do it. An example of two entrepreneurs, Debbi and Randy Fields, who together run Mrs. Fields Cookies, is the subject of Integrative Case I.1, "Mrs. Fields' Secret Ingredient."

In Canada and the United States the average full-time working person can expect to put in about 2000 hours per year on the job and to take ten to fifteen days of paid vacation per year. In some other countries, especially those newly industrialized, total hours worked can still be well over 2000 and a six-day work week is not uncommon. Exhibit 4.2 compares working time for male industrial workers and shows that there is substantial variation in hours worked across countries.

For example, in the developing economy of Korea, the 899 hours worked over and above those worked on average in the United States means the Korean worker is putting in almost two hours a day more than his U.S. counterpart (working ten-hour versus eight-hour days) from Monday to Friday *and* working an eight-hour day on Saturday. Add to this the fact that fifteen less days of vacation are taken by the Korean worker and you can see that the Korean industrial worker is on the job almost all the time.

In other countries, however, the number of hours worked is even less than in the U.S. and Canada and more vacation days are taken. Where you live in the world therefore affects how hard you can expect to work.

In North America, regular office hours typically start between 8 and 9 in the morning and end between 4 and 5 at night, with an hour off for lunch. These hours are worked with minor variations from Monday to Friday by many people, as is demonstrated by the morning and afternoon rush hours of people commuting to and from work.

Flextime is an attempt to make it easier for employees to commute, by setting a core time of the day when all must be at work, for example 10 a.m. to 3 p.m., but allowing flexibility in the other three hours of the workday. Individual employees might choose to work from 7 a.m. to 3 p.m., 10 a.m. to 6 p.m., or whatever particular times best suit their own schedule and lifestyle. As long as the total hours worked are as required by the company and all work the core period—in order to allow easy communication within the organization and with customers and suppliers—the flextime system functions well.

Flextime Allowing employees to choose to some extent the hours that they will work.

EXHIBIT 4.2 AVERAGE HOURS WORKED AND
VACATION TAKEN PER YEAR FOR MALE
INDUSTRIAL WORKERS

COUNTRY	AVERAGE HOURS WORKED PER YEAR	VACATION DAYS ACTUALLY TAKEN PER YEAR
Korea	2833	4.5
Japan	2180	9.6
Great Britain	1941	22.5
United States	1934	19.5
West Germany	1652	30.2
France	1649	25.0

SOURCE: Table selected from THE CHAEBOL: KOREA'S NEW INDUSTRIAL MIGHT by Richard M. Steers, Yoo Keun Shin, and Gerardo R. Ungson, p. 96. Copyright © 1989. Reprinted by permission of HarperCollins Publishers Inc.

NOTE: *Chaebol* means Korean patrimonial bureaucracy.

But many people do not work in offices, and therefore work different hours. Grocery stores are now open until midnight, or even all night, seven days a week. Shops in malls open at 9 or 10 a.m. and remain open until 9 at night, Monday to Friday, with shorter hours on Saturday and Sunday. In hospitals there must be doctors and nurses and their supporting X-ray and laboratory services available 24 hours a day. Restaurants may open late in the day for the dinner trade and remain open until 2 a.m. Factories often produce a product 12 or 16 hours a day. When dictated by the nature of the manufacturing process, they will remain functioning continuously. Oil refineries, nuclear power plants, and other continuous process technologies are of this type (see the B&B Containers case at the end of this chapter for another example).

Many factories and mines, as well as service organizations, divide the day into pieces, or shifts, and determine the activities that need to be completed during each shift. In a grocery store, shelves are often stocked at night, from midnight until 7 a.m., when customers are either absent because the store is closed or not present in large numbers. In an office building the cleaning staff arrive at 7 p.m. when most office personnel have gone home, and work into the early morning hours. In a factory, machine servicing may take place from midnight until 7 a.m. so that all machines are operational for the next 17 hours. In a hospital, only a skeleton staff is left to maintain minimal service at night. Most surgeries and tests are scheduled for the day, leaving only emergency work for the night.

Some common shifts worked are the day, evening, "graveyard," 10- or 12-hour, and split shifts. The day shift is a typical office day, and is often prized by shift workers because it allows them to work "normal" hours. Friends and family are more likely to be working during the day, so everyone is on the same schedule. Socializing, eating, and even sleeping is then easier. The evening shift runs from 4 p.m. to midnight or thereabouts. Working this shift allows the person to sleep during the night, but makes family dinners and socialization more difficult. On the other hand, the daytime is available for personal errands and activities.

The graveyard shift runs from midnight to 8 a.m. and got its name because of how quiet it usually is during the early morning hours. Most of the city is asleep and at work it may be lonely and quiet. This shift is hard on the worker because sleep in the day is difficult due to daylight, street noise, and interruptions such as the telephone and doorbell. Meals are difficult because others are eating dinner when the graveyard shift worker's day is just starting. Also, the shift worker's personal body-clock may be out-of-sync, resulting in physical stress. Possibly the hardest part of a graveyard shift is the weekend, if the worker starts to readjust to day hours only to return to night work. While shift work can pay slightly higher than normal for the job, and may often be the only job made available to a beginning employee, it is hard on a person's physical and psychological well-being. Workers on day, evening, and graveyard shifts are often rotated through the different shifts to spread the costs and benefits among everyone.

Those on ten-hour shifts work four days a week, with rotating days off, whereas twelve-hour shifts divide the day into two halves, and are usually worked on a three-days-on, four-days-off type of schedule. These are both **compressed work weeks**. Having several days off is an advantage, though 12 hours of work at a stretch can be very demanding in some occupations and for some individuals. Split-shifts require the worker to work for a few hours, take unpaid time off, and then return to work for several more hours. City bus drivers often have split-shifts, especially those drivers with low seniority, working the morning and evening rush hours and having free time around noon when the public's demand for bus travel is lower.

Compressed work weeks
The total weekly hours of work are compressed into three or four longer-than-usual days.

JOB DESIGN

There are four main approaches to the design of jobs (see Exhibit 4.3). The *engineering approach* is based on work in industrial engineering and scientific management. Its aim is to simplify jobs so that it becomes easy to find and train workers that can do those jobs. The efficiency of the work is the goal of the engineering approach to job design. The *ergonomics approach* is based on how humans process information and how their basic biology and physiology affect perception and physical movement. Its aim is to improve the fit between person and task so that the reliability of performance is enhanced and the person doing the job experiences less fatigue and stress. The *biological approach* to job design is based on work dealing with how people react to the physical conditions experienced in the workplace. Its aim is to reduce the physical stress and strain on the worker so that employee comfort is increased. The *psychological approach* to job design is based on work dealing with how people think about their jobs, the meaning of the job, and why the job is important. Its aims are to improve the worker's job satisfaction, motivation to do the job, involvement in the job, and job performance.

Each of these four approaches to job design focuses on a different outcome of work. Each has its own costs and benefits. The manager in an organization could not attempt to use all four approaches at the same time because their recommendations can conflict. For example, jobs can be simplified and made easy for a worker to accomplish adequate and reliable performance. But then these jobs are not likely to offer the depth and challenge that some workers require. Similarly, workers can be provided with the equipment and physical space that improve their comfort, but the organization must pay for that comfort. The design of jobs must be seen as requiring trade-offs between organizational and individual benefits.

We will now examine each of the four approaches to job design in greater detail.

EXHIBIT 4.3   APPROACHES TO JOB DESIGN

APPROACH	EXAMPLES OF RECOMMENDATIONS	FOCUS ON
Engineering	Use work simplification, specialization, time and motion study	Efficiency
Ergonomics	Develop equipment and jobs that are simple, safe, and reliable, and that minimize mental requirements of the worker	System reliability
Biological	Improve seating positions, lessen strength demands, reduce noise distractions	Employee comfort
Psychological	Enhance autonomy, skill and task variety, feedback from the task and others	Satisfaction, motivation

SOURCE: Adapted with permission from Stephen P. Robbins (1989), ORGANIZATIONAL BEHAVIOR: Concepts, Controversies, and Applications, 4/E, © 1989, p. 215. Reprinted by permission of Prentice-Hall, Inc., Englewood Cliffs, N.J. Research concerning these four approaches is examined by Michael Campion and Paul Thayer (1985, 1987) and by Michael Campion (1988).

Engineering

Scientific management, work simplification, and time and motion study (see Exhibit 1.5) are the sources of this approach. The engineering method concentrates on the job itself, and not on the person doing the job. It attempts to make the job easier to perform in order to obtain greater efficiency and reliability, make it easier to find people who can perform the job, and simplify training. One result is that the **job content** is reduced. The word processor operator with a job simplified in content is expected, for example, to spend a large amount of time at the computer entering and editing documents. Any physical and psychological effects on the people doing the job are of secondary importance. Workers are seen mechanistically, as interchangeable parts needed to do the work.

Job content   The tasks required in a job.

Ergonomics

This is the study of persons in their working environment and is concerned with the fit between the person and the machine. Here the person is considered in the performance of the work, but mostly in the sense of reducing errors that humans are likely to make. The attention and concentration requirements of jobs are designed so that the job does not demand too much of the worker's mental capabilities and basic human abilities.

Common ergonomic approaches are the design of parts that can be inserted only one way, machines that can be operated only in the most efficient manner, and dials that can be easily read. When a job is designed well ergonomically the reliability of job performance should be enhanced. The worker should make fewer mistakes and have fewer job-related accidents. Also, the individual worker should experience less fatigue, stress, mental overload, and boredom on the job (Campion, 1988).

Biological

This approach focuses on the physical comfort and well-being of the person doing the job and on the physical characteristics of the workplace. **Job conditions** concern where and how the work is done and in what physical environment. Exposure to physical risk is also a component of job conditions. For example, this chapter's *Overboard* cartoon suggests that Boof the Pirate cannot handle the risk inherent in being the helmsman of the ship.

Job conditions Where and how the work is done and in what physical environment.

SOURCE: OVERBOARD © Universal Press Syndicate. Reprinted with permission. All rights reserved.

The biological design of jobs and workplaces has been broken down into the five characteristics of privacy, lighting, air quality, noise, and space (Field & Phillips, 1991).

Privacy   This characteristic concerns visual and speech privacy as well as the physical accessibility of the office. Open-plan or landscaped offices are less private than traditional enclosed offices. Their walls are usually room dividers that can be moved as necessary. Offices are areas of the floor enclosed by dividers and usually do not have a door. The person working in an open office can typically be easily seen and heard, and is readily accessible. Open-plan workspaces may also be made up of workstations or carrels. In accounting firms, a large number of carrels in a sizeable room is called a "bullpen."

When Greg Oldham (1988) studied the reactions of employees to the design of offices, he found that employees felt they were less crowded, had greater task and communication privacy, and were more satisfied with their offices when they moved from one open office to another open office with more space or more separating partitions. These effects were not the same for everyone but were greater for those employees with higher needs for privacy.

Lighting   Natural light is preferred to artificial light by most people. Natural light contains the full spectrum of colours, and is perceived as warmer and brighter than artificial lighting. Fluorescent lighting can flicker, hum, and cause headaches. There are fluorescent tubes available that are called "full spectrum" because their design produces light that is 93% the same as natural light. Incandescent lights produce a more "yellow" light than most fluorescents. They are useful for desks because the light can be flexibly directed by the individual. This is an advantage because people at work like to be able to control the amount of light in their workspace.

Artificial lights can also be concentrated in an array to make a bright panel that mimics the intensity of natural outdoor light. Such a panel can be useful in controlling a form of depression, called seasonal affective disorder, caused in some individuals by a lack of light. Artificial light can also be used to help people working at night in offices or factories to control their body clocks. The body can be fooled into switching night for day, which helps the person to work more effectively at night. This night-for-day technique is used by zoos to deceive nocturnal animals into being active in the day when visitors are present.

Air Quality   This is one of the most important biological effects on the worker. Because many office towers are sealed, fresh air is supplied only through the heating, ventilating, and air conditioning (HVAC) system. Air temperatures are often not controllable in individual offices, so that some employees feel too hot and others too cool to work effectively.

The increasing numbers of computers, laser printers, photocopiers, and fax machines in an office release more chemicals into the air and therefore require a greater supply of fresh air. When air flow is restricted, contaminants can build up in the air causing allergic and medical reactions among employees.

This is known as **sick building syndrome**. One definition of this syndrome is "When more than 20 percent of the people working in [the building] complain of headaches, dizzy spells, sore throats, itchy eyes, nausea, skin irritations or coughs, and when workers get better 12 to 24 hours after leaving the building" (Farrar & Murray, 1993, p. 72).

To reduce the effects of poor office air quality the following prescriptions apply:

- The heating, ventilating and air-conditioning system needs to be examined and cleaned, especially to eliminate molds growing in the ventilation system itself (a cause of the potentially fatal Legionnaires' disease);
- Molds and mildews on walls and other surfaces must be cleaned;
- More fresh air needs to be drawn into the building;
- Fresh air intakes must be located away from exhausted air and outdoor pollutants;
- Tobacco smoke needs to be reduced or eliminated inside the building;
- Since paint, glue, and new cloth used in office screens and new carpets all give off vapours and gases, these need to be "cooked" off when installed by heating the building to high levels and venting the gases to the outside;
- The use of insecticides and volatile cleaners inside the building must be reduced.

Noise   Noise makes concentration difficult, and again is increasing in offices along with the number of office machines and the density of people working in the office. Noise can be reduced by installing noise absorbent ceiling, wall, and floor coverings. Another solution is to build walls and partitions that will shield workers from ambient noise. The addition of a white noise generator is also a possibility. A white noise generator emits sounds that are not distracting in themselves, but that effectively mask the auditory clutter in the office. An example of a white noise generator in the home is a machine that projects sounds of waves or rain. With such a generator operating in the office the conversations of others will be heard but the words spoken will be harder to make out. Such conversations will therefore be less distracting.

A more active and high-tech approach is **active noise control**. Here a microphone is placed near the source of a repetitive noise, the sounds picked up are digitally analyzed and an anti-noise is generated by a speaker. This anti-noise is made to be out of phase with the original noise so that the two cancel each other out. Noise here is not masked or baffled, but eliminated. For high-noise workplaces where hearing damage is a possibility, special anti-noise headsets can be worn (Morantz, 1992).

Space   Uncomfortable furniture, inappropriately sized work surfaces, sharp-cornered desks, and bookcases with the top shelves out of reach are all symptoms of a poor physical support system. People differ widely in their physical characteristics and equipment designed for the "average" person suits almost no one. The trend towards a more diverse work force also increases the need for the careful design of office furnishings and work equipment. For example, a farm combine needs to be designed so that it can be operated as easily by a smaller woman as by a larger man.

Sick building syndrome

When the environment inside a building is such that more than 20% of the people working in it complain of headaches and other forms of sickness. Usually caused by poor indoor air quality.

Active noise control

Anti-noise is electronically produced to cancel out repetitive noise.

Similarly, the adjustability and flexibility of office furnishings is becoming more and more important. The comfort, efficiency, and health of employees are key factors that are influenced by the design of the worker's physical space and equipment used.

One important new area of equipment design is that of computer monitors and keyboards. With many employees now sitting in front of video display terminals (VDTs) for long periods of time, the radiation they emit is a health concern. There are now low radiation monitors available for office use. Typing faster and faster on computer keyboards while having few rest breaks is causing repetitive stress disorders such as carpal tunnel syndrome and arm and wrist tendonitis. Several low stress, flexible keyboards have been designed that require far less finger muscle energy than conventional keyboards and can be split and rotated so that the user's hands are not in stressful positions (e.g., see Churbuck, 1993; Walmsley, 1992).

Psychological

In this approach to job design, the mental state of the worker is considered in the performance of the task. Job enlargement, job enrichment, job rotation, Motivator-Hygiene Theory, and the Job Characteristics Model are all forms of this approach.

Job Enlargement

Job enlargement refers to the addition of tasks to a job. The result is an increase in the job's **horizontal loading**. The greater the number of different tasks, the greater the job's horizontal loading, or range. When tasks are added that add variety to the work and help to break up the day, enlargement is a useful approach. However, if the tasks added are seen by job holders as "more of the same," the enlarged job will not likely increase the worker's motivation to perform the work.

Horizontal loading The number of different tasks a job requires.

An important aspect of job enlargement is a particular job's level of **job relationships.** This refers to the number of people with whom the job holder interacts, who these people are (clients, suppliers, customers, etc.) and how long these interactions typically last. For example, a telephone operator or person waiting on restaurant tables is in constant contact with the general public and, has a job high in number of relationships, but these last a short time. The more frequent the number of contacts and the briefer their duration, the more the job is horizontally loaded.

Job relationships The people with whom the job holder interacts.

Job Enrichment

This approach builds motivational factors into a job, making the job more complex and challenging. Enriched jobs are expected to increase the job holder's motivation to perform, especially if the worker is seeking more of a challenge. Enriched jobs may have increased authority, supervision, management, and decision-making responsibilities. The more these elements exist in a job the higher is its **vertical loading**.

Vertical loading The amount of authority, supervision, management and decision making responsibilities in a job.

An example of job enrichment for a travel agent would be to allow the agent to plan and book all the elements of a particular client's trips. Space would be booked on an airplane, the car rental arranged and a hotel room booked that met the distinctive needs of the client. The agent would deal with any changes or problems that arose, and would have the responsibility of making sure the client was satisfied with the travel arrangements and outcomes. The preparation of expense account statements, frequent flyer reward tickets, and personal holiday travel could also be added to the agent's job responsibilities.

Job Rotation

Job rotation allows the movement of people between jobs. This can help to reduce the boredom associated with performing any one job for a long period of time. In a factory with a number of assembly jobs, personnel can be moved between the jobs on a fixed rotation or on an "as-requested" basis. Rotation could occur at the end of a relatively long period of time performing one job, a month for example, or could occur on a daily basis. Job rotation is not limited to factory or service jobs. Professionals can be "seconded" from their home organization to help another organization for a fixed period. An executive might, for instance, be given four months away from the home organization to work with the United Way on its yearly campaign.

One benefit of job rotation is that it has a group cooperative emphasis. Personnel rotated through jobs build personal relationships with others while learning what the others do in their work. A bank management trainee could, for example, expect to rotate through a number of different functional areas in bank branches, through branches of different sizes and serving different clienteles, before being assigned to head office.

In Canada job rotation is thought of as something to be built into the job. In Japan, job rotation is quite a normal event. While Canadians are generally used to fixed designs in their daily life, Japanese workers are used to flexibility. This chapter's *A Rose by Any Other Name* feature explores this concept in more depth.

A ROSE BY ANY OTHER NAME

The Japanese way of carrying out a task is based on the principle of *interactive heterogeneity*, while the American way is based on the principle of categorized and specialized heterogeneity.

The principle of interactive heterogeneity has deep roots. While Greek philosophers and European scholars were writing books on social organization and interaction, the Japanese were developing and refining their principles of interaction and expressing them in architectural spatial composition, garden design and floral arts. European architecture was based on principles of unity by similarity and repetition, opposition, tension, and extension. Windows of the same shape are repeated. Each space and each mass has a boundary, identity, and a permanently specialized function such as a dining room or a bedroom. Masses oppose one another. Spaces oppose one another. And mass opposes space. Tension between points generate lines, and extension of a surface or a line generates shafts of space. ... Similarly European and American management is based on the principles of boundary, identity, specialization, opposition, tension, and extension.

In contrast, in the traditional Japanese gardens and floral art, repetition of the same form is avoided, and different shapes, colors, and materials are combined to interact and enhance the individuality of each element. ... In traditional Japanese houses, boundaries can be removed and space becomes a continuous flow, and each space is convertible. The paper partitions between rooms can be removed to provide a continuous space. The outer shell of the house, mostly consisting of sliding wooden boards, can be opened to make the outdoor come into the indoor. One can sit in the house and hear birds sing, smell the flowers in the garden, and look at the mountain. The garden can recess under the roof of the house, and the floor can protrude into the garden. A river may flow under the house. ... Furthermore, in the traditional Japanese houses, a room can serve as a dining room if a table is placed, a bedroom if mattresses are laid, and a playroom if all furniture is removed. The principles of continuity and convertibility make job rotation quite natural and logical for Japanese people.

If you are a manager in Japan, the five employees are like five rocks in a Japanese garden. Their shapes are different, and they interact in a mutually beneficial way. They know one another's skills and idiosyncrasies, and they interact together to do the whole job. This is the principle of interactive heterogeneity, and this is why it is better to give the whole job to the whole group and let them figure out how to do it.

SOURCE: Quoted from Magoroh Maruyama (1992), "Changing dimensions in international business," *Academy of Management Executive* 6(3): 89. Reprinted by permission of the Academy of Management. Also see Magoroh Maruyama (1993), "Mindscapes, individuals, and cultures in management," *Journal of Management Inquiry* 2: 140-155.

Motivator-Hygiene Theory

Frederick Herzberg (1966, 1968) developed the **motivator-hygiene theory** of job design. This theory states that satisfaction and dissatisfaction with a job are not opposite ends of one scale but two separate scales. To provide satisfaction, a job must have what Herzberg called *motivators*. These factors must be designed into the job itself. Motivators include factors such as recognition, challenging work, responsibility, and opportunities for achievement and individual growth and development. To prevent dissatisfaction, a job must have certain *hygiene factors*. The job must provide enough money and security, working conditions that are environmentally pleasant and safe, agreeable supervision and interpersonal relations, and be free of organizational policies and methods that are irritating.

Motivator-hygiene theory
A theory of job design that satisfaction and dissatisfaction with a job are not opposite ends of one scale but two separate scales.

The Job Characteristics Model

Exhibit 4.4 shows the job characteristics model developed by Richard Hackman and Greg Oldham. This model shows how the characteristics of a job are likely to affect the performance of the job holder (Hackman and others, 1975; Hackman & Oldham, 1980). An important aspect of this model is that the motivating potential of a job is considered.

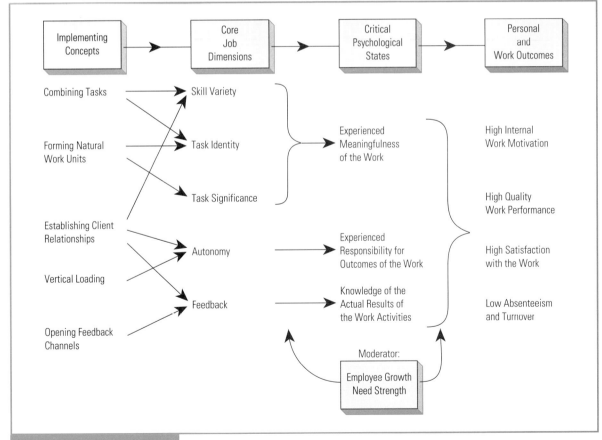

EXHIBIT 4.4

The Job Characteristics Model

SOURCE: Reprinted from J. Richard Hackman, Greg R. Oldham, Robert Janson, and Kenneth Purdy (1975), "A new strategy for job enrichment." Copyright 1975 by the Regents of the University of California. Reprinted from the *California Management Review*, Vol. 17, No. 4, p. 62. By permission of The Regents.

The way a job is structured is hypothesized to affect the people who have that job. Five core job dimensions identified by Hackman and Oldham are:

1. *Skill Variety:* the number of skills necessary to do the job;
2. *Task Identity:* the degree to which the whole job is done by one worker;
3. *Task Significance:* the importance of the job to other people's lives;
4. *Autonomy:* the freedom to do the job in the way desired by the worker;
5. *Feedback:* information about job performance from the job itself (by observation of the product, for example) or from co-workers.

EXPERIENCE IS THE BEST TEACHER

In 1974 I joined the University of Toronto's Faculty of Management Studies to start my doctoral studies in Organization Behaviour. Before that, I had done some professional work in Kenya and Alberta in personnel training, especially supervisory and management development. I was always attracted to the study of jobs, their content and context, for at least two reasons. First, I expected that better understanding of job content would lead to more systematic selection and effective training for improved employee skills, knowledge, and abilities. Second, better knowledge about jobs would help researchers and practitioners to delineate those job attributes related to employee attitudes, behaviour, motivation, and performance.

I read the literature relating to various aspects of job analysis, job enrichment, and job design. In the end, I decided to use the Hackman and Oldham model as the basis for my research because at the time it was (and still is): (i) the most theoretically complete and well grounded; (ii) more integrative with objective job dimensions, employee psychological states, and individual differences; and (iii) developed with a reliable and valid instrument (the Job Diagnostic Survey) for the measurement of jobs, psychological states, individual differences, and outcome variables such as satisfaction, internal motivation, and quality of performance.

However, the Hackman and Oldham model lacked a conceptual framework linking the job to the wider organizational context within which jobs are performed (e.g.,

Moses N. Kiggundu teaches at Carleton University's School of Business in Ottawa, Ontario.

group dynamics, structures, technology). This was important to me because I wanted to understand jobs and their properties, not in their own right, but as part of the larger organizational arrangements which affect employee attitudes, behaviour, and performance.

Drawing on socio-technical systems theory and organization theory, I developed the concept of task interdependence in the hope that it would provide the necessary conceptual link between the individually based job design and the wider organizational context (see M.N. Kiggundu, 1983, "Task interdependence and job design: Test of a theory," *Organizational Behavior and Human Performance* 31: 145-172).

After my doctoral studies, my active research interests and professional work became more macro in orientation, focusing on the relationships between jobs, employee reactions, and teams, structure, technology, and supervision. Today, most of my work involves investigating problems of organization and management in developing and modernizing countries (see M.N. Kiggundu, 1989, *Managing Organizations in Developing Countries: An Operational and Strategic Approach*, West Hartford, CT: Kumarian Press). As before, the job is the starting point, but the focus is now more on the organizational and institutional arrangements including the wider context—economic, political, sociocultural, technological—within which jobs, people, and groups operate in functionally interdependent relationships.

The model states that these five core dimensions of a job affect the psychological state of the individual worker. Psychological state in turn affects personal and work outcomes. The outcomes considered in the model are internal work motivation, quality of work performance, satisfaction with the work, and absenteeism and turnover. The basic prediction of the model is that jobs that are higher on the five core job dimensions will create positive psychological states that will then result in beneficial personal and work outcomes.

Specifically, the combination of skill variety, task identity, and task significance is thought to lead to a psychological state labelled "experienced meaningfulness of the work." The more skills that are required to do the job, the more the whole job is performed by the same worker, and the more the performance of the job makes a difference to other people's lives, the more it is likely to be experienced as meaningful. A doctor working the emergency ward of a downtown hospital will have to use many different skills over the course of a 12-hour shift. For some patients the doctor is the only health care professional that they will see (high task identity). Task significance is high because, at least for some patients, the doctor's actions can mean the difference between life and death.

Autonomy is expected in the job characteristics model to lead to the psychological state of "experienced responsibility for outcomes of the work." The person at work who is free to make choices regarding what to do and how to do it is also likely to feel responsible for the decisions made. The emergency room physician decides how to treat patients and bears the responsibility for what happens to them.

Feedback on the job performed will lead to "knowledge of the actual results of the work activities." Sometimes doctors prescribe medication to a patient and never find out what difference the medicine made or even if the patient actually took the medication. In the emergency room medication is likely to be prescribed and administered; then the patient's status is monitored. Feedback from blood samples, blood pressure readings, etc., as well as the patient's own reports all provide knowledge of the results of actions taken by the emergency room physician.

The model proposes that the relationship between core job dimensions and work outcomes is affected by the employee's "growth need strength" (GNS). GNS is a person's basic desire to better herself. An employee might have a low growth need strength and not desire a motivating job. He might be quite content to work in a job low on the five core job dimensions and to experience low meaningfulness, low responsibility, and low knowledge of work results. In that case, even a job high in the five core job dimensions would not be motivational for that individual. Work outcomes are therefore not likely to be high.

Yitzhak Fried and Gerry Ferris (1987) reviewed almost 200 studies of the model. They assessed the model's validity, and found modest support for it. Job characteristics were related to both psychological and behavioural outcomes. They also found that the individual difference characteristic of growth need strength, as predicted, did affect the relationship between job characteristics and performance. For two further perspectives on the validity of the job characteristics model, see this chapter's *On the One Hand* feature.

There are two other variables thought to affect (or moderate) the relationship between job characteristics and performance (Hackman & Oldham, 1980). First, the theory supposes that if the knowledge and skills required to do a job are not present, then even a job high on the core dimensions is not likely to result in better work outcomes. The job can be challenging, but a person who feels unable to effectively perform the job will not feel challenged. For example, a student who has yet to take integral calculus but who registers in an astronomy course that requires that particular knowledge and skill (in order to calculate satellite orbits) will not be motivated to perform well. Even if the course is designed so that the student is challenged and is provided with autonomy and feedback, the basic knowledge that student requires to perform is missing.

ON THE ONE HAND...

This review of the job characteristics theory has shown that the initial promise has not been confirmed by later research. It has been a good theory in the sense of generating a great deal of research but, unfortunately, the negative findings from many studies have not yet led to constructive alterations. Analysis of the results from studies testing the theory indicated that the theory has weak support for its propositions that are related to job satisfaction and intrinsic motivation. It has not been shown capable of predicting individual productivity. The job characteristics are not well-defined or independent and there is some evidence showing that it omits important predictors of job satisfaction such as skill-utilization. Some of the important features of the theory are potentially discriminatory. Lacking strong evidence which shows that growth need strength is independent of work experiences, the restriction of job enrichment interventions to those who measure high on growth need strength could deny a considerable number of employees the opportunity to increase their job satisfaction. Overall, the support for the job characteristics is weak and hence the unqualified recommendation of the job characteristics model is unjustified.

SOURCE: Excerpt from Gordon E. O'Brien (1982), "Evaluation of the job characteristics theory of work attitudes and performance," *Australian Journal of Psychology* 34: 398-399.

ON THE OTHER HAND...

The JCM has suggested that in order to improve psychological and behavioral outcomes at work, all five core job characteristics should be developed. The present results appear to suggest that although all of the five core job characteristics are associated with positive outcomes, specific outcomes are associated only or primarily with some of these job characteristics rather than with others. This further implies that different organizational goals could be operationalized through the development of specific task dimensions. In order to improve performance, the organization might choose to allocate resources for the development of task identity and job feedback. Absenteeism may be reduced through the development of skill variety, autonomy, and job feedback. Finally, attitudinal or psychological outcomes could be improved by focusing primarily on skill variety, task significance, autonomy, and job feedback.

Furthermore, because job feedback is associated with all of the psychological and behavioral measures investigated, the development of this task dimension potentially could benefit the organization more than the development of any one of the remaining task dimensions. The JCM implies that the success of a job design intervention is contingent upon both contextual factors in the work environment and job content factors—as well as whether the job characteristics meet the individual's personal desire to grow (i.e., GNS). Our results provide partial support for this implication.

SOURCE: Excerpt from Yitzhak Fried and Gerald R. Ferris (1987), "The validity of the Job Characteristics Model: A review and Meta-analysis," *Personnel Psychology* 40: 314.

The second factor is "context" satisfactions. If the context of work (biological factors) is disagreeable, then the individual worker will probably not be motivated by the job's characteristics. Working outside on the construction of a building when it is 40 degrees below zero may serve to lower both critical psychological states and personal and work outcomes. Even a motivating job can lose its appeal when the employee is cold.

While these two moderators of the job characteristics and performance relationship make intuitive sense, there is as yet little empirical evidence testing their validity.

The job characteristics model serves as the theoretical foundation for the job diagnostic survey (JDS), a questionnaire that examines a job's five dimensions in order to determine its motivating potential (see Hackman & Oldham, 1974).

Motivating potential score (MPS) is defined as:

$$\frac{\text{Skill Variety} + \text{Task Identity} + \text{Task Significance}}{3} \times \text{Autonomy} \times \text{Job Feedback}$$

Using seven-point scales where 1 is low and 7 is high, the maximum MPS is 7^3 or 343. The average MPS for a variety of jobs has been determined to be 128 (Oldham and others, 1979).

If a job is determined to be low on MPS, an examination of the levels of the five factors may identify one that is relatively low and therefore a candidate for change. It is important to remember that MPS is a measure of the characteristics of the job itself, not of how any particular person might perceive the dimensions of her job. Job redesign, then, is a general concept. A more specific concept of motivation would be altering a job to better fit a particular person, or modifying a person's perceptions of a job so that it is seen as more motivating.

A job may be redesigned by working on the implementing concepts that affect the particular job dimensions to be changed (see Exhibit 4.4).

Combining tasks to be performed is a way to increase both skill variety and task identity. By building bigger jobs out of smaller ones the resulting job will both require more skills and do a larger piece of the total work.

Sometimes the work to be done comes in "clumps." A car dealership might be in the business of selling new cars, selling used cars, and of performing service/warranty work on the cars it sells. These three aspects of the one business divide naturally into three clumps. Sales personnel often specialize in selling new or used cars, but not both. Mechanics fix cars but do not usually sell them. Travel agents often specialize in selling either business travel or holiday travel, because the nature of the two jobs is quite different.

Work units can be formed that follow these natural work clusters, thereby increasing task identity and task significance (because the formation of natural work units allows the individual to see the whole job being done and the difference it makes). For example, travel agents who work on corporate accounts usually book all of a client's travel and see the importance of their work to that person's job.

Building up relationships with clients helps to increase skill variety, autonomy, and feedback. Sometimes travel agents are formed into teams that serve a particular group of corporate clients. The team of agents deals with a few corporate accounts, specifically the people from those organizations that are travelling on business. Over time the members of the travel agent team get to know the travellers, their likes and dislikes, and how different trips were experienced. They can therefore see the effects of their work more easily than an airline reservations agent who never sees or communicates with a particular customer more than once.

Vertical loading can also enrich a job so that the job holder has more autonomy and responsibility for work outcomes. A sales clerk at Mark's Work Wearhouse, for instance, could be given responsibility for ordering clothing for several product categories and tracking sales and customer response to the product.

The amount of feedback generated by a job can be increased by opening feedback channels. Clients can be asked to report on their experiences. Comment cards are often used for this purpose. Feedback can come from supervisors or from devices used to perform the work. For instance, supermarket checkout scanners can be programmed to report on the number of items scanned in a given period.

Job description

A summary of the tasks and role behaviours for a particular job.

After the job has been designed, a **job description** is created, which is a summary of the tasks and role behaviours for the particular job. A person hired into a job will often be given or will seek a job description so that he has a better idea of what will be expected of him.

Integrative Views

To this point we have discussed four main approaches to the design of jobs. Exhibit 4.5 provides a summary of the factors relevant to each of these approaches in the form of a multimethod job design questionnaire.

EXHIBIT 4.5   MULTIMETHOD JOB DESIGN QUESTIONNAIRE (MJDQ)

This questionnaire is designed so that individual workers can indicate the extent to which each of the following statements is descriptive of their job. The common scale used is: (1) strongly agree, (2) agree, (3) neither agree nor disagree, (4) disagree, (5) strongly disagree, and (blank) don't know or not applicable. The questionnaire's four parts each focus on one of the four main approaches to job design.

Psychological Job Design Factors

1. *Autonomy.* The job allows freedom, independence, or discretion in work scheduling, sequence, methods, procedures, quality control, or other decision making.

2. *Intrinsic job feedback.* The work activities themselves provide direct and clear information as to the effectiveness (e.g., quality and quantity) of your job performance.

3. *Extrinsic job feedback.* Other people in the organization, such as managers and co-workers, provide information as to the effectiveness (e.g., quality and quantity) of your job performance.

4. *Social interaction.* The job provides for positive social interaction such as team work or co-worker assistance.

5. *Task/goal clarity.* The job duties, requirements, and goals are clear and specific.

6. *Task variety.* The job has a variety of duties, tasks, and activities.

7. *Task identity.* The job requires completion of a whole and identifiable piece of work. It gives you a chance to do an entire piece of work from beginning to end.

8. *Ability/skill level requirements.* The job requires a high level of knowledge, skills, and abilities.

9. *Ability/skill variety.* The job requires a variety of knowledge, skills, and abilities.

10. *Task significance.* The job is significant and important compared with other jobs in the organization.

11. *Growth/learning.* The job allows opportunities for learning and growth in competence and proficiency.

12. *Promotion.* There are opportunities for advancement to higher level jobs.

13. *Achievement.* The job provides for feelings of achievement and task accomplishment.

14. *Participation.* The job allows participation in work-related decision making.

15. *Communication.* The job has access to relevant communication channels and information flows.

16. *Pay adequacy.* The pay on this job is adequate compared with the job requirements and with the pay in similar jobs.

17. *Recognition.* The job provides acknowledgment and recognition from others.

18. *Job security.* People on this job have high job security.

Engineering Job Design Factors

19. *Job specialization.* The job is highly specialized in terms of purpose, tasks, or activities.

20. *Specialization of tools and procedures.* The tools, procedures, materials, and so forth used on this job are highly specialized in terms of purpose.

21. *Task simplification.* The tasks are simple and uncomplicated.

22. *Single activities.* The job requires you to do only one task or activity at a time.

23. *Skill simplification.* The job requires relatively little skill and training time.

24. *Repetition.* The job requires performing the same activity (or activities) repeatedly.

25. *Spare time.* There is very little spare time between activities on this job.

26. *Automation.* Many of the activities of this job are automated or assisted by automation.

Biological Job Design Factors

27. *Strength.* The job requires fairly little muscular strength.

28. *Lifting.* The job requires fairly little lifting and/or the lifting is of very light weights.

29. *Endurance.* The job requires fairly little muscular endurance.

30. *Seating.* The seating arrangements on the job are adequate (e.g., ample opportunities to sit, comfortable chairs, good postural support, etc.).

31. *Size differences.* The workplace allows for all size differences between people in terms of clearance, reach, eye height, leg room, and so forth.

32. *Wrist movement.* The job allows the wrists to remain straight without excessive movement.

33. *Noise.* The workplace is free from excessive noise.

34. *Climate.* The climate at the workplace is comfortable in terms of temperature and humidity and it is free of excessive dust and fumes.

35. *Work breaks.* There is adequate time for work breaks given the demands of the job.

36. *Shift work.* The job does not require shift work or excessive overtime.

Ergonomic Job Design Factors

37. *Lighting.* The lighting in the workplace is adequate and free from glare.

38. *Displays.* The displays, gauges, meters, and computerized equipment on this job are easy to read and understand.

39. *Programs.* The programs in the computerized equipment on this job are easy to learn and use.

40. *Other equipment.* The other equipment (all types) used on this job is easy to learn and use.

41. *Printed job materials.* The printed materials used on this job are easy to read and interpret.

42. *Workplace layout.* The workplace is laid out so that you can see and hear well to perform the job.

43. *Information input requirements.* The amount of information you must attend to in order to perform this job is fairly minimal.

44. *Information output requirements.* The amount of information you must put out on this job, in terms of both action and communication, is fairly minimal.

45. *Information processing requirements.* The amount of information you must process, in terms of thinking and problem solving, is fairly minimal.

46. *Memory requirements.* The amount of information you must remember on this job is fairly minimal.

47. *Stress.* There is relatively little stress on this job.

48. *Boredom.* The chances of boredom on this job are fairly small.

SOURCE: Adapted from Michael A. Campion (1988), "Interdisciplinary approaches to job design: A constructive replication with extensions," *Journal of Applied Psychology* 73: 480-481. Copyright © 1988 by the American Psychological Association. Adapted/reprinted by permission.

There are also integrative views of jobs that examine the relationship between the job and the worker and how they influence each other. Two integrative perspectives are socio-technical systems theory and the integrated model of task design.

Socio-technical Systems Approach

According to the **socio-technical systems** approach, job design is a function of the relationship between the social system of which each person is a part and the technical system used to get the work done. (See this chapter's *A Little Knowledge* feature.) They must be considered together instead of separately. Albert Cherns (1987) has designed 10 principles of socio-technical design.

Socio-technical systems approach Job design is a function of the relationship between the social system and the technical system used to get the work done.

A LITTLE KNOWLEDGE

A classic example of how technology changed the social system of work in a coal mine is given by Eric Trist and Mr. Ken Bamforth (1951). They described how the technology of gathering coal in a deep mine had changed and how those changes had altered social interactions among workers. With the oldest hand-got method, miners worked in small groups on a short wall of coal, sharing the dangers and the pay for the amount of coal they mined. The long-wall method transplanted factory techniques underground, using machines to cut the coal and conveyor belts to move it. Miners did not identify with the large groups they worked in and pay was for the specific task performed. There was little social interaction or group feeling, an important element when these men were working miles underground in dangerous conditions. Miners were unhappy with this method and conflict increased. The composite long-wall method reintroduced work groups and incentive pay, while retaining the new machines. This method integrated both technology and a social system, thereby lessening conflict.

SOURCE: See Eric L. Trist and Ken W. Barnforth (1951), "Some social and psychological consequences of the longwall method of coal-getting," *Human Relations* 4: 3-38.

---

1. *Compatibility.* The first principle, and the most important, is that decisions about how to design an organization's structure and processes must be made considering technical and social reasons at the same time. Social and technical factors at work must be jointly considered, integrated, and compatible. No expert opinion should be accepted without challenging its assumptions. Decisions should be made by informed consensus instead of by political methods or by power.

2. *Minimal critical specification.* Task design should identify the parts of the task that are absolutely essential to be performed, and no more. When there is too much specification of exactly what to do and how to do it, creativity and flexibility are lost. The person in the job is constrained by the rules of how to act. Alternatives to how each job may be done should be generated, and problems with each alternative examined. The cost of fixing those problems can then be estimated before determining the best way to design the performance of the job.

   This principle also applies to the specification of what personnel should be assigned to what jobs. If tasks are assigned to teams as a whole and job assignment within the team is left to the team itself, flexibility of task/job design is enhanced. "The extent to which teams can assume responsibility given the right conditions surprises even those who wished it" (Cherns, 1987, p. 156).

3. *Variance control.* Variations in raw materials or technical processes should not be exported from one organizational unit to another. Variance needs to be controlled within each unit so that the next unit has less fluctuation to deal with.

4. *Boundary location.* Organizational boundaries should not be created (or located) where they will restrict the sharing of information. Knowledge that is gained about processes, tasks, and customers should be shared with those who can benefit. Creating boundaries between those who are in a position to share their learning will disrupt the effective operation of the organization.

5. *Information flow.* Information in organizations is used to control the actions of others, to create organizational records of actions already taken, and to communicate actions planned. "Information for action should be directed first to those whose task it is to act. This holds for action to control variances ... It is no use holding an individual or a team responsible for any function and doling

out information about its performance in arrear [after the fact] and through a higher authority. Under those conditions, the individual or team cannot have ownership of the performance" (Cherns, 1987, p. 157).

6. *Power and authority.* The individuals and teams in organizations are given responsibilities to carry out. They should also be given the power to acquire the tools and materials needed to do the job. As well, they need the authority to perform their job in the way they think best. When responsibility is given to an individual or team but power and authority are withheld, the result is likely to be lack of confidence or resentment of those with the power.

7. *Multifunctionality.* Organizational adaptation to the environment can be done either by adding new roles and pieces to the organization's structure, or by expanding existing roles. The problem with adding new roles is that the organization becomes more complex, more rigid, and less able to change in the future. It is better to enlarge existing roles, to make them multi-functional. In this way individuals and groups are able to deal with more complexity in the environment without adding to the complexity of the organization's structure.

8. *Support congruence.* Organizational support systems should be placed where they can help those who are doing the key work of the organization. When support systems take on an importance of their own that has no direct connection to the work, there is incongruence. For example, when the corporate finance department looks to serve its own goals first and not the units it is designed to support, the cart is before the horse. Reward systems in socio-technical designs pay the worker for what she knows rather than for what she does, on the assumption that it is the worker's knowledge and capacity to act when required that counts.

9. *Transitional organization.* When the organization is undergoing structural and job design change, the old organization, the new organization, and the organization in transition should each be considered. Transition should not be seen as an inconvenience to be minimized but as a crucial step that must be planned and carefully managed. Will workers be retrained or laid off? Who will take training opportunities and how will workers be selected for training? These are important questions. The answers arrived at will affect the new organization. If the transitional organization is insensitive to the human impacts of job changes, the new organization will be less effective.

10. *Incompletion.* The principle here is that change in jobs and systems is not an interim state between an initial stable state and an ending stable state. Rather, job and social change is continuous. This principle is also known as the "Forth Bridge principle," because painters of the bridge over the Forth estuary in Scotland never finish. By the time they reach one end it is time to start painting again at the other. When we accept the principle of incompletion, we can understand job redesign not as the task of a special group but as the job of the operating team itself. The team has the power and authority to perform its task, the capacity to add functions as required and to change itself as necessary.

Integrated Model of Task Design

Ricky Griffin (1987) has developed an integrated model of task design (Exhibit 4.6) that shows how job factors affect the behaviours of individual workers. In this model the task is the particular work to be done, the job is a set of related tasks, and the job holder's role is the set of behaviours expected of the individual holding the job. The characteristics of the task, the physical and social setting of the job, and personal traits affect a person's perceptions of the task, job, and role.

EXHIBIT 4.6

Integrated Model of Task Design

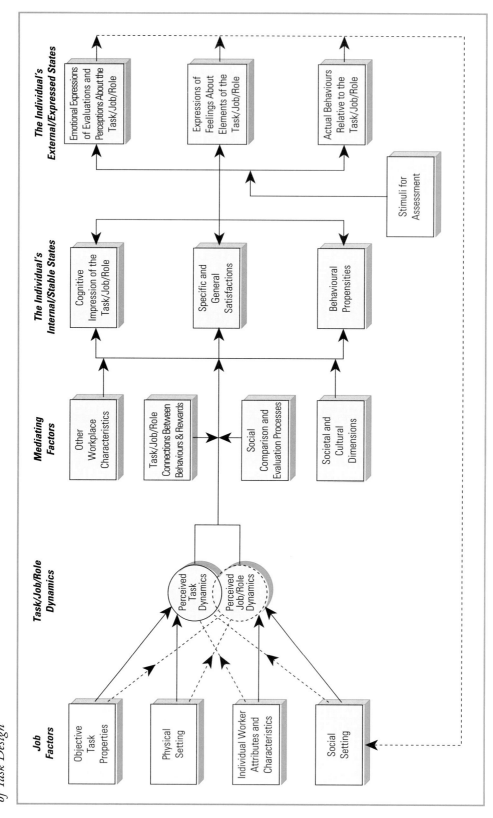

Source: Adapted from Ricky W. Griffin (1987). "Toward an integrated theory of task design," in Larry L. Cummings and Barry M. Staw, Eds., *Research in Organizational Behavior* 9: 79-120. Greenwich, CT: JAI Press, p.111. Reprinted with permission.

These perceptions are further modified (or mediated) by the connection between be-haviour and rewards, personal comparisons with others, and the individual worker's culture. The perceptions lead to "stable internal states" that consist of an individual's conception of the task, the job, and the role; feelings about them; and a predisposition to certain actions in that task, job, and role. Finally, as events happen on the job, a person reacts with emo-tional expressions and actual behaviours relating to the task, job, and role, which then feed back to affect actual job factors.

In this model actual job factors are perceived by the individual worker. A travel agent, for example, considers her work environment and set of tasks. Her perceptions contribute directly to what she thinks of her job and role of travel agent; how satisfied she is in her job; and how she might act while doing her work. Actual actions are then taken and feelings ex-pressed about parts of the job ("I hate making bookings with that airline") or about the job itself ("I love being in the travel business").

CONCLUSION

Organizations seeking to redesign jobs can use the job characteristics approach, the job enrichment approach, Japanese-style management (Theory J), the socio-technical model or, indeed, any other philosophy of how jobs should be designed. A summary of the four ap-proaches just mentioned is shown in Exhibit 4.7.
These first four chapters complete Part I. We have examined the study of organizations, their environments, their structures and technologies, their cultures and socialization practices, and the way they divide their work into jobs. While people affect and are affected by all these facets of organizations, we have yet to study people as individuals.

Each one of us brings a unique set of abilities, types of knowledge, personality traits, perceptions, and attitudes into an organization. These individual differences need to be ex-amined so that we can understand how they in turn influence communication, group for-mation and behaviour, motivation, decision making, and the processes of interpersonal power, politics, and conflict.

CHAPTER SUMMARY

The nature of work has changed over time. The Agricultural Revolution created the stability of place and food supply that allowed people to develop and fill a wide number of specialist jobs. The Industrial Revolution encouraged people in large numbers to leave the coun-tryside and concentrate in cities where factories were located. Lately, the information rev-olution is having wide-ranging effects on how and where people work, how they interact with others, and what they produce.

Information workers are engaged in the manipulation and production of informa-tion. They use the new tools of computers, fax, and cellular communications. Computers and databases are being linked up worldwide to allow the information worker to work from any place and connect with anyone at any time.

There are four main approaches to the design of jobs: engineering, ergonomics, biological, and psychological. The engineering approach to job design concentrates on the job itself and attempts to make the job easier to perform. The ergonomics approach is concerned with the fit between the person and the machine. The biological approach to job design focuses on the physical comfort and well-being of the person doing the job and on the physical char-acteristics of the workplace. Biological approaches are becoming increasingly important in dealing with physical and environmental stresses due to work. The psychological approach to job design concentrates on the mental state of the worker in the performance of the task. Psychological approaches to the design of jobs are job enlargement, job enrichment, job rotation, motivator-hygiene theory, and the job characteristics model.

EXHIBIT 4.7   FOUR APPROACHES TO JOB DESIGN

	DESCRIPTION	MOTIVATIONAL ASSUMPTIONS	CRITICAL TECHNIQUES
Job Enrichment	Based on motivation-hygiene theory. Focuses on changes in job content.	Two different needs are involved: increasing motivation and reducing dissatisfaction. Factors involved in increasing motivation relate to human characteristics; factors involved in reducing dissatisfaction relate to pain avoidance.	• Direct feedback • Direct contact with client • Opportunities to learn more job-related skills • The opportunity for each person to schedule his or her own work • Unique expertise • Control over resources • Direct communications • Personal accountability
Job Characteristics	Based on job characteristics research. Focuses on job content.	Work motivation is based on three psychological states: the knowledge of results, experienced responsibility, and experienced meaningfulness. These are achieved through five core job characteristics; task significance, skill variety, autonomy, task identity, and job feedback.	• Combining tasks • Forming natural unity of work • Establishing client relationships • Using vertical loading • Opening feedback channels
Japanese-Style Management	Based on Japanese experience. Deals with organizational, job, and managerial factors.	Motivation is based on "wa" (teamwork) or family-like norms and the organizational culture.	• Intensive socialization • Lifetime employment • Competitive education • Job rotation and slow promotion • Behaviour evaluation • Work-group task assignments • Nonspecialized career paths • Open communication • Consultational decision making • Concern for employees • Compensation
Quality-of-Worklife Approaches (Socio-technical Model)	Based on a variety of experiences in many countries and many types of organizations.	Motivation is based on jobs assigned according to socio-technical criteria and the capacity of individuals to make choices in designing their work.	• Technical systems changes • Job changes • Participation/consultation • Structural changes • Pay/reward systems • Compressed shift schedules • Training and recruitment • The operating philosophy statement • Collective agreement modifications • Group management

Source: Cunningham & Eberle (1990). Adapted, excerpted and reprinted, by permission of publisher, from PERSONNEL, February 1990. © 1990 American Management Association, New York. All rights reserved.

QUESTIONS FOR REVIEW

1. What are the five factors considered in the job characteristics model? How could a manager attempt to make a job more motivational by using this model?

2. Teaching is a job involved with the transmission and processing of information. How will the information revolution affect the job of teacher?

3. How much attention do you think a manager should focus on the biological aspects of job design?

4. What do you see as the main trends for work in the future? Will Canada's population continue to migrate to the cities and away from the countryside? If so, what will the impact be on how we work and where we work?

5. Why would a person want to be rotated through jobs or to have an enriched or enlarged job? Why would a person not want job rotation, enrichment, or enlargement?

SELF-DIAGNOSTIC EXERCISE 4.1

Design Your Own Job

Answer the following questions by thinking of what the psychological job design would be for your ideal job. Score 0 if the description is totally wrong for your ideal job, 5 if it is a perfect description, and 1, 2, 3, or 4 if the description is somewhere in between.

1. I will have the opportunity to use a wide variety of skills on the job.
2. I will have the chance to do the whole job from start to finish.
3. Doing this job makes a difference to people's lives.
4. I will be able to work on my own in this job.
5. I will be able to find out how well I am doing on this job.
6. The job can only be done by someone who has a variety of skills.
7. This job can be done by one person.
8. I will have the opportunity to do important work in this job.
9. The job is one that is not closely supervised by another person.
10. The job provides direct feedback to the job holder about performance.
11. To perform effectively, a person doing this job needs to have a set of skills.
12. The job holder can do all the parts of the task by himself or herself.
13. The job is one that is important to me and others.
14. The person in this job can make job related decisions by himself.
15. The holder of this job will know how well the task is being performed.

Now add up your scores for each of the five core job dimensions of the job characteristics model.

Your Ideal Job:

Skill Variety: $\dfrac{\text{(Questions } 1 + 6 + 11)}{3}$ = _____

Task Identity: $\dfrac{\text{(Questions } 2 + 7 + 12)}{3}$ = _____

Task Significance: $\dfrac{(\text{Questions } 3 + 8 + 13)}{3}$ = _____

Autonomy: $\dfrac{(\text{Questions } 4 + 9 + 14)}{3}$ = _____

Feedback: $\dfrac{(\text{Questions } 5 + 10 + 15)}{3}$ = _____

Calculate your ideal job's Motivating Potential Score and determine which of the five factors is least and most important to you.

$$MPS = \dfrac{\text{Skill Variety} + \text{Task Identity} + \text{Task Significance}}{3} \times \text{Autonomy} \times \text{Job Feedback}$$

Ideal Job MPS = _____

Now think of the job that you expect to get upon graduation and answer the questions again with that job in mind.

Expected Job:

Skill Variety: $\dfrac{(\text{Questions } 1 + 6 + 11)}{3}$ = _____

Task Identity: $\dfrac{(\text{Questions } 2 + 7 + 12)}{3}$ = _____

Task Significance: $\dfrac{(\text{Questions } 3 + 8 + 13)}{3}$ = _____

Autonomy: $\dfrac{(\text{Questions } 4 + 9 + 14)}{3}$ = _____

Feedback: $\dfrac{(\text{Questions } 5 + 10 + 15)}{3}$ = _____

$$MPS = \dfrac{\text{Skill Variety} + \text{Task Identity} + \text{Task Significance}}{3} \times \text{Autonomy} \times \text{Job Feedback}$$

Expected Job MPS = _____

Compare the scores of your ideal and expected jobs and identify any areas of mismatch. How could your expected job be made to match more closely the characteristics you have identified of your ideal job?

EXPERIENTIAL EXERCISE 4.1

The Best and Worst Jobs in the Class

1. Divide into groups of five or six.

2. Each person is to describe either the best or worst job they have ever had using the following four job design approaches:

   a) *Engineering.* How simplified was the work? How specialized? Was time and motion study used to engineer the work?

   b) *Ergonomics.* How simple and safe was it to work with the job's machines in terms of their controls, labels, dials, and lights?

   c) *Biological factors.* How was your privacy, office or workspace lighting, the freshness of the air, and surrounding noise? What were the conditions of the physical workspace?

   d) *Psychological factors.* What was the job's range? Was there job rotation? Were there any attempts to enrich the job? How much autonomy did you have to do the work the way you thought best? What skill variety, task identity, and task significance did the job have? How did you get feedback on your job performance?

3. Of the jobs in your group, which is the best and which is the worst? Does everyone agree? Report the best and the worst jobs to the class as a whole, then when all the best and worst have been described, take a vote to determine who has had the overall best and worst jobs.

SELF-GUIDED LEARNING ACTIVITY

The best way to find out about a job you're interested in is to go out and talk to someone who is currently doing the job. One way to find that person is to get your local yellow pages and look up the businesses that do the kind of work that you want to do. Find one that is within easy travel distance and call the company. Usually an operator or administrative assistant will answer. All you have to do is tell that person your name, that you are a student at your college/university, and that for a course project you need to interview someone doing the particular kind of work that you wish to study. Get the recommended job holder's name, then call and ask for a half-hour interview at the person's office to talk about the job. You might find this method of "cold calling" somewhat scary, but business people are interested in telling students about what they do and in sharing their expertise. If you have some trouble at first don't give up, but keep trying and call several more businesses. At the interview have some questions prepared about the job that will help get your discussion started.

CASE 4.1

MANAGER'S CASE FILE: THE CASE OF THE MISSING STAFFER

Carrie had just been informed that she was not getting a replacement for her editorial assistant who had just left for a better job with a competing publisher. Her supervisor had told her, "You'll just have to divide the work among your other staffers. With the hiring and salary freezes in effect, there's nothing else we can do. Try to make the best of it."

"Easy for you to say," she thought to herself. "My people are overworked now and not getting compensation for it. They're going to love this."

The following Monday Carrie called her staff members together for an informal meeting. "As you all know," she began, "there is a hiring freeze on, so Cynthia is not going to be replaced. Over the weekend I divided Cynthia's job responsibilities into eight categories, and each of you will be responsible for one area of her job. I know that is a lot of work, but if we all work together, we'll be able to handle it. And when the freeze is lifted, we'll get a new person to assume Cynthia's work. In the meantime, if any of you have a problem with your assignment, please come to see me and we'll try to work something out."

As Carrie passed out the assignments, she heard the grumbling. She had given the choice assignments to her favorite workers and the routine tasks to the others. She reasoned that the best workers should have the best assignments. She had not considered that what she thought to be the best assignments would not be appreciated by the persons to whom she gave them.

The next day, she found Martin waiting for her in her office when she came in. "Martin, what can I do for you?" she asked, although she already suspected what Martin wanted, or rather didn't want.

"Why did you assign the press lunches to me?" he asked. "I can't stand being bored by someone's speech. Can't you give this one to someone else?"

"I thought you would like the press lunches," Carrie said. "You're always trying new restaurants and you like meeting people; I thought you'd jump to get this one."

The next person at her door was George. "Just because my wife drags me everywhere on my vacation, don't think I enjoy it. Can't you reassign the traveling interviews?"

And so it went all day. Carrie attempted to juggle and switch assignments until she thought she'd go crazy. Finally, she stepped outside her office and said, "Enough already! I've tried to accommodate you all, and it can't be done. Take the assignments I've given you and do your best with them."

Her staff members were so shocked by Carrie's uncharacteristic outburst that they were quiet for the rest of the day. But the next day the tradeoffs began.

"I know you hate the traveling interviews, George," Alan began, "I'll do them if you take the proofreading."

"Proofreading is worse. I'll trade with you anyway. Maybe I can get Rose Marie to trade the proofreading for the research work. I'd like that."

"You have got to be nuts," Rose Marie said to George. "I like research, and I'm not trading. Maybe you can trade with Martin for the press lunches. You only have to go once or twice a week. It can't be that bad."

When several voices started to get loud, Carrie came out of her office to see what the fuss was about.

For a moment everyone was quiet. Then, everyone started to talk at once. When Carrie finally discovered what was going on, she was upset. "Half the staff seems to be happy with their trades," she thought. "But what do I do with the other half? I can't have half the staff in revolt."

SOURCE: Reprinted, by permission of publisher, from SUPERVISORY MANAGEMENT, December 1985. © 1985 American Management Association, New York. All rights reserved.

Questions

1. Could Carrie have reassigned the work better?
2. Is there a solution that will be acceptable to the staff?
3. How can Carrie get the staff to work better as a team?

B & B CONTAINERS

B&B Containers is a Canadian producer of two products—steel drums and plastic buckets. The entire operation is housed in one building of 42 000 square feet (see Exhibit 4.8) and is run by a general manager.

The Steel Drum Division employs 14 unionized workers and a foreman. Two employees take sheets of steel and place them onto the production line, on which 10-, 25-, or 45-gallon drums are manufactured. The drums are used for gasoline and oil storage, the transportation of honey, nickel ore, toxic chemicals, and water. To manufacture the drums, a steel sheet is sent into a rolling machine where it is shaped into a cylinder and then pressure welded. The drum then proceeds on rollers to the flanger, where its ends are curled back to aid in the later attachment of drum ends. Next, the drum goes through a swedger, which slips inside the barrel and stretches the steel at the appropriate spots to produce two or three support ribs in the drum. If the inside of the drum is to be painted, the welded seam is pressure tested, the drum moves to the interior painting machine, and then proceeds through an oven to dry the paint. Next stop is the seamer, where one or two operators place pre-made ends onto the drum. These drum ends are manufactured from steel disks and their inside surfaces are painted independently of the drum itself. The end stamping machine produces both tops and bottoms and requires one employee to operate the machine. An operator then checks the weld seams of unlined drums and ensures that the ends have been properly attached. A chimer can then attach steel rings onto the ends of the drums in order to provide more strength. Chime rings must be installed on drums that will contain toxic chemicals or pesticides. The drum's exterior may then be painted in up to three different colours before passing through a drying oven and a cooling chamber. Drums requiring silkscreening are painted by two operators. All drums are loaded directly onto a truck at one of two loading docks.

Due to the presence of the open-ended ovens, the facility tends to become very hot during muggy summer days. When it gets too hot, the plant manager gets ice cream cones for drum-making employees, who then take a short break together. The machinery is old and not highly automated, operating on an eight-hour-day, five-day-week schedule. When the production line is stopped for a coffee break or lunch, or for an ice cream break, employees shut down the line and leave the manufacturing area to socialize either in the cafeteria or near the loading dock. There is very low turnover in the Steel Drum Division, with employees having three to twelve years tenure.

The Plastics Bucket Division consists of two bucket making machines, one lid making machine and a three-colour printing press. The buckets are used for a variety of purposes including storage of foodstuffs, paints, peanut butter, and bulk oil. The bucket and lid making machines each cost $1 million while the printing press cost $100 000. Plastic pellets used in bucket production are stored in large, tall, outdoor silos and are pumped into inside storage tanks where they warm up to room temperature. Pellets are then pumped through a network of pipes to the bucket and lid making machines. Through the addition of coloured pellets, buckets as well as lids can be produced in a variety of colours. There is a foreman and five unionized employees on during the day shift, which is composed of a lead hand, three employees on the machines, and one printer. There are four employees on during the other two shifts as the printing press runs only during the day, while the bucket and lid making machines are staffed 24 hours a day, six days a week, closing on Sunday.

The bucket machine drops out a bucket every 17.85 seconds. The operator picks it up and adds a handle, then puts the bucket on a cooling ring so that it cools in a cylindrical shape. Twelve cooling rings are located on the edge of a large revolving table. The operator leaves the bucket on the cooling ring until the revolving table brings it back around. The operator then places the cooled bucket on the flaming stand which removes any excess wax from the surface so that ink will not run when the bucket is printed. After flaming, the operator stacks the bucket onto pallets containing 120 buckets.

Lid production is a similar process, a lid dropping out of the lid machine every 18 seconds. The operator then places the lid onto a revolving table containing twelve cooling rings. When cooled, an O-ring sealing gasket is permanently embedded by

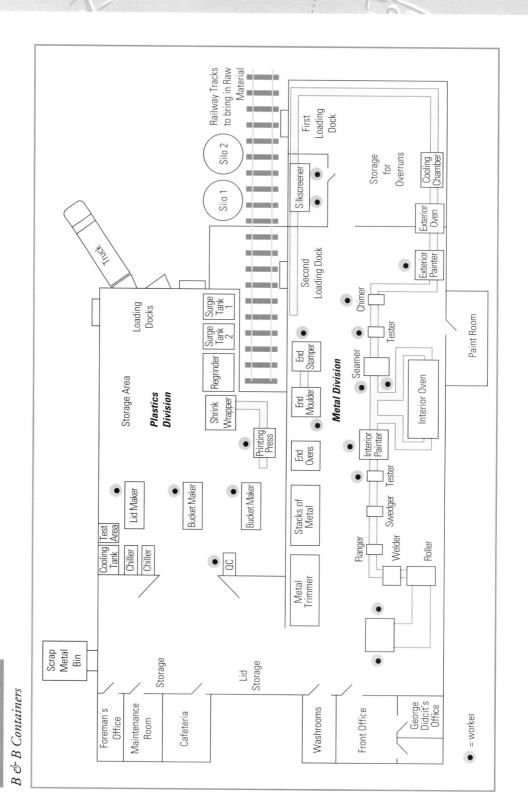

EXHIBIT 4.2

B & B Containers

machine into the lid and the lid is then flamed. The operator stacks lids onto pallets of 240 lids. Since more buckets are made than lids, some lids must currently be purchased from another factory. It is the job of the lead hand to take away full pallets of buckets and lids, to perform quality control tests and to relieve the operators during their coffee breaks, washroom breaks, and lunch break. Coffee breaks total one-half hour per shift and the lunch break is one-half hour per shift. Beyond these breaks, operators can leave their stations for only a very limited amount of time to contact the lead hand. The printing press operator prints the buckets four at a time. This operator may stop production completely while taking a coffee break, when restacking the finished products, or if the machine needs resetting. Not all buckets go through the printing press, as many buckets simply have labels attached to them by the customer.

The Plastics Division is fairly noisy, but not as noisy as the Metal Division. The bucket and lid machines are large and separated, so that communication between the shift workers is very difficult. It is cooler in Plastics than in the Metal Division, maintaining an even and pleasant temperature all year. The Plastics Division is clean, but does smell slightly of hot plastics. The turnover in this division is much higher than in the Metal Division and appears to be rising. Also, there was a recent problem with one of the bucket machines. The machines must warm up for approximately two hours on Monday morning before they are usable, but it appears that an operator turned on the machine before it was completely warm and a $1200 screw feeder broke as a result. An old lid-making machine has recently been purchased. It will be delivered in one month. It should take a month to set it up and then the Plastics Division will have two bucket makers and two lid makers operational.

SOURCE. ©1990 by Richard Field and Greg Paton

Questions

1. Would you rather work in the Plastics Division or the Metal Division?

2. Is the technology of the Metal Division small batch, large batch/mass production, or continuous process? What is the Plastics Division technology?

3. How will the job of lead hand in the Plastics Division change when the second lid-making machine becomes operational?

4. The machines in the Plastics Division can be physically moved within the Plastics area. How would you position the machines when the new lid-making machine becomes operational?

REFERENCES

Beazley, Mitchell (Editor) (1979). *The Joy of Knowledge: History and Culture 1*, Second Revised Edition. London: Mitchell Beazley Encyclopaedias Limited.

Campion, Michael A. (1988). "Interdisciplinary approaches to job design: A constructive replication with extensions." *Journal of Applied Psychology* 73: 467-481.

Campion, Michael A., & Paul W. Thayer (1985). "Development and field evaluation of an interdisciplinary measure of job design." *Journal of Applied Psychology* 70: 29-43.

Campion, Michael A., & Paul W. Thayer (1987). "Job design: Approaches, outcomes, and trade-offs." *Organizational Dynamics* 15(3): 66-79.

Caudron, Shari (1992). "Working at home pays off." *Personnel Journal*, November 1992, pp. 40-49.

Cherns, Albert (1987). "Principles of sociotechnical design revisited." *Human Relations* 40: 153-162.

Churbuck, David C. (1993). "My aching hands!" *Forbes*, December 20, 1993, p. 246.

Cunningham, J. Barton, & Ted Eberle (1990). "A guide to job enrichment and redesign." *Personnel* 67(2): 56-61.

Farrar, Alice, & Linda J. Murray (1993). "How to stay well in a sick building." *Working Woman*, January 1993, p. 72.

Field, Richard H.G., & Nelson Phillips (1992). "The environmental crisis in the office: Why aren't managers managing the office environment?" *Journal of General Management*, Autumn 1992, 18(1): 35-50.

Fisher, Anne B. (1992). "Welcome to the age of overwork." *Fortune*, November 30, 1992, pp. 64-71.

Fried, Yitzhak, & Gerald R. Ferris (1987). "The validity of the Job Characteristics Model: A review and meta-analysis." *Personnel Psychology* 40: 287-322.

Goeudevert, Daniel (1993). "Age of reasons." *International Management*, May 1993, p. 68.

Griffin, Ricky W. (1987). "Toward an integrated theory of task design." In Larry L. Cummings & Barry M. Staw (Eds.), *Research in Organizational Behavior* Greenwich, CT: JAI Press, pp. 79-120.

Hackman, J. Richard & Greg R. Oldham (1974). "The Job Diagnostic Survey: An instrument for the diagnosis of jobs and the evaluation of job redesign projects." *Catalog of Selected Documents in Psychology* 4: 148 (MS. No. 810).

Hackman, J. Richard & Greg R. Oldham (1980). *Work Redesign*. Reading, MA: Addison-Wesley.

Hackman, J. Richard, Greg R. Oldham, Robert Janson, & Kenneth Purdy (1975). "A new strategy for job enrichment." *California Management Review* 17(4): 57-71.

Herzberg, Frederick I. (1966). *Work and the Nature of Man.* Cleveland: World.

Herzberg, Frederick I. (1968). "One more time: How do you motivate employees?" *Harvard Business Review* 46(1): 53-62.

Jenkins, Anthony (1992). "I heard it in the salt mine." The *Globe and Mail*, January 18, 1992, p. D3.

Kiggundu, Moses N. (1983). "Task interdependence and job design: Test of a theory." *Organizational Behavior and Human Performance* 31: 145-172.

Kiggundu, Moses N. (1989). *Managing Organizations in Developing Countries: An Operational and Strategic Approach.* West Hartford, CT: Kumarian Press.

Maruyama, Magoroh (1992). "Changing dimensions in international business." *Academy of Management Executive* 6(3): 88-96.

Maruyama, Magoroh (1993). "Mindscapes, individuals, and cultures in management." *Journal of Management Inquiry* 2: 140-155.

McInnes, Craig (1992). "A night in the life of No. 5." The *Globe and Mail*, February 15, 1992, p. D3.

Morantz, Alan (1992). "The quiet revolution." *Canadian Business*, June 1992, pp. 55-60.

O'Brien, Gordon E. (1982). "Evaluation of the job characteristics theory of work attitudes and performance." *Australian Journal of Psychology* 34: 383-401.

Oldham, Greg R. (1988). "Effects of changes in workspace partitions and spatial density on employee reactions: A quasi-experiment." *Journal of Applied Psychology* 73: 253-258.

Oldham, Greg R., J. Richard Hackman, & Lee P. Stepina (1979). "Norms for the job diagnostic survey." *Catalog of Selected Documents in Psychology* 9: 14 (MS. No. 1819).

Robbins, Stephen P. (1989). *Organizational Behavior: Concepts, Controversies, and Applications.* 4th edition. Englewood Cliffs, NJ: Prentice Hall.

Steers, Richard M., Yoo Keun Shin, & Gerardo R. Ungson (1989). *The Chaebol: Korea's New Industrial Might.* New York: Ballinger Publishing Company.

Trist, Eric L., & Ken W. Bamforth (1951). "Some social and psychological consequences of the longwall method of coal-getting." *Human Relations* 4: 3-38.

Walmsley, Ann (1992). "Posture perfect." *Report on Business Magazine*, September 1992, pp. 95-97.

FURTHER READING

An interesting novel that offers informed speculation about the lives and jobs of early human groups is the book by Jean M. Auel (1984), *The Clan of the Cave Bear*, New York: Bantam Books.

An autobiographical chapter by Frederick Herzberg is titled "Happiness and unhappiness: A brief autobiography." It is found in Arthur G. Bedeian (Ed.), *Management Laureates: A Collection of Autobiographical Essays*, Volume 2, Greenwich, CT: JAI Press.

For a good look at the importance of offices and their design, see Suzyn Ornstein (1989), "The hidden influences of office design," *Academy of Management Executive* 3(2): 144-147. Another interesting article on offices and office design is that of Philip J. Stone and Robert Luchetti (1985), "Your office is where you are," *Harvard Business Review* 64(2): 102-117. A book that offers a more complete discussion of office space allocation from an architect's viewpoint is by Thomas Walton (1988), *Architecture and the Corporation*, New York: Macmillan. Also see "The physical environment of work setting: Effects on task performance, interpersonal relations, and job satisfaction" by Robert A. Baron, in Volume 16, 1994, *Research in Organizational Behavior*.

To better understand the jobs required in cities, look into the computer program SimCity 2000, by Maxis Corp. This update of the classic SimCity program allows you to build your own city and make decisions about housing and services. The program allows you to zone areas of your city for various uses and has a political aspect as well, in that legislation can be passed on specific issues.

A practical look at the benefits and problems of telecommuting is given in "Sending them home to work: Telecommuting," *Business Quarterly*, Spring 1993, pages 104-109, by Jocelyne Côté-O'Hara.

A study that found that growth need strength and context satisfactions did not moderate the relationship between job characteristics and work outcomes is described in "Growth need strength and context satisfactions as moderators of the relations of the Job Characteristics Model," by Robert B. Tiegs, Lois E. Tetrick, and Yitzhak Fried (1992), *Journal of Management* 18: 575-593. On the measurement of job characteristics, see Jacqueline R. Idaszak and Fritz Drasgow (1987), "A revision of the Job Diagnostic Survey: Elimination of a measurement artifact," *Journal of Applied Psychology* 72: 69-74.

MRS. FIELDS' SECRET INGREDIENT

Part of the late Buckminster Fuller's genius was his capacity to transform a technology from the merely new to the truly useful by creating a new form to take advantage of its characteristics. Fuller's geodesic designs, for instance, endowed plastic with practical value as a building material. His structures, if not always eye-appealing, still achieved elegance—as mathematicians use the word to connote simplicity—of function. Once, reacting to someone's suggestion that a new technology be applied to an old process in a particularly awkward way, Fuller said dismissively, "That would be like putting an outboard motor on a skyscraper."

Introducing microcomputers with spreadsheet and word-processing software to a company originally designed around paper technology amounts to the same thing. If the form of the company doesn't change, the computer, like the outboard, is just a doodad. Faster long division and speedier typing don't move a company into the information age.

But Randy Fields has created something entirely new—*a* shape if not *the* shape, of business organizations to come. It gives top management a dimension of personal control over dispersed operations that small companies otherwise find impossible to achieve. It projects a founder's vision into parts of a company that have long ago outgrown his or her ability to reach in person.

In the structure that Fields is building, computers don't just speed up old administrative management processes. They alter the process. Management, in the Fields organizational paradigm, becomes less administration and more inspiration. The management hierarchy of the company *feels* almost flat.

What's the successful computer-age business going to look like in the not-very-distant future? Something like Randy Fields' concept—which is, in a word—neat.

What makes it neat, right out of the oven, is where he's doing it. Randy Fields, age 40, is married to Debbi Fields, who turns 31 this month, and together they run Mrs. Fields Cookies, of Park City, Utah (see "A Tale of Two Companies," *INC.*, July 1984). They project that by year end, their business will comprise nearly 500 company-owned stores in 37 states selling what Debbi calls a "feel-good feeling." That sounds a little hokey. A lot of her cookie talk does. "Good enough never is," she likes to remind the people around her.

But there's nothing hokey about the 18.5% that Mrs. Fields Inc. earned on cookie sales of $87 million last year, up from $72.6 million a year earlier.

Won't the cookie craze pass? people often ask Debbi. "I think that's very doubtful ... I mean," she says, "if [they are] fresh, warm, and wonderful and make you feel good, are you going to stop buying cookies?"

Maybe not, but the trick for her and her husband is to see that people keep buying them from Mrs. Fields, not David's Cookies, Blue Chip Cookies, the Original Great Chocolate Chip Cookie, or the dozens of regional and local competitors. Keeping the cookies consistently fresh, warm, and wonderful at nearly 500 retail cookie stores spread over the United States and five other countries can't be simple or easy. Worse, keeping smiles on the faces of the nearly 4500 mostly young store employees—not to mention keeping them productive and honest—is a bigger chore than most companies would dare to take on alone.

Most don't; they franchise, which is one way to bring responsibility and accountability down to the store level in a far-flung, multi-store organization. For this, the franchisor trades off revenues and profits that would otherwise be his and a large measure of flexibility. Because its terms are defined by contract, the relationship between franchisor and franchisee is more static than dynamic, difficult to alter as the market and the business change.

Mrs. Fields Cookies, despite its size, has not franchised—persuasive evidence itself that the Fieldses have built something unusual. Randy Fields believes that no other U.S. food retailer with so many outlets has dared to retain this degree of direct, day-to-day control of its stores. And Mrs. Fields Cookies does it with a headquarters staff of just 115 people. That's approximately one staffer to every five stores—piddling compared with other companies with far fewer stores to manage. When the company bought La Petite

Boulangerie from PepsiCo earlier this year, for instance, the soft-drink giant had 53 headquarters staff people to administer the French baker/sandwich shop chain's 119 stores. Randy needed just four weeks to cut the number to 3 people.

On paper, Mrs. Fields Cookies *looks* almost conventional. In action, however, because of the way information flows between levels, it *feels* almost flat.

On paper, between Richard Lui running the Pier 39 Mrs. Fields in San Francisco and Debbi herself in Park City, there are several apparently traditional layers of hierarchy: an area sales manager, a district sales manager, a regional director of operations, a vice-president of operations. In practice, though, Debbi is as handy to Lui—and to every other store manager—as the telephone and personal computer in the back room of his store.

On a typical morning at Pier 39, Lui unlocks the store, calls up the Day Planner program on his Tandy computer, plugs in today's sales projection (based on year-earlier sales adjusted for growth), and answers a couple of questions the program puts to him. What day of the week is it? What type of day: normal day, sale day, school day, holiday, other?

Say, for instance, it's Tuesday, a school day. The computer goes back to the Pier 39 store's hour-by-hour, product-by-product performance on the last three school-day Tuesdays. Based on what you did then, the Day Planner tells him, here's what you'll have to do today, hour by hour, product by product, to meet your sales projection. It tells him how many customers he'll need each hour and how much he'll have to sell them. It tells him how many batches of cookie dough he'll have to mix and when to mix them to meet the demand and to minimize leftovers. He could make these estimates himself if he wanted to take the time. The computer makes them for him.

Each hour, as the day progresses, Lui keeps the computer informed of his progress. Currently he enters the numbers manually, but new cash registers that automatically feed hourly data to the computer, eliminating the manual update, are already in some stores. The computer in turn revises the hourly projections and makes suggestions. The customer count is OK, it might observe, but your average check is down. Are your crew members doing enough suggestive selling? If, on the other hand, the computer indicates that the customer count is down, that may suggest the manager will want to do some sampling—chum for customers up and down the pier with a tray of free cookie pieces or try something else, whatever he likes, to lure people into the store. Sometimes, if sales are just slightly down, the machine's revised projections will actually exceed the original on the assumption that greater selling effort will more than compensate for the small deficit. On the other hand, the program isn't blind to reality. It recognizes a bad day and diminishes its hourly sales projections and baking estimates accordingly.

Hourly sales goals?

Well, when Debbi was running *her* store, *she* set hourly sales goals. Her managers should, too, she thinks. Rather than enforce the practice through dicta, Randy has embedded the notion in the software that each store manager relies on. Do managers find the machine's suggestions intrusive? Not Lui. "It's a tool for me," he says.

Several times a week, Lui talks with Debbi. Well, he doesn't exactly talk *with* her, but he hears from her. He makes a daily phone call to Park City to check his computerized PhoneMail messages, and as often as not there's something from Mrs. Fields herself. If she's upset about some problem, Lui hears her sounding upset. If it's something she's breathlessly exuberant about, which is more often the case, he gets an earful of that, too. Whether the news is good or bad, how much better to hear it from the boss herself than to get a memo in the mail the next week.

By the same token, if Lui has something to say to Debbi, he uses the computer. It's right there, handy. He calls up the FormMail program, types his message, and the next morning, it's on Debbi's desk. She promises an answer, from her or her staff, within 48 hours. On the morning I spent with her, among the dozen or so messages she got was one from the crew at a Berkeley, Calif., store making their case for higher wages there and another from the manager of a store in Brookline, Mass., which has been struggling recently. We've finally gotten ourselves squared away, was the gist of the note, so please come visit. (Last year Debbi logged around 350 000 commercial air miles visiting stores.)

Here are some other things Lui's computer can do for him.

- Help him schedule crew. He plugs his daily sales projection for two weeks hence into a scheduling program that incorporates as its standards the times Debbi herself takes to perform the mixing, dropping, and baking chores. The program gives him back its best guess of how many people with which skill levels he'll need during which hours. A process that done manually consumed almost an hour now takes up just a fraction of that time.

- Help him interview crew applicants. He calls up his interview program, seats the applicant at the keyboard, and has him or her answer a series of questions. Based on the answers given by past hirees, the machine suggests to Lui which candidates will succeed or fail. It's still his choice. And any applicant, before a hire, will still get an audition—something to see how he or she performs in public. Maybe Lui will send the hopeful out on a sampling mission.

- Help with personnel administration. Say he hires the applicant. He informs the machine, which generates a personnel folder and a payroll entry in Park City, and a few months later comes back to remind Lui that he hasn't submitted the initial evaluation (also by computer), which is now slightly past due. It administers the written part of the skills test and updates the records with the results. The entire Mrs. Fields personnel manual will soon be on the computer so that 500 store managers won't forget to delete old pages and insert revised ones every time a change is made.

- Help with maintenance. A mixer isn't working, so the manager punches up the repair program on the computer. It asks him some questions, such as: is the plug in the wall? If the questions don't prompt a fix, the computer sends a repair request to Park City telling the staff there which machine is broken, its maintenance history, and which vendor to call. It sends a copy of the work order back to the store. When the work gets done, the store signs off by computer, and the vendor's bill gets paid.

That's a lot of technology applied to something as basic as a cookie store, but Randy had two objectives in mind.

He wanted to keep his wife in frequent, personal, two-way contact with hundreds of managers whose stores she couldn't possibly visit often enough. "The people who work in the stores," says Debbi, "are my customers. Staying in touch with them is the most important thing I can do."

It's no accident, even if Lui isn't consciously aware of why he does what he does, that he runs his store just about the same way that Debbi ran her first one 10 years ago. Even when she isn't there, she's there—in the standards built into his scheduling program, in the hourly goals, in the sampling and suggestive selling, on the phone. The technology has "leveraged," to use Randy's term, Debbi's ability to project her influence into more stores than she could ever reach effectively without it.

Second, Randy wanted to keep store managers managing, not sweating the paperwork. "In retailing," he says, "the goal is to keep people close to people. Whatever gets in the way of that—administration, telephones, ordering, and so on—is the enemy." If an administrative chore can be automated, it should be.

Store managers benefit from a continuing exchange of information. Of course, Park City learns what every store is doing daily—from sales to staffing to training to hires to repairs—and how it uses that information we'll get to in a minute. From the store managers' perspective, however, the important thing is that the information they provide keeps coming back to them, reorganized to make it useful. The hour-by-hour sales projections and projected customer counts that managers use to pace their days reflect their own experiences. Soon, for instance, the computer will take their weekly inventory reports and sales projections and generate supply orders that managers will only have to confirm or correct—more administrative time saved. With their little computers in the back room, store managers give, but they also receive.

What technology can do for operations it can also do for administration.

"We're all driven by Randy's philosophy that he wants the organization to be as flat as possible," says Paul Quinn, the company's director of management information systems (MIS).

"There are a few things," says controller Lynn Quilter, "that Randy dislikes about growth ... He hates the thought of drowning in people so that he can't walk in and know exactly what each person does ... The second thing that drives him nuts is paper."

"The objective," says Randy, "is to leverage people—to get them to act when we have 1000 stores the same way they acted when we had 30."

He has this theory that large organizations, organizations with lots of people, are, per se, inferior to small ones. Good people join a growing business because it offers them an opportunity to be creative. As the company grows, these people find they're tied up managing the latest hires. Creativity suffers. Entropy sets in. Randy uses technology to keep entropy at bay.

He began by automating rote clerical chores and by minimizing data-entry effort. Machines can sort and file faster than people, and sorting and filing is deadly dull work, anyway. Lately he's pushed the organization toward automated exception reporting for the same reason. Machines can compare actual results with expected results and flag the anomalies, which are all management really cares about anyway. And within a few years, Randy expects to go much further in his battle against bureaucracy by developing artificial-intelligence aids to the running of the business.

Understand that it's not equipment advances—state-of-the-art hardware—that's pushing Mrs. Fields Cookies toward management frontiers. The machines the company uses are strictly off the shelf: an IBM minicomputer connected to inexpensive personal computers. It is, instead, Randy's ability to create an elegant, functional software architecture. He has, of course, had an advantage that the leader of an older, more established company would not have. Because Mrs. Fields is still a young enough company, he doesn't have to shape his automated management system to a preexisting structure. Every new idea doesn't confront the opposition of some bureaucratic fiefdom's survival instinct. Rather, the people part and the technology part of the Fields organization are developing simultaneously, each shaped by the same philosophy.

You see this congruence at corporate headquarters and in the company's operational management organization.

Between Debbi as chief executive officer and the individual store managers is what seems on paper to be a conventional reporting structure with several layers of management. But there's an additional box on the organization chart. It's not another management layer. It transcends layers, changing the way information flows between them and even changing the functions of the layers.

The box consists of a group of seven so-called store controllers, working in Park City from the daily store reports and weekly inventory reports. They ride hard on the numbers. If a store's sales are dramatically off, the store controller covering that geographical region will be the first to know it. If there's a discrepancy between the inventory report, the daily report of batches of cookies baked, and the sales report, the controller will be the first to find it. (It is possible for a smart thief to steal judiciously for about a week from a Mrs. Fields store.) "We're a check on operations," says store controller Wendy Phelps, but she's far more than just a check. She's the other half of a manager's head.

Since she's on top of the numbers, the area, district, and regional managers don't have to be—not to the same degree, at any rate. "We want managers to be with people, not with problems," says Debbi. It's hard, Randy says, to find managers who are good with both people and numbers. People people, he thinks, should be in the field, with numbers people backing them up—but not second-guessing them. Here's where the company takes a meaningful twist.

Problems aren't reported up the organization just so solutions can flow back down. Instead, store controllers work at levels as low as they can. They go to the store manager if he's the one to fix a discrepancy, a missing report, for instance. Forget chain of command. "I'm very efficiency minded," says Randy.

So the technology gives the company an almost real-time look at the minutiae of its operations, and the organizational structure—putting function ahead of conventional protocol—keeps it from choking on this abundance of data.

Some managers would have problems with a system that operates without their daily intervention. They wouldn't be comfortable, and they wouldn't stay at Mrs. Fields. Those who do stay can manage people instead of paper.

If administrative bureaucracies can grow out of control, so can technology bureaucracies. A couple of principles, ruthlessly adhered to, keep both simple at Mrs. Fields.

The first is that if a machine can do it, a machine *should* do it. "People," says Randy, "should do only that which people can do. It's demeaning for people to do what machines can do. ... Can machines manage people? No. Machines have no feelie-touchies, none of that chemistry that flows between two people."

The other rule, the one that keeps the technological monster itself in check, is that the company will have but one data base. Everything—cookie sales, payroll records, suppliers' invoices, inventory reports, utility charges—goes into the same data base. And whatever anybody needs to know has to come out of it.

Don't enforce this rule, and, says Randy, "the next thing you know you have 48 different programs that can't talk to each other." Technology grown rampant.

Having a single data base means, first, that nobody has to waste time filing triplicate forms or answering the same questions twice. "We capture the data just once," says controller Quilter.

Second, it means that the system itself can do most of the rote work that people used to do. Take orders for chocolate, for instance. The computer gets the weekly inventory report. It already knows the sales projection. So let the computer order the chocolate chips. Give the store manager a copy of the order on his screen so he can correct any errors, but why take his time to generate the order when he's got better things to do—like teaching someone to sell. Or, take it further. The machine generates the order. The supplier delivers the chips to the store and bills the corporate office. A clerk in the office now has to compare the order, the invoice, and what the store says it got. Do they all match? Yes. She tells the computer to write a check. The more stores you have, the more clerks it takes. Why not let the computer do the matching? In fact, if everything fits, why get people involved at all? Let people handle the exceptions. Now the clerk, says MIS director Quinn, instead of a processor becomes a mini-controller, someone who uses his brain.

The ordering process doesn't happen that way yet at Mrs. Fields, although it probably will soon as Randy continues to press for more exception reporting. You can see where he's going with this concept.

"Eventually," he says, "even the anomalies become normal." The exceptions themselves, and a person's response to them, assume a pattern. Why not, says Randy, have the computer watch the person for a while? "Then the machine can say, 'I have found an anomaly. I've been watching you, and I think this is what you would do. Shall I do it for you, yes or no. If yes, I'll do it, follow up, and so on. If no, what do you want me to do?'" It would work for the low-level function—administering accounts payable, for instance. And it would work at higher levels as well. "If," Randy says, "I can ask the computer now where are we making the most money and where are we making the least and then make a decision about where not to build new stores, why shouldn't that sort of thing be on automatic pilot too? 'Based on performance,' it will say, 'we shouldn't be building any more stores in East Jibip. Want me to tell [real-estate manager] Mike [Murphy]?' We're six months away from being able to do that."

The ability to look at the company, which is what the data base really is, at a level of abstraction appropriate to the looker, is the third advantage of a single data base—even if it never moves into artificial-intelligence functions. It means that Debbi Fields and Richard Lui are both looking at the same world, but in ways that are meaningful to each of them.

The hurdle to be overcome before you can use technology to its best advantage—and that isn't equivalent to just hanging an outboard motor on a skyscraper, as Buckminster Fuller said—isn't technical in the hardware sense. Randy buys only what he calls plain vanilla hardware. And it isn't financial. For all its relative sophistication in computer systems, Mrs. Fields spends just 0.49% of sales on data processing, much of which is returned in higher productivity.

Much more important, Randy says, is having a consistent vision of what you want to *accomplish* with the technology. Which functions do you want to control? What do you want your organization chart to look like? In what ways do you want to leverage the CEO's vision? "Imagination. We imagine what it is we want," says Randy. "We aren't constrained by the limits of what technology can do. We just say, 'What does your day look like? What would you *like* it to look like?'" He adds, "If you don't have your paradigm in mind, you have no way of knowing whether each little step is taking you closer to or further from your goal."

For instance, he inaugurated the daily store report with the opening of store number two in 1978. The important thing was the creation of the report—which is the fundamental data-gathering activity in the company—not its transmission mode. That can change, and has. First transmission was by Fax, then by telephone touch tone, and only recently by computer modem.

Having a consistent vision means, Randy says, that he could have described as far back as 1978, when he first began to create it, the system that exists today.

But he doesn't mean the machines or how they're wired together. "MIS in this company," he says, "has always had to serve two masters. First, control. Rapid growth without control equals disaster. We needed to keep improving control over our stores. And second, information that leads to control also leads to better decision making. To the extent that the information is then provided to the store and field-management level, the decisions that are made there are better, and they are more easily made.

"That has been our consistent vision."

SOURCE: Excerpted from Tom Richman, "Mrs. Fields' secret ingredient," *INC.* Magazine, October 1987. Reprinted with permission, Inc magazine, October 1987. Copyright © 1987 by Goldhirsh Group, Inc., 38 Commercial Wharf, Boston, MA 02110.

PART

2

WORKING
WITH PEOPLE

Part II of the text continues to follow the new entrant to the organization. Each chapter in Part II answers questions about the people of the organization and how to work with them.

Chapter 5 answers questions about how individuals in an organization are the same and different, and how these individual differences can be expected to affect organizational functioning and interpersonal behaviour. This chapter answers questions about biological characteristics such as age, sex, and physical capacities, and psychological characteristics such as personality and attitudes. Chapter 6 continues with the examination of an individual difference, that of perception. Each person sees the world in a way that is somewhat different from the next person.

Now that our new organizational entrant has a grasp of the organization and the people in it, the next questions to be addressed are how to deal with the other people of the organization. Chapters 7 and 8 look at the

elements of communicating with others, as well as managing and motivating them. Management and communication occur between a manager and a member, but also occur between a manager and several members and between different managers. Chapter 9 focuses on groups, teams, and intergroup relationships. Chapter 10 on the subject of leadership follows this discussion of groups because leading a group entails more than managing it.

The last two chapters of Part II examine processes in organizations, how organizations work and how their members interrelate. To understand organizations our new member needs to know not just how they are at one point in time but how they operate over time. The former is the static view and the latter is the dynamic view. Chapter 11 discusses how decisions are made at the individual, group, and organizational levels, while Chapter 12 investigates processes of power, politics, and conflict. Understanding these is crucial to effective functioning in an organization.

CHAPTER

5

INDIVIDUAL DIFFERENCES: BIOLOGICAL AND PSYCHOLOGICAL

CHAPTER OUTLINE

Biological Individual Differences

   Race

   Sex

   Physical Characteristics

   Age

   Intelligence

Psychological Individual Differences

   Gender

   Personality

   Attitudes

Conclusion

QUESTIONS TO CONSIDER

- *How are people at work the same or different in their biological and psychological characteristics?*

- *How are people at work the same or different in what they believe, think, feel, and value?*

- *What are the effects of job satisfaction?*

Individual differences (ID's) are the variables that may be used to distinguish between people. The two broad categories of individual difference are biological and psychological. Biological differences include race, sex, physical characteristics, age, and intelligence. Psychological differences include gender, personality, and attitudes.

An almost continual argument has gone on about the relative contribution of genes (nature) and environment (nurture) to the traits and behaviour of people. Some have taken the position that humans are born *tabula rasa*, or with a mind like a blank slate. The slate is filled, and the person's individuality formed, through each person's particular experiences and learning. This is the extreme nurture position. Others believe that individuality is pre-coded and determined by genetic makeup. This is the extreme nature position. Research has shown that both nature and nurture are important in understanding human behaviour (Plomin, 1989).

The relative contributions of nature and nurture to each biological or psychological attribute are not necessarily well known, but it is important to realize that both have influence and that they may influence each other. For example, the environment affects how genes are manifested. Think of genetically equivalent corn seeds planted in poor or rich soil. Though the genes allow a certain development of the corn plant, the local environment can stunt or nourish its growth, resulting in plants that look different, although they are still genetically equal. In the human family nutrition and health care provide the poor or rich soil for the developing child. Genes do not fix behaviour but establish a range of possible experiences that environments can provide (Weinberg, 1989).

In this chapter we will first explore biological individual differences. These are critically important in the workplace because our physical characteristics have a direct impact on how we work and the effectiveness of our work performance. For instance, we expect firefighters to be strong enough to carry a person from a burning building. But it is important when using individual differences as predictors of effective work performance to be sure that the characteristic is truly relevant to the work. In the past it was assumed, for example, that a firefighter had to be male in order to fulfill the strength requirements of that job. A more direct approach today is to determine how much weight a firefighter should be able to carry and *then* to determine if each firefighter, regardless of sex, is able to bear that load.

Another example of the biological basis for organizational behaviour is the design of our workplaces. Humans are social animals. We like to be near one another. Our workplaces are places of social gathering. At work we do not like to be socially isolated from others. Also, humans have evolved to have excellent eyesight and the ability to process great amounts of visual information. We therefore care a great deal about the design, colours, and layout of where we work. If our eyesight were less well developed and our hearing more advanced (as is the case for dogs), our workplaces would be less colourful and quieter.

After discussing biological individual differences we will examine psychological ID's. These include gender, personality, and attitudes. Differences of how people think of themselves, how they tend to act in work situations and how they feel about work are important for our understanding of how effective people are at work. We know, for instance, that people have different attitudes toward their jobs—some are satisfied and some are not. Job satisfaction has effects on such work behaviours as attendance and intentions to quit.

BIOLOGICAL INDIVIDUAL DIFFERENCES

Humans today are of the genus *Homo* and the species *Sapiens*. We are predators. We have a highly developed binocular vision focused forward. Our sense of smell has become less important to us than our vision. We are marked by upright posture, articulate speech, superior mental development, an approximately vertical forehead, and a rounded back of the skull. We live in social structures and have highly dependent infants who need years of care before they are able to take care of themselves.

Sex

For mammals (and that of course includes humans), the basic body plan is female and stays that way until told otherwise by masculine hormones (Konner, 1982). More males than females are conceived than are born, and more males are born than females. Males are more likely to die before reproducing. The conclusion is that though larger and stronger as adults, males are more physically vulnerable than females (Jacklin, 1989).

In the normal curves for height shown below, though the male average is higher than that of the female average, there are clearly parts of the female normal curve that are to the right of parts of the male normal curve.

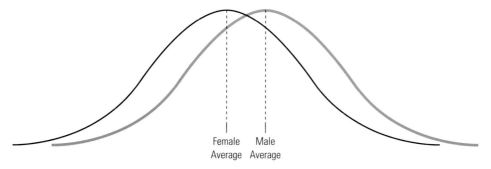

This means that there are many females who are taller, heavier, and stronger than some males. The same would be true for the other characteristics showing differences between males and females. While the average for one sex may be higher than the average for the other sex, the more the two distributions for the characteristic overlap the lower is the likelihood of an accurate prediction about one male and one female.

The observer of high-level sport may tend to disagree with this argument that males and females, as individuals, may not be very different, because the best male swimmers and runners (for example) are faster than the best female swimmers and runners. But these athletes have capabilities far above that of the average person and would be found at the extreme right tail of the population distribution for that skill. Even with a high degree of distribution overlap, at the tail of the distribution males (in this case) will be to the right of females. An organizational implication of this fact is described in this chapter's *Seeing is Believing* feature.

The key to understanding individual differences in organizations is to focus on the individual's characteristics. Differences between means in the population as a whole are usually not relevant in organizations.

Physical Characteristics

Genes do not fix behaviour or a person's characteristics, but establish a range of possibilities that are affected by the environment. For example, in the last 20 years, because of improvements in health, hygiene, and nutrition, average human height has increased by three to four inches (see *On the One Hand* for a discussion about the malleability of nature). Also, genes do not always determine our destiny. Physical characteristics such as weight, height, hair colour and style, eye colour, body shape, appearance, and physical defects such as shortsightedness can all be changed.

Peoples of the world.

SEEING IS BELIEVING

The job of a firefighter can be dirty and dangerous, but it offers comradeship, the knowledge of helping others, and good pay. There are so many people interested in becoming firefighters in Toronto that the Toronto Fire Department can select only the best and brightest recruits. This means that only those individuals performing at the very right hand side of the performance curve are hired.

In order to improve their chances, potential firefighters are training for both the physical side of the tests and the knowledge side. But women are finding it difficult to be hired. Even though some women are able to meet the standards of physical performance set for a firefighter (just as only some men are), such as being able to carry a 90.72-kilogram (200-lb) weight down a ladder, a woman in top condition still finds it difficult to physically outperform a man in top condition. Essentially, in this high performance job screening, biological differences between males and females are making the difference in who is hired.

But what is fair? Should the top women be hired even though they don't perform quite as well on the physical tests as the top men? Would that be discriminating against the men who would have been hired had the women not been hired?

SOURCE: Based on information in Craig McInnes (1992), "A night in the life of No. 5," The *Globe and Mail*, February 15, 1992, p. D3.

ON THE ONE HAND...

In an interesting article, William Angoff of the Educational Testing Service argues that the debate over whether intelligence is largely genetically or environmentally determined is not the real issue. What is important, according to Angoff, is whether intelligence can be changed.

The first point he makes is that inherited characteristics, even those with high heritability such as height, have shown dramatic change over several generations and even within the last generation. For example, British and American adolescent children are over six inches taller today than children of a similar age 100 years ago. More recently, a study of 898 American-born Japanese children in California found they were taller and heavier than the children in Japan. Therefore, if height is changeable due to environmental factors, then perhaps intelligence, which is acknowledged to be less a product of genes than is height, may also be changed by environment. His point is that genes are not necessarily deterministic: there is not necessarily a fixed and permanent gene blueprint for the development of inherited traits.

Further, Angoff goes on to point out that "some environmentally acquired habits and attitudes are extremely resistant to change. These include not only the physically addictive habits like smoking, drinking, and drug addiction, but also racial, national, and religious prejudices; attitudes toward crime, money, and marriage; attitudes of authoritarianism, and even voting behavior" (p. 715). So the key issue for debate in his opinion is not Nature versus Nurture, but what traits are amenable to change. Angoff feels that aptitude and intelligence are subject to change if cognitive training begins early in life and continues for an extended period in a supportive and motivating environment.

SOURCE: Based on information in William H. Angoff (1988), "The Nature-Nurture debate, aptitudes, and group differences, *American Psychologist* 43: 713-720.

Three dimensions of physical performance have been found to be important at work. They are muscular strength, endurance, and movement quality. A summary of these dimensions is presented in Exhibit 5.1. This chapter's *Overboard* cartoon humorously illustrates that Nate the pirate has high capabilities in muscular tension and power.

EXHIBIT 5.1   DIMENSIONS OF PHYSICAL PERFORMANCE

MUSCULAR STRENGTH

Muscular Tension:	requires exerting muscular force against objects. It is used to push, pull, lift, lower, and carry objects or materials.
Muscular Power:	requires exerting muscular force quickly.
Muscular Endurance:	requires exerting muscular force continuously over time while resisting fatigue.

CARDIOVASCULAR ENDURANCE

Cardiovascular Endurance:	requires sustaining physical activity that results in increased heart rate.

MOVEMENT QUALITY

Flexibility:	requires flexing or extending the body limbs to work in awkward or contorted positions.
Balance:	requires maintaining the body in a stable position, including resisting forces that cause loss of stability.
Coordination:	requires sequencing movements of the arms, legs, and/or body to result in skilled action.

SOURCE: Joyce Hogan (1991), Structure of physical performance in occupational tasks, *Journal of Applied Psychology* 76: 498. Copyright © 1991 by the American Psychological Association. Reprinted by permission.

SOURCE: OVERBOARD © Universal Press Syndicate. Reprinted with permission. All rights reserved.

Age

The body has a genetically coded structure that sets the timetable for its maturation (Konner, 1982). It must be noted, however, that to mature properly the body needs sufficient energy, protein, and minerals from the environment. Children learn to walk at approximately the same age, 10 to 15 months, and acquire a language (it doesn't matter which) between 18 and 28 months of age. Ego development and moral judgment are also, along with many other human traits, a product of maturation.

Later in life there is a decline in physical abilities as the body loses calcium and mass, though the onset of this decline is also a product of genetics and environment. People differ at all ages in how well they can hear, see, smell, taste, and touch, though decrement in these abilities also usually occurs later in life.

Age and intelligence may be related. Fluid intelligence (problem solving ability) peaks in the late teens and early 20s (Flynn, 1987), but crystallized intelligence (general information) may peak as late as age 60 because of the lifelong addition of experiences and information.

Many jobs have physical and mental requirements that can be met by almost all adult men and women in the usual working span of 18 to 65 years of age. In these jobs the decline in physical ability that normally occurs with age is not relevant to job performance. But there are jobs with physical and/or mental requirements that are typically best met by workers of a given age. Jobs requiring heavy lifting and carrying, for example, are normally filled by young adults.

On the other hand, jobs are sometimes segregated by age for reasons other than job performance. At Proteus Rainwear Limited (Young, 1989) there were two different groups of mostly female workers. In the work wear group there was a heavy and steady work load, and the pay was by piece rate. Here workers were generally older with family obligations. In the group making handbags and toiletry bags pay was by piece rate and employees came and went with the level of the work load. These workers tended to be younger and unmarried. The younger workers who did not have a family to support were not allowed to occupy the jobs with a more stable income. These were reserved for the older workers.

This same effect can be observed in jobs which have suffered waves of layoffs. Unions customarily insist that workers laid-off be those with the least amount of time on the job. These workers are ordinarily also the youngest. When a wave of new workers is hired the organization will then find itself with a younger and an older group of employees.

Intelligence

Richard Weinberg (1989) asked people in general the question: "What is intelligence?" They said it is composed of three main factors: (1) Practical problem-solving ability; (2) Verbal ability; and (3) Social intelligence (how to get along with others).

Psychologists have determined other models of intelligence. Raymond B. Cattell (1965) considered general intelligence to be composed of fluid and crystallized intelligence. Louis L. Thurstone (1938) conducted mathematical factor analysis on human test data to determine seven primary mental abilities. These were verbal comprehension, perceptual speed, ability to compute numbers, word fluency, inductive reasoning, memory, and spatial aptitude.

J. Paul Guilford (1967) went further, dividing intelligence into 120 unique intellectual abilities. Five mental operations (cognition, memory, divergent thinking, convergent thinking, and evaluation) are applied to four possible contents (figural, symbolic, semantic, and behavioural), resulting in six possible products (units, classes, relations, systems, transformations, and implications). For example, is 2 + 3 less than 4 or greater than 4? To answer this question requires convergent thinking applied to figural content to produce a relation. Tests of intelligence may be devised for each of these separate abilities.

The most common intelligence tests are the Stanford-Binet IQ test and the Wechsler Adult Intelligence Scale (WAIS). The Intelligence Quotient (IQ) is defined as mental age divided by chronological age, and gives one statistic that is meant to represent overall intelligence. By setting the average score for a population at 100 and the standard deviation (here a measure of the dispersion of intelligence scores) at 15, a normal distribution of intelligence would be as shown on the following page.

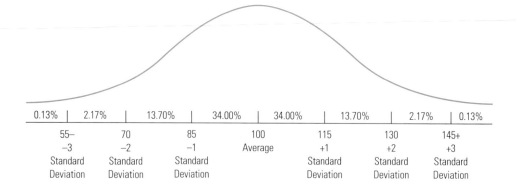

0.13%	2.17%	13.70%	34.00%	34.00%	13.70%	2.17%	0.13%
55–	70	85	100	115	130	145+	
−3	−2	−1	Average	+1	+2	+3	
Standard Deviation	Standard Deviation	Standard Deviation		Standard Deviation	Standard Deviation	Standard Deviation	

By definition, then, 68 of 100 people would fall within one standard deviation of the average. Almost 14 out of 100 people would be expected to fall between 116 and 130 and just over 2 people of 100 would have measured IQ's over 130.

The practical implications for high IQ people are that: above 130 they find school easy and can succeed in virtually any occupation; above 140 their adult achievements are so clear that they fill the pages of *American Men of Science* and *Who's Who*; above 150 they begin to duplicate the life histories of the famous geniuses who have made creative contributions to our civilization (Flynn, 1987, p. 187). Of course this does not mean that having a high IQ will necessarily lead to high achievement. Other factors such as family background, experience, and amount of effort exerted, among others, will also be important.

g The factor of general intelligence.

s Any one of a number of specific factors of intelligence.

Analyses of the answers to intelligence tests have resulted in two further views of intelligence. Spearman's two factor theory proposes a factor of general intelligence, **g**, and a specific factor **s** that measures intelligence for a particular test. While general intelligence cannot be improved in the short term, specific test intelligence can. For example, one study found that coaching for aptitude tests raised scores by an average of .43 standard deviations (Kulik and others, 1984).

Three tests that can be studied for and that the student may encounter are the GMAT (Graduate Management Admissions Test), the LSAT (Law School Admissions Test), and the MCAT (Medical College Admissions Test). While general intelligence is partly responsible for performance on these tests, test performance will also be affected by test intelligence. Each test has specific types of questions, an answer format, and some knowledge that is assumed. To improve the test intelligence of aspiring business, law, and medical students a large test preparation industry has developed. This includes test preparation manuals and test preparation seminars.

What then is intelligence? The best answer is that it is a general factor and then any number of specific mental abilities. These may be named and tested for, but it should be remembered that the names created for specific aspects of intelligence are only labels given by testers and do not necessarily relate directly to one part of the brain. Thinking of intelligence in this way means that while some people may be very intelligent overall they may be less intelligent in some specific areas of ability. Similarly, some people may be very intelligent in some specific abilities but of lower than average overall intelligence.

The argument has been made about intellectual ability that there are two different types of thinking. A person who is left-brain dominant is expected to be a more analytic, deductive, and logical thinker. The right-brain dominant individual is expected to be more intuitive, holistic, and inductive in his thinking (Hayes & Allinson, 1994). A listing of the separate functions of the brain's left and right hemispheres is shown as Exhibit 5.2 (see page 178).

Stratified systems theory

A person's cognitive level should be an important factor in determining the hierarchical level they come to occupy in the organization.

A specific cognitive mental ability that has been suggested is the degree to which a person thinks in concrete or abstract terms. This ability has formed the foundation for **stratified systems theory**. The basic idea in this theory is that a person's cognitive level

EXPERIENCE IS THE BEST TEACHER

This is an exciting time for researchers interested in the underpinnings of individual differences in human behavioural development. There is growing appreciation for the contribution of genetic factors to variations in general intelligence, special mental abilities, personality traits and mental disorders. In recent years, new evidence has demonstrated genetic influences on behaviours as diverse as vocational interests, job satisfaction and social attitudes. Genetic influences on vocational interests are, for example, evidenced by increased resemblance between individuals with relatively high proportions of common genes, as compared with less closely related individuals, or non-relatives living together. At the same time, increased attention is being directed toward understanding how environmental factors affect development. In particular, efforts are underway toward distinguishing between environmental events that uniquely affect family members and lead to differences among them, from shared environmental events that are associated with similarities among family members. Two children in the same family may, for example, share religious beliefs due to a common rearing. However, exposure to different teachers and classmates may be associated with differences in school attitudes and selected social behaviours.

Nancy L. Segal is a professor at the Department of Psychology, California State University at Fullerton. For an example of her work with the Minnesota twin study group, see Bouchard, Lykken, McGue, Segal, and Tellegen (1990), published in Science, 250: 223-228.

Individual differences researchers make use of naturally occurring human "experiments." These include twin and adoption designs. These methods are able to disentangle the relative influences of genetic and environmental factors with respect to behaviours of interest. In contrast, studies of intact families do not offer this advantage because the effects of genes and environments are completely confounded. Second marriages may, however, generate informative kinships, such as unrelated siblings reared together or half-siblings. My own work has included studies of twins reared together and apart, with an emphasis on social relationships. A study of individual differences in bereavement, using identical and fraternal twins who have lost co-twins and other relatives, is in progress.

Important advances and refinements in research design and methodology promise to yield numerous compelling findings in the near future. Twin and family designs are, for example, being usefully combined in studies of behavioural and physical variation. Developments in molecular genetics should assist in identifying associations between DNA differences and behavioural traits. The increasingly interdisciplinary climate of the individual differences field is a powerful testimony to the many complex and fascinating aspects of human behaviour.

---

should be an important factor in determining the hierarchical level they come to occupy in the organization. For further information on this approach, see this chapter's *If You Can't Ride Two Horses At Once, You Shouldn't Be in the Circus* feature.

There is clear evidence that IQ is determined genetically, at least in part (Bouchard & McGue, 1981). A good estimate for the genetic contribution to intelligence is 50% to 70% (Bouchard and others, 1990; Plomin, 1989; Weinberg, 1989). The other influences on intelligence are the environment and organic factors. The environment might include such factors as the amount of stimulation received by a child, the toys available for play, and culture exposed to as a child. An example of an organic factor is any drugs taken by the mother while the child is developing in the uterus.

A political and scientific controversy has developed in the last 30 years over the relative intelligence of different races. One argument that can be marshalled against any racial differences in actual intelligence is that measured intelligence differences could be due to

EXHIBIT 5.2   SEPARATE FUNCTIONS OF THE
TWO SIDES OF THE BRAIN

LEFT HEMISPHERE *(RIGHT SIDE OF BODY)*	RIGHT HEMISPHERE *(LEFT SIDE OF BODY)*
Speech/Verbal	Spatial/Musical
Logical, Mathematical	Holistic
Linear, Detailed	Artistic, Symbolic
Sequential	Simultaneous
Controlled	Emotional
Intellectual	Intuitive, Creative
Dominant	Minor (Quiet)
Worldly	Spiritual
Active	Receptive
Analytic	Synthetic, Gestalt
Reading, Writing, Naming	Facial Recognition
Sequential Ordering	Simultaneous Comprehension
Perception of Significant Order	Perception of Abstract Patterns
Complex Motor Sequences	Recognition of Complex Figures

Source: Robert J. Trotter (1976), "The other hemisphere," *Science News*, April 3, 1976, p. 219. Reprinted with permission from SCIENCE NEWS, the weekly newsmagazine of science, copyright 1976 by Science Service, Inc. For an application of the left/right brain concept to management, see Henry Mintzberg (1981), "Planning on the left side and managing on the right," *Harvard Business Review*, January/February 1981, pp. 50-58.

IF YOU CAN'T RIDE TWO HORSES AT ONCE, YOU SHOULDN'T BE IN THE CIRCUS

Canadian-born management consultant Elliott Jaques has developed a theory of management based on a person's level of cognitive thinking ability. His first point is that organizations should be structured into layers. These are defined by the "target completion time of the longest task, project or program" for the roles of organizational members at that level. Jaques has determined that there are six natural levels of time orientation for jobs. Level one contains jobs with a time orientation of three months or less. At level two tasks might take up to a year to complete. The time horizon is up to two years for level three and five years for level four. Long-term programs of ten years duration are located at level five, and twenty years at level six. Jaques' second point is that people vary in their ability to think in concrete or abstract terms. Those who are able to consider problems and process information in more complex and abstract ways are also able to think about how decisions might unfold in the future. They are there-

fore mentally equipped to operate effectively at the higher levels of organizational time orientation.

Therefore, in the terms of Jaques' stratified systems theory, the individual difference of cognitive thinking level is a determinant of success at a given organizational level. In other words: "Each person has an inherent potential for cognitive development and is thus equipped to rise only so high, and no higher, in an organization" (Ross, 1992, p. 47). The manager who can't consider multiple streams of information and how they might interact in the long run is not equipped for upper levels of management where time horizons are longer.

These principles have been used to restructure organizations into time-horizon layers and to match managers' cognitive levels to their layer in the hierarchy. At Canadian Tire Acceptance Ltd. of Welland, Ontario, restructuring and staff changes have led to revenue increases of $73 million in three years.

SOURCE: Based on information in Alexander Ross (1992), "The long view of leadership," *Canadian Business*, May 1992, pp. 46-51.

the test used. For example, IQ-test-measured intelligence has risen dramatically in the last 30 years, but there has been no corresponding rise in overall performance by the population (Flynn, 1987). The conclusion must be that the population as a whole is not getting smarter, even though IQ test results say that is the case.

What then, are these tests measuring if not intelligence? Flynn's conclusion is that intelligence tests are not measuring intelligence but some other factors that are weakly related to intelligence. IQ tests may be measuring culture differences between groups. Therefore, measured differences in IQ between groups are not likely to be actual differences in intelligence.

PSYCHOLOGICAL INDIVIDUAL DIFFERENCES

To this point in the chapter we have examined the primarily biological side of how people are the same and different from one another. Now we turn to the psychological side. Three main differences between people in how they think, feel, and act are gender, personality, and attitudes.

Gender

We saw in Chapter 3 that cultures differ in how they answer basic questions about the meaning and purpose of life. What it means to be male and female is taught in cultures around the world (Konner, 1982). Gender is more than a person's biological sex, it is the sex role taught in a particular culture.

For example, one study found that 27 of 33 world cultures sampled attempted to get more nurturance out of girls than boys and none attempted the reverse, and that 70 of 82 cultures gave boys more training in self-reliance than girls and none attempted the reverse (Barry and others, 1957). A study of children in six cultures—the U.S.A.; Mexico; Kenya; India; Japan; and the Philippines—by Beatrice Whiting and John Whiting (1975) found that boys were more aggressive than girls within each culture. This is the genetic influence. However, they also found that the girls of some cultures were more aggressive than the boys other cultures. This is the cultural/environment influence.

Parents treat boys and girls differently. Hugh Lytton and David Romney (1991) analyzed 172 published studies of how parents socialize their children. They found that in North America both parents encouraged sex-typed activities, though these differences decreased as the child grows up. They also found that in other Western countries boys received more physical punishment than did girls. Significantly, fathers treated boys and girls more differently than did mothers.

Male and female managers are more similar than different. It has been found that men and women become more similar the more time they spend in management (Dipboye, 1987). There is an argument, however, that in general the management style of women will be more consensus-building than that of males. This could be the result of a female's socialization, emphasizing nurturing and emotional connection with others. Tips for how women in particular could tap these natural skills are offered in this chapter's *A Word to the Wise* feature. Of course, these tips apply as well to empathetic and caring men.

Personality

Personality is a stable set of tendencies and characteristics that determine those commonalities and differences in people's psychological behaviour (thoughts, feelings, and actions) that have continuity in time and that may not be easily understood as the sole result of the social and biological pressures of the moment (Salvatore Maddi, 1989, p. 8).

Personality A stable set of tendencies and characteristics that determine those commonalities and differences in people's psychological behaviour that have continuity in time and that may not be easily understood as the sole result of the social and biological pressures of the moment.

A WORD TO THE WISE

TAP YOUR NATURAL MANAGERIAL SKILLS

1. Trust your senses. Women can be vulnerable to doubts about following their own instincts in the workplace. But although the way we handle situations may be different from the way men do, different can often be *right*. Powerful women tend to have faith in their decision-making abilities, and that makes them even more powerful within their organizations.

2. Gather outside support, particularly from women who may be dealing with similar gender issues in their own organizations. Women's natural affiliative skills—and the difficulties we often face in the workplace—make creating a "reality check" network essential.

3. The more you attain, the more you can help other women. Being a mentor to younger professionals helps to legitimize the roles of all women in the work force, says Columbia, Maryland, psychologist Susan Rockwell Campbell, Ph.D. She notes that a younger woman's reputation can be enhanced—and her progress accelerated—by an alliance with an established and respected leader.

4. Create a special niche. Women who specialize early in their careers develop "expert power," according to Campbell. "They are treated," she says, "with more respect and are perceived by others as having power and leadership capabilities."

5. If you find yourself in a situation where women are being treated inappropriately, band together and fight to change the status quo. But remember, an ability to tolerate frustration can work to your advantage because large-scale change takes place extremely slowly.

6. Make it clear to others that your achievements—and your mistakes—belong to you alone. Do not be limited by those who would stereotype your actions.

7. Finally, be sympathetic to other women managers—both to their successes and to their failures. *Never* let any successful woman be referred to as "a bitch," and don't allow professional criticism of a female manager to deteriorate into a critique of her clothing choices or attractiveness. When you feel tempted to do this, think about whether you would subject a male leader to such an irrelevant and superficial standard.

SOURCE: Excerpted and reprinted with permission from Susan Merrell (1993), "When a woman manages the company," *New Woman*, January 1993, p. 116.

Many aspects of personality have been studied to determine how people are different and how those differences affect attitudes and behaviour. Scientists have proposed several theories of personality. It must be remembered that these theories and names of personality characteristics are for our convenience when thinking about personality. They do not necessarily relate directly to physical structures inside a person. Three theories of personality are psychoanalytic, humanistic, and traits.

Psychoanalytic Theory   Sigmund Freud was a psychiatrist who worked in Vienna in the 1900s. He considered personality the result of unconscious conflict between a person's **id**—their source of energy, their **ego**, which exerts control over the id, and their **superego**, or conscience (see Freud, 1976). A person with a dominant id would be impatient, quick tempered, and uncontrolled. An ego-dominant person would be controlled, realistic, and pragmatic. A person who feels guilty and is worried about what others think would be dominated by the superego.

In 1928 Carl Jung, a student of Freud's, proposed a theory of psychological types. In his theory people can differ on how they acquire information from the environment (by sensing or by intuition), by how they make decisions (by thinking or by feeling), by their focus of attention (extroversion or introversion), and by how they orient themselves to the outer world (by judging it or by being open to it). The Myers-Briggs Type Indicator (MBTI: Myers, 1987) measures these four dimensions and produces a set of 16 personality types.

id   A person's source of energy.

ego   Exerts control over the id.

superego   A person's conscience.

For our purposes in this text we will discuss only the four broad personality types obtained by crossing sensing/intuition with thinking/feeling (see Exhibit 5.3). Sensing/Thinkers tend to be practical and analytical. Sensing/Feelers tend to be sympathetic and friendly. Intuitive/Feelers tend to be enthusiastic and insightful. Intuitive/Thinkers tend to be logical and analytical.

EXHIBIT 5.3   EFFECTS OF COMBINATIONS OF PERCEPTION AND JUDGMENT

People who prefer:	ST SENSING & THINKING	SF SENSING & FEELING	NF INTUITION & FEELING	NT INTUITION & THINKING
focus their attention on:	Realities	Realities	Possibilities	Possibilities
and handle these with:	Objective analysis	Personal warmth	Personal warmth	Objective analysis
thus they tend to become:	Practical & analytical	Sympathetic & friendly	Enthusiastic & insightful	Logical & analytical
and find scope for their abilities in:	Technical skills with objects and facts	Practical help & services for people	Understanding & communicating with people	Theoretical & technical developments

for example:	Applied science
	Business
	  administration
	Banking
	Law enforcement
	Production
	Construction
		Health care
		Community service
		Teaching
		Supervision
		Religious service
		Office work
		Sales
			Behavioral science
			  research
			Literature
			Art & music
			Religious service
			Health care
			Teaching
				Physical science
				  research
				Management
				Computers
				Law
				Engineering
				Technical work

S Sensing

One way to "find out" is to use your sensing function. Your eyes, ears, and other senses tell you what is actually there and actually happening, both inside and outside of yourself. Sensing is especially useful for appreciating the realities of a situation. Sensing types tend to accept and work with what is "given" in the here-and-now, and thus become realistic and practical. They are good at remembering and working with a great number of facts.

N Intuition

The other way to find out is through intuition, which shows you the meanings, relationships, and possibilities that go beyond the information from your senses. Intuition looks at the big picture and tries to grasp the essential patterns. If you like intuition, you grow expert at seeing new possibilities and new ways of doing things. Intuitive types value imagination and inspirations.

T Thinking

One way to decide is through your thinking. Thinking predicts the logical consequences of any particular choice or action. When you use thinking you decide objectively, on the basis of cause and effect, and make decisions by analyzing and weighing the evidence, even including unpleasant facts. People with a preference for thinking seek an objective standard of truth. They are frequently good at analyzing what is wrong with something.

F Feeling

The other way to decide is through your feeling. Feeling considers what is important to you or to other people (without requiring that it be logical) and decides on the basis of person-centred values. When making a decision for yourself, you ask how much you care, or how much personal investment you have, for each of the alternatives. Those with a preference for feeling enjoy dealing with people and tend to become sympathetic, appreciative, and tactful. (It is important to understand that the word "feeling," when used here, means making decisions based on values; it does not refer to your feelings or emotions.)

This way of measuring and interpreting personality can be useful in organizations because it illustrates how people are different and how those differences are of benefit to the organization. For example, Myers (1987, p. 26) lists ways that personality types need each other.

Intuitive types need sensing types:
- To bring up pertinent facts;
- To face the realities of the current situation;
- To apply experience to problems;
- To read the fine print in a contract;
- To focus on what needs attention now;
- To keep track of essentials;
- To face difficulties with realism;
- To stay aware of the joys of the present.

Sensing types need intuitive types:
- To bring up new possibilities;
- To read the signs of coming change;
- To focus on preparing for the future;
- To keep the big picture in mind;
- To anticipate trends;
- To show that the joys of the future are worth working for.

Feeling types need thinking types:
- To analyze consequences and implications;
- To organize;
- To find the flaws in advance;
- To reform what needs reforming;
- To hold consistently to a policy;
- To weigh "the law and the evidence";
- To fire people when necessary;
- To stand firm against opposition.

Thinking types need feeling types:
- To persuade;
- To conciliate;
- To forecast how others will feel;
- To arouse enthusiasm;
- To teach;
- To sell;
- To appreciate what is right;
- To appreciate the thinker.[1]

Humanistic Theory The Theory X/Theory Y approach of Douglas McGregor (1960) can serve to categorize how people think about the basic motivations of others. Some managers take the point of view that others value work for its own sake and do not have

---

[1] Reproduced by special permission of the Publisher, Consulting Psychologists Press, Inc., Palo Alto, CA 94303 from *Introduction to Type* by Isabel Briggs Myers. Copyright ©1987 by Consulting Psychologists Press, Inc.. All rights reserved. Further reproduction is prohibited without the Publisher's written consent.

to be monitored closely. This is the humanistic Theory Y view. Other managers might take the Theory X perspective that people basically don't want to work, and that employees have to be watched continually to make sure they keep to their jobs. Theory X/Y has been used as a tool to understand the attitudes and actions of managers. It can also be used in organizational training to sensitize managers to their basic theory of personality in the hopes of moving all managers to the more humanistic Theory Y outlook. This approach, however, may be culturally constrained. Theory X/Y relies on the cultural value of individualism, which may hold in North America but is less true for people in South East Asia (Hofstede, 1987).

Trait Theory   This approach focuses on particular observable personality characteristics or traits. Similar to the nature/nurture debate, an argument has raged over the relative influence on a person's behaviour of the person's traits and the situation the person is in. Some have argued that traits determine behaviour and some have taken the position that the situation constrains personal behaviour. The answer is, of course, that both traits and the situation interact to affect behaviour.

Douglas Kenrick and David Funder (1988) make the point that people do differ in their personalities and that these differences do influence their behaviour. They also provided several examples of how personality traits and the situation interact.

1. In relevant situations traits can influence behaviour. In a threatening situation a person who is anxious is liable to fidget, break into a cold sweat, or run from the scene.

2. A person's traits can change the situation. An individual who is aggressive can act in a way that causes conflict with others. The aggressive subordinate in a performance review may make statements to the manager that inflame the situation and cause the manager to react with defensiveness or aggression.

3. People with different traits will choose different situations. Those who are introverted, for example, will often choose to be in a quiet place like a library instead of a noisy place like a party.

4. Traits can change with persistent exposure to a situation. Going to college and living in the student environment has been found to change a person to be less conservative.

5. Personality traits are more easily expressed in some situations than others. It is easier to "be yourself" at a picnic than at a funeral. The picnic has fewer rules about how to behave than does the funeral. Extroverts and introverts would act similarly at a funeral but would be expected to act quite differently at a picnic.

An example of the interaction of a personality trait and the situation is Machiavellianism. Niccòlo Machiavelli (1467-1527) lived in Florence, Italy during the Italian renaissance and wrote the classic book *The Prince* as a handbook to power for the local ruling family, the Medici. Another book, *The Discourses*, details checks and balances on power but is less well known. Today we think of Machiavelli as one concerned with gaining and keeping power and in using power with little moral constraint. Those who are high on Machiavellianism (as measured by the Mach V Attitude Inventory: Christie & Geis, 1970) are considered more likely to modify their tactics depending on the particular work situation they face (see Exhibit 5.4). Support for this hypothesis has been found in a test of sales persons (Shultz, 1993).

EXHIBIT 5.4   PREDICTED TACTICS OF THOSE HIGH AND LOW ON MACHIAVELLIANISM

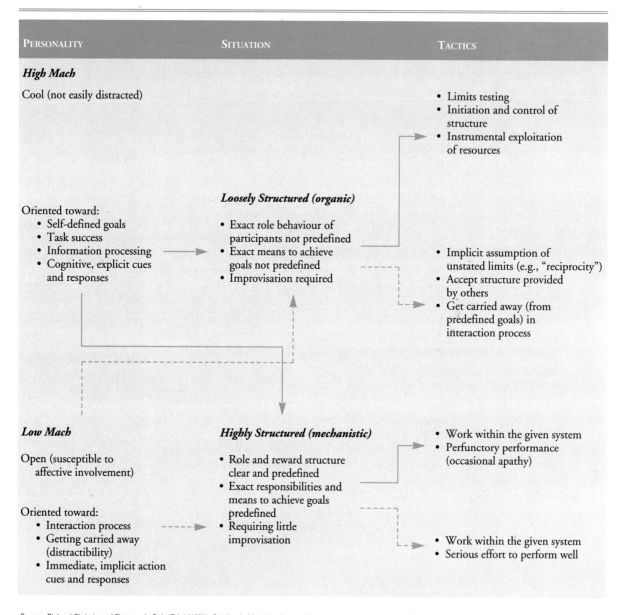

PERSONALITY	SITUATION	TACTICS

High Mach

Cool (not easily distracted)

Oriented toward:
- Self-defined goals
- Task success
- Information processing
- Cognitive, explicit cues and responses

Loosely Structured (organic)
- Exact role behaviour of participants not predefined
- Exact means to achieve goals not predefined
- Improvisation required

- Limits testing
- Initiation and control of structure
- Instrumental exploitation of resources

- Implicit assumption of unstated limits (e.g., "reciprocity")
- Accept structure provided by others
- Get carried away (from predefined goals) in interaction process

Low Mach

Open (susceptible to affective involvement)

Oriented toward:
- Interaction process
- Getting carried away (distractibility)
- Immediate, implicit action cues and responses

Highly Structured (mechanistic)
- Role and reward structure clear and predefined
- Exact responsibilities and means to achieve goals predefined
- Requiring little improvisation

- Work within the given system
- Perfunctory performance (occasional apathy)

- Work within the given system
- Serious effort to perform well

SOURCE: Richard Christie and Florence L. Geis (Eds.) (1970), *Studies in Machiavellianism.* New York: Academic Press, p. 351. Reprinted by permission.

Two well-known tests of personality traits are the Minnesota Multiphasic Personality Inventory (MMPI-2) and Cattell's 16 Personality Factor Questionnaire (16PF). The MMPI-2 consists of 566 true/false questions and measures a large number of personality traits. It is mainly used by clinical psychologists to measure psychological disturbance. The 16PF (see Exhibit 5.5) measures more commonly understood aspects of personality.

EXHIBIT 5.5   FACTORS MEASURED BY THE 16 PERSONALITY
FACTOR QUESTIONNAIRE

FACTOR	DESCRIPTION OF PERSON WITH A LOW SCORE	DESCRIPTION OF PERSON WITH A HIGH SCORE
A	RESERVED, cool, detached, aloof	WARMHEARTED, easygoing, participating, outgoing
B	CONCRETE THINKER, practically minded	ABSTRACT THINKER, intellectual interests
C	AFFECTED BY FEELINGS, emotionally less stable	EMOTIONALLY STABLE, faces reality, calm, mature
E	SUBMISSIVE, mild, accommodating	ASSERTIVE, dominant, aggressive, competitive
F	SOBER, prudent, serious, taciturn	HAPPY-GO-LUCKY, impulsively lively, enthusiastic
G	EXPEDIENT, disregards rules, feels few obligations	CONSCIENTIOUS, persevering, moralistic, straight-laced
H	SHY, restrained, timid, threat-sensitive	VENTURESOME, socially bold, uninhibited, spontaneous
I	TOUGH-MINDED, self-reliant, realistic, no-nonsense	TENDER-MINDED, gentle, over protected, sensitive
L	TRUSTING, adaptable, free of jealousy, easy to get along with	SUSPICIOUS, self-opinionated, hard to fool
M	PRACTICAL, careful, conventional, regulated by external realities	IMAGINATIVE, wrapped up in inner urgencies, careless of practical matters, bohemian
N	FORTHRIGHT, natural, artless, unpretentious	SHREWD, calculating, worldly, penetrating
O	SELF-ASSURED, confident, complacent	APPREHENSIVE, self-reproaching, worrying, troubled
Q_1	CONSERVATIVE, respecting established ideas, tolerant of traditional difficulties	EXPERIMENTING, liberal, analytical, free-thinking
Q_2	GROUP-DEPENDENT, a 'joiner' and good follower	SELF-SUFFICIENT, prefers own decisions, resourceful
Q_3	UNDISCIPLINED SELF-CONFLICT, follows own urges, careless of social rules	CONTROLLED, socially precise, compulsive, following self-image
Q_4	RELAXED, tranquil, composed	TENSE, frustrated, driven, overwrought

SOURCE: Vivian Shakleton and Clive Fletcher (1984), *Individual Differences: Theories and Applications.* London: Methuen and Company, p. 55.

After years of research, a model of personality as composed of five main factors has emerged (Digman, 1990; Barrick & Mount, 1991). The five broad personality traits are:

- *Extroversion/Introversion.* Extroverts are oriented toward the outer world of other people and activities. Introverts are oriented toward the inner world of their own thoughts and feelings.
- *Friendliness/Hostility.* Friendly people are open to interaction with others and expect positive results. Hostile people look for and expect confrontation.
- *Conscientiousness (or Will).* A conscientious person is responsible, performing actions that were agreed to.
- *Neuroticism/Emotional Stability.* An emotionally stable person has a firm grasp on the reality of situations. Such an individual reacts in a steady way, not riding a rollercoaster of emotions.
- *Intellect.* This factor is composed of inquiring intellect, openness to new feelings and thoughts, cultural and creative interests. It has also been thought of as creativity. A test of personal creativity is presented as this chapter's self-diagnostic exercise.

These five broad traits have been found in studies conducted in the United States, Germany, Israel, and Japan, indicating a cross-cultural consistency for human personality. A study conducted in the Philippines found the first four factors and a fifth factor that instead of Intellect could better be called Culture or Openness.

Influences on Personality   Four main influences on an individual's personality are genetic/biological, social, cultural, and situational factors.

Genetic effects on personality The idea that personality is partly a function of a person's genes.

The study of **genetic effects on personality** is accomplished by assessing identical twins that are brought up by different families. One such study (Bouchard and others, 1990: see *A Little Knowledge*) found identical twins reared apart are about as similar as identical twins reared together "on multiple measures of personality and temperament, occupational and leisure-time interests, and social attitudes" (p. 223). Heredity therefore has an effect on an individual's personality.

Estimates are that 50% of extroversion and neuroticism (Plomin, 1989) and 50% of conscientiousness is inherited (Henderson, 1982). For schizophrenia, the disorder of personality marked by the disconnection of thoughts, feelings, and actions, genetic influence is approximately 8%.

You're not seeing double! Sets of identical twin girls at the Twins Day Festival.

A LITTLE KNOWLEDGE

The Minnesota study of twins reared apart has investigated more than 100 sets of twins or triplets that were raised in different homes. Separated early in life due to family misfortune, these twins spent their formative years apart and were reunited as adults. The research team based at the Institute of Human Genetics at the University of Minnesota seeks to study all cases of twins that were reared apart, and is active in trying to find more cases of reared-apart twins from around the world. In the study each twin completes 50 hours of medical and psychological assessment. Measures are made of personality traits, occupational interests, mental ability and IQ. A life history interview determines the family environment in which the twin was raised. A psychiatric interview and sexual life history interview is also part of the assessment process.

In this particular study, 56 sets of identical twins were studied (this includes two sets of male identical triplets that were reared apart). These individuals were labeled MZA in the study, for monozygotic apart, indicating they come from one ovum that split into two (or three), producing two (or three) genetically equivalent people. The average age of these twins was 41 years, they spent an average of only 5 months together before they were separated, were reared apart, and were reunited as adults.

Results of this study are that genetic factors exert a strong effect on the behaviour of the person. The researchers conclude that the effect of the home environment was negligible for many psychological traits. IQ was found to be 70% determined by genes, but material possessions and the cultural level in the adoptive home were also significantly related to IQ. Their overall conclusion is that "The genes sing a prehistoric song that today should sometimes be resisted but which it would be foolish to ignore" (p. 228).

SOURCE: Based on information in Bouchard and others (1990).

Heredity also affects the body's chemistry. Chemicals in the body can also affect personality. As Melvin Konner says: "two individuals who differ genetically in metabolic characteristics controlling behavioral tendencies will, if raised in identical environments with identical resources and training, grow up to act and think and feel differently" (1982, p. 105).

Culture and social class affects personality via group membership and socialization experiences. The family has an effect on a person's personality, but members of one family will often be dissimilar. Siblings will be unalike because of differences in genetic makeup and birth order (Toman, 1969), the age of the child when an event occurs (for example a death in the family, divorce), the child's gender, the child's physical appearance (attractive children are often favoured), and experiences that are unique to the individual (Hoffman, 1991).

Situational influences on personality include temporary body conditions such as fatigue and ingested chemicals. Examples of chemicals consumed are the caffeine in coffee, mood altering drugs such as stimulants and depressants, and performance altering drugs such as steroids.

Personality Assessment   A major method of surveying personality is self-assessment through questionnaires. Self-assessment is useful as a way of gaining self knowledge (and knowledge of others), but is likely to be valid only to the extent the individual responds honestly. Self-assessment tests of personality can easily be faked and so are less useful for the selection of employees.

Personality may also be analyzed by personal interview, watching a person work, or by using a projective test. Needs tests, for example, have often been projective. In the **thematic apperception test** (or TAT) a person is asked to read a story or look at a picture. Then the individual is asked to explain what she thinks is happening. The test is projective because the person's own inner needs are thought to be projected into the description given. The TAT provides a measure of individual need for achievement, need for affiliation, and need for power.

Thematic apperception test (TAT) A projective test used to measure an individual's needs for achievement, affiliation, and power.

Attitudes

Beliefs

Values

Feelings

Attitudes

Beliefs are what an individual accepts to be true without questioning. Beliefs that endure over time are called **values**. **Feelings** are sentiments or the emotional component of beliefs. Beliefs plus feelings make up an individual's **attitudes** (Tesser & Shaffer, 1990).

For example, a belief accepted without questioning (especially in some cultures) is that managers should make the decisions. This becomes over time a value, that a "good" manager is one who makes the decisions that are required. A related feeling could be that "this manager makes me uneasy because he keeps asking me what I would do." The resulting attitude might then be "I don't like working for my manager."

The primary purpose of attitudes is knowledge of how to act with respect to another person or object. This essentially means an evaluation of whether to approach or avoid the object. Three other functions of attitudes (Tesser & Shaffer, 1990) are ego defensive, social-adjustive, and value expressive.

Ego defensive attitudes
Provide the means to cope with intrapsychic conflict.

Ego defensive attitudes provide the means to cope with intrapsychic conflict. One example of an ego defensive attitude is the rationalization of behaviours. The attitude here serves as an explanation to the self of why some action was taken—"I cut back his hours because he's not very friendly to the customers." **Social-adjustive attitudes** change as the person and others engage in normal interaction—"I really can't stand to be around that person." **Value-expressive attitudes** serve to express the person's own internal values—"Smoking is wrong for the smoker and others around the smoker."

Social-adjustive attitudes
Change as the person and others engage in normal interaction.

Beliefs and values are influenced by both genetics and environment. One study of work values found they were 40% influenced by genetic factors (Keller and others, 1992). *Traditionalism,* the tendency to follow rules and authority and to believe in high moral standards, has been estimated to be 50% influenced by genes (Plomin, 1989).

Value-expressive attitudes Serve to express the person's own internal values.

Feelings may also have a biological basis. Paul MacLean (1990) has proposed that the human brain (like those of other advanced mammals) has three levels that were founded in different evolutionary periods. This **triune brain** is composed first of the reptilian brain (in humans the *corpus striatum* and related structures) which controls movement and instinctive behaviours. The old mammalian brain was added later in evolution, arising with the evolution of early mammals. In humans this is the limbic system that gives emotional colouring to behaviours. The new mammalian brain was added last and is the human neocortex, which allows a stream of thought and complex mental functioning.

Triune brain The concept that the human brain is composed of three structures laid down over the course of millions of years of evolution.

Melvin Konner (1972, p. 150) provides us with a wonderful description of how a person's smile may or may not involve feelings.

> Thus, the human smile—a gesture of joy, a gesture of greeting, a gesture of submission, a gesture of deception, occasionally even a gesture of contempt—involves, or at least can involve, all three portions of the triune brain. The sudden smile in greeting a welcome acquaintance toward whom we feel very little may be no different in neural control from the friendly or aggressive displays of lizards and robins. The slowly spreading smile on the face of a parent watching a loved child take its first steps depends, in all likelihood, on a normally functioning limbic system, that invention of the early mammals. And the presumably less authentic, endlessly repeated "stewardess smile" could probably not be effected without the more advanced portions of the cerebral cortex.

The behaviour of people in organizations is a central concern of those who live and work in organizations. Attitudes are important in organizations because they affect behaviour. People may act non-rationally, that is, without conscious thought or by habit. In this case the attitude/behaviour link is direct. When acting rationally individuals form an intention to behave that is created from an attitude toward the anticipated behaviour and subjective norms. This behavioural intention is then linked to the behaviour (Tesser & Shaffer, 1990), as shown in the model that follows.

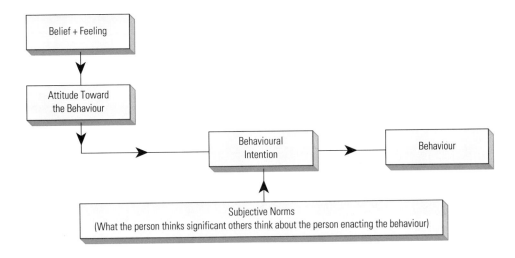

The best predictor of a person's behaviour is that individual's behavioural intention. Three parts of work attitudes are therefore: the *affective*—what the person feels about work; the *cognitive*—what the person thinks about work; and the *intentional*—what actions are intended.

Affective Component of Attitude   Job satisfaction is caused by the work environment and by the worker as an individual. For example, Richard Arvey and colleagues (1989) found that job satisfaction was 30% the result of genetic factors. In a later report Arvey and his colleagues (1991) put forward their tentative hunch "that person factors account for between 10 and 30% of the variance in job satisfaction, that 40-60% of the variance is associated with situational factors, and that interactive elements account for between 10 and 20%" (p. 377). One situational factor (among many) that affects job satisfaction has been found to be wage inequality and dispersion. The greater the dispersion of wages, in general, the lower is satisfaction with those wages (Pfeffer & Langton, 1993).

There are several ways of measuring feelings toward work. One such measure is the Minnesota Satisfaction Questionnaire (MSQ), shown as Exhibit 5.6. A common measure used in academic studies of worker satisfaction is the Job Descriptive Index (JDI) (Smith and others, 1969). The JDI asks workers to rate their work, the people at work, supervision, pay, and promotion opportunities and policies. Because job dissatisfaction often leads to thoughts of quitting and the intention to quit, these feelings about work have important organizational implications. The Organizational Commitment Questionnaire (Mowday and others, 1979) measures these feelings and intentions.

A comparative study of American and Japanese work attitudes is described in this chapter's *A Rose by Any Other Name.*

Cognitive Component of Attitude   Leon Festinger (1957) proposed a theory of cognitive dissonance that described what might happen when an individual is faced with an inconsistency between a thought and an action. For example, a clerical worker might find the job of sorting mail in an office building to be boring, but be asked by the boss to tell a new recruit that it was interesting work. If the mail sorter did so, his first attitude and later action would not agree. Festinger proposed that such dissonance would have to be resolved.

EXHIBIT 5.6   MINNESOTA SATISFACTION QUESTIONNAIRE

Ask yourself: How satisfied am I with this aspect of my job?

VS	=	I am very satisfied with this aspect of my job.
S	=	I am satisfied with this aspect of my job.
N	=	I can't decide whether I am satisfied or not with this aspect of my job.
DS	=	I am dissatisfied with this aspect of my job.
VDS	=	I am very dissatisfied with this aspect of my job.

On my present job, this is how I feel about:

		VS	S	N	DS	VDS
1.	Being able to keep busy all the time.	☐	☐	☐	☐	☐
2.	The chance to work alone on the job.	☐	☐	☐	☐	☐
3.	The chance to do different things from time to time.	☐	☐	☐	☐	☐
4.	The chance to be "somebody" in the community.	☐	☐	☐	☐	☐
5.	The way my boss handles the staff.	☐	☐	☐	☐	☐
6.	The competence of my supervisor in making decisions.	☐	☐	☐	☐	☐
7.	Being able to do things that don't go against my conscience.	☐	☐	☐	☐	☐
8.	The way my job provides for steady employment.	☐	☐	☐	☐	☐
9.	The chance to do things for other people.	☐	☐	☐	☐	☐
10.	The chance to tell people what to do.	☐	☐	☐	☐	☐
11.	The chance to do something that makes use of my abilities.	☐	☐	☐	☐	☐
12.	The way company policies are put into practice.	☐	☐	☐	☐	☐
13.	My pay and the amount of work I do.	☐	☐	☐	☐	☐
14.	The chances for advancement on this job.	☐	☐	☐	☐	☐
15.	The freedom to use my own judgment.	☐	☐	☐	☐	☐
16.	The chance to try my own methods of doing the job.	☐	☐	☐	☐	☐
17.	The working conditions.	☐	☐	☐	☐	☐
18.	The way my co-workers get along with each other.	☐	☐	☐	☐	☐
19.	The praise I get for doing a good job.	☐	☐	☐	☐	☐
20.	The feeling of accomplishment I get from the job.	☐	☐	☐	☐	☐

SOURCE: Reprinted from David J. Weiss, Rene V. Dawis, George W. England, & Lloyd H. Lofquist (1967), *Manual for the Minnesota Satisfaction Questionnaire*, Minnesota Studies in Vocational Rehabilitation, Vol. 22, Minneapolis: University of Minnesota Industrial Relations Center. Reprinted by permission.

A ROSE BY ANY OTHER NAME

Given the economic success of Japan and the well-known Theory J career system of the Japanese, James Lincoln and his colleagues decided to examine the work attitudes of Japanese and American manufacturing employees. Between 1981 and 1983 they surveyed 106 factories in central Indiana of the United States and the Kanagawa Prefecture of Japan (capital Yokohama). Over 8000 employees participated in the survey. Surprisingly, they found that American employees reported either the same or more commitment to the organization and higher job satisfaction. Responses to the specific questions asked are shown below.

Organizational Commitment Questions	U.S. Mean	Japan Mean	Was there a significant difference between countries?
Overall measure of organizational commitment	2.13	2.04	Yes
I am willing to work harder than I have to in order to help this company succeed (1 = strongly disagree, 5 = strongly agree)	3.91	3.44	Yes
I would take any job in order to continue working for this company (same answer codes)	3.12	3.07	No
My values and the values of this company are quite similar (same answer codes)	3.15	2.68	Yes
I am proud to work for this company (same codes)	3.70	3.51	Yes
I would turn down another job for more pay in order to stay with this company (same codes)	2.71	2.68	No
I feel very little loyalty to this company (1 = strongly agree, 5 = strongly disagree)	3.45	3.40	No

Job Satisfaction Questions	U.S. Mean	Japan Mean	Was there a significant difference between countries?
Overall measure of job satisfaction	1.54	0.96	Yes
All in all, how satisfied would you say you are with your job (0 = not at all, 4 = very)	2.95	2.12	Yes
If a good friend of yours told you that he or she was interested in working at a job like yours at this company, what would you say? (0 = would advise against it, 1 = would have second thoughts, 2 = would recommend it)	1.52	0.91	Yes
Knowing what you know now, if you had to decide all over again whether to take the job you now have, what would you decide? (0 = would not take job again, 1 = would have some second thoughts, 2 = would take job again)	1.61	0.84	Yes
How much does your job measure up to the kind of job you wanted when you first took it? (0 = not what I wanted, 1 = somewhat, 2 = what I wanted)	1.20	0.43	Yes

Analyzing their results further, they found that job satisfaction was a cause of organizational commitment, but that the reverse was not true. Then, controlling statistically for reported levels of job satisfaction, they found Japanese commitment to the organization was higher than American commitment. The lower reported job satisfaction by Japanese workers may have been because their expectations are high, which when not realized result in lower satisfaction. Or, alternatively, there may have been cross-cultural effects in questionnaire responses to job satisfaction because Japanese tend to see "the glass as half-empty" whereas Americans tend to see "the glass as half-full."

Source: James R. Lincoln (1989), "Employee work attitudes and management practice in the U.S. and Japan: Evidence from a large comparative survey," *California Management Review*, Fall 1989, p. 91. Table ©1989 by the Regents of the University of California. Reprinted by permission of the Regents. See also Lincoln and Kalleberg (1985), "Work organization and workforce commitment: A study of plants and employees in the U.S. and Japan," *American Sociological Review* 50: 744.

There are, however, many ways for a person to reduce cognitive dissonance. A person might take any of the following actions.

- Forget about the inconsistency or ignore it as unimportant. Dissonant acts are likely to induce cognitive change only when they relate to the person's self-concept.
- Seek information that makes actions and attitudes seem more consistent. This information is useful to rationalize away the dissonance. A consumer who purchases a new and expensive CD player might have conflicting thoughts about enjoying the player but missing the money. Information about the quality and features of the CD player might then be scrutinized to rationalize the purchase.
- Distort or change the perception of the situation and actions taken. Memory will be adjusted to reduce the inconsistency between thought and action.
- Separate actions and attitudes in the mind. By compartmentalizing them, inconsistencies can be avoided.
- Change the attitude about the event. The mail sorter in the above example might actually come to believe that the job is more interesting than he thought. In this case performing the behaviour has caused a change in attitude.
- Leave the situation. This method of reducing cognitive dissonance is likely when dissonance has built up over time and leaving is relatively easy. It may also be used when an attitude-behaviour inconsistency is too large to reduce by the above methods.

Cognitive dissonance is useful in understanding what a person thinks about work. But there is no way of knowing, given what a person thinks, which course of action that particular person might follow.

Intentional Component of Attitude   Individuals differ in how attitudes held affect their behavioural intentions. Job dissatisfaction is liable to result in the intention to quit for people that see a high probability of finding another job, that have skills easily transportable between jobs, that are younger with fewer situational constraints on their behaviour (for example car and house payments, children to support, etc.), or that have a high self concept. A model of behavioural intentions to quit a job is shown in Exhibit 13.5 (Chapter 13).

Four categories of response to job dissatisfaction are exit, voice, loyalty, and neglect (Farrell, 1983; Rusbult & Lowery, 1985), shown in Exhibit 5.7. *Exit* is an active but destructive option because it does not improve conditions for those still on the job. *Voice* is the active and constructive attempt to improve conditions by discussing work related problems. *Loyalty* is the passive acceptance of organizational conditions and hoping that change for the better will occur. *Neglect* is both passive and destructive because the person essentially "gives up" on the organization and making the workplace any better. Absenteeism and becoming part of the organization's "deadwood" are likely results of this reaction to job dissatisfaction.

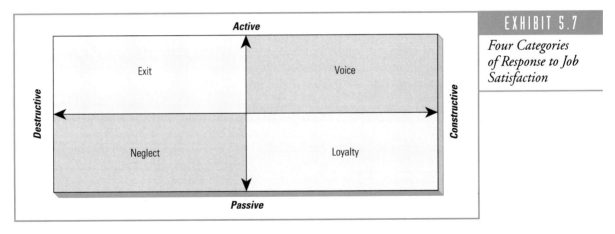

SOURCE: Reprinted from Caryl Rusbult and David Lowery (1985), "When bureaucrats get the blues: Responses to dissatisfaction among federal employees," *Journal of Applied Social Psychology* 15: 83. Reprinted with permission of V.H. Winston & Son, Inc.

EXHIBIT 5.7

Four Categories of Response to Job Satisfaction

CONCLUSION

This chapter has laid the foundation for understanding how people at work are the same and how they are different. An important message of this chapter is that, at the deepest levels of being human, we are all much the same.

But we are all different as well. Each of us is an individual with a biological, social, cultural, family, and experience background that has made us into a unique person. It is crucial to recognize the similarities and the differences of individuals at work.

When we meet new people at work we often take them as they are, fully formed, without thinking of how they came to be that way. Only later, with those few who become closer friends, is personal history and background experience revealed, allowing a better and deeper understanding of the underlying causes for their values, thoughts and actions.

This chapter's case is an autobiography that we hope the student of the nature-nurture debate finds interesting. It offers a useful way to think about and discuss the multiple influences that go into the making of one individual.

The next chapter continues our examination of individual differences. People are not only different in who they are but also in how they perceive, interpret, and evaluate those around them. First, Chapter 6 will focus on perception—how individuals perceive their environment, what effects there are on their perceptions, and how they form evaluations and attributions about other people. It is an important area for study because job and career success is due in large measure to how each of us is perceived and evaluated by others. Second, Chapter 6 will examine the process of performance appraisal. These reviews are an important aspect of a manager's job. We will consider methods of performance appraisal and possible limits to their effective use.

CHAPTER SUMMARY

To understand people at work it is necessary to consider how they are the same or different from each other. The study of these factors is the study of individual differences. The two main areas of difference are the biological and the psychological.

First, people differ from one another in their basic biological characteristics. From an organizational standpoint it is important to consider when these biological differences between individuals are crucial factors in that person's job performance and when these differences are immaterial. When crucial, a person's individual characteristics can be measured with assessment tests.

Second, people differ from one another in their psychological characteristics. Three main differences between people in how they think, feel, and act are gender, personality, and attitudes. Gender has to do with the sex roles a person is taught while growing up. There is some debate over the degree to which gender makes a difference in how managers in organizations act, how effective they are, and in how others evaluate them. Three theories of personality are the psychoanalytic, the humanistic, and traits. The "Big Five" model of personality proposes that there are five central traits required to understand personality. They are extroversion/introversion, friendliness/hostility, conscientiousness, neuroticism/emotional stability, and intellect. Individual differences can also affect a person's attitudes toward work. Three parts of work attitudes are the affective—what the person feels about work (for example job satisfaction); the cognitive—what the person thinks about work; and the intentional—what actions are intended.

QUESTIONS FOR REVIEW

1. What is the evidence about how similar men and women are in their attitudes and behaviours as managers in the workplace?

2. Give an example of cognitive dissonance and how it might motivate the organizational member to take action.

3. When might a particular individual difference make a difference to organizational performance? Is hiring based on a measure of that difference an acceptable form of discrimination?

4. Are assessment tests accurate enough to use to discriminate between people's biological and psychological characteristics? If most every test is subject to some level of error in measurement, and such error might mean that a particular individual is not hired or placed into a job for which they are in fact qualified, should the test be used?

5. How important is job satisfaction? What outcomes or behaviours might it predict?

SELF-DIAGNOSTIC EXERCISE 5.1

How Creative are You?

How creative are you? The following test helps you to determine if you have the personality traits, attitudes, values, motivations, and interests that make up creativity. It is based on several years' study of attributes possessed by men and women in a variety of fields and occupations who think and act creatively.

For each statement write in the appropriate letter:

A = *Agree;*   **B** = *In-Between or Don't Know;*   **C** = *Disagree*

Be as frank as possible. Try not to second-guess how a creative person might respond.

____ **1.** I always work with a great deal of certainty that I am following the correct procedure for solving a particular problem.

____ **2.** It would be a waste of time for me to ask questions if I had no hope of obtaining answers.

____ **3.** I concentrate harder on whatever interests me than do most people.

____ **4.** I feel that a logical step-by-step method is best for solving problems.

____ **5.** In groups I occasionally voice opinions that seem to turn some people off.

____ **6.** I spend a great deal of time thinking about what others think of me.

____ **7.** It is more important for me to do what I believe to be right than to try to win the approval of others.

____ **8.** People who seem uncertain about things lose my respect.

____ **9.** More than other people, I need to have things interesting and exciting.

____ **10.** I know how to keep my inner impulses in check.

____ **11.** I am able to stick with difficult problems over extended periods of time.

____ **12.** On occasion I get overly enthusiastic.

____ **13.** I often get my best ideas when doing nothing in particular.

____ **14.** I rely on intuitive hunches and the feeling of "rightness" or "wrongness" when moving toward the solution of a problem.

____ **15.** When problem solving, I work faster when analyzing the problem and slower when synthesizing the information I have gathered.

____ **16.** I sometimes get a kick out of breaking the rules and doing things I am not supposed to do.

____ **17.** I like hobbies that involve collecting things.

____ **18.** Daydreaming has provided the impetus for many of my more important projects.

____ **19.** I like people who are objective and rational.

____ **20.** If I had to choose from two occupations other than the one I now have, I would rather be a physician than an explorer.

____ **21.** I can get along more easily with people if they belong to about the same social and business class as myself.

____ **22.** I have a high degree of aesthetic sensitivity.

____ **23.** I am driven to achieve high status and power in life.

____ **24.** I like people who are most sure of their conclusions.

____ **25.** Inspiration has nothing to do with the successful solution of problems.

____ **26.** When I am in an argument, my greatest pleasure would be for the person who disagrees with me to become a friend, even at the price of sacrificing my point of view.

____ **27.** I am much more interested in coming up with new ideas than in trying to sell them to others.

____ **28.** I would enjoy spending an entire day alone, just "chewing the mental cud."

____ **29.** I tend to avoid situations in which I might feel inferior.

____ **30.** In evaluating information, the source is more important to me than the content.

____ **31.** I resent things being uncertain and unpredictable.

____ **32.** I like people who follow the rule, "business before pleasure."

____ **33.** Self-respect is much more important than the respect of others.

____ **34.** I feel that people who strive for perfection are unwise.

____ **35.** I prefer to work with others in a team effort rather than solo.

____ **36.** I like work in which I must influence others.

____ **37.** Many problems that I encounter in life cannot be resolved in terms of right or wrong solutions.

_____ **38.** It is important for me to have a place for everything and everything in its place.

_____ **39.** Writers who use strange and unusual words merely want to show off.

40. Below is a list of terms that describe people. Choose 10 words that best characterize you.

energetic ☐	factual ☐	courageous ☐
persuasive ☐	open-minded ☐	efficient ☐
observant ☐	tactful ☐	helpful ☐
fashionable ☐	inhibited ☐	perceptive ☐
self-confident ☐	enthusiastic ☐	quick ☐
persevering ☐	innovative ☐	good-natured ☐
original ☐	poised ☐	thorough ☐
cautious ☐	acquisitive ☐	impulsive ☐
habit-bound ☐	practical ☐	determined ☐
resourceful ☐	alert ☐	realistic ☐
egotistical ☐	curious ☐	modest ☐
independent ☐	organized ☐	involved ☐
stern ☐	unemotional ☐	absent-minded ☐
predictable ☐	clear-thinking ☐	flexible ☐
formal ☐	understanding ☐	sociable ☐
informal ☐	dynamic ☐	well-liked ☐
dedicated ☐	self-demanding ☐	restless ☐
forward-looking ☐	polished ☐	retiring ☐

How do you rate?

To compute your score, circle and add up the values assigned to each item. The values are as follows:

	A Agree	B In-Between or Don't Know	C Disagree		A Agree	B In-Between or Don't Know	C Disagree
1.	0	1	2	**10.**	1	0	3
2.	0	1	2	**11.**	4	1	0
3.	4	1	0	**12.**	3	0	-1
4.	-2	0	3	**13.**	2	1	0
5.	2	1	0	**14.**	4	0	-2
6.	-1	0	3	**15.**	-1	0	2
7.	3	0	-1	**16.**	2	1	0
8.	0	1	2	**17.**	0	1	2
9.	3	0	-1	**18.**	3	0	-1

	A Agree	B In-Between or Don't Know	C Disagree		A Agree	B In-Between or Don't Know	C Disagree
19.	0	1	2	30.	-2	0	3
20.	0	1	2	31.	0	1	2
21.	0	1	2	32.	0	1	2
22.	3	0	-1	33.	3	0	-1
23.	0	1	2	34.	-1	0	2
24.	-1	0	2	35.	0	1	2
25.	0	1	3	36.	1	2	3
26.	-1	0	2	37.	2	1	0
27.	2	1	0	38.	0	1	2
28.	2	0	-1	39.	-1	0	2
29.	0	1	2				

40. *The following have values of 2:*

energetic	dynamic	perceptive	dedicated
resourceful	flexible	innovative	courageous
original	observant	self-demanding	curious
enthusiastic	independent	persevering	involved

The following have values of 1:

self-confident	determined	informal	forward-looking
thorough	restless	alert	open-minded

The rest have values of 0.

95 – 116	Exceptionally Creative
65 – 94	Very Creative
40 – 64	Above Average
20 – 39	Average
10 – 19	Below Average
Below 10	Noncreative

Ways to Become More Creative

If you scored below your expectations, don't despair. By learning new attitudes, values, and ways of approaching and solving problems, you can considerably enhance your creative powers. Here are some ways to increase your creative ability:

- *Keep track of your ideas at all times.* Carry a notebook wherever you go, and keep it at your bedside. Ideas come at strange times, frequently when we least expect them, and they may never come again. Listen to your hunches and intuitions, particularly during moments of relaxation, before going to sleep or upon awakening.

- *Pose new questions every day.* An inquiring mind is a creatively active mind. It is also a mind that constantly enlarges the area of its awareness.
- *Avoid rigid, set patterns of doing things.* Overcome fixed ideas and look for new viewpoints; try new ways. Attempt to find several solutions to each problem and develop the ability to drop one idea in favour of another.
- *Be open and receptive to ideas, others' as well as yours.* New ideas are fragile—listen positively to them. Seize on tentative, half-formed concepts and possibilities: A new idea seldom arrives as a complete ready-made package. Freely entertain apparently wild, farfetched or even silly ideas.
- *Be alert in observation.* Look for similarities, differences, and unique and distinguishing features in objects, situations, processes and ideas. The more new associations and relationships you can form, the greater are your chances of coming up with really creative and original combinations and solutions.
- *Engage in hobbies.* Try ones that allow you to construct or produce something with your hands. This allows you to relax and enhances the creative problem-solving abilities so useful in your work. Also, keep your brain trim by playing games and doing puzzles and exercises.
- *Improve your sense of humour and laugh easily.* This helps you to put yourself and your problems into proper perspective. Humour relieves tension, and you are more creative when you are relaxed.
- *Adopt a risk-taking attitude.* Nothing is more fatal to creativity than fear of failure. Heed management consultant Chester Barnard's advice: "To try and fail is at least to learn. To fail to try is to suffer the inestimable loss of what might have been."

Note: It is important to remember that while the results of this test will be suggestive of your own creativity, this test as used here should not be considered a valid scientific instrument.

Source: Copyright © 1981 Eugene Raudsepp, President, Princeton Creative Research, Inc., 10 Nassau Street, P.O. Box 122, Princeton, New Jersey 08540, U.S.A. Reprinted by permission of Eugene Raudsepp.

EXPERIENTIAL EXERCISE 5.1

Role Play of Case 5.1

The class instructor can play the role of Herbie, and select two students to play Ron and Shirley. Then the instructor, based on input from the rest of the class on what to do, can role-play the scenario described in this case. For example, the class might suggest a one-on-one meeting between Herbie and Ron, with Shirley absent. The instructor would then ask the student playing Shirley to step outside the classroom for a moment, then actually have the meeting with Ron.

Alternatively, the class instructor can divide the class into groups of three, with the roles of Herbie, Ron, and Shirley assigned to group members. Then the student playing "Herbie" (who in this case could be female), can role play her plan to stop the feud. The students playing Ron and Shirley act out their parts within the scenario as described.

EXPERIENTIAL EXERCISE 5.2

Social Expressivity Card Game

The trait of self-monitoring is the degree to which individuals scrutinize their own social behaviour. The social skills inventory (see Riggio, 1986, for sample items) has been devised to measure individual differences in the seven basic social skills listed below.

- *Emotional expressivity* — the ability to express emotions
- *Emotional sensitivity* — the ability to understand the emotions of others
- *Emotional control* — the ability to control the expression of emotions, either by not showing emotions or by showing false emotions
- *Social expressivity* — the ability to speak easily with others, for example, at parties and with strangers
- *Social sensitivity* — the ability to understand what others say and the norms of social behaviour, paying attention to what others say
- *Social control* — the ability to play different social roles in different situations
- *Social manipulation* — the ability to use other people to get what is wanted.

This exercise will provide an opportunity to test your own emotional expressivity, emotional sensitivity, and emotional control.

First, create a list of emotions that people express towards others (for example, love, hate, disgust, etc.). Second, assign one emotion to each value in a deck of playing cards: one each to the numbers 2 through 10, one to the Jack, one to the Queen, one to the King, one to the Ace, and one to the Joker. Third, divide into groups of five, each with a pack of playing cards.

Then deal five cards face down to each person. The person to the left of the dealer picks one card/emotion to express, selects one of the other five people in the group as the target of the emotion, and then, without using any words, expresses the emotion.

The target guesses what the expressed emotion was. If the target can't guess or is wrong, anyone in the group can guess at the displayed emotion.

Everyone should take several turns expressing and receiving the expressed emotions of others. At the end of the game it is interesting to note which emotions were the easiest and most difficult to express and/or to receive, and if there was any emotion that was consistently misinterpreted by the receiver.

SOURCE: Adapted from a game described in James M. Johnson (Editor), (1972), *Instructional Strategies and Curriculum Units for Secondary Behavioral Sciences*, Plattsburgh, New York: State University of New York, pp. 111-112.

SELF-GUIDED LEARNING ACTIVITY

This chapter has provided a basic understanding of how individuals differ. You might now like to explore your own personality, interests, attitudes, and abilities in greater depth. The student counselling centre at most colleges and universities normally offers personal testing. The benefit of this analysis is that you will receive a report that can offer new information about yourself and an idea of what career is best suited to your interests or abilities. Private psychologists and corporations such as the YMCA/YWCA also offer diagnostic services, usually for a fee, in the areas of personality testing, career interests, and individual skills and abilities.

CASE 5.1

MANAGER'S CASE FILE: A WOMAN IN THE HOUSE

"Herbie, Tom's transfer is official. You'll need to start the ball rolling on hiring a replacement," Stu advised. "The sooner you can find someone, the better."

"O.K., boss, I'll let personnel know right away," Herbie Victor replied.

As supervisor of the production planning group, Herbie was responsible for selecting Tom's successor. The three planning positions were traditionally held by men, but Herbie found himself interviewing several women for the position. As the latest female candidate left his office, Ron Bridges, one of the planners, stuck his head in the door. "You've interviewed a bunch of women, Herbie. You really wouldn't do that to us, would you?"

"Do what, Ron?"

"Hire a woman planner. A woman just couldn't do the job."

"Why, Ron, I never thought you were a male chauvinist," Herbie kidded. Both men laughed.

A few days later, Herbie did decide to hire a woman—Shirley Edwards, a recent college graduate with a degree in math. When Herbie took her around to meet the others in the department, Ron mumbled, "Hello." He said he'd like to talk to Shirley but had a deadline to meet. "I'll drop by later," he added, "after I turn in this job." However, the afternoon found Ron working intently on his next project.

Shirley quickly caught on to the work, but Ron's attitude toward her continued to be icy. This bothered Herbie, but he felt that the problem would eventually disappear. Ron would just have to get used to working with a woman.

When Shirley had been in the position about six weeks, Herbie stopped by her desk to see how she felt about the job. "Oh, I'm very pleased," she replied. "This is the kind of work I've always wanted to do."

"Well, good. I've been pleased with your progress. If you keep on, you'll be a real asset to the planning group." As Herbie walked back to his office, he noticed Ron scowling. Ron obviously had overheard his conversation with Shirley.

Thereafter, the situation grew more and more unpleasant. Herbie frequently heard Ron and Shirley arguing. Once he heard the other planner tell Ron to give Shirley a break. "She's really a good worker, Ron," he said, "I don't see why you can't be nice to her." Finally, Stu summoned Herbie to his office to discuss the civil war that was raging in Herbie's department.

Stu told Herbie that the planners' feud had to stop. Because of it, the production planning group had missed two deadlines in the past two weeks. "Shirley seems capable enough, but I'm not sure that having her on staff is worth all this aggravation," Stu concluded.

Herbie didn't know what to do next. He wanted to keep Shirley, not only because she was a good worker, but also because she would have excellent grounds to level a discrimination charge if he fired her. But he just couldn't think of a way to make peace between her and Ron.

SOURCE: Reprinted, by permission of publisher, from SUPERVISORY MANAGEMENT, June 1985. © 1985 American Management Association, New York. All rights reserved.

Questions

1. How can Herbie stop the feud and get production back on schedule?

2. What could he have done to prevent the crisis from occurring in the first place?

3. How can he overcome the poor impression that Ron's behaviour has given Shirley?

UNHOLY TOLEDO

My father, of whom I am very proud, was required to quit school at the end of the fourth grade to go to work on his father's farm. In 1902, at the age of fifteen, he left the farm because he could no longer suffer his autocratic and authoritarian father.

Upon leaving the farm in central Ohio, my father went to the big city of Toledo, Ohio, where he obtained a job as a railroad worker. He began working on the railroad in about 1902 or 1903 and continued until he had saved enough money, probably $100 or so, to buy a poolroom. In 1902, unskilled railroad workers earned $9 per week, so saving $100 most likely required him to work overtime and make many personal sacrifices. He used the earnings from the poolroom to buy three slot machines. Thus, his career as an entrepreneur was launched.

Because of the competition from the "syndicate," it was necessary for him to place the slot machines in restaurants, poolrooms, after-hours joints, speakeasies and cafes on the outskirts of Toledo. When he placed the slots closer to the center of town, the syndicate would physically destroy them to protect its turf. Thus, he spent his early years as an entrepreneur, driving a Model A ford on mud roads, back and forth across the northern part of Ohio to service the slots and collect revenues. His "locations" could be as far as forty miles apart. A forty mile trip on a mud road might take as long as an hour and a half. My mother, Mary, would often ride with him to keep him company and to prevent him from falling asleep. To pass the time, she would frequently sing the popular songs of the day to him.

My father's business thrived, and he expanded into pinball machines, which were different from today's pinball machines. It cost a nickel to play a pinball machine, and one could possibly win as much as $2 or $3 in a given play. My father was moderately successful, and thus we enjoyed middle-class economic status. However, I was raised in a blue-collar neighborhood as my parents found themselves uncomfortable around more affluent and more educated people. Prior to my birth, and after my father had become somewhat successful, he and my mother moved to an affluent section of Toledo, Westmoreland. The neighbors snubbed my mother and gossiped about my father's business and the kind of people who came to our house. My father saw them as "blue bloods," and thought they didn't appreciate what it took for a poor boy to make good. To him, these people really didn't believe in the "American way." Consequently, my parents moved back to a working-class neighborhood on the east side of Toledo where my sisters and I were raised. My father's success was sufficient to put my two sisters and me through university and to leave my mother a sufficient amount of funds for her remaining years after his accidental death at the age of seventy.

My mother, whose maiden name was Mary Kinn, and of whom I am equally proud, was born in 1902 on a farm near Fostoria, Ohio. She was the youngest of eleven children. Her mother died when she was ten, and her father when she was fifteen. She and her brothers and sisters sold the farm and divided the proceeds equally. At the age of fifteen, she moved to Tiffin, Ohio, where she took a room with a family and spent her inheritance obtaining a diploma for secretarial and bookkeeping skills. At the age of about seventeen, she moved to Toledo, where she took an apartment with a number of other young women. They were carefree, fun-loving young women who were referred to in those days as "flappers," although my mother would never admit to it. Nevertheless, her stories, and the stories about her in the "roaring twenties" belied her denial.

From this brief description of my parents' background, you can see that I was endowed with two role models of industriousness, risk taking, and courage. It took a lot of courage for these young people to leave the farm and come to the big city, then known as "Unholy Toledo," while still in their teens. My mother was very nurturing. My father was strongly achievement-oriented, hard-driving, and very intolerant of

SOURCE: Robert J. House (1993), "Slow learner and late bloomer," In Arthur G. Bedeian (Editor), *Management Laureates: A Collection of Autobiographical Essays* (Volume 2, pp. 39-78). San Francisco: JAI Press. Excerpted and reprinted with permission of the publisher.

laziness and dishonesty. From him I learned three things: achievement motivation, the importance of controlling one's own destiny, and honesty. While my father was small, five-foot-four, and quite a gentle man, he didn't take any guff from anyone. He said it was necessary to stand on your own two feet or you'd get knocked over. From my mother I learned nurturance, hard work, respect for honesty and for the less fortunate, and humor. She loved to tell and listen to jokes, play cards (bridge and gin rummy), entertain, and party.

If you've read any of Damon Runyon, or if you've seen the play or the movie *Guys and Dolls*, you'll have a good idea of what life was like for me as a child growing up in Toledo. It was a Runyonesque environment. Toledo was a wide-open city. People would come to Toledo from Chicago, Cleveland, Detroit, Columbus and all the small farm towns to have a good time. Gambling houses, poolhalls and bars were open around the clock. Anybody who wanted "action" could find it in Toledo. By virtue of my father's occupation, the people whom the family knew were either small-time gamblers or people who, like my father, ran gambling businesses: numbers, racetracks, gambling houses, pinballs, "floating" card games, and slots. These were exciting times with exciting people. Many lived a roller coaster life of up and down; win at the track or the tables one day, lose the next. Borrow a hundred and make good your marker (IOU) as promised. Welchers could never borrow a second time—the word got around. Consequently, for the most part, these were honest people who lived and worked at night and slept most of the day. While my father was not a show-off, he had a dry sense of humor and enjoyed having a good time. My mother also liked to "kick up her heels," as she would say. She was a bit of an "Auntie Mame" type.

To give you an idea of the kind of environment in which I was raised, I'll recount a few incidents that occurred in my childhood and early adolescence.

There were a number of guys who hung out at my father's shop, where he repaired the slots; at a local bar and restaurant entitled "The Main Street Grill;" at the pool hall next door to my dad's shop, which he sold after he got into the slot machine business; at Charlie Bones' cigar store, where Bones ran a numbers book; or at Tuffy La Marche's cigar shop, where he ran an around-the-clock poker game. To pass the time, these guys would kibbitz, play gin rummy, poker, pool, bunker (a dice game), liar's dice, or bet on the horses, athletic games, or boxing matches. They would bet on almost anything, including the weather—or even which way a bird sitting on a telephone wire would fly!

Most of the guys had monikers. There was my dad, "Little Louie," Tuffy La Marche, Sam "Potatoes" Papata, Charlie "Bones" Bennett, Two Shirt Sam, Billy "The Belly" Grubowsky, Johnny "The Nose" Suzor, and Big Rollie. Because my last name was House, all of the guys with whom I hung out would refer to me by a number of monikers, such as "Domicile Dan," "Sammy Shack," "Izzy Igloo," "Gabby Garage," "Railroad Terminal Tom," or my favorite, "Tony Tepee."

Two Shirt Sam got his moniker because he always wore a light blue shirt and brown trousers. We all assumed that he had at least two shirts, and that they were the same. One day, Potatoes visited Two Shirt at his apartment. He opened the closet to find that Two Shirt actually had fifteen identical blue shirts and six identical pairs of brown trousers. He said it made life simpler for him in the morning. Everyone liked Two Shirt Sam, so the way he dressed didn't make much difference. From Two Shirt I learned that it was important and satisfying to "be yourself."

One day when the family was vacationing in Florida, Charlie Bones and Tuffy La Marche came to visit in Charlie's big yellow Cadillac convertible. We all piled into his car for a ride. As we were going down the road, parallel to an intercostal canal, a speedboat passed us by. Tuffy said, "Charlie, I'll bet you $500 you can't beat the boat to the bridge." Charlie said, "I'll bet you this car against your boat." Tuffy said, "You're on," and Charlie hit the accelerator. My mother screamed, "Don't do this, you damn fools, we have two kids in the car." My sister and I yelled in excitement, "Go Charlie, Go!" I'm sure my memory is tainted by retrospective enhancement, but I can recall my sister and I looking over the backseat of the car as we cleared the bridge. I swear we just made it. The overhanging gate was coming down, and the back wheels of the car cleared the bridge by about five feet before the drawbridge opened!

The next day, Charlie came to visit again. He said, "Let's go for a ride. I swear I'll behave." We went down to the dock where Tuffy's boat, which Charlie Bones had just won, was moored. There was a man there with a blow torch. He said, "OK, Mr. Bennett?" Bones said yes, and the man proceeded to remove the names "Fluffy and Tuffy" from the stern of the boat. Fluffy was short for Florence, Tuffy's girlfriend. Tuffy and Bones remained lifelong friends. From this incident, I learned how important it was to make good on your wager and not take a loss personally.

Gert, a young woman on whom Charlie Bones had a crush, made beer in her apartment during the Prohibition era. One night, the beer was bottled and stacked in her bathroom. Evidently, she didn't have the formula right. The beer fermented and dripped into the apartment below. The tenants called the police and Gert was arrested. Bones bailed her out, to the tune of much razzing, hooting, and laughing from the cops and clerks at the police station, even though he didn't really have to do it. "Hey, Charlie, doesn't your girlfriend even know how to make hooch?" That's when Charlie won Gert's heart. The lesson I learned from this was that loyalty and friendship are not only of value in their own right but sometimes also get rewarded. Loyalty and friendship paid off for Charlie.

My father always told us not to gamble. He said you can never beat the house. However, he did not discourage me from betting on skill. He taught me to shoot pool when I was about twelve years old. After I learned how to hold a cue, line up the shot, draw, follow, and put a little spin on the ball, he told me he didn't want to catch me playing pool unless I played for at least a quarter or so a game. I said, "But Dad, you always tell us never to gamble." He said, "You'll never be a good pool player if you don't play for money. If you don't have a little something on the game, you'll never know whether or not the other guy is really trying. If he's not trying, there's no satisfaction in winning. You're betting on your skill. Gambling is betting on the horses, the numbers, dice or the roulette wheel." Further, he said, "Outwardly, you've gotta be graceful when you lose, but deep down you have to feel it. You show me a good loser and I'll show you a loser."

At that time, men either wore suits, sweaters, or sport shirts. Sports jackets and blazers had not come into style yet. Dad said, "If you're in a strange town, and you want to find the racetrack, look for a guy whose jacket doesn't match his pants. Follow him and he'll take you to the track. He can afford to bet on the nags, but he can't afford a full suit." From these incidents I learned the importance of developing skill and not wishing or hoping fruitlessly that "one day my horse will come in a winner."

My first real accomplishment came at the age of sixteen. I won the Toledo Junior Pocket Billiards Championship. One of my best friends, Bill Murphy, was the runner-up and almost beat me in the finals. Murph (known as "the Thermometer" because he was six-three, skinny and occasionally wore a red tie) was a better pool player than me. I remember how I won it, however. First, I practiced hard, so I knew my game was as good as it could be at the time. I concentrated hard on every shot; I would make sure that my stance and my bridge (the hand that supports the cue stick) were just right. I lined up the ball carefully, took several practice strokes, calculated the weight of the stroke—that is, how hard to hit the ball—and the position on the table where I wanted the cue ball to stop after sinking the object ball. For a really good pool player, all of this wouldn't be necessary. Pool players like "Fast Eddie" in *The Hustler,* or his opponent, "Detroit Fats" (the real character after whom the fictional character "Minnesota Fats" was named) would do all of this intuitively and quickly. I learned a lot from that experience. Do your homework (practice), stick with the fundamentals, and concentrate.

Let me tell you how this all came about. The pool hall proprietor and owner was Huey Heal. Huey had been the three-rail billiard champion of the world in 1932. Three-rail billiards is not a hustler's game. It's a gentleman's game. The game requires a player to hit three rails with the cue ball before completing the shot by hitting two object balls. This is a very difficult game requiring a mastery of angles, English (spin), and geometry, as well as having a very powerful stroke and a good eye.

When Huey took over Holtz's pool hall, the tables sat on a cold cement floor. The paint was peeling off the walls, and the place was generally run-down. Only the tables were kept in good condition. Holtz's Pool Hall was a sleaze box if there ever was one. The regulars that hung out there were among the worst of the hustlers. If it hadn't been for Huey Heal, my friends and I might have come under the influence of these people. Fortunately, a few months after we started visiting Holtz's Pool Hall, Huey took over as proprietor.

Huey said to my friends and me, "This is going to be a gentleman's billiard parlor. No foul language, no irresponsible behavior, and no spitting on the floor." He then spat on the floor and said, "That's the last goober you'll ever see on this floor." Soon after, he installed floor tiling, painted the walls, put in a lunch counter, and hired two women to cook and serve short-order meals. He said that when you're in the presence of women, you behave like gentlemen. He then made his deal. He said, "If you young men will live up to these standards, I'll teach you how to be first-rate pool players." For us, this was like a dream come true—having a former world billiards champion for your coach.

He replaced several of the straight pool and snooker tables with billiard tables. Soon we noticed a change in clientele. The rummy hustlers who previously spent time at Holtz's were gone. Their behavior wasn't appropriate and they couldn't take the cleanliness of the place. I think it made them nervous. In their place were a number of elderly gentlemen, usually around fifty years of age or older, who were well-dressed and mannerly. They were frequently accompanied by their wives, who would watch them play in the tournaments that Huey established. Consequently, a significant part of my adolescent environment was changed for the better, due to Huey Heal. Huey diverted me from an ill-spent youth to a misspent youth.

REFERENCES

Angoff, William H. (1988). "The Nature-Nurture debate, aptitudes, and group differences." *American Psychologist* 43: 713-720.

Arvey, Richard D., Thomas J. Bouchard, Jr., Nancy L. Segal, & Lauren M. Abraham (1989). "Job satisfaction: Environmental and genetic components." *Journal of Applied Psychology* 74: 187-192.

Arvey, Richard D., Gary W. Carter, & Deborah K. Buerkley (1991). "Job satisfaction: Dispositional and situational influences." In Cary L. Cooper and Ivan T. Robertson (Eds), *International Review of Industrial and Organizational Psychology* (Volume 6, pp. 359-383). London: John Wiley & Sons Ltd.

Barrick, Murray R., & Michael K. Mount (1991). "The big five personality dimensions and job performance: A meta-analysis." *Personnel Psychology* 44: 1-26.

Barry, Herbert, III, Margaret K. Bacon, & Irvin L. Child (1957). "A cross-cultural survey of some sex differences in socialization." *Journal of Abnormal and Social Psychology* 55: 327-332.

Bouchard, Thomas J., Jr., David T. Lykken, Matthew McGue, Nancy L. Segal, & Auke Tellegen (1990). "Sources of human psychological differences: The Minnesota study of twins reared apart." *Science* 250: 223-228.

Bouchard, Thomas J., Jr., & Matthew McGue (1981). "Familial studies of intelligence: A review." *Science* 212: 1055-1059.

Cattell, Raymond B. (1965). *The Scientific Analysis of Personality.* Harmondsworth: Penguin.

Christie, Richard, & Florence L. Geis (1970). Chapter 17: "Implications and speculations." In Richard Christie and Florence L. Geis (Eds.), *Studies in Machiavellianism.* New York: Academic Press.

Cohn, Lawrence D. (1991). "Sex differences in the course of personality development: A meta-analysis." *Psychological Bulletin* 109: 252-266.

Digman, John M. (1990). "Personality structure: Emergence of the five-factor model." *Annual Review of Psychology* 41: 417-440.

Dipboye, Robert L. (1987). "Problems and progress of women in management." In Karen Shallcross Koziara, Michael H. Moskow, & Lucretia Dewey Tanner (Eds.), *Working Women: Past, Present, Future* Washington, D.C.: Industrial Research Association Series, The Bureau of National Affairs, Inc., pp. 118-153.

Farrell, Dan (1983). "Exit, voice, loyalty, and neglect as responses to job dissatisfaction: A multidimensional scaling study." *Academy of Management Journal* 26: 596-607.

Festinger, Leon (1957). *A Theory of Cognitive Dissonance.* Stanford, CA: Stanford University Press.

Flynn, James R. (1987). "Massive IQ gains in 14 nations: What IQ tests really measure." *Psychological Bulletin* 101: 171-191.

Freud, Sigmund (1976). *Complete Psychological Works:* Standard edition, Sigmund Freud (Editor), James Strachey (Translator). London: Hogarth.

Guilford, Joy Paul (1967). *The Nature of Human Intelligence.* New York: McGraw-Hill.

Hayes, John, & Christopher W. Allinson (1994). "Cognitive style and its relevance for management practice." *British Journal of Management* 5: 53-71.

Henderson, Norman D. (1982). "Human behavior genetics." *Annual Review of Psychology* 33: 403-440.

Hofstede, Geert (1987). "The applicability of McGregor's theories in South East Asia." *The Journal of Management Development* 8(3): 9-18.

Hoffman, Lois W. (1991). "The influence of the family environment on personality: Accounting for sibling differences." *Psychological Bulletin* 110: 187-203.

Hogan, Joyce (1991). "Structure of physical performance in occupational tasks." *Journal of Applied Psychology* 76: 495-507.

House, Robert J. (1993). "Slow learner and late bloomer." In Arthur G. Bedeian (Ed.), *Management Laureates: A Collection of Autobiographical Essays* (Volume 2, pp. 39-78). Greenwich, CT: JAI Press.

Hyde, Janet S., & Marcia C. Linn (1988). "Gender differences in verbal ability: A meta-analysis." *Psychological Bulletin* 104: 53-69.

Jacklin, Carol N. (1989). "Female and male: Issues of gender." *American Psychologist* 44: 127-133.

Johnson, James M. (Editor) (1972). *Instructional Strategies and Curriculum Units for Secondary Behavioral Sciences.* Plattsburgh, New York: State University of New York.

Jung, Carl G. (1928). "Psychological types." In Boris Semeonoff (Ed.) (1966) *Personality Assessment*, (pp. 75-88). Harmondsworth: Penguin.

Keller, Lauren M., Thomas J. Bouchard, Jr., Richard D. Arvey, Nancy L. Segal, & Rene V. Dawis (1992). "Work values: Genetic and environmental influences." *Journal of Applied Psychology* 77: 79-88.

Kenrick, Douglas T., & David C. Funder (1988). "Profiting from controversy: Lessons from the person-situation debate." *American Psychologist* 43: 23-34.

Konner, Melvin (1982). *The Tangled Wing: Biological Constraints on the Human Spirit.* New York: Holt, Rinehart and Winston.

Kulik, James A., Robert L. Bangert-Drowns, & Chen-Lin C. Kulik (1984). "Effectiveness of coaching for aptitude tests." *Psychological Bulletin* 95: 179-188.

Lincoln, James R. (1989). "Employee work attitudes and management practice in the U.S. and Japan: Evidence from a large comparative survey." *California Management Review*, Fall 1989, 89-106.

Lincoln, James R., & Arne L. Kalleberg (1985). "Work organization and workforce commitment: A study of plants and employees in the U.S. and Japan." *American Sociological Review* 50: 738-760.

Lytton, Hugh, & David M. Romney (1991). "Parents' differential socialization of boys and girls: A meta-analysis." *Psychological Bulletin* 109: 267-296.

Maccoby, Eleanor E., & Carol N. Jacklin (1974). *The Psychology of Sex Differences.* Stanford, CA: Stanford University Press.

Machiavelli, Niccolò *The Prince.* Translated by Leo Paul S. de Alvarez. Dallas: University of Dallas Press.

Machiavelli, Niccolò *The Discourses.* London: Routledge & Paul.

MacLean, Paul D. (1990). *The Triune Brain in Evolution: Role in Paleocerebral Functions.* New York: Plenum Press.

Maddi, Salvatore R. (1989). *Personality Theories: A Comparative Analysis,* 5th edition. Chicago, IL: Dorsey Press.

McGregor, Douglas M. (1960). *The Human Side of Enterprise.* New York: McGraw-Hill.

McInnes, Craig (1992). "A night in the life of No. 5." The *Globe and Mail,* February 15, 1992, p. D3.

Merrell, Susan (1993). "When a woman manages the company." *New Woman,* January 1993, pp. 112-117.

Mintzberg, Henry (1981). "Planning on the left side and managing on the right." *Harvard Business Review,* January/February 1981, pp. 50-58.

Mowday, Richard T., Richard M. Steers, & Lyman W. Porter (1979). "The measure of organizational commitment." *Journal of Vocational Behavior* 14: 224-247.

Myers, Isabel B. (1987). *Introduction to Type.* Palo Alto, CA: Consulting Psychologists Press, Inc.

Pfeffer, Jeffrey, and Nancy Langton (1993). "The effect of wage disperion of satisfaction, productivity, and working collaboratively: Evidence from college and university faculty." *Administrative Science Quarterly* 38: 382-407.

Plomin, Robert (1989). "Environment and genes: Determinants of behavior." *American Psychologist* 44: 105-111.

Riggio, Ronald E. (1986). "Assessment of basic social skills." *Journal of Personality and Social Psychology* 51: 649-660.

Ross, Alexander (1992). "The long view of leadership." *Canadian Business,* May 1992, pp. 46-51.

Rossi, Alice, & Peter Rossi (1977). "Body time and social time: Mood patterns by menstrual cycle phase and day of the week." *Social Science Research* 6: 273-308.

Rusbult, Caryl, & David Lowery (1985). "When bureaucrats get the blues: Responses to dissatisfaction among federal employees." *Journal of Applied Social Psychology* 15: 80-103.

Shakleton, Vivian, & Clive Fletcher (1984). *Individual Differences: Theories and Applications.* London: Methuen.

Shultz, Clifford J., II (1993). "Situational and dispositional predictors of performance: A test of the hypothesized Machiavellianism X structure interaction among sales persons." *Journal of Applied Social Psychology* 23: 478-498.

Smith, Patricia C., Lorne M. Kendall, and Charles L. Hulin (1969). *The Measurement of Satisfaction in Work and Retirement.* Chicago: Rand McNally. The complete forms, scoring key, instructions and norms can be obtained from the Department of Psychology, Bowling Green State University, Bowling Green, OH 43404.

Tesser, Abraham, & David R. Shaffer (1990). "Attitudes and attitude change." *Annual Review of Psychology* 41: 479-523.

Thurstone, Louis L. (1938). *Primary Mental Abilities.* Chicago: University of Chicago Press.

Toman, Walter (1969). *Family Constellation: Its Effects on Personality and Social Behavior,* 2nd edition. New York: Springer Publishing Company.

Trotter, Robert J. (1976). "The other hemisphere." *Science News* 109: 218-223.

Weiss, David J., Rene V. Dawis, George W. England, & Lloyd H. Lofquist (1967). *Manual for the Minnesota Satisfaction Questionnaire, Minnesota Studies in Vocational Rehabilitation,* Vol. 22. Minneapolis: University of Minnesota Industrial Relations Center.

Weinberg, Richard A. (1989). "Intelligence and IQ." *American Psychologist* 44: 98-104.

Whiting, Beatrice B., & John W.M. Whiting (1975). *Children of Six Cultures.* Cambridge, MA: Harvard University Press.

Young, Ed (1989). "On the naming of the Rose: Interests and multiple meanings as elements of organizational culture." *Organization Studies* 10: 187-206.

FURTHER READING

For an interesting look at the biological bases of human behaviour that follows the line of Melvin Konner's (1982) book, see Jerome H. Barkow (1991), "Precis of Darwin, sex and status: Biological approaches to mind and culture," *Behavioral and Brain Sciences* 14: 295-301. On Nature-Nurture, see Robert Plomin and Gerald E. McClearn (Eds.), 1993, *Nature-Nurture and Psychology*, published in Hyattsville, MD by the American Psychological Association and Robert Plomin & C.S. Bergeman (1991), "The nature of nurture: Genetic influence on 'environmental' measures," *Behavioral and Brain Sciences* 14: 373-386. Research on gender differences in personality or abilities is presented in A. Feingold (1988), "Cognitive gender differences are disappearing," *American Psychologist* 43: 95-103 and Janet S. Hyde (1990), "Meta-analysis and the psychology of gender differences," *Signs: Journal of Women in Culture and Society* 16: 55-73.

A fascinating book on the socialization of children is by Beatrice Blyth Whiting and Carolyn Pope Edwards (1988), titled "Children of Different Worlds: The Formation of Social Behavior." It is published by Harvard University Press. One important finding is that children in different cultures learn different behaviours because they are socialized by adults in one culture and by other children in another culture.

There have been several large-scale investigations studying twins. A special section in Volume 54 (1983) of the journal *Child Development* contains reports from five separate twin projects. See David A. Hay and Pauline J. O'Brien (1983), "The La Trobe twin study: A genetic approach to the structure and development of cognition in twin children," *Child Development* 54: 317-330; Joseph M. Horn, "The Texas adoption project: Adopted children and their intellectual resemblance to biological and adoptive parents" on pages 268-275; Robert Plomin and J.C. DeFries, "The Colorado adoption project," pages 276-289; Sandra Scarr and Richard A. Weinberg, "The Minnesota adoption studies: Genetic differences and malleability," pages 260-267; and Ronald S. Wilson, "The Louisville twin study: Developmental synchronies in behavior," pages 298-316.

A more recent article reporting results of the Minnesota Twin Study is by Auke Tellegen, David T. Lykken, Thomas J. Bouchard, Kimerly J. Wilcox, Nancy L. Segal, and Stephen Rich (1988), "Personality similarity in twins reared apart and together," *Journal of Personality and Social Psychology* 54: 1031-1039. Another interesting article is that of Eric Turkheimer (1991), "Individual and group differences in adoption studies of IQ," *Psychological Bulletin* 110: 392-405.

Need for achievement can be measured with the TAT or a questionnaire. A study of their relative validity is by William D. Spangler (1992), "Validity of questionnaire and TAT measures of need for achievement: Two meta-analyses," *Psychological Bulletin* 112: 140-154.

An interesting study in the *Journal of Applied Psychology* examines differences and similarities in values among managers in the United States, Hong Kong, and the People's Republic of China. This research used a questionnaire specifically designed to measure more Eastern values. See David A. Ralston, David J. Gustafson, Priscilla M. Elsass, Fanny Cheung, and Robert H. Terpstra's article titled "Eastern Values: A comparison of managers in the United States, Hong Kong, and the People's Republic of China", 1992, Volume 77, pages 664-671.

The March-April 1993 edition of *Business Horizons* is devoted to the examination of issues of importance to women in the workplace. One article by E. Holly Buttner examines the traits shared by female and male entrepreneurs. It is titled "Female entrepreneurs: How far have they come?"

PERCEPTION AND PERFORMANCE EVALUATION

CHAPTER OUTLINE

The Perception Process

    Environmental Stimuli and Observation

    Perceptual Selection

    Perceptual Organization

    Perception

    Interpretation

    Response

Performance Evaluation

    Methods of Performance Evaluation

    Errors in Performance Evaluation

Conclusion

QUESTIONS TO CONSIDER

- How do people perceive the world?

- How are people the same or different in how and what they perceive?

- How is an individual at work perceived and evaluated?

- What evaluation errors are possible and what can be done about them?

A central question about perception concerns the nature of reality. Is there one physical reality in the world that people find out about through their perceptions? If so, knowledge mirrors the real world. Or are there multiple realities, with each of us living in the world as we individually perceive it? If so, what knowledge is depends on how the physical world is understood by each person.

As an example, people studying elephants in the African wild thought it very mysterious that widely separated elephants would suddenly converge at a place where other elephants were meeting or were in distress. Only when it was discovered that elephants could make very low frequency sounds that travel long distances and are inaudible to the human ear did this behaviour make sense. The physical stimuli, here low frequency sounds, clearly exist in the world—but until recently they were not part of the world of the people who study elephants.

The point of view taken here is that there is one physical world but that each of us experiences it differently. There are therefore multiple created realities. One cannot be chosen over another as more real, or as corresponding more closely to the physical "real world," because each reality corresponds more closely in some areas and less closely in others.

It is important to recognize that each person lives in a separate experienced reality. A grandson might understand quite easily how his grandmother cannot hear or see very well. He knows that to communicate effectively with her it is necessary to speak loudly and to write using larger letters. But that same grandson might be less ready to understand why another person sees discriminatory practices in hiring, promotion, and job treatment when to him the discrimination does not exist. Each person experiences a somewhat different reality. It is important to try to see the other person's perceived reality.

Virtual reality (VR)
A computer generated simulation of a reality into which people can immerse themselves.

By now, most people have heard about **virtual reality** (VR). Using a computer hooked up to small television screens built into a helmet, a person can be immersed into a reality created by the computer program. The television screens are mounted directly in front of the viewer's eyes and create an imaginary three-dimensional world. The participant wears special gloves or a body suit with motion sensors connected to the computer. These allow the participant to walk, look around, and even manipulate objects in the constructed reality.

Virtual reality has had an immediate impact in video games, but has business uses as well. Five particular applications (from Carr, 1992) are as follows.

1. When mistakes in training would be costly—the use of flight simulators and combat simulations.
2. When the real environment cannot be experienced by humans—outer space, dangerous workplaces, buildings not yet built, environments at the atomic level.
3. To build interfaces that make intuitive sense—instead of computer icons, virtual file cabinets could be "opened" and the contents examined.
4. To make training situations really "real"—examples are architects designing buildings, and sales people dealing with VR clients.
5. To make perceptible the imperceptible—VR could be used to show group members someone else's feelings or the outcomes of a group interaction. For example, as a group becomes more cohesive, VR spheres, each of a different colour and representing a different group member, would be seen to come closer together in space.

THE PERCEPTION PROCESS
Environmental Stimuli and Observation

Sensory overload Occurs when there are too many stimuli for a person's senses to process.

A model of the perception process is shown as Exhibit 6.1. The environment is full of stimuli—things, sounds, movements, electromagnetic radiation—and we as humans are only able to sense a small part of those stimuli. When they are too great in level or number, **sensory overload** causes perception to be lessened.

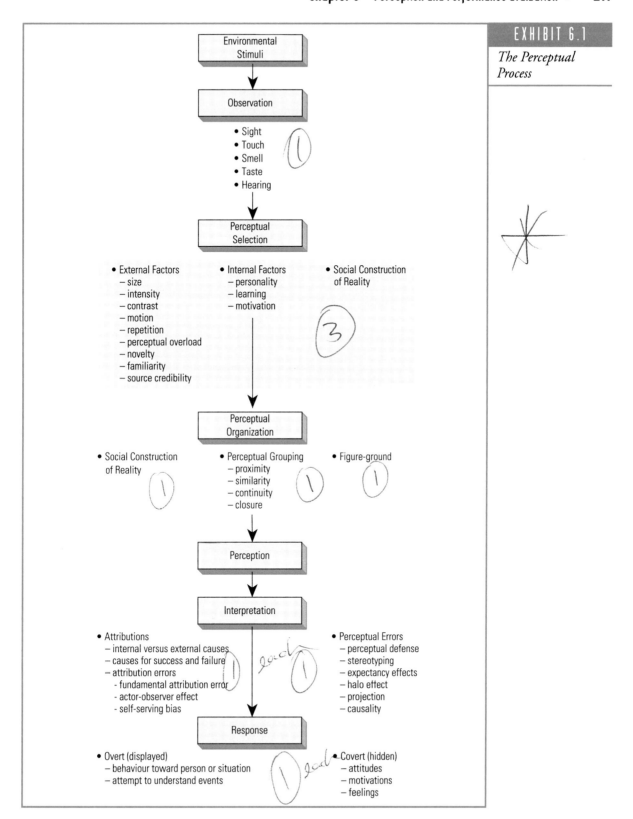

EXHIBIT 6.1

The Perceptual Process

Environmental
Stimuli

Observation

- Sight
- Touch
- Smell
- Taste
- Hearing

Perceptual
Selection

- External Factors
  - size
  - intensity
  - contrast
  - motion
  - repetition
  - perceptual overload
  - novelty
  - familiarity
  - source credibility

- Internal Factors
  - personality
  - learning
  - motivation

- Social Construction of Reality

Perceptual
Organization

- Social Construction of Reality

- Perceptual Grouping
  - proximity
  - similarity
  - continuity
  - closure

- Figure-ground

Perception

Interpretation

- Attributions
  - internal versus external causes
  - causes for success and failure
  - attribution errors
    - fundamental attribution error
    - actor-observer effect
    - self-serving bias

- Perceptual Errors
  - perceptual defense
  - stereotyping
  - expectancy effects
  - halo effect
  - projection
  - causality

Response

- Overt (displayed)
  - behaviour toward person or situation
  - attempt to understand events

- Covert (hidden)
  - attitudes
  - motivations
  - feelings

Biologically, humans have evolved to favour the visual and touch senses. Our brains are capable of quickly processing information from these senses but we are not as good at smelling, tasting, and hearing as other animals. It has long been known that dogs, for example, have a very well developed sense of smell. Dogs can also hear higher frequency sounds than can humans, elephants (as previously discussed) can hear lower frequency sounds, and pigeons can sense the earth's electromagnetic lines of force (they have a substance in their brain that is magnetic).

Even between people there is normal variation in the ability to taste, smell, hear, see, and feel. For example, to have 20/20 vision means that the individual can see objects 20 feet distant as if they were 20 feet distant. But some people can actually see better than this "perfect vision." A person with 20/15 vision can see objects at 20 feet as if they were only at 15 feet. Of course, there are also sense defects such as colour blindness that do not allow what we consider to be normal discrimination between colours.

Having normal ability to sense is clearly important for the performance of some jobs. Airline pilots and ferry boat captains often must, as a basic requirement of being hired and keeping the job, have natural 20/20 vision. This means that environmental sense aids such as contact lenses or eyeglasses are not required to bring actual vision up to the 20/20 standard. Wine tasters require a keen sense of taste, fragrance designers need a good sense of smell, musicians and singers must have good hearing, and surgeons, to be effective, need a finely developed sense of touch. There are many jobs, of course, that require only normal sense capability and allow corrective devices to bring a particular sense up to the levels required for the job (e.g., Anderson, 1989).

We should remember that not all senses are necessarily required for every job. This chapter's *Overboard* cartoon humorously illustrates that the job of pirate captain may be one where good vision is a liability! A switchboard operator may be able to perform perfectly well even if blind. A manufactured goods inspector may not need to hear. A proofreader may be able to perform that task with only one hand or no hands at all.

The ability to sense can be affected by the environment. For instance, long exposure to loud noises damages hearing. Workers in noisy conditions are therefore required to wear ear plugs or ear guards. These allow normal frequency speech to be heard but loud noises at other frequencies are blocked. The intense light of an arc weld can quickly damage a welder's eyesight. They must therefore wear protective face shields. The protection of workers' senses and the safety of workers' lives are the focus of job safety programs.

Perceptual Selection

Given that only some of the stimuli in the environment are sensed, perceptual selection then limits what will be perceived. Three broad categories of perceptual selection are external factors, internal factors, and the social construction of reality (Berger & Luckmann, 1967).

External Factors

Fairly obviously, **size** is important in being seen—larger objects are more likely to be seen than those that are smaller. But there are ways to make even large objects, such as a ship at sea, less visible. Camouflage, using paint and nets, can help to disguise from the perceiver the ship's presence. Conversely, large full-page ads in the newspaper are an advertising organization's attempt to have the potential customer see and pay attention to a client organization's message.

Objects of higher **intensity** are more visible and therefore more likely to be perceived. For example, bold words on a typeset page stand out, as do back-lit billboards.

Objects that do not fit with their surroundings or are unexpected, such as an expletive not deleted from a manager's conversation are in **contrast** to their surroundings and therefore more likely to be noticed.

Motion also makes people and things more noticeable. This principle is used in billboards that have internal sections that rotate to show three different messages and in electronic signs with moving words or pictures.

Repetition can make a message more likely to be perceived. This concept is used by advertisers who show the same commercial on television many times. **Perceptual overload** may occur when a person has perceived so many messages and stimuli that it is no longer possible to keep track of them all.

Novel stimuli are likely to be perceived *because of* their newness. For example, a consumer may pay particular attention to a television advertisement the first time it is noticed on TV. Its novelty helps it to be perceived.

Familiarity can help make perception easier. For example, an experienced professional football quarterback can "see" the field and the opposition players better than a person who doesn't know football. For a cross-cultural example of this effect, see *A Rose by Any Other Name*.

Source credibility also affects what is perceived. Sources low in credibility are less likely to be able to make an impression on the perceiver. They are not given as much attention as high credibility sources. For example, the Dean of a college addressing students will generally be listened to and heard to a greater degree than would a lower status member of the organization.

Internal Factors

An individual's personality, learning, and motivation are individual difference factors that will influence the selection of environmental stimuli. For example, an employee with a personality high on need for affiliation (the need to be with others) listening to a speech by the corporation's president will tend to hear best the parts of the speech about getting together and being part of the team. An employee high on the need for power will hear best the parts about taking charge and beating the competition. An employee high on the need for achievement (McClelland, 1961) will hear best the parts about doing better and the setting of challenging goals. Is it any wonder that when discussing the speech over coffee the three will not agree on what they have just heard?

Size   An important factor in perceptual selection. Larger objects are more likely to be seen than those that are smaller.

Intensity   Objects that are more visible are more likely to be perceived.

Contrast   Objects dissimilar to their surroundings are more likely to be noticed.

Motion   Objects that are moving are more noticeable.

Repetition   A message is more likely to be perceived if it is encountered numerous times.

Perceptual overload Occurs when a person has perceived so many messages and stimuli that it is not possible to keep track of them all.

Novel stimuli   Are perceived because of their newness.

Perceptual familiarity It is easier to see the familiar than the unfamiliar.

Source credibility Sources that are low in credibility make less of an impression on the perceiver.

A ROSE BY ANY OTHER NAME

When I first visited Australia I went for a walk in Sydney and stumbled upon a cricket match in progress. Here were two people batting and eleven people fielding on a very large oval expanse of grass (later I found out this is called the "pitch"). While I could tell that one team was throwing the ball (actually, "bowling," a peculiar over arm/straight arm delivery) and the person with the bat was trying to hit it, I couldn't understand anything else. I watched for over an hour and every now and then the fielding side would suddenly jump up and get excited, and a new batter would come in. But I couldn't figure out what was going on.

From this I learned that to be able to really see what was happening, it was important to learn the rules. Without knowledge of the rules and objectives of the game it was extremely difficult to figure out what was happening. Later in Australia I learned to understand and appreciate cricket and the differences between international "Test" matches and one-day games.

Upon my return to Canada, I had occasion to visit the University of Toronto. There, in the centre of the university grounds where I had many times seen a large oval field surrounded by a traffic circle, I saw for the first time a cricket pitch! It took a visit to another country to give me the knowledge of cricket so that I could see the University of Toronto pitch that had been so clearly there all along.

Source: Richard Field.

Perceptual learning

People learn to pay attention to the stimuli in the environment that are important for job performance.

Learning also allows for the selective perception of those stimuli in the environment that are important for job performance. The football quarterback from our previous example is taught, or learns, what to look for when on the field. While learning focuses perceptions, learning can turn out to be helpful or harmful. For example, Karl Weick (1988, p. 311) has said that: "Specialists can do a few things well, which means that they search the world to see if it needs what they can do. If it doesn't, they do nothing else because they see nothing else."

An example of the effect of learning on perception would be the lyrics to Billy Joel's song "We Didn't Start the Fire." In this song a wide assortment of historical events are very briefly mentioned. A listener to this song, especially at first, should hear clearly only those names and events that are already known and understood by the listener. Even after listening many times there are names and events mentioned that may not be recognized because the listener simply has not learned who and what these people and events are.

Another example of how perception is affected by the words we have available to describe what we experience is given in Exhibit 6.2.

Perceptual motivation

People tend to perceive what they want to.

Motivation also affects what an individual will perceive. For example, a person looking for a job will listen and watch for any information about new jobs and opportunities. This chapter's experiential exercise provides readers with an opportunity to use their powers of observation. When a person is motivated to see, what is there to be seen?

Social Construction of Reality in Perceptual Selection

People are often unsure of what they are seeing, hearing, feeling, tasting, and touching, and seek out others to compare their sensory experiences. One person might ask another the question: "Do you hear a high-pitched noise? or "Do you smell that?" When a person at an office feels cold, she might look at what others are wearing and ask others about how cold they feel the office is. The point here is that what is perceptually selected is due in part to what others are perceiving. People as a group can create their own reality where they perceive some parts of the physical world and ignore other parts.

EXHIBIT 6.2   PERCEPTION AND LANGUAGE: INUKTITUT WORDS FOR SNOW

What a person sees is affected by experience and the words that person has available to describe events or experiences. For example, the Inuit language of Inuktitut has a number of words that describe different types of snow.

aniugaviniq	very hard, compressed and frozen snow	*matsaaq*	half-melted snow
apijaq	snow covered by bad weather	*natiruvaaq*	drifting snow
apigiannagaut	the first snowfall of autumn	*pukak*	crystalline snow that breaks down and separates like salt
katakartanaq	snow with a hard crust that gives way underfoot	*qannialaaq*	light falling snow
kavisilaq	snow roughened by rain or frost	*qiasuqaq*	snow that has thawed and refrozen with an ice surface
kinirtaq	compact, damp snow		
mannguq	melting snow	*qiqumaaq*	snow whose surface has frozen after a light spring thaw
masak	wet falling snow		

SOURCE: Indian Affairs & Northern Development Canada (1990). *Indians and Inuit of Canada.* Ottawa: Supply and Services Canada, p. 16. Reproduced with the permission of the Minister of Supply and Services Canada.

Perceptual Organization

Once stimuli have been selected there is a sensemaking of the perceptions. Perceptual organization is this "making sense" of what is perceived. Processes active here are the social construction of reality, perceptual grouping, and figure-ground.

Social Construction of Reality in Perceptual Organization   Important in the sensemaking process of an individual is how others are making sense of the same environment. The television series "Mission: Impossible" often fooled their target person into believing in a reality that the MI team had constructed. If everyone else in a social situation believes in a certain reality, a newcomer to the situation is likely to as well.

A good example of a social construction of physical reality is star constellations. The Big Dipper and the Southern Cross do not really exist though the individual stars do. People of some cultures are taught to see the stars in these patterns against the background of the other stars and the night sky. In other cultures the very same stars become parts of other constellations/star groupings.

Perceptual Grouping   Humans tend to group together people and objects that appear close together. If on the first day at a new job the new organizational member were to join a group of co-workers for lunch—even if he knew none of them previously—other workers eating lunch would tend to see a group and the new recruit as part of it. Thus, **proximity** to co-workers can lead to perceptual grouping on the part of other observers.

Similarity to others also helps a person be seen as part of the group. If so-called "interview clothes" are worn to a college class by one student when everyone else is wearing their regular "going-to-class clothes," that student is likely to be seen as less similar to the group. The dressed-up student may even feel less a part of the group and somewhat ill-at-ease.

Perceptual continuity refers to the way we tend to see events separated in time as part of a pattern. Motion pictures are perhaps the best physical example of this—we see a moving picture even though the reality is that 24 pictures are projected per second onto the screen. In organizations, individuals tend to see patterns in the actions of others even if no pattern exists.

We know the spoon is all in one piece, but our eyes deceive us.

Proximity   Nearness of one object to another can lead observers to perceptually group the objects together.

Similarity   Objects that are alike tend to be perceived as part of a group.

Perceptual continuity People tend to see events as related over time.

Perceptual closure

A missing piece of a picture, story, or action can be supplied by the person doing the perceiving.

The principle of **perceptual closure** is often illustrated by a circle having a small gap—people see the whole circle and not the gap, perceptually filling in the missing part. Sales organizations use this principle by showing a potential customer his needs, how the product fills that need, and then leaving the customer to supply closure and purchase the product.

Figure-Ground   Images that can be perceived in two ways (for example a picture of a vase that can also be seen as the profiles of two faces looking at each other) illustrate the **figure-ground** principle of perceptual organization. The figure is up-front, on-stage, and noticed against the background or ground. When sitting in a large classroom a student is part of the group (the ground). The professor is usually the object of everyone's attention—the figure. When the student is asked by the professor to comment on the lecture or to answer a question, the student becomes the object of everyone's attention, and moves from being part of the ground to the figure.

Figure-ground   A principle of perceptual organization that people tend to see one object (the figure) on a background of other objects (the ground).

Those who want to be noticed in organizations can act or dress in a way to make themselves stand out. Being noticed in a positive way is a good start towards better opportunities at work. Conversely, some people make it their business *not* to be noticed. Examples here are the undercover police officer on surveillance, the bureaucrat marking time until retirement, the sales person who wants to enter an office building without being stopped by security. These people learn how to blend into the background and avoid becoming the figure in someone else's perception.

Perception

From the vast number of environmental stimuli in the world, only some are sensed. Of those that are sensed only some are actually selected and noticed by the individual. Those that are noticed are grouped together and organized, in order to make them more internally consistent. These processes result in the perception of the environment.

On a personal level, how one is perceived is important because the next steps in the perceptual process are the interpretations made about and responses to that person. The manipulation and control of how one is perceived is **impression management**.

Impression management

The manipulation and control of how one is perceived.

Exhibit 6.3 shows Heather Cooper's painting "The Lion and the Lamb." Cooper wrote that "I painted this work to convey the dilemma of a woman in business. How am I perceived, lion or lamb? Later, I found out that this dilemma was shared, not just by people but by corporations" (1987, p. 58). Organizations, especially those that need acceptance by their environment (see the Strategic Constituencies and Legitimacy models of Exhibit 1.3), are interested in their image and how they are perceived by individuals and other organizations.

Interpretation

Having formed a perception, an individual will then make an interpretation of the perception. That is, the person will decide what it means. Attributions will be made about behaviours and errors in interpretation will be made at times.

Attributions

To answer "What it means" or "What's going on here?" a person will examine the behaviour of another (or the self) and try to determine if that person's actions (e.g., appearance, task performance) were due to internal factors or the external factors of the situation

EXHIBIT 6.3

The Lion and the Lamb

SOURCE: *"The Lion and the Lamb"* © 1975 by Heather J. Cooper. Oil on board, 13 by 15 inches. Used by permission, Heather Cooper Communication by Design, Ltd., Toronto.

(Weiner, 1985). A second determination is whether the action was due to stable or unstable causes. Unstable causes are seen as more likely to change in the future (Weiner and others, 1971).

Performance on the job or on an exam could be attributed to ability, task difficulty, effort, or luck (see below).

	Internal	External
Stable	Ability	Task Difficulty
Unstable	Effort	Luck

For example, if a student were to select parts of a course to study for a final exam and happened to do well because those parts were actually examined, the student might be overheard telling a friend she "lucked out." But if that same student were to study hard and yet found the exam difficult, she might tell a friend it was "a bear." In this case the student is attributing her results to the difficulty of the task.

Three questions may be asked of anyone's behaviour to determine the cause of the outcome:

1. Is the behaviour consistent with the individual's behaviour over time? Consistent behaviour is attributed more to internal causes. For example, a student who typically receives A's on weekly course assignments in Marketing would be likely to attribute that result to effort or ability. An inconsistent result, such as an 'F' on a Marketing assignment, could be attributed to bad luck or the unexpected difficulty of the task.

2. Is the behaviour distinctive? That is, does the person perform the behaviour across situations or more in one situation than in another? Behaviour that is distinctive to a particular situation is attributed more to unstable causes. A student who performs well in all courses but one could attribute that result to lack of effort or bad luck.

3. Is the behaviour common, are others doing it, is there a consensus? Behaviour that is in agreement with everyone else's (if all class members did poorly on a test, for example) will likely be attributed more to external causes. In organizations, behaviour by members can be expected to be high in consensus when the organizations have strong cultures, are structured in a mechanistic manner, or have rules about the behaviour expected in a given situation.

> *Before moving on in this chapter, we suggest that you take a moment to complete the self-diagnostic exercise found at the end of the chapter*

Fundamental attribution error The tendency of people to underestimate the influence of the situation and overestimate the influence of individual characteristics on behaviour.

Attribution Errors There are, however, common errors made in attributing the behaviour of the self and others. One is called the **fundamental attribution error** (Kelley, 1973; Kelley & Michela, 1980). This is defined as the tendency of people to underestimate the influence of the situation and overestimate the influence of individual characteristics on behaviour. A person who gets on an elevator at the ground floor and pushes "2" might be thought of by others as lazy. But these observers would be in error when the actual cause of the behaviour was an overcrowded stairway.

Actor-observer effect People tend to see their own behaviour as due to the situation and others' behaviour as due more to internal and stable traits.

A second attribution error is the **actor-observer effect**. People tend to see their own behaviour as due to the situation and others' behaviour as due more to internal and stable traits. The person pushing the second floor button usually is *not* making self-attributions about stable traits like "I am one lazy guy," but is thinking something like "I'm pretty tired today and just don't have the energy to climb the stairs"—a situational cause of behaviour.

Self-serving bias People tend to give themselves any benefit of doubt when evaluating their own behaviours.

The third attribution error is the **self-serving bias**. A person tends to give the benefit of any doubt to the self. For example, people tend to attribute a good result on an exam or performance appraisal to internal causes and a poor result to external causes. People are ready to take credit for success and make excuses for failure.

Taking all these factors into account, then, we can reasonably expect that in an organizational performance review the manager and the employee will make different attributions about the same employee behaviour. They create two realities of what happened. One is the manager's reality. The other is the organizational member's reality. The performance appraisal is often an occasion for the manager and employee to attempt to negotiate these two realities into one shared reality.

Perceptual Errors   Besides attributional errors, perceptual errors may be made when interpreting a formed perception. These are perceptual defense, stereotyping, expectancy, the halo effect, projection, and causality.

Perceptual defense is the inability to perceive that which is threatening to the perceiver. For example, a person performing poorly at work may be unable to see what is obvious to everyone else and may in fact misinterpret or not hear the warnings about job performance made by the manager. A consequence of perceptual defense is that employees that are fired often express shock and maintain that they were never told about this poor performance. Managers therefore must document fully any warnings and low performance appraisals received by the employee.

Stereotyping is the assignment of traits and characteristics to an individual based on that person's membership in a larger group. Stereotypes exist for age, sex (see Kelly and others, 1993), race, culture, socio-economic status, the types of jobs that should be held by various groups in the population, as well as a multitude of other factors. Stereotypes are errors because while they may have some accuracy for a group as a whole they do not necessarily apply to any one individual. For example, an age stereotype could be that people over the age of 55 are in general less physically capable than people in their 20s. Important advice about avoiding age stereotyping is offered in this chapter's *A Word to the Wise*.

Perceptual defense
The inability to perceive that which is threatening to the perceiver.

Stereotyping   The assignment of traits and characteristics to an individual based on that person's membership in a larger group.

A WORD TO THE WISE

An elderly man goes into a pharmacy, accompanied by his much younger niece. The pharmacist fills his prescription, directing the instructions to the young woman, not the man.

An elderly woman in a wheelchair remarks to a relative pushing her down a hospital corridor, "At some point the smarter ones catch on that you're not blind, deaf and stupid. You're an old woman in a wheelchair."

Although they represent a growing segment of our population, elder individuals are still sometimes victims of stereotypes. Many studies show that senior members of our population are perceived to be less competent and more dependent than younger people in some situations and that these stereotypes can have a profound influence on social life and health.

Stereotypes have a significant impact on how people communicate with the elderly, says Dr. Ellen Ryan, a professor of psychiatry and director of McMaster's Office of Gerontological Studies, who, with her colleagues, has been exploring this issue.

"For example, in a conversation a young person might assume that he or she has no interests in common with an elder individual, or that the older person prefers to talk about the past," says Dr. Ryan. "Frequently, too, we observe that a younger person will think, 'I must speak loudly because this person has a hearing problem.'"

Dr. Ryan says that in nursing homes in particular there is a tendency for some people to use "baby talk"—high-pitched, exaggerated speech—to speak to older people. "Those kinds of behaviour convey a lack of respect, or, at the very least, send the message that the older per-

son is childlike," says Dr. Ryan. Unfortunately, the attitude implicit in such behaviours reinforces older people's own negative stereotypes.

"Older people have lived with the same stereotypes about aging that everyone has," says Dr. Ryan. "They're expecting some decline in their health, their capabilities and their level of independence and so, if they are treated as though their memory is fading or as though they can't take care of themselves, they see it as evidence that the decline has begun."

In some cases, older individuals will avoid social situations in order to avoid receiving stereotypical treatment. However, the lack of social interaction weakens their conversational skills, which in turn reinforces the stereotypes.

"If an older person receives only one negative communication among many other positive ones, it doesn't have a debilitating effect," says Dr. Ryan. "But if the person experiences a series of negative encounters, it can have a major impact on self-esteem."

The loss of self-esteem can, in turn, have an effect on physical health. Studies in Germany and North America suggest that nursing home residents who conform to the stereotypes tend to die sooner than those who object to being stereotyped. These residents tend to have an innate feistiness and to use their sense of humour to make it clear they will not be condescended to.

Based on such evidence, says Dr. Ryan, elders of all dispositions can develop strategies to prevent being patronized. They can form discussion groups with other elders to share ways of coping, and they can learn how to prevent a condescending attitude before it starts.

For example, an older individual who prefers to have a family member accompany him or her on visits to the doctor or when shopping or banking, perhaps to help with translation or to jog memory, might find it useful to set ground rules at the beginning of a transaction. If the elder explains to the doctor why the third party is there and makes it clear that he or she would like to be addressed directly, the doctor is more likely to comply.

SOURCE: Excerpted and reprinted with permission from Cheryl MacDonald (1993), "Shedding stereotypes," *McMaster Times* 8(3): 14.

EXHIBIT 6.4

Expectancy Model of Attributions

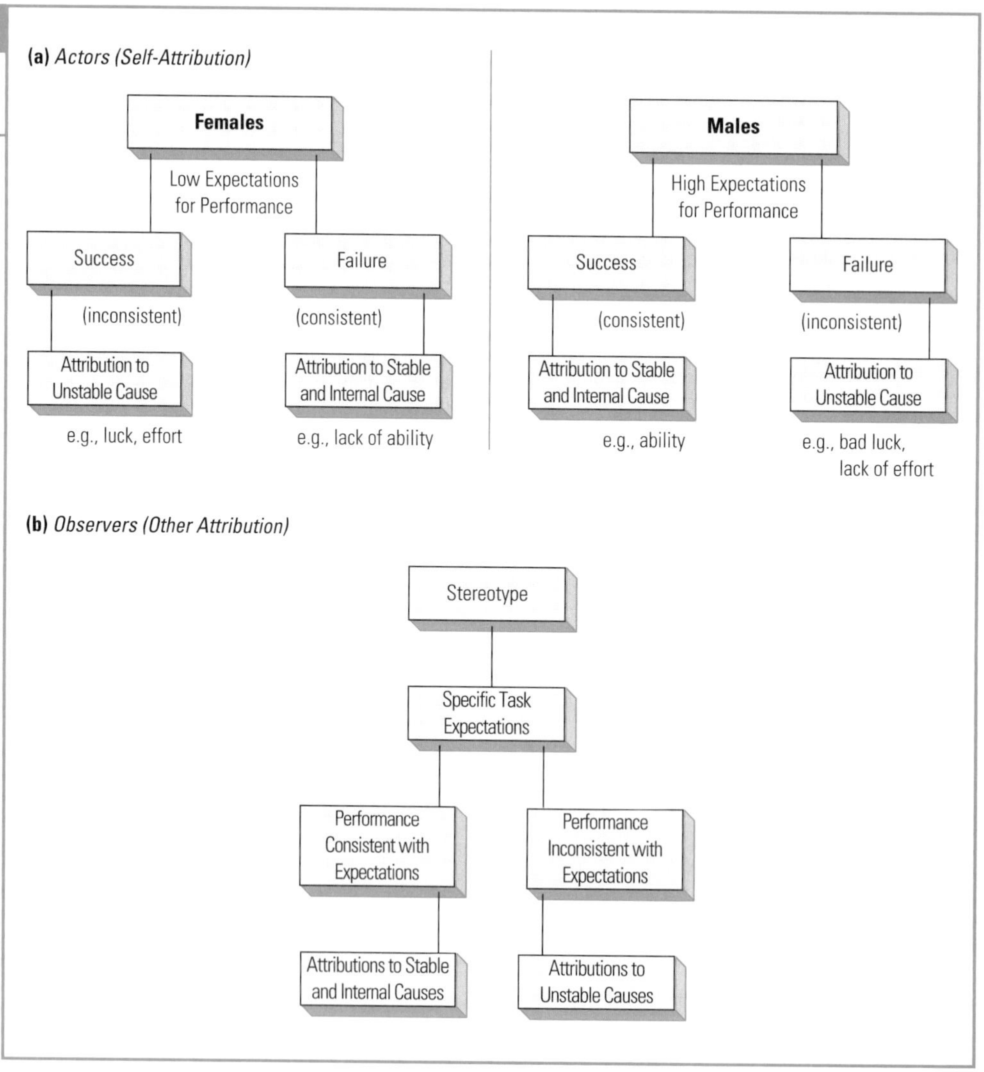

(a) *Actors (Self-Attribution)*

Females — Low Expectations for Performance
- Success (inconsistent) → Attribution to Unstable Cause — e.g., luck, effort
- Failure (consistent) → Attribution to Stable and Internal Cause — e.g., lack of ability

Males — High Expectations for Performance
- Success (consistent) → Attribution to Stable and Internal Cause — e.g., ability
- Failure (inconsistent) → Attribution to Unstable Cause — e.g., bad luck, lack of effort

(b) *Observers (Other Attribution)*

Stereotype → Specific Task Expectations
- Performance Consistent with Expectations → Attributions to Stable and Internal Causes
- Performance Inconsistent with Expectations → Attributions to Unstable Causes

SOURCE: Kay Deaux (1984), "From individual differences to social categories: Analysis of a decade's research on gender," *American Psychologist* 39: 106, 111. Copyright © 1984 by the American Psychological Association. Reprinted by permission.

Stereotypes and expectancy effects can interact to affect attributions. For example, Exhibit 6.4(a) shows that males and females given a task stereotypically seen as a "male task" (for example, fixing an engine) may well differ on their own expectations for performance and attributions of success or failure. In one experiment, even when actual performance on a task did not differ, males evaluated their own performance as better and claimed less luck and more ability (Deaux, 1984).

It is important to note the importance of the task stereotype on attributions by observers (see Exhibit 6.4(b)). The impact of sex and task on attributions loses its power when actual information about the performance of an individual (male or female) is available (Deaux, 1984).

Expectancy effects are not confined to sex stereotypes. The Self-Fulfilling Prophecy (SFP: Rosenthal & Jacobson, 1968) is an expectation about another person's behaviour that when communicated to that person, actually causes the behaviour that was expected. SFP operates best when expectations about individual student performance are given to a teacher before the students are personally known. Then the teacher's behaviours towards the students help to create the very student behaviours that were expected, even if the initial expectations were false. These SFP expectations may also operate in the workplace between managers and organization members (Field & Van Seters, 1988).

Expectancy in perception is also a function of socialization. We see what we learn to expect to see. An interesting example of this phenomenon is discussed in the feature *A Little Knowledge*.

The influence of our system of thought on how we think and perceive is shown by the French philosopher Michel Foucault, who in the introduction to his 1970 book *The Order of Things* quotes a passage from the Argentinian writer Jorge Luis Borges, which in turn quotes "a certain Chinese encyclopedia." It divides animals into the following categories: (a) belonging to the Emperor, (b) embalmed, (c) tame, (d) sucking pigs, (e) sirens, (f) fabulous,

Expectancy effect

The concept that expectations about another person's behaviour can, when communicated to that person, actually cause the behaviour that was expected.

A LITTLE KNOWLEDGE

In an experiment designed to determine if people see what they expect to see, Jerome Bruner and Leo Postman showed 28 experimental subjects playing cards for very brief periods of time. But all the cards were not "normal." The experimenters made up six trick playing cards—the three and four of hearts were coloured black, the two and six of spades were red, the ace of diamonds was black, and the six of clubs was red. Normal cards were the five and ace of hearts (red) and the five and seven of spades (black).

The researchers found that normal cards were, on average, recognized with only 28 milliseconds of exposure but the incongruous cards required an average of 114 milliseconds to recognize them for what they were. Almost all subjects dealt with the incongruous stimulus by allowing form or colour to dominate their perception. For example, faced with a red six of spades the subject would report seeing either a six of spades (form bound) or the six of hearts (colour bound). Other reactions to the unusual cards were compromise (for example, one subject saw a red spade as coloured purple), disruption, and finally recognition.

Disruption was "a gross failure of the subject to organize the perceptual field" (p. 218). The subject undergoing disruption can lose confidence and become perceptually confused, unable to tell what is being seen. The most disrupted subject in the experiment said, in response to a red spade: "I can't make the suit out whatever it is. It didn't even look like a card that time. I don't know what color it is now or whether it's a spade or a heart. I'm not even sure now what a spade looks like! My God!" (p. 218).

SOURCE: Based on information contained in Jerome S. Bruner and Leo Postman (1949), "On the perception of incongruity: A paradigm," *Journal of Personality* 18: 206-223.

(g) stray dogs, (h) included in the present classification, (i) frenzied, (j) innumerable, (k) drawn with a very fine camelhair brush, (l) *et cetera*, (m) having just broken the water pitcher, and (n) that from a long way off look like flies.

Foucault (1970, p. xv) says "In the wonderment of this taxonomy, the thing we apprehend in one great leap, the thing that, by means of the fable, is demonstrated as the exotic charm of another system of thought, is the limitation of our own, the stark impossibility of thinking *that*."

The **halo effect** in perception is the tendency to let one overall impression colour specific interpretations. A manager impressed with the fact a new employee graduated from a top-ranked university sees the person in a positive light (or halo) and interprets that person's actions and other personal characteristics more positively than may be justified. Negative halo is also possible.

Projection is the tendency by people to see their own traits and characteristics in others, even if those traits are not present.

Finally, the **causality perceptual error** is the tendency to see events as related, or caused, even when there is no connection between them. For example, a manager may see an employee's late arrival at the workplace as evidence of that employee's poor quality work even though there may be no actual connection (for a particular job) between lateness and quality.

Halo effect The tendency to let one overall impression colour specific interpretations.

Projection The tendency by people to see their own traits and characteristics in others, even if not present.

Causality perceptual error The tendency to see events as related or caused, even when there is no connection between them.

Response

The response to a perceptual interpretation can be overt or covert. Covert (or hidden) responses to perceptions include attitudes, motivations, and feelings. Interestingly, even feelings can be social constructions as people seek out others to provide information about how they should feel in a given situation. Overt (or displayed) behaviour may be linked to covert responses, but does not have to be. For example, emotional behaviour may be "put on" or displayed for the benefit of an audience (Gergen, 1985), but not actually felt.

People who are in a situation that is puzzling to them will try to gather information to clarify the situation. Karl Weick (1985) has written about times when people are in situations that handicap them perceptually because they do not have access to a full set of sensory data. For example, the air traffic controller sitting alone at a radar scope, the nuclear power plant technician who sees only the dials and gauges monitoring the reactor, or the market analyst who sits at a computer terminal studying sales data but who does not visit a supermarket—all these people lack the opportunity to build a socially perceived reality, a consensus of what is happening.

Without this social consensus, a worker is liable to seek more information (but of the wrong kind) and get into a state of total confusion where crises can occur. A model of this process is shown below.

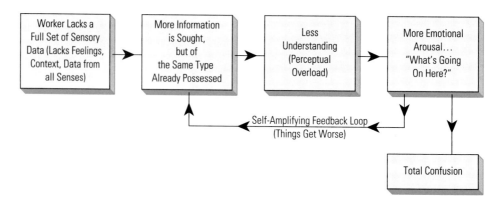

Professor Weick suggests that people seek to understand events through five mechanisms. They (1) *effectuate*—do something and see what happens; (2) *triangulate*—use different sources of information about the same issue or problem in order to find what is common and therefore probably true; (3) *affiliate*—compare what they see with what someone else sees and then negotiate the reality; (4) *deliberate*—formulate ideas and reach conclusions by reducing the amount of data processed; and (5) *consolidate*—put events into a context, a system of order (or disorder) that makes sense.

The implication for organizations is that systems must be designed so that when a crisis is in the making, and people turn to these five actions, the information gathered and reality created will tend to support the correct course of action to avoid a disaster. For example, air traffic controllers can work in pairs and be provided with multiple sources of data about the airplanes under their control. A real example of perceptual problems and organizational and personal disaster is to be found at the end of this chapter in the Tenerife Air Disaster case.

Weick has gone further in understanding and describing how people consolidate information into a system of order that helps them to make sense of and operate effectively within their workplace. Analyzing the operations of United States Navy Nimitz class aircraft carriers, Karl Weick and Karlene Roberts (1993) have put forward the concepts of *collective mind* and *heedful interrelating*. "Collective mind" is a term used to describe the fact that in complex systems made up of individuals, each person contributes a part of understanding the whole system. When everyone has the same understanding of the whole, they have a collective mind that is complex enough to deal with the complexity of the system. For example, "the men in the tower ... monitor and give instructions to incoming and departing aircraft. Simultaneously, the men on the landing signal officers' platform do the same thing. They are backed up by the men in Air Operations who monitor and instruct aircraft at some distance from the ship" (p. 362).

People having a collective mind engage in "heedful interrelating" when they understand that the system consists of connected actions by themselves and others, they decide what actions to take based on this understanding, and they subordinate their actions to the system as a whole. Weick and Roberts argue that as heedful interrelating increases, complex events can be better understood and organizational errors will decrease. For an example of the loss of this heedful interrelating, see this chapter's *If You Can't Ride Two Horses at Once, You Shouldn't Be in the Circus* feature.

PERFORMANCE EVALUATION

Job performance is the employee's actual contribution, in terms of both quality and quantity, to the organization's tasks and to the development of the employee's potential to contribute in the future. **Performance evaluation** is the determination or measurement of an individual's performance by one or more members of the organization.

Methods of Performance Evaluation

There are many ways to measure performance. A useful way to order them is by their relative emphasis on the traits or the behaviours of the person being rated. The following ten methods of performance evaluation are ordered in general from those that focus mainly on personal traits to those that focus mainly on job behaviours.

Trait scales are very commonly used. Employees are rated on a numeric scale that orders the degree to which the employee possesses the given trait from low to high. The traits that are measured are determined by each organization and are presumably directly related

Job performance The employee's actual contribution, in terms of both quality and quantity, to the organization's tasks and to the development of the employee's potential to contribute in the future.

Performance evaluation The determination or measurement of an individual's job performance by one or more members of the organization.

Trait scales A method of performance evaluation. Employees are rated on a numeric scale that orders the degree to which the employee possesses a given trait.

The Mann Gulch fire disaster occurred on August 5, 1949 in Montana. Fifteen "smokejumpers" parachuted near to a fire and prepared to fight it with the help of one forest ranger on the ground. Within two hours 13 men died in the fire. In Karl Weick's analysis of what happened, based on a reconstruction of the disaster in Norman Maclean's 1992 book "Young Men and Fire," he makes the case that the crew at Mann Gulch was a minimal organization that suffered a sudden loss of meaning.

The crew had an experienced leader and a second in command. Other crew members followed their directions in fighting fires. But while marching toward the fire, the crew leader suddenly noticed the fire had crossed from the south to the north side of Mann Gulch and was moving toward them. He then ordered the crew to turn around and head up a steep hill on an angle towards the top of the ridge. As the fire gained quickly on them, the crew leader yelled at the crew to drop their fire-fighting tools. He then lit a fire in front of them in the tall grass through which they were moving and ordered them to lie down in the newly burned area in the grass.

But the group had at this point lost their organization. By throwing away their tools they had also lost their roles as firefighters. Seeing their leader set a fire and order them to lie down in its ashes likely caused them to lose the sense that the leader knew what he was doing. Now without any structure the group disintegrated and that precipitated panic. Fifteen of the group ran for the top of the ridge but only two made it through a small crevice and were able to save themselves. The crew leader survived by lying down in the area burned by his escape fire and letting the fire pass by him.

Weick's analysis shows that loss of sensemaking ability and loss of structure were both important conditions leading to the disaster. With loss of group structure the world as experienced by the crew became less ordered, less rational and understandable, and more frightening. Under these conditions rational thought became more difficult. If the structure of the group had been maintained the disaster could have been averted.

Source: Based on information in Karl E. Weick (1993) "The collapse of sensemaking in organizations: The Mann Gulch disaster," *Administrative Science Quarterly* 38: 628-652.

Performance appraisal interview A meeting between a manager and a subordinate used to communicate the manager's evaluation of the subordinate's job performance and to help the employee focus on where and how to improve performance.

Ranking of job performance Employees are listed from the best to the worst in terms of their job performance.

Paired comparison of job performance Compares every person against every other on each characteristic being rated.

to performance. The composition of the rating form is of critical importance because it sends a clear message to employees of what the organization thinks is important in an employee. There is no generally accepted best length for trait scales, though 3-point, 5-point, and 7-point lengths are very commonly used by organizations.

In most organizations managers rate employees on a performance evaluation form, then conduct a **performance appraisal interview** with the employee. The purpose of this meeting is to communicate the manager's decisions and to help the employee focus on where and how to improve performance. Because pay increases, bonuses, or promotion possibilities are usually tied to performance, both managers and employees can be defensive and the chance to learn how to improve performance may be lost.

To avoid this problem, one organization, the Johnsonville Foods Company, used a form that asked the employee to rate self-performance. That person's coach (similar to a manager) used the same form to rate the employee's performance on 17 categories of behaviour important for the success of the company (see the *Seeing is Believing* feature).

Ranking employees from the best to the worst can be an effective method of performance evaluation if there are not too many trait categories or personnel to be ranked. The ranks are typically combined (usually averaged) to determine an overall ranking of employees.

The **paired comparison** method of evaluating job performance evaluates every person against every other on each characteristic being rated. This is a time consuming process, especially with a large number of persons and characteristics to be compared. However, computer programs do exist to facilitate the comparisons and the determination of the overall ranking of best to worst.

SEEING IS BELIEVING

JOHNSONVILLE FOODS COMPANY PERFORMANCE-SHARE EVALUATION FORM

In this profit sharing program, employees rated themselves using a 1 to 9 scale on 17 specific categories of behaviour divided into the three general categories of performance, teamwork, and personal development. Scores of 3, 4, and 5 are average; scores of 1 and 2 are low and require a short explanation, as do high scores of 6 to 9. The employee's coach also fills out the form for the person and they discuss their ratings. The rule for agreement is that the overall point total must agree within 9 points, then the two totals are averaged to reach a final score. Final scores are put into a forced distribution that determines the amount of profit sharing to be awarded to each employee.

Distribution of employee performance	poor: 5% or less	below average: 20% of employees	average: 50%	better than average: 20% of employees	top 5% of employees
Percent of profit sharing bonus allocated	75%	90%	100%	110%	125%

JOHNSONVILLE FOODS, INC.
COMPANY PERFORMANCE-SHARE
EVALUATION FORM

Please check one: _____ Self _____ Coach

I. PERFORMANCE

A. Customer Satisfaction
How do I rate the quality of the work I do? Do I contribute my best to producing a product to be proud of—one that I would purchase or encourage someone else to purchase?   *Score* _____

B. Cost-Effectiveness
To what extent do I perform my job in a cost-effective manner? Do I strive to work smarter? To work more productively with fewer errors? To complete my job functions in a timely manner, eliminating overtime when possible? To reduce waste where possible in all departments?   *Score* _____

C. Attitude
To what extent do I have a positive attitude toward my personal, department, and company goals as expressed by my actions, feelings, and thoughts? Do I like to come to work? Am I thoughtful and considerate toward fellow members? Do I work to promote better attitudes? Do I demonstrate company loyalty?   *Score* _____

D. Responsibility
To what extent do I take responsibility for my own job? Do I accept a challenge? Do I willingly take on or look for additional responsibilities? Do I work independently of supervision?   *Score* _____

E. Ideas
To what extent have I offered ideas and suggestions for improvements? Do I suggest better ways of doing things instead of just complaining?   *Score* _____

(continued on next page)

F. Problem Solver/Preventer

To what extent have I contributed to solving or preventing problems? Do I anticipate problem situations and try to avoid them? Do I push-pull when necessary? Do I keep an open line of communication?

Score _____

G. Safety

To what extent do my actions show my concern for safety for myself and others? Do I alert coworkers to unsafe procedures? Do I alert my coach to unsafe conditions in my department?

Score _____

H. Quality Image

To what extent have I displayed a high-quality image in my appearance, language, personal hygiene, and working environment?

Score _____

II. PERFORMANCE

A. Contribution to Groups

How would I rate my contribution to my department's performance? Am I aware of department goals? Do I contribute to a team? Do I communicate with team members?

Score _____

B. Communication

To what extent do I keep others informed to prevent problems from occurring? Do I work to promote communication between plants and departments? Do I relay information to the next shift? Do I speak up at meetings and let my opinions and feelings be known?

Score _____

C. Willingness to Work Together

To what extent am I willing to share the responsibility of getting the work done? Do I voluntarily assist others to obtain results? Do I demonstrate a desire to accomplish department goals? Do I complete paperwork accurately and thoroughly and work toward a smooth flow of information throughout the company? Am I willing to share in any overtime?

Score _____

D. Attendance and Timeliness

Do I contribute to the team by being present and on time for work (including after breaks and lunch)? Do I realize the inconvenience and hardship caused by my absence or tardiness?

Score _____

II. PERSONAL DEVELOPMENT

A. To what extent am I actively involved in lifelong learning? Taking classes is not the only way to learn. Other ways include use of our resource center or libraries for reading books, articles, etc.

Score _____

B. Do I improve my job performance by applying what I have learned?

Score _____

C. Do I ask questions pertaining to my job and other jobs too?

Score _____

D. Do I try to better myself not only through work but in all aspects of my life?

Score _____

E. Do I seek information about our industry?

Score _____

TOTAL POINTS: _____

SOURCE: Reprinted by permission of *Harvard Business Review*. An exhibit from "How I learned to let my workers lead" by Ralph Stayer, November/December 1990. Copyright © 1990 by the President and Fellows of Harvard College; all rights reserved.

The **descriptive essay** is a very common appraisal method. The manager responds to a set of trait/behaviour statements (for example: "Is dependable," "Deals well with clients") by writing a short paragraph describing the person's performance since the last evaluation. Essays are flexible but require more interpretation than numeric ratings or rankings.

A **forced distribution** is used when a manager has many employees to rate and wants to show the differences between them. This method is similar to ranking but allows less precise differentiation between individuals. For instance, the manager does not have to determine who is 14th best and who is 15th best but may rate both these employees in the "below average" category. As one example of the use of this method, the Johnsonville Foods performance evaluation system uses a forced distribution to allocate performance bonus money once individual employee ratings are completed.

The **behavioural checklist** lists areas of performance and specific behaviours expected of someone at each level of performance. The rater scans the behaviour descriptions for each category and chooses the one that seems to describe the employee best. A tongue-in-cheek example of a behavioural checklist for the job of superhero is shown as Exhibit 6.5.

A **weighted checklist** rates performance using the same method as the behavioural checklist, but the performance categories are then weighted. For superheroes, the five performance areas might be weighted as follows:

quality of work and capability = 3;
initiative and communication = 2; and
promptness = 1.

Descriptive essay
A method of evaluating job performance in which the manager describes the subordinate's performance.

Forced distribution
Assigns a certain number (or percentage) of employees to each category of job performance.

Behavioural checklist
Lists performance areas and specific behaviours expected at each job performance level.

Weighted checklist   A behavioural checklist with weights assigned to each performance area.

EXHIBIT 6.5   BEHAVIOURAL CHECKLIST FOR SUPERHERO
PERFORMANCE APPRAISAL

NUMERIC SCORE	5	4	3	2	1
AREA OF PERFORMANCE	FAR IN EXCESS OF JOB REQUIREMENTS	EXCEEDS JOB REQUIREMENTS	MEETS JOB REQUIREMENTS	NEEDS IMPROVEMENT	DOES NOT MEET MINIMUM REQUIREMENTS
Quality of work	Leaps tall buildings in a single bound	Leaps tall buildings with running start	Can leap short buildings if prodded	Bumps into buildings	Cannot recognize buildings
Promptness	Is faster than a speeding bullet	Is as fast as a speeding bullet	Would you believe a slow bullet?	Misfires frequently	Wounds self when when handling guns
Initiative	Is stronger than a locomotive	Is as strong as a bull elephant	Almost as strong as a bull	Shoots the bull	Smells like a bull
Capability	Walks on water	Keeps head above water	Washes with water	Drinks water	Passes water in emergencies
Communication	Talks with God	Talks with the angels	Talks with self	Argues with self	Loses arguments with self

SOURCE: Reprinted from Terence R. Mitchell and James R. Larson, Jr. (1987), PEOPLE IN ORGANIZATIONS, © 1987. Third Edition, New York: McGraw-Hill Book Company, p. 491. Reproduced with permission of McGraw-Hill, Inc.

Then each performance rating from 1 (= does not meet minimum requirements) to 5 (= far in excess of job requirements) would be multiplied by the performance weight for that area in order to compute the individual superhero's overall performance rating.

The **critical incidents** method requires the rater to record critical job behaviours exhibited by the employee as they happen. These critical incidents are then stored until the time of performance appraisal. Then they are reviewed before making a rating. A critical incident might be, for example, when an employee dealt particularly well with an irate customer or when being late for work meant the store could not be opened on time. There is no reason why a manager could not share critical incidents with employees as they happen. They would, however, still be stored and retrieved for the performance appraisal.

Behaviourally anchored rating scales (BARS) are a generalized set of critical incident descriptions for each job in an organization. The process of creating BARS is difficult and time-consuming. First, the important aspects of job performance must be identified. Then, many individuals holding each job must be interviewed in order to build up a set of critical incidents for that job. These incidents must then be ordered and the resultant scales checked for their descriptive validity—that is, do they describe each job well? The resulting scales, a different set for each job in the organization, are useful for making it clear to employees what behaviours are descriptive for each level of performance. To use BAR scales a manager would examine each scale in turn before deciding which critical incident is most descriptive of the employee's typical behaviour.

Critical incidents

Important job events that can be recorded and stored until it is time to evaluate an employee's performance.

Behaviourally anchored rating scales (BARS)

A set of descriptions created for each job in an organization that specify in detail what behaviour is expected for each level of performance in a given job.

Errors in Performance Evaluation

Because the evaluation of performance relies on the perceptions of people, there are a number of perceptual errors that can occur in the rating process. The 11 steps of the performance evaluation process and the possible errors that might occur at each step are shown in Exhibit 6.6. This exhibit is from work done by Professor Bill Cooper at Queen's University.

The first step in rating performance is the observation of the ratee's (employee's) actions. We already know that observation is not simply seeing the events of the real world but depends on perceptual selection, organization, and interpretation. There are several errors possible at this stage.

Selection   In terms of selection, one potential error is that only a few employee behaviours are taken as indicating overall performance. Recording critical incidents is a rating method designed to overcome this problem. Exceptional performances, both good and bad, are recorded for later input into the performance review.

Organization   It must also be recognized that those who rate the performance of others may construct a reality that they then rate. Timothy Judge and Gerald Ferris (1993) have noted that "Traditional conceptualizations of the performance-rating process imply that performance is a knowable and observable objective reality and that performance ratings are reasonable reflections of that reality" (p. 97). But "only quite recently has performance-rating theory recognized ... that supervisors' ratings of subordinates' performance may be a socially constructed reality" (p. 97).

Interpretation   Another error is that early judgments by the manager can affect subsequent perceptions of the employee. People tend to seek information that confirms their early judgments. *Stereotyping* of individuals, especially with respect to the sex role of a given job, also acts as an early judgment and restricts full observation. Perceptual defense

Exhibit 6.6   The Performance Evaluation Process

Action	Possible Errors
1. Observation of actions	Primacy, recency, projection, early explicit judgments affect later information, perceptual defense, inadequate sample of behaviours, stereotyping
2. Observation encoding, aggregation, and storage in short-term memory	Central traits, implicit personality theory
3. Short-term memory decay	Loss of information
4. Transfer to long-term memory and aggregation	Discounting and confirmationist biases
5. Long-term memory decay	Loss of information
6. Presentation of categories to be rated	Categories might not be connected to important aspects of job performance
7. Observation and impression retrieval from long-term memory	Salient aspects retrieved first, halo
8. Recognition of observations and impressions relevant to rating categories	Expectancy, similarity to rater, hits noticed more than misses
9. Comparison of observations and impressions to rater's standards	Strictness, leniency, central tendency
10. Incorporation of extraneous considerations	Attributions, politics
11. Rating	Traits regarded as more important to job performance than behaviours when the reverse is actually the case (or vice-versa)

Source: William H. Cooper (1981), "Ubiquitous halo," *Psychological Bulletin* 90: 236. Copyright © 1981 by the American Psychological Association. Adapted by permission.

is another way raters miss actual actions. *Projection*, however, is the process of the rater seeing a personal weakness in others when it is not really present in the ratee (the person being rated). *Primacy* is the tendency for people to remember more clearly events that happen first—hence the importance of first impressions both in meeting people and in job performance. *Recency* is the overweighting of the employee's performance in the last few weeks or months before an evaluation. Organizations can train raters to be aware of and reduce the occurrence of these errors.

Step two is the encoding, combining, and storage in short-term memory of observations. This process is subject to error as managers cannot remember every detail about employee performance, and the rater relies on a personally held (implicit) theory of personality and what traits are most important. To avoid these errors raters need to be trained to perceive each trait independently of others.

At step three there is a loss of information in short-term memory. Written notes about performance and reviews more frequent than once a year are methods used to combat this error.

To remember events over some significant amount of time people must transfer their short-term memories into long-term memory (step four). Because short-term memories about an individual employee may not be consistent with long-term memories already present about that person, there is a tendency for only new memories that confirm existing long-term memories to be added to the long-term store.

Step five shows the loss of information through the gradual decay of long-term memory. Categories to be rated are then presented to the rater (step six). The most important possible error at this step is that the categories may not in fact be relevant to job performance. Organizations must be very careful to discover the traits and behaviours critical to job performance for each job in the organization.

At step seven, the rater recalls observations and impressions relevant to each category to be appraised. Potential errors here are that exceptional aspects of the ratee and the ratee's performance are retrieved first and these may then colour or halo other less easily recalled observations. One way to reduce halo is to use ratings from more than one rater. Ratings can come from the manager and the employee or from more than one manager. Self-ratings can be a useful way for employees to objectively review their own performance. An example of multiple-manager rating is auditors who work on a number of audit teams and are rated by each team leader.

Then at step eight, recalled observations and impressions are matched to the rating categories. Likely errors here are those of: (a) expectancy—the rater finds observations that fit the expected pattern; (b) hits are noticed more than misses—agreements with prior expectations are given more weight than disagreements; and (c) similarity to rater—the rater is more likely to make job performance observations that fit the rater's own personality and performance strengths and weaknesses. By making the rater aware of these perceptual errors their impact can be reduced.

The rater then compares the recalled observations and impressions to the scales used to rate performance (step nine). Simple numeric scales are subject to the errors of strictness, leniency, and central tendency (all employees are rated either very low, very high, or in the middle regardless of performance).

Steps ten and eleven in the performance evaluation process are perhaps the most interesting, because they explicitly recognize that there is more to a performance rating than performance. The two extraneous considerations that will be examined here are the attributional process and the politics of the performance appraisal.

Attributions   The model shown as Exhibit 6.7 shows how there are several links and possible biases between the observation of behaviour and the manager's response, which here includes the manager's evaluation of employee performance. The first link between observations and attributions are social and informational factors that have been discussed previously: distinctiveness, consistency, and consensus. The causal attribution is then made. Given the attribution made by the manager about *why* the behaviour occurred, the actual response may then not follow logically but can be affected by the costs of various actions perceived by the manager.

Costs considered could include: (1) what happened due to the subordinate's action—punishments/evaluations are harsher when negative outcomes occurred; (2) apologies offered by the subordinate—managers often act leniently toward those who apologize; (3) the social context—a subordinate who is a leader or who is well-liked by the work group will attract higher ratings from the manager; (4) manager-subordinate interdependence—subordinates are given higher ratings when the manager is dependent on the work and support of the subordinate; and (5) the costs/benefits of the manager's possible responses—managers will be practical and act to some degree in the way they perceive as best for themselves, their subordinates, and their departments.

EXHIBIT 6.7

The Attribution Process in Performance Evaluation

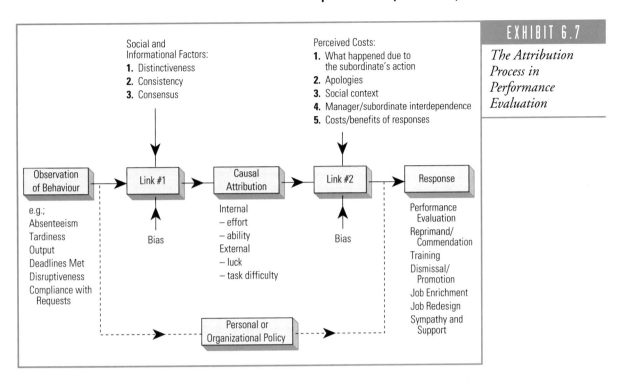

SOURCE: Adapted from Terence R. Mitchell (1982), "Attributions and actions: A note of caution," *Journal of Management* 8: 67. Reprinted by permission.

Finally, a personal or organizational policy may act to circumvent this attributional process. In effect, the manager's hands may be tied and regardless of personal attributions the response may be dictated by policy.

Politics of Performance Evaluation   Clinton Longnecker and his colleagues (1987) interviewed 60 upper-level executives about the performance evaluation process. They found that executives admit that evaluations are sometimes affected by political considerations and by conditions in the organization as a whole. The executives interviewed also explained why a particular employee's ratings might be inflated or deflated (see Exhibit 6.8).

These findings help to explain why pay and performance are sometimes not well related (Markham, 1988). Though organizations may consider that members performing well should be paid more, managers doing the performance evaluations are liable to either make perceptual errors or choose to include attributional and political factors in the performance evaluation process that weakens the connection between pay and performance. For a look at CEO pay and performance, see *On the One Hand*.

Are there other organizational conditions that weaken the link between pay and performance? While it depends on the particular organization, its structure and culture, the answer is yes. Three reasons why pay and performance may be weakly related are as follows.

1. People are paid to join the organization. At times a person's job is less important than the fact that that particular person be seen as part of the company.
2. People are paid an entry salary required by the market for their services, whether or not they can actually return that degree of performance to the organization.

3. People who have been with an organization for many years and whose skills are not easily transported to another firm may be paid less than deserved because they have little choice but to accept it.

A person who seeks to use these factors to advantage in obtaining high pay should obtain a unique set of skills, these should be scarce in the market, and be desired by the organization.

EXHIBIT 6.8   PERFORMANCE EVALUATION POLITICS

A. Politics as Part of Performance Evaluation

- Political considerations were nearly always part of executive evaluative processes
- Politics played a role in the evaluation process because:
  - executives took into consideration the daily interpersonal dynamics between them and their subordinates
  - the formal appraisal process results in a permanent written document
  - the formal appraisal can have considerable impact on the subordinate's career and advancement

B. Organizational Factors that Influence the Degree of Performance Appraisal Politics

- The economic health and growth potential of the organization
- The extent to which top management supported and, more importantly, did or did not practice political tactics when appraising their own subordinates
- The extent to which executives sincerely believed that appraisal was a necessary and worthwhile management practice or just a bureaucratic exercise
- The extent to which executives believed that their written assessment of their subordinates would be evaluated and scrutinized by their superiors
- The extent to which an organization was willing to train and coach its managers to use and maintain the performance appraisal system
- The degree to which the appraisal process was openly discussed among both executives and subordinates
- The extent to which executives believed the appraisal process became more political at higher levels of the organizational hierarchy

C. Why Ratings are Inflated

- Executives inflated the appraisal to provide ratings that would effectively maintain or increase the subordinate's level of performance (the primary concern was not the accuracy of the ratings)

- Inflated ratings occur primarily on the overall performance rating, as opposed to the individual appraisal items
- Executive justification for inflating the appraisal:
  - to maximize the merit increases a subordinate would be eligible to receive, especially when the merit ceiling was considered low; to protect or encourage a subordinate whose performance was suffering because of personal problems (feeling sorry for a subordinate also resulted in an inflated appraisal)
  - to avoid hanging dirty laundry out in public if the performance appraisal would be reviewed by people outside the organization
  - to avoid creating a written record of poor performance that would become a permanent part of a subordinate's personnel file
  - to avoid a confrontation with a subordinate with whom the manager had recently had difficulties
  - to give a break to a subordinate who had improved during the latter part of the performance period
  - to promote a subordinate "up and out" when the subordinate was performing poorly or did not fit in the department

D. Why Ratings are Deflated

- Executives indicated that they were very hesitant consciously to deflate a subordinate's ratings because of potential problems associated with such a tactic
- Nevertheless, they sometimes deflated appraisals
  - to shock a subordinate back on to a higher performance track
  - to teach a rebellious subordinate a lesson about who is in charge
  - to send a message to a subordinate that he or she should consider leaving the organization
  - to build a strongly documented record of poor performance that could speed up the termination process

---

SOURCE: Clinton O. Longnecker, Henry P. Sims, Jr., and Dennis A. Gioia (1987), "Behind the mask: The politics of employee appraisal," *Academy of Management Executive* 1: 183-193. Reprinted by permission. Also see Dennis A. Gioia and Clinton O. Longnecker, 1994, "Delving into the dark side: The politics of executive appraisal," *Organizational Dynamics* 22(3): 47-58.

ON THE ONE HAND ...

Some maintain that CEO pay is too high. The CEO of a large American corporation earns about $1.2 million a year in pay and bonus, with stock options worth about another $.8 million a year. This amount of pay has tripled in the last ten years, widening the gap with the lowest level workers in the organization, whose pay has not kept up with inflation. Further, if the CEO is fired, a "golden parachute" of at least three times annual pay softens the blow. Critics also point out that the pay of American CEO's is much higher than for those of foreign companies. One study found that average total compensation in the U.S. was two-thirds higher than that of the next highest nation. Canada's executive pay averaged just over $400,000 (in U.S. dollars), in fourth place among the seven nations studied. Another argument that is made is that CEO pay does not relate to CEO performance. This position was supported by a Jeffrey Kerr and Richard Bettis (1987) study. Using CEO salary data from *Business Week* surveys for 78 companies, they found that a corporation's stock price and CEO salary and bonuses were not linked.

SOURCES: Based on information in *Business Week*, "Executive Pay," March 30, 1992, pp. 52-58; Frances Mitsutka (1992), "The biggest headache money can buy," *Canadian Business*, July 1992, pp. 50-54; and Jeffrey Kerr and Richard A. Bettis (1987), "Boards of directors, top management compensation, and shareholder returns," *Academy of Management Journal* 30: 645-664.

ON THE OTHER HAND ...

An article by Sidney Finkelstein and Donald Hambrick (1988) argues that CEO compensation is complex and that looking at it in only one way can lead to the conclusion that it is a pay system out of control. They argue that there are several determinants of a CEO's compensation. One is market factors. The limited supply and high demand for CEO talent creates a market with a high price for CEO's. Also, companies seek to create equitable pay for their CEO's as compared to other companies, which tends to raise overall pay levels. CEO pay can also be an inducement to those at the Vice-President level to work hard and compete for the CEO job. Finally, the CEO job can be a difficult one and since the CEO can make a big difference to company performance, pay should reflect that potential impact.

The second determinant of CEO compensation is political factors. Board members set or approve CEO pay and they have complex preferences and motives. Their own status can be reflected on by the status and pay of the corporation's CEO. A third determinant of CEO pay is as a motivational tool. Pay compensates for the long hours and high stress endured by CEO's, is a symbolic reward, and may direct the CEO's effort in the direction desired by the Board.

SOURCE: Based on information in Sidney Finkelstein and Donald C. Hambrick (1988), "Chief executive compensation: A synthesis and reconciliation," *Strategic Management Journal* 9: 543-558.

CONCLUSION

We have now completed our discussion of how people in organizations perceive their environments and in turn are perceived by others. Next we turn to the topic of communication in organizations. There may be no more important topic in all of organizational behaviour, because the process of communicating with others is central to so many activities of people in organizations. The perceptual process of socially constructing reality depends on communication with others. Performance evaluation is usually communicated between two or more people, and is sometimes negotiated. Communication skill is also an important individual difference. Some people are better at communicating than others. Since effective communication is a skill that can be learned, Chapter 7 will discuss how to effectively communicate with others.

CHAPTER SUMMARY

The point of view taken in this chapter is that there is one physical world but that each of us perceives it differently and experiences it differently. There are therefore multiple created realities with each person living in a separate reality.

The process of perceiving the environment is affected by external factors such as object size and intensity; internal factors of an individual's personality, learning, and motivation; and how social reality is constructed between people by comparing their sensory experiences. Stimuli that are perceived and selected for notice are then organized so that they make sense. The formed perception is then interpreted. Errors in attributions and perception can occur at this stage. The last stage of the perceptual process is the displayed (overt) or hidden (covert) response to a perceptual interpretation.

The process of perception is crucially important to organizations because people need to make sense of their world and to take action based on their interpretation. When the organizational world as experienced fails to "make sense" then the social connections between organizational members can break down and cause a crisis.

This chapter also considered the perception and evaluation of another's performance in the organization. This common and vital component of organizational life shows how perceptual processes apply in everyday practice.

QUESTIONS FOR REVIEW

1. Make a case that there is only one physical world and that we each perceive it in the same way.

2. How do individuals construct a social reality for themselves? Why would they do so? How does the constructed reality then affect them?

3. Explain Karl Weick's ideas about collective mind and heedful interrelating. Under what conditions are they necessary?

4. Why is it necessary to evaluate a person's organizational performance? What are the drawbacks and potential flaws in performance appraisal?

5. What are the organizational applications of virtual reality that go beyond its use in toys and games? What are the implications of organizational members working in these artificially created realities for the way work is done and for human relationships?

SELF-DIAGNOSTIC EXERCISE 6.1

Rate yourself and then a friend on each of the following 20 traits.

SELF			FRIEND		
Serious	Cheerful	Depends on situation	Serious	Cheerful	Depends on situation
Subjective	Analytic	Depends on situation	Subjective	Analytic	Depends on situation
Future-oriented	Present-oriented	Depends on situation	Future-oriented	Present-oriented	Depends on situation
Energetic	Relaxed	Depends on situation	Energetic	Relaxed	Depends on situation
Unassuming	Self-asserting	Depends on situation	Unassuming	Self-asserting	Depends on situation
Lenient	Firm	Depends on situation	Lenient	Firm	Depends on situation
Reserved	Emotionally expressive	Depends on situation	Reserved	Emotionally expressive	Depends on situation
Dignified	Casual	Depends on situation	Dignified	Casual	Depends on situation
Realistic	Idealistic	Depends on situation	Realistic	Idealistic	Depends on situation
Intense	Calm	Depends on situation	Intense	Calm	Depends on situation
Skeptical,	Trusting	Depends on situation	Skeptical	Trusting	Depends on situation
Quiet	Talkative	Depends on situation	Quiet	Talkative	Depends on situation
Cultivated	Natural	Depends on situation	Cultivated	Natural	Depends on situation
Sensitive	Tough-minded	Depends on situation	Sensitive	Tough-minded	Depends on situation
Self-sufficient	Sociable	Depends on situation	Self-sufficient	Sociable	Depends on situation
Steady	Flexible	Depends on situation	Steady	Flexible	Depends on situation
Dominant	Deferential	Depends on situation	Dominant	Deferential	Depends on situation
Cautious	Bold	Depends on situation	Cautious	Bold	Depends on situation
Uninhibited	Self-controlled	Depends on situation	Uninhibited	Self-controlled	Depends on situation
Conscientious	Happy-go-lucky	Depends on situation	Conscientious	Happy-go-lucky	Depends on situation

SOURCE: Richard E. Nisbett, Craig Caputo, Patricia Legant, and Jeanne Marecek (1973), "Behavior as seen by the actor and as seen by the observer," *Journal of Personality and Social Psychology* 27: 161. Copyright © 1973 by the American Psychological Association. Adapted by permission.

EXPERIENTIAL EXERCISE 6.1

Office Perception

The Chairman's Office

The chairman's office was on the second floor; that is, it was not on the top floor of the building, but it occupied a position that in many ways was intermediate and central. Hanging on the walls of the chairman's room were (a) his own painting, (b) pictures that had been there before him and were the property of the organization, (c) pictures that were more organizational in nature and served to illustrate and embellish the company. To complete the description of its appearance and aesthetic, the room contained two beautiful plants; a small table apparently haphazardly scattered with publications displaying the organization's products and premises together with publicity material from other organizations; a low cupboard of light-coloured wood, which was, in fact, a filing cabinet; a small bookcase containing some objects; a computer, a telephone, a tape recorder, and the organization's logo, all arranged on the desk top; and finally a sofa and two small armchairs. The walls were painted off-white.

The chairman often left his door half open when he was alone. The chairman's desk stood immediately opposite the door to one side and on the left of the room between his armchair and armchairs for his guests. The desk, which held the objects previously described, was usually strewn with file folders, publications, and memoranda. When seated, the chairman was directly in front of his visitor(s). To their right, between two French windows that opened onto a small balcony, hung a painting of an elderly woman; she had a proud, soft but determined expression on her face and she was painted sitting in aristocratic surroundings. The painting dated back a number of years, but was not as old as one might have thought from the woman's clothing, the posture of the sitter, and the painter's style. It was a portrait of the current chairman's maternal grandmother.

Opposite the chairman, above the sofa and the low table with the magazines, hung a large picture which belonged to the organization. This very large abstract painting, which was executed with considerable style, covered the entire wall. The previous chairman had placed it on the wall where it now hung. It was an extremely expensive picture: The money spent on it could have been used to decorate several other offices. Next, against the wall by the door were the bookcase and (above it) a large photograph of the organization's bottling and bottle-boxing production line. This photograph documented one of the company's historical facts: the first assembly line to be invented, designed, and built by the organization. A section of this line could be seen in the photograph: two rollerways, one for bottling, the other, moving in the opposite direction, for boxing. Striking poses around this section of the production line—photographed half-length and with their eyes fixed on the camera—were the previous chairman, the two owners, and an engineer, all wearing jackets and ties, and the technician and three workers in overalls. The same picture was reproduced in the organization's brochures and could also be seen—as a photograph—hanging in the corridor leading to the conference room. The original photograph in the chairman's office was slightly yellowed and faded. It had been taken by a professional photographer, as was evident from the embossed stamp in the lower left-hand corner.

A large plant and a small picture completed the decorations for this wall. The small picture was a figurative-abstract graphic work by a well-known artist, purchased previously as an investment by one of the owners on the suggestion of a friend who ran an art gallery. The picture had pleased the owner, but aroused the curiosity and admiration of the chairman and others, who were uncertain about its meaning and unsure that they would have hung it in that place. The picture was worth a great deal of money.

Finally, on the wall behind the chairman's desk, but slightly to one side of it, were pictures that he found useful for his day-to-day work: large sheets of paper with messages (in blue, red, green, and black) written in capital letters.

The Secretary's Office

At the left side of a small corridor was the chairman's office; to the right was his secretary's office. This smaller room was long and narrow, and it had a window at the end. When visitors entered the room they saw a filing cabinet; on the left side was a desk that divided the room almost in half and occupied a large part of it. On the desk were arranged a telephone, a computer, a typewriter, a small plant, diaries, various items of stationery, and a framed snapshot of the secretary's family. Opposite the desk was a large office-style cabinet full of files, dossiers, and so forth. A poster showing a nude sketch by a late Viennese artist hung on the wall between the secretary's chair and the photocopier.

Pinned up alongside the poster was a photograph of the secretary's two smiling children. The space around the desk was cramped; one could stretch out to get a pencil, or rest on a corner to write one's signature, but things were ordered in such a way that, after a fruitless search for a form that could have been filed in any number of ways, one had to ask where it was kept. For the visitor, confusion seemed to reign: a confusion of plants, family photographs, piled up forms and folders, filing cabinets, machinery, locked drawers, and unlocked drawers. Everyone had to knock to ask permission to enter her office; unlike the chairman, the secretary rarely left her door open.

1. What are the similarities and differences between the chairman's and the secretary's office?
2. What impressions would a visitor obtain when meeting with the chairman in his office?
3. How would interaction likely proceed when entering the secretary's office?
4. What is the importance of the pictures on the walls in the two offices?
5. How might these offices change with a new chairman or a new secretary?

SOURCE: Excerpted from Antonio Strati (1992), "Aesthetic understanding of organizational life," *Academy of Management Review* 17: 570-574. Reproduced with permission of the author and the Academy of Management.

SELF-GUIDED LEARNING ACTIVITY

How are you seen by others? One way to find out is to ask the key people in your life to describe how they see you and their attributions about why you act as you do. For work purposes, you can dress up in your interview clothes and do a practice interview with either someone in the job already or with an employment counsellor at your college or university's placement office. After the interview ask how you were perceived and compare perceptions with the image that you would like to project to others.

MANAGER'S CASE FILE:
"I DESERVE A BIGGER RAISE"

Ellen Richards supervised 30 stenographers in the automobile claims department of a large insurance company. She spent much of her time assigning dictation to the staffers who handled correspondence arising out of accident claims against the company. Some of this correspondence was fairly routine, but other letters, involving litigation, were quite complicated.

As a rule, Ellen gave the most difficult dictation to the more experienced stenographers she knew could handle it. From time to time she overheard some of the workers complain that they got only the toughest jobs while others got the easiest ones. When Ellen first became a supervisor, such grumbling used to bother her. But now she felt that no matter what she did, it was impossible to please everybody.

She tried to remind herself of this as it became time to announce the annual merit raises. She used her records on attendance, lateness, and daily letter output to determine the size of each raise. After she had made her decisions, Ellen called each person to her desk individually to tell the employee the amount of the raise. When she was through, the staffers started comparing notes as usual. After the buzzing died down, she could see that some of them looked angry or unhappy.

The next day, Annette Simmons came up to Ellen's desk, obviously upset. "Ellen," she said, trying to control her voice, "could you please tell me why Jason got a bigger raise than I did? I have had very few absences and I'm never late. You often compliment me on my work, and you give me some of the hardest assignments." Ellen got out her records and looked at them. "You're a good worker, Annette," she said, "but your letter output is just a little below average. If you could raise your output, next time I'm sure you'll get a bigger raise."

"But I get the hardest dictation," Annette said angrily. "And when Gene came to our section, you put him next to me and told me to help him until he got familiar with the work. I don't mind helping somebody new, but he still interrupts me with questions about things he should know by now. Don't you take things like that into consideration before deciding how much of a raise I deserve?"

"In a section as large as ours," Ellen explained, "I have to use objective standards like output and attendance to determine each person's raise. Here, productivity is everything. I'm sorry you're upset because I know how helpful you are to the less experienced workers, and I know how much they appreciate your giving them a hand."

"Evidently they're the only ones who appreciate my giving them a hand. From now on, I'll just attend to my own work." With that, Annette turned away and went back to her desk before Ellen could say anything.

Ellen watched Annette and knew that she had the beginning of what could turn into a big problem for herself, the department, even the company. "But she'll bounce back," Ellen thought. "She's always had such a good attitude."

Later that afternoon when Gene asked Annette a question about the work, Ellen heard Annette snap back at him, "Don't bother me with your questions. I've got my own work to do. I have to raise my letter output, and I don't have time for you any more. If you have any questions, ask the supervisor."

SOURCE: Reprinted, by permission of publisher, from MANAGEMENT SOLUTIONS, June 1986. © 1986 American Management Association, New York. All rights reserved.

Questions

1. Other than productivity and attendance, on what should Ellen base her evaluations?

2. How could Ellen have better handled this situation?

3. What can Ellen do now to appease Annette?

CASE 6.2

THE TENERIFE AIRPORT DISASTER

On March 27, 1977 a bomb exploded about noon local time in the concession area of Las Palmas airport on Grand Canary island off the coast of Africa, injuring two people. Responsibility was claimed by a group seeking Canary Island independence from Spain. Since a telephone call tipped police to look for a second bomb, the Las Palmas airport was closed.

A Royal Dutch Airlines charter flight, KLM 4805, was en route to Las Palmas from Holland with 234 passengers on board and 14 crew members. After Las Palmas was closed, KLM 4805 was rerouted to Los Rodeos airport on the island of Santa Cruz de Tenerife, about 25 minutes by air from Las Palmas. KLM 4805 arrived at 13:38 Greenwich mean time, joining Boeing 737 and 727 aircraft that were also rerouted to Los Rodeos.

The KLM captain was Jacob Louis Veldhuyzen van Zanten, age 50. His total flying time was 11 700 hours with 1,545 of that on 747s. The co-pilot Klass Meurs, 32, had 9200 hours of flight experience but only 95 hours on 747s. The flight engineer Willem Schreuder, age 48, had 15 210 hours of flight experience and 540 hours on 747s. Captain van Zanten was one of KLM's senior pilots. He was KLM's chief flying instructor, had been a flying instructor for more than 10 years, and had certified co-pilot Meurs to fly on the Boeing 747 aircraft. On simulated training flights Captain van Zanten would act as the air traffic controller and issue takeoff clearances to the pilot trainee. In these simulated flights it was common for no communications at all to take place and for simulated takeoff to take place without clearance from an external controller.

Because the month of March was coming to an end, the KLM's Dutch crew was approaching its maximum allowed duty time for the month. Changes in Dutch law had set strict limits on the amount of allowable duty time, and the aircraft's captain was forbidden to exceed that limit. Since the formula for computing duty time was very complicated and could not be performed on the airplane, Captain van Zanten spoke by radio to Amsterdam to ask about his crew's duty status. He was informed that he could return to Amsterdam that night if he were able to leave Las Palmas Airport (on the Grand Canary Island) by early that evening. Head office would send a telex to Las Palmas Airport if there was a problem with duty times.

While on the ground at Los Rodeos Airport (Tenerife) KLM passengers disembarked and 55 500 liters of aviation fuel were pumped into the KLM's fuel tanks, enough to get the plane from Los Rodeos to Las Palmas, and then on to Amsterdam.

A Pan American charter flight, Pan Am 1736, was en route to Las Palmas from Los Angeles and New York. On board the Boeing 747 aircraft were 16 crew and 380 passengers bound for a 14-day cruise in the Mediterranean. When Las Palmas airport was closed, Pan Am 1736 requested permission to circle Las Palmas until it reopened (they had enough fuel for this) but were told by Spanish air traffic controllers to land at Los Rodeos Airport. This they did, landing at 14:15, with passengers staying on board. The captain of the Pan Am flight, Victor F. Grubbs, was 56 years old, had 21 043 hours of flight experience and 564 hours on 747s. His co-pilot was Robert L. Bragg, age 39, with 10 800 hours of flight experience and 2796 hours experience on 747s. The flight engineer, George W. Warns was 46 and had 15 210 hours flight experience and 559 on 747s. When Las Palmas airport reopened, Pan Am 1736 attempted to leave Los Rodeos but was blocked by the KLM aircraft. The taxi strip at Los Rodeos was blocked by other aircraft diverted from Las Palmas, so the Pan Am flight had to wait.

The Los Rodeos airport (see Exhibit 6.9) is at an altitude of 2073 feet (632 meters) and is located in a hollow between mountains. The runway is over two miles long (11 154 feet or 3400 meters). The weather is changeable, with frequent low-lying clouds that hamper visibility and moving clouds that can cause sudden and radical changes in visibility. At Los Rodeos (Tenerife), air traffic controllers had no ground radar, they were shorthanded, they did not often handle 747s, and they were working in English—not their normal working language of Spanish. Also, the runway centerline lights were out of service—in poor visibility larger aircraft may not be allowed to take off because keeping in the center of the runway can be difficult. Also, because of the congestion on the Los Rodeos taxiway, controllers had their normal routines for the moving of airplanes disrupted. Because exits C1 and C2 from the taxiway were blocked by aircraft, controllers in the tower engaged in the non-standard procedure of carrying out taxiing maneuvers on the active runway.

Los Rodeos Airport

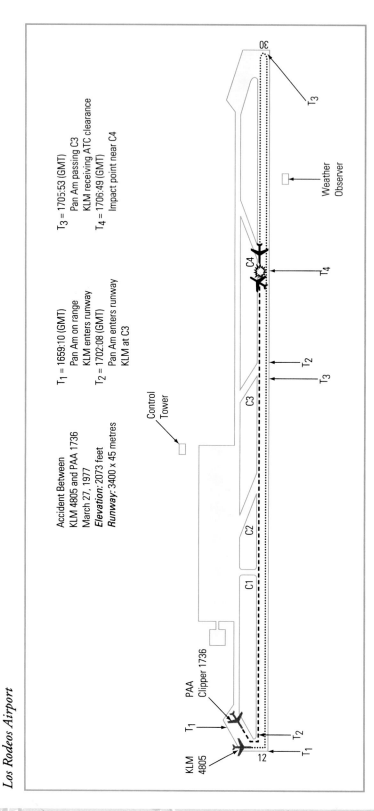

Accident Between
KLM 4805 and PAA 1736
March 27, 1977
Elevation: 2073 feet
Runway: 3400 x 45 metres

T_1 = 1659:10 (GMT)
Pan Am on range
KLM enters runway
T_2 = 1702:08 (GMT)
Pan Am enters runway
KLM at C3

T_3 = 1705:53 (GMT)
Pan Am passing C3
KLM receiving ATC clearance
T_4 = 1706:49 (GMT)
Impact point near C4

SOURCE: P.A. Roitsch, G.L. Babcock, and W.W. Edmunds (1979). *Human Factors Report on the Tenerife Accident*, Washington, D.C.: Air Line Pilots Association, p. 30, Appendix 1. Reproduced by permission of the Air Line Pilots Association.

Here is what happened next.

Time	Event
1645	Runway visibility was 2000 to 3000 meters with intermittent light rain and fog at a distance.
1650	Runway visibility was 2000 to 3000 meters with light rain and fog patches.
1659:10	KLM 4805 enters runway and begins to travel down the runway (from left to right on the map). They were to take exit C4 onto the taxiway, then turn around and wait to take off (from right to left on the map). Pan Am 1736 requested permission to wait where they were parked until the KLM had taken off. This permission was denied and the Pan Am Captain Victor Grubbs, instead of entering into a negotiation with the Spanish controller, prepares to taxi down the active runway. The controller told Pan Am to exit at C3, then proceed down the taxiway and get in line behind the KLM in preparation for takeoff.
1702	Runway visibility was 300 meters with light rain and fog patches. The Pan Am needed 800 meters runway visibility to take off if centerline lights were not working.
1702:08	Pan Am enters runway; KLM is at C3. A cloud moving down the runway between the Pan Am and the KLM prevented them from seeing each other.
1704:26.4	Pan Am identified exit C1, using a little map they had of the airport in the cockpit. KLM missed exit C4 and therefore had to travel to the end of the runway and execute a difficult 180 degree turn to get into position for takeoff. Problems were accumulating on the KLM pilot and co-pilot and after this turn was completed the KLM crew may have relaxed, then felt a desire to be airborne.
1705:22.0	Pan Am identified exit C2.
1705:44.6	KLM reports ready for takeoff.
1705:53	Pan Am passing exit C3 where the air traffic controller had asked them to turn off the main runway. The width of exit C3 was not great enough for a 747 aircraft to make a sharp left turn into C3, then a sharp right turn onto the taxiway. Pan Am may therefore have decided not to attempt these turns but to take exit C4 onto the taxiway. Alternatively, Pan Am may have missed seeing exit C3 because they were inside a cloud.
1705:53.41 to 1706:08.9	Tower – "KLM eight seven zero five -uh- you are cleared to the Papa Beacon, climb to and maintain flight level niner zero, right turn after takeoff, proceed with heading four zero until intercepting the three two five radial from Las Palmas VOR"
1706:09.61 to 1706:17.79	KLM – "Ah, Roger Sir, we are cleared to the Papa Beacon, flight to level nine zero until intercepting the three two five. We are now at takeoff." Shortly after this transmission ended, at 1706:19.35 Pan Am Captain Grubbs says "No, uh."
1706:11.08	Brakes in the KLM were released while clearance for takeoff was being asked for.
1706:11.70	KLM begins to move.
1706:12.25	Captain van Zanten said "Let's go ... check thrust."
1706:17.17	KLM lift had begun (the plane started to lift into the air).
1706:18.19 to 1706:21.79	Tower – "O.K. ... Stand by for takeoff, I will call you." [A squeal in the KLM cockpit starts at 1706:19.39 and ends at 1706:22.06]. The tower is not expecting the KLM to take off as the controller had not yet given clearance.
1706:19.35	Pan Am Copilot Bragg says "We are still taxiing down the runway, the Clipper one seven three six." This radio transmission caused the shrill noise in the KLM cockpit that made the tower's order to "Stand by for takeoff" harder to hear.

Time	Event
1706:21.92	Pan Am requests to communicate with the tower - "Clipper one seven three six."
1706:25.47 to 1706:28.89	Tower – "Ah - Papa Alpha one seven three six report the runway clear." [This was audible in the KLM cockpit.]
1706:29.59	Pan Am – "O.K., will report when we're clear." [This was audible in the KLM cockpit.]
1706:32.43	KLM Flight Engineer Willem Schreuder says "Is he not clear, then?"
1706:34.10	KLM Captain van Zanten says "What do you say?"
1706:34.15	Pan Am Captain Grubbs says "Yup."
1706:34.70	KLM Flight Engineer Schreuder says "Is he not clear that Pan American?"
1706:35.70	KLM Captain van Zanten says "Oh, yes" (emphatically)
1706:39.5	Pan Am sees the approaching lights of the KLM through the fog. Captain Grubbs turns to the left and speeds up in an attempt to get off the runway.
	KLM Captain van Zanten sees the Pan Am and attempts to fly over it, leaving a streak of metal from the plane's tail embedded in the runway.
1706:49	Impact point near C4.
	The nose gear of the KLM passed over the top of the Pan Am, but the #3 engine took off part of the Pan Am upper lounge. The KLM main landing gear smashed into the side of the Pan Am.
	The KLM continued over the Pan Am, then crashed on the runway. It's fuel caught fire, enveloping the aircraft in flames. All 248 persons on board the KLM were killed. The accident was not immediately visible from the control tower, where they only heard one explosion followed by another. Five fire trucks were dispatched. The fire crews initially could not find the fire because of the fog. Upon finding the KLM in flames, the fire crews then became aware of another fire further in the fog. Thinking it was part of the KLM and investigating, they discovered the Pan Am and, because the KLM could not be saved, rushed all fire fighting equipment over to the Pan AM.
1707	People on the Pan Am who were able to find an exit jumped to the ground from a 20-foot height. The airplane was evacuated in about one minute. Fire crews arrived and fought the fire, being successful in keeping some on-board fuel from igniting. Of the 396 people on board the Pan Am, 335 died.
1710	Runway visibility was 1000 meters with intermittent rain and fog patches.

SOURCES: David M. North (1977), "Crash investigation focuses on tapes," *Aviation Week & Space Technology*, April 4, 1977, pp. 33, 37; *Aviation Week & Space Technology* (1978), "Spaniards analyze Tenerife accident," November 20, 1978, pp. 113-121; *Aviation Week & Space Technology* (1978), "Clearances cited in Tenerife collision," November 27, 1978, pp. 67-74; P.A. Roitsch, G.L. Babcock, and W.W. Edmunds (1979), *Human Factors Report on the Tenerife Accident,* Washington, D.C.: Airline Pilots Association; Karl E. Weick (1990), "The vulnerable system: An analysis of the Tenerife air disaster," *Journal of Management* 16: 571-593. The Weick (1990) article provides an interesting organizational behaviour analysis of the Tenerife disaster.

Questions

1. Using the perception model of Exhibit 6.1, describe the possible perceptual causes of the accident.

2. What other factors contributed to the accident?

REFERENCES

Anderson, Julia (1989). "How technology brings blind people into the workplace." *Harvard Business Review* 67(2): 36, 38, 40.

Aviation Week & Space Technology (1978). "Spaniards analyze Tenerife accident." November 20, 1978, pp. 113-121.

Aviation Week & Space Technology (1978). "Clearances cited in Tenerife collision." November 27, 1978, pp. 67-74.

Berger, Peter L., & Thomas Luckmann (1967). *The Social Construction of Reality: A Treatise in the Sociology of Knowledge.* Garden City, NY: Doubleday.

Bruner, Jerome S., & Leo Postman (1949). "On the perception of incongruity: A paradigm." *Journal of Personality* 18: 206-223.

Business Week (1992). "Executive pay." March 30, 1992, pp. 52-58.

Carr, Clay (1992). "Is virtual reality virtually here?" *Training and Development*, October 1992, 37-41.

Cooper, Heather J. (1987). *Carnaval Perpétuel: A Collection of Works by Heather Cooper.* Toronto: Le Carnaval Perpétuel.

Cooper, William H. (1981). "Ubiquitous halo." *Psychological Bulletin* 90: 218-244.

Deaux, Kay (1984). "From individual differences to social categories: Analysis of a decade's research on gender." *American Psychologist* 39: 105-116.

Field, Richard H.G., & David A. Van Seters (1988). "Management By Expectations: The power of positive prophecy." *Journal of General Management* 14: 19-33.

Finkelstein, Sidney, & Donald C. Hambrick (1988). "Chief executive compensation: A synthesis and reconciliation." *Strategic Management Journal* 9: 543-558.

Foucault, Michel (1970). *The Order of Things.* New York: Pantheon Books, Random House.

Gergen, Kenneth J. (1985). "The social constructionist movement in modern psychology." *American Psychologist* 40: 266-275.

Gioia, Dennis A., & Clinton O. Longnecker (1994). "Delving into the dark side: The politics of executive appraisal." *Organizational Dynamics* 22(3): 47-58.

Hellriegel, Don, John W. Slocum, Jr., & Richard W. Woodman (1992). *Organizational Behavior*, 6th edition. St. Paul, MN: West Publishing Company.

Indian and Northern Development Canada (1990). *Indians and Inuit of Canada.* Ottawa: Supply and Services Canada.

Judge, Timothy A., & Gerald R. Ferris (1993). "Social context of performance evaluation decisions." *Academy of Management Journal* 36: 80-105.

Kelley, Harold H. (1973). "The processes of causal attribution." *American Psychologist* 28: 107-128.

Kelley, Harold H., & John L. Michela (1980). "Attribution theory and research." *Annual Review of Psychology* 31: 457-501.

Kelly, Eileen P., Amy Oakes Young, & Lawrence S. Clark (1993). "Sex stereotyping in the workplace: A manager's guide." *Business Horizons* 36(2): 23-29.

Kerr, Jeffrey, & Richard A. Bettis (1987). "Boards of directors, top management compensation, and shareholder returns." *Academy of Management Journal* 30: 645-664.

Longnecker, Clinton O., Henry P. Sims, Jr., & Dennis A. Gioia (1987). "Behind the mask: The politics of employee appraisal." *Academy of Management Executive* 1: 183-193.

MacDonald, Cheryl (1993). "Shedding stereotypes." *McMaster Times* 8(3): 14.

Maclean, Norman (1992). *Young Men and Fire.* Chicago: University of Chicago Press.

Markham, Steven E. (1988). "Pay-for-performance dilemma revisited: Empirical example of the importance of group effects." *Journal of Applied Psychology* 73: 172-180.

McClelland, David C. (1961). *The Achieving Society.* Princeton, NJ: Van Nostrand.

Mitchell, Terence R. (1982). "Attributions and actions: A note of caution." *Journal of Management* 8: 65-74.

Mitchell, Terence R., & James R. Larson, Jr. (1987). *People in Organizations,* Third Edition. New York: McGraw-Hill Book Company.

Mitsutka, Frances (1992). "The biggest headache money can buy." *Canadian Business,* July 1992, pp. 50-54.

Nisbett, Richard E., Craig Caputo, Patricia Legant, and Jeanne Marecek (1973). "Behavior as seen by the actor and as seen by the observer." *Journal of Personality and Social Psychology* 27: 154-164.

North, David M. (1977). "Crash investigation focuses on tapes." *Aviation Week & Space Technology,* April 4, 1977, pp. 33, 37.

Roitsch, P.A., G.L. Babcock, & W.W. Edmunds (1979). *Human Factors Report on the Tenerife Accident.* Washington, D.C.: Airline Pilots Association.

Rosenthal, Robert, & Lenore Jacobson (1968). *Pygmalion in the Classroom.* New York: Holt, Rinehart & Winston.

Stayer, Ralph (1990). "How I learned to let my workers lead." *Harvard Business Review* 68(6): 66-83.

Strati, Antonio (1992). "Aesthetic understanding of organizational life." *Academy of Management Review* 17: 568-581.

Weick, Karl E. (1985). "Cosmos vs. chaos: Sense and nonsense in electronic contexts." *Organizational Dynamics* 14(2): 51-64.

Weick, Karl E. (1990). "The vulnerable system: An analysis of the Tenerife air disaster." *Journal of Management* 16: 571-593.

Weick, Karl E. (1993). "The collapse of sensemaking in organizations: The Mann Gulch disaster." *Administrative Science Quarterly* 38: 628-652.

Weick, Karl E., & Karlene H. Roberts (1993). "Collective mind in organizations: Heedful interrelating on flight decks." *Administrative Science Quarterly* 38: 357-381.

Weiner, Bernard (1985). "An attributional theory of achievement motivation and emotion." *Psychological Review* 92: 548-573.

Weiner, Bernard, Irene Freize, Andy Kukla, Linda Reed, Stanley Rest, & Robert M. Rosenbaum (1971). "Perceiving the causes of success and failure." In Edward E. Jones, David E. Kanhouse, Harold H. Kelley, Richard E. Nisbett, Stuart Valins, & Bernard Weiner (Eds.), *Attribution: Perceiving the Causes of Behavior* (pp. 95-120). Morristown, NJ: General Learning Press.

FURTHER READING

A general look at virtual reality is found in "Virtual Reality" by Howard Rheingold, published in 1991 by Summit Books of New York.

Two articles in a March-April 1993 *Business Horizons* special issue on women in the workplace that deal with attitudes and stereotyping are: Crystal L. Owen and William D. Todor "Attitudes toward women as managers: Still the same" and "Sex stereotyping in the workplace: A manager's guide" by Eileen P. Kelly, Amy Oakes Young, and Lawrence S. Clark.

An interesting though complex study on the CEO pay-performance question is that of Henry L. Tosi, Jr. and Luis R. Gomez-Mejia (1989), "The decoupling of CEO pay and performance: An agency theory perspective," *Administrative Science Quarterly* 34: 169-189.

For a further look at how organizations act in a crisis, see Karl E. Weick's 1988 article titled "Enacted sensemaking in crisis situations," *Journal of Management Studies* 25: 305-317. Other interesting articles in this subject area are "Dyads and triads at 35,000 feet: Factors affecting group process and aircrew performance," *American Psychologist* 39: 885-893 by H. Clayton Foushee; and "The textual approach: Risk and blame in disaster sensemaking" by Robert P. Gephart, Jr. of the University of Alberta, found in the *Academy of Management Journal*, 1993, 38: 1465-1514.

CHAPTER

7

COMMUNICATION

CHAPTER OUTLINE

Verbal and Non-verbal Communication

Influences on Communication

   Physical Aspects of Communication

   Personal Factors Influencing the Communication Process

Improving Communication

   The Resume and Job Interview

   Listening and Responding

Conclusion

QUESTIONS TO CONSIDER

- *What is communication?*

- *How does communication work?*

- *What are the forms of communication and influences on communication?*

- *What are the barriers that exist to effective communication?*

- *How can people at work improve their communications, both verbal and non-verbal?*

It is likely that there is nothing more important to the effective functioning of organizations than communication. Almost everything that is done, how people relate, and how an organization's culture is created involves people communicating with other people. The study of communication is of the utmost importance for anyone who wishes to understand how organizations function and how to be more personally effective in organizations.

We will consider four views of organizational communication in this chapter. They are the psychological, systems-interaction, interpretive-symbolic, and mechanistic perspectives, summarized in Exhibit 7.1.

EXHIBIT 7.1   FOUR PERSPECTIVES ON ORGANIZATIONAL COMMUNICATION

PERSPECTIVE	FOCUS	ASSUMPTIONS
Mechanistic	Message transmission over a channel	There is a linear connection between communicators
		Communication occurs as a chain, the weakest link of which affects communication effectiveness
		Messages are concrete "things" with properties that can be measured
		Communication can be broken down into smaller and smaller units (message bits)
Psychological	How characteristics of individuals affect their communication	Attitudes, cognitions, and perceptions are conceptual filters that affect what information is processed and how it is processed
		The receiver of communication does the filtering
		The informational environment is important in determining communication effectiveness
Interpretive-Symbolic	Role taking	Communication is not only an outcome but can also serve to create and shape the social reality. Communication leads to the creation of shared meanings
		Organizational culture develops from consensual meanings and then serves to shape the next generation of consensual meanings
		Cultural factors are strong influences on the interpretive process
Systems-Interaction	Sequences of communication behaviour between people	The pattern of messages is more important than any one message
		Communication is an act of participation

SOURCE: Based on information in Krone and others (1987)

We saw in Chapter 6 how stimuli from the environment pass through an individual's physical and cognitive filters as those stimuli are perceived and interpreted. Communication is affected by these perceptual and psychological processes. This *psychological* perspective of communication will be briefly considered in this chapter.

Communication can also be considered as an act of participation between people (Krone and others, 1987). What is important in this *systems-interaction* perspective is the sequences and patterns of communication between people. This perspective is useful when considering how a manager and subordinate conduct a performance review, how union and management teams bargain over the terms of a new contract, and how conflict can escalate when groups differ on goals. These topics, as they relate to communication, will be touched on in this chapter. They will be discussed in more detail in Chapter 12.

While the organization's work is performed by individuals and groups, it is communication that is required to plan and coordinate that work. While individuals must be motivated to work, managers help to organize the work, and leaders determine the work that needs to be done, none of these activities would be possible without communication. The lifeblood of the organization is communication: information is carried to all parts of the organization so that decisions and actions may be taken. This is the *mechanistic* perspective on communication. It will be the primary focus of this chapter.

A model of the communication process with a mechanistic perspective is shown as Exhibit 7.2. In this model communication is the transmission of information using verbal and non-verbal signals from a sender to a receiver. Starting with a sender, a message is created and then transmitted over a channel, which is the way the message is delivered. The receiver must then use the perceptual processes described in Chapter 6 to first receive and then decode the message to create a meaning. Noise in this process may make the message difficult to receive or interpret, and perceptual errors may distort the message or its intended meaning.

In two-way communication the receiver then becomes a sender and encodes feedback to the message as decoded and interpreted, not necessarily the message that was initially intended. A channel is then selected for the transmission of feedback to the initial sender.

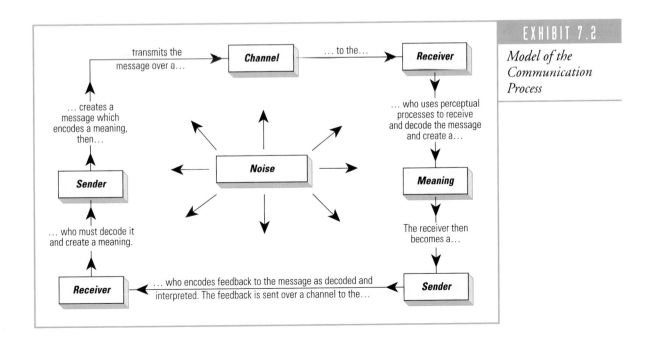

EXHIBIT 7.2

Model of the Communication Process

This message is decoded and its meaning created. Throughout this process noise in transmission can make reception more difficult. The process of communicating has effects on the sender, the receiver, and the functioning of the organization.

Mechanistic communication emphasizes the verbal and routine messages needed to solve the organization's structured, routine, and programmed problems. It can follow the form of an argument. The emphasis is on yes versus no answers, the use of logic, separating facts from conjectures, detecting fallacies in an argument, and winning the argument (Weick & Browning, 1986).

The fourth communication perspective is the *interpretive-symbolic*. This view emphasizes how communication leads to the creation of shared meanings. These shared meanings create the organization's culture, which helps to shape further meaning. Chapter 3 discussed this process in some detail. Organizational culture is partially created by the shared talk of its members. Examples of shared talk given were the language used; myths, sagas, legends, and folktales recounted; and organizational stories told by one member to another. The interpretive-symbolic perspective will be studied further in this chapter.

Narration and storytelling is used by organizational members to capture complex experiences that are combinations of sense, emotion, reason, and imagination. They are a mix of verbal and non-verbal communications, and are used to deal with the complexity of social realities. Stories connect facts and store complex summaries of events, motives, and meanings in retrievable form (Weick & Browning, 1986) so that events and actions in the organization may be understood.

This type of communication is not so much structured as it creates a structure. The process of **structuration** (Ranson and others, 1980) acts to constrain future interactions and interpretations. The telling of narratives and stories in the organization helps to create the organization's culture (Smircich & Morgan, 1982) which then, in turn, affects the behaviour of organizational members.

While the sender of a message may be transmitting a particular meaning to another person, there are other times when the meaning of the communicator's message does not become clear until the message is transmitted. This is **enacted** meaning. According to Karl Weick (see his 1987 book chapter), a person enacting meaning might say "How do I know what I mean until I hear what I say?" This is communication as narration or discourse, communication that creates meaning. For example, in the **Management By Wandering Around** style (Peters & Austin, 1985), a manager who walks around the organization, talking and listening, looking at activities and being looked at by others, is communicating that the members of the organization are important and that what they have to say is important. Without directly saying so, the manager's actions have communicated.

Actions and decisions taken by the organization, what the organization cares about and what its values are, all these create meaning that becomes part of the organization's culture and may then form the basis for stories that summarize the organization's culture. This chapter's *Seeing is Believing* feature examines storytelling in the real, though fictitiously named, Gold Corporation.

Structuration   The process of both being affected by a structure and affecting the structure. Structure affects behaviour but behaviour also affects the structure that will, in turn, affect behaviour.

Enactment   The process of dealing with the environment creates the environment.

Management By Wandering Around (MBWA)   The manager gets out of the office and into the field where, by talking and listening in an unstructured way, she is exposed to organizational events and makes decisions as situations arise.

VERBAL AND NON-VERBAL COMMUNICATION

The verbal and non-verbal aspects of communication may be theoretically distinct from each other, but in practice they are usually combined. A wholly verbal message could be a computer-generated voice on a telephone voice-mail system, if the designers of the voice have eliminated the non-verbal tones and inflections that we have learned to listen for. But even here such a voice usually has a "sex" and an "ethnicity" and so has a non-verbal part to it. A wholly non-verbal message could consist, for example, of a look, a wink, a nod, a smile, a touch, or the utterance of a non-word ("mmm...").

SEEING IS BELIEVING

David Boje (1991) studied the stories told at Gold Corporation, a 35-year-old manufacturer of office supplies with 300 employees and sales of over $50 million annually. Boje tape recorded everyday organizational conversations among seven executives and 23 managers, customers, and vendors, then converted these recordings into line-numbered transcripts. These were then analyzed to find evidence of the performance of organizational stories in the conversation.

Boje found that stories were not simply told, from beginning to end, in order to make the story's moral clear to all who heard it. Instead, he found that the performance of stories was an exchange between organizational members that served to reference, recount, or interpret the meaning of past experience, or to challenge the meaning of a past or anticipated experience. Also, and importantly, Boje concluded that the story text (how the story goes) and its performance (how the story is told) are two sides of the same coin. In performing a story the teller can choose which parts of the text to abbreviate, which to accentuate, and what interpretation is to be made. Therefore, storytelling was found to be an important part of effective communication in organizations. As Boje says:

"These stakeholders tune into stories as real-time data and tell stories to predict, empower, and even fashion change. Customers, vendors, salespeople, and executives in this office-supply distribution company performed stories not only to make sense of their setting but to negotiate alternative interpretations and to accommodate new precedents for decision and action. They tell stories about the past, present, and future to make sense of and manage their struggles with their environment (p. 124)."

We have already described how communication in organizations helps to create the organization's culture. Communication also creates the climate for further organizational communication. Messages about autonomy of individuals, structure, rewards, and the consideration, warmth, and support displayed by members create the conditions for future communications. How these messages are sent, called the meta-message, is also an important influence on the communication climate. For example, a manager could send out a memo to "all staff" describing his new "open-door" policy. The message is that he will be available for discussions and consultations, but the meta-message is "don't bother me—I'm really too busy."

Verbal communication is dependent on the language used to convert meaning into word symbols, slang available in the language, sayings that are understood, like a cultural story, to evoke a particular meaning, and specialized technical words. The following description of the rules of cricket is definitely written in English, but unless you understand the game, it makes no sense at all!

> You have two sides, one out in the field and one in. Each man that's in the side that's in goes out and when he's out he comes in and the next man goes in until he's out. When they are all out the side that's out comes in and the side that's been in goes out and tries to get those coming in out. Sometimes you get men still in and not out. When both sides have been in and out twice, including the not outs, that's the end of the game.

Each of the world's languages (and there are thousands) has words and a grammar that allow some meanings to be easily captured but that make the expression of other meanings more difficult. The aboriginal peoples of North America and Australia, for instance, generally had no real way to translate the European concept of land ownership into their native languages, and so could not grasp the concept so well accepted by the Europeans.

The English language is remarkably flexible; new words, acronyms, and words from other languages are continually being added so that it is continuously evolving (see Case 7.2). Japanese, in contrast, uses one way of phonetic writing for old Japanese words, another phonetic writing style for new "foreign" words, as well as Chinese ideographs.

Shaking hands is an important non-verbal gesture.

Non-verbal communication (NVC) helps the expression of emotions and attitudes toward another person and it helps people to present their own personalities. NVC is also a means to regulate the communication interaction between people—for example a sharp intake of breath in a conversation means "I have something to say" (Argyle, 1975). The following description of nonverbal communication in Japan shows just how important these cues can be.

> Persons who are obviously foreigners in Japan often experience a strange situation: On entering a place where they expect to be served, e.g., a department store, they tend to become "invisible" to the sales personnel. The latter are often loath to start an interaction because they know from experience that foreigners rarely speak Japanese. This can cause them no end of trouble and often makes it necessary to call for a translator, if one is available. They will thus tend to avoid eye contact by studiously looking somewhere else. However, I found after a while that they all had a kind of "lighthouse look" which would sweep across the room to check if the troublesome foreigner was still around. It suddenly occurred to me to bow relatively deeply at the very moment when the saleslady's gaze was passing me. And, sure enough, it did then elicit a reflex reaction: she now had to bow as well, thereby acknowledging my presence and the subsequent obligation to serve me (Morsbach 1988, p. 197).

Non-verbal cues may be organized into seven categories (Knapp, 1978; Baird & Wieting, 1979): the environment, proxemics, postures, gestures, facial expressions, eye behaviour, and vocalics.

The Environment   This is the physical setting in which the communication takes place. It includes the temperature, lighting, colour of the room, the arrangement of furniture, and the attractiveness of the surroundings. Also encompassed are time cues, including time spent waiting, time spent communicating, and evidence that the other has much or little time.

Proxemics   Proxemics is the placement of one person's body relative to someone else's body. Proxemic rules are well understood in every culture, though they vary dramatically between cultures. Middle-eastern cultures favour low interpersonal distance during communication and a direct face-to-face orientation. Anglo North Americans favour a medium interpersonal distance and Japanese a greater distance (presumably due to the necessity of more space for bowing without knocking heads).

Postures   NVC postures have been made famous by books about how to "read" another person's non-verbal posture. For example, leaning toward a speaker can indicate interest and arms folded across the chest can be a sign of being closed to the speaker's ideas.

Gestures   Extremely important in understanding and being understood, gestures add meaning and emotion to communication. Hand, head, and arm gestures are a way to send a message or to add impact to a verbal message. Handshaking, which initially was intended to demonstrate that the hand was not holding a weapon, has evolved into an almost universally understood gesture of friendship. Handshaking is very complex in its variations even within a culture—secret handshakes still exist to help members of a group identify each other—and has major variations between cultures. This chapter's *A Rose by Any Other Name* feature discusses how gestures differ across cultures.

Facial Expressions   Smiling is a universal human means of communication. Various tilts of the head and eyebrow movements are used, often without conscious thought, as a message or as an addition to a verbal message. Cross-culturally, there is little disagreement about the interpretation of expressions of fear, anger, disgust, sadness, or enjoyment (Ekman, 1993).

A ROSE BY ANY OTHER NAME

THE MEANING OF GESTURES AROUND THE WORLD

Nodding the head up and down: As we all know, signals "yes," and shaking it back and forth means "no." In Bulgaria, parts of Greece, Turkey, Iran, and Bengal it is the *reverse.*

Tapping the head with the forefinger: In Argentina and Peru it can mean "I'm thinking." If the tapping is done near the temple, it can mean "That's very intelligent." In North America and other places it can either mean "that person is very intelligent," or "that person is crazy." It all depends on the statement accompanying the gestures. In Holland, if the finger is tapped to the center of *the forehead* it means "He's crazy."

Winking with one eyelid: Among Americans and Europeans signifies some shared secret, but it is regarded as impolite in Hong Kong. In the United States it is also a rather bold, flirtatious gesture, but in Australia it is improper to wink at women.

Pinching the earlobe with the thumb and forefinger: In Brazil is a way of expressing appreciation, as when you wish to signal you have enjoyed a meal. Some Brazilians, to add further emphasis, will reach around over the top of the head and grasp the opposite earlobe.

Rotating the forefinger around in front of the ear: In the United States it usually connotes that someone or something is "crazy"; yet in Argentina, it can be a signal to indicate "You have a telephone call." In the United States the customary way to signal a telephone call is holding an imaginary telephone to the ear or to hold the hand near the ear and stiffly extend the thumb and little finger outward as if to emulate the shape of a phone receiver.

Nose tap: In England means confidentiality, as in "Don't spread this around." In Italy it is more of a friendly warning: "Watch out. Take care."

Cheek screw: Is primarily an Italian gesture of praise, as when observing a pretty girl. Here the extended forefinger is rotated, or turned into the cheek. It is rarely seen or understood—with this meaning—outside of Italy. In Germany, it has an entirely different message: "That's crazy."

Cheek stroke: In Greece, Italy, and Spain means "attractive," and would be one way of signaling "I see a pretty girl." In the United States it can also be a sign of contemplation, as if saying "That's interesting—let me think about that."

The teeth flick: involves placing the thumbnail under the upper teeth and then flicking the thumb and fist outward. It is now primarily an Italian gesture meaning anger or a curse or the equivalent of saying "You are nothing!"

The chin flick: involves brushing the fingernails of one hand under the chin and then continuing in an outward motion, away from the chin. In France and Northern Italy it means "Get lost. You are annoying me." In Southern Italy it is negative but not insulting. It could mean "There is nothing," or "no," or "I cannot."

The OK signal: where the thumb and forefinger form a simple circle, in most societies means "everything is fine," but in France it means "zero" or "worthless," and in Japan it is the signal for "money." In a host of other countries it is considered a very rude gesture.

The thumbs up gesture: is used when hitch-hiking in North America, but in some countries the upright thumb is considered an insult.

Pointing with the index finger: is considered impolite in Japan and China where they favor using the whole open hand. Malaysians prefer pointing with the thumb rather than the forefinger. Among native American Indians it is considered impolite to point with the fingers. Instead, they use pointed lips or their chins.

Extending the forefinger and little finger, like horns, while keeping the other fingers in a fist: At the University of Texas, this represents the horns of a longhorn steer, the school symbol. This same "horn" gesture in Italy means someone is being cuckolded. In some African countries, it is seen as casting a spell or a curse, and in Brazil it means "good luck."

Pointing with your toes: In Thailand the head is considered almost sacred and the foot is considered lowly and inferior. While it seems unreasonable that any of us might be in a situation where we would—or even could—point our toes at someone's head, in Thailand this would be the most grievous insult possible. Another taboo would be putting your feet on a desk or any other piece of furniture.

SOURCE: Axtell, Roger E. (1991), *Gestures: the Do's and Taboo's of Body Language Around the World,* pp. 60-76, 101-107, New York: John Wiley & Sons, Inc. © 1991 by Roger E. Axtell. Reprinted by permission of John Wiley & Sons, Inc.

When communicating by computer message, various symbols have been devised to show the expression that goes along with a written comment. For example, :-) is a smile (look at it sideways), 8-) the smile of a person wearing glasses, :-(is a frown, ;-) a wink, 8-] a state of bliss, and :-^ means the comment was made tongue-in-cheek. Called **emoticons**, they are becoming more and more complex. For instance %*} means very drunk, :-(o) is the symbol for yelling, and a nun might sign her e-mail with the +<:-) emoticon.

Acronyms are also used on computer message networks to pass along non-verbals in the message. ROFL means "Rolling on the Floor Laughing", IMHO is the acronym for "in my humble opinion", TIC is "tongue in cheek", (g) is the symbol for a grin, BTW is "by the way", FWIW is "for what it's worth, OTOH is "on the other hand", and GR&D means "Grinning, Running, & Ducking". One interesting side effect when communicating by computer is that the lack of inhibition can promote strong statements of feeling and opinion. The use of swear words, insults, and name-calling is called "flaming" (Siegel and others, 1986).

Emoticons Combinations of regular alphabet letters and special symbols, usually looked at sideways, that are inserted into electronic mail to indicate the sender's emotions.

Eye Behaviour　　It is said that "the eyes are a window to the soul." Eye contact and where a person is looking are used as strong indicators of interest and enthusiasm. There are many rules within a culture that regulate eye contact. For example, think of the norms for eye contact on a bus, when shaking hands, or when kissing.

Vocalics　　The pitch and pitch variations (how high or low the voice sounds), volume, inflection, enunciation (how the sounds in words are pronounced), and the rate of speech are all used to add meaning. In English, for example, a question is usually signaled by an upward inflection at the end of a sentence. In Australia, however, such an inflection does not always signal a question. This can cause confusion even between English speakers.

Vocalics are often used to show emotion (Baird & Wieting, 1979), as shown in the list below.

- Affection: low pitch, softness, slow rate, regular rhythm, slurred enunciations.
- Anger: loud, fast rate, high pitch, irregular inflection, clipped enunciation.
- Boredom: moderate volume, pitch and rate; monotone inflection.
- Joy: loud volume, high pitch, fast rate, upward inflection, regular rhythm.
- Sadness: soft volume, slow rate, low pitch, downward inflection, slurred enunciation.

As these are not cultural universals, one should expect that different cultures will have arrived at different combinations of vocalics to show common human emotions.

All seven categories of non-verbal cues can be observed in this picture. Find an example of each one.

INFLUENCES ON COMMUNICATION

Communication is affected by both physical and personal factors. Physical aspects of communication include office furnishings and layout; how networks for communication are structured; the direction of communication within those networks; and the media selected for the message (Fulk & Boyd, 1991). The personal side to communication is marked by individual style; differences between males and females; and differences between cultures. As we examine each of these factors, it will be useful for readers to think of examples from their own experience that illustrate how communication was made either more or less effective.

Physical Aspects of Communication

Office Furnishing and Layout

The overall design of a building can serve to define how its inhabitants will interact. If, for example, executives are all located on one floor, usually higher up in a building than other workers, they will tend to see and talk to each other more than the people working directly for them. Employees will usually feel distant from these executives. They will speak of them using company jargon, saying "the 14th floor," for instance, as jargon for the executive group and will venture onto the executive floor only when absolutely necessary. If the actual 14th floor is quiet, with closed doors, deep carpeting, and a receptionist just outside the elevator, few employees will wish to disturb the seeming peace with the message of a problem. Better to write a memo or telephone, most would think.

On the other hand, if people work close to each other and physical offices are such that they must see each other and bump into each other as they go about their work day, differences between them are minimized and communication is made both easier and more likely. The same is true of cafeterias, elevators, and meeting rooms. The greater the separation of organization members into separate physical areas, the more difficult communication is made between members.

In Chapter 6 we discussed perception and the power of managing the first impressions of others, especially through the clothes that one wears. A person's work station, cubicle, desk, or office can also send out strong messages, intended or unintended, about the occupant. First and foremost in importance is the concept of "turf" or home ground. An individual's personal space in the organization is his home turf, where he is most at home and most powerful. How communication proceeds will likely be very different if it takes place in the office of the higher authority individual, the lower authority person, or in a "neutral ground" conference room.

Office furnishings and their arrangement can also affect communication. When two people sit across a desk from each other the situation is formal: a job interview, a performance review, a review of progress on a project, etc. Here the physical situation is a clear reminder to both parties that communication is to be formal, with differences in position and power recognized. In a larger office there is often a couch, arm chairs, and a coffee table grouped together. When people sit down at this location for a meeting, the message is that communication will be more informal, less direct, and less likely to have immediate consequences. Offices can therefore be arranged for different kinds of communication in different situations.

Office furnishings also send messages, by themselves, to those entering. Large organizations assign office furniture by the organizational rank of the occupant. Those at the bottom of the hierarchy in North American organizations will usually share an office or a large room with several others. They will have little private space and furnishings will be inexpensive. As one moves up the hierarchy personal space increases and furnishings become more expensive. Desks which were all metal at the lowest positions become simulated wood construction, then wood veneer, then solid wood or wood and glass. At the highest ranks executives may not even have desks, preferring to imply that they have risen above such needs (Korda, 1975).

Personal possessions brought to the office are potent communicators about the owner. They speak to others about what the owner finds important and will be interpreted by others as a message. Their quality, first, suggests organizational level. Framed photographs, especially enlargements hung on a wall, indicate taste and a willingness to spend money to achieve quality, attributes not found with posters thumbtacked to the wall. Pictures of family, hobbies, and the like send a message of what the person cares about and how she spends her time outside the office. Important here is the realization that how an office is "dressed," both in furnishings and their placement and in personal possessions, will tell visitors to that office what to expect from the occupant.

Networks

People in organizations are linked together in communication networks that allow members to communicate with certain other members. Perhaps we are most familiar with the *all channel* network of a small group, where everyone can communicate to everyone else in the group. Another common network is the *inverted "Y,"* the normal hierarchy wherein each member communicates to the person above and the person(s) below, but levels are not skipped when communicating up or down the organization. Three other networks that have been studied are the wheel, the chain, and the circle. These are shown in Exhibit 7.3 for a five-person group.

EXHIBIT 7.3

Communication Network Characteristics

Network Diagram					
Network	Wheel	"Y"	Chain	Circle	All Channel
Average Member Satisfaction	Low	Low	Moderate	High	High
Leadership Emergence	Center	Center	Center	No Pattern	No Pattern
Centralization	High	High	Moderate	Low	Low
Errors with Simple Tasks	Low	Low	Moderate	Higher	Higher
Organizational Example	Taxi Dispatch	Hierarchy in Manufacturing Organization	Assembly Line	24-Hour Shift Workers	Interacting Groups

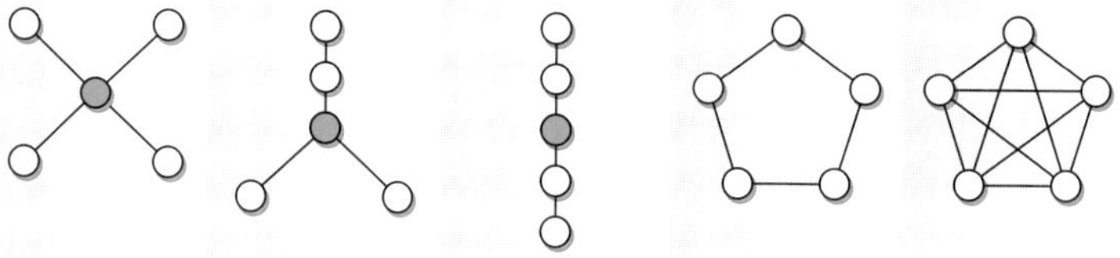

SOURCE: Based on information in Bavelas (1950), Leavitt (1951), and Shaw (1964).

In the *wheel network* a central person can communicate to each other person, but they cannot talk to each other except through the centre. A taxi dispatcher, for instance, occupies the centre of a wheel and has a high degree of central control over information. However, drivers who equip themselves with cellular telephones and take pick-up calls directly from their regular customers can bypass the dispatcher by creating their own communication network.

In a *chain network*, individuals can communicate only to the two people next to them in the chain (or only one other person for the person at the end of the chain). For example, people on an assembly line may be restricted in who they can talk to by their physical location on the line. A *circle network* is a closed chain and may be illustrated by workers dividing a 24-hour shift. Each person coming on shift meets the worker they are replacing and when going off shift meets the one who is their replacement.

Network research began with individuals working on artificial tasks in behavioural laboratories (for example Bavelas, 1950; Leavitt, 1951), where the centralization of networks was examined for its effects on leadership emergence and member satisfaction.

Now that computer communication networks are becoming more important both within and across organizations, a person's link into the network is a real and important consideration. The person at the hub of a wheel network, the network manager, can expect to be very satisfied with communications and to assume a position of leadership within the network, even though average member satisfaction with communication may be low. While it is theoretically possible for all members of a computer network to send messages to all others (the all-channel network), such a system is inefficient when there are a large number people on the network.

Direction of Communication Within Networks

Communication may be vertical (up or down the organization's hierarchy), lateral, or diagonal. Vertical communication is marked in North America by **filtering**. The filtering process is one in which communicators decide what information to send and what to withhold. In the upward direction, information is summarized and codified so that only a part of the whole is transmitted. When filtering is effective it helps to reduce **information overload**, the problem of having too much information to be able to cognitively understand it all.

Filtering Process whereby information is summarized, codified, or withheld so that only a part of the whole is transmitted.

Information overload The problem of having too much information to be able to cognitively understand it all.

A manager and his colleague communicate in the control room of a mill.

A computer printout, for example, that details all the sales results for 100 stores can be too much for one person to easily comprehend. Instead, a cover page listing of only those branches that are over or under budgeted sales by more than 10% is a filter (called an exception report) than can make comprehension easier. But upward filtering can make communication less effective when subordinates pass along the good news about organizational activities and results while withholding the bad. Downward filtering occurs when important information is withheld from lower-level subordinates. The result is that they do not know the "big picture" and decision making is more difficult.

Lateral communications among people at the same level in the organization are useful for increasing coordination between individuals and departments. Diagonal communication crosses both horizontal and vertical boundaries. Diagonal communication is uncommon in mechanistic organizations, where it is seen as outside the normal vertical and horizontal flows of information, and therefore a threat to the established communication system. Diagonal flows of information would be more common and more accepted in organic organizations.

But communications can flow across all levels and boundaries via the **grapevine**. This is an informal network that can use any or all media available (i.e., face-to-face, computer messaging, telex, etc.), operating outside the usual bounds of the organization. Communications on the grapevine can take the form of gossip (Noon & Delbridge, 1993), and may, when unchecked, give rise to rumours. **Rumour** as a form of communication has certainly existed for many thousands of years. Case 7.1 offers a chance to discuss how best to deal with a rumour in an organization.

Grapevine An informal network for communication within and outside of the organization.

Rumour Unverified information circulating by the grapevine in an organization.

Media

Media convey data *and* meaning (Sitkin and others, 1992). Each medium has its own **meta-message**, the larger message. For instance, on receipt of a telegram the message is attended to on the level of its meaning and on the meta-level of how it was sent. A telegram implies great importance and urgency.

An electronic mail, or **e-mail**, message sent by a computer network or a telex can imply a more routine transmission of information and less urgency for reply. Leaving a message on a telephone answering machine or voice mail system implies that the matter is of some urgency, less formal, and that a personal reply is required.

Because faxed messages are a newer medium, etiquette is still being established. At the moment faxing is used for the transmission of both urgent and routine material. A cutting edge use of fax technology is fax broadcasting. The originator of the fax can send a message to a service company, which then broadcasts the message to as many as 1600 fax machines at the same time (see Gutman, 1994). The benefit of this medium is that everyone who needs to receive a fax gets it at the same time. This can be crucial for time sensitive material such as stock market analysis distributed to customers via fax. The company last on the list of 200 subscribers to a stock market newsletter does not want to wait for over two hours to receive the latest news.

Mail is definitely seen as the least urgent of media. A letter delivered by mail is formal, bearing a true signature and being a recognized legal document. Registered mail is one of the most formal methods of message delivery, as proof of message receipt is provided. With registered mail the receiver cannot lie and say the message was lost in the mail or that the fax was garbled in transmission.

Personal delivery of a letter is the most formal communication method. Delivery by courier still implies that great time urgency is felt by the sender. Couriered documents are usually bulky or legal documents and usually do not demand an immediate reply.

Meta-message The larger message within which the smaller message is contained.

E-mail Electronic mail sent by a computer network.

The telephone has been an informal medium that implies that personal contact is important in the sending of the message. The message sender has had control in when to initiate this contact. The message receiver has often been willing to give the telephone message priority over a face-to-face meeting. We have likely all had the experience of talking to someone who interrupts the conversation to answer the telephone! But advances in telecommunications technology have changed the relationship between the caller and the called. Call display, call block, call return, and other services mean that the person called can now know who called, block some incoming calls, and return calls from an unknown source (see this chapter's *A Little Knowledge* feature for more information).

A LITTLE KNOWLEDGE

I am on the phone or away from my desk

Once it was as simple as this. I sat at my desk. The phone rang. I answered it. It is a memory I have tried to erase.

Now when the phone rings, I first read the number on my Caller I.D. and decide whether to pick it up. If I'm on the phone already, I see the incoming call and decide who is more important, the person I'm talking to or the person I could talk to. I triage and hit the "drop" button, sacrificing line one for line two. Or I conference the new one in. They talk. I hit "mute" to chat with a deskmate, then "hold" to take line three.

Sometimes I let the calls go unanswered, then scroll through my messages in voice mail, deleting some with a satisfying terminality, saving others. I retrieve messages from airports and planes, punching in encrypted number sequences, wielding an entirely unfamiliar phone with the same deftness as I would my own.

There are occasions when I hear my pre-programmed personalized phone ring from across the room. I come running too late to see the number on Caller I.D., and the caller doesn't leave a message. So I hit "answer call," which immediately dials back the number that just dialed me. "You called?" I ask innocently, as if I do not recognize the inherent belligerence of the act. Or perhaps a caller irritates. I program that number into "Call block," meaning that whenever they phone again a computer politely informs them that I will not be taking their call. Sure, they can try another number, but I have forwarded my calls from my office to my home, putting identical voice mail messages on each phone to obscure my true whereabouts. The calls bounce from one to the other in a fruitless loop. The notion that a telephone number corresponds to a physical location has been irrevocably shattered. I could be anywhere.

These new telephone services are not simple gadgets. They are the basis of a revolutionary shift in power from the caller to the called.

Take my voice mail. It functions like a real secretary, only better. A real secretary would give away far too much information, eroding whatever slim advantage I have over the person interrupting my day: "Mr. Gladwell is on the phone." "Mr. Gladwell is at lunch until 2 o'clock." A real secretary might crack under the relentless charm of some stranger and reveal critical details of where I am and when I'll be back. Voice mail cannot do that. It is unalterably unambiguous. "I am on the phone or away from my desk," my message says, which is as functionally tautological as "I am at work or I am not at work," "I may answer your call or I may not answer your call."

Caller I.D. takes me one step further. As the numbers roll across my screen, I purge the undesirable. 301-234-7645 is a man who crossed me once. I will never pick up that call. 703-332-8355 is my real estate agent. 202-443-1130 brings a moment of uncertainty. The 443 summons the image of an old girlfriend, the 1130 is the suffix of my mother's number. The numerated images merge in a brief, Oedipal moment.

There are those who do not understand these changes. Some civil libertarians fret that Caller I.D. will sacrifice the anonymity of those who want to leak important information, an objection that manages to overlook both the invention of the pay phone and the fact that no one other than the ten journalists still writing about the Warren Commission ever gets anonymous calls.

Nor does the phone company fully comprehend what all this means. The reason the phone company likes Caller I.D. is that it permits the public correction of those who would use the phone improperly, exposing those who would hide behind the anonymity of a phone call. By the same reasoning, phone companies have promoted the abomination known as call waiting, which permits any incoming caller to hijack any ongoing phone conversation with impunity. Their goal is to break down the barriers of the conventional phone call, to make telephone conversation as unstructured and fluid as face-to-face conversation, to let participants come and go freely.

They are totally wrong. The true appeal of advances in phone technology is that they permit us to move in exactly the opposite direction—to use the phone to erect new barriers, to get closer to our phones and farther from those who would use them to get to us.

It is a notion rich with paradox. My voice mail liberates me from the neatly stacked rows of messages on a receptionist's desk and from the blinking black box in the hallway of my apartment. It means my messages have ceased to have any physical reality and spring ex nihilo from any receiver anywhere. But it also means that I can never escape my messages. So long as there is a pay phone within sight or a cellular phone in my pocket they are always with me, swirling about in electronic hyperspace.

Why is this so appealing? Perhaps it is that I am selfishly searching for a more perfectly asymmetrical conversation, where others call and I reap the ego gratification of them having called. Perhaps it is that I am obsessively searching for relief from the anxiety associated with not knowing who is trying to reach me without making the commitment to actually take any calls. Or perhaps it is something even more basic than this. Maybe I just don't like telephones and would prefer to reserve my most important communications for something more real and more personal.

Take fax machines, for example. I have three separate numbers ....

SOURCE: Malcolm Gladwell (1992), "Speed dialer," *The New Republic* 207(25): 9-10. Reprinted by permission of The New Republic.

The widespread use of cellular telephone and computerized communication networks has now changed the nature of the telephone as a work aid. The telephone is losing its personal and immediate impact and becoming a more formal tool. More routine work is done by cellular phone. People can be reached wherever they are, even around the world.

For example, a salesperson on the road can use a cellular phone in the car to contact buyers, suppliers, and a support person at head office who is tied into the computer systems that track orders and deliveries (Falvey, 1989). The telephone is used as a tool to get the latest information to the salesperson, to schedule appointments, and to relay data on orders and information on clients back to head office. The sales agent is using the telephone not as an informal way to chat but as an indispensable tool to perform the work.

Because some cellular communications are over public airwaves and are not scrambled, the information relayed is non-confidential and therefore must become more guarded and formal. Cellular telephones are also used to connect with computer modems, creating the cellular computer, able to connect to home-office programs and databases without hard telephone links; and to fax machines so that faxes may be received anywhere cellular service is provided.

Teleconferencing

A meeting held between people who are in different locations.

Teleconferencing is a method in use to connect a small to large number of people so that they can talk together. Fax machines can also be connected so that documents can be distributed to everyone in the conference at once. Teleconferencing can save organizations money by reducing travel costs. It can also be a strategic method used by organizations to reach their employees, customers, and clients (Warshaw, 1993).

The final medium of communication that we will discuss is the face-to-face meeting. As previously mentioned, such a meeting can be formal or informal, vertical, horizontal, or diagonal, but it is always the richest communication medium. Here the full play of verbal and non-verbal cues is available to both sender and receiver.

Meetings of course take place in offices and boardrooms, but many are the more informal meetings in the hallways at work (by chance or by design), breakfast, lunch, or dinner meetings, and discussions that take place at "the club" or on the golf course. These more informal meetings should not be underestimated for their importance to activities at work, for it is here that many relationships are built and deals are made.

Organizational members who are (or have been) excluded from such meetings by their sex, age, or race are discriminated against because they do not have the same opportunities to communicate as do others. This discrimination can be as simple as the men at a meeting taking a washroom break and continuing to discuss business while in the washroom, when women present at the meeting are excluded. Even if washroom discussions were not planned, those excluded have every right to feel left out of the full communication process.

Communication media have different capacities for carrying the cultural values of the organization. Exhibit 7.4 illustrates how four diverse communication media can function as symbols of cultural values or as the carriers of symbolic meaning.

EXHIBIT 7.4   ILLUSTRATIONS OF SYMBOL CARRYING CAPACITIES OF MEDIA

COMMUNICATION MEDIUM AND FUNCTION	FREQUENTLY CITED CULTURAL VALUES		
	WE ARE INNOVATIVE	WE ARE EFFICIENT	WE CARE ABOUT TREATING OUR EMPLOYEES WELL AND FAIRLY
Written materials as symbol	Use of latest desktop publishing features in producing written materials Use of clearly innovative designs (e.g., layout or materials)	Time sheets with quarter-hour increments Formal MBO planning and review procedures Simple, inexpensive formats and materials	Written "Employee Bill of Rights" Formal due process procedures Photos of low-level employees in corporate annual reports
Written materials as the carrier of symbolic meaning	Pictures of innovative products or modern facilities Description of comparative statistics on innovation (e.g., number of patents)	Graphs and pictures to depict cost savings Description of productivity measures(e.g., comparison of output per employee)	Inclusion of stories illustrating company actions on behalf of employees Analysis of equity data and comparative benefits offered employees
Electronic mail (e-mail) as symbol	Use of latest equipment to signify leading-edge procedures Paper-free "office of the future"	Group mail lists and community files "Paper free" office	Universal access and standardization illustrate status equality
Electronic mail as the carrier of symbolic meaning	Permits ready access to entire user group regardless of schedules (i.e., communication is asynchronous)	Meeting announcements Asynchronous communication To handle routine announcements and asynchronous communication	Personalized message from executives could be prepared by secretary Permits rapid deployment of apparently personal message

(continued on next page)

COMMUNICATION MEDIUM AND FUNCTION	FREQUENTLY CITED CULTURAL VALUES		
	WE ARE INNOVATIVE	WE ARE EFFICIENT	WE CARE ABOUT TREATING OUR EMPLOYEES WELL AND FAIRLY
Large group meetings as symbol	High-tech presentation modes Training or conferences via TV networks with satellite links	Use of agenda techniques Group process techniques	Personal time allocated by executives Demonstrates high level of concern (e.g., after a crisis) Ceremonial leader sessions, "roasts," or retirement dinners
Large group meetings as the carrier of symbolic meaning	Facilitates idea generation and exchange	Facilitates rapid development of shared understanding of efficiency goals and standards	Opportunity to gripe and to get response to personal questions Permits choreographed demonstration of concern One-way nonverbal expression of attitudes
Face-to-face meetings as symbol	Leader in novel communication or socialization practices (e.g., mentoring)	Ad hoc meetings in the hall Very brief time allotments Use of agendas for meeting	Personal attention to individual Personal time allocation by executive Ceremonial review, condolence calls
Face-to-face meetings as the carrier of symbolic meaning	Permits free-flowing idea exchange Nonpublic, reversible setting for revealing "trial balloon" ideas	Useful for in-process tailoring of information to individual needs	Opportunity for one-on-one exchange Facilitates off-the-record disclosures Permits nonverbal exchange Use of stories to illustrate concern

SOURCE: Adapted/Reprinted from Sim B. Sitkin, Kathleen M. Sutcliffe, and John R. Barrios-Choplin (1992), "A dual-capacity model of communication media choice in organizations," *Human Communication Research* 18: 574-575. Reprinted by permission of the International Communication Association.

Robert Lengel and Richard Daft (1988) studied the selection of different communication media for different messages. They ordered different communication media on a continuum of their richness—their capacity to convey information. Lengel and Daft hypothesized that communication would be most effective when rich media are used for nonroutine organizational messages and when lean media are used to transmit routine messages (see Exhibit 7.5).

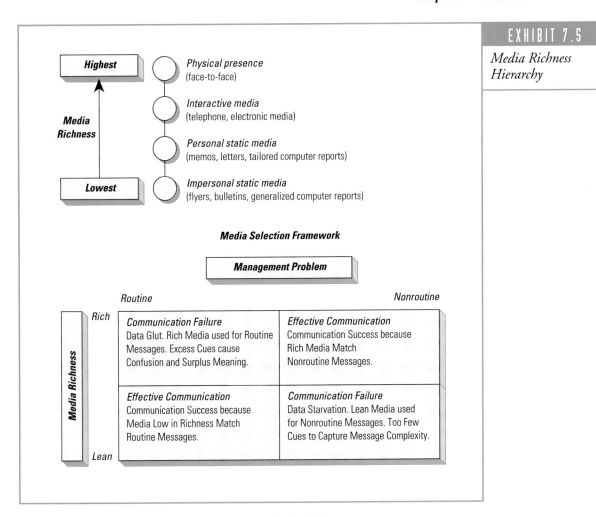

EXHIBIT 7.5

Media Richness Hierarchy

SOURCE: Lengel & Daft (1988), pp. 226 & 227. Reprinted by permission of the Academy of Management.

In their study of 95 managers in a petrochemical company, they found that high performing managers were more sensitive to the media they used for the message they had to send than were low performing managers. Their conclusion was that media selection is an important skill for executives, one that can be learned in order to improve organizational performance.

Personal Factors Influencing the Communication Process

Individuals differ in how they communicate because of their culture, their gender, and how they have learned to perceive the world. First, cultures differ not only in their verbal languages, but their non-verbal languages as well. As we saw earlier in this chapter, there are a variety of gestures that are only used in certain cultures or whose meaning changes between cultures.

But just as no one knows more than a small percentage of all the world's languages, no one knows how to interpret gestures in all the world's cultures. A person can only learn to communicate verbally and non-verbally with experience in a given culture. Even among the predominantly English-speaking nations of the world there are many variations in the words used. For example, what in Canada and the United States is called a toilet is in Australia a dunny and in England often called a loo.

As we saw in Chapter 5, because of differences in socialization, females are, on average, better than males at communicating with others. While males growing up in Canada and the U.S. are generally encouraged to *do things* with other males, especially games and sports, females are generally encouraged to *talk about things* and build relationships. This can be an advantage for females when communication is important, but selection and promotion systems in organizations that discriminate against females will lessen this advantage. Communication between males and females can be made more difficult if the individuals are using a different basis for understanding events and relationships.

Neuro-linguistic pro-gramming (NLP) The idea that people differ on how they interpret the world that surrounds them. Some people rely on feeling, some on visual cues, and some on hearing.

Neuro-linguistic programming (NLP) takes this perspective further, in that people are thought to differ on the basis of their interpretation of the world that surrounds them. In this theory it is proposed that some people rely on feeling, some on visual cues, and some on hearing. When communicating they tend to show which system is in use by word references to one of these senses.

For example, when the message is "I understand you," a person who relies on feelings might say "What you are saying feels right to me," a person using more visual sensing might instead say "I see what you are saying," whereas a person relying on the auditory sense might say "I hear you clearly" (Bandler & Grinder, 1979). The thinking in NLP is that more effective communication and better understanding between two people can be facilitated when they use a consistent basis for talking about their world.

IMPROVING COMMUNICATION

There is no doubt that skill at communication is one of the most important factors in both being hired into an organization and in being effective once in the organization. Exhibit 7.6 lists the factors that personnel managers in 1983 considered important in helping a graduate obtain employment. They rated oral and written communication skills ahead of other important factors such as work experience and technical competence.

These skills are still important today. A 1993 survey of 56 recruiters from *Fortune 500* organizations found that student interview performance was the most important factor in evaluating both schools and their students (Kane, 1993). This factor was rated more important than the previous work experience of students and student grade point averages. The factor rated as most critical to student performance in the interview was communication skills.

Overall, what were these recruiters looking for in an MBA student? The top three factors were strong interpersonal skills, strong communication skills, and team oriented skills. These were rated ahead of job experience and technical skills (Kane, 1993, Table 1). This was true for recruiters looking for people to fill general management positions, commissioned sales positions, and also for functional area positions in operations, finance, accounting, or marketing.

Public speaking is an important oral communication skill. Speaking in front of groups is widely regarded as one of the most difficult and stress producing situations that is commonly faced in business. And yet everyone, at one time or another, will have to make a public speech. Accordingly, speaking in the classroom is the subject of this chapter's *On the One Hand* feature.

EXHIBIT 7.6   FACTORS CONSIDERED IMPORTANT IN
OBTAINING EMPLOYMENT, 1983

Following are the rankings in 1983 of factors and skills considered important by personnel managers in helping business graduates to obtain employment

RANK/SCORE	FACTOR/SKILL	SCORE
1.	Oral communication skills	6.294
2.	Written communication skills	6.176
3.	Work experience	5.706
4.	Energy level (enthusiasm)	5.706
5.	Technical competence	5.647
6.	Persistence/determination	5.529
7.	Dress/grooming	5.235
8.	Personality	5.118
9.	Resume	5.118
10.	Appearance	5.000
11.	Poise	4.882
12.	Specific degree held (finance, marketing, (accounting, etc.)	4.867
13.	Grade point average	4.235
14.	Letters of recommendation	4.059
15.	Interview skills	4.059
16.	Accreditation of the school/college	3.941
17.	Social graces	3.824
18.	Physical characteristics	3.647
19.	School attended	2.941

SOURCE: Benson (1983), p. 63. Adapted/Reprinted, by permission of publisher, from PERSONNEL, July-August 1983. © 1983 American Management Association, New York. All rights reserved.

This section of the chapter will present important advice on how to improve your communications skills. We hope that these points will help you to obtain the job you desire and to be successful in that job. The categories we will discuss are: (1) The resume and job interview; and (2) listening and responding.

The Resume and Job Interview

In times of job shortages and high unemployment, company personnel specialists may receive hundreds of applications for one advertised job. Their task is to sort through this tall stack of resumes in order to find the few individuals who will be called in for a personal interview. It is clear, then, that your resume must stand out enough that your strengths are noticed. The key parts of the resume are who I am, what I can do, where I have worked and studied, when this work and studying took place, and why the employer should interview me.

1. Who I am: Name, address, and telephone numbers are included here.
2. What I can do: List your skills and abilities, along with what work you can do to help the employer now and in the longer run.
3. Where I have worked and studied: Describe your job experience, what you learned, actions you took on the job, schooling, degrees, diplomas and awards, key courses taken or major field of study.
4. When this work and studying took place: Do not leave any gaps in schooling and work uncovered.
5. Why the employer should interview me. Explain why you can bring something extra to the job, how you can make a positive difference to the employer's organization.

A covering letter must be sent along with the resume. This chapter's *A Word to the Wise* feature presents an excerpt from Margot Northey's 1986 book "Impact: A Guide to Business Communication," which offers explicit and useful guidelines for the job applicant. For both the resume and covering letter, it can be helpful to use a word processing program that checks spelling and grammar so that small but glaring errors do not slip through the proofreading process.

ON THE ONE HAND . . .

The following words of a business student tell what it felt like to make a three minute speech to a class.

"The day of the speech was a day that I didn't want to see at all. Throughout that day, all that occupied my mind was the speech. As three o'clock came near, I began to feel the pressure building up inside of me. When the time came to present my speech I felt like crawling under a giant rock to hide away so no one could find me. However, there was no stopping now and besides, everyone had to go through with it. While writing my name on the board, I felt all eyes on me and didn't want to turn around to face the fourteen sets of fixed eyes. To my surprise everyone was attentive and ready to hear me speak. As I began to talk, I felt everything going wrong from stuttering and forgetting parts of the speech, to feeling a hot red flush across my face. Those three minutes were the slowest moving minutes that I have ever seen go by. However, as the speech progressed I became more comfortable with myself and the audience in front of me. If you can see that they are interested in your speech and there is good eye contact, then the fear can easily be overcome. The greatest relief was to finally finish the speech and sit back to relax and watch others experience similar feelings. It was as if someone had released all the pressure out of me. To conclude, all I can say is don't be nervous, get up to the front of the class and think of everyone as your friends. Believe me, all the stress that I went through on account of a three minute speech was not worth it."

ON THE OTHER HAND . . .

It is important to realize that you will be nervous, that you may feel sweaty, short of breath, and even hear your heart pounding; but your audience will not see you as being as nervous as you feel! Use your nervous tension to work for you, as a way to add spark and life to the beginning of your talk, and expect that as you keep talking you will relax and will feel less nervous. Prepare your speech, but don't read it word-for-word. Keep some spontaneity in your presentation and make eye contact with your audience—they are with you and want you to succeed. Use some motion and gestures to enliven your talk. Also, pay attention to how much time has gone by since you began, because time can seem to go more slowly or more quickly when you are speaking—it depends on the person. With practice, speaking in front of a group will become less daunting and even enjoyable, though some nervousness can be expected even for seasoned speakers.

For further detailed tips about speechmaking, see the book by Brent Filson (1991). Some of his ideas are to know yourself and your audience, to be yourself, to use the question and answer session after your speech to make some of your points, and to sell the one main idea that you want your audience to leave with.

A WORD TO THE WISE

THE COVERING LETTER

A covering letter should do more than state "Here's my application and resume." It should be the primary attention-getter, making the reader want to examine the resume. Can you imagine a prospective employer, with a stack of applications on the desk, wanting to read the following applicant's resume?

> *Dear Sir:*
>
> *I am applying for the job in your sales department, which you advertised. I am graduating from college this year and would like a job in sales. The enclosed resume gives my qualifications for that kind of work. I hope you will think I am suitable and that I will hear from you soon.*
>
> *Yours truly,*

Not only is this an I-centred letter but it provides no particular reason for the employer to hire the applicant. Your covering letter must do a better job. Aside from what you say, the way you say it matters: a well-written letter reveals important communications skills.

The following guidelines for a covering letter, like those for other letters, are not hard-and-fast rules. Applicants should not be like cookie-cutters, producing identical products. Feel free to express your own personality, as long as you remember the reason for writing and the reader you hope to influence.

1. *Get the reader's attention.* Try to say something that will make the reader want to read on. This could be an outstanding qualification or a reason for your interest in the firm. Here are some examples:

   The article on your firm in Canadian Business suggested that you may be expanding. Are you looking for a dynamic sales person?

   As a prize-winning English student, I believe my skill as a writer would be a useful attribute in your public affairs department.

   Name-dropping is another attention getter: if someone respected by the employer has suggested you make the application or is willing to vouch for you, mention the person right at the beginning; for example, "Arthur Stone suggested I get in touch with you," or "Arthur Stone has told me that your company regularly hires students as summer office help."

2. *State your purpose.* You want the reader to know early in the letter that you are applying for a job. Don't beat around the bush and merely imply that you want

employment—be specific. If you are responding to an advertised opening; say so. If your application is unsolicited, indicate the type of work you are applying for. Remember that a reader who is uncertain about your purpose is unlikely to act.

3. *Give a brief summation of your selling points.* You may create a second paragraph for this part, but keep it as short as possible. A covering letter should not exceed a page. The shorter the better—as long as it creates interest in you. Here are some tips:

   - Link your skills to the employer's needs. Don't just restate part of your resume, but adapt it to the company or organization. Focus not on how the job would help you but on how you can help the employer. If you were a surveyor looking for summer help, which sentence from a surveying student would appeal to you most?

     _ *I would like to work for a surveyor this summer to up-grade my qualifications and gain some practical experience.*

     _ *I believe the courses in surveying I have taken will help me to make a useful contribution to your summer surveying work.*

   - *Sell yourself without seeming egotistical.* This may seem a tall order, but you can emphasize strengths in a sincere way. First of all, don't boast. State your attributes simply, without exaggeration or a lot of intensifying adjectives. For example, instead of saying "I am extremely responsible," or "I can fill completely all your expectations" (a statement which presumes you can read the employer's mind), reveal why you can do the job well. In other words, try to use facts that speak for themselves rather than make claims:

     ✗ *I have extraordinary talent in mathematics.*
     ✓ *"I have consistently achieved high marks in mathematics."*
     ✗ *I am a very good salesperson.*
     ✓ *Last summer, although one of the youngest salespeople in the store, I had the second highest sales total.*

   - *Try to bury the "I's".* When writing an application letter, it's impossible to avoid using "I" repeatedly. After all, the letter is about you. You can make the first-person pronoun less prominent, however, by placing something in front of it. Rather than putting it in a position of emphasis at the beginning of the sentence, bury it in the middle.

✗ *I worked for an accountancy firm last summer.*

✓ *Last summer I worked for an accountancy firm.*

You needn't switch the order in all instances, but you can easily prevent a string of "I" beginnings.

- *Place any weaknesses in a subordinate position.* Most of the time your covering letter or resume will not mention the weak areas of your background. In an advertised job opening, however, you may be asked to provide specific information that is not a selling point for you—information such as present employment or work experience in a specific field. If you must include something you don't want to emphasize, try putting it in a subordinate position clause, with a main clause emphasizing a more positive point.

  ✗ *"Unfortunately I have never worked in a job requiring accounting"*

  ✓ *"Although I have not had an accounting job, I have taken four accounting courses, and have the knowledge to perform well in your office."*

- *Don't apologize.* If you don't think you can do a specific job, don't apply for it. If you think you can, be confident in outlining your qualifications. Avoid apologetic phrases, such as "I'm sorry," "I regret," or "unfortunately" when referring to your background or skills.

4. *Ask for an interview.* Applicants often forget to take this step. But since an interview is usually an essential stage in the hiring process, you need to press for one. You can indicate specific days or times when you will be available.

As a general practice, mention that you will telephone the employer rather than ask the employer to get in touch with you. Unless your application is one of hundreds routinely received (for example, an application for a summer job with a government department or with a large manufacturing plant), such a telephone call will not be considered a nuisance. As long as you are polite, you will appear eager rather than pushy.

Source: Northey (1986), pp. 128-130. Reproduced by permission of Prentice Hall Canada, Inc.

The most important advice for achieving effective communication in any business writing, including the resume and covering letter, is to plan what information you wish to transmit, to organize it so that the receiver can order it in "chunks" that are more easily processed, and to use language that can be understood by the intended target of your message. The writer who has trouble getting started should look at the tip given in this chapter's *Overboard* cartoon.

While content in any message is of primary importance, presentation is vital as well. One without the other means either that your message will attract little attention because of poor presentation or that it will be discounted because it lacks depth and meaning. Therefore, any report, letter, or resume must effectively balance these two sides—the verbal message and the non-verbal message.

The job interview is the next step in receiving a job offer. The interview is a decision making meeting. First impressions are critical. Dress appropriately for the job under consideration and be prepared to answer the interviewer's difficult questions.

Know your resume inside-out, since it is often the starting point for the interview. You should also know something about the company and why you want to work there. A list of 10 factors considered important by organizational recruiters in evaluating student's interview performance is shown as Exhibit 7.7. Note again that the most critical factor in student interview performance was communication skills.

Finally, the interviewee needs to be aware of the script for the interview. There is a generalized sequence of events that will occur and that you can prepare for. An interview script for a professional job in Canada most likely includes shaking hands while saying hello, sitting down and getting comfortable, polite social conversation about the weather or hobbies, then questions/answers related to the job and the interviewee, questions asked by the interviewee, and shaking hands while saying goodbye.

EXHIBIT 7.7   EVALUATING STUDENTS' INTERVIEW
PERFORMANCES

MEAN SCORE	
4.82	Communication skills
4.52	Presentation skills
4.49	Energy and enthusiasm
4.29	Confidence
4.21	Self-knowledge/goals
4.04	Eye contact
3.93	Appearance
3.80	Questions asked by the student
3.64	Posture
3.63	Knowledge of that organization

NOTE: These ratings were made on a scale of 1 ="Not important at all"; 2 ="Slightly important";
3 ="Moderately important"; 4 ="Very important"; and 5 ="Extremely important".

SOURCE: Kane (1993), p. 68. Reprinted from *Business Horizons*, January-February 1993. Copyright © 1993 by the Foundation for the School of
Business at Indiana University. Used with permission.

It is important to note that the interviewee can be proactive in the interview. There is no
rule that the interviewer is proactive, asking most of the questions, while the interviewee is reactive, responding to questions asked. The interview should be thought of as a meeting of equals.
The interviewer is looking for someone to hire and the interviewee is looking for a job.

Listening and Responding

There are several barriers potentially standing in the way of effective communication. While
the sender is encoding and transmitting the message, there is a great amount of noise that
makes it difficult for the receiver to accurately decode and understand the message sent. The
effective communicator must try to reduce or eliminate these barriers so that the message
gets through and is understood by the receiver.

Mechanical and Physical Barriers   These include the following:

- Physical noises, static and drop-outs (blanked-out spaces in the message due to transmission errors).
- Time zone differences. Between Toronto and London, England the eight-hour time difference means that at the start of work in Toronto at 9 a.m., people in London have already left the office; by 5 p.m. in Toronto it is 1 a.m. in London. Obviously, to converse on the telephone someone must stay late or arrive early.
- Most telephones today do not transmit pictures of the persons conversing. The visual cues that allow one to "read" another's face and use non-verbals to help receive the whole message are therefore missing. Picturephones are now available in the marketplace, but their use is not widespread. Advances in computer technology have allowed moving pictures on these phones. This is accomplished by sending, after the initial image, only the part of the picture that is changing. It is likely that when fiber-optic cables are commonly installed, picturephones will be in common use.
- On some long distance telephone calls transmitted by satellite an echo of the speaker's own voice can be heard. Communication is arduous because it is difficult to talk and listen to yourself at the same time.
- On telephone calls to the other side of the world messages must travel over 40 000 kilometres up to a satellite, then the same distance back to earth, plus land-line distances. This can cause a time-lag of one-third of a second between one person speaking and the other hearing. A break is often taken as a cue to speak in the conversation. Consequently, these delays can trick both parties into talking at the same time.

Information Overload   When confronted by too much information the receiver can become overwhelmed and unable to receive the message sent. Computer networks are now global and messages may pile up in one's computer "electronic mailbox" causing what has been termed **In-box gridlock** (Pearl, 1993). The reader confronted with many messages may skim their contents on the VDT screen and pay scant attention to their contents. Also, computer network users have developed a number of commonly used abbreviations and acronyms that can be obscure at first. For example, what does AtDhVaAnNkCsE mean in a message? It may take more than one look to see "Thanks in Advance."

In-box gridlock   When a person's incoming e-mail becomes overwhelming.

Fatigue   Because it is hard work to listen to a great deal of information, after some time the mind begins to wander and the message is missed. People speaking to groups should remember the saying that "the mind can absorb only what the seat can endure." The message should be kept somewhat shorter than the endurance of the audience.

Time Pressure   When under pressure to complete a task or move on to another task the listener is likely to pay less attention to the communicated message. Pressure must be reduced or the message resent when the receiver is more able to listen.

Selective Listening   A listener's motivation affects what is heard. The sender needs to restate the message several ways and to anticipate the receiver's motivation in order to maximize the chances that the message will get through.

Status   Status differences between the sender and receiver can affect communication. A high status person may not listen as carefully to one of lower status, whereas in the reverse situation the low status person is likely to listen very carefully. For example, in a performance review the employee being appraised can be expected to be very intent on the manager's message, at least until the amount of the salary increase has been mentioned, at which point many employees will "tune out."

Value Judgments   A listener who makes a negative judgment about the personal characteristics of the sender ("What a jerk!") is then not in a position to hear the rest of the sender's message.

Source Credibility   A sender with low credibility is less likely to be listened to than a highly credible source. Try to listen to the message no matter what the source and then make a determination of the credibility of the message, not the source.

Besides acknowledging communication barriers, the second factor in improving listening and responding skills is to work at listening to others. Since listening is a skill that can be developed, with practice and effort at listening, communication effectiveness will be increased. A list of ten ways to be a more effective listener is shown as Exhibit 7.8.

Thirdly, a listener can consider how to reply to the message of a sender. The key to effective response is to learn how and when to use different styles of response. There are at least nine possible responses that may be used, each effective in some circumstances (Cherrington, 1989).

1. Trying to change the behaviour of the other person is an effective strategy when the other has asked for help and advice.

2. Pacifying the other with reassurances that the message has been heard and understood is useful when the other is most upset about not being listened to or having been ignored.

3. Reframing the message (e.g., "What you mean is ...") is an effective way to make sure both parties to the communication understand the same message.

4. Probing and problem solving is a good way to get information to solve a problem.

5. Confronting the other is effective when conflict must be dealt with.

6. Being open in an attempt to get more information from the other (e.g., "Tell me more") is an effective strategy when the message has only been partially sent or understood.

7. Reflecting and paraphrasing what the other person has said, by summarizing and restating the message as heard and understood, is a good way for the sender to correct any errors or misinterpretations and to know that the message has been heard.

8. Passing judgment and evaluating the other's statement is a common response to another's message. In the early stages of communication this can block understanding, but a judgment may be called for as each side's position is clarified.

9. Being silent. In his book "What They (still) Don't Teach you at Harvard Business School," Mark McCormack (1990) makes clear the importance of silence in business communications. He says that by remaining quiet after having stated your position, even through those (seemingly) long and uncomfortable pauses, the other person is motivated to talk to fill the silence. When the other person talks and you listen you get more information and learn more. Also, when you are asked to state your opinion, the ability to bite your tongue for a few moments lets you collect your thoughts and say only what you mean to.

EXHIBIT 7.8   PRINCIPLES OF EFFECTIVE LISTENING

PRINCIPLE	THE GOOD LISTENER	THE BAD LISTENER
1. *Look for areas of interest.*	Seeks personal enlightenment and/or information; entertains new topics as potentially interesting.	Tunes out dry subjects; narrowly defines what is interesting.
2. *Overlook errors of delivery.*	Attends to meaning and content; ignores delivery errors while being sensitive to any messages in them.	Ignores if delivery is poor; misses messages because of personal attributes of the communicator.
3. *Postpone judgment.*	Avoids quick judgments; waits until comprehension of the core message is complete.	Quickly evaluates and passes judgment; inflexible regarding contrary messages.
4. *Listen for ideas.*	Listens for ideas and themes. Identifies the main points.	Listens for facts and details.
5. *Take notes.*	Takes careful notes and uses a variety of note taking or recording schemes depending on the speaker.	Takes incomplete notes using one system.
6. *Be actively responsive*	Responds frequently with nods, "uh-huhs," etc.; shows active body state; works at listening.	Passive demeanor; few or no responses; little energy output.
7. *Resist distractions.*	Resists being distracted; longer concentration span; places loaded words in perspective.	Easily distracted; focuses on loaded or emotional words; short concentration span.
8. *Challenge your mind.*	Uses difficult material to stimulate the mind; seeks to enlarge understanding.	Avoids difficult material; does not seek to broaden knowledge base.
9. *Capitalize on mind speed.*	Uses listening time to summarize and anticipate the message; attends to implicit messages as well as explicit messages.	Daydreams with slow speakers; becomes preoccupied with other thoughts.
10. *Assist and encourage the speaker.*	Asks for clarifying information or examples; uses reflecting phrases; helps to rephrase the idea.	Interrupts; asks trivial questions; makes distracting comments.

SOURCE: From David J. Cherrington (1989), ORGANIZATIONAL BEHAVIOR: THE MANAGEMENT OF INDIVIDUAL AND ORGANIZATIONAL PERFORMANCE, p. 577. Copyright © 1989 by Allyn & Bacon. Reprinted with permission.

CONCLUSION

Communication is the lifeblood of any organization. Without effective communication members do not know what actions to take or how effective their actions have been. Though the prescriptions for communicating effectively seem straightforward, their implementation is difficult. Communication is a skill that is learned. Practice is required to improve the ability to communicate well. Managers, because they deal with other organizational members on a regular basis, need to be good communicators.

But managers must do more than communicate with others. They have a set of organizational roles to perform. These roles and what managers do are considered first in Chapter 8. Then, it is important to consider how managers try to encourage others at work to act in ways that help the organization to accomplish its objectives. This is the question of motivation, the second focus of Chapter 8.

CHAPTER SUMMARY

It is likely that there is nothing more important to the effective functioning of organizations than communication. There are four ways of conceptualizing organizational communication. The first is the psychological, that communication is affected by the perceptual and psychological processes of people at work. The second is the systems-interaction view. Here communication is seen as the sequences and patterns of interaction between people. The third view of organizational communication is the mechanistic perspective. In it, information is transmitted using verbal and non-verbal signals from a sender to a receiver and then, in two-way communication, back to the sender. Mechanistic communication emphasizes the verbal and routine messages needed to solve the organization's structured, routine, and programmed problems. The fourth communication perspective is the interpretive-symbolic. This view emphasizes how communication leads to the creation of shared meanings as narration and storytelling are used by organizational members to capture complex experiences that are combinations of sense, emotion, reason, and imagination. The organization's nonroutine problems may be dealt with using interpretive-symbolic communications. Learning to communicate effectively in organizations is important both for personal reasons of getting and keeping a job, and for organizational reasons of efficiency and effectiveness.

QUESTIONS FOR REVIEW

1. How can a person in an organization manage the non-verbal messages that they send?

2. What would be the preferred medium for asking the boss for a raise?

3. What are the most important barriers to effective communication?

4. How could a person go about learning to be a more effective communicator?

5. How can a company encourage the use of both interpretive-symbolic kinds of communication for nonroutine problems and mechanistic communication for routine problems?

SELF-DIAGNOSTIC EXERCISE 7.1

The Business Jargon Test

In the business world new terms are constantly being invented to describe new kinds of actions, or to put a new slant on the old ways. To stay on top of what is going on around you, it is important to learn the jargon. Match the terms below to the definitions and find out how well you know the word on the street.

1. gender revenge

2. formica parachute

3. bleeding edge

4. phone lag

5. ear candy

6. zircon in the rough

7. bag of snakes

8. golden handcuffs

9. firing line

10. naked to your enemies

11. Canadian complaint

12. Infostructure

13. Speed money

14. "it is difficult"

15. empty suit

a) the system of people, computers, faxes, cellular phones and voice mail used to receive information

b) an acquisition full of nasty surprises

c) when your mentor gets fired

d) a Japanese expression meaning "no"

e) when global management causes people on the other side of the world to call you at 3 a.m.

f) foreign investment that limits the power of the locals to make decisions

g) a bribe paid to ease the passage of goods

h) a catchy but vacuous platitude designed to appeal to the sentiments of the listener

i) very generous pay and benefits that bind the receiver to the company

j) unemployment insurance

k) the dividing line between a management layer that no longer exists and the one above it

l) someone who seems modestly talented, and is

m) the final remark you make that gets you fired

n) the coming triumph of women at work

o) someone who dresses well and creates the appearance of leadership while actually doing little of substance

SOURCE: Based on definitions appearing in Olive (1990). The correct pairings are: 1n, 2j, 3k, 4e, 5h, 6l, 7b, 8i, 9m, 10c, 11f, 12a, 13g, 14d, 15o.

EXPERIENTIAL EXERCISE 7.1

Preparing for the Interview

An employment interview is meant to be an occasion for communicating information between the representative of an organization and a prospective employee. It is not an adversarial relationship in which each side tries to trick the other. From the interviewee side it looks like the company is all-powerful, making decisions regarding who to hire from on high. But from the company interviewer's point of view, it is difficult to find people who will fit in and benefit the organization. Questions asked in interviews are designed to elicit information about the interviewee so that a decision—a choice of who, if anyone, to hire—can be made. In order to help you prepare for the employment interview, we have listed below a number of questions that you may be asked. Divide into groups of three, have one person ask a question, another answer as they would in an interview, and the third provide feedback on the answer. Rotate these roles so that everyone has a chance to ask, answer, and provide feedback. The more seriously you take this exercise, the more you are likely to learn about your interviewing skills and which questions you find most difficult to answer.

Questions

1. What are your goals in life?
2. Where do you hope to be five years from now?
3. Why did you select this company for an interview?
4. How much money would you expect if you were offered this position?
5. Is money or the job more important to you?
6. When do you expect to get married?
7. Are you willing to relocate from our head office to our other locations?
8. Are you willing to travel on the job?
9. What is the course you enjoyed the most at college or university? Why?
10. What is the course you enjoyed the least? Why?
11. What is your greatest weakness?
12. When you have children, how do you plan to allocate your time to home and work?
13. What is more important to you: work or family?
14. Why do you think you would be successful in this organization?
15. Tell me about the worst boss you have had.
16. What kind of work are you most interested in doing?
17. Have you ever quit a job or been fired? What happened?
18. Why did you choose to attend this college/university?
19. Why did you choose the major that you did?
20. What type of person do you find you just can't get along with?
21. When can you start work? If not right away, why not?

22. Do you see this job as a stepping stone to another one in another organization?

23. If you get this job, how long do you expect to stay with our organization?

24. What book has had the most impact on your life? Why?

25. What can you do for our organization?

SOURCE: Inspired by "The awful interview," developed by Donald D. Bowen, in Lewicki and others (1988), pp. 268-270; and by "Questions employers often ask," p. 539 of Rachman and Mescon (1979).

EXPERIENTIAL **EXERCISE 7.2**

Listed below are communication situations at the work place that can be very difficult to manage effectively. Form into groups of three and role play discussions between co-workers. It is important to be creative in your playing of the roles and to go beyond the easy or simple answer of what each person might say. Explore what might happen as their discussion continues. The third person in the group should observe their interaction and any communication problems that are encountered. Switch roles with each scenario that you role play.

1. At the yearly performance appraisal interview, the subordinate does not agree with the manager's decision to give an average performance rating and an average salary increase.

2. The manager is criticizing the subordinate's handling of an irate customer because the subordinate argued loudly with the customer. The subordinate is still upset because of the customer's insulting attitude and use of language.

3. The employee is being fired but does not understand why—no one said anything before about poor performance. The manager maintains that the poor performance was discussed and that this has been going on for some time.

4. The manager and employee were discussing a business account when the manager was called out of the office for a few moments. Letters relating to confidential customer and employee material have been left on the manager's desk. When the manager returns to the office, it seems the employee is engaged in reading these letters upside-down as they sit on the manager's desk. The manager confronts the employee about this ethical breach.

5. A co-worker has just offered to tell another a secret on the condition that it may not be told to anyone else. Should the other listen to the secret?

6. One co-worker has just asked another "what you really think of me as a person." Should the second co-worker take this as free rein to tell the first exactly what is thought, even if it is not positive?

It is a good idea to consider these communication situations before they are confronted in actual organizations. Thinking about them in advance helps a person to prepare to act in the way that he or she has decided is best.

EXPERIENTIAL EXERCISE 7.3

Baseball: An Exercise in Exploring Cross-Cultural Communication

Introduction

Obviously there are problems when we try to communicate with people who speak a different language. But the language problems are merely the tip of the iceberg, because many of the problems we experience in communicating with people from a different society arise in connection with everyday issues—things we normally take for granted. The following activity is designed to give you a feeling for the kinds of things that can make communication difficult.

Procedure

1. The instructor will divide the class into (1) teams of 5 to 10 Canadian students, and (2) one or more teams of up to six foreign students.
2. The Canadian students have the task of teaching the game of baseball to the foreign students. The groups will meet for the time designated (usually 20-30 minutes) and plan for how they will explain baseball to the foreign students. The objective is to help the foreign students understand the game well enough so that they can attend and enjoy a baseball game. In making their explanation, the students may use the blackboard to draw any diagrams they wish. One of the group members should be appointed to make the presentation. A time limit for the presentation should be decided beforehand.
3. The other team should ask questions whenever they find the presentation confusing or unclear. In addition to their own questions, the listeners may want to ask about the following:
   - What is the infield fly rule?
   - When does a foul ball count as a strike?
   - How are a batter's official at-bats computed?
   - Why is it that sometimes a batter can go to bat but no "at-bat" is credited?
   - When is a team likely to sacrifice, steal, bunt, hit-and-run?
4. Presentations are usually limited to 10 minutes per group. Or one group can present until they encounter problems, then another group can be asked to help them out.
5. As a class, discuss the following questions:
   - What did it feel like to try to communicate the intricacies of baseball to the other team?
   - When did communication tend to break down?
   - How did the foreign students feel as the Canadian students made their presentation? What was effective from their perspective?
   - How did this conversation typify the experience that foreign students have had with Canadians?

Options

Any well-known sport can be substituted for baseball. Foreign students could reverse the roles in the exercise and explain a game familiar to them but unfamiliar to Canadians.

SOURCE: Adapted from an original exercise created by Donald D. Bowen, The University of Tulsa. Reprinted by permission.

SELF-GUIDED LEARNING ACTIVITY

To write a resume and covering letter that will help you to get the job you want, a good place to start is your business reference library or the business section of your local bookstore. You will find a number of books that offer sample resumes and resume preparation tips. Because everyone's background is different there is no one best way to prepare a resume; it's best to look at a number of books and then choose the one that offers advice that makes the most sense to you. One useful book is *The Damn Good Resume Guide* by Yana Parker. The next step is to think about your long-term career plans (see this text's Chapter 14 on Careers) and how your first job fits with those plans. A useful book in this area is the latest edition of *What Color is Your Parachute?*, which you can also find at the bookstore. Then sit down and hand write or keyboard a resume and a covering letter. You should ask for help and advice on the resume and letter as you prepare revisions, and expect that many drafts will be necessary (five or more) before you have said what you want to say in the way you want to say it. Your friends, parents, employers, teachers, and guidance centre counsellors can all offer useful advice. Then the resume is ready for inputting (if you wrote it by hand) and formatting. At this stage you need to work on layout, paper type and colour, and the elimination of any typographical errors. The final document should be accurate and send a strong message of the care and effort that you have put into its creation. The covering letter should be of the same quality as the resume. Useful guides to resumes and covering letters are the books by Richard H. Beatty, *175 High-Impact Cover Letters* and *The Resume Kit*, published by John Wiley and Sons, Inc.

MANAGER'S CASE FILE:
I HEARD A RUMOUR

Denise Cotton transferred to another department after settling a sexual harassment suit against her former supervisor, Milton Burke. Since both had retained their jobs with the company, Denise felt that she would be more comfortable working in a different area where she would have no contact with Milton. Management had cleared the way so that her transfer would be effective immediately after the suit was settled.

Denise had been a conscientious, reliable employee and her new supervisor, Lisa Duran, was happy to have Denise on her staff. Although Denise was slow to pick up the new routine, Lisa coached her along with promising results. However, after about two months on the new job, Denise began having trouble with her productivity.

Lisa was concerned about Denise's performance, but she decided to give her a little time before discussing the situation. Then, one day, a possible explanation for Denise's declining performance surfaced.

Lisa was eating lunch with another supervisor at the company, Anita Grant. As usual, the two managers had agreed not to discuss any work problems. But then, over coffee, Anita asked Denise a question.

"Don't you have a former employee of Milton working for you?" Anita asked.

"Yes, I do," said Lisa. "What about her?"

"Well, I heard that Milton's been at it again," Anita said. "I heard that he got one of his employees pregnant and there's been some talk about the two weeks that Denise took off just before the suit was settled. It was suggested that perhaps there was more than harassment going on."

"I don't believe it," Lisa said. "Denise is a good kid. But if she's heard any of the talk, it could explain why she's been having trouble lately. Thanks for the tip," Lisa said, deciding not to discuss the rumour further.

As soon as Denise returned from lunch, Lisa asked to speak with her privately.

"I've just heard a rumour," Lisa started gently. "I was wondering if you'd heard it, too. Your performance has been off, and I thought that that might be what's been bothering you."

"Which version have you heard?" Denise asked. "There seem to be several different angles to the story: One has me pregnant, another says I've had an abortion. It goes on and on."

"What I've heard doesn't matter, Denise," Lisa said. "What matters is how it's affecting you."

"I can't stand it anymore," Denise said. "Every time I hear whispering, I assume it's about me. I see the looks people are giving me. It seems clear that everyone believes the rumours and are adding a few new details when they pass it on. I can't concentrate on my work; I'm not sleeping well at night. The worst is that none of the rumours is true. I took two weeks off to keep from dealing with Milton. What I did during those two weeks seems to be everyone else's concern, but it's none of anyone's business. I wish people would leave it alone. I don't know what to do about it."

"Why don't you take the rest of the day off and relax," Lisa said. "I want to think about this and decide about the best course of action for us to take. Don't worry. We'll put an end to this once and for all," Lisa said, adding a confidence she didn't feel.

After Denise had left, Lisa tried to determine what to do. Riding out the rumours until they died down would take too much time and she didn't think that Denise would last that long. And if more talk about Milton arose in the future, the whole matter would be rehashed again. Giving Denise some time off would only add fuel to the fire. Any kind of general announcement might lend credence to the rumours.

As Lisa left the office for the day, she was still undecided as to what to do.

SOURCE: Written by Grace Lander. Reprinted, by permission of publisher, from MANAGEMENT SOLUTIONS, December 1988. © 1988 American Management Association, New York. All rights reserved.

Questions

1. What can Lisa do to stop the rumours from circulating?

2. How can Lisa help Denise to cope with the situation?

3. What, if anything, should be done with Milton?

WORDS: SAY WHAT YOU MEAN, MEAN WHAT YOU SAY

"Sometime between when I was a kid and now," says comedian George Carlin with mock bewilderment, "operations became 'surgical procedures,' sneakers became 'athletic footwear,' theatres became 'performing arts centres,' and the dump became 'the landfill site!'"

He pronounces each euphemism slowly to stress its artificial elegance, and his long list of new names for familiar words sends his audience into gales of laughter.

Carlin and his audience are laughing at one (and the one most ridiculed) of the many forces that act on language to change its vocabulary and style of expression. Carlin might as easily have noted that over his lifetime "raising children" has become "parenting," committee chairmen have become "chairpersons" or "chairs," handicapped people have become "persons with disabilities," and members of his own age group became "baby boomers," some of whom went on to become "yuppies" who may consider a "user-friendly PC" to be part of their professional "lifestyle."

These are symptoms of the social influences on language: modifications we make in the way we speak by introducing euphemisms, slang, jargon, new words, and new meanings for old words into the language. This ongoing metamorphosis provides an interesting perspective on cultural history.

Most grammars and handbooks on style warn the would-be writer away from most of these "corrupting" influences, especially the euphemism. H.W. Fowler, whose *Modern English Usage* has been acknowledged as the final authority on style and usage for more than 60 years, is perhaps the most withering in his analysis of the euphemism. Citing its heyday as the Victorian era, "when the dead were *the departed*, or *no longer living*, pregnant women were *in an interesting condition*, novelists wrote d—d for damned and G-d for God," Fowler notes, "We are less mealy-mouthed now."

Nonetheless, we continue to use "the mild or vague or periphrastic expression [roundabout way of speaking] as a substitute for blunt precision or disagreeable truth" even though it may make us seem mealy-mouthed and even though its effectiveness can only be short-term. As Fowler says, "euphemism is a will-o'-the-wisp forever eluding pursuit; each new word becomes in turn as explicit as its predecessors and has to be replaced."

Consequently we have an abundance of expressions for certain concepts, some lending prestige ("janitors" became "custodians" and then "stationary engineers") and some concealing the meaning of what Victoria Fromkin and Robert Rodman in *An Introduction to Language* call "taboo words." Fromkin and Rodman list close to 20 euphemisms for urination, such as "seeing a man about a dog," and an even greater number for sexual intercourse, from "making love" to "playing hospital."

But as Fowler points out, "In the present century euphemism has been employed less in finding discreet terms for what is indelicate than as a protective device for governments and as a token of a new approach to psychological and sociological problems." Thus, a war can be called a "police action" or a "strategic defense," aid to the poor is called a "welfare program," backward or troublesome children are called "maladjusted."

Slang and jargon are other corruptions that grammarians and stylists tend to deplore. Slang expressions are invented by demographic groups to create a language understood only by those who are fashionably in the know. In the '60s, young people went to "love-ins" and "sit-ins," not public rallies, and they talked about being "spaced out" or "ripped off" or having a "hang-up." So eager was the general population to be identified with this group that its slang is familiar to most people today, and many of these expressions are so common as to be almost respectable.

And so important is the influence of slang that "it was thought necessary to give the returning Vietnam prisoners of war a glossary of 86 new slang words and phrases, from *acid* to *zonked*. The words on this list—prepared by the Air Force—had come into use during only five years" (*An Introduction to Language*).

Slang of more recent times likewise reflects the currently dominant group, yuppies (an acronym for "young upwardly mobile professionals") who may be DINKs (dual income, no kids), probably drive a BMW (called, affectionately, the "Beemer") and may be guilty of NIMBY ("not in my backyard") when it comes to plans for subsidized housing. Deriving new words from acronyms is a particularly popular influence on morphology, or the formation of words, today—groups like MADD (Mothers Against Drunk Driving) and HANDS (Hamilton AIDS Network for Dialogue and Support) want the acronym to make as much sense as the title it's derived from.

The jargon we import into our everyday conversation is somewhat more revealing of our current preoccupations. For instance, today many people are familiar with quite a bit of the jargon of computer technology, to the extent that descriptions of "hands-on" experience or inviting "input" from a group need not have any reference to computers. We also apply the jargon of business ("cash flow," "bottom line," "profit margin") to other areas and are quite comfortable with the rarefied terminology of disciplines such as health, fitness and psychology (10 years ago, did you know the meaning of "aerobic exercise," "myocardial infarction" and "self-actualization"?).

Even more revealing of an age is the way terms are broadened or modified to ease discussion of new social patterns. The preoccupation of the current generation with child-rearing has spawned terms unfamiliar a decade ago when the word "parent" referred only to a person, not an activity, "day care" was "babysitting" and mothers and fathers didn't worry about "quality time."

And because the state of the environment is a pressing concern, our language is sprinkled with previously unheard-of terms such as "non-recyclable" and "ozone-friendly," and we talk about a manufacturer "going green."

Most revealing, perhaps, of cultural preoccupations is the kind of terminology we consciously introduce into everyday language out of regard for a lobby group. Sensitivity to the plight of a disenfranchised racial group motivated the socially aware to avoid all the then-familiar colloquial terms in favor of "Negro" and eventually to call them "blacks," their own preference. Today, people with physical or mental handicaps prefer to be referred to as "persons with disabilities," so that the emphasis is on their personhood.

"If sexism and racism are diseases, words are often the germs that spread them," says Jeremiah Creedon in an article in the *Utne Reader*. "The cure of choice today is verbal modification. Rather than altering what we believe, we are encouraged to alter what we say. The idea is that we will end up adopting the desired beliefs anyway—won over not by argument but by the unconscious effect of our corrected vocabularies."

The question of sexism in language has prompted a flurry of books and articles, ranging from advice about using gender-neutral pronouns like "they" and "he/she" to whole dictionaries like Mary Daly's *Webster's First New Intergalactic Wickedary of the English Language*. A teacher of feminist ethics at Boston College, Daly coins new words and redefines old ones in her attempt to rid the English language of its patriarchal and heterosexual biases. For example, she invents *gynergy* to mean "the female energy which both comprehends and creates who we are."

Grammarians and language purists have raised some protests over these efforts; while agreeing that terms such as "girl Friday" are undesirable and while applauding "firefighter," "flight attendant" and "staffing" as substitutes for "fireman," "stewardess" and "manning," some have complained that a person is not a "chair" (the preferred substitute for "chairman") and that advice not to use "he" as the neutral pronoun amounts to policing the language, or, at least, upsetting it unnecessarily. "Undoubtedly grammar rebels against *their*," harrumphs Fowler earlier in the century, "and the reason for using it is clearly the reluctance to recognize that, though the reference may be to both sexes, the right shortening of the cumbersome *he or she, his or her,* etc., is *he* or *him* or *his*."

In response to modern purists, Fromkin and Rodman observe, "the prescriptivists are bound to fail. Language is vigorous and dynamic and constantly changing. All languages and dialects are expressive, complete, and logical, as much so as they were 200 or 2000 years ago."

The proof of the statement? Today's father does not say, like Shakespeare's Lear, "How sharper than a serpent's tooth it is/To have a thankless child!"; instead, he sighs, "Parenting can be a downer sometimes."

SOURCE: Welstead (1991). Reprinted by permission of the *McMaster Times*.

Questions

1. What are the slang and jargon words of the last few years?

2. Would people in their 40s know these words?

3. What euphemisms, the use of a mild word or expression for more direct description, are popular today? Why do we need to use euphemisms instead of speaking more plainly and directly?

REFERENCES

Argyle, Michael (1975). *Bodily Communication.* New York: International Universities Press.

Axtell, Roger E. (1991). *Gestures: The Do's and Taboo's of Body Language Around the World.* New York: John Wiley & Sons, Inc.

Baird, John G., & Gretchen K. Wieting (1979). "Nonverbal communication can be a motivational tool." *Personnel Journal,* September 1979, pp. 607-610.

Bandler, Richard, & John Grinder (1979). *Frogs into Princes: Neurolinguistic Programming.* Moab, UT: Real People Press.

Bavelas, Alex (1950). "Communication patterns in task-oriented groups." *The Journal of the Acoustical Society of America* 22: 725-730.

Beatty, Richard H. (1992). *175 High-impact Cover Letters.* New York: John Wiley and Sons, Inc.

Beatty, Richard H. (1984). *The Resume Kit.* New York: John Wiley and Sons, Inc.

Benson, Gary L. (1983). "On the campus: How well do business schools prepare graduates for the business world?" *Personnel,* July-August 1983, pp. 61-65.

Boje, David M. (1991). "The storytelling organization: A study of story performance in an office-supply firm." *Administrative Science Quarterly* 36: 106-126.

Bowen, Donald D. (1988). "The awful interview." In Roy J. Lewicki, Donald D. Bowen, Douglas T. Hall, & Francine S. Hall (Eds.), *Experiences in Management and Organizational Behavior* (3rd edition), pp. 268-270. New York: John Wiley & Sons, Inc.

Cherrington, David J. (1989). *Organizational Behavior: The Management of Individual and Organizational Performance.* Needham Heights, MA: Allyn & Bacon.

Ekman, Paul (1993). "Facial expression and emotion." *American Psychologist* 48: 384-392.

Falvey, Jack (1989). "Car phones become the sales force's fifth wheel." *Wall Street Journal,* July 27, 1989.

Filson, Brent (1991). *Executive Speeches: 51 CEOs Tell You How to do Yours.* Williamstown, Mass.: Williamstown Publishing Co.

Fulk, Janet & Brian Boyd (1991). "Emerging theories of communication in organizations." *Journal of Management* 17: 407-446.

Gladwell, Malcolm (1992). "Speed dialer." *The New Republic* 207(25): 9-10.

Gutman, Dan (1994). "Flying high: Fax broadcasting helps a new airline get off the ground." *Success,* March 1994, p. 53.

Kane, Kimberly F. (1993). "MBAs: A recruiter's-eye view." *Business Horizons* 36(1): 65-71.

Knapp, Mark (1978). *Nonverbal Communication in Human Interaction,* 2nd edition. New York: Holt, Rinehart & Winston.

Korda, Michael (1975). *Power! How to Get It, How to Use It.* New York: Random House, Inc.

Krone, Kathleen J., Fredric M. Jablin, & Linda L. Putnam (1987). "Communication theory and organizational communication: Multiple perspectives." In Fredric M. Jablin, Linda L. Putnam, Karlene H. Roberts, and Lyman W. Porter (Eds.), *Handbook of Organizational Communication: An Interdisciplinary Perspective* (pp. 18-40). Newbury Park, CA: Sage Publications, Inc.

Leavitt, Harold J. (1951). "Some effects of certain communication patterns on group performance." *Journal of Abnormal and Social Psychology* 46: 38-50.

Lengel, Robert H., & Richard L. Daft (1988). "The selection of communication media as an executive skill." *Academy of Management Executive* 2: 225-232.

McCormack, Mark H. (1990). *What They (still) Don't Teach You at Harvard Business School: Selling More, Managing Better, and Getting the Job Done in the '90s.* New York: Bantam Books.

Morsbach, Helmut (1988). "Nonverbal communication and hierarchical relationships: The case of bowing in Japan." In Fernando Poyatos (Ed.), *Cross-cultural Perspectives in Nonverbal Communication* (pp. 189-199). Toronto: C.J. Hogrefe.

Noon, Mike, & Rick Delbridge (1993). "News from behind my hand: Gossip in organizations." *Organization Studies* 14: 23-36.

Northey, Margot (1986). *Impact: A Guide to Business Communication.* Scarborough, Ontario: Prentice Hall Canada, Inc.

Olive, David (1990). "The secret language of sharks." *Report on Business Magazine*, October 1990, pp. 80-83. Also see David Olive (1990), *White Knights and Poison Pills: A Cynic's Dictionary of Business Jargon.* Toronto: Key Porter Books Limited.

Pearl, Jayne A. (1993). "The e-mail quandary." *Management Review* 82(7): 48-51.

Peters, Tom J., & Nancy Austin (1985). *A Passion for Excellence.* New York: Random House.

Rachman, David J., & Michael H. Mescon (1979). *Business Today,* 2nd edition. New York: Random House.

Ranson, Stewart, C.R. (Bob) Hinings, & Royston Greenwood. (1980). "The structuring of organization structures." *Administrative Science Quarterly* 25: 1-17.

Shaw, Marvin E. (1964). "Communication networks." In Leonard Berkowitz (Ed.), *Advances in Experimental Social Psychology* (pp. 111-147). New York: Academic Press.

Siegel, Jane, Vitaly Dubrovsky, Sara Kiesler, & Timothy W. McGuire (1986). "Group processes in computer-mediated communication." *Organizational Behavior and Human Decision Processes* 37: 157-187.

Sitkin, Sim B., Kathleen M. Sutcliffe, & John R. Barrios-Choplin (1992). "A dual-capacity model of communication media choice in organizations." *Human Communication Research* 18: 563-598.

Smircich, Linda, & Gareth Morgan (1982). "Leadership: The management of meaning." *Journal of Applied Behavioral Science* 18: 257-273.

Warshaw, Michael (1993). "Giant killer." *Success,* January/February 1993, p. 36.

Weick, Karl E. (1987). "Theorizing about organizational communication." In Fredric M. Jablin, Linda L. Putnam, Karlene H. Roberts, and Lyman W. Porter (Eds.), *Handbook of Organizational Communication: An Interdisciplinary Perspective* (pp. 97-122). Newbury Park, CA: Sage Publications, Inc.

Weick, Karl E., & Larry D. Browning (1986). "Argument and narration in organizational communication." *Journal of Management* 12: 243-259.

Welstead, Susan (1991). "Words: Say what you mean, mean what you say." *McMaster Times,* Winter 1991, pp. 26-27.

FURTHER READING

For more information on the technology of communication, see the edited book of 13 chapters titled *Organizations and Communication Technology.* It was edited by Janet Fulk and Charles Steinfield and published in 1990 by Sage Publications, Inc.

Karl Weick and Larry Browning (1986) discuss argument and narration as two types of communication. Argument is a way to present the facts; narration can present the emotions and feelings that go along with those facts. An article that combines argument and narration in the telling of a story about academic dishonesty is by Richard H.G. Field, 1993, and is titled "The case of the purloined journal article, or on being at the receiving end of academic dishonesty." It can be found in the *Journal of Management Inquiry* 2: 317-324.

The software program *What They Don't Teach You at Harvard Business School* is based on Mark McCormack's 1984 book and is a simulation of a sports management company. At the time of writing it is available for an educational price of $29.95 USD from Strategic Management Group, 3624 Market Street, University City Science Center, Philadelphia, PA 19104; telephone 215-387-4000.

Eliminating sexist language in the workplace is the focus of the article "Benefiting from nonsexist language in the workplace" by Bill Daily and Miriam Finch in the March-April 1993 issue of *Business Horizons.*

A very useful article dealing with resumes and on-campus interviews is by Fredric M. Jablin and Vernon D. Miller, "The on-campus job screening interview" pages 17-48 of Beverly Davenport Sypher (Ed.), *Case Studies in Organizational Communication* (1990), New York: The Guilford Press. Also see their article "Interviewer and applicant questioning behavior in employment interviews" in *Management Communication Quarterly* 4: 51-86.

For brief but comprehensive looks at more effective communication across cultures, see Mary Munter's (1993) *Business Horizons* article titled "Cross-cultural communication for managers," May-June 1993, pages 69-77; the article by Ronald E. Dulek, John S. Fielden, and John S. Hill titled "International communication: An executive primer," in *Business Horizons,* January-February 1991, pages 20-25; and "Communicating to a diverse Europe" by James E. McLauchlin in the January-February 1993 issue of *Business Horizons,* pages 54-56. More in-depth treatment is offered by Roger E. Axtell in his books *Do's and Taboos in International Trade, Do's and Taboos Around the World, The Do's and Taboos of Hosting International Visitors, The Do's and Taboos of International Trade: A Small Business Primer,* and *The Do's and Taboos of Public Speaking: How to get those Butterflies Flying in Formation.* All are published by John Wiley and Sons, Inc.

Communication between men and women has been compared to cross-cultural communication, with the same attendant difficulties. Deborah Tannen's 1990 book *You Just Don't Understand: Women and Men in Conversation* takes the view that there are gender differences in ways of speaking. Advice is given on how to communicate across the gender divide. The book was published in New York by William Morrow and Company, Inc.

CHAPTER

8

MANAGERSHIP AND MOTIVATION

CHAPTER OUTLINE

Managerial Roles

The Nature of Managerial Work

Motivation

   Needs/Personality/Interests

   Motives

   Cognitive Choice

   Intentions

   Goals

   Self-Regulation

Reward Systems

Conclusion

QUESTIONS TO CONSIDER

- What is a manager?
- What does a manager do?
- How can a manager motivate others to get tasks performed?
- What is self-management?
- How are people rewarded?

Many people in organizations are called upon to manage others. Instead of actually doing the organization's work—for example waiting on tables, writing computer programs, operating a drilling rig—the manager's job is to help others to do their work. While managers sometimes actually do the organization's work, a full-time manager is separated by vertical division of labour from the front-line workers. The job of manager is therefore different from the job of worker. The objective of this chapter is to examine managership—doing the job of a manager—and the ways a manager can influence what gets done in the organization and how it gets done.

Before reading about what managers do, we suggest you try the self-diagnostic exercise at the end of this chapter, to discover your own motivation to manage.

MANAGERIAL ROLES

Is there one way to manage? In the past, when organizations were considered to be bureaucracies, effectiveness was defined as how well the work was done (this is the internal process model). Managership was quite simply defined as the ability to *plan* operations, *organize* the work and the work force, *staff* jobs appropriately and at the right cost, and to *control* what work was done and how it was done.

More recently is has become clear that there is more than one way for organizations to define effectiveness. Besides the internal process model, organizations may determine effectiveness by the human relations model, the open systems model, or the rational goal model (see Chapter 1, Exhibit 1.3 for a review of these models of organizational effectiveness).

To understand how these models are similar to and different from one another, two different underlying dimensions may be considered. The first is the organization's internal versus external focus. An organization with an internal focus will be inward-looking; an externally focused organization will be outward-looking. The second dimension is the organization's emphasis on flexibility versus control. Flexibility allows faster change whereas control allows a firmer grasp on current operations.

In each of these dimensions there is a competing value. Will the organization choose more flexibility and therefore give up control, or more control but sacrifice flexibility? The organization cannot have both flexibility and control at the same time. Likewise, will the organization be more internally or externally focused?

When these two dimensions are drawn orthogonal (at right angles) to each other, the four models of organizational effectiveness can be plotted (see Exhibit 8.1). The internal process model emphasizes internal focus and control. The human relations model is oriented to the organization's internal development of its people so that they can be more flexible workers in the future. The open systems model is focused toward flexible interaction with the external environment. Finally, the rational goal model has as its aim the maximization of output (by control) for acceptance by the external environment.

Now that the basic framework for this competing values framework of organizational effectiveness has been described, eight different managerial roles within it can be specified. Each of these eight managerial roles relates to the degree of emphasis the organization places on flexibility or control, and on the organization's internal or external orientation. Each role also has three competencies related to it that are required by the manager performing that role.

The **coordinator** role is most like that of the classical manager—competencies are planning, organizing, and controlling. The manager is dependable, reliable, and maintains structure. In the **monitor** role the manager is technically expert and receives, evaluates, and reacts to information about internal organizational processes. These first two roles are subsumed within the internal process model.

Coordinator Managerial role involving planning, organizing, and controlling.

Monitor Managerial role involving receiving, evaluating, and reacting to information about internal organizational processes.

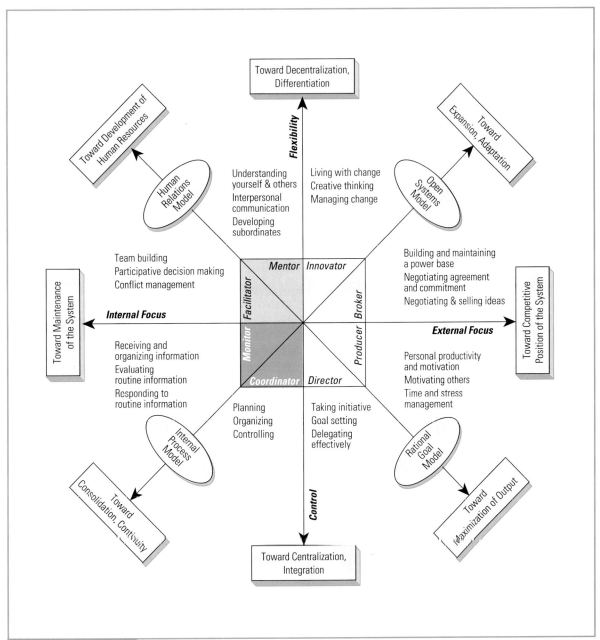

SOURCE: Robert E. Quinn (1988), *Beyond Rational Management: Mastering the Paradoxes and Competing Demands of High Performance*. San Francisco: Jossey-Bass, Inc., pp. 48 and 86. Used with permission. Also based on information in Robert E. Quinn, Sue R. Faerman, Michael P. Thompson, and Michael R. McGrath (1990), *Becoming a Master Manager: A Competency Framework*, New York: John Wiley & Sons, Inc. pp. 13 and 15.

EXHIBIT 8.1

Eight Managerial Roles in the Competing Values Framework

The director and producer roles of the rational goal model focus on the manager's attempts to maximize organizational output. These roles are especially important when the manager is dealing with subordinates and attempting to motivate their behaviour toward the accomplishment of organizational goals. The **director** sets goals and delegates tasks in the attempt to best organize and guide the work. The **producer** manager is more likely to be actively involved in the organization's work while attempting to motivate employees to produce more output in less time. For example, the manager of a travel agency who continues to sell travel to personal and corporate clients fits well into the producer role.

Managers operating in organizations with an open systems model of effectiveness are more used to change and are more oriented to external relations with the people and organizations that accept the organization's product. The **broker** builds a base of power inside and outside the organization and engages in a great deal of discussion and negotiation with others. The **innovator** is more oriented to being flexible, thinking creatively, and managing the constant change that is required in this type of organization.

Managers in organizations subscribing to the human relations model are oriented towards the development of their people, as individuals and in teams. In the **mentor** role the manager attempts to help subordinates develop as individuals, to understand themselves and others, and to learn to communicate well with others. More highly developed employees will be capable of greater flexibility as the organization and its environment change. The **facilitator** role is more group oriented, with the manager acting as a team builder, helping to manage conflict within and between groups, and helping the group to make decisions. The role of facilitator and manager of groups will be discussed more fully in Chapter 9.

These eight managerial roles are a useful starting point for understanding what managers do. A particular manager may concentrate activities in only one of the eight roles. But the other roles will also compete for attention because effectiveness cannot be fully described by only one orientation. Therefore, someone who expects to engage in management can expect to engage in all of the competencies listed in Exhibit 8.1, although possibly at different times and in different organizations.

Director Managerial role involving setting goals and delegating tasks in the attempt to best organize and guide the work.

Producer Managerial role requiring active involvement in the organization's work while attempting to motivate employees to produce more output in less time.

Broker Managerial role involving building a base of power inside and outside the organization and engaging in discussion and negotiation with others.

Innovator Managerial role involving flexibility, creative thinking, and managing constant change.

Mentor Managerial role involving helping subordinates to develop as individuals, to understand themselves and others, and to learn to communicate well with others.

Facilitator Role of the manager as a group oriented team builder, helping to manage conflict within and between groups, and helping the group to make decisions.

Which of the roles in the competing values framework is this manager exhibiting?

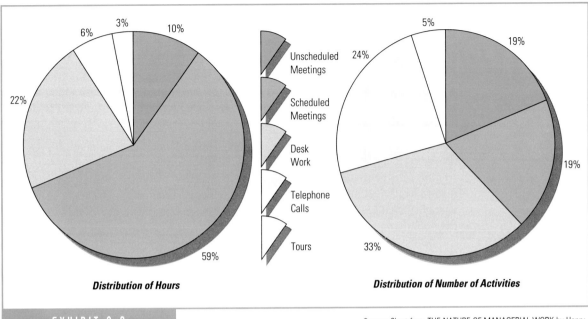

Distribution of Hours

Unscheduled Meetings
Scheduled Meetings
Desk Work
Telephone Calls
Tours

Distribution of Number of Activities

SOURCE: Chart from THE NATURE OF MANAGERIAL WORK by Henry Mintzberg, p. 39. Copyright © 1973 by Henry Mintzberg. Reprinted by permission of HarperCollins Publishers

EXHIBIT 8.2

The Nature of Managerial Work

THE NATURE OF MANAGERIAL WORK

What is it like to be a manager? Henry Mintzberg (1973) studied the nature of the manager's job by observing five chief executives, each for a one-week period. He found six defining characteristics of managerial work.

1. "The manager performs a great quantity of work at an unrelenting pace." Work was long and constant. After office hours, managers read material related to work.

2. "Managerial activity is characterized by variety, fragmentation, and brevity." Many unscheduled meetings, telephone calls, and reactions to the day's crises produced a day broken into a large number of activities of short duration. Exhibit 8.2 shows how the managers Mintzberg observed spent their hours and the activities they performed. Note the relatively large percentage of telephone calls and unscheduled meetings (24% and 19% respectively) but the low percentage of hours these activities consumed (6% and 10% respectively).

3. "Managers prefer issues that are current, specific, and ad hoc." They preferred to deal with issues in real-time, at the present moment and on-the-spot. Their choice was to take action at the time they were confronted with the problem.

4. "The manager sits between the organization and a network of contacts." An important activity was to communicate with a wide variety of people outside the organization. Clients, suppliers, peers, outside experts and officials of other organizations had to be interfaced with because they supply information relevant to the operation of the organization.

5. "The manager demonstrates a strong preference for the verbal media—using the telephone and meetings in preference to the mail." Building and maintaining a personal relationship with others both inside and outside the organization is crucial, and requires personal contact.

6. "Despite the preponderance of obligations, managers appeared to be able to control their own affairs." The manager has to react to requests and communications and must attend meetings, but can choose over the longer term how to spend his time.

Mintzberg then compared what people in general *think* a manager does with the reality he observed (1975). He identified four myths about managerial work.

First, the myth exists that the manager is a reflective, systematic planner, but in fact they tend to work at an unrelenting pace, their activities are brief with high variety, and they are strongly action oriented, disliking reflection. Managers simply do not spend a great deal of time pondering the future.

Second, even though people think the effective manager has no regular duties to perform, the fact is that there are rituals and ceremonies, negotiations, and regular contacts with individuals in the organization's environment that the manager must maintain. Managers do have routine activities to attend to.

Third is the myth that the senior manager needs summarized information provided in written form. While there is no doubt the "executive summary" of one written page at the beginning of a report is popular with managers, the fact is that managers strongly favour the verbal media. They like to talk to people face to face.

The fourth and final myth identified by Mintzberg is that management is a science. Even though organizational scientists have accumulated a great deal of knowledge about organizations, the fact is that managers are more likely to use their judgment and intuition to solve problems. Overall then, what people think managers do with their day and how they make decisions is not congruent with the reality.

The nature of the managerial job differs by culture and country. In Canada and the United States the manager is considered more of an equal by those lower in the organizational hierarchy. The manager is therefore not expected to have all the knowledge required to make all decisions, or indeed even to make all work decisions. In Japan the manager is more of a father figure to the group, is seen as more knowledgeable and in control, and takes a personal interest in both the work and personal lives of employees. Exhibit 8.3 supplies one example of how the manager's job is seen in different countries.

MOTIVATION

The motivation of individuals at work is one of the most important jobs of a manager. What makes someone come to work and apply effort towards getting the task accomplished? What makes someone decide *not* to come to work?

Managers need to understand the different forces that act on an individual. Then the question of how to exert influence on those forces may be addressed. At that point the manager can attempt to influence the behaviour of organizational members so that it is directed towards accomplishing the organization's tasks.

Motivation The attention paid, effort exerted, and persistence of behaviour.

Motivation can be defined as the attention paid, effort exerted, and persistence of behaviour. A number of theories of human motivation have been proposed over the years. We will briefly review some of them in this chapter. These motivation theories, like all theories, are composed of variables considered to be important in understanding the phenomenon in question. For motivation theories the variables are what people at work pay attention to, what they exert effort toward, and how long they persist in a certain behaviour.

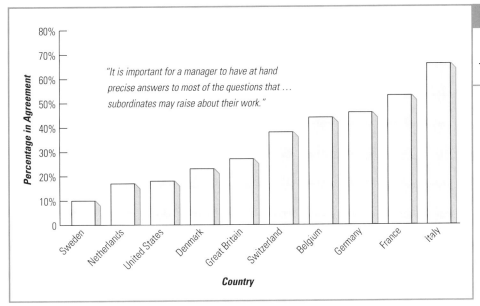

FIGURE 8.3

The Managerial Job in Different Countries

"It is important for a manager to have at hand precise answers to most of the questions that … subordinates may raise about their work."

SOURCE: From André Laurent (1983), "The cultural diversity of western conceptions of management," *International Studies of Management and Organization* 13: 86. Reprinted by permission of the publisher, M.E. Sharpe, Inc., Armonk, N.Y.

The variables in these motivation theories can be called **constructs**. This makes it clear that people have invented, or constructed them. Motivation, for example, is a construct. It is a useful device to think about why people do what they do.

In a major review of work motivation, Ruth Kanfer (1992) has ordered motivation constructs from those that are the most distant from actual behaviour to those that are closest to exhibited behaviour. The most distant (for example, genetics and heredity) are called *distal constructs* and the closest (such as self-regulation and goals) are called *proximal constructs*. Her ordering of motivation constructs is shown as Exhibit 8.4.

The most distal construct that can serve to explain motivation is genetics and heredity. An individual's genetic makeup can be a basic explanation for how he acts. But there are many other factors influencing action that are more proximal than genetics/heredity.

These have to do with: (1) a person's needs, personality, and interests; (2) inherent human motives; (3) decisions and choices that a person makes; (4) formulated intentions for action; (5) goals that a person sets; and (6) self-regulation of action based on recognition of the results of previous actions.

The more distal constructs of needs, personality, interests, and motives influence the intermediate process of cognitive choice. Choices then form the basis for an individual's intentions and goals. It is these more proximal constructs of intentions and goals that then relate more directly to action.

Also shown in Exhibit 8.4 are the names of motivation theories that have been developed for each level of motivation construct. Theories that are closer to behaviour (more proximate) should, when tested, be supported more strongly than theories that are farther (more distal) from human behaviour. The setting of goals and self-reinforcement of behaviour, as the motivation theories most proximate to behaviour, are therefore expected to provide good explanations of the actual actions of people.

Construct A variable that has been invented in order to help develop a theory or understand a phenomenon.

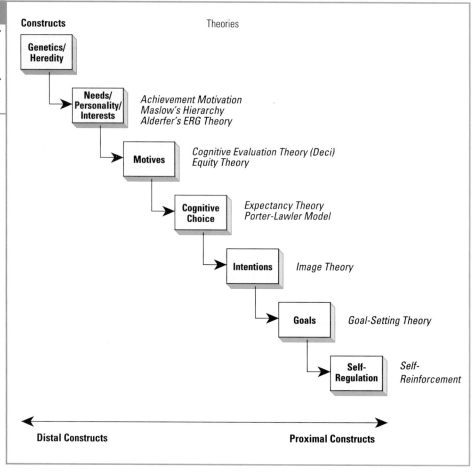

Source: Adapted from Figure 1.1 on p. 4 of Ruth Kanfer (1992), "Work motivation: New directions in theory and research." In Cary L. Cooper and Ivan T. Robertson (Eds.), *International Review of Industrial and Organizational Psychology* (Volume 7, pp. 1-53). Copyright © 1992 by John Wiley & Sons Ltd. Reprinted by permission of John Wiley & Sons, Ltd.

Theories that deal with intentions for action should predict the goals that a person sets, the next most proximate construct, better than they predict actual behaviour. The most distal theories of needs and motives should predict choice, but not necessarily behaviour. Choice and behaviour are expected to be strongly linked only when a choice, once made, can easily lead to the chosen action.

We will now examine selected theories of motivation, starting with the most distal and working our way towards those most proximate to behaviour.

Needs/Personality/Interests

Maslow's Hierarchy

In what is probably the most widely described theory of human motivation, Abraham Maslow (1943) proposed that humans have a built-in set of five basic needs, and that these needs form a hierarchy. Maslow described the five needs (from lowest to highest) as physiological—

the most basic human need for air, food, and water; safety—the need to be safe from physical and psychological harm; social—the need to be accepted, loved, and to belong to a social system; esteem—the need for recognition and prestige given by others; and self-actualization—the need to become the best that one is capable of becoming and to be self-fulfilled.

In this theory each lower need in the hierarchy must be satisfied before the next higher level need takes effect. To use this model of human needs, a manager attempting to build a group at work would want the esteem needs of group members to be dominant. The manager would therefore have to make sure that physiological and safety needs were met. This would be done by paying a living wage and providing a safe and secure work environment.

Maslow also proposed that when a lower-level need was not fulfilled it would again be activated. An individual at work who is concerned with the recognition of others has her esteem needs activated. If this job were lost the person would be expected to revert back to the physiological need to obtain food. She would then be unconcerned with esteem.

Maslow's hierarchy is a useful though very broad way of understanding the behaviour of people. There are certainly exceptions to the fixed movement up and down the hierarchy of needs. An example is the starving artist who fulfills the self-actualization need but not physiological needs. A second example is people who injure themselves because of unmet social needs. Also, more than one category of need could affect an individual's behaviour at a given time. People at work could, for instance, be concerned with social and esteem needs at the same time.

In addition, it is clear that Maslow's hierarchy relies on the Anglo-American cultural emphasis on the individual. Other cultures may have different hierarchies of needs. For example, in the People's Republic of China the group is of great importance to the individual. Belonging is therefore the primary need (see *A Rose by Any Other Name*). It cannot, therefore, be assumed that people from all the cultures of the world share the same basic built-in needs. Need hierarchies can be expected to vary by culture depending on each culture's values.

The manager of organizational members from different cultural backgrounds has to remember that everyone does not share the same way of looking at and understanding a situation. Their needs may be different even in the exact same work conditions. The "Moosajees, Limited" case at the end of this chapter provides a chance to analyze the needs of people from another culture.

Furthermore, the argument has been put forward that Maslow's hierarchy is gender biased (Cullen, 1994). In this way of thinking the hierarchy can be seen to reflect the values of a hierarchical social order. This is a male-oriented way of thinking; women, it is claimed, think more in terms of webs of relationships with others (Gilligan, 1982).

McClelland's Theory of Needs

A second theory of needs is by David McClelland (1961). In this theory individuals are thought to vary in their drive to gratify six basic human needs. These are the need for achievement, power, affiliation, independence, esteem, and security. The need for achievement has been extensively studied. The theory is that people will accomplish the most when they have a high need for achievement. They will select goals that are medium in difficulty: challenging but not impossible goals. Those low in need for achievement will select goals that are either low in difficulty and easy to accomplish or very high in difficulty. Failure to achieve such extreme goals would therefore be expected.

One other interesting finding of McClelland's work is that need for achievement varies among nations (1961, p. 100). On a practical level, McClelland has proposed that the populace of entire nations (or portions of a nation's populace) could be trained to be higher

A ROSE BY ANY OTHER NAME

Research by Edwin Nevis in the People's Republic of China (PRC) shows that human needs are not invariant across cultures. In the PRC, where there is a cultural emphasis on belonging to the group and seeing yourself as part of the larger whole, the basic and most primary need is that of belonging. Whereas Maslow's hierarchy in Anglo American cultures is topped by individual self-actualization, in the PRC the top of the hierarchy is self-actualization in the service of society. The individual is not dominant, as in Canada and the United States, but subordinate to the society as a whole. Maslow's hierarchy for the PRC would therefore look like the following:

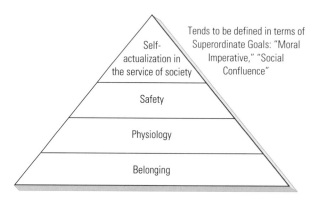

To understand what basic human needs are likely to motivate behaviour at work, then, a manager must first know the culture that has influenced a person's need development and what needs are most important in that culture. People who were raised with the needs of one culture and work in another culture are likely to have a mixed set of needs that do not completely match either culture. To understand the needs of these people is a challenge for the manager.

SOURCE: Based on information in Edwin C. Nevis (1983), "Using an American perspective in understanding another culture: Toward a hierarchy of needs for the People's Republic of China," *The Journal of Applied Behavioral Science* 19: 256.

on need for achievement. Then, over time, these needs would manifest themselves as people chose more difficult goals and worked to achieve those goals. The economy of a whole region could be positively influenced in this way.

ERG Theory

Another theory of human needs and motivation is Clayton Alderfer's (1972) theory that the three basic human needs are Existence, Relatedness, and Growth. For this reason it is called ERG Theory. Existence includes the basic physical, safety, and security needs. Relatedness needs involve a person's relationship with others on the job and off. Growth needs consist of the needs for self-esteem and self-actualization. ERG theory does not assume a hierarchy of these three needs but that all three levels might be important at the same time.

Alderfer also proposed that the less the higher order needs are satisfied the more important will be lower order needs. Therefore, if a job were low in satisfactions of relatedness and growth needs, individuals in those jobs would be expected to focus on the satisfaction of existence needs. For many jobs this would be job security and money. Using ERG theory, then, a manager could attempt to increase the job's relatedness and growth satisfactions (see Chapter 4 on job design) instead of responding to an employee's expressed existence needs. Basically, this approach would be to make the job more interesting and socially satisfying instead of providing more money.

Motives

Cognitive Evaluation Theory

Under some experimental conditions extrinsic rewards can reduce the individual's perceived amount of intrinsic rewards. That is, rewards that are external to the task—a good example is money—can reduce the amount of rewards generated by the task itself—for example a feeling of accomplishment or enjoyment of performing the task (Deci, 1975; Deci & Ryan, 1985).

Equity Theory

One way that people at work examine their situation is by comparing what they put into and get out of the job to the inputs and outcomes of another. Inputs could be hours worked, education, experience, etc. Outcomes could be money, status, job level, etc. The theory presented by J. Stacey Adams (1963, 1965) presents this comparison in the form of a ratio:

$$\frac{\text{Outcomes}_{\text{self}}}{\text{Inputs}_{\text{self}}} : \frac{\text{Outcomes}_{\text{other}}}{\text{Inputs}_{\text{other}}}$$

If the ratio of self inputs to outcomes is similar to the ratio of the comparison other's inputs to outcomes, equity (or harmony) is not disturbed. However, when inequity is perceived to exist the individual perceiving the inequity is motivated to restore balance. Note that this is an individual's *perception* of inequality. Others could well see the same situation as being equitable. People can restore equity in many ways.

If the self outcomes-to-inputs ratio is less than that of the comparison other, the person could seek more outcomes (typically more pay); reduce inputs into the job (work less hard, take longer breaks); attempt to reduce the other's outcomes ("If you can't pay us the same, then pay him less"); decide that the other really has more inputs that balance the equation; decide that the comparison is being made with the wrong person (change the comparison other in the equity equation); or quit the job.

Employees often feel a strong need for equity. Managers seek to create a social situation where inequity is not felt, at least by those employees the manager wishes to keep on the job. What is important is the feeling of equity and not the absolute value of inputs or outcomes. Even professional baseball players earning two million dollars a year can genuinely feel mistreated when comparisons with their peers show their situation to be inequitable.

Salaries and benefits in North America are often kept secret in order that the information necessary to determine equity is not available to the individual. This **pay secrecy** is often not possible, however, for government or union jobs where pay rates are known. In Japan and Korea pay increases are not usually widely different for different members of a work group.

Pay secrecy When people at work do not know the salaries and benefits of others employed by the organization or of others employed in similar jobs with other organizations.

Keeping everyone at the same level earning about the same pay means that equity and harmony are maintained. Slow promotion in these Far East cultures allows the truly superior performers to be recognized over the long term. By then all members of the group have come to the same conclusion that the inputs of these superior performers are indeed greater than the inputs of others.

If the ratio of outcomes to inputs for the self turns out to be greater than that for the other, this overpayment inequity can be resolved by working harder or changing the perceived level of self inputs. In an individualistic work culture it does not usually take long for someone in overpayment inequity to decide that the level of self inputs is actually higher than previously thought and for internal balance to be restored. Someone else at work may perceive inequity, however!

Cognitive Choice

Cognitive Having to do with the mind.

This way of looking at managership is based on the **cognitive** approach, that how a person thinks about their work situation will affect their behaviour. The cognitive approaches to managership that will be examined here are expectancy theory and the Porter-Lawler extension to expectancy theory.

Expectancy Theory

Formulated by Victor Vroom (1964), expectancy theory is a theory of cognitive choice. It proposes that each individual at work examines his own personal work situation and makes a decision about how much effort to exert in the pursuit of work success. The formula for this calculation is

$$\text{Effort} = \text{E} \; \Sigma \; \text{I} \bullet \text{V}$$

Effort The amount of force exerted by an individual.

In this formula **effort** is the motivation of the worker to exert effort on the job. Effort, here the dependent variable, is predicted by the other variables. E is the worker's **expectancy** that effort will result in job performance. Expectancies are probabilities, ranging from 0 to 1, that effort will result in performance. I is the **instrumentality** of job performance to a work or non-work outcome. Instrumentalities can range from -1 to +1. They indicate the connection perceived in the mind of the individual worker that performance will lead to a given outcome. An instrumentality of +1 would mean that performance is certain to lead to the outcome. For example, a real estate agent selling a house is certain to receive a commission. The instrumentality between these two events is therefore +1.

Expectancy The employee's perception of the probability that effort will result in performance.

An instrumentality of -1 means that performance ensures another outcome is certain *not* to occur. For example, when a contractor completes a building on time, a late penalty will not be invoked. The instrumentality between on-time building completion and late penalty is -1.

Instrumentality The connection perceived in the mind of the individual worker that performance will lead to a given outcome.

Instrumentalities equal to or near zero mean that essentially no connection is perceived between job performance and outcomes. They in effect become zero in the expectancy equation and do not affect the decision about work effort.

Valence The anticipated satisfaction of an outcome.

V is the **valence** or anticipated satisfaction of an outcome. Valences can be positive or negative, small or large, and are attached to each outcome considered by the individual. When expectancy theory is represented in equation form, valences are often defined to vary between -10 and +10. This choice of units is arbitrary. Large anticipated satisfactions (high positive valences) and large anticipated dissatisfactions (high negative valences) when multiplied by associated instrumentalities and performance expectancy will have a large effect on the motivation to exert effort on the job.

The Σ (capital sigma: the summation sign) indicates that effort is affected by a range of possible work and non-work outcomes that might result from job performance. It is very important to recognize that it is the individual who decides what outcomes are related to job performance and what valences and instrumentalities to assign to each of the outcomes. Finally, examining the expectancy theory equation, it is clear that if expectancy is low, then no matter what outcomes are considered and how high their valences, effort is predicted to be low.

As an example of the operation of expectancy theory, think of an individual worker who considers important job-related outcomes to be an increase in salary, keeping the job, time spent with the family, and anticipated fatigue.

	Expectancy		Instrumentality	Valence	Outcome
			.7 ———————	+7	Salary Increase
			1.0 ———————	+10	Keeping the Job
Effort =	(.8)	Σ	-.6 ———————	+8	Family Time
			.5 ———————	-5	Anticipated Fatigue

For this person there are both positive and negative anticipated satisfactions that would result from job performance. The connection (instrumentality) between working hard and receiving a valued (V = +7) increase in salary is fairly strong at .7. But the connection between working hard and keeping the job is even stronger at 1.0. Working hard is moderately strongly connected to a decrease in time spent with family and to increased fatigue. The expectancy that working hard will lead to job performance is high, .8, or an 80% chance.

Summing the expectancy theory variables,

$$\text{Effort} = (.8)\times[(.7)(+7)+(1.0)(+10)+(-.6)(+8)+(.5)(-5)] = 6.08$$

we find that the overall motivation to exert a great deal of job effort is positive. For this person the benefits of working hard outweigh the costs.

The same person also considers the costs and benefits of working fairly easily. Outcomes and valences are the same, but the instrumentalities between working easily and outcomes change. As well, the expectancy that working easily will lead to job performance has dropped to .2. Note that the two expectancies add up to 1.0. There are no other possibilities considered—the choice is to work hard or to work easily.

	Expectancy		Instrumentality	Valence	Outcome
			.2 ———————	+7	Salary Increase
			.5 ———————	+10	Keeping the Job
Effort =	(.2)	Σ	.8 ———————	+8	Family Time
			-.8 ———————	-5	Anticipated Fatigue

Summing the expectancy theory variables,

$$\text{Effort} = (.2)\times[(.2)(+7)+(.5)(+10)+(.8)(+8)+(-.8)(-5)] = 3.36$$

we find that the motivation to work easily, while positive, is just over half the motivation to work hard. Expectancy theory would predict that this individual will choose to work hard on the job.

To use expectancy theory in an attempt to increase each individual worker's motivation to exert effort, a manager can focus on each of the theory's components.

1. The manager can aim to increase the worker's expectancy that effort will result in performance. Success on the job will increase E (and failure will lower it), as will job related training and the provision of the tools needed to do the job. The individual at work needs to see that performance is possible. Also, performance must be accurately perceived and measured (Chapter 6) for the individual worker to maintain a high Effort-leads-to-Performance expectancy.

2. The manager can find out what outcomes each person considers important, whether they are positively or negatively valued, and how they are affected by work performance. Perhaps these outcomes and values can be reevaluated based on the manager's knowledge of the experiences of other employees. For example the chances of a promotion may be higher than an employee thinks and the benefits of the promotion may be higher than anticipated by the employee. Also, the manager may know of other outcomes resulting from work performance that would be valued by the employee. Managers usually have at their disposal a variety of rewards that go beyond those anticipated by the employee. These can be made available as outcomes that will follow (with high instrumentality) work performance.

3. Finally, the manager can attempt to increase the valence of outcomes that are closely tied to job performance and to increase the instrumentality of outcomes that have high valence for the individual. Perhaps an employee can be convinced that the rewards available from work have more value (to the employee) than previously thought.

The Porter-Lawler Model

Lyman Porter and Edward Lawler (1968) extended expectancy theory. In their model, shown as Exhibit 8.5, Effort leads to Performance, but this link is moderated by the person's role perceptions and abilities and traits. A person lacking the ability to type, for example, would expect that effort and performance on a typing task would not be strongly linked. A person's role—the set of behaviours expected by others—will also affect the link between effort and performance. (Roles will be examined in more detail in Chapter 9.)

Performance leads to rewards—both intrinsic rewards that result from the work itself and extrinsic rewards that come from outside the work. More rewards are more satisfying, but perceived inequity in the amount of rewards will lower felt satisfaction.

There are two feedback loops in the model. Performance directly affects the future perception that effort leads to performance and rewards. Reward satisfaction affects the value of the reward as people can have enough of a given reward. This is called **satiation**. For example, praise is a reward given by managers, but over time a person can have enough praise. It can lose its value to the individual if it is not accompanied by other rewards such as promotions, raises in pay or new job duties.

The Porter-Lawler model is a useful extension to expectancy theory because it recognizes the individual nature of motivation but adds to that the importance of social roles and social comparisons.

Intentions

The major theory that relates to the construct of intentions is image theory (Beach, 1990). Image theory states that when individuals compare their current state to a projection of where they would like to be, the discrepancy will motivate action toward the image. Image theory is a theory of decision making and is discussed in Chapter 11.

Satiation The condition of an individual having had enough of a given stimulus, outcome, or reward.

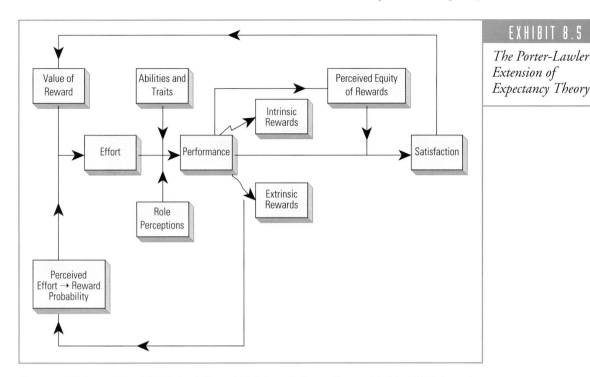

SOURCE: Lyman W. Porter and Edward E. Lawler (1968), *Managerial Attitudes and Performance*, Homewood, IL: Richard D. Irwin, Inc., p. 165. Reprinted with permission.

EXHIBIT 8.5

The Porter-Lawler Extension of Expectancy Theory

Goals

The theory of goal setting (for example Locke, 1968) is straightforward and formed of four parts: (1) difficult goals will produce higher performance than easy goals; (2) specific difficult goals will produce higher performance than will no goals or "I'll do my best" kinds of goals; (3) goal setting with feedback on goal attainment will produce higher performance than goal setting alone; and (4) employee participation in goal setting will help to produce higher performance than no participation when goals that are set participatively are higher than assigned goals.

Research evidence (Tubbs, 1986; Mento and others, 1987) strongly supports points (1) and (2) above. There is good evidence for point (4) (Tubbs, 1986), and some support for point (3) (Tubbs, 1986; Pritchard and others, 1988).

An early but still useful model for the managerial use of goal setting (Latham & Locke, 1979) is shown as Exhibit 8.6. In this model the manager works to set a specific and difficult goal at either the individual or group level so that subsequent employee effort can be directed toward high organizational performance. Not to be forgotten, however, are the organizational supports that are necessary to enable high performance to occur. Simply setting a difficult and challenging goal is not enough; employees must have the ability and resources required to do the job.

Some organizations have instituted formal goal setting procedures for use organization-wide. These plans, called **Management By Objectives (MBO)**, can be effective if the goals set are specific and difficult, are accepted by organizational members, and feedback is provided about goal accomplishment.

Management By Objectives (MBO)

A goal-setting plan whereby managers and subordinates discuss together the subordinate's goals and objectives for the next performance period. Rewards are usually tied to reaching these objectives.

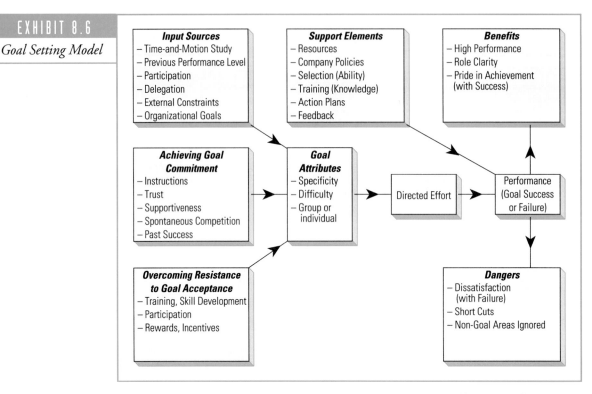

Source: Latham & Locke (1979). Reprinted, by permission of publisher, from ORGANIZATIONAL DYNAMICS, Autumn 1979. © 1979 American Management Association, New York. All rights reserved.

Individuals can, of course, use goal setting principles to manage themselves. The interested reader might like to try setting a specific and difficult goal and then charting progress toward it. The key is to select a goal that is not too far in the future and to be very specific about exactly what the goal is. A student's goal of carefully reading class notes and text chapters from 6 to 10 p.m. on Tuesday night before the test on Wednesday is a better goal, for example, than to get an "A" grade in the course. For a self-test of goal setting, see the exercise included at the end of this chapter.

Setting goals for oneself doesn't always work, though. The pirate in this chapter's *Overboard* cartoon has been working on his own motivation by listening to tape recordings of motivational speakers and setting goals for himself. His only problem is that in his line of work being in a group is necessary for individual success!

Source: OVERBOARD © Universal Press Syndicate. Reprinted with permission. All rights reserved.

A later goal model, also by Gary Latham and Ed Locke (Locke & Latham, 1990a,b,c) is called the high performance cycle and is shown in Exhibit 8.7. In this model high and challenging goals on meaningful tasks (along with the individual's generalized sense of competence and that effort will result in performance—called *self-efficacy*) lead to performance, rewards, and satisfaction.

Moderators to performance are variables that will make some people more or less capable of performing. For example, task performance will be more difficult without the necessary ability, commitment, or feedback. Mediators, on the other hand, are variables that affect how the performance is carried out. In this model the mediators are the motivation of the organizational member, the degree of persistence, and the specific strategies used for task accomplishment.

The high performance cycle shares some similarities to the Porter-Lawler expectancy theory. There is one main difference, however. In the expectancy model a manager attempts to affect how the employee thinks about the work and the decision of how much effort to expend. But in the high performance cycle the manager places performance demands on the employee and then through the model's moderators and mediators attempts to make high performance more possible. In both models, however, as well as those theories that focus on a person's behaviour, the use of rewards by managers is important.

Self-Regulation

Cognitive choice theories of motivation are concerned with what a person thinks about. Self-regulation theories are interested in actual behaviour. These two approaches are contrasted in this chapter's *On the One Hand* feature.

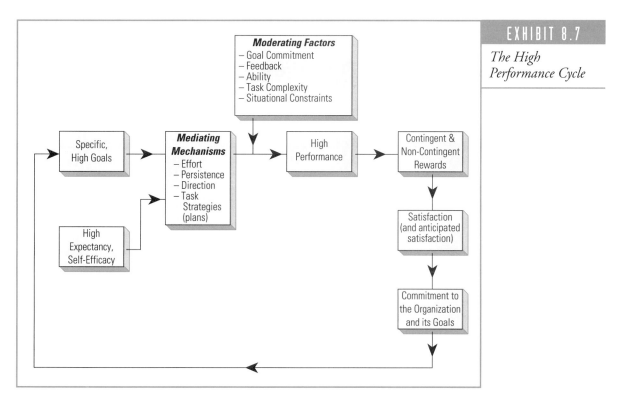

EXHIBIT 8.7

*The High
Performance Cycle*

Source: Reprinted with permission from Edwin A. Locke and Gary P. Latham (1990), "Work motivation and satisfaction: Light at the end of the tunnel," *Psychological Science* 1: 244. Reprinted by permission of Cambridge University Press.

We will now examine how behaviour is learned and how to make desirable work behaviours more likely and less desirable behaviours less likely. Concepts of classical conditioning, operant conditioning, negative reinforcement, punishment, self-reinforcement, and social learning will be investigated as ways to help a manager understand and possibly control the behaviours of individuals at work.

Classical Conditioning

Before scientists of human behaviour discovered the principles of operant conditioning, the Russian scientist Ivan Pavlov demonstrated that the sound of a bell could make a dog salivate. First, Pavlov rang the bell while food powder was placed in the mouth of the dog. Then, after a series of these pairings of food and the bell, the dog learned to salivate (which, of course, is the dog's natural response to food) at the sound of the bell, whether or not food was actually present. Humans as well as dogs can be conditioned to salivate at the sound of a dinner bell, but there are also occasions when classical conditioning is found in the workplace.

The lunch bell or factory whistle at quitting time can produce the conditioned responses of salivating/eating or leaving the factory. The sound of a warning horn on a forklift truck, if paired with the adrenaline released into the body to help avoid danger, can later produce the adrenaline push even when danger is not present. If the air quality in an office building is poor and gives people headaches, the act of going to the office can trigger the headache even before the poor air quality has had an actual physical effect.

Operant Conditioning

Shaping   The shaping of behaviour requires that a target end behaviour is known and that the person (or animal) being shaped can exhibit successive approximations to that end behaviour. For example, a salesperson may be taught how to deal with customers by working with a trainer. This instructor has a predetermined image of the desired sales behaviour in mind. The trainer rewards the trainee when a customer is served in a way that is closer to the ideal than was the service to the previous customer. For shaping to be successful, the person being shaped must be able to generate the target behaviour and must value the reward being offered to learn the new behaviour.

O N   T H E   O N E   H A N D . . .

Ahmed Ashour of Alexandria University and Gary Johns of Concordia University in Montreal examined how a leader's [or manager's] influence on subordinate motivation could be exerted through the use of rewards and punishments. They hypothesized that higher rewards contingent on desired behaviour would increase subordinate motivation; more intense punishments, also contingent on behaviour, would reduce the subordinate's motivation to engage in the undesirable behaviour, and that the leader/manager's use of fixed or variable ratio reinforcement schedules would generate more intense subordinate motivation than other schedules. They go on to examine the constraints on the use of reinforcements and punishments at work. The view put forward in this article is that a manager's influence on subordinate motivation can be well understood by looking at the manager's use of rewards and punishments.

SOURCE: Ahmed S. Ashour and Gary Johns (1983), "Leader influence through operant principles: A theoretical and methodological framework," *Human Relations* 36: 603-626.

ON THE OTHER HAND...

In a review of organizational behaviour articles, Martin Evans of the University of Toronto proposes that individual motivation is best understood as a cognitive process. The individual is thought to set goals and compare feedback on performance to the goal, and then to evaluate any discrepancy by making attributions about the causes of performance. The decision made of *why* the goal/performance discrepancy exists then affects satisfaction with performance and the individual's overall estimate that the goal can be reached. This decision then feeds back to affect the new goal and acceptance of the new goal. Though Evans also notes that the consequences of performance also affect the goals set and goal acceptance, there is a decidedly cognitive slant to his understanding of motivation at work.

SOURCE: Martin G. Evans (1986), "Organizational behavior: The central role of motivation," *Journal of Management* 12: 203-222.

Reinforcement Theory   In reinforcement theory a certain behaviour (the operant) by the subject is followed by a positive stimulus (the reward) or a negative stimulus (the punishment) in order to make the behaviour more likely or less likely. The general and most important principle of reinforcement theory is that people will do what they are rewarded for doing and will avoid doing what they are punished for doing. This principle is well-known and many examples can be given to illustrate that rewarded behaviour is more likely to occur in the future.

A simple example is why a person goes to work. What is the reward for attendance? One answer is usually the money paid for attendance. But some jobs are not paid positions. These include volunteer work in a hospital or serving on the board of directors of a charity. Whether a position is paid or unpaid, it may provide such rewards as membership in a work group, doing interesting work, or providing learning and experience that will be valuable in a future job. Without a reward for being a member of an organization or group, people simply stop attending (unless there is a punishment for absence). The thoughts of several prominent executives in Canada on the issue of motivating others without relying exclusively on money as a reward are found in Exhibit 8.8.

An important point that needs to be remembered is that what is rewarding or punishing is decided on by each individual person. Even a boss that screams obscenities at employees (most people would find that punishing) could be perceived as rewarding by someone.

A great deal of research has been done by psychologists on how best to reinforce behaviour, in terms of the amount and timing of rewards. A strong finding is that rewards and punishments have their greatest effect when they closely follow behaviour. When the separation between behaviour and outcomes is too long, the connection between behaviour and stimulus can be lost.

Other work has shown that different **schedules of reinforcement** affect how quickly a behaviour is learned and how long it takes before it disappears when it is no longer rewarded (called **extinction**). Four reinforcement schedules are fixed interval, fixed ratio, variable interval, and variable ratio.

An example of **fixed interval** is being paid once a month on the last day of the month. A fixed interval schedule of reinforcement will reward a person for being present on the day the reward is due.

An example of a **fixed ratio** reinforcement plan is being paid a piece rate of 50 cents for every unit produced. The ratio in this case is fixed at 1:1. If a $10 bonus were paid to an employee for every tenth customer who applies for a company credit card the ratio

Schedules of reinforcement   Plans of timing and frequency in the rewarding of behaviour.

Extinction   The process of not rewarding a behaviour so that it will cease to be exhibited.

Fixed interval reinforcement schedule The reinforcer is given after a precise interval of time has elapsed since the last reinforcement.

Fixed ratio reinforcement schedule The reinforcer is given after every nth occurrence of the desired behaviour. N may be one or a number greater than one.

EXHIBIT 8.8 ADVICE FROM CANADIAN EXECUTIVES ON MOTIVATING EMPLOYEES

The Question:

Times are tough. How do I motivate my people without money or promotions?

The Answers:

Luckily, money's important but it's not top of the list. In my experience, people value independence, responsibility and a chance to grow.

Rosey Brenan, Rodon Communications.

The way to motivate when money and promotions are scarce is the same as when money and promotions are abundant—respect and recognition.

Equity is critical—employees want fair treatment for everyone (that includes you, the boss). Contribution should be what counts, not position or politics.

Employees want to know what's expected of them, so give direction, honest feedback and training.

Motivation's an individual thing so don't assume; ask employees what turns their crank.

Wayne Hanna, Coopers & Lybrand Consulting Group.

Managers and employees need more praise than they're getting. Effective praise is sincere, specific, frequent, appropriate, and timely.

Get creative to add challenge. Use job-title changes, job rotations and job re-definitions.

Carla Furlong, Furlong & Associates.

Let people know their work is valued in little ways that really count. Remember their birthdays. Send anniversary and sympathy cards. Take everyone out for pizza. Bring in some home cooking. Lunch with someone new every day.

Wayne McKay, Wayne McKay & Associates.

Show them how their work contributes to the organization's goal/mission. Include staff in planning and decision-making.

Dugal Smith, Partner, Price Waterhouse.

In the final analysis, remember that you don't motivate people, they motivate themselves. The most you can do—and the operative word here is do—is create a motivating environment.

Harriett Lemer, Einblau & Associates.

SOURCE: Excerpted with permission from Carla Furlong (1993), "A million dollars worth of advice," *B.C. Business*, April 1993, pp. 79, 81.

Variable interval reinforcement schedule

The reinforcer is given at varying and unpredictable times. The time between reinforcements averages out to a pre-set interval.

Variable ratio reinforcement schedule

The reinforcer is given after a varying and unpredictable number of times that the behaviour occurs.

Token reinforcement plan

Symbolic items (tokens) are given as rewards for desired behaviour.

would be fixed at 1:10. It would be paid immediately after the tenth order. A fixed ratio schedule will motivate a person to work hard when the reward is near ("Only three more orders to go!") but not when the reward has just been obtained.

A company could be concerned about employees being at work by 8 a.m. It could pay a $20 bonus to every employee at work by 8 a.m. on a given day. If this bonus were awarded *on average* once in every five days it would be a **variable interval** reinforcement schedule.

A **variable ratio** schedule would allocate a reward on an average of once for every x times that the behaviour being rewarded were to occur. For example, a salesperson could be paid a $10 bonus for every 25 customers contacted, but the bonus could be paid at any time, not just after the 25th customer. It might be paid after the 10th and 40th customers. The average, however, would be that for every 25 customers the bonus would be paid once. A popular example of the variable ratio reward schedule is that of a slot machine, which is programmed to pay jackpots on a determined frequency (unknown to the gambler) but could pay a jackpot twice in succession. Think how effective slot machines would be if they operated on a fixed ratio schedule! Variable interval and variable ratio reinforcement schedules make the behaviour more constant because the person does not know which behaviour will be the one to be rewarded.

Organizations often provide reinforcements using what is called a **token reinforcement plan**. In this plan a token (it could be a poker chip, a "point," or any other symbolic item) is given after the desired behaviour. Tokens are accumulated and then turned in for a product or service that has value to the person being rewarded. For example, mental health organizations often put patients on a token plan to control their behaviour—patients then buy food, magazines, etc. with the tokens. Airlines use these principles with their frequent flier plans—here the tokens are "points" which may be turned in later for air travel. However, like all token reinforcement plans, when stopped the behaviour being rewarded will likely stop as well (see Kohn, 1993). In technical terms the behaviour will "extinguish." This is one dilemma faced by airlines over their frequent flier plans—once started they are hard to stop.

Though the effects of reinforcement and different schedules of reinforcement are well-known to managers in organizations, their use could be planned much better. For example, paying people their salary once a month by direct bank deposit is efficient and effective in the accounting sense, but the reward potential of that payment is mostly lost. A classic article in organizational behaviour is that by Steve Kerr (1975) of the University of Southern California, entitled "On the folly of rewarding A, while hoping for B" (see this chapter's *A Little Knowledge* feature). His main point is that it can be very clear to organizations what behaviour is being rewarded, yet people in the organization persist in hoping that another behaviour will be exhibited by organizational members. Reinforcement theory can help the manager in an organization to understand just what is being rewarded. The manager's job will then be to decide if the rewarded behaviour is the one desired.

Sometimes rewards have unintended consequences. This point is made in Tom Watson Jr.'s 1963 book about IBM.

> The moral is drawn from a story by the Danish philosopher, Søren Kierkegaard. He told of a man on the coast of Zealand who liked to watch the wild ducks fly south in great flocks each fall. Out of charity, he took to putting feed for them in a nearby pond. After a while some of the ducks no longer bothered to fly south; they wintered in Denmark on what he fed them. In time they flew less and less. When the wild ducks returned, the others would circle up to greet them but then head back to their feeding grounds on the pond. After three or four years they grew so lazy and fat that they found difficulty in flying at all. Kierkegaard drew his point—you can make wild ducks tame, but you can never make tame ducks wild again. One might also add that the duck who is tamed will never go anywhere anymore. We are convinced that any business needs its wild ducks. And in I.B.M. we try not to tame them. (pp. 27-28)

Negative Reinforcement

When a behaviour causes a negative stimulus to be removed, that stimulus is a negative reinforcer. For example, in Japan's Hell Camp (Phalon, 1984) employees wear several "badges of shame"—ribbons that each list a personal weakness. During the camp, employees engage in often humiliating exercises. Then, as they demonstrate their strengths, the ribbons are removed one by one. The ribbon is a negative stimulus that the person is trying to remove by behaving appropriately, so it is a negative reinforcer.

Negative reinforcement When a person learns to act to remove a negative stimulus.

Punishment

Sometimes a behaviour by an organizational member is not desired, but not rewarding it will not lead to its extinction. In this case there is some other reward that is reinforcing the undesired behaviour. Therefore, to stop the behaviour a punishment is applied. A punishment is an outcome that is negatively valued by the person. For example, factory time clocks are often programmed to print the time of worker arrival on the time card. When the employee is late the time is printed in red ink and the employee is "docked" 1/4 hour of pay (for example) as a punishment. The red ink is the signal of the punishment.

In some provinces, when drivers violate the rules of the road and are apprehended, the government may apply "points" to their licenses. This earning of points is a punishment for inappropriate behaviour. When enough points are earned the punishment escalates.

Punishment The application of a negative stimulus to stop an unwanted behaviour.

A LITTLE KNOWLEDGE

What is the hoped for behaviour and what is actually being rewarded? Steven Kerr gives us a series of examples that show how we (societies, organizations, and individuals) reward one thing while hoping for another. Cases in point:

1. In politics the citizens of a country want the candidates to be clear about what their policies and proposed programs are, but will elect only those candidates that are *not* clear about what will be done.

2. In war, the soldier on the front line wants to go home. But when soldiers are asked to complete a time limited tour of duty (as was the case for the American soldiers in Viet Nam) the way to go home was to survive until the end of the tour (not necessarily to win the war!). To get home, then, the individual soldier was rewarded for avoiding combat, not winning the war.

3. In medicine, a doctor can theoretically make two kinds of error. The doctor can label a sick person well or a well person sick. With medical costs rising, society as a whole may want to accept some of the first kind of error until symptoms are strong enough that the error is uncovered. But for the physician the reward system encourages the doctor to avoid pronouncing a sick person well (What if the patient dies! Think of the malpractice suit!) and to err on the side of pronouncing a well person sick (better safe than sorry, and the patient can be billed for the tests that are made to make sure).

4. In organizations such as orphanages, the hope is that the organization will place its children with good homes and keep the number of children in the institution at a very low level. But the orphanage is given a budget that is based on the number of children who are actually living in the facility— encouraging the manager to increase the number of children in residence.

5. An insurance organization wants to pay claims in a timely and accurate manner, while holding down the number of complaint letters received by policy holders. When paying surgical claims it can often be difficult for the claims clerk to decide which surgical procedure, each having a different claim payment, was performed. In order to avoid a letter of protest for paying on the procedure with a lower claim amount (the surgeon's staff is unlikely to protest if the insurance company pays too much) and to keep to the target of paying claims within two days of receipt, the clerk pays for the more costly procedure. While it looks like claims are being handled properly, the reality is that the insurance company is paying too much. Behaviour that fits the reward system is chosen even if it is not the most effective behaviour for the organization as a whole.

SOURCE: Based on information in Steven Kerr (1975), "On the folly of rewarding A, while hoping for B," *Academy of Management Journal* 18: 769-783.

Fines may be levied or the license may be revoked. But when a defined period of time has elapsed, some of these points are removed from the driver's record. This is a negative reinforcement. Presumably the driver is behaving appropriately (that is, not receiving any more points) and so is rewarded by the loss of points.

Punishment can be a good way to stop the occurrence of an unwanted behaviour, but has some undesirable side effects. For this reason punishment should only be used when the behaviour is one that must be immediately stopped. Examples are unsafe working practices or physical violence between two workers.

One side effect of punishment is that the person being punished can associate the negative consequence with the punisher and may later react against the punisher, someone else, or the company. This side effect is not to be taken lightly. People at work who learn to dislike someone who punishes them can become violent. They may take their anger out on the supervisor, co-workers, themselves, or even innocent bystanders.

Another punishment side effect is that the undesirable behaviour will tend to reoccur when the punisher is absent or the person punished feels there is little chance of being caught. So, for example, a person pumping gasoline may know it is against the safety rules to smoke a cigarette near the pumps and would be fired for doing so, but may smoke anyway if the manager is absent. Under punishment, "while the cat's away the mice will play."

To punish effectively, the manager must punish immediately after the undesired behaviour. The desired behaviour must be made clear so that the employee knows what *to do* not just what *not* to do. Finally, it is the action that should be punished and not the person.

Self-Reinforcement

An individual can reward or punish himself depending on his own behaviour. For example, some people who are struggling to get through a dry textbook will say to themselves something like "I'll get to the end of this chapter, then take 20 minutes off to watch TV." The behaviour is reading and reaching the goal and the reward is watching TV.

Self-reinforcement
A person applying rewards and punishments to his or her own behaviour.

Self-reward can be a very effective tool used by participants in organizations to control their own behaviour. But it is necessary that the rules set linking behaviour and rewards are strictly held. Many people cannot keep to their own rules and start cheating either on the behaviour (flipping the pages instead of reading them) or on the reward (20 minutes stretches to an hour). People also engage in self-punishment, but again there can be negative consequences—for example a lessening of the self-concept as the punisher is the self.

Social Learning

People learn what to do, what works and what doesn't work not only by what happens when they try different behaviours, but by watching others. This can also be called **modeling**. It is a very important form of learning because mistakes do not have to be made before they are corrected and effective behaviours do not have to be learned bit by bit over time. People can learn effective behaviours all at once in great leaps by watching what others do. They can see the whole behaviour all at once. Also, they learn vicariously (not directly) by watching others so they do not receive the rewards or the punishments that the other may obtain.

Modeling   Learning by watching others

The most crucial element in social learning is the role model. Managers can model effective behaviour themselves. For instance, the manager of a life insurance agency could take a new recruit on a series of sales calls to show how the selling is done. Or the manager could create two-person teams of a junior and a senior person so that the junior can learn by watching the other. Rookie police officers are often assigned to more senior colleagues in this way. They learn by doing and by watching. Of course, if the role model is showing what the manager would consider to be the "wrong" way to act, social learning in this instance will not be effective from the manager's point of view.

REWARD SYSTEMS

People at work are concerned with rewards—what they receive as a consequence of a certain behaviour. Managers therefore must understand the importance of rewards in the workplace, the many different types of rewards, and how rewards are made.

In an interesting book on management, Michael LeBoeuf (1985) writes that the greatest management principle in the world is "The Things That Get Rewarded Get Done!" He says that the magic question of management is "What is being rewarded?" LeBoeuf has distilled his thinking about the management of rewards into the ten strategies shown as Exhibit 8.9.

What rewards are available to the manager? While most people would immediately think of only a few major work rewards—pay, promotion, the chance to do interesting tasks—there is a wide variety of possible work rewards. The list presented in

Dr. Nancy Greer of the British Columbia Systems Corporation receives a corporate commendation.

EXHIBIT 8.9   TEN STRATEGIES OF REWARDING

1. Reward solid solutions instead of quick fixes.
2. Reward risk taking instead of risk evading.
3. Reward applied creativity instead of mindless conformity.
4. Reward decisive action instead of paralysis by analysis.
5. Reward smart work instead of busywork.
6. Reward simplification instead of needless complication.
7. Reward quietly effective behaviour instead of squeaking joints.
8. Reward quality work instead of fast work.
9. Reward loyalty instead of turnover.
10. Reward working together instead of working against.

SOURCE: Based on information in Michael LeBoeuf (1985), *The Greatest Management Principle in the World*, New York: Putnam Publishing Group.

Exhibit 8.10 is only a start! While some of these rewards are typically not tied to job performance—for example a base salary can be contingent on attendance or organizational membership—others can be contingent on performance. Managers need to:

- Determine what is currently being rewarded;
- Decide what work performance should be rewarded;
- Develop a wide variety of rewards that can be awarded at the manager's discretion (that is, the manager controls the reward);
- Reward desired behaviour within the context of the social situation at work.

Reward system   A set of rules regarding how rewards are earned and paid.

Managers in organizations will often create a **reward system**, especially for the allocation of pay and benefits. These systems are a set of rules regarding how rewards are earned and paid. An important point to remember when considering any system is that if one person can create it, another can figure out how to beat it (see the feature *Seeing is Believing* for an example of this in a gas plant). Managers have to avoid being caught up in a cycle of adding more rules to the system only to have someone else find the "loophole" to beat the system, which necessitates the addition of still more rules and so on.

Unintended consequences   Behaviours in reaction to a reward system that were not anticipated by the system's designer.

Pay systems always have intended consequences (the behaviours and outcomes they are designed to reward) and **unintended consequences** (the other behaviours that are actually rewarded). Both intended and unintended consequences need to be carefully monitored for a reward system to be effective.

Job evaluation   A determination of the requirements of a job.

In order to determine the relative worth or contribution of a job to the organization as a whole, a **job evaluation** may be undertaken. Evaluations are then used, at least in part, as input to determine the pay associated with a job. Four methods of job evaluation are: job ranking; job classification; factor comparison; and the point method (Bartley, 1981).

Job ranking is the simplest method of the four. Job descriptions are compared for all jobs in the organization and an overall ranked list is created. One drawback to this approach is that the relative worth of each job is difficult to determine.

Job classification methods attempt to classify jobs based on the amount of skill and responsibility required. Jobs are then ordered from highest to lowest. Pay is allocated in greater amounts for jobs higher in the classification.

The *factor comparison* method begins by determining the important job factors for any job. Common factors are those of the mental, skill, and physical requirements of the job, responsibility, and working conditions. Then key jobs are identified for the organization and

EXHIBIT 8.10   REWARDS AVAILABLE FROM ORGANIZATIONS

CONSUMABLES	STATUS SYMBOLS	MONEY AND BENEFITS	SOCIAL	BETTER WORK/ TIME OFF WORK
Coffee-break treats	Desk accessories	Money	Friendly greetings	Job with more responsibility
Free lunches	Personal computer	Stocks	Informal recognition	Job rotation
Food baskets	Wall plaques	Stock options	Formal acknowledge-ment of achievement	Early time off with pay
Easter hams	Company car	Movie passes		
Paid dinners for the family	Watches	Trading stamps (green stamps)	Feedback about performance	Extended breaks
Company picnics	Trophies	Paid-up insurance policies	Solicitation of suggestions	Extended lunch period
After-work wine and cheese parties	Commendations		Solicitation of advice	Personal time off with pay
	Rings/tie pins	Dinner theatre/ sports tickets	Compliment on work progress	Work on personal project on company time
	Sales prizes such as home appliances	Vacation trips	Recognition in com-pany newsletter	Use of company ma-chinery or facilities for personal projects
	Clothing, especially symbolic clothing	Coupons redeemable at local stores	Pat on the back	Use of company recreation facilities
	Club privileges	Profit sharing	Verbal or nonverbal recognition or praise	Special assignments
	Office with a window	Company literature		
	Piped-in music or office stereo	Tickets to popular speakers or lecturers		
	Redecoration of work environment	Membership in book club, magazine subscriptions		
	Private office			

SOURCE: Adapted with permission from Fred Luthans and Robert Kreitner (1985), *Organizational Behavior Modification and Beyond: An Operant and Social Learning Approach*, Glenview, IL: Scott, Foresman and Company, p. 127. © 1985 Scott Foresman & Co. Reprinted by permission of HarperCollins Publishers.

these are ranked against each factor. Through a process of discussion and evaluation, monetary values are assigned to each factor. For example, the mental requirements of one key job might be determined to be worth $4/hour, the skill requirements $2.50/hour, etc. Then other jobs in the organization are broken down into their levels of each of the job factors and the monetary values for those factors are added up, resulting in a pay level for each job.

The *point method* (Hay, 1948) is similar in that job factors are identified and described, then points are assigned to these factors. Each job in the organization is then evaluated for its level of each job factor, points are summed, and point totals are linked to pay levels. Higher point totals for a job mean higher pay for the person in that job.

Some newer approaches to reward systems are cafeteria-style fringe benefits, all-salaried teams, skill-based pay, and profit sharing. The **cafeteria-style fringe benefits** approach gives employees a budget and allows them to select the benefits they most want from a "menu" of possibilities. The advantage of this approach is that each person can select the benefit of most value depending on her circumstances. A young single person might select extra vacation days, a parent of young children a dental plan, and an older worker with adult children higher contributions to the company pension plan. While such choice of benefits might not motivate job effort or performance, it could make the individual worker more satisfied, less stressed, and therefore be more likely to attend work and stay in the job.

Cafeteria-style fringe benefits Employees are given a budget and are allowed to select the benefits they most want from a menu of possibilities.

SEEING IS BELIEVING

SEÑOR PAYROLL

Larry and I were Junior Engineers in the gas plant, which means that we were clerks. Junior Engineers were beneath the notice of everyone except the Mexican laborers at the plant. To them we were the visible form of a distant, unknowable paymaster. We were Señor payroll.

Those Mexicans were great workmen: the aristocrats among them were the stokers, big men who worked Herculean eight-hour shifts in the fierce heat of the retorts. They scooped coal with huge shovels and hurled it with uncanny aim at tiny doors. The stokers worked stripped to the waist, and there was pride and dignity in them. Few men could do such work, and they were the few.

The company paid its men only twice a month, on the fifth and on the twentieth. To a Mexican, this was absurd. What man with money will make it last 15 days? If he hoarded money beyond the spending of three days, he was a miser—and when, Señor, did the blood of Spain flow in the veins of misers? Hence it was the custom for our stokers to appear every third or fourth day to draw the money due to them. There was a certain elasticity in the Company rules, and Larry and I sent the necessary forms to the Main Office and received an "advance" against a man's paycheck. Then, one day, Downtown sent a memo that an advance against wages was only to be made in the case of a genuine emergency.

We had no sooner posted the notice when in came stoker Juan Garcia. He asked for an advance and I pointed to the notice and explained that the Company would pay only if someone was ill or if money was urgently needed for some other good reason. In the next hour two other stokers came in, looked at the notice, had it explained and walked solemnly out; then no more came. What we did not know was that Juan Garcia had spread the word and that every Mexican in the plant was explaining the order to every other Mexican. "To get the money now, the wife must be sick. There must be medicine for the baby."

The next morning Juan Garcia's wife was practically dying, Pete Mendoza's mother would hardly last the day, there was a veritable epidemic among children and, just for variety, there was one sick father. We always suspected that the old man was really sick; no Mexican would otherwise have thought of him. At any rate, nobody paid Larry and me to examine private lives; we made out our forms with an added line describing the "genuine emergency." Our people got paid.

That went on for a week. Then came a new order that employees would be paid ONLY on the fifth and the 20th of the month. Exceptions would be made only in the case of employees leaving the service of the Company. The notice went up on the board and we explained its significance to Juan Garcia. In the morning he was back. "I am quitting this company for a different job. You pay me now?" We argued that it was a good company but in the end we paid off, because Juan Garcia quit. And so did Gonzales, Mendoza, Obregon, Ayala and Ortez, the best stokers, men who could not be replaced. The next day, when the foreman was wringing his hands and asking the Almighty if he was personally supposed to shovel this coal, there in the employment line stood Garcia, Mendoza and the others—waiting to be hired. We hired them, of course. There was nothing else to do.

Every day we had a line of resigning stokers, and another line of stokers seeking work. Our paperwork became very complicated. At the Main Office they were jumping up and down. Our phone rang early and often. Out of chaos, Downtown issued another order. I read it and whistled. Larry looked at it and said, "It is going to be very quiet around here." The order read: "Hereafter, no employee who resigns may be rehired within a period of 30 days." Juan Garcia was due for another resignation, and when he came in we showed him the order and explained that standing in line the next day would do him no good if he resigned today. "Thirty days is a long time, Juan."

It was a grave matter and he took time to reflect on it. So did Gonzales, Mendoza, Ayala and Ortez. Ultimately, however, they were all back—and all resigned. We did our best to dissuade them and we were sad about the parting. This time it was for keeps and they shook hands with us solemnly. In the morning, however, they were all back in line. With the utmost gravity, Juan Garcia informed me that he was a stoker looking for a job. "No dice, Juan" I said. "Come back in 30 days. I warned you." His eyes looked straight into mine without a flicker. "There is some mistake, Señor," he said. "I am Manuel Hernandez. I work as the stoker in Pueblo, in Santa Fe, in many places." I stared back at him, remembering the sick wife and the babies without medicine, the mother-in-law in the hospital, the many resignations and the re-hirings. I knew that there was a gas plant in Pueblo, and that there wasn't any in Santa Fe; but who was I to argue with a man about his own name? A stoker is a stoker.

So I hired him. I hired Gonzalez, too, who swore that his name was Carrera, and Ayala, who had shamelessly become Smith. Three days later the resigning started. Within a week our payroll read like a history of Latin America. Everyone was on it: Lopez and Obregon, Villa, Diaz, Batista, Gomez, and even San Martin and Bolivar. Finally, Larry and I, growing weary of staring at familiar faces and writing unfamiliar names, went to the Superintendent and told him the whole story. He tried not to grin, and said, "Damned nonsense!"

The next day the orders were taken down. We called our most prominent stokers into the office and pointed to the board. No rules any more. "The next time we hire you *hombres*," Larry said grimly, "come in under the names you like best, because that's the way you are going to stay on the books." They looked at us and they looked at the board; then for the first time in the long duel, their teeth flashed white. "*Si, Señores*," they said. And so it was.

On **all-salaried teams** everyone is paid a salary instead of some members being on salary and some paid on an hourly basis. The advantage here is that a greater sense of cohesion is created along with the willingness to share tasks.

Employees on a **skill-based pay** plan are paid a base hourly rate and an additional amount per hour for each job skill they have mastered, whether the skill is currently used or not. This plan promotes flexibility, job rotation, and the constant upgrading of skills.

Finally, there are many different types of **profit sharing** plans that exist for allocating a portion of company profits to its members. The purpose of these plans is to enhance the employee's identification with the company's overall objective by providing the employee a stake in the profits.

The above four approaches can be very effective if the manager continually keeps in mind the key questions: "What behaviour is being rewarded?" and "Is that the behaviour that I wish to encourage?"

While reward systems are important, as we have discussed, a manager cannot concentrate on only one area of motivation. The manager must view the employee as a whole person whose behaviour is affected by factors at home, at work, and in the society. At the middle management level self-managing teams are taking over some of the manager's tasks of supervising others and processing information. This has led to a reduction in the ranks of middle managers and new ways of getting things done. The new manager is more of a leader, coach, or internal consultant, shares information and decision making, and looks for results (Dumaine, 1993). An evaluation of the basic requirements for a manager are to be found in this chapter's *A Word to the Wise* feature.

All-salaried teams

Everyone on a team is paid a salary instead of some members being on salary and some paid on an hourly basis.

Skill-based pay plan

Employees are paid a base hourly rate and an additional amount per hour for each job skill they have mastered, whether the skill is currently used or not.

Profit sharing   A plan for allocating a portion of company profits to its members.

CONCLUSION

In this chapter we have examined management and motivation at primarily the individual and dyadic (manager-subordinate) levels. Here we conclude our discussion about individuals—how people are the same and different in who and what they are and in how they perceive and evaluate their environment. While there is no question that organizations are made up of individuals and that it is individuals who make decisions and take actions on behalf of their organization, people in organizations are often part of a group. The importance of groups and group behaviour is the topic which we now turn to in Chapter 9.

CHAPTER SUMMARY

Managers in organizations can take upon themselves different roles. Eight managerial roles are those of coordinator, monitor, director, producer, broker, innovator, mentor, and facilitator. Each of these roles is expected to be most useful in different organizational circumstances and using different ways of measuring organizational effectiveness.

Managers typically perform a great quantity of work at an unrelenting pace. Their daily activity is full of unscheduled meetings, telephone calls, and reactions to the day's crises, producing a varied, fragmented, and hectic day. They do, however, have some control over the structure of what they do, especially in the longer term. Managers prefer to deal with issues on-the-spot. They communicate with a wide variety of people outside the organization, usually over the telephone and in meetings. One of the most important jobs of a manager is to motivate organizational members to apply effort towards accomplishing the organization's task. Theories of motivation may be used by a manager toward this end. Theories have been constructed that deal with a person's needs, personality, and interests; inherent human motives; the decisions and choices that a person makes; a person's formulated intentions for action; goals that a person sets; and individual self-regulation of action based on recognition of the results of previous actions. Managers may also devise reward systems in their efforts to help direct action and effort toward achieving organizational goals.

A WORD TO THE WISE

Looking back from the year 2000, I believe that the 1990s will be seen in management circles as the decade of the flat company. By that, I do not mean that I am predicting a change in terminology from today's "limited company," public or otherwise. Nor am I making reference to property concerns or off-shoots of the Flat Earth Society. I am talking about organisational structures — more specifically, about the changes that information technology will bring to bear on them in the course of the next 10 years.

Until recently, developments in IT were restricted largely to building computers that could crunch ever more numbers ever faster. We are now seeing something different. Systems can currently provide a range of alternatives which give the manager a set of choices by risk, resources, and potential benefits. They can carry out the most complex and realistic "what if" tests, assessing what can happen to a business if it tries differing strategies. They can even run simulations which are so detailed and complicated that they allow realistic "creations" of products and substances which do not exist. In effect, the advances in systems are not just quantitative. They permit completely new ways of thinking about, and carrying out, all the tasks of business.

Systems can provide management with immediate, complete decision support facilities — all the information necessary to decide which course of action to pursue, with all the attached risks and benefits quantified, at the touch of a button.

In practice, this will result in role changes for large chunks of what have traditionally been managerial positions. Instead of being either a keeper of data or a transmission belt for orders, the manager will become the decision maker, following the overall outlines of previously decided main corporate strategy.

This will result in far slimmer management structures. It will mean that only two levels of management are required — one level which selects long-term strategies and finds the people to effect them, and one level which deals with operational opportunities and motivates and leads the staff members who will accomplish them.

These developments make possible the long-time dream of business structures: organisations which are lean, but flexible and resilient to marketplace changes, even in the largest of companies.

All managers will, of course, have to be "IT fluent." This does not mean that every manager will need to know how to build or operate systems, but he or she will need to understand their potential and how to make use of them. The manager will thus have a far broader focus and greater flexibility than has previously been the case. He or she will need to be a far more complete business person than ever before.

However, the basic requirements of a manager will still be there. Everyone who has reached a certain level in any organisation has their own personal yardstick of what they are looking for in their managers. I look for 10 qualities, which I list here in no particular order of merit.

The first is to have lots of energy. There are many bad decisions made, and many decisions that are not made at all, simply because the person responsible was too tired to handle things effectively. British Airways is a service business, operating around the clock worldwide, seven days a week. A manager without a great deal of energy quickly starts to look frayed around the edges.

Second, good managers must be totally willing to commit themselves emotionally. Traditionally in Britain we have considered it a bad show to be seen to be emotionally enthusiastic when it comes to business issues. But emotional commitment helps other people to identify and participate, as well as giving them a good reason to associate. It is a key part of what most people unashamedly call charisma.

Third, managers must have the desire to excel. Anyone who does not have a strong desire to do well—to pursue personal, professional excellence—or who feels no need for compliments, will certainly not be a good manager. They have to have the desire to be good simply because it gives them satisfaction, quite apart from any resulting financial benefits.

Fourth, he or she must have the ability to take delight from the success of others — the kind of person who enjoys basking in the warmth of success that they have helped engender, without seeking personal credit.

Fifth, a manager must possess a good state of health.

This ties in with the need for energy and emotional commitment. Without a healthy physique, neither is possible.

The sixth quality is a genuine liking for people, without being excessively outgoing. I am interested in managers who can relate to people easily and without condescension, who can learn from them and enjoy their quirks and foibles.

Seventh, it is essential to have a good self image. By that, I do not mean egotists, but people who have a solid, sensible estimate of their own worth and understand what they are good at and what they are bad at. Good managers will have many people working for them who are smarter and more able at their craft than the managers themselves: So they must understand their own strengths and be comfortable with who they are.

Eighth, managers should appreciate, but not be dominated by the need for analysis. We have many people in this country who will be happy to write dozens of pages of good, clear analysis, but never wish to come to, or effect, a decision. Business decisions still have much of gut feeling and experience as well as the analytical about them.

The ninth requirement is a belief in the ultimate business efficacy of probity, that being truthful pays off.

Tenth and last on my list is the possession of a usefully alert and curious mind with a fair degree of commonsense.

Given people with these 10 characteristics, any business worth its salt should be able to provide the experience and training to help them move forward effectively. They may not be IT literate today, but they will have the ability to be so tomorrow. While it is the systems that will make the flat company possible, it is these people who will make it successful.

SOURCE: By Sir Colin Marshall, "Flat, not flatulent," in *Management Today*, April 1990, p. 5. Sir Colin is Chief Executive and Chairman of British Airways.

QUESTIONS FOR REVIEW

1. How many roles can a manager take on? Is it necessary to focus in on one or two, or can one manager show parts of all eight managerial roles?

2. What is it like to be a manager of other people at work? How would your description of managerial work change if you were to describe being a manager in different countries and cultures?

3. There are several theories of motivation that could be of use in explaining or controlling a person's behaviour at work. Which theory do you think would be of the most practical use for motivating another person?

4. Which theory of motivation would be of the most use for motivating yourself? Is your answer the same as for question 3 above? If not, explain the difference in your two choices.

5. Given enough time, could a manager devise a reward system that resulted in intended effects with no unintended effects? What would it be like to work under such a system? What would the costs and benefits be of such a plan?

SELF-DIAGNOSTIC EXERCISE 8.1

How Motivated to Manage Are You?

Complete this instrument by circling the number for each item that represents your best estimate of your current level.

0 = well below average
5 = average
10 = well above average

1. Favourable attitude toward authority   *0 1 2 3 4 5 6 7 8 9 10*

2. Desire to compete   *0 1 2 3 4 5 6 7 8 9 10*

3. Assertive motivation   *0 1 2 3 4 5 6 7 8 9 10*

4. Desire to exercise power   *0 1 2 3 4 5 6 7 8 9 10*

5. Desire for a distinctive position   *0 1 2 3 4 5 6 7 8 9 10*

6. A sense of responsibility   *0 1 2 3 4 5 6 7 8 9 10*

Now rate the appeal of these different job characteristics:

7. Relatively small span of control / Large span of control

0	*1*	*2*	*3*	*4*	*5*	*6*	*7*	*8*	*9*	*10*

8. Small number of subordinates / Large number of subordinates

0	*1*	*2*	*3*	*4*	*5*	*6*	*7*	*8*	*9*	*10*

9. High technical/engineering component / High people/budgetary component

0	*1*	*2*	*3*	*4*	*5*	*6*	*7*	*8*	*9*	*10*

10. Maintain "hands-on" expertise / Surround oneself with technical experts

0	*1*	*2*	*3*	*4*	*5*	*6*	*7*	*8*	*9*	*10*

11. Limited number of activities per day / As many as 200 activities per day

0	*1*	*2*	*3*	*4*	*5*	*6*	*7*	*8*	*9*	*10*

12. Few interruptions / Many interruptions

0	*1*	*2*	*3*	*4*	*5*	*6*	*7*	*8*	*9*	*10*

13. Time for reading, analyzing / Time for interactions

0	*1*	*2*	*3*	*4*	*5*	*6*	*7*	*8*	*9*	*10*

14. Serve as facilitator to staff / Serve as "boss" to staff

0	*1*	*2*	*3*	*4*	*5*	*6*	*7*	*8*	*9*	*10*

15. Career progression—Increase in technical expertise / Career progression—Managerial advancement

0	*1*	*2*	*3*	*4*	*5*	*6*	*7*	*8*	*9*	*10*

16. Little exercise of power is required   Much intervention in the lives of others

0	1	2	3	4	5	6	7	8	9	10

17. Lower stress position   Higher stress position

0	1	2	3	4	5	6	7	8	9	10

Sum all the circled numbers to determine
YOUR TOTAL MOTIVATION TO MANAGE = _____

Now compare your score to that of others in your class or people who are already successful managers. Are you motivated to be a manager?

SOURCE: Adapted from Dennis P. Slevin (1989), *The Whole Manager: How to Increase your Professional and Personal Effectiveness*, New York: AMACOM, pp. 208, 218.

NOTE: This test is meant to be used as a guide to thinking about your motivation to manage. It does not measure your managerial skills or how successful you may be as a manager.

EXPERIENTIAL EXERCISE 8.1

Boggle Goal Setting

Have you ever played the game Boggle™ by Parker Brothers? Here is a game that you can try to show the effects of goal setting.

First, learn the rules.

1. ***Goal.***   The object of the game is to list, within the time limit of three minutes, as many correct words as possible for each board of 16 jumbled letters.
2. ***Procedure.***   To play you need a pencil and paper and a timer. Start the timer and then look at the letter board for words of not less than three letters. Write down each word as you find it. Words are formed by the use of adjoining letters and must join in the proper sequence to spell a word. They may join horizontally, vertically, or diagonally, to the left, right, or up and down, but no one letter may be used more than once within a single word. Boards 1 through 3 below show how three words can be formed using the adjoining letters S, O, L, and I.

BOARD 1   BOARD 2

BOARD 3

Board 4 shows an incorrect use of the same letters. "SOILS" cannot be formed here because there is only one adjoining "S", and it cannot be used twice in one word.

BOARD 4

Try your skill at finding the hidden words in the arrangement of letters used in the above examples. There are at least 70 words including "trails," "armor" and "prose" which are made up of properly joined letters. Maybe you can find more.

3. **Types of words.**   Any word (noun, adjective, adverb, etc.), plural of, any form of, or tense is acceptable as long as it can be found in a standard English dictionary. Proper names, abbreviations, and words spelled with apostrophes or hyphens are not acceptable. Words within words are permissible; for example spare, spa, par, are, spar, pare.

4. **Scoring.**   When the three minutes are up, you must stop writing and count the number of acceptable words you have found. To assign points to words, count one point for each three or four letter word, two points for a five letter word, three points for a six letter word, five points for a seven letter word, and 11 points for words with eight or more letters.

Now try this board for practice. Give yourself three minutes and find all the words you can. When you are done, add up the number of words you found and their point value.

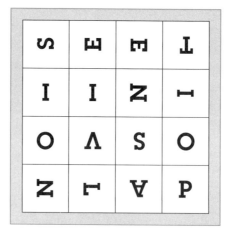

BOARD 5

Now, set a specific and challenging goal for yourself. Board 5 above has 33 words worth a total of 35 points as does Board 6, shown below. Before you set the timer again to try Board 6, set your goal. You might also like to know that a sample of undergraduate business students given three minutes found, on average, 7 words in each of these two boards.

BOARD 6

How did you do? With that feedback about your performance, you can revise your goal. Remember to make it specific and challenging. Here are two more boards that you can try. Board 7 has 29 words and 35 points while Board 8 has 33 words and 36 points. Again, a sample of students given three minutes found an average of 7 words in each of these two boards.

BOARD 7

BOARD 8

Did you find that setting a specific and challenging goal helped you to find more words? You might also like to think about how your goal setting would have gone if you were not allowed to count your words and points but simply were asked to move on to the next board. Without feedback it can be difficult to maintain the task motivation provided by setting goals.

Your instructor has more boards that can be used for in-class exercises. Now that you know how to play you are ready to see how other motivational factors affect performance on this word finding game.

Source: Exercise © 1992 by Richard Field. The Boggle instructions are copyrighted by Parker Brothers.

SELF-GUIDED LEARNING ACTIVITY

People at work can manage up the hierarchy as well as down. If you use this upside-down way of looking at management, ask yourself what behaviours you would like from your boss, what situation she is in, and what personal characteristics affect your boss' behaviour. Then you can use the principles discussed in this chapter to affect your boss' actions toward you.

To work on your own self-motivation and self-management, go to your local bookstore and look in the business books section for motivational tapes and motivational books. Some people find that these resources can help them to better control their own behaviour.

Another interesting activity is to go to a seminar and listen to a motivational speaker—you can find these people at sales conferences for the real estate sales, life insurance sales, and home sales industries. They can be fun to listen to but the key is to try and learn enough to make a lasting change for the better in your life. It's easy to feel good when listening to a motivational speaker but the challenge is to work at positive change.

MANAGER'S CASE FILE:
THE LONG WEEKENDS

"Where's Jennifer?" Joan asked. "She's supposed to be helping me with this project."

"She had to go to her doctor's office this morning for some tests," Henry said.

"I should have known; it's Friday, isn't it?" Joan said sarcastically.

"What does that mean?" Henry asked.

"Haven't you noticed that she's out more often on Fridays and Mondays than any other day?" Joan said. "It's not that she's not really sick," Joan added, "it's just that it seems to happen so conveniently around the weekend."

Jennifer's supervisor, Karen Gross, had also noticed that Jennifer was out sick primarily on Mondays and Fridays. She knew that Jennifer had problems with her health and that she had not taken any days to which she was not entitled. Jennifer had been with the company for many years and had accrued a large amount of sick days. However, Jennifer's habit of scheduling doctor's appointments on Mondays and Fridays was upsetting to the other members of the staff with whom she worked on group projects and Jennifer's input was invaluable because of her long experience with the company. When Jennifer was out sick, the other members of the project group felt that they were treading water, awaiting her return.

When Jennifer returned to work the next week, Karen called her into her office to discuss the situation.

"Jennifer," Karen began, "I really don't know what to say. You always present a doctor's note, and I know you don't take days off unnecessarily, but it's becoming more and more difficult to keep my staff motivated when you're out sick. Is it possible for you to schedule your different tests all in the same week and get them over with?"

"I wish I could," Jennifer answered. "My family doctor is in his office most of the week; it's the specialists who make it so difficult to schedule appointments.

"Besides, I have the time coming to me. I appreciate your position, though, but I don't know what I can do about it," Jennifer said.

"I was considering decreasing your responsibilities," Karen said. "That way if you're out, work on the projects can continue uninterrupted. It's true you've done so many of these projects that you seem to be able to solve any problem we come up against. But I can't have the work coming to a halt or the staffers working overtime to make up the difference when you return. I can slowly remove you from the projects, giving the others the chance to learn how to work without you."

"I hate the idea," Jennifer said. "I love doing the projects; I've been doing them for years. I'd be lost doing anything else."

"Okay, Jennifer, don't get upset," Karen said. "I'll try to come up with something else over the weekend. Let's talk again on Monday."

"Oh," Jennifer said, "I forgot. I won't be in Monday. I have a doctor's appointment."

SOURCE: Reprinted, by permission of publisher, from MANAGEMENT SOLUTIONS, July 1988. © 1988 American Management Association, New York. All rights reserved.

Questions

1. What can Karen do to encourage her staffers to depend more on themselves and less on Jennifer in resolving project problems?

2. What options, besides decreasing Jennifer's responsibilities on the projects, does Karen have?

3. Granted, Jennifer is truly sick. But how much disruption to workflow should Karen be expected to accept?

MOOSAJEES, LIMITED

The management group of Moosajees, Limited of Ceylon [now Sri Lanka] was concerned with increasing the company's production of combed or hackled coconut fiber for export. A major problem, as the company saw it, was not to increase the number of employees, for space limitations prevented this. Rather, the management believed ways should be devised to secure increased productivity from individual workers. However, the attitude of Ceylonese employees raised certain difficulties, and conventional methods of stimulating productivity had not proved successful.

Coconuts are stripped of their husks, split, and dried into copra, which is shipped abroad to be processed into oil; this export is one of Ceylon's major foreign exchange sources. In recent years, other coconut products, such as fibers, have found expanding markets. Increased demand for fibers had led to Moosajees' concern with worker productivity.

Moosajees was one of Ceylon's major exporters of fiber. The company had a processing plant in Colombo, the country's capital. Recovery of fiber from the husks of coconuts was done at various mills, mainly situated to the north and northeast of Colombo in the coconut producing areas. The fiber was delivered to Moosajees, which, as shippers, stored, sorted, graded, baled, and exported the commodity. The company received two kinds of fibers: mattress and bristle. The latter type, distinguished by its longer staple, could be further processed by combing or hackling. It was then tied into bundles and was used in the production of fiber brushes.

For the purpose of combing or hackling brush fiber, it had been customary in Ceylon to use women. Moosajees employed more than 300 women for this purpose. The women were paid on a piece rate, on the basis of a hundred-weight (112 pounds) of fiber hackled. Rates varied according to the quality hackled but had risen in recent years from Rupees 5/50 to Rupees 8/50 per hundredweight for the upper quality limit.

As payment was on a piece-rate basis and because of local customs and attitudes, Moosajees had never kept a strict check on attendance or on the exact number of hours worked each day by women employees. Many women living in the neighborhood of the warehouse came to work in their spare time. They worked as long as they felt like it, returning home to prepare meals or attend to their children, or when they were bored with the rather unpleasant and tiring hackling process.

Under the demand situation that prevailed for a long period, the company had been content to accept these conditions for work for its female operatives. Although production could not be effectively organized, this had not been particularly significant. Hackling was a hand operation not involving machinery. Normal daylight was adequate for the combers and hacklers, weather conditions in Colombo required little more than a roof on the hackling building, and the irregular output of the women actually made checking their production fairly simple, since it combined to produce a fairly steady, if limited, yield. No timekeeping records were necessary; normal security precautions for the entire warehouse were sufficient; and everybody seemed satisfied.

However, two things occurred that made increased production important. The first of these was an increase in foreign demand for hackled fibers, which Moosajees was anxious to meet since the company's management was considerably more profit-oriented than were its women employees. Secondly, a continuing decline in Ceylon's foreign exchange position had concerned the government and led it to encourage those companies in the export trade to do what they could to expand sales abroad. Moosajees had, therefore, both economic and patriotic reasons for producing more hackled fiber.

The most obvious way to increase output was to hire more employees. Since Ceylon has a chronic unemployment problem, it was not difficult to find women who were willing to work. However, limitations of space prevented any significant expansion in the company's labor force. Moreover, the country's labor laws prohibited the use of female workers in a night shift, so that operating two or three shifts was impossible. If, as an alternative, the company displaced less productive workers in favor of new ones who might be more productive, the result was likely to be difficulties with the government department of labor or with labor organizers. Since the company had never developed production norms that it could enforce, dismissal of an employee for what Moosajees might consider low production would not necessarily be accepted as adequate cause.

The company recognized that one solution might be to work toward the development of production standards and that this should be prefaced by enforcement of attendance and of working hours. An attempt to do this, however, merely led to strong resentment and expressions of annoyance. Any effort to attract women outside normal working hours seemed also destined to failure, since most of the female work force were married and occupied with home duties at those times.

The next step taken was to increase payment for fiber hackled, in the hope that this would lead to greater output. Somewhat to the surprise of the Moosajees management, however, the result was not increased production but poor attendance. Apparently, while Moosajees had not established production norms or tasks for the workers, they themselves had developed earning objectives of their own. When this objective was reached, the employee merely failed to report for work. If an increase in the piece rate made it possible to secure the objective in less time, then the employee saw little reason to put in more time to earn more than she wanted.

Moosajees management was considering what it might do. Better enforcement of hours and attendance records was a long-run objective and pretty clearly one that could not be implemented at this time. As the consumption level of the Ceylonese rose, it seemed reasonable to assume that increased consumer goods wants would be developed and that the desire to meet these wants would lead to an interest in higher earning, but this, too, was in the future. Appeals to produce more goods because of the country's situation and the requirement of higher export sales were suggested; however, the management doubted that the typical female worker would be very moved by patriotism. Ceylon had been independent only since 1948, and national fervor was strongest among intellectuals and government employees. Such workers as Moosajees employed were concerned with little more than food, shelter, clothing, and some relatively simple pleasures.

SOURCE: Reprinted by permission of Stanford University Graduate School of Business, © 1963 by the Board of Trustees of the Leland Stanford Junior University.

Questions

1. Where on Maslow's hierarchy of needs would you place the workers?

2. How can goal setting theory be used in this situation to understand both management plans and the workers' response?

3. What social and cultural factors must management be aware of in attempting to motivate the workforce?

4. What would you recommend Moosajees management do next to try to increase levels of production?

REFERENCES

Adams, J. Stacey (1963). "Toward an understanding of inequity." *Journal of Abnormal and Social Psychology* 67: 422-436.

Adams, J. Stacey (1965). "Inequity in social exchange." In Leonard Berkowitz (Ed.), *Advances in Experimental Social Psychology* Vol. 2, pp. 267-299. New York: Academic Press.

Alderfer, Clayton P. (1972). *Existence, Relatedness, and Growth: Human Needs in Organizational Settings.* New York: The Free Press.

Ashour, Ahmed S., & Gary Johns (1983). "Leader influence through operant principles: A theoretical and methodological framework." *Human Relations* 36: 603-626.

Bartley, Douglas (1981). *Job Evaluation.* Reading, MA: Addison-Wesley.

Barrett, William E. (1943). *Señor payroll.* Harold Ober Associates Incorporated.

Beach, Lee Roy (1990). *Image Theory: Decision Making in Personal and Organizational Contexts.* New York: Wiley.

Cullen, Dallas (1994). "Feminism, management and self-actualization." *Gender, Work and Organization* 1(3): in press.

Deci, Edward L. (1975). *Intrinsic Motivation.* New York: Plenum Press.

Deci, Edward L., & Richard M. Ryan (1985). *Intrinsic Motivation and Self-Determination in Human Behavior.* New York: Plenum Press.

Dumaine, Brian (1993). "The new non-manager managers." *Fortune,* February 22, 1993, pp. 80-84.

Evans, Martin G. (1986). "Organizational behavior: The central role of motivation." *Journal of Management* 12: 203-222.

Furlong, Carla (1993). "A million dollars worth of advice." *B.C. Business,* April 1993, pp. 79-84.

Gilligan, Carol (1982). *In a Different Voice: Psychological Theory and Women's Development.* Cambridge, MA: Harvard University Press.

Hay, Edward N. (1948). "Creating factor comparison key scales by the per cent method." *Journal of Applied Psychology* 32: 456-464.

Kanfer, Ruth (1992). "Work motivation: New directions in theory and research." In Cary L. Cooper and Ivan T. Robertson (Eds.), *International Review of Industrial and Organizational Psychology* Volume 7, pp. 1-53. London: John Wiley & Sons Ltd.

Kerr, Steven (1975). "On the folly of rewarding A, while hoping for B." *Academy of Management Journal* 18: 769-783.

Kohn, Alfie (1993). "Why incentive plans cannot work." *Harvard Business Review,* September/October 1993, pp. 54-63.

Latham, Gary A., & Edwin P. Locke (1979). "Goal-setting—A motivational technique that works." *Organizational Dynamics* 8(2): 68-80.

Laurent, André (1983). "The cultural diversity of western conceptions of management." *International Studies of Management and Organization* 13: 75-96.

LeBoeuf, Michael (1987). *The Greatest Management Principle in the World.* New York: Berkeley Publishing.

Locke, Edwin A. (1968). "Toward a theory of task motivation and incentives." *Organizational Behavior and Human Performance* 3: 157-189.

Locke, Edwin A., & Gary P. Latham (1990a). "Work motivation: The high performance cycle." In Uwe Kleinbeck, Hans-Henning Quast, Henk Thierry, & Hartmut Häcker (Eds.), *Work Motivation,* pp. 3-25. Hillsdale, NJ: Lawrence Erlbaum Associates Publishers.

Locke, Edwin A., & Gary P. Latham (1990b). *A Theory of Goal Setting & Task Performance.* Englewood Cliffs, NJ: Prentice Hall, Inc.

Locke, Edwin A., & Gary P. Latham (1990c). "Work motivation and satisfaction: Light at the end of the tunnel." *Psychological Science* 1: 240-246.

Luthans, Fred & Robert Kreitner (1985). *Organizational Behavior Modification and Beyond: An Operant and Social Learning Approach.* Glenview, IL: Scott, Foresman.

Maslow, Abraham H. (1943). "A theory of human motivation." *Psychological Review* 50: 370-396.

McClelland, David C. (1961). *The Achieving Society.* Princeton, NJ: Van Nostrand.

Mento, Anthony J., Robert P. Steel, & Ronald J. Karren (1987). "A meta-analytic study of the effects of goal setting on task performance: 1966-1984." *Organizational Behavior and Human Decision Processes* 39: 52-83.

Mintzberg, Henry (1973). *The Nature of Managerial Work.* New York: Harper & Row Publishers, Inc.

Mintzberg, Henry (1975). "The manager's job: Folklore and fact." *Harvard Business Review* 53(4): 49-61.

Nevis, Edwin C. (1983). "Using an American perspective in understanding another culture: Toward a hierarchy of needs for the People's Republic of China." *The Journal of Applied Behavioral Science* 19: 249-264.

Phalon, Richard (1984). "Hell camp." *Forbes,* June 18, 1984, Volume 133(14): 56-58.

Porter, Lyman W., & Edward E. Lawler (1968). *Managerial Attitudes and Performance.* Homewood, IL: Richard D. Irwin, Inc.

Pritchard, Robert D., Steven D. Jones, Philip L. Roth, Karla K. Stuebing, & Steven E. Ekeberg (1988). "Effects of group feedback, goal setting, and incentives on organizational productivity." *Journal of Applied Psychology* 73: 337-358.

Quinn, Robert E. (1988). *Beyond Rational Management: Mastering the Paradoxes and Competing Demands of High Performance.* San Francisco: Jossey-Bass, Inc.

Quinn, Robert E., Sue R. Faerman, Michael P. Thompson, & Michael R. McGrath (1990). *Becoming a Master Manager: A Competency Framework.* New York: John Wiley & Sons, Inc.

Slevin, Dennis P. (1989). *The Whole Manager: How to Increase your Professional and Personal Effectiveness.* New York: AMACOM.

Tubbs, Mark E. (1986). "Goal setting: A meta-analytic examination of the empirical evidence." *Journal of Applied Psychology* 71. 474-483.

Vroom, Victor H. (1964). *Work and Motivation.* New York: John Wiley & Sons, Inc.

Watson, Tom J., Jr. (1963). *A Business and its Beliefs: The Ideas that Helped Build IBM.* New York: McGraw-Hill.

FURTHER READING

Two summary articles on motivation are: Raymond A. Katzell & Donna E. Thompson (1990), "Work motivation: Theory and practice," *American Psychologist* 45: 144-153; and Frank J. Landy & Warren S. Becker (1987), "Motivation theory reconsidered," *Research in Organizational Behavior* 9: 1-38. A summary article on goal setting is that of James C. Naylor and Daniel R. Ilgen (1984), "Goal setting: A theoretical analysis of a motivational technology," *Research in Organizational Behavior* 6: 95-140.

A further criticism of Maslow's need hierarchy, especially the definition of self-actualization, is given by Francis Heylighten (1992), "A cognitive-systemic reconstruction of Maslow's theory of self-actualization," *Behavioral Science* 37: 39-59.

For a classic article on expectancy theories, see Terrence R. Mitchell (1974), "Expectancy models of job satisfaction, occupational preference, and effort: A theoretical, methodological, and empirical appraisal," *Psychological Bulletin* 81: 1053-1077. A newer look at expectancy theory is that of Lynn E. Miller and Joseph E. Grush (1988), "Improving predictions in expectancy theory research: Effects of personality, expectancies, and norms," *Academy of Management Journal* 31: 107-122.

The effects of pay inequity in professional baseball and basketball are examined in Joe Harder's 1992 article "Play for pay: Effects of inequity in a pay-for-performance context," *Administrative Science Quarterly* 37: 321-335.

An interesting and important article on goal setting that shows how theories can be put into a competitive test to determine which is better at explaining the facts is that of Gary P. Latham, Miriam Erez, and Edwin A. Locke (1988), "Resolving scientific disputes by the joint design of crucial experiments by the antagonists: Application to the Erez-Latham dispute regarding participation in goal setting," *Journal of Applied Psychology* 73: 753-772.

Responses to Kohn's 1993 article "Why incentive plans cannot work" are found on pages 37 to 53 of the November/December 1993 issue of the *Harvard Business Review* in the article "Rethinking rewards."

While we often think of a manager influencing the behaviour of a first-level employee, every manager has a manager at the next higher level in the organization's hierarchy. It would be a mistake to think that because a person *is* a manager that person knows all there is to know about management and can be left to do the job. An exploration of this is offered by Clinton O. Longnecker and Dennis A. Gioia (1991), "SMR Forum: Ten myths of managing managers," *Sloan Management Review*, Fall 1991, pages 81-90. A look at how top managers came to be the way they are is given by David B.P. Sims in his 1993 *British Journal of Management* article titled "The formation of top managers: a discourse analysis of five managerial autobiographies," found in Volume 4, pages 57-68.

A two-cassette audio program by Peter B. Vaill of George Washington University is titled *Permanent White Water: The Realities, Myths, Paradoxes, and Dilemmas of Managing Organizations*, and examines the problems that managers confront daily. Published in 1992, it is available from Jossey-Bass.

A useful article about the difficulties of managing others and having to make hard choices about their lives is "The hard work of being a soft manager," by William H. Peace, published in the *Harvard Business Review* in the November/December 1991 issue, pages 40-47.

Finally, an interesting article that deals with the positive reinforcement that we can get from small successes is that of Karl E. Weick (1984), "Small wins: Redefining the scale of social problems," *American Psychologist* 39: 40-49.

CHAPTER 9

GROUPS AND INTERGROUP BEHAVIOUR

CHAPTER OUTLINE

Types of Groups

Work Group Effectiveness

   Organizational Context

   Work Group Design

   Internal Group Processes

   *Strategies for External Integration and
   Boundary Maintenance*

The Management of Groups in Organizations

Conclusion

QUESTIONS TO CONSIDER

- *Is it common to work in a group?*

- *What types of groups are there?*

- *What kinds of groups are there in
  organizations?*

- *What are the characteristics of groups?*

- *What processes are there in groups?*

- *How do groups work together?*

When a new recruit enters an organization for the first time, he is confronted with an ordered system. The organization has work to do, jobs and a structure have been created to do the work, and people have been brought into the organization to do those jobs. While some individuals can remain independent in their completion of the work assigned to them (for example: the artist who works alone; the contractor who performs the job having little contact with others), usually people are either formed into groups or form themselves into groups. As John Levine and Richard Moreland (1990, p. 621) have written: "Much of the world's work is done by small groups." Almost without doubt, everyone will find themselves at some point in life as the member of a work group.

In this chapter we will describe the different types of groups that exist, both inside and outside work organizations, and then focus on the organizational context, design, and processes in work groups that influence their effectiveness. Finally, we will look at the management of small groups in organizations and suggestions for making groups more effective in organizations.

TYPES OF GROUPS

Work group A group with social systems and boundaries that separate it from other individuals and groups, and having different roles for different task members.

Social group A group that has no task.

Reference group A group used for comparison.

Coacting group Individuals in the group each perform individual tasks, but there is no group task.

Freestanding group A group which does not have an organizational context.

Team A group composed of a small number of people with complementary skills who are committed to a common purpose, set of performance goals, and approach for which they hold themselves mutually accountable.

According to Richard Hackman (1987), there are five basic types of group. The first is the true **work group**, which is a real group with social systems, boundaries that separate it from other individuals and groups, and different roles (sets of expected behaviours) for different task members. The work group also has one or more tasks to perform and it operates within the context of an organization. It is part of the organization and is affected by the organization's culture, task, systems, structure, etc.

Another type of group is the **social group**, which has no task. An example of this group would be a group of people who get together for coffee in the afternoons. **Reference groups** are used for comparisons—for example a police officer in Toronto might compare herself to officers in other cities of Ontario, but there is no intact social system that binds them together into a social or work group. **Coacting groups** are formed of individuals performing individual tasks, with no group task. For example, twenty professors at a university might be grouped into a Department and seen as a group by those outside the coacting departmental group, but each professor would teach and research as an individual. The last type of group is the **freestanding group**, which does not have an organizational context. A group of people who rent land from a city and share in its cultivation but who are not part of a co-operative, a company, or a kibbutz, are a group but without an organization surrounding them.

While all five group types are important for understanding human behaviour, we will restrict ourselves here to discussing only work groups in organizations.

Very often work groups are called teams, and in this text we will use the terms *group* and *team* interchangeably. Some authors, however, draw a distinction between groups and teams. In this way of thinking a **team** is a small number of people with complementary skills who are committed to a common purpose, set of performance goals, and approach for which they hold themselves mutually accountable (Katzenbach & Smith, 1993, p. 112). The distinction between groups and teams is that a work group's performance is affected by what each group member does individually whereas a team's performance depends on both individual performance and the joint performance of its members.

WORK GROUP EFFECTIVENESS

Work group effectiveness is composed of three parts. The first is the **performance** of the group as rated by the team itself and by the outsiders-who receive the team's output. The second is the team's **viability** in the future. Viability is the team's long term effectiveness, its ability to work together, and its ability to adapt to changing organizational and environmental conditions. The third part of work group effectiveness is the **satisfaction** of the work group's members.

The relative importance of these three effectiveness components is certain to vary for specific teams in their unique circumstances. For example, a professional baseball team may have as its only goal to win the World Series, whereas members of a professional orchestra may care most about their ability to work together in the future. There is no one best way to weight these three group effectiveness factors. Their relative importance will change from group to group and over time, depending on the organization and the group itself.

Three influences on work group effectiveness are the organizational context that surrounds the group, the way the work group is designed, and internal and external group processes. This last category is what goes on in the group as it does its work. A model of work group effectiveness is presented as Exhibit 9.1. We will be working through these important factors of work group effectiveness by examining Exhibit 9.1 in some detail.

Organizational context can affect group design which may in turn affect group processes and then effectiveness. In addition, however, the organizational context and the design of the work group can each have a substantial and direct effect on group effectiveness.

For example, a professional accounting firm may decide to equip its auditors with fast notebook computers that are connected by cellular modems to auditing data bases and expert system auditing programs at head office. This decision makes a direct impact on the auditing team's effectiveness through task design and technology.

Similarly, an accounting firm may decide to keep teams together over a series of audits, thereby increasing the team's life span. This work group design decision will have an effect on team performance and the satisfaction of team members. Work group members will probably get to know one another quite well. If they become cohesive, communication will likely be easier and satisfaction with the group should be high.

An alternative design for auditors would be to break up audit teams on the completion of each audit. New teams would be formed from the "pool" of available auditors. This method allows group composition to be designed for each audit. Group members who do not get along on a personal level would only have to work together for a short time.

Organizational Context

Organization Structure   Work groups are part of the larger organization. They are therefore affected by its design, culture, and systems. These organizational context factors are likely to have especially strong effects on newly formed groups because new group members are open to outside influences as they begin to create their team's internal and external processes.

An organically structured organization would likely allow a great deal of work group autonomy in how the work was performed as long as relations with other corporate groups were maintained and the users of the group's output were satisfied. A group in a mechanistic organization would more likely be routinely guided by directives from above.

Performance Outcomes of ability and effort.

Viability The team or work group's long term effectiveness, its ability to work together, and its ability to adapt to changing organizational and environmental conditions.

Satisfaction An attitude of being content.

These basketball players are members of performing groups that were created to compete with each other.

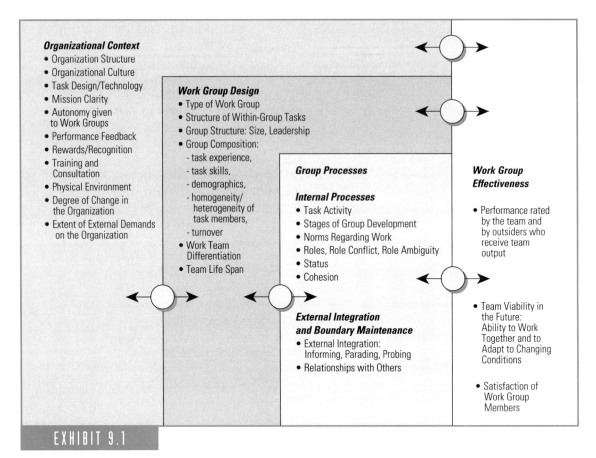

Sources: Adapted from Eric Sundstrom, Kenneth P. DeMeuse, and David Futrell (1990), "Work teams: Applications and effectiveness," *American Psychologist* 45: 122. Copyright 1990 by the American Psychological Association. Adapted by permission. Also adapted from Deborah Gladstein Ancona (1990), "Outward bound: Strategies for team survival in an organization," *Academy of Management Journal* 33: 362. Reprinted by the permission of the Academy of Management. Also based on ideas and information in J. Richard Hackman (1987), "The design of work teams," in Jay W. Lorsch (Ed.), *Handbook of organizational behavior*, Englewood Cliffs, NJ: Prentice Hall, Inc. pp. 315-342; Deborah Gladstein (1984), "Groups in context: A model of task group effectiveness," *Administrative Science Quarterly* 29: 499-517; and Paul S. Goodman, Elizabeth Ravlin, and Marshall Schminke (1987), "Understanding groups in organizations," *Research in Organizational Behavior* 9: 121-173.

Organizational Culture   The cultural profile of a company (see Exhibit 3.6) will affect how groups in that culture operate. For example, an organization with a Tough-Guy/Macho culture will probably have cohesive groups that interact a great deal. People in these kinds of organizations need social support that can best be provided by a closely-knit team. Teams should be less common in a Process culture as individuals focus more on doing their own jobs and are less concerned about the jobs of others.

Task Design and Technology   The methods and machines used to perform the group's task will affect how the group is designed, how it functions, and its ultimate effectiveness. The performance of a team can be directly affected by changing the tools it has available to do its work.

Mission Clarity   The more clear the mission at the organizational level, the more clear group tasks and goals will be. The organization's mission must be communicated down to the group level.

Autonomy Given to Work Groups   More autonomous groups are able to design their own work, provide their own internal group leadership, and determine how the group's task is divided among group members.

Performance Feedback   More feedback to the group about its performance allows the group to adjust its design and its processes in order to be more effective. One study of five organizational units at a U.S. Air Force base (Pritchard and others, 1988) found that group-level feedback increased productivity by an average of 50%.

Rewards and Recognition Given to the Group   Rewards for group activity and performance are more effective at strengthening identification and membership with the group than are individual rewards. An individualistic organization will find it difficult to have effective groups due to its reward structure.

Training and Consultation   Groups in organizations need training and consultation/coaching to help them improve their internal processes and external relations. Group members need to learn both technical job requirements and how to work with others in a group. People cannot simply be put into a group and expected to perform well. Working in a group presents its own challenges and opportunities. Training is required to help group members to accept the challenges and seek opportunities.

Physical Environment   Groups can be possessive of their physical space. By establishing a territory and defending it against outsiders the group can protect valuable resources, improve its own living and working conditions, gain a sense of privacy, control social interactions, become more cohesive, and express its social identity (Levine & Moreland, 1990). The organization can therefore have a direct effect on a group by controlling the group's work area.

For instance, a basketball team could be provided living space all together in one house away from other residences on a college campus. This control over their physical space should increase team interaction and team cohesion. If less cohesion were desired, team members could be encouraged to live on and off campus with other students who are not on the basketball team.

The organizational control of where the group works also affects its performance. Sales territories, for instance, can be established to allow high sales or force poor performance.

The Degree of Change in the Organization   High rates of organizational change can cause instability within work groups due to changes in organizational policies and personnel.

The Extent of External Demands on the Organization   Greater external demands will mean that a group will need to be more externally focused. High environmental volatility will need to be matched by flexible and adaptable groups.

Work Group Design

Anyone who has been a member of a class project or case analysis group likely already knows that the way a group is initially set up affects how the group works and how well it performs. The job given to the group, its number of members, how similar the members are to each other and how long the group expects to work together are all important design factors.

The design factors that have important influences on group processes and effectiveness are type of work group, task structure, group structure, group member composition, work team differentiation, and team life span.

Type of Work Group   First in importance to a group's functioning is what the group does. **Top management teams** are composed of the people at the top of the organizational hierarchy. They create the organization's strategy and set its direction. **Task forces** are temporary groups created to solve a particular problem or complete a task. An example is a team that travels across the country to different bank branches and installs a new computer system in each branch.

Professional support groups are designed to help others either inside or outside the organization to do their jobs. Examples are a small business consulting unit and an internal team that helps an organization to make effective changes to its structure. **Performing groups** put on a performance (an orchestra or theatre group), perform an activity (a surgical team in a hospital), or compete with other groups (sports teams, combat teams in the army).

Human service teams are staffed by people who are grouped together to help others. Examples are teaching, social assistance, and the provision of emergency relief by an organization like the Red Cross. **Customer service teams** are organized to sell the organization's product to its customers and/or to make sure the product works correctly for the customer. Last, but certainly not least in importance are **production teams** that make the organization's product.

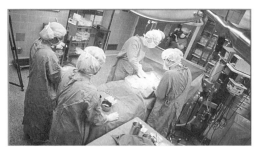

This surgical team is a performing group put together to perform an activity–the operation on the patient.

Structure of Within-Group Tasks   It is important to note that even within one type of group there may be different tasks to perform. Some group members may be asked to perform highly structured and repetitive work such as typing a report or computing spreadsheets. Others may be assigned more unique and creative work such as designing a marketing plan and its presentation. Task differences within a group create differences between group members.

Group Structure   Two key structural factors of a group are its size and its leadership.

Paul Hare (1981) has summarized the effects of **group size** on group members. His main findings are that the larger the group, the less satisfied its members generally are; group performance is generally enhanced with the addition of more members, but each new member brings smaller and smaller performance gains to the group; and that larger groups will split into subgroups and have non-participators.

Satisfaction in a larger group declines because the number of relationships possible in a group increases rapidly as size increases, making it harder to know everyone in the group. The time available to each group member for communication also decreases as group size increases. As well, the gap in the amount of participation between the most frequent participator and the other group members grows wider. These factors make participation in the group more difficult and lower member satisfaction.

The best group size will depend on the nature of the task, but smaller is probably better. Hackman (1987) has suggested that groups should be slightly *smaller* than the task requires. One study (Yetton & Bottger, 1983) found that interacting groups showed no improvements in performance beyond four members.

Top management team
The people at the top of the organizational hierarchy.

Task force   A temporary group created to solve a particular problem or to complete a particular task.

Professional support group   A group whose job it is to help others either inside or outside the organization to do their jobs.

Performing group
A group that puts on a performance, performs an activity, or competes with other groups.

Human service team
People who are grouped together to help others.

Customer service team
A group organized to sell the organization's product to its customers and/or to make sure the product works correctly for the customer.

Production team   Makes the organization's product.

Group size   The number of members in a group.

EXPERIENCE IS THE BEST TEACHER

Much of organizational theory focuses on similarities between groups. Theories such as population ecology argue that groups or organizations tend to become similar over time, imitating those that are successful. Theories of organizational culture tend to assume that organizations have one culture which all organizational members share and follow. But what about those companies, groups, or individuals who are different?

Some of the most interesting research I have encountered, and which I have participated in, deals with these "outliers": groups or organizations that differ from the norm. By studying those that are different, we can learn about alternate ways of doing business or operating organizations, which might in fact be more profitable or personally satisfying than the traditional forms we are used to. It is ironic that much business education is designed to produce future entrepreneurs

Fiona McQuarrie is an Assistant Professor at the University of Prince Edward Island.

and innovators, but at the same time encourages us to copy traditional organizational forms and structures. It is the individuals or companies who think of new ideas, who conduct themselves differently, and who challenge the norms that keep businesses growing and adapting.

Also, by studying groups that are different, we may in fact be introducing ourselves to companies that will set trends and be models for others in the future. The Body Shop, for example, began as a deliberate attempt to provide an alternative to established cosmetic products, but its founder, Anita Roddick, also made other choices simply because she did not know how such operations were "supposed" to be done. It is that kind of thinking and creativity that businesses thrive on, and looking at groups and organizations who are different is a very good way to foster that sort of daring.

The lowered level of member effort in a larger group is called **free-riding** (Harkins & Szymanski, 1989) or **social loafing** (Albanese & Van Fleet, 1985; Kidwell & Bennett, 1993). Group members do not exert as much effort toward task accomplishment when in a group as they do when alone. This lessening of effort could be due to a loss of individual motivation when in a group (Shepperd, 1993).

It has been found that this phenomenon can be reduced or eliminated by making the individual group member's contribution more unique and identifiable and by evaluating that contribution (Levine & Moreland, 1990). Also, one study that examined social loafing for American managerial trainees and those from the People's Republic of China (Earley, 1989) discovered social loafing for the individualistic culture of America but not in the collectivistic culture of China. Therefore, societal culture (and presumably organizational culture) affects a person's social loafing behaviour.

Since a group may be designed with varying degrees of organizational autonomy, the leadership of the group can also be created structurally—the group may be led by an external manager, by an internal coach/supervisor, or have no formal leader. Leadership structure affects how group members relate to each other, make decisions and interact with other groups and individuals in the organization.

Group Composition   Of critical importance to work group effectiveness are the task experience and task skills of group members, turnover in the group, and demographics of the individual members of the group.

Demographics are the age, sex, personality traits, job and life background, and other descriptive characteristics of group members. These factors together describe what group members bring to the team and how that team is likely to operate in the organization.

Free-riding   One or more individuals in a group reducing effort below that which would have been exerted if not in the group.

Social loafing   When group members do not exert as much effort toward task accomplishment when in a group as they do when alone.

Demographics   The age, sex, personality traits, job and life background, and other descriptive characteristics of group members.

For example, a restaurant having a serving staff composed of all middle-aged women can expect differences in the way food is served compared to a serving staff composed of all male college students in their early 20s.

There are now occurring in North America large-scale changes in the demographics of the work force (O'Reilly, 1990) as the baby boom generation ages and there are fewer new workers to replace them as they retire. Also, as more females and individuals of different cultures enter the North American work force, groups will become more heterogeneous (the group members will be different from one another) and, by definition, less homogeneous. The Canadian manager will often have a multicultural and mixed-gender work group. To effectively manage the task accomplishment of this diversity in the work force requires sensitivity to different cultural values and expectations and the maintenance of a social situation that can be shared by all group members.

In Canada and the United States women are making up a larger percentage of the total work force and are beginning to enter traditionally male occupations in greater numbers, though women still occupy in large numbers traditional female jobs and part-time work. Some think (for example Sargent & Stupak, 1989) that the North American work culture is shifting from the male-oriented cultural values of individualism and independence to the more female orientation of interdependence and harmony at work.

On the other hand, managers in the Far East—Japan and Korea for example—are more paternalistic. Managers in these cultures take the role of the father figure at work. The father is to be obeyed in these cultures. The manager-as-father is expected to be interested in and to influence the worker's whole life, both at work and at home. Since it is very important that no one disturb the harmony of the work place (in Japan the *wa*, in Korea the *inhwa*), a large part of the manager's job is to maintain harmony. Unfortunately, at least from an Anglo North American perspective, to maintain harmony women at work are treated as more temporary employees. They are generally expected to work for only five years or so until they get married and then resign their jobs in order to take care of their family.

Heterogeneity in group membership can help the group understand different perspectives and ways of accomplishing the group's task. However, heterogeneity can also hinder the group's performance in times of crisis or rapid change (Bettenhausen, 1991) since different viewpoints are less easy to integrate than homogeneous perspectives.

Joe DiStefano and Martha Maznevski of the University of Western Ontario have examined the performance of homogeneous versus culturally diverse work groups. They found that culturally diverse groups can outperform homogeneous groups but only if they are trained to recognize and then use their differences to advantage (Perkins, 1993). Another study of diverse versus homogenous groups (Watson and others, 1993) found that diversity was costly in the short run but an advantage to group creativity in the longer run.

Task experience and **task skills** can help group members to accomplish a task, but can also limit how group members see problems and their solutions. A person's background will be a strong influence on how that person sees their work world.

Group **turnover** can keep levels of task experience low, increase the amount of training time needed in the group, and lessen group friendships and familiarity that can make the group's activities predictable. On the other hand turnover can serve to bring in fresh ideas and perspectives that can help a group to stay out of predictable routines.

Work Team Differentiation   The more different organizational groups are from each other the more difficult will be interaction between the groups, since ways of thinking and acting will be less likely to be shared.

Team Life Span   Some teams such as task forces have a limited life span and team members know when the team will be disbanded. This knowledge can affect internal group processes and the actions of group members. For example, some group members may put

---

Heterogeneity   Mixed demographics in group membership.

Task experience   Background and knowledge about a particular task.

Task skills   The ability to accomplish a task.

Turnover   The rate at which members leave a group or organization.

off conflict and not attempt to resolve differences within the group because the group will soon be disbanded. Others may compress the normal time scale of human interaction into the time that is available. They may show a "live for today for tomorrow we are apart" attitude and behaviour. Teams that are ongoing will tend to have more stable patterns of interaction among group members as there is no predictable end to the group's activities.

Internal Group Processes

In the process of doing their work, groups organize themselves internally to perform task activity and group maintenance activity. Expectations about behaviour, called norms, are created about being a member of the group and doing the group's work. Members are either assigned or adopt different roles. Status is given in different degrees to each group member, and members feel some sense of cohesion toward the group.

Task Activity   Groups can be at the same place at the same time. An example is a quality circle discussing how to lower the team's production costs while producing a higher quality product. We commonly think of a group as working all together in a particular place, but there are other possibilities (Johansen and others, 1991). For example, groups can operate at a different place at the same time. Team members who are in different cities can be connected together by a conference telephone call, screen sharing on computers in different sites, or (in the future) sharing a virtual reality (VR) meeting place. A VR computer-generated conference room would be experienced by each team member as if all other team members were in the room, even though they are not. Desktop video conferencing is now in operation. For example, at Bell Canada, project participants can see each other in a corner of their computer screens (Blackwell, 1993). Each participant's computer has a small camera attached to the top of the monitor. While the images are in black and white and a little fuzzy, the picture is live and in real-time.

Groups can function at the same place but at a different time. Examples are team rooms where members come and go on their own schedules and stations for shift work (such as a nursing station in a hospital) where members rotate in and out of the team station on different shifts.

Groups can also work at a different place and at a different time. One example is a group that communicates by voice mail (recorded telephone messages) or by different time computer conferencing and computer mail. As more work gets done by telecommuting, groups may become more virtual as well (for example, see Mason, 1993).

Stages of Group Development   As a new group comes together, its members are faced with a dilemma. People *do* want to belong to groups. "Groups can provide a comforting refuge for members in a hostile or threatening world. Rites, rituals, and social roles provide continuity and order. The group's common goal provides a sense of purpose, and self-selection homogenizes membership" (Bettenhausen, 1991, p. 348). But people also want to maintain their independent identities—they *do not* want to be submerged into the group (although this would be much less the case in group-oriented societies such as China and Japan).

This is only the first of several dilemmas faced by an individual in a group as the group works towards its goals and objectives. Therefore, the stages of group activity—how a group changes over time—are of central importance to the understanding of group processes and group effectiveness.

An early model of the stages of group development is that groups proceed through the five stages of forming, storming, norming, performing, and adjourning (Tuckman, 1965; Tuckman & Jensen, 1977). At the *forming* stage group members get to know one another and the limits of the group. It is clear that the group forming stage is important because members forming a group typically reach quick agreement on how to perform the task (Hackman, 1987; Bettenhausen & Murnighan 1985, 1991). The *storming* stage is marked by conflict over interpersonal and task issues and resistance to group influence. *Norming* then follows. At this time the group creates its group roles and standards of behaviour. Once these earlier issues have been resolved the *performing* stage begins. Finally, the group breaks up at the *adjourning* stage. Though this model was based on therapy groups whose group goal was to explore and improve the self, it has been used as a model to understand the stages of group development in organizations.

Other models of group development contend that groups do not progress through stages in a linear fashion. For example, Connie Gersick (1988, 1989) found that the task groups she studied had a half-way transition point in their development. At the half-way point in their limited life span these groups dramatically reoriented their way of doing the work. Gordon Burnand (1990) asserts that therapy groups confront six problems about the group and its members; these problems are dealt with in a cyclical fashion, not in a linear and orderly way. Further discussion of Gersick's and Burnand's work on group development phases is discussed in this chapter's *On the One Hand* feature.

A useful model of seven stages of work team performance is the Drexler/Sibbet team performance model (Drexler and others, 1988), reproduced as Exhibit 9.2 on page 338. Each stage in their model is an issue that teams have to come to grips with as they move through the formative stages of team development. Teams are not seen as always moving sequentially through these stages, though. The question at each stage is always present in the working of the team.

At six of the stages there is a primary question that must be addressed. If these questions are resolved well then the team is prepared to deal effectively with the next stage. The "resolved" behaviours shown in the model are the competencies of high performing teams. Unresolved behaviours indicate the question at that stage has not been well answered. More work is necessary for the team at that stage.

The seven stages of the Drexler/Sibbet model are as follows.

1. *Orientation*—Why am I here? People wonder whether or not they will fit in and be accepted by others. They need an answer to continue on with the team.
2. *Trust Building*—Who are you? People want to know about the others they will work with. What do they expect, what are they good at, what do they want from the group? Sharing information builds trust and free exchange in the group.
3. *Goal/Role Clarification*—What are we doing? What are the team's goals and what is each member's role in accomplishing those goals? People in the team want assumptions made explicit.
4. *Commitment*—How will we do it? At this stage the team moves from discussing what to do to discussing exactly how to do it. Resources, people, and time must be allocated.
5. *Implementation*—Who does what, when, where? Teams at this stage start actually doing their work. Timing, scheduling, and execution of tasks are predominant.
6. *High Performance*—A team that masters its methods of operating can become more flexible in responding to the environment. Goals can change as the team adapts as required.
7. *Renewal*—Why continue? People can get tired, group members change, continuing to perform the task can lose its appeal. Team members confront the question of why the group should continue as it has.

ON THE ONE HAND...

Connie Gersick of UCLA studied the phases of group development of time limited task teams for her doctoral dissertation at Yale University. In a report of her findings (Gersick, 1988) she explained that her eight subject groups did not progress through Tuckman's theoretical sequence of forming, storming, norming, and performing. "Instead, every group exhibited a distinctive approach to its task as soon as it commenced and stayed with that approach through a period of inertia [stability] that lasted for half its allotted time" (Gersick, 1988, p. 16). Then, at the half-way point each group underwent a series of changes that created a new way for the group to do its work. For the last half of their allotted time the groups concentrated on carrying through the plans they had made at their transition point. Therefore, *time* was an important element in the development of task groups with deadlines. Gersick saw their development as marked by **"punctuated equilibrium"**—a time when the normal procedures for group operation were suddenly changed in a revolutionary (not evolutionary) way.

Punctuated equilibrium

A revolutionary change in a system's stable state that leads to a new and different stable state.

SOURCE: Based on information in Connie J.G. Gersick (1988), "Time and transition in work teams: Toward a new model of group development," *Academy of Management Journal* 31: 9-41. Two follow-ups to this report are Connie J.G. Gersick (1989), "Marking time: Predictable transitions in task groups," *Academy of Management Journal* 32: 274-309; and Connie J.G. Gersick (1994), "Pacing strategic change: The case of a new venture," *Academy of Management Journal* 37: 9-45.

ON THE OTHER HAND...

Gordon Burnand of England described how therapy groups tend to follow six phases of group development as they work through six basic questions that any group might face. These questions are:

- *The certainty problem.* Group members want to know what to do and what is expected of them;

- *The freedom problem.* Group members have to deal with the dependence they feel in their relationship with the leader and the group;

- *The reward problem.* Members want to find out what the group can offer that is good for the self;

- *The other's good state problem.* Members want to find out how to help other group members get into a good state;

- *The unity problem.* Members want to decide how the group will relate to outsiders;

- *The fairness problem.* Group members want to decide how to achieve fairness in the group's activities for all group members.

Burnand thinks that groups do not deal with these problems in a neatly ordered progression from the first to the last problem. Instead, in making the transition from one problem to the next the group focuses first on the next problem, then finds its resolution difficult and shifts attention back to the earlier (already resolved) problem before finally confronting the next problem again. For example, having obtained certainty about what to do in the group, feelings of loss of freedom and dependence emerge, but when these are explored the question of certainty is again opened up. Only when certainty is again dealt with can the freedom problem be solved. Therefore, therapy groups can be expected to undergo a series of transitions in how they work as these problems are addressed.

SOURCE: Based on information in Gordon Burnand (1990), "Group development phases as working through six fundamental human problems," *Small Group Research* 21: 255-273.

Stages of Team Performance

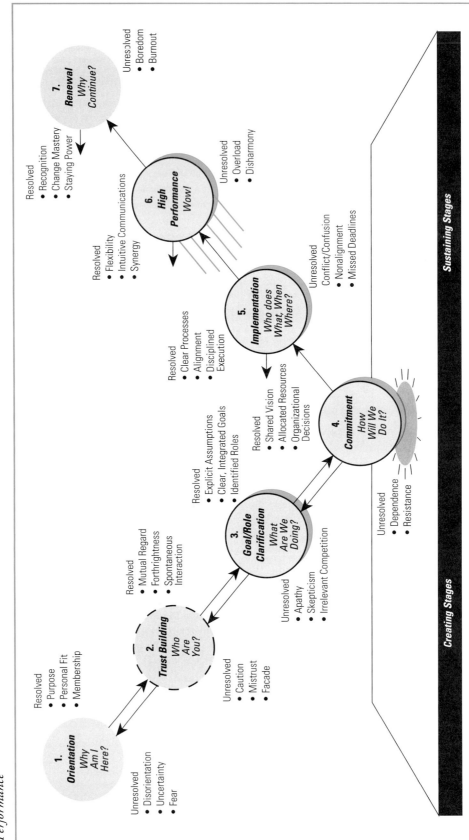

1. Orientation — *Why Am I Here?*

Resolved
• Purpose
• Personal Fit
• Membership

Unresolved
• Disorientation
• Uncertainty
• Fear

2. Trust Building — *Who Are You?*

Resolved
• Mutual Regard
• Forthrightness
• Spontaneous Interaction

Unresolved
• Caution
• Mistrust
• Facade

3. Goal/Role Clarification — *What Are We Doing?*

Resolved
• Explicit Assumptions
• Clear, Integrated Goals
• Identified Roles

Unresolved
• Apathy
• Skepticism
• Irrelevant Competition

4. Commitment — *How Will We Do It?*

Resolved
• Shared Vision
• Allocated Resources
• Organizational Decisions

Unresolved
• Dependence
• Resistance

5. Implementation — *Who does What, When Where?*

Resolved
• Clear Processes
• Alignment
• Disciplined Execution

Unresolved
• Conflict/Confusion
• Nonalignment
• Missed Deadlines

6. High Performance — *Wow!*

Resolved
• Flexibility
• Intuitive Communications
• Synergy

Unresolved
• Overload
• Disharmony

7. Renewal — *Why Continue?*

Resolved
• Recognition
• Change Mastery
• Staying Power

Unresolved
• Boredom
• Burnout

Creating Stages

Sustaining Stages

The Drexler/Sibbet model is a very useful tool, or map, for guiding the creation and performance of teams in organizations. It shows many of the issues that are confronted in teams and what behaviours are likely if these issues remain unresolved.

Norms   A **norm** is a set of expected attitudes, beliefs and behaviours that define how a group member is expected to think or act (Goodman and others, 1987). Descriptive norms identify what most people do in a given situation. Injunctive norms indicate what behaviour is generally approved of in the society (Reno and others, 1993). To be considered a norm these expectations should be held by most group members and should be enforced. When a person deviates from the norm there is a punishment. In this chapter's *Overboard* cartoon Seahawk is being reminded of his group's norm about performance.

Norm   A set of expected attitudes, beliefs, and behaviours that define how a group member is expected to think or act.

Norms common to most groups deal with sharing the rewards or costs of group membership, preventing conflicts among group members, regulating contacts with outsiders, and expressing a group's core values (Levine & Moreland, 1990).

Daniel Feldman (1984) has examined how norms develop at work and when they are likely to be enforced (Exhibit 9.3). Commitment to the group's task is increased when the act of committing to the group and its task is clearly stated, cannot be changed, is made in public, and is done freely (Goodman and others, 1987). Violation of group norms will lead to conflict with the norm violator, more communication directed at the violator about the norm and expected behaviour, and eventual rejection from the group.

EXHIBIT 9.3   THE DEVELOPMENT AND ENFORCEMENT OF GROUP NORMS

How group norms develop:

1. Explicit statements by supervisors or co-workers about expected behaviour.

2. Critical events in the group's history help to establish precedents about expected behaviour.

3. Primacy. The first behaviour pattern that emerges in a group often becomes a group norm about expected behaviour.

4. Carry-over behaviours from past situations. Individuals bring norms with them from their other work groups, organizations or cultures.

Norms are likely to be enforced if they:

1. Facilitate group survival, keeping the group together and protecting it from other groups. Behaviour that threatens the group is punished.

2. Simplify, make predictable, what behaviour is expected of group members. Norms help group members to predict and anticipate the actions of other group members.

3. Help the group avoid embarrassing interpersonal problems. Norms of behaviour help to make sure no one's self-image or "face" is damaged.

4. Express the central values of the group and clarify what is distinctive about the group's identity (i.e., who we, as a group, are).

SOURCE: Adapted and reprinted from Daniel C. Feldman (1984), "The development and enforcement of group norms," *Academy of Management Review* 9: 47-53.

However, the consequences of norm violation do depend on the violator's level in the organizational hierarchy. A norm violator of higher level will suffer fewer consequences. A group's leader is allowed more flexibility to violate group norms. Peripheral norms in a group are less central and less important to group survival. They may be violated with less penalty than central norms. Finally, the consequences of norm violation depend on the member's previous behaviour in the group. Those who have accepted the group's norms and acted in accordance with them have "credit" with the group (Hollander, 1958, 1961, 1964). This credit is used up as norm violation occurs.

It is very important to note that norms only describe what is expected of a group member—not that the group's way is necessarily the *right* or *best* way. For example, members of a professional baseball team may be expected to wear a jacket and tie when travelling. This norm likely has little or no impact on game performance, but a recruit will be told of the right clothes to wear on the road. Deviation from this norm would typically be punished by the levy of a fine.

An example of norm operation at the University of Glasgow business school is shown as Exhibit 9.4. It makes an interesting exercise to compare that school's norms of how students should act to the norms of another school. Remember, one is not "right" and the other "wrong". Norms are only agreements on what is expected from a group member. To examine the norms of a small group in more detail, the experiential exercise at the end of this chapter asks the group member to compare with fellow group members the appropriateness of a number of different possible behaviours.

General group and business norms also differ significantly between countries. While it is easy for those raised in Canada and the United States to think that their standards of polite business behaviour are the "right" way to act, other countries have their own business norms. For example, a common theme in Eastern countries is the importance of the group to the individual and the importance of building a relationship with another person *before* discussing business. In contrast, business in Anglo North America is often conducted first, then the relationship is built.

In Arab countries, hospitality is not a simple courtesy but a basic ingredient in strengthening ties to the all-important group. As Neil Chesanow (1985, p. 121) says in his fascinating book about doing business in the nations of the world:

> When you're offered something by an Arab colleague—coffee, tea, a soft drink, nuts or dates, an invitation to dinner, a gift—in the office or out, politeness dictates that you should accept it. Whether or not you want it is irrelevant. It's the *symbolic meaning* of an offer and its acceptance that matters, not the content of the offer or your desire to receive it.

Script Norms about a sequence of behaviours.

Norms about a sequence of behaviours can be called a **script** (Abelson, 1981; Lord & Kernan, 1987). An example of a script that most people share is how to act in the first few minutes of a job interview—meeting, shaking hands, sitting down and waiting for the interviewer to "break the ice" by talking about sports or the weather.

In many countries the scripts for normal business interaction can be quite different from the Anglo North American script. For example, the occupant of an Arab office will sit on the floor in the centre of the room surrounded by people who have come to see him. He will not talk to each person in turn and then dismiss them, as would be expected in the United States. Instead, he will talk to each person for some time, finally returning to the first person he spoke to. Interaction is not linear but cyclical (Chesanow, 1985).

Chesanow offers specific advice about the script to be followed when visiting an Arab business associate (pages 79, 132-133).

> You may shake hands with an Arab several times in one day, each time you're apart for a while and remeet. Exchange greetings as you shake hands, and continue shaking until greetings are done, which may take several minutes. Arabs rarely say anything concisely. A simple "hello" is too abrupt in the elaborately flowery Arabic style of expression; it lacks sincerity and warmth.

EXHIBIT 9.4   NORMS AND SANCTIONS IN A MASTER OF BUSINESS
ADMINISTRATION PROGRAMME

The part time Masters degree programme in Business Administration lasts three years. Each participant is therefore a member of one of the three large Year Groups, but additionally is a member of a smaller Syndicate Group. The latter operate as task-orientated, face-to-face primary groups. In these small groups, group norms are formed and established. These norms then control the behaviour of members. Deviant members are brought into line by the application of punishment mechanisms. Norms operating within the small Syndicate Group include the following:

- Keep up with the reading;
- Contribute positively to the discussions;
- Don't go isolate— i.e., participate, don't "shut-off;"
- Obtain or arrange copies of any handouts for absent members;
- Support each group member.

Syndicate members who did not contribute were at first gently reprimanded, for example, by being accused of having a hectic social life or by having criticism levelled at them ("nice of you to turn up"). Embarrassment was used as a major sanction. Continued failure by the student to behave in accordance with group norms led to them initially being temporarily, but deliberately, excluded from discussions and conversations. The group would go to a different pub at lunch without telling the "deviant." Further failure to conform would lead to exclusion from the group. This was done by the sanctions on the member becoming more regular, and being imposed with increasing magnitude, so that the attachment of the individual to the group would be reduced to the extent that it would be negative. At this point he or she would resign from the group. Embarrassment, reprimand, and exclusion were the main sanctions available to members of the Syndicate groups.

The large Year Group which consisted of some fifty students and met regularly in a lecture hall also had its own norms:

- Listen quietly and attentively—let the lecturer "bang on" [drone away] about his particular subject;
- Behave courteously—don't shout the lecturer down or walk out even if you feel he is talking rubbish [garbage];
- Relatively static seating pattern;
- Ask brief questions, don't give mini-lectures, make relevant contributions;
- If you're late apologize to the lecturer, if you have to leave early get the lecturer's permission;
- However old and mature you may be as a manager, in the classroom the lecturer (however young he may be) is superior to you;
- No smoking in the large group.

The sanctions available to members of the large Year Group to enforce these norms were not as strong as those available within the smaller Syndicate groups. Expulsion from the Year Group was not open to students since only the Department could exclude the student if he had failed the exams or else not paid his fees. The group did show disapproval of the behaviour of its members at times by visual and verbal displays of apathy, boredom, or restlessness. Shuffling, sighing, groaning, and students talking to each other while the deviant delivered a mini-lecture were frequent. If these sanctions failed, students would have an open discussion about the behaviour of the offender, within his earshot, in the coffee queue [line] during the intermission. It was agreed that these sanctions were not however particularly effective.

SOURCE: David A. Buchanan and Andrzej A. Huczynski (1985), *Organizational Behaviour: An Introductory Text* (pp. 177-178). London: Prentice Hall International (UK) Ltd. Reprinted by permission of Prentice Hall International (UK) Ltd.

A typical greeting might begin:

"Good morning. How are you? Things are fine with me. I'm in good health. Are you? I hope so. Yes? Ah, that's good. It's a pleasure to meet you [or see you again]. The weather's hot today, isn't it? Does it bother you? I don't find it that uncomfortable. I was at my hotel, and now I'm on my way to..."

It goes on and on. You shake hands all the while.

Americans have an aggressive handshake. We grip firmly and shake for three or four strokes. The Arab handshake is gentle and limp. Don't squeeze too hard. Hold an Arab's hand loosely. The actual shaking is light, with only a slight up-and-down movement, never a pump.

Arabs are conscious of rank and expect their protocols to be observed. Shake hands with the most important person in an office first. You'll spot him easily, as he'll be sitting in the middle of the room, surrounded by other guests who pay him visible obeisance. If you're accompanied by a local interpreter or agent, he'll point out the person of highest rank.

Regardless of your sex, it's the duty of the guest to extend his hand to the host.

If the room is crowded, no matter. After shaking hands with the host, you must greet and shake hands with each guest in turn. A general nod to the others in the room is rude. Pros work the room in sections, taking care not to leave anyone out, even though the guests may have nothing to do with business and you may not know who they are.

As you shake hands and convey a greeting, maintain eye contact throughout. Eye contact is a sign of sincerity.

Everyone rises when a new guest enters the room, waits for him to shake hands with and greet the host, and then prepares to be greeted and shaken hands with in turn. Rising is a sign of respect. If other guests arrive after you, and those in the room stand up as they enter, so should you.

You may see some Arabs use both hands to shake hands, with the four hands gently clasped into a ball. This gesture is usually used with old friends, not new acquaintnces. But follow your host's lead. If he clasps your right hand with both of his, cover them with your left hand. (Reprinted with the permission of Rawson Associates, an imprint of Macmillan Publishing Company from *The World Class Executive* by Neil Chesanow. © 1985 by Neil Chesanow.)

Role A set of shared expectations about who in the group is to do what under what circumstances.

Roles   **Roles** are sets of shared expectations about who in the group is to do what under what circumstances. Common roles in groups (according to Levine & Moreland, 1990) are those of leader, newcomer, and scapegoat. The scapegoat is the person in the group who accepts the group's punishment for things that go wrong. Group members may also take on different task roles, maintenance roles, or self-oriented roles (Benne & Sheats, 1948). These are described in Exhibit 9.5. It can be very interesting and instructive to examine your own actions in different groups and see which of these roles you tend to give or accept.

There are several conflicts than can occur because of the roles people are given or seek. **Person-role conflict** occurs when there is a mismatch between the core values of the person and the behaviours expected of that person in the role. A person with strong ethical principles who sells an inferior product for an inflated price would likely experience this kind of role conflict.

Person-role conflict Occurs when there is a mismatch between the core values of the person and the behaviours expected of that person in the role.

Role expectations conflict exists when some behaviours expected of the role occupant are difficult for the person holding that role to enact. For example, a group leader may be very confident and comfortable when interacting in the small group but uncomfortable when required to represent the group to others.

Role expectations conflict Exists when some behaviours expected of the role occupant are difficult for the person holding that role to enact.

Multiple role sender conflict occurs when a person is expected to fill different roles at the same time, even when the expectations of these roles conflict. The role of first level supervisor, for example, is subject to this type of role conflict. The people below the supervisor in the hierarchy expect the supervisor to be one of them and take their point of view whereas those higher up the organization's hierarchy expect the supervisor to act like management.

Multiple role sender conflict Occurs when a person is expected to fill different roles at the same time, even when the expectations of these roles conflict.

Sex discrimination and sexual harassment can occur because of role conflict. Women who are in non-traditional roles (such as a welder in a shipyard or a partner in a national accounting firm) may be subject to harassment because of their "violation" of the male work role. Males may see such women as "asking for" harassment. Sexual harassment in this case can operate as a form of punishment to try to force the women to quit and stay in their traditional roles. Sexual desire is not here the point of such male-female contact.

EXHIBIT 9.5 SOME COMMON GROUP ROLES

TASK ROLES	
Initiator-contributor	Suggests new ideas to solve a group problem or new ways for the group to organize for the task.
Information seeker/Information giver	Deals with information and facts about the group's task.
Opinion seeker/Opinion giver	Deals with the group's values regarding its task.
Elaborator	Goes into detail about how group plans would work.
Coordinator	Coordinates group activities.
Orienter	Keeps the group focused on its goals.
Evaluator	Compares group accomplishment to a standard.
Energizer	Tries to keep up the group's energy level.
Recorder	Acts as the memory of the group.

MAINTENANCE ROLES	
Encourager	Praises and encourages group members.
Harmonizer	Tries to keep relations between group members harmonious.
Compromiser	Offers to compromise own position to keep the group harmonious.
Gatekeeper	Facilitates the participation of others in the group.
Standard setter	Sets or applies standards to the group's work.
Group observer/commentator	Supplies the group with observations of its procedures.
Follower	Goes along with the group.

SELF-ORIENTED ROLES	
Aggressor	Attacks the group.
Blocker	Disagrees with the group and revives old issues for discussion.
Recognition seeker	Seeks personal honour in the group.
Self-confessor	Uses the group as a setting for inappropriate talk about the self.
Clown	Displays non-involvement with the group.
Dominator	Attempts to manipulate the group and dominate others.
Help seeker	Looks for sympathy from others.
Special interest pleader	Speaks for some other "group" while masking own wants.

SOURCE: Based on information in Kenneth D. Benne and Paul Sheats (1948), "Functional roles of group members," *Journal of Social Issues* 4(2): 41-49.

Instead, sexual behaviour is the means used by males to try to force the woman back into what the males see as her "place." Such harassment is not about sexual desire but about power and social control.

An example of sex discrimination at work is that of a Price Waterhouse manager who, after she was denied a promotion to partner, claimed that she was intentionally discriminated against on the basis of illegal sex stereotypes (see Fiske, 1993). Women at Price-Waterhouse made up only one percent of all partners.

Interrole conflict occurs when a person has multiple roles to play and role demands are such that it is difficult to perform well in each one. A common interrole conflict is that between employee/group member and spouse/parent. Each of these roles demands time and energy. Sometimes there is not enough of either to satisfy the requirements of both roles. Different cultures resolve this particular interrole conflict in different ways. While Anglo North American businessmen usually put business before family, a Latin American businessman may miss business appointments because, to him, family comes first (Chesanow, 1985). Anglo North American businesswomen often face a very strong interrole conflict because family demands can be stronger than they are for a businessman in their culture.

Role ambiguity is uncertainty regarding what actions, duties and relationships are required for a certain job role. Some individuals are quite tolerant of ambiguity. They do not mind working in uncertain conditions. Others, however, need clearly defined job roles and will seek out certainty if it is lacking. Self-diagnostic exercise 9.1 at the end of this chapter provides an instrument that can be used to examine role conflict and ambiguity in a job.

Status   A person's **status** within a group is affected by the individual's organizational level and job, the roles played in a group, and how well group norms are adhered to. In North America, status is generally reflected by the size and location of the person's office, the quality and type of office furnishings, and a more formal form of address.

Status systems can be much more elaborate and formalized in other countries. North Americans easily recognize the status of sitting at the head of the table, but Japanese know the relative status in their system of the other places at the table as well. In Japan the place of honour is known and recognized by all in meeting rooms, restaurants, elevators, trains, and even automobiles (Yaginuma & Kennedy, 1986). An example of this cross-cultural difference in norms and status is shown in *A Rose by Any Other Name*.

Cohesion   Group **cohesion** is a measure of the attraction to the group by the group's members. The Group Attitude Scale (Evans & Jarvis, 1986), self-diagnostic exercise 9.2 at the end of this chapter, can be used to measure cohesion. To increase cohesion in a group it is necessary to put people together in a group, have them spend time together and be near one another (this is called **propinquity**), have them communicate with each other and conform to group norms (Sundstrom and others, 1990), have them experience success as a group and the rewards that come from that success, and have them like one another by promoting their real or perceived similarity to each other (Levine & Moreland, 1985).

In an interesting study of group cohesion, Patti and Peter Adler followed a college basketball team for five years to find out what affected loyalty to the team. A review of this study can be found in the feature *A Little Knowledge*.

Cohesion is important in groups because higher cohesion lowers turnover and amplifies norms about group performance. Therefore, if a team has a norm that they will do well at their task, greater cohesion will strengthen the group's resolve to succeed. Conversely, greater cohesion can serve to limit performance if that is the group's norm.

Interrole conflict   Occurs when a person has multiple roles to play and role demands are such that it is difficult to perform well in each one.

Role ambiguity
Uncertainty regarding what actions, duties and relationships are required for a certain job role.

Status   Relative standing within a group.

Cohesion   The attraction to the group by the group's members.

Propinquity   Physical proximity.

A ROSE BY ANY OTHER NAME

The reporter walked into the small room and sat on one of two vinyl couches. The others were already there, sipping tea. From the office-furniture company had come the director, the director's son and the chief salesman. They sat on one side of the coffee table. Facing them were Mr. N the intermediary, his assistant and now the reporter.

Mr. A, the intermediary's intermediary, sat at a separate chair at the head of the coffee table.

Round three of the office-furniture negotiations was about to begin.

The reporter was there to buy a desk, a chair and a filing cabinet. "Get yourself some office furniture," the reporter's superiors had said vaguely, before he left Canada to open a new office in Tokyo. "You know. A desk, a chair, a filing cabinet - that sort of thing."

But the reporter had found buying office furniture more difficult than he had imagined. He could not find a store that sold office furniture. And while he could say "desk" and "chair" and "how much?" in Japanese, he did not know the words for "filing cabinet" or "don't you have anything cheaper?"

So the reporter had turned to Mr. A. Mr. A's company had business dealings with the reporter's newspaper. And, in the matter of office furniture, Mr. A knew exactly what to do. He introduced the reporter to Mr. N.

Mr. N did not sell office furniture, but did know people in the business. So, over a period of two weeks, rounds one and two of the office-furniture talks had been held. Tea was drunk, pleasantries exchanged, bargaining positions sketched out.

Round three was to be make-or-break, the first time for buyer and seller to meet face-to-face. But the reporter felt confident; he had stayed up late the night before, reading his office-furniture catalogue.

The reported opened his catalogue and indicated the desk he wanted. The salesman, the director and the three intermediaries conferred. Yes, they said, that would be fine.

The reporter indicated the filing cabinet he wanted. Another conference. Yes, that too would be fine.

The chair was the sticking point. The reporter had opted for the cheapest chair in the catalogue. "That one," said the reporter, pointing to the cheap chair. The others looked embarrassed.

"That is a student's chair," said Mr. A. "You are not a student."

The reporter was puzzled. Was the chair too small? Too light-weight?

Mr. A assured the reporter that this was not the point.

"How will it look to visitors," he said, "when they come to see you? If they see you sitting in a student's chair, they will think your company is not important."

The reporter felt abashed. He had not thought of that. The chief salesman, the director, Mr. A and Mr. N agreed on a chair they thought suitable for the reporter. The chair had arms and one lever. It was decided that a two-lever chair would be pretentious. Only presidents had two-lever chairs.

"What kind of couch would you like?" asked Mr. A. The reporter had not thought about a couch. Why would he need a couch?

"For your visitors," said Mr. A reproachfully. "You will need a vinyl couch and a coffee table and two chairs to have tea and negotiations with your visitors."

The reporter felt foolish. Of course. Where would his visitors drink their tea? They couldn't all fit in his one-lever chair. He chose a couch.

"And of course, the rug," said Mr. A. The reporter knew he was trapped. What if the visitors, whoever they might be, wanted to remove their shoes while sitting on his couch drinking tea? Their feet would get cold on bare linoleum.

He pointed to the cheapest, a sample in electric blue.

"Not a very good quality for an important newspaper," said Mr. A smoothly. "Try this one." He pointed to a brown sample. "The Wall Street Journal uses that." The reporter hung his head and agreed. Tea was sipped. And the office furniture talks were adjourned until the following Tuesday.

SOURCE: Reprinted from Thomas Walkom (1985), "Humble dickering for furniture," The *Globe and Mail.* November 14, 1985, p. A8.

A LITTLE KNOWLEDGE

Patti and Peter Adler studied the development of loyalty to a team by following a college basketball team in the south central United States. This was a high-performing team that over four years won four times as many games as they lost in the National Collegiate Athletic Association's Division I. From 1980 to 1985 Peter Adler was an assistant coach of the team and Patti Adler interacted with team members and worked with Peter to record and understand each day's events. Each day they would look for different categories of structures and processes in the team and how they occurred and influenced each other. They found that there were five key elements that affected loyalty to the organization.

1. *Domination.* The head coach had a high level of control over much of the players' lives. He controlled the food they ate, where and how they lived, their playing time, courses taken at the university, their daily schedule during the season, and had a direct impact on their likely success in their future career (if they made it) as professional basketball players. This socialization reduced their individuality and made each player into a member of the group.

2. *Identification.* Players identified strongly with the team. They represented the team on campus and on road trips and were rewarded for it. The group of players, coaches, and trainers spent time together, travelled together, and wore uniforms. A family atmosphere was developed where the player and the group became one—almost a family—and the team's loyalty to the head coach was matched by his loyalty to the players.

3. *Commitment.* New recruits to the team attended a formal and ritualistic meeting where they signed a letter of agreement to join the team. They were given team equipment at the signing to indicate their new status as a team member.

4. *Integration.* There was high cohesion in the group. Players spent summers on campus in an athletic dormitory that was physically isolated from other students on campus. They were encouraged to develop harmony within the group and an adversarial attitude toward outsiders.

5. *Goal alignment.* The individual's and the organization's goals were one. Winning games helped the coach achieve his goals and the players to achieve their goals.

SOURCE: Based on information in Patricia A. Adler and Peter Adler (1988), "Intense loyalty in organizations: A case study of college athletics," *Administrative Science Quarterly* 33: 401-417.

Strategies for External Integration and Boundary Maintenance

Besides what goes on inside groups and teams, work groups have boundaries that separate them from other individuals and groups. The boundary is useful to the group because it is a marker of who is inside the group and who is not. Without a clear boundary the social system of the group would be more difficult to maintain since group members would not have a clear idea of who the members were, the norms of the group, and the roles played by group members. Boundary maintenance, then, is comprised of activities that clarify for everyone, both those inside and those outside the group, the limits of the group. External integration refers to activities that groups use to relate to individuals and groups outside the group's boundary. While internal group processes are important factors in work group effectiveness, so too are external relations.

External Integration

Deborah Ancona (1990) has examined the strategies organizational teams use to relate to outsiders. She found that the groups she studied used the strategies of: *informing*—making sure that others know of the group's intentions; *parading*—showing the group's existence and abilities to outsiders so that they know of the team and are more likely to support it in the organization; and *probing*—taking an active role in talking to those outside the group, finding out their needs and how they could interact with the group. In the particular situation studied these three strategies were not equally successful. Therefore, in order to be effective, organizational groups need to consider how they will deal with others in their social network.

Relationships with Others   These can be competitive or cooperative. A group can choose to exchange resources with outsiders, form alliances, merge with them, imitate the other, or use the other group as a basis for social comparison (Levine & Moreland, 1990). But a great deal of study of the relationships between groups has shown that people in one group regularly produce an intergroup bias such that group members are favoured over the members of other groups (Messick & Mackie, 1989). Jerome Barkow of Dalhousie University has nicely summarized this process. He wrote (1991, p. 300) that:

> We human beings regularly form into ingroups that believe ourselves superior to outgroups, we effortlessly grow hostile toward and prejudiced against outgroup members, we meet external threat with increased internal solidarity and cooperativeness, we punish those who decamp from the ingroup ("traitors") with conspicuous viciousness, we permit behavior toward outsiders that would be penalized were it directed toward insiders, and so forth.

In general, people perceive other groups to be more homogeneous than their own group. Because of day-to-day interaction with individuals in their own group, differences between ingroup members are noticed. However, when the work group is in the minority compared to the organization as a whole the ingroup tends to be seen as more homogeneous. In other words, "We are alike and they are different from us" (Messick & Mackie, 1989). Groups need to consider their relationships with outsiders and be aware of the tendency for an in-group bias to occur.

THE MANAGEMENT OF GROUPS IN ORGANIZATIONS

While much of the world's work is done by small groups, they are not automatically or universally effective. Groups can waste time, develop and enforce a norm of low productivity, make bad decisions, and cause conflict (Hackman, 1987). Further, each type of organizational work group, because of the kind of work it does, is subject to a different risk that could lead to poor performance (see Exhibit 9.6). Each group type, however, has a corresponding opportunity for high performance.

In order to help create more effective work groups, Richard Hackman (1987) has identified four steps a manager may take.

The first is *prework*. The manager identifies what work is required by the organization, whether a group is really required, and the amount and type of authority (for example manager-led, self-managing, or self-governing) to be given to the group. Because there are multiple ways to get from a starting point to a goal (the concept of equifinality), a manager cannot know if a team's chosen course is worse or better than the course that the manager would have selected. Therefore, managers should help design the group and involve themselves at the start of a group's life and at the middle (if the group has a limited time span) but not at other times.

The second step to building effective groups is *creating performance conditions*. The group's structure must be designed and the group provided with the necessary organizational resources and support for the group to perform effectively. Special attention should be paid at this step to the physical facilities and equipment to be used by the group. Setting

---

EXHIBIT 9.6　SPECIAL RISKS AND OPPORTUNITIES
FOR WORK TEAMS

GROUP TYPE	RISKS	OPPORTUNITIES
Top Management Teams	Underbounded; absence of organizational context	Self-designing; influence over key organizational conditions
Task Forces	Team and work both new	Clear purpose and deadline
Professional Support Groups	Dependency on others for work	Using and honing professional expertise
Performing Groups	Skimpy organizational supports	Play that is fueled by competition and/or audiences
Human Service Teams	Emotional drain; struggle for control	Inherent significance of helping people
Customer Service Teams	Loss of involvement with parent organization	Bridging between parent organization and its customers
Production Teams	Retreat into technology; insulation from end users	Continuity of work; ability to hone both the team design and the product

SOURCE: Reprinted from J. Richard Hackman (1990), "Creating more effective work groups in organizations," in J. Richard Hackman (Ed.) *Groups That Work (And Those That Don't): Creating Conditions for Effective Teamwork*, San Francisco: Jossey-Bass, Inc., p. 489. Reprinted by permission of Jossey-Bass, Inc.

---

up a space in the organization to be used exclusively by the team and putting the required tools and machines into that space for the sole use of the team are of great importance in getting the group off to a good start.

The third step is *forming and building the team*. The manager's job here is to help the group to establish its processes for action both inside and outside the group, to help the group to define its task and methods for task accomplishment, and to assist with the creation of group norms and roles.

The last step is *providing continuing assistance to the group* by offering training as required, solving problems as they arise, and supplying needed resources. Team training can attempt to improve interpersonal processes, goal setting, role definition, and problem solving (Sundstrom and others, 1990).

For example, one way to help people learn about groups and the processes in groups is to take them away from their usual organizational life and confront them with new challenges that can only be successfully met by a team. One such training method is described in this chapter's *Seeing is Believing* feature. Because task failure in a group can have negative effects on cohesion and group activity and result in a downward spiral of group performance, initial and continued group success is important. Teams must therefore be helped to perform at all four of these steps in order to avoid the experience of failure.

The *A Word to the Wise* feature in this chapter is a review by Paul Thorne of ways to make work groups more effective. His thoughts on what he calls the 7 R's of groups are valuable advice to those who hope to make the work teams in their organizations more effective. Another approach is that of Tom Peters (1991), who advises that managers must be careful not to let project teams become committees (see Exhibit 9.7).

SEEING IS BELIEVING

The Colorado Outward Bound School is an organization that offers courses in management development and group process. In "The Wilderness Lab" (1984), Janet Long describes her participation in one such adventure training program designed to help people learn how groups work together. First, participants were bussed out into the wilds of Colorado where they stayed for the five-day program. They were divided into small groups and given a group identity—Long's group was the "Coyotes." Everyone was blindfolded and all Coyotes had to find one another using only animal sounds. The Coyote "howl" of her group, though it sounds a lot like summer camp as a child, helped her group to be cohesive and to develop ways of telling who was in the group and who was not.

Then came exercises designed to develop trust (climbing a ladder on the side of a tree and falling backwards into the hands of fellow group members), to show that a mix of skills and abilities is needed in any group (group members had to scale a sheer 4-metre wooden wall with a platform on the back side), and to demonstrate that a group has to work on its process—the *how* of how the job is done (the group had to get across a pit dug in the ground with only minimal equipment).

At the end of the five days cohesion within the Coyotes was high. They then worked with a similar group, the Beavers, to learn to work across group lines as well as within them. Later, before heading home, each person spent some time alone to think about how the lessons learned about groups could be transferred back to their regular jobs.

Source: Based on information in Janet W. Long (1984), "The wilderness lab," *Training and Development Journal* 38(5): 58-69. Also see Janet W. Long (1987), "The wilderness lab comes of age," *Training and Development Journal* 41(3): 30-39; and Lynne Sanford (1993), "Triumph over fear: How adventure training turns managers into leaders," *Success*, March 1993, pp. 46, 47. For further information about the Colorado Outward Bound School, contact them at 945 Pennsylvania Street, Denver Colorado 80203-3198, Telephone 303-837-0880.

A WORD TO THE WISE

Management fashions and conventions move and shift like Mexican waves around the business arena. Right now, teams are in. Teamwork goes with empowerment. It is central to total quality management. It is the deliverer of 'time compression,' sometimes known as getting things done faster.

Speed is of the essence now. New products are 'hothoused' to hit the market ahead of rivals through teaming up marketing, design, engineering, and manufacturing all at once, rather than one after another. This can improve results greatly, but works only if the team works.

A team is a more complex creature than most people imagine. For it to work as a problem-solving tool it must address seven fundamentals: 'the *7 R's* of *raison d'être*, rules, roles, relationships, rituals, rewards and results.

First, a team has to have a *raison d'être*. Unless there is a purpose, there is nothing to combine, to focus, to create a sense of being more than individuals casually interacting. The lack of a genuine reason for existing often leads to the failure of quality circles and consultative committees. The purpose and function of the team must be clear to all.

A team has to have *rules*. Without them, team members' behaviour becomes unpredictable. The rules can be formal or informal, extensive or singular, static or ever-changing, newly minted or time honoured. Anyone wishing to be part of a team and contribute to its activities must obey the rules and be prepared to make the personal concessions required for continued membership.

Invariably when teams are formed, members assume different *roles*. Some people naturally behave in certain ways whatever team they join, according to R.M. Belbin, a British social psychologist. Team members who consistently get elected leader or secretary are invariably people who go out of their way to play the role of coordinator.

The roles of task leader (father) and emotional leader (mother) are both necessary for effective team functioning. Belbin showed that performance varied clearly as a result of diverse role-playing. Too many members playing just one or two roles can reduce teams to bodies that become anything from inert to violently self-defeating.

Like it or not, in among this defined team rigour is the undergrowth of *relationships*. People form relationships within teams that can help the team perform or stick together. They can also divide the team and defeat its best endeavour. Relationships need to be understood if team functioning is to be followed or measured. But many are hard to read and can change in a few moments, as the political value of alliances waxes and wanes during the life of the team.

Rituals often describe rules in action, but they are more than this. They are the aspects of behaviour that people offer to others to show they belong. Rituals confirm the right of team membership. They acquire a life of their own. People who do not follow team rituals soon look and feel out of place. Rituals include such features as timing. How many teams meet regularly whether or not there is anything to do? What would happen if one member turned up in bare feet? Suppose a newcomer tried to take over the leadership. Rituals subtly control team membership, keeping it comfortable.

Rewards are the pay-off for team membership. However, seldom are rewards the same for each team member. Esteem or power needs could be satisfied where the team has prestige or the role has high value. Membership itself could be a reward, it could protect from attack, enlarge the individual's range and depth of impact or increase the sophistication of decisions.

Ultimately, this produces the *result*, the added value of a first-rate team effort that could not be achieved by individuals operating independently. Occasionally it can be disastrous. 'Group think' has proved both overtly risky and overburdened by convention.

In the end, teams produce well only where they draw the benefit of all individuals' input and at the same time use it to add greater value. The results come from a complicated human process - and its complexity is always underestimated.

So think on the "7 Rs". How many are working for your team? How many against?

Source: Paul Thorne (1992), "Hit squads," *International Management*, February 1992, p. 56. Reprinted by permission of International Management © Reed Business Publishing 1992.

EXHIBIT 9.7   DON'T LET PROJECT TEAMS BECOME COMMITTEES

1. Set goals and deadlines for key subsystem tests—this keeps people focused on the task and steps towards its completion.

2. Insist on 100 percent assignment to the team—keeps team members concentration on the task of the team, not on other work or organizational roles.

3. Place key functions on board the team from the outset—its too late to try to add them later when you find they are needed.

4. Give members authority to commit their function—it is important that team members don't have to go back and forth to get approval from their functional boss. This slows things down and dilutes responsibility.

5. Keep team-member destiny in the hands of the project leader—the project leader must have the ability to reward and punish.

6. Make careers a string of projects—then each project is important to the person's long-term success.

7. Live together—put team members in the same place so that they can be around each other and see each other often.

8. Remember the social element—don't forget that play is a part of work.

9. Allow outsiders in—to bring in new viewpoints and ideas.

10. Construct self-contained systems—so that the team does not have to rely on anyone else for project completion.

11. Permit the teams to pick their own leader—leadership can't be forced on them.

12. Honour project leadership skills—project success requires more than technical skills.

SOURCE: Based on information in Tom Peters (1991), "Get innovative or get dead (Part 2)," *California Management Review*, Winter 1991, 33(2): 9-23.

CONCLUSION

Now that we have examined work group effectiveness and the management of groups in organizations we can turn to the leadership of individuals and groups at work. Leadership is more than management, it deals with ways of influencing organizational members so that they will *want* to help the leader and the organization to achieve their goals.

CHAPTER SUMMARY

Work groups in organizations are called teams when the group's performance depends on both individual performance and the joint performance of its members. There are several factors that affect work group (or team) performance. The context within which the group works in the organization, its design, and the processes it uses to accomplish its work all have an impact on work group effectiveness.

Of critical importance to a group's effectiveness is how it is initially designed. Elements of group design are the type of work group, its task and group structure, the composition of group membership, how different the organization's work groups are from one another, and the anticipated life span of the group. A group's effectiveness is also expected to be influenced by the way the group is organized to do its work. Important factors in group organization are shared expectations among group members about behaviour (norms), shared expectations about who in the group is to do what under what circumstances (roles), and shared expectations about the relative standing among the members of the group (status). Norms, roles, and status are all essential for the internal functioning of the group. But to be effective, groups must also consider how to deal with other groups and individuals in their social network.

QUESTIONS FOR REVIEW

1. Many organizations around the world are reorganizing themselves into a form that is less hierarchical and more team-based. What are the expected benefits of such a reorganization? What are the likely costs?

2. Some large organizations have found that breaking into smaller units has had beneficial effects on creativity, customer relations, and more effective intragroup relationships. Why would this be the case?

3. Why is conflict between groups a common occurrence? When is such conflict likely to have positive outcomes for the organization as a whole and when is it likely to have negative outcomes?

4. How could the manager of a group structure the group's task and activities to encourage high group cohesiveness? Under what conditions would high cohesiveness be beneficial to the organization?

5. What steps might a manager take to create an effective group?

SELF-DIAGNOSTIC EXERCISE 9.1

Role Conflict and Role Ambiguity

Think of a job you have held or are currently holding and answer the following statements. Then calculate total scores for the role conflict and role ambiguity for you in that job.

Role Conflict

		A poor description of my job					A good description of my job	
1.	I have to do things that should be done differently	1	2	3	4	5	6	7
2.	Lack of policies and guidlines to help me	1	2	3	4	5	6	7
3.	I work under incompatible policies and guidelines	1	2	3	4	5	6	7
4.	I have to buck a rule or policy in order to carry out an assignment	1	2	3	4	5	6	7
5.	I work with two or more groups who operate quite differently	1	2	3	4	5	6	7
6.	I receive incompatible requests from two or more people	1	2	3	4	5	6	7
7.	I do things that are apt to be accepted by one person and not accepted by others	1	2	3	4	5	6	7
8.	I receive an assignment without adequate resources and materials to execute it	1	2	3	4	5	6	7
9.	I work on unnecessary things	1	2	3	4	5	6	7
10.	I have to work under vague directives or orders	1	2	3	4	5	6	7

Total Score for Role Conflict: _____

Higher scores indicate higher role conflict for the job.

Role Ambiguity

		A poor description of my job					A good description of my job	
1.	I feel certain about how much authority I have	7	6	5	4	3	2	1
2.	Clear, planned goals and objectives exist for my job	7	6	5	4	3	2	1
3.	I know that I have divided my time properly	7	6	5	4	3	2	1

4.	I know what my responsibilities are	7	6	5	4	3	2	1
5.	I feel certain how I will be evaluated for a raise or promotion	7	6	5	4	3	2	1
6.	I have just the right amount of work to do	7	6	5	4	3	2	1
7.	I am able to act the same regardless of the group I am with	7	6	5	4	3	2	1
8.	I know exactly what is expected of me	7	6	5	4	3	2	1
9.	Explanation is clear of what has to be done	7	6	5	4	3	2	1
10.	I perform work that suits my values	7	6	5	4	3	2	1

Total Score for Role Ambiguity: _____

Lower scores indicate lower role ambiguity for the job.

NOTE: It is important to remember that while the results of this test will be suggestive of your own role conflict and role ambiguity, this test as used here should not be considered a valid scientific instrument.

SOURCE: John R Rizzo, Robert J. House, and Sidney I. Lirtzman (1970), "Role conflict and ambiguity in complex organizations," *Administrative Science Quarterly* 15:156. Reprinted by permission of Administrative Science Quarterly.

SELF-DIAGNOSTIC EXERCISE 9.2

The Group Attitude Scale

Think of a group of which you are a member and answer the following 20 questions to measure your attraction to that group.

		Agree								*Disagree*
1.	I want to remain a member of this group	1	2	3	4	5	6	7	8	9
2.	I like my group	1	2	3	4	5	6	7	8	9
3.	I look forward to coming to the group	1	2	3	4	5	6	7	8	9
4.	I don't care what happens in this group	1	2	3	4	5	6	7	8	9
5.	I feel involved in what is happening in my group	1	2	3	4	5	6	7	8	9
6.	If I could drop out of the group now, I would	1	2	3	4	5	6	7	8	9
7.	I dread coming to this group	1	2	3	4	5	6	7	8	9
8.	I wish it were possible for the group to end now	1	2	3	4	5	6	7	8	9

		Agree								*Disagree*
9.	I am dissatisfied with the group	1	2	3	4	5	6	7	8	9
10.	If it were possible to move to another group at this time, I would	1	2	3	4	5	6	7	8	9
11.	I feel included in the group	1	2	3	4	5	6	7	8	9
12.	In spite of individual differences, a feeling of unity exists in my group	1	2	3	4	5	6	7	8	9
13.	Compared to other groups I know of, I feel my group is better than most	1	2	3	4	5	6	7	8	9
14.	I do not feel a part of the group's activities	1	2	3	4	5	6	7	8	9
15.	I feel it would make a difference to the group if I were not here	1	2	3	4	5	6	7	8	9
16.	If I were told my group would not meet today, I would feel badly	1	2	3	4	5	6	7	8	9
17.	I feel distant from the group	1	2	3	4	5	6	7	8	9
18.	It makes a difference to me how this group turns out	1	2	3	4	5	6	7	8	9
19.	I feel my absence would not matter to the group	1	2	3	4	5	6	7	8	9
20.	I would not feel badly if I had to miss a meeting of this group	1	2	3	4	5	6	7	8	9

Scoring:

Add your scores from the following statements.

Item	*Score*
4	_____
6	_____
7	_____
8	_____
9	_____
10	_____
14	_____
17	_____
19	_____
20	_____
Subtotal:	_____

For the following items, subtract your score from 10 to obtain a revised score. For example, if your score for item 2 was 8, the revised score would be 10-8=2.

Item	Score
1	_____
2	_____
3	_____
5	_____
11	_____
12	_____
13	_____
15	_____
16	_____
18	_____

Subtotal: _____

Now add the two subtotals to create your overall score: _____

Then compare your score to others in your class. Your scores and those of your classmates will be suggestive of your own group attitudes and will provide a useful basis for class discussion. However, this test as used here should not be considered a valid scientific instrument.

Source: Nancy J. Evans and Paul A. Jarvis (1986), "The group attitude scale: A measure of attraction to group," *Small Group Behavior* 17:207. Copyright © 1986 by Sage Publications, Inc. Reprinted by permission of Sage Publications, Inc.

EXPERIENTIAL EXERCISE 9.1

Group Norms

Step 1

Form groups of five. Imagine your group's task is to study an actual organization, write a report on your findings, and present these findings to the rest of the class. Complete the following questionnaire about your group.

Given below is a list of behaviours. Without consulting the other members of your new group, please indicate how appropriate or inappropriate you think it would be as a norm for the group. Write in the number that shows your best estimate of how the group would feel. Write a "5" if the behaviour is definitely appropriate as a norm, write a "4" if the behaviour is somewhat appropriate, a "3" if it is questionable, a "2" if it is somewhat inappropriate, and a "1" if it is definitely inappropriate.

_____   1. Said little or nothing in most meetings.

_____   2. Talked about the details of her sex life.

_____   3. Brought up problems he had with others who weren't in the group.

_____   4. Kissed another group member.

_____   5. Asked for reactions or feedback (how do you see me in this group?).

_____   6. Talked mostly about what was going on in the group.

_____   7. Frequently joked.

_____   8. Pleaded for help.

_____   9. Challenged another members' remarks.

_____   10. Said she was not getting anything from being in the group.

_____   11. Described his reactions to what was taking place in the group.

_____   12. Highlighted opposition among ideas.

_____   13. Formed a contract with another member about the use of each other's resources in meeting both their needs and goals.

_____   14. Refused to be bound by a group decision.

_____   15. Asked for the goal to be clarified.

_____   16. Noted competition in the group and asked how it could be reduced.

_____   17. Gave advice to other group members about what to do.

_____   18. Interrupted a dialogue going on between two members.

_____   19. Told another member that she was unlikable.

_____   20. Was often absent.

_____   21. Shouted with anger at another member.

_____   22. With strong feelings, told another member how likable he was.

_____   23. Tried to manipulate the group to get her own way.

_____   24. Hit another group member.

_____   25. Acted indifferently to other members.

_____   26. Dominated the group's discussion for more than one session.

_____   27. Encouraged other group members to react to the topic being discussed.

_____   28. Tried to convince members of the rightness of a certain point of view.

_____   29. Talked a lot without showing his real feelings.

_____   30. Told the group off, saying that it was worthless.

_____   31. Showed she had no intention of changing her behaviour.

_____   32. Resisted the suggestions of other members on procedures.

_____   33. Commented that the decision-making procedure was not appropriate to the nature of the decision.

_____   34. Asked that the causes of a group problem be analyzed.

_____   35. Expressed affection for several group members.

Step 2

Discuss your answers to the questions with the other members of the group. Where are the areas of most agreement and disagreement?

Step 3

Return to the main classroom and report back to the large group on the findings in your small groups. Are there common areas of agreement or disagreement between the groups?

NOTE: This exercise can also be used with actual work groups. Group members would individually complete the questionnaire, then meet to discuss their answers.

SOURCE: David W. Johnson and Frank P. Johnson (1975), *Joining Together: Group Theory and Group Skills* (pp. 250-251). Englewood Cliffs, NJ: Prentice Hall, Inc. Reprinted with permission.

SELF-GUIDED LEARNING ACTIVITY

Go to a city or town council meeting that is open to the public and take along Exhibit 9.5. As you watch the meeting ignore the content of what council members are saying. Instead, look for the roles different members are playing. Who on council is focused on the task roles, who is playing the maintenance roles, and who is self-oriented? How do members playing different roles relate to each other? How effective is the council at making decisions? Are the roles played by council members helping or hindering its effectiveness?

CASE 9.1

MANAGER'S CASE FILE: SHORT SHIFT

Until yesterday, George had often told himself that his luckiest break since making foreman was the day Smitty got elected union steward. Smitty was easy to talk to, and he was someone George felt he could trust. Each made concessions, so that in the year since Smitty had been elected, he hadn't filed one grievance and George hadn't had to discipline one worker. Moreover, production was higher than ever.

But a few months ago, the staffers—Smitty included—had slipped into the habit of knocking off early to wash up. They stayed outside the shop and talked until a minute before closing time, then came back to punch out just at 4:30. There was nothing wrong with shutting down four or five minutes early. Management expected that. But, little by little, they had been leaving earlier until now they'd worked it up to 15 minutes. George first became aware of this a couple of months ago and had meant to talk to Smitty about it, but then several more pressing problems came up and he just hadn't gotten around to it.

The real trouble came yesterday when Ed Barnes, the plant manager, dropped into George's office around three o'clock to discuss plans for new storage facilities. At four o'clock, Ed was still there, and George began to worry that he might walk out of the office just as the workers started going to the washrooms. Ed was a stickler for the rules. George got so edgy watching the clock that he finally told Ed he had to check something outside and would be right back.

He looked around frantically for Smitty and finally asked one of the women where he was. He was told that Smitty had left a couple of hours ago. Just as he was wondering whether or not he should warn the workers that the big boss was on the floor, he had to go back to answer his phone. As George hung up, Ed looked at his watch. "Holy smoke," he said, "I've got to get out of here. Work on these figures, will you, George, and let me have them tomorrow morning." Ed

walked out on the floor just as the workers were leaving for the washrooms. He paused a moment and seemed puzzled, but he didn't say anything. George had no doubt that he would have plenty to say to his immediate boss, Sid Trumbull.

The only thing George could do now was to phone Smitty at home that night and ask him to get the staffers back in line the very next day. George started to call Smitty at five o'clock. When ten o'clock came and there was still no answer, his wife made him stop and go to bed.

Not that he slept much. Nevertheless, the next day he got to the plant early. The instant he saw Smitty, he shouted "Where the devil were you yesterday? Just when I need you most, you goof off early and stay out all night. Next thing, I suppose, the staffers will be taking off at three o'clock. Well, from now on, no one leaves before 4:30."

Smitty was red in the face. "Now, hold on, George. I asked you last week if I could leave early yesterday so I could drive my mother to my sister's house and you said it was okay. You know it's a long trip; I didn't get back until midnight. Furthermore, since you want to play the big boss, so what if everybody washes up on company time. They get dirty on company time, don't they?" He turned on his heels and walked off.

Seething, George locked himself in his office for the rest of the day working on the figures Ed wanted. He had a hard time concentrating. He knew Sid was going to call him on the carpet, and he just wished he'd get it over with.

When George finally completed Ed's figures, he looked at the clock. It was 4:10 and still no call from Sid. If his luck held, he might be able to nail this down before it came. At 4:15 George started for Ed's office. He stopped the first person he saw heading toward the washroom, but Smitty was on top of him before he'd finished ordering the man back to his machine.

"George, I guess I'll have to file a grievance. You don't have a very good case, though, because this has been going on for quite a while." He stopped. "Come on, why not let it go? We can work something out."

Questions

1. Does George have a good case should this problem reach arbitration?

2. What should George say to Smitty?

3. How can George prevent such situations in the future?

FAB SWEETS LIMITED

ORGANIZATIONAL SETTING

FAB Sweets Limited is a manufacturer of high quality sweets [candies]. The company is a medium-sized, family-owned, partially unionized and highly successful confectionery producer in the north of England. The case study is set within a single department in the factory where acute problems were experienced.

BACKGROUND TO THE CASE

The department (hereafter called "HB") produces and packs over 40 lines of hard-boiled sweets on a batch-production system. It is organized in two adjacent areas, one for production staffed by men and one for packing staffed by women. The areas are sep-

arated by a physical barrier, allowing the packing room to be air conditioned and protected from the humidity resulting from production. Management believed this was necessary to stop the sweets from sweating (thus sticking to their wrappers) during storage. Each room has a chargehand and a supervisor who reports to the department manager, who himself is responsible to the factory manager. In total, 37 people work in the department (25 in production, 12 in packing), the majority of whom are skilled employees. Training takes place on the job, and it normally takes two years to acquire the skills necessary to complete all the production tasks. Exhibit 9.8 presents an outline of the physical layout of the department and the work-flow.

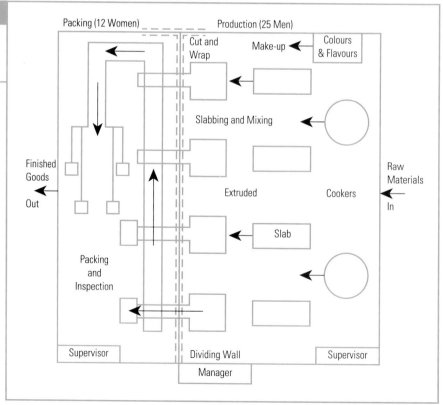

EXHIBIT 9.8

The HB department: Physical layout and work flow

Packing (12 Women) Production (25 Men)

Cut and Wrap — Make-up — Colours & Flavours

Slabbing and Mixing

Finished Goods Out

Extruded   Cookers   Raw Materials In

Slab

Packing and Inspection

Supervisor   Dividing Wall   Supervisor

Manager

THE HB DEPARTMENT: PHYSICAL LAYOUT AND WORK FLOW

The production process is essentially quite simple. Raw materials, principally sugar, are boiled to a set temperature, with "cooking time" varying from line to line. The resulting batches are worked on by employees who fold and manipulate them so as to create the required texture, while adding colouring and flavourings ("slabbing" and "mixing"). Different batches are moulded together to create the flavor mixes and patterns required ("make up"). The batch, which by now is quite cool, is then extruded through a machine which cuts it into sweets of individual size. Some products at this stage are automatically wrapped and then passed by conveyor belt to the packing room where they are inspected, bagged, and boxed ready for dispatch to retail and wholesale outlets. Other products progress unwrapped into the packing room where they are fed into a wrapping machine, inspected, bagged and dispatched. Several different product lines can be produced at the same time. The most skilled and critical tasks occur early in the process; these include "cooking" mixtures for different products and "make up" (for example, for striped mints). These skills are gradually learned until the operator is able to "feel" the correct finish for each of the 40 lines. All the tasks are highly interdependent such that any one individual's performance affects the ease with which the next person down the line can successfully achieve his/her part of the production process. Although the work appears quite simple and the management of the process straightforward, the department nevertheless experienced acute problems. These are outlined below.

THE PROBLEM

In objective terms the problems in HB were manifest in a high level of labor turnover, six new managers in eight years, production which consistently fell below targets based on work study standards, and high levels of scrap. The department was known as the worst in the factory, and its problems were variously characterized in terms of "attitude," "atmosphere," and "climate." Moreover, employees had few decision-making responsibilities, low motivation, low job satisfaction, and received little information on their performance. Finally there were interpersonal problems between the employees in the production and packing rooms, between the two supervisors, and also among the operators, and there were a number of dissatisfactions relating to grading and payment levels.

EXPERIENCE OF THE METHOD OF WORKING

To understand how HB works and how people experienced their work, it is necessary to recognize the strong drive throughout the organization for production. Departmental managers are judged primarily in terms of their production levels (against targets) and the efficiency (against work study standards) at which they perform. In HB this pressure was transmitted to the two supervisors. In practice, production levels were the number of batches of sweets processed, and efficiency was the ratio of batches produced to hours used by direct labor.

The production supervisor responded to the pressure for production in a number of ways. First, in an attempt to maximize production, he always allocated people to the jobs at which they performed best. He also determined the cooker speeds. In effect, this set the pace of work for both production and packing. Buffer stocks were not possible in production because the sweets needed processing before they cooled down. If he was falling behind his target, the supervisor responded by speeding up the pace of work. In addition, he regarded his job purely in terms of processing batches, and ignored problems in the packing room which may in fact have resulted directly from his actions or from those of his staff. The supervisory role thus involved allocating people to tasks, setting machine speeds (and hence the pace of work), organizing reliefs and breaks, monitoring hygiene, safety and quality standards, maintaining discipline and recording data for the management information systems. The chargehand undertook these responsibilities in the absence of a supervisor, spending the rest of his time on production.

The men in production complained that they were bored with always doing the same jobs, especially as some were physically harder than others (for example, "slabbing" involved manual manipulation of batches of up to 50 kilograms). Several claimed that their greater efforts should receive financial recognition.

Furthermore, this rigidity of task allocation was in direct conflict with the grading system which was designed to encourage flexibility. To be on the top rate of pay in the department, an operator had to be capable of performing all the skills for all the lines and hence be able to cover any job. Training schedules matched this. In practice, however, people rarely used more than one or two of their skills. The others decayed through disuse. All the staff recognized that the grading system was at odds with how the department actually worked and tended to be dissatisfied with both.

The production supervisor's strict control over the pace of work also proved suboptimal in other ways. For example, he sometimes pushed the pace to a level regarded as impossible by the staff. Whether this was true or self-fulfilling is a moot point—the net result was an increase in the level of scrap. Also he ignored the wishes of the staff to work less hard in the afternoon when they were tired: again scrap resulted. In addition the feeling was widespread among the men in production that management and supervision organized the work badly and would do better if they took advice from the shop floor. Their own perceived lack of control over the job led them to abrogate responsibility when things went wrong ("We told them so!"). And finally, although the processes of production were highly interdependent, operators adopted an insular perspective and the necessary cooperation between workers was rarely evident, and then only on the basis of personal favors between friends.

The equivalent pressure on the packing supervisor was to pack the sweets efficiently. As her section could pack no more than was produced, her only manipulable variable was hours worked. Thus to increase her efficiency she could only transfer the packers to "other work" within her room (for example cleaning) or to another department.

The packers for their part resented being asked to work flat out when HB was busy, only to be moved elsewhere when things were slacker. As described above, their own work flow was basically controlled by the speed at which the men were producing. When in difficulty, direct appeals to the men to slow down were unsuccessful and so they channeled their complaints through their supervisor. Because of the insular perspective adopted by the production supervisor (in ra-

tional support of his own targets), her approaches were usually ignored ("It's my job to produce sweets"), and the resulting intersupervisory conflict took up much of the department manager's time. In addition the packing room was very crowded and interpersonal conflicts were common.

Finally, production problems throughout the factory were created by seasonal peaks and troughs in the market demand for sweets. These "busy" and "slack" periods differed between production departments. In order to cope with market demands the production planning department transferred staff, on a temporary basis, between production departments. In HB this typically meant that, when they were busy, "unskilled" employees were drafted in to help, whereas when demand was low HB employees were transferred to other departments where they were usually given the worst jobs. Both of these solutions were resented by the employees in HB.

This description of the department is completed when one recognizes the complications involved in scheduling over 40 product lines through complex machinery, all of it over 10 years old. In fact, breakdowns and interruptions to smooth working were common. The effects of these on the possible levels of production were poorly understood and in any case few operators were aware of their targets or of their subsequent performance. More immediately the breakdowns were a source of continual conflict between the department and the maintenance engineers responsible to an engineering manager. The department laid the blame on poor maintenance, the engineers on abuse or lack of care by production workers in handling the machinery. Much management time was spent in negotiating "blame" for breakdowns and time allowances resulting since this affected efficiency figures. Not surprisingly, perhaps, the factory-wide image of the department was very poor on almost all counts, and its status was low.

PARTICIPANT'S DIAGNOSES OF THE PROBLEMS

Shopfloor employees, chargehands, supervisors, the department manager and senior management were agreed that much was wrong in HB. However, there was no coherent view of the causes and what should be done to make improvements. Many shopfloor employees placed the blame on supervision and management for their lack of technical and planning expertise, and their low consideration for subordinates. The production supervisor favored a solution in terms of "getting rid of the trouble-makers," by transferring or sacking [firing] his nominated culprits. The de-

partment manager wanted to introduce a senior supervisor to handle the conflicts between the production and packing supervisors and further support the pressure for production. The factory manager thought the way work was organized and managed might be at the core of the difficulties.

SOURCE: Case prepared by Nigel J. Kemp, Chris W. Clegg, and Toby D. Wall (1985). In Chris W. Clegg, Nigel J. Kemp, and Karen Legge (Eds.), *Case Studies in Organizational Behavior* (pp. 17-22). London, England: Harper & Row Publishers Ltd.

Questions

1. What is the problem in the HB department?

2. Use your understanding of groups and intergroup processes to analyze the HB department and its relationship with FAB Sweets as a whole.

3. What would you recommend the HB department manager do now?

REFERENCES

Abelson, Robert P. (1981). "Psychological status of the script concept." *American Psychologist* 36: 715-729.

Adler, Patricia A., & Peter Adler (1988). "Intense loyalty in organizations: A case study of college athletics." *Administrative Science Quarterly* 33: 401-417.

Albanese, Robert, & David D. Van Fleet (1985). "Rational behavior in groups: The free riding tendency." *Academy of Management Review* 10: 244-255.

Ancona, Deborah Gladstein (1990). "Outward bound: Strategies for team survival in an organization." *Academy of Management Journal* 33: 334-365.

Barkow, Jerome H. (1991). "Precis of Darwin, sex and status: Biological approaches to mind and culture." *Behavioral and Brain Sciences* 14: 295-301.

Benne, Kenneth D., & Paul Sheats (1948). "Functional roles of group members." *Journal of Social Issues* 4(2): 41-49.

Bettenhausen, Kenneth L. (1991). "Five years of groups research: What we have learned and what needs to be addressed." *Journal of Management* 17: 345-381.

Bettenhausen, Kenneth L., & J. Keith Murnighan (1985). "The emergence of norms in competitive decision-making groups." *Administrative Science Quarterly* 30: 350-372.

Bettenhausen, Kenneth L., & J. Keith Murnighan (1991). "The development of an intragroup norm and the effects of interpersonal and structural challenges." *Administrative Science Quarterly* 36: 20-35.

Blackwell, Gerry (1993). "Intimacy on the cheap." *Canadian Business.* November, 1993, pages 89-92.

Buchanan, David A., & Andrzej A. Huczynski (1985). *Organizational Behaviour: An Introductory Text.* London: Prentice Hall International (UK) Ltd.

Burnand, Gordon (1990). "Group development phases as working through six fundamental human problems." *Small Group Research* 21: 255-273.

Chesanow, Neil (1985). *The World-class Executive.* New York: Rawson Associates.

Drexler, Allan B., David Sibbet, & Russell H. Forrester (1988). "The team performance model." In W. Brendan Reddy & Kaleel Jamison (Eds.), *Team Building: Blueprints for Productivity and Satisfaction* (pp. 46-61). San Diego, CA: National Training Laboratory, Institute for Behavioral Sciences.

Earley, P. Christopher (1989). "Social loafing and collectivism: A comparison of the United States and the People's Republic of China." *Administrative Science Quarterly* 34: 565-581.

Evans, Nancy J., & Paul A. Jarvis (1986). "The group attitude scale: A measure of attraction to group." *Small Group Behavior* 17: 203-216.

Feldman, Daniel C. (1984). "The development and enforcement of group norms." *Academy of Management Review* 9: 47-53.

Fiske, Susan T. (1993). "Controlling other people: The impact of power on stereotyping." *American Psychologist* 48: 621-628.

Gersick, Connie J.G. (1988). "Time and transition in work teams: Toward a new model of group development." *Academy of Management Journal* 31: 9-41.

Gersick, Connie J.G. (1989). "Marking time: Predictable transitions in task groups." *Academy of Management Journal* 32: 274-309.

Gersick, Connie J.G. (1994). "Pacing strategic change: The case of a new venture." *Academy of Management Journal* 37: 9-45.

Gladstein, Deborah (1984). "Groups in context: A model of task group effectiveness." *Administrative Science Quarterly* 29: 499-517.

Goodman, Paul S., Elizabeth Ravlin, & Marshall Schminke (1987). "Understanding groups in organizations." *Research in Organizational Behavior* 9: 121-173.

Hackman, J. Richard (1987). "The design of work teams." In Jay W. Lorsch (Ed.), *Handbook of Organizational Behavior* (pp. 315-342). Englewood Cliffs, NJ: Prentice Hall, Inc.

Hackman, Richard (1990). "Creating more effective work groups in organizations." In J. Richard Hackman (Ed.) *Groups that Work (And Those That Don't): Creating Conditions for Effective Teamwork* (pp. 479-504). San Francisco: Jossey-Bass, Inc.

Hare, A. Paul (1981). "Group size." *American Behavioral Scientist* 24: 695-708.

Harkins, Stephen G., & Kate Szymanski (1989). "Social loafing and group evaluation." *Journal of Personality and Social Psychology* 56: 934-941.

Hollander, Edwin P. (1958). "Conformity, status, and idiosyncrasy credit." *Psychological Review* 65: 117-127.

Hollander, Edwin P. (1961). "Some effects of perceived status on responses to innovative behavior." *Journal of Abnormal Social Psychology* 63: 247-250.

Hollander, Edwin P. (1964). *Leaders, Groups, and Influence.* New York: Oxford University Press.

Johansen, Robert, David Sibbet, Suzyn Benson, Alexia Martin, Robert Mittman, & Paul Saffo (1991). *Leading Business Teams: How Teams Can Use Technology and Group Process Tools to Enhance Performance.* New York: John Wiley & Sons, Inc.

Johnson, David W., & Frank P. Johnson (1975). *Joining Together: Group Theory and Group Skills.* Englewood Cliffs, NJ: Prentice Hall, Inc. Revised edition 1987.

Katzenbach, Jon R., & Douglas K. Smith (1993). "The discipline of teams." *Harvard Business Review,* March/April 1993, pp. 111-120.

Kemp, Nigel J., Chris W. Clegg, & Toby D. Wall (1985). "Job design: Fab Sweets Ltd." In Chris W. Clegg, Nigel J. Kemp, & Karen Legge (Eds.), *Case Studies in Organizational Behavior* (pp. 17-22). London: Harper & Row, Publishers.

Kidwell, Roland E., Jr., & Nathan Bennett (1993). "Employee propensity to withhold effort: A conceptual model to intersect three avenues of research." *Academy of Management Review* 18: 429-456.

Levine, John M., & Richard L. Moreland (1985). "Innovation and socialization in small groups." In S. Moscovici, G. Mugny, & E. Van Avermaet (Eds.), *Perspectives on Minority Influence* (pp. 143-169). Cambridge: Cambridge University Press.

Levine, John M., & Richard L. Moreland (1990). "Progress in small group research." *Annual Review of Psychology* 41: 585-634.

Long, Janet W. (1984). "The wilderness lab." *Training and Development Journal* 38(5): 58-69.

Long, Janet W. (1987). "The wilderness lab comes of age." *Training and Development Journal* 41(3): 30-39.

Lord, Robert G., & Mary C. Kernan (1987). "Scripts as determinants of purposeful behavior in organizations." *Academy of Management Review* 12: 265-277.

Mason, Julie Cohen (1993). "Workplace 2000: The death of 9 to 5?" *Management Review*, January 1993, pages 14 to 18.

Messick, David M., & Diane M. Mackie (1989). "Intergroup relations." *Annual Review of Psychology* 40: 45-81.

O'Reilly, Charles A. (1990). "Organizational behavior: Where we've been, where we're going." *Annual Review of Psychology* 42: 427-458.

Perkins, Anne G. (1993). "Briefings from the editors: Diversity." *Harvard Business Review*, September/October 1993, p. 14.

Peters, Tom (1991). "Get innovative or get dead (Part 2)." *California Management Review*, Winter 1991, 33(2): 9-23. Also see Tom Peters (1990), "Get innovative or get dead (Part 1)," *California Management Review*, Fall 1990, 33(1), 9-26.

Pritchard, Robert D., Steven D. Jones, Philip L. Roth, Karla K. Steubing, & Steven E. Ekeberg (1988). "Effects of group feedback, goal setting, and incentives on organizational productivity." *Journal of Applied Psychology* 73: 337-358.

Reno, Raymond R., Robert B. Cialdini, & Carl A. Kallgren (1993). "The transsituational influence of social norms." *Journal of Personality and Social Psychology* 64: 104-112.

Rizzo, John R., Robert J. House, & Sidney I. Lirtzman (1970). "Role conflict and ambiguity in complex organizations." *Administrative Science Quarterly* 15: 150-163.

Sanford, Lynne (1993). "Triumph over fear: How adventure training turns managers into leaders." *Success*, March 1993, pp. 46, 47.

Sargent, Alice G., & Ronald J. Stupak (1989). "Managing in the '90s: The androgynous manager." *Training and Development Journal*, December 1989, pp. 29-35.

Shepperd, James A. (1993). "Productivity loss in performance groups: A motivation analysis." *Psychological Bulletin* 113: 67-81.

Sundstrom, Eric, Kenneth P. DeMeuse, & David Futrell (1990). "Work teams: Applications and effectiveness." *American Psychologist* 45: 120-133.

Thorne, Paul (1992). "Hit squads." *International Management*, February 1992, p. 56.

Tuckman, Bruce W. (1965). "Developmental sequence in small groups." *Psychological Bulletin* 63: 384-399.

Tuckman, Bruce W., & Mary Ann C. Jensen (1977). "Stages of small-group development revisited." *Group & Organization Studies* 2: 419-427.

Walkom, Thomas (1985). "Humble dickering for furniture." Toronto: *The Globe and Mail*, November 14, 1985, p. A8.

Watson, Warren E., Kamalesh Kumar, & Larry K. Michaelsen (1993). "Cultural diversity's impact on interaction process and performance:

Comparing homogeneous and diverse task groups." *Academy of Management Journal* 36: 590-602.

Yaginuma, Mikie, & Rick Kennedy
(1986). "Life is so simple when you know your place: A quick guide to Japanese etiquette." *Intersect*, May 1986, pp. 35-39.

Yetton, Philip, & Preston Bottger
(1983). "The relationships among group size, member ability, social decision schemes, and performance." *Organizational Behavior and Human Performance* 32: 145-159.

FURTHER READING

A review of groups in organizations is provided in the article by Deborah Gladstein Ancona (1987), "Groups in organizations: Extending laboratory models," in Clyde Hendrick (Ed.), *Annual Review of Personality and Social Psychology: Group Processes and Intergroup Relations* (pp. 207-230), Newbury Park, CA: Sage Publications. A book that makes the distinction between groups at work and teams is titled *The Wisdom of Teams: Creating the High-performance Organization*. By Jon R. Katzenbach and Douglas K. Smith, it was published in 1993 by Harvard Business School Press.

A practical approach to getting people to work together as a team is discussed in the 1992 book *Leading the Team Organization* by Dean W. Tjosvold of Simon Fraser University and Mary M. Tjosvold, published by Lexington Books. How team-based management works at XEL Communications Inc. is the subject of John Case's article "What the experts forgot to mention," in the September 1993 issue of *Inc.* magazine, pages 66 to 79.

More information on the Drexler/Sibbet Team Performance™ System is available from Quality Team Performance, 13205 Moran Drive, N. Potomac, MD 20878; Drexler & Associates, Inc., Route 1, Box 131-A, Rockbridge Baths, VA 24473; or Graphic Guides Inc., 832 Folsom Street, Suite 810, San Francisco CA 94107. A training program is available for teams that uses the Team Performance framework and measures team performance using the Team Performance Inventory.

You may be interested in looking up an article that provides an interesting look at the habitual behaviour of work groups. See Connie J.G. Gersick and J. Richard Hackman (1990), "Habitual routines in task-performing groups," *Organizational Behavior and Human Decision Processes* 47: 65-97.

For a look at the relationship of teams and culture, see Lee G. Bolman and Terrence E. Deal (1992), "What makes a team work?", *Organizational Dynamics*, 21(2), 34-44.

Amanda Sinclair has written an article that discusses how teams don't always work as we would like. She makes the point that "teams are frequently used to camouflage coercion under the pretense of maintaining cohesion; conceal conflict under the guise of consensus; convert conformity into a semblance of creativity; give unilateral decisions a co-determinist seal of approval; delay action in the supposed interests of consultation; legitimize lack of leadership; and disguise expedient arguments and personal agendas." See "The tyranny of a team ideology" in *Organization Studies*, 1992, 13(4), pages 611-626.

For further information about the Price Waterhouse versus Ann B. Hopkins case that went all the way to the Supreme Court of the United States, see the article by Eileen P. Kelly, Amy Oakes Young, and Lawrence S. Clark (1993), "Sex stereotyping in the workplace: A manager's guide," *Business Horizons* 36(2): 23-29. This article describes the case and its resolution. It also includes the legal references for court decisions.

For a further look at scripts and how people might use them to learn from others, see Dennis A. Gioia and Charles C. Manz (1985), "Linking cognition and behavior: A script processing interpretation of vicarious learning," *Academy of Management Review* 10: 527-539.

Articles that could help with the analysis of the Fab Sweets case are: Nigel J. Kemp, Toby D. Wall, Chris W. Clegg, and J.L. Cordery (1983), "Autonomous work groups in a greenfield site: A comparative study," *Journal of Occupational Psychology* 56: 271-288; and Toby D. Wall, Nigel J. Kemp, Paul R. Jackson, and Chris W. Clegg (1986), "Outcomes of autonomous workgroups: A long-term field experiment," *Academy of Management Journal* 29: 280-304. For some discussion of what was done at Fab Sweets, see Toby D. Wall, and Chris W. Clegg (1981), "A longitudinal field study of group work redesign," *Journal of Occupational Behavior* 2: 31-49.

An article that is about the wood harvesting industry and shows the interrelationship between the task, the technology, and the group is by the University of Toronto's Harvey F. Kolodny and Carleton's Moses N. Kiggundu (1980), "Toward the development of a sociotechnical systems model in woodlands mechanical harvesting," *Human Relations* 33: 623-645. Another look at teams and sociotechnical systems is the 1992 book *All Teams are Not Created Equal: How Employee Empowerment Really Works* by Lyman D. Ketchum and Eric L. Trist, Newbury Park, CA: Sage.

CHAPTER 10

LEADERSHIP

CHAPTER OUTLINE

The History of Leadership Thought

How Leadership Operates

    By Who the Leader Is

    By What the Leader Does

    By the Relationship Between the Leader and the Follower

Perceptions of Leaders

Leadership Considerations

    Ethical Leadership

    Leadership of Ethics

    Leading People from Diverse Cultures

    Leader Succession

    Leadership of Self-Managed Groups

Conclusion

QUESTIONS TO CONSIDER

- What is the difference between managership and leadership?

- What is leadership?

- How does a person in an organization lead others?

- How can people lead themselves?

- How are leaders perceived?

- What is ethical leadership and the leadership of ethics?

Leadership has been studied for thousands of years. It is therefore not surprising that there are many ways of examining leadership and of considering how leadership works in organizations. In this chapter we will discuss several approaches to the study of leadership. Our aim is to show the richness and complexity of the field without being exhaustive in covering every theory of leadership in detail. Besides presenting leadership theory, we will outline what these theories have to say to someone who is, or wishes to be, in a leadership role.

Leadership is a social relationship between two or more people in which the leader influences the social knowledge, goal acceptance, and actions of the follower.

It is important to note in this definition the importance of a relationship in a social setting. Leaders do not exist in isolation, they affect others. Leaders affect social knowledge by helping to create a social reality. This reality includes what is "known," what a leader and group decide are their "facts" in the world they experience, and how the leader and members are to relate and interact with each other and with outsiders.

Leaders also affect the goal acceptance and actions of followers by helping to create the goals that will be pursued and ensuring that followers accept goals as legitimate and relevant to themselves. Goal acceptance is internalized by the follower. The follower accepts the leader's goals. Extrinsic rewards offered by others are not critical influences on follower behaviour.

There is a difference between leadership and managership. A simple and catchy phrase that summarizes this difference is that "managers are people who do things right and leaders are people who do the right thing" (Bennis & Nanus, 1985, p.21). That is, managers tend to take a goal or organizational procedure as a given and then try to accomplish it in the best way possible. Their focus is on *means*, or how the work is done more than the *ends*, or what the goal is. Doing the right thing implies that leaders influence the selection of goals and what will be done more than how it is done.

A more detailed look at the differences between managership and leadership is found in Dale McConkey's 1989 article titled "Are you an administrator, a manager, or a leader?" McConkey looks explicitly at these three organizational roles (see this chapter's Self-Diagnostic Exercise for a summary). The *administrator* carries out organizational policies but does not make or change the policy. The *manager* can have some influence on policy and on how activities are carried out, and is most concerned with efficiency. The *leader* is more concerned with the organization's effectiveness than its policies and sets out to create the conditions that will allow the organization to be effective.

THE HISTORY OF LEADERSHIP THOUGHT

With this definition of leadership in mind, and before we examine in detail the operation of leadership, let's briefly look at the history of thinking about leadership. Exhibit 10.1 showing the streams of leadership thought is useful for understanding how thinking about leadership has changed over the last 100 years. It shows ten "eras," or times when leadership thought was centred on a particular approach. Periods within an era show more minor divisions within the broader perspective signified by an era.

The first is that of personality. At this time, notably in the late 1800s, effective leadership was thought to reside within the person. "Leaders are born, not made" is a saying that well summarizes this way of thinking. An organization would look for a leader who possessed the qualities essential for leadership. These qualities, even if known, could not be taught.

A significant amount of effort was expended in attempting to determine what these key leadership qualities, or traits, were. But effective leaders were found to differ from one another on a great variety of traits, and so leadership began also to be considered as influence over others, through power and persuasion. This stream of thought was joined by two

---

Leadership   A social relationship between two or more people in which the leader influences the social knowledge, goal acceptance, and actions of the follower.

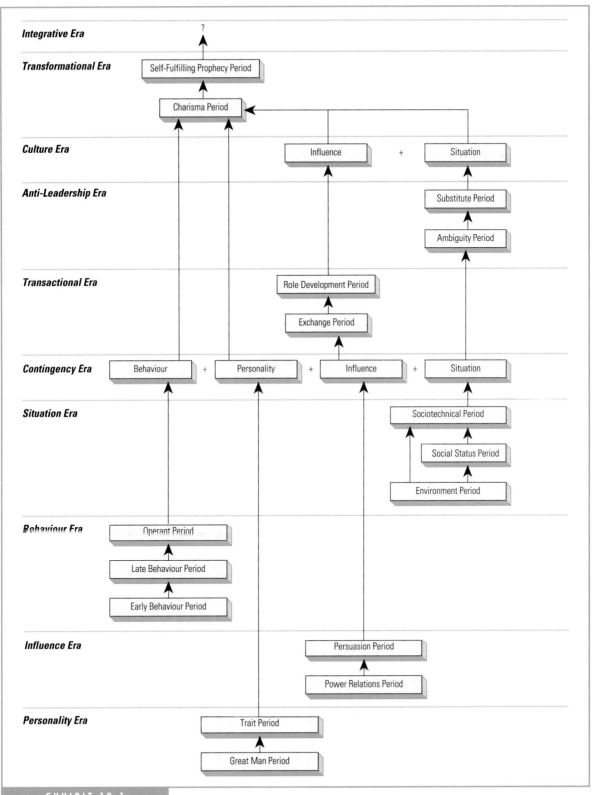

EXHIBIT 10.1

Streams of Leadership Thought

SOURCE: David A. Van Seters and Richard H.G. Field (1990), "The evolution of leadership theory," *Journal of Organizational Change Management* 3(3): page 33. Reprinted by permission of MCB University Press Limited.

others: the behaviour era when the leader's actions and rewarding of followers was of prime importance and the situation era when social status and group role, environmental, and sociotechnical influences on the leader were brought into the analysis of leader effectiveness.

These four separate streams of leadership thought came, in the 1960s and 1970s, to be of joint importance to understanding leadership in organizations. The **contingency** era took the general approach that different leader behaviours influenced followers and were effective depending on the situation. There was no one way to act that was always considered to be best. The most appropriate leader behaviour was contingent on the situation (which included the personality of the leader and the leader's group members). Adding to this contingent outlook the exchange relationship between leader and members, that is, their agreed upon roles, rewards, and interaction, was more fully developed in the transactional era.

In the late 1970s, a crisis occurred in the study of leadership. In this so-called "Anti-leadership" era, a number of authors questioned the study of leadership and whether leaders did, in fact, make a difference to the performance of organizations. Perhaps the beginning of this era of leadership study was signaled by an article titled "The ambiguity of leadership" by a well-known and influential organizational scholar, Jeffrey Pfeffer (1977).

Pfeffer posed three problems for those who would study leadership:

1. It is not clear exactly what behaviours are indicative of leadership;
2. Leaders in organizations may have only small effects on organizational performance because they are selected from individuals very similar to each other, because there are many situational constraints on their actions, and because organizational performance is affected by many factors that are outside the leader's control;
3. Organizational members may be promoted to leadership positions not based on their performance or ability but on irrelevant factors such as social status.

Pfeffer went on to argue that leaders may actually be symbols in that they represent how an organization achieves its outcomes, even if leaders have no effect themselves. People in organizations, according to this view, need to attribute organizational actions and outcomes to a person, and that person is the symbolic leader. As illustrated in *On the One Hand,* organizational scientists are still engaged in a debate about the effects of leadership. The perspective taken in this chapter is that leaders do indeed make a difference.

Next, it was pointed out that elements of the leadership situation could substitute for active leadership by an individual leader (Kerr & Jermier, 1978; Jon Howell & Peter Dorfman, 1981, 1986). For example, work tasks that are intrinsically satisfying to a leader's subordinates can substitute for a leader's behaviour that attempts to create a satisfying leader-member relationship (Kerr & Jermier, 1978). Another example is that the task expertise of professionals means that less (or no) leader task direction is required.

It was also proposed that there are situational variables that neutralize or supplement effective leadership (Howell & Dorfman, 1986). Neutralizers make leadership impossible while supplements add to the leader's ability to influence subordinates. An example of a neutralizer would be a leader's lack of task knowledge—leader direction of subordinate actions is simply not possible. A leadership supplement would be feedback on job performance from the task itself. In this case leader feedback on task performance could still have an effect on the subordinate, but so too could direct task feedback.

It is certainly true that the situation can have strong effects on the relationship between leader actions and organizational outcomes. But leaders may themselves create substitutes and supplements in the situation and so have an indirect influence on subordinates (Howell and others, 1990).

Leader influence on the social situation in an organization was a critical component of the next era of leadership thought. Flourishing in the mid-1980s (for example Schein, 1985) leaders were seen as the creators and maintainers of an organization's culture (see Chapter 3).

Contingency theory

The theory that there is no consistently appropriate best action for all situations. Instead, what is most effective will depend on some other variable or combination of variables.

ON THE ONE HAND ...

In an important article, James Meindl, Sanford Ehrlich, and Janet Dukerich provided a strong set of evidence in support of the attributional view of leadership, that people use the concept of leadership as an explanation for complex organizational events. Their findings from six separate studies were that:

1. Titles of Wall Street Journal articles made attributions to leadership when organizational performances were either very good or very bad;

2. Students writing doctoral dissertations were more interested in leadership when the general economy was either good or bad;

3. Articles in business magazines deal more with leadership when the nation's economy is improving;

4. Undergraduate students asked to rate the importance of the leader in a short case about organizational sales improvement used the organization's leader as an explanation to a greater degree when outcomes were large and positive;

5. In an experiment similar to study number 4, students attributed both high and low organizational performance to leadership;

6. Students tended to attribute larger positive and negative outcomes more to leadership than to other possible causes.

SOURCE: From James R. Meindl, Sanford B. Ehrlich, and Janet M. Dukerich (1985), "The romance of leadership," *Administrative Science Quarterly* 30: 78-102.

ON THE OTHER HAND ...

In a test designed to determine if leadership is more than an attributional phenomenon and really does make a difference to the performance of organizations, Alan Thomas of the Manchester Business School studied 12 large United Kingdom retailing firms. Using twenty years of data on sales, profits, net assets, and the periods of office of each organizational leader, Thomas found that the effect of leadership was constrained by the size of the firm. When performance was considered between companies, the variation in their performance was mostly due to the size of the companies, not their leadership. But when the effects of company size were taken out of the analysis, differences in firm leadership had a substantial impact on profit and sales. His conclusion was that "First, leader differences do account for performance variations within firms to a substantial degree, and second, these impacts are generally insufficient to outweigh the inbuilt differences among firms that largely account for performance variation among firms" (p. 399).

SOURCE: Based on Alan Berkeley Thomas (1988), "Does leadership make a difference to organizational performance?" *Administrative Science Quarterly* 33: 388-400.

This concept helped to bring about the next era of leadership study, that of transformational leadership. Here the focus was not on the transactions between leader and member but on how the organizational member was transformed or changed by the leader. The influence of a leader's personality once again became prominent. The concept of personal charisma, though dormant for long periods in the study of leadership, was revived. Leader expectations and their effects on subordinates (for example, a leader who expects high performance may cause high performance) were also part of this focus on the leader as transforming subordinates.

Pierre Trudeau in 1968 was a charismatic leader who made a difference in Canada by being different.

The last stage in the evolution of leadership theory identified in Exhibit 10.1 is named "the integrative era." This name is meant to indicate that the streams of leadership thought are coming together and that each major stream will have an influence on the understanding of leadership in organizations. We will now discuss organizational leadership by examining three areas: who the leader is; what the leader does; and the relationship between leader and followers.

HOW LEADERSHIP OPERATES
Leadership By Who the Leader Is

Research on leader traits did tend to get bogged down in the study of a seemingly inexhaustible number of possible traits that helped to predict effective leadership in only certain situations. However, a review by Gary Yukl (1989b) concluded that while certain traits can make leader effectiveness more likely, the importance of a given trait will depend on the leadership situation. Yukl's list of traits and skills characteristic of successful leaders is shown as Exhibit 10.2.

Another look at the essential qualities necessary in a leader is offered in this chapter's *A Word to the Wise.*

The emergence of a leader in a group has been found to be at least partially a function of individual differences such as sex, personality, high verbal participation, and seniority (Levine & Moreland, 1990).

EXHIBIT 10.2   TRAITS AND SKILLS MOST FREQUENTLY CHARACTERISTIC OF SUCCESSFUL LEADERS

TRAITS	SKILLS
Adaptable to situations	Clever (intelligent)
Alert to social environment	Conceptually skilled
Ambitious and achievement-oriented	Creative
Assertive	Diplomatic and tactful
Cooperative	Fluent in speaking
Decisive	Knowledgeable about group task
Dependable	Organized (administrative ability)
Dominant (desire to influence others)	Persuasive
Energetic (high activity level)	Socially skilled
Persistent	
Self-confident	
Tolerant of stress	
Willing to assume responsibility	

SOURCE: Gary A. Yukl, LEADERSHIP IN ORGANIZATIONS, 2e, © 1989, p. 176. Reprinted by permission of Prentice Hall, Englewood Cliffs, New Jersey.

A WORD TO THE WISE

Before turning to some specific qualities in a successful leader I would like to make one general point. I believe that it is fundamentally important for a leader to have a credo or belief in what he stands for and in the organisation, formation or body in which he is a leader.

I suspect everyone has his own list of the general qualities necessary in a leader. Here are mine:

Personality and Character. Great leaders have the strength of character and personality to inspire confidence and to gain the trust of others. Clearly this is a personal thing but it can be developed by experience and training. I would emphasise that leaders do not have to be roaring extroverts to be successful. Some very charismatic leaders have been just quietly confident, although they had the ability to communicate.

Courage. Field Marshal Slim said, "Courage is the greatest of all virtues for without it there are no other virtues." Although he was talking about both physical and moral courage, it was moral courage on which he laid the greatest emphasis. Indeed, I believe that moral courage is the single most important quality for a successful leader.

It is the courage to do what you believe to be right without bothering about the consequences for yourself. The funny thing is that the more you use your moral courage on small issues the easier it becomes to use it on big things, but the reverse is equally true. The less you use it on small things the more difficult it becomes to use it on big issues. Physical courage is, of course, the reverse and is more like a bank account. The more you use it the more likely it is to become overdrawn.

Willpower. A leader has to learn to dominate events and never allow these events to get the better of him and this determination or willpower concerns not only rival organisations or, in the case of armed forces, the enemy, but equally colleagues and allies.

Knowledge. This means knowledge not only of your profession but equally of the men under your command. Knowing them well and being known to them is vital if you are to gain their confidence. As a newly-joined platoon commander, after every one of my first few muster parades, the company sergeant major always asked me about a particular soldier. I was never able to answer him satisfactorily. Eventually I plucked up the courage to ask him what he meant and why he was always asking me these questions. He said, "I watch you on muster parade, Sir, and you inspect the men very thoroughly, their belts, their boots and their weapons but you don't look them in the eye. Every morning you must look your soldiers in the eye and that will tell you how they feel and if they have a problem." It was outstanding advice and done in a way that made me never forget it.

Initiative. This is, of course, a fundamentally important quality in any walk of life but nowhere more so than on the battlefield. I can do no better in this context than to quote Field Marshal Slim: "Here one comes up against a conflict between determination, fixity of purpose and flexibility. There is always the danger that determination becomes plain obstinacy and flexibility, mere vacillation. If you can hold within yourself the balance between these two—strength of will and flexibility of mind—you will be well on the road to becoming a leader in a big way."

In conclusion I would add two final qualities. They are unselfishness and showing that you enjoy being a leader. In summary, to quote General Sir John Hackett: "Successful military leadership is impossible without the leader's total engagement in the task in hand and to the group committed to his care for its discharge." For all I know, this may be so not only in the military but in other spheres as well.

SOURCE: From a quote by General Sir Peter Inge, Chief of the General Staff of the United Kingdom. Quoted in Simon Caulkin (1993), "The lust for leadership," *Management Today*, November 1993, p. 43.

One theory of leadership, **Cognitive Resource Theory** (Fiedler, 1986; Fiedler & Garcia, 1987), reasonably proposes that leader intelligence and technical knowledge are important determinants of the quality of the leader's plans, decisions, and actions. The theory goes on to state that when leaders are in situations of low interpersonal stress (i.e., they have supportive groups) they use their intelligence but when under high interpersonal stress they use their experience, not their intelligence. Therefore, when under stress it is not intelligence that should predict effectiveness but experience.

Cognitive resource theory
Proposes that leader intelligence and technical knowledge are important determinants of the quality of the leader's plans, decisions, and actions.

Another possibility, however, is that it is the leader's rational processing of information that breaks down under high stress and not the leader's use of her intelligence (Lord & Hall, 1992).

According to cognitive resource theory relatively bright leaders should use their intelligence and tell group members what to do, whereas the less bright leaders should listen to their group members in order to perform well on the task (Fiedler & House, 1988).

Leadership by What the Leader Does

Before the Second World War there was an increase in autocratic leadership—rule by one person—in Italy and Germany. To study some of the effects of this autocratic leadership, three researchers at the University of Iowa, Kurt Lewin, Ronald Lippitt, and Ralph White (1939), created an experiment that manipulated the leader behaviours in a group of adolescent boys.

Initiating structure
The degree to which a leader structures the task, provides direction, and defines the leader and subordinate roles in the group and the group's goals.

In one group the leader acted democratically, allowing the boys to decide their activities while at their group meeting. Another leader acted autocratically, telling his group of boys what they would do at their meeting (unknown to the boys, they were told to do what the previous group had democratically decided upon). A third leader was meant to act democratically but actually provided little guidance or direction to his group. This type of leadership behaviour was termed *laissez-faire*, from the French for "let act," and meaning to leave alone. The researchers found that the boys preferred the democratic leadership and were more likely to work independently on their chosen tasks even when the leader was absent (on purpose) from the group.

Consideration
The degree to which a leader is friendly and supportive in dealing with subordinates.

After the war, research in leadership behaviour began to focus on determining the dimensions of leader behaviour. A program of research at Ohio State University (for example Stogdill & Coons, 1957) identified two separate dimensions. The first is **initiating structure**, the degree to which a leader structures the task, provides direction, and defines the leader and subordinate roles in the group and the group's goals. The second dimension is **consideration**, the degree to which a leader is friendly and supportive in dealing with subordinates.

Task-oriented behaviour
The group leader or manager's focus on the task.

At the University of Michigan, researchers were attempting to determine the leader behaviours that distinguished between ineffective and effective leaders. They found that **task-oriented behaviour** (similar to initiating structure) and **relationship-oriented behaviour** (similar to consideration) were two important categories of leader behaviour. Effective leaders engaged in more planning and coordinating of the task than in performing it, and did not ignore the importance of building and maintaining the leader-subordinate relationship.

Relationship-oriented behaviour The leader or manager's focus on interpersonal relationships in the group.

These two research streams both suggested that task and relationship behaviours are important to effective leadership. This conclusion is now widely accepted and managers/leaders have been encouraged to pay attention to both task and relationships in order to be effective (for example Blake & McCanse, 1991; see Exhibit 10.3). A research program in Japan during this same time period (Misumi & Peterson, 1985) created a theory of leadership based on the leader **performance function** (forming and reaching group goals) and the **maintenance function** (preserving the social stability of the group). Given the similarities in leadership behaviour theory across two diverse cultures, we can be sure that these two general categories of leadership behaviours are important to effective leadership.

Performance function
The group leader's behaviours of forming and reaching group goals.

Maintenance function
The group leader's behaviours that preserve the social stability of the group.

EXHIBIT 10.3

The Leadership Grid®

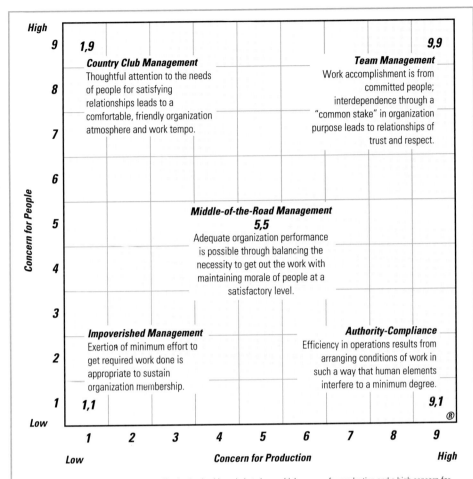

Blake and McCanse argue that the most effective leadership style is to have a high concern for production and a high concern for people. This ideal form is called the "9,9" Team Management style. Other less effective styles are the "1,9" Country Club management, the "9,1" Authority-Compliance style, and the mid-level "5,5" Middle-of-the-Road management style. The least effective approach is thought to be the "1,1" approach, called Impoverished Management. Two other possible styles are the 9+9 Paternalistic "father knows best" management and Opportunistic "what's in it for me" management.

STYLE DEFINITIONS

1,1 *Impoverished management*, often referred to as laissez-faire leadership. Leaders in this position have little concern for people or productivity, avoid taking sides, and stay out of conflicts. They do just enough to get by.

1,9 *Country Club management.* Managers in this position have great concern for people and little concern for production. They try to avoid conflicts and concentrate on being well liked. To them the task is less important than good interpersonal relations. Their goal is to keep people happy. (This is a soft Theory X approach and not a sound human relations approach.)

9,1 *Authority/Obedience.* Managers in this position have great concern for production and little concern for people. They desire tight control in order to get tasks done efficiently. They consider creativity and human relations to be unnecessary.

5,5 *Organization Man management*, often termed middle-of-the-road leadership. Leaders in this position have medium concern for people and production. They attempt to balance their concern for both people and production, but are not committed to either.

9+9 *Paternalistic "father knows best" management*, a style in which reward is promised for compliance and punishment threatened for non-compliance.

Opp *Opportunistic "what's in it for me" management*, in which the style utilized depends on which style the leader feels will return him or her the greatest self-benefit.

9,9 *Team management.* This style of leadership is considered to be ideal. Such managers have great concern for both people and production. They work to motivate employees to reach their highest levels of accomplishment. They are flexible and responsive to change, and they understand the need to change.

SOURCE: The Leadership Grid® Figure from *Leadership Dilemmas—Grid Solutions*, by Robert R. Blake and Anne Adams McCanse (formerly the Managerial Grid Figure by Robert R. Blake and Jane S. Mouton) Houston: Gulf Publishing Company, P. 29. Copyright © 1991, by Scientific Methods, Inc. Style definitions from Robert R. Blake and Jane S. Mouton. *The Managerial Grid III* (Houston: Gulf Publishing Company, copyright © 1985), chapters 1-7 as modified here. Reproduced by permission of the owners.

There are more fine-grained approaches to understanding what a leader does (for example Yukl, 1989b). Several of these will be discussed later in this chapter.

A third category of leader behaviour found to be important by the University of Michigan researchers was allowing **participation** by subordinates in decisions affecting the group. But should subordinates be involved in every decision? What if time is short or subordinates do not share the organization's goals to be achieved in solving a particular problem? Two researchers examined these questions (and others) and developed the theory that leaders should vary the amount of subordinate participation in decisions depending on the particular circumstances of each decision. This theory was one of the first contingency theories of leadership. It focused on only one leader behaviour, that of subordinate participation allowed in decisions. This theory came to be called the Vroom-Yetton model (1973), named after Victor Vroom and Philip Yetton.

Participation

Involvement by subordinates in the decision making process.

The Vroom-Yetton Model

The Vroom-Yetton model considered that leaders could use five different decision methods. In the first, called AI to indicate autocratic method number one, the leader makes a decision without the aid of subordinates. Using method AII the leader obtains necessary information from subordinates and then makes the decision. Method CI (C for consultative) allows more subordinate information as the leader consults with each subordinate individually before making a decision. Even more participation is encouraged with method CII as subordinates are consulted as a group, though the leader retains the right to make the final decision. With the GII process (G stands for Group; method GI is used for decisions affecting a leader and only one subordinate) the leader acts as the chair of a group discussion where the aim is to obtain a consensus on the decision's solution.

Factors in the decision situation to be assessed by a leader were: (1) the problem's quality requirement—whether or not decision quality is important for the particular problem being considered; (2) the leader's information relevant to the problem; (3) problem structure—for example, whether the way to find the solution was well-known; (4) the importance of subordinate acceptance of the decision; (5) the likelihood that subordinates would accept a decision made autocratically by the leader; (6) whether subordinates share the organization's goals regarding the problem; and (7) whether it is likely that subordinates would prefer different solutions to the problem and would conflict with each other over these solutions.

The Vroom-Yetton model has generally been represented as a decision tree that showed, for each combination of problem attributes, which decision method (or set of methods) was prescribed by the model as likely to be most effective. Research has been supportive of the model's prescriptions (for example Vroom & Jago, 1978; Field, 1982), but the model does consider only the participation aspect of leader behaviour. A revision of this model by Victor Vroom and Art Jago (1988) will be discussed in Chapter 11 on decision making.

Situational Leadership Theory

A second contingency theory of leadership was called the life-cycle theory by its developers, Paul Hersey and Kenneth Blanchard (1969). According to the theory, a leader should adjust the degree of task orientation and relationship orientation exhibited toward followers to match the maturity of those followers.

Hersey and Blanchard's theory is now called situational leadership theory (Hersey & Blanchard, 1988). It proposes that subordinate readiness to complete the task (subordinate maturity) is determined by subordinates' achievement motivation, ability and willingness to assume responsibility, and education and experience relevant to the task.

If readiness is low, the leader should be highly task directive but low on relationship orientation. This is called **directing** because the subordinate is new to the task and needs specific instructions and close task supervision most of all.

As follower readiness increases as the subordinate gains task experience and confidence, the leader should add high relationship behaviour to high task behaviour. This is called **coaching**, as the subordinate is now ready for more explanation of the how and why of task performance.

At the next stage of follower readiness the leader can drop high task orientation while maintaining high relationship behaviour. Called **supporting**, the follower now needs less task direction and is ready to contribute to task decisions.

The final stage of follower readiness is marked by a subordinate requiring neither high leader task nor high relationship behaviour. This leader behaviour is called **delegating** because readiness is high and the leader can give the subordinate responsibility for making and implementing decisions.

Situational leadership theory requires a leader to be able to diagnose follower maturity and vary relationship and task oriented behaviour for different followers at different times. Though the theory makes intuitive sense, evidence concerning the theory's validity is sparse. One study (Vecchio, 1987), however, did find that low consideration and high structuring was an effective strategy for low-maturity employees.

Directing The group leader tells subordinates how to accomplish the task.

Coaching The group leader helps the subordinate to understand the task and how best to perform it.

Supporting The group leader provides social assistance to followers while they engage in accomplishing the task.

Delegating The group leader gives subordinates responsibility for making and implementing decisions about how best to perform the task.

Fiedler's Contingency Theory

One of the first contingency theories of leadership was developed by Fred Fiedler (1967). A key part of Fiedler's theory is the measurement of a leader's personality by the Least-Preferred Coworker (LPC) scale. This measurement tool asks a leader to think of the actual person with whom he or she would least like to work, and then to answer a set of questions describing that least-preferred coworker.

A second key part of the theory is the favourability to the leader of the group social situation. An example of a favourable situation would be when leader-member relations are good, the task is structured, and the leader has strong power from the formal position. Fiedler proposed that a leader is most likely to have an effective group when the leader's personality matches the favourability to the leader of the group social situation.

When the situation is very favourable, low-LPC leaders (they are assumed to be task oriented) should be more effective than high-LPC leaders. High-LPC leaders are assumed to be relationship oriented. In situations of moderate favourability, high-LPC leaders are predicted to have the most effective groups. When the situation is very unfavourable it is again the low-LPC leader who, in this worst of all situations, can be most effective.

Fiedler's contingency model can be prescriptive. A leader could attempt to alter the situation to make it fit the leader's own LPC. This is called the leader match concept (Fiedler & Chemers, 1984). Alternatively, an organization could choose a leader with an LPC appropriate to a group situation.

Though summaries of research on Fiedler's contingency model (called meta-analyses) have provided support for some of the model's predictions (Strube & Garcia, 1981; Peters and others, 1985) the model has been severely criticized (see Yukl, 1989b, pages 197-198).

The major problem is the connection between leader personality (LPC) and leader behaviour (task versus relationship orientation). Yukl (1989b, p. 198) concluded that "initial enthusiasm for the model has waned over the years, and it no longer is believed to have much utility for understanding leadership effectiveness."

Path-Goal Theory

The final contingency theory of leadership discussed here proposes that leaders, in order to be effective, should vary their behaviour depending on the personal goals of each follower. Based on expectancy theory (Chapter 8), path-goal theory is so called because the leader's role is to clarify for subordinates the path to desired goals. Based on early work by Martin Evans (1970) of the University of Toronto, the theory was developed by Bob House (1971) and then extended by House and Terry Mitchell (1974).

Path-goal theory states that leaders can exhibit four types of behaviour: directive (similar to task oriented); supportive (similar to relationship oriented); achievement oriented (appealing to a follower's inherent need to achieve); and participative. The contingency in this theory is that particular leadership behaviours should be used to complement, or fill in, what is missing from the work situation in order to enhance follower motivation, satisfaction, and performance.

For example, in a case where the subordinate's task is well structured, the work group is cohesive and provides necessary social support, the subordinate has a high need for achievement and is experienced enough to both wish to and be able to participate in task-related decisions, path-goal theory would direct the leader *not* to be directive and supportive. In this case direction and support are not missing from the work situation. They are supplied by the task itself and by co-workers. Instead, the leader should be achievement-oriented and participative.

In order to determine the leadership behaviours required, a leader needs to analyze two factors. The first is attributes of the work environment. These include the task, the formal authority system, and the primary work group. The second is attributes of each individual subordinate. These include ability, experience, personal goals and needs, and locus of control. Subordinates with an internal locus of control believe that they influence events and have an impact on others. Those with an external locus feel little control over their lives (Rotter, 1966).

After this analysis, the leader must make it clear to subordinates that effective performance will result in the attainment of their desired goals. This clarifies the performance-leads-to-outcome link of expectancy theory and would help followers to achieve their goals. Goal achievement strengthens the effort-leads-to-performance link of expectancy theory.

The leader may be directive (which includes coaching), supportive, achievement oriented, and participative as required by the situation's contingency factors. Path-goal theory suggests that the outcome of this approach to leadership will be high subordinate motivation to exert effort towards task accomplishment, performance, acceptance of the leader, and job satisfaction.

Path-goal theory can be very complex because it specifies a particular set of leader behaviours as most effective for a particular situation and subordinate. Though parts of the theory have been studied, Yukl (1989b) concluded that the theory has not yet been adequately tested.

Leadership Through the Leader-Follower Relationship

Path-goal theory specifies a **transactional** relationship between leader and followers; that is, the leader and followers enter into a transaction, with subordinates exchanging performance for rewards. A second type of leader-follower relationship is **transformational**.

Transactional theory of leadership The group leader and members engage in an exchange relationship where members provide time and effort in return for certain benefits allocated by the leader.

Transformational theory of leadership The group leader changes the follower's needs and values, self-esteem, self-expectation of work success, and heightens the follower's motivation to exert extra work effort.

Here, the leader causes subordinates to change their values, goals, needs, and aspirations—to be transformed. We will now examine transactional and transformational relationships between leaders and followers.

One transactional theory, originally called vertical dyad linkage theory (Dansereau and others, 1975; Graen & Cashman, 1975; Graen & Scandura, 1987) and now called **leader-member exchange** (LMX), makes explicit the fact that leaders may develop different relationships with different subordinates. Instead of an average style of leadership for all group members, leaders may develop a close working relationship with some members, called the in-group, and a less close relationship with the others, called the out-group (Graen & Uhl-Bien, 1991).

From the in-group, leaders receive greater cooperation, willingness to work longer hours, willingness to be part of the decision-making process, and loyalty. For this, leaders exchange organizational rewards under the leader's control, such as more interesting work, higher pay, a better office or working conditions, and a better chance for promotion. For the out-group, leaders exchange normal organizational pay and rewards for regular job commitment and working hours. This theory is not so much prescriptive—that leaders should create different exchange relationships with different subordinates, but descriptive—that such differentiation can occur.

The 1991 review of LMX theory (Graen & Uhl-Bien, 1991) proposes that the leader-member relationship can have three possible phases. In the initial testing phase the leader and the subordinate evaluate what each can bring to the exchange relationship. Changes in the subordinate's role are negotiated by the leader and subordinate in cycles of greater levels of exchange. This first phase is transactional in nature. The second phase that may be reached is marked by greater mutual trust, loyalty, and respect for one another by the manager and the member. In the third phase "exchange based on self-interest is transformed into mutual commitment to the mission and objectives of the work unit" (Yukl & Van Fleet, 1992, p. 162). This third phase is transformational in nature.

Transformational views of leadership focus on the leader-follower relationship, specifically on how the leader changes the follower's needs and values, self-esteem, self-expectation of work success, and heightened motivation to exert extra work effort. We will consider three transformational approaches: leadership and performance beyond expectations; the self-fulfilling prophecy leader model; and charismatic leadership in organizations.

> **Leader-member exchange (LMX)** A theory of leadership that makes explicit the fact that leaders may develop different relationships with different subordinates.

Leadership and Performance Beyond Expectations

This model by Bernard Bass (1985, 1993) includes both the "normal" transactional process between a leader and follower and transformational processes. The leader increases the follower's subjective probabilities of success through confidence building. The values of the follower's outcomes are increased by the leader's expanding the range and number of the follower's needs, elevating the follower's needs to a higher level in Maslow's hierarchy, and by going beyond the follower's self-interests. Supporting these leader actions are changes in the surrounding organizational culture.

Together, these transactions and transformations can result in the subordinate's heightened motivation to exert extra effort and the resultant performance beyond expectations. Evidence in support of Bass' model has been found by Jane Howell and Bruce Avolio in their 1993 study of 78 managers.

The Self-Fulfilling Prophecy Leader Model

This approach to transformational leadership (Field, 1989: See Exhibit 10.4) sees the leader's expectations of member performance as central to the member's actions and performance.

Its basic principle is that high leader expectations will result in leader behaviours that will cause the very performance expected. Essentially, the leader's prophecy about subordinate performance is self-fulfilling.

In the model, leader expectations are initially influenced by member and leader characteristics (for example the intelligence of the member, the experience of the leader). These then influence leader behaviours, such as the difficulty of the work given to the member, the feedback given about task performance, and allowing the subordinate to interact with the leader. Leader behaviours are then proposed to affect the member's self-concept and self-expectancy that effort will result in effective performance. These self-expectancies then affect motivation and performance. Performance feeds back to influence future leader expectations about the member and the member's characteristics (such as performance history).

EXHIBIT 10.4

The Self-Fulfilling Prophecy Leader Model

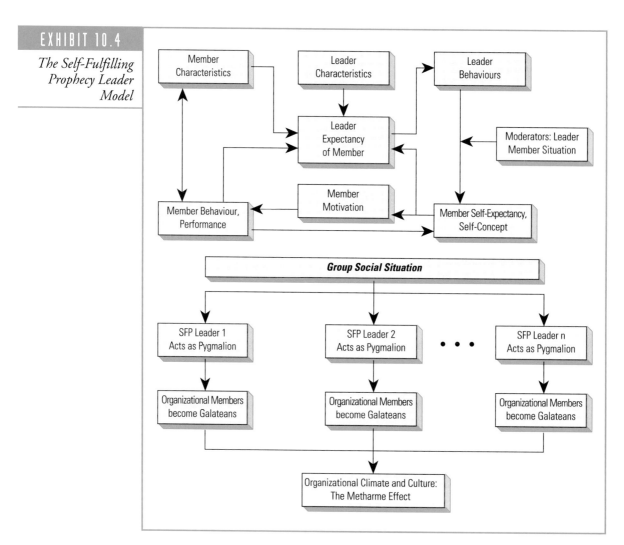

SOURCE: Richard H.G. Field (1989), "The Self-Fulfilling Prophecy Leader: Achieving the Metharme effect," *Journal of Management Studies* 26: 151-175.

The importance of this model is that leader expectations can change the way the member acts and thinks about the self. This has been called the Pygmalion effect, named after the King of Cyprus in Greek mythology. In this myth, Pygmalion carved a statue of a woman that was so beautiful he fell in love with it, and began to treat it as if it were alive. This caused Aphrodite, the goddess of love, to bring the statue to life as Galatea. Pygmalion and she were married, and together they had a daughter named Metharme.

Exhibit 10.4 shows how these leader and member expectations become part of the group's social situation—what to expect from a person in the work group becomes part of the group's constructed reality. If expectations are positive then members of that group can act as Pygmalions toward others, who can then become inspired Galateans and create an organizational climate and culture of high positive expectations.

For an illustration of how the Pygmalion effect may have operated at Olivetti, see this chapter's *Seeing is Believing* feature.

SEEING IS BELIEVING

When Carlo De Benedetti set out to revive the ailing Olivetti, one of the first things he did was raise prices. Most executives would have done the opposite. After all, don't lower prices attract customers?

"Normally, when you lose money, you cut prices," explains De Benedetti. "But then you have a losing attitude. We were discounting our products. We were always 10 percent to 15 percent lower than the competition, not because we were more clever (or had lower costs), but because we were shyer. I increased the prices by 15 percent.

Immediately, the volume increased. The Olivetti people began to believe in themselves when they stopped discounting.

"I gave a little courage to the company," De Benedetti says.

Customers don't want to buy from a loser, and De Benedetti's move signaled a winning attitude. When the Olivetti staff began living up to new positive expectations, customers responded. Why?

The reason is simple: It's the Pygmalion Effect, based on the premise that our behavior reflects others' expectations. According to Greek mythology, King Pygmalion of Cyprus sculpted his version of the perfect woman in ivory, then fell in love with it. Aphrodite, goddess of love, gave life to Pygmalion's statue.

Harvard University's Robert Rosenthal began noticing the effect when he tested the power of expectation on lab rats. Rosenthal told half of his unsuspecting college students they were training "maze bright" rats, a more intelligent strain. The other half were told they had ordinary rats. It sounds crazy, but the "maze bright" rats outperformed the others.

Rosenthal proved his theory of self-fulfilling prophecies with humans as well. In an eight-month experiment, students randomly labeled as "intellectual bloomers" really did flourish. Student achievement, he found, had less to do with ability than with the way teachers pigeonholed them.

EXPECT EMPLOYEE PERFORMANCE

The same phenomenon works in business. When managers believe their staff is competent, employees are not only more effective, they also find their jobs more rewarding. Self-confidence has a proven influence on performance—people do as well as they believe they can.

De Benedetti knew that, and his belief in people paved the way for Olivetti's dynamic renewal course. "I don't believe in being condemned to be a loser or being blessed to be a winner," he says. "You have to gain your day every morning. As long as you are convinced you can do it, it is feasible."

The Pygmalion Effect also helped turn around General Electric's refrigerator plant in Louisville, Kentucky. When Don Kelley, manager of production and operations, arrived there, he found defensive foremen and disillusioned line managers. For years, quality had been sacrificed, and everyone knew it.

Facing low morale and poor quality, he chose to accentuate the positive. Kelley installed traffic lights in the aisle to register end-of-line audits. If quality fell below standard, the red light came on and the line stopped until quality increased. He assured hourly workers there would be no penalty when the line was down.

"We didn't want to turn the quality around at the expense of the operators," he says. "We didn't want any negativity associated with quality."

Some were concerned about sabotage. But Kelley's expectations insured that it never happened. He trusted the employees and believed in their desire to produce quality. Because he anticipated responsible behavior, he got it.

To make the Pygmalion Effect work for you, pick a product and set out to be the best in quality or service. Create high standards, and let employees know you believe they can live up to them.

Think Pygmalion. People succeed if someone they respect thinks they can. Be vocal about expecting people to be competent, and they will be.

SOURCE: Bob Waterman (1988), "The Pygmalion effect," *Success*, October 1988, p. 8. Reprinted by permission.

Charismatic Leadership

Studied in the past as a means of organizational control (e.g., Weber, 1946), charisma—the gift of being able to inspire followers—is now seen as an important means by which leaders transform their followers.

A model of charismatic leadership in organizations is presented as Exhibit 10.5. In this complicated model by Kimberly Boal and John Bryson (1988) the primary role of the charismatic leader is to create a world that is perceived and felt by the follower to be real. The leader acts at the group level to create a shared reality and agreement on how to see and understand the group's world (it's interpretative scheme).

Phenomenological world
The world as experienced and constructed by an individual.

Once accepted as the individual's and group's reality, this **phenomenological world** affects the perceptions and feelings of the follower based on shared interpretive schemes. Specifically affected are:

- Commitment to the leader—trust in the leader, loyalty to the leader, unquestioning acceptance of and obedience to the leader;
- Arousal of the follower's needs;
- Acceptance by the follower of challenging goals;
- Enhanced follower self-esteem; and
- Enhanced performance expectations on the part of the follower.

In addition, the phenomenological world affects both the behaviour of the follower (as he seeks to emulate the leader's value system) and the consequences of the follower's behaviour. Follower performance is effective if aroused behaviour is appropriate to the demands of the task and in agreement with behavioural norms in the group.

Charismatic leaders are proposed to be unusually high in dominance, self-confidence, the need for influence, and in belief in their own values. They act to create these effects by: having a vision of what could be and then stating goals in support of that vision; building their own image as the leader; arousing needs in followers; and communicating high performance expectations and confidence in followers.

Of course, because charismatic leaders are acting within an organization, the characteristics of followers and of the task and environment will have effects on the extent to which charismatic leader behaviours change the perceptions, feelings, and behaviours of followers. A study of personality and charisma in the U.S. Presidency is summarized in the feature *A Little Knowledge*.

Charisma can be used to transform followers in positive or negative ways. There is no reason why a charismatic leader should have only positive organizational results. In a 1992 interview study of 25 charismatic leaders in large Canadian companies, Jane Howell of

EXHIBIT 10.5

*Charismatic Leadership
in Organizations*

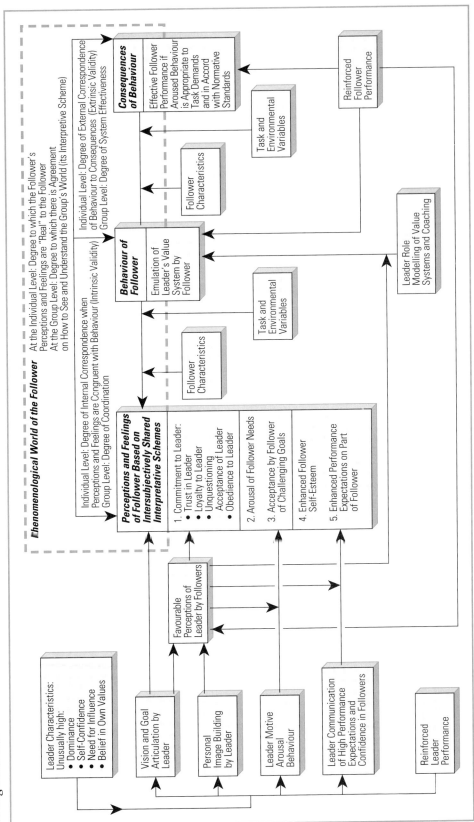

Phenomenological World of the Follower

At the Individual Level: Degree to which the Follower's Perceptions and Feelings are "Real" to the Follower
At the Group Level: Degree to which there is Agreement on How to See and Understand the Group's World (its Interpretive Scheme)

Individual Level: Degree of External Correspondence of Behaviour to Consequences (Extrinsic Validity)
Group Level: Degree of System Effectiveness

Individual Level: Degree of Internal Correspondence Perceptions and Feelings are Congruent with Behaviour (Intrinsic Validity)
Group Level: Degree of Coordination

Consequences of Behaviour

Effective Follower Performance if Aroused Behaviour is Appropriate to Task Demands and in Accord with Normative Standards

Task and Environmental Variables

Follower Characteristics

Reinforced Follower Performance

Behaviour of Follower

Emulation of Leader's Value System by Follower

Task and Environmental Variables

Follower Characteristics

Leader Role Modelling of Value Systems and Coaching

Perceptions and Feelings of Follower Based on Intersubjectively Shared Interpretative Schemes

1. Commitment to Leader:
   • Trust in Leader
   • Loyalty to Leader
   • Unquestioning Acceptance of Leader
   • Obedience to Leader
2. Arousal of Follower Needs
3. Acceptance by Follower of Challenging Goals
4. Enhanced Follower Self-Esteem
5. Enhanced Performance Expectations on Part of Follower

Leader Characteristics: Unusually high:
   • Dominance
   • Self-Confidence
   • Need for Influence
   • Belief in Own Values

Vision and Goal Articulation by Leader

Personal Image Building by Leader

Leader Motive Arousal Behaviour

Leader Communication of High Performance Expectations and Confidence in Followers

Reinforced Leader Performance

Favourable Perceptions of Leader by Followers

SOURCE: Adapted from Kimberly B. Boal and John M. Bryson (1988), "Charismatic leadership: A phenomenological and structural approach," pp. 20–21. Reprinted with the permission of Lexington Books, an imprint of Macmillan, Inc., from EMERGING LEADERSHIP VISTAS by James Gerald Hunt, B. Rajaram Baliga, H. Peter Dachler, and Chester A. Schriesheim, editors. Copyright © 1988 by Lexington Books. This figure was in turn adapted from Figure 11 on p. 206 of Robert J. House (1977), "A 1976 theory of charismatic leadership," in James G. Hunt & Larry L. Larson (Eds.), *Leadership: The Cutting Edge* (pp. 189–207), Carbondale, IL: Southern Illinois University Press. Copyright © 1977 by Southern Illinois University Press.; and based in part on ideas in Brickman (1978).

One study examined the influence of leader personality and charisma on the effectiveness of 31 United States presidents and concluded that, contrary to the view that context largely determines individual behaviour, personality and charisma do make a difference.

The argument of the theory of charisma put forward was that "such charismatic leaders affect followers in ways that are quantitatively greater and qualitatively different than the effects specified by past leadership theories. Charismatic leaders transform the needs, values, preferences, and aspirations of followers. These leaders motivate followers to make significant personal sacrifices in the interest of some mission and to perform above and beyond the call of duty. Followers become less motivated by self-interest and more motivated to serve the interests of the larger collective" (p. 364).

To test the effects of charisma in the U.S. presidency, the authors collected a great deal of information about each president's first term of office—his motives, charisma, and performance. Using a complex statistical model to test the effects of motives and charisma on performance (among other tests), they found that "charisma was strongly and positively related to presidential direct action, presidential subjective performance, presidential economic performance, and presidential social performance" (p. 384).

One conclusion of the study about the motives of presidents was that "presidential leaders do make a difference. They achieve both positive and negative substantive effects by enacting the power motive and by departing from societal motive norms. Such leaders are transcendental—they transcend the ethos of their times—and make a difference by being different" (p. 389).

SOURCE: Robert J. House, William D. Spangler, and James Woycke (1991), "Personality and charisma in the U.S. presidency: A psychological theory of leader effectiveness," *Administrative Science Quarterly* 36: 364-396.

the University of Western Ontario and Bruce Avolio of the State University of New York at Binghamton compared ethical charismatic leaders to unethical charismatic leaders. The ethical/unethical judgment was made by analyzing interview transcripts and looking for "whether the leader attacked moral abuses, confronted and resolved dilemmas, encouraged pursuits of ideals, cultivated an ethically responsible culture, and fostered and rewarded those with moral integrity" (p. 44). Their study results are shown as Exhibit 10.6. Ethical charismatic leaders convert followers into leaders in their own right. "Unethical charismatic leaders select or produce obedient, dependent, and compliant followers" (p. 49).

A model by David Nadler and Michael Tushman (Exhibit 10.7) shows how charismatic and instrumental leadership can be combined. In this model charismatic leadership is defined as consisting of envisioning, enabling, and energizing behaviours.

Envisioning is the articulation by the leader of a compelling vision, setting high expectations for followers, and modeling consistent behaviours for followers. Enabling is composed of expressing personal support, empathizing with followers, and expressing confidence in others. Energizing others is accomplished by demonstrating personal excitement about the mission, expressing personal confidence that it can be achieved, and using success experiences to help others to feel that progress is being made.

These charismatic behaviours are supplemented by the instrumental actions of structuring tasks and rewards, controlling the actions of others, and rewarding appropriate actions by followers.

Finally, in this model leadership is extended and developed throughout the organization in three ways. The first is to leverage the senior team. An executive team is developed that can supplement and extend the influence of the main organizational leader. Secondly, senior

EXHIBIT 10.6   INDIVIDUAL QUALITIES OF ETHICAL AND UNETHICAL CHARISMATIC LEADERS

UNETHICAL CHARISMATIC LEADER	ETHICAL CHARISMATIC LEADER
• Uses power only for personal gain or impact	• Uses power to serve others
• Promotes own personal vision	• Aligns vision with followers' needs and aspirations
• Censures critical or opposing views	• Considers and learns from criticism
• Demands own decisions be accepted without question	• Stimulates followers to think independently and to question the leader's view
• One-way communication	• Open, two-way communication
• Insensitive to followers' needs	• Coaches, develops, and supports followers; shares recognition with others
• Relies on convenient external moral standards to satisfy self-interests	• Relies on internal moral standards to satisfy organizational and societal interests

SOURCE: Jane M. Howell and Bruce J. Avolio (1992), "The ethics of charismatic leadership: Submission or liberation?" *Academy of Management Executive* 6(2): 45. Reproduced by permission of the Academy of Management.

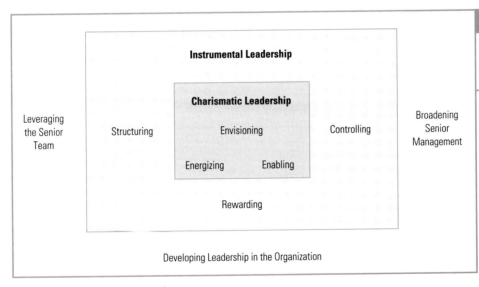

EXHIBIT 10.7

Institutionalizing the Leadership of Change

SOURCE: David A. Nadler and Michael L. Tushman (1990). Copyright ©1990 by the Regents of the University of California. Reprinted from the *California Management Review,* 32(2). By permission of The Regents.

management is broadened. More individuals are brought into the senior group and their influence is increased. Thirdly, leadership is developed throughout the organization by encouraging those at all levels, not just at the top or in the senior team, to take action when necessary.

Leaders in organizations need to remember their role in creating meaning and the interpretations given to events occurring in the organization. A vision of the organization's direction must be communicated to others and must be consistent with the actions taken. Joseph Bower and Martha Weinberg (1988) argue that a critical skill in this process is **statecraft**, which is "the use of persuasion and informal authority to mobilize coalitions to accomplish goals" (p. 40).

Statecraft has six key elements that any organizational leader must consider.

Statecraft The use of persuasion and informal authority to encourage coalitions to accomplish goals.

1. The leader's messages in words and actions must be consistent. Leaders must walk like they talk so that there is no confusion about the leader's true message.

2. The support of subordinates is necessary if the leader's vision of the organization is to become a reality. Therefore, it is critical for the leader to find subordinates that can help to develop plans in support of the vision and that will be part of the coalition of organization members who are supporting the accomplishment of the leader's vision.

3. Since the leader's vision usually means change for the organization, it is critical for the leader to support the individuals in the coalition that are supporting change so that they can influence others who are not so supportive of the proposed organizational changes.

4. Leaders using the skill of statecraft have to choose carefully the issues that they personally consider. Key issues cannot be delegated, but routine operating issues must be delegated.

5. Leaders must develop connections with a diverse array of people both inside and outside the organization. These contacts help the leader to understand the organization's environment and to plan strategy for the organization.

6. It is as important to know when not to act as when to act. Effective leaders can resist the temptation to act when the organization is functioning well.

This ends our discussion of how leadership operates in organizations. We have looked at the effects of who the leader is, what the leader does, and the relationship between the leader and the follower. Gary Yukl of the State University of New York has summarized and integrated many of these approaches to leadership into one conceptual framework, shown as Exhibit 10.8. This framework is a very useful guide to understanding leadership in organizations.

There is one aspect of leadership, however, that we have yet to discuss. After the actual operation of leadership in organizations, it is the perception of leadership that is important. A leader must consider not only what is done but what is perceived.

PERCEPTIONS OF LEADERS

Does Alex Tilley, pictured here with Susan Tilley in their famous Tilley hats, match your mental image of a corporate leader?

Because people in organizations try to understand their environment and what occurs around them in the organization, and because they tend to seek rational explanations for events, organizational outcomes are often attributed to leadership in the organization (Calder, 1977). Leaders therefore need to understand that even when events are such that actual leader influence on outcomes has been low, others will see a higher level of leader influence on these outcomes (see this chapter's *Overboard* for a humorous example). This phenomenon may be used by leaders to take credit for success even when positive outcomes were due to other factors, but it will be difficult for leaders to avoid the blame for failures even when caused by external factors.

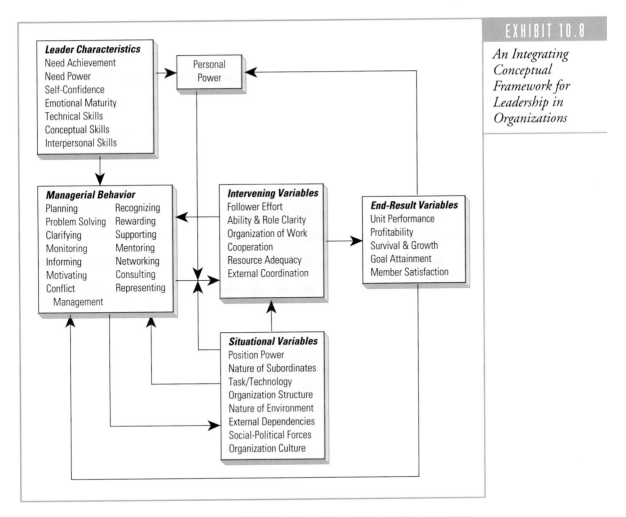

EXHIBIT 10.8

An Integrating Conceptual Framework for Leadership in Organizations

SOURCE: Reprinted from Gary A. Yukl (1989a), "Managerial leadership: A review of theory and research," *Journal of Management* 15:274.

People in organizations develop in their minds an **implicit theory of leadership** (for example Phillips & Lord, 1986), describing how an effective leader should act, and a **leader prototype** (Bass & Avolio, 1989) or mental image of what characteristics an effective leader should have. Organizational members asked to select a person for a particular leadership position or asked to evaluate the performance of a leader in a given task situation can be expected to compare a leader or leader candidate to these mental images of leaders. This is an important process because often it is not actual leadership ability or effectiveness that forms the basis for the judgment, but the degree of match, or "fit," with the image of what a leader "looks like" and what a leader does.

Mental images of leaders can be created by the media of a societal culture, people within a culture, and by a specific organizational culture. For example, one article (Chen & Meindl, 1991) examined how the press constructed and reconstructed the image of Donald Burr of the People Express airline as the company's fortunes rose and fell.

Implicit theory of leadership A theory held in people's minds of how an effective leader should act.

Leader prototype A mental image of what characteristics an effective leader should have.

What is considered effective leadership will also vary between societal cultures. An example of what is expected of American and Japanese CEOs is shown in this chapter's cross-cultural feature, *A Rose by Any Other Name.*

Finally, what is seen as effective leadership is sure to vary between different organizational cultures. Members of a Tough-Guy, Macho culture (Exhibit 3.6), for example, are sure to compare their leadership to different standards than those used by members of a Process culture.

A ROSE BY ANY OTHER NAME

AMERICAN AND JAPANESE CEOs: A COMPARISON OF A TYPICAL DAY

American		*Japanese*
Mr. Mann, president of Eastern Oil, begins his day with a cup of coffee.	6:30 a.m.	
To beat traffic he leaves early for work.	7:15	
Along the way he uses his mini cassette recorder to dictate instructions to his secretary and employees.	7:15-7:45	
Mr. Mann's mobile phone rings as he pulls into Eastern Oil. His refinery production manager tells of an oil leak at the Indonesia plant. The manager wants instructions on what to do next. The president says he will call him back with a plan of action.	7:45-8:00	
Mr. Mann has his secretary call in all necessary personnel for an 8:30 meeting and his assistant gathers all related files.	8:00 a.m.	Mr. Nakamura, president of Congee Oil, begins his day with a limousine ride.
He asks the legal department about legal problems that could result from the spill.	8:20-8:30	
He briefs subordinates on what is known so far about the spill.	8:30-8:50	
	9:00	Mr. Nakamura arrives. He proceeds to have tea and read the newspaper.
The legal staff submits reports on what can and should be done.	9:00-9:15	
Mr. Mann meets with plant and design engineers and discusses suggestions on how to contain the oil spill.	9:17-10:00	

American		Japanese
The VP of marketing and communications says the press is calling for a story. She wants to know what the angle should be.	10:03	
The Indonesia plant manager calls back, asking what the plan of attack is.	10:10-10:25	
The plant engineers at headquarters decide to shut down the plant until the leak is contained.	10:31-10:47	
The accounting department is asked how much the plant shutdown will cost. The comptroller says he will have the figures in an hour.	10:55-11:15	
	10:00 a.m.-12:00 noon	He meets with subordinates to discuss why the planned effort in the South China Sea isn't working.
		(Earlier the CEO was made aware of the problem and informed his subordinates indirectly of his solution. The subordinates then met together and developed a consensus of opinion on the solution.) At the same time, the subordinates, already aware that there has been an oil leak at an Indonesian plant, do not mention the leak to the CEO. Rather, their staff makes a considerable effort to develop an appropriate response plan to the leak problem.
The Indonesia plant manager calls back, saying that only the affected area of the plant has been shut down, so production will continue at 60 percent capacity.	11:30	
Mr. Mann holds another meeting with the chief assistants to get an update on the situation.	11:45 a.m.-12:15 p.m	
He has a hurried lunch while talking on the phone to the legal department about insurance clauses.	12:15-12:30	
	12:15 p.m.-12:30 p.m.	The subordinates and staff inform Mr. Nakamura of the oil leak and the plan of action already in place to address the problem. Mr. Nakamura acknowledges the information and compliments the staff on their quick action.
At this point Mr. Mann already has had many times as many meetings as his Japanese counterpart in half the time. The remainder of his day is a mirror image of his morning.	12:30	
	12:30-2:30	He meets with an MITI (Ministry of International Trade and Industry) representative for lunch to discuss long-term production goals.
	3:00-5:50	He meets with two department heads to discuss the 25-year plan for the Yokohama refinery.
Mr. Mann finishes his day, having had a grand total of 18 meetings, 20 phone calls, 2 vending machine meals, and a late night at the office.	9:45 p.m.	
	5:30 p.m.-1:00 a.m.	Mr. Nakamura has cocktails with a supplier, followed by dinner and evening entertainment at a private restaurant club in the Ginza.

Source: Doktor (1990). Reprinted, by permission of publisher, from ORGANIZATIONAL DYNAMICS, Winter 1990. © 1990 American Management Association, New York. All rights reserved. For a look at the operation of leadership in China, see John R. Schermerhorn, Jr., and Mee-Kau Nyaw (1990), "Managerial leadership in Chinese industrial enterprises," *International Studies of Management & Organization* 20: 9-21.

One of the most important applications of this area of leadership perception is the perceptions of men and women as leaders. Are men and women evaluated differently with respect to leadership, not because of their abilities and performance but because of their sex? To address this question we must first determine if men and women leaders in organizations behave differently.

In terms of initiating structure and showing consideration, one review (Dobbins & Platz, 1986) found no difference in the amounts of these behaviours shown by male and female leaders. While this review did find that male leaders were rated as more effective than female leaders, this result did not hold for studies conducted in organizational settings. The implication is that males in artificial experiments were rated as more effective leaders simply because they were male, but that in real on-going organizations, where performance could be observed over a longer time period and where there were many other factors operating (the group, the reward system, etc.), the sex of the leader lost its power to predict effectiveness ratings.

A later review (Eagly & Johnson, 1990) found that in organizational studies female and male leaders did not differ in their interpersonally oriented style or task-oriented style. However, women did tend to adopt a more democratic or participative leadership style compared to the more autocratic or directive style adopted by the men studied. It may be that women leaders are using their better verbal ability and enculturation to be nurturant and to encourage more participation by their group. The effectiveness of this more participative approach is, according to a contingency perspective, likely to vary depending on the particular task and leadership situation. However, it may also be that female leaders use a more democratic/participative style because of a lower evaluation of their leadership when they act in a more autocratic/directive style.

A review of many studies examining sex and leader evaluation offered the following summary:

> Although this research showed only a small overall tendency for subjects to evaluate female leaders less favorably than male leaders, this tendency was more pronounced under certain circumstances. Specifically, women in leadership positions were devalued relative to their male counterparts when leadership was carried out in stereotypically masculine styles, particularly when this style was autocratic or directive. In addition, the devaluation of women was greater when leaders occupied male-dominated roles and when evaluators were men (Eagly and others, 1992, p. 3).

Therefore, the answer to the question posed previously is a qualified yes. Male and female leaders do show some slight differences in behaviour; there is a small tendency for female leaders to be evaluated less favourably than male leaders. Leaders of both sexes should be aware of the importance of leadership perceptions in evaluations of their effectiveness.

LEADERSHIP CONSIDERATIONS

There are several specific areas of organizational leadership that need to be considered by those who either are leaders or wish to become leaders. We will discuss ethical leadership, the leadership of ethics, leading people from diverse cultures, leader succession, and the leadership of self-managed groups.

Ethical Leadership

Ethical leadership is the way a particular leader acts within ethical guidelines, however set. Ethical leaders use their power to serve others and to further the mission, values, and goals of the organization. Unethical leaders use their power to further their own personal vision and goals.

Stories abound of the unethical acts of top level leaders. Misuse of the organization's resources, insider trading in stocks based on confidential information, and sexual impropriety are a few common occurrences. Why do leaders act in this way? Are these actions taken by those who have no moral code to guide them? Or are these people under pressure to compete at any cost?

In an interesting article titled "The Bathsheba syndrome: The ethical failure of successful leaders," Dean Ludwig and Clinton Longnecker (1993) argue that it is not only unprincipled leaders or those under heavy competitive pressure who act unethically. They make the point that it can be the very success of leaders that gives them the power and resources that can cause them to take actions that are obviously unethical.

The **Bathsheba syndrome** is named after King David of Israel and his affair with Bathsheba, the wife of one of his army officers. It describes how a leader's success can cause unethical acts that the leader knows to be wrong. About these leaders Ludwig and Longnecker (1993, p. 267) write that:

> Just at the moment of seemingly "having it all," they have thrown it all away by engaging in an activity which is wrong, which they know is wrong, which they know would lead to their downfall if discovered, and which they mistakenly believe they have the power to conceal.

Bathsheba syndrome

Named after King David of Israel and his affair with Bathsheba. It describes how a leader's success can cause unethical acts that the leader knows to be wrong.

How does this come about? Ludwig and Longnecker argue that when the leader becomes successful, he is given privileged access to information and the control over organizational resources. These are given for a reason. They are tools with which the leader keeps in touch with events in and outside the organization and which the leader uses to set and revise the organization's strategy. But a leader might come to think that these tools of top leadership are in fact rewards for past successes. The leader may relax and enjoy the privileges and control of the position. When the leader succumbs to the temptations which abound at the top, he loses strategic focus. The job of leader is not being done.

Often these unethical actions can be covered up using the power that comes with the position. This then reinforces the leader's belief in a personal ability to control outcomes. Further unethical actions are then taken. The leader may come to see himself as "above the law" with respect to the rules of the organization. Information about these actions is kept from those lower in the hierarchy. Power is wielded to force others to accept these abuses. Those who complain are likely to be removed from their positions.

The lesson in the Bathsheba syndrome is that everyone is susceptible to the temptations that come with power and control. It is not just the unprincipled who take advantage of being on top. Ludwig and Longnecker's advice is for the leader to lead a balanced life of work and family. In this way the leader is less likely to lose touch with reality. It is also critical for the leader to remember that privilege and status were given to do the job and not as a reward.

Leadership of Ethics

The leadership of ethics refers to the leader's actions to help set ethical guidelines and to encourage their use in organizational decision making (the subject of Chapter 11). Because leaders help to create the social knowledge in an organization they must concern themselves with acting ethically and creating the conditions that encourage others to act in an ethical manner.

Acting ethically is critically important. Organizational members must see the leader as responsible and credible if they are to act ethically themselves. Joseph Rost and

Anthony Smith (1992) describe the credible leader as caring, competent, demonstrating courage, and exhibiting composure (grace under pressure) and character (integrity, trustworthiness, and honesty).

To create ethical awareness and the conditions for ethical actions, the leader needs to take three actions. First, a code of ethical conduct should be created. Second, ethical and unethical actions must be made explicit. Ethical "gray areas" must be discussed and clarified. Third, the leader must be willing to reward ethical behaviour and punish unethical behaviour.

An example of the leadership of ethics is the Academy of Management's (*Academy of Management Journal*, 1992) formal statement of the ethical conduct required of its members (see Exhibit 10.9). In terms of the advancement of managerial knowledge, the Academy's code states that "Academy member research should be done honestly, have a clear purpose, show respect for the rights of all individuals and organizations, efficiently use resources, and advance knowledge in the field" (Academy of Management, 1992, p. 1137).

More specifically, the ethical code requires that the conducting and reporting of research be rigorous in the design, execution, and analysis of studies, and in the interpretation of results. Also, informed consent must be obtained from research participants. Potential subjects must be told enough about the study to be able to make an informed choice about whether or not to participate. They must be capable of making such a choice (that is, they must be adults with adult mental functioning), and given the free right to withdraw from the study without penalty.

Exhibit 10.9 THE ACADEMY OF MANAGEMENT CODE OF ETHICAL CONDUCT

CREDO

We believe in discovering, sharing, and applying managerial knowledge.

PREAMBLE

Our professional goals are to enhance the learning of students, colleagues, and others and to improve the effectiveness of organizations through our teaching, research, and practice of management. We have five major responsibilities.

- *To our students*—Relationships with students require respect, fairness, and caring, along with recognition of our commitment to the subject matter and to teaching excellence.

- *To managerial knowledge*—Prudence in research design, human subject use, confidentiality, result reporting, and proper attribution of work is a necessity.

- *To the Academy of Management and the larger professional environment*—Support of the Academy's mission and objectives, service to the Academy and our institutions, and the recognition of the dignity and personal worth of colleagues is required.

- *To both managers and the practice of management*—Exchange of ideas and information between the academic and organizational communities is essential.

- *To all people with whom we live and work in the world community*—Sensitivity to other people, to diverse cultures, to the needs of the poor and disadvantaged, to ethical issues, and to newly emerging ethical dilemmas is required.

SOURCE: Reprinted by permission of the Academy of Management. Academy of Management (1990), "The Academy of Management code of ethical conduct," *Academy of Management Journal* 33: 901. The remainder of this article explains each of the above points in depth.

Leading People from Diverse Cultures

Leaders cannot simply assume that everyone at work or in the leader's group shares the same cultural background. As we have seen in Chapter 3, differences in cultural approaches to fundamental human issues will cause people in the same situation to perceive it differently and react to the situation in ways different from others. The more diversity exists among group members (the more heterogeneous they are) the more the leader, to be effective, will have to treat each person as an individual. The approach must be more individualistic and less reliant on a common leader style for all followers.

Leader Succession

Leader succession is important for organizations and for leaders themselves (for example Day & Lord, 1988; Heller, 1989). Organizations often create a **succession plan**, a list of the organization's managers and leaders and which persons could fill positions above them in the organization's hierarchy. Such a plan can be useful because it can identify areas where no successor is ready within the organization and potential successors who are ready but may have no opening to fill for many years. The succession plan can also note the experience and training that possible successors would need in order to be ready to assume the leadership role.

    Individual leaders need to consider succession from their own point of view. They should examine what positions they are now ready for, what experience and training they need for other positions, and how to develop subordinates so that one is ready for succession to their own position!

Succession plan A list of the organization's senior personnel specifying when each is expected to be ready to be promoted to the next higher positions in the hierarchy.

Leadership of Self-Managed Groups

A further leadership consideration is the leadership of self-managed groups. Many groups in organizations manage their own functioning, including how the work is done and allocated, and even the selection, pay, and performance appraisals of group members. Though such groups are self-managed, they are tied into the organization through an external leader, who has the difficult problem of deciding how to lead a group that is managing itself.

    This problem has been expressed by Charles Manz and Henry Sims (1984) as the problem of "searching for the 'unleader.'" These authors later studied a factory using self-managing work teams (Manz & Sims, 1987). They concluded that the most important role of the external leader is to lead others to lead themselves. A set of self-leadership strategies were developed in their 1989 book, and are shown as Exhibit 10.10.

CONCLUSION

Leadership exists at all levels of the organization as leaders influence the social knowledge, goals, and actions of others. This influence often occurs through the decisions that are made. In fact, some scholars who study organizations think that an understanding of how decisions are made is central to understanding organizations. The actions that are taken by organizations can be thought of as a direct outcome of decisions that are made. Decision making at the individual, group, and organizational levels is therefore the subject of our next chapter.

EXHIBIT 10.10   SELF-LEADERSHIP STRATEGIES

| BEHAVIOURAL FOCUSED STRATEGIES | |
BEHAVIOUR	STRATEGY
Self-Set Goals	Setting goals for your own work efforts.
Management of Cues	Arranging and altering cues in the work environment to facilitate your desired personal behaviours.
Rehearsal	Physical or mental practice of work activities before you actually perform them.
Self-Observation	Observing and gathering information about your own specific behaviours that you have targeted for change.
Self-Reward	Providing yourself with personally valued rewards for completing desirable behaviours.
Self-Punishment	Administering punishments to yourself for behaving in undesirable ways (this strategy is generally not very effective).

| COGNITIVE FOCUSED STRATEGIES | |
BEHAVIOUR	STRATEGY
Building Natural Rewards into Tasks	Self-redesign of where and how you do your work to increase the level of natural rewards in your job. Natural rewards that are part of, rather than separate from, the work (i.e., the work, like a hobby, becomes the reward) result from activities that cause you to feel: a sense of *competence*, a sense of *self-control*, or a sense of *purpose*.
Focusing Thinking on Natural Rewards	Purposely focusing your thinking on the naturally rewarding features of your work.
Establishing Constructive Thought Patterns	Establishing constructive and effective habits or patterns in your thinking (e.g., a tendency to search for opportunities rather than obstacles embedded in challenges) by managing your *beliefs* and *assumptions, mental imagery,* and *internal self-talk*.

SOURCE: Charles C. Manz & Henry P. Sims, Jr. (1989), *SuperLeadership: Leading Others to Lead Themselves* (p. 45). Englewood Cliffs, NJ: Prentice Hall, Inc. For a further look at self-leadership and a model of thought self-leadership, see Chris P. Neck and Charles C. Manz (1992), "Thought self-leadership: The influence of self-talk and mental imagery on performance," *Journal of Organizational Behavior* 13: 681-699. A book that offers advice on self-leadership strategies and methods of learning how to be an effective self-leader is *Mastering Self-Leadership: Empowering Yourself for Personal Excellence*, by Charles C. Manz, published by Prentice Hall in 1992.

CHAPTER SUMMARY

Leadership is about influence within a social relationship. Leaders affect what followers "know" about a social situation, they affect the goals that followers choose to pursue, and they affect what followers do. While managers are concerned with how the work is done, leaders are concerned with what work is to be done. Managers take a goal and then try to accomplish it in the best way possible, while leaders are more concerned with what the goal is in the first place.

Thinking about leadership has changed several times over the years. From a focus on personality and traits, leadership began to also be considered as influence over others through power and persuasion. Then the leader's behaviours toward followers were considered to be of prime importance, though it was later recognized that the leader behaviour likely to be most effective would depend on the particular situation.

In recent years there has been a change from leadership seen as a transaction between leader and follower to how the organizational member was transformed or changed by the leader. Three transformational approaches are leadership and performance beyond expectations; the self-fulfilling prophecy leader model; and charismatic leadership in organizations. In each of these the leader's beliefs, values, and actions help to change the follower's needs, values, and social world. It is also important to consider how leaders are perceived. People in organizations develop in their minds an implicit theory of leadership (by which they explain how an effective leader should act) and a mental image of what characteristics an effective leader should have.

QUESTIONS FOR REVIEW

1. What is the difference between transactional and transformational approaches to the understanding of leadership?

2. Does leadership make a difference to organizational performance? Or are differences seen merely attributed to top level leadership?

3. Where does leadership reside in an organization? Is it concentrated at the top of the hierarchy because of status, role, and organizational legitimacy, or is leadership dispersed throughout the organization to any member who wishes to be a leader?

4. Why do people feel more intensely toward a charismatic leader, both positively and negatively, than toward an organizational manager?

5. Does leadership have to involve a social relationship between two or more people? Could a person be a leader even without any followers?

SELF-DIAGNOSTIC EXERCISE 10.1

Do you think like an administrator, a manager, or a leader? To find out, circle the way you think you would approach each of the organizational issues that follow. When you are finished, add up the total number of times you circled the description for the administrator, the manager, and the leader.

	Administrator	*Manager*	*Leader*
Rewarding Subordinates:	Get just what the policy provides for	Fair pay for fair work	Major rewards for major results/ accomplishments
Decision-Making Basis:	The decision is made by the policy/procedure	Stick with policy except where exceptions are fully justified	Special circumstances require different decisions
Strategic Orientation:	Internal	Internal except when major external events intervene	External

	Administrator	Manager	Leader
Innovation/ Creativity:	Change is threatening	Tries to plan out major changes	Improvements come through change
Handling Variables:	One variable at a time	Handles multiple variables if not too complex	Balances/blends multiple, complex variables
Efficiency/ Effectiveness:	Covers every detail in depth	Doing things right	Doing the right things
Time Frame for Thinking:	Short-range. Month to month, year to year	Medium-range 2-4 years	Strategic 5-10 years
Big vs. Small Picture:	Concentrates on details	Details as they fit into a system	Concepts and a big picture
Organization Structure:	Bureaucratic, many levels	Traditional	Flat, few levels
Security Level:	Low, protect my rear	Average, except when things go wrong	Very secure and confident
Management Atmosphere:	You can't fight City Hall	Your progress depends on you	Win-win atmosphere
Policies:	Cast in concrete, takes an Act of God to change	Exceptions can be made but must be heavily justified	Use only as a guide to most actions
People:	Emphasis on controls most actions	Emphasizes team effort	Lead by example
Change:	Maintain status quo, don't rock the boat or make waves	Changes made if major problems dictate or when pressure builds up	Change is encouraged continuously
Conflict:	Avoid conflicts at any cost	Address if they become major	Recognizes they will occur—concentrates on resolving them for improvements
Subordinate Loyalty:	Is to the policy	Mixed between the policy and the manager	Is to the leader
Risk Taking:	Avoids at all costs	Accepts minimal risk	Encourages planned risk taking
Information Sharing:	Little	Need to know basis	Open and frank
Approach to Problems:	Avoid like the plague	Solve as they develop —reactive	Problems are normal part of the job— proactive

	Administrator	Manager	Leader
Handling Mistakes:	Protect my rear and offer excuses, pin the guilty	Emphasize why it happened, not who caused it	Learn from them, don't dwell on them once solved
Authority:	Emphasizes formal authority and power	Authority goes with the position	Maximum use of informal authority
Basis of Loyalty:	Demand it	Earn it	Willingly given by subordinates
Planning Approach:	Knee-jerk reactions, short range	Long and short range	Concentrates on strategies and the long range
Primary Drive:	Power	Mixture of power and achievement	Achievement
Delegation:	Has limited authority so is limited delegator	Delegates clear-cut authority to match responsibility	Delegates extensively with minimal controls
Controls:	Extensive and often excessive to protect my rear	Tailored closely to the delegation	The minimal necessary to stay in control
Subordinate Initiative:	Poor, follow the leader and policy	Prepares and follows a plan	Forces people to take responsibility and exercise it
Resources:	Emphasizes amount spent, not returns	Tries to blend both	Emphasizes returns
Communicating:	Top down and internal	Seeks organized methods	Promotes and facilitates two-way communications and external communications
Networking:	Empire builder, isolationist	Concentrates on internal networks	Promotes both internal and external networks
Clock Watching or Hours Worked	9 to 5	As required by workload	Results are the important thing, not the hours
Results vs. Potential:	Works below potential	Strives to achieve potential	Achieves full potential
Organizational Emphasis:	Rigid and proscribed	Emphasizes the formal organization	Emphasizes the informal organization
Chain of Command:	Rigidly adhered to	Detailed list for observing	Observed only for major policies and problems
Primary Skill Requirements:	Technical and processing	Human and technical	Conceptual and human

	Administrator	*Manager*	*Leader*
Public Dealt With:	Internal and limited	Primarily internal	Primarily external
Using Information:	Overwhelmed by too much	Uses what is required for decisions, for what is being done (reactive)	Highly selective, determines which is significant and what should be done (proactive)
Use of Intuition:	Little, follow the policy	Some, but tends to act based on hard facts	Extensively, with data used as a check and balance
Team Building:	Clones	Based on the skills required by the job	Picks people with complementary skills
Strategic Directions:	Little, handles day-to-day matters as they develop	Concentrates on doing things better within current mission and markets	Determines major directions, what is most important, then leads the team there—new missions, new markets
Total:	_____	_____	_____

(out of 40 points total)

SOURCE: Dale D. McConkey (1989, pp. 19-20). Reprinted from *Business Horizons*, September-October 1989. Copyright © 1993 by the Foundation for the School of Business at Indiana University. Used with permission.

EXPERIENTIAL EXERCISE 10.1

Skilled Warriors of Old

> *Their wariness was as that of one*
> *Crossing a river in winter;*
> *Their caution was as that of one*
> *In fear of all around.*
> *They were as serious as guests,*
> *Relaxed as ice at the melting point.*
> *Simple as uncarved wood,*
> *Open as the valleys,*
> *They were inscrutable as murky water.*

This poem can be applied to contemporary issues in organizations if the word "Warriors" is replaced with "Leaders." Form into small groups of four or five and discuss the following questions.

1. What is meant by each line?
2. How does each line apply to present day leaders?
3. What advice can be obtained from reading this poem?

SOURCE: (A quote from the TAO TE CHING) From MASTERING THE ART OF WAR, translated & edited by Thomas Cleary. ©
1989 by Thomas Cleary. Reprinted by arrangement with Shambhala Publications Inc., 300 Massachusetts Ave., Boston,
MA 02115.

SELF-GUIDED LEARNING ACTIVITY

Thinking about leadership has been an activity through the ages. It is worthwhile to examine the advice offered by the ancient writers. A good place to start is *The Art of War*, written in Chinese about 2500 years ago by Sun Tzu (translated by Thomas Cleary, Shambhala Publications Inc., 1988). The book is well worth the time and effort invested in it by a student of leadership. Follow this up with *Mastering the Art of War* (translated and edited by Thomas Cleary, Shambhala Publications Inc., 1989). These two books will give the reader a wealth of ideas that are applicable to modern-day organizations and leadership situations.

The Book of Five Rings was written in Japanese in 1643 by Miyamoto Musashi (translated by Thomas Cleary, Shambhala Publications Inc., 1993). It takes an approach more focused on the individual warrior and the qualities of perseverance, insight, self-understanding, and the importance of swift but unhurried action. More recent works that follow in this tradition are *Leadership Secrets of Attila the Hun* by Wess Roberts, Warner Books Inc., 1985 and *Victory Secrets of Attila the Hun* by Wess Roberts, 1993. Though Attila himself did not write about his experiences, these books are very readable accounts of his life and times and the lessons there to be learned.

A useful article about leadership is based on the lessons of Oriental masters; see W. Chan Kim and Renée A. Mauborgne, "Parables of Leadership," in the July-August 1992 *Harvard Business Review*, pages 123-128. See also the article by Simon Fraser University's Rosalie Tung, "Strategic management thought in East Asia," *Organizational Dynamics*, Spring 1994, pp. 55-65.

MANAGER'S CASE FILE:
A QUESTION OF LOYALTY

Rodney Lutwig never worked overtime. It was his responsibility to pick up his kids from the day-care center on his way home from work. Rodney's wife brought them to the center on her way to work in the morning. The system had always worked out well because Rodney had opted for the early shift at work and left at four o'clock, thereby missing the heavy traffic, and was able to pick up his kids by five o'clock. His wife, Amanda, didn't start work until 10 o'clock, when her shop opened, so she was able to drop the kids off in the morning at about nine o'clock. She worked late, however, and never got home before eight o'clock at night.

Rodney had just been promoted to senior technician and placed on Tony Ortega's staff. He was grateful to his former supervisor, Gene Kowalski, because Gene had brought him into the business, taught him everything he knew, encouraged him to take a class at the local college for some additional technical training, gave him an important project where he could utilize his newly acquired expertise, and recommended him for the promotion to his new department.

After Rodney had been on the job for only two weeks, Gene stopped him on his way out to lunch.

"Rodney, am I glad to see you," Gene said. "I need to ask you for a favor."

"What's up?" Rodney asked.

"Well, we've been having trouble replacing you and I was wondering if you couldn't give me a hand with the project you were working on."

"I'd love to help you out, Gene, but I'm working on an important project and I really don't have the time," Rodney said. "Couldn't you get someone else to give you a hand? Or why don't you get some temporary help until you find a permanent replacement?"

"By the time I can train someone, you could have the work done," Gene said. "Couldn't you come in a little earlier in the morning, or maybe take a short lunch break? It wouldn't be for very long; I'm sure I'll get someone soon."

So Rodney began to take a half hour for lunch and work the other half hour for Gene, trying to make a dent in the project work. After a couple of days, he began to work through his lunch hour, taking bites out of his sandwich as he went. When he returned to his job in the afternoon, his stomach was upset and his nerves were on edge. Within a few weeks, as the work continued to back up, Rodney started to come in a half hour earlier in the morning to get a jump on the work.

Another week had gone by and Tony called Rodney into his office. "I've tried to be patient," Tony started. "I know you feel indebted to Gene for all he's done for you, but your work here is suffering. I'm going to have to ask you to stop working for Gene and concentrate on your work here. However, if you want to work for Gene after four o'clock, that's fine by me."

"But I have to pick up my kids by five o'clock," Rodney exclaimed. "I have to leave by four."

"I'm sorry, Rodney, that's the way it has to be."

"Do it for just one more week," Gene said when Rodney told him what Tony had said. "I'll explain it all to Tony."

"Okay," Rodney said, "but just for one more week."

"I understand your problem," Tony said when Gene approached him, "but it's affecting Rodney's work. He's very loyal to you and grateful for all the help you've given him, but he has responsibilities here. He's working on a very important project, and he needs to devote his full attention to it. He has to be on his toes, but he comes back from lunch very anxious and irritable. You'll just have to find someone else."

"But it was his project," Gene said, becoming upset. "He's the only one in my department who has the expertise to work on it."

"He *was* in your department," Tony said controlling his temper. "He's in my department now."

"He's in your department on my recommendation!" Gene flared. "I was the one to get him the extra training he needed to qualify for the promotion and to complete the project he was working on. I don't have anybody else who knows all about the project."

"Well, then, you'd better get someone," Tony said angrily.

The next morning Rodney came in early to work on the project. Gene was in an all-day project meeting and hadn't seen Rodney to relate the conversation he had had with Tony. At lunch time, Rodney again returned to his old department to continue work. About a half hour later, one of his co-workers came looking for him.

"Hey, Rodney, she said. "Mr. Ortega was looking for you. When I told him you were here, he blew up. I think you'd better talk to him."

Source: Reprinted, by permission of publisher, from MANAGEMENT SOLUTIONS, June 1987. © 1987 American Management Association, New York. All rights reserved.

Questions

1. How much loyalty can a supervisor ask?

2. What can be done to ease the tension between the two managers?

3. What can be done to get both projects completed?

THE ART OF WAR

*S*un Tzu was a warrior/philosopher of China in the 6th century B.C. His book of strategy in war has been studied for well over two thousand years, and still has many useful and practical insights for the current student of business. Form into small groups and discuss what each of the following selections means and how each would apply to a modern-day work organization.

1. **Strategic Assessments**

   A military operation involves deception. Even though you are competent, appear to be incompetent. Though effective, appear to be ineffective.

2. **Doing Battle**

   Those who use the military skillfully do not raise troops twice and do not provide food three times.

3. **Planning a Siege**

   So there are five ways of knowing who will win. Those who know when to fight and when not to fight are victorious. Those who discern when to use many or few troops are victorious. Those whose upper and lower ranks have the same desire are victorious. Those who face the unprepared with preparation are victorious. Those whose generals are able and are not constrained by their governments are victorious. These five are the ways to know who will win.

4. **Formation**

   Therefore the victories of good warriors are not noted for cleverness or bravery. Therefore their victories in battle are not flukes. Their victories are not flukes because they position themselves where they will surely win, prevailing over those who have already lost.

5. **Force**

   Order and disorder are a matter of organization, courage and cowardice are a matter of momentum, strength and weakness are a matter of formation.

6. **Emptiness and Fullness**

   So assess them to find out their plans, both the successful ones and the failures. Incite them to action in order to find out the patterns of their movement and rest.

7. **Armed Struggle**

   An ancient book of military order says, "Words are not heard, so cymbals and drums are made. Owing to lack of visibility, banners and flags are made." Cymbals, drums, banners and flags are used to focus and unify people's ears and eyes. Once people are unified, the brave cannot proceed alone, the timid cannot retreat alone—this is the rule for employing a group.

8. **Adaptations**

   Therefore there are five traits that are dangerous in generals: Those who are ready to die can be killed; those who are intent on living can be captured; those who are quick to anger can be shamed; those who are puritanical can be disgraced; those who love people can be troubled.

9. **Manoeuvering Armies**

   To be violent at first and wind up fearing one's people is the epitome of ineptitude.

10. **Terrain**

    If you are so nice to them [your soldiers] that you cannot employ them, so kind to them that you cannot command them, so casual with them that you cannot establish order, they are like spoiled children, useless.

11. **Nine Grounds**

    Confront them with annihilation, and they will then survive; plunge them into a deadly situation, and they will then live. When people fall into danger, they are then able to strive for victory.

12. *Fire Attack*

A government should not mobilize an army out of anger, military leaders should not provoke war out of wrath. Act when it is beneficial, desist if it is not. Anger can revert to joy, wrath can revert to delight, but a nation destroyed cannot be returned to existence, and the dead cannot be restored to life. Therefore an enlightened government is careful about this, a good military leadership is alert to this. This is the way to secure a nation and keep the armed forces whole.

13. *On the Use of Spies*

One cannot use spies without sagacity and knowledge, one cannot use spies without humanity and justice, one cannot get the truth from spies without subtlety. This is a very delicate matter indeed. Spies are useful everywhere.

SOURCE: From THE ART OF WAR, by Sun Tzu, translated by Thomas Cleary. © 1988 by Thomas Cleary. Reprinted by arrangement with Shambhala Publications Inc., 300 Massachusetts Ave., Boston, MA 02115.

REFERENCES

Academy of Management (1990). "The Academy of Management code of ethical conduct." *Academy of Management Journal* 33: 901-908.

Academy of Management (1992). "The Academy of Management code of ethical conduct." *Academy of Management Journal* 35: 1135-1142.

Bass, Bernard M. (1985). *Leadership and Performance Beyond Expectations.* New York: Free Press.

Bass, Bernard M., & Bruce J. Avolio (1993). *Improving Organizational Effectiveness Through Transformational Leadership.* Thousand Oaks, CA: Sage Publications, Inc.

Bass, Bernard M., & Bruce J. Avolio (1989). "Potential biases in leadership measures: How prototypes, leniency, and general satisfaction relate to ratings and rankings of transformational and transactional leadership constructs." *Educational and Psychological Measurement* 49: 509-527.

Bennis, Warren, & Bert Nanus (1985). *Leaders: The Strategies for Taking Charge.* New York: Harper and Row.

Blake, Robert R., & Anne Adams McCanse (1991). *Leadership Dilemmas—Grid Solutions.* Houston: Gulf Publishing Company.

Blake, Robert R., & Jane Srygley Mouton (1985). *The Managerial Grid III: The Key to Leadership Excellence.* Houston: Gulf Publishing Company.

Boal, Kimberly B., & John M. Bryson (1988). "Charismatic leadership: A phenomenological and structural approach." In James G. Hunt, B. Rajaram Baliga, H. Peter Dachler, & Chester A. Schriesheim (Eds.), *Emerging Leadership Vistas* (pp. 11-28). Lexington, MA: D.C. Heath and Company.

Bower, Joseph Lyon, & Martha Wagner Weinberg (1988). "Statecraft, strategy, and corporate leadership." *California Management Review*, 30(2), 39-56.

Brickman, Philip (1978). "Is it real?" In John H. Harvey, William John Ickes, & Robert F. Kidd (Eds.), *New Directions in Attribution Research*, Vol. 2 (pp. 5-34). Hillsdale, NJ: Lawrence Erlbaum Associates.

Calder, Bobby J. (1977). "An attribution theory of leadership." In Barry M. Staw & Gerald R. Salancik (Eds.), *New Directions in Organizational Behavior* (pp. 179-204). Chicago: St. Clair.

Caulkin, Simon (1993). "The lust for leadership." *Management Today*, November 1993, pp. 38-43.

Chen, Chao C., & James R. Meindl (1991). "The construction of leadership images in the popular press: The case of Donald Burr and People Express." *Administrative Science Quarterly* 36: 521-551.

Dansereau, Fred, Jr., George Graen, & William J. Haga (1975). "A vertical dyad linkage approach to leadership within formal organizations: A longitudinal investigation of the role making process." *Organizational Behavior and Human Performance* 13: 46-78.

Day, David V., & Robert G. Lord (1988). "Executive leadership and organizational performance: Suggestions for a new theory and methodology." *Journal of Management* 14: 453-464.

Dobbins, Gregory H., & Stephanie J. Platz (1986). "Sex differences in leadership: How real are they?" *Academy of Management Review* 11: 118-127.

Doktor, Robert H. (1990). "Asian and American CEOs: A comparative study." *Organizational Dynamics* 18(3): 46-56.

Eagly, Alice H., & Blair T. Johnson (1990). "Gender and leadership style: A meta-analysis." *Psychological Bulletin* 108: 233-256.

Eagly, Alice H., Mona G. Makhijani, & Bruce G. Klonsky (1992). "Gender and the evaluation of leaders: A meta-analysis." *Psychological Bulletin* 111: 3-22.

Evans, Martin G. (1970). "The effects of supervisory behavior on the path-goal relationship." *Organizational Behavior and Human Performance* 5: 277-298.

Fiedler, Fred E. (1967). *A Theory of Leadership Effectiveness.* New York: McGraw-Hill.

Fiedler, Fred E. (1986). "The contribution of cognitive resources and behavior to organizational performance." *Journal of Applied Social Psychology* 16: 532-548.

Fiedler, Fred E., & Martin M. Chemers (1984). *Improving Leadership Effectiveness: The Leader Match Concept,* 2nd edition. New York: John Wiley & Sons Inc.

Fiedler, Fred E., & Joe E. Garcia (1987). *New Approaches to Leadership: Cognitive Resources and Organizational Performance.* New York: John Wiley & Sons Inc.

Fiedler, Fred E., & Robert J. House (1988). "Leadership theory and research: A report of progress." In Cary L. Cooper & Ivan T. Robertson (Eds.), *International Review of Industrial and Organizational Psychology* (pp. 73-92). New York: John Wiley & Sons Inc.

Field, Richard H.G. (1982). "A test of the Vroom-Yetton normative model of leadership." *Journal of Applied Psychology* 67: 523-532.

Field, Richard H.G. (1989). "The self-fulfilling prophecy leader: Achieving the Metharme effect." *Journal of Management Studies* 26: 151-175.

Graen, George B., & James F. Cashman (1975). "A role-making model of leadership in formal organizations: A developmental approach." In James G. Hunt & Larry L. Larson (Eds.), *Leadership Frontiers* (pp. 143-165). Kent, Ohio: The Comparative Administration Research Institute, Graduate School of Business Administration, Kent State University.

Graen, George B., & Terri A. Scandura (1987). "Toward a psychology of dyadic organizing." *Research in Organizational Behavior* 9: 175-208.

Graen, George B., & M. Uhl-Bien (1991). "The transformation of work group professionals into self-managing and partially self-designing contributors: Toward a theory of leadership-making." *Journal of Management Systems* 3(3): 33-48.

Heller, Trudy (1989). "Conversion processes in leadership succession: A case study." *Journal of Applied Behavioral Science* 25: 65-77.

Hersey, Paul, & Kenneth Blanchard (1969). "Life-cycle theory of leadership." *Training and Development Journal* 23: 26-34.

Hersey, Paul, & Kenneth Blanchard (1988). *Management of Organizational Behavior: Utilizing Human Resources.* 5th edition. Englewood Cliffs, NJ: Prentice Hall.

House, Robert J. (1971). "A path-goal theory of leader effectiveness." *Administrative Science Quarterly* 16: 321-339.

House, Robert J. (1977). "A 1976 theory of charismatic leadership." In James G. Hunt & Larry L. Larson (Eds.), *Leadership: The Cutting Edge* (pp. 189-207). Carbondale, IL: Southern Illinois University Press.

House, Robert J., & Terence R. Mitchell (1974). "Path-goal theory of leadership." *Journal of Contemporary Business* 3(4): 81-97.

House, Robert J., William D. Spangler, & James Woycke (1991). "Personality and charisma in the U.S. presidency: A psychological theory of leader effectiveness." *Administrative Science Quarterly* 36: 364-396.

Howell, Jane M., & Bruce J. Avolio (1992). "The ethics of charismatic leadership: Submission or liberation?" *Academy of Management Executive* 6(2): 43-54.

Howell, Jane M., & Bruce J. Avolio (1993). "Transformational leadership, transactional leadership, locus of control, and support for innovation: Key predictors of consolidated-business-unit performance." *Journal of Applied Psychology* 78: 891-902.

Howell, Jon P., & Peter W. Dorfman (1981). "Substitutes for leadership: Test of a construct." *Academy of Management Journal* 24: 714-728.

Howell, Jon P., & Peter W. Dorfman (1986). "Leadership and substitutes for leadership among professional and non-professional workers." *Journal of Applied Behavioral Science* 22: 29-46.

Howell, Jon P., David E. Bowen, Peter W. Dorfman, Steven Kerr, & Philip M. Podsakoff (1990). "Substitutes for leadership: Effective alternatives to ineffective leadership." *Organizational Dynamics* 19(1): 21-38.

Kerr, Stephen, & John Jermier (1978). "Substitutes for leadership: Their meaning and measurement." *Organizational Behavior and Human Performance* 22: 375-403.

Levine, John M., & Richard L. Moreland (1990). "Progress in small group research." *Annual Review of Psychology* 41: 585-634.

Lewin, Kurt, Ronald Lippitt, & Ralph K. White (1939). "Patterns of aggressive behavior in experimentally created social climates." *Journal of Social Psychology* 10: 271-301.

Lord, Robert G., & Rosalie J. Hall (1992). "Contemporary views of leadership and individual differences." *Leadership Quarterly* 3: 137-157.

Ludwig, Dean C., & Clinton O. Longnecker (1993). "The Bathsheba syndrome: The ethical failure of successful leaders." *Journal of Business Ethics* 12: 265-273.

Manz, Charles C. (1992). *Mastering Self-Leadership: Empowering Yourself for Personal Excellence.* Englewood Cliffs, NJ: Prentice Hall.

Manz, Charles C., & Henry P. Sims, Jr. (1984). "Searching for the 'Unleader': Organizational member views on leading self-managed groups." *Human Relations* 37: 409-424.

Manz, Charles C., & Henry P. Sims, Jr. (1987). "Leading workers to lead themselves: The external leadership of self-managing work teams." *Administrative Science Quarterly* 32: 106-128.

Manz, Charles C., & Henry P. Sims, Jr. (1989). *SuperLeadership: Leading Others to Lead Themselves.* Englewood Cliffs, NJ: Prentice Hall, Inc.

McConkey, Dale D. (1989). "Are you an administrator, a manager, or a leader?" *Business Horizons,* September-October 1989, pp. 15-21.

Meindl, James R., Sanford B. Ehrlich, & Janet M. Dukerich (1985). "The romance of leadership." *Administrative Science Quarterly* 30: 78-102.

Misumi, Jyuji, & Mark F. Peterson (1985). "The Performance-Maintenance (PM) theory of leadership: Review of a Japanese research program." *Administrative Science Quarterly* 30: 198-223.

Nadler, David A., & Michael L. Tushman (1990). "Beyond the charismatic leader: Leadership and organizational change." *California Management Review* 32(2): 77-97.

Neck, Chris P., & Charles C. Manz (1992). "Thought self-leadership: The influence of self-talk and mental imagery on performance." *Journal of Organizational Behavior* 13: 681-699.

Peters, Lawrence H., Darrell D. Hartke, & John T. Pohlmann (1985). "Fiedler's contingency theory of leadership: An application of the meta-analysis procedures of Schmidt and Hunter." *Psychological Bulletin* 97: 274-285.

Pfeffer, Jeffrey (1977). "The ambiguity of leadership." *Academy of Management Review* 2: 104-112.

Phillips, James S., & Robert G. Lord (1986). "Notes on the practical and theoretical consequences of implicit leadership theories for the future of leadership measurement." *Journal of Management* 12: 31-41.

Rost, Joseph, & Anthony Smith (1992). "Leadership: A postindustrial approach." *European Management Journal* 10: 193-201.

Rotter, Julian B. (1966). "Generalized expectancies for internal versus external control of reinforcement." *Psychological Monographs* 80: Whole number 609.

Schein, Edgar H. (1985). *Organizational Culture and Leadership: A Dynamic View*. San Francisco: Jossey-Bass Inc.

Schermerhorn, John, R., Jr., & Mee-Kau Nyaw (1990). "Managerial leadership in Chinese industrial enterprises." *International Studies of Management & Organization* 20: 9-21.

Stogdill, Ralph M., & Alvin E. Coons (Eds.) (1957). *Leader Behavior: Its Description and Measurement*. Columbus: Ohio, Bureau of Business Research, Ohio State University.

Strube, Michael J., & Joseph E. Garcia (1981). "A meta-analytic investigation of Fiedler's contingency model of leadership effectiveness." *Psychological Bulletin* 90: 307-321.

Thomas, Alan Berkeley (1988). "Does leadership make a difference to organizational performance?" *Administrative Science Quarterly* 33: 388-400.

Tzu, Sun (1988). *The Art of War*. Translated by Thomas Cleary. Boston: Shambhala Publications, Inc.

Van Seters, David A., & Richard H.G. Field (1990). "The evolution of leadership theory." *Journal of Organizational Change Management* 3(3): 29-45.

Vecchio, Robert P. (1987). "Situational leadership theory: An examination of a prescriptive theory." *Journal of Applied Psychology* 72: 444-451.

Vroom, Victor H., & Arthur G. Jago (1978). "On the validity of the Vroom-Yetton model." *Journal of Applied Psychology* 63: 151-162.

Vroom, Victor H., & Arthur G. Jago (1988). *The New Leadership: Managing Participation in Organizations*. Englewood Cliffs, N.J.: Prentice Hall, Inc.

Vroom, Victor H., & Philip W. Yetton (1973). *Leadership and Decision Making*. Pittsburgh: University of Pittsburgh Press.

Waterman, Bob (1988). "The Pygmalion effect." *Success*, October 1988, page 8.

Weber, Max (1946). "The sociology of charismatic authority." In H.H. Mills & C.W. Mills (Editors and translators) from Max Weber, *Essays in Sociology*, New York: Oxford University Press.

Yukl, Gary A. (1989a). "Managerial leadership: A review of theory and research." *Journal of Management* 15: 251-289. This article is a good place to start for an in-depth review of the leadership literature.

Yukl, Gary A. (1989b). *Leadership in Organizations*, 2nd ed. Englewood Cliffs, N.J.: Prentice Hall.

Yukl, Gary A. & David D. Van Fleet (1992). "Theory and research on leadership in organizations." In Marvin D. Dunnette and Leaetta M. Hough (Eds.) *Handbook of Industrial and Organizational Psychology* (Second edition, Volume 3, pp. 147-197). This chapter is an update of Gary Yukl's 1989(a) leadership review.

FURTHER READING

An overview of leadership research is offered by James G. Hunt (1993) in his book *Leadership: A New Synthesis,* Thousand Oaks, CA: Sage Publications.

For a discussion of how organizations can help to create transformational leaders through recruitment, training, and organization design, see Bernard M. Bass (1990), "From transactional to transformational leadership: Learning to share the vision," *Organizational Dynamics* 18(3): 19-31. A follow-up book edited by Bernard M. Bass and Bruce J. Avolio is titled *Improving Organizational Effectiveness through Transformational Leadership*, published in 1993 by Sage Publications, Inc.

Two articles by McGill's Jay Conger look at the concept of "empowerment"—the transfer of power from the leader to subordinates; and the importance of communicating the leader's vision. See Jay A. Conger (1989), "Leadership: The art of empowering others," *Academy of Management Executive* 3: 17-24; and Jay A. Conger (1991), "Inspiring others: The language of leadership," *Academy of Management Executive* 5(1): 31-45.

A practical look at how leader emergence differs by gender is found in the article by Gregory H. Dobbins, William S. Long, Esther J. Dedrick, and Tanya Cheer Clemons (1990), "The role of self-monitoring and gender on leader emergence: A laboratory and field study," *Journal of Management* 16: 609-618. Also see Judith B. Rosener (1990), "Ways women lead," *Harvard Business Review*, November/December 1990, 119-125; and "Men, women & leadership" by Sharon Nelton in the May 1991 issue of *Nation's Business*. Leadership and diversity are examined in Ann M. Morrison's 1992 book *The New Leaders: Guidelines on Leadership Diversity in America,* published by Jossey-Bass.

Two articles that deal with leadership as a system of beliefs and its influence on social practice are by Marta B. Calás and Linda Smircich. See their 1988 article "Reading leadership as a form of cultural analysis" in James Gerald Hunt, B. Rajaram Baliga, H. Peter Dachler, & Chester A. Schriesheim (Eds.), *Emerging Leadership Vistas*, pages 201-226, Lexington Books. Also see their 1991 article "Voicing seduction to silence leadership" in *Organization Studies* 12: 567-602.

A book-length treatment of the interrelationship of leadership and the self-fulfilling prophecy in organizations is by Dov Eden (1990), *Pygmalion in Management: Productivity as a Self-Fulfilling Prophecy,* Lexington, MA: D.C. Heath and Company. An article that offers a managerial viewpoint on how to use positive expectations in the workplace to improve performance is by Richard H.G. Field and David A. Van Seters (1988), "Management by Expectations (MBE): The power of positive prophecy," *Journal of General Management* 14: 19-33.

Articles of interest on the topic of ethics and leadership are: Ronald B. Morgan (1993), "Self- and co-worker perceptions of ethics and their relationships to leadership and salary," *Academy of Management Journal* 36: 200-214; Georges Enderle (1987), "Some perspectives of managerial ethical leadership," *Journal of Business Ethics* 6: 657-663; and Patrick E. Murphy (1989), "Creating ethical corporate structures," *Sloan Management Review* 30(2): 81-87.

An article that concludes that individuals can be trained to exhibit charismatic leader behaviour—implying that charisma is not so much a personality characteristic as a behaviour—is that by University of Western Ontario's Jane M. Howell and UBC's Peter J. Frost (1989), "A laboratory study of charismatic leadership," *Organizational Behavior and Human Decision Processes* 43: 243-269.

Manfred F.R. Kets de Vries is well known for his examination of leadership based on psychoanalytic principles. A book of essays on the psychology of leadership is his *Leaders, Fools, and Impostors*, published in 1993 by Jossey-Bass. This book also includes a number of case studies that are used to illustrate the concepts discussed. Two articles of particular interest in which Kets de Vries examines needs and dependence in the leader-follower relationship are "The dark side of CEO succession," *Harvard Business Review*, January/February 1988, pages 56-60; and "Leaders who self-destruct: The causes and cures," in *Organizational Dynamics*, 1989, Volume 17(4): pages 5-17. The first article offers an interesting look at problems of life at the top of organizations, while the second examines what causes some leaders to "derail" at the top of the organization.

CHAPTER 11

DECISION MAKING

CHAPTER OUTLINE

Rational and Expert Models of Information Processing

    At the Individual Level

    At the Group Level

    At the Organizational Level

Ethics in Decision Making

    At the Individual Level

    At the Group Level

    At the Organizational Level

Improving Decision Making

    At the Individual Level

    At the Group Level

    At the Organizational Level

Conclusion

QUESTIONS TO CONSIDER

- What types of decisions are there?

- How can an individual make good decisions?

- How can a group make good decisions?

- What are the factors influencing organizational decision making?

- How can organizations promote ethical decision making?

- How does a person make a decision when confronted with an ethical dilemma?

- What are the common errors in decision making at the individual, group, and organizational levels?

Leaders make decisions in organizations, but decision making is not restricted to those who are leaders. All the members of an organization have to make decisions as part of their normal job activities. How to speak to a customer, whether or not to give a discount to close a sale, approving further investment in the development of a new product, and how late to work one evening—all these are decisions that an individual has to make. Work groups also make decisions. These might concern what products to promote for sale, how to improve customer service, how to eliminate flaws and improve the quality and reliability of a consumer good, or what actions the group will take in response to a critical situation. Finally, decisions are made at the organizational level that affect the policies, strategies, and actions of the organization as a whole. In this chapter we will examine decision making in organizations at the levels of the individual, the group, and the organization.

There are three areas of organizational decision making that we will consider. The first is the distinction between rational and expert models of information processing. This is the difference between what can be thought of as the "best" way to decide and how people in organizations actually decide. The second area we will consider is how ethical criteria can be included in the making of decisions. Thirdly, we will explore some known techniques for improving the quality of decision making in organizations.

RATIONAL AND EXPERT MODELS OF INFORMATION PROCESSING
At the Individual Level

Rational model of decision making

The view that decisions can be made based on logic to determine the optimal decision.

For tasks that have an answer, the **rational model of decision making** can be used to determine the optimal decision. For instance, a person who seeks the shortest route between home and work can determine what roads to use on the way to work. Using this model (Exhibit 11.1) the problem is first identified—what roads to use. Then the objectives are defined—to find the shortest route. A predecision is made (Wedley & Field, 1984) concerning who to involve in the problem and how the decision will be made. The decision maker may ask a friend, consult a map on his own, or decide to experiment with different routes.

Alternatives are then generated such that no possible route is left unconsidered. This is called an exhaustive search. Then a choice is made of the best alternative, here the shortest route. What remains is to implement the choice by actually driving to work on the roads chosen. Finally, as a last step, the decision maker must follow up on the decision by considering how well it is working over time. If roads close or new roads open, alternatives will change and a new decision will be required.

But the rational model can become complicated by a mix of objectives. Perhaps the criterion for the decision is not simply to choose the shortest route. Multiple criteria might be to balance the comfort of the drive, the length of the route, and the time taken to drive it. Now, in order to be rational, the decision maker must assign weights to each of these three criteria. The weights are how important each is compared to the others. Given these weights a new optimal route can be chosen. While the decision still appears to fit the rational model, assumptions have now been built into the solution. Criterion weights are assumptions because they are based on the values and preferences of the decision maker.

Even problem identification makes presumptions on rationality. One might ask, why travel to work in the first place? Perhaps the work could be done from home or another location. Or why assume that travel must be on roads in a vehicle? The individual might be able to walk to work or bike to work on special paths.

Programmed decisions

Decisions routinely made in an organization that have a structured and repetitive method of analysis and choice of alternative.

The point we are making here is that even decisions that have an answer and that may be made with the rational model have assumptions built in. These assumptions deal with the way the problem is identified and the way objectives are defined. Even routinely made and **programmed** decisions have assumptions built in. For example, determining whether a

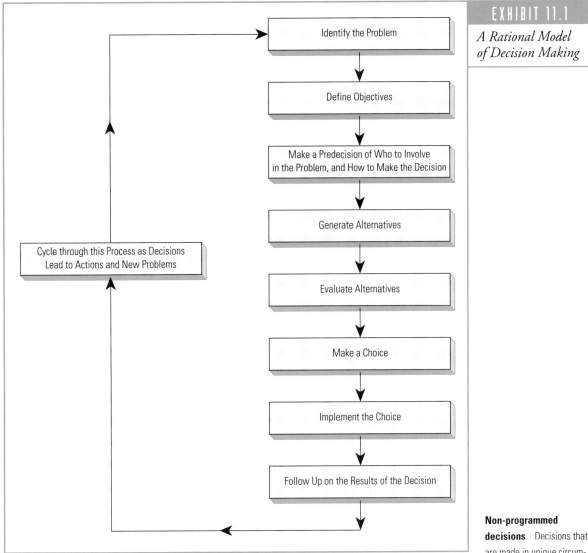

EXHIBIT 11.1

A Rational Model of Decision Making

Non-programmed decisions Decisions that are made in unique circumstances. Their analysis has not yet been routinized.

Expert model The way people in organizations actually go about information processing and decision making, generating and exploring only a limited number of decision alternatives and then using their pre-existing knowledge and simple rules of thumb to make a decision.

Heuristic A rule of thumb about how to approach a problem or how to go about solving it.

client has accumulated enough frequent flyer points to receive a frequent flyer bonus is a programmed decision. The assumptions in this example are the levels at which points qualify for free flights and the number of points needed to qualify for other non-travel prizes.

But sometimes problems do not have one answer. Some are more open-ended. There may be no one answer that could be described as "correct." For instance, how should a new Reebok running shoe be advertised? Creativity may be required to generate problems, objectives, and alternatives. These types of task are **non-programmed** in that they cannot (at least not yet) be programmed onto a computer for machine consideration of alternatives and choice. For non-programmed tasks it is much more difficult to even attempt to appear rational. Here the assumptions of the decision maker are much more visible.

Individuals in organizations can decide rationally, but more often they use an **expert model** of information processing (see Lord & Maher, 1990). They generate and explore only a limited number of decision alternatives. They use their pre-existing knowledge and simple "rules of thumb," called **heuristics**, to make a decision. An example of a decision heuristic used to solve an organizational problem is depicted in this chapter's *Overboard* cartoon.

Bounded rationality
Recognizes that decision makers usually do not have complete information as required by the rational model of decision making. Decisions made are bounded by this lack of information.

Satisficing   The decision maker chooses the first alternative that meets to a satisfactory degree the requirements of the problem.

Nonrational decision
A decision that does not follow the rational model, but is instead based on intuition or "gut feel."

Irrational decision
A decision not based on rationality or non-rationality, but may instead be based on emotion.

Decision makers also act with incomplete information. The Nobel prize-winner Herbert Simon (1976) called this **bounded rationality**. Simon also coined the term **satisficing** to describe the decision maker's choice of the first alternative that meets, to a satisfactory degree, the requirements of the problem.

People in organizations sometimes make decisions based on their intuition. This is usually called deciding by "gut feel." These intuitive decisions may be seen as **nonrational** because they do not follow the traditional rational model. Using intuition, hunches or guesses can be an effective way to decide when the sub-conscious brain provides the conscious brain with information (see, for example, Solomon, 1990).

Using emotion in decision making is quite often seen as **irrational** (for example Simon, 1989). This is the case when work values do not accept emotion as an acceptable foundation for decisions. However, some scholars of decision making argue that emotionality is an acceptable basis for making decisions. They contend that what seems to be boundedly rational decision behaviour may instead be emotionally rational (Mumby & Putnam, 1992). Therefore, the question of what is rational depends on the values of the organizational decision maker.

There are a number of errors that reduce the pure rationality of an individual's decisions. We will discuss five of these errors. The first general category of errors is in how information is perceived and processed. A second type of error occurs because of how a problem is presented—that is, by how it is framed. The third type of error that we will discuss is the automatic and intuitive decision making described in image theory. A fourth error is the escalation of an individual's commitment to a losing course of action. Finally, a fifth type of decision error is the reliance by individuals on scripted behaviour instead of on cognitive decision making.

Information Perception and Processing

People are prone to certain errors when perceiving and analyzing their world. Exhibit 11.2 presents a comprehensive list of these individual biases in decision making. For example, people remember events that are recent or more vivid in their memory. Also, they fail to pay enough attention to the effects of chance or sample size when evaluating the importance of data. For example, people understand chance occurrences very little. Many people think that if "heads" comes up on a coin seven times in a row, for instance, the chance of a "tail" on the next coin toss is greater than .5. This is also called the gambler's fallacy.

Some logical problems are difficult for people to solve because they just don't make intuitive sense. The logical answer fails to agree with what a person feels "should" be the case. For example, if a bullet is dropped from a height of four feet just as another bullet is fired across a level field from a gun four feet above the ground, which bullet hits first? If a wooden cube is 2.5 cm. long on each side, how many form a cube 5 cm. along each edge? The answers are that the bullets hit at the same time, and 8 cubes are needed. Sometimes physical reality and intuitive sense do not agree.

Exhibit 11.2   Biases in Individual Decision Making

Bias	Description
1. *Biases due to ease of recall*	Individuals judge events that are more easily recalled from memory to be more numerous than events of equal frequency whose instances are less easily recalled.
2. *Biases due to the way a memory search is conducted*	Individuals are biased in their assessments of the frequency of events based upon the way their memory structure affects the search process.
3. *Biases due to illusory correlation*	Individuals tend to overestimate the probability of two events co-occurring when their memory recall finds that the two events have occurred together in the past.
4. *Insensitivity to base rates*	Individuals tend to ignore base rates (how often an event is likely to occur) when any other information about the event is provided.
5. *Insensitivity to sample size*	Individuals frequently fail to appreciate the role of sample size in evaluating the accuracy of sample information.
6. *Misconceptions of chance*	Individuals expect that a sequence of events generated from a random process will be representative of the underlying process, even when the sequence is too short for those expectations to be statistically valid.
7. *Regression to the mean*	Individuals fail to note the statistical fact that extreme events tend to regress to the mean on subsequent trials.
8. *Insufficient adjustment*	Individuals make estimates from an initial value (based on past events, random assignment, or whatever else is accessible) and make insufficient adjustments from that estimate.
9. *Conjunctive and disjunctive events bias*	Individuals tend to overestimate the probability of events that occur together (conjunctive events) and underestimate the probability of events that occur separately (disjunctive events)
10. *Overconfidence*	Individuals tend to be overconfident of the accuracy of their judgment when they answer moderately to extremely difficult questions.
11. *The confirmation trap*	Individuals tend to seek confirmatory information for what they think is true and exclude disconfirming information from their search process.
12. *Hindsight*	After finding out whether or not an event occurred, individuals tend to overestimate the degree to which they would have predicted the event without the benefit of hindsight.

Source: Excerpted/Adapted from Chapter 2 of Max H. Bazerman (1994), *Judgment in managerial decision making,* 3rd edition (pp. 45-46). New York: John Wiley & Sons, Inc. © 1994 by John Wiley & Sons, Inc. Reprinted by permission of John Wiley & Sons, Inc.

Two other biases to which individuals are subject are called the confirmation trap and hindsight bias. When falling into the confirmation trap, decision makers look for information that supports what they think is true. Also, they do not look for information that would refute their decision. With hindsight bias, people are likely to overestimate the degree to which they would predict an outcome once they have been informed that the outcome has indeed occurred. Hindsight can be 20/20 vision.

Framing

Framing How a question is put to individuals can determine how they will decide.

Individual choices in decision situations can be affected by the **framing** of the question. Developed by Daniel Kahneman and Amos Tversky (1982, 1984), this concept states that individuals will avoid risk in order to hold onto a gain and will seek risk in order to avoid a loss.

For example (from Bazerman, 1984), consider the following two decision situations. A car manufacturer is in difficulty. It appears that three plants will have to be closed and 6000 employees laid off. Two options have been formulated.

1. *Plan A:* Will save 1 of 3 manufacturing plants and 2000 jobs.
   Plan B: Has a 1/3 probability of saving all 3 plants and all 6000 jobs, but has a 2/3 probability of saving no plants and no jobs. Which plan would you select? About 80% of individuals choose Plan A.

2. *Plan C:* Will result in the loss of 2 of the 3 plants and 4000 jobs.
   Plan D: Has a 2/3 probability of resulting in the loss of all 3 plants and all 6000 jobs, but has a 1/3 probability of losing no plants and no jobs. Which plan would you select? About 80% of individuals choose Plan D.

But Plan D is the same as Plan B! Framing is therefore a boundary condition to pure rationality in decision making.

The above example also illustrates the normative and descriptive sides of decision making. A normative decision is what people should do while a descriptive decision is what people actually do. While an expected value analysis of Plans A & C and B & D show that they are equivalent, people do not really make choices based simply on expected values.

Image Theory

Image theory (Beach, 1990; Beach & Mitchell, 1990) proposes that a decision maker will compare her current image of a project with its trajectory image. The current image is the project's status as presently perceived. The trajectory image is the future state of the project towards which the decision maker is striving. Image theory proposes that when little difference is perceived between current and trajectory images, decision making will be automatic and intuitive. There will be limited analysis of information relating to the project.

When decision makers experience a discrepancy between current and trajectory images, they are then thought to be more likely to engage in controlled and thorough decision processes. However, image theory states that there are two conditions making it less likely that discrepancy between current and trajectory images will be noticed.

The first is that only limited progress towards the trajectory image is likely required to make it and the current image seem compatible. The second is that people are biased in how they search for and process information. They are likely to search for and also be more sensitive to information that indicates the current and trajectory images are in accord.

Escalation of Commitment

The fourth category of individual bias in decision making that we will discuss is **escalation of commitment** to a losing course of action. While it is clear why an individual would become more committed to a decision whose outcomes are positive, why does commitment sometimes increase when outcomes are negative? For example, bank loan officers reviewing poor loan decisions, a project team evaluating lack of progress, and an investment analyst examining declining prices of stocks purchased may all increase their commitment to their initial decision.

Barry Staw and Jerry Ross (1987, 1989) found that objective characteristics of a project were important in determining future commitment to the project. For example, large early losses can cause a project to be abandoned whereas small losses can be endured. As small losses become larger the total loss builds until so much is committed that people will seek future risk to try to avoid the certain loss. If the individual decision maker determines that early losses are due to a temporary problem and that further investment is likely to ensure a good return, then project commitment is likely to increase.

Psychological factors can also cause an individual decision maker to escalate commitment. When sunk costs are not seen as already spent and gone forever the decision maker may invest further to justify his own earlier action. Decision makers tend to become more committed to a course of action when their decision is: explicit and unambiguous; irrevocable; made freely; personally important; made publicly; and made a number of times.

Escalation of commitment
Commitment to a losing course of action that increases when outcomes are negative.

EXPERIENCE IS THE BEST TEACHER

I trace my interest in decision making to my days as a law student, when I was pursuing studies to which I had aspired since childhood but with which I had become disillusioned. I wondered then how I could have become so enamoured of a discipline for which it was increasingly obvious that I was unsuited. Much like someone who has invested considerable effort to see a much anticipated film, however, only to discover that they should have stayed home, I was determined to finish what I had started. Instead of leaving law school to explore my options, I stayed the course and spent several years becoming qualified for a profession that I had no desire to join. I knew then how Groucho Marx felt, in not wanting to join any club that would have him as a member.

At least my time in law school was not entirely wasted, as I was able to reflect on my career options, which is something that I did not do earlier. I eventually ended up studying organizational behaviour. My doctoral dissertation was on the topic of decision making, and focused on why people are often reluctant to abandon losing courses of action. This behaviour has been described as throwing good money after bad, or as having "too much invested to quit." My faculty advisers at Yale would often claim, although I was never quite sure whether they were

joking, that people chose dissertation topics on the basis of the extent to which they could personally relate to the topic. Joke or not, I often think that my interest in escalating commitment, and in decision making in general, stems at least in part from my earlier experience in making a less than optimal career choice.

The consequences of this and other questionable decisions is a reminder to me of the significance of decision making as a field of study. Knowledge of the processes by which good decisions are made, for example, may not guarantee successful outcomes but can at least shift the odds in your favour. In a world characterized by high-velocity social and economic change, the practical importance of the study of decision making is hard to overstate.

Glen Whyte is an Associate Professor at the Faculty of Management, University of Toronto. His work has appeared in numerous management and organizational journals. For one example, see his 1993 article "Escalating commitment in individual and group decision making: A prospect theory approach," Organizational Behavior and Human Decision Processes, Volume 54, pages 430-455. Also see McKay (1994)

Scripts

Script Norms about a sequence of behaviours.

Our final category of individual decision making bias is that of scripts. "Human problem solving is basically a form of means-ends analysis that aims at discovering a process description of the path that leads to a desired goal" (Simon, 1981, p. 223). These solution paths become encoded in the mind as a generalized sequence of events, which is called a **script**. Scripts wear "conceptual ruts" into the mind which, like wagons that wore physical ruts into stone streets, make it easier to travel that path but harder to get out of the ruts.

Blake Ashforth and Yitzhak Fried (1988) argue that a script can therefore generate behaviour and decision making that is relatively "mindless." That is, with little conscious thought and little or no real problem solving. Much behaviour in organizations is based on scripts that fall within the subordinate's normal range of actions. Conscious decision making is therefore only triggered when something happens that is out of the ordinary. But even non-routine decisions can be broken down into pieces to which the decision maker can apply general procedures. Therefore, scripts may be used even in unusual situations.

Stress can also cause a decision maker to fall back on a previously learned script. This threat-rigidity response can make change more difficult for individuals, groups, and organizations. It is explored in more detail in this chapter's *If You Can't Ride Two Horses at Once, You Shouldn't Be in the Circus* feature.

A last and important point made by Ashforth and Fried is that a situation only partially perceived can trigger a script, which then takes over the decision maker's perceptions, filling in any perceptual gaps that exist. Routines that are learned very well can make thinking about the situation that actually exists more difficult. This can have significant effects on organizational performance (for an example, see Gersick & Hackman, 1990, pp. 65-67).

IF YOU CAN'T RIDE TWO HORSES AT ONCE, YOU SHOULDN'T BE IN THE CIRCUS

Barry Staw, Lance Sandelands, and Jane Dutton make the case that reactions to threat are similar for individuals, groups and organizations. The overall rule that they proposed is that under threat information processing is reduced so that decision making becomes easier. Responses are restricted and become more rigid. This is called the "threat-rigidity effect." For individuals, threat creates psychological stress and anxiety which results in restriction in information processing and the tendency to emit well-learned responses. These help performance when they are appropriate to the threat situation but are harmful when inappropriate.

At the group level, an external threat that the group feels can be met increases cohesiveness, leadership support, and pressure for conformity within the group. Consensus is sought by restricting information, and ignoring creative solutions and people not in tune with the rest of the group. An external threat that the group feels cannot be met causes leadership instability and a loosening of control.

At the organizational level an adverse environmental condition causes an overload of communication channels, reliance on prior knowledge, and a reduction in communication complexity. The result of these is a restriction in information processing. Threat also tends to centralize authority and increase formalization. There is a "mechanistic shift" when under threat for the organization to be more tightly controlled. Efforts may also be made to achieve increased efficiency by controlling costs.

Threat leads to restricted information processing, more rigid decision making, and the emitting of well-learned responses for individuals, groups, and organizations. The structural response, however, differs by level. Organizations under threat become more mechanistic in structure and more controlled. Groups become more controlled when success is foreseen but less controlled when failure in dealing with the threat is anticipated. Individuals under threat can lose their linkages with others and fall back on primitive forms of personal reaction to the threat.

SOURCE: Based on information in Barry M. Staw, Lance E. Sandelands, and Jane E. Dutton (1981), "Threat-rigidity effects in organizational behavior: A multilevel analysis," *Administrative Science Quarterly* 26: 501-524.

At the Group Level

There are three main factors that are known to affect how groups make decisions (Davis, 1992). They are the individual preferences and opinions of group members; the format for group interaction and constraints on interaction; and other procedural rules or norms affecting the group.

It is difficult to have a truly free discussion in groups because social norms, status, structure, the size of the group, and past experience all affect the group's talk about a problem. Procedural routines of the group can also serve to define what the group will do. For instance, an agenda is a procedural routine that schedules the discussion. The agenda can determine who speaks and in what order. It can therefore be a procedural routine that restricts group discussion.

The way that decision preferences become known—through voting or consensus-seeking behaviour—is another such procedural routine. Majority vote, veto, unanimous consensus, or consensus as defined by the group's leader are all rules that restrict group discussion (Tjosvold & Field, 1983).

For example, group discussion that proceeds from more senior to more junior members and ends with a decision made by show-of-hands voting can constrain the less secure and more junior members of the group from speaking their minds and even in voting their actual preferences (for example Asch, 1956).

This chapter's *A Rose by Any Other Name* feature examines differences in group decision routines in Japan and in the West. Among other points it illustrates how even junior members of a Japanese team have input into the group's decisions.

Because of these pressures in groups, decisions made can be subject to some bounds on pure rationality. We will briefly discuss four such bounds: groupthink, the Abilene paradox, group shifts of opinion, and group level escalation of commitment.

Groupthink

Irving Janis (1982) coined the term **groupthink** to describe how highly cohesive groups can overestimate the strengths of the group. This can result in an illusion of the invulnerability of the group and a belief in the inherent morality of the group. The group becomes closed-minded about the decision under consideration, engaging in collective rationalizations about the decision and in stereotyping out-groups. Pressures experienced within the group create group uniformity of opinion. There is self-censorship by individuals and the illusion that the group is in unanimous agreement. Direct pressure is put on dissenters to agree with the group. Self-appointed "mindguards" shield the group from contradictory information.

Groupthink The process by which highly cohesive groups can overestimate the strengths of the group.

One method that can be used to promote open discussion is **constructive controversy**. Group members are provided with discussion rules that encourage everyone to make their opinions known. Conflict that focuses on different approaches to problem solution is promoted. Discussion rules used to promote a constructive controversy discussion are, from Johnson and Johnson (1992):

Constructive controversy A method of group decision making designed to promote information sharing.

1. Be critical of ideas, not people.
2. Focus on making the best possible decision, not on winning.
3. Encourage everyone to participate in the discussion.
4. Listen to everyone's ideas, even if you do not agree.
5. Restate what someone has said if their point is not clear to you.
6. Bring out the ideas and facts supporting both sides of the argument and then try to integrate them.
7. Try to understand both sides of the issue under discussion.
8. Change your mind if the evidence clearly indicates that you should do so.

A ROSE BY ANY OTHER NAME

Robert Ballon of Sophia University in Tokyo makes the case that decision making in Japanese industry is a totally different process from decision making in the West. Whereas in the West decision making is *linear*, in Japan it is *circular*.

In Western linear decision making the decision maker originates the problem, then eliminates all but one alternative course of action. Once the decision is made it is implemented by others. Therefore, a gap exists between the decision and its implementation. The making of the decision is quick, but implementation is long.

In Japanese circular decision making the manager is not concerned with a problem's comprehension (to understand it) but its apprehension (to take it for what it is). He takes action in reaction to reality and as a response to a necessity. The Japanese manager is not concerned with the rationality of the decision but its implementation, because he recognizes that a decision does not change reality, only implementation does. To change a decision really means to make another decision, but has the reality been changed? He does not seek to take action that, *if implemented*, would change reality, but to react to the reality that is. The Japanese manager is less concerned with the flow of authority and more concerned with the flow of work, and knowledge is not valued as much as experience.

Since decision and performance are understood in Japan as one move, while the decision process may be long, implementation is quick. The circular process occurs because consensus in Japan is not a consensus of *ideas* but of action. Because the decision and the implementation are interdependent, consensus is highly dynamic, evolving and changing with the implementation itself. The physical conditions in which this circular decision making occur are illustrated by the typical open-office layout shown in Exhibit 11.3, which illustrates how section heads sit and work with their group members instead of making decisions that are then passed down to them.

EXHIBIT 11.3

Typical Layout of a Japanese Administrative Department (With Two Sections)

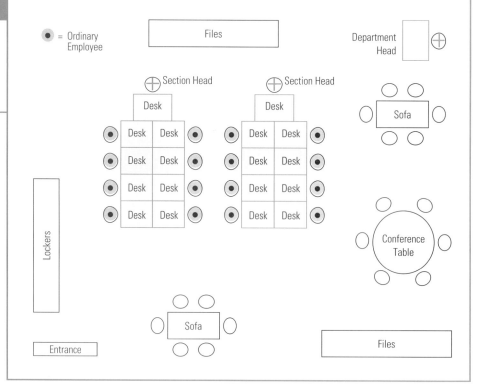

Source: From Ballon (1990), p. 12.

THERE ARE FOUR ELEMENTS OF THE CIRCULAR JAPANESE DECISION:

nemawashi — laying the groundwork, getting support, piecing together a compromise that everyone can live with. This is a process that continues even as the other processes unfold.

uchi-awase — the ironing out of differences, the concern with the concrete details of implementation. Before a decision is made it must be clear to all how it will be implemented, for once made implementation must begin. Decision and action are two sides of the same coin. One cannot occur without the other. As implementation details are considered, more nemawashi may be required to keep working on an evolving compromise. The compromise keeps changing as the implications of how the decision will be implemented are understood.

kaigi — managers get together and make their consensus official by getting together. No formal declaration of a decision is made, but by discussing the decision they agree to it.

ringi-sho — the circulation of a document to all parties concerned, collecting the imprint of the manager's seals [a personal device used for signing a document] which indicate that they have been informed in writing and state their readiness for action. If at this point a manager does not agree with the plan, then nemawashi has failed and he may simply withhold the document from further circulation. If all endorse the decision/action, implementation begins immediately.

SOURCE: Adapted from Robert J. Ballon (1990), *Decision Making in Japanese Industry.* Sophia University Institute of Comparative Culture, Business Series No. 132, Tokyo, Japan: Sophia University. Reprinted by permission. Another interesting article on this topic is Basadur (1992).

The Abilene Paradox

In a classic article about group decision making, Jerry Harvey (1988) makes a case for what he calls the **Abilene paradox**. The paradox is that groups can fail to manage the basic agreement of its members and end up taking an action that no one individual wants! Further, they end up achieving results that are the opposite to their intentions.

The Abilene paradox was named after a trip Dr. Harvey took with his wife and her parents from Coleman, Texas to Abilene on a hot July afternoon. Driving an older car without air conditioning, the 170-kilometre round trip took four hours, including dinner. Back in Coleman, it turned out that no one really wanted to go in the first place. They were in agreement, but their inability to manage that agreement led them to do the opposite of what everyone wanted. The Abilene group privately agreed they would rather stay home, sip lemonade and play dominoes, but they failed to communicate that agreement to each other. Being polite, they agreed to go on the trip because it seemed everyone else wanted to. As a result of the undesired action, each person experienced anger, frustration, irritation, and dissatisfaction with the group.

Dr. Harvey argues that people in organizations take the "trip to Abilene" and do the opposite of what they really want to do for three reasons. The first is action anxiety—the fear to act in the way that can be seen as the most appropriate. The second is negative fantasies—dwelling on the projected negative consequences of acting in the way they want to but not considering the risk of inaction. The third reason is fear of separation from the group—of being ostracized or fired.

To avoid the Abilene paradox, people in organizations need to know what they really want to do, they need to clarify for themselves the real risks of action versus inaction, and they need to confront others by owning up to their own beliefs and feelings without telling others what they must be believing and feeling.

Abilene paradox That groups can fail to manage the basic agreement of their members and end up taking an action that no one individual wants.

Group Shifts of Opinion

This was originally called the "risky shift" (Stoner, 1961, 1968). It has been defined as occurring "when an initial tendency of group members toward a given direction is enhanced following group discussion" (Isenberg, 1986, p. 1141). It is now called **group-induced attitude polarization**. Daniel Isenberg offers two major explanations for this phenomenon.

Group-induced attitude polarization When an initial tendency of group members toward a given direction is enhanced following group discussion.

1. Social Comparison Processes People are motivated to both perceive and present themselves in a socially desirable light. When members of a group do this, those on the less desirable side of an issue change their opinion to be more socially desirable. The result is an average shift in the direction of greater perceived social value.

2. Persuasive Argumentation Theory An individual's position on an issue is influenced by the number and persuasiveness of the arguments that the person can recall and their perceived validity and novelty. Arguments raised in a group can polarize scattered individual opinions so that opinions become more alike. It seems, therefore, that attitude polarization is simply a characteristic of how groups make decisions.

Group decisions can be more risky, more cautious, or less dispersed than the average of individual decisions (Davis, 1992). These effects may be explained by considering that group discussion serves to moderate individual framing effects (Bazerman, 1984). For instance, if an initial problem scenario is negatively framed, the risky choices made by individuals will be moderated by the group discussion as it examines the problem from both positive and negative sides. A cautious group shift will then be found. Conversely, in a positively framed situation the cautious choices of individuals will be moderated by the group discussion and a risky group shift will be found.

Group Level Escalation of Commitment

In a group situation, escalation is more likely under several conditions: when the decision maker does not want others to know about the losing course of action or is concerned with saving face, when project failure would threaten the decision maker's social identity, and when there are social rewards for persistence and eventual success.

Group versus Individual Decision Making

Now that we have examined individual and group decision making, we are in a position to compare the assets and liabilities of each. Group decisions can be either less or more effective than those made by individuals.

Perhaps one of the most important factors affecting the quality of a group decision is the nature of the problem. Those problems that need to be considered as a whole and cannot be broken down into pieces without losing the essence of the problem are best left to individuals working on their own. But any problem that requires more time and effort than can be supplied by one individual is likely to be more effectively solved by a group. When problems can be separated into component parts, the special skills and talents of group members can be applied to the parts to which they are most suited.

Another advantage of group problem solving is that group members jointly explore a problem, understand how it was analyzed and why a certain decision was reached. This can benefit implementation of decision actions and acceptance of the decision reached.

Groups are likely to make better decisions than individuals when group members bring a diverse fund of knowledge to a problem. Groups usually do better in an absolute sense than individuals working on their own (Davis, 1992). Also, joint exploration by group members of their individual assumptions can be of benefit to the group's problem analysis and decision. An experiential exercise that allows comparison of group to individual problem solving is provided at the end of this chapter. It is the "Mist Ridge" exercise.

While there are advantages to group problem solving, there are disadvantages as well. One is **process losses**. As members are added to a group there are more and more possible relationships among the members. This increases the likelihood that subgroups will form. Subgrouping, if not based on task or problem lines, can tend to make more difficult the sharing of ideas and information among group members.

Process losses The decrease in group performance as members are added to the group.

Also, the larger the decision making group the less time is available for each member in open discussion. This means that some members will not contribute their ideas to the group as much as others. Depending on the knowledge of the more silent member, the group's decision quality can be lower than its potential. Because adding members increases the group's knowledge base but increases process losses, adding to a group beyond four or five members usually has little positive influence on decision quality.

When a group has **diversity** in membership it is heterogeneous. One advantage of diversity is that a wider range of individual perspectives is available and a greater number of different ideas will be generated. Creativity, innovation, and group problem solving may be improved, along with organizational flexibility (Cox & Blake, 1991). But a disadvantage to heterogeneity is that there may be a lack of cohesion within the group and difficulty in group members understanding each other. The skills and abilities of a group's leader, if one exists, are important factors in how a group's size and membership become assets or liabilities in group problem solving. Leaders with training in methods of decision making that are appropriate for different tasks, and who have enough conflict handling and group participation skills, can make groups more effective.

Diversity Heterogeneity in group membership.

At the Organizational Level

While it is the individuals and groups in organizations that make decisions, the organization itself provides a context for those decisions and actions.

An early and important view that the rational model of decision making was not used in organizations was made by Charles Lindblom (1959). He argued the rational model assumes intellectual capabilities that individuals do not have, that complete information is rarely available and that there is time and money to explore all options though neither is available. Lindblom pointed out that people in organizations **muddle through** by making decisions that are a series of successive limited comparisons of the present state of the organization to possible future states. Each new decision is therefore affected by all the organization's decisions that have gone before.

Muddling through The argument that people in organizations make decisions that are a series of successive limited comparisons of the present state of the organization to possible future states.

Somewhat later Michael Cohen, James March, and Johan Olsen (1972) described their **garbage can model of organizational decision making**. While they agreed that problems in organizations can be defined and solved in a series of orderly steps (problem→ alternatives→ evaluation→ choice), they also suggested that things are not always so straightforward. Sometimes "an organization is a collection of choices looking for problems, issues and feelings looking for decision situations in which they might be aired, solutions looking for issues to which they might be the answer, and decision makers looking for work" (Cohen and others, 1972, p. 2).

Garbage can model of organizational decision making A model of organizational decision making that sees the organization as choices looking for problems, issues and feelings looking for decision situations, solutions looking for issues, and decision makers looking for work.

To better understand decision making in such a "garbage can" organization, consider decision making as an unusual game of soccer. In this game the soccer balls are problems, the field is the organization, and a decision is made when a goal is scored.

Consider a round, sloped, multi-goal soccer field on which individuals play soccer. Many different people (but not everyone) can join the game (or leave it) at different times. Some people can throw balls into the game or remove them. Individuals while they are in the game try to kick whatever ball comes near them in the direction of goals they like and away from goals that they wish to avoid. The slope of the field produces a bias in how the balls fall and what goals are reached ... (March and Romelaer, 1976, p. 276).

A study of organizational decision making that found elements of muddling through and garbage cans was by Henry Mintzberg and colleagues (1976). They studied 25 non-programmed, strategic decisions that took place over several years. Examples of decisions studied are an airline choosing new jet aircraft, a consulting firm negotiating a merger, and a hospital instituting a new form of treatment. They found that the decision situation was ambiguous with few givens, that individuals gathered information and developed alternatives simultaneously, and that a series of small choices added up to make a major decision. Further, decision making did not progress from start to finish without hitting barriers (called interrupts) that caused the organization to cycle back to a previous point in the decision making process.

Exhibit 11.4 shows three phases of organizational decision making. At the identification phase the organization usually has little understanding of the decision it faces or the route to the solution. The development phase is marked by a search for ready-made solutions. If these are unavailable or unfound then a custom solution is designed or a ready-made solution is modified. The selection phase was not found to involve setting of choice criteria, evaluating alternatives based on the criteria, and making a choice. Instead, it was a multi-staged, iterative process. It began with an initial screening of alternatives because of time and cognitive constraints. Evaluation/choice was based on judgment or bargaining. Then an authorization was sought from a higher level in the organization's hierarchy.

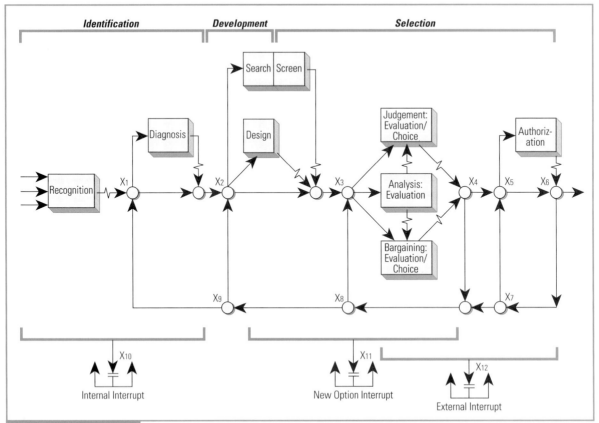

EXHIBIT 11.4

A General Model of the Strategic Decision Process

Source: Reprinted from "The structure of 'unstructured' decision processes" by Henry Mintzberg, Duru Raisinghani, and André Théorêt published in *Administrative Science Quarterly*, 21(2), June 1976 by permission of the Administrative Science Quarterly. Copyright © 1976 by Administrative Science Quarterly.

Interrupts could force the decision back to the identification, development, or selection phases. For instance, the discovery of a new option could send decision making back to the searching and screening of options. Or, if the new option was sufficiently attractive, a new option could speed the decision to a conclusion. External interrupts could be new constraints confronted in the selection phase, for example outside forces blocking a solution.

Escalation of commitment has been found to be caused by organizational forces as well as social, psychological, and perceived project economics (Ross & Staw, 1986). This escalation process is modeled in Exhibit 11.5. An organizational example is found in this chapter's *A Little Knowledge* feature.

The final point that we will make about bounded rationality in organizational decision making is that knowledge and information may themselves be constructed or enacted. People in the organization can create their own reality which then affects their decisions. We usually think of information as objective knowledge and uncertainty as a lack of objective knowledge. But "when we acknowledge the socially constructed nature of information, the focus is shifted from the utility and validity of information to its meaning and the motivation this meaning gives rise to" (Feldman, 1988, p. 87).

The implication is information is not always objective, and can be controlled or distorted. Sometimes organizational members create information and knowledge. Therefore, the person who is able to identify a problem and define it and who can set the premises (or constraints) for a solution can control the decisions and actions of others.

ETHICS IN DECISION MAKING

There are several ways of theorizing about whether or not a given decision is ethical. A broad approach is to compare teleological and deontological moral philosophies (Ferrell and others, 1989). These two approaches are normative. They specify how a person *should* make an ethical decision.

Teleological philosophies determine the moral "worth" of a behaviour by examining its consequences. For instance **utilitarianism** selects the alternative with the greatest good for the greatest number of people as the most moral. "Utilitarian theories are either act or rule utilitarian. An individual acting in line with an *act* utilitarian approach bases decisions solely on their outcomes or consequences, selecting the act which provides the greatest social good. The decision maker following a *rule* utilitarian philosophy evaluates the rule under which the action falls. Following a chosen rule may not lead to the greatest benefit in every situation, but over the long term the rule will result in decisions that lead to the greatest societal benefit" (Premeaux & Mondy, 1993, p. 350). **Egoism** determines the most moral act as the one with the most positive consequences for the individual.

Deontological philosophies examine the moral obligations or commitments that should be necessary for proper conduct. Examples of these are concepts of justice and the basic rights of individuals. The **theory of rights** proposes that individuals have the right to free consent, to privacy, to freedom of conscience, to free speech, and to the due process of law. The **theory of justice** declares that decisions should be based on equity, fairness, and impartiality.

> Individuals should receive differential treatment only when the basis of the treatment is related to the goals and tasks of the organization. The theory of justice further holds that rules should be administered fairly and impartially enforced. Finally, individuals must not be held responsible for matters over which they have no control and injured individuals should be compensated for their injuries by those responsible (Premeaux & Mondy, 1993, p. 350).

There are also descriptive approaches to understanding ethical decision making in organizations. These specify how a person, group, or organization *does* make an ethical decision. We will now consider ethical decision making at the individual, group, and organizational levels.

Teleological philosophies Determine the moral worth of a behaviour by examining its consequences.

Utilitarianism Selects as most moral the alternative with the greatest good for the greatest number of people.

Egoism Determines the most moral act as the one with the most positive consequences for the individual.

Deontological philosophies Examine the moral obligations or commitments that should be necessary for proper conduct.

Theory of rights Proposes that individuals have the right to free consent, to privacy, to freedom of conscience, to free speech, and to due process of law.

Theory of justice Declares that decisions should be based on equity, fairness, and impartiality.

A LITTLE KNOWLEDGE

On April 13, 1966 the Long Island Lighting Company (LILCO) announced plans to build a nuclear power plant in Shoreham, New York. With an estimated cost of $75 million, a 540 megawatt capacity, and a 1973 completion date, LILCO was excited to be entering the nuclear power age of electricity generation. Little did they know that twenty-three years later the plant would still not be operating, would have cost over five billion dollars, and that the plant would be sold to the state of New York.

What happened? How did LILCO get deeper and deeper into a project that seemed straightforward (after all, other nuclear power plants were being built and opened) but ended a failure? Jerry Ross and Barry Staw have examined this case and use their model of organizational escalation of commitment to a losing course of action to understand what went so terribly wrong at Shoreham.

First, initial project economics looked good. However, these estimates of building costs, the cost of capital needed to build the plant, projected revenues from sales of generated electricity, the estimated demand for electricity in 1973, and prices of alternative energy sources such as oil and coal were, by necessity, very imprecise. No one really knew how much oil would cost in 1973 or 1980, or what interest rates would be. Once the project was approved, based on these initial estimates of project economics, bad news started to come in. In 1967 public resistance to LILCO's other planned nuclear plant at Lloyd Harbor caused its abandonment. Resistance then turned to the Shoreham plant. Public hearings were long lasting and contentious, causing unforeseen delays in the granting of the plant's construction permit. When finally granted in 1973, the original completion date, LILCO had already spent $77 million, more than the original estimate for the plant! These negative results, however, were not overwhelming or so unambiguous that they could not be explained away and the project continued. Construction began.

By 1979 the plant's estimated cost was $1300 million. Now psychological and social forces of commitment helped to keep the project moving along. Problems were attributed to the environmental actions of outsiders and

Shoreham managers seemed overconfident about their ability to build the plant on time and on budget. The March 28, 1979 Three Mile Island nuclear accident in Pennsylvania caused new public concern about Shoreham and on June 4, 1979 there was a large public demonstration against the Shoreham plant. In defense, LILCO's chairman appeared in television advertisements extolling the benefits of the Shoreham plant. These public pronouncements may have served to publicly commit LILCO to continuing with Shoreham. Another social force for continuing was that other utilities were successfully building and operating nuclear plants. Though project economics now looked less positive, this decrease was more than made up for by the increase in project commitment caused by psychological and social variables.

By November 1983 construction of the plant was completed and testing was to begin. However, organizational forces had now started to build both in opposition and in support of the Shoreham plant. In opposition, local governments, sensitive to the concerns of their citizens, asked the Nuclear Regulatory Commission (NRC) about the area's evacuation plan. In support, LILCO was hiring personnel with nuclear experience, other interest groups promoting nuclear power were supporting LILCO's efforts, and so much money had now been spent on the Shoreham nuclear plant (almost $4 billion) that Shoreham was a key part of LILCO's future: the company was now being bet on the Shoreham plant opening.

Testing started in January, 1985, but on April 25, 1986 the Chernobyl nuclear power plant in the Ukraine suffered a catastrophic failure. In 1987 state and county governments refused to cooperate with the development of evacuation plans. Though other institutional forces were still strong to continue with the plant and the NRC granted a full operating power license to LILCO for the Shoreham plant, it was instead sold in 1989 to the state of New York. Psychological and social forces supporting its opening had by this point been drastically reduced, and project economics had again become important. Tax write-offs and future rate increases offered by the state of New York for LILCO's other generating plants had made it possible for LILCO to finally get out of its escalating commitment to Shoreham.

SOURCE: Ross and Staw (1993).

SOURCE: Reprinted from Barry M. Staw and Jerry Ross (1989). "Understanding behavior in escalation situations." *Science*, Volume 246, October 13, 1989, p. 219. Copyright © 1989 by the AAAS.

EXHIBIT 11.5

Escalation of Commitment to a Losing Course of Action

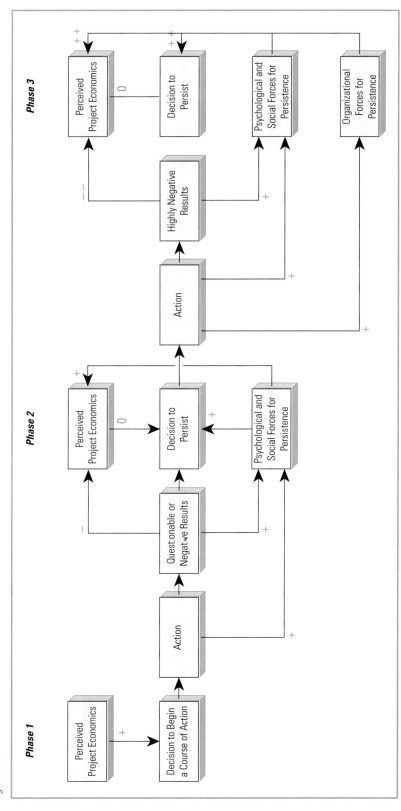

At the Individual Level

When faced with a decision having moral implications, how does an individual decide what to do? Alan Waterman (1988) described two approaches that are used to determine what is moral. They are the taxonomic and the cognitive-developmental.

The Taxonomic Approach

The taxonomic approach divides individuals into four categories using the two criteria of relativism and idealism (Exhibit 11.6). Relativism is whether or not an individual believes it possible to create and use universal moral rules when coming to a decision about a moral question. The high idealist believes that desirable consequences will always occur if the "right" course of action is followed. The low idealist believes that even with the right choice, undesirable consequences can accompany desirable ones.

The four categories describing ethical positions are Absolutists, Exceptionists, Subjectivists, and Situationalists. Absolutists believe in universal moral laws that can be used to determine what is ethical. For example, an employee of an organization may be asked by a customs officer for a bribe so that the organization's goods pass easily and quickly through customs. This is known to happen in some countries. The person taking an absolutist position could decide that the bribe is in effect a form of stealing, and that since stealing is always wrong the bribe should not be offered.

Exceptionists believe that moral absolutes are guides to moral judgments, but are open to exceptions when more desirable outcomes are likely. In our bribery example the moral law against stealing applies, but could be overridden if the item being imported is important medical equipment that will save many lives. In that case the moral imperative to save lives when possible would take precedence.

Subjectivists reject universal moral rules. Instead, moral decisions are based on personal preferences and values. If the person going through customs is not offended by the bribe and, for example, considers it a cost of doing business in that country, then the bribe would be paid.

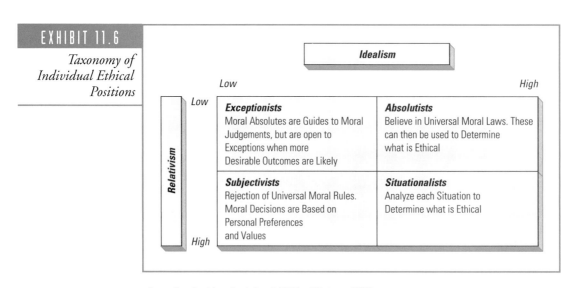

EXHIBIT 11.6

Taxonomy of Individual Ethical Positions

Source: Based on information in Forsyth (1980) and Waterman (1988).

Situationalists analyze each situation to determine what is ethical. Is the bribe against company policy? Is it against the laws of the country where the bribe is being sought and/or against the laws of the home country? Is the bribe a significant amount? Would the costs of not bribing, such as delays, extra transportation charges, etc., be greater than the bribe being asked? Questions like these would be asked by the situationalist to decide what is the ethical response.

People at work therefore are likely to differ in how they analyze an ethical dilemma and on the basis of their choice. A questionnaire designed to help students examine their own positions in this ethical taxonomy is included as this chapter's Self-Diagnostic Exercise. For an example of an ethical dilemma, see this chapter's feature *On the One Hand*.

The Cognitive-Developmental Approach

The cognitive-developmental approach of Lawrence Kohlberg (1969) proposes that individuals progress through six stages of moral development (see Exhibit 11.7). Each stage has its own moral logic. Higher stages are presumed to reflect increased cognitive sophistication and complexity. Therefore, according to Kohlberg, what is considered to be "right" by an individual making an ethical choice depends on that person's stage of moral development.

O N   T H E   O N E   H A N D . . .

TRAVEL FAIR

You have just earned your M.B.A. and are beginning a new job in a large organization. The area manager's position requires that you supervise the work of five field officers. The position demands a great deal of travel, and for the first few months you will be working closely with a new colleague, Joe, who will help you "learn the ropes." Things are going well until it comes time to fill out the travel reimbursement voucher. Joe explains that your actual expenses must not be written in and as a general rule to add in an extra 10 percent to what you really spent. Also, any extraordinary expenses that do not fall under lodging, meals, or travel can be written off under "taxi fares." You question Joe further and finally he says, "Don't worry about it. This is the way we all do it. The difference between what you spend and what you report is yours. These are figures everybody uses. If you start reporting differently you could get us all in trouble. Besides, the per diem allowance is not enough to cover all your expenses when you stay in a major city. The hotel usually takes up the total per diem allowance, and you have to use your own money to be able to eat. But when you report the way I've shown you, you'll make enough money off the cheaper trips to be able to cover the costs of the more expensive ones."

SOURCE: "Travel Fair," written by Cathy Ridyard, appears in James R. Glenn, Jr. (1986), Ethics in Decision Making (pp. 29-30). Copyright © 1986 by James R. Glenn, Jr. Reprinted by permission of John Wiley & Sons, Inc.

O N   T H E   O T H E R   H A N D . . .

On the one hand, taking the exceptionist position, everyone else seems to be over-reporting some expenses. Also, group norms are such that penalties may apply to someone who breaks the informal rules. It seems that the moral rule against stealing can be overlooked in this case.

On the other hand, reporting expenses that are fictitious is stealing money from the company. Even if at other times true expenses are greater than reimbursed by the company, the one case when reported expenses are greater than actual expenses is stealing. The absolutist position therefore is that this over-reporting, even once, is wrong.

What would you do in such a situation?

Exhibit 11.7   Six Stages of Moral Development

	STAGE	WHAT IS CONSIDERED TO BE RIGHT	REASONS FOR DOING RIGHT	SOCIAL PERSPECTIVE OF STAGE
LEVEL ONE — PRECONVENTIONAL *(based on egoism)*				
Stage One	Obedience and punishment orientation	Sticking to rules to avoid physical punishment. Obedience for its own sake.	Avoidance of punishment and the superior power of authorities	Egocentric point of view
Stage Two	Instrumental purpose and exchange	Following rules only when it is in one's immediate interest. Right is an equal exchange, a fair deal.	To serve one's own needs where others have interests too.	Concrete individualistic perspective.
LEVEL TWO — CONVENTIONAL *(based on benevolence)*				
Stage Three	Interpersonal accord, conformity, mutual expectations	Stereotypical "good" behaviour. Living up to what is expected by people close to you.	The need to be a good person in your own eyes and in the eyes of others.	Perspective of the individual in relationships with other individuals.
Stage Four	Social accord and system maintenance	Fulfilling duties and obligations to which you have agreed. Upholding laws except in extreme cases where they conflict with fixed social duties. Contributing to the society, group.	To keep the institution going as a whole, to avoid the breakdown of the system	Differentiates societal point of view from interpersonal agreement or motives.
LEVEL THREE — PRINCIPLED *(based on principle)*				
Stage Five	Social contract and individual rights	Being aware that people hold a variety of values; that rules are relative to the group. Upholding rules because they are the social contract. Upholding nonrelative values and rights regardless of majority opinion.	Obligation to law for the welfare of all.	Prior-to-society perspective: values and rights exist prior to social attachments and contracts.
Stage Six	Universal ethical principles	Following self-chosen ethical principles. When laws violate these principles, act in accord with principles.	Belief in universal moral principles and a sense of personal commitment to them	Perspective of a moral point of view.

SOURCE: Adapted from Linda Klebe Trevino (1986) and Lawrence Kohlberg (1976), "Moral stages and moralization: The cognitive-developmental approach," In Thomas Lickona (Ed.), *Moral Development and Behavior: Theory, Research, and Social Issues* (pp. 34-35), New York: Holt, Rinehart and Winston. Reprinted by permission of Thomas Lickona and the Academy of Management.

Carol Gilligan (1982), however, sees Kohlberg's stages as reflecting more the male experience of ethics based on justice and rights than ethics based on care and responsibility. In Gilligan's developmental model, which may apply to men as well as women, Stage 1 is characterized by caring for the self to ensure survival. During the transition to Stage 2 this judgment is criticized as selfish. At Stage 2 the individual accepts the responsibility of caring for the dependent and unequal. A disequilibrium may then result between care for the self and care for others that when resolved allows the individual to move to Stage 3 of moral development. At this stage the interconnection of the self and the other is realized and that care enhances both others and the self. Both Kohlberg's and Gilligan's approaches recognize that individuals differ in their moral development. This then affects the ethical component of their decisions.

At the Group Level

The constructionist/interactional approach to moral decision making considers that there are no natural principles of justice, and that moral decision making is based on agreements that people in social groups construct among themselves (Waterman, 1988). Therefore, in this group perspective to ethical decision making, moral actions are affected by more than individual moral predispositions but also by social agreements of the "right" way to act.

At the Organizational Level

Consider the Challenger space shuttle disaster, the nuclear devastation at Chernobyl, and the tragedy at Bhopal. Were these "normal" accidents (Perrow, 1984; Weick, 1987) due to inherent flaws in organizational decision making? Or did individual decision makers act unethically? To examine these questions we need to consider the ethical climates within the organizations before they experienced these catastrophes.

The space shuttle Challenger explodes on January 28, 1986.

Bart Victor and John Cullen (1988) identified nine theoretical types of ethical climates in organization (see Exhibit 11.8). They describe three ethical criteria that organizations are based on. These are egoism (maximizing self-interest), benevolence (maximizing joint interest), and adherence to principle (also called deontology). Note that these three levels are the same levels used in Kohlberg's taxonomy shown in Exhibit 11.7.

Locus of analysis specifies the group looked to by members of an organization for their definition of ethical decision criteria. The members of an organization using an individual locus of analysis would look to their own personal ethics for guidance. In an organization having a local locus a person would look to the work group. Cosmopolitan organizational members would find ethical guidance from the social system outside the organization itself. Examples would be a professional association or law society.

The important point Victor and Cullen make is that organizations have ethical climates, and that these climates can differ both across organizations and within organizations.

For example, the ethical code of Shell Canada is shown in this chapter's *Seeing is Believing* feature. This code explicitly forbids Shell employees from engaging in bribery. For Shell there is no clash between money and morality because the ethical decision of what to do when asked for a bribe has already been answered.

IMPROVING DECISION MAKING
At the Individual Level

In order to break out of their conceptual ruts, individuals (and groups) often need to use creativity exercises and specific decision techniques to enhance their creativity (see Exhibit 11.9).

To improve personal decision making a manager can explore how she has made decisions in the past and the resources that are available to her. One approach to improving the predecision—the decision of how to make the decision—is detailed further in this chapter's *A Word to the Wise* feature.

EXHIBIT 11.8

Typical Decision Criteria for Nine Theoretical Types of Ethical Climate

Ethical Criterion	Locus of Analysis		
	Individual	Local	Cosmopolitan
Egoism	Self-Interest	Company Profit	Efficiency
Benevolence	Friendship	Team Interest	Social Responsibility
Principle	Personal Morality	Company Rules and Procedures	Laws and Professional Codes

SOURCE: Reprinted from "The organizational bases of ethical work climates" by Bart Victor and John B. Cullen published in *Administrative Science Quarterly* Volume 33(1), March 1988, by permission of Administrative Science Quarterly. Copyright © 1988 by Administrative Science Quarterly.

There are of course many aids available for rational decision making in organizations. Decision support systems help to present the information required for a decision. Operations research methods can determine optimal solutions given the particular problem statement and variable values.

Expert systems are computer-based decision aids that offer advice or solutions for problems in a particular area that is comparable to the advice of a human expert (Holsapple & Whinston, 1987). Composed of a knowledge base that may be represented as rules, an inference engine that uses these rules and problem information supplied by the user to

Expert systems

Computer-based decision aids that offer advice or solutions for problems in a particular area that are comparable to the advice of a human expert.

SEEING IS BELIEVING

This excerpt from the ethical code of Shell Canada illustrates how the organization attempts to make clear to its members the ethical criteria that should guide their decision making.

SHELL CANADA CODE OF ETHICS

Value Shell Canada employees must continue to demonstrate a commitment to ethical business practices and behaviour in all business relationships in order to safeguard the Company's reputation and credibility. No one in the Company, regardless of his or her position, is ever expected to commit an unethical or illegal act or to instruct other employees to do so.

More specifically, Shell employees must be guided by the following ethics:

Accounting and Auditing Procedures and Controls
Every transaction between the Company and those with whom it deals and every payment, receipt, asset, and liability must be reflected on the books of the Company promptly, accurately and in the normal financial reporting channels.

Conflict of Interest No employee may have a personal or business interest which conflicts with the Company's interest.

Gifts and Entertainment Employees and their families should neither give nor receive gifts or entertainment that could in any way influence company business dealings.

Confidential Information Employees must protect the Company's confidential business information against loss, theft or misuse which could jeopardize the Company's competitive position in the marketplace.

Insider Trading No employee will trade in securities of Shell Canada or any other company if he/she has knowledge of confidential information that could influence the market price or value of such securities.

Political Contributions Neither the Company, nor any representatives acting on its behalf, will provide financial support to political parties.

Use of Company Assets Use of Company assets for personal gain or benefit is prohibited.

Bribery The Company and its employees will not indulge in bribery or knowingly be associated with any transaction involving bribery.

Canadian Competition Law Employees are expected to conduct the Company's operations according to the laws of the countries in which the Company conducts its business. Particular attention should be paid to the competition laws which are intended to ensure and maintain competition in the market place and to deal with prohibited trade practices. Details of the Competition Act of Canada are contained in the Company's Competition Law handbook (copies are available from Legal).

SOURCE: Excerpted from a Shell Canada pamphlet for employees, entitled "Code of Ethics". Reprinted by permission of Shell Canada.

NOTE: A discussion of the use of ethical codes in business is to be found in Earl A. Molander (1987), "A paradigm for design, promulgation and enforcement of ethical codes," *Journal of Business Ethics* 6: 619-631.

The pamphlet goes on to describe how this ethical code will be implemented in the Company, and who is accountable for the administration of the Code of Ethics. Company employees are asked to sign a sepa- *rate page stating that they have read and understood the Code of Ethics and are willing to comply with them. This signed document is then added to the employee's personnel file.*

EXHIBIT 11.9   TECHNIQUES FOR GENERATING CREATIVE SOLUTIONS

TECHNIQUE	DESCRIPTION	PROBLEM/SITUATION WHEN MOST APPROPRIATE
Brainstorming	Group members generate as many new ideas as possible. Members are non-judgmental of ideas and attempt to build on the ideas of other group members.	Problem is open-ended; Problem is well defined; Simple solution is sought; Problem is easily understood; Problem has more than one acceptable solution; Participants are able and willing to freewheel and emphasize the positive.
Free association	Symbols that are related to the problem are written down. These symbols may be words or pictures. They are then combined and associated to generate new ways of seeing the problem.	Same as brainstorming. The desired result is one or more simple, feasible, creative solutions to a well defined problem that is well understood.
Reverse brainstorming	Group members engage in critical thinking about the problem. Their objective is to identify the components of the problem	Problem is open-ended; Problem is ill defined; Simple solution is sought; Problem is not well understood; Problem has more than one acceptable solution; Participants are initially unable to freewheel or to emphasize the positive aspects of a problem.
Edisonian (named after Thomas Edison)	Extensive trial-and-error experiments are conducted.	Same as reverse brainstorming. The desired result is the analysis of faults, failure modes, things to be corrected in an area that may be incompletely understood.
Synectics	A two-stage approach that uses analogies and metaphors to make the familiar strange and the strange familiar. An attempt is made to see the problem from different points of view.	Problem is open-ended; Problem is fairly well defined; A complex illogical solution may be sought; Problem is fairly well understood; Problem has one best solution; Participants are able to emphasize the bizarre, to analogize, and to emphasize the positive aspects of the problem. The result desired is a "far-out" solution that may be toned down if desired.
Checklists; attribute listing	The properties and attributes of objects or products are listed.	Problem need not be open-ended; Problem is well defined and well understood; Problem has several acceptable solutions, but one best solution; Participants are able to visualize combinations and attributes; Attributes are well defined; Combinations and variations are meaningful.
Morphological analysis	A structured approach that examines all possible combinations of object and problem attributes.	Same as checklists and attribute listing. The result desired is that new combinations of forms, shapes, or means will be discovered.
Collective notebook	Group members maintain a diary with their ideas about a problem. The notebooks are collected and summarized. The summaries are used as input to future discussions.	Problem may be either open or closed-ended; Problem is well defined; Simple, logical solution is sought; One best solution is desired; The technology or discipline being studied is well-known; A logical process may be followed to reach a solution; An algorithmic approach may be taken to solution.
Scientific method	A problem-solving approach is used to test hypotheses about the cause of the problem.	Same as collective notebook. A far-out solution is not desired; the bits and pieces of the problem are laying around, waiting to be properly assembled.
Value engineering	Incremental changes are made that can be shown to increase product value or decrease costs.	Problem is closed ended; Problem is well-defined; A best, logical solution is desired; An engineered solution that can be immediately put into effect is desired; The technology or discipline being studied is highly refined. The result desired is incremental change in form, type, or process.

SOURCE: Table of creative solution techniques adapted from William E. Souder and Robert W. Ziegler (1977), "A review of creativity and problem solving techniques," *Research Management*, July 1977, p. 40. By permission of the authors and publisher. The technique of mind mapping can also be used to help individual or group creativity. See Joseph V. Anderson (1993), "Mind mapping: A tool for creative thinking," in the January-February issue of *Business Horizons*, pp. 41-46.

make a recommendation, and a user interface, expert systems are in use today to solve practical problems. One system, called *Prospector* (Duda and others, 1979) can help to find ore deposits by analyzing geological data. Another, called *Auditor*, is designed to help accounting audit teams to do their work.

Expert systems codify knowledge that is then readily available to others. They are not subject to logic errors. Also, they are capable of dealing with very complex situations that can overwhelm the cognitive capacities of an individual. But they cannot be creative and can do no better than the best of the expert which they model. We can expect to see many more expert systems developed for use in organizations over the next few years.

Another category of expert system is the new product category of business management software (see Austin, 1993). For example, *ManagePro for Windows* offers help in planning projects and monitoring completion. It also allows the user to input notes about staff and to later retrieve summarized information. The program *Negotiator Pro* provides help in negotiating. *The Idea Generator Plus* is a management software program that interactively works with the user in seven different ways to come up with creative solutions to problems.

Three methods have been found to help an individual avoid escalating commitment to a losing course of action (Simonson & Staw, 1992). The first is to outline at the start of a project the minimum goals that, if not achieved, will lead to a change in policy. This method helps to make clear to the decision maker when targets are not reached. It increases the legitimacy of withdrawal because the decision maker sets the conditions for withdrawal at the outset. It also helps to increase the planning done for alternative courses of action that may be pursued.

The second method is to make decision makers accountable for their decision *process* and not the decision result. When evaluation is based on the effectiveness of the decision process, decision makers feel less responsible for losses. They are therefore less likely to spend more organizational resources in the hope of turning around the situation and achieving a favourable outcome.

Threat reduction is the third method of reducing decision escalation. When the threat of negative outcomes is reduced the decision maker is less concerned with self-justification of the initial decision or justifying the decision to others.

A WORD TO THE WISE

DECIDING TO DECIDE:
10 QUESTIONS TO EASE THE TASK

Many managers find decision making difficult. They are smart and diligent, but when it comes to settling on a course of action, they resort to delaying tactics, or they blame others to duck responsibility. Below are 10 questions to ask yourself in order to help you overcome your block.

1. Do I have to make this decision alone?
2. What is the basic issue that I must address and resolve?
3. Do I have all the information I need?
4. Who, inside or outside my firm, can I consult?
5. How have I handled similar issues in the past? Would I do anything differently?
6. Do I have a track record of making poor decisions? If so, what has been responsible for it? Is it something I can change?
7. Do I rely too heavily—or not heavily enough—on experts' opinions?
8. If the stakes appear too high, is there a compromise that I can settle on as a safety net?
9. Whose style of decision making do I admire, and why?
10. If I were to set my alarm clock to ring in 10 minutes, what would my immediate decision be?

SOURCE: Reprinted with permission from Adele Scheele (1993), "Deciding to decide: 10 questions to ease the task," *Working Woman*, January 1993, p. 22. This column is included in her book *Career Strategies for the Working Woman* (1994), published by Simon & Schuster Trade Paperbacks.

At the Group Level

Brainstorming A method of group idea generation.

Nominal groups
A method of generating ideas by having individuals write down as many ideas about a problem or issue as they can and then combining these individual lists across all the members of a group.

Production blocking
Group factors that act to limit the contributions of group members.

Evaluation apprehension
When group members are hesitant to contribute their ideas because of concern about how those ideas will be evaluated by other group members.

Groupware Group decision support software used to facilitate group decisions made in electronic decision rooms.

Improved nominal group technique (INGT)
Designed to avoid some of the problems groups encounter when making decisions in face-to-face meetings.

Delphi technique Group decision method that asks experts in a structured and cyclical way for their wisdom about a particular problem.

One of the first methods devised to improve the number and creativity of group-generated ideas was **brainstorming** (Osborn, 1957). The rules of brainstorming are simple. The more ideas the better, the wilder the ideas the better, group members are encouraged to combine and modify the ideas given by others, and no idea, no matter how odd it seems, is to be criticized. In the brainstorming process the evaluation of ideas occurs later.

While there is no doubt that brainstorming in groups can be a good way to generate ideas, some researchers wondered if the equivalent number of individuals could create more ideas than a brainstorming group (Taylor and others, 1958). Called **nominal groups** because they were groups in name only, they did indeed come up with more unique ideas than brainstorming groups of equivalent size. It was also found that the number of ideas generated per person in brainstorming groups declined with increasing group size.

One reason for these declining returns is that as size increases there is less time for each member to state ideas. This is **production blocking**. A second reason is that group members, especially those of lower status, are concerned about how other group members will receive their ideas. This is **evaluation apprehension**.

These problems can be overcome if the individuals in brainstorming groups do not conduct a face-to-face meeting, but instead meet in a special electronic decision room. Equipped with personal computers networked together and coordinated by group decision support software called **groupware**, production blocking effects are lessened because all members can communicate at once. The computer software sends each person's ideas to the others. Evaluation apprehension is lessened because each person's identity is concealed—only their ideas are transmitted (Gallupe and others, 1992).

Computer-mediated groupware (see Kirkpatrick, 1993) can also be used for group decision making, often with an individual that is not a group member acting as a facilitator. The benefits of discussion via the keyboard and screen can help a group to make decisions under conditions of conflict when free discussion would be unproductive.

Electronic decision rooms are currently in use. In one case nine senior managers of Metropolitan Life Insurance Co. met to plan company strategy at the Executive Decision Centre at Queen's University. The estimate is that they were able to accomplish in one day what normally would have taken up to five (Blackwell, 1993).

The **improved nominal group technique** or INGT (Fox, 1989) is a refinement of the original nominal group technique of decision making (Delbecq and others, 1975). It is designed to avoid some of the problems groups encounter when making decisions in face-to-face meetings (see Exhibit 11.10). For effective use the group's leader must be trained in the INGT methodology. Group members must accept in advance that group decision making will not follow standard methods of "open" discussion and voting until a majority opinion is achieved. If these prescriptions are followed the negative feelings of being pressured by the group or of losing the argument may be avoided.

Another technique for group decision making was developed by the Rand Corporation. This was named the **Delphi technique** after the Delphic oracles in Ancient Greece who were sought out for their prophecies about the future. The modern Delphi technique also asks experts for their wisdom about a particular problem.

When using this method experts are individually presented with the problem. Then their thoughts and recommendations are collected and summarized by a facilitator who sends the summaries back out to the experts. The experts send their comments on each others' ideas and proposed solutions back to the facilitator who looks for an emerging consensus of opinion. This process repeats until a consensus emerges. When performed by mail the Delphi process can be extremely slow. Newer global computer-messaging networks and fax communications have made quick Delphi decision making a possibility.

EXHIBIT 11.10   IMPROVED NOMINAL GROUP TECHNIQUE

1. Assure anonymity of input by contributors so that individuals do not censor their own ideas.

   ↓

2. Define realistically what the group is attempting to accomplish when it meets.

   ↓

3. Collect and distribute inputs before a meeting so that ideas can be considered by all group members.

   ↓

4. Put all inputs on display in a group meeting room, maintain the display throughout the meeting, and defer in-depth evaluation of the items.

   ↓

5. Make sure there is opportunity for discussion on all display items before voting begins.

   ↓

6. Limit the group's discussion to clarification and the presentation of pros and cons of each display item.

   ↓

7. Allow a single, unexplained objection to block any proposed change to items on display.

   ↓

8. Always use anonymous voting to rank the ideas in their order of preference.

   ↓

9. Provide the opportunity to explore voting results so that discussion may be reopened when necessary and a second vote taken.

   ↓

10. The group's decision is the highest ranking idea.

SOURCE: Based on information in Fox (1989).

A method of group decision making that seeks to incorporate all points of view while avoiding voting or bargaining is **group consensus**. Using this method it is important that all group members freely give their own opinions and ask for the opinions of others. The emphasis is on understanding all points of view rather than on seeking support for one's own opinion, criticizing the opinions of others, confronting others, or winning the argument. Conflict with others is not sought or avoided; instead the reasons for any conflict are explored. Consensus is reached when, even though the decision may not be exactly what is wanted, each person in the group can accept the group's decision and support its implementation.

Consensus mapping (Hart and others, 1985) is a decision technique that is designed to help a group deal with a complex problem by organizing ideas generated by the group into categories and then producing a map of how the categories are linked. The map is the guide to how a problem can be solved and how subgroups are involved in the problem's solution.

An expert system that summarizes organizational behaviour knowledge about participation in decision making is the **Vroom-Jago model** (Vroom & Jago, 1988a,b). To use the model a group's leader would describe 12 characteristics of the decision situation (see Field and others, 1990). Then the computer program provides advice on how autocratic, consultative, or participative to be when making the decision. The Vroom-Jago model is sensitive to requirements of decision quality, required acceptance of the decision by subordinates, and time pressures for making a quick decision.

The model's rules are complex, but using the program is easy. It allows the leader to easily analyze a decision situation and conduct "what if" analyses to determine how the model's recommendations would change given a different analysis of the situation.

Group consensus
A method of group decision making that seeks to incorporate all points of view while avoiding voting or bargaining.

Consensus mapping
A decision technique that is designed to help a group deal with a complex problem by organizing ideas generated by the group into categories and then producing a map of how the categories are linked.

Vroom-Jago model   An expert system that summarizes organizational behaviour knowledge about participation in decision making.

At the Organizational Level

Organizations that actively consider the ethical dimension to decision making can improve decisions made by its members in three ways. First, when decision makers pay more attention to the people affected by decisions they are more likely to see potential conflict in its early stages and to avoid costly mistakes. Second, ethical decision making takes the long-run perspective. Third, having and observing ethical principles enhances the credibility of the organization because the basis of decisions made is less likely to change from day-to-day (Enderle, 1987).

Many organizations have addressed ethical issues by creating codes of conduct. They have also installed ethics "hot lines" where employees can report ethical concerns and receive advice about how to deal with ethical dilemmas. Taking ethical actions is often difficult in times of economic downturn, especially if the organization values results over how those results were achieved. It is important that unethical actions are not rewarded with money and promotions, thereby encouraging employees to engage in those acts.

Staw and Ross (1987) considered how organizations could reduce escalation of commitment at the organizational level. One strategy dealt with project costs. The idea was to gather outside data on the project's success from multiple sources so that feedback would be unambiguous. Any phase-out costs, they suggested, should also be considered earlier rather than later in the decision process. Staw and Ross also proposed that organizations could rotate administrators in charge of a project, have different individuals evaluate a project's success, and provide excuses for project failure and reduce the penalties for failure so as to reduce the psychological and social supports for escalation. Finally, making the project less central to the organization can lessen organizational factors that increase the likelihood of escalation.

CONCLUSION

This ends our discussion of decision making in organizations. But we still have to consider the forces in organizations that affect the process of decision making. Chapter 12 will examine power: the capacity to influence. Decisions, once made, have to be implemented. The process of influence, or politics, is a second focus of that chapter. We will also explore the conflicts that can occur in organizations when an attempt to exert influence meets with resistance.

CHAPTER SUMMARY

For tasks that have an answer the rational model of decision making can be used to determine the optimal decision. The steps of this model are to: 1) identify the problem; 2) define the objectives to be met; 3) make a predecision of who to involve in the problem and how to make the decision; 4) generate alternatives; 5) evaluate those alternatives; 6) make a choice from among the alternatives; then 7) implement the choice and 8) follow up on the results of the decision. As decisions lead to actions and the discovery of new problems another cycle of the rational model is begun.

But the people in organizations who make decisions do not always follow the rational model. Instead, using an expert model of information processing, they generate and explore only a limited number of decision alternatives and use their pre-existing knowledge and simple rules of thumb to make a decision. Members of organizations may also make decisions that are based on intuition (nonrational) and on emotion (irrational).

Group decisions can be either less or more effective than those made by individuals. Processes that are known to impede effective group decisions are groupthink, the Abilene paradox, and escalation of commitment.

Organizations are increasingly concerned about their members making ethical decisions. One response has been to develop codes of conduct so that individual decision makers with different moral standards and bases of moral judgment will have a consistent basis for their decisions. Decision making in the organization can be improved by using creativity training, decision support systems and expert systems, and group methods such as brainstorming, Delphi decision making, and computerized group decision rooms.

QUESTIONS FOR REVIEW

1. How does an organization decide on a code of conduct? Should the organization follow its code when the laws and expectations about how business is done in another country contradict the organization's code?

2. Examine your own choice of which college or university to attend. To what extent did your decision follow the rational, non-rational, or irrational approaches?

3. Describe the Abilene paradox. Have you ever taken a so-called "trip to Abilene" when in a group?

4. What is a decision heuristic? What are examples of decision heuristics that a manager might use?

5. Why would an organization wish to rent an electronic decision room when almost every organization has a conference room or access to the conference facilities at a hotel?

SELF-DIAGNOSTIC **EXERCISE 11.1**

The Ethics Position Questionnaire

Instructions

You will find a series of general statements listed below. Each represents a commonly held opinion and there are no right or wrong answers. You will probably disagree with some items and agree with others. We are interested in the extent to which you agree or disagree with such matters of opinion.

Please read each statement carefully. Then indicate the extent to which you agree or disagree by placing in front of the statement the number corresponding to your feelings, where:

1 = Completely disagree
2 = Largely disagree
3 = Moderately disagree
4 = Slightly disagree
5 = Neither agree nor disagree
6 = Slightly agree
7 = Moderately agree
8 = Largely agree
9 = Completely agree

_____ 1. A person should make certain that their actions never intentionally harm another even to a small degree.

_____ 2. Risks to another should never be tolerated, irrespective of how small the risks might be.

_____ 3. The existence of potential harm to others is always wrong, irrespective of the benefits to be gained.

_____ 4. One should never psychologically or physically harm another person.

_____ 5. One should not perform an action which might in any way threaten the dignity and welfare of another individual.

_____ 6. If an action could harm an innocent other, then it should not be done.

_____ 7. Deciding whether or not to perform an act by balancing the positive consequences of the act against the negative consequences of the act is immoral.

_____ 8. The dignity and welfare of people should be the most important concern in any society.

_____ 9. It is never necessary to sacrifice the welfare of others.

_____ 10. Moral actions are those which closely match ideals of the most "perfect" action.

_____ 11. There are no ethical principles that are so important that they should be a part of any code of ethics.

_____ 12. What is ethical varies from one situation and society to another.

_____ 13. Moral standards should be seen as being individualistic; what one person considers to be moral may be judged to be immoral by another person.

_____ 14. Different types of moralities cannot be compared as to "rightness."

_____ 15. Questions of what is ethical for everyone can never be resolved since what is moral or immoral is up to the individual.

_____ 16. Moral standards are simply _personal_ rules which indicate how a person should behave, and are not to be applied in making judgments of others.

_____ 17. Ethical considerations in interpersonal relations are so complex that individuals should be allowed to formulate their own individual codes.

_____ 18. Rigidly codifying an ethical position that prevents certain types of actions could stand in the way of better human relations and adjustment.

_____ 19. No rule concerning lying can be formulated; whether a lie is permissible or not permissible totally depends upon the situation.

_____ 20. Whether a lie is judged to be moral or immoral depends on the circumstances surrounding the action.

Scoring

Your idealism score is the average of your answers for items 1 through 10. The mean of items 11 through 20 is your relativism score.

NOTE: It is important to remember that while the results of this test will be suggestive of your ethics position, this test as used here should not be considered a valid scientific instrument.

SOURCE: Donelson R. Forsyth (1980). "A taxonomy of ethical ideologies." _Journal of Personality and Social Psychology_ 39: 178. Copyright © 1980 by the American Psychological Association. Reprinted by permission of the American Psychological Association.

EXPERIENTIAL EXERCISE 11.1

The booklet "Ethics and You" produced by the Chartered Accountants of Alberta lists five examples of ethical concern. They are: (1) conflicts of interest; (2) confidentiality; (3) integrity of company information; (4) gifts from suppliers; and (5) turning a blind eye to the dishonest or unacceptable actions of others.

Here are common ethical dilemmas that you may be confronted with in an organization. Consider each one and first decide which category of ethical concern each one fits into. Then decide what you would do in each case. Finally, using the ethical models discussed in this chapter, examine the underlying reasons for your choices.

1. You know someone responsible for money in an organization is stealing from the company, but the organization as a whole is finally doing well because of this person. What do you do?
2. You see a colleague taking home office supplies such as pens and stationery.
3. You are doing 4-hour gas transmission tests for an oil company, but now that it is busy your boss has told you to spin the recording chart so that the 4-hour test is completed in 20 minutes. What do you do?
4. You are filling out your time sheet and are tempted to put down more hours than you actually worked.
5. You are paying an employee minimum wage when you know that it is hard to live on that wage. Should you give the employee a raise?
6. When the invigilator of an exam leaves the room, other students start to pass around answers. Since the course is graded on the curve, do you cheat too so that you are not disadvantaged by their resulting higher grades?
7. You are in charge of hiring in a small organization. One candidate is average and could do the job, but another is very good, potentially better than you. Who would you hire?
8. You are attracted to your secretary and you think the feelings are mutual. Do you ask your secretary out to dinner?
9. You were having lunch with your boss when the information was let slip that a colleague of yours was going to be fired. The colleague is your good friend who you know is about to buy a new car. Should you tell your colleague your inside knowledge?
10. It's December 20th and you arrive home to find that a company you buy from has sent you a cheese and fruit gift basket. It's quite large and is probably worth about $50. Should you send it back, tell your boss, give it to charity, or simply keep it?

EXPERIENTIAL EXERCISE 11.2

Mist Ridge

It is approximately 9 a.m. on August 23, and you and four friends are about to set off on an all day hike in the mountains of Southwestern Alberta. Having driven southwest from Calgary, Alberta, you have arrived at Kananaskis Provincial Park, located on the boundary between British Columbia and Alberta. Just off Highway 40, you turn into the Mist Creek

Misty Range,
Kananaskis country

day-use area and have just parked the car. You can see a sign indicating the beginning of the Mist Ridge trail, which you have selected for your hike, but you know that from there on the trail proceeds along unmarked paths and logging roads. You can also see another sign that allows campfires only in designated rest areas.

Since it is mid-week, few others should be on the Mist Ridge trail. You and your friends are looking forward to an enjoyable day walking the long grass and rock ridge as it is usually dry and sunny at this time of the year, when a mere few kilometres away across the valley Mist Mountain can be covered in rain clouds. Hiking from the parking lot to the ridge, then along the whole top of the ridge to Rickert's Pass, and then returning at ground level alongside the Mist Creek is, at minimum, an eight hour trip. In guidebooks it is classified as a long day hike covering a total distance of 23 kilometres with a height gain of 808 metres and a maximum elevation of 2515 metres.

The weather at the moment is cool but not cold, and the sun is beaming down, beginning to heat the air. In general, the climate of Southwestern Alberta is cold continental, having long cold winters and cool summers, though summers do have brief hot spells. Annual precipitation peaks in the summer and thunderstorms occur regularly. Hikers at this time of year must be prepared for rain or cold weather. Snow has been known to fall by the middle of August in this area, with accumulations on the ground of up to 20 centimetres. Also, the weather can be somewhat changeable and unpredictable. What starts out as a warm, sunny morning could easily change into a cold, snowy afternoon. Therefore, experienced hikers will make sure that they have adequate reserve clothing for the rain or snow that could develop. It is also known that temperatures are expected to be cooler at the top of the ridge, as temperatures decrease, in general, 2 degrees Celsius for every 300 metres of altitude.

There are a few dangers to watch out for during your hike. If you get soaked crossing a river, loss of body heat may result in hypothermia, even when temperatures are above freezing. Death from hypothermia is quite possible within a few hours of the first symptoms if proper care is not taken. On the other hand, the exertions of walking and climbing will probably cause you to sweat. Dehydration can increase your chance of sunstroke and hypothermia. In terms of animals, you may encounter a bear looking for berries. While bear attacks on humans are not common, they are not unusual either. It is also possible that elk or moose may be encountered. These large plant eaters are not usually dangerous to humans, but should be avoided during the mating season. There are also some insects to be considered. Ticks can carry Rocky Mountain Spotted Fever, which can be fatal if left untreated. Bees can also be dangerous if the person stung has a strong allergic reaction.

You are all currently dressed in warm clothes including wool socks and sturdy hiking boots, and each person has a day pack in which to carry those items that you deem necessary.

Part I: Individual Decision

There are 15 items listed below. Before you set out on your hike your task is to rank these items according to their general importance for a hiker, not for you specifically. Rank the items from 1, the most important, to 15, the least important. No ties are allowed. You might want to consider "If a hiker was allowed to take only one item, what would it be?" That item would be ranked number 1. Then, "If a hiker was allowed only one more item, what would it be?" That item would rank number 2. Write your rankings in the column below titled "Your Ranking." It is important to remember that the decisions that you are making are for your group as a whole and should not be influenced by factors affecting you as an individual.

Items	Your Ranking	Group Ranking	Expert Ranking	Your Score	Group Score
Canteen with water	____	____	____	____	____
Matches	____	____	____	____	____
Compass	____	____	____	____	____
Hat	____	____	____	____	____
Repair kit (includes short length of cord, string, duct tape, and shoelaces)	____	____	____	____	____
First aid kit (includes blister protection and aspirin)	____	____	____	____	____
Five Sleeping bags	____	____	____	____	____
Sunglasses	____	____	____	____	____
Flashlight	____	____	____	____	____
Topographic map and Kananaskis Country Trail guide book	____	____	____	____	____
Food	____	____	____	____	____
5-person tent with waterproof fly	____	____	____	____	____
Sunscreen	____	____	____	____	____
Rain gear	____	____	____	____	____
Insect repellent	____	____	____	____	____

Part II: Group Decision

Now form into groups. Take a few minutes to examine and discuss your individual assumptions before you begin to discuss how to rank specific items. Use constructive controversy decision rules to guide your decision method and rank the 15 items again. To refresh your memory, they are: (1) be critical of ideas, not people; (2) focus on making the best possible decision, not on winning; (3) encourage everyone to participate in the discussion; (4) listen to everyone's ideas, even if you do not agree; (5) restate what someone has said if their point is not clear to you; (6) bring out the ideas and facts supporting both sides of the argument and then try to integrate them; (7) try to understand both sides of the issue under discussion; and (8) change your mind if the evidence clearly indicates that you should do so (from Johnson & Johnson, 1992).

Write your group's answers into the "Group Ranking" column.

Part III: Scoring

Your instructor will inform you of how experts have ranked these 15 items. Write these rankings into the column titled "Expert Ranking." To calculate your personal score, calculate for each of the 15 items the absolute difference between your ranking and the expert's ranking, then sum these 15 absolute value differences. Determine your group's score in the same manner. Write these scores and summary statistics into the spaces below.

Your total score _____

Average of the individual scores in your group _____

Your group's total score _____

Number of individuals in your group having a lower score than your group's total score _____

SELF-GUIDED LEARNING ACTIVITY

The destruction on January 28, 1986 of the space shuttle *Challenger* provoked a great deal of study of the decision making process surrounding its launch. The interested reader could start with William H. Starbuck and Frances J. Milliken (1988), "*Challenger:* Fine-tuning the odds until something breaks," *Journal of Management Studies* 25: 319-340 and the article by Diane Vaughan (1990), "Autonomy, interdependence, and social control: NASA and the space shuttle *Challenger,*" *Administrative Science Quarterly* 35: 225-257.

For an examination of the individual ethical implications of the launch decision, see the speech by Roger Boisjoly reprinted in *Books and Religion,* March/April 1987: 3-4, 12-13; the article by M. Cash Matthews (1987), "Whistleblowing: Acts of courage are often discouraged," *Business and Society Review,* Fall 1977: 40-44; and the case by Russell P. Boisjoly, Ellen Foster Curtis, and Eugene Mellican (1989), "Roger Boisjoly and the Challenger disaster: The ethical dimensions," *Journal of Business Ethics* 8: 217-230.

Two other cases on the *Challenger* launch are "Anatomy of a tragedy" from IEEE *Spectrum,* February 1987, 24(2): 44-51; and Robert Marx, Charles Stubbart, Virginia Traub, and Michael Cavanaugh (1987), "The NASA space shuttle disaster: A case study," *Journal of Management Case Studies* 3: 300-318.

Two articles dealing with changes made to NASA's decision making process are "NASA's challenge: Ending isolation at the top," *Fortune,* 12 May 1986, pp. 26-28; and "NASA overhauls shuttle launch decision process," *Aviation Week and Space Technology,* 23 May 1988, pp. 20-21.

A look back at the impact on NASA of *Challenger* is provided in Mary Helen Brown's article "Past and present images of *Challenger* in NASA's organizational culture," pages 111-124 of Beverly Davenport Sypher (Ed.), *Case Studies in Organizational Communication* (1990), New York: The Guilford Press.

MANAGER'S CASE FILE: THE LETTER OF RECOMMENDATION

Tom Straat needed a letter of reference to show a prospective employer the next morning. He begged Karen Gross, a supervisor at his former employer's company, to write the letter for him.

"Please, Karen," he said, "I need this letter to get the job."

"I'd help you out," Karen replied somewhat reluctantly, "but I wasn't your supervisor. I'm not in a position to recommend you."

Karen was hoping that Tom would let her off the hook. She knew that Tom wasn't a good employee. He was lazy and avoided work as often as possible. He was an expert at dodging assignments and getting a co-worker to "help" him with some of his tasks.

"You know my former supervisor wouldn't give me a good recommendation. He never liked me anyway; that's why I left the company. I suppose I could sue if he gave me a bad recommendation, but I think this way is better. What do you say, Karen, will you help me?"

Feeling as if Tom would sue someone if she didn't give him a recommendation, Karen agreed to write the letter.

"Great," Tom replied. "By the way, I need it by this afternoon so I can give it in tomorrow morning. I'll be back around four o'clock."

Karen felt trapped. She had to write a letter to satisfy Tom but she did not want to mislead a prospective employer either. To top it off, she had about two hours.

Finally, after giving it a good deal of thought, Karen wrote the letter. Hoping it would pass Tom's inspection while alerting the interviewer, she used ambiguous phrases like, "It saddened me that we were never able to utilize his full potential" and "I cannot recommend this person too highly."

When Tom came for the letter, he read it and responded enthusiastically, "This is terrific. It will tell the interviewer just what kind of employee I am." "I hope so," Karen thought. "Good luck," she said.

SOURCE: Reprinted, by permission of the publisher, from MANAGEMENT SOLUTIONS, October 1988. © 1988 American Management Association, New York. All rights reserved.

Questions

1. Under the circumstances, did Karen do the right thing?

2. What other options did she have?

3. Did Karen compromise her ethics?

CRADLE TOYS, INC.

Alicia Thomas was clearing off her desk with more than the usual Friday enthusiasm. On Monday she would be going to the Toy Manufacturers National Show and Convention and it was a real feather in her cap to be going. Vice-presidents in her company, Cradle Toys, vied all year long for the honor (and fun) of attending, and here she was, a mere department head. "Well," she thought, "why not? I deserve it after the bang-up job my department did marketing that hard-to-love **Snugglepuss** toy. There's probably not a baby in the country that doesn't have that ugly stuffed cat in its crib."

"Hey, Alicia," said Skip Young, the head of toy development and "father" of **Snugglepuss**, as he stuck his head in her office, "I hear you got invited to the convention."

"Yeah, Skip, I'm leaving Monday." It was hard not to grin.

"Well, it's no surprise to me that our venerable leader has the good judgment to see that he's accompanied by the best-looking woman at Cradle. I've always heard he has an eye for the ladies."

"Skip, get out of here. I've got to finish this before I can leave."

"I'm going, but you watch yourself. I hear ole Tom's way with the ladies is as practiced as his eye for pickin' 'em."

"I hear you've been spending too much time in singles bars. Now I believe it. Get thee to a bar and let me get my work done, you clown."

Alicia couldn't help liking Skip even if he did create **Snugglepuss** and a host of other nearly unmarketable toys. After you scratched Skip's very carefully contrived bachelor's veneer, you found a man who sincerely liked women as people.

Skip's comments suddenly gave Alicia a sinking feeling. What if Skip was trying to warn her? Tom Deaton did have a reputation as a ladies' man and she was the only department head in recent memory to be selected to go. "This is crazy," she thought. "Tom Deaton treats me the same as every other department head. I've had little contact with him except across the table at departmental meetings and he certainly didn't single me out. He took great pains to point out to me that I was chosen for turning **Snugglepuss** into a marketing success and because I would be considered for promotion in the near future. He said he may even recommend me for his position. Upper management just wants to get a look at me, see how I handle myself. When he said, 'Oh, I may recommend you for my position,' could he have really been saying, 'Be nice, and I'll help you'?"

SOURCE: Written by Susan Smith Purdy. Appeared in James R. Glenn, Jr. (1986), *Ethics in Decision Making*, Copyright © 1986 by James R. Glenn, Jr. Reprinted by permission of John Wiley & Sons, Inc.

Questions

1. What should Alicia do now?

2. If Alicia does go to the convention, how should she act toward Tom?

3. Assume Alicia went to the convention and Tom acted professionally. But on Alicia's return, office gossip has it that Alicia and Tom had an affair. What should she do now?

REFERENCES

Anderson, Joseph V. (1993). "Mind mapping: A tool for creative thinking." *Business Horizons,* January-February 1993, pp. 41-46.

Asch, Solomon E. (1956). "Studies of independence and conformity: A minority of one against a unanimous majority." *Psychological Monographs* 70(9): 1-70. (Whole No. 416).

Ashforth, Blake E., & Yitzhak Fried (1988). "The mindlessness of organizational behaviors." *Human Relations* 41: 305-329.

Austin, Nancy K. (1993). "MBA-in-a-box." *Working Woman,* November 1993, pp. 29-32.

Ballon, Robert J. (1990). *Decision Making in Japanese Industry.* Sophia University Institute of Comparative Culture, Business Series No. 132. Tokyo, Japan: Sophia University. Available from Sophia University Institute of Comparative Culture, 4 Yonbancho, Chiyoda-ku, Tokyo 102, Japan.

Basadur, Min (1992). "Managing creativity: A Japanese model." *Academy of Management Executive* 6(2): 29-42.

Bazerman, Max H. (1984). "The relevance of Kahneman and Tversky's concept of framing to organizational behaviour." *Journal of Management* 10: 333-343.

Bazerman, Max H. (1994). *Managerial Decision Making* (third edition). New York: John Wiley & Sons, Inc.

Beach, Lee Roy (1990). *Image Theory: Decision Making in Personal and Organizational Contexts.* Chichester, England: Wiley.

Beach, Lee Roy, & Terence R. Mitchell (1990). "Image theory: A behavioral theory of decision making in organizations." In Barry M. Staw and Larry L. Cummings (Eds.), *Research in Organizational Behavior* (Volume 12, pp.1-41). Greenwich, CT: JAI Press.

Blackwell, Gerry (1993). "You, too, can be an Einstein." *Canadian Business,* May 1993, pp. 66-69.

Cohen, Michael D., James G. March & Johan P. Olsen (1972). "A garbage can model of organizational choice." *Administrative Science Quarterly* 17: 1-25.

Cox, Taylor & Stacey Blake (1991). Managing cultural diversity: Implications for organizational competitiveness." *The Executive* 5: 45-56.

Davis, James H. (1992). "Some compelling intuitions about group consensus decisions, theoretical and empirical research, and interpersonal aggregation phenomena: Selected examples, 1950-1990." *Organizational Behavior and Human Decision Processes* 52: 3-38.

Delbecq, André L., Andrew H. Van de Ven, & David Gustafson (1975). *Group techniques: A guide to nominal and Delphi processes.* Glenview, IL: Scott, Foresman.

Duda, Richard, John Gaschnig, & Peter Hart (1979). "Model design in the Prospector consultant system for mineral exploration." In Donald Michie (Ed.), *Expert Systems in the Micro-electronic Age* (pp. 153-167). Edinburgh: Edinburgh University Press.

Enderle, Georges (1987). "Some perspectives on managerial ethical leadership." *Journal of Business Ethics* 6: 657-663.

Feldman, Steven P. (1988). "Secrecy, information, and politics: An essay on organizational decision making." *Human Relations* 41: 73-90.

Ferrell, O.C., Larry G. Gresham, & John Fraedrich (1989). "A synthesis of ethical decision models for marketing." *Journal of Macromarketing* 9: 55-64.

Field, Richard H.G., Peter C. Read, & Jordan J. Louviere (1990). "The effect of situation attributes on decision method choice in the Vroom-Jago model of participation in decision making." *Leadership Quarterly* 1: 165-176.

Forsyth, Donelson R. (1980). "A taxonomy of ethical ideologies." *Journal of Personality and Social Psychology* 39: 175-184.

Fox, William F. (1989). "Anonymity and other keys to successful problem-solving meetings." *National Productivity Review* 8(2): 145-156.

Gallupe, R. Brent, Alan R. Dennis, William H. Cooper, Joseph S. Valacich, Lana M. Bastianutti, & Jay F. Nunamaker, Jr. (1992). "Electronic brainstorming and group size." *Academy of Management Journal* 35: 350-369.

Gersick, Connie J.G., & J. Richard Hackman (1990). "Habitual routines in task-performing groups." *Organizational Behavior and Human Decision Processes* 47: 65-97.

Gilligan, Carol (1982). *In a Different Voice: Psychological Theory and Women's Development.* Cambridge, MA: Harvard University Press.

Glenn, James R., Jr. (1986). *Ethics in Decision Making.* New York: John Wiley & Sons, Inc.

Hart, Stuart, Mark Boroush, Gordon Enk, & William Hornick (1985). "Managing complexity through consensus mapping: Technology for the structuring of group decisions." *Academy of Management Review* 10: 587-600.

Harvey, Jerry B. (1988). "The Abilene paradox: The management of agreement." *Organizational Dynamics* 17(1): 17-37. For commentary on this article see Rosabeth Moss Kanter (1988), "An Abilene defense: Commentary one," pp. 37-40, and Arthur Elliott Carlisle (1988), "An Abilene defense: Commentary two," pp. 40-43.

Holsapple, Clyde W., & Andrew B. Whinston (1987). *Business Expert Systems.* Homewood, IL: Irwin.

Isenberg, Daniel J. (1986). "Group polarization: A critical review and meta-analysis." *Journal of Personality and Social Psychology* 50: 1141-1151.

Janis, Irving L. (1982). *Groupthink: Psychological Studies of Policy Decisions and Fiascoes* (2nd edition). Boston: Houghton Mifflin.

Johnson, David W., & Roger T. Johnson (1992). *Cooperation and Competition: Intellectual Challenge in the Classroom.* Edina, MN: Interaction Book.

Kahneman, Daniel, & Amos Tversky (1982). "Psychology of preferences." *Scientific American* 247: 161-173.

Kahneman, Daniel, & Amos Tversky (1984). "Choices, values, and frames." *American Psychologist* 39: 341-350.

Kirkpatrick, David (1993). "Groupware goes boom." *Fortune.* December 27, 1993, pp. 99-106.

Kohlberg, Lawrence (1976). "Moral stage and moralization: The cognitive-developmental approach." In Thomas Lickona (Ed.), *Moral Development and Behavior: Theory, Research, and Social Issues* (pp. 31-53). New York: Holt, Rinehart and Winston.

Lindblom, Charles E. (1959). "The science of 'muddling through.'" *Public Administration Review* 19: 79-88.

Lord, Robert G., & Karen J. Maher (1990). "Alternative information-processing models and their implications for theory, research, and practice." *Academy of Management Review* 15: 9-28.

March, James G., & Pierre J. Romelaer (1976). "Position and presence in the drift of decisions." In James G. March & Johan P. Olsen (Eds.), *Ambiguity and Choice in Organizations* (pp. 251-276). Bergen: Universitetsforlaget.

McKay, Shona (1994). "When good people make bad choices." *Canadian Business*, February 1994, pp. 52-55.

Mintzberg, Henry, Duru Raisinghani, and André Théorêt (1976). "The structure of 'unstructured' decision processes." *Administrative Science Quarterly* 21: 246-275.

Molander, Earl A. (1987). "A paradigm for design, promulgation and enforcement of ethical codes." *Journal of Business Ethics* 6: 619-631.

Mumby, Dennis K., & Linda L. Putnam (1992). "The politics of emotion: A feminist reading of bounded rationality." *Academy of Management Review* 17: 465-486.

Osborn, Alex F. (1957). *Applied Imagination: Principles and Procedures of Creative Problem-solving.* New York: Scribner.

Perrow, Charles (1984). *Normal Accidents.* New York: Basic Books.

Premeaux, Shane, & R. Wayne Mondy (1993). "Linking management behavior to ethical philosophy." *Journal of Business Ethics* 12: 349-357.

Ross, Jerry, & Barry M. Staw (1986). "Expo 86: An escalation prototype." *Administrative Science Quarterly* 31: 274-297.

Ross, Jerry, & Barry M. Staw (1993). "Organizational escalation and exit: Lessons from the Shoreham nuclear power plant." *Academy of Management Journal* 36: 701-732.

Scheele, Adele (1993). "Deciding to decide: 10 questions to ease the task." *Working Woman,* January 1993, p. 22.

Scheele, Adele (1994). *Career Strategies for the Working Woman.* Simon & Schuster Trade Paperbacks.

Simon, Herbert A. (1976). *Administrative Behavior* (3rd edition). New York: The Free Press.

Simon, Herbert A. (1981). *The Sciences of the Artificial* (2nd edition). Cambridge, MA: MIT Press.

Simon, Herbert A. (1989). "Making management decisions: The role of intuition and emotion." In W.H. Agor (Ed.), *Intuition in Organizations* (pp. 23-39). Newbury Park, CA: Sage.

Simonson, Hamar, & Barry M. Staw (1992). "Deescalation strategies: A comparison of techniques for reducing commitment to losing courses of action." *Journal of Applied Psychology* 77: 419-426.

Solomon, Charlene Marmer (1990). "What an idea: Creativity training." *Personnel Journal*, May 1990, pp. 65-71.

Souder, William E., & Robert W. Ziegler (1977). "A review of creativity and problem solving techniques." *Research Management*, July 1977, pp. 34-42.

Staw, Barry M., & Jerry Ross (1987). "Behavior in escalation situations: Antecedents, prototypes, and solutions." *Research in Organizational Behavior* 9: 39-78.

Staw, Barry M., & Jerry Ross (1989). "Understanding behavior in escalation situations." *Science* 246: 216-220.

Staw, Barry M., Lance E. Sandelands, & Jane E. Dutton (1981). "Threat-rigidity effects in organizational behavior: A multilevel analysis." *Administrative Science Quarterly* 26: 501-524.

Stoner, James A.F. (1961). "A comparison of individual and group decisions involving risk." Unpublished master's thesis, Massachusetts Institute of Technology, Cambridge MA.

Stoner, James A.F. (1968). "Risky and cautious shifts in group decisions: The influence of widely held values." *Journal of Experimental Social Psychology* 4: 442-459.

Taylor, Donald W., Paul C. Berry, & Clifford H. Block (1958). "Does group participation when using brainstorming facilitate or inhibit creative thinking?" *Administrative Science Quarterly* 3: 23-47.

Tjosvold, Dean, & Richard H.G. Field (1983). "Effects of social context on consensus and majority vote decision making." *Academy of Management Journal* 26: 500-506.

Trevino, Linda Klebe (1986). "Ethical decision making in organizations: A person-situation interactionist model." *Academy of Management Review* 11: 601-617.

Victor, Bart & John B. Cullen (1988). "The organizational bases of ethical work climates." *Administrative Science Quarterly* 33: 101-125.

Vroom, Victor H., & Arthur G. Jago (1988a). *The New Leadership: Managing Participation in Organizations.* Englewood Cliffs, N.J.: Prentice Hall, Inc.

Vroom, Victor H., & Arthur G. Jago (1988b). "Managing participation: A critical dimension of leadership." *Journal of Management Development* 7(5): 32-42.

Waterman, Alan S. (1988). "On the uses of psychological theory and research in the process of ethical inquiry." *Psychological Bulletin* 103: 283-298.

Wedley, William C., and Richard H.G. Field (1984). "A predecision support system." *Academy of Management Review* 9: 696-703.

Weick, Karl E. (1987). "Organizational culture as a source of high reliability." *California Management Review,* Winter 1987, pp. 112-127.

Whyte, Glen (1993). "Escalating commitment in individual and group decision making: A prospect theory approach." *Organizational Behavior and Human Decision Processes* 54: 430-455.

FURTHER READING

A relatively recent technique designed to aid group decision making is called the stepladder technique. Group members are added one at a time to the discussion of the problem so that new ideas can be combined with prior thinking. See Steven G. Rogelberg, Janet L. Barnes-Farrell, and Charles A. Lowe (1992), "The stepladder technique: An alternative group structure facilitating effective group decision making," *Journal of Applied Psychology* 77: 730-737.

For a new look at groupthink, see the article "Beyond fiasco: A reappraisal of the groupthink phenomenon and a new model of group decision processes," published in 1993 in *Psychological Bulletin,* 113: 533-552, by Ramon J. Aldag and Sally Riggs Ruller.

Interesting articles about ethics in organizations are those by Michael W. Small (1993), "Ethics in business and administration: An international and historical perspective," *Journal of Business Ethics* 12: 293-300; Barry M. Staw and Eugene W. Szwajkowski (1975), "The scarcity-munificence component of organizational environments and the commission of illegal acts," *Administrative Science Quarterly* 20: 345-354; Thomas M. Jones (1991), "Ethical decision making by individuals in organizations: An issue-contingent model," *Academy of Management Review* 16: 366-395; and Sir Adrian Cadbury (1987), "Ethical managers make their own rules," *Harvard Business Review,* September/October 1987, pages 69-73. Ethical behaviour in Russia is described in "Unethical business behavior in post-Communist Russia: Origins and Trends," *Business Ethics Quarterly,* 1994, Volume 4.

The argument that men and women differ in their use of reasoning based on justice versus care is explored in Nancy A. Clopton and Gwendolyn T. Sorell's 1993 article "Gender differences in moral reasoning: Stable or situational?" published in *Psychology of Women Quarterly* 17: 85-101. They argue that differences in moral reasoning are not due to stable gender characteristics but are instead a function of the kinds of dilemmas that men and women tend to encounter.

Two articles that describe Victor and Cullen's work on the ethical climates of organizations are Bart Victor and John B. Cullen (1987), "A theory and measure of ethical climate in organizations," In William C. Frederick (Ed.), *Research in Corporate Social Performance and Policy* (pp. 51-71), Greenwich, CT: JAI Press; and John B. Cullen, Bart Victor, and Carroll Stephens (1989), "An ethical weather report: Assessing the organization's ethical climate," *Organizational Dynamics* 18(2): 50-62.

For further information on electronic meetings, see J.F. Nunamaker, Jr., Lynda M. Applegate, and Benn R. Konsynski (1988), "Computer-aided deliberation: Model management and group decision support," *Operations Research* 36: 826-848; Alan R. Dennis, Joey F. George, L.M. Jessup, J.F. Nunamaker, Jr., and Douglas R. Vogel (1988), "Information technology to support electronic meetings," *MIS Quarterly* 11: 591-624; and J.F. Nunamaker, Jr., Alan R. Dennis, Joseph S. Valacich, Douglas R. Vogel, and Joey F. George (1991), "Electronic meeting systems to support group work," *Communications of the ACM* 34(7): 40-61. Two other related articles are R. Brent Gallupe, Lana M. Bastianutti, and William H. Cooper (1991), "Unblocking brainstorms," *Journal of Applied Psychology* 76: 137-142; and R. Brent Gallupe, William H. Cooper, Mary-Liz Grisé, and Lana M. Bastianutti (1994), "Blocking electronic brainstorms," *Journal of Applied Psychology* 79: 77-86.

A software package that allows you to make decisions as the CEO of a real-life corporation is BusinessWeek's *Business Advantage*, available from Strategic Management Group Inc., 3624 Market Street, Philadelphia, PA 19104 (215-387-4000). The program *Expert Choice* is software for multi-criteria decision making. It is based on Thomas Saaty's work on analytical hierarchy processes, and is available from Analytical Power Tools, Palisade Corporation, 31 Decker Road, Newfield, NY 14867 (800-432-7475).

The work of Henry Mintzberg (1976) is followed up by Mark P. Kriger and Louis B. Barnes in their 1992 article "Organizational decision-making as hierarchical levels of drama," *Journal of Management Studies* 29: 439-457.

An interesting and provocative book that aims to help improve personal creativity is by Roger von Oech (1990), titled *A Whack on the Side of the Head: How You Can Be More Creative*. New York: Warner Books.

CHAPTER 12

POWER, POLITICS, AND CONFLICT

CHAPTER OUTLINE

Power

  Individual Power

  Group and Department Power

  Organizational Power

Organizational Politics

Conflict

  The Creation and Management of Conflict

Conclusion

QUESTIONS TO CONSIDER

- *What is power?*
- *How is power acquired by individuals, departments, and organizations?*
- *What are the types of power?*
- *What is politics?*
- *What are examples of politics in organizations?*
- *What is conflict?*
- *What are the costs and benefits of conflict?*
- *How can conflict be created and managed?*

Organizations are created in order to accomplish a goal—to get things done. Decisions are made and communicated to those whose action is required in order to reach the goal. While it may be assumed that a decision once communicated will be carried out, everyday experience in organizations tells us that this assumption does not always hold. There are times when decisions are resisted by simply ignoring them, for instance, or by lobbying support from others that allows the resistance to be maintained. The first part of this chapter will examine power in organizations, and how it is gained and maintained.

As we have seen in Chapter 11 on decision making, decisions made in organizations do not always follow the rational model. Similarly, the actions taken in organizations are not always rational, with goals consistent across organization participants and rational decisions made to improve the efficiency and effectiveness of organizational outcomes. Instead, organizations can be political systems having a number of competing goals. Decisions can be made and actions taken by individuals and coalitions of individuals based on their own determinations of what is best for the organization and for themselves. The political processes in organizations will be the second focus of this chapter.

Finally, in the third part of the chapter we will examine conflict in organizations and the management of conflict. Organizations may be seen as rational systems which experience conflict only when breakdowns occur in that rationality. They may also be seen to encourage conflict as a way to determine the organization's best course of action. When organizational members holding different views about the organization's goals are allowed, or even encouraged to conflict, the organization maintains its flexibility and increases its ability to change.

Power The capacity to influence the attitudes or behaviour of others.

Power, politics, and conflict are interrelated concepts. **Power** is the capacity to influence the attitudes or behaviour of others. It is a relationship between two parties (which could be individuals, groups, organizations, or even countries) that serves to define the interactions of the parties.

For example, while a manager may have the institutionalized right to fire a subordinate or have that person transferred to another organizational unit, that power is not necessarily exercised. It is the *capacity* to fire or transfer, known to both the manager and the subordinate, that affects their relationship and interactions.

Politics The process in organizations of one person exerting influence over another.

Organizational **politics** is the process of one person exerting influence over another. Politics is the exchange relationship as acted out in the day-to-day forum of the organization. Politics and influence depends on the power relationship between the parties involved.

Conflict Occurs in organizations when an influence attempt is resisted.

Conflict in organizations occurs when the influence attempt is resisted, likely because of different preferences or goals of the parties involved, or because the influence would change the power dynamics between the parties involved.

POWER

How does a person get things done in an organization? The capacity to influence, or power, is a function of individual, group, and department factors. It is also a function of the structure, systems, culture, and environment of the organization as a whole.

Individual Power

Five bases of individual power were identified by John French and Bertram Raven (1959) as:

- *Coercive power:* based on the ability to punish or apply sanctions to another's behaviour;
- *Expert power:* based on possessed knowledge and expertise relevant to the job or task at hand;

- *Positional power:* based on organizational position, hierarchical level and status (also called legitimate power);
- *Referent power:* based on the attractiveness of the powerholder to the other person in the relationship;
- *Reward power:* based on the ability to provide rewards or benefits to another person.

Because power is the capacity in a relationship to influence the other, these bases of power are dynamic—that is, they may be expected to change over time—and they depend on the perceptions of the parties in the relationship. Coercive power, for example, is given to the powerholder by the other who wishes to avoid the punishment or sanctions. Similarly, if expertise is not recognized by others, it cannot be a source of power over them.

Expert power can be created by the acquisition of knowledge and making it unavailable to others. A group can set up a system of testing for knowledge and awarding credentials. The accountancy, legal, and medical professions are examples. These self-set credentials are then made a requirement for the practice of a profession. In this way expertise can be captured and expert power limited to those who have been credentialled.

Legitimate power depends on hierarchical level and the right of the powerholder to exercise that power. Referent power is given to the powerholder by the person who is attracted to the other. Reward power depends on the other person's interest in the rewards that are available.

A sixth source of individual power is **information power** (Raven & Kruglanski, 1975): the possession of information important to the organization or having access to information. Data base and network managers usually have information power because of their control over the flow of information. Secretaries, though usually low on legitimate power, can be high on information power. This occurs when they control access to decision makers or to information—either formally in files or informally via the grapevine.

Finally, **connection power** (Hersey & Blanchard, 1988) has been noted as the power that comes from position in a network of work relationships. The more connections with other people at work, the more people known, the greater one's ability to get things done. Networking is a way to gain connection power. Networking can be done at formal meetings whose purpose is to meet similar others or on an informal basis at clubs or the Chamber of Commerce. Interest in networking has risen in recent years, especially among women.

Any relationship of power can be examined using these bases of power as a way to better understanding the interactions between two or more people at work. An example of the use of power in the Canadian Army is given in this chapter's *Seeing is Believing* feature. This explicitly illustrates how one individual can use different sources of power in a given organizational situation.

Some of these forms of power can be shared by allowing participation in decision making, or distributed by delegating power to others. This sharing or distributing of power is called **empowerment** (Hollander & Offerman, 1990).

In order to gain power at work, which is necessary to perform the job effectively, an individual could examine this list of seven power sources and determine how to increase each one.

For example, a manager's coercive power is increased when necessary sanctions are actually applied. The use of a punishment makes it salient in the minds of the others in the power relationship, whereas a refusal to punish can effectively remove this kind of power from the manager's power repertoire.

Expert power can be increased by on-the-job experience, and is relatively greater when few other individuals at work have the same knowledge. The more scarce is the expertise, the more that expertise is a source of power. Training, certificate programs, degrees, and professional designations can all increase expert power. The more critical such knowledge and skill is to the organization's effective functioning, the greater is the power given to the holders of such expertise.

Information power
The possession of information or having access to information that is important to the organization.

Connection power
The power that comes from position in a network of work relationships.

Empowerment The sharing or distribution of power.

S E E I N G   I S   B E L I E V I N G

THE FIFTY DOLLAR WAR BOND

During World War II, many people in Canada purchased fifty-dollar war bonds, in order to help the war effort. My job in the artillery was to send signals from a forward observation post back to the 25 pounder field guns. It was said that our artillery shells cost $50, so we often said "There goes another fifty dollar war bond" when we fired a shell at a target.

One day near the end of the war we were up in a farmhouse attic in Germany, observing the Germans who were in a line of trees about a quarter of a mile away. In the middle of the field between us and the Germans was one solitary German soldier, acting as an outpost sentry, lying in the field getting a suntan. Our Captain thought the German was being very nervy, so he ordered one round of artillery gunfire at this man. You could hear our gun fire, "thunk," then "whish" as it came in and "wham!" as it hit the ground and exploded about 30 yards from this guy. He wasn't hurt because when he heard the shell coming he jumped into his trench in the ground. The Captain ordered a round correcting for line and distance, and it hit almost in line with the German's trench but about 40 yards short. The next round was ordered, "thunk," and the German hopped into his trench before it hit close by. When the smoke and dust cleared, there was our friend out on the side of his trench, lying down having a suntan. Our Captain now ordered one round troop fire, four guns firing

one-two-three-four. When the smoke cleared, there he was, lying down and still getting his tan. So now one round gun fire, four guns firing all at once. Crash! The four rounds hit and smoke and dust were everywhere. "That's scared him now," said the Captain, but there was our guy when the smoke cleared, lying down in the sun. So the Captain calls a Mike target—a battery of eight guns firing five rounds each—at this one man.

Forty rounds came in. There was noise, smoke, and geysers of dirt. It took three or four minutes for the smoke to clear, and as the last smoke drifted away, there, sitting on the side of the slit trench, thumbing his nose at everybody, is our friend. Well, the Captain is so fed up, he called a Yoke target—a whole regiment of 24 guns firing five rounds at this man. All Hell broke loose as these 120 rounds hit, and when it was all over, that guy got up on the side of his trench, took out a newspaper, and started reading it! Our Captain had gotten so caught up in his power and the defiance of this one man, he had spent $8,550 (in 1945 dollars) of the Canadian public's money trying to make him stay in his trench.

Before the Captain could spend any more money, the Germans retaliated—they had figured out where we were by this point—by firing mortar bombs at the roof above our heads. So we all scrambled out of there as fast as we could, leaving our German friend to get his suntan in peace.

SOURCE: Excerpted from Richard Dudley Field, "The fifty dollar war bond," in the manuscript of his book titled *One Man's War*. Reprinted with permission.

A classic example of the creation of expert power was given by Michael Crozier (1964). In a French factory the maintenance workers were the only people in the factory who knew how to fix the machines used in production. This skill was guarded by keeping their knowledge "in their heads" and not letting production workers or supervisors know how to fix or maintain the machines. Their sole possession of this skill gave them power over the machine operators, who, because they were paid on a piece-rate plan, were dependent on the maintenance workers for their earnings.

Legitimate power can of course be increased by promotion and moving up the organization's hierarchy. The careful use of status symbols and organizational dress can help make clear to other members of the organization the individual's position in the hierarchy. This also makes clear the legitimate power that comes with that position.

Referent power can be increased by emphasizing goals and values held in common with others and how these joint goals may be attained by working together. A manager may also be able to increase referent power over time by selecting subordinates willing to give the manager referent power over them.

Reward power is normally part of a manager's power portfolio. This can be increased by making it clear to subordinates what rewards are controlled by the manager and available for dispersal (see Exhibit 8.10). Subordinates have reward power too. Typical subordinate rewards are support of the manager, willingness to take on undesirable tasks, and the willingness to work long hours or unscheduled hours.

An increase in information power can be created if an individual works at gathering information from a number of sources and is able to use that information at critical times to improve organizational decision making.

Connection power is often built by rotating personnel through a number of organizational departments so that more people come to know each other. These people can later deal on a more personal level when business requires that they interact. Connection power goes beyond the bounds of the organization. It is important to develop relationships and connections with customers and suppliers as well as with those inside the organization.

Group and Department Power

Subunit Power

Power accrues to subunits in organizations and of course to the individuals in those subunits (Hickson and others, 1971; Hinings and others, 1974). There are three main ways that this occurs.

First, subunits that cope with critical organizational problems and the uncertainties in organizational performance obtain more power. This coping may be done by the prevention of uncertainty—using information to predict future trends, or by absorbing uncertainty—taking action after the event.

Secondly, subunits that are not easily substituted for by other personnel obtain more power. Non-substitutability is enhanced when there are few alternatives and personnel are not easily replaced.

Thirdly, units or departments that are central to the flow of the organization's work obtain more power. Centrality is increased when the subunit's actions are pervasively linked to the work of other units and the subunit's actions are felt quickly and strongly in the organization's final outputs.

Gerry Salancik and Jeffrey Pfeffer (1977) note that subunit power can be a positive for the organization. It can be used to enhance the survival of the unit by gaining control over scarce and critical organizational resources, placing allies in key positions, and helping to define organizational problems to be faced and policies to be followed.

Subunits who gain structural power are good at coping with uncertainty, are non-substitutable, control information, and create for themselves a central position in the flow of the organization's work (Lachman, 1989).

Coalitions

In a work group each individual's bases of power and total power are usually well understood by the other workers. Individuals can join together to form a **coalition** where the interests of coalition members become intertwined. The power of each individual is pooled within the coalition, increasing its power relative to other individuals in the work unit. Such a group can become a **dominant coalition** (Pfeffer, 1981), with more power than any other coalition.

Other coalitions may try to oppose the dominant coalition and a **power struggle** may take place. Henry Mintzberg (1983) has identified several power base games. In the **sponsorship game** subordinates attach themselves to a superior in the hopes of rising in the

Coalition   A joining of organizational members to promote joint interests.

Dominant coalition   The coalition of organizational members with more power than any other coalition.

Power struggle   When coalitions try to oppose the dominant coalition of an organization.

Sponsorship game Subordinates attach themselves to a superior in the hopes of rising in the organization's hierarchy as the sponsor is promoted.

Alliance game

Organizational peers band together and support each other.

Empire building game

An individual or group attempts to become more important in the organization by adding personnel, increasing the budget controlled or physical space, and gaining control over more areas of organizational decisions.

organization's hierarchy as the sponsor is promoted. The **alliance game** is played more with peers who band together and support each other. In the **empire building game** an individual or group attempts to become more important in the organization by adding personnel, increasing the budget controlled or physical space, and gaining control over more areas of organizational decisions.

An interesting form of coalition in the work group is that of the romantic couple. When a couple forms a power coalition other members of the work group must treat them as a unit because what is said to one can be expected to be repeated to the other. Also, a conflict with one may come to include the other partner in the couple.

Lisa Mainiero (1986) has reviewed the impact of organizational romances on power. In her model, shown as Exhibit 12.1, there are three possible domains of social exchange in a relationship of power. The first is the task domain of how the job is done, time worked, the types of tasks assigned, etc. The second is the career domain of job evaluations, promotions and career advancement. The third is the personal domain of affection, sex, and companionship.

EXHIBIT 12.1

Model of Power Dynamics in Organizational Romances

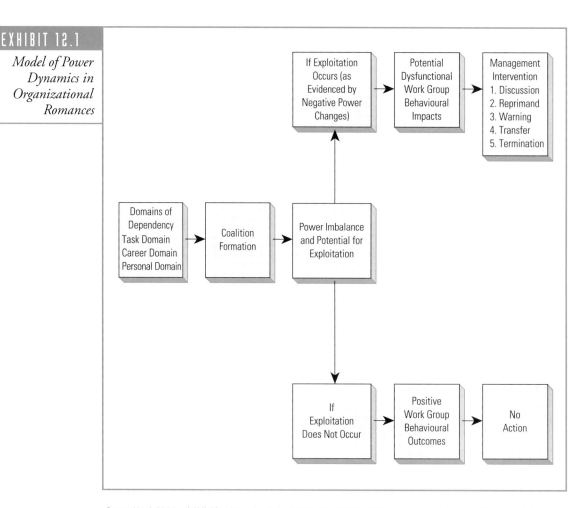

SOURCE: Lisa A. Mainiero (1986), "A review and analysis of power dynamics in organizational romances," *Academy of Management Review* 11: 759. Reprinted by permission.

In Mainiero's model a romantic coalition at work can have dysfunctional effects on the work group as a whole. Work group members may fear the potential for cross-domain social exchange. Specifically, they may fear that resources in the personal domain will be exchanged for task and career domain outcomes. This concern is especially salient when the two members of the couple are from different hierarchical levels and there is an organizational power imbalance between them.

Exploitation of the relationship, marked by changes in power behaviour such as promotion of the lower level person, the flaunting of power by either party, or task assignment reallocations of the lower level person can create negative outcomes for the work group. These negative outcomes can include distorted communications in the work group, lower morale, lower performance, and social disapproval or even hostility toward the members of the couple, including sabotage of their work.

If these negative outcomes occur, management will have to intervene by discussing the problem, reprimanding, warning, transferring, or terminating one or both members of the couple. The person with the least power in the couple can expect to be the primary target of these management interventions.

Mainiero hypothesizes that not all couples at work have power imbalances or exploitation of the relationship. In such cases no management action to restore group functioning would be required. One important key seems to be maintaining the boundaries between personal and organizational roles. When these boundaries are crossed, the potential for negative outcomes increases.

It can be argued that when the participants in organizational romances are not balanced in power that any actions that fall outside the normal work role are inappropriate. The reasoning is that when one party is of significantly higher organizational status and authority than the other party, true consent to the relationship is not possible. The person of low power is not in a position to make a free choice.

While participants in an organizational romance may attempt to keep their coalition a secret, co-workers often notice the telltale signs of a romance. These may include the two seen away from work together, spending long lunches together, spending a great deal of time chatting at work, or having intense discussions behind closed doors.

EXPERIENCE IS THE BEST TEACHER

I became interested in the subject areas of power, politics, and conflict when I began interviewing women on the issues that stymied their career advancement. Several women told me, "I'm so sick and tired of hearing about all the barriers that women face. My advice to you is to study the tough issues — the ones that no one talks about — like what are the political ramifications of becoming involved with a coworker romantically." I thought about the comments of these women and decided they were giving me good advice. So rather than studying "women's issues"

per se [as such], I decided to approach the subject backwards by examining the factors that affected women's progress in organizations — namely power, politics, conflict — and then to assess their ramifications for working women (as well as their male counterparts).

Lisa Mainiero received her Ph.D. from Yale University. She is a professor at Fairfield University and active in the field of management consulting and organizational development. Photograph by David M. Mangini.

Organizational Power

The French philosopher Michel Foucault (1982) noted that power relationships are institutionalized. They are codified into a system. He argued that for a relationship of power to exist the persons in the relationship must be free to choose their own course. Control of one over the other is not absolute—that is not power—but one is influenced to act by the other.

When a power relationship is established a system of differentiations is also set up that defines how one person is different from the other. This creates a condition of power and allows the exercise of power by one over the other. In organizations, such differentiations could be based on hierarchy, department, function, ownership, etc. For example, using the hierarchy differentiation, the manager is in opposition to the subordinate. The exercise of power by the manager over the subordinate is made legitimate by the differentiation between them that has been created. An example of a department differentiation is production versus sales. In one organization the power condition may be that production people make the rules, sales follows their decisions. A function differentiation is line versus staff; in ownership, family versus management.

In organizations, power relations can take three forms: market control; bureaucratic control; and clan control (Ouchi, 1980).

With a system of **market control**, organizations rely on prices as the means of exchange. Between organizations the way prices are set indicates the power relationship that exists. If prices are set by one organization and presented to the other in a "take it or leave it" fashion, power is exercised by the first organization over the second. In a more equal power relationship, both organizations may enter into bargaining to determine a price for the exchange that is acceptable to both. Even within an organization, goods and services may be "purchased" using "soft money" by one department or division from another. The way prices are set can be both an indicator of power and a determinant of power. If the purchasing department is allowed to seek outside suppliers then the power of the supplying department is lowered.

Bureaucratic control is established by a system of rules and by specifying who in the organization has the legal authority to make decisions and require compliance.

The system of **clan control** is marked by the reliance on traditions. Power is given to the family and clan, not for reasons of efficiency or effectiveness, but because of shared values and the belief that that is how power should be allocated. Family businesses often rely on clan control. Family members are given positions of authority more for who they are than for what they know or can do.

Large organizations have power over their environment because of their impact on the social system and the economy. When the Chrysler corporation sought U.S. government loan guarantees in order to stay in business, the costs of the loan had to be weighed against the costs of unemployment insurance and the potential failures of parts suppliers. Large organizations also lobby governments in order to obtain contracts, and even to change laws to be more congruent with their interests.

Small organizations usually have little power because each one has only a minor impact on the environment. The banding together of small organizations into associations is a response designed to increase the power of each small organization by the creation of one larger organization that represents them. In the airline industry, an association of travel agencies can negotiate lower prices or higher commissions that small independent agencies cannot.

A final point about power in organizations is that power and influence are changeable and adjustable. The power relationship is not fixed, but changes with the people of the organization and with changes in the environment. Foucault (1982, p. 792) wrote that:

> The exercise of power is not a naked fact, an institutional right, nor is it a structure which holds out or is smashed: it is elaborated, transformed, organized; it endows itself with processes which are more or less adjusted to the situation.

Market control
Organizations rely on prices as the means of exchange.

Bureaucratic control
A system of rules specifying who in the organization has the legal authority to make decisions and require compliance.

Clan control Power given to the family and clan because of shared values and beliefs that that is how power should be allocated.

How power adjusts and changes is one aspect of politics. Power, the capacity to influence, creates politics, the influence process. The influence process can then affect the nature of the power relationship itself. There is therefore a circular relationship as power creates politics which affects power.

ORGANIZATIONAL POLITICS

Behaviour in the normal authority relationship of formal roles regulated by organizational norms and goals is not considered to be political (Farrell & Petersen, 1982). Instead, political behaviour exists in the informal structures of the organization.

Therefore, while a look at an organization chart would show formal authority relationships and interactions, it would not show the informal relationships and behaviours that are characteristic of organizational politics.

For a humourous look at how scientists might try to use politics to influence manuscript reviewers, see this chapter's *On the One Hand* feature.

Dan Farrell and James Petersen (1982) have prepared a typology, or categorization, of political behaviour in organizations (Exhibit 12.2). There are three dimensions to this typology: (1) where the behaviour occurs—inside or outside the organization; (2) the direction of attempted influence—vertical or lateral; and (3) the legitimacy or illegitimacy of the political behaviour—illegitimate behaviours are considered to threaten the organization and central agreements about the "rules of the game."

Most political behaviours are expected to fall in Cell I, consisting of legitimate-internal-vertical actions such as: direct voice—trying to achieve personal outcomes by asking directly; complaining to the manager or supervisor; going "over the head" of the immediate boss by bypassing the hierarchical chain of command; and practicing obstructionism—not doing the work, ignoring requests, missing deadlines on purpose, and the like.

	Legitimate		**Illegitimate**	
	Vertical	*Lateral*	*Vertical*	*Lateral*
Internal	**I** Direct Voice Complain to Supervisor Bypassing Chain of Command Obstructionism	**II** Coalition Forming Exchanging Favours Reprisals	**V** Sabotage Symbolic Protests Mutinies Riots	**VI** Threat
External	**III** Lawsuits	**IV** Talk with Counterpart from Another Organization Outside Professional Activity	**VII** Whistleblowing Scapegoating	**VIII** Organizational Duplicity Defections

EXHIBIT 12.2

A Typology of Political Behaviour in Organizations

SOURCE: Adapted from Dan Farrell and James C. Petersen (1982), "Patterns of political behavior in organizations," *Academy of Management Review* 7: 407. Adapted/reprinted by permission.

ON THE ONE HAND ...

The business of science is serious. Scientists are hard-nosed people concerned more about their work and making new discoveries than with publishing the results. But when they do write up their results, only the best work gets by the tough review process and ends up being published. A scientist lets the work speak for itself and wouldn't dream of playing political games in the vain attempt to influence equally hard-nosed reviewers and editors.

ON THE OTHER HAND ...

Recently several books have been written in our area about how to publish. They are very predictable tomes which emphasize mundane things like originality of the idea, methodological soundness of the study, practical and theoretical significance, and so on. It is almost as if the authors of these books really believe that manuscripts are accepted for publication on the basis of their quality. Nothing could be further from the truth. While the content of the manuscript is certainly not devoid of salience, the actual publication fate of a manuscript rests with an obscure and arcane source of influence: the footnote. Yes, the footnote. It is this small but powerful weapon which dictates the fate of most manuscripts. Footnotes are carefully crafted messages designed to manipulate the reviewer into accepting the manuscript for publication. A footnote is the only way an author can communicate directly to the reviewer. In the manuscript itself the reader has to *infer* the quality of the research based upon what is read. But the footnote is different, for here the author can state, not imply, and can proclaim, not intimate. By judiciously presenting a footnote, the author might influence the reviewer to accept the manuscript prior to even having read the paper. Let us now examine some of the more selectively composed footnotes through which authors attempt to influence reviewers.

This first one is my personal favourite: "The author would like to thank President Ronald Reagan, Pope John Paul II, Carl Sagan, Albert Einstein, Madame Curie, Aristotle, and three anonymous Nobel Prize laureates for reviewing previous drafts of this manuscript." Now, what is a reviewer likely to think after reading this? "Who am I to reject this manuscript after such noted *personae* have already blessed it?" Right? And guess what—that is precisely why the footnote was written!

How about this one: "This manuscript is the author's Presidential Address to the LXVII International Congress of Truth Discovery and Assertion. Interested readers may refer to the original text which has been cast in bronze and placed upon the cornerstone of Congress headquarters, Geneva, Switzerland." Pretty impressive, 'eh? Are you going to flush this manuscript? Hardly.

Here's another one: "This manuscript is based upon a grant received from the Intergalactic Research Academy for Excellence in Scientific Advancement, Grant #A13725 N4 LQ627, funded for $14,882,641. However, the findings reported by the authors do not necessarily represent an official policy endorsement by the Academy." I'm so relieved. Are you going to reject a manuscript that was supported by a level of funding exceeding the Gross National Product of Lichtenstein? I doubt it.

And finally, we are sometimes offered this gem: "This manuscript received the Outstanding Paper Award at the Centennial Exposition of Meritorious Scholars—21st Century, held in Perth Amboy, New Jersey." Real subtle, wouldn't you say?

But let's be fair. Why do authors write them? Because they are the only professionally legitimate means authors have to proselytize themselves.

SOURCE: Excerpted from Paul M. Muchinsky (1986). "Footnotes as influence attempts." *The Industrial Psychologist* 23(2): 42-43. Reprinted by permission of the Society of Industrial and Organizational Psychology.

But politics doesn't always work from lower to higher in the hierarchy. Managers have developed the fine art of saying no to requests by subordinates (see Exhibit 12.3), by appealing to organizational goals and rules, entitlement, or equity; by claiming "it's for your own good;" or by giving no reason at all. Obstructionism clearly can work down the hierarchy as well as up, as managers sometimes say no by stalling or avoiding giving an answer until the subordinate simply gives up.

EXHIBIT 12.3   THE ART OF SAYING NO

Subordinates can obstruct the directives of their manager by, among other methods, "working to rule," purposely limiting their effort to the minimum required, and withholding critical information from their manager. But Dafna Izraeli and Todd Jick describe the other side of the obstructionist coin, how managers can obstruct the requests and plans of their subordinates. They call this the "Art of Saying No" to requests by subordinates. This is a good example of how power can work both ways. Here are some of the tactics a manager might use.

I. In this first group of ways of saying no, a reason is given. The arbitrary nature of these answers is shown in brackets after each quote.

The reason is:
1. Based on organizational goal accomplishment or organizational rules and procedures
    "We can't afford it"
    [But it's really a question of priorities.]
    "It's against company policy"
    [But policy can be changed.]

2. You are not entitled to receive what you have asked for (i.e., a raise, a promotion)
    "You are not old enough"
    [But what is old enough? And by then will I be too old?]
    "You are not senior enough"
    [But I could be made senior enough.]

3. An appeal is made to equity and fairness
    "Granting your request will create a precedent—everyone else will want it too"

[But if they deserve it too they should get it too.]
"Granting your request will mean that others will have less"
[But does that have to be true? Maybe the others should have less.]

4. It's for your own good
    "You think you'll like it but you won't"
    [But how can you know?]
    "You don't want to be seen as a trouble-maker"
    [But who says granting my request will make me seen as a trouble maker?]

II. In this second group of ways of saying no, a reason is not given. The real answer is shown in brackets after each quote.

1. An explicit no is given but without an explanation
    "No you can't have it"
    [And I either don't want to or don't have to tell you why.]

2. When the refusal is implicit by avoidance of giving an answer or by stalling
    "I'll look into it"
    [I won't look into it.]
    "You look into it"
    [It will cost you to look into it and then I'll say "I'll look into it".]
    "I'll get back to you"
    [I won't get back to you: "Don't call us, we'll call you."]
    "Wait a while until things settle down"
    [It's not going to happen.]

SOURCE: Based partly on information in Dafna M. Izraeli and Todd D. Jick (1986), "The art of saying no: Linking power to culture," *Organization Studies* 7: 171-192.

These Cell I types of politics are expected to be more frequent in mechanistic organizations where the chain of command and rules are formalized and authority flows mostly along hierarchical lines. In more organic organizations, political behaviours are expected to fall more under Cell II of the typology: the formation of coalitions, the exchanging of favours, and reprisals to punish the undesired actions of others.

Abraham Zaleznik (1990, p. 19) has noted that family businesses often exhibit this kind of political behaviour. In his words:

> Some types of businesses do breed politics, family business being a notorious example. These situations, in which people tend to spend excessive time building and maintaining coalitions, resemble elective politics. Control of the organization depends on the ability to create alignments of power. The net result, however, is to arrive at innocuous decisions that create the least divisiveness within the ruling alliance. Divisive decisions put the alliance at risk. One of the reasons for the high mortality rate of family businesses is that coalition politics allows incompetence to gain the upper hand. The exception, of course, is where one family member dominates through either ownership or force of personality. During the time of that person's dominance the situation returns to one of command, but if later succession to power results in fostering alliances and coalition politics, the business will be in danger. One way to address the problem is to institute integrity of command and marry competence with power.

Another case of coalition formation is that of organizational entrepreneurs who must secretly build a base of support for a new idea or product before going to the formal funding committees and asking for a budget. An intriguing description of such processes describes the organizational entrepreneur as having to "lie, cheat, and steal" to develop a new product for the organization (Cornwall & Perlman, 1990).

These actions are not considered unethical but political. The entrepreneur lies by using words carefully and not telling everything to others in the organization. Information is deliberately withheld or distorted to achieve the entrepreneur's purpose. Cheating is the bending or breaking of bureaucratic rules, often on the principle that it is easier to obtain a pardon than permission. Stealing is the obtaining of people, money, or time from other projects in the organization, often with the implicit (but not explicit) consent of others in the organization.

But what are the most effective internal and legitimate political behaviours? Gary Yukl and Bruce Tracey (1992) conducted a study of influence tactics used with subordinates, peers, and hierarchical superiors by the managers of five large companies. Their results, shown as Exhibit 12.4, show that rational persuasion, inspirational appeal, and consultation were the most effective influence tactics for the managers studied. Coalition, legitimating, and pressure were the least effective. Ingratiation and exchange were not effective strategies for influencing superiors but were moderately effective for influencing subordinates and peers.

EXHIBIT 12.4   INFLUENCE TACTICS LISTED FROM MOST EFFECTIVE TO LEAST EFFECTIVE

TACTIC	DEFINITION
Rational persuasion	The person uses logical arguments and factual evidence to persuade you that a proposal or request is viable and likely to result in the attainment of task objectives.
Inspirational appeal	The person makes a request or proposal that arouses enthusiasm by appealing to your values, ideals, and aspirations or by increasing your confidence that you can do it.
Consultation	The person seeks your participation in planning a strategy, activity, or change for which your support and assistance are desired, or the person is willing to modify a proposal to deal with your concerns and suggestions.
Ingratiation	The person seeks to get you in a good mood or to think favourably of him or her before asking you to do something.
Exchange	The person offers an exchange of favours, indicates willingness to reciprocate at a later time, or promises you a share of the benefits if you help accomplish a task.
Personal appeal	The person appeals to your feelings of loyalty and friendship toward him or her before asking you to do something.
Coalition	The person seeks the aid of others to persuade you to do something or uses the support of others as a reason for you to agree also.
Legitimating	The person seeks to establish the legitimacy of a request by claiming the authority or right to make it or by verifying that it is consistent with organizational policies, rules, practices, or traditions.
Pressure	The person uses demands, threats, or persistent reminders to influence you to do what he or she wants.

SOURCE: Reprinted from Gary Yukl and J. Bruce Tracey (1992), "Consequences of influence tactics used with subordinates, peers, and the boss," *Journal of Applied Psychology* 77: 526. Copyright © 1992 by the American Psychological Association. Reprinted by permission.

Yukl and Tracey also proposed a model for the selection of a particular influence tactic for a particular relationship. Exhibit 12.5 shows the factors that are likely to affect both the political tactic chosen and its effectiveness. The tactic chosen must be appropriate to the situation and its effectiveness depends at least in part on the skill of the influence agent. One implication of this model is that effective political influence is a skill that can be learned. Political skill in organizations, like other skills, can therefore be expected to vary between managers.

Moving on to Cells III and IV of Exhibit 12.2, legitimate external political behaviours would be lawsuits and discussions with others outside the organization. The filing of a lawsuit is external politics directed vertically. Such lawsuits might be for discrimination in hiring or promotion, for lapses in on-the-job safety, or for unfair dismissal. Engaging in outside professional activity such as professional organizations or associations, conventions, etc., or establishing communication links with outside individuals is lateral political behaviour.

Before we go on to discuss illegitimate politics, is it necessary to be involved in organizational politics? Some people may consider that it is possible to remain aloof from such political "games," to ignore the politics that goes on and just stick to doing one's job in the best way that one can.

According to Jeffrey Davidson (1988) and Donald Hathaway (1992) the problem with this approach is that organizational politics will occur with or without the organizational member's involvement. Refusing to play the political game simply makes that person unaware and vulnerable.

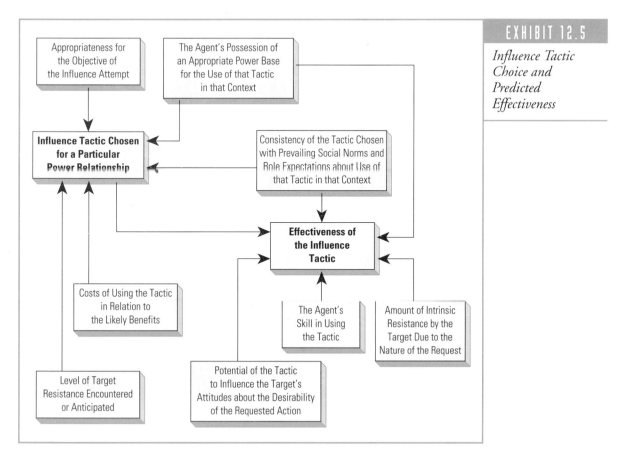

EXHIBIT 12.5

Influence Tactic Choice and Predicted Effectiveness

Appropriateness for the Objective of the Influence Attempt

The Agent's Possession of an Appropriate Power Base for the Use of that Tactic in that Context

Influence Tactic Chosen for a Particular Power Relationship

Consistency of the Tactic Chosen with Prevailing Social Norms and Role Expectations about Use of that Tactic in that Context

Effectiveness of the Influence Tactic

Costs of Using the Tactic in Relation to the Likely Benefits

The Agent's Skill in Using the Tactic

Amount of Intrinsic Resistance by the Target Due to the Nature of the Request

Level of Target Resistance Encountered or Anticipated

Potential of the Tactic to Influence the Target's Attitudes about the Desirability of the Requested Action

Source: Based on information in Yukl & Tracey (1992).

The politics of listening to colleagues.

Whistleblowing

The political behaviour of challenging the authority structure of the organization.

Scapegoating The symbolic shifting of blame by power holders from themselves onto someone who is not at fault.

Davidson recommends an active approach to politics based on watching, listening, and learning. He suggests that the political player watch who works together and who lunches together to determine the coalitions at work, then listen to what people talk about to figure out what is important to them and what they value. His advice to the organizational member is to go out for lunches, dinners, and for drinks (there is no need to ingest alcohol). The key is to avoid being isolated from others by eating lunch at the office desk and always going home directly after work. Get others to talk, listen, and learn from them. Adversaries at work are important too. Davidson advises that special attention should be paid to what they care about so that they can be understood and dealt with in the political arena.

Hathaway advises that relationships be developed, teams worked on, allies obtained and a mentor found. Having friends and exchanging favours is as important as competing with others. Since political skills are learned, Hathaway believes they must be actively developed to help the member of an organization be effective.

The message here is that the workplace is not a simple place where work is done and rewards follow directly and appropriately to those who deserve them. In order to get the job done, to be properly recognized and rewarded, and at times, even to hold on to the job, it is necessary to be political.

Illegitimate internal political behaviours include sabotage and protests as well as the more dramatic mutinies and riots (Cell V). Laterally, the making of threats is illegitimate because threats of harm to an individual's physical or job well-being go over the bounds of the employment contract (Cell VI). Providing work for remuneration does not anticipate potential harm to the self.

Externally, organizational members may "blow the whistle" on actions by others in the organization (Cell VII). **Whistleblowing** is a challenge to the authority structure, a challenge that must be met by power holders in that structure. A review of the literature on whistle-blowing by Janet Near and Marcia Miceli (1987) concluded that retaliation will occur against the whistle-blower and that the greater is the challenge to the authority structure, the greater is the likelihood of retaliation and the magnitude of such retaliation.

While whistleblowers in the organizational hierarchy generally make their charges on those higher up, **scapegoating** is the symbolic shifting of blame by power holders from themselves onto someone who is not at fault. Giuseppe Bonazzi (1983) studied the process of scapegoating by examining cases from Italian and French government. He found that when an error is discovered, power holders deny responsibility and find a culprit at the lowest possible level that is as far away as possible from their own level. People and organizations external to the offending organization then demand that the real culprit be found at the top, among the power-holders themselves. A scapegoat is then found at the lowest hierarchical level with sufficient external credibility: the scapegoat's organizational role must appear to have a connection to the occurrence of the error or accident *and* the scapegoat must be high enough in the hierarchy to match the severity of the consequences of the error.

Bonazzi contends that scapegoating is used in three distinct sets of circumstances, namely: (1) when power-holders perceive an external challenge to the prestige and respectability of their institution; (2) to intimidate others and to increase their own power; or (3) as a way to redefine their own social image by blaming someone in the organization who exhibits conduct that the power-holders have now deemed to be unacceptable. It is not hard to imagine that being selected as a scapegoating target would lead to resistance and conflict, one of the possible outcomes of the influence attempt.

Cell VIII describes the political behaviour of defection: abandoning the organization, possibly with knowledge of trade secrets and future plans; and duplicity, which may include industrial espionage and the selling of organizational secrets.

CONFLICT

We have seen that the members of an organization, when in a power relationship with other members, seek to exert influence over these others through the use of politics. But sometimes that influence is resisted. Perhaps the power relationship itself is in question—that is, at least one of the parties is seeking to redefine the relationship. Or, alternatively, the goals of the parties are not aligned—the preferences or goals of one party differ from those of the other party, and both sets of goals cannot be realized at the same time. When either of these situations occurs, the parties are in conflict (Lewicki and others, 1992; Lewicki & Spencer, 1992).

Molson workers in Toronto go on strike to exert influence on the company.

Conflict can be thought of as a dysfunction in the normal cooperative state of the organization, because goals *should* be linked. In this way of thinking about organizations, there is a common goal shared by all and every member helps every other member to achieve that goal (or set of common goals).

But as we saw in the garbage can model of decision making in organizations, there are many goals and many players who are busy "kicking balls (problems) towards the goals they like and away from the goals they don't like." Organizations, then, can also be thought of as arenas for staging conflicts with conflict as the essence of what the organization is (Pondy, 1992).

In this way of thinking, conflict is not a byproduct of normal operations or an unintended and unwanted consequence of day-to-day activities, but the way the organization: (1) makes choices for future action; (2) makes changes in power relationships; and (3) keeps itself flexible and adaptive.

Making Choices for Future Action   Managers, in this metaphor for how the organization works, organize and referee the bouts. They set up the conditions for conflict to occur and then watch to see who wins (Pondy, 1992).

Changing Power Relationships   A conflict between two parties has as its objective and outcome the redefinition of the power relationship that links them (Foucault, 1982). The redefined power relationship then acts as the basis for future influence.

Maintaining Flexibility   If one side of a pair of tendencies (for example risk taking versus risk avoiding; or creativity versus efficiency) were to become dominant, the organization would settle into a way of thinking and operating that would be difficult to change. By building in diversity and institutionalizing conflict between these competing ways of thinking and operating, the organization keeps the flexibility it needs to adapt to changing conditions and to survive (Pondy, 1992). Also, organizational subunits that deal with critical elements of the environment have the power to win power struggles and then gain the resources they need to help the organization cope with the environment as it changes (Pfeffer, 1981).

Conflict is therefore to be expected in organizations when goals are negatively (competitively) linked, just as cooperation can be expected when goals are positively linked (Tjosvold, 1984, 1993).

When a conflict situation arises, the decision of how to react is an important one. Kenneth Thomas (1977, 1992) has noted five possibilities for dealing with conflict:

1. *Competing:* When the parties involved try to achieve their own goals with little or no concern for the goals or interests of the other party. Conflict is seen as a one must win and one must lose situation.
2. *Collaborating:* When each of the parties in the conflict attempts to find a solution that satisfies the goals of all parties involved—conflict is defined as a search for a win-win solution.

3. *Compromising:* When there is no clear winner and loser, but each party to the conflict gives up something. Neither party achieves all their goals.

4. *Avoiding:* When one or both parties refuses to recognize that conflict exists or refuses to become involved in an attempt to resolve the conflict. Avoidance may be accomplished by the physical separation of the parties involved or by suppressing any open display of conflict. Neither party's goals are addressed—there is no change in the underlying situation causing the conflict.

5. *Accommodating:* When one party to the conflict places the goals of the other party above its own interests. Conflict is dealt with by one party giving in to the other.

Situations appropriate for the use of each method of handling conflict are listed in Exhibit 12.6.

EXHIBIT 12.6 CONFLICT HANDLING MODES

CONFLICT-HANDLING MODE	APPROPRIATE SITUATIONS
Competing (Dominating)	1. When quick, decisive action is vital—e.g., emergencies. 2. On important issues where unpopular actions need implementation—cost cutting, discipline. 3. On issues vital to organizational welfare when you know you are right. 4. Against people who take advantage of noncompetitive behaviour.
Collaborating (Integrating)	1. To find an integrative solution when both sets of concerns are too important to be compromised. 2. When your objective is to learn. 3. To merge insights from people with different perspectives. 4. To gain commitment by incorporating concerns into a consensus. 5. To work through feelings which have interfered with a relationship.
Compromising	1. When goals are important, but not worth the effort or potential disruption of more assertive modes. 2. When opponents with equal power are committed to mutually exclusive goals. 3. To achieve temporary settlements of complex issues. 4. To arrive at expedient solutions under time pressure. 5. As a backup when collaboration or competition is unsuccessful.
Avoiding	1. When an issue is trivial, or more important issues are pressing. 2. When you perceive no chance of satisfying your concerns. 3. When potential disruption outweighs the benefits of resolution. 4. To let people cool down and regain perspective. 5. When gathering information supersedes an immediate decision. 6. When others can resolve the conflict more effectively. 7. When issues seem tangential or symptomatic of other issues.
Accommodating (Obliging)	1. When you find you are wrong—to allow a better position to be heard, to learn, and to show your reasonableness. 2. When issues are more important to others than yourself—to satisfy others and maintain cooperation. 3. To build social credits for later issues. 4. To minimize a loss when you are outmatched and losing. 5. When harmony and stability are especially important. 6. To allow subordinates to develop by learning from mistakes.

Source: Adapted from Kenneth W. Thomas (1977), "Toward multi-dimensional values in teaching: The example of conflict behaviors," *Academy of Management Review* 2: 487. Adapted/reprinted with permission.

It should be recognized that conflict may also be used as a political tactic. For instance, competing may be selected as a strategy to win a conflict over an accommodator. Confrontation may be used, especially in public situations, to cause embarrassment and stress for the other party and more influence for the confronting party. On the other hand, avoidance of public confrontation and conflict may be used as a tactic designed to look like the avoider has "given up," when a dominating strategy is actually being followed behind the scene. Finally, the tactic of **stonewalling**, simply refusing to discuss a conflict or compromise in the slightest, is a dominating tactic that can be used to frustrate the other party and perhaps cause them to act in a way that will end up damaging their own position.

Stonewalling The conflict tactic of simply refusing to discuss an issue in conflict or to compromise in the slightest.

The list in Exhibit 12.6 presumes that the manager of conflict has the skills to use each of these methods when appropriate and the personal capacity to choose the necessary method in a particular situation. But individuals in organizations differ in their styles of handling interpersonal conflict.

One dimension of individual difference is concern for others (also called cooperativeness), while another is concern for self (also called assertiveness: Ruble & Thomas, 1976). The style favoured by each combination of concern for others versus self is shown in Exhibit 12.7. This chapter's Self-Diagnostic Exercise provides a short questionnaire to help you to consider your own predisposition towards using the five conflict-handling styles.

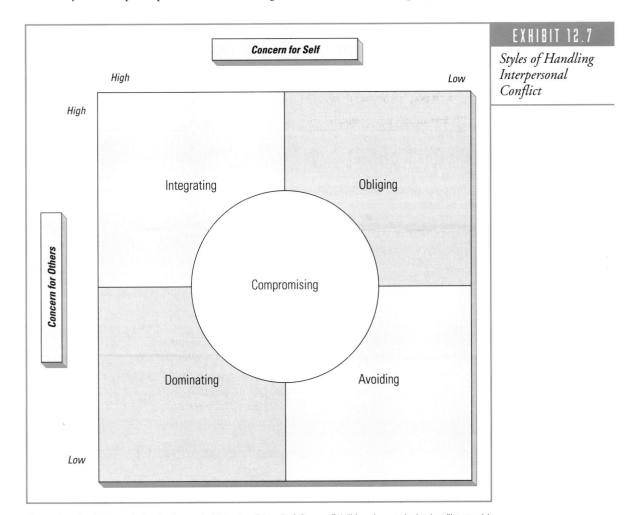

EXHIBIT 12.7

Styles of Handling Interpersonal Conflict

SOURCE: Reproduced with permission of authors and publisher from Rahim, A., & Bonoma, T.V. "Managing organizational conflict: a model for diagnosis and intervention." *Psychological Reports*, 1979, 44, 1323-1344. © *Psychological Reports*, 1979.

The Creation and Management of Conflict

There are times when conflict and controversy are beneficial to the organization: when creativity is required; when there are only sufficient resources to support some proposed projects but not all; when it is important to find the best performers possible; and when training for future stressful and conflict-ridden situations is required.

To create conflict, managers in organizations have several tools at their disposal. One is to select individuals who are not afraid of conflict and confrontation. A second is to make the situation one of competition—for example, set up teams that compete directly with one another (product development teams, for example), and select a winner from all the teams. In budget allocation, completely fund the projects of the winners and give nothing to the losers instead of giving every team some funding but not all they had requested. A third is to create a reward structure, either individual or team based, that rewards winning.

Though conflict can be constructive, it can also be destructive. The creation of winners and losers can damage effective communication. It can cause rival camps to be set up within the organization. Conflict can also make organization members focus too much on playing the political games required to win the next battle instead of concentrating on working cooperatively with other organizational members so that the organization as a whole is more effective. Several ways of reducing conflict or managing conflict are available to the manager.

Structural Changes   Conflict between groups is common in organizations. Often caused by task interdependence and differences in goals and perceptions, predictable changes are known to occur within each group and between groups.

Within each group there is greater cohesion between group members, a lack of tolerance of members deviating from group norms and goals and an emphasis on winning the conflict. A leader is likely to be selected or to emerge who is skilled at handling conflict.

Between groups there is stereotyping of the member group as "all good" and the other group as "all bad." There is less communication between groups that is aimed at resolving the conflict, and less accurate perceptions of the other group.

Mechanisms for resolving these intergroup conflicts include (Neilsen, 1972):

1. Lessening the interdependence between the groups. Physical separation of groups can reduce their conflict. The separation of their work flows by buffering—the creation of inventory between the units so their work flow is less interdependent—will also reduce conflict.

2. Authoritative command from someone in the organization's hierarchy above both the groups. Essentially, an order is given to cooperate.

3. The use of integrators and boundary spanners who can effectively communicate the positions of both groups. These people need to be able to "speak the language" of their own group and the other group.

4. Direct confrontation and negotiation. For an example of how these processes might depend on both masculine and feminine managerial attributes, see this chapter's *A Little Knowledge* feature.

Superordinate goal

A goal that can only be accomplished by two groups working together.

5. The creation of interdependent tasks and goals superordinate to both groups—tasks that can only be accomplished by working together. Given a **superordinate goal,** individuals or groups will redefine their conflict as harmful to their own goal, in this case the larger goal.

A LITTLE KNOWLEDGE

"Andro is Greek for male; *gyne* is Greek for female. The new value set calls for each person to have a blend of values—competence and compassion, action and introspection. Such a blend mixes together two sets of values:

- The so-called masculine characteristics that managers will need to continue to exhibit—dominance, independence, a direct achievement style, a reverence for rational, analytical problem solving, a valuing of verbal behaviour, and a competitive strategic approach;
- The so-called feminine characteristics—concern for relationships, a valuing of expressive behaviour, attention to nonverbal behaviour, the ability to accommodate and mediate, and a vicarious achievement style (enjoying the development of others).

Androgynous behaviour can enhance a range of managerial functions, including the following:

- Conducting performance appraisals;
- Building, developing, and maintaining team effectiveness;
- Assisting in the career development of employees;
- Using a variety of decision-making styles;
- Dealing with conflict;
- Responding to new ideas;
- Dealing with stress."

Therefore, a comparison of the traditional manager to the new style androgynous manager can be made in the following way:

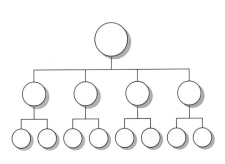

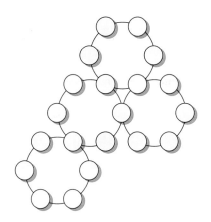

Traditional Manager

New-Style Androgynous Manager

- Do as I say, not as I do
- Rational
- Eliminates complexity; has all the answers
- Compartmentalized experimentation permitted only in an R&D setting
- Standard operating procedures; highly bureaucratic
- Chain of command
- Conformity

- Models good interpersonal relationships
- Rational and intuitive
- Comfortable with uncertainty and complexity
- Experiments; organization embraces errors
- Fairness; core set of values; deals with individuals
- Networks
- Diversity

SOURCE: Excerpted and adapted from Alice G. Sargent and Ronald J. Stupak (1989), "Managing in the '90s: The androgynous manager." Reprinted from the *Training and Development Journal.* Copyright © December 1989, the American Society for Training and Development. Reprinted with permission. All rights reserved.

Reward Systems When conflict is caused by competition for a limited pool of rewards the rewards available can be expanded so that all who qualify for a reward are able to obtain it. Or rewards can be allocated on the basis of individual accomplishment and not based on comparison to the achievements of other individuals. Reward systems can be designed to reward group effort and achievement rather than the individual, in order to encourage cooperation between group members.

Individual Knowledge and Skills When conflict occurs because members of the organization have different backgrounds, different values because of different socialization experiences, or different time spans of feedback from their work, exposure to these differences by cross-training or job rotation can help to reduce the conflict. Interpersonal communications skills can be taught so that small disagreements are dealt with as they arise and therefore do not accumulate over time into major conflicts. One such skill that can be learned is **assertiveness** (see Exhibit 12.8).

Assertiveness Direct speaking about your own needs, feelings, and goals without being aggressive or hurtful toward another.

EXHIBIT 12.8 CHARACTERISTICS OF NONASSERTIVE, AGGRESSIVE, AND ASSERTIVE BEHAVIOUR

	NONASSERTIVE BEHAVIOUR	AGGRESSIVE BEHAVIOUR	ASSERTIVE BEHAVIOUR
Feelings and consequences typical for the person (sender) whose actions are nonassertive, aggressive, or assertive	Self-denying	Self-enhancing at expense of another	Self-enhancing
	Inhibited	Self-enhancing at expense of another	Expressive
	Hurt, anxious	Expressive	Feels good about self
	Allows others to choose	Chooses for others	Chooses for self
	Does not achieve desired goal	Achieves desired goal by hurting others	May achieve desired goal
Likely consequences for the person toward whom the action is directed (receiver)	Guilty or angry	Self-denying	Self-enhancing
	Depreciates sender	Hurt, defensive, humiliated	Expressive
	Achieves desired goal at sender's expense	Does not achieve desired goal	May achieve desired goal

SOURCE: From *Your Perfect Right: A Guide to Assertive Living* (Sixth Edition) © 1990 by Robert E. Alberti and Michael L. Emmons. Reproduced for Prentice-Hall Canada, Inc. by permission of Impact Publishers, Inc., P.O. Box 1094, San Luis Obispo, CA 93406. Further reproduction prohibited.

Assertive behaviour is direct speaking about your own needs, feelings, and goals. It tells the other party what you think, feel, and want without being aggressive or hurtful. Likewise, assertiveness is not self-sacrifice, denial, and the avoidance of the conflict situation.

Donald Bowen (1988) lists eight principles of assertiveness.

1. Share your feelings with the other person in a statement beginning with the word "I". This tells the other what you are thinking, feeling, or what your goals are.
2. Don't discount yourself and don't discount others. Be straightforward in your statements and avoid qualifiers such as "I'm no expert on this, but ..."
3. Don't be wishy-washy. Make your statements clear, direct, and to the point.
4. Be specific in feedback and criticism. Provide the other with specific and constructive comments instead of generalizations.
5. Use neutral, nonexplosive language. Aggressive language can provoke an aggressive response from others, simply in defense of themselves.
6. Be cooperative, open and receptive to others—they may know something you don't. Instead of assuming there is a problem, ask about the facts of the situation.
7. Confront unpleasant situations immediately (or at least as soon as practicable). Deal with hurts or frustrations before they build up to the point where you explode in an angry outburst.
8. Make sure your nonverbal communication is congruent with your words. Being assertive means that you do not send mixed messages—both what you say and how you say it must match for the message to come across clearly.

An assertive approach to dealing with workplace conflict is offered by Richard Greene, in his 1988 article "Seven steps to winning a fight." He says the employee in conflict with the boss must do these things. Select the appropriate time for the meeting; be direct; don't go in angry; clarify the issues; know that when a loss is inevitable it is time to give up; keep in mind that there is no problem that does not have a solution; and remember that the boss' goals must be considered as well as your own goals.

Conflict Resolution Methods   A key way to resolve work conflict is by **negotiation**. Mark McCormack (1984) advises that any business dispute should be seen as the beginning of a negotiation and that "Once two parties have acknowledged in some way that they can both benefit from agreement—which is usually the stage at which a negotiation begins—it is inexcusable, barring unforeseen circumstances, not to reach one" (p. 156).

Negotiation A method of conflict resolution.

Roger Fisher and William Ury (1983) describe four key points in what they call principled negotiation. They are: (1) separate the *people* from the problem; (2) focus on *interests* not positions; (3) generate a variety of possible *options* before making a decision; and (4) ensure that the result is based on *objective criteria*.

Further advice about negotiations is given by Mark McCormack in this chapter's *A Word to the Wise* feature. This chapter's *Overboard* cartoon shows how negotiations work on the pirate ship *Revenge*.

Besides the actual parties to a negotiation, there are different roles that can be played by a third party (Raiffa, 1982). Facilitators act to bring the disputants together, and can also serve as counselors in an attempt to help one or both sides understand the source of the conflict and how to deal with it. Mediators help the parties in conflict to find an agreement. Arbitrators examine both sides of a dispute and then either suggest a solution or select a decision. For instance, major league baseball uses a system of final offer arbitration in which the arbitrator must select either management's salary offer to a player or that player's own suggestion (made via his agent). Finally, rules manipulators have the authority to alter the process of negotiation in order to reach a decision.

A WORD TO THE WISE

WATCHING PEOPLE/REACHING PEOPLE: MY SEVEN-STEP PLAN

Obviously, there aren't 7 steps or 70 steps or 700 steps to learning to read people by opening up your senses. That's the whole point: If it were that categorical it could be learned in a classroom. Nevertheless, what I can say categorically is that learning to read people involves a few basic fundamentals:

STEP 1: Listen Aggressively

Listen not only to what someone is saying but to how he is saying it. People tend to tell you a lot more than they mean to. Keep pausing—a slightly uncomfortable silence will make them say even more.

STEP 2: Observe Aggressively

Have you ever said to yourself when watching a talk show or a news interview, "Oh, that person's nervous," or "Aha! That question made him uncomfortable"?

You don't need to read a book on body language to interpret certain motions or gestures or to "hear" the statement someone may be making simply by the way he or she is dressed.

STEP 3: Talk Less

You will automatically learn more, hear more, see more—and make fewer blunders. Everyone can talk less and almost everyone should be talking less.

Ask questions and then don't begin to answer them yourself.

STEP 4: Take a Second Look at First Impressions

I usually go with my first impressions, but only after I've carefully scrutinized them. Some sort of "thinking out" or contemplative process has to take place between your initial impression and your acceptance of it as a tenet of a relationship.

Muhammed Ali once said to me, "I'm more famous than Jesus Christ" (a line he perhaps borrowed from the Beatles). I was appalled at the statement, dismissed it as braggadocio, and let it go at that. But months later for some reason I got to thinking about it and started counting up all the Moslem, Hindu, and other non-Christian

countries in which Ali was extremely well known. The statement was still braggadocio, but I realized it was also possibly true.

STEP 5: Take Time to Use What You've Learned

If you're about to make a presentation or a phone call, take a moment to think about what you know and what reaction you want. From what you know of the other person, what can you say or do to be most likely to get it?

STEP 6: Be Discreet

Discretion is the better part of reading people. The idea of using what you have learned properly is not to tell them how insecure you think they are or to point out all the things you have perceptively intuited that they may be doing wrong. If you let them know what you know, you will blow any chance of using your own insight effectively.

You don't owe anyone an insight into yourself for every insight you have into him. Remember, you can only use what you've learned if he's learned less about you.

The surest way to let people in on your own security quotient is to tell them all about your accomplishments. Let people learn of your qualities and achievements from someone else.

STEP 7: Be Detached

If you can force yourself to step back from any business situation, particularly one that is heating up, your powers of observation will automatically increase. When the other person gets a little hot under the collar, he or she is going to be more revealing than at almost any other time. If you come back with an equally heated response, you will not only be less observant, you will be revealing just as much about yourself.

I am practically a missionary for the importance of acting rather than reacting in any business situation.

Acting rather than reacting allows you really to use what you have learned. It allows you to convert perceptions into controls. By reacting, by failing to step back first, you are probably throwing this powerful advantage away.

If you don't react you will never overreact. You will be the controller rather than the controllee.

SOURCE: From WHAT THEY DON'T TEACH YOU AT HARVARD BUSINESS SCHOOL by Mark McCormack. Copyright © 1984 by Book Views, Inc. Used by permission of Bantam Books, a division of Bantam Doubleday Dell Publishing Group, Inc.

The accepted social rules for negotiation and bargaining certainly differ between countries and cultures. In most Canadian and U.S. supermarkets it would be unthinkable to start bargaining with the cashier over the price of eggs. But in many farmers markets around the world, including those in North America, bargaining is possible.

In many countries, bargaining is not only possible but a way for the seller and the shopper to begin and then maintain a personal relationship. In such countries the anonymous shopper and cashier are not considered an appropriate way to do business. Therefore, to refuse to bargain can be seen as insulting, because the buyer is implicitly refusing to enter into a relationship with the seller. An example of the difficulties of cross-cultural negotiation is given in this chapter's *A Rose by Any Other Name*.

A ROSE BY ANY OTHER NAME

Professor John Pfeiffer has conducted extensive studies of cross-cultural negotiations between Americans and Japanese. This work could easily be interpreted to include Canadians as well. He has found that there are a number of cultural differences in negotiating styles that make it difficult for the two sides to understand each other. Specifically, he found that:

1. Americans prefer to work quickly while the Japanese prefer a more drawn-out process that explores in detail the product they are buying or selling.

2. While Americans prefer about 10 minutes of light personal conversation before getting down to business—any more is seen as wasting time—for the Japanese such conversation is an essential element in the bargaining process because it builds the personal relationships that are what is really being negotiated. The more important the deal and the dealers, the longer the personal talk, which may last for an hour, a morning, or more.

3. Nonverbal communications can be cross-culturally misinterpreted. In Japan a child is taught to look down when being scolded to show how they have been humbled and shamed. In America a child being scolded is taught to look directly at their scolder to show they are paying attention. When adult Japanese and Americans negotiate the Japanese looking down can be perceived as shiftiness while to the Japanese, American eye-to-eye contact can be seen as impolite and insensitive.

4. To maintain harmony, Japanese will avoid saying "no" directly, by asking a question, changing the subject, promising to answer later, leaving the room, or simply remaining silent—even for long periods of time. To an American such silence, along with a lack of eye contact, can be puzzling and uninterpretable. To give up negotiations at this point misinterprets the Japanese avoidance of saying "no" with a willingness to abandon negotiations.

SOURCE: Pfeiffer (1988).

CONCLUSION

We have now reached the end of Part II of this text—"Working with People." We have discussed how people are the same and different, how we perceive, communicate, and evaluate each other. We have examined what motivates people to take the actions they do, and how a manager could use theories and principles of motivation when working with organizational subordinates. We have investigated the formation and operation of groups in the workplace. The processes of leadership and decision making were also analyzed. Lastly, in the current chapter, the importance of power, politics, and conflict were explored.

The Part II ending case describes a real-life decision situation at the Knowledge Engineering Group of the Mutual Life Assurance Company of Canada, based in Waterloo, Ontario. Concepts and theories from the last eight chapters of this text will be useful tools for the analysis of this case.

The next chapter, Chapter 13, is the first of three that comprise Part III of this text— "What the Future Holds." The topics of these chapters are Stress, Careers, and Change.

Fortunately or unfortunately, the future does hold stress for all of us. Our next chapter considers the topic of stress in organizations. We will examine the nature of stress and how it operates, the common sources of stress, and the results of stress. Chapter 13 will also examine how stress reactions can be effectively managed to reduce their impact on individuals and the organizations of which they are a part. Career management is important for everyone. Chapter 14 describes theories of careers and gives advice to the person interested in overseeing her own career. Change is inevitable for individuals, groups, and whole organizations. Theories of change and change methods at these three levels are discussed in Chapter 15.

CHAPTER SUMMARY

Power is the capacity of one person to influence the attitudes or behaviour of others. Individual power may be based on coercion, expertise, hierarchical position, relationship attraction, rewards, access to or possession of important information, or connections with others. Organizational politics is the process of one person exerting influence over another outside the bounds of the normal authority relationship of formal roles regulated by organizational norms and goals. Political influence tactics can be those of: rational persuasion; inspirational appeal; consultation; ingratiation; exchange; coalition forming; establishing the legitimacy of a request; and exerting pressure.

Politics cannot be avoided in organizations. Every member of an organization needs to know about and be able to engage in different political behaviours in order to be effective. Conflict occurs in organizations when an influence attempt is resisted. Conflict may be seen as evidence that the organization is not operating in a rational manner. But organizations can also be seen as arenas for staging conflicts. In this case conflict is intended as the way the organization makes choices for future action, makes changes in power relationships and keeps itself flexible and adaptive. At an individual level there are five possibilities for dealing with conflict: Competing, collaborating, compromising, avoiding, and accommodating. Each of these is thought to be an effective strategy in specific situations.

QUESTIONS FOR REVIEW

1. Does power corrupt and absolute power corrupt absolutely?

2. Why would a manager in an organization want to accumulate power?

3. What forms of political behaviour have been found to be effectively used in at least one organization?

4. If an organizational member were predisposed to avoid conflict, how could that person be trained to deal with a dominator?

5. Describe three methods that have been created to allow conflict to be formally recognized, confronted, and dealt with.

SELF-DIAGNOSTIC EXERCISE 12.1

Your Primary Conflict Handling Style

Instructions: Indicate your level of agreement or disagreement for each of the 15 items below.

		Disagree				*Agree*
1.	I exchange accurate information with my boss to solve a problem together	1	2	(3)	4	5
2.	I use my influence to get my ideas accepted	1	2	3	(4)	5
3.	I try to find a middle course to resolve an impasse	1	2	3	(4)	5
4.	I usually accommodate the wishes of my boss	1	2	3	(4)	5
5.	I attempt to avoid being "put on the spot" and try to keep my conflict with my boss to myself	1	2	3	4	(5)
6.	I usually propose a middle ground for breaking deadlocks	1	2	(3)	4	5
7.	I use my authority to make a decision in my favour	1	2	3	(4)	5
8.	I usually avoid open discussion of my differences with my boss	1	2	3	(4)	(5)
9.	I often go along with the suggestions of my boss	1	2	3	(4)	5
10.	I try to bring all our concerns out in the open so that the issues can be resolved in the best possible way	1	(2)	3	4	5
11.	I use "give and take" so that a compromise can be made	1	2	3	(4)	5
12.	I try to keep my disagreement with my boss to myself in order to avoid hard feelings	1	2	3	(4)	5
13.	I try to satisfy the expectations of my boss	1	2	3	4	(5)
14.	I try to work with my boss for a proper understanding of a problem	1	2	(3)	4	5
15.	I sometimes use my power to win a competitive situation	1	2	3	(4)	5

Scoring

Integrating   Item 1 _3_ + Item 10 _2_ + Item 14 _3_ = _8_

Avoiding   Item 5 _5_ + Item 8 _5_ + Item 12 _4_ = _14_

Dominating   Item 2 _4_ + Item 7 _4_ + Item 15 _4_ = _12_

Obliging   Item 4 _4_ + Item 9 _4_ + Item 13 _5_ = _13_

Compromising   Item 3 _4_ + Item 6 _3_ + Item 11 _4_ = _11_

The category with the highest total score is your primary conflict handling style.

SOURCE: M. Afzalur Rahim (1983). "A measure of styles of handling interpersonal conflict." *Academy of Management Journal* 26: 368-376. Reprinted by permission.

NOTE: This shortened version of the Rahim Organizational Conflict Inventory-II is included here to encourage you to think about your own conflict handling styles. This shortened version cannot be expected to be as scientifically valid as the full 28-item Inventory.

EXPERIENTIAL EXERCISE 12.1

Role Play

1. Read Case 12.1. The class instructor can select two students (male or female) to play the roles of Tom and Joe. The students should act out the role play until the instructor calls a halt. Then the rest of the class should comment on the role play and critique it in a constructive way. Opinions should be solicited from the rest of the class on what to do next. Then two other students can be selected or can volunteer to take on the roles of Tom and Joe, and the role-play can continue. This process of role-playing followed by critique and suggestions, then further role play can continue for as many cycles as time and interest allow.

EXPERIENTIAL EXERCISE 12.2

The Ugli Orange Case

The purpose of this case exercise is to play the roles of Dr. Roland and Dr. Jones, who are about to engage in a negotiation with the owner of a number of Ugli oranges for the right to purchase those oranges.

It is important that the student *not* read any further information about this role play, because in class students will be assigned one of the two roles to play, and it is necessary that each student have read only the one role assigned.

• STOP reading here until informed by your instructor which role to read •

Step 1   Form groups of three members. One person will be Dr. Roland, one will be Dr. Jones, and the third will be the observer.

Step 2   Dr. Roland reads his/her role, Dr. Jones reads his/her role, and the observer reads both role descriptions.

Step 3   The instructor will announce:
"I am Mr./Ms. Cardoza, the owner of the remaining Ugli oranges. My fruit export firm is based in South America. My country does not have diplomatic relations with your country, although we do have strong trade relations. Please spend about 10 minutes meeting with the other firm's representative and decide on a course of action. Then pick a spokesperson who will tell me:

1. What do you plan to do?
2. If you want to buy the oranges, what price will you offer?
3. To whom and how will the oranges be delivered?

Step 4   The group observers will report on how the solutions were reached, how bargaining proceeded, and how the two role players interacted.

ROLE OF DR. JONES

You are Dr. J.W. Jones, a biological research scientist employed by a pharmaceutical firm. You have recently developed a synthetic chemical useful for curing and preventing Rudosen. Rudosen is a disease contracted by pregnant women. If not caught in the first four weeks of pregnancy, the disease causes serious brain, eye, and ear damage to the unborn child. Recently there has been an outbreak of Rudosen in your geographical area, and several thousand women have contracted the disease. You have found, with volunteer patients, that your recently developed synthetic serum cures Rudosen in its early stages. Unfortunately, the serum is made from the juice of the Ugli orange, which is a very rare fruit. Only a small quantity (approximately 4000) of these oranges were produced last season. No additional Ugli oranges will be available until next season, which will be too late to cure the present Rudosen victims.

You've demonstrated that your synthetic serum is in no way harmful to pregnant women. Consequently, there are no side effects. The serum has been approved for use by pregnant women in both Canada and the United States as a cure for Rudosen. Unfortunately, the present outbreak was unexpected, and your firm had not planned on having the compound serum available for six months. Your firm holds the international patent on the synthetic serum, and it is expected to be a highly profitable product when it is generally available to the public.

You have recently been informed on good evidence that a certain R.H. Cardoza, a South American fruit exporter, is in possession of 3000 Ugli oranges in good condition. If you could obtain the juice of all 3000 you would be able to both cure present victims and provide sufficient inoculation for the remaining pregnant women in your area. No other area currently has a Rudosen threat.

You have recently been informed that Dr. P.W. Roland is also urgently seeking Ugli oranges and is also aware of Cardoza's possession of the 3000 available. Dr. Roland is employed by a competing pharmaceutical firm and has been working on biological warfare research for the past several years. There is a great deal of industrial espionage in the pharmaceutical industry. Over the past several years, Dr. Roland's firm and yours have sued each other for infringement of patent rights and espionage law violations several times.

You've been authorized by your firm to approach R.H. Cardoza to purchase 3000 Ugli oranges. You have been told that they will be sold to the highest bidder. Your firm has authorized you to bid as high as $250 000 to obtain the juice of the 3000 available oranges.

ROLE OF DR. ROLAND

You are Dr. P.W. Roland. You work as a research biologist for a pharmaceutical firm. The firm is under contract with the government to do research on methods to combat enemy uses of biological warfare.

Recently, several World War II experimental nerve gas bombs were moved from the United States to a small island just off the U.S. coast in the Pacific. In the process of transporting them, two of the bombs developed a leak. The leak is presently controlled by government scientists, who believe that the gas will permeate the bomb chambers within two weeks. They know of no method of preventing the gas from getting into the atmosphere and spreading to other islands, and very likely to the west coast as well. If this occurs, it is likely that several thousand people will incur serious brain damage or die.

You've developed a synthetic vapor that will neutralize the nerve gas if it is injected into the bomb chamber before the gas leaks out. The vapor is made with a chemical taken from the rind of the Ugli orange, a very rare fruit. Unfortunately, only 4000 of these oranges were produced this season.

You've been informed on good evidence that a certain R.H. Cardoza, a fruit exporter in South America, is in possession of 3000 Ugli oranges. The chemicals from the rinds of all 3000 oranges would be sufficient to neutralize the gas if the serum is developed and injected efficiently. You have also been informed that the rinds of these oranges are in good condition.

You have also been informed that Dr. J.W. Jones is also urgently seeking purchase of Ugli oranges, and is aware of Cardoza's possession of the 3000 available. Dr. Jones works for a firm with which your firm is highly competitive. There is a great deal of industrial espionage in the pharmaceutical industry. Over the years, your firm and Dr. Jones' have sued each other for violations of industrial espionage laws and infringement of patent rights several times. Litigation on two suits is still in process.

The federal government has asked your firm for assistance. You've been authorized by your firm to approach R.H. Cardoza to purchase 3000 Ugli oranges. You have been told that they will be sold to the highest bidder. Your firm has authorized you to bid as high as $250 000 to obtain the rind of the oranges.

Before approaching Cardoza, you have decided to talk to Dr. Jones to influence Jones not to prevent you from purchasing the oranges.

SELF-GUIDED LEARNING ACTIVITY

Perhaps the best source of information on gaining power, the use of politics, and dealing with conflict are the biographies of famous people. These books give a fascinating and usually detailed account of how the person made it to the top of his or her profession. It can be instructive to examine their stories to experience vicariously the problems, setbacks, and conflicts they experienced before they achieved ultimate success.

MANAGER'S CASE FILE: THE MEMO

An interoffice memo was sent to all departments at Techco, Inc. noting that there had been complaints over employees taking advantage of visits to the medical department as an excuse to leave their work stations. To control the situation, a new procedure was being adopted.

In the future, employees would need a pass signed by their supervisor stating the reason for the visit. After completion of the visit, the medical department attendant would sign the pass, and it would be returned to the supervisor.

When Tom Garner, manager of the materials management group, announced the new procedure at a meeting with his employees, he noticed some uneasiness and a lot of eye contact among the employees, but no one spoke. The next day, however, Tom got some feedback from Joe Hart, the department's top employee. Joe was the natural leader among the employees, and his relationship with Tom was one of mutual respect, but this was clearly a confrontation as he faced Tom across the manager's desk.

"Listen," Joe said, his voice tight. "A lot of us are mad about this medical thing. None of us is ripping off Techco, and we figure it's nobody's business why we want to go to medical. Tom, it's like we're back in kindergarten."

"Look, Joe," Tom said, "it wasn't my idea, but some of the other managers lodged complaints about the amount of time their employees were spending away from their desks. Most of them had reported to the medical office, and during this time production was down and it slowed the entire department. It was felt that some of these employees had gone to medical just to get away from the job for a while."

"That's at the other departments, Tom," Joe explained. "That wasn't us, and you know it."

"I know no one in this department has been taking advantage," Tom replied. "But I've got to follow procedure just like everyone else. We can't have different rules for the different departments. It's really not such a big deal."

"It is to us," Joe said over his shoulder as he walked back to his work station.

Within two days it was clear that the employees at Techco were not holding still for the new procedure. The medical department's usual patient load of 25 people a day had slowed to a trickle. But absenteeism throughout the plant broke all records. Illness seemed to have felled a high percentage of employees who were using sick days to "see their own doctors."

On the morning of the fourth day, Tom stood in his office door looking at the overflowing desks and empty chairs in his department. Purchase orders and inventory control records were piled high. Productivity was at a standstill, and Tom knew that it was the same in other parts of the plant. It was emptier than when employees went to medical at will.

For Tom, there was another thing at stake besides the bottom line at Techco, Inc. He was in line for a vice-presidency, and he wouldn't have a chance if he couldn't keep his own department operating. He knew that something had to be done—and done fast if his own chance for promotion wasn't to be lost. When he tried to talk to his employees about it, they claimed that they were "just following procedure." Since they were taking sick days that were due them, Tom wondered what he could do to get his employees to come to work.

SOURCE: Reprinted, by permission of publisher, from MANAGEMENT SOLUTIONS, September 1987. © 1987 American Management Association, New York. All rights reserved.

Questions

1. How could Tom have better handled the announcement meeting?

2. How should Tom have handled the confrontation with Joe and what can he do now to rectify the situation?

CASE 12.2

SQUARING OFF À LA FORESTIÈRE

When environmentalists and logging companies confront each other, the battleground is usually deep in old-growth forests in British Columbia.

The combatants often wear the colours of MacMillan Bloedel Ltd., the biggest forest products company in the province, or the Western Canada Wilderness Committee, the primary environmental action group fighting to save old-growth forests.

One recent evening—instead of squaring off on a logging road—representatives of the two groups met in a downtown Vancouver restaurant over dinner. Two of the forest company's public relations people and two directors of the wilderness committee gathered around the table.

Scott Alexander of MacMillan Bloedel organized the meeting. "I hear stories all the time," he said, "about other parts of the world, that there is a lot more contact between the industry and environmental organizers. In B.C., we don't talk to each other except through [the media]. We scream at each other across the barricades."

The warring groups find much to scream about. The activists despise the large companies' forest practices—logging roads that crisscross mountain sides, the large bare patches left after clearcutting and the replanting that replaces complex ecosystems of interdependent plant, animal and insect life with mainly single-species tree farms.

The company folk are livid about what they consider to be the interference of the activists—blockades set up on logging roads and public pressure that leads politicians to tighten regulations and customers to demand chlorine-free paper or wood harvested in a selection rather than clearcut fashion.

The environmental groups have added another dimension to the fray, by forming alliances with forest company workers, convincing many of them that their jobs will disappear if all the old-growth forest—natural forest that is largely untouched by logging—that can be harvested is cut. The environmental groups also stress their view that more jobs can and should be generated from the province's primary industry.

These were some of the items on the agenda the night the two sides met over dinner. For more than two hours, rhetoric and invective flew across the table. But between the insults and harangues, Paul George and Joe Foy of the wilderness committee and Mr. Alexander and Dennis Fitzgerald of MacMillan Bloedel did manage to trade some information, clarify some misunderstandings and find a bit—albeit a very small patch—of common ground.

Following is some of that discussion, edited for length (MB represents the two company spokesmen, and WC, the wilderness committee representatives):

MB: You've been quoted as saying there should be no more clearcutting in British Columbia; that was a BCTV report about a year and a half ago. Are you still of that mind?

WC: Yeah.

MB: No clearcutting at all?

WC: No, in small little patches. Clearcutting, what we're talking about, is these huge giant things.

MB: What's an acceptable size clearcut?

WC: It depends, it's site specific.

MB: We've got common ground there.

WC: Yeah but you guys are so far out of scale, you're a hundred times larger than they should be.

MB: A hundred times?

WC: I think two or three hectares that's the maximum, in a little narrow strip. And natural regeneration, we don't believe in planting. We think it's wasteful, costs a whole bunch of money. We believe you can really do it through natural regeneration. If it's done right you don't have to [replant]. You can see it in natural blowdowns. You must read the stuff. It isn't me inventing some weird, brand-new idea, this is coming out of the scientific community.

MB: Let me get back to you 'cause I have been judging you and the wilderness committee on a clip I saw maybe two years ago.

WC: And I said no clearcutting?

MB: Yeah.

WC: I want to see that clip.

MB: I'll send it to you. You see that's the problem with some of this stuff and if there's no other reason to get together it is to clear up that stuff. Another one was you saying there would be no old-growth logging in British Columbia. Did you say that?

WC: Well some day for sure. We're going to run out of it.

MB: [Do we have to stop] old-growth logging now?

WC: I think it's coming very close to the time when we have to move into husbanding our second-growth resource.

MB: That's an evasive answer. Give a clear yes or no. Should there be old-growth logging in B.C. right now?

WC: Only in a selection way on the coast. We should continue old-growth forests by selection, slow, long rotations, we can maintain that forest in an old-growth state forever. It doesn't mean hammering it with technology the way we are now. And we have certain enclaves of ancient forests we want to leave as benchmarks.

MB: We've got a common ground there.

WC: Then we want a whole other bunch of forests that are managed where you harvest them but keep them in an old-growth state—you keep these snag trees for the birds, you take out logs, come back every 10 to 15 years, take a tree here or there, and you use human intelligence to improve the stands. And you make a lot of money because this kind of product, some of the fine-grained stuff, is valuable. You know how valuable it is.

MB: You're suggesting all this stuff that we can do—the 'we,' I take it, is not MacMillan Bloedel, it's what society can do.

WC: Society. MacMillan Bloedel can't do that because you're tied into a system where you get maximum profit from doing the way you're doing it now. And you can't break out of it.

Even if you personally wanted to, it takes societal change. The people have to understand that. So we're trying to go to the average Joe and say, 'Hey, we can't expect so much from the environment.' We're into using all the resources less, everybody cutting back.

MB: Does that mean that people who work in the woods are going to have to earn less money?

WC: Of course. Eventually when the old growth's gone they're going to—

MB: No, I mean now.

WC: Yes.

MB: Can we maintain the wage rates that we're paying people to work in the woods now?

WC: I don't think so, not [at the rate] that M and B's paying.

MB: What are we going to be paying? Cut 'em in half? If they make $28 an hour now gross wages, what do you think is a sustainable level?

WC: Well I think we have to start, first of all, going to this other way [of logging]. The horse loggers I know make pretty good, $100 to $110 a day. The people up on Cortes Island [east of Campbell River at the north end of the Straight of Georgia] who've gone to selection logging are making more now, they said, than they made with M and B.

MB: Is this going to follow, for everybody everywhere?

Over the past decade, the B.C. forest industry's production of wood, pulp and paper has soared while employment has plummeted. IWA Canada, which represents most of the workers in the woods and the lumber mills, says total hours for its members are now just half of what they were 10 years ago. Workers in the pulp and paper industry have been hit by similar losses.

MB: What do you figure is the root cause of the job loss, 'cause we get blamed for that? What do you think they're doing wrong?

WC: I think the trees are undervalued. I think you're sitting on the best in the province, they're not going to open bid.

MB: Open bid? To the Japanese or within B.C.?

WC: Open bid within B.C. I feel strongly about that. We may pull that off 'cause Washington State would like to see that, too. The Forests Minister said that we might have problems with GATT trying to shut down raw log exports, but Washington State has teamed up with B.C. and we've got a chance to keep that closed. The problem is, if you can buy my house for $50, you can afford to pulp it; but if you have to buy my house on the open market, you couldn't. If you sever the integrated companies so that one group logs, the other manufactures, and the manufacturers bid on an open B.C. log market, you will get the right value for the wood and that will mean more jobs.

MB: Something that distresses me: When times are as tough as they are, I think people polarize more, it gets nastier, it gets tougher and I don't like the feeling that engenders.

WC: Stop fighting, stop financing the hate groups, stop bringing Ron Arnold into your picture. *[Mr. Arnold is a U.S. consultant said to be linked with the Unification Church of Reverend Sun Myung Moon.]*

MB: Stop mislabelling them. Ron Arnold—he's not in our equation, he's never been in our equation.

WC: I was at a forestry meeting three years ago and he was the keynote speaker.

MB: I've learned more about Ron Arnold reading in *The Vancouver Sun* and listening to [environmental activist] Pauline McCrory than I have in any dealings I've had with Ron Arnold.

WC: Well how much money do you put into the Forestry Alliance, the pseudo-environment groups and the Share groups? I mean, I'll honestly tell you about our stuff, what we do.

MB: When you say we're somehow linked up with the Moonies—

WC: I didn't say that. I said Ron Arnold is the thought behind the Share groups. He is the person who has promulgated them. You guys were down there for that conference in Reno.

[A 1988 conference of 400 people examined the principle of multiple use of land.] How much money do you put in?

MB: I don't know.

WC: Can you find it out for me?

MB: Yeah, I can find out.

WC: And who's paying Claude Richmond's ticket?

MB: I don't know, Ministry of Forests?

WC: Not any more.
[Mr. Richmond, former B.C. forests minister, has been hired by B.C. forest products companies to represent them at the United Nations environmental conference in Rio in June.]

WC: Like [when you] say, we're Earth First [a U.S.-based radical environmental action group], that's the same old ... Do you think we're Earth First?

MB: No. Do you think we're Share and Ron Arnold?

WC: But I read it in [*The Vancouver Sun*. You] said "Earth First is an arm of the wilderness committee." I mean, who the hell wants to eat with somebody who says total falsehoods, lies—

MB: You say we're hooked up with Ron Arnold, that's the same shit, man.

WC: I'm not saying you're hooked up with Ron Arnold, I'm saying you believe his philosophy.

MB: What's his philosophy, just in a nutshell?

WC: It's called the wise-use philosophy, that every piece of land was put here for man to use, and all the environmentalists have a hidden agenda, lock everything away and throw away the key and not have anybody working.

So the people who are now fighting for their jobs must have a hidden agenda too, to open up every place to logging, to use widely, even the parks. And he said you have to start a grassroots movement, get industry to finance a whole bunch of different groups—you don't have just one. The environmentalists have lots of different groups, you know, Friends of Clayoquot Sound and so on, so we should have Share the Rock, Forestry Alliance, Scientists for Wise Use, a million different organizations, all pretending they're grass-roots environmental groups but really the funding comes from multinationals and the agenda is to keep them clearcutting, keep the companies doing exactly the same thing they're doing now.

MB: Have we been successful in getting P.R. points in the past three or four years?

WC: Oh yeah, for sure. You've still got your tree farm license, you're still out there, still clearcutting just like ever. You haven't changed a damn bit. You're better and better at saying, "Hey, we used to do it the bad way." But we can go out to areas that you cut yesterday—same goddamn way, same way it was always done.

————————————

WC: If you guys could get Southam to use recycled newsprint—

MB: Why is it a good thing to use recycled?

WC: It's a psychological commitment, a statement that we don't have to cut as many trees down.

MB: Not in B.C. it isn't. The use of recycled newsprint saves space in landfills. It's not going to affect one iota the number of trees we cut.

WC: Yes it is. When I have visitors from other countries, they ask "what can I do to save B.C. rain forests?" and the first thing I tell them is to use recycled newsprint.

MB: No, no, think back to "Recycle this envelope and save a tree"—that's one of the mythologies on the West Coast. Back East, they take whole trees and put 'em in pulp. On the West Coast, we don't do that.

WC: You pulp a lot of good sawlogs. Come on now. You should go out to your plant and see what's going on there. They put lots of sawlog quality into pulp, because pulp is high now and sawlogs are not worth much.

MB: That's a point of dispute.

————————————

WC: You guys are just basically the janitors in the outfit. You're trying to clean up after the dirty deal that's happening to the people in B.C. Okay, I look you right in the eye now: I think it's reprehensible; I think that you sending out that we're Earth Firsters—you know it's wrong—and you'll do anything to try to smear us because that's your job. And you have no power in your company over any policy to change, to go to selection logging or do anything positive. You can only protect the status quo and that's why this is the last dinner I'll have with you.

MB: Your self-righteousness, it—

WC: Yes, really, it is. You go out and see—you're destroying the land with these clearcuts. I could show you areas, it wasn't to be cut and they cut it anyway and you say, "Well I feel so bad about that but I can't do anything, I'm working for a big multinational." We don't want them around here. We don't need them. We can run this place—

MB: Who's "we"?

WC: A whole bunch of people, a big, big coalition building up against corporate ripoff, which has not provided jobs—you promised to provide jobs.

MB: I hope you'll have a look at your printers who print your books because some of those guys 20 years ago employed a whole lot more people than they do now and they can get your books out so people can afford them. You're always on the industry for not providing jobs.

WC: You've got massive land. We can prove it'll make more jobs.

MB: You should do that.

WC: Already they've taken 5 per cent from the TFLs *[taken from large companies' tree farm licenses and given to the province's small business forest program a few years ago]*—it's provided a hell of a lot of jobs.

MB: What's the forestry record there? You guys looked at that? What's the replanting record on the small business program?

WC: You're trying to get evidence, trying to say, that taking away your clearcut privilege in British Columbia is a bad idea because other people don't manage it as well. I think that small industry provides a lot more jobs, because they do it carefully, they don't go to grapple yarders.

MB: I think part of what's at issue here is that we ascribe values and beliefs to people without benefit of dealing with the people directly. I think that's part of why we're at loggerheads so much and that personally distresses me so much. I think there have to be more things like this [dinner] rather than fewer. You say this is the last one.

WC: I'll eat with the president, someone who's got power in your organization, anybody who can really make change. My job is to try to get environmental change, to get a better way of logging, to preserve bio-diversity through big wilderness areas.

MB: How will you go about doing that?

WC: Public education and research. We've got the Carmanah Research Station. Why don't you put $10 000 or $100 000 into [that]? We've already found a whole bunch of insects, a whole bunch of bio-diversity nobody even knew was up there.

MB: When is this going to be published in the scientific journals for the scientists?

WC: A lot of it's already been published.

MB: Would you do this again?

WC: [Joy Foy] I find it totally absolutely useless. I want to go back and work with the volunteers, I think you're an okay guy [but] you couldn't pay me enough to do what you're doing. (At that point, Mr. Foy left the restaurant.)

MB: (To Paul George) Would you do this again?

WC: No, absolutely not. You guys, we have nothing in common, it's useless.

MB: If you were running MB from this position of power—

WC: I wouldn't run it, I would cut it up, I'd dissolve it. They've been given a chance, a social contract with the province and the workers and I think that kind of arrangement no longer works for the 1990s or the 21st century.

A GLOSSARY OF ENTRÉES

Clearcutting—Complete removal of all growth from a specified area at one time.

Selection logging—Harvesting only mature trees, usually the oldest and largest, one at a time or in small groups and removing deformed and less desirable trees to leave more room for the good ones to grow.

Selective logging—Taking only the best trees.

Old growth—Natural forest, largely untouched.

Ancient forest—Never-logged, untouched forest.

Horse loggers—Use horses to drag selection logged trees out of the forest; less damaging to the remaining growth than tractors or cables.

B.C. Forest Alliance—An industry-sponsored group established [in 1991] to build public confidence in the industry's performance through broad public involvement and education.

B.C.Share—A coalition of community-based groups, originally established by the industry, to promote shared use of the forest resource in their area rather than preservation in parks or wilderness areas.

Tree farm license—A 25-year license to manage a large tract of Crown or private forest lands.

Open bid—Allows companies to buy logs from other companies or independent loggers as opposed to buying them from the government.

SOURCE: Case written by Patricia Lush. *The Globe and Mail,* April 4, 1992, p. B22. Reprinted by permission of the Globe and Mail.

Questions

1. Analyze the power bases of MacMillan Bloedel and the Wilderness Committee, and then the power of the representatives of these two organizations.

2. How would you characterize the discussion? Are the individuals sharing information, problem solving, or talking past each other? Is one side engaging in more information sharing and problem solving than the other side?

3. What evidence of political games can you find in this discussion?

4. Are the representatives of MacMillan Bloedel and the Wilderness committee in conflict?

5. How has future interaction between MacMillan Bloedel and the Wilderness Committee changed because of this meeting? Is conflict more or less likely? Have the perceptions and attitudes of the individuals involved changed in any way due to this meeting? How has this meeting affected the levels of stress felt by the individuals involved?

6. Is this meeting likely to provoke change in either the organizations involved or the individuals that represent the organizations?

REFERENCES

Alberti, Robert E., & Michael L. Emmons (1990). *Your Perfect Right: A Guide to Assertive Living.* 6th edition. San Luis Obispo, CA: Impact Publishers.

Bonazzi, Giuseppe (1983). "Scapegoating in complex organizations: The results of a comparative study of symbolic blame-giving in Italian and French public administration." *Organization Studies* 4: 1-18.

Bowen, Donald D. (1988). "Toward a viable concept of assertiveness." In Roy J. Lewicki, Donald D. Bowen, Douglas T. Hall, & Francine S. Hall (Eds.) *Experiences in Management and Organizational Behavior* (pp. 332-335), 3rd edition. New York: John Wiley & Sons, Inc.

Cornwall, Jeffrey R., & Baron Perlman (1990). *Organizational Entrepreneurship.* Homewood, IL: Irwin.

Crozier, Michael (1964). *The Bureaucratic Phenomenon.* Chicago: University of Chicago Press.

Davidson, Jeffrey P. (1988). *Blow Your Own Horn: How to Market Yourself and Your Career.* New York: Amacom Books.

Farrell, Dan & James C. Petersen (1982). "Patterns of political behavior in organizations." *Academy of Management Review* 7: 403-412.

Field, Richard Dudley (1988). *One Man's War.* Unpublished manuscript.

Fisher, Roger & William Ury (1983). *Getting to Yes: Negotiating Agreement Without Giving In.* Boston: Houghton Mifflin.

Foucault, Michel (1982). "The subject and power." *Critical Inquiry* 8: 777-795.

French, John R.P., Jr., & Bertram H. Raven (1959). "The bases of social power." In Douglas Cartwright (Ed.) *Studies in Social Power* (pp. 150-167). Ann Arbor, MI: University of Michigan, Institute for Social Research.

Greene, Richard (1988). "Seven steps to winning a fight." *Forbes,* July 25, 1988, Volume 142(2): 200-201.

Hathaway, Donald B. (1992). "The political office." *CMA Magazine,* April 1992, p. 35.

Hersey, Paul & Kenneth H. Blanchard (1988). *Management of Organizational Behavior: Utilizing Human Resources.* 5th edition. Englewood Cliffs, NJ: Prentice Hall, Inc.

Hickson, David J., Christopher R. Hinings, Charles A. Lee, Rodney E. Schneck, & Johannes M. Pennings (1971). "A strategic contingencies' theory of intraorganizational power." *Administrative Science Quarterly* 16: 216-229.

Hinings, Christopher R., David J. Hickson, Johannes M. Pennings, & Rodney E. Schneck (1974). "Structural conditions of intraorganizational power." *Administrative Science Quarterly* 19: 22-44.

Hollander, Edwin P., & Lynn R. Offerman (1990). "Power and leadership in organizations: Relationships in transition." *American Psychologist* 45: 179-189.

Izraeli, Dafna M., & Todd D. Jick (1986). "The art of saying no: Linking power to culture." *Organization Studies* 7: 171-192.

Lachman, Ran (1989). "Power from what? A reexamination of its relationship with structural conditions." *Administrative Science Quarterly* 34: 231-251.

Lewicki, Roy J., & Gay Spencer (1992). "Conflict and negotiation in organizations: Introduction and overview." *Journal of Business* 13: 205-207.

Lewicki, Roy J., Stephen E. Weiss, & David Lewin (1992). "Models of conflict, negotiation and third party intervention: A review and synthesis." *Journal of Organizational Behavior* 13: 209-252.

Lush, Patricia (1992). "Squaring off à la forestière." The *Globe and Mail*, April 4, 1992, p. B22.

Mainiero, Lisa A. (1986). "A review and analysis of power dynamics in organizational romances." *Academy of Management Review* 11: 750-762.

McCormack, Mark H. (1984). *What They Don't Teach You at Harvard Business School*. New York: Bantam Books.

Mintzberg, Henry (1983). *Power In and Around Organizations*. Englewood Cliffs, NJ: Prentice Hall, Inc.

Muchinsky, Paul M. (1986). "Footnotes as influence attempts." *The Industrial Psychologist* 23(2): 42-45.

Near, Janet P., & Marcia P. Miceli (1987). "Whistle-blowers in organizations: Dissidents or reformers?" *Research in Organizational Behavior* 9: 321-368.

Neilsen, Eric H. (1972). "Understanding and managing conflict." In Jay W. Lorsch & Paul R. Lawrence (Eds.), *Managing Group and Intergroup Relations* (pp. 329-343). Homewood, IL: Irwin and Dorsey.

Ouchi, William G. (1980). "Markets, bureaucracies, and clans." *Administrative Science Quarterly* 25: 129-141.

Pfeffer, Jeffrey (1981). *Power in Organizations*. Marshfield, MA: Pitman Publishing.

Pfeiffer, John (1988). "How not to lose the trade wars by cultural gaffes." *Smithsonian*, January 1988, Volume 18(10): 145-156.

Pondy, Louis R. (1992). "Reflections on organizational conflict." *Journal of Business* 13: 257-261.

Rahim, M. Afzalur (1983). "A measure of styles of handling interpersonal conflict." *Academy of Management Journal* 26: 368-376.

Rahim, Afzalur, & Thomas V. Bonoma (1979). "Managing organizational conflict: A model for diagnosis and intervention." *Psychological Reports* 44: 1323-1344.

Raiffa, Howard (1982). *The Art and Science of Negotiation*. Cambridge, MA: Harvard University Press.

Raven, Bertram H., & Arie W. Kruglanski (1970). "Conflict and power." In Paul G. Swingle (Ed.), *The Structure of Conflict* (pp. 69-109). New York: Academic Press.

Ruble, Thomas L. & Kenneth W. Thomas (1976). "Support for a two-dimensional model of conflict behavior." *Organizational Behavior and Human Performance* 16: 143-155.

Salancik, Gerald R., & Jeffrey Pfeffer (1977). "Who gets power—and how they hold on to it: A strategic-contingency model of power." *Organizational Dynamics* 5(3): 3-21.

Sargent, Alice G., & Ronald J. Stupak (1989). "Managing in the '90s: The androgynous manager." *Training and Development Journal*, December 1989, 29-35.

Thomas, Kenneth W. (1977). "Toward multi-dimensional values in teaching: The example of conflict behaviors." *Academy of Management Review* 2: 484-490.

Thomas, Kenneth W. (1992). "Conflict and negotiation processes in organizations." In Marvin D. Dunnette and Leaetta M. Hough (Eds.) *Handbook of Industrial and Organizational Psychology* (2nd edition, Volume 3, pp. 651-717). Palo Alto, CA: Consulting Psychologists Press.

Tjosvold, Dean (1984). "Cooperation theory and organizations." *Human Relations* 37: 743-767.

Tjosvold, Dean (1993). *Learning to Manage Conflict: Getting People to Work Together Productively.* New York: Lexington Books.

Yukl, Gary, & J. Bruce Tracey (1992). "Consequences of influence tactics used with subordinates, peers, and the boss." *Journal of Applied Psychology* 77: 525-535.

Zaleznik, Abraham (1990). "The leadership gap." *Academy of Management Executive* 4: 7-22.

FURTHER READING

A book length look at power in organizations by Stanford University's Jeffrey Pfeffer is titled *Managing with Power*, and was published in 1992 by Boston's Harvard Business School Press. Pfeffer discusses the sources of power, strategies and tactics for employing power effectively, and the dynamics of power—how power is lost and how organizations change.

One of the first manuals aimed at increasing the political survival skills of women in organizations was *Games Mother Never Taught You: Corporate Gamesmanship for Women* by Betty Lehan Harragan, published in 1977 by Rawson, Wade Publishers, Inc. Still a useful guide, Harragan's premise is that males learn the competitive rules of business from childhood games such as football and baseball while females were learning more cooperative rules from what were seen as more traditionally female childhood games. An academic work on gender and empowerment is Lisa Mainiero's 1986 article in the *Administrative Science Quarterly* titled "Coping with powerlessness: The relationship of gender and job dependency to empowerment-strategy usage." It is found in Volume 31, pages 633-653.

Prescriptions on managing relationships at work are located in the article by David R. Eyler and Andrea P. Baridon (1992), "Managing sexual attraction in the workplace," *Business Quarterly*, Winter 1992, pp. 19-26.

An intriguing look at the effect of native culture and values on methods of organization and the politics in newly formed native corporations is provided by Gary C. Anders and Kathleen K. Anders in their 1986 article titled "Incompatible goals in unconventional organization: The politics of Alaska native corporations," from *Organization Studies* 7: 213-233.

The article "Perceptions of organizational politics" is a useful place to start to examine the factors that affect whether or not an individual sees politics at work. It is in the *Journal of Management*, Volume 18, pages 93-116.

For a discussion of whistle blowing and the strategies an individual could use to change unethical behaviour within an organization see Richard P. Nielsen (1989), "Changing unethical organizational behavior," *Academy of Management Executive* 3(2): 123-130.

This book on negotiation takes the position that most managers tend to behave irrationally in negotiations. It goes on to examine how to avoid this by focusing on the other person's behaviour. See Max H. Bazerman and Margaret A. Neale (1991), *Negotiating Rationally*, New York: Free Press. Also see Margaret A. Neale and Max H. Bazerman (1992),

"Negotiating rationally: the power and impact of the negotiator's frame," in *Academy of Management Executive* 6(3): 42-51. Dealing with others who try to manipulate you can be difficult. A book that offers advice in this area is *Hidden Agendas* by Marlin S. Potash with Susan Meltsner (1990), published by Delacorte Press.

A book that examines four factors of management style is by Robert Benfari, titled *Understanding Your Management Style: Beyond the Myers-Briggs Type Indicator,* published in 1991 by The Free Press. The four factors discussed are how we perceive and judge the world around us, our motivations, how conflict is handled, and how power is used.

MUTUAL LIFE ASSURANCE COMPANY OF CANADA: THE KNOWLEDGE ENGINEERING GROUP

By June 1990, the first production expert system at Mutual Life Assurance Company of Canada (Mutual) had been in use for almost four months. Brian Cooper, leader of the Knowledge Engineering Group (KEG) which had developed the Group Quotes expert system ("Quality Underwriting-Intelligent Calculations" or "QU-IC") wondered what the future should hold for further expert systems development at Mutual.

Senior management, thanks to the information sessions Bill Yeo, Vice President-Information Systems, had arranged for KEG to conduct, seemed to understand the potential for expert systems and seemed eager to move forward. Mutual was in the last stages of purchasing a mainframe expert system shell that should facilitate the embedding of expert systems logic into traditional applications and enable expert systems to become a part of mainstream data processing.

KEG now consisted of five experienced and capable knowledge engineers, but did not yet have a major new application to develop. Should the group focus on finding major new applications? Should they concentrate on bringing expert systems into the mainstream of data processing? Should they make expert systems an available tool for end user computing? Should they do all of these things? What was the best way to proceed?

THE MUTUAL GROUP

The Mutual Group is a broad-based group of financial services companies, active in life and health insurance, investments, financial management and counselling, property management, and oil and gas exploration. In 1989 it had assets of $12.5 billion, revenues of $3.3 billion, net income of $125 million and more than 2800 employees. The Mutual Life Assurance Company of Canada is the lead company of the group providing life and health insurance, reinsurance, annuities,

RRSPs, pensions, mortgages, real estate financing and corporate lending. According to *Canadian Business,* the Mutual Group was the sixth largest life insurance company in Canada in 1989[1].

INFORMATION SYSTEMS AT MUTUAL

The Information Systems (IS) division at Mutual Life had an objective to stay at the forefront of relevant technology, and had committed significant resources to research and development, often ahead of many of its competitors. As a result, Mutual often used IS as a way to recruit top quality people. There was a great deal of movement from IS to the other divisions in the company, so there was good understanding and support of IS throughout the organization.

A staff of more than 300 worked in the IS division at The Mutual Group's head office in Waterloo, Ontario. (The organizational structure of the division is shown in Exhibit 1.)

Industry cost studies typically showed that Mutual spent a greater proportion of its general and administrative expenses on data processing than its competitors of a similar size, and that, overall, general and administrative expenses were lower than those of similar firms. Mutual users were involved in every aspect of the development process. Developers were organized into resource teams by lines of business. Users determined development priorities and were clearly the owners of the systems that were developed. The development process always included JAD sessions (Joint Application Design) among users and developers. End user computing had been encouraged since the late 1970s.

Employees who had experience in other organizations found that the tool-kit that Mutual used for systems development had a much higher degree of integration than was the norm in the industry. In 1985,

---

SOURCE: This case was prepared by Betty Vandenbosch, under the direction of Professor Peter C. Bell of the Western Business School. Copyright © 1990, The University of Western Ontario.

EXHIBIT 1   INFORMATION SYSTEMS DIVISION DEPARTMENTS

DEPARTMENT	RESPONSIBILITY	HEADCOUNT
Computer Systems	Mainframe Applications Development	175
Micro-Computer Centre*	PC-based Systems (mostly agent support)	21
Computer Operations	Day-to-day running of systems	21
Telecommunications Services	Voice and data network	18
Technical Services	Operating Systems support	20
Support Services	Bridge between technical services and developers; Data Entry	35
Personal Computing Centre	End user computing and remote user support	32

* KEG reports to the executive responsible for the Micro-Computer Centre.

Mutual began using a tool to automate several aspects of the systems analysis and design process including helping systems professionals develop systems diagrams and models, validate design data, prototype screens and reports before coding, and create user- and system-related documentation. The IS division found that automating analysis and design allowed production of more thorough and consistent designs, which resulted in better quality systems.[2]

A successfully piloted document image processing system illustrated how new technology was typically introduced at Mutual. Bill Yeo and the interested user group agreed that the time had come to experiment so they invested in the system. They shared the cost so that the first user would not be burdened with learning costs that would ultimately benefit the entire organization. An article about the system appeared in *Computing Canada* in July 1989.[3]

EXPERT SYSTEMS AT MUTUAL

David Blackburn, a senior systems engineer at Mutual Life, became interested in expert systems in 1984 and was soon joined by Brian Cooper. Both had come from Support Services, and began by doing a lot of reading about the technology. As soon as they were convinced that expert systems might hold

promise for Mutual, they surveyed senior managers to find a place to try the new technology. The Mutual Financial Planning subsidiary (MFP) appeared to have a problem that was amenable to an expert systems solution.

MFP consisted of eight offices across the country, each with a few executive financial planners responsible for providing individuals with customized tax and investment advice. The expert system, called FAST (Financial Analysis Support Tool), was designed to support the financial analysis component of the planning process.

Mutual ordered two Xerox LISP machines in August of 1985 and purchased an expert system shell called KEE from Intellicorp Inc. The machines arrived in early 1986, and Dave and Brian, together with Kam Lafontaine, an expert planner, started immediately. Dave thought they probably rewrote FAST three times as they experimented with a number of approaches.

Typically the team would meet and discuss the system and financial planning until they had filled a white board full of notes. Dave and Brian would work on that for a day or two, at which time the team would get back together, review progress, and fill in the gaps that had appeared on the white board as a result of the features that had been implemented. There was always more work on the white board, but they never tried to implement all of the ideas before having Kam come back for another look at the progress they had made. The idea was to keep the iterative process going and never implement so much that they would hesitate to retrace their steps.

While the FAST system was being developed, Xerox announced that it would no longer support the LISP machines Mutual was using. KEG then ordered Sun workstations to replace the Xerox equipment, and were forced to convert all the software already developed.

The FAST system was ready for implementation in mid-1988 after about 250 days of development time (each day of development time was estimated to cost between $300 and $500). Unfortunately, by that time, the window of opportunity had closed, and FAST was no longer a high priority—executive financial planners had been shifted into a much greater agent support role and could no longer justify the expense of FAST, which was designed for a more sophisticated planning process.

Although the system was in production for only a short time, the participants learned a great deal about how to develop expert systems during the process—an important objective at the outset. While they were converting the system from Xerox to Sun equipment, the group was already looking for another application of expert systems technology. They found Group Quotes.

QUOTATIONS IN THE GROUP INSURANCE DIVISION

In 1987, the underwriting group in the Group Insurance division realized they had to improve the systems support available for the quotation process. What were once straightforward quotation calculations for group clients, had evolved into complicated, time-consuming, number-crunching procedures. Over the years, the quotation procedures manual had become incredibly complicated and full of special exceptions as a consequence of the increasingly competitive environment Group Insurance faced.

The underwriters were doing a remarkable job using a patchwork of support tools consisting of a mainframe application, APL programs designed by

Group actuaries, PC programs and many many manual calculations. The underwriters were limited in their ability to undertake "what if" analyses because the turnaround required by brokers and the sales force was short while the turnaround provided by the system was long. In addition, it was difficult for underwriters to thoroughly research unusual requests because most of their time was spent on rate calculation.

An expert system was conceived to make the difficult and time-consuming rate calculation aspect of the underwriters' job easier, and to produce client quotes more quickly. The objective was to integrate all of the data and procedures required for the entire quotation process.

The first step was to build a prototype to prove that the expert system was a viable solution. A single benefit, the Long Term Disability benefit, was chosen because it was considered to be one of the most difficult to support. The prototype was demonstrated to the senior people in the underwriting group who were anxious to see the progress that had been made. Bill Yeo also arranged a technology session to showcase QU-IC to the senior executives of the company. KEG believed that the process of demonstrating the system as often as possible was important to maintain a high level of commitment throughout the project.

In March 1989, the *Financial Post* reported that executive vice-president David MacIntosh told the annual meeting that the company would spend $250 000 on an expert systems project. The pressure to perform was on. Once the prototype was approved, development of QU-IC took about a year with a team of two full-time and three part-time developers working with two experts.

Brian described the development as follows:

> The quotation process was the most complicated thing I hope I ever try to program. It was riddled with exceptions and special cases. It was not exhaustively documented or consistently applied from underwriter to underwriter. There were so many variables and special cases that I doubt we would ever have been able to write specifications for this system. At times it seemed we would never get it right (as we iterated over and over and over) but we did it and the result is better than I think we really expected or hoped it would be.

One of the real challenges was to make the quotation system a "white" rather than a "black box"; just to output a final rate would not have been acceptable. The process had to be transparent, giving the underwriter access to the calculations throughout. In addition, the expertise of senior underwriters had to be built in.

Another difficult aspect of QU-IC's development was the testing and validation phase. About a month's worth of historical case studies were tried using the system and the results compared to the underwriters' actual recommendations. These cases then formed the basis of a test system to allow ongoing validation as QU-IC inevitably was enhanced.

QU-IC asked underwriters to describe the benefit requested by the prospective group, the type of business the group was, the age, sex, income and job titles of all group members, past benefit programs, and the claims history. From this information, QU-IC calculated rates that should be charged for the policy, and checked for and noted any unusual situations that should be brought to the underwriter's attention (for example: good or bad claim experience for specific benefits, or an unusual age distribution in the group). The underwriter then used the reports from the analysis to investigate and tune the rate—there were literally hundreds of ways the underwriter could introduce discretionary changes into the pricing procedure.

Nine Sun workstations (each costing about $18 000) were purchased in late 1989 for the group quotes system which went into full operation in February 1990.

By June, the fourteen underwriters in the group had processed over five hundred quotations using QU-IC. Mutual now owned twenty-two Sun work stations, fifteen for use in Group Quotes and seven for development.

Only four months after its implementation, the underwriters believed that developing quotes using QU-IC was both faster and more effective than the old way. Typically, it took about three years for an underwriter to become proficient (turnover in the financial services industry averaged about 10% annually and the average cost of an underwriter, including salary, benefits, office space and supplies, was about $51 000), but with QU-IC underwriters with one year of experience were doing the same work as three-year underwriters. In addition, rate calculations that used to take up to two or three days to complete now took about an hour. Underwriters were now able to review more scenarios and undertake more research to produce more informative quotations.

THE KNOWLEDGE ENGINEERING GROUP (KEG)

In June 1990, KEG consisted of five people: David Blackburn, Rick Schmidt and Brian Cooper with traditional DP backgrounds, and Janice McGuire and David Sibson from the Micro-Computer centre.

Brian had a clear idea of the kinds of people that made the best knowledge engineers. He believed that people skills were more important than technical skills, but anyone attracted to KEG would have to have an innate interest in the technology: "After all, technical skills were crucial so that the developers could learn the new technology quickly, and provide early results to the users when they began developing systems." David Sibson and Janice McGuire had learned from the more experienced members of the team, acting somewhat like apprentices initially. As Janice said, "I spend a lot of time experimenting and looking at other people's code."

Up to now, KEG had been interested primarily in providing computerized support to people who did extensive analysis and would benefit from a system that adapted to their way of working. KEG had not been interested in propagating the expert's special knowledge to an army of clerks, but rather, in boosting the expert's performance and effectiveness with a highly tailored and powerful analysis support tool.

KEG had developed a standardized approach to investigating and developing expert systems. The group believed that an iterative process employing rapid prototyping with constant feedback was the key to success; the application expert had to be involved throughout.

Typically, the development process began with a study to investigate the merits of employing expert systems technology in a particular situation. This phase involved spending two weeks sitting beside a person currently doing the work to understand exactly what was done. With this understanding, the knowledge engineer would work with the managers involved to decide if the application showed promise as an expert system. If it did, a prototype would be built. During the prototype development phase, which lasted from six to eight weeks, the user would be involved about half-time. The prototype either proved or disproved the potential of the concept. If the users and the KEG felt the prototype had merit, they discussed it in detail with the ultimate users of the system using the prototype to demonstrate the potential of the system. After approval of the prototype, the team would begin to build the production system.

KEG had undertaken about twenty studies and developed six prototypes by the middle of 1990. Often the study phase determined that an expert system was not the most appropriate solution. Sometimes a prototype would be built for the sole purpose of researching a difficult problem, with the intention of using traditional software development techniques once the problem was understood.

In June, decisions were being made on a group renewal system, which would be an add-on to QU-IC, and a dental claim system. The latter would be an expert systems component of a traditional system designed to lessen the manual intervention required to process dental claims.

CHALLENGES FACING KEG

Brian Cooper believed KEG faced a major decision point in determining its future focus. As he saw it, they had three opportunities: undertake more projects like QU-IC and FAST, integrate expert systems tools and techniques into mainstream data processing, and help users build their own "non-critical" applications. Should they pursue all three avenues or just one or two?

FINDING MORE PROJECTS

To leverage their specialized abilities in building complex analysis systems, KEG wanted to find more applications like QU-IC and FAST. Applications would have to be ill-defined (to justify the iterative development style), important or strategic (to justify the exotic development and delivery environment) and manually intense. (It would have to be really hard for someone to do the job, or the system would probably not be cost justified.)

While it might be possible to continue to search out new applications and convince users to allow development, it seemed more effective to try to educate users about the potential of expert systems and try to encourage them to start coming to KEG with their needs.

KEG had already spend a great deal of time building awareness about expert systems, and advertising QU-IC's success throughout the organization, but found it a long and slow process to get the organization up to speed. There just wasn't anyone beating a path to KEG's door to have work done (as was the case for the rest of IS). In fact, KEG was the only development group in IS that did not face a development backlog of daunting proportions.

BRINGING EXPERT SYSTEMS INTO MAINSTREAM DP

Brian believed the challenge in bringing expert systems into mainstream data processing was one of changing the mind set of the more than one hundred and seventy-five developers to convince them to abandon what had worked for them in the past, and take the risk of adopting a new methodology. The developers would then have to convince the ultimate decision makers in the user community to use the system. KEG also had to prove the dependability and maintainability of the new technology: Mutual could not afford to have the flaky and the unproven in their traditional DP shop. The company could not operate without reliable systems and had come to depend on IS to provide them with just that.

The second aspect was one of ongoing application support. So far, KEG had undertaken all systems support and data administration for QU-IC because the skills to deal with QU-IC as a regular production system were not yet in Computer Operations. No wonder; QU-IC used a new technology, and workstations that no one else in the company was using. However, as more applications were developed, KEG could no longer go on supporting the operational aspects of implemented systems.

How far and how hard should KEG push? Brian wanted to see some of the useful expert systems tools and techniques adopted in IS. IS management also felt this way and had decided to purchase ADS, a mainframe-based expert systems shell, to enable expert systems logic to be embedded into traditional applications. At the same time, Brian believed that expert systems would remain an important niche in data processing—a niche that could provide a real advantage over competitors, but not a way to develop "bread and butter" kinds of applications.

END USER EXPERT SYSTEMS

KEG knew that most organizations experimenting with expert systems were using a different approach from Mutual. Rather than looking for complex analytical tasks, many companies were developing many simple applications or providing simple expert systems technology to end users to develop their own "non critical" applications. Should KEG do this at Mutual? What would the resource requirements be? Were the skills of the members of KEG "right" for this sort of effort?

QU-IC had proven that expert systems were a viable development technology that could provide Mutual with significant benefits. The challenge now facing KEG was to determine how to proceed to realize the full potential of expert systems technology.

---

1 Jan Matthews, "Pacesetting Service Firms." *Canadian Business,* July 1990, p. 60.

2 Cindy Trudel, "CASE tool delivers an assist." *Computing Canada,* May 25, 1989, p. 28.

3 Gerry Blackwell, "Future for document image processing remains uncertain." *Computing Canada,* July 6, 1989, p. 35, 42.

PART

3

WHAT THE FUTURE HOLDS

Through the first 12 chapters of this text we have been following a new entrant to an organization and answering the questions that he might ask about the organization's structure, culture, people, and interactions. Now we return to a focus on the individual. What will it be like to work in one or more organizations over the long term? What can be expected? Chapter 13 discusses the stresses that will likely be encountered, both the positive kind of stress and the negative kind. Careers from both the individual's and the organization's point of view are the subject of Chapter 14. Finally, Chapter 15 examines the theory and practice of change at the individual, group, and organizational levels. Change is a certainty and our organizational entrant needs to be aware of the types of change as well as the management of change.

CHAPTER

13

STRESS

CHAPTER OUTLINE

Stressors

   Stressors Outside the Organization

   Stressors Produced by the Organizational Structure and Systems

   Stressors in the Physical Environment

   Group Factors Affecting Stress

   Individual Factors Affecting Stress

Perceived Stress

Responses to Stress

Consequences of Stress

Managing Stress

   Altering the Stressors Themselves

   Altering the Stress Moderators

   Lessening the Individual's Responses to Stress

   Alleviating the Consequences of Stress

Conclusion

QUESTIONS TO CONSIDER

- *What is stress?*
- *What are common sources of stress?*
- *What are the results of stress and how can they be managed?*

The individual living and working in an organization is going to be subjected to stressors. To name but a few, these are factors dealing with the job, the organization, and co-workers. But whether or not these stressors result in strain on that person's physiological or psychological functioning will depend on how the stressors are perceived. It is important to be clear that stress is not simply due to the work environment or a particular employee. It is a relationship between the two (Edwards, 1992). Our discussion of stress in this chapter will emphasize that what is stressful for one person may not be stressful for another.

A useful definition of stress by Jeffrey Edwards (1992) emphasizes its contingent nature. **Stress,** he claims, is a discrepancy between an employee's perceived state and desired state (provided that the discrepancy is considered important by that person).

Any condition of how work is done, the circumstances of the work, or the work itself could be a source of stress. But stress should not always be seen as something to be avoided. If a goal is set, then the person setting the goal recognizes the discrepancy between where she is at present and where she would like to be in the future. Goal setting is therefore a way to create stress. Such positive stress, or eustress, can help the individual to accomplish her goals. This makes common sense when we think of our accomplishments in life. Graduating from high school, competing in a sport and winning a championship, passing a music exam—all these desired goals and outcomes usually involve some level of perceived stress.

Of course, if there is no stress—a person may, for example, be satisfied with a result that is easily within his capabilities—performance may also be comparatively low. This relationship is illustrated in Exhibit 13.1. Also indicated in this exhibit is the idea that performance improves as stress increases until optimal performance is reached. After that point, adding further stress results in distress and a decline in performance. What is important to remember about this diagram is that some stress can be beneficial, too much can harm performance, and that the stress/performance curve will be different for each individual in each work situation.

We are now ready to examine a more detailed model of stress in organizations, shown as Exhibit 13.2. Here we see that stressors of various kinds lead first to stress as perceived by an individual. This stress leads in turn to physiological, psychological, and behavioural responses of the individual. These responses then have consequences both for the individual person and the organization.

Stress A discrepancy between an employee's perceived state and desired state, provided that the discrepancy is considered important by that person.

Positive stress can be expected by the bride and groom on their wedding day. Marriage rates as the seventh highest social readjustment in a person's life (see Exhibit 13.3)

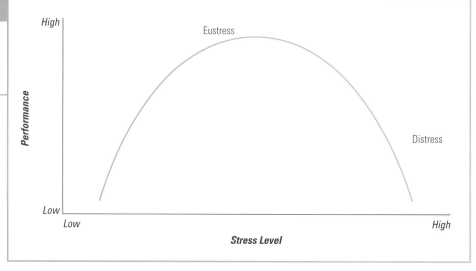

EXHIBIT 13.1

The Curvilinear Relationship Between Stress and Performance

EXHIBIT 13.2   STRESS IN ORGANIZATIONS

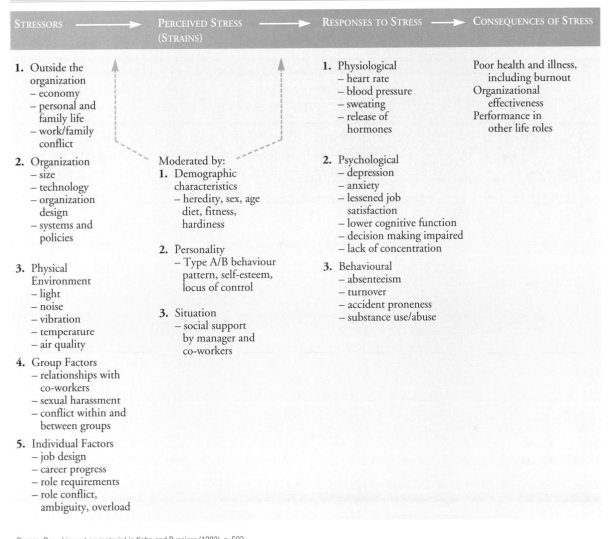

STRESSORS →	PERCEIVED STRESS (STRAINS) →	RESPONSES TO STRESS →	CONSEQUENCES OF STRESS
1. Outside the organization – economy – personal and family life – work/family conflict		1. Physiological – heart rate – blood pressure – sweating – release of hormones	Poor health and illness, including burnout Organizational effectiveness Performance in other life roles
2. Organization – size – technology – organization design – systems and policies	Moderated by: 1. Demographic characteristics – heredity, sex, age diet, fitness, hardiness	2. Psychological – depression – anxiety – lessened job satisfaction – lower cognitive function – decision making impaired – lack of concentration	
3. Physical Environment – light – noise – vibration – temperature – air quality	2. Personality – Type A/B behaviour pattern, self-esteem, locus of control 3. Situation – social support by manager and co-workers	3. Behavioural – absenteeism – turnover – accident proneness – substance use/abuse	
4. Group Factors – relationships with co-workers – sexual harassment – conflict within and between groups			
5. Individual Factors – job design – career progress – role requirements – role conflict, ambiguity, overload			

SOURCE: Based in part on material in Kahn and Byosiere (1992), p. 592.

There is a set of moderators that can alter the relationship between stressors and perceived stress or between perceived stress and responses to stress. These **moderator variables** help to explain how people can differentially perceive the amount of stress in a situation, or how their responses to stress can be different even if the same amount of stress is perceived. We will now explore more fully each of the major variables in this stress model.

Moderator variables

Variables that can alter the relationship between independent and dependent variables.

STRESSORS

There is a wide range of stressors that can affect the stress perceived by a person in a work organization. These stressors can be found outside the organization itself, in the way the organization is structured and operates, in the worker's physical environment, in the worker's group, or in factors specific to the individual at work.

Stressors Outside the Organization

Conditions outside the organization can affect the stress felt by organizational members. When a country is at war, is affected by internal conflicts and riots, or is suffering through a drought or an economic depression—these conditions and others like them can affect the country's workers. Lack of control over a situation and uncertainty about what will happen next are stressors that typically cannot be influenced by an individual.

On a smaller scale, it has been shown that it is no longer possible to separate the effects of home life on work and of work life on the home (e.g., Frone and others, 1992; Higgins & Duxbury, 1992). When there is conflict and unhappiness at home, the stress that is felt very often carries over from the home to the workplace. Also important is the increase in work-family conflict in Canadian families (see this chapter's *A Little Knowledge* feature). Rising taxes and other costs have impelled more and more Canadian families to have both the wife and the husband earning income. In these families less time and energy may be available by both spouses to give to the family and to each other. Stress and conflict are often the result.

Stressors Produced by the Organizational Structure and Systems

Organizational size can be a stressor. Large organizations, especially those that are very large, can create a sense of helplessness to create change or to influence the organization. Such feelings can be stressful.

Similarly, the technology used by an organization to produce its product or provide its service can be a source of employee stress. For example, vehicle assembly lines in an automotive plant often involve repetitive work where the worker's actions are controlled by the assembly line instead of the reverse.

This is described in a fascinating way in Ben Hamper's 1991 book *Rivethead*.

I was assigned to the cab shop, an area more commonly known to its inhabitants as "the jungle." The noise level was deafening. The [man] working right across from me was Roy. Our jobs were identical: install splash shields, pencil rods, and assorted nuts and bolts in the rear end of Chevy Blazers. To accomplish this, we worked on a portion of the line where the cabs would rise up on an elevated track. Once the cabs were about five feet off the ground, we'd have to duck inside the rear wheel wells and bust a little ass. We adjusted to the heat and grew accustomed to the noise. After awhile, we even got used to the claustrophobia of the wheel wells. The one thing we couldn't escape was the monotony of our new jobs. Every minute, every hour, every truck, and every movement totaled nothing but a plodding replica of the one that had gone before.

An organization's design can also affect employee stress. Mechanistic organizations can create in some employees the sense of being controlled by the organization as a machine. In contrast, organically structured organizations can create more of a sense of being a part of the organization as a living thing.

It must be realized, however, that while an organization's design can be a stressor, whether or not a particular employee will perceive stress due to that design will be affected by other factors. In this case personality might be a factor that influences the type of organization structure found to be stressful. For example, a person who likes order and certainty would probably find an organic organization stressful and a mechanistic organization much less so.

A LITTLE KNOWLEDGE

Work-family conflict occurs when an individual has to perform multiple roles, such as worker, spouse, and parent. Each of these roles imposes demands on their incumbents requiring time, energy and commitment. The cumulative demands of multiple roles can result in role strain of two types: overload and interference. Overload exists when the total demands on time and energy are too great to perform the roles adequately or comfortably. Interference occurs when conflicting demands make it difficult to fulfil the requirements of multiple roles. This commonly occurs because many work and family activities must be performed during the same time periods in different physical locations.

How big is the problem in Canada? Recent estimates suggest that at least one quarter of the human resource challenges faced by Canadian organizations are the result of employees having to manage dual responsibilities at home and at work. A survey conducted by Christopher Higgins, Catherine Lee and Linda Duxbury gathered responses from over 24 000 public and private sector employees. They found that:

- Forty percent of working mothers and 25% of working fathers are experiencing high levels of work-family conflict.
- Half of the parents surveyed reported high levels of difficulty in managing their family time.
- Fifty percent of working mothers and 36% of working fathers report high levels of stress.
- Forty percent of working mothers and 25% of working fathers report high levels of depressed mood.
- Less than half of the parents surveyed were highly satisfied with their present lifestyle.

Although there is increasing recognition of the problems faced by working parents and employees with elder-care responsibilities, the research indicates that the majority of Canadian firms have not responded to the changing needs of an increasingly diverse work force. Despite the oft-expressed interest in supporting families, the actual practices of most North American companies lag behind. The majority of Canadian employees today are feeling the burden of combining work and dependent care in a climate that has been unresponsive to the realities of work and family life. Flexible work arrangements are rare and most employees (their data suggests about 65% of the work force) still work a fixed "9 to 5" type day.

There are several reasons for corporate inaction on work and family issues. First, in a time of cost-cutting, restructuring and downsizing, many companies view family concerns as something that should be addressed in better economic times. The recession has also meant that many organizations have not had to address work and family issues because they have occurred in the context of a labour surplus. Employees who perceive that they can be easily replaced are competing for jobs, and are often willing to make sacrifices such as working long hours and overtime to ensure job security.

Second, many companies still do not see the connection between work and family issues and the bottom line. The lack of information on flexible work arrangements, child and dependent-care options, as well as the lack of documented evidence that such involvement will have a positive impact on the bottom line, deters many employers from implementing family benefits. Unless management understands why family benefits and flexible work arrangements make sense from a business standpoint, many managers will be reluctant to support them.

Third, the majority of corporate decision makers are from the diminishing "traditional family." Without personal experience or employees' input, management remains unaware of the problems and its impact on performance and employees.

What then, is the cost of continuing to operate in the traditional fashion now practised by organizations? While both the potential costs and benefits of new policies are admittedly unclear, the price of not changing is hardly obscure. Workers who have difficulties balancing work and family demands are more likely to quit their jobs, be less productive, arrive late, be absent from work, and suffer poorer physical and mental health. Working parents, in particular, need flexibility in working hours and working days in order to attend to sick children, family crises, and gaps in child-care arrangements. If human resource policies are not made more responsive, employees at all levels will continue to bear the major brunt of work and family conflict.

SOURCE: Summary prepared by Linda Duxbury, Associate Professor, School of Business, Carleton University. © 1993 by Linda Duxbury.

EXPERIENCE IS THE BEST TEACHER

Why did I, a chemical engineer with a Ph.D. in Management Sciences get interested in the area of work-family conflict and stress? Quite simply, it was to try and find solutions to problems that I was having, my husband was having, and most of our friends were experiencing balancing competing work and family demands. At the end of each work day I was exhausted from trying to find time for everything ... my husband, my 3-year-old daughter ... my students ... my administrative responsibilities and my research. Most of the time I was feeling guilty. If I worked long hours on my research I felt that I was neglecting my family. If I spent the time with my husband or my child I felt resentful because of sacrifices I felt I was making to my career and jealous of my male colleagues with "wives at home." I was in a "no-win" situation.

I have been doing research in this area now for 6 years. With my colleagues Dr. Christopher Higgins at the University of Western Ontario and Dr. Catherine Lee at the University of Ottawa I have completed a major survey on Balancing Work and Family in Canada (survey data on 24 000 Canadians and interviews on 1000 employees and 530 couples). What have I learned? That I am not alone. That the majority of working Canadians share my problems. In fact, my research would suggest that I am better off than the majority of working mothers in Canada today. I have a job with a high

Linda Duxbury received her Bachelor of Engineering degree from the Faculty of Engineering Co-operative Program at the University of Waterloo, and her Masters and Doctorate degrees from the same faculty. To further explore her work, see Balancing Work and Family: A Study of the Canadian Work Force, coauthored by Duxbury, Chris Higgins, and Catherine Lee, published by the University of Western Ontario.

degree of autonomy and control, flexible working hours, and the ability to work from home when necessary. I also have enough money to allow me to buy goods and services to help me balance competing work and family demands.

My research has led me to believe that dramatic changes are needed in Canada with respect to human resource policies. As a true engineer I believe that organizations will only change when faced with empirical evidence to support the need for change. My mission has, therefore, become one of conducting research which will show organizational and government decision makers that inability to balance work and family demands has a negative impact on the "bottom line."

Particularly frightening to me is the fact that Statistics Canada data indicates that approximately two-thirds of women under 40 who have reached the upper levels in Canadian corporations and institutions are childless, while virtually all men in leadership positions are fathers. If organizations and governments continue to send the message to women that a demanding work life is incompatible with a satisfying family life, we are in danger of creating a society where more and more leaders have traded family for career success. The price of business success should not be disinterest in the family. Nor should the price of having a family be the abandonment of professional ambition.

The reward and control systems in place and policies used to make decisions can likewise become a source of stress. When layoffs are made in order from the least senior to the most senior staff, this policy can be both a source of stress among those of low seniority and a relief of stress for high seniority employees.

An organization's system of promotions can be a source of stress. In a study of 1883 jobs in 100 single-site California establishments (between the years 1965 and 1979), it was found that 16 of the 100 establishments had no promotion paths (Baron and others, 1986). Employees of these organizations had no career path at all. They were hired at the entry level and there they stayed. Workers with aspirations for promotion would likely feel blocked and therefore stressed.

In the other 84 organizations studied the researchers found that male dominated jobs were more likely to be organized into promotion ladders than were traditional female secretarial and clerical jobs. Nearly 80% of the promotion ladders were completely segregated by sex. Also, in ladders having both sexes represented at the bottom rung it seemed that promotion prospects for females were limited because lower level production jobs were linked to all-male managerial jobs. Women seeking to join the management ranks would be subject to stressors produced by sex-segregated systems of promotion.

Stressors in the Physical Environment

In Chapter 4 on Job Design we discussed how physical aspects of doing the work and conditions experienced by the worker can affect that person's motivation. These physical conditions are also direct stressors. Returning to the example of the vehicle factory, conditions can be so noisy that communication with co-workers is difficult or impossible. Also, the work can be physically draining and is done in hot, dusty, and dimly-lit places.

Any working environment that exposes the worker to extremes is stressful. For example, extremes of light, noise, temperature, significant vibration, and of air low in oxygen or high in contaminants are all stressful. Common work examples would be firefighting, underground mining, and the operation of heavy construction equipment.

Poor indoor air quality in energy efficient (but not necessarily work efficient) sealed window office buildings can be a source of employee stress. Poor air quality can cause employee headaches, fatigue, sickness, asthma, and even cancer (Farrar & Murray, 1993).

The perception of exposure to physical and chemical risks can also result in stress. The effects of worry and uncertainty about being exposed to toxicities at work can lead to increased worker anxiety, fatalism, depression, and lowered self-esteem (see Roberts, 1993). For example, workers in factories using toxic chemicals such as chlorine gas have reported going home after work and feeling a tightness in the chest. There is no easy way to know if the tightness is serious and work related or a normal human problem such as indigestion. People who work around x-ray machines can worry about their long-term radiation exposure. Those who work in coal and asbestos mines are justified in worrying about damage to their lungs from small particles present in workplace air.

Group Factors Affecting Stress

Conflict within and between groups can be a significant source of organizational stress, as can poor relations with co-workers. For an example at the Saturn Company automobile assembly plant, see this chapter's *Seeing is Believing* feature.

Now that many organizations are downsizing, many work groups are becoming self-managed. The position of supervisor is being integrated into the team itself. Interestingly, one study by James Barker (1993) of a company he called "ISE Communications" found that self-managing teams caused stress for team members, especially for new hires on probationary contracts. The self-managed teams created more rules than existed before in the hierarchical system of control, they enforced the rules more stringently, and were ever-watchful for rule violations. For instance, Sharon was a single mother who had problems arriving for work on time at 7 a.m. When she showed up late one day "the team reacted in the same way a shift supervisor in ISE's old system might have. The team confronted Sharon immediately and directly. They told her that they were very upset that she was late. They bluntly told her how much they had suffered from having to work short-handed. Stung by the criticism of her peers, Sharon began to cry" (p. 431).

The effects of stress are showing on workers and management alike at Saturn Corporation's automobile factory in Spring Hill, Tennessee. This new plant was designed to be team-oriented, with a joint management-union structure. The initial group of 3200 Saturn workers was selected from over 16 000 United Auto Worker union members employed at General Motors. They were given extensive training in team and cooperative work methods as well as in production methods. However, customer demand for the Saturn subcompacts has been strong, resulting in over a year of 50 hour workweeks and longer for Saturn employees. This strain has resulted in felt stress by the initial group of workers. They have begun to tire from the demands placed on them. Other workers have therefore had to be hired to help ease the load. Also, in order to satisfy demand for Saturns, the company has planned the addition of a third shift.

These two pressures have resulting in the hiring of thousands of new workers. Most of these new hires have come from workers laid off at other General Motors plants. But these new employees have not received the training offered to earlier hires. Their total training hours is down to 175 hours each from the 700 hours given to the initial group of Saturn workers. And the training of the new workers has emphasized production techniques and not the team skills that are so central to Saturn's success and reputation for high quality. Also, newer employees, transferring to the Saturn plant after having been laid off from another GM job, are often less accepting of the close ties between management and the UAW union at Saturn.

These factors have combined to create a workplace suffering from the effects of stress. Conflicts between management, workers, and their union are on the increase. The Saturn workplace was designed to be team-oriented and cooperative. Will the stresses of a tired group of original workers, and of new workers who have been laid off by management once already and who have not been given the extensive training required for team-oriented work, cause a breakdown in the system? Will the effects of workplace stress cause the new Saturn plant to become like other more traditional automobile factories?

SOURCE: Based on information in "Saturn: Labor's love lost?" *Business Week*, February 8, 1993, pp. 122, 124. For further information see "Is Saturn competitive?" by Robert R.Rehder, in the March-April 1994 issue of *Business Horizons*, pp. 7-15.

Barker found that constantly being watched by the group for norm violation had an effect on the workers. He stated that "To a person, the older team workers told me that they felt much more stress in the team environment than they had under the old ISE system. The newer members also complained of the constant strain of self-management" (p. 432). Barker goes on to mention that the self-management concept has been called "management by stress" (Parker & Slaughter, 1988).

Sexual harassment

Discrimination on the basis of gender. Behaviour which is not acceptable to the recipient and to which the recipient has not consented.

Another source of stress at the group level is **sexual harassment**. Essentially discrimination on the basis of gender, sexual harassment has been defined by Frederick Day (1992) as behaviour which is not acceptable to the recipient and to which the recipient has not consented. Though sexual harassment is possible between individuals of the same gender and the same or different sexual preference, most cases of sexual harassment fit the mold of a man sexually harassing a woman.

How common is such harassment? One study found that "as many as one of every two women will be subjected to some form of harassment during her academic or working life" (Fitzgerald, 1993, p. 1071). Sexual harassment occurs in the pink collar occupations of secretaries, office workers, and clerks and in occupations ranging from blue collar industrial to white collar professional.

Two broad categories of sexual harassment (from Day, 1992) are:

1. Demanding sexual favours in exchange for a job, a promotion, a course grade, a raise, a certain work assignment, or any other benefit or work outcome;
2. Sexual touching, non-sexual but inappropriate touching, sexually explicit or vulgar jokes or remarks, abusive language or sexual innuendo, leering, posting sexual magazine photographs or cartoons, and writing graffiti of a sexual nature.

Graphic examples of how these types of sexual harassment operated in one Florida shipyard are given in an article by Susan Fiske (1993). Women at the shipyard were teased, touched, humiliated, sexually evaluated, and propositioned by male co-workers.

Harassing behaviour and the conflict that may result can be a significant source of stress felt by the victim, which may then result in lowered work performance. When harassment becomes intolerable the victim may escape the situation by absenteeism or by involuntarily leaving the job.

Individual Factors Affecting Stress

This last set of factors are stressors that affect a particular individual at work. Elements of the job's design may affect only one person and not the work group as a whole. Career progress can also create stress. For example, **underpromotion**, the feeling of being unduly delayed in career progress, is undoubtedly a common source of stress. On the other hand, **overpromotion** can also cause stress. When a person is promoted too quickly into a job for which he is unready or underqualified, he may feel that failure is imminent and may even fear losing the job. Going back to our definition of stress, whenever there is a perceived imbalance and that imbalance is important, stress can result. Of course, **layoff** from a job is usually a source of stress. An example of middle management layoff in Japan is our *A Rose by Any Other Name* feature in this chapter.

Underpromotion The feeling of being unduly delayed in career progress.

Overpromotion When a person is promoted too quickly into a job for which he or she is unready or underqualified.

Layoff Temporary or permanent job loss as a result of downsizing for structural or economic reasons.

A ROSE BY ANY OTHER NAME

We are accustomed to hearing about how Japan has "lifetime employment" for its middle-managers, or "salarymen." Though never true for the smaller firms in Japan's economy, the larger enterprises were able to guarantee lifetime job security for its white-collar workers. Now, however, the economic downturn that has begun to affect the Japanese economy has meant that these larger firms are asking some of their salarymen to resign.

In Canada and the West being asked to resign would be a severe blow, but to a Japanese salaryman it is catastrophic. His whole career has been built with one organization, all his experience is related to that one company, and his self-image is constructed in large part by his connection to the company. Friends and family provide him status and respect partly based on his job and title in his organization.

Besides the economic loss of income there is the loss of self-esteem and social status that comes from losing connection to the work group. His wife also loses the basis for her social status in the community. To lose all this is to lose more than just a job but a way of being.

And finding an equivalent job in another large organization is difficult. These organizations typically do not hire older generalists from a competitor, but instead hire young graduates and train them in the company's ways.

Salarymen in Japan who lose their jobs may try to hide that fact from their family or find an excuse that will allow them to explain why they are no longer working. In this way they can attempt to save face in their time of upheaval.

SOURCE: Based on information in Kumiko Makihara (1993), "The agony of a salaryman," *Time*, May 24, 1993, p. 46.

Work role A set of expectations about what is required in a particular job.

The **work role** can also be a potential stressor (for a humourous example, see this chapter's *Overboard* cartoon).

Role overload occurs when the individual either tries to do too much or is given more work than she can cope with. Especially in times of downsizing, when companies are thinning their work force in order to attempt to save on personnel costs, the job duties of laid-off employees will be reassigned to others. The resulting accumulation of duties can eventually overwhelm the ability of some workers to cope.

Role overload Occurs when an individual either tries to do too much or is given too big a workload.

Role ambiguity can also create stress. The person in the job role is subject to role ambiguity when it is unclear what job duties are most important, which deadlines are most critical or, in some cases, which demands to attend to from two different bosses. Also, progress on the job or in a training program is sometimes not evaluated on a regular basis. This can cause employees or trainees to feel unsure about their performance. Role ambiguity is the result.

Role conflict can also come about. Of the three main types of role conflict, the first is **approach-approach conflict**. This occurs when two opportunities are attractive but both cannot be accepted. The employee with the time and money to attend only one business conference of two available has to make a choice. But any choice means that one opportunity must be foregone, causing approach-approach conflict.

Approach-approach conflict Occurs when two opportunities are attractive but both cannot be accepted.

The second type of role conflict, **approach-avoidance conflict**, occurs when a job role is attractive but threatening at the same time. The chance to give a presentation to the president of the company, to have your work noticed, is desirable. But what if the talk goes badly? Would that harm your chances for promotion? This kind of push-pull conflict can cause the employee to become "frozen" like a deer in a car's headlights, unable to move or make a choice.

Approach-avoidance conflict Occurs when a job role is attractive but threatening at the same time.

Thirdly, **avoidance-avoidance conflict** occurs when the member of an organization must choose between two actions, but both are anticipated to have negative consequences. For example, bad news must be passed along to the boss, yet the employee knows the news will result in undesirable actions by the boss. But if the bad news is *not* communicated the boss will eventually find out and there will be other negative outcomes to face. In this case the conflict is one of wanting to avoid both of the certain negative outcomes but being unable to do so.

Avoidance-avoidance conflict Occurs when one of two actions must be taken but both are anticipated to have negative consequences.

PERCEIVED STRESS

Strain The effects of stress.

Given the abundance of workplace stressors that we have considered, why is everyone not in a constant state of shock? The reason is that not everyone will react to given stressors in the same way. Some will not perceive stress. They will therefore not experience **strain** due to the stressors that do exist. Some, even when stress is perceived, will not react to it. Each person is unique in their demographic characteristics such as heredity, sex, age, diet, fitness, and hardiness. Some people are simply more able to withstand the stresses under which they live and work.

For example, assault troops in the armies of the world are invariably young and healthy, with high levels of fitness. These characteristics allow them to carry heavy loads over long distances and engage the enemy at the end of a march.

Heredity causes some individuals to be stronger and hardier than others. When organizations select individuals that have these characteristics, the stressors present in an organizational situation may not be significant for those so selected.

Personality is another factor that can moderate the relationship between a stressor being present and stress being perceived. One important personality characteristic is called Type A/B Behaviour Pattern (see, for example, Ganster and others, 1991). This classification is based on early work in medicine linking personality to susceptibility to heart attack. It was found that those people who could be classified as Type A were hard-driving, felt time pressured, and tried to accomplish too much in too little time. Behaviourally, the Type A individual would always seem to be in a hurry. While conversing the Type A would likely interrupt another to finish the other's sentences (presumably to save time).

The Type B person, in contrast, would be more relaxed, less in a hurry, and more willing to take time. Given these descriptions, it is not surprising to find that Type A's are more at risk of health breakdowns. Type B's either do not expose themselves to as many potentially stressful situations, feel less stress even when in those situations, or do not respond to stress in the same way.

Other personality characteristics thought to moderate the

$$\text{stressor} \longrightarrow \text{perceived stress} \longrightarrow \text{stress response}$$

relationship are self-esteem and what is called *locus of control*. People with a strong sense of self (high self esteem) and who feel in control of events (internal locus of control) are predicted to be less affected by stressors. They are also predicted to respond less to the stress that is perceived. The more a person feels out-of-control and/or unable to make required changes, the stronger the links should be between stressors, perceived stress, and stress reactions.

In this latter case, the individual is under strain and yet feels that he cannot do anything about it. An air traffic controller, for example, has to guide aircraft using radio and radar tools. When the radio is full of static because of sunspot activity and the radar does not display aircraft information in a way that is easily understandable, the controller is likely to feel helpless to improve the situation.

Finally, the stress relationship shown in Exhibit 13.2 is moderated by aspects of the social situation at work. When the manager and co-workers offer their support in dealing with stress it is easier to handle than being left alone to cope. Examples of high stress jobs are air traffic controlling, policing, and fire fighting. The stresses of these jobs can be intense, with lives literally on the line.

Air traffic controllers, though not personally at risk of losing their lives, worry about causing an "aluminum shower" and seeing the results on the news that night. Police and fire fighters can encounter dangerous situations in the course of their work. One way of dealing with the stresses of personal danger is for them to form close social bonds with their peers. The social support found among those who intimately know the dangers of the job can make the stress more bearable.

It can be difficult for people in these types of jobs to discuss with their families the daily pressures that they experience. One reason for this is that family members usually lack similar job experience. This makes communication difficult. Another reason is that workers in dangerous jobs do not want their family members to worry about their safety. In these high stress jobs, social support is necessary yet can come mostly from co-workers.

Air traffic controllers working near Moncton , New Brunswick.

Ironically, time spent away from the family in social situations with co-workers can add to the individual's total perceived stress. The social support of co-workers can lessen perceived job stress, but the time taken for this social support decreases the amount of time spent with the family. This can increase the conflict between work and family life, increasing family stress.

RESPONSES TO STRESS

Fight or flight

Physiological reaction to perceived danger, in which the body prepares itself to fight or run.

Human biology has predisposed us to two reactions when danger is perceived: **fight or flight**. Using this survival mechanism, the body prepares itself to either fight or run by releasing adrenaline, catecholamines, and other hormones into the bloodstream and moving more blood into the body's extremities to make the muscles work more effectively. The heart rate and blood pressure rise as well.

These *physiological responses* are also triggered by the less than life-or-death events in the workplace such as a meeting with the boss about a raise, getting into an argument with a client, or preparing to give a speech in public. Therefore, perceived stress affects our body chemistry and physiological response. Because our bodies have this built-in reaction to perceived stress, we tax our bodies when under stress. These reactions are meant to help survival in the event that extra physical response is required. They are not the norm for average daily functioning.

When stress is constant or unremitting the physiological effects of stress will accumulate. The body needs to come back to a normal state of functioning to rest and recover. If recovery does not occur then physiologically an exhaustion occurs. Chemicals in the body build up, the heart works harder to keep up with the body's requirements, and sleep may be disturbed. These events make the stress recovery problem even worse. One study of 989 managers in the United Kingdom found that 68% reported they had suffered from disturbed sleep patterns in the last three months (Wilsher, 1993).

Sleep loss makes it harder to pay attention, decreases the motivation to attend to details, and impairs memory (Adler, 1992). These dysfunctions can have serious repercussions in the workplace. One example is the British Airways maintenance worker who, at 4 a.m., replaced a cockpit windshield with screws that were too short. Later on the airplane was flying at 17 000 feet when "the windshield popped out and the pilot was nearly sucked out of the plane" (Gibb-Clark, 1993). A simple test of sleep deprivation is that "When your head is nodding, you are so impaired you can't understand how impaired you are" (David Dinges, quoted in Adler, 1992, p. 23).

Continued stress can lead to problems of coronary artery disease and high blood pressure, coronary heart disease and heart attack, stomach ulcers, and any number of other physical ailments.

The idea that stressful events in one's life "add up" to cause illness was studied by Thomas Holmes and Richard Rahe (1967). They produced a "Social Readjustment Rating Scale" to measure the cumulative effects of stresses that people encounter in their lives (see Exhibit 13.3). In this scale each life event has a stress score attached. Interestingly, even positive events such as getting married or the birth of a child can be significant life stressors. People add their total stress points for a one year period. Those with scores of 300 and higher are calculated to have a high health risk. They have at least a 70% chance of a major illness in the following year.

Beyond the physiological, there are also *psychological responses* to stress. Depression and anxiety can be the result of the body's tension and constant preparedness for the fight or flight that is seldom required. Sleeplessness, when a part of the physical stress reaction, can help cause psychological reactions of depression and anxiety. Sleeplessness can also impair cognitive functioning. Losing concentration and having difficulties making decisions are examples. Job dissatisfaction is also a likely psychological response to stress.

EXHIBIT 13.3   THE SOCIAL READJUSTMENT RATING SCALE

RANK	LIFE EVENT	MEAN VALUE
1	Death of spouse	100
2	Divorce	73
3	Marital separation	65
4	Court conviction and detention in jail	63
5	Death of close family member	63
6	Personal injury or illness	53
7	Marriage	50
8	Fired at work or expelled from school	47
9	Marital reconciliation	45
10	Retirement	45
11	Major change in the health of a family member	44
12	Pregnancy	40
13	Sexual difficulties	39
14	Birth or adoption of a new family member	39
15	Major business readjustment or change	39
16	Major change in financial state	38
17	Death of a close friend	37
18	Changing to a different line of work or major	36
19	Change in the number of arguments with spouse or girlfriend/boyfriend	35
20	Getting a large mortgage or loan	31
21	Defaulting on a mortgage or loan	30
22	Major change in responsibilities at work	29
23	Son or daughter leaving home	29
24	Trouble with in-laws	29
25	Outstanding personal achievement	28
26	Spouse getting a job or losing a job	26
27	Starting or finishing formal schooling	26
28	Major change in living conditions	25
29	Major change in personal habits	24
30	Trouble with supervisor at work	23
31	Major change in working hours or conditions	20
32	Change in residence	20
33	Change of school attended	20
34	Major change in recreation activity	19
35	Major change in church activities	19
36	Major change in social activities	18
37	Obtaining a small mortgage or loan	17
38	Change in sleeping habits	16
39	Change in number of family get-togethers	15
40	Change in eating habits	15
41	Vacation	13
42	Christmas or major religious holiday	11
43	Minor violations of the law and encounters with police	11

NOTE: The scale may be completed by circling the mean stress value to the right of each life event if the event has happened to you in the past year. If an event has happened to you more than once, multiply the mean stress value by the number of occurrences in the past year. Then total all the values to obtain your total stress score for the year. A score of 300 or more indicates a high probability of suffering a stress-related illness in the next year. It is important to remember that while the results of this test will be suggestive of your own life stress, this test as used here should not be considered a valid scientific instrument.

SOURCE: Adapted/reprinted from Thomas H. Holmes and Richard H. Rahe (1967), "The social readjustment rating scale," *Journal of Psychosomatic Research*, 11: 216. Reprinted with permission from *Journal of Psychosomatic Research*, Volume 11, 1967, Pergamon Press Ltd. Oxford, England.

These physiological and psychological responses to stress may also lead to or occur with *behavioural responses*. This is what the stressed person does. Absenteeism and turnover are two possible actions. Absenteeism is a short-term solution to avoiding the stressful situation. Turnover is a more long-term solution. An extensive list of affective, psychological, physical, and behavioural reactions to stress are shown in Exhibit 13.4.

It is clear that there are other forces acting on people making choices about holding on to or leaving a job. One model of the employee turnover process, Exhibit 13.5, shows how forces interact from the organizational, individual, and economic labour market levels.

The bottom left corner of this model notes that there are alternative forms of withdrawal behaviour besides actual turnover. Included here might be accident proneness (being hurt is a socially acceptable way to get out of the job) and substance use/abuse. Employees might get drunk at work or away from work as a way to withdraw from the situation. Or to

---

EXHIBIT 13.4   EXAMPLES OF REACTIONS TO STRESS

AFFECTIVE (SATISFACTION WITH ...)	PSYCHOLOGICAL	PHYSICAL
Kind of work	Anxiety	Headaches
Amount of work	Alienation	Sleep loss
Physical work conditions	Low self-esteem	Skin disorders
Co-workers	Neuroses	Stomach ulcers
Supervision	Depression	High cholesterol
Career	Psychosomatic symptoms	level
Compensation	Boredom	High blood pressure
Company	Mental fatigue	Heart disease
Leisure activities	Lost concentration	Perspiration
Life	Anger	Diarrhea
		Physical fatigue

BEHAVIOURAL

PERSONAL	NONPERFORMANCE	PERFORMANCE (CHANGE IN ...)
Nicotine use	Absenteeism	Quantity
Alcohol use	Lateness	Quality
Caffeine use	Turnover	Timeliness
"Soft" drug use	Early retirement	Efficiency
"Hard" drug use	Sabotage	Decision making ability
Conflict	Theft	Coordination with others
Aggression	Job actions — e.g., strikes	Materials waste
Suicide	Grievance filing	Safety practices
Legal violations	Low participation	Record keeping
Poor sexual relations	Complaining	Organization effectiveness

SOURCE: Randall B. Dunham (1984), *Organizational Behavior: People and Processes in Management*, Homewood, IL: Richard D. Irwin, Inc., page 439. Reprinted by permission of Richard D. Irwin, Inc.

avoid the stressful situation they might take hallucinogens such as LSD or other mind and sense-altering drugs such as morphine, cocaine, heroin, THC, marijuana, or hashish.

One study of employee substance abuse and on-the-job behaviours (Lehman & Simpson, 1992) found that while substance abusers did not differ from nonusers on positive work behaviours, they had significantly more psychological and physical withdrawal and also more antagonistic behaviours.

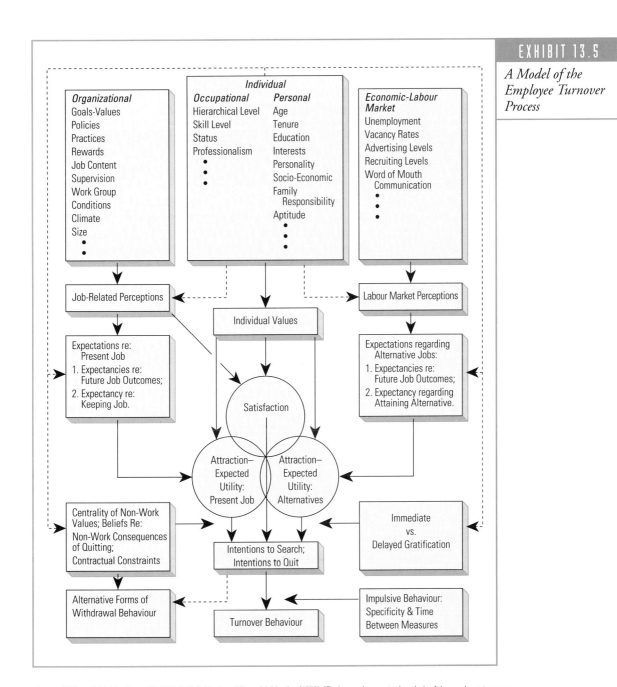

EXHIBIT 13.5

A Model of the Employee Turnover Process

SOURCE: William H. Mobley, Roger W. Griffeth, H. H. Hand, and Bruce M. Meglino (1979), "Review and conceptual analysis of the employee turnover process," *Psychological Bulletin* 86: 517. Copyright © 1979 by the American Psychological Association. Reprinted by permission.

Drug use was found to increase absenteeism, accidents, turnover, worker's compensation claims, and medical insurance claims. Cast in Hirschman's (1970) terms, these employees chose Exit (leaving the organization) and Neglect (psychological and physical withdrawal from work) over the more positive choices of Loyalty (waiting out the hard times while hoping conditions improve) or Voice (active behaviours trying to improve the organization).

CONSEQUENCES OF STRESS

As we have discussed, a person's response to stress can be physiological, psychological, and behavioural. These in turn can lead to poor health, illness, and "burnout" (Lee & Ashforth, 1993).

Burnout is a term that means the person: (1) feels emotionally exhausted; (2) depersonalizes others; and (3) has a sense of lower personal accomplishment (Maslach, 1982).

Emotional exhaustion is characterized by a lack of energy and a feeling that there are no more emotional resources left to draw on. Workers dealing with clients feel unable to give of themselves any more.

The depersonalization of others is marked by seeing others as objects and not persons. The worker builds a "wall" around himself and doesn't let personal feelings about others intrude into the work situation. Clients may be seen stereotypically. The student may be seen as a number. A hospital patient may be described as a symptom, for example, the "broken leg" in the emergency room.

Diminished personal accomplishment occurs when the organizational member feels less competent at work and less able to deal with others at work.

Burnout is more likely for individuals with a high frequency of interpersonal contact at work and with a high intensity of interpersonal contact (Cordes & Dougherty, 1993). People in these "helping professions," for example social workers, teachers, doctors, and nurses, are especially susceptible to burnout. Their contact with others is both frequent and intense.

Individuals who choose to enter the helping professions are often susceptible to burnout because they *do* care about their job and the people they are trying to help. They may have entered the profession to make a difference, to be a person who cares about and helps others. Because they care, they invest emotional energy in their client and co-worker relationships. Then they find that they cannot save (or even help) everyone, and that the demands on them continue without pause.

The emergency room physician or neonatal intensive care unit nurse, for example, deals with a great deal of human suffering every day. Some patients are saved, some die, and some are helped but not enough to prevent them from dying. No matter what the outcome, each new day brings more patients and more suffering. The emotional energy of the worker declines and, possibly as a self-protective mechanism, clients are depersonalized. Then the realization may set in that the helping professional has become the uncaring professional that she did not want to be. This can lead to the third component of burnout, the feeling of diminished competence at work and the inability to effectively deal with others at work (Cordes & Dougherty, 1993; Leiter & Maslach, 1988).

Emotional exhaustion is predicted to be moderately likely for individuals in jobs of lower frequency interpersonal contact or lower intensity of interpersonal contact (Cordes & Dougherty, 1993). Examples of these jobs would be receptionist or librarian (high frequency of contact but low intensity) and lawyer or fire fighter (low frequency of contact but high intensity). People in occupations with both low frequency and low intensity of interpersonal contact (e.g., research scientist, forest ranger) are predicted to be least likely to suffer emotional exhaustion due to their job role.

Burnout A reaction to stress characterized by emotional exhaustion, the depersonalization of others, and a sense of lower personal accomplishment.

As people at work become "burned out," they will be less able to effectively perform their jobs. Those who can escape the stressful situation will do so. They may quit, transfer out, or work hard to be promoted out of the situation. For example, the doctor who becomes a hospital administrator may not have to deal with patients face-to-face.

Those who cannot escape the situation because of economic pressures, lack of other opportunities, or the like (see Exhibit 13.5), will stay burned out. These people are likely to be less effective in their work role. A spillover of the effects of stress may then occur from their work role to their other life roles. A person overwhelmed at work is liable to bring negative feelings home. Stress is therefore important in the total context of a person's life and must be managed in life as a whole.

MANAGING STRESS

There are four possible ways in which stress or stress consequences can be prevented or lessened (based on Kahn & Byosiere 1992, and Ivancevich and others, 1990).

1. Alter the stressors themselves and as perceived by the individual.
2. Alter the moderators of the stressors $\longrightarrow$ perceived stress $\longrightarrow$ stress responses relationship so that the stressors $\longrightarrow$ perceived stress link is weakened and/or the perceived stress $\longrightarrow$ stress responses link is weakened.
3. Lessen the individual's responses to stress.
4. Alleviate the consequences of stress.

Altering the Stressors Themselves

People can make choices of where to live, what type of job to have, and what lifestyle to pursue. The Bay Street stockbroker in Toronto who quits a high-paying but high stress job to move out to the country is a noteworthy enough occurrence to make the newspapers. Another approach is to try to balance work and family life so that stress in one has less chance of moving across the work-family interface to affect the other.

At the organizational level, workers can be given more information and control over their work lives so that events, rather than happening *to* the worker, happen more by the individual's own choice . For example, principles of job design can be used to redesign jobs so that the individual has control over the job and how it is done. Flextime programs allow the organizational member to choose what hours to work. Such choices can alleviate stress by allowing the individual to choose hours that provide a better fit with other life commitments. Likewise, some organizations offer "personal days" off. With these days the employee can tend to personal business that is difficult to accomplish after normal working hours or on the weekend.

Selection and placement programs can give a realistic job preview of the good and bad points of a job. The worker can also be given some ability to choose between jobs that are available.

The employee's work area can be created so that there is some individual control over lighting, heating, air supply, task seating, etc. The more choices and control, the more job stress is expected to be lessened.

The organization can lessen an individual's perceived stress by providing support services such as on-site daycare for children and/or elders. Other services that may be offered to lessen the stress in employee's lives are tax and financial planning newsletters and workshops, retirement counselling, and the like.

Finally, training programs can teach the skills required to do a job so that the employee is more able to cope. When people know what to do, how to use the job's machines and tools, and are trained in how to react in crisis and/or stressful situations, they are more likely to take action.

Altering the Stress Moderators

Actions in this category fall into the areas of making the person more hardy, more physically able to deal with stress and to make the situation more supportive. Participative decision making, for example, builds social support into the decision making process. Co-worker relationships can be enhanced by providing opportunities for socialization outside of work. Some organizations use sabbaticals and time away from regular work responsibilities as a way to recharge the batteries of employees. This is one way to try to avoid job burnout, especially in the helping professions. Time away from client relationships can help the worker to reaffirm her commitment to the profession.

Lessening Responses to Stress

There are many forms of stress management programs. These are designed to either lessen the perception of stress or to lessen the effects of stress that is felt. One of the most popular programs is based on exercise, diet, and employee health and fitness (see *A Word to the Wise*). Organizations have installed gyms in the organization's building and even hired instructors to form and lead exercise classes before work, at lunch, or after normal working hours. Some organizations have pursued a middle course of reimbursing employees for fitness club memberships or exercise class expenses.

Other programs that can be useful in alleviating stress, at least for some individuals, are meditation, relaxation techniques such as stretching and visualization of calm experiences, and time management. This last approach can be especially helpful if a person is suffering from role overload and is trying to do too much in the limited time available. Time management is not a cure-all, however, as is illustrated in this chapter's *On the One Hand* feature.

Cognitive approaches to dealing with stress include bio-feedback and goal setting. With bio-feedback the employee is able to learn more about his own physiological responses as machines monitor blood pressure, skin electricity, sweating, heart rate, and sometimes even brain waves. One computer program takes physiological measurements as input and displays an animated hot air balloon on the video screen. The patient watches the balloon and tries to make it fall. The higher the balloon the more stress is felt. By learning how to control the balloon, the person learns to control his own biological processes and felt stress.

Using goal setting to manage stress, workers can learn to make plans and back-up plans to use when the initial plan goes awry. Goals can be set for both the long and the short run so that employees can learn to consider what outcomes are most important to them, and how best to go about achieving those outcomes.

Another approach to help reduce stress is to encourage office humour. A little humour and poking fun at office practices can help to improve productivity, facilitate teamwork, boost office morale, and help employees deal with job stress (Caudron, 1992).

Alleviating the Consequences of Stress

Illicit drug or alcohol abuse is estimated to be a problem for over 10% of Canadians, and 11% report that they know someone at work with a drug or alcohol problem (Layng & Perras, 1992).

A WORD TO THE WISE

Medical doctor Walter Bortz has found that there is a strong similarity between the changes in the human body due to physical inactivity and the changes that we think are due to aging. His point is that we expect to age—to become more physically fragile, to lose bone and muscle mass, and to be less capable and more dependent on others. This expectation of what aging is helps to cause the lack of physical activity that then leads to these very effects! His prescriptions for remaining healthy and fully functional even as we age are to keep active, to eat and sleep well, and to maintain independence. Specifically, he suggests that it is important to:

1. *Get exercise*—make it a regular part of your routine and make sure that it is vigorous enough to work the cardiovascular and musculoskeletal systems.
2. *Have a good diet*—eat fruit, grains, vegetables and lean meat. A return to natural foods will help your body to be healthy and strong.
3. *Get enough sleep*—make sure to get the rest and the sleep that your body requires to repair and regenerate itself.
4. *Have a sense of humour*—a positive attitude and sense of humour about the daily trials and tribulations of life will go a long way toward lessening stress levels.
5. *Set goals*—by setting goals and taking on challenges that force you to keep active, you slow the aging caused by inactivity.
6. *Retain your independence*—we all need to feel that we are masters of our own lives. By relying on yourself and not on others for your well-being you create a sense of self-efficacy that will help you deal with life's problems.
7. *Increase involvement*—get involved with other people and important causes. It is by being involved that you create a reason for being and a sense of your own importance in the world.
8. *Maintain energy*—the key here is not to slow down, to keep going. If a person assumes that slowing down is a part of getting older, then that will become a self-fulfilling prophecy.

SOURCE: Based on information in Walter Bortz (1992), "Use it or lose it," *The Saturday Evening Post.* November/December 1992, pp. 62, 64, 82. Also see Walter Bortz (1990), *We Live Too Short and Die Too Long,* New York: Bantam.

Employee Assistance Plans (EAPs) are a good way to allow employees suffering stress reactions to begin to learn how to manage those reactions. The best approach is for an organization to provide confidential counselling for all the problems that are likely to arise. Examples are alcohol dependency, drug addiction, marital or family difficulties, and on-the-job conflicts with subordinates, co-workers, or superiors. Career counselling, testing, and suicide prevention hotlines are sometimes also offered as a resource to employees. Besides being comprehensive and confidential, EAPs work well when the counsellors do not take sides—neither management's nor the employee's. Involvement of the employee's family members is also often important in dealing with substance abuse or other problems (Coshan, 1992). However, for EAPs to be effective, they must be publicized so that employees know that help is available.

Employee Assistance Plans (EAPs) Programs of counselling and treatment offered by organizations to employees suffering stress reactions as a way for them to begin to learn how to manage those reactions.

CONCLUSION

In this chapter we have seen how stress can be caused by factors in the workplace. Each of us will experience stress at work and stress in our personal life. In the next chapter we will examine how an individual's life and career is liable to go through predictable stages, and we provide some hints about how to go about career management. Chapter 14 will offer theories about careers as well as practical advice of critical importance for the management of your organizational life. We will study career stages, career planning, problems that may be faced, as well as the process of getting a first full-time career related job.

ON THE ONE HAND ...

One approach to dealing with stress is that of *Time Management*. To manage time a person could set out a plan of what needs to be done. Then work is done in accordance with the plan. For example, here is a time management plan to try.

1. *Set daily goals.* Be precise in what you wish to accomplish, set intermediate goals that can be accomplished in the short to medium term, and order your goals by priority.
2. Purchase and keep a daily organizer that keeps track of your daily goals, your appointments, important telephone and fax numbers, etc. Keep it with you at all times and update it continually so that you have your plan and activities directly in front of you.
3. *Set aside time to plan.* At the end of each day, take a few minutes to revise your daily goals and to plan your agenda for the next day. In this way you will wake up the next morning with a clear plan of what you wish to accomplish.
4. *Do high priority items first.* Stick to your plan of what to do in what order. Don't be tempted by yourself or others to leave the more important goals until the last while "cleaning up a number of details" and less important items in your agenda. By working on the high priority items first they will get your attention and get done. The lower priority items will either disappear from your list (they resolved themselves or were actually not that important) or will become higher priority.
5. *Only look at a piece of paper once.* Don't waste time going over memos and documents more than once. Take action and then move on.
6. *Keep to your schedule.* It is tempting to overreact to what others define as a "crisis" that needs your immediate attention by abandoning all your carefully laid out plans and schedules and dealing with the crisis. But many so-called crises can actually wait or can be dealt with by others.
7. *Learn to say no and mean it.* The greatest drain on your time is doing things for others that are not a high priority for you. When you make a decision about what you will do and will not do, stick to it.

ON THE OTHER HAND ...

Miami Herald *columnist Dave Barry has described in excruciatingly funny detail what actually happens to our well thought out plans. Here, in his own words, is his time management plan.*

The key to my efficiency is my daily schedule, a miracle of smart planning and split-second timing:

DAILY SCHEDULE

6:00 A.M.— Alarm goes off.

6:10, 6:20, 6:30, 6:40, 6:50 A.M.— Alarm goes off.

7:00 A.M.— Wake up and mentally review Plan of Action for accomplishing Today's Target Tasks.

7:10 A.M.— Alarm goes off.

7:11 A.M.— Open bedroom door and greet dogs.
Note: I always allow at least ten minutes for this, because dogs have the same IQ as artichokes, and thus when they see me close the door at night—even though they've seen me do this approximately 1,300 times—they are certain they'll never see me again, and consequently they give me an insanely joyful welcome comparable to the one given to the Allied forces when they liberated Paris, the difference being that the Parisians were slightly less likely, in their enthusiasm, to pee on your feet.

7:21 A.M.— Wake up child.

7:25 A.M.— Commence bathroom activities, including intense 12-minute inspection and tentative probing of impending nose zit.

7:45 A.M.— Wake up child.

7:48 A.M.— Prepare breakfast of modern, easy-to-prepare, nutrition-free food substances, such as Waffles In A Can.

7:50 A.M.— Wake up child.

8:00 A.M.— Read newspaper. Save time by skipping stories whose headlines contain any of the following words: NATO, ECONOMY, DOLLAR, MIDEAST, ENVIRONMENT, FEDERAL, OZONE, ASIA, PRESIDENT, CONGRESS, NUCLEAR, and CANCER. If running late, go directly to comics.

8:03 A.M.— Wake up child.

8:06 A.M.— Feed child quick breakfast consisting of cereal advertised on Saturday-morning television cartoon shows, such as Sug-a-Rama with Lumps o'Honey ("The Cereal That Makes Your Attention Span Even Shorter").

8:12 A.M.— Rush to car and drive child to school, learning en route that child's Science Fair project, which child has never mentioned, is due that morning.

8:23 A.M.— Arrive at school with completed Science Fair project, entitled "Objects Found in 1984 Jeep Ashtray."

8:25 A.M.— Drive to office, turning "dead time" in car to productive use by examining nose zit in rearview mirror and making helpful corrective gestures at other drivers.

9:07 A.M.— Arrive at office and immediately plunge into the hectic but invigorating task of getting coffee.

9:14 A.M.— Meet with co-workers to review issues left unresolved from previous day concerning pathetic state of Miami dolphin defense.

9:37 A.M.— Coffee.

9:43 A.M.— Receive phone call from school official wondering how come child is not wearing shoes.

9:49 A.M.— Turn on word processor in preparation for day's highest-priority Target Task, writing humor column due several days earlier.

9:51 A.M.— Coffee.

10:20 A.M.— Stop in office of colleague for briefing concerning the story about the Polish airliner that crashed in a cemetery. (NOTE: They recovered 11 000 bodies.)

10:56 A.M.— Lunch.

11:27 A.M.— Back to work on humor column. Develop strong opening phrase: "One thing that has always struck me as very funny is ..." Sink back in chair in exhaustion due to creative effort.

11:34 A.M.— Lunch.

12:22 P.M.— Review Polish airliner story with various colleagues.

1:34 P.M.— Revise opening phrase to read: "A very funny thing, and one that lends itself quite naturally to being the topic of a humor column, is ..."

2:05 P.M.— Lunch.

2:42 P.M.— Come up with very strong new opening phrase: "If you're going to write a funny column, probably the easiest topic you could pick is ..."

3:32 P.M.— Coffee.

3:51 P.M.— Nose zit update.

4:23 P.M.— Brief additional colleagues on Polish airliner matter.

4:47 P.M.— Lunch.

5:08 P.M.— Make final revisions to opening column phrase ("A humor-column topic so obvious that it practically writes itself is ...").

5:27 P.M.— Explain to editor that only minor "fine-tuning" remains and column will definitely be finished by next day or following summer at latest.

6:39 P.M.— Arrive home to insanely joyful greeting from dogs, who, believing themselves abandoned forever, spent entire day throwing up in despair.

7:22 P.M.— Finish cleanup and commence quiet, intimate, romantic microwave pizza dinner with spouse.

7:23 P.M.— Receive phone call from school official with talent for sarcasm, inquiring about any possible plans in near future to pick up child.

7:52 P.M.— Return home with child to discover that dogs, grief-stricken over most recent departure, have managed to get pizza smears as high as seven feet up on living-room walls.

8:51 P.M.— Enjoy wholesome fast-food family dinner at Cholesterol Castle.

9:47 P.M.— Return home and enjoy emotional dog reunion resulting in several hairline fractures.

10:23 P.M.— Put child to bed and experience touching parental moment when, just as he is falling asleep, child remembers that on following day he is supposed to come to school in authentic costume of Yap islander.

10:32 P.M.— Nose zit update.

10:47 P.M.— Lunch.

11:00 P.M.— Turn on late news.

11:01 P.M.— Turn off late news when announcer uses word "nuclear."

11:02 P.M.— Sex life.

11:03 P.M.— Think about Target Tasks for tomorrow. Lots to do. Got column to write. Got developing nose zit. Got dogs to kill. Better set alarm for 6:00 A.M. sharp.

SOURCE: Dave Barry's Daily Schedule from *Dave Barry Turns 40* (1991), New York: Ballantine Books, pap. 99-103. © 1990 by Dave Barry. Reproduced by permission of Dave Barry.

CHAPTER SUMMARY

People in organizations are subject to stressors of various kinds. These can come from outside the organization, from the organization's structure and its systems, from the physical environment at work, from interpersonal relationships at work, or from the job role. Any or all of these factors can lead to stress as perceived by an individual.

When stress is felt it can cause physiological, psychological, and behavioural responses in the individual. Physiological responses are changes to the body's chemistry, heart rate, blood pressure, etc., in preparation for "fight or flight." Psychological responses can include depression, anxiety, and impairment of cognitive functioning. Potential behavioural responses are absenteeism, turnover, drug use, accident proneness, and sickness, among others. These then have consequences both for the individual and the organization.

But there is a set of moderators that can alter the relationship between stressors and perceived stress or between perceived stress and responses to stress. Examples of these moderators are youthfulness, hardiness, and certain aspects of personality. These moderators help to explain how people can differentially perceive the amount of stress in a situation, or how their responses to stress can be different even if the same amount of stress is felt.

There are four possible points at which stress or stress consequences can be prevented or lessened. The first is to reduce the amount and severity of the stressors themselves or how they are perceived by the individual. The second is to alter the moderators of the stressors-stress response link. The aim of this approach is to make the person more able to deal with the stressors that are present so that not as much actual stress is felt. The third is to alter the individual's responses to stress. Examples are meditation, relaxation, and time management. The fourth is to alleviate the consequences of stress. Employee counselling is one approach to help the organizational member learn to deal with the stress that is felt and its negative outcomes.

QUESTIONS FOR REVIEW

1. List some of the ways that individuals in organizations purposely add to the amount of stress in their work lives.

2. When people take on too much the stress they feel can be so debilitating that they are unable to make progress on any of their commitments. What can a person do in this case?

3. Why is it important that employee assistance plans be confidential?

4. An individual at work is overloaded, mentally exhausted, and physically run down. But, refusing to quit, things only go from bad to worse. Why does this happen?

5. How do stress in a person's home life and stress in that same person's work life affect each other?

SELF-DIAGNOSTIC EXERCISE 13.1

How High is Your Stress Threshold?

The following test can give you an indication of how well you react to stress. Answer the 11 questions and then score your results.

1. When competing for an important engagement or for a promotion, do you:
   a) Go about it with full enthusiasm without worry?
   b) Worry about how your success will be viewed by others?
   c) Feel that you must succeed at all costs, and become depressed if you don't?
   d) Fail to approach the challenge with full enthusiasm because you are wasting energy by worrying?

2. When meeting new group members or joining a new firm, do you:
   a) Feel nervous and sweaty?
   b) Have no feeling one way or the other and, in fact, are sort of bored?
   c) Worry about how the people will feel about you?
   d) Feel relaxed and sort of excited?

3. First thing in the morning, do you feel:
   a) Nervous in wondering expectation as to what the day will hold for you?
   b) Wide awake and looking forward to what the day will hold for you?
   c) Anxious as to what you have to do today and how you are going to get it all done?
   d) No different from any other day, since all days are the same?

4. When you have high expectations of a partner, peer, or spouse, do you:
   a) Feel you are expecting too much from him or her?
   b) Try to convince yourself that you should listen to all points of view and then back off from your strong position if you are shown to be wrong?
   c) Insist that your way is the only way and that the other person should abide by your demands?
   d) After hearing the other person's point of view, usually find yourself saying that he or she must be right, and then give in?

5. When scheduling an engagement or organizing an important project, do you:
   a) Approach the project in an organized and systematic manner?
   b) Find it difficult to get started, but stay with the project until it is completed?
   c) Find yourself procrastinating and continually postponing the start of the project?
   d) Become nervous and have the feeling that you will not be able to complete the project?

6. When dealing with entry-level staff or people new to your group, do you find yourself:
   a) Impatient with their questions?
   b) Unconcerned with their questions and concerns?
   c) Wishing the meeting was over so that you can get on with your own "to do" list?
   d) Listening to all that is being said and trying to help them handle their problems?

7. When a new member of your firm or group does something you don't like, do you:
   a) React in a calm manner and help him learn the best way?
   b) Ignore the situation and go on with your normal work?
   c) Lose your temper but don't say anything to anyone?
   d) Lose your temper and yell at him?

8. After a long day at work, do you, before going to sleep:
   a) Have lots of thoughts running through your head about this day and the next day, and find it difficult to fall asleep?
   b) Find it difficult to relax and fall asleep?
   c) Feel not tired?
   d) Feel tired and find it easy to fall asleep?

9. When challenged by a critical event or client, do you respond:
   a) Almost always effectively?
   b) Sometimes effectively?
   c) Rarely effectively?
   d) Almost never effectively?

10. Do you smoke:
    a) Not at all?
    b) Less than 10 cigarettes a day?
    c) Less than 20 cigarettes a day?
    d) 20 or more cigarettes a day?

11. Is your intake of alcohol:
    a) Frequent and heavy?
    b) Frequent but not heavy?
    c) Occasional (not more than 3 days per week)?
    d) Light (only a small amount)?

Analysis:

	Response			
Question	a	b	c	d
1	+5	-1	+4	-2
2	-4	-1	-2	+5
3	-2	+5	-3	-1
4	+5	-1	-4	-2
5	+4	-1	-2	-3

| | *Response* | | | |
Question	a	b	c	d
6	-4	-1	-3	+5
7	+5	-1	-5	-3
8	-4	-2	-1	+3
9	+5	+2	-2	-4
10	+5	+2	+1	-4
11	-4	-2	+1	+5

If your score totals:

45 or more: You are free of excess stress
20 to 44:   You are freer from stress than the average person
2 to 19:   You are somewhat overstressed but still within the "safe" zone
Below 2:   You are definitely overstressed.

Remember, in interpreting these stress threshold results, this test as used here should not be considered a valid scientific instrument. The results should be used as input into your own considerations of how you deal with stress and how you will plan to deal with stress in the future.

SOURCE: From Jay N. Nisberg and Wayne A. Label (1984), "How to cope with stress," The Practical Accountant, March 1984, pp. 68-69. Reprinted with permission from *The Practical Accountant.* Copyright © 1989 Faulkner & Gray Inc.

SELF-DIAGNOSTIC EXERCISE 13.2

Fear of Success/Fear of Failure

Take the following test for an indication of whether or not you have, or to what extent you have, a fear of success or a fear of failure. Try to answer the questions as accurately and objectively as possible for you—don't answer as you think you "should." Remember, while the results will be suggestive of your own fear of success or failure, this test as used here should not be considered a valid scientific instrument. Take the results as input into your own considerations of your fear of success and fear of failure. To further discuss the test results and your own interpretations of them, see a trained psychologist.

In the first column, answer **A** for agree, **B** for in-between or don't know, and **C** for disagree.

Test A
Column 1   Column 2

_____   _____   1. When things seem to be going really well for me, I get uneasy because I know it won't last.

_____   _____   2. I find that I measure up to the standards I've set for myself most of the time.

Column 1	Column 2	
_____	_____	3. I find it difficult to tell my friends that I excel at something.
_____	_____	4. It is important for me to be liked by people holding positions of higher status and power.
_____	_____	5. When I win a competitive game, I feel a little sorry for the other player.
_____	_____	6. When I have to ask others for help, I feel I'm imposing on them.
_____	_____	7. Although I may experience occasional difficulty doing so, I generally finish essential projects.
_____	_____	8. When I think I've been too forceful in making a point with a colleague, I get worried that I might have made my colleague feel unfriendly toward me.
_____	_____	9. When others compliment me on my work, I feel they are being insincere.
_____	_____	10. When I complete an important piece of work, I am usually satisfied with the result.
_____	_____	11. When engaged in competitive games, I make more mistakes near the end than at the beginning.
_____	_____	12. When my boss praises my work, I wonder whether I can live up to my boss' expectations in the future.
_____	_____	13. At times I believe I have gotten as far in my career as I have because of good luck and not because I deserved to succeed.
_____	_____	14. It is more important to win a game than to enjoy it.
_____	_____	15. I often daydream about accomplishing something that no one else ever has.
_____	_____	16. I like being the centre of attention in a social gathering.
_____	_____	17. Most of my colleagues are secretly pleased when I get into trouble.
_____	_____	18. I'm skillful at most things I try.
_____	_____	19. When I make a decision, I usually stick with it.
_____	_____	20. I often get excited when I start a new project, but it gets stale rather quickly.
_____	_____	21. I often feel let down after completing an important project.
_____	_____	22. At times my accomplishments amaze me because I feel that I rarely put in the effort that I could.

Column 1	Column 2	
_____	_____	23. When I hear about the accomplishments of others, I tend to think about how little I have accomplished.
_____	_____	24. I'm not influenced one way or another by persuasive people.
_____	_____	25. When a project seems to be going well, I often get scared that I'll do something to botch it.
Total	_____	

Test B

Answer in the first column **A** for agree, **B** for in-between or don't know, and **C** for disagree.

Column 1	Column 2	
_____	_____	1. The surest way to be disappointed is to want something too much.
_____	_____	2. I seldom consult my associates before deciding to go ahead with a project.
_____	_____	3. When I decide to go after something, I usually get it.
_____	_____	4. Before I decide what procedures to use in my work, I like to ask my peers for advice.
_____	_____	5. I sometimes downgrade my abilities so that my boss won't expect too much from me.
_____	_____	6. When someone I know succeeds at something, I often feel I could have done as well, or better.
_____	_____	7. I don't mind having to ask others for help.
_____	_____	8. I seldom participate in competitive games.
_____	_____	9. When I have to complete an important project in a hurry, I get so upset that I can't concentrate on it.
_____	_____	10. Most of the time I feel that I do things as well as I can.
_____	_____	11. I prefer to settle for less than I want rather than get into an argument.
_____	_____	12. I dislike people who look out for themselves first.
_____	_____	13. When I commit myself to something, I go through with it.
_____	_____	14. I can easily concentrate on a task for a long period of time.
_____	_____	15. When I sit down to solve a problem, I often get distracted and my thoughts drift off to other things.

Column 1	Column 2	
____	____	16. My work tends to pile up so much that I have difficulty completing all of it.
____	____	17. I have little trouble saying no to people.
____	____	18. I like to explore subject areas in which I have little knowledge.
____	____	19. I have what it takes to be a success in my chosen field.
____	____	20. When developing a new idea, I often tend to get stuck at a certain point.
____	____	21. I like to avoid situations that could pose conflicts.
____	____	22. Even when I have good ideas, I frequently don't follow through on them.
____	____	23. I don't mind working on difficult problems, even when I'm not sure I can figure them out.
____	____	24. When I am in a heated discussion, my mind often goes blank.
____	____	25. When starting to work on an important project, I often find many other things that need to be taken care of first
Total	____	

Scoring:

Now record in the *second column* for each test the numeric value for each question that corresponds to your letter answer. Total these numeric scores for each test.

Test A: Fear of Success

Question	A	B	C	Question	A	B	C
	Answer				*Answer*		
1	-1	0	2	14	2	1	-1
2	2	0	-1	15	3	0	-2
3	-1	0	1	16	2	1	-1
4	-1	0	1	17	-1	0	1
5	1	0	-1	18	2	1	-1
6	-2	1	2	19	3	0	-2
7	3	0	-2	20	-2	1	2
8	-2	1	2	21	-1	0	1
9	-1	0	1	22	-1	0	1
10	2	0	-1	23	-2	0	2
11	-2	0	2	24	3	1	-2
12	-2	0	2	25	-1	0	2
13	-2	1	2				

Test B: Fear of Failure

Question	Answer A	B	C	Question	Answer A	B	C
1	-2	1	2	14	2	0	-2
2	1	0	-1	15	-2	0	2
3	3	1	-2	16	0	1	2
4	-1	0	1	17	2	1	-1
5	-2	0	2	18	3	0	-2
6	3	0	-2	19	3	0	-2
7	2	1	-1	20	-1	0	1
8	-2	1	2	21	-2	0	1
9	-2	0	2	22	-2	0	2
10	2	1	-1	23	3	0	-2
11	-2	0	2	24	-3	0	3
12	-2	1	2	25	-3	0	3
13	3	0	-3				

Interpretation:

Fear of Success

A score of 28 to 47 indicates that you have no problem with "fear of success." You are likely to be strongly achievement-oriented and like to come up a winner. You take commitments and persevere with projects until successful. You take pride in your talents and have full confidence in yourself. Although you are independent-minded and assertive, your relationships with others are trustful and open.

If you scored 4 to 28, you have a tendency to aspire to unrealistically high standards, and are not always satisfied with your achievements. You prefer win/win rather than win/lose situations. You are concerned about what others think of you and want to be liked by everybody. Because of a fluctuating self-esteem you periodically lapse into self-critical ruminations about your ability to succeed. You have some trouble making decisions and sticking with them. The limelight is not for you, and you scorn those who want to be the "life of the party." Because you have a moderate fear of success, you're not functioning fully up to your potential.

A score of -25 to 4 indicates that you want to win but frequently lose. You tend to be overly passive and withdrawn, preferring to take the back seat in competitive situations. Because of your excessive need to be liked, you refrain from arguments and contests of will. You lack self-confidence and you seldom give yourself the credit you deserve for your accomplishments. You tend to be somewhat distrustful of other people's motives and feel that human nature cannot always be relied upon. Fear of success definitely hampers you.

A score of -36 to -25 means that "fear of success" is definitely a problem for you. Too unassertive and self-effacing, you consider modesty a virtue. You are never satisfied with your achievements, and frequently manage to snatch defeat from victory. Doubtful about whether you have any luck at all, you tend to worry about the future. Because you're too concerned about others' opinions of you, you frequently play the doormat, although you resent the role. You neither give nor receive compliments.

Fear of Failure

A score of 35 to 54 indicates that you are seldom troubled with thoughts of failure. Indeed, you move toward objectives with full confidence, acting as if it is impossible for you to fail. You stick with difficult tasks and seldom give up on problems. You rarely compare your achievements with those of others; when you do, you usually feel you could have done better. Your self-reliance and self-trust enable you to remain unperturbed in challenging situations.

A score between 8 and 35 says that you are sometimes overly cautious and hesitant, and even entertain doubts about reaching goals. You have trouble concentrating even when something important is at stake. Before you act on your ideas, you feel compelled to enlist others' opinions and evaluations of your plans. If they don't approve or encourage you, you frequently give up on your plans.

A score of -25 to 8 suggests a marked fear of failure in many areas. You lack self-confidence and have an unrealistically low image of yourself. You tend to avoid important tasks and busy yourself with the tried and true. Competitive situations are anathema, as well as being with people you don't know. In meetings, you feel that everyone else has more witty and knowledgeable things to say than you do, and you tend generally to act in a timid and embarrassed way. Your aspirations are low and you hesitate to take any risks.

A score between -47 and -25 shows a complete lack of self-confidence. You avoid challenges, preferring to stick with routine, familiar tasks. With other people, you seek timid accommodation and dislike those who are boisterously self-assertive. Because you fear failure so much, you have anti-success attitudes and feel that those who climb the ladder of success will find that the top isn't resting on anything.

Analysis:

Now think about your own behaviour and whether or not you think the test results have given a reasonably accurate portrayal of yourself. If you are not satisfied with where you are, consider what you can do to reduce your fear of success and/or fear of failure. Please note that while the results of this test will be suggestive of your own fear of success and fear of failure, this test as used here should not be considered a valid scientific instrument. If you think that your results for this test need to be explored further, it is advisable that you contact the student counselling office at your university or college, or a psychologist trained in work testing, training, and counselling.

SOURCE: Reprinted by permission of Chemical Engineering, McGraw-Hill, Inc. from Eugene Raudsepp, (1988), "Overcoming barriers to career success," *Chemical Engineering*, November 7, 1988, pp. 101-104.

EXPERIENTIAL EXERCISE 13.1

Deborah Dwyer and Daniel Ganster (1991) have studied the effects of job control on employee attendance and satisfaction. This exercise is designed to allow you to evaluate the degree of control you have on your job, and then to compare your experiences of job attendance and satisfaction with those of your classmates.

Step 1. Individually complete the job control scale.
Step 2. Form into classroom groups of 5 or 6.
Step 3. Discuss the results of the job control scale in your group. Also discuss the linkages you see between job control and your experience of job attendance and satisfaction on your job.
Step 4. Each group reports its findings back to the main group.

The Job Control Scale

Below are listed a number of statements which could be used to describe a job. Please read each statement carefully and indicate the extent to which each is an accurate or an inaccurate description of *your* job by writing a number in front of each statement.

1 = Very Little
2 = Little
3 = A Moderate Amount
4 = Much
5 = Very Much

_____ 1. How much control do you have over the variety of methods you use in completing your work?

_____ 2. How much can you choose among a variety of tasks or projects to do?

_____ 3. How much control do you have personally over the quality of your work?

_____ 4. How much can you generally predict the amount of work you will have to do on any given day?

_____ 5. How much control do you have personally over how much work you get done?

_____ 6. How much control do you have over how quickly or slowly you have to work?

_____ 7. How much control do you have over the scheduling and duration of your rest breaks?

_____ 8. How much control do you have over when you come to work and leave?

_____ 9. How much control do you have over when you take vacations or days off?

_____ 10. How much are you able to predict what the results of decisions you make on the job will be?

_____ 11. How much are you able to decorate, rearrange, or personalize your work area?

_____ 12. How much can you control the physical conditions of your work station (lighting, temperature)?

_____ 13. How much control do you have over how you do your work?

_____ 14. How much can you control when and how much you interact with others at work?

_____ 15. How much influence do you have over the policies and procedures in your work unit?

_____ 16. How much control do you have over the sources of information you need to do your job?

_____ 17. How much are things that affect you at work predictable, even if you can't directly control them?

_____ 18. How much control do you have over the amount of resources (tools, material) you get?

_____ 19. How much can you control the number of times you are interrupted while you work?

_____ 20. How much control do you have over the amount you earn at your job?

_____ 21. How much control do you have over how your work is evaluated?

_____ 22. In general, how much overall control do you have over work and work-related matters?

This scale has one main factor—that of job control. Add up your answers for the 22 questions to find your average job control score. While your results are useful as data for input into a class discussion about job control and stress, this test as used here should not be considered a valid scientific instrument.

SOURCE: The job control scale is reprinted from Deborah J. Dwyer and Daniel C. Ganster (1991), "The effects of job demands and control on employee attendance and satisfaction," _Journal of Organizational Behavior_ 12: 608. Reprinted by permission of John Wiley & Sons, Ltd.

SELF-GUIDED LEARNING ACTIVITY

To look further into the concept of burnout and how burnout is measured, you might wish to look for a copy of the 1982 book by Christina Maslach titled _Burnout—The Cost of Caring_. The companion _Maslach Burnout Inventory_ (MBI) is a widely known tool used to measure burnout. By Christina Maslach and Susan E. Jackson, it consists of 22 items measuring three subscales: Emotional Exhaustion, Personal Accomplishment, and Depersonalization. The MBI can be used to help counsel people to reduce their symptoms of burnout by changing their job conditions. It is available to psychologists from Consulting Psychologists Press. A second useful book is _Preventing Job Burnout_ by Beverly A. Potter (1987), also published by Consulting Psychologists Press. It provides exercises, activities, and programs designed to help the reader avoid job burnout. These two books in combination can help you to evaluate your own career plans, how susceptible people are to burnout in your chosen career, and what actions you might take to beat job burnout.

CASE 13.1

MANAGER'S CASE FILE: IN THE FAST LANE

Paul Brock had been with Daylight Enterprises for 14 years. During that time, he had performed his job well: He kept his current accounts up to date and satisfied with his service, he brought in new clients on a regular basis, and he kept himself appraised of the latest developments in his field by attending conferences and expositions. All in all, Paul Brock was a very busy man. But lately Paul seemed more busy than usual.

Paul's colleagues noticed that he was always rushing off somewhere to see a client, to check on an account, to catch a plane, or to confer with his boss, John Spivak. They wondered how he could keep up such a hectic pace.

"I don't know how he does it," Bill said. "He never seems to sit still for a minute."

"And he plays as hard as he works," Jose added. "He takes his kids to little league, he's on the bowling team, and he plays handball."

"You think he could be on something?" Bill asked quietly.

"No, not Paul," Jose said. Both managers were quiet for a moment, then Jose noted, "His eyes have been red a lot. I just thought it was jet lag."

"He always seems to have a cold, too," Bill said. "He goes through a lot of tissues with his sniffles."

"Do you think we should say something to the boss?" Jose asked.

"No," Bill said. "We can't go to him with just suspicions. Suppose we're wrong. We might get Paul in trouble."

"Maybe you're right," Jose agreed. "But I'm going to keep one eye on Paul just the same."

The next Wednesday Paul came to work looking awful, like he hadn't slept in days. His eyes were red, and he was practically dragging himself in. When Bill and Jose noticed Paul's condition, they agreed to approach him together after they gave him a chance to get settled in his office.

However, when the two went into Paul's office, he looked alert and energetic.

"Just out a little late last night," Paul said in response to their questions about his condition. "Some eye drops will take care of the redness, and I'm ready for a new day," he said as he wiped his nose.

"You've had that cold for a long time, Paul," Jose said. "Shouldn't you see a doctor?"

"Nonsense, it's just a little cold. It's nothing to worry about."

"Well, to be honest, Paul," Bill began and looked at Jose, "we were wondering if you were using something to pep you up. You've been running around so much lately that it has to be taking its toll."

"What are you two trying to say?" Paul asked.

"We're worried about you, Paul," Jose said. "From everything we've noticed, it appears as if you've been taking drugs." All three men looked shocked that the words had actually been said. Paul was the first to recover.

"Look, just because I've got more on the ball than you do is no reason to accuse me of taking drugs," Paul said. "Get a few nosebleeds and everybody comes down on you! You two are just jealous because I've got more accounts and make more money than you do."

"Take it easy, Paul," Bill said. "We're just concerned...."

"There's no need to be concerned with anything other than your own business," Paul shot back.

Jose and Bill knew that they were getting nowhere with Paul, so they left him and went into Bill's office to talk over what, if anything, they should do.

Source: Reprinted, by permission of publisher, from MANAGEMENT SOLUTIONS, September 1988. © 1988 American Management Association, New York. All rights reserved.

Questions

1. Should Bill and Jose tell their boss about their suspicions?

2. Provided that John Spivak believes Bill and Jose, what should he do about Paul?

3. If Paul does not admit to a drug habit, is there anything that can be done for him?

CASE 13.2

FRANK PEPPER

Frank Pepper is a 55-year-old owner of a successful and growing business in Edmonton. Frank has put a lot of work into this company, and now has land, building, and $500 000 of equipment as assets. He employs five office staff and about ten full-time production workers, along with 30 to 40 semi-permanent unskilled laborers. In the first month of business twelve years ago sales were zero, whereas now they are into the millions per month. Barring unforeseen circumstances, July 1987 should be the best month ever with over 4 million dollars in sales.

It was a hot summer day in Edmonton, July 31, 1987, and Frank was looking at the monthly sales while contemplating the future. He wasn't sure how much longer he wanted to remain in this business. Frank's partner is 42 years old, and will no doubt take over the company one day. Frank likened taxes to a mosquito bite, "The more you scratch, the more you itch; the more you earn, the more the government wants." The Government of Alberta always seemed to have new rules and regulations that appeared to be there only to make life a little bit harder for Frank.

Frank was sick and tired of his taxes going to Eastern Canada. He was also upset with the fact that companies in his business in Eastern Canada were making money hand over fist, because of the present boom in economic conditions there. Frank is contemplating selling his business and moving to a warmer climate such as Bermuda to spend the rest of his days in a warm and quiet place.

It is 2:00 Friday afternoon, and Frank decides to call it a day. As he leaves his office and heads for his car it starts to rain. He looks up to see that a thunderstorm is brewing. As he drives away from his building, he thinks to himself "We've sure been having a lot of thunderstorms lately."

A short time later a tornado ripped through Edmonton, leaving a trail of death and destruction from the city's south end through its eastern edge. While no one was killed at Frank's business, Frank returned that night to find his building demolished, inventory smashed, and equipment damaged. Frank rolled up his sleeves. He had a lot of work to do.

Questions

1. Which is more stressful, the continuing stress felt by Frank of taxes and government rules, or the sudden change created by having the tornado destroy much of Frank's hard assets?

2. Will Frank retire now? If you think he will retire, what are your reasons? If you think he will not retire now, what has changed for Frank?

3. Could Frank have planned for a disaster such as the tornado? Would such planning have helped him in coping?

REFERENCES

Adler, Tina (1992). "Sleep loss impairs attention—and more." *APA Monitor* 24(9): 22-23.

Barker, James R. (1993). "Tightening the iron cage: Concertive control in self-managing teams." *Administrative Science Quarterly* 38: 408-437.

Baron, James N., Alison Davis-Blake, & William Bielby (1986). "The structure of opportunity: How promotion ladders vary within and among organizations." *Administrative Science Quarterly* 31: 248-273.

Barry, Dave (1991). *Dave Barry Turns 40.* New York: Ballantine Books.

Bortz, Walter (1990). *We Live Too Short and Die Too Long.* New York: Bantam.

Bortz, Walter (1992). "Use it or lose it." *The Saturday Evening Post.* November/December 1992, pp. 62, 64, 82.

Business Week (1993). "Saturn: Labor's love lost?" February 8, 1993, pp. 122, 124.

Caudron, Shari (1992). "Humor is healthy in the workplace." *Personnel Journal,* June 1992, pp. 63-68.

Cordes, Cynthia L., & Thomas W. Dougherty (1993). "A review and an integration of research on job burnout." *Academy of Management Review* 18: 621-656.

Coshan, Margaret (1992). "An EAP can be part of the solution." *Canadian Business Review,* Summer 1992, 22-24.

Day, Frederick A. (1992). "Sexual harassment." *Law Now,* September 1992, 17(1), 13-14.

Dunham, Randall B. (1984). *Organizational Behavior: People and Processes in Management.* Homewood, IL: Richard D. Irwin, Inc.

Dwyer, Deborah J., & Daniel C. Ganster (1991). "The effects of job demands and control on employee attendance and satisfaction." *Journal of Organizational Behavior* 12: 595-608.

Edwards, Jeffrey R. (1992). "A cybernetic theory of stress, coping, and well-being in organizations." *Academy of Management Review* 17: 238-274.

Farrar, Alice, & Linda J. Murray (1993). "How to stay well in a sick building." *Working Woman,* January 1993, p. 72.

Fiske, Susan T. (1993). "Controlling other people: The impact of power on stereotyping." *American Psychologist* 48: 621-628.

Fitzgerald, Louise F. (1993). "Sexual harassment: Violence against women in the workplace." *American Psychologist* 48: 1070-1076.

Frone, Michael R., Marcia Russell, & M. Lynne Cooper (1992). "Antecedents and outcomes of work-family conflict: Testing a model of the work-family interface." *Journal of Applied Psychology* 77: 65-78.

Ganster, Daniel C., John Schaubroeck, Wesley E. Sime, & Bronston T. Mayes (1991). "The nomological validity of the Type A personality among employed adults." *Journal of Applied Psychology* 76: 143-168.

Gibb-Clark, Margot (1993). "Shift work can be hazardous to your health." The *Globe and Mail,* April 5, 1993, p. B5.

Hamper, Ben (1991). *Rivethead: Tales from the Assembly Line.* New York: Warner Books.

Higgins, Christopher A., & Linda E. Duxbury (1992). "Work-family conflict: A comparison of dual-career and traditional-career men." *Journal of Organizational Behavior* 13: 389-411.

Hirschman, Albert O. (1970). *Exit, Voice and Loyalty: Responses to Decline in Firms, Organizations, and States.* Cambridge, MA: Harvard University Press.

Holmes, Thomas H., & Richard H. Rahe (1967). "The social readjustment rating scale." *Journal of Psychosomatic Research* 11: 213-218.

Ivancevich, John M., Michael T. Matteson, Sara M. Freedman, & James S. Phillips (1990). "Worksite stress management interventions." *American Psychologist* 45: 252-261.

Kahn, Robert L., & Philippe Byosiere (1992). "Stress in organizations." In Marvin D. Dunnette and Leaetta M. Hough (Eds.), *Handbook of Industrial and Organizational Psychology,* Second Edition (Volume 3, pp. 571-650). Palo Alto, CA: Consulting Psychologists Press, Inc.

Layng, Sanderson, & Jacques Perras (1992). "Promoting a drug-free workplace." *Canadian Business Review,* Summer 1992, pp. 19-21.

Lee, Raymond T., & Blake E. Ashforth (1993). "A further examination of managerial burnout: Toward an integrated model." *Journal of Organizational Behavior* 14: 3-20.

Leiter, Michael P., & Christina Maslach (1988). "The impact of interpersonal environment on burnout and organizational commitment." *Journal of Organizational Behavior* 9: 297-308.

Lehman, Wayne E.K., & D. Dwayne Simpson (1992). "Employee substance use and on-the-job behaviors." *Journal of Applied Psychology* 77: 309-321.

Makihara, Kumiko (1993). "The agony of a salaryman." *Time,* May 24, 1993, p. 46.

Maslach, Christina (1982). *Burnout: The Cost of Caring.* Englewood Cliffs, NJ: Prentice Hall.

Mobley, William H., Roger W. Griffeth, H. H. Hand, and Bruce M. Meglino (1979). "Review and conceptual analysis of the employee turnover process." *Psychological Bulletin* 86: 493-522.

Nisberg, Jay N., & Wayne A. Label (1984). "How to cope with stress." *The Practical Accountant,* March 1984, pp. 65-70.

Parker, Mike, and Jane Slaughter (1988). *Choosing Sides: Unions and the Team Concept.* Boston: South End Press.

Potter, Beverly A. (1987). *Preventing Job Burnout.* Palo Alto, CA: Consulting Psychologists Press.

Raudsepp, Eugene (1988). "Overcoming barriers to career success." *Chemical Engineering.* November 7, 1988, pp. 101-104.

Rehder, Robert R. (1994). "Is Saturn competitive?" *Business Horizons,* March-April 1994, pp. 7-15.

Roberts, J. Timmons (1993). "Psychosocial effects of workplace hazardous exposures: Theoretical synthesis and preliminary findings." *Social Problems* 40: 74-89.

Wilsher, Peter (1993). "The mixed-up manager." *Management Today,* October 1993, pp. 34-40.

FURTHER READING

A theoretical look at stress models is offered by Joe R. Eulberg, Jerr A. Weekley, and Rabi S. Bhagat in their 1988 paper titled "Models of stress in organizational research: A metatheoretical perspective," published in the journal *Human Relations,* Volume 41, pages 331-350.

For further information on the measurement of stress, see the article by Michael H. Birnbaum and Yass Sotoodeh (1991), titled "Measurement of stress: Scaling the magnitudes of life changes," published in *Psychological Science* 2: 236-243.

Balancing work and family life can be difficult. An article that looks into this issue is Douglas T. Hall's (1990) "Promoting work/family balance: An organization change approach," in *Organizational Dynamics*, Winter 1990, pp. 5-18.

A discussion of harassment at work that goes beyond the issue of sexual harassment is by Terry Morehead Dworkin, "Harassment in the 1990s," in *Business Horizons*, March-April 1993.

AIDS in the workplace is an issue of growing concern. For a featured review of the issues, see *Business Week*, February 1, 1993, "Why AIDS policy must be a special policy: Fear and misunderstanding of the virus can disrupt a workplace."

CHAPTER 14

CAREERS

CHAPTER OUTLINE

Life Stages

Careers in Organizations

   Career Stages and Career Movement

   Career Systems

   Organizational Approaches to the
   International Assignment

   Discrimination

Managing Your Career

   The Career Edge

   Choosing a Career

   Selecting a First Job

   Goals For Success

   Breaking the Glass Ceiling

   Mentors

   The Dual-Career Couple

   The International Assignment

Conclusion

QUESTIONS TO CONSIDER

- What is a career?

- How can a career be chosen?

- What are the typical career steps or stages?

- What is success?

- Does the definition of success vary depending on the person?

- How do people plan for their career?

- What problems do members of organizations face because of their age, sex, and race?

- What do organizational members need to know about international (cross-cultural) assignments?

There are two main ways to think about a person's career. One is the generally accepted idea that people choose an occupation to engage in over a period of time. For example, a person could be a career soldier, IBM employee, computer programmer/analyst, or work in the life insurance industry. Given such a career, a person could work for one organization or several and could move up the hierarchy of an organization by being promoted. The jobs this person has are linked by the organization worked in or by the type of work that is done. When a major transition takes place the person goes through a career change, say from computer programmer to law school student and then lawyer, or from life insurance executive to owner of a travel agency.

The benefit of this way of conceptualizing a career and career changes is that the transitions in one's working life are thought of as explicit events. To change careers is to make a change in one's life. Such change can be stressful and difficult to accomplish, so making a career change should not be undertaken lightly. It is also very important to note that those who will begin their careers in the 1990s can expect to have a series of careers, or changes from one major occupation or pursuit to another. One important reason for this career changing will be the fast pace of technological and social change.

An initial degree or diploma from a university or college will likely serve as an entry into a first job. For example, a business degree may help a new graduate to obtain a job as a stockbroker or accountant. But a person graduating in the 1990s should not expect to be in that job or career path the rest of her life. As society and organizations change, new career opportunities will open up, other careers will be in decline, and some careers will change in significant ways. A major shift in a person's career should therefore be expected not just once but several times over that individual's 30 to 40 year working life.

This is an important realization. It is still important to learn a technical skill or ability in order to be able to perform well on a first job. But it is ever more important to learn how to learn. Also important is to learn how to be flexible and to see learning as a lifelong activity. It is no longer possible for most people to learn one skill and to rely on only that one skill for a lifetime of work.

The second way of defining a career is based on the work of Douglas Hall (1976). His point of view is that a career is a person's course, or progress through life, or history. It is both a way of making a livelihood and a means of advancing oneself.

The benefit of thinking of careers in this way is that all parts of a person's work related experience, even across different professions or occupations, can be seen as a whole. The career is all the work a person does in his life. All work relates to and informs all other work. Hall (1976) makes several important points about careers seen in this way.

1. A career does not imply success or failure. A person can have a career in one job and need not advance up the hierarchy.
2. The career is made up of both what is done and how one feels about it.
3. Career success or failure is best assessed by the person in the career rather than by others. Outside parties cannot evaluate for others how well they are doing.

Viewing a career in this way allows us to think easily about the interaction of work life and home life. As the next section will show, both these areas of life can follow predictable patterns of change based on age and sex.

LIFE STAGES

Men and women can be seen to, in general, go through the same set of key life experiences: Birth, marriage, having a family, working in and outside the home over the course of their lives, and death. But there are differences between women and men due to biological function and to cultural socialization that affect how these life events will occur and will be experienced.

While the development patterns of men and women consist of the same steps, it has been suggested (Gilligan, 1982) that these steps may be experienced in a different order by the two sexes. Gilligan's argument has been summarized as follows:

> Men's development begins with separation and individuation, emphasizes achievement and accomplishments, eventually explores intimacy and connections with others, and finally views others as equally important to the self. For women, the developmental pattern is reversed. Women's development begins with the assumption of connectedness and interdependence, gradually explores means of separation and individuation, allows women to achieve and chart accomplishments as individuals, and then gradually allows women to view their contributions as of equal importance to that of others (Powell & Mainiero, 1992, p. 217).

There are fairly predictable stages of male adult development (Levinson and others, 1978), though not all men can be expected to pass through these stages in exactly the same way. For men, the ages 17 to 22 are a time to work and learn, to prepare for entry into the adult world. Up to the age of about 30 years old is a time for exploring and making choices about relationships and work. About age 30 there comes the time for a transition into a period of stability, settling down, and possibly raising a family.

There is the potential for an age 30 crisis. Early choices may be revised before it is too late. Divorce, change of jobs, going back to school to retrain, or making a major shift from one career track to another are all possible.

The next transition can occur somewhere between the ages of 41 to 45. An aging body that is (usually) incapable of performing with the strength and endurance of the 20s, hair graying or thinning—these are some of the signals that may trigger a mid-life crisis. The man in crisis may try to regain lost youth and what he missed when he was younger. At this age a man typically confronts his own mortality, the fact that he will die. He may also have to confront the fact that his career goals may not be attained. The man at this transition stage may see himself as not only getting old but as failing to achieve his objectives. He also tends to think that he has little time to correct the situation.

After this transition and possible crisis period comes a time of maturity and wisdom, of balance between work and the rest of life, and the acceptance of aging. The last transition occurs at retirement, to either the pursuit of a hobby, emphasis on home life, or the movement into a new career or business.

Women are seen to have a concern for career *and* a concern for relationships and others (Powell & Mainiero, 1992). For women, one of these two concerns may be primary at one point in time or the woman may try to strike a balance between the two. If one concern was primary early on, then the other factor will likely be emphasized later on. A woman who stresses career to the age of 30 or so may then emphasize family. A woman who has children and raises them early in life may then emphasize work and career when the children have grown more independent.

Generally, for women the late teens to early 20s are a time to focus on formulating adult commitments, while the 40s on are a time to gain more independence and a focus on self-identity (Bardwick, 1980).

An important biological constraint faced by women is the ability to bear children. Older women may find it more difficult to become pregnant and may run out of time to have more than one or two children. While a man in his 30s without children may be concerned about work, establishing himself, and becoming successful, a woman in her 30s without children may be considering her own biology. Her time to make a choice about children is more limited than for a man the same age.

CAREERS IN ORGANIZATIONS
Career Stages and Career Movement

Like the stages of life, careers have been found to have predictable stages (Levinson, 1986). Edgar Schein (1991) discussed seven of these.

1. *Pre-entry and entry.* The interview process, becoming acquainted with the organization and being pre-socialized into it. For different views of this process, see this chapter's *Overboard* cartoon.
2. *Basic training and initiation.* Going through whatever probationary period and rites of inclusion that mark new membership in the group.
3. *First regular assignment.* A critical time for the new member. Success here will be crucial for later success. The new member is granted some responsibility, and the "ropes" are learned.
4. *Second assignment.* This point marks the fully accepted member.
5. *Granting of tenure.* The individual is made a "permanent" member.
6. *Termination and exit.* Any rites of passage from inside to outside the organization occur at this stage.
7. *Post-exit.* The individual is no longer a part of the organization.

Vertical career movement
Moving up and down the hierarchy as rank and level is achieved or lost.

Lateral career movement
Movement across the functions performed within the organization.

Radial career movement
Occurs when the person becomes more or less on the inside of the organization.

Besides passage through these stages, Schein considered three types of career movement. A person could move in the **vertical** direction, up and down the hierarchy. The second type of career movement is **lateral**, that is, movement across the functions performed within the organization—for example sales, marketing, and production. Many job rotation plans provide this lateral movement in preparation for future movement either vertically or radially.

Radial movement, the third type of career movement, occurs when the person becomes more or less on the "inside" of the organization. While vertical career movement is "up and down" the organization's hierarchy, and lateral movement is "side to side" across one level of the hierarchy, radial movement is "from out to in" or "from in to out." The person moving radially inward is becoming more of an organizational "insider," moving closer to those that have organizational power. Radial movement may be combined with vertical career movement as an organizational member becomes one of the dominant coalition or ruling elite.

Career Systems

Organizations are often interested in linking jobs together into career and promotion ladders. This helps to make it clear how jobs are related and how an employee could expect to move through a series of jobs over time (e.g., Baron and others, 1986). These are **career systems**.

Jeffrey Sonnenfeld and Maury Peiperl (1988) have constructed a model of four different career systems. Their model is based on the concepts of supply flow and assignment flow.

Supply flow is the openness of the career system to the external labour market at other than entry levels. With an external supply flow staff may be recruited by an organization as required. A professional baseball team might, for example, sign a free agent to fill a particular position on the team. A university requiring a senior professor to hold a chair of accounting might look to the professors already working in other universities and attempt to hire one of them away from her current employer.

Assignment flow is the criteria by which individuals are chosen for assignments and whether promotion decisions are based primarily on individual or group contribution. On baseball teams and in universities assignments are usually made to the individual, though teamwork may be required to get the job done. Promotion and pay are based principally on individual performance.

The four categories of career system are the academy, club, baseball team, and fortress. Their properties are summarized in Exhibit 14.1 and examples of industries using these systems are shown in Exhibit 14.2.

The *academy* is like a modern guild. Entry is in early career and the organization's focus is on developing and retaining staff over their careers. There are elaborate career paths and internal job ladders.

The *club*'s focus is on the early career entry of members, on their retention and equality of treatment over a long career. Reliability of performance and organizational commitment are emphasized.

The organization using a *baseball team* style of career system emphasizes the recruitment at all career stages of experts to fill specific job needs. There is high turnover and individuals can follow a career among many employers.

Finally, the organization with a *fortress* approach to careers recruits as necessary for survival, exit is by layoff or early retirement, and the development of personnel is limited to the people seen as critical to continued survival. Jobs are linked, but generalists are required because change is a constant.

As organizations downsize in their efforts to cope with recessionary times, the fortress approach to careers is becoming more common. When cost cutting results in layoffs by seniority, the academy and club systems are compromised. Junior members who are forced to leave the organization learn that their development and retention or training and equality of treatment with more senior employees are not high priorities for the organization. Those members not laid off and new members hired when times improve are therefore likely to see the career system as a fortress.

The virtual organization is becoming a more common organizational form. In it organizations contract work out to other organizations and individuals (they form a loosely coupled system) in a varying pattern depending on contracts and job requirements. In these virtual organizations the baseball team career system is common. Professionals are hired as necessary for particular jobs, then move on, managing their own careers by moving from organization to organization.

Career systems

An organization's plan for how employees can be expected to move through a series of jobs over time.

EXHIBIT 14.1   CAREER SYSTEM PROPERTIES

	ACADEMIES	CLUBS	BASEBALL TEAMS	FORTRESSES
Strategic Mission Career:	Analyzers	Defenders	Prospectors	Reactors
	Development	Retention	Recruitment	Retrenchment
System	Firm-specific	Firm-specific	Celebrity talent/expertise	Turnaround expertise
Priority	Functional specialists	Generalists	Specialists	Flexible generalists
Supply Flow	Exclusive entry at early career	Emphasis on early career entry	Entry throughout career stages	Entry limited to recruitment of turn-around expertise and cheap replacement labour
	Exit at retirement	Exit at retirement	Exit through push due to poor individual performance or pull of outside opportunities	Exit due to poor corporate performance: layoffs/ dismissals, early retirements
Assignment Flow	Individual contribution	Group contribution	Individual contribution	Group contribution
	Internal tournament drives advancement through job ladders	Corporate service	Internal and external contest for advancement	Corporate sacrifice
		Loyalty/Length of service		Willingness to change
			Performance always at peak	Survival under stress
		Special assignments		
		Relocations		
		Age grading		
Training and Development	Constant retraining with job moves	Training for general enrichment	Very little training due to portability of skill	No training due to financial hardship and high turnover

SOURCE: Reprinted with permission from Jeffrey A. Sonnenfeld and Maury A. Peiperl (1988), "Staffing policy as a strategic response: A typology of career systems," *Academy of Management Review* 13: 595.

Organizational Approaches to the International Assignment

There are three different views that organizations might use when preparing their employees for international operations (Perlmutter, 1969).

1. *The ethnocentric view* assumes that all other countries are similar and the home country's ways are best;
2. *The polycentric view* sees each country and its operations as unique, geographic decentralization is promoted;
3. *The geocentric view* recognizes similarities and dissimilarities between countries, but uses a global strategy to target the whole world as a market.

The polycentric view likely allows individuals the best chance to adjust on an international assignment. Previous overseas experience, cross-cultural skills, and cross-cultural

EXHIBIT 14.2

Examples of Four Career System Models

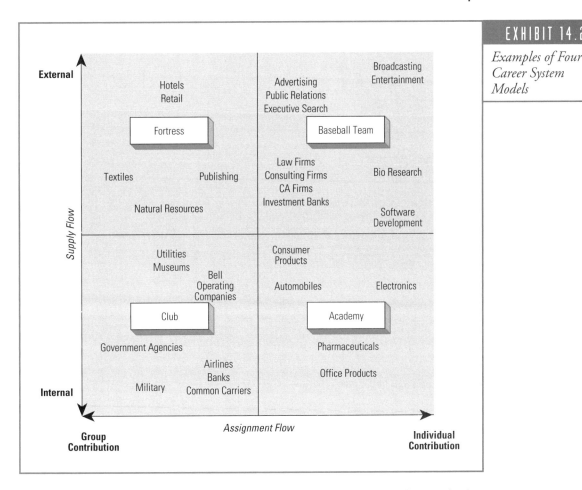

SOURCE: Reprinted with permission from Jeffrey A. Sonnenfeld and Maury A. Peiperl (1988), "Staffing policy as a strategic response: A typology of career systems," *Academy of Management Review* 13: 592.

training will help the adjustment process (Black and others, 1991). Training in language, customs, and how people think in the other culture can be effective (Black & Mendenhall, 1990). Magoroh Maruyama has examined some of these processes. He notes that

> The principles, styles, and methods of management are affected by mind patterns, which may vary from individual to individual and from culture to culture. As the cultural heterogeneity increases, managers become aware of some new phenomena:
>
> *1.* That management principles and methods must be adapted both to the cultural heterogeneity within the office and to the local culture;
>
> *2.* That there are significant individual differences within each culture;
>
> *3.* That some managers and workers from the local culture may look excellent if judged by the criteria of the superior from a foreign culture, but they may be cultural deviants who reject their own culture, and whose credibility may be very high among foreigners but very low among their compatriots;
>
> *4.* That those who appreciate both local and foreign cultures are a valuable asset (1985, p. 126).

Taking cross-cultural training to the extreme, Maruyama notes that

> Some Korean firms have very thorough training programs. An example is the use of "culture houses." An employee who will be sent to Germany, for example, is put in a "German house" where he is confined until he is able to eat, live, and sleep like a German (1992, p. 94).

Examples of different approaches to multicultural management are described in this chapter's *A Rose by Any Other Name* feature.

Discrimination

Glass ceiling A subtle barrier to vertical career movement that is transparent, yet still exists, especially for women and minorities.

It has been proposed that women and minorities face a **glass ceiling** that limits their vertical career movement. It is "a barrier so subtle that it is transparent, yet so strong that it prevents women and minorities from moving up in the management hierarchy" (Morrison & Von Glinow, 1990, p. 200).

A ROSE BY ANY OTHER NAME

Using Hofstede's five dimensions of Individualism/Collectivism, Power Distance, Uncertainty Avoidance, Masculinity/Femininity, and Long versus Short Time Orientation, Peter Smith (a professor in England) has analyzed how certain organizational behaviour concepts are likely to be understood in different cultures.

For example, when negotiating across cultures Smith notes that "most commentators characterize the behaviour of more individualist Western negotiators as 'rational and task-centred,' in contrast to those from more collectivist national cultures, where the state of relationship between the negotiating parties becomes an increasingly important factor" (p. 45).

However, in the East taking a longer-term view of benefits might be seen as rational. Japanese will tend to avoid saying 'no' and use long periods of silence during negotiations to convey lack of agreement. They are more interested in determining if the other party is worthy of their trust. Contracts, therefore, can be seen as exhibiting a lack of trust. Explicit contract terms are likely not to be seen as binding by Japanese, who are negotiating a good faith relationship rather than a set of specific actions.

In terms of *multicultural management*, Smith notes that "US-owned ventures were found to attempt most strongly to introduce the procedures and policies obtaining within the parent company" whereas the Japanese organizations were found to be willing "to adapt to whatever they judge to work best in local circumstances" (p. 45).

The training and career development of employees sent abroad varied by home country as well. Japanese placements abroad quite often last 5 or more years and are rather frequently preceded by substantial training input, often with a more extensive emphasis on language training. US placements are more typically for 1-2 years, and 68% of those placed received no training. US firms quite often also expressed the view that training could not be justified, because the employee might not stay with the firm (p. 47).

The Japanese reliance on internal promotion and long-term service allows for a longer-term approach to international experience for managers.

Smith concludes that "Working effectively across cultures is therefore not simply a matter of applying the skills found to be most effective within the culture of one's country or organization. It requires also that one can understand and cope with the processes of communication and decision-making in settings where these are achieved in a different manner" (p. 48).

SOURCE: Based on information in Peter B. Smith (1992), "Organizational behaviour and national cultures," *British Journal of Management* 3: 39-51.

Ann Morrison and Mary Ann Von Glinow (1990) discuss three theories that purport to explain the glass ceiling effect. The first is that women and minorities possess some kind of handicap that selects them out of the running for top management jobs. That is, they might be less well educated, less experienced, or somehow less capable than white men. However, the evidence is that women are not significantly different as managers than are men. The second theory is that white men in power are biased and are holding back women and minorities. Morrison and Von Glinow find evidence that this is true. Women and minorities may be held back by being refused consideration for top management jobs, denied deserved promotions, and not provided with the type of work and experience that is necessary for promotion, among other things. Thirdly, it is theorized that there is structural discrimination built into the social system against women and minorities. Again, they find support for this theory.

Women and minorities can be seen as tokens in the organization. Women can find performing effectively difficult when they are a few among many men (Kanter, 1977). Minorities can be excluded from the informal work groups whose membership is necessary for high performance. Further, minorities often have to be culturally changeable, learning and moving between their home culture and the culture in the office.

The result of these barriers is that: (1) lateral movement can be restricted as women and minorities are confined to a set of secondary jobs not so critical to the organization; (2) radial movement is limited due to membership exclusions; and (3) vertical movement is possible only up to the glass ceiling.

To remedy this problem, Morrison and Von Glinow propose as a first step that organizations increase their numbers of women and minorities. This would lessen the problems of tokenism and would help to make organizational members aware of the skills and abilities of these people as individuals. Then, as the numbers of women and minorities in the organization increased, they would have social support and role models available. Finally, the organization can learn to capitalize on its multicultural diversity as a competitive advantage.

For further information on the topics of diversity and discrimination, see this chapter's *On the One Hand* feature.

While there is no doubt that men hold the vast majority of upper management positions (Fisher, 1992), there is some evidence that career progression is affected more by other factors than by sex (Stroh and others, 1992). These authors found that gaining work force experience, investing in human capital by obtaining education and training, being high in family power (the importance of a person's career within the family) and being in an industry of employment that pays well had a greater impact on salary progression and geographic mobility than did sex.

However, they also found that women managers' salaries were increasing at a lower rate than men's, that women were moving for their careers less often, and that they were turning down more job transfers than were men. In an interview study of 30 women holding middle management positions in 15 *Fortune 500* companies, factors both assisting and hindering their career development were identified (see Exhibit 14.3).

While sex discrimination is less likely for men than women, everyone has some personal characteristic or factor that *could* be used as the basis for discriminatory exclusion. For example, sex, race, cultural background, schools attended, clubs of which one is a member, or sexual orientation could be used by one group to discriminate against a given individual. Everyone therefore needs to be aware of discrimination at work.

MANAGING YOUR CAREER

The points made in Exhibit 14.3, though made by women in middle management, apply equally to men. Everyone needs to pay attention to managing their own career.

Given that the work world is becoming more culturally diverse, the workplace must become more diverse as well. But to achieve that diversity is not as easy as setting out to hire more individuals from an under-represented race or gender. To use such an approach would likely be a form of "reverse discrimination" against the majority of current employees—in many cases white males.

So what is an employer seeking to increase workforce diversity to do? The best answer is to make more efforts to get job applications from a variety of sources, including those where minority people are likely to be. By increasing the pool of candidates and making the pool more culturally, racially, and gender diverse, there is a better chance that the most qualified candidate for a position will be from a minority group. Then the person hired will be the best among those who applied, and neither discrimination nor reverse discrimination will have taken place.

But what if women and minorities don't bother to apply because they think their chances of being hired are small? And once hired, what about retaining them in their jobs? An approach to these problems is to work in the community to encourage skill development and the attitude that jobs will be open to women and minorities, especially in job areas not seen as traditionally held by them.

For example, Ontario Hydro has encouraged its female engineers to reach out into their communities and promote science education to girls in public school. Such educational preparation is necessary to gain admittance to engineering programs at university. Hydro has also examined its own barriers to hiring and promotion as well as sexual harassment in the workplace, with intent to encourage women to stay with engineering as a career.

But the obstacles in the way of women aspiring to engineering careers can be formidable. While Ontario Hydro is encouraging science education for girls and is promoting diversity and the elimination of sexual discrimination for its female engineers, they can only hire women engineers who graduate. There are other barriers that female engineering students will face before they can graduate. At Canadian universities only 14% of engineering students are female; 2% of full-time engineering faculty members are women; and 3% of the registered engineers in Canada are female. Attitudes of predominantly male students, professors, and graduates can be sexist, creating an unwelcome atmosphere for the small minority of females in their midst. One female engineering graduate left the profession and later said "what I never learned to deal with was the constant frustration that I felt because there was no support, no mentors, nobody who believed in me" (McKay, 1992, p. 42). Clearly, to encourage women to enter into engineering careers and then to stay, support programs will be necessary.

Such support programs could take the form of special scholarships in engineering available only to women, places in engineering faculties set aside for women, and courses in engineering faculties directed more towards subjects of interest to women. Are such efforts and programs justified, or do they constitute a form of reverse discrimination? What about the males who do not qualify for scholarships simply because they are male? Or the "extra" few places in an engineering school set aside for women that could have been filled by men with higher grades in mathematics and science out of high school? On the one hand it is a good idea to lessen the current effects of discrimination and to promote sex diversity in the engineering field. But on the other hand, can it be done without discriminating against males?

SOURCE: Based on information in Jane Easter Bahls (1993), "Playing fair," *Entrepreneur*, January 1993, pp. 234-239 and in Shona McKay (1992), "Boys' club," *Report on Business Magazine* 9(3): 37-44. For further information see Ann M. Morrison (1992), "Developing diversity in organizations," *Business Quarterly* 57(1): 42-48.

The Career Edge

It is vitally important when preparing for a successful career to have a plan of what to do and how to accomplish it. Given that there is competition for most jobs, what will your "edge" be over the others? Perhaps it will be education, schools attended, courses taken, relevant work experience, experience in student organizations, or a second or

EXHIBIT 14.3   FACTORS THAT HELP OR HINDER WOMEN'S CAREERS

FACTORS IDENTIFIED BY WOMEN MANAGERS AS ASSISTING THEIR CAREER DEVELOPMENT	FACTORS IDENTIFIED BY WOMEN MANAGERS AS HINDERING THEIR CAREER DEVELOPMENT
1. *Educational credentials* — a bachelor's degree, an MBA, and additional management training.	1. *Bosses who did not guide or encourage career progression.*
2. *Working hard, long hours* — on average these women reported working almost 54 hours per week, and travelling an average of 41 days per year.	2. *Sex discrimination* — being paid less, having a smaller budget to work with, obtaining fewer job-related benefits, being excluded from some activities seen as "male" (e.g., golf games, fishing trips).
3. *Having a mentor to provide guidance and advice* — 90% of these women had a mentor.	3. *Lack of political savvy* — exclusion from the "old boy" power networks (an inclusion factor) meant it was harder to get the job done.
4. *Good interpersonal skills* — communication, decision making, and conflict management skills.	4. *Lack of career strategy* — not having a long-term plan, putting the husband's career first.
5. *Demonstrating competence on the job.*	
6. *A willingness to take risks.*	

SOURCE: Based on information in Rose Mary Wentling (1992).

third language (see McGarvey & Smith, 1994). Or your edge might be experience as a volunteer for a charity or social service organization or the ability to manage diversity at work (see *Seeing is Believing*). It is useful to plan early on where you want to go, then decide what must be done to get there. The cliché that without a goal, any direction is the right one, is still true.

SEEING IS BELIEVING

As immigration into Canada from different parts of the world continues, and the sources of new immigrants continues to change, the Canada of the future will become more diverse and multicultural. To manage this diversity, managers will have to learn how to be flexible.

At the garment manufacturer S.R. Gent (Canada) Inc. of Mississauga, Ontario, managing director Bob Wood and the plant manager, Bob Vallender, have had to learn how to deal with a workforce that was once mainly Italian but now spans 16 ethnic groups.

Without showing favouritism to any one group, Wood and Vallender have tried to be flexible within the rules that they have set. Muslims are required to pray by their faith, but at Gent praying is allowed only during regular breaks. Special foot basins have been provided for the Muslims to wash their feet. Similarly, one woman from the Punjab in India was promoted even though she would never look Wood and Vallender in the eye. But because of their sensitivity to different cultures, they realized that such behaviour did not indicate a lack of confidence but instead deference to their authority.

It is important to understand multiple cultures and to be adaptable to different cultural needs, within the basic constraints of the business, in order to effectively manage diversity. In the Canada of the future, success in a managerial career will depend in large part on such skills.

Source: Based on Nicholas Bradbury (1989), "Strategies: The faces of change," *Canadian Business*, October 1989, 133-136.

Choosing a Career

In the board game called *Careers* each player has to decide at the beginning of the game what his objectives will be. The player has to allocate 60 points among the three goals of money ($), fame (★), and love (♥). During the play of the game, points in these categories are accumulated by going through various experiences such as getting a job, going to college, getting married, etc.

The beauty of this game is that the winner is the first person to achieve their goals, whatever they are. A player could choose to seek only one objective, for instance only money, while ignoring fame and love, or a mix of the objectives could be chosen. There is no mix of goals that is by definition any better than any other mix. Another feature of this game is that each time the game is played a player can decide on a different mix of goals. If last time the player sought only money, this time the contestant might decide to see how the game gets on when love is the only object.

In real life, choices are very similar, except that we only get one play of the game. "Should I seek the job/career that pays the most money?" "Should I put my family first?" "How do I balance needs for money, family, and recognition?" Making these choices is not easy, but there are some resources available to help a person to decide.

The first step is to find out more about oneself and the kinds of jobs that exist. There are many self-help books available, from the popular *What Color is Your Parachute?* to the dry *Canadian Classification and Dictionary of Occupations*. Many colleges and universities offer counselling services, as do many private organizations, to help people examine themselves and the types of jobs that are available.

One test, the Edwards Personal Preference Schedule, compares the testee's answers to questions regarding activity preferences (for example, would you rather go swimming or bowling?) to the answers given by people in various occupations. The testee's answer pattern is matched to the patterns from different occupations and similarities are noted. This test is not one of aptitude (what the testee is likely to be good at) or skill (what the testee can do). Instead, it gives an indication of whether or not the person completing the test would tend to "fit in," in terms of interests, with members of different occupations.

Other similar tests are the Strong Vocational Interest Inventory, the Kuder Preference Record, and the Vocational Preference Inventory. Taken along with other tests measuring intelligence and ability, professional career counsellors can make educated guesses regarding what careers might fit the individual.

One theory of vocational choice is based on this idea that a person will choose a work environment and be successful in it when it matches his or her own personality. The principles of this theory (from Holland, 1985) are that:

1. The choice of a vocation is an expression of personality.
2. Interest inventories are personality inventories.
3. Vocational stereotypes (that is, our knowledge of what people in various occupations are like) have reliable and important psychological and sociological meanings.
4. The members of a vocation have similar personalities and similar histories of personal development.
5. Being similar, people in a vocational group will create particular environments for their vocation.
6. Vocational satisfaction, stability, and achievement depend on the congruence between one's personality and the environment in which one works.

Holland theorizes that there are six personality types (see Exhibit 14.4), and that the shorter the distance between any two types, the more similar they are. Different personality types are thought to be suited for different occupational environments (Exhibit 14.5).

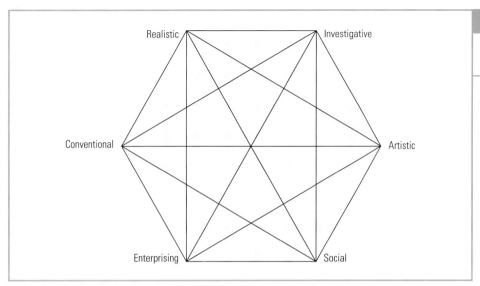

SOURCE: Reprinted from John L. Holland (1985), Making vocational choices: *A Theory of Vocational Personalities and Work Environments*, 2nd ed. Englewood Cliffs, NJ: Prentice Hall, Inc., p. 29.

EXHIBIT 14.4
Holland's RIASEC Career Type Model

EXHIBIT 14.5   PERSONALITY TYPE DESCRIPTIONS IN HOLLAND'S CAREER TYPE MODEL

PERSONALITY TYPES	TYPICAL OCCUPATIONS
1. *Realistic:* Involves the use of tools and machines, physical activities that require skill and/or strength and coordination.	Auto and airplane mechanic, carpentry, construction, surveying, engineer, machinist, electrician
2. *Investigative:* Involves the observation, organization, and understanding of physical and social phenomena.	Research scientist, writer of scientific articles, research worker, all scientific disciplines such as anthropologist, chemist, physicist, etc.
3. *Artistic:* Involves self-expression, artistic creation, expression of feelings, working on individual projects.	Author, musician, poet, commercial artist, composer, cartoonist, singer, symphony conductor
4. *Social:* Involves interpersonal activities, being with others, informing and training others	Teacher, vocational counsellor, social work or psychiatric case worker, speech therapist, clinical psychologist
5. *Enterprising:* Involves verbal activities used to influence others, to obtain power and status, being where the action is.	Advertising executive, real estate sales, sports promotion, store buyer, businessperson, entrepreneur, speculator, television producer
6. *Conventional:* Involves structured activities that are ordered by rules, following others, going by the book.	Bookkeeper, accountant, tax expert, financial analyst, banking

SOURCE: Based on information in John L. Holland (1985), Making vocational choices: *A Theory of Vocational Personalities and Work Environments*, 2nd ed. Englewood Cliffs, NJ: Prentice Hall, Inc.

Research on Holland's model has generally been supportive (e.g., Spokane, 1985), and some evidence of its transferability to another culture has been found (Khan & Alvi, 1985).

One study of Holland's model tracked 3612 four-year college graduates in the United States who were employed full-time from two to four years after graduation and who had completed a careers interest test while in high school (Prediger & Vansickle, 1992). These individuals were grouped into 51 occupations and their interest scores averaged within an occupation. Locations on Holland's hexagon for the 51 occupations are shown in Exhibit 14.6.

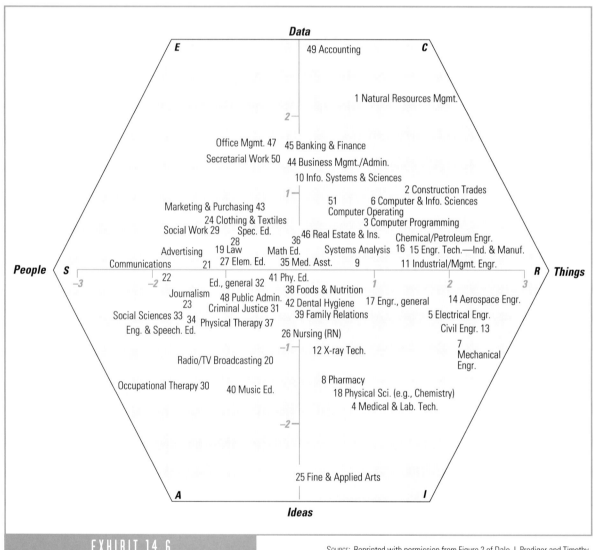

EXHIBIT 14.6	

Hexagon Locations for 51 Occupational Groups

Source: Reprinted with permission from Figure 2 of Dale J. Prediger and Timothy R. Vansickle (1992), "Locating occupations on Holland's Hexagon: Beyond RIASEC," *Journal of Vocational Behavior* 40: 118.

EXPERIENCE IS THE BEST TEACHER

Interest in careers, and related concepts of career management and career development, emerged in the 1970s and 80s—a time when organizations were growing and societal values supporting upward mobility were high. White collar and professional employees pursued careers; blue-collar workers held jobs. The concept of a career has typically been applied to women and men in jobs offering prospects of advancement. More recently, definitions of a career have broadened; a *career* is the pattern of work-related experiences that span the course of a person's life.

There are two aspects of a career. One, the objective aspect, refers to the job titles and job changes a person has undertaken during his/her own working life. These can be seen on one's resume. The second, the subjective aspect, involves the person's feelings, attitudes and values as he/she acquires various work-related experiences. These changes occur within the person. The subjective element suggests that individual employees have their own unique criteria for evaluating their careers and are therefore the best judges of how successful their careers have been. As a consequence, individuals

Dr. Burke is a professor at York University's Faculty of Administrative Studies. He is internationally known for his work on stress, careers, and women in the workplace.

are likely to use different success criteria as they themselves change and as social values change.

Both individuals and their employing organizations have a stake in careers. *Career management* refers to individual initiatives such as setting of personal career goals, planning appropriate job and educational activities to prepare oneself for advancement, and developing strategies for achieving one's career goals. *Career development,* on the other hand, refers to programs and policies initiated by the organization to support advancement. These include such things as the use of assessment centres, career planning workshops and formal mentoring programs.

Although organizations in the 1990s are growing less quickly, and in some cases even shrinking, the relevance of career management remains high. Individuals need to anticipate more frequent career changes now than ever before. This places a premium on life-long learning, personal flexibility and resilience. The influx of non-traditional professionals into the workforce—women, visible minorities, the handicapped, native people—have also changed the nature of careers, increasing the diversity of their patterns.

Selecting a First Job

Selection of a first job is crucial because of its impact on later career experiences. Early success in challenging assignments can lead to the opportunity to take on further challenges. Continued success will usually mean higher visibility in the organization, promotion, opportunities for training and further education, and possibly even being put on the "fast track." Senior members of organizations are continually scanning and evaluating those below them in the hierarchy, and being successful means that the person will be noticed.

Similarly, if a first job does not suit a person's interests or abilities, it may prove difficult to succeed in it. There is also the opportunity cost to consider in the selection of a first job. Once in a job it can be difficult and costly to find another. Working full time restricts the time available to look for another job. It can be difficult to arrange interviews, since they must be scheduled outside work hours or at lunch.

Of course, to get that first important job it is usually necessary to perform well in a job interview. Tips for interview success are offered in this chapter's *A Word to the Wise* feature.

A WORD TO THE WISE

The following tips should help you to do well in your job interviews.

1. **Before the interview**
   - Plan your arrival at the interview location. Arriving late or out of breath from a last-minute run to arrive on time is almost certain to end your chances of being hired.
   - Prepare yourself: your clothes, resume, grooming, knowledge of company background, your objectives for this job and for your career.

2. **During the interview**
   - Say hello and shake hands while introductions are made. Offer your hand if the interviewer does not offer first.
   - Wait to be asked to take a seat, then put away your coat and make yourself comfortable.
   - Ask for the interviewer's business card. This helps to make the interviewer's name perfectly clear and provides you with her or his business address, which you will require later.
   - Do not smoke even if the interviewer does. If you are being interviewed on organizational premises others may see you smoking and this may hurt your chances of being offered the job.
   - Politely decline offers of tea or coffee. Keep your mind focused on the interview, not on beverages.
   - Expect some polite discussion of your hobbies or personal background before moving on to questions about the job and your interest in it.
   - Be open and honest, giving the interviewer a good understanding of your strengths and abilities. Do not hide any weaknesses in your background but do not bring them up either.
   - Ask relevant questions about the job, the organization and the industry. Ask questions about both the long term and the short term.

   - When the subject of money comes up, do not name any figure, but say you expect to be paid at a level commensurate with the job requirements and your own experience and skills. Naming a dollar figure that is too high will let you out of the running for the job, whereas naming a figure that is too low could lead to your own feelings of salary inequity if you are hired.

3. **At the end of the interview**
   - Thank the interviewer.
   - Don't be afraid to ask what the next step is in the interview process. If the next step is a final decision, ask to be offered the job. A salesperson must ask for the order, and since you are selling yourself (figuratively, of course), you must ask to be hired.

4. **After the interview**
   - Immediately make notes on the company, the discussion, and any information you have learned about the next steps in the interview process. If you are interviewing many organizations these notes will prove invaluable later on when your memory of all the companies is jumbled and hazy. If you are called back to the organization for a second or third interview these notes will refresh your memory of who you met and what was said. The interviewer took notes after your meeting, so you should too.
   - Send a thank you letter to the interviewer about a week later. If you would not be receptive to a job offer, politely say that you have decided to seek other opportunities. If you are interested in receiving an offer, make it clear that you are interested in the job and note how you believe that your talents would fit in well with the needs of the organization.
   - Wait for an offer before discussing salary or benefits. With your offers in hand you are in a position to make a choice or to negotiate.

While it is important to dress well for a job interview, it is also important, once hired, to project an image that is appropriate for the job on a daily basis. Many bankers would not find it unreasonable, for instance, to give a loan against future income so that an individual might purchase a work wardrobe. This is an investment that is likely to pay itself back many times over. When selecting clothes, pay particular attention to the successful people in the organization that are one level above you. One approach would be to find out where they buy their clothes, to go there, and then be "dressed" by the professional clothiers.

It is important in many professions to dress up one level so that when the time for promotion comes the candidate appears to "fit in". Also, the aspirant to the top organizational levels should not get lazy or too thrifty with accessories. Shoes, socks, briefcase, gloves, scarf, watch, and jewelry all send messages to others. For example, upper level executives usually know about different brands of watches and what each kind costs. These seemingly small nuances can make a big difference to a career. For further tips on "dressing for success," for both women and men, see Molloy (1975, 1977).

Also important is whether one's job is in the line or on the staff. Organizations will differ in how internal career ladders operate. In some a line job is necessary to move up to the highest levels of the hierarchy. In other organizations it is the reverse. Jobs that are central to the key activities of the organization are always more important than jobs that can be seen as more peripheral.

Another issue in the selection of a first job is the company itself. In their determination of the best companies to work for in America, Robert Levering and Milton Moskowitz (1993) focused on six important criteria. These were: "pay and benefits, opportunities for advancement, job security, pride in work and the company, the degree of openness and fairness, and the level of camaraderie among employees" (p. 26). Levering and Moskowitz found that the company worked for makes a big difference to a person's working life.

One of the companies chosen as the top 100 to work for in Canada is The Body Shop (Innes and others, 1991). The president of The Body Shop in Canada, Margot Franssen, describes her company as being of "the third type."

> There are three company types in this world. First, there are companies that are managed by their accountants and consider business to be war; corporate responsibility is the last consideration taken. Second, we have those companies that are a bit more astute when it comes to public perception; they believe that business is part sport and part war, and are driven by their marketing departments. These companies are good at talking the talk of being a caring company but cannot or will not walk the talk. And finally, there are those companies that have real integrity; they have the reputation for doing the right and honorable thing even when no one is looking. They do care about running a profitable, healthy business, but they understand that there is more to running a company than watching the bottom line. They are driven by their values and by basic human understanding. They do not believe that business is a war to win at all costs or a game to be played without severe consequences. Instead, it is an adjunct of life, and no matter how much we try, it cannot be contained within a nine to five framework. The pursuit of profits is not the driving force for these companies. They are not propelled by the single-minded desire to make more money, but by the need to fulfil their vision, to satisfy a craving to make a difference to people and the world" (Franssen, 1993, p. 16).

Goals for Success

To this point we have assumed that everyone aims to be successful. But what is success for one person might be considered as failure by another. Like the *Careers* game, success is a measure of how well your achievements match your life and career goals.

There are several important points to consider about success. First, in a career, how much progress up the hierarchy is desirable? We commonly think of the organization as structured like a pyramid, with the president and chief executive officer at the top. This metaphor is useful here because it illustrates the declining number of positions as one ascends the hierarchy. Because competition for these positions is intense, and the quality of the competition increases as one moves higher, sacrifices are required to reach the top.

Margot Franssen, President of The Body Shop Canada.

The person wishing to reach the top must be willing to work extremely hard and long hours, to travel, often be willing to relocate, and sometimes to work on weekends and in the evenings at home. With this kind of commitment, there are fewer hours and less energy available for other goals. For example, if a person works from 8 a.m. to 8 p.m Monday to Friday, time with children will be limited during the week and will be concentrated on the weekends. There will always be people at work who have no family or who have full-time assistance at home. Competing with them for a limited number of higher level jobs can be difficult.

It must also be considered that the skills required for success will differ by organizational level. While entry-level jobs usually require proficiency at a skill—such as knowledge of the stock market, how to perform an audit, or how to program a computer—higher level jobs will require a different set of skills. Stock brokers and accountants, as they move up the hierarchy, need to be able to attract clients and retain their business. Computer programmers need to be able to supervise others and to relate effectively with client users. To be ready for promotion and effective performance at the new level means that the new skills needed must be learned before promotion is attained.

Breaking the Glass Ceiling

Reaching the top is an upstream battle.

Ann Morrison and others (1987) determined six lessons for success by interviewing 76 women and analyzing their experiences. The executive woman must channel her efforts to meet each of these issues.

LESSON 1: Learn the Ropes   It is imperative to listen to others, to network, and to determine the rules and expectations necessary to your organizational survival.

LESSON 2: Take Control of Your Career   Instead of relying on the system, human resource professionals, or a mentor, it is necessary that you take control of your own career. Seek out and ask for the jobs that will lead to the top while avoiding critical career mistakes.

LESSON 3: Build Confidence   Develop the self-confidence that will allow you to acquire the confidence of others. It may be necessary to take on risky assignments (and make sure they succeed) and to become successful at outside activities.

LESSON 4: Rely on Others   No one can do all the job alone. It is important to develop and use a network of supporters in your career. These include mentors, bosses, and role models as well as subordinates.

LESSON 5: Go for the Bottom Line   A focus on results will not be wasted. The right actions must be taken and with good results. While a sole emphasis on performance is not all that is required to achieve success, it is a strong prerequisite.

LESSON 6: Integrate Life and Work   It can be difficult to compete with others who devote a majority of their time to work without doing the same. Sacrifices may be necessary in order to achieve success, with career coming first and other life responsibilities fitting in to the time remaining.

Mentors

A mentor is someone older and more experienced, who is willing to provide career guidance and social support to a younger protégé. The mentor relationship can be beneficial to both parties.

The mentor contributes to the development of young managerial talent in the organization, experiences satisfaction through helping another and through the protégé's career successes, and receives confirmation of his importance and status from the protégé (Kram, 1983).

The protégé obtains career benefits that may include sponsorship within the organization, increased exposure and visibility to senior management, help in receiving challenging assignments, coaching in "learning the ropes" of how to achieve in the organization, and protection from others in the organization that might want to harm the protégé's career (Kram, 1983). There are also social support benefits for the protégé. These include the friendship and counselling of the senior person, a role model to emulate, and the security of being accepted as an important organizational member.

The benefits for a junior member in an organization are so strong and varied that it would be wise to be open to developing such a mentor-protégé relationship. But there are potential costs as well.

First, a typical mentor-protégé relationship goes through the four phases of initiation, cultivation, separation, and redefinition (Exhibit 14.7). The separation phase is one with potential for conflict as the protégé seeks independence and more equal relationship with the former mentor.

Second, mentors may have enemies in the organization who dare not confront the senior person. They may instead attack that person's protégés who are less able to defend themselves.

Third, potential female protégés confront distinctive mentoring problems. One study of 510 employees of research and development organizations in the Southeastern United States (Ragins & Cotton, 1993) found that while women were the same as men in their intentions to mentor, they anticipated more drawbacks to becoming a mentor. This, along with the fact that women are currently less well represented in senior management, may mean that female mentors are in short supply. While senior male-junior female mentor-protégé relationships certainly occur, they are not without their own special problems. Other employees in the organization are almost certain to question whether sexual relations are involved. This perception, even when unfounded, can make the female protégé's relationship with a male mentor more difficult.

The Dual-Career Couple

Four different kinds of relationships of couples with careers have been identified (Hall & Hall, 1979).

1. *Accommodators:* one person emphasizes work life, the other is the opposite, emphasizing the home life—they accomodate each other;
2. *Allies:* both are focused primarily on work and agree to let the home be deemphasized, or both are primarily focused on the home;
3. *Adversaries:* each person in the couple wants to emphasize work and career, but also wants a well-ordered home and a family. They conflict over who will do the home.
4. *Acrobats:* both emphasize work and the home.

EXHIBIT 14.7   PHASES OF THE MENTOR RELATIONSHIP

PHASE	DEFINITION	TURNING POINTS*
Initiation	A period of six months to a year during which time the relationship gets started and begins to have importance for both managers.	• Fantasies become concrete expectations. • Expectations are met; senior manager provides coaching, challenging work, visibility; junior manager provides technical assistance, respect, and desire to be coached. • There are opportunities for interaction around work tasks.
Cultivation	A period of two to five years during which time the range of career and psychosocial functions provided expand to a maximum.	• Both individuals continue to benefit from the relationship. • Opportunities for meaningful and more frequent interaction increase. • Emotional bond deepens and intimacy increases.
Separation	A period of six months to two years after a significant change in the structural role relationship and/or in the emotional experience of the relationship.	• Junior manager no longer wants guidance but rather the opportunity to work more autonomously. • Senior manager faces midlife crisis and is less available to provide mentoring functions. • Job rotation or promotion limits opportunities for continued interaction; career and psychosocial functions can no longer be provided. • Blocked opportunity creates resentment and hostility that disrupts positive interaction.
Redefinition	An indefinite period after the separation phase, during which time the relationship is ended or takes on significantly different characteristics, making it a more peerlike friendship.	• Stresses of separation diminish, and new relationships are formed. • The mentor relationship is no longer needed in its previous form. • Resentment and anger diminish; gratitude and appreciation increase. • Peer status is achieved.

* Examples of the most frequently observed psychological and organizational factors that cause movement into the current relationship phase.

SOURCE: Reprinted by permission from Kathy E. Kram (1983), "Phases of the mentor relationship," *Academy of Management Journal* 26: 608-625.

The "traditional" family structure of the male busy in the organization and the female busy at home is changing (Frone and others, 1992). At the present time in Canada this accommodator model does not account for the majority of dual-career couples. In fact, the 1991 Canadian census indicated that only 13% of families fit the traditional accommodator model where the male is the income earner; the same census found that 65% of husband and wife families were dual-income (Duxbury, 1993).

Interestingly, a study of men in dual-career relationships found that male workers in an accommodator relationship were more stressed than men in relationships with women who worked for pay outside the home. Apparently the advantages of extra income allowed the couple to pay for home services that neither had to perform themselves, and the women in these relationships were more fulfilled with their life at work (Higgins & Duxbury, 1992).

While few men as yet see marriage or a family as a constraint on the emphasis they place on their careers (Powell & Mainiero, 1992), women, because they physically bear the children, often face family constraints.

A woman who wishes to care for her young family herself faces a career interruption from which it may be difficult to recover. Required job skills may change so quickly that retraining is necessary.

Women who wish to breastfeed a newborn after returning to work from maternity leave, may well find such feedings difficult. On-site daycare at work would be required. Many large corporations in Canada provide such facilities, but smaller organizations, especially in highly competitive times, may well find such an expense prohibitive.

The International Assignment

With the increased globalization of business, more people are being asked to work for a period of time in another culture. On an international assignment managers tend to learn how to be a better manager, a tolerance for ambiguity, the ability to see multiple perspectives, and the ability to work with and manage others, but not technical skills (Business International Corporation, 1978). In some organizations success on international assignments is a prerequisite for a promotion to the ranks of senior management.

Many people on international assignment find adjustment difficult—for an example see this chapter's *A Little Knowledge* feature. One study (Black and others, 1991) reported that between 16% and 40% of all American employees sent overseas return from their assignments early. Each premature return was estimated to cost a firm $100 000. This last section dealing with careers will consider the cross-cultural assignment and how to manage it.

When moving to a different culture, a common **culture shock cycle** of moods may be expected (Exhibit 14.8). At first the mood is high and positive. In this phase, called the *tourist* phase (Copeland & Griggs, 1985), the traveller is excited, may be visiting the local sights of interest, and be busy taking pictures. Then, as time passes, mood declines as differences between the home culture and the visited culture are encountered on a daily basis. Telephones may not work or may operate differently, language difficulties may cause frustration, and so on. This *crisis* phase can be marked by blaming the host culture for its values and how things are done, blaming the organization for getting the manager into this mess, and even blaming one's spouse for not being sufficiently supportive.

Culture shock cycle

The cycle of moods experienced over time that may be expected when moving between cultures.

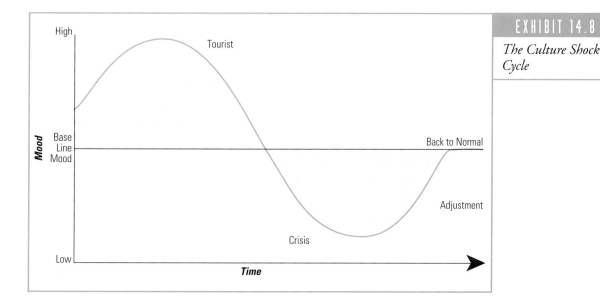

EXHIBIT 14.8

The Culture Shock Cycle

A LITTLE KNOWLEDGE

In Mexico, at a business lunch—*la comida*—the point is to establish a relationship that then forms the basis for business dealings. What then, are the rules?

1. *It will begin late.* Mexicans eat a large breakfast and a light dinner. Their main meal of the day is the lunch in the late afternoon. In this they are similar to many Europeans. Besides eating late in the day, Mexicans may well be late for the scheduled start of the luncheon. Business delays, heavy traffic in the larger cities such as Mexico City, and less of a sense that time must be kept with great accuracy means that lateness is to be expected and not apologized for.

2. *It will last a long time.* Like the French, food is not seen by a Mexican as simply something to be consumed to keep the body fuelled, but an important event. Cocktails, appetizers, a main course with wine or more cocktails, dessert and coffee are all to be expected. The food and drink is to be savoured, appreciated, and commented on. Mexican specialties and delicacies are especially important to appreciate, as it will show your Mexican colleagues that you understand and value their culture.

3. *Very little business will be discussed.* Because the point is to establish and then build a personal relationship which is vital to a subsequent business relationship, business is last on the agenda. Expect to comment on and discuss everything but business and be sure to show your knowledge and appreciation of Mexican music, architecture, and history.

4. *You will be watched.* Mexican society is more structured by class than is Canada's, and top executives are more likely to come from the ruling class. They will be sophisticated about manners and etiquette, and will expect you to be accomplished in these arts as well. Because Mexico is male-oriented or macho, in order to be taken seriously female managers have to be especially careful to keep the relationship on a formal business level.

The following advice from Neil Chesanow for business-women is worth noting.

> An effective way to discourage passes from foreign men—particularly Latin men—is to wear an engagement ring with a diamond of impressive size. If you don't own one, try to borrow one. A wedding ring won't work. In the fast lane of global commerce, American women who are married are thought to be beyond love and ripe for sexual adventure, or so many non-American men like to think. An engagement ring indicates that you have a fiancé not a husband, and, by definition, are more in love. A good-size stone says that your fiancé is affluent. Love and money are serious setbacks to men who contemplate making sexual overtures. Foreign men fear rejection no less than Americans.

Sources: Based on information in David Lida (1992), "The three-tequila lunch," The *Globe and Mail Destinations Business Traveler*, May 1992, pp. 37-43, and Neil Chesanow (1985, p. 67), *The World-Class Executive*, New York: Rawson Associates.

Expatriate ghetto A compound, building, or cluster of housing units inhabited by people from other countries where the norms, values, and ways of life of the local culture may be avoided.

Going native The adoption of many of the foreign culture's values and ways of behaving.

Integrating The combination of values and behaviours from both home and foreign cultures.

The next phase is one of *adjustment*. In this phase mood gradually recovers. Adjustment may be achieved in three distinct ways. One is by avoiding the local culture as much as possible, for example by living in an **expatriate ghetto** using the home culture. Another is by **going native** and adopting many of the foreign culture's values. A third is by **integrating** home and foreign cultures, learning from both.

Adjustment after arrival is thought to be influenced by the individual's sense of self-efficacy, relation skills, and perception skills. Work roles, the degree of cultural novelty of the organization, social support, and logistical help all affect adjustment. Finally, non-work factors such as the novelty of the new culture and family adjustment are important influences on how well the manager settles in to the new culture (Black and others, 1991).

In the final phase of the culture shock cycle the traveller recovers a *back-to-normal* mood. Culture shock has been presented here as occurring in four distinct phases. But shock may reoccur. Jonathan Rauch (1992) describes how this might work for an international business manager in Japan.

Step 1. Arrival.
Step 2. This place is so different!
Step 3. This place is really just like home!
Step 4. Formation of conclusion: "Now I think I understand this place."
Step 5. Collapse of conclusion; too many exceptions.
Step 6. Repeat from Step 2.

Culture shock is certainly possible when one moves within a country, but across cultures. Minnie Aodla Freeman (1978), an Inuit from Cape Hope Island in James Bay, describes her shock on entering a life among the Qallunaat (the white people):

> My first ride in a car left me speechless. There were cars and more cars everywhere I looked; some were moving, some were parked. How does the man who is driving know when to stop and when to go? Does he count to a certain number? Or does the other car let him know? The blinking red light on the car ahead of us meant nothing to me. (p. 17)

Interestingly, moving back into the home culture and organization may cause **reentry shock** (see Southerst, 1992). The home country's weaknesses are seen more fully and the strengths of the foreign country's culture may be missed. At work, the skills leaned in the international assignment and the manager's personal growth may not be valued or recognized. While others have changed during the time the international manager was away, these others may expect the international manager to be the same. Further, the job returned to may be less critical to the organization than the job left behind. Reentry will be made easier if the transition back to the home country is carefully planned and if contact between the home office and the returning individual was maintained throughout the time away.

Reentry shock Culture shock caused by moving back into the home culture and organization.

If the person sent on international assignment is a man with a wife and family, the greatest culture shock may be experienced by the wife (D'Orazio, 1981). While the husband has work and support systems in the new culture, and the children have school, the woman at home has to deal more in the local language and with the less educated groups of the new culture. Working for pay may not be allowed, the transient nature of the appointment can make it hard to find new friends, and her husband may be able to provide even less support than he did back home (D'Orazio, 1981). Further stresses that may be anticipated are that her husband will likely be away from home a great deal and could find himself in situations ripe for temptations of various kinds.

In her descriptions of the culture shock awaiting foreign executive's wives in Tokyo, Nancy D'Orazio notes that a career-oriented woman needs to get a job, but then confronts the male-oriented Japanese society *and* being a foreigner. It is difficult to "go native" in Tokyo, she writes, because the non-Japanese is never allowed to be a member of the club.

Detailing the pros and cons of life in Tokyo, D'Orazio asserts that:

- Tokyo is an ugly, crowded city, but there are some beautiful parks, gardens and cycling paths.
- There are unzoned dirty grey concrete buildings, but there are beautiful old Japanese houses tucked here and there.
- Traffic jams are abominable, but fast and efficient public transportation is available.
- Cinder block walls surround everything, but behind the walls are lovely private Japanese gardens.

- Men spit, urinate, and vomit on the streets, but the city is cleanly swept and very safe relative to other large cities.
- There is a bureaucracy of endless rules, but a Japanese society is disciplined and predictable.
- On the subway at rush hour, when department store shopping or walking along the street there is a herd mentality where there are no rules, but, person to person, the Japanese are polite and helpful people.
- The foreigner will never be a part of Japanese society, but there is a wealth of culture and tradition to enjoy.

In order to lessen culture shock for the foreign executive's wife in Tokyo, Nancy D'Orazio makes six suggestions.

1. A welcome by the company and introduction to other wives would help lessen loneliness.
2. A greeter should be made available to explain foods, housing, shopping, etc.
3. A Westerner familiar with Tokyo must help with house-hunting, since Tokyo is not zoned and one needs to consider carefully where to live.
4. It is important to learn the Japanese culture and protocol.
5. It is compulsory to learn some Japanese.
6. Any Japanese household staff must be oriented to Western social and business customs. For example, a Western hostess may act as a maid by taking coats, getting drinks, etc., but she does not expect to be treated as one!

It would also undoubtedly be useful for both the foreign executive and his spouse to become familiar with a few general rules of business etiquette in Japan (see Exhibit 14.9).

If the person being sent overseas is a woman, she may encounter difficulties as well as opportunities. Mariann Jelinek and Nancy Adler (1988) note that many companies have been hesitant to send women overseas. The companies fear foreign prejudice, the safety of the woman worker, or that the woman being sent overseas would turn down the opportunity because of her husband's job.

Though many countries are much more male dominated than Canada, and women managers are rare in those countries, their male managers are usually able to deal with a North American female manager. In Japan, for example, the female expatriate manager is seen as neither a woman nor a man, but as a **gaijin** (a foreigner; see Adler 1987).

Gaijin Japanese word meaning "foreigner."

Jelinek and Adler (1988) argue that women are excellent choices for international assignments because of their good interpersonal and communications skills. And women want these assignments. In one study (Adler, 1986) of 1129 female MBA graduates from Canada, the United States, and Europe, 84% reported that they would like to take on an international assignment. But women are not being given the same chance to work abroad as are men. Another study by Nancy Adler (1984) found that only 3% of those sent abroad were female. Women will need to counter the fears of upper management about their chances of international success if they are to gain international experience.

CONCLUSION

We have seen how stress can be caused by changes in a person's life, and how an individual's life and career are liable to go through predictable stages. In the next chapter we will examine processes of change at the individual, group, and organizational levels. There is nothing so constant as change. We must strive to understand change so that we are prepared for the future.

EXHIBIT 14.9   GENERAL BUSINESS ETIQUETTE IN JAPAN

1. The customary form of greeting is a bow from the waist, although most Japanese expect to shake hands with a Westerner. To bow, place your heels together and hold your palms at your sides if a man. Women, again place heels together but fold hands over each other at thigh-level. Bow as low as and as long as your counterpart.

2. Exchange business cards after being introduced. Have your cards printed with English on one side and Japanese on the other. Offer your card with both hands, Japanese side up, and take time to read your new acquaintance's card.

3. It is traditional to address a Japanese person by his or her family name, followed by the honorific suffix "—san", but you may also address most Japanese western-style (Mr., Mrs. or Miss, followed by the family name). People in high positions may be addressed by their titles only. For example, "Shacho-san" for Mr. President.

4. Punctuality is expected for both business and social events. Make prior appointments and be on time. First meetings are very important and will set the tone of future relationships.

5. Show respect for age, status and/or seniority. Introduce a person of lower rank to someone of higher rank, and indicate their relationship to yourself, or position within their company.

6. Try to arrange a formal introduction to someone within the company with which you want to do business. The person doing the introduction assumes a responsibility for the action of the other parties.

7. A sense of harmony ("wa") is important for all relationships. Avoid direct confrontation or causing public embarrassment to your counterpart. Japanese will usually avoid saying "no" directly and may instead use such phrases as "I'll try" or "that may be difficult."

8. Do not show impatience with the Japanese method of reaching a decision through consensus. Negotiations may take longer than are common in the West, but once a decision is reached, implementation is usually swift and cooperative.

9. Consider it a great honour to be invited to a Japanese home. Remove your shoes before entering and place them together pointing toward the outside. It is customary to bring an inexpensive gift, such as food or wine, when visiting a home. Wrap your gift in pastel coloured paper or have it wrapped locally, and offer your present with both hands. It is not advisable to bring flowers, as some flowers may have ceremonial connotations.

SOURCE: Reprinted with permission from *Backgrounder Japan*, a publication of the Asia Pacific Foundation of Canada Information Series. © 1993 Asia Pacific Foundation of Canada. For further information contact: Asia Pacific Foundation of Canada, 666-999 Canada Place, Vancouver BC V6C 3E1.

CHAPTER SUMMARY

One way to think about a career is that it is an occupation engaged in over a period of time. The benefit of this way of conceptualizing a career is that career changes can be thought of as explicit events. A second way of defining a career is that it is a person's course through life. The benefit of this approach is that there is no simple way to define career success or failure.

Men and women go through the same set of key life experiences but they differ in the pattern of those events. Like the stages of life, careers have been found to have predictable stages. These are career entry, initiation into the organization, the first regular assignment, the second assignment, granting of tenure, termination and exit, and no longer being a part of the organization.

There are three types of career movement. Lateral movement can occur with job rotation, vertical movement up the hierarchy with promotion, and inward radial movement when an individual becomes more on the "inside" of the organization. People in organizations, especially women and minorities, may face discrimination in their careers. Barriers may be encountered that restrict lateral movement to a set of secondary jobs not so critical to the organization; that limit radial movement due to membership exclusions; and that allow vertical movement only up to the glass ceiling.

Everyone needs to manage their own career, deciding what career to enter into and what kind of success to pursue. The selection of a company to work for and the crucial first job, the decision to work for oneself, the finding of a helpful mentor, all are important decisions that must be made by the individual. Other issues that may be confronted in a career are being part of a dual-career couple and being sent on an international assignment.

QUESTIONS FOR REVIEW

1. How should an organization prepare individuals for an international assignment? What is the culture shock cycle and how can its effects be lessened?

2. Describe the ways that dual-career couples can choose to manage their two careers?

3. What can individuals and organizations do to reduce discrimination in hiring and promotion?

4. How can women's and men's life experiences, in general, be expected to be the same and how can they be expected to differ?

5. How can a person plan for a career in an organization?

SELF-DIAGNOSTIC EXERCISE 14.1

Career Assessment Test

Circle the answer that best describes your feelings about each statement.

SA = Strongly Agree   A = Agree   D = Disagree   SD = Strongly Disagree

1. I would like to accumulate a personal fortune to prove to myself and others that I am competent.	SA	A	D	SD
2. A career that provides a maximum variety of types of assignments and work projects is important to me.	SA	A	D	SD
3. It is important for me to remain in one geographical location rather than move because of a promotion or new job assignment.	SA	A	D	SD
4. It is important for me to be identified by my occupation.	SA	A	D	SD
5. I find most organizations to be restrictive and intrusive.	SA	A	D	SD
6. Being able to use my skills and talents in the service of an important cause is important to me.	SA	A	D	SD
7. Remaining in my area of expertise rather than being promoted into general management is important to me.	SA	A	D	SD

8. My main concern in life is to be competent in my area of expertise.   SA   A   D   SD

9. Seeing others change because of my efforts is important to me.   SA   A   D   SD

10. To rise to a position in general management is important to me.   SA   A   D   SD

11. A career that permits a maximum of freedom and autonomy to choose my own work, hours, and so forth, is important to me.   SA   A   D   SD

12. I like to see others change because of my efforts.   SA   A   D   SD

13. I do not want to be constrained by either an organization or the business world.   SA   A   D   SD

14. I am willing to sacrifice some of my autonomy to stabilize my total life situation.   SA   A   D   SD

15. The chance to pursue my own lifestyle and not be constrained by the rules of an organization is important to me.   SA   A   D   SD

16. To be recognized by my title and status is important to me.   SA   A   D   SD

17. The use of my skills in building a new business enterprise is important to me.   SA   A   D   SD

18. A career that gives me a great deal of flexibility is important to me.   SA   A   D   SD

19. An organization that will provide security through guaranteed work, benefits, a good retirement, and so forth, is important to me.   SA   A   D   SD

20. I want to achieve a position that gives me the opportunity to combine analytical competence with supervision of people.   SA   A   D   SD

21. An organization that will give me long-run stability is important to me.   SA   A   D   SD

22. I would leave my company rather than be promoted out of my area of expertise.   SA   A   D   SD

23. An endless variety of challenges in my career is important to me.   SA   A   D   SD

24. I have always sought a career in which I could be of service to others.   SA   A   D   SD

25. I like to be identified with a particular organization and the prestige that accompanies that organization.   SA   A   D   SD

26. I have been motivated throughout my career (or will be) by the number of products that I have been directly involved in creating.   SA   A   D   SD

27. Becoming highly specialized and highly competent in some specific functional or technical area is important to me.   SA A D SD

28. The use of my interpersonal and helping skills in the service of others is important to me.   SA A D SD

29. I want a career that allows me to meet my basic needs through helping others.   SA A D SD

30. Remaining in my present geographical location rather than moving because of a promotion is important to me.   SA A D SD

31. I will accept a management position only if it is in my area of expertise.   SA A D SD

32. Being identified with a powerful or prestigious employer is important to me.   SA A D SD

33. I see myself less as a generalist as opposed to being committed to one specific area of expertise.   SA A D SD

34. To be in a position in general management is important to me.   SA A D SD

35. I want others to identify me by my organization and my job title.   SA A D SD

36. I would like to reach a level of responsibility in an organization where my decisions really make a difference.   SA A D SD

37. To be able to create or build something that is entirely my own product or idea is important to me.   SA A D SD

38. An endless variety of challenges is what I really want from my career.   SA A D SD

39. I have been motivated throughout my career (or can see myself being motivated) by using my talents in a variety of different areas of work.   SA A D SD

40. During my career I will be mainly concerned with my own sense of freedom and autonomy.   SA A D SD

41. The process of supervising, influencing, leading and controlling people at all levels is important to me.   SA A D SD

42. Remaining in my specialized area, as opposed to being promoted out of my area of expertise, is important to me.   SA A D SD

43. The excitement of participating in many areas of work will be the underlying motivation behind my career.   SA A D SD

44. A career that is free from organization restriction is important to me.   SA A D SD

Scoring:

Score your responses by writing the number that corresponds to your response (SA = 4, A = 3, D = 2, SD = 1) to each question in the space next to the item number.

1 _____   2 _____   3 _____   4 _____   5 _____   6 _____

7 _____   8 _____   9 _____   10 _____   11 _____   12 _____

13 _____   14 _____   15 _____   16 _____   17 _____   18 _____

19 _____   20 _____   21 _____   22 _____   23 _____   24 _____

25 _____   26 _____   27 _____   28 _____   29 _____   30 _____

31 _____   32 _____   33 _____   34 _____   35 _____   36 _____

37 _____   38 _____   39 _____   40 _____   41 _____   42 _____

43 _____   44 _____

Now obtain subscale scores by adding your scores on the items indicated for each subscale and then dividing by the number of items in that subscale.

Technical competence: You organize your career around the challenge of the actual work you're doing.

Items 7 + 8 + 22 + 27 + 31 + 33 + 42   divided by 7 = _____

Autonomy: You value freedom and independence

Items 5 + 11 + 13 + 15 + 23 + 40 + 44   divided by 7 = _____

Service: You're concerned with helping others or working on an important cause.

Items 6 + 9 + 12 + 24 + 28 + 29   divided by 6 = _____

Identity: You're concerned with status, prestige, and titles in your work.

Items 4 + 16 + 25 + 32 + 35   divided by 5 = _____

Variety: You seek an endless variety of new and different challenges.

Items 2 + 18 + 38 + 39 + 43   divided by 5 = _____

Managerial competence: You like to solve problems and want to lead and control others.

Items 10 + 20 + 34 + 36 + 41   divided by 5 = _____

Security: You want stability and career security.

Items 3 + 14 + 19 + 21 + 30   divided by 5 = _____

Creativity: You have a strong need to create something of your own.

Items 1 + 17 + 26 + 37   divided by 4 = _____

Interpretation:

These eight career anchors are clues to your motives, values, and self-perceived competencies. The higher your score on a given anchor the stronger is your self-perceived emphasis in that career direction. You could use your set of anchor scores to determine what jobs would be likely to fit your own pattern. Alternatively, if you have a particular career in mind, how well do its attributes fit your career anchor pattern? Remember, however, that there is no one best set of anchor scores for every person or job—higher does not mean better. It is also important to remember that while the results will be suggestive of your own career motives, this test as used here should not be considered a valid scientific instrument.

SOURCE: Adapted/Reprinted by permission of the publisher, from Thomas J. DeLong, "Reexamining the career anchor model," PERSONNEL, May-June 1982, pp. 56-57. © 1982 American Management Association, New York. All rights reserved.

EXPERIENTIAL EXERCISE 14.1

Marriage/Career Expectations

The purpose of this exercise is to explore career and marriage expectations. Students should complete the appropriate questionnaire outside of class. In class, mixed-sex groups of four to six members are formed to discuss their responses to the questionnaires. Specifically, discuss the following:

- Which items caused the most disagreement?
- What did you learn about your career and marriage expectations?

Then groups report to the whole class on items of most disagreement.

MARRIAGE CAREER EXPECTATION INVENTORY
Female Form

Strongly Agree		*Neutral*		*Strongly Disagree*
1	*2*	*3*	*4*	*5*

_____ **1.** It will be preferable for my husband to have at least as much as or more education than I do.

_____ **2.** I expect to fully develop my career and for my husband to encourage me.

_____ **3.** If I am not employed, I will do all the housework; if I am employed, I will expect my husband to help somewhat.

_____ **4.** I expect to stay home full-time with our children.

_____ **5.** It is preferable for my husband to make most of the financial decisions, regardless of whether (and how much) income I bring to the household.

_____ 6. Weekends will be time for my husband to relax, watch TV, etc., and I will strive to keep distractions (i.e., visitors, children) to a minimum for him.

_____ 7. Substitute mothers can do an excellent job and will take care of our children while I work.

_____ 8. I expect to have the major responsibility of raising our children, regardless of whether I am employed or not.

_____ 9. If there is a disagreement which we cannot resolve, I think the wife should most often give in to the husband.

_____ 10. I expect to take some vacations either a) by myself, or b) with my husband, but no children.

_____ 11. I may not want children, since I want to develop my career.

_____ 12. I expect to be able to continue my education if I wish, even if we have children.

_____ 13. I expect to be able to go out in the evening with my friends.

_____ 14. Yard work and fix-it tasks will mainly be done by my husband.

_____ 15. If my husband gets an excellent job offer elsewhere, I will expect to pick up and move to the new place. Therefore, his career will be more important than mine.

_____ 16. I expect that my husband will at some times have to put his career before our family, but I will not.

MARRIAGE CAREER EXPECTATION INVENTORY
Male Form

Strongly Agree		*Neutral*		*Strongly Disagree*
1	*2*	*3*	*4*	*5*

_____ 1. It will be preferable for me to have at least as much as or more education than my wife.

_____ 2. I expect my wife to fully develop her career and I will encourage her.

_____ 3. If my wife is not employed, I will expect her to do all the housework; if she is employed I will help somewhat.

_____ 4. I expect my wife to stay home full-time with our children.

_____ 5. It is preferable for me to make most of the financial decisions, regardless of whether (and how much) income is brought into the household by my wife.

_____ 6. Weekends will be time for me to relax, watch TV, etc., and I expect my wife to keep distractions (i.e., visitors, children) to a minimum for me.

_____ 7. Substitute mothers can do an excellent job and will take care of our children while my wife works.

_____ 8. I expect my wife to have the major responsibility for raising our children, regardless of whether she is employed or not.

_____ 9. If there is a disagreement which we cannot resolve, I think the wife should most often give in to the husband.

_____ 10. I expect to take some vacations either a) by myself, or b) with my wife, but no children.

_____ 11. We may not want children since I want my wife to develop her career.

_____ 12. I expect my wife to be able to continue her education if she wishes, even if we have children.

_____ 13. I expect my wife to be able to go out in the evening with her friends, as I do with mine.

_____ 14. Yard work and fix-it tasks will mainly be done by me.

_____ 15. If I get an excellent job offer elsewhere, I will expect my wife to pick up and move to the new place. Therefore, my career will be more important than hers.

_____ 16. I expect at some times to put my career before our family, but my wife will not.

EXPERIENTIAL EXERCISE 14.2

The Lifeboat Drill

Step 1: Groups of 7 to 9 persons are formed.

Step 2: The situation: The group is on a small sailboat that is taking on water. There is one small lifeboat, but it can only hold three people. The others must stay on the sailboat and will not be saved.

Step 3: Five minutes are allowed for the group members to individually prepare a statement of why he or she should be saved. For the purpose of this exercise, it is not permitted to argue that another should be saved but only to argue as strongly as you can for yourself.

Step 4: Each group member takes three minutes to present his or her case and argue that he or she should be saved.

Step 5: The group as a whole votes on which three people on the lifeboat should be saved. No one is allowed to vote for themselves. The three people with the most votes are saved.

Step 6: In the group discuss why those three gave the most compelling reasons for being saved.

EXPERIENTIAL EXERCISE 14.3

Old Age

The object of this exercise is for each person in the class to conduct an interview with a person over 60 and then to report their findings either in class or in a short paper.

First, in class, a timeline dated from 1920 to 1995 is drawn the length of the blackboard. The class as a whole provides input to mark on the time line the major events and inventions that have had an impact on people who have lived through those years. Each person should make a copy of the timeline for their notes.

Second, also in class, students divide into groups to write questions that they would like to ask older people. The questions are combined to form one list that has the categories of: childhood; dating, marriage and family; career; the effect of world events; lifestyle changes; societal attitudes; the interviewee looking back on his/her life; and the interviewee's advice to the student.

Third, students divide into pairs and practice interviewing, using the class list of questions. Interview technique may then be demonstrated by some of the pairs for the rest of the class.

Fourth, students adapt the class list of questions and conduct an interview outside of class with someone over the age of 60.

Finally, results of the interview are reported either by a written assignment or by class discussion.

SOURCE: Based on Peggy Brick (1985), "The life cycle." In Ludy T. Benjamin, Jr., & Kathleen D. Lowman (Eds.), *Activities Handbook for the Teaching of Psychology* (pp. 128-130). Washington, D.C.: American Psychological Association.

SELF-GUIDED LEARNING ACTIVITY

In this activity, you will have to pretend that you have lived to the age of 70, and have passed on. Now your objective is to write your own obituary. To get started, think about who was important in your life, what were the key events (looking back from the future, of course), and what impacts you had on the world at large and on other people's lives. Once your obituary is finished, examine it to see what you have valued the most.

CASE 14.1

MANAGER'S CASE FILE: MAILROOM MAYHEM

John Miller, a mailroom supervisor, has a big problem on his hands. A few years ago he started selecting a protégé from among his subordinates. Whenever a particularly bright person came to work in the mailroom, John would take him or her under his wing. He'd encourage the individual to go for more education and even arrange for a loan to pay for it. He'd take his protégé to lunch and explain company history and politics. He'd give the employee all the easy mail runs and train the individual to take over in an emergency or in John's absence.

Sometimes, all this paid off. Some of his protégés went on to bigger and better things, and they gave John a lot of the credit for it. The last couple of protégés, however, have gotten nothing but swelled heads. These protégés lorded their position over the others by coming to work late and running up high absence rates. Resentment in the mailroom ran high, and the mail operation suffered. John ultimately had to fire the last two protégés.

Both times, John went to his supervisor and friend, Mel Fisher, the head of shipping, and said, "Mel, I don't know what happened. I did everything I could to train and help the youngster."

Now, John has another protégé. However, this time is the worst. One of John's subordinates, Ralph, went to Mel the other day to complain about how unfair it was to the others. They were doing all the hard work while the latest protégé, George, was slacking off more than the other ones ever did. The mailroom workers had tried to complain about it, but John wouldn't listen. Mel talked to John about the situation, but John assured him that it was just sour grapes—that the other employees had no ambition and that they were lazy, to boot. He said George was the only one he could train to take over in an emergency. Mel accepted John's explanation and did nothing about the complaint.

Mel knew that part of the reason he was not involving himself was his friendship with John. But Mel also believed that his supervisors should be left to run their shops as they thought best.

Now there is real trouble. After a telephone call from the office manager, Mel called John into his office. John's other subordinates, led by Ralph, had gotten up a petition detailing their complaint about the unfair distribution of work, and they had sent the petition to Mel's boss, the office manager. He had read Mel the riot act. John was to be ordered to straighten out the situation. In the meantime, a note from the office manager would be sent to the mailroom workers who had contacted him assuring them that he was taking steps to deal with their complaint.

Mel and John, of course, feel that their authority has been undermined. John is even talking about quitting rather than going back to the mailroom.

SOURCE: Reprinted, by permission of publisher, from SUPERVISORY MANAGEMENT, April 1985. © 1985 American Management Association, New York. All rights reserved.

Questions

1. What should John do now to save face and regain control of the mailroom?

2. Is John justified in bringing along bright subordinates? If so, how could he have handled their training better?

3. How should Mel have handled the complaint from John's subordinates in the first place?

THE CARPENTER CASE

Tom and Jane Carpenter are a young couple living comfortably in a New England town in the United States.

They have three children, Mary 11, Jerry 6, and Ann 3.

Tom works in the headquarters of a manufacturing company as an executive in the engineering department. He has a high salary, by company standards, and up until now has been satisfied with his job. A quiet, handsome man of about 36 years, he is intelligent, sensitive, ambitious, and known as "a good family man." He has the respect of his colleagues and subordinates. The upper echelons of management regard him as a promising candidate for senior management in this company. Tom is considered a practical man, able to take the changes in life with a basic optimism and adaptability that appear to give him a maturity beyond his years. He likes the material wealth and comfort that his years of conscientious work have produced. He enjoys his status in the company which has an excellent name in its field, being considered one of the most progressive and future-minded of U.S. companies of this type.

If Tom is the practical member of the family, Jane is the "dreamer." She is a pretty, energetic woman of thirty, a good wife and mother and an active member of several committees and voluntary groups. She is strongly attached to both her family and her parents who are in their early sixties and live in a nearby town. She is sincerely interested in many good causes and always finds the time and energy to devote to them. While she is not a very practical woman by nature, her enthusiasm for her projects is admired by her many friends.

Tom and Jane married early and struggled together for several years until they were able to achieve the comfortable life they now have. Their marital life has been happy and more or less undisturbed, and through the struggle of their earlier years they were able to develop between themselves a rewarding relationship. Although they have traveled to several parts of the U.S. with and without the children, neither Tom nor Jane had traveled abroad until two years ago. At that time Tom, together with three other executives, was sent to Latin America to explore the possibilities of setting up four new plants in different countries in Latin America.

Both Tom and Jane have been feeling more and more relaxed in the past years, since many of their dreams have been realized. They have a good family, financial security and many friends. They are especially proud of their new home, recently finished. Jane has worked hard to find the furniture and the interior decorations they wanted and now her dream house seems completed. They have both been so far generally satisfied with their children, who are well adjusted to their present environment. There have been certain problems with Mary, who is a very sensitive and shy girl, and with Jerry, who has had some difficulties adapting in school. But these were very minor problems and they have not disturbed seriously the otherwise happy family life.

Despite this very satisfactory picture of family life, there have recently been more and more occasions when Tom and Jane have felt (each one without admitting it to the other) that something is "missing."

More and more, Tom thinks that his life has become a comfortable routine. The new tasks he is given have less "challenge" and "adventure." For a long while he has been satisfied that his career had a steady development through the years. The time of anxiety and uncertainty has passed, but also with it the time of excitement and the inner feeling of searching and moving. He has begun to feel that he needs a change and it was at that time that he was sent for four months to Latin America. Tom felt that this trip was one of the

SOURCE: This case was prepared by Foulie Psalidas-Perlmutter, Ph.D. Professor Psalidas-Perlmutter is a member of the faculty in the Graduate Professional Development Program on Dynamics of Organization, School of Arts & Sciences, University of Pennsylvania. The case is reproduced here with her permission. Copyright © by Foulie Psalidas-Perlmutter.

most interesting and rewarding events of his whole life. Being away for the first time from his family for such a long period, he missed them and he was disappointed because the wives were not allowed to accompany their husbands on that trip. But the prospects of building up their company in Latin America have been attractive and he found that he liked to travel, to meet new people, to become acquainted with different ways of living, to be more a part of the "world" and of events outside of their home town. The three other executives who took the trip with him had about the same feelings as he had. Each seemed to be a little "weary" of being "a little fish" at headquarters. The possibility of being a pioneer in the Latin American division to be created was an exciting prospect. Tom somehow felt reluctant to communicate to Jane all his satisfaction and his thoughts about that trip, as well as the fact that he was hoping to be chosen from among the executives to be responsible for setting up the plants in Latin America.

In a different way, but with the same feeling of restlessness and discontent, there are times now that Jane feels that the pleasant, well-organized life she has is lacking the excitement of unpredictability. She divides her time between many activities, but finds herself at times dreaming about the world outside of her home town. She wonders at times, like Tom, whether their life has not become too settled, an almost unaltered routine, but unlike Tom, she checks herself by asking the simple question that, after all, isn't this what life really is?

When Tom came home with the news that Mr. Abbott, the president of the company, had offered him the key position in the Latin America operation, she was pleased to hear of the high esteem his superiors had for Tom. Actually, Jane too had been wondering for some time what could be the result of Tom's trip to Latin America. Although she would have liked to have been able to go with him at that time, the idea that they would have had to leave the children for such a long time forced her to exclude absolutely the possibility of her going, even if the wives of the executives had been allowed to go with them. After that, she used to wonder at times whether the company would choose him, if the decision was made. At that time the idea of having to move to a new environment was not an unpleasant one.

Now that the offer was a firm one, with a high salary, cost of living expenses, and opportunity for travel throughout Latin America, she began to have some fears. As Tom talked excitedly about the challenging tasks he would have, her fears seemed to increase. She began to feel more and more that they had little to gain from this experience as regards their family and their life. It was a big step forward in Tom's career, to be sure, but Jane felt that Tom would be successful wherever he was. On the present job, Tom and she shared so much time together, while in the new job, as she understood it, Tom would have to travel a great deal. She was very unhappy and ashamed about her fears as opposed to Tom's enthusiasm and obvious willingness to venture ahead.

One evening she tried to sit down by herself and figure out why this new job was not so attractive to her. There was some urgency for Tom to make up his mind within a week, and she felt the need to understand what this decision to move abroad meant for her and for her family.

She tried to be honest with herself. She naturally had fears about moving to a new environment which was strange and where people spoke another language. She knew that the climate was very different and she believed that the living conditions were likely to offer fewer comforts. She would be far from her friends and her parents. Their furniture would have to be stored, and their new house rented or sold, since it was not clear how many years Tom would need to get the four new plants going.

She felt she would be isolated because she did not think that they could have a close contact with the local people for a long time. Whatever she had heard so far about the personality of the Latin Americans made her fear that close friendships would be difficult to achieve, at least for some time, because she had the impression that they were rather temperamental and unstable. Although she admitted to herself that this impression was based on hearsay and fiction, she somehow could not avoid believing it. She had also heard that there was a great deal of anti-American feeling in the country where they would first live. Furthermore, she wondered whether the sanitary conditions would be dangerous to the health of the children. The company had little experience in Latin

America, so it would be likely that they would have to find their own way and learn, probably by hard experience, how to get along in these countries.

She realized that what disturbed her more than anything else was probably that Tom was going to travel a lot. Then she would probably have to face a great deal of the problems of their adaptation there alone, while up until this time they had always shared whatever problems they had to face and they supported each other in finding solutions. This also meant that Tom would see more places, meet more people, in general he would enjoy more, and probably get more satisfaction out of the whole experience than she and the children would. She was distressed to realize that she was already resentful toward him for that and angry because she could sense that, although he was discussing the problem with her, he had already made up his mind.

Jane kept these fears more or less to herself, but she did communicate to Tom her reluctance to go and gave as one of her main reasons her worry about the effect this move was going to have on the education of their children as well as on their health.

Tom sensed most of Jane's fears and he reacted to her expressed doubts by saying that he thought that the children could adapt after a while and that the experience would be a very good one for them. They could learn a new language and they could make new friends after a while. As for themselves, he had the best of memories from his own trip and he believed that they were both going to find this new experience an enriching and rewarding one. He did not underestimate the difficulties involved, but he expressed the belief that they were capable of overcoming them, while enjoying all the advantages that living abroad would offer them.

Inwardly Tom was disappointed with Jane's negative reactions and the difficulties she seemed to be having. He had always believed her to be a woman of courage endowed with curiosity and interest in the world outside. In times of crisis previously in their life, she had always proved to be strong and supportive and she had always shown a spirit of adventure and willingness to go ahead. It was a painful surprise for him to realize that this spirit would operate only in the security of the familiar environment, while a more profound change seemed to appear to Jane as a great threat to herself and her family. He had hoped that she would back him in this decision which was so important to his career. Nevertheless, he maintained his confidence in her and he believed that she would change her mind in time. He called a Berlitz school nearby and made plans for both of them to take Spanish lessons.

When Jane's parents came to visit during this period of time, Jane told them of the company's offer to Tom. Her father, who had been ailing for some time, was visibly depressed by the news. Her mother said that this was going to be a great experience for them, "a chance of a lifetime," as she put it. Jane knew that her mother had always regretted not being able to travel abroad. Now she was thrilled that the children were given the opportunity and she promised to come and visit them in Latin America if Tom accepted the job.

DINNER WITH MR. ABBOTT

A few days later, Tom's boss, Mr. Abbott, invited Tom and Jane for dinner, saying that he always talked over a new job abroad with both husband and wife, because he felt that it was very important to take into consideration how the wife felt. Jane had many fears about this dinner. First, she resented being "looked over" by Mr. Abbott who, until now, had not really spent much time with them socially. Second, she did not want to reveal her doubts to Tom's boss, who had a reputation for making quick judgments about people, often not very favorable.

This dinner turned out to be a very pleasant one. Mrs. Abbott helped to put everyone at ease throughout the dinner, talking about her pleasant experience abroad when Mr. Abbott was managing director of a subsidiary branch in Europe. Mrs. Abbott had enjoyed Paris and Rome, but she admitted that she knew little about life in cities like Buenos Aires and Rio.

Mr. Abbott finally turned to Jane and said: "Well, we are very glad you are taking the news of this new assignment for Tom so well. I know you realize what an opportunity this job will be for him. It is a real challenge for him, far greater than what he can get here, you know." Tom hurriedly answered for Jane, who was about to reply to Mr. Abbott: "Jane is really a born traveller. I know that she is looking forward to this. She has already found out how she can take lessons in Spanish." Mr. Abbott seemed pleased. He said: "That is really fine. You know, Tom, that ours is becoming an international company. There will be few opportunities for executives at headquarters whose overseas experience is limited. Our policy is to create a management team which could base its decisions on actual experience abroad. Of course, having the kind of wife who is willing to take the risk of going off to the jungle is quite an asset. You are a lucky man, Tom."

While Jane joined in the laughter, she was inwardly very angry. That night, she and Tom had a quarrel which continued for the next few days. Jane resented the fact that the whole discussion was conducted as though Tom had already accepted the job,

as well as the fact that she was not given a chance to talk about Tom's work with Mr. Abbott. Tom insisted that Mr. Abbott was not the kind of man to whom one could reveal any doubts about a decision of the company. Discussing the problem the next day with the children confused Tom and Jane more, because the children's reaction was not clear. Mary was unwilling to go, Jerry and Ann seemed excited, but it was more because of the thrill they felt than because they really understood the issue. By now Jane was finding it difficult to sleep, and Tom said that a formal decision was required by next Monday.

They had a long weekend to think over the decision and give a final answer to Mr. Abbott on Monday.

Questions

1. What are the pros and cons of Tom's accepting this assignment to Latin America? Do Tom and Jane see the pros and cons the same way?

2. How should Tom and Jane go about discussing this issue? Is there a way to consider this opportunity without Tom and Jane becoming increasingly angry at each other? [A role play of Tom and Jane's positions may be a good idea. Try switching the roles, though, so that a male plays Jane's position and a female plays Tom's position.]

3. Is it true that Mr. Abbott does not want to hear or see any of Jane's uncertainties? What would he do if he knew she had her doubts?

4. What will it be like for the Carpenters and their three children if they do go to Latin America for an extended period? Do you see any problems on the horizon?

5. Are there any other alternatives other than the whole family going or staying? Should Jane and the children stay in their home while Tom goes away for an extended period?

REFERENCES

Adler, Nancy J. (1984). "Women in international management: Where are they?" *California Management Review* 26(4), Summer 1984, pp. 78-89.

Adler, Nancy J. (1986). "Do MBAs want international careers?" *International Journal of Intercultural Relations* 10(3): 277-300.

Adler, Nancy J. (1987). "Pacific basin managers: A *gaijin*, not a woman." *Human Resource Management* 26(2): 169-192.

Asia Pacific Foundation of Canada Information Series (1993). *Backgrounder Japan.* Vancouver: Asia Pacific Foundation of Canada.

Bahls, Jane Easter. (1993). "Playing fair." *Entrepreneur*, January 1993, 234-239.

Bardwick, Judith M. (1980). "The seasons of a woman's life." In Dorothy G. McGuigan (Ed.), *Women's Lives: New theory, Research, and Policy* (pp. 35-58). Ann Arbor, MI: University of Michigan Center for Continuing Education of Women.

Baron, James N., Alison Davis-Blake, & William Bielby (1986). "The structure of opportunity: How promotion ladders vary within and among organizations." *Administrative Science Quarterly* 31: 248-273.

Black, J. Stewart, & Mark Mendenhall (1990). "Cross-cultural training effectiveness: A review and a theoretical framework for future research." *Academy of Management Review* 15: 113-136.

Black, J. Stewart, Mark Mendenhall, & Gary Oddou (1991). "Toward a comprehensive model of international adjustment: An integration of multiple theoretical perspectives." *Academy of Management Review* 16: 291-317.

Bradbury, Nicholas (1989). "Strategies: The faces of change." *Canadian Business*, October 1989, 133-136.

Brick, Peggy (1985). "The life cycle." In Ludy T. Benjamin, Jr., & Kathleen D. Lowman (Eds.), *Activities Handbook for the Teaching of Psychology* (pp. 128-130). Washington, D.C.: American Psychological Association.

Business International Corporation (1978). "Successful repatriation demands attention, care, and a dash of ingenuity." *Business International* 15(9), March 3, 1978, pp. 57-65.

Chesanow, Neil (1985). *The World-class Executive.* New York: Rawson Associates.

Copeland, Lennie, and Lewis Griggs (1985). *Going International: How to Make Friends and Deal Effectively in the Global Marketplace* New York: Random House, Inc.

D'Orazio, Nancy (1981). *Foreign Executives' Wives in Tokyo.* Tokyo: Sophia University Institute of Comparative Culture Business Series Bulletin No. 82.

DeLong, Thomas J. (1982). "Reexamining the career anchor model." *Personnel*, May-June 1982, pp. 50-61.

Duxbury, Linda (1993). Personal communication to Richard Field.

Fisher, Anne B. (1992). "When will women get to the top?" *Fortune*, September 21, 1992, pp. 44-56.

Franssen, Margot (1993). "Beyond profits." *Business Quarterly*, Autumn 1993, pp. 15-20.

Freeman, Minnie Aodla (1978). *Life Among the Qallunaat.* Edmonton: Hurtig Publishers.

Frone, Michael R., Marcia Russell, & M. Lynne Cooper (1992). "Antecedents and outcomes of work-family conflict: Testing a model of the work-family interface." *Journal of Applied Psychology* 77: 65-78.

Gilligan, Carol (1982). *In a Different Voice: Psychological Theory and Women's Development.* Cambridge, MA: Harvard University Press.

Hall, Douglas T. (1976). *Careers in Organizations.* Pacific Palisades, CA: Goodyear.

Hall, Francine S., and Douglas T. Hall (1979). *The Two-career Couple.* Reading, MA: Addison-Wesley.

Higgins, Christopher A., and Linda E. Duxbury (1992). "Work-family conflict: A comparison of dual-career and traditional-career men." *Journal of Organizational Behavior* 13: 389-411.

Holland, John L. (1985). *Making Vocational Choices: A Theory of Vocational Personalities and Work Environments*, 2nd ed. Englewood Cliffs, NJ: Prentice Hall, Inc.

Innes, Eva, Jim Lyon, & Jim Harris (1991). *The Financial Post 100 Best Companies to Work For In Canada.* Toronto: HarperCollins Publishers.

Jelinek, Mariann, & Nancy J. Adler (1988). "Women: World-class managers for global competition." *Academy of Management Executive* 2(1): 11-19.

Kanter, Rosabeth Moss (1977). *Men and Women of the Corporation.* New York: Basic Books.

Khan, Sar B., & Sabir A. Alvi (1985). "A study of the validity of Holland's theory in a non-Western culture." *Journal of Vocational Behavior* 26: 132-146.

Kram, Kathy E. (1983). "Phases of the mentor relationship." *Academy of Management Journal* 26: 608-625.

Levering, Robert, & Milton Moskowitz (1993). "The ten best companies to work for in America." *Business and Society Review*, August 1993, pp. 26-38.

Levinson, Daniel J. (1986). "A conception of adult development." *American Psychologist* 41: 3-13.

Levinson, Daniel J., with Charlotte N. Darrow, Edward B. Klein, Maria H. Levinson, and Braxton McKee (1978). *The Seasons of a Man's Life.* New York: Alfred A. Knopf.

Lida, David (1992). "The three-tequila lunch." The *Globe and Mail Destinations Business Traveler*, May 1992, pp. 37-43.

Maruyama, Magoroh (1985). "Mindscapes: How to understand specific situations in international management." *Asia Pacific Journal of Management* 2: 125-149.

Maruyama, Magoroh (1992). "Changing dimensions in international business." *Academy of Management Executive* 6(3): 88-96.

McGarvey, Robert, & Scott Smith (1994). "Speaking in tongues." *Training*, January 1994, pp. 113-116.

McKay, Shona (1992). "Boys' club." *Report on Business Magazine* 9(3): 37-44.

Molloy, John T. (1975). *Dress for Success.* New York: P.H. Wyden.

Molloy, John T. (1977). *The Woman's Dress for Success Book.* Chicago: Follet Publishing Company.

Morrison, Ann M. (1992). "Developing diversity in organizations." *Business Quarterly* 57(1): 42-48.

Morrison, Ann M., & Mary Ann Von Glinow (1990). "Women and minorities in management." *American Psychologist* 45: 200-208.

Morrison, Ann M., Randall P. White, Ellen Van Velsor, and the Center for Creative Leadership (1987). *Breaking the Glass Ceiling: Can Women Reach the Top of America's Largest Corporations?* Reading, MA: Addison-Wesley.

Perlmutter, Howard (1969). "The tortuous evolution of the multinational corporation." *Columbia Journal of World Business*, Jan/Feb 1969, pp. 9-18.

Powell, Gary N., and Lisa A. Mainiero (1992). "Cross-currents in the river of time: Conceptualizing the complexities of women's careers." *Journal of Management* 18: 215-237.

Prediger, Dale J., & Timothy R. Vansickle (1992). "Locating occupations on Holland's Hexagon: Beyond RIASEC." *Journal of Vocational Behavior* 40: 111-128.

Ragins, Belle Rose, & John L. Cotton (1993). "Gender and willingness to mentor in organizations." *Journal of Management* 19: 97-111.

Rauch, Jonathan (1992). *The Outnation: A Search for the Soul of Japan.* Boston: Harvard Business School Press.

Schein, Edgar H. (1991). "The individual, the organization, and the career: A conceptual scheme." In David A. Kolb, Irwin M. Rubin, & Joyce S. Osland (Eds.), *The Organizational Behavior Reader* (pp. 128-145). Englewood Cliffs, NJ: Prentice Hall, Inc.

Smith, Peter B. (1992). "Organizational behaviour and national cultures." *British Journal of Management* 3: 39-51.

Sonnenfeld, Jeffrey A., & Maury A. Peiperl (1988). "Staffing policy as a strategic response: A typology of career systems." *Academy of Management Review* 13: 588-600.

Southerst, John (1992). "There goes the future." *Canadian Business*, October 1992, pp. 98-105.

Spokane, Arnold R. (1985). "A review of research on person-environment congruence in Holland's theory of careers." *Journal of Vocational Behavior* 26: 306-343.

Stroh, Linda K., Jeanne M. Brett, & Anne H. Reilly (1992). "All the right stuff: A comparison of female and male managers' career progression." *Journal of Applied Psychology* 77: 251-260.

Wentling, Rose Mary (1992). "Women in middle management: Their career development and aspirations." *Business Horizons*, January-February 1992, pp. 47-54.

Further Reading

For a review of careers, see Suzyn Ornstein and Lynn A. Isabella (1993), "Making sense of careers: A review of 1989-1992," *Journal of Management*, Volume 19: 243-267.

John Holland's career interest inventory, called the Holland Self-Directed Search (SDS) Form R, is available from Psychological Assessment Resources, Inc., PO Box 998, Odessa Florida. A computer version asks the questions, calculates the RIASEC score and Holland code, and searches for compatible occupations. Canadian editions in English and French are available that are based on the Canadian Classification and Dictionary of Occupations (CCDO). This evaluation tool may be available at your college or university's counselling or career placement office. They may also have available a range of guidance and counselling instruments such as the Edwards Personal Preference Schedule and the Educational Testing Service's interactive career planning program. The System of Interactive Guidance and Information, called SIGI, compares your own test results and values to different occupations in order to provide you with suggestions about which occupations might best fit your own attributes. Career counselling by mail is available from National Computer Systems, Inc., P.O. Box 1416, Minnetonka, MN 55440. Their multiple-choice test can be purchased and completed at home, then mailed back to be scored.

General works of interest on careers are Jeffrey H. Greenhaus (1987), *Career Management*, Chicago: Dryden Press; Edgar H. Schein (1987), "Individuals and careers," in Jay W. Lorsch (Ed.), *Handbook of Organizational Behavior* (pp. 155-171), Englewood Cliffs, NJ: Prentice Hall, Inc.; and Gail Sheehy's *Passages*, 1976, published in New York by E.P. Dutton. A book on managerial careers is by the University of Toronto's Hugh Gunz (1989), *Careers and Corporate Cultures: Managerial Mobility in Large Corporations*, New York: Basil Blackwell Inc.

The March-April 1993 edition of *Business Horizons* is devoted to the examination of issues of importance to women in the workplace. An article of interest on the glass ceiling is "Cracks in the glass: The silent competence of women" by Dan R. Dalton and Idalene F. Kesner. The issues of a woman/woman mentoring relationship are discussed in Victoria A. Parker and Kathy E. Kram's article "Women mentoring women: Creating conditions for connection". The Body Shop International was started by Anita Roddick in 1976 and is now well known for its socially responsible values. For further information on The Body Shop see the article "'You don't necessarily have to be charismatic ....'" An interview with Anita Roddick and reflections on charismatic processes in the Body Shop International," by Jeannie Gaines in *Leadership Quarterly* 4: 347-359.

Books on cross-cultural training are available from Intercultural Press, P.O. Box 768, Yarmouth ME 04096. Their telephone number is (207) 846-5168. Films on the international assignment are the *Going International* series by Copeland Griggs Productions, 3454 Sacramento Street, San Franciso CA 94118. Telephone them at (415) 921-4410. The titles of the four films in the series are "Bridging the Culture Gap," Managing the Overseas Assignment," "Beyond Culture Shock," and "Welcome Home, Stranger." The book that accompanies this series is *Going International: How to Make Friends and Deal Effectively in the Global Marketplace* by Lennie Copeland and Lewis Griggs, Random House 1985.

Also of interest: *The Travelers' Guide to Asian Customs and Manners* by Kevin Chambers, Meadowbrook 1988; , a series of guides by Nancy L. Braganti and Elizabeth Devine on customs and manners, published by St. Martin's Press—*The Travelers' Guide to Latin American Customs and Manners, The Travelers' Guide to European Customs and Manners*, and *The Travelers' Guide to Middle Eastern and North African Customs and Manners; Hidden Differences: Doing Business with the Japanese,* by Edward T. Hall and Mildred Reed Hall, Anchor Press/Doubleday, 1987; *How to do Business with the Japanese: A Strategy for Success,* by Mark Zimmerman, Random House of Canada, 1985; and *The International Businesswoman: A Guide to Success in the Global Marketplace* by Marlene L. Rossman, Praeger, 1986.

A videotape program which presents the role of the spouse on an international assignment is *A Portable Life*, available from McGill University, Instructional Communication Centre, 815 Sherbrooke Street West, Montreal, Quebec H3A 2K6 (Telephone 514-392-8031). Another important work, from Nancy Adler at McGill University, is the 1993 book *Competitive Frontiers: Women Managers in a Global Economy*, co-edited with Dafna N. Izraeli, published by Blackwell.

Other works of interest are Nicolas Bouvier (1992), *The Japanese Chronicles*, published by Mercury House, translated by Anne Dickerson. For a good overview of doing business in the East and a discussion of the importance of "face," see John A. Reeder (1987), "When west meets east: Cultural aspects of doing business in Asia," *Business Horizons*, January-February 1987, pp. 69-74. Also see "A Miss Manners guide to doing business in Europe" by John Hill and Ronald Dulek in the July-August 1993 issue of *Business Horizons*, pages 48-53. An article by Simon Fraser University's Rosalie Tung (1987) in the May *Academy of Management Executive*, pages 117-125, lists reasons expatriate assignments fail. Also see Rosalie L. Tung (1988), *The New Expatriates: Managing Human Resources Abroad*, published in Cambridge, Massachusetts by Ballinger. Finally, on China, see the book by Randall E. Stross (1990), *Bulls in the China Shop and Other Sino-American Business Encounters*, New York: Pantheon; and the article "Managing in China: Expatriate experiences and training recommendations" in *Business Horizons* 1990, Volume 33(3), pages 23-29.

CHAPTER 15

CHANGE

CHAPTER OUTLINE

Organization Development

   How OD Has Changed

   Five Factors of Change: The Organizational Work Setting

   Two Types of Change

   Three Levels of Change

   OD Methods and Techniques

Putting it All Together: A Model of Organizational Performance and Change

Conclusion

QUESTIONS TO CONSIDER

- *What is change?*
- *How do people, groups, and organizations change?*
- *What methods are there for managing change in individuals, groups, and organizations?*
- *Who manages change?*

Proactive change
Undertaken to make the organization, its systems, and/or its people more effective in dealing with demands from its environment.

Reactive change Change that is typically undertaken in response to environmental demands.

Incremental change
Is linear, orderly, slow, and ongoing, and does not question the basic nature of the system or of the organization.

Quantum change
Is discontinuous, chaotic, fast, and temporary, marked by a shift in how the organization and its people think about themselves and how they do business.

Chaos theory States that natural systems are very complex and unstable, with interconnections so widespread and subtle that even very small changes in system variables can cause very large changes in the end result.

Butterfly effect The concept that minute changes in system variables at one point in time can cause very large changes in the end result that is experienced.

Complexity In systems theory the concept that systems must be thought of in terms of how the parts interact with the whole.

Leverage The concept that small and well-focused actions can have large effects on a system.

Organizations, systems, and the people in them are constantly undergoing change. Therefore, change should be seen as the rule rather than the exception in organizational life. However, as often as not, changes at work are viewed with fear and suspicion. Facilitating change is therefore a big part of a manager's job.

There are two main ways of categorizing change. The first way defines change as either proactive or reactive. **Proactive change** is usually undertaken in order to make the organization, its systems, and/or its people more effective in dealing with demands from its environment. Such demands may be either existing or anticipated (Porras & Robertson, 1992), but the drive to change comes from within the organization. **Reactive change** is typically undertaken in response to environmental demands. Reactive change is adaptive—that is, it is aimed at making the organization better able to deal with its environment. In this case, the drive to change comes from outside the organization.

The second change dimension looks at whether change is incremental or quantum. **Incremental changes** do not question the basic nature of the system or of the organization. Incremental change is linear, orderly, slow, and ongoing (Mirvis, 1990), although small changes may over time accumulate to create large effects (e.g., Weick 1984). **Quantum change,** by contrast, is discontinuous, chaotic, fast, and temporary (e.g., Goss and others, 1993). It is marked by a shift in paradigm (Kuhn, 1970)—how the organization and its people think about themselves, their organization, and how they do business. Quantum change is the sudden and radical punctuation of the normal equilibrium. The linear path suddenly veers away from its earlier direction. The shift can be called a catastrophe, a punctuation in the equilibrium, an upheaval, or a paradigm shift.

incremental change path ———— *quantum change* ———— *new incremental change path*

Chaos theory (Gleick, 1987) is useful in understanding quantum change. This theory states that natural systems are very complex and unstable. Interconnections are so widespread and subtle that even very small changes in system variables can cause very large changes in the end result. This has been called the **butterfly effect**. The butterfly effect was first noticed in computer simulations of weather systems. Very small differences in initial conditions led to large changes in the weather patterns predicted by the model. The name originates from the concept that a butterfly fluttering its wings in Texas could trigger a storm in Alberta.

Chaos theory, as it relates to organizations, has given us two very important concepts (Freeman, 1992). The first is that the links between actions and outcomes is characterized by **complexity**. This view states that breaking a system down into its parts and looking for simple and direct cause-effect relationships will not be fruitful. The organization must be thought of in terms of how its parts interact with the whole. The second is that small and well-focused actions can have large effects on the system. This is the concept of **leverage**.

Combining the two change dimensions (proactive/reactive and quantum/incremental) results in four categories of change. These are transformational, revolutionary, evolutionary, and developmental (see Exhibit 15.1). For further discussion of change categories see Nadler and Tushman (1990) and Porras and Robertson (1992).

Transformational Change Transformational change is both proactive and quantum. The organization may go through a period of death and rebirth, arising phoenix-like from its own ashes. The organization is transformed by design from what it was, how its members thought and acted, into a new organization with qualitatively different methods. In this approach organizations have to match the complex adaptive systems found in nature in order to cope with the newly chaotic business environment (Freeman, 1992).

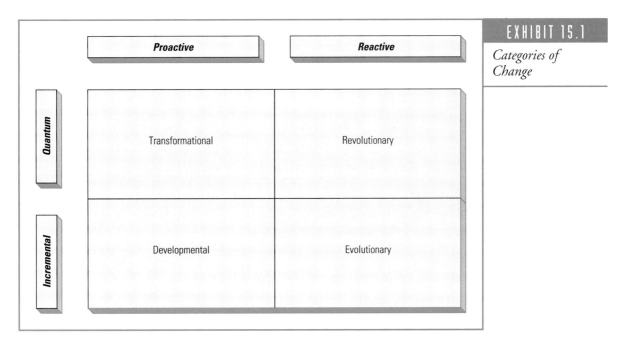

EXHIBIT 15.1

Categories of Change

One reason transformational change is needed is that organizations can be limited by their own successes. Tom Peters (1990, p. 18) wrote that "success is the product of deep grooves. Deep grooves destroy adaptability." The better the organization becomes at a particular way of operating, or the more successful a particular product becomes, the more likely it is that this success will lead to entrenched ways of operating and thinking that will hinder future adaptability. Danny Miller of the University of Montreal and McGill University has termed this "The Icarus Paradox" (1992), that exceptional companies bring about their own downfall by being, in essence, too successful. To transform the organization, techniques must be used with the intent to break out of these grooves, to break the organization's frame—its way of thinking and operating (Mirvis, 1990).

Revolutionary Change   This type of change is quantum but reactive. Organizations have to adapt to chance events that have large effects on their environment. Those who fail to make the major changes necessary will likely cease to operate. Required for success are revolutionaries with a qualitatively different conception of the organization and its environment who can win control and force massive and quick change. Manufacturers of inexpensive watches had to make the fundamental shift from mechanical to electronic watches in order to survive when physics made the quantum leap to transistors and integrated circuits.

Evolutionary Change   Evolutionary change is reactive and incremental. Organizations undergoing this type of change must mimic the adaptive methods found in nature. David Freeman describes this type of change as follows:

> In general, the complex adaptive systems found in nature contain individual agents that network to create self-managed but highly organized behavior; respond to feedback from the environment and adjust their behavior accordingly; learn from experience and embed that learning in the very structure of the system; and reap the advantages of specialization without getting stuck in rigidity" (1992, p. 32).

Developmental Change This category of change is proactive and incremental. The organization's aim is to develop in small, step-by-step increases, so that at each step it is slightly better than it was before. Many of the methods used by organizations for their own improvement fall into this change category.

ORGANIZATION DEVELOPMENT

There are several definitions of Organization Development (OD). Ronald Clement (1992) defines it as "the use of behavioral science ideas to improve both organizational effectiveness and employee well-being" (p. 6). Michael Beer and Anna Walton take a developmental approach to OD. They define it as "the theory and practice of managing the continual adaptation of internal organizational arrangements to changes in the external environment" (1987, p. 340). Jerry Porras and Peter Robertson offer a more formal definition of **organizational development** as "a set of behavioral science-based theories, values, strategies, and techniques aimed at the planned change of the organizational work setting for the purpose of enhancing individual development and improving organizational performance, through the alteration of organizational members' on-the-job behaviors" (1992, p. 722). Key elements of these definitions are that OD:

- Uses behavioural science theory and methods;
- Plans and manages change; and
- Targets change at the individual, the group, the work setting, and the organization as a whole.

Organizational development A set of behavioural science-based theories, values, strategies, and techniques aimed at the planned change of the organizational work setting for the purpose of enhancing individual development and improving organizational performance, through the alteration of organizational members' on-the-job behaviours.

How OD Has Changed

The definition of OD has changed over the years. Philip Mirvis (1988) makes the point that OD itself has changed in response to changes in society. Exhibit 15.2 summarizes these changes.

It is important to review how OD has refashioned itself over the years so that we can see how tightly interwoven are societal changes, organizational behaviour theories, and the application of behavioural science theories to the improvement of individual, group, and organizational functioning. We will then be in a position to see how events of the 1990s, for instance global competition and the impact of information technology, will affect the practice of OD.

Founding Principles: 1950s-1960s In its founding years OD was a philosophy of how change should take place and a value system of what the end results of change should look like. The individual was especially valued. Behavioural science principles were used by an external change agent who formed a collaborative enterprise with the learner. The focus was on taking action and measuring the results (e.g., McLaughlin & Thorpe, 1993; Whyte, 1989, 1991).

Socio-cultural Framework: 1950s-1960s Change was expected in the long term because this post-World War II period was one of affluence and growth in Canada and the United States. Organizations had the resources to pay external change agents to manage change. Relationships were long-term because society as a whole was stable. One example of this stability was that interest rates were low and relatively unchanging. Before computers became widely available bank rates might change only twice a year, not weekly as is now the case. One reason for this is that prior to computers individual bank employees had to manually calculate and record interest on deposits. Job shifting and mass layoffs were not the norm during this period.

Exhibit 15.2   Changes in Organization Development: 1950 to 2000

	Founding Principles: 1950s-1960s	Socio-cultural Framework: 1950s-1960s	Transitional Times: 1970s	Major Philosophic Shifts: 1980s	Socio-cultural Framework: 1980s	Integration for the 1990s and Beyond
Time Focus	Long-term orientation	Stable tenure of leaders, managers, employees	Unpredictable tenure of leaders, managers, and employees—short-term focus	Long- and short-term intervention	Greater managerial and consultant sophistication in matching depth of intervention with perceived need for change	Long-term focus: (1) OD to introduce strategic planning and/or (2) OD integrated with strategic plans and long-term goals
Knowledge Orientation	Applied behavioural science	Seminal principles taught and understood from shared beliefs	Changing beliefs; perceived importance of pragmatism	Inclusion of principles from behavioural science, systems theory, and anthropology, with emphasis on socio-technical systems, and organization culture analysis	Changing workforce demographics; more ethnic/gender diversity; greater need to understand information-age technologies	Integration of the principles from the 1980s, with an emphasis on processes that enhance content (task) capabilities
Change Agent	External, process-oriented consultation	Stability of change agents trained in process consultation	Shift to short-term focus & short-term contracts	External and internal consultants; task and process orientations	Increased sophistication and legitimacy of internal OD departments	Greater use of both internal and external OD consultants to assist with process variables essential to adaptation and survival
Who Manages the Change Effort	Change effort managed from top	Affluence, resource availability; hierarchical organizations; leaders believed in new era	Leadership focus toward bottom line	Middle managers and top executives jointly managing change	More knowledge workers; information more decentralized; fewer hierarchies of the industrial age	Client groups cross traditional organizational boundaries and functions; change effort managed throughout, with top managers involved; assist managers in understanding/integrating roles

	FOUNDING PRINCIPLES: 1950S-1960S	SOCIO-CULTURAL FRAMEWORK: 1950S-1960S	TRANSITIONAL TIMES: 1970S	MAJOR PHILOSOPHIC SHIFTS: 1980S	SOCIO-CULTURAL FRAMEWORK: 1980S	INTEGRATION FOR THE 1990S AND BEYOND
Methodology	Action research	Evolution of qualitative methods in social sciences	Shift to focus on quantitative methods	Multiple methodologies; action research, ethnomethodology	Broader definitions of empirical research	Continued use of multiple methodologies integrated into the overall OD effort
OD Change Agent/ Manager Relationship	Collaborative-emphasis	Stability enabled ability to form long-term relationships	Quick fix: short term, bottom-line contracts	Collaborations confrontation, attention to politics and power	Greater understanding of hierarchical and consensus-based dimensions of power; increasing attention to non-Western approaches to management (e.g., Japanese)	Collaboration through broader integration of various leverage points within the organization

SOURCE: Adapted from Jyotsna Sanzgiri & Jonathan Z. Gottlieb (1992), "Philosophic and pragmatic influences on the practice of organization development, 1950-2000," *Organizational Dynamics* 21(2): p. 65. Adapted/excerpted, by permission of publisher, from ORGANIZATIONAL DYNAMICS, Autumn 1992. © 1992 American Management Association, New York. All rights reserved.

Transitional Times: The 1970s   The seventies was a time of more rapid social change. Baby boom students began to graduate from colleges and universities in large numbers. There was social unrest in the United States due to that country's involvement in Vietnam. Civil rights unrest in the U.S. was also widespread, with rioting and looting often seen on the nightly news, both in the U.S. and in Canada. Computerization meant that the pace of change accelerated. It also allowed the emergence of quantitative methods, since mathematical calculations could now be performed quickly and easily.

Organizations came to be dominated by numbers and analysis. In this quantitative environment, Organization Development was seen by many managers as too soft, too "touchy-feely." Money markets became more volatile. Job switching came to be expected. Loyalty between employer and employee declined. A widespread questioning of values occurred. Sexual mores were changing with the widespread availability of the birth control pill (and before AIDS became a threat). The ethical and moral standards of leaders came into question. There was a general movement towards pragmatism. Getting a practical job in order to make money was widely accepted. OD came to be seen in this period as a set of technologies to be applied as a quick fix for the short term.

Socio-cultural Framework: The 1980s   The 1980s saw a strong movement to the information age. The personal computer was introduced and increased fantastically in power from the start of the decade to its end while decreasing fantastically in price. As personal computers became more common in the workplace, information was decentralized away from the Information Systems department and its mainframe computer to the individual user.

Hierarchies flattened as workers became more knowledge-oriented and professional. The microchip has accelerated the pace of change. New products, ways of organizing, and ways of communicating changed the very nature of how business was done.

Immigration from non-traditional source countries into Canada and the large-scale entry of college-educated women into the workforce dramatically changed the demographics of the 1980s workplace as compared to the 1950s.

The phenomenal success of electronic and automotive products from Japan provided the impetus for Western management to study non-Western approaches. Global competition and Eastern success made openness to new philosophies and systems possible (see *A Rose by Any Other Name*). Behavioural science in turn became more open and receptive to anthropological concepts of culture.

Major Philosophic Shifts: The 1980s   In the 1980s OD became a legitimate part of the ongoing work of the organization (Mirvis, 1988). Multiple methodologies came to be used as qualitative methods were added to the well-known quantitative methods. Action research made a comeback as change agents took a more collaborative approach with the client. It was recognized that technology was no longer something that could be dumped on others without their involvement. A wry comment by the well-known sociologist and OD practitioner William Foote Whyte illustrates this point:

> It is important, nevertheless, to recognize the costs of these earlier misguided attempts at technology transfer. [The agency] invested enormous sums of money and years of work by highly educated personnel to demonstrate to farmers how they could cut the value of their crops in half (1991, p. 173).

Time focus became both short and long term. OD change agents came to be brought into the organization to implement both short-term skill training and longer-term process and system changes.

Integration for the 1990s and Beyond   In the 1990s OD has become more crucial, more collaborative, and more complex (Sanzgiri & Gottlieb, 1992).

Firstly, OD is more crucial because it is now used to develop an organization's strategic plan and/or to change the organization to meet the plan. OD has taken on a policy emphasis that goes beyond how to do things better to what the organization needs to do.

Secondly, OD is more collaborative because internal and external change agents work with clients from all organizational levels across traditional boundaries. The change agent and manager have a collaborative relationship. They attempt to discover jointly where change can be implemented in the organization so that its positive effects are leveraged into change in other parts. The change agent, whether an external consultant, an internal consultant, or a manager, has to consider how best to do the job. Rules of thumb for the change agent are offered in this chapter's *A Word to the Wise* feature.

Thirdly, OD is more complex because multiple OD methods that focus on tasks and processes are used throughout the organization. The OD practitioner has a broad palette of OD methods available for use. To portray this complexity, we have included here (quoted, with minor changes, from French & Bell 1990) descriptions of thirteen separate families of OD interventions.

1. *Diagnostic Activities:* Fact-finding activities designed to ascertain the state of the system, the status of a problem, the "way things are." Available methods range from projective devices such as "build a collage that represents for you your place in this organization" to the more traditional data collection methods of interviews, questionnaires, surveys, and meetings.

A ROSE BY ANY OTHER NAME

Alfred Jaeger of McGill University's Faculty of Management has argued that most Organizational Development techniques have underlying values. Using the culture elements of Geert Hofstede (see Chapter 3), Jaeger claims that Organization Development methods can be seen as being:

- Low on power distance (less powerful members of the organization should not accept that power is distributed unequally or accept the orders of those in power);

- Moderate on individualism-collectivism (people should look out for both themselves and their family, acting as both individuals and as members of groups);

- High on femininity (people should value caring for others, maintaining warm personal relationships, solidarity with others, and the quality of how life is lived);

- Low on uncertainty avoidance (people should not want to avoid situations where their behaviour is unspecified—they should not mind unstructured situations).

In addition, we could expect that OD has a long term orientation.

Jaeger makes the point that in countries where OD values tend to match the country's cultural values OD methods are more likely to find acceptance. The chart below shows how the values of some countries tend to be more or less in accord with OD values. Note that in general Nordic values match OD values the most. This may help to explain why many OD approaches have found their greatest acceptance in the Nordic countries.

Specific OD techniques may also vary in effectiveness depending on how the specific values underlying the technique match the cultural values of the country where they are being applied. The point here is that the OD practitioner and change agent must not assume that all OD methods will operate in the same way in every country.

For example, an OD method such as Management By Objectives (MBO) requires managers and subordinates to negotiate with each other about task objectives on the assumption that the manager and the subordinate are of equal power. This would not be possible in countries with high power distance where managers are expected to be different from their subordinates. In India, for example, the manager is expected to make the decisions that need to be made. To ask the subordinate for an opinion would open the manager to ridicule for being weak and indecisive. Management By Objectives should therefore work less well in India than in Canada.

Cultural values different from OD values   *Cultural values similar to OD values*

◄ – ►

Belgium	Australia	Finland	Denmark
Brazil	Canada	Ireland	Norway
Greece	France	Israel	Sweden
Hong Kong	Germany	Netherlands	
Italy	Great Britain		
Japan	Switzerland		
Mexico	United States		
Pakistan	Thailand		

SOURCE: Based in part on information in Alfred M. Jaeger (1986), "Organizational development and national culture: Where's the fit?" *Academy of Management Review* 11: 178-190.

A WORD TO THE WISE

RULES OF THUMB FOR CHANGE AGENTS

If you are attempting to get others to change, here are some tips to help you be more effective. These are useful guides whether you are a consultant, an OD practitioner in your organization, or even a manager trying to make changes in your own department.

RULE NUMBER 1:
Stay Alive.

This first rule is vital because if you lose your job or your credibility, then you can have no impact on a system. Do what you have to do but keep in mind the necessity of holding on to your power to make change in the future. Staying alive "means going with the flow even while swimming against it."

RULE NUMBER 2:
Start Where the System Is.

For the change agent to be effective, he has to come to a deep understanding of how the client sees the organizational situation. Outside ways of thinking and diagnosing problems may be effective, but only after the change agent has a complete understanding of the organization and the situation from the client's point of view.

RULE NUMBER 3:
Never Work Uphill.

Work in a way that makes change easier instead of more difficult. Find the most promising area of the organization to work in and start there. Don't put in a system-wide change that will make some people happy and others angry. The angry ones will make your work more difficult later on. Have a plan of what you want to accomplish, but be flexible regarding how. Let the organization and its members guide your actions, but don't be afraid to make tough choices when they are required. And finally, avoid win-lose scenarios. If you win the other person loses, and if you lose, you lose big.

RULE NUMBER 4:
Innovation Requires a Good Idea, Initiative, and a Few Friends.

Without friends both inside and outside the organization it will be difficult to implement your good ideas, even with a great deal of personal initiative. It is necessary to build relationships with others who can help you and who you can help in turn.

RULE NUMBER 5:
Load Experiments for Success.

An experiment means that the outcome is not certain. But there is no reason why an experimental change cannot be conducted in the place and with the conditions most likely to result in a positive outcome. If middle managers are to engage in team-building, start with the managers most receptive to team ideas. If a new production process is to be implemented, start with the best and most adaptive production area.

RULE NUMBER 6:
Light Many Fires.

Organizations are composed of interconnected subsystems. When change in one of these subsystems is attempted, interaction with other unchanged subsystems can force the changing subsystem back into place. Therefore, change must occur simultaneously in all the organization's parts. One important subsystem that resists change may be enough to stop change in the organization as a whole.

RULE NUMBER 7:
Keep an Optimistic Bias.

It is too easy to focus on the negative experiences of the past. Look to the positive and create a new and positive present that can be the foundation for a better future.

RULE NUMBER 8:
Capture the Moment.

Use all your training and experience to make a difference at the moment when making that difference is possible. The essence of this rule is that you must be open to the situation and to your own knowledge so that your intervention is on time and on target.

SOURCE: Based on information in Herbert A. Shepard (1985), "Rules of thumb for change agents," *OD Practitioner*, December 1985, pp. 1-5.

An Outward Bound team-building activity. See also Chapter 9's "Seeing is Believing" feature.

2. *Team-Building Activities:* Activities designed to enhance the effective operation of system teams. They may relate to task issues, such as the way things are done, or the skills and resource allocations needed to do the job; or they may relate to the nature and quality of the relationships among team members or between members and the leader. Again, a wide range of activities is possible. In addition, consideration is given to the different kinds of teams that may exist in the organization, such as formal work teams, temporary task force teams, newly constituted teams, and cross-functional teams.

3. *Intergroup Activities:* Activities designed to improve effectiveness of interdependent groups. They focus on joint activities and the output of the groups considered as a single system rather than as two subsystems. When two groups are involved, the activities are generally designated *intergroup* or *interface* activities; when more than two groups are involved, the activities are often called *organizational mirroring*.

4. *Survey Feedback Activities:* These are related to and similar to the diagnostic activities mentioned, in that they are a large component of those activities. However, they are important enough in their own right to be considered separately. These activities centre on actively working the data produced by a survey and designing action plans based on the survey data.

5. *Education and Training Activities:* Activities designed to improve the skills, abilities, and knowledge of individuals. There are several activities available and several approaches possible. For example, the individual can be educated in isolation from her own work group (say, in a T-group comprised of strangers), or in relation to the work group (say, when a work team learns how to manage interpersonal conflict). The activities may be directed toward technical skills required for effective task performance or toward improving interpersonal competence. For example, activities may be used to explore leadership issues, responsibilities and functions of group members, decision making, problem solving, goal setting and planning, and so forth.

6. *Technostructural or Structural Activities:* Activities designed to improve the effectiveness of the technical or structural inputs and constraints affecting individuals or groups. The activities may take the form of (a) experimenting with new organization structures and evaluating their effectiveness in terms of specific goals or (b) devising new ways to bring technical resources to bear on problems. Included in these activities are certain forms of job enrichment, management by objectives, sociotechnical systems, collateral organizations, and physical settings interventions.

7. *Process Consultation Activities:* Activities on the part of the consultant that help the client to see, understand, and then act on the processes that are taking place in the client's environment. These activities perhaps more accurately describe an approach, a consulting mode in which the client is given insight into the human processes in organizations and taught skills in diagnosing and managing them. Primary emphasis is on processes such as communications, leader and member roles in groups, problem solving and decision making, group norms and group growth, leadership and authority, and intergroup cooperation and competition.

8. *Grid Organization Development Activities:* Activities invented and franchised by Robert Blake and Jane Mouton (1985), which constitute a six-phase change model involving the total organization. Internal resources are developed to conduct most of the programs, which may take from three to five years to complete. The model starts with upgrading individual managers' skills and leadership abilities, moves to team improvement activities, then to

intergroup relations activities. Later phases include corporate planning for improvement, developing implementation tactics, and concluding with an evaluation phase assessing change in the organization culture and looking toward future directions.

9. *Third-Party Peacemaking Activities:* Activities conducted by a skilled consultant (the third party), which are designed to help the other two parties to deal with their interpersonal conflict. They are based on confrontation tactics and an understanding of the processes involved in conflict and conflict resolution.

10. *Coaching and Counselling Activities:* Activities that entail the consultant or other organization members working with individuals to help them (a) define learning goals; (b) learn how others see their behaviour; and (c) learn new modes of behaviour to see if these help them to achieve their goals better. A central feature of this activity is the nonevaluative feedback given by others to an individual. A second feature is the joint exploration of alternative behaviours.

11. *Life- and Career-Planning Activities:* Activities that enable individuals to focus on their life and career objectives and how they might go about achieving them. Structured activities lead to life and career inventories, discussions of goals and objectives, and assessments of capabilities, needed additional training, and areas of strength and deficiency.

12. *Planning and Goal-Setting Activities:* Activities that include theory and experience in planning and goal setting, utilizing problem-solving models, planning paradigms, ideal organization versus real organization "discrepancy" models, and the like. The goal of all of them is to improve these skills at the levels of the individual, group, and total organization.

13. *Strategic Management Activities:* Activities that help key policymakers reflect systematically on their organization's basic mission and goals and environmental demands, threats, and opportunities and engage in long-range action planning of both a reactive and proactive nature. These activities direct attention in two important directions: outside the organization to a consideration of the environment, and away from the present to the future.[1]

To this point we have discussed in general what OD is, how it has changed over the years as society has changed, and how for organizations it has become more crucial, more collaborative, and more complex. We will now present a specific model of OD over five different work settings, two types of change, and three levels of change. Specific OD methods that may be used will then be described.

Five Factors of Change: The Organizational Work Setting

A very useful model of organization development has been created by Jerry Porras and Peter Robinson (1992). A modification of it is shown as Exhibit 15.3. This model illustrates how the organizational work setting can be divided into five parts, all of which fall under and are influenced by the organization's environment. They are: (1) vision; (2) organizing arrangements; (3) social factors; (4) physical setting; and (5) technology. Each part is a separate area that can be addressed by organizational change interventions.

---

[1] From Wendell French and Cecil Bell (1990), *Organization Development: Behavioral Science Interventions for Organization Improvement* (4th edition, pp. 117-119), © 1990 Prentice Hall, Inc. Adapted/reprinted by permission of Prentice Hall, Inc., Englewood Cliffs, New Jersey.

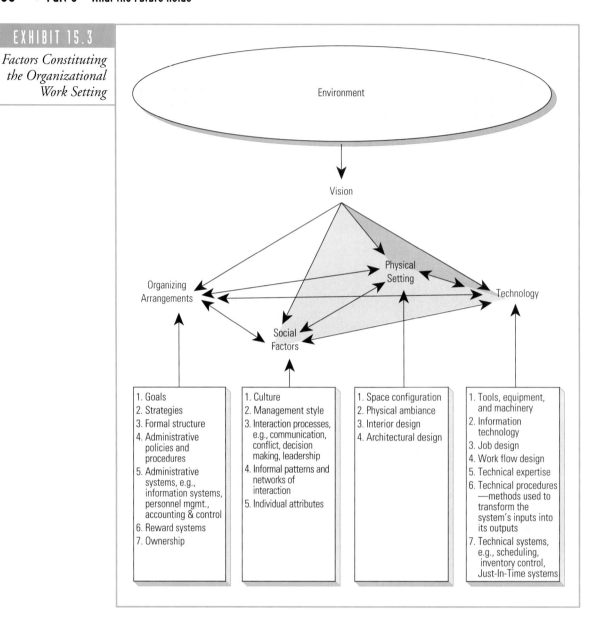

Vision

Vision is affected by the core values and beliefs of the organization (see Chapter 3). In the medium term of 5 to 20 years, it directs the formation of the organization's mission—what it hopes to do. In the long run, it has to do with why the organization was created, its enduring purpose, and the major contribution that the organization expects to make within the next 100 years. In terms of communication, vision is the description of what the organization hopes to do that brings its mission to life.

Organizing Arrangements

These facets of the organization have to do with how the work is ordered, planned, and parcelled out. They have to do as well with the methods and systems of doing the work, not the people who do the work. Goals and strategies for accomplishing the work (Chapter 8), the organization's structure (Chapter 2), policies, procedures, and systems (Chapter 6 on performance evaluation, Chapter 8 on goals, Chapter 14 on careers) are all elements of how the work is organized. Ownership (Chapter 1) is also an important component that can affect the operation of the organization.

Social Factors

This aspect of the organizational work setting has to do with how people interact and relate. Subcomponents are organizational culture (Chapter 3); management style (Chapter 8); interaction processes of communication (Chapter 7); conflict (Chapter 12); decision making (Chapter 11); leadership (Chapter 10); informal patterns and networks of interaction (Chapter 9); individual attributes, such as individual differences (Chapter 5); perception (Chapter 6); and stress (Chapter 13).

Physical Setting

These factors deal with the real physical structures used by an organization. Of interest are how the building itself and its architectural design affect people working within it (e.g., Chapter 4 on job design). Also considered are the interior design (elements of this are discussed in Chapter 7 on communication), physical ambiance (for example Chapter 9 on groups and Chapter 7 regarding non-verbal communication), and how the physical space is configured (e.g., Chapter 9).

Technology

This last factor of the work setting includes all the elements of how the job is designed (Chapter 4), the tools and information used, and how the organizational system's inputs are turned into its outputs.

How frequently are these different approaches to change used? In an examination of 72 field studies of organizational change (described in Porras & Robinson, 1992) organizing arrangements interventions were found in 43% of these studies, social factors interventions in 40%, while 15% involved technological interventions, and 13% involved interventions into the physical setting. In terms of outcome, 40% of the time an OD intervention was positive, 50% of the time there was no change, and in 10% of the cases there was a negative change.

Two Types of Change

Task (or content) change aims to create a specific result. For example, a skill is learned, two groups become more able to cooperate with each other, or a new group decision room is constructed. The change is a task to be accomplished, and is completed when the task is done.

Process change aims to make a difference in how an activity is carried out. Decisions might be made lower in the hierarchy, information to these decision makers could be made available on personal computers located throughout a factory floor, or goal setting procedures could be altered throughout the organization. For a humourous look at an attempt at process change, see this chapter's *Overboard* cartoon.

Three Levels of Change

There are three levels of change in organizations: individual, group/intergroup, and organization. Individual change is aimed at one person. Examples are learning to manage stress, to set goals, or to guide one's career. At the group level change can target relationships within a group, how to be a better leader or manager, negotiating with others, or how groups can use technology to make a higher quality product. How groups relate to each other and manage their interdependence is a topic of intergroup change. Lastly, change can be targeted at the level of the organization as a whole. Examples would be an organization's mission and vision, culture, or socialization practices.

The Change Cube

As we have seen, there are three dimensions of change. The *factor dimension* has five components: vision, organizing arrangements, social factors, the physical setting, and technology. The *types of change* dimension has two categories: task and process. The third dimension that describes *where change takes place* addresses the three levels of individual, group/intergroup, and the organization as a whole. These dimensions may be combined into the change cube shown as Exhibit 15.4. Each cell of the cube represents a particular kind of change at a specific level, type, and factor.

Specific organizational development methods and techniques are shown in the "exploded" change cube of Exhibit 15.5 (page 600). We now turn to a discussion of some of these specific OD methods.

OD Methods and Techniques
At the Individual Level

The aim of **career planning** is to produce a specific plan of what to do to enhance the likelihood of an individual's career success and satisfaction. **Life planning** widens the objective to the subject's life as a whole. It is concerned with how to create a method that will allow the on-going evaluation of the individual's life and changes that may be required.

Stranger T-groups (the "T" stands for training) are formed of people who don't know one another. The group facilitator does not give the group an objective, but lets the group deal with issues as they come up. These issues are expected to be expressed in questions such as "Why are we here?" "What are we going to do now?" "Who is going to take charge if the facilitator won't?" and "How will we get along with each other?" T-groups are meant to help individuals better understand themselves, to learn to diagnose group characteristics, and to be more effective as leaders (Mirvis, 1990).

Career planning
The production of a specific plan of what to do to enhance the likelihood of an individual's career success and satisfaction.

Life planning The production of a specific plan of what to do to enhance the likelihood of an individual's satisfaction with life as a whole.

Stranger T-groups
Training groups whose objective is to help individuals better understand themselves, to learn to diagnose group characteristics, and to be more effective leaders. Participants do not know one another prior to the group's formation.

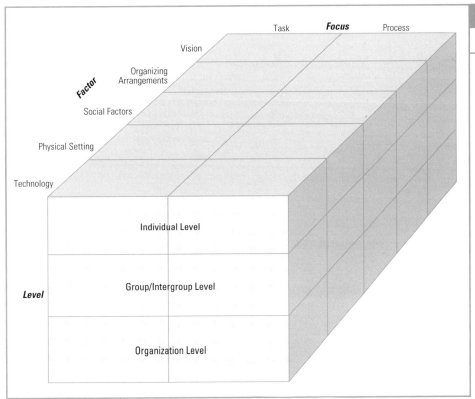

EXHIBIT 15.4

The Change Cube

Grid Organizational Development is a six-step program. The first step occurs at the individual level. Managers learn the basic concepts of the Grid Program. They also examine their own individual skills in team development, communication, and problem solving.

At the Group/Intergroup Level

Grid OD Phase II aims to help managers and their subordinates to work together more effectively. The manager aims to develop a "9,9" Team Management relationship with the group (see Exhibit 10.3). The objective of Grid OD Phase III is intergroup development—the reduction of conflict and increase in cooperation between groups. **Survey feedback** is a method used to gather information from groups on their perception of the group's task and what might be done to accomplish it. This information, usually gathered anonymously from group members, serves as input for decisions about how the organization should be changed.

Force field analysis is a technique used to identify all the forces in support of change and all those opposing change. Each major variable is drawn with an arrow whose length and thickness indicates the magnitude of that variable's force for or against change. When the entire force field is drawn a picture exists of all the change forces and what the net force is likely to be for or against change. Then specific forces can be targeted so that overall change can occur.

Quality circles are groups formed to identify specific problems in the work environment and to propose solutions to those problems. They are usually voluntary, have a membership of 5 to 12, and meet every two to four weeks (Steel & Jennings, 1992). Formal recommendations are made to management about proposed problem solutions. While expectations were initially high for quality circle performance, actual results were not as encouraging. A problem exists when Q-circles are seen as a "quick-fix," circle leaders are not given the training they require in how to manage the group, and authority structures

Grid Organizational Development A six-step program with the objective of improving the functioning and interactions of the individuals and groups of the organization and the organization as a whole.

Survey feedback A method used to gather information from groups on the current organizational situation and what might be done about it.

Force field analysis A technique used to identify all the forces in support of change and all those opposing change.

Quality circles Groups formed to identify specific problems in the work environment and to propose solutions to those problems.

EXHIBIT 15.5

Layers of the Change Cube

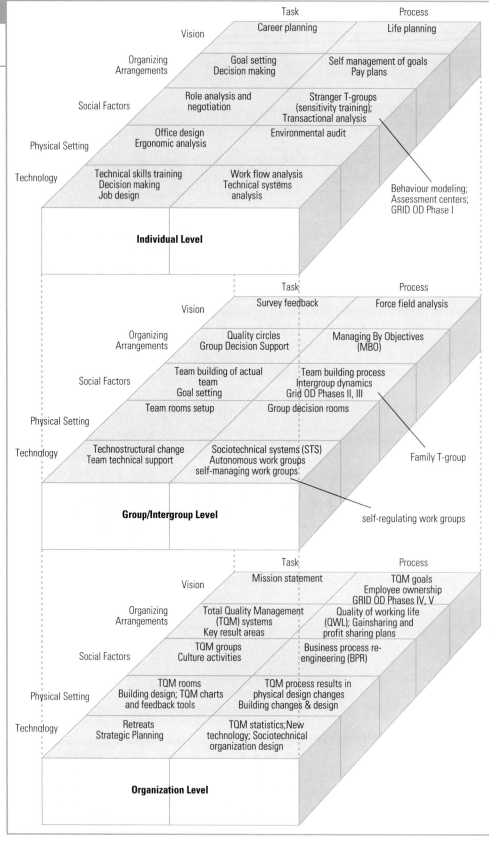

Individual Level

	Task	Process
Vision	Career planning	Life planning
Organizing Arrangements	Goal setting Decision making	Self management of goals Pay plans
Social Factors	Role analysis and negotiation	Stranger T-groups (sensitivity training); Transactional analysis
Physical Setting	Office design Ergonomic analysis	Environmental audit
Technology	Technical skills training Decision making Job design	Work flow analysis Technical systems analysis

Behaviour modeling; Assessment centers; GRID OD Phase I

Group/Intergroup Level

	Task	Process
Vision	Survey feedback	Force field analysis
Organizing Arrangements	Quality circles Group Decision Support	Managing By Objectives (MBO)
Social Factors	Team building of actual team Goal setting	Team building process Intergroup dynamics Grid OD Phases II, III
Physical Setting	Team rooms setup	Group decision rooms
Technology	Technostructural change Team technical support	Sociotechnical systems (STS) Autonomous work groups self-managing work groups

Family T-group

self-regulating work groups

Organization Level

	Task	Process
Vision	Mission statement	TQM goals Employee ownership GRID OD Phases IV, V
Organizing Arrangements	Total Quality Management (TQM) systems Key result areas	Quality of working life (QWL); Gainsharing and profit sharing plans
Social Factors	TQM groups Culture activities	Business process re-engineering (BPR)
Physical Setting	TQM rooms Building design; TQM charts and feedback tools	TQM process results in physical design changes Building changes & design
Technology	Retreats Strategic Planning	TQM statistics; New technology; Sociotechnical organization design

are not in place allowing for group ideas to go up the hierarchy and authority to come down (Mirvis, 1990). It has also been found that Q-circles are likely to have a survival crisis between the second and third years of operation (Steel & Jennings, 1992).

Team building uses theory about groups and group processes (Chapter 9) to help to create more effectively functioning groups. One approach is to seek to improve working relationships by disclosing the internal frames of reference of group members (Mitchell, 1986). Group members using this method would share information regarding their orientation towards work, their backgrounds, past experiences, and current job and life attitudes.

Another approach has been used by Hostess Frito-Lay Co. of Mississauga Ontario (Solomon, 1993). They used a simulation training board game called *Self-managed Work Teams: A Business Simulation*, produced by People Tech Products of Toronto. In the game, groups of five participants take on the roles of the members of a newly formed team charged with producing, installing, and servicing a new product. They learn during the game about working together as a team and the importance of working with other teams.

A **family T-group** is made up of organizational members who know one another and are attempting to learn more about each other and how to work together. The purpose is to explore feelings and processes in the group. Unlike a stranger T-group, the family T-group is expected to transfer their training and learning as a group back to the workplace (e.g., Baldwin & Ford, 1988).

Self-managing work groups are also called autonomous work groups or self-regulating work groups. They are based on socio-technical systems theory. The basic concept is that the social and the technical system should not be worked on separately but jointly optimized. Core characteristics of these groups are (from Steel & Jennings, 1992):

1. The group is responsible for the whole of the group's task;
2. The group has the authority to make and implement its own decisions;
3. Focus will be more on problems with group output;
4. Group members will be trained in group process skills and performing multiple tasks, and will be paid based more on what they know than on what they actually do on a given day;
5. Leadership is by the group itself or by facilitators/coaches who do not manage or lead traditionally but help group members to do the group's leadership work themselves.

At the Organization Level

Organizations often seek to create a **mission statement** that will codify their jointly accepted vision for the future. Then, to have an impact, it must be accepted and used as a basis for organizational actions. Otherwise the mission statement will likely hang unnoticed on the organization's walls. Mission statements can be one outcome of the **retreat** process. Organizational members come together, usually outside the physical bounds of the workplace, to discuss the future. Strategic planning could be another outcome of a retreat. An off-site location is important so that individuals can leave behind their day-to-day operational concerns to concentrate more on the long run.

In a similar vein, Grid OD Phase IV deals with the setting of organizational goals and what the organization should look like in the future. In Grid OD Phase V organizational efforts are made to make those goals a reality. The last Grid phase is to stabilize the goals that have been achieved while determining where more effort is still necessary.

Likert System 4 is an organization-wide method used to analyze and develop a plan for organizational change (Likert, 1967). Likert's System 4 chart of organizational characteristics (see Exhibit 15.6) is used to measure an organization's leadership, motivational methods, communication patterns and characteristics, the style of interaction between members of the organization, how decisions are made, the establishment of and resistance

Team building Theory about groups and group processes is used to help to create more effectively functioning groups.

Family T-group A training group made up of organizational members who know one another and are attempting to learn more about each other and how to work together.

Self-managing work groups Work groups that are responsible for the whole of the group's task, have the authority to make and implement their own decisions, and may do their own training, hiring, and leading.

Mission statement A codification of an organization's jointly accepted vision for the future.

Retreat Organizational members come together, usually outside the physical bounds of the workplace, to discuss the future.

Likert System 4 An organization-wide method used to analyze and develop a plan for organizational change.

EXHIBIT 15.6   LIKERT'S SYSTEM 1 TO 4 PROFILE
OF ORGANIZATIONAL CHARACTERISTICS

	EXPLOITIVE AUTHORITATIVE SYSTEM 1	BENEVOLENT AUTHORITATIVE SYSTEM 2	CONSULTATIVE SYSTEM 3	PARTICIPATIVE GROUP SYSTEM 4
LEADERSHIP				
How much confidence is shown in subordinates?	None	Condescending	Substantial	Complete
How free do subordinates feel to talk about job tasks with their superior?	Not at all	Not very	Rather free	Completely
Are subordinates' ideas sought and constructively used?	Seldom	Sometimes	Usually	Always
MOTIVATION				
What kind of motivators, rewards, and punishments are used?	Fear, threats, punishment, occasional rewards	Rewards and some actual or potential punishment	Rewards, occasional punishment, and some involvement	Economic rewards based on group set goals
Where is responsibility felt for achieving organization's goals?	Mostly at top	Top and middle	Most personnel, especially those at the top	At all levels
COMMUNICATION				
How much communication is aimed at achieving organization's objectives?	Very little	Little	Quite a bit	Much with both individuals & groups
What is the direction of information flow?	Downward	Mostly downward	Down and up	Down, up and sideways with peers
How is downward communication accepted by subordinates?	Viewed with great suspicion	May or may not be viewed with suspicion	Often accepted but may be viewed with caution	Generally accepted, but if not, openly and candidly questioned
How accurate is upward communication?	Inaccurate	Unpopular info. restricted	Some unpopular info. flows	Accurate
How well do superiors know problems faced by subordinates?	Know little	Some knowledge	Quite well	Very well

	EXPLOITIVE AUTHORITATIVE SYSTEM 1	BENEVOLENT AUTHORITATIVE SYSTEM 2	CONSULTATIVE SYSTEM 3	PARTICIPATIVE GROUP SYSTEM 4
INTERACTION				
How do superiors and subordinates interact?	Little, with distrust	Little, with caution	Moderate	Extensive
How much cooperative teamwork is there?	None	Relatively little	A moderate amount	A substantial amount
DECISIONS				
At what level are decisions formally made?	Mostly at top	Policy at top, some delegation	Broad policy at top, more delegation	Throughout but well integrated
Are decision makers aware of problems at lower levels in the organization?	Often unaware	Sometimes aware	Moderately aware	Generally well aware
Where is technical and professional knowledge used in decision making obtained?	From top management	From upper and middle management	From upper, middle and lower management	From all levels
Are subordinates involved in decisions related to their work?	Not at all	Occasionally consulted	Generally consulted	Fully involved
What does the decision-making process contribute to motivation?	Nothing, often weakens it	Relatively little	Some contribution	Substantial contribution
GOALS				
How are organizational goals established?	Orders issued	Orders, some comment invited	After discussion, by orders	By group participation (except in emergencies)
How much covert resistance to goals is present?	Strong resistance	Moderate resistance	Some resistance at times	Little or none

	EXPLOITIVE AUTHORITATIVE SYSTEM 1	BENEVOLENT AUTHORITATIVE SYSTEM 2	CONSULTATIVE SYSTEM 3	PARTICIPATIVE GROUP SYSTEM 4
CONTROL				
How concentrated are review and control functions?	Highly at top I I I I I	Relatively highly at top I I I I I	Moderate delegation to lower levels I I I I I	Quite widely shared I I I I I
Is there an informal organization resisting the formal one?	Yes I I I I I	Usually I I I I I	Sometimes I I I I I	No—same goals as formal I I I I I
What are cost, productivity, and other control data used for?	Policing, punishment I I I I I	Reward and punishment I I I I I	Reward—some self-guidance I I I I I	Self-guidance problem-solving I I I I I

SOURCE: Adapted/reprinted from Rensis Likert (1967), *The Human Organization: Its Management and Value,* New York: McGraw-Hill. Reprinted with permission.

Profit sharing A reward system designed to share any profits among organizational members.

Gainsharing A bonus system based on the mutual sharing of the financial gains of improved productivity.

Business Process Re-engineering (BPR) A philosophy of management that stresses the key concept that companies should refocus themselves around the processes they use to get the product or service to the customer.

Total Quality Management (TQM) A family of OD intervention techniques that includes: quality circles; group processes and goals; statistical techniques; the use of new technologies, production methods, and processes; and work group facilities.

to organizational goals, and how control over organizational activities is achieved. When questions relating to these areas are answered an organizational profile is created. This profile is then compared to the profile of the organization as it could be or should be. The differences between the two profiles indicate areas for change.

Profit sharing and **gainsharing** plans are reward systems designed to share among organizational members the fruits of the organization's work. Profit sharing plans rely on formal statements of profit, and then divide that profit among plan participants. Gainsharing provides bonuses based on the financial gains of improved productivity.

Business Process Re-engineering is a philosophy of management that stresses the key concept that companies should refocus themselves around the processes they use to get the product or service to the customer (*The Economist,* 1994). Old ways of structuring by function such as manufacturing, sales, or marketing should be eliminated. Responsibility and decision making is not done by middle managers, who are bypassed, but by heterogeneous teams of workers who actually make the product or provide the service.

Total Quality Management (TQM) is an entire family of OD intervention techniques. These include: quality circles; group processes and goals; statistical techniques (see Exhibit 15.7); the use of new technologies, production methods, and processes; and work group facilities. TQM, also called Total Quality Control, makes organizational commitment to quality the organization's top priority.

Formal academic studies of TQM are scarce to this point in time. There has been worldwide acceptance of TQM concepts by organizations (For insight into how some cash-strapped Canadian hospitals have been using TQM, see this chapter's *Seeing is Believing* feature.) But the results of implementing TQM have not been all positive. There is evidence that some organizations may adopt TQM for the appearance of quality (and not quality itself), to emulate their larger competitors who already have TQM, or to gain prestige (Judge & Ferris, 1993). Prestige may be at stake because TQM is a "hot" new method of organizational improvement. Many managers want to get on the TQM bandwagon whether or not they want to play the TQM tune. This chapter's *On the One Hand* feature offers two views of the success of TQM.

EXHIBIT 15.7

Continuous Improvement Process (CIP) Tools

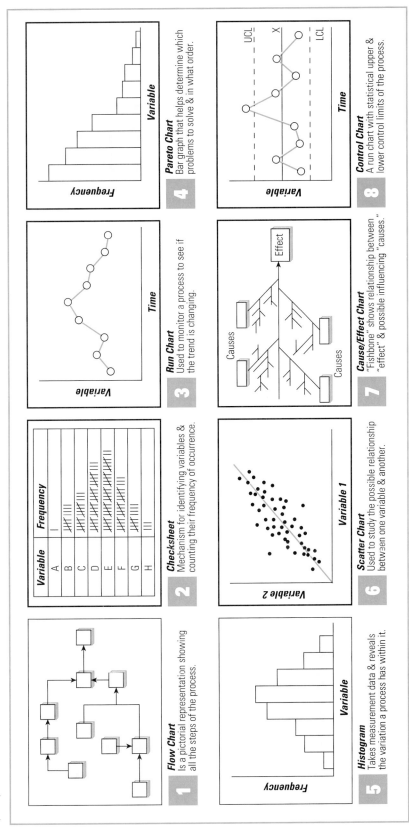

1 Flow Chart
Is a pictorial representation showing all the steps of the process.

2 Checksheet
Mechanism for identifying variables & counting their frequency of occurrence.

Variable	Frequency
A	I
B	III IIII
C	III IIII IIII
D	III IIII IIII IIII
E	III IIII IIII IIII
F	III IIII IIII
G	III IIII IIII
H	III

3 Run Chart
Used to monitor a process to see if the trend is changing.

4 Pareto Chart
Bar graph that helps determine which problems to solve & in what order.

5 Histogram
Takes measurement data & reveals the variation a process has within it.

6 Scatter Chart
Used to study the possible relationship between one variable & another.

7 Cause/Effect Chart
"Fishbone" shows relationship between "effect" & possible influencing "causes."

8 Control Chart
A run chart with statistical upper & lower control limits of the process.

Source: David Graves (1993), "Forget the myths and get on with TQM—Fast," *National Productivity Review*, Summer 1993, p. 309. Reprinted with permission from National Productivity Review, Volume 12 Number 3, Summer 1993, Copyright 1993 by Executive Enterprises, Inc., 22 West 21st Street, New York, NY 10010-6990. ALL RIGHTS RESERVED.

SEEING IS BELIEVING

Costs of health care in Canada are rising rapidly. Some provinces are spending more than one third of their total budget on health care. What is the cause? It is Canada's aging population (which in the near future is expected to keep on aging). Health care costs are higher for older than younger people, and the baby boom bulge is now at middle-age. As this large group of "boomers" gets older health care costs are expected to keep on rising. One government action has been to reduce hospital budgets.

Hospitals have responded with the closure of beds and laying off of hospital staff. These changes can lead to increased waiting times for patients to be admitted for treatment. Hospitals have also been closed or merged in order to save administrative expenses. But these changes are not enough and have had some negative side effects. Some hospitals are now turning to Total Quality approaches to save money and improve patient care.

At St. Michael's hospital in Toronto Dr. Michael Guerriere, the vice-president of clinical affairs, is working to improve the hospital's administrative system and save money. One project was to adapt the hospital's computer record system. Letters about patients from hospital physicians sent to general practitioners are now handled more quickly. Estimated savings for St. Michael's are in the order of $100 000 per year.

Don Schurman, president of the University of Alberta Hospital in Edmonton, is implementing Continuous Quality Improvement (CQI) to improve patient care, cut the costs of providing the care, and also improve working conditions for hospital staff. One initiative is to provide doctors with complete data on the costs for the treatment of each patient. Doctors can then compare notes on how patients with similar conditions were treated by different doctors. The costs of each approach can also be compared. The expectation is that if a lower cost treatment is found to be just as effective or more effective than a higher cost treatment, then cost savings can be made.

Another approach has been to form quality improvement groups variously composed of doctors, nurses, dieticians, physiotherapists, support technicians, and clerical staff. These groups then examine a particular patient care issue from all angles and attempt to find the problems in the system that impede the quality of care, raise costs, or restrict caregiver satisfaction.

The Princess Margaret Hospital in Toronto is Canada's largest cancer treatment centre. A CQI program was started there in June of 1990. An important component of the program was to find out about patient concerns and perceptions of the care being given. One prominent concern of patients was the time lag between first coming to the hospital and the beginning of radiation treatment. This key indicator is now being monitored. Change efforts are focusing on reducing the average number of waiting days experienced by patients.

SOURCES: Based on information in Bruce Little (1992), "Curing what ails system," *The Globe and Mail,* January 18, 1992, pp. A1, A6; Tim Warner (1991), "Implementing continuous quality improvement in a hospital," *Business Quarterly,* Autumn 1991, pp. 42-45; and Judith MacBride-King (1993), "Prescription for change: An interview on improving Canada's health care system with Donald P. Schurman, President, University of Alberta Hospitals," *Canadian Business Review* 20(2): 6-14.

ON THE ONE HAND ...

On the one hand, a 1991 A.T. Kearney study found that 80% of companies in Canada were planning or had Total Quality Management already in place. Japan offers its Deming Prizes to recognize outstanding quality processes. The United States has created the Baldridge award to commend companies for their quality efforts and outcomes. Canada now has its own quality award, the National Quality Institute's Canada Award for Business Excellence. There are many quality improvement success stories. Pratt and Whitney Canada Ltd. has used quality methods to halve new product development time. AMP of Canada Ltd. has achieved an "as promised" on-time delivery rate of its electric and electronic components of 98% to 99%. Steelcase Canada Limited has used quality methods to cut inventory in two manufacturing areas by 50%.

O N   T H E   O T H E R   H A N D ...

There is a good deal of evidence that quality programs in Western companies are failing. Of the Canadian companies surveyed in the 1991 A.T. Kearney study with quality programs in place, only one-third reported appreciable positive results. In an A.T. Kearney study of 100 British firms only 20% believed that their quality programs had produced "tangible results." One reason for such a high failure rate may be that companies are creating quality departments that are isolated from the company's key processes. Cross-functional teams must be created that focus on the processes that produce the company's goods or services. Quality cannot be isolated from processes in a quality department.

Instead, quality must be a part of everyone's way of normally doing business.

A second reason for TQM failure is that change is a long-run process. Results are not likely to be quick. One estimate is that seven years are required before tangible results are seen. Quality in the long run is part of the Japanese culture, where quality programs have had their most dramatic success, but is less part of the Western culture. Workers in the West may not adapt well to the idea that change will be continuous and that the goals set in a quality program will keep changing. Quality programs may therefore start well but gradually grind to a halt as worker momentum falters.

Eugene Polistuk (left) of Celestica Inc. and Steve Delaney of Ford Electronics Manufacturing Coporation receive the National Quality Institute's Canada Award for Business Excellence.

SOURCES: Based on information in Céline Bak (1992), "Lessons from the veterans of TQM," *Canadian Business Review,* Winter 1992, pp. 17-19; and in *The Economist,* "The cracks in quality," April 18, 1992, pp.67-68.

TQM has encountered opposition by organizational members who fear that it is just a new management fad. This can be called the **OD flavour-of-the-month phenomenon**. Having experienced the fad cycle of adoption-disappointment-discontinuation (Steel & Jennings, 1992), these managers are leery of adopting a new OD method until it has proved its worth elsewhere. As Lieutenant Russ Farmer of the USS Theodore Roosevelt aircraft carrier put it: "There's a big fear of this being another touchy-feely program" (Borrus, 1991, p. 134). If top management does not commit to TQM in the longer term (at least five to seven years) and change the corporate culture, then TQM will likely not succeed.

TQM change is large in scale, affecting the whole organization. To understand why, examine the Total Quality Management philosophy that is shown in Exhibit 15.8.

Another important element of TQM is the definition of just what quality is. Management guru Peter Drucker made the point brilliantly when he said:

> Contrary to what most manufacturers believe, a product is not "quality" because it is hard to make and costs a lot of money. That is incompetence. Customers pay only for what is of use to them and gives them value. Nothing else is "quality" (1985, p. 21).

Conceptions of what quality is vary around the world. In Japan quality and artistic standards are tied closely together. The tea ceremony and how to properly fold a kimono are but two common examples of how important it is to the Japanese to perform an activity in the right way. For a further look at concepts of Japanese and American quality, see this chapter's *A Little Knowledge* feature.

Quality is complicated. David Garvin (1984) defined product quality as consisting of the product's performance, features, reliability, conformance to standards, durability, serviceability (including speed and courtesy of repair personnel), aesthetics (the product's appeal to human senses), and quality as perceived by the customer. According to Berry and others (1990), service quality consists of the appearance of the facilities and equipment, the dependability and accuracy of service; the server's willingness to help the customer and the promptness of service; the knowledge and courtesy of staff; and a high degree of caring about the customer.

OD flavour-of-the-month phenomenon

The tendency for management of organizations to seek quick fixes of organizational problems, and when encountering difficulty to flock to the next quick fix offered by consultants and organizational gurus.

EXHIBIT 15.8   ELEMENTS OF TOTAL QUALITY MANAGEMENT (TQM)
PHILOSOPHY

ELEMENT	DEFINITION
1. *Changing the Corporate Culture*	• All employees assume responsibility for quality
2. *Top Management Commitment*	• Active quality leadership by top management
3. *Problem-Solving Training*	• Employee training in quality-analysis tools
4. *Continuous Process Improvement*	• Expanding conceptualization of business processes and focus on their continuous improvement
5. *Measurement Bias*	• Emphasis on measurement and evaluation of organizational processes
6. *Employee Empowerment*	• Empowerment of employees to take action when quality problems are detected
7. *Quality Engineering*	• Design and testing of prototypes to produce robust products
8. *Supplier-Relations Management*	• Proactive supplier relations and prequalifying sources of supply
9. *Cross-Functional Problem Solving*	• Cross-functional teams analyzing and solving cross-functional quality problems
10. *Customer Relationship Management*	• Continuing focus on internal and external customer preferences
11. *Quality Policy Deployment*	• Treating quality improvement as a strategic objective

Over the years the way quality has been defined has changed. Ray Gehani (1993) discussed nine historical approaches to quality and the person or organization with which each is most identified.

1. *Inspected quality* (Frederick W. Taylor). Quality is inspected into the product by identifying and discarding or fixing items of lower quality.

2. *Process-control quality* (W. Edwards Deming). Control needs to be achieved over the production process in order to reduce variations that reduce quality. The ISO 9000 standard is a set of rules designed to measure if processes are under control. Companies may attempt to comply with the standard as a way to improve their product quality.

3. *Quality Management* (Joseph Juran). Quality improvement needs to be made a central part of the organization's business plan.

4. *Total Quality Control* (Armand Feigenbaum). Quality is determined by the customer.

5. *Preventive Quality* (Kaoru Ishikawa). Identify causes of quality problems and fix them. Remember that the next process is your customer.

6. *Design Quality* (Genichi Taguchi). Design quality into the product so that the failure rate is low.

7. *Quality Cost* (Philip Crosby). It is cheaper to do the job right the first time. Aim for zero defects.

8. *Competitive Quality* (David Kearns). Quality can be used as a competitive weapon in the marketplace. Benchmarking is important—learn how the best make their products or deliver their services.

9. *Innovative Quality* (Sony Corp.). Create new products the customer has not yet thought of, for example the Walkman.

A LITTLE KNOWLEDGE

A classic and fascinating book about Japan and the United States is "A Daughter of the Samurai" by Etsu Inagaki Sugimoto. Madame Sugimoto's father was a samurai in Japan, and she was raised in Japan in the late 1800s. Her brother lived in the United States and arranged a marriage for her with an American of Japanese descent. Madame Sugimoto moved to San Francisco in the early 1900s to marry her intended husband and to live with him. Later in life she looked back on the significant changes she had experienced going from feudal Japan to industrial America. Her book was published in 1926, before the outbreak of the Second World War, and well before North Americans came to know of Japan's ability to produce high quality goods.

In this excerpt from her book, we hear from her about the Japanese people's love for quality. This feeling for quality has not been lost in the years since 1900. As you read this passage, think about average Canadians' outlook on the quality of their work and their pride in their work. Compare that to the quality outlook of the Japanese labourer. Also consider the relatively recent Canadian and American emphasis on quality programs in the workplace (Total Quality Management, Continuous Quality Improvement, etc.). How well do the philosophies of those programs fit the mindsets of the local worker in Japan and in Canada?

A few days after, I went down to Matsuo's store [in San Francisco] and he showed me whole shelves of articles called Japanese, the sight of which would have filled any inhabitant of Japan with a puzzled wonder as to what the strange European articles could be. They were all marked, "Made in Japan." Matsuo said that they had been designed by Americans, in shapes suitable for use in this country, then made to order in Japanese factories and shipped direct to America, without having been seen in Japan outside the factory. That troubled me, but Matsuo shrugged his shoulders.

"As long as Americans want them, design them, order them, and are satisfied, there will be merchants to supply," he said.

"But they are not Japanese things."

"No," he replied. "But genuine things do not sell. People think they are too frail and not gay enough." Then he added slowly, "The only remedy is in education; and that will have to begin here."

That night I lay awake a long time, thinking. Of course, artistic, appreciative persons are few in comparison to the masses who like heavy vases of green and gold, boxes of cheap lacquer, and gay fans with pictures of a laughing girl with flower hairpins. "But if Japan lowers her artistic standards," I sighed, "what can she hope for from the world? All that she has, or is, comes from her art ideals and her pride. Ambition, workmanship, courtesy— all are folded within those two words."

I once knew a workman—one who was paid by the job, not the hour—to voluntarily undo half a day's work, at the cost of much heavy lifting, just to alter, by a few inches, the position of a stepping-stone in a garden. After it was placed to his satisfaction, he wiped the perspiration from his face, then took out his tiny pipe and squatted down, near by, to waste still more unpaid-for-time in gazing at the re-set stone, with pleasure and satisfaction in every line of his kindly old face.

As I thought of the old man, I wondered if it was worth while to exchange the delight of heart-pride in one's work for—*anything*. My mind mounted from the gardener to workman, teacher, statesman. It is the same with all. To degrade one's pride—to loose one's hold on the best, after having had it—is death to the soul growth of man or nation.

A final question. What did Matsuo mean when he said "The only remedy is in education; and that will have to begin here"?

Source: Quote from Etsu Inagaki Sugimoto (1926/1966), *A Daughter of the Samurai*, Rutland, VT. and Tokyo: Charles E. Tuttle Co., pp. 194-195.

David Graves (1993) identified what he called the two myths about TQM. The first was that top management must lead the change process. In Graves' point of view change requires a person at some level who has a vision of what the organization could become. Such a person has been called a "champion of change" (Howell & Higgins, 1990a,b), and found to be persistent, self-confident, energetic, and a risk taker. Such champions express a vision that captivates others, pursue unconventional action plans, develop others' potential, and give recognition to others (Howell & Higgins, 1990a). The champion of change needs to get other organizational members on-side to adopt the change and to overcome the resistance of the rest.

EXHIBIT 15.9 STEPS IN THE TOTAL QUALITY MANAGEMENT (TQM) PROCESS

Step 1
Set up Quality Council to oversee the TQM process.

Step 2
Create an index to measure the company's performance – it is this index which is then the target of the TQM process.

Step 3
List the processes within the company – how things are done.

Step 4
Prioritize these processes in terms of which have the most impact on the company's performance.

Step 5
Assign employees who work in each process to a Continuous Process Improvement (CPI) group.

Step 6
Teach those groups TQM philosophy and tools (see Exhibits 15.7 and 15.8).

Step 7
Understand the process by preparing a flow chart.

Step 8
Measure the process.

Step 9
Develop a cause/effect chart, identify underlying causes that lead to diminished performance of the process, and then make changes to the process.

Step 10
Measure the impact of the intervention using a process run chart.

Step 11
Dissolve the Continuous Process Improvement group but continue to monitor the process,

Step 12
Report regularly to the Quality Council regarding process.

Step 13
Confirm the cumulative impact of all CPI groups on the index of company performance. Customers and employees should be more satisfied.

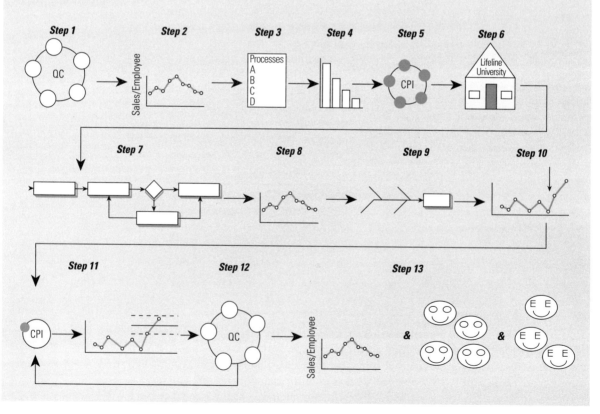

SOURCE: Adapted from David Graves (1993), "Forget the myths and get on with TQM—Fast," *National Productivity Review*, Summer 1993, pp. 310-311. Reprinted with permission from National Productivity Review, Volume 12 Number 3, Summer 1993, Copyright 1993 by Executive Enterprises, Inc., 22 West 21st Street, New York, NY 10010-6990. ALL RIGHTS RESERVED.

Graves' second TQM myth was that a comprehensive TQM strategy is required before the organization embarks on change, and that the strategy is executed faithfully. In fact, says Graves, people in organizations just are not that exact. The point is to just get started. Steps of the TQM process are shown as Exhibit 15.9.

PUTTING IT ALL TOGETHER:
A MODEL OF ORGANIZATIONAL PERFORMANCE AND CHANGE

Now that we have examined the nature of change and the different kinds of OD interventions that exist, we may look at a model of organizational performance and change. The model by Warner Burke and George Litwin (1992) shown as Exhibit 15.10, is a useful one. It makes it clear that many of the elements of organizational functioning that we have discussed in this text are interrelated and jointly affect the bottom line of performance.

Starting at the top of the model, it is important to note that it is the external environment that is the first cause of change. Organizations can be reactive or proactive with their environment, but in either case must exist in relationship to their environment. In the world of the 1990s the external environment is in a state of flux. The rate of change is accelerating. This means that change is more likely to be necessary than ever before.

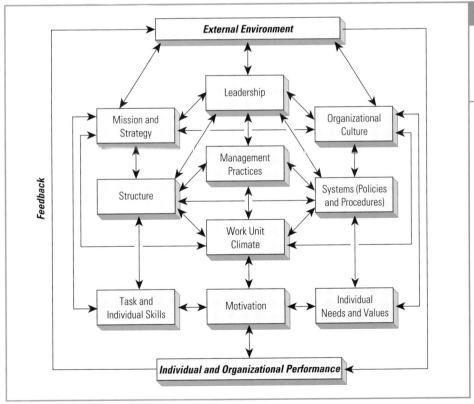

EXHIBIT 15.10

A Model of Organizational Performance and Change

Source: W. Warner Burke and George H. Litwin (1992), "A causal model of organizational performance and change," *Journal of Management* 18: 528. Reprinted by permission.

Learning organization

An organization capable of embracing change on a continuous basis at the individual, group, and organizational levels.

In order to manage change what is required is a **learning organization**. In one view (Kiernan, 1993), the learning organization requires:

- A continuous improvement culture.
- The ability to embrace change.
- That the people of the organization engage in life-long learning.
- That front-line employees are involved in gathering information about the environment and the organization's relationship with elements of the environment.
- That learning take place at the level of the group instead of necessarily at the individual level—learning must be related to the group's task.

The learning organization's philosophy, management practices, employee actions, customer relations, and approach to change are summarized and compared to other ways that organizations deal with their experience in Exhibit 15.11.

The next elements of the model are the organization's leadership, its mission and strategy, and its culture. Leaders must decide how the organization should relate to its external environment. They then need to foster the mission/strategy and culture that will help the organization to adapt. This upper part of the model is transformational in nature. Changes at this level are fundamental and have great leverage. Small modifications can have large results.

The bottom part of the model follows upper-level decisions and actions. It is more transactional in nature. Structure is selected to enable the organization's mission and strategy to be accomplished. Management practices follow leadership decisions. Systems are conceived that reflect the culture that has been formed. Work unit climate is the perception individuals have of how their local work unit is managed. This climate affects individual motivation which, along with individual skills, needs, and values and the structure of tasks to be performed, affect individual and organizational performance.

This is a systems model. Arrows indicate the direct relationships between the variables. Double ended arrows signify that such relationships work both ways. For instance, leadership directly affects management practices which in turn affect leadership. But even though there are no arrows directly connecting every variable in the model to every other, we can assume that such connections really do exist. Organizations are complicated and a change in one place is sure to reverberate through the system. Change is not a simple phenomenon. Peter Senge has said (1990) that while managers may *think* they understand cause and effect in their organizations, the links between variables are much more complex than they think.

Managers in the 1990s have to balance change in both the "soft" areas of the organization, such as culture, leadership, and innovation, and the "hard" areas such as structure, tasks, and policies. This idea is further explored in this chapter's *If You Can't Ride Two Horses At Once, You Shouldn't Be in the Circus* feature (page 614).

CONCLUSION

Managers must be able to effectively deal with complexity and change. Organizations are not simple, with easy-to-understand cause-effect relationships. "As Senge puts it, the scientific managers of today must be researchers who study their own organizations" (Freeman, 1992, p. 38). Organizational development is no longer the province of specialists or consultants. It is the task of every manager. Integrative Case III.1 deals with the operations of Whitbread Merseyside, a brewery in the United Kingdom. The change concepts discussed in this chapter should prove to be useful instruments with which to analyze the case.

In the last chapter of this text we will consider what organizations are likely to be like in the near future and changes that can be expected in the work force. We will also reflect on modernist and postmodernist methods now being used to study organizations. The manager of the future will have to have a well-developed tool-kit of organizational science methods in order to be effective in the more complex and turbulent years ahead.

EXHIBIT 15.11   ORGANIZATIONAL APPROACHES TO EXPERIENCE

	KNOWING	UNDERSTANDING	THINKING	LEARNING
Philosophy	Dedication to the one best way: • Predictable • Controlled • Efficient	Dedication to strong cultural values which guide strategy and action.	A view of business as a series of problems. If it's broke, fix it fast.	Examining, enhancing, and improving every business experience, including how we experience.
Management Practices	Maintain control through rules and regulations, "by the book."	Clarify, communicate, reinforce the company culture.	Identify and isolate problems, collect data, implement solutions.	Encourage experiments, facilitate examination, promote constructive dissent, model learning, acknowledge failures.
Employees	Follow the rules, don't ask why.	Use corporate values as guides to behaviour.	Enthusiastically embrace and enact programmed solutions.	Gather and use information; constructively dissent.
Customers	Must believe the company knows best.	Believe company values insure a positive experience.	Are considered a problem to be solved.	Are part of a teaching/learning relationship, with open, continuous dialogue.
Change	Incremental, must be a fine tuning of "the best way."	Only within the organization's way of seeing and understanding itself.	Implemented through problem-solving programs, which are seen as providing quick fixes.	Part of the continuous process of experience/examine/hypothesize/experiment/experience.

IF YOU CAN'T RIDE TWO HORSES AT ONCE,
YOU SHOULDN'T BE IN THE CIRCUS

Management must be based on a dynamic balance between its hard and soft aspects, working together to create a balance in tension. The following Yin/Yang model of management is based on interviews with individuals in 15 organizations. This model illustrates how management's soft cycle must be balanced with its hard framework.

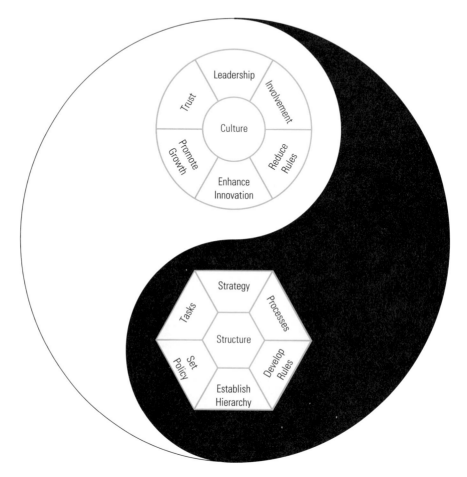

In the soft cycle, culture is considered the central medium and key ingredient which provides the enabling condition to sustain the other six soft-cycle managerial keys. Leadership is shown at the top of the circle because before the cycle can begin to move, there must be strong leadership input as to what the organization's values and beliefs will be. Trust and involvement are shown flanking culture and leadership because they are intrinsically linked to them. It is impossible to develop a strong culture and implement visionary leadership without trust and involvement from organizational members. The remaining three attributes of reducing rules, promoting employee growth, and enhancing innovation are effective when used in conjunction with the first four principles. These seven soft-cycle keys have a synergistic effect on one another. By improving one area there is a corresponding improvement in other areas.

The hard management framework's central component is organizational structure. It provides the base upon which the other keys rest. Strategy is found at the top of the hexagon because it provides the overall direction for the organization. Tasks and processes flank strategy and represent tactics as well as the information and decision systems which are used to carry out the organization's strategy. Policy, rules and procedures, and hierarchy provide the underlying support necessary to the first four keys of the hard side of management.

Source: David A. Van Seters and Richard H.G. Field (1991), "Restoring the balance in management practice." University of Alberta working paper.

EXPERIENCE IS THE BEST TEACHER

Going to college in the 1960s, becoming interested in organizational change was a natural development, for the world seemed to be in upheaval. Technological developments such as the computer were first beginning to reach the factory and the office; social technologies such as the birth control pill were beginning to redefine the role of women; and the re-

building of the economies of those countries defeated in World War II, such as Germany and Japan, were beginning to make them formidable global competitors, thereby reshaping global competition.

Furthermore, the generation that came of age in the 1960s and then entered the workplace was one of the first whose formative experiences or organizational life came from the college campus rather than the military. This provided a powerful force to begin to change organizations in more democratic, collegial, participative rather than hierarchical directions. Many of the themes of student movements on college campuses in the 1960s later became important themes in management in the 1980s. I think this is no accident.

Now, in the 1990s, change is on everyone's mind, from governments that are privatizing industry all over the world to companies that are reshaping their structures in order to be more competitive. This is why my newest book, *The Challenge of Organizational Change: How People Experience it and Manage it*, by myself, Barry Stein, and Todd Jick, published in 1992 by Free Press, again takes up this important theme, but in a world context.

Rosabeth Moss Kanter is the Class of 1960 Professor of Business Administration at the Harvard University Graduate School of Business Administration. Her work on organizational change is known worldwide. The book Kanter mentions discusses many examples of actual organizations undergoing change. The first part deals with emergent change, the second with forced change, and the third with engineered change.

CHAPTER SUMMARY

Organizations, systems, and the people in them are constantly undergoing change. There are four main types of change in organizations. Transformational change is proactive and quantum. The organization seeks to remake itself. Revolutionary change is quantum but reactive. Events outside the organization force it to be remade. Evolutionary change is reactive and incremental. The organization changes over time in small ways to match changes occurring in its environment. Developmental change is proactive and incremental. Here the organization seeks to make the small changes that make it better able to compete.

Organizational development (OD) is a wide-ranging set of behavioural science-based theories, values, strategies, and techniques developed to aid the planned change of the organizational work setting. The focus of OD has shifted over the years as behavioural science theories have themselves changed emphasis. OD is now more complex, more collaborative, and more crucial to the organization. Five areas of the organization that may be the target of OD interventions are the organization's vision, its organizing arrangements, social factors of the work setting, the physical setting of the workplace, and the technology used to accomplish the organization's work. Change efforts targeted on any of these five areas might focus specifically on altering a specific task or content area to create a specific result or on the process of how an activity is carried out. Changes can be aimed at the individual, the group and intergroup relationships, or at the level of the organization as a whole. An important family of OD intervention techniques is Total Quality Management. These make organizational commitment to quality the organization's top priority.

Managers must be able to effectively deal with complexity and change. Organizations are not simple with easy-to-understand cause-effect relationships. Organizational development is no longer the province of specialists or consultants. It is the task of every manager.

QUESTIONS FOR REVIEW

1. Why do organization development methods tend to reflect current conditions in society?

2. What problems might be encountered by an external change agent who is planning to implement a transformational change of the organization?

3. In your opinion, are Total Quality Management and Business Process Reengineering the serious change tools for the 1990s or are they destined to be remembered as fads since gone out of fashion?

4. Which level of change, individual, group/intergroup, or organizational is likely to be the hardest in which to implement change?

5. How transferable do you think OD techniques would be to different countries and corporate cultures around the world?

SELF-DIAGNOSTIC EXERCISE 15.1

One technique that is used to analyze the likelihood of personal or organizational change is Kurt Lewin's "Force Field Analysis." Here is how to try it out for yourself. First, choose an area in your own life that you have been considering changing. For example, you might have thought about quitting smoking or changing jobs. Second, take a blank sheet of paper and draw a line horizontally across the page at the middle of the page. This is the balance point. Third, think about the forces that are operating on you that are in support of the change. For each force for change draw an arrow pushing the balance point upward (toward change). The length and thickness of the arrows should be different for the various forces in support of change. Longer and thicker arrows represent greater force for change.

Now think about the forces that are resisting change. What are the reasons why it is difficult to make changes? Again draw a set of arrows representing these forces, with thicker and longer arrows showing the forces against change. These arrows are drawn so that they are pushing the balance point downward (against change). The diagram below has been provided as a convenience for your first force field analysis.

Finally, examine the total set of forces acting on you both for and against change. Whichever set is greater should act to shift the balance point, either toward a change in your actions or further entrenching your current behaviours. Forces for change that are many and strong but resisted by a like number of powerful forces resistant to change indicate a system in stress. In this case there are intense forces on both sides but the change that would reduce the stress is not occurring.

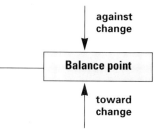

EXPERIENTIAL EXERCISE 15.1

Common Supervisory Problems

Managers and supervisors confront common problems in their relationships with subordinates. The purpose of this exercise is to examine some of these problems and to begin to learn how to deal with them.

Step 1: The class as a whole will create a list of common supervisory problems. The instructor will write this list on the chalkboard or on a flip-chart. A beginning to this list of problems is:

- The poorly performing subordinate
- Dealing with paid staff and volunteers in the same office
- The employee who is continually late for work
- The staff member who must be fired because of documented poor performance
- Two staff members who just don't like each other but have to work together
- An employee who is coming to work under the influence of a drug or alcohol
- An employee who has had to take a great deal of time off to help with problems at home with the children.
- A subordinate who is being overwhelmed with work and is missing deadlines and appointments, even though others are able to effectively handle similar work loads
- A staff member who refuses to accept responsibility for delegated work and keeps coming back to the supervisor for decisions about what to do next.

Step 2: The class as a whole will discuss some of these problems, how they come about, and how to deal with them.

Step 3: Two volunteers come to the front of the class and role play one of the problems. The instructor will assign the manager and subordinate roles and the problem to be role played.

Step 4: After discussing what was done well in the role play, the class will break into groups of four. Two persons in each group will take the manager and subordinate roles and role play one of the problem situations. The two observers will then comment on their approach. It is especially important to comment on what could be done more effectively to deal with the problem in the future. Then switch roles in the group and role play and discuss other problem situations.

SELF-GUIDED LEARNING ACTIVITY

Mark Twain had a useful approach to personal change. First he created a list of important traits he wanted to have. The list was put in a book with one page for each week of the year. Then every day he marked off how many times his actions were consistent or inconsistent with those traits. Over time, by rewarding himself with a check mark or punishing himself with an "X," he was able to change himself into the man he hoped to become. Perhaps this approach would work for others. What is required is a good idea of what kind of person you would like to be and the willingness to work towards your goal.

CASE 15.1

MANAGER'S CASE FILE: CHANGES FOR BETTER OR WORSE

When the position of department supervisor opened up at Business Works, Inc., Joe Hayes, the senior and most qualified staff member in the department, was promoted to fill the vacancy. For the first four months, he ran the department well, having no problems with former co-workers or meeting production schedules. About this time, the company implemented plans to expand their services and eight new workers were added to Joe's staff. Most of them were fresh out of school and eager to make their mark on the world.

While the new staffers were being oriented into the department, production fell off somewhat but not enough to cause serious problems. Joe had expected this. As he told one of the older staffers, "It's just until they get the hang of things." And in a few weeks' time, Joe's prediction of a return to normal came to pass. It was shortly after this that one of the new staffers approached him with an idea.

"Joe," Mike began, "I want to run an idea by you. I think it would speed up the paperwork that we have to do with the production jobs."

Joe saw the validity of the idea so he decided to give it a try. "Let's try it out on a small scale at first," he said to Mike, "just in your group and see how it works."

Mike became excited and promised to do his best to make the idea work.

As the new process began to prove itself, Joe expanded its use to the other work groups and was pleased to see production moving more quickly.

Some of the older workers were skeptical at first. They were used to the old way of doing things. However, at Joe's insistence that they at least give the new idea a try, and its having proved itself in one work group, they relented and began to use the new process. Over time, they agreed that Mike had had a good idea and were happy that their work had become somewhat easier.

Seeing the success of the new process and being encouraged to go to Joe with new ideas, more of the younger staffers came forward to offer suggestions. Joe listened to and considered all the ideas of his staff members, rejecting those he felt had a low probability of success and spot-testing those he felt had a good chance of working. At times, he had as many as three groups each testing out a different idea.

Having received praise from upper management for having the foresight and flexibility to implement the systems that proved themselves, Joe was unprepared for the meeting his older workers had requested.

Four of the senior staff members entered Joe's office at the agreed upon time. "We represent the senior members of the department," Shane, the appointed spokesman, said, "and we've come to protest your new work methods."

"Go ahead," Joe said, "I'm listening."

Encouraged, Shane began, "While we agreed to try out Mike's idea, we just can't keep up with all the changes you're making. It's becoming confusing. One department is doing things one way; another department is doing the same thing a different way. You've got so many ideas running at once that everything is starting to come out backwards. That last idea didn't even work on a large scale; it set us back three weeks. The only reason it didn't set us further behind is that we went back to using the old system before the situation got too far out of hand. We want you to go back to the old ways of doing things. We always managed to get the work out on time. We don't want to implement anymore of these darned changes."

"Admittedly, that one idea was bad judgment on my part," Joe confessed, "but some of these ideas are really better ways of doing things. It's just a matter of trying them out and incorporating them if they work."

"We like our work just the way it is," Shane said, "and since we get the work out on time, although not ahead of schedule, we don't see why you would try to force us to change."

After they had said all they came to say, the staffers left Joe's office and returned to work. Joe had assured them that he would try to work something out to everyone's satisfaction. Actually, Joe didn't know what to do. If he discontinued considering changes in methods, Joe could lose his credibility, and the younger staffers would be frustrated and consider leaving the company. On the other hand, Joe didn't want the older workers to feel displaced. He felt that resentment would grow between the two groups and he wondered what he could do that would satisfy everyone.

Questions:

1. Is there any way Joe could satisfy both groups of workers?

2. How could Joe get the older workers to use some of the new ideas?

3. How can Joe keep resentment from growing between the two groups?

THE LIMORA COMMUNITY HEALTH CENTRE AND THE LIMORA HOSPITAL

The Limora Community Health Centre (LCHC) is located in Tanzania (Africa) and is part of a 280-bed hospital. LCHC is headquartered in its own building which is located in the Limora Hospital compound.

Limora is a Lutheran church hospital and is one of three Lutheran hospitals in the diocese, all of which are answerable to Bishop Marizin, the Diocesan Bishop. The Director of LCHC is Dr. Jan MacDonald, an expatriate who was born in Scotland and trained there as a family physician. Dr. MacDonald has been living and working at Limora for the past 10 years. He started working at Limora Hospital but after three years was asked to become Director of LCHC and to take complete responsibility for the program.

In the years prior to MacDonald becoming director, the community health program had a series of directors, the majority of which stayed for very short periods of time. A number of the former directors did not have any real interest or experience in primary health care and took the position mainly because they were asked to do so. The result was that for several years the community health program was in a state of "organizational drift." Staff turnover at LCHC was extremely high prior to MacDonald becoming director and the Centre continues to have difficulty retaining personnel. Many of the nursing staff at LCHC stay for a short time and then request a transfer to work back at the hospital. One of the former staff members commented:

> The work at the Centre was interesting, but you always felt that everyone was on a different wavelength. There wasn't any sense that people were working together as a team. LCHC seems to lack the necessary organizational glue to hold it together.
>
> At the hospital we all share the same values, e.g., good quality patient care. At the Centre there were too many surprises! None of us really knew what we were supposed to be doing. I came out of a hospital environment, and I never really knew what we were supposed to be doing in the Community Health Centre. It was all sort of vague and indefinite. People started

out with great enthusiasm but got discouraged quickly and ended up transferring back to work in the hospital or finding a job somewhere else.

There didn't seem to be very much commitment among the staff to the work at the Centre. Maybe this was because we never received an orientation or proper training for the jobs we were supposed to be doing. Several of us who came from the same village were hired, and we were expected to get on with the job.

It took me about three weeks before I began to catch on, but by that time, I had become very discouraged. I had no idea how the various parts of the job were supposed to come together.

I was never told exactly what my job was or what my duties were … everything was pretty vague and unpredictable. The most frustrating part was when we went out to the village to try to organize the local people. It was like "the blind leading the blind." It's no wonder that we had so little success. It became pretty discouraging after a while.

I don't know if I just wasn't the right person for the job or did not receive the proper training. My supervisor gave me a good evaluation after three months, but I don't know why. I didn't feel I was doing a good job, but the supervisor gave everyone a good evaluation. She was very nice, and I don't think she wanted to hurt anyone's feelings or get people mad at her.

The result was that everyone in her unit got exactly the same evaluation, so the evaluation didn't really mean anything. There was one exception.

One staff member who worked extremely hard all the time got the supervisor annoyed with her two weeks before her evaluation. It was a personal thing and really didn't have anything to do with her work, but it counted against her nevertheless. Any confidence I had in the system up to then was destroyed.

There was an ongoing struggle between the hospital and the LCHC for available physical and human resources. Land Rovers, which were obtained for the work of the community health unit, would end up being used by the hospital. There were a lot of times when we couldn't go out because our vehicles were being used for hospital business. There was also a fierce competition for the best nurses. The hospital matron wanted to use the best nurses in the hospital, and everyone was afraid of her, so she got the pick of the new graduates out of the Limora nursing school.

There was a lot of conflict between Dr. Taturo, the doctor in charge of the hospital, and Dr. Jan MacDonald, the Director of LCHC, over budgetary matters—LCHC is funded by money from a variety of external funding organizations. All the money goes into the hospital budget from where it is supposed to get reallocated. However, LCHC never knows where it stands financially because the hospital has been unable to provide it with a complete accounting statement on a regular basis. LCHC has tried keeping its own record of expenditures and receivables but some of these are only estimates because some of the invoices go directly to the hospital accounting department as do a lot of the cheques from the granting agencies. The inability of hospital accounting to provide LCHC with a satisfactory break-out of the budget has resulted in a deteriorating relationship between the hospital and LCHC, which is characterized by increasingly poor communication between the two units.

A further problem has developed around Dr. Kiganda, the Associate Director of the hospital, who has been seconded to LCHC for two days per week. Dr. Kiganda is a surgeon who also has a Master's Degree in Primary Health Care (PHC). Dr. Kiganda believed the work of the Centre is extremely impor-tant and that it will ultimately reduce the number of patients coming to the hospital for treatment for various recurring illnesses.

Other doctors at the hospital do not share Dr. Kiganda's view and believe that many of the resources going to LCHC would be better utilized by the hospital, including Dr. Kiganda's time. Whenever the hospital is short staffed or there is an emergency, there is a great deal of pressure on Dr. Kiganda to fill in even if he is scheduled to be working at the Centre. There is added pressure for Dr. Kiganda to be available whenever the doctor in charge of the hospital is called away on business. There are many remarks made such as: "Where is Dr. Kiganda? He is supposed to be here in the hospital when we need him, not running around the countryside. He needs to get his priorities straight."

Staff at LCHC say that they do not have the power to take local initiatives without the power of higher authorities, especially the Bishop. The Bishop, for his part, says that staff have the power to take whatever initiatives are required, but they have failed to do so.

Communication within the hospital and between the hospital and the community health centre has become strained, and there appears to be a great deal of unresolved conflict within and between the two organizations. The poor communication and the unresolved conflict are contributing to poor morale and low motivation among employees in the two units with the result that neither unit is operating as effectively or efficiently as it should.

Dr. MacDonald and Dr. Taturo both recognize the need for changes, and the Bishop has invited your group to carry out an OD intervention to assist in bringing about the required changes.

SOURCE: Copyright © 1989 by Dr. Carl Garry and Loraine Spencer Garry. Prepared for the Instituto Superiore di Sanità (Italian National Institute of Health), ICHM Course in Rome.

Questions

1. What theoretical approach will your group use to analyze the need for change and to develop a change plan?

2. Assume that you have called a meeting with Bishop Marizin, Dr. Taturo, and Dr. MacDonald. What do you hope to accomplish in this meeting? What will be the agenda?

3. What should be done about the staffing policies of the hospital and the community health centre, the use of the Land Rovers, and the integrated budgets of the hospital and the centre?

4. What is your plan for Dr. Kiganda? Should he be part of any meetings?

REFERENCES

Bak, Céline (1992). "Lessons from the veterans of TQM." *Canadian Business Review*, Winter 1992, pp. 17-19.

Baldwin, Timothy T., & J. Kevin Ford (1988). "Transfer of training: A review and directions for future research." *Personnel Psychology* 41: 63-104.

Beer, Michael, & Anna Elise Walton (1987). "Organizational change and development." *Annual Review of Psychology* 38: 339-367.

Berry, Leonard L., Valarie A. Zeithaml, & A. Parasuraman (1990). "Five imperatives for improving service quality." *Sloan Management Review* 31(4): 29-38.

Blake, Robert R., & Jane Srygley Mouton (1985). *The Managerial Grid III: The Key to Leadership Excellence*. Houston: Gulf Publishing Company.

Borrus, Amy (1991). "The Navy tries to get its ship in shape." *Business Week*, October 25, 1991, p. 134.

Burke, W. Warner, & George H. Litwin (1992). "A causal model of organizational performance and change." *Journal of Management* 18: 523-545.

Clement, Ronald W. (1992). "The changing face of Organizational Development: Views of a manager-turned-academic." *Business Horizons* 35(3): 6-12.

Drucker, Peter F. (1985). "Entrepreneurial strategies." *California Management Review*, Winter 1985, 27(2): 9-25.

Economist, The (1992). "The cracks in quality," April 18, 1992, pp. 67-68.

Economist, The (1994). "Re-engineering Europe." February 26, 1994, pp. 63-64.

Freeman, David H. (1992). "Is management still a science?" *Harvard Business Review*, November/December, pp. 26-38.

French, Wendell L., & Cecil H. Bell, Jr. (1990). *Organization Development: Behavioral Science Interventions for Organization Improvement* (4th edition). Englewood Cliffs, NJ: Prentice Hall, Inc.

Garvin, David A. (1984), "What does 'product quality' really mean?" *Sloan Management Review* 26(1): 25-43.

Gehani, R. Ray (1993). "Quality value-chain: a meta-synthesis of frontiers of quality movement." *Academy of Management Executive* 7(2): 29-42.

Gleick, James (1987). *Chaos: Making a New Science*. New York: Viking.

Goss, Tracy, Richard Pascale, & Anthony Athos (1993). "The reinvention roller coaster: Risking the present for a powerful future." *Harvard Business Review*, November-December 1993, pp. 97-108.

Graves, David (1993). "Forget the myths and get on with TQM—Fast." *National Productivity Review* 12: 301-311.

Howell, Jane M., & Christopher A. Higgins (1990a). "Champions of change: Identifying, understanding, and supporting champions of technological innovations." *Organizational Dynamics*, Summer 1990, pp. 40-55.

Howell, Jane M., & Christopher A. Higgins (1990b). "Champions of technological innovation." *Administrative Science Quarterly* 35: 317-341.

Jaeger, Alfred M. (1986). "Organizational development and national culture: Where's the fit?" *Academy of Management Review* 11: 178-190.

Judge, Timothy A., & Gerald R. Ferris (1993). "Social context of performance evaluation decisions." *Academy of Management Journal* 36: 80-105.

Kanter, Rosabeth Moss, Barry A. Stein, & Todd Jick (1992). *The Challenge of Organizational Change: How People Experience it and Manage it.* New York: The Free Press.

Kiernan, Matthew J. (1993). "The new strategic architecture: Learning to compete in the twenty-first century." *Academy of Management Executive* 7(1): 7-21.

Kuhn, Thomas S. (1970). *The Structure of Scientific Revolutions.* Second edition. Chicago: University of Chicago Press.

Likert, Rensis (1967). *The Human Organization: Its Management and Value.* New York: McGraw-Hill.

Little, Bruce (1992). "Curing what ails system." The *Globe and Mail,* January 18, 1992, pp. A1, A6.

MacBride-King, Judith (1993). "Prescription for change: An interview on improving Canada's health care system. With Donald P. Schurman, President, University of Alberta Hospitals." *Canadian Business Review* 20(2): 6-14.

McGill, Michael E., & John W. Slocum, Jr. (1993). "Unlearning the organization." *Organizational Dynamics* 22(2): 67-79.

McLaughlin, Hugh, & Richard Thorpe (1993). "Action learning—A paradigm in emergence: the problems facing a challenge to traditional management education and development." *British Journal of Management* 4: 19-27.

Miller, Danny (1992). "The Icarus Paradox: How exceptional companies bring about their own downfall." *Business Horizons,* January-February 1992, pp. 24-34.

Mirvis, Philip H. (1988). "Organization development: Part I—An evolutionary perspective." In William A. Pasmore and Richard W. Woodman (Eds.), *Research in Organizational Change and Development* (Volume 2, pp. 1-57). Greenwich, CT: JAI Press.

Mirvis, Philip H. (1990). "Organization development: Part II—A revolutionary perspective." In William A. Pasmore and Richard W. Woodman (Eds.), *Research in Organizational Change and Development,* (Volume 4, pp. 1-66). Greenwich, CT: JAI Press.

Mitchell, Rex (1986). "Team building by disclosure of internal frames of reference." *Journal of Applied Behavioral Science* 22: 15-28.

Nadler, David A., & Michael L. Tushman (1990). "Beyond the charismatic leader: Leadership and organizational change." *California Management Review,* Winter 1990, 32(2): 77-97.

Peters, Tom (1990). "Get innovative or get dead (Part 1)." *California Management Review,* Fall 1990, 33(1): 9-26. Also see the second part to this article by Tom Peters (1991), "Get innovative or get dead (Part 2)." *California Management Review,* Winter 1991, 33(2): 9-23.

Porras, Jerry I., & Peter Robertson (1992). "Organizational development: Theory, practice, and research." In Marvin D. Dunnette and Leaetta M. Hough (Eds.), *Handbook of Industrial and Organizational Psychology,* Second Edition (Volume 3, pp. 719-822). Palo Alto, CA: Consulting Psychologists Press, Inc.

Sanzgiri, Jyotsna, & Jonathan Z. Gottlieb (1992). "Philosophic and pragmatic influences on the practice of organization development, 1950-2000." *Organizational Dynamics* 21(2): 57-69.

Senge, Peter M. (1990). "The leader's new work: Building learning organizations." *Sloan Management Review,* Fall, 1990, pp. 7-23.

Shepard, Herbert A. (1985). "Rules of thumb for change agents." *OD Practitioner,* December 1985, 17(4):1-5.

Solomon, Charlene Marmer (1993). "Simulation training builds teams through experience." *Personnel Journal*, June 1993, pp. 100-108.

Steel, Robert P., & Kenneth R. Jennings (1992). "Quality improvement technologies for the 90s: New directions for research and theory." *Research in Organizational Change and Development* 6: 1-36.

Sugimoto, Etsu Inagaki (1926/1966). *A Daughter of the Samurai.* Rutland, VT. and Tokyo: Charles E. Tuttle Co.

Van Seters, David A., & Richard H.G. Field (1991). "Restoring the balance in management practice." University of Alberta working paper.

Warner, Tim (1991). "Implementing continuous quality improvement in a hospital." *Business Quarterly*, Autumn 1991, pp. 42-45.

Weick, Karl E. (1984). "Small wins: Redefining the scale of social problems." *American Psychologist* 39: 40-49.

Whyte, William Foote (1989). "Advancing scientific knowledge through participatory action research." *Sociological Forum* 4: 367-385.

Whyte, William Foote (1991). "Participation strategies in agricultural R & D." In William Foote Whyte (Ed.) *Participatory Action Research* (pp. 169-178). Beverly Hills, CA: Sage.

FURTHER READING

An interesting look at organizational change is by David Kearns and David A. Nadler (1992), *Prophets in the Dark: How Xerox Reinvented Itself and Beat Back the Japanese*, New York: HarperCollins. That OD may be led by internal consultants is discussed in "Restructuring for survival—the Navistar case" by Chet Borucki and Carole K. Barnett, published in *The Executive*, February, 1990, pages 36-49. A fascinating and detailed look at the implementation of Total Quality at Alcoa is Peter J. Kolesar's 1993 article titled "Vision, values, milestones: Paul O'Neill starts total quality at Alcoa," published in the *California Management Review*, Volume 35(3), pages 133-165.

For further reading on chaos theory as it applies to psychology, see "Chaos, self-organization, and psychology" by Scott Barton in the January 1994 issue of *American Psychologist*, pages 5-14.

The cultural relativity of OD is discussed in Risto Tainio and Timo Santalainen (1984), "Some evidence for the cultural relativity of organizational development programs," *Journal of Applied Behavioral Science* 20: 93-111.

A recent book by Gareth Morgan of York University in Toronto is *Imaginization: The Art of Creative Management*, published by Sage. The use of creative imagery is shown as an approach to the management of change.

Three pioneers of the quality movement are W. Edwards Deming in the area of Process-control quality, Joseph Juran in Quality Management, and Kaoru Ishikawa on Preventive Quality. Three of their representative books are: W. Edwards Deming (1988), *Out of the Crisis*, Cambridge, Mass.: Massachusetts Institute of Technology, Center for Advanced Engineering Study; Joseph M. Juran (1988), *Juran on Planning for Quality*, New York: Free Press; and Kaoru Ishikawa (1985), *What is Total Quality Control? The Japanese Way*, Englewood Cliffs, NJ: Prentice Hall. For background on W. Edwards Deming, see the book by Cecilia S. Kilian (1992) titled *The World of W. Edwards Deming*, 2nd Edition, published in Knoxville,

Tennessee by SPC Press, Inc. A fourth quality pioneer is Genichi Taguchi in the area of design quality. For more information see the article by Genichi Taguchi and Don Clausing (1990), "Robust quality," *Harvard Business Review* 68(1): 65-75.

To explore the two sides of the Total Quality Management argument—does it work or not—see Selwyn W. Becker (1993), "TQM does work: Ten reasons why misguided attempts fail," *Management Review*, May 1993, pp. 30-33; Oren Harari (1993), "Ten reasons why TQM doesn't work," *Management Review*, January 1993, pp. 33-38; and Oren Harari (1993), "The eleventh reason why TQM doesn't work," *Management Review*, May 1993, pp. 31-36. A discussion of how TQM can fail in large part because of the organization's culture is given by Gervase R. Bushe of Simon Fraser University in his 1988 article, "Cultural contradictions of statistical process quality control in American manufacturing organizations," published in the *Journal of Management*, 14: 19-31.

The book *Employee Involvement and Total Quality Management,* published in 1992 by Jossey-Bass, explores trends in these two areas of organizational development. The authors are Edward E. Lawler, III, Susan Albers Mohram, and Gerald E. Ledford, Jr. Further information on quality circles is given by Ricky W. Griffin (1988), "Consequences of quality circles in an industrial setting: A longitudinal assessment," *Academy of Management Journal* 31: 338-358, and Dianna T. Sheffield, Lynn Godkin, and Richard Drapeau (1993), "An industry-specific study of factors contributing to the maintenance and longevity of quality circles," *British Journal of Management* 4: 47-55.

A model of culture, leadership, and TQM is presented by Concordia University's David A. Waldman (1993), in "A theoretical consideration of leadership and Total Quality Management," *Leadership Quarterly* 4: 65-80.

Kaizen is a Japanese word meaning continual improvement. See the book by Masaaki Imai (1986) titled *Kaizen: The Key to Japan's Competitive Success,* published in New York by Random House.

An instrument useful for measuring eight critical factors of quality management is presented in Appendix A of Jayant V. Saraph, P. George Benson, and Roger G. Schroeder (1989), "An instrument for measuring the critical factors of quality management," *Decision Sciences* 20: 810-829.

Further references on quality management are: Lloyd Dobyns & Clare Crawford-Mason (1991), *Quality or Else: The Revolution in World Business*, Boston: Houghton Mifflin Company, Jon Woronoff (1992), *The Japanese Management Mystique: The Reality Behind the Myth*, Chicago: Probus Publishing; William F. Roth, Jr. (1992), *A Systems Approach to Quality Improvement*, New York: Praeger Publishers; Warren H. Schmidt and Jerome P. Finnigan (1992), *The Race Without a Finish Line: America's Quest for Total Quality*, San Francisco: Jossey-Bass; Thomas H. Berry (1991), *Managing the Total Quality Transformation,* New York: McGraw-Hill; H. Gitlow (1989), *Tools and Methods for the Improvement of Quality*, New York: Irwin; Ted Cocheu (1993), *Making Quality Happen*, San Francisco: Jossey-Bass; and David A. Garvin (1987), *Managing Quality: The Strategic and Competitive Edge*, New York: The Free Press.

Two textbooks on Total Quality Management are Vincent K. Omachonu and Joel E. Ross (1994), *Principles of Total Quality* , Delray Beach, FL: St. Lucie Press; and James W. Dean, Jr. & James R. Evans (1994), *Total Quality: Management, Organization & Strategy*, St. Paul, MN: West Publishing.

Two TQM videos titled *Quality or Else* and *Prophet of Quality* are available from Films, Incorporated, 5547 North Ravenswood, Chicago IL 60640-1199, telephone 800-323-4222.

The manual *ISO 9001, The Standard Companion*, is available from ISO Easy, P.O. Box 21, Middletown, NJ 07748. It describes the standard in plain English.

WHITBREAD MERSEYSIDE

In December 1981 Mr. Bernard King, Managing Director of Whitbread West Pennines, met with Len Oliver, the newly appointed general manager of Whitbread Merseyside, to discuss the troubled state of affairs in the company's Merseyside operations. Plagued by strikes, a history of poor brewery management and a recent rapid decline in sales volume and market share, the Merseyside company was considered to be one of Whitbread's most serious problem areas. Mr. King presented his view of the situation to Len Oliver.

We can't just throw up our hands and say 'Liverpool is unmanageable.' We earn a lot of money there and we could be earning a lot more. What you've got to do, Len, is break the mould. Business as usual is not good enough. I'll support you—but how you do it is up to you.

THE COMPANY

Whitbread and Company was established in 1742 when Samuel Whitbread founded a brewery bearing his name in London. The company gradually expanded to become a national brewer, and by the 1980s it operated twenty breweries and forty-one distribution depots in the United Kingdom as well as 7000 pubs and more than 100 Beefeater steak houses. The company also played a role in the wine, spirits, and soft drinks industries in the U.K. Sales in the year ending February 28, 1981 were £782 million and net profits were £60 million. Since 1978, growth in sales had been approximately 11% per year while profits had increased an average of 16% per annum.

Whitbread's operations were managed as nine regional companies, listed in Exhibit 1. The West Pennines company consisted of three sites, Liverpool, Salford and Blackburn (Shadsworth), which combined distribution and production operations, and five separate distribution depots. Whitbread Merseyside (Liverpool based) was a subunit of Whitbread West Pennines, comprising Whitbread's Liverpool operation and depots in Birkenhead (across the Mersey River from the Liverpool brewery) and in Llandudno, North Wales.

Bernard King became Managing Director of Whitbread West Pennines in June 1981, having spent the previous six years running the company's soft drink operations. He inherited a situation which was considered by many observers to be an industrial relations nightmare, with profit performance significantly below standard. Peter Watkins, the general manager of Whitbread Merseyside when Bernard arrived, explained some of the origins of the company's industrial relations problems to his new boss:

When you realize that not so long ago Liverpool dock workers were kept in cages, with a chosen few allowed out to unload ships for the day, you begin to understand why the Liverpool workers and their unions are so militant. They are tough, smart (often smarter than the managers who are trying to control them), and a number of them are waging an ideological war to overthrow the capitalist system. The result of this has been that many major British union disputes, particularly dock and transport disputes, have begun in Liverpool and then spread to the rest of the country.

Whitbread's history of labour problems here is a long one. Our employees belong to the Merseyside branch of the Transport and General Worker's Union (the 'T and G'), which is reputed to be the toughest branch of a tough union. The full time union official who runs Merseyside is a strong character who more than once has forced a firm out of business. In the late 1960's we went through a major struggle with him and the T and G to have the third man eliminated from our delivery fleet. In the early 1970's the issue was our use of hired transport. We wanted to maintain a fleet of trucks and employees capable of meeting our base monthly load, and use hired transport to meet our seasonal peaks. The union felt we should staff to meet our peak loads on a year round basis. These are just two of the struggles we've had over the years, and both were long acrimonious disputes involving intermittent work stoppages and slow downs, and demanding a huge amount of management time.

We have also added to our own problems. In 1972, for instance, senior Whitbread management announced that over the next several years a number of regional breweries, including Liverpool, would be closed. The result was that many of our older, stable employees left the company and were replaced by younger, more transient people. However, one year later the order was rescinded. The growth of lager beer had significantly exceeded market projections, which meant that the breweries would stay open after all. Then, in quick succession in 1973 and 1974, it was again announced that the breweries would be closed, and then that they would stay open.

This vacillation was the result of differences of opinion concerning the appropriate size of a new brewery which the company was planning to build at Samlesbury, near Blackburn. Production planners wanted this to be a very large, efficient brewery, which would absorb the capacity of small local breweries like Liverpool, Blackburn and Salford, and it was their intentions which led to the second closure announcement. However, the marketers in Whitbread believed that the existence of these local breweries was very important to British beer drinkers who didn't want to drink a standardized product, but something which had been brewed locally to local tastes. In the end it appears to have been a draw, as the Blackburn brewery was closed in 1978 after Samlesbury opened, but Liverpool and Salford are still in operation. The uncertainty generated by the whole exercise definitely hurt our relationship with the unions.

More recently, Bernard, we have tried to put in place wealth creation schemes which would result in profit sharing for hourly paid workers. Unfortunately, your predecessor put a plan in place in 1978, the region's peak year, and most workers gained nothing because profits have never recovered to 1978 levels. The unions wasted no time in convincing them that it was just another management ploy to get more work for no extra pay. To make matters worse, the workers in the Samlesbury plant, which exports 50% of its volume to healthier regions, have benefitted, so now the workers we were most interested in, like those in Liverpool, have an extra grudge against us.

After his first six months as Managing Director (which included two major strikes in Liverpool and a temporary brewery closure because of quality problems), Bernard King concluded that management changes were needed if the region were to progress. He decided to place Peter Watkins in charge of the Blackburn operations, where he had spent much of his early career, and to look for a new man to run Whitbread Merseyside. What he wanted, he said, was someone "big, strong, and dumb enough to accept the job."

LEN OLIVER

Len Oliver was recommended to Bernard King by a Whitbread manager who knew Len and thought he could do the job in Liverpool. Len had joined Whitbread in 1976 in a senior distribution post after spending 17 years with a major British food products company where he was primarily involved in distribution and industrial relations issues. After a few years as Distribution Manager, a job which involved solving a number of serious industrial relations issues, Len had been appointed general manager of Whitbread's Sheffield operations. He commented:

When I arrived in Sheffield in 1978, the business had been growing nicely and a new management structure had just been put into place. I was told not to make any major changes for 12 months, to let everyone get used to the new structure and to me. Unfortunately, volumes started to fall in 1979—it wasn't just our problem, it was the whole industry—and I couldn't just sit still. I started cutting people, and in the end I reduced the original level of 400 employees to approximately 300.

Before taking over Whitbread Merseyside, Len Oliver met separately with Bernard King to learn more about the recent industrial relations situation in Liverpool. Bernard described the situation as follows:

> I had not been in my job two days when the Shadsworth brewery went on strike. I did not get good advice from my local managers on this issue, but in the end, after a two week walk out, the T and G came back to work without gaining anything. I learned a lot about the union from that strike, and they learned that I don't back down. Then there was the Liverpool strike. Although the brewery has only 20 employees, the strike spread to the 40 workers in the packaging operation, and they jointly picketed our distribution centres, effectively shutting down all of Whitbread Merseyside. At one point, it appeared that our Samlesbury plant would also be picketed, which would have been a disaster of major proportions.
>
> This strike, and the second one which followed it (a total of six weeks), were a major test of will between ourselves, the union, and Whitbread senior management in London. They were precipitated by two new managers that Peter Watkins had hired to try to restore order and supervisory morale in the brewery. We suspended five hard core troublemakers whom the new managers had seen, in spite of repeated warnings, in a pub during working hours. The suspension was followed by an investigation, that ultimately led to their dismissal. During the investigation the union officials said to us "are you really sure you want to go through with this?" We could have backed down, as we had so many times before, but we decided that the time had come to take a stand, to support our first line managers.
>
> At one point during the second strike, I was called to London to meet senior Whitbread managers, who told me that I should give the union of-

ficials whatever they wanted, so the strike could be ended. I replied that, if they forced me to do that, I would have to resign. It was a rather tense meeting, but I did not concede. As the strike dragged into November, however, we decided that perhaps we should permanently close the brewery. When I announced this to Merseyside management, they objected and said that they felt the union would yield, as they now finally understood that we were serious. They were right and two days later the workers returned to work, minus the infamous five.

LEN OLIVER'S FIRST WEEK

Len Oliver began his new job in Liverpool on January 5, 1982. From the first day, he made a point of being very visible and accessible, talking formally and informally to his managers, union officials, and hourly paid workers. He explained to everyone that he came with no preconceived notions about what should be done at Liverpool, but when he did decide, they would be told openly and clearly. This message was received with skepticism by the union leaders, who were convinced that Oliver had been sent to Merseyside to close the brewery, and intended to give both him and Whitbread a very hard time if he tried to do so.

During the first week, Len's focus was twofold; to gain an understanding of the business situation facing Whitbread Merseyside, and to make an assessment of the individuals he would be working with. (An organization chart is presented in Exhibit 2.) A recently completed report (see Appendix) suggested that the company's market share decline was the result of high prices, underinvestment in pubs, not taking advantage of a trend to cask beer[1], and stiff competition from local brewers. The market share decline was apparent in both the free trade business (sales to pubs not allied to any brewer) and the tied trade business (pubs owned by Whitbread). In spite of the fact that he had no personal experience at developing or managing pubs, Len was somewhat disturbed after discussing the report with the free trade and tied trade managers. He commented:

---

[1] Cask beer was made the "old fashioned way," which meant that it was conditioned in the cask rather than in the brewery, and dispensed in the pub with a hand pump.

The free trade manager does not believe that we have a problem. He seems to think that we have a God given right to survive. Unfortunately, he's been here a long time and his attitudes will be difficult to change. I think he sees himself as the number two manager in Merseyside, but he does not appear to me to be a good manager of people.

The tied trade manager, on the other hand, has only been here about eight months and is new to the brewing business. In spite of this, he's a very independent character and his position seems to be "I've got pubs to run and I know what I'm doing." However, I hear that the pub managers dislike and distrust him as he is very aggressive, openly runs checks on their honesty, and insists they are in their pubs virtually all the time. His drive is to reduce costs in general and overheads in particular.

Len also examined volume and profit figures during his first week in Liverpool and these confirmed his belief that the Merseyside operation was earning approximately 50% less than it should have been. As shown in Exhibit 3, volume sold in the Merseyside region had fallen from 356 000 barrels to approximately 250 000 barrels in a 2-year period. Part of this decline was due to a transfer of business to Whitbread's take home division, but most of it was due to declining trading conditions and the 1981 strikes. The Liverpool brewery was operating at approximately 60% of its 300 000 barrel per year capacity, and beers which it could not produce were shipped in from other Whitbread breweries.

Further probing revealed the employment figures presented in Exhibit 4.

After examining these figures, Len commented:

In spite of the fact that they have laid off 157 people here since the volume decline began in 1979, there are still far too many. Based on my Sheffield experience, I would say that this operation should be run with about 300 people. I am not just talking about a reduction in weekly paid employees; there are about 70 middle level managers in this operation, and that's about 30 too many! One of the most blatant offenders is the distribution operation.

We initially grew into this area by acquisition, and we still have too many depots, too many trucks, too many people. Naturally, I have talked with the distribution manager. He is very apprehensive; he knows he has problems. He strikes me as an honest man; he's genuinely concerned about Whitbread Merseyside and Liverpool's severe problems, but he's not getting the job done. I was told before I came here that I'd probably have to replace him, but I'm not sure if that's the best move. The problem is complex because we can't simply combine our various depots. The union has negotiated different restrictive practices in each location, which means such things as manning levels, overtime rules, and the organization of work are different in Birkenhead than they are in Liverpool, even though one is just across the river from the other.

The one area that clearly is not overstaffed is the brewery. It was reduced from 30 to 20 hourly employees in the last round of cuts, and that is the minimum they can get by with. Due to a quality problem prior to my arrival, the brewery was shut for a time, and a new head brewer and number two brewer were brought in. Although new to the job, the head brewer has worked in this brewery before and appears competent. He reports to Samlesbury in terms of the quality of the product he makes, cleanliness standards, and so on, but to me with respect to issues relating to his workforce.

The problem with the brewery is the incredible resentment that resides there. They hate every manager up to and including Bernard King for firing their five ringleaders, and they hate me because I'm the new boss and because I was put in here by Bernard King. They could start another strike at any time on the slightest pretext.

I should also mention that when quality problems temporarily closed the Liverpool brewery, we shipped in beer from other Whitbread breweries and our local customers didn't notice the difference. Another marketing myth destroyed! And there is certainly enough excess capacity at Samlesbury to absorb the total Liverpool production. We don't need this Liverpool brewery!

At the end of his first week in Liverpool, Len took a few minutes to talk about his personal situation and the need for change at Merseyside.

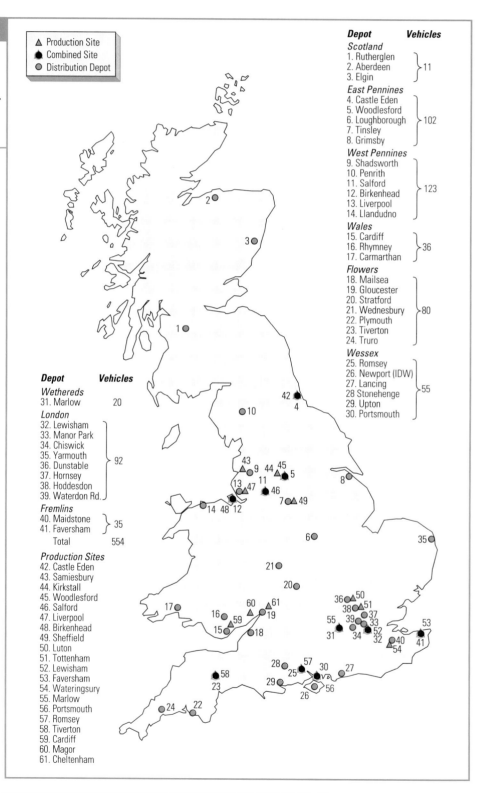

EXHIBIT 1

Distribution Depots and Production Sites Within the U.K. Whitbread & Company PLC as at 1st March 1981

△ Production Site
⬟ Combined Site
⬤ Distribution Depot

Depot	Vehicles
Scotland	
1. Rutherglen	
2. Aberdeen	11
3. Elgin	
East Pennines	
4. Castle Eden	
5. Woodlesford	
6. Loughborough	102
7. Tinsley	
8. Grimsby	
West Pennines	
9. Shadsworth	
10. Penrith	
11. Salford	
12. Birkenhead	123
13. Liverpool	
14. Llandudno	
Wales	
15. Cardiff	
16. Rhymney	36
17. Carmarthan	
Flowers	
18. Mailsea	
19. Gloucester	
20. Stratford	
21. Wednesbury	80
22. Plymouth	
23. Tiverton	
24. Truro	
Wessex	
25. Romsey	
26. Newport (IDW)	
27. Lancing	
28. Stonehenge	55
29. Upton	
30. Portsmouth	

Depot	Vehicles
Wethereds	
31. Marlow	20
London	
32. Lewisham	
33. Manor Park	
34. Chiswick	
35. Yarmouth	
36. Dunstable	92
37. Hornsey	
38. Hoddesdon	
39. Waterdon Rd.	
Fremlins	
40. Maidstone	35
41. Faversham	
Total	554

Production Sites
42. Castle Eden
43. Samiesbury
44. Kirkstall
45. Woodlesford
46. Salford
47. Liverpool
48. Birkenhead
49. Sheffield
50. Luton
51. Tottenham
52. Lewisham
53. Faversham
54. Wateringsury
55. Marlow
56. Portsmouth
57. Romsey
58. Tiverton
59. Cardiff
60. Magor
61. Cheltenham

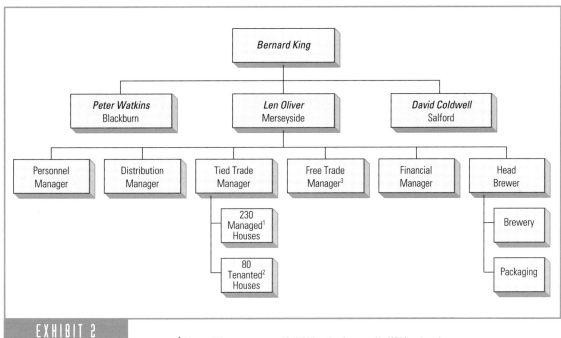

EXHIBIT 2

Whitbread Merseyside Organization Chart

[1] Managed Houses were owned by Whitbread and managed by Whitbread employees.

[2] Tenanted Houses were owned by Whitbread and managed by entrepreneurs who leased the pubs from the company.

[3] Free Houses were pubs not owned by a brewer, and free to buy from whatever supplier they wished.

It's a good thing I'm here without my family, because I'm spending 15 hours a day on the job, and it looks as if it will continue that way for some time. I am eating with managers every night, and then we usually go out for a few drinks. Although the managers are being quite protective of one another, I don't detect any jealousy of me—I don't think any of them wanted this job! In fact the personnel manager, who appears competent, had already arranged a transfer to Samlesbury before my arrival. It takes effect in about a month's time, but I could probably stop it if I wanted to ...

I have talked directly with the union leaders. There are two key guys. The full time union official is the incredibly tough character that Bernard first met in the Shadsworth dispute and then again in the Liverpool battles. He is 62 years old and has lost his last two fights with Bernard—I wonder if he's getting tired. It could be expensive to find out, of course. The other man is the full time union convenor, a company employee, who is 57. He is reputed to have been a firebrand in his youth, but has settled a little now. Of course the young shop stewards below him are as tough and militant now as he was in earlier years.

My style is not to sit around. Bernard is expecting me to create changes, so is the union, so are my managers. I don't think next week is too early to begin.

EXHIBIT 3   WHITBREAD MERSEYSIDE PERFORMANCE
(FEBRUARY 28 YEAR END)

YEAR	VOLUME (000 BARRELS)	PROFIT (£000)
1977-78	365	N
1978-79	355	4824
1979-80	356	5524
1980-81	308	6000
1981-82 (est.)	250	4800

EXHIBIT 4   WHITBREAD MERSEYSIDE 1981 YEAR END EMPLOYMENT

	WEEKLY PAID	MONTHLY PAID	TOTAL
Production (Brewery and Packaging)	68	20	88
Cellar Service	—	36	36
Tied Trade	19	38	57
Free Trade	—	16	16
Distribution	161	62	223
Administration	9	18	27
TOTAL	257	190	447

Appendix

ANALYSIS OF MARKET SHARE LOSS

Between 1978 and 1981 our share in the North West has declined from 18.26% to 16.36%, representing a 21% volume decline.

Whitbread Market Share—North West

	1978	1979*	1980	1981
Total beer	18.26%	19.08%	17.86%	16.36%
Tied trade	20.36%	21.48%	19.94%	18.60%
Free trade	14.71%	16.19%	15.29%	13.73%

* Increased share due to Tetley strike

The decline is due to a number of factors working together rather than any single factor.

A. TIED TRADE

1. House Location

In West Pennines, 41% of the volume loss is accounted for by the Liverpool Managed Houses. Sixty-six of these houses (1/4 of the Estate) represented 50% of the managed loss. The principal reasons for the decline in these houses were: thirty-two due to non trading factors such as urban redevelopment, recession, and industrial decline; eighteen due to high prices; and sixteen due to miscellaneous factors. In addition, the recent growth of unemployment in Merseyside is concentrated in areas of Whitbread strengths (e.g., Ellesmere Port where we have a 44% share). Whitbread also has above average presence in the inner city area (19% of the total), which has experienced above average growth in unemployment.

2. Investment

Compared with our major competitors, Whitbread has under-invested in the tied estate. For example, between 1976 and 1980 Allied spend 64% more on its pubs. Bass 48% more on its. As a consequence, a large proportion of our estate is untidy and unattractive.

Tied Trade Investment 1976-1980

	Per Tied House (£)	Gross Spending (£)
Allied	3500	127M
Courage	2300	60M
Bass	2200	89M
Whitbread	1300	46M

3. Pricing

Whitbread has been one of the price leaders in the North West for 1 1/2-2 years. At retail prices, we have been up to 8p per pint more expensive than the local brewers. For example, in 1979 the difference between Whitbread and Boddingtons was 1p/pint. In the two years of recession since then, the difference has been 5p/pint. Combined with the under-investment, the Whitbread pub will be perceived as offering a lower value for money package.

4. Cask Beer

Between 1969 and 1979, the cask beer market grew by 26%. By 1980 cask beer had grown to 20.7% of the market at a time when the total beer market was declining. Whitbread West Pennines' share of the draught market in 1979/80 was 13.4%, but our share of cask beer was estimated at only 1.3% (representing 1.7% of our draught volume). Cask beer represented about 75% of the local brewer volumes and, amongst the nationals, Bass had 25% of its volume in cask, Allied 15% of its volume in cask.

5. Local Brewers' Performance

We estimate that our share loss has been gained by the local brewers in the North West (e.g., Local 1.4% down, Nationals 5.6% down 1980 v. 1981). The major reasons whey the locals have performed better are covered previously, but in addition we feel that the locals have achieved a better image partly as a result of price, signage, etc., and also because the consumer has developed a "small and local is best" philosophy. Local brewery brands consistently outperform national brands in terms of product preference.

B. FREE TRADE

1. Small Accounts

In order to improve our Free Trade profitability, we have closed our 0-20 barrel per year accounts. As a result we have shed 12 000 barrels from the business, most of which we planned to transfer to wholesalers. However, we would estimate that more than 50% of the transferred volume has been lost from the business. Our current intention is to evaluate the closure of 20-50 barrel accounts, which would put at risk a further 22 000 barrels. There is evidence that other brewers, notably Bass, are accepting small accounts closed by Whitbread.

2. Price

Price is playing an increasing part in consumer choice. Up to 1980, Free Trade accounts would equalise their retail prices regardless of the wholesale price. More recently, however, the retail prices now reflect the wholesale price and consequently, as Whitbread has been a price leader, the consumer has decided on the lower priced alternative on the same bar. The wholesale price differences, especially against the local brewers, have been significant.

PART

4

EPILOGUE

There is only one chapter in the epilogue to this text. Part III examined what we know will happen to the new organizational entrant over the course of a career. Now Part IV deals with what might happen in the future. What are organizations going to look like, how will they be structured? How will the people in organizations of the future be different from the people of today? Also examined in this last chapter are the tools, both theoretical and statistical, that will be useful for organizational members in their evaluation and assimilation of new knowledge about organizations. Finally, we will look at different approaches to organizational science that have the promise to provide new ways to think about organizations and the people in them.

CHAPTER 16

ORGANIZATIONAL
BEHAVIOUR IN THE FUTURE

CHAPTER OUTLINE

Organizations in the Future: Towards the Year 2000

   The Work Force

   The Nature of Organizations

The Methods of Organizational Science

   Theory

   Boundary Conditions

   Theory Testing

Other Approaches to Organizational Science

   Modernism and Postmodernism

   Critical Theory

   Poststructuralism

   Feminist Research

Conclusion

QUESTIONS TO CONSIDER

- *What are organizations and management going to be like in the next ten years?*

- *What does one need to know to become an educated consumer of management literature?*

- *What is a theory, what is a hypothesis?*

- *How are theories tested?*

- *What are the forms of management knowledge that will be commonly encountered in the future?*

- *How does one make judgments about the validity of new findings about organizations?*

In this chapter we will examine current and future forces acting on organizations and the changes that may occur. Knowledge about organizations is developing at an increasing rate, and there are many ways of approaching the subject. This chapter will also examine the various methods used to study organizations and their members.

ORGANIZATIONS IN THE FUTURE: TOWARDS THE YEAR 2000
The Work Force

The composition of the work force in both Canada and the United States will likely undergo major changes in the near future. Three critical factors to consider are baby boom demographics, the sex composition of work force participants, and the inclusion of minorities.

Baby Boom Demographics

Because of the large numbers of babies born in Canada from 1946 to 1961, as people started or added to their families following the second world war, a "bulge" of population was created. These large numbers of "boomers" had an impact on primary, secondary, and college/university expansion, then entered the work force in large numbers. With the end of the boom, though, fewer births mean that fewer young people will be entering the job market (Offerman & Gowing, 1990). The overall size of the labour force will therefore increase at a slower rate.

In the year 2000, baby boomers will be aged 39 to 54. The oldest will be starting to retire, others will be holding on to high-level positions. Competition among them will be stiff for the top management jobs. Whereas one person in twenty could expect in 1987 to be promoted into top management, only one in fifty can expect such a promotion in the year 2001 (Offerman & Gowing, 1990).

As the boomers age, organizations will have to pay more attention to dealing with older workers. The average age of people working in organizations should rise. Current attitudes towards older workers can be positive because these workers tend to be loyal, productive, and have good work habits. But older employees can also be perceived as being lower in flexibility and adaptability. Ageism will become more of an issue in organizations.

As boomers retire from the work force in the years 2000 to 2026, openings will be created. A person born in 1977 will be 34 when the first and 49 when the last of the boomers is 65 years old. When the large bulge of boomer workers leaves the work force there will be fewer workers available to replace them. Therefore, there should be good opportunities for promotion as organizations seek replacements.

Women have been entering the work force in large numbers. Notable is the fact that women with small children are now more strongly represented in the work place. One 1989 study found that maternal employment in two-parent families with school-aged children was 71% and rising somewhat each year (Offerman & Gowing, 1990). Opportunities for women should increase as the older segment of the work force starts to retire. These workers in the management and executive ranks are currently mostly male. The percentage of males should decline as time goes by and women, who make up more of the younger workers, move up the organizational ladder.

The work force will also become more racially and ethnically diverse. When the number of people entering the job market shrinks and boomers retire, there will likely be a need for more new workers than are available. Immigration into Canada from diverse countries and cultures is one source of new labour. This means that the Canadian organization of the future is likely to become even more diverse than is presently the case.

Managing that diversity and being able to understand the nature of culture and different cultural answers to common questions about life will be an important skill. Many of the concepts covered in Chapter 14 on managing international assignments will be applicable to the challenges of managing an international or culturally diverse work force. This chapter's *A Word to the Wise* gives tips on the traits thought to be necessary for managers in the twenty-first century.

A WORD TO THE WISE

TEN TRAITS PERSONIFYING THE MANAGER OF THE 21ST CENTURY

By learning to apply the following specific behavior traits, one is on the way to joining the ranks of the "new breed" of XXI Century managers:

1. *Generalization.* Generalization is the ability to use a limited number of general ideas to integrate a large number of specific ideas. Generalization allows one to maintain a nonabsolutist belief system because, if one can integrate ideas, even an incongruous one does not threaten the entire belief system.

2. *Intuition.* Intuition is an instantaneous cognitive process in which one recognizes familiar patterns in order to combine isolated bits of data and experience into an integrated picture. Through intuition, flexibility is greatly enhanced and life, then, can be experienced innovatively.

3. *Networking.* Networking is defined as the ability to define problems by forming categories to see how individual problems interrelate. The result is that you are able to see the old in a brand new way and gain a universal perspective.

4. *Creative problem analysis.* Creative problem analysis is the ability to use multiple approaches to find a solution. This is an outgrowth of openness: being receptive to new ideas permits us to entertain multiple or opposing points of view, simultaneously. This inner dialectic permits us to make a choice that represents the best idea. That choice making, in turn, is linked to using a number of approaches to problem solving. It's an infinite loop of cybernetic qualities.

5. *Ambiguity.* This ability to simultaneously entertain opposing points of view—to accept ambiguity—and to select the best answer emergent from those, is a capacity that evolves from internal anchors. It is the stability and independence gained from becoming inner directed, that permit one to consider ideas that oppose one another in order to choose the best one.

6. *Novelty.* Novelty is the ability to counteract the basic conservatism of the human mind—its thoughts, attitudes, and patterns that persist beyond their need. This ability can be developed by paying attention to feelings of surprise when a particular fact does not fit a prior understanding and then by highlighting, rather than denying, that novelty. This perceptual view allows us to imagine new possibilities and to see the world with fresh eyes.

7. *Structure.* Structure is based on the ability to establish information systems to create order and harmony out of entropy and, in so doing, direct attention away from the routine and mundane. Freed from the routine, the mind is open to innovative perspectives and can embrace the capacity to wonder—curiosity. It is this curiosity that makes one susceptible to new ideas and to the use of the technology that makes the novel possible. With well-structured information systems, the human mind is able to keep moving.

8. *Responsiveness.* Responsiveness means systematically and continually gleaning information about an organization's performance in both time-sequenced-linear and intuitive ways. In order to be responsive to both external and internal environments and to discard false facts without threatening the entire belief system, one must possess a nonabsolutist belief system.

9. *Discretion.* Discretionary powers are essential to define problems, develop alternative solutions, make decisions, and communicate change to entire organizations. This is dependent, in large measure, upon a well-developed sense of optimism and hopefulness—in short—idealism, the ability to view the world as it might be.

10. *Action.* Action can be defined as placing thinking and doing in close concert. It also involves analyzing a problem, in light of the experience gained while attempting to solve that problem. Idealism is a fundamental component of action—one must believe in one's ability to make some impact on the world. By applying idealism through action, one gains a sense of direction and control and develops the stick-to-itiveness the modern world demands.

SOURCE: Gerald Baxter and Nancy Kerber Baxter (1986), "Einstein's advice on work in the next century," *Personnel Journal*, April 1986, pp.14-19.

The Nature of Organizations

In the late 1980s and early 1990s we saw several trends. These included more business failures, more downsizing of the numbers of employees (also called rightsizing or negative growth), a good deal of merger and acquisition activity, the expanding service sector, and a move to a more global economy (Offerman & Gowing, 1990). These trends are likely to continue in the near future. Two other important trends are an increasing pressure for the social responsibility of organizations and the rapid development of information technology.

The importance of the global economy is that organizations can no longer consider only their own product made for a local market. It used to be possible for a company to ignore production costs and labour rates in other countries because taxes, legal barriers to imports, and transportation logistics and costs made imported goods difficult to obtain and more expensive than local products. But legal barriers to trade and import duties are lessening with free trade agreements such as NAFTA (North American Free Trade Agreement), the European Common Market, and GATT (General Agreement on Tariffs and Trade). Transportation costs, especially for high value items, are a lower percentage of their total price. One result of all this is that it is harder to see who a company's competitors are. A manufacturing firm is in competition not just with the company down the street or in another province, but with companies around the world. The global economy means that companies cannot be satisfied with being the best in their local area but must strive to be the best in the world.

Mergers and acquisitions are stimulated by the global economy because organizations seek the size and expertise that can provide global competitiveness. To compete globally often means having a presence in many countries. Legal and accounting firms are now in the process of merging because their services must be globally available for clients with a global presence.

There is also a global pressure on organizations to be socially responsible. The earth and its finite resources must be guarded so that people and organizations in the future will experience conditions similar to or better than those of today. An organization that promotes these values is the Body Shop International. Here, from its in-house publication *This is The Body Shop* (Summer, 1993, p.1), as quoted by Gaines (1993, p. 357), is a list of six Body Shop values.

1. The success of The Body Shop proves that profits and principles can go hand in hand, and that business can be a force for social change.
2. We address the concerns and needs of our customers. Our products look to the traditions of the past for inspiration, with ingredients that are backed by centuries of safe human usage.
3. We want to put back more than we take out. This is only possible if we respect the planet and the life it supports.
4. Our products express our ideals; we won't test on animals and we ethically source our ingredients to reward primary producers in the majority world.
5. We try to make work a meaningful, pleasurable challenge for staff.
6. Our business is a celebration of life; we will never take anything about it for granted. We must always challenge our success.

Pressure for social responsibility is experienced globally because information about organizational actions is available world-wide. Organizations, especially multinationals, must consider how their actions will be seen and interpreted around the world. Consumers of organizational products are increasingly active in exerting market and social pressure on organizations. For example, a British Columbia forestry company that logs an old-growth forest and uses the logs in the making of newsprint may find itself the subject of an environmental boycott of its products.

Information technology is likely to have an increasingly powerful effect on the way organizations operate. Computers are quickly becoming more powerful. Databases are growing in size, complexity, and easy availability. CD-ROM technology has allowed huge amounts of information to be accessed by the users of personal computers. Global connections on the **"information superhighway"** allow fast and easy connections between individuals and corporations. Data and ideas are shared quickly, easing the barriers of time and space.

For example, a worldwide consulting firm can post messages on a company network about new contracts open for bid. Managers can pull together information for a bid by accessing databases of old bids for other similar projects and of relevant new information. E-mail messages can then be sent calling for applications to join the project team, and team members' resumes from an employee database can be added to the bid. The bid proposal can be quickly put together and then posted on the network with a call for comments and criticism. The updated proposal then benefits from the thinking of organizational members from around the world, and all this can take place over a weekend (see Kirkpatrick, 1993). Once the contract is obtained, the global network can be used as a resource when problems are encountered, information is needed, or issues need to be discussed. Information technology allows this consultancy firm to access all its resources and be more competitive and more effective.

One new organizational form will be the **boundaryless company**, also called the virtual corporation. The idea here is that the traditional vertical hierarchy will be replaced by horizontal networks. Traditional functions will be linked through interfunctional teams, and strategic alliances will be created with suppliers, customers, and even competitors (Hirschhorn & Gilmore, 1992). For a terrific example of how the virtual organization can work in practice, see the article by Ricardo Semler (1994).

Though middle management layoffs have flattened organizations, their basic structures have been left intact (Byrne and others, 1993). The virtual corporation—virtual as in virtual reality or a computer's virtual memory—will be very different in structure. These corporations of the future may be seen as a temporary network of companies that are extremely flexible, that come together to exploit fast-changing opportunities.

Roger Nagel (1993) summarizes these points as follows:

> Each participating company contributes what it is best at. Because these businesses are chosen for their leadership in one area only, opportunities will be created for organizations of all sizes, from one-man consultancies upwards. By carefully selecting each partner, it will be possible to create a "best of everything" enterprise. As projects develop, so the virtual corporation will evolve, shedding and gaining partners as appropriate, always maintaining the optimum configuration. When the project is complete, the corporation will be disbanded (p. 64).

Virtual corporations have the following key attributes (Byrne and others, 1993).

1. *Technology* — reliance on information networks that link members of the alliance.
2. *Excellence* — each company brings to the alliance what it does the best.
3. *Opportunism* — relationships are less permanent and formal; each company continually scans the environment for new opportunities.
4. *Trust* — each company is dependent on the other, and so must trust in the other's actions.
5. *No borders* — lowered boundaries between customers, suppliers, and competitors.

The boundaryless company is not, however, a simple solution to new environmental conditions. Employees would need to become more flexible, negotiating their organizational role and relationships with others. Such negotiations may even take place within the organization. Internal company departments will find themselves in competition with outside

---

Information superhighway Also called the infobahn. The growing interconnectedness of information sources and information users.

Boundaryless company (virtual corporation) Reflects the idea that the traditional vertical hierarchy of organizations will be replaced by horizontal networks. The organization will accomplish its work by forming agreements with suppliers, customers, and competitors. What is inside and what is outside the organization will become fuzzy.

suppliers. They will have to learn to treat others in their own organization as customers and be as good as their external competitors (Markham, 1993). The benefits of organizational and worker flexibility will depend "on maintaining a creative tension among widely different but complementary skills and points of view" (Hirschhorn & Gilmore, 1992, p. 106).

Workers in such organizations may find that they are no longer employed on a regular, continuing basis. So called "non-standard" workers will be self-employed, on contract, or working part-time. Estimates are that in the early 1990s more than 30% of Canadians with paid jobs were in this group, and their numbers are growing (Williamson, 1993). Companies will **outsource** their work instead of providing jobs-for-life, and will gain the benefits of flexibility (see the *If You Can't Ride Two Horses At Once, You Shouldn't Be in the Circus* feature).

Outsourcing The practice of sending some of the organization's work to others outside its boundaries.

Work at home will become more common in the 1990's.

These organizations will obtain whatever skills are needed when they are needed, while spending less on pay and benefits (Williamson, 1993). Individuals who can be flexible and rely on their skills to make a living could do very well in such conditions. Of course, more virtual corporations and outsourcing will mean less security for employees. When income is less certain, stress is likely to increase.

In the new flexible and chaotic world of work, there are new realities to be faced by both men and women. Here are some general tips (from Sherman, 1993).

IF YOU CAN'T RIDE TWO HORSES AT ONCE, YOU SHOULDN'T BE IN THE CIRCUS

In Chapter 15 we saw that quality of a product or service can be a source of competitive advantage. Quality leads to customer satisfaction and lower costs. But while the gap between product quality (durability, conformance to specifications, on-time delivery) has been closing between North America and Japan, the next area of competition may be on flexibility.

With product quality taken as a given, companies that can respond quickly to customers by changing fast while keeping costs low will be more competitive. The concept is that manufacturing follows a swift progression from product quality (doing it right) through product reliability (always doing it right) to flexibility (the addition of variety and speed to quality and reliability). Factories engage in "agile production" by being small and modular, using robotics and programmable machinery.

One example of a company already pursuing the flexibility strategy is *Kao Corp*, Japan's largest soap and cosmetics company. Using **economies of scope** and

Economies of scope
The advantage gained by producing a wide variety of products.

not just economies of scale, a large factory (scale) can produce many different types of products (scope). By gathering volumes of data on product sales, competitor moves, consumer test marketing, production and purchasing, and research and development, among others, Kao Corp's aim is to maximize the whole company's response to customer demand.

The flexibility strategy may also be pursued by manufacturers of large complex machinery, such as automobiles. In this case production lines are able to make many models, each with many different options. Changeover from one model to another need not take a great deal of time or require the production line to be stopped for more than one shift. Such flexibility allows the car manufacturer to make the model ordered by the customer in a short amount of time. High or low sales of a particular market can be adapted to. The object is to split the market into small segments and to avoid mass production while manufacturing for the smaller market segments.

SOURCE: Based on information contained in Thomas A. Stewart (1992), "Brace yourself for Japan's hot new strategy," *Fortune*, September 21, 1992, pp. 62-74.

1. Each person will have to take responsibility for his own career. The individual will need to take stock of his skills and add to them every year. Everyone should have an answer to the question of what they would do if they lost their job tomorrow.

2. The old career path is no more. As middle management is lessened there are fewer rungs on the corporate ladder. This means that jobs in functional areas are again of importance.

3. Knowledge and adaptability are newly important. It is necessary to be flexible, to be able to adapt quickly to new work settings and culture, and to unlearn old and outdated ways of thinking and acting.

4. With fewer middle managers and more employee empowerment, teamwork will replace hierarchy as the primary way of organizing. People will move in and out of jobs as their skills are needed on a project basis.

5. Leaders will have to build relationships with their team members, investing in members in order to gain returns from their involvement.

Exhibit 16.1 summarizes and adds to these ideas in Tom Peters' view of organizations in the future.

THE METHODS OF ORGANIZATIONAL SCIENCE

Learning about organizations is a lifelong endeavour. To be effective in organizations, either as an employee or self-employed, you will need to learn continually about recent changes in organizational forms and practices. Sometimes this learning will be through formal courses, perhaps for an advanced degree. Sometimes it will take place in seminars on management topics. And sometimes, perhaps even most often, your continuing education will take place on your own. The student of organizations will read about organizations and organizational behaviour in books, academic or practitioner journals, business magazines, and newspapers.

Given this emphasis on continual and independent learning, it is important that you become familiar with the basic tools and methods used in management research, so as to be able to make your own informed judgments about that research. In this next section we will examine the concepts of theory and theory testing using a normal science (or positivistic) model. Then we will briefly examine ethics in science.

Theory

What is a theory? When we don't know exactly how things work, a theory is a description of how we think they work. While in physics there are several "laws" for how things work—such as the law of gravity—in the study of organizations there are no such laws. We therefore seek to create theories that will describe how we think events in organizations do work. Some of these descriptions are more interesting than others. For an elaboration, see this chapter's *A Little Knowledge* feature.

A theory description links things that can vary, called **independent variables**, with other things that are proposed to be affected by those independent variables. This latter group is comprised of **dependent variables**. For example, an incentive pay plan may be designed so that a bonus of 20% of cumulative salary is paid at the end of a specified contract. The idea is that more people will stay until the contract is completed if the bonus is payable only at that time but lost altogether if the person terminates the contract early. The independent variable here is the 20% bonus and the dependent variable is the person's quitting early or staying to the end of the contract.

Independent variables
The factors in a theory that are proposed to vary.

Dependent variables
The factors in a theory that are proposed to be affected by variation in the independent variables.

EXHIBIT 16.1

Organizations in the Future

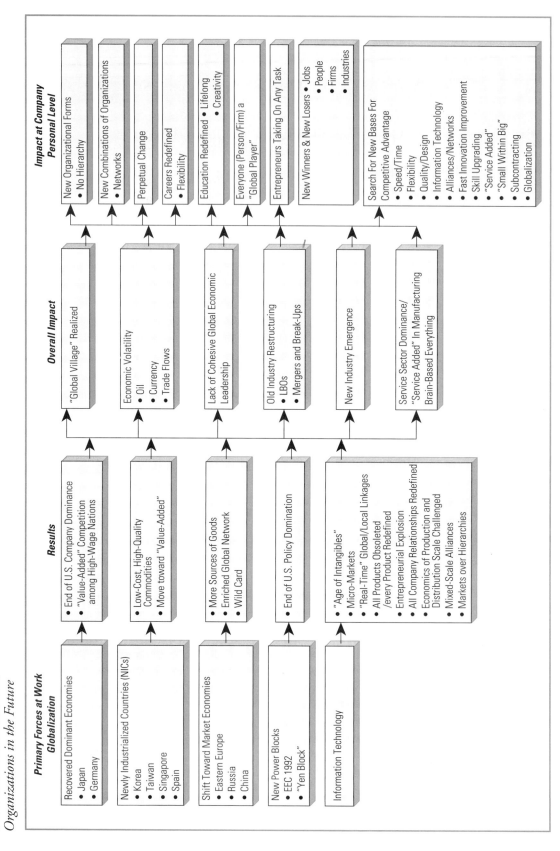

Primary Forces at Work
Globalization

Recovered Dominant Economies
• Japan
• Germany

Newly Industrialized Countries (NICs)
• Korea
• Taiwan
• Singapore
• Spain

Shift Toward Market Economies
• Eastern Europe
• Russia
• China

New Power Blocks
• EEC 1992
• "Yen Block"

Information Technology

Results

• End of U.S. Company Dominance
• "Value-Added" Competition among High-Wage Nations

• Low-Cost, High-Quality Commodities
• Move toward "Value-Added"

• More Sources of Goods
• Enriched Global Network
• Wild Card

• End of U.S. Policy Domination

• "Age of Intangibles"
• Micro-Markets
• "Real-Time" Global/Local Linkages
• All Products Obsoleted /every Product Redefined
• Entrepreneurial Explosion
• All Company Relationships Redefined
• Economics of Production and Distribution Scale Challenged
• Mixed-Scale Alliances
• Markets over Hierarchies

Overall Impact

"Global Village" Realized

Economic Volatility
• Oil
• Currency
• Trade Flows

Lack of Cohesive Global Economic Leadership

Old Industry Restructuring
• LBOs
• Mergers and Break-Ups

New Industry Emergence

Service Sector Dominance/ "Service Added" In Manufacturing Brain-Based Everything

Impact at Company
Personal Level

New Organizational Forms
• No Hierarchy

New Combinations of Organizations
• Networks

Perpetual Change

Careers Redefined
• Flexibility

Education Redefined • Lifelong
• Creativity

Everyone (Person/Firm) a "Global Player"

Entrepreneurs Taking On Any Task

New Winners & New Losers • Jobs
• People
• Firms
• Industries

Search For New Bases For Competitive Advantage
• Speed/Time
• Flexibility
• Quality/Design
• Information Technology
• Alliances/Networks
• Fast Innovation Improvement
• Skill Upgrading
• "Service Added"
• "Small Within Big"
• Subcontracting
• Globalization

A LITTLE KNOWLEDGE

What makes a theory interesting? Why are people in general fascinated by black holes, dinosaur extinction, and Einstein's theory that time is not an absolute? In a classic article that is interesting in its own right, Murray Davis has shown what makes theories interesting. Interesting theories, he claims, deny certain assumptions that their audience makes, while non-interesting theories assert that the assumptions made by their audience are correct. Why are scientists concerned about making their theories "interesting?" Because science and the construction of "truth" is a social enterprise. The amount of money provided for research and the status given the researcher/theorist are contingent on the general acceptance and widespread interest of the theories presented. Here, then, is Davis' list of what makes a theory interesting along with current examples of how each might apply in a management/organizational context.

1. *Organization:* What seems to be a disorganized (unstructured) phenomenon is in reality an organized (structured) phenomenon. For example, what appears to be a competitive market turns out really to be an oligopoly with price fixing. Or the reverse, that what seems to be an organized (structured) phenomenon is in reality a disorganized (unstructured) phenomenon.

2. *Composition:* What seem to be assorted heterogeneous phenomena are in reality composed of a single element (or the reverse). For instance, men and women are found to be more similar than different.

3. *Abstraction:* What seems to be an individual phenomenon is in reality a holistic phenomenon (or the reverse). Unemployment, for example, may be seen more as a matter of organizational choice than as an individual choice.

4. *Generalization:* What seems to be a local phenomenon is in reality a general phenomenon (or the reverse). Layoffs, for instance, seen as a Canadian/American problem, are now occurring more broadly in Japan, Russia, Europe, etc.

5. *Stabilization:* What seems to be a stable and unchanging phenomenon is in reality an unstable and changing phenomenon (or the reverse). For example the balance of power between unions and management, which was seen to be stable, is now shifting away from unions and towards management.

6. *Function:* What seems to be a phenomenon that functions ineffectively as a means for the attainment of an end is in reality a phenomenon that functions effectively (or the reverse). For instance, hierarchical organizations, so effective in times of stability, are found to be ineffective in rapidly changing environments.

7. *Evaluation:* What seems to be a bad phenomenon is in reality a good phenomenon (or the reverse, what seems to be a good phenomenon is in reality a bad phenomenon). Turnover, often seen as an organizational problem, can be seen as good for the organization as long as the less effective employees are the ones leaving.

8. *Co-relation:* What seem to be unrelated (independent) phenomena are in reality correlated (interdependent) phenomena (or the reverse). The actions of small organizations, each of which is too small to have any effect on the economy as a whole, in total have a large effect.

9. *Co-existence:* What seem to be phenomena which can exist together are in reality phenomena which cannot exist together (or the reverse). Individuals at work with widely different cultures and values can work together, each subordinating his culture to some extent to the overarching organizational culture.

10. *Co-variation:* What seems to be a positive co-variation between phenomena is in reality a negative co-variation between phenomena (or the reverse). It was commonly assumed that higher quality and higher costs of manufacturing went together. New approaches to quality management find that higher quality is associated with lower cost.

11. *Opposition:* What seem to be dissimilar phenomena are in reality similar (nearly identical) phenomena (or the reverse). For instance, union leaders and company managers are seen to be completely opposite to one another, but can be found to act similarly to each other.

12. *Causation:* What seems to be the independent phenomenon (variable) in a causal relation is in reality the dependent phenomenon (variable) (or the reverse). At one time it was thought that work control by managers caused poor worker performance, but it has now been shown that poor worker performance causes the manager to exert greater work control.

SOURCE: Twelve principles are from Murray S. Davis (1971) "That's interesting! Towards a phenomenology of sociology and a sociology of phenomenology," *Philosophy of the Social Sciences* 1: 309-344. Also see Murray S. Davis (1986), "'That's Classic!' The phenomenology and rhetoric of successful social theories," *Philosophy of the Social Sciences* 16: 285-301.

Independent and dependent variables and the relationships that are proposed between them form a cluster, a grouping, or a net. Try to visualize a section of a fishing net, with the knots being variables and the rope between two knots signifying the relationship between the two variables. Organizational scholars often call this metaphor the **nomological net** of a theory, meaning its rule-based net of relationships between variables.

Nomological net A network of rule-based relationships between variables in a theory.

There are other types of variables that we have encountered on our journey through this text and the theories of organizational behaviour. **Intervening variables** are proposed as intermediate links between independent and dependent variables (see the Job Characteristics Model). **Moderator variables** act to alter the relationship between independent and dependent variables. For example, there might be a leader supportive behaviour and subordinate satisfaction link for inexperienced subordinates but not for experienced subordinates. Here subordinate experience would be a moderator.

Intervening variables Intermediate links between independent and dependent variables.

All these ways of describing theoretical variables and their links are tools used by organizational scientists as they try to make sense of what is going on in organizations. Kurt Lewin said that "there is nothing so practical as a good theory." The reason is that a theory helps us to organize our thoughts and gives direction to what we might do—which variables to influence—in different situations.

Moderator variables Variables that can alter the relationship between independent and dependent variables.

For example, let us say that a car broke down on the owner's way to work. Without any working theory of cars and how they work, what could the owner do? The answer is nothing, except wait at the roadside for help, for someone to come along with a theory about what is wrong with the car.

If the car won't move there are several questions that may be asked of this theory. Data can then be gathered to test if these questions are right or wrong. These questions could be: Is there gas in the car? Is the carburetor "flooded" with gas so that air cannot be properly mixed in? Are the sparkplugs sparking? Is the transmission broken so that engine power cannot be transmitted to the wheels?

Each of these questions, and of course there could be many more, is an hypothesis. A **hypothesis** is basically a guess about what could be going on—in this example, with the car. Data is gathered to test each hypothesis before it is ruled as right, wrong, or that there is insufficient evidence to support or refute it. In our car example, one hypothesis could be that the gas tank is empty. Data on this could be gathered by checking the gas gauge. The theory is therefore useful as a guide to action.

Hypotheses Best guesses of the relationship that might exist between the independent and dependent variables of a theory.

One purpose of this text has been to put forward a range of theories that help us to explain the behaviour of people in organizations. With the understanding that each one can be useful in certain circumstances, the student of organizations can be like the driver of a car who knows car theories. When an organization breaks down, instead of waiting at the metaphorical side of the road for a mechanic—here the organizational consultant—the student of organizations knows the questions to ask to begin the process of fixing the organization. The theories that we have discussed in this text are the tools in the manager's tool box.

Boundary Conditions

All theories are right and wrong at the same time. This seemingly contradictory and confusing statement illustrates the fact that theories are useful in particular circumstances. The car theory described so far would be wrong for electric powered vehicles, but there are other vehicles and other situations for which it would be "right," or at least right enough to be of use.

The theories of organizational science are the same—they are right in certain circumstances and situations where they predict well or help us to explain what might be going on or going wrong. They are wrong for other circumstances and situations. The problem is that the more a theory tries to explain all contingencies and events the more it becomes too complex and cumbersome to practically use. And when a theory explains well only a small set of events it is too limited for use in many different situations. In this latter case the theory is said to be not generalizable. Theories that try for the middle are appropriately called mid-range theories.

There is not necessarily a significant relationship between the estimated usefulness of organizational theories and their estimated scientific validity (Exhibit 16.2). Using a theory in specific conditions for a specific purpose is quite a different issue from evaluating its validity—how "true" the theory is. If a theory is useful in practice, the fact of its not being proven scientifically will likely matter little to practising managers.

One boundary condition of organizational behaviour theories that is coming under increasing scrutiny is their cross-cultural relevance. Geert Hofstede (1993) argues that management theories are not universal. The act of being a manager and managing others takes place differently and is perceived differently in diverse countries. How families work, schooling, politics, government, and religion—all these factors will influence the process of management. These differences must be recognized so that theories can be developed that are appropriate to each country.

An organizational example is that in Japan workers are controlled more by their peer group than by their manager. In France worker and manager are from different social classes (Hofstede, 1993). Superior-subordinate relationships can therefore be expected to be quite different in Japan from those in France. Theories that attempt to describe superior-subordinate relations are also likely to be quite different depending on whether the theory originates in Japan or in France.

For recommendations of how organizational behaviour scholars should make their theories more relevant to management in other countries, see *A Rose by Any Other Name*.

Theory Testing

Organizational scientists are interested in creating and testing theories about how things work in organizations. These tests often try to determine how well the theory describes or explains real events in organizations. The results of these tests can improve the theory itself, knowledge about when it is more and less useful, and our cumulative knowledge about organizations.

Research methods tend to fall into two main groups: the qualitative and the quantitative. Qualitative methods generally aim to create theory and to come to a detailed understanding about organizational phenomena and how they interrelate in a specific organization. The qualitative researcher usually "lives" in an organization for a long period of time, often a year or more, to obtain a deep and wide grounding for the theory that is developed.

Quantitative methods generally aim to test theory and to understand a specific phenomenon. The quantitative researcher usually analyzes data from a large number of organizations in order to come to an understanding that applies to organizations in general.

Qualitative and quantitative research are not mutually exclusive methods, but can be combined by one or more researchers studying a phenomenon. This is called **triangulation** (Jick, 1979). Its benefit is that the same phenomenon can be studied from several vantage points. Weaknesses in some methods are compensated for by the strengths of other methods.

Triangulation The use of research methods to study the same phenomenon from several vantage points.

A ROSE BY ANY OTHER NAME

Knowledge about organizational behaviour is very Western oriented. Most scholars have been trained in the West and most organization science journals and books are published in English in the West. But people in diverse cultures around the world think, act, and feel very differently when confronted with the basic problems of society. Therefore, theories developed in one culture cannot be assumed to operate in another culture (for examples, see Smith, 1992). The following list of recommendations by Nakiye Avdan Boyacigiller and Nancy J. Adler is meant to show scholars of organizational behaviour that they have to pay more attention to the international relevance of their theories. In this table it can be safely assumed that references to the United States can also apply in a broad sense to developed countries of the "West."

Recommendations for a More Internationally Relevant Organizational Science

Recommendations	Significance
Reflection	
• Explicitly address the influence of cultural values on how we conceptualize organization phenomena and construct organization theories.	• Helps scholars uncover neglected, overemphasized, and overgeneralized aspects of theories.
• Examine the extent to which the organizational sciences reflect U.S. cultural values.	• Increases scholars' understanding of American culture and its impact on their perceptions, thoughts, and scholarship.
Action Steps for Individual Researchers	
• State the cultural and geographical domain of theories and research, as well as indicate other locales in which they apply.	• Minimizes implicit universalism
• Indicate the national and cultural characteristics of research samples.	• Assists readers of the research to recognize potential limitations.
• Research management systems outside the United States.	• Creates new theoretical and methodological approaches not predicated on American assumptions.
• Study non-U.S. management systems on their own terms (idiographic research); develop thick descriptions of organizational phenomena and the contexts in which they are embedded.	• Increases the organizational forms and contexts with which scholars are familiar, as well as increasing their understanding of the uniqueness of U.S. organization forms.
• Create more multinational and multicultural research teams.	• Facilitates recognition of cultural biases in theory development.
• Use non-U.S. settings to frame theoretical and methodological approaches.	• Expands domain of organizational theories.
• Take sabbaticals in foreign countries.	• Increases scholars' understanding of cultures and their own cultures, including providing personal thick descriptions of the foreign sabbatical culture.
Organizational Changes	
• Journal editors, reviewers, and scholars should question one another regarding their cultural assumptions and research domains.	• Rewarding careful exposition of the geographical and cultural domain will check implicit universalism.

- Expand editorial boards to include global representation and expertise.

- Consider forming "global lines of business," strategic alliances, and networks among academic organizations worldwide.

- Select leaders of academic management organizations from multiple nations.

- Increases the perspectives represented, both substantively and symbolically.

- Facilitates internationalization, and, thus, contributes to future relevance.

- Increases perspective and knowledge bases represented, thus facilitating frame-breaking change.

SOURCE: Nakiye Avdan Boyacigiller and Nancy J. Adler (1991), "The parochial dinosaur: Organizational science in a global context," *Academy of Management Review* 16: 279-280. Reprinted by permission of the Academy of Management.

EXHIBIT 16.2 ESTIMATED USEFULNESS IN APPLICATION AND ESTIMATED SCIENTIFIC VALIDITY OF 32 ORGANIZATIONAL SCIENCE THEORIES

ESTIMATED USEFULNESS IN APPLICATION	ESTIMATED SCIENTIFIC VALIDITY		
	LOW	MIXED	HIGH
High	• Theory of System 4 and 4T	• Behaviour modification and operant learning • Sociotechnical systems theory	• Job Characteristics theory • Goal setting theory • Achievement motivation • Role-motivation theory
Questionable	• Contingency theory of organization • Motivation-hygiene theory • Theory X and theory Y • Theory of bureaucratic demise • Classical management theory	• Contingency theory of leadership • Goal-congruence theory • Theory of strategy and structure • Influence-power continuum theory	• Expectancy theories • Decision tree theory of participative leadership • Theory of bureaucracy
Low	• Need hierarchy theory • Technological determinism • Technology in a comparative framework • Mechanistic and organic systems theory • Leadership pattern choice theory	• Psychological open-systems theory • Path-goal theory • Sociological open-systems theory • Group-focused systems theory	• Decision making concepts and constructs • Equity theory • Control theory • Vertical-dyad linkage theory

Source: John B. Miner (1984), "The validity and usefulness of theories in an emerging organizational science," *Academy of Management Review* 9: 300. Reprinted by permission of the Academy of Management. In a related work, Miner (1990) found that the perceived goodness of a theory was found to be a function of the perceiver's values.

Notes: This table is based on a survey conducted in 1977 of 35 knowledgeable organizational behaviour scholars. There was not a significant relationship between the estimated scientific validity of a theory and its estimated usefulness in application. This table points out that some theories are seen to be very useful for helping organizations to do their work, but have not necessarily been tested and scientifically validated; while other theories are scientifically valid but perhaps of less day-to-day utility in organizations. In this latter category are theories such as Equity Theory (Chapter 8) and Vertical dyad linkage theory (Chapter 10) which may describe well what is occurring in organizations without necessarily making prescriptions about how to use that knowledge. Some theories are seen as having low validity and low utility in organizations, but even here such theories as Maslow's hierarchy (Chapter 8) and the theory of mechanistic/organic structures (Chapter 2) are part of everyday managerial thinking. Those fortunate few theories that have attracted supportive evidence of scientific validity *and* that are seen as useful in practice, for example Goal Setting Theory (Chapter 8), are generally seen as "true" by both managers and academics.

Organizational research requires a plan. Exhibit 16.3 presents the stages in the quantitative research process. (Qualitative research methods are briefly explored in a later section dealing with other approaches to organizational science.)

The basic elements of a plan for quantitative research are to:

- Describe the theory's variables and their connections (what you think is really happening);
- Define the constructs of the theory (what you intend to measure);
- Specify hypotheses (these are questions you intend to ask of the theory);
- Decide how you will measure the theory's constructs (questionnaires, observations, interviews, etc.);
- Make measurements and code these into data;
- Analyze the data and test hypotheses;
- Interpret the results and come to conclusions about the theory.

Each student of organizations and organizational participant is a potential consumer of the results of such research. Therefore, it is important for everyone to be able to make informed judgments about the quality of the research being conducted. It is also important that the consumer of organizational knowledge be able to critically evaluate what the results and conclusions of research have to say about the theory being tested.

EXHIBIT 16.3   STAGES IN THE RESEARCH PROCESS

1. *Organizational problems and research questions.* The first requirement is to convert ambiguous problems into researchable questions. See Balsley & Clover (1988: Chapter 3); Sekaran (1984: Chapter 2).

2. *Hypotheses for addressing the research question.* Need to frame questions into testable hypotheses. For advice on how to create hypotheses from literature reviews, see Sekaran (1984: pp. 25-41); on meta-analysis, see Schmitt and Klimoski (1991: Chapter 12).

3. *Strategies.* The decision must be made of how to test the hypotheses. Will an experiment be conducted in the laboratory or in the field, or will data be gathered by a survey? See Stone (1978: Chapter 7) for details and a chart (page 116) comparing strengths and weaknesses of different strategies.

4. *Designs.* The design of the test is created to allow the researcher to capture variation of interest. The design plans the data that will be gathered that will allow a test of the hypotheses.

5. *Operationalizing constructs.* The variables specified in hypotheses must be measured. How this occurs is the operationalization of the theoretical constructs. See Stone (1978: Chapter 5).

6. *Carrying out the plan.* The plan must now be carried out. Practical issues must be considered such as how to

gain entry into an organization, contracts, training assistants, and budgeting time and money. For further details, see Gay and Diehl (1991: Chapter 3).

7. *Converting observations into data.* This process is crucial to the results of a study and often very time consuming. Issues to consider are methods of data coding, entry and storage, and how data will be transformed into summary variables. See Gay and Diehl (1991: Chapter 13).

8. *Data analyses.* Statistical techniques used must correspond to the properties of the data and to the hypotheses being tested. Statistical analysis is a way of determining the strength of an effect and the likelihood it was discovered by chance. Therefore, statistics must not be used blindly, but must fit the data and question being asked of it. For basic statistics, see Jaeger (1990).

9. *Conclusions and interpretations of results.* A key stage of the research where the investigator attempts to determine what the results mean.

10. *Communicating results, conclusions, and recommendations.* The idea here is to write directly and simply to your audience. See Balsley and Clover (1988: Chapter 16 "Writing Research Reports"); Witzling and Greenstreet (1989: Chapters 1, 2, and 7); and Tufte's *The Visual Display of Quantitative Information* (1983: Chapters 1, 2, 5, and 9).

SOURCE: David A. Harrison (1993). "Why can't you use just one textbook for this class?!" The *Academy of Management Research Methods Division Newsletter*, 8(1): 9-12 and 8(2): 14-16.

Neither theories nor the results of tests of theories should be accepted as true without questioning. In science, as in other endeavours, there are cases of cheating in published research. Perhaps the most famous case of possible cheating in organizational science is that of Sir Cyril Burt, a British psychologist who studied intelligence. One charge against him is that he fraudulently reported results supporting his theories. However, a review of this case by Bert Green (1992) concludes that "the charge of deliberately falsifying data can neither be established nor disproved with certitude" (p. 331). Green's review is the subject of this chapter's *On the One Hand* feature.

Theory Description and Hypotheses   The first step in testing a theory is to describe the theory in some detail, specifying variables and their connections. Second, hypotheses are developed that describe exactly what relationships are to be expected. A hypothesis is basically a guess about what could be going on. They may be written in the form of a **null hypothesis**,

Null hypothesis   A hypothesis written in a form that describes no relationship between two variables.

ON THE ONE HAND ...

Cyril Burt was a well-known British psychologist who, five years after his death in 1971, was accused of scientific fraud. Studying the genetic basis of intelligence, Burt used his position as chief psychologist for the London County Council to give intelligence tests to school children. Burt collected data on siblings and twins and computed correlations of their intelligence scores. Higher correlations between twins, especially identical twins, he hypothesized, would provide evidence for heredity as a basis for intelligence.

But there were irregularities in these correlations. A correlation might appear in two different articles by Burt with the same value but a different sample size. After these suspicions were raised, an attempt was made to find the two assistants, Miss Howard and Miss Conway, that Burt acknowledged as helping him to collect his data. But they could not be found. This led some to question Burt's methods and the allegation in the *Sunday Times* (of London) that Burt invented his twin data (and his two assistants). Then a biography of Burt was published by Leslie Hearnshaw (*Cyril Burt, Psychologist*, 1979, Cornell University Press) that supported some of these charges, added others, and caused irreparable damage to Burt's reputation.

Recently, however, two books have been published that review the evidence for and against Burt. One book is by Ronald Fletcher (1991), *Science, Ideology, and the Media: The Cyril Burt Scandal*, by Transaction Publishers. This work examines the role of the media in publicizing the Burt "fraud." In Robert Joynson's book *The Burt Affair*, published in 1989 by Routledge of London, the charges

against Burt are separated into three categories: 1. that he misrepresented the history of the development of the factor analytic technique; 2. that he reported kinship correlations that he had made up himself; and 3. that his data are of low quality.

On the first charge Burt is found guilty, but no more guilty than many other scientists who seek to promote their own reputations while ignoring the contributions of others.

On the second charge the point is made that calculating correlation coefficients in the days before computers and electronic calculators had to be done by hand and took several hours, not the seconds of today. Burt may have added cases to his data base and updated that number without recalculating the correlation. Regarding his two assistants, while they have not been found, evidence that they did exist has been uncovered, meaning that Burt did not invent them after all. The conclusion was reached that inconsistencies in Burt's data could be explained in several different ways. Given the time elapsed and in the absense of Burt's records (many were lost in the London Blitz of the Second World War, others were burned after his death), no conclusion is possible.

On the third charge, that his data are of low quality, Burt can be found guilty if standards of today are used. Some of his methods could not be replicated, he used statistical transformations that are not in wide use today, and he failed to keep good records of his research. But using the standards of the 1920s and 1930s, when the data collection began, he cannot be found guilty. Overall, then, the case against Burt cannot be proven.

SOURCE: Based on information in Bert F. Green (1992), "Exposé or smear? The Burt affair," *Psychological Science* 3: 328-331.

Alternative hypothesis
A hypothesis written to be in opposition to the null hypothesis.

Instrument A tool used to gather data from subjects. Could be a physical device or a questionnaire.

Reliability A measure of how consistent multiple measurements are of a phenomenon.

Validity An indicator of how well an instrument is measuring what the investigator thinks is being measured.

Sample size The number of subjects selected for study from a population.

Descriptive statistics Statistics that describe the characteristics of the data.

Mode A descriptive statistic of the value of the variable that occurs the most frequently in a sample.

Median A descriptive statistic of the middle value of the measurements taken of a variable in a sample.

Mean The average value of a variable in a sample.

Variance A descriptive statistical measure of how much the measurements of a variable from a sample are alike. Variance is the sum of the squared differences between each data point and the mean, divided by the number of data points minus one.

Standard deviation The square root of the variance.

that is, in a form that describes no relationship between two variables. For example, if a researcher thought that increasing organizational rewards are positively linked to higher performance, the null hypothesis might be:

H_o: There is no relationship between organizational rewards and individual performance.

The researcher is basically trying to disprove this null hypothesis. The **alternative hypothesis** would be:

H_a: There is a positive relationship between organizational rewards and individual performance.

Data is gathered to test each hypothesis before it is ruled as right, wrong, or that there is insufficient evidence to support or refute it. Evidence for or against the theory may be gathered in a number of ways (see Exhibit 16.4). Interviews, questionnaires, observation of behaviour, or using supplementary data are all methods in use.

Measurement The variables of a theory must be measured. Questionnaires are often used because they provide hard data—in effect, numbers, about a variable. Also, once a questionnaire has been created (it can also be called an **instrument**), other researchers can use it in their own studies. A questionnaire should be reliable and valid.

Reliability describes how consistent multiple measurements will be. If a person were to stand on an electronic weigh scale three times, how similar would the readings be? The more reliable the scale, the more similar the readings.

Validity describes how well what is being measured is what is thought to be measured. For example, an intelligence test may be reliable in that it tends to give similar measures over time for the same person, but not valid because it is measuring something else besides intelligence. It might be measuring test response speed, test anxiety, or culture in addition to intelligence.

Using measurement tools, data is gathered from a sample of subjects that represent a population (called the **sample size**), or from every individual in the population. Two kinds of statistics are used as tools. One is descriptive statistics, used to describe the characteristics of either the sample or the population. The other is inferential statistics. With this type of statistics, tests are performed on a sample of data to determine how representative that sample is likely to be of the population as a whole. If measurements are made on an entire population there is no need for inferential statistics.

Descriptive statistics describe the characteristics of the data. Measures of central tendency are the **mode** (the value of the variable that occurs the most frequently), the **median** (the middle value of the variable of all the measurements taken), and the **mean** (the average value of the variable).

To describe the variability of the data, which tells us how much the observations vary around the mean, the statistics of **variance** and **standard deviation** may be computed. Variance, S^2, is the sum of the squared differences between each data point and the mean, divided by the number of data points minus one. Standard deviation is defined as the square root of the variance.

Standard deviations are useful statistics because they can be used to tell us where an individual falls compared to the distribution of all individuals in the population. In a normal distribution of data points, 68% of all observations will fall within one standard deviation of the mean. Ninety-five percent of all observations will fall within two standard deviations of the mean. The remaining five percent of observations will fall in the "tails" of the distribution, either more that two standard deviations above the mean or more than two standard deviations below the mean.

EXHIBIT 16.4   DATA COLLECTION METHODS COMPARED

METHOD	MAJOR ADVANTAGES	MAJOR POTENTIAL PROBLEMS
Interviews	1. Adaptive—allows data collection on a range of possible subjects 2. Source of "rich" data—reflects the complexity of the "real world" 3. Empathic—interviewer can begin to understand the interviewee 4. Process of interviewing can build rapport between interviewer and interviewee	1. Can be expensive 2. Interviewer can bias responses 3. Coding/interpretation problems—unstructured data can be difficult to code for further analysis 4. Self-report bias is possible—the interviewee can report data to make herself look good to the interviewer
Questionnaires	1. Responses can be quantified and easily summarized 2. Easy to use with large samples 3. Relatively inexpensive 4. Can obtain a large volume of data	1. Nonempathic—the questioner and the respondent never meet 2. Predetermined questions may miss important issues 3. Data may be over-interpreted—some results will occur by chance and yet be interpreted as important 4. There may be a response bias in that those who choose to reply to a questionnaire (the sample) may be unrepresentative of the population as a whole
Observations	1. Collects data on behaviour rather than reports of behaviour 2. Done in real-time, not based on retrospective recall 3. Adaptive—the researcher can change the focus of observations at any time	1. There may be difficulty in interpreting and coding the data that is gathered 2. Sample is likely to be small which makes generalization from the results more difficult 3. Possible reliability problems due to observer bias—the observer could see what he wants to see 4. Expensive because of the time involved
Secondary Data/ Unobtrusive Measures	1. Nonreactive—no response bias 2. High face validity 3. Easily quantified	1. Access/retrieval is possibly a problem 2. Potential validity problems if data collected are based on self-reports (i.e., corporate annual reports) 3. Possible coding and interpretation problems when data are not directly related to the issue being studied

SOURCE: Adapted from David A. Nadler (1977), *Feedback and Organization Development: Using Data-Based Methods.* Table 7.1. © 1977 by Addison-Wesley Publishing Company, Inc. Reprinted with permission of the publisher.

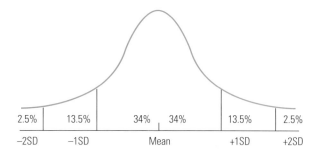

2.5% | 13.5% | 34% | 34% | 13.5% | 2.5%

−2SD   −1SD   Mean   +1SD   +2SD

Correlation coefficient
A measure of the direction and strength of the relationship between two variables.

Causality The determination of the direction of influence between two or more variables.

Inferential statistics
Used to determine if an effect or relationship can be called statistically significant.

Significance level The number of chances in 100 that the result of a statistical test occurred by chance.

Effect size A measure of the strength of a relationship between variables, and how well a theory explains an organizational phenomenon.

Type I error An inferential error made when an effect or relationship between variables is said to have been found even though it does not exist in reality.

Type II error An inferential error made when an effect or relationship between variables is denied, even though it really does exist.

When two variables are measured, the correlation between them may be computed. The **correlation coefficient** is a measure of the direction and strength of the relationship between the two variables. If the relationship is positive, when one variable increases the other tends to increase as well. In this case the correlation coefficient r might be +.30. With a negative relationship when one variable increases the other variable decreases. In this case r might be -.30. Correlation measures relationship but not **causality**. Other methods must be used to determine if one variable directly influences or causes the variation in the other variable.

Inferential statistics are used to determine if an effect or relationship can be called statistically significant. A standard is set of what the odds are that the result found happened by chance, then the actual result found is compared to this standard.

The odds that the result found happened by chance is called the **significance level**. It is usually set at p = .01, p = .05, or p = .10. Here p stands for probability and the numbers after the decimal for the number of chances in 100 that the results found occurred by chance. So, for example, a correlation between two variables of .30 found with a sample size of 70 and a p value of .05 means that if the data were to be gathered 100 times, in 5 of those times the result would occur by chance. If a result were found to be significant at a p value of .01, the result would be expected to occur by chance only 1 time in 100 tests. For any one test, however, the result *could* simply be due to chance.

Effect size is a measure of the strength of a relationship between variables or how well a theory explains an organizational phenomenon. Effect size is different from statistical significance and is important because it is a measure of whether or not what is found is of any real and practical importance. For example, in a test between two independent means a medium effect would be a difference of one-half a standard deviation (Cohen, 1992). A medium effect should be visible to a careful observer of the data. That is, in our previous example of a test between two independent means, a person looking at the data describing the two means should see the difference just by looking (without calculating the actual statistics). An effect size of r = .10 is considered a small effect, r = .30 is a medium effect, and r = .50 is a large effect.

Two types of inferential errors may occur. The first is when an effect or relationship is said to have been found even though it does not exist in reality. This is called a **Type I error**. The other type of error is to deny that an effect or relationship exists, even though it really does exist. This is a **Type II error**. Current methods of testing psychological and organizational theories tend to make more Type II errors because scientists wish to avoid the mistake of claiming a relationship has been found when it is in fact not real (the Type I error).

Gregory Kimble (1990) has described the process of testing a theory.

The assessment of a psychological theory is like a jury trial. There is a defendant (a theory) who is accused of being guilty (a good theory). A verdict of guilty requires rejection of the null hypothesis (innocent 'til proven guilty) at a high level of confidence (beyond a reasonable doubt). Whatever the verdict, two types of error are possible: a Type I error, where the jury finds a truly innocent person (bad theory) guilty (erroneously confirmed), and a Type II error where the jury finds a truly guilty person (good theory) innocent (not confirmed). Type II errors are more frequent because the circumstances are more apt to make them happen. The decisions of a jury are based on an array of considerations involving things like motive, opportunity, and access to the resources needed to commit the crime. In addition they entail auxiliary decisions about the credibility of witnesses, the capabilities of the opposing attorneys, and mitigating circumstances. The verdict of *not* not-guilty represents the judgment that, in the light of all these factors, it seems certain that the defendant, and no one else, must be the criminal. Reasonable doubts about any of them are grounds for acquittal.

In theory testing the case is similar. The verdict of innocent (not a good theory) is handed down when the theory does not make sense, when measurement tools are not reliable and valid, when the capabilities of the theory's supporters are not as strong as its critics, and when the circumstances of the theory's testing are far removed from the situation where the theory is meant to be applicable.

Ralph Rosnow and Robert Rosenthal (1989) have examined the Type I/Type II issue in some detail. This issue is crucially important because it explains why organizational scientists can have trouble finding support for their theories. The methods currently in use are often just not powerful enough (Cohen, 1990) to reduce Type II errors to the same level as Type I errors.

Exhibit 16.5 lists the ratios of Type II to Type I error rates for various sample sizes, three effect sizes, and the two common significance levels of .05 and .10 (called the alpha level). Note that effect size, significance level, and sample size are related. Also note in this exhibit that for the sample size of N = 50, a medium effect (r = .30) and a p value of .05, Type II errors are nine times more likely to occur than Type I errors! This means that with such a small sample it is much more likely that statistical inference will find no effect, even when one is really there to be found. Such tests do not have a large enough sample size to find medium effects that are there. In this case the sample size needs to be increased to N = 200 before the chances are even between Type I and Type II errors.

There is a story of a somewhat inebriated person who was looking for car keys under a lamp post. Asked where the keys were dropped, the drunk pointed to a dark parking lot and said "Over there." "Then why are you looking here?" the drunk was asked. "Because the light's better here" was the reply. Alluding to this story, Rosnow and Rosenthal (1989, p. 1278) stated that, "Given a typical medium-sized effect …, it would appear that psychological experimenters seemingly choose to work, or are forced to work by logistic constraints, in 'dimly lit' rather than in 'brightly lit' situations." In other words, the drunk is looking in the wrong place, but where the light is best; experimenters work in the right place, but without sufficient light to find anything. Neither is right.

The solution is for researchers to create tests of higher power. Power of .80 means there is an 80% chance of finding an effect if it is present. Exhibit 16.6 lists the sample sizes required for power = .80 for several different statistical tests. The main point of this table as used in this text is to point out the sizes of sample required to have a good chance of finding evidence of a phenomenon, assuming it is a moderately strong phenomenon (effect size is medium) and that the significance test used is set at p = .05. If an organizational scientist were testing the correlation between an independent variable and a dependent variable (test 2), the sample size required is N = 85. In other words, 85 independent observations would be required. Many tests do not gather that many observations and therefore do not have a good chance of finding evidence of the phenomenon. The analyst of organizational research should therefore be wary of tests with small sample sizes and low power.

Note that for the above conditions, except that the effect is small, the sample size required jumps to 783! Organizational scientists can use this table to decide for a given phenomenon and statistical test how large a sample they should collect.

EXHIBIT 16.5 RATIOS OF TYPE II TO TYPE I ERROR RATES FOR VARIOUS SAMPLE SIZES, EFFECT SIZES, AND SIGNIFICANCE LEVELS (TWO-TAILED)

| | EFFECT SIZES AND SIGNIFICANCE LEVELS | | | | | |
| | R = .10 | | R = .30 | | R = .50 | |
N	.05	.10	.05	.10	.05	.10
10	19	9	17	8	13	5
20	19	9	15	6	7	2
30	18	8	13	5	3	1
40	18	8	10	4	2	—
50	18	8	9	3	—	—
100	17	7	3	—	—	—
200	14	6	—	—	—	—
300	12	5	—	—	—	—
400	10	4	—	—	—	—
500	8	3	—	—	—	—
600	6	2	—	—	—	—
700	5	2	—	—	—	—
800	4	1	—	—	—	—
900	3	—	—	—	—	—
1000	2	—	—	—	—	—

NOTE: Entries are to nearest integer; missing values < 1.

SOURCE: Ralph L. Rosnow and Robert Rosenthal (1989), "Statistical procedures and the justification of knowledge in psychological science," *American Psychologist* 44: 1278. Copyright 1989 by the American Psychological Association. Reprinted by permission.

EXPLANATORY NOTE:

To create relatively even chances of both types of error the organizational scientist would want to select a sample size that is large enough, given the expected size of the effect and significance level chosen. The table above lists how many more times likely is a Type II error than a Type I error for given sample sizes, effect sizes, and significance levels. The dashes represent cases where the Type I error is *more* likely than a Type II error. So, if the phenomenon being studied was just a small effect (r = .10, it's hard to find), and the significance level chosen was p = .05 (a typical level), the scientist should make over 1000 observations to make the chances of Type II/Type I errors roughly equal. For a medium effect (r = .30), 200 observations would be required.

Meta-analysis A statistical method of combining and testing the empirical results from a number of studies.

One way to lessen our reliance on the test of significance from a single study is to combine a number of empirical results in a new test called a **meta-analysis**. Because in any study or experiment there are measurement errors, sampling errors, and other errors that can affect the results, meta-analysis averages these errors out over a number of studies. This allows a good estimate to be found of the true population value of the effect under study (Schmidt, 1992). In a meta-analysis each individual study is a single data point. No study is therefore relied upon to tell the whole truth about a phenomenon.

Interpretation   Even when a statistical test result is significant, the question must be addressed of what the result means. With a very large sample size even very small effects can be found to be "significant," meaning that they are not likely to have occurred by chance. But is the result meaningful? Does knowing the result help to make a difference in how a manager decides to act? The answer to this question is likely to be determined by the size of the effect. Larger effects explain more behaviour than do small effects.

EXHIBIT 16.6   NECESSARY SAMPLE SIZE FOR POWER OF .80
FOR THREE EFFECT SIZES AND ALPHA LEVELS

| | ALPHA | | | | | | | | |
| | .01 | | | .05 | | | .10 | | |
TEST	SMALL	MED	LARGE	SMALL	MED	LARGE	SMALL	MED	LARGE
1. *Mean dif*	586	95	38	393	64	26	310	50	20
2. *Sig r*	1163	125	41	783	85	28	617	68	22
3. *r dif*	2339	263	96	1573	177	66	1240	140	52
4. *P = .5*	1165	127	44	783	85	30	616	67	23
5. *P dif*	584	93	36	392	63	25	309	49	19
6. *Chi-square*									
1 df	1168	130	38	785	87	26	618	69	25
2 df	1388	154	56	964	107	39	771	86	31
3 df	1546	172	62	1090	121	44	880	98	35
4 df	1675	186	67	1194	133	48	968	108	39
5 df	1787	199	71	1293	143	51	1045	116	42
6 df	1887	210	75	1362	151	54	1113	124	45
7. *ANOVA*									
2 groups	586	95	38	393	64	26	310	50	20
3 groups	464	76	30	322	52	21	258	41	17
4 groups	388	63	25	274	45	18	221	36	15
5 groups	336	55	22	240	39	16	193	32	13
6 groups	299	49	20	215	35	14	174	28	12
7 groups	271	44	18	195	32	13	159	26	11
8. *Mult R*									
2 ind var	698	97	45	481	67	30			
3 ind var	780	108	50	547	76	34			
4 ind var	841	118	55	599	84	38			
5 ind var	901	126	59	645	91	42			
6 ind var	953	134	63	686	97	45			
7 ind var	998	141	66	726	102	48			
8 ind var	1039	147	69	757	107	50			

NOTE: *Test 1* is a test for a difference between two independent sample means.

Test 2 is a test for a significant correlation between two variables.

Test 3 is a test for the difference between two population correlations.

Test 4 is a test to determine if half of a population of paired differences are positive.

Test 5 tests the difference between two independent population proportions.

Test 6 tests the degree of association of variables in a contingency table.

Test 7 is an Analysis of Variance used to examine the variance in a dependent variable accounted for by two or more groups (the independent variable is group membership).

Test 8 is a Multiple R test of significance in a multiple regression analysis with two or more independent variables.

SOURCE: Jacob Cohen (1992), "A power primer," *Psychological Bulletin* 112: 158. Copyright 1992 by the American Psychological Association. Reprinted by permission.

Another way organizational scientists attempt to measure the importance of an effect is by examining the variance explained. If, for example, a correlation coefficient of .30 was found between rewarding good performance and product quality, the interpretation could be put forward that the amount of variation of quality explained by rewards was 9% (.30 squared), or not much. The implication is that 91% of the variation in quality is unaccounted for.

But this method of interpreting results can grossly underestimate the magnitude of a relationship. Daniel Ozer (1985) has shown that the absolute value of a correlation coefficient is directly interpretable as an effect size indicator. In other words, r = .30 is a medium effect. Robert Abelson (1985) demonstrated that even small effects can accumulate over many occurrences to amount to an important result. For example, if a decision making theory allowed a 1% improvement in the quality of a manager's decisions, the impact on any one decision would be small. But accumulated over a series of decisions or over a career the theory would be shown to be useful.

The point we are making here is that interpretation of study results must be done carefully. In the behavioural sciences there is "a strong cult of overconfident empiricism … an excessive faith in data as the direct source of scientific truths and an inadequate appreciation of how misleading most social science data are when accepted at face value and interpreted naively" (Schmidt, 1992, p. 1179).

OTHER APPROACHES TO ORGANIZATIONAL SCIENCE

To this point in the text we have taken a mostly modernist point-of-view. Essentially, this approach assumes that the organization and its environment is real and that it can be measured and acted upon. But there are other ways of thinking and understanding organizations. We will now examine several of these approaches and compare them to modernism.

Kenneth Gergen (1992) discusses three ways of approaching the study of organizations. The first is **romanticism**. Here the basic principle is that people have a deep interior where there exists their unique capacities and characteristics that define them as individuals. The human soul, genius, inspiration, creativity, the power of the human will—all these are to be found deep inside a person. This romanticist perspective is still found in the arts, literature, and religion, but less commonly in theories of organizations. Exceptions would be theories of fundamental human needs (e.g., Maslow, 1943) and charismatic leadership theory (House, 1977), among others. But Gergen notes that "In the intellectual world most particularly, romanticist voices largely speak from the margins. The chief replacement for the romanticist world-view is the modernist" (p. 210).

Romanticism The point of view that people have a deep interior where there exists their unique capacities and characteristics that define them as individuals.

Modernism and Postmodernism

Modernism is characterized by Gergen as:

Modernism The currently dominant scientific viewpoint that believes in progress and the powers of reason and observation, and whose objective is a search for fundamentals or essentials.

1. Belief in the powers of reason and observation;
2. A search for fundamentals or essentials;
3. A faith in progress and designs for society that work for all;
4. Using the machine as the predominant metaphor for understanding— for example the organization as a machine.

While modernism is still strongly rooted as a way of seeing the world and thinking about the organizations and people in it, postmodernism offers another perspective.

Postmodernism does not attempt to build all-encompassing theories of causal relationships between variables, but instead examines the social world from multiple perspectives. There is not expected to be central knowledge for all, but knowledge from perspectives based on a person's class, race, gender, or other characteristics. The Postmodern approach challenges and seeks to expose existing beliefs. Concepts that are accepted as natural in modernism (hierarchical power, for example) are challenged. Reality is seen to emerge through a process of people constructing it.

Postmodernism is important as a new way of looking at organizations, a way that will become more familiar as postmodern culture becomes more prevalent in society as a whole. Stewart Clegg has said that "for students growing up today, in the 1990s, postmodern culture saturates their whole mature life" (Boje, 1993). Clegg also makes the point that postmodernism can be useful for managers. His reason is that the United States' experience (and we can assume Canada's as well) is very modernist while other cultures are not. To better understand other cultures, then, postmodern approaches offer a useful training ground.

Comparing modernism to postmodernism we can examine several dimensions as discussed by Gibson Burrell and Gareth Morgan of York University in Toronto (Burrell & Morgan, 1979). These describe how organizational scientists make assumptions about organizations and people in them, and how research should be carried out.

Regarding the essence of the phenomenon being studied (its ontology), modernism takes a **realist** approach, that society has a real, concrete existence. The postmodern view is **nominalism**, the belief that social reality is a product of the interactions of the participants. There can be many social realities.

In terms of how we know (epistemology), the modernist view is that of **positivism**, that it is possible to reflect the world as it is. The post-modern **anti-positivism** assumes that the observer affects what is seen.

Human nature in positivism is **deterministic**. People are assumed to be restricted in how they will act by their background. Human nature in postmodernism is **voluntaristic**. People are seen as flexible and able to make choices about their own actions.

Modernistic methodology (how we study and produce knowledge) is **nomothetic** — it presumes that there are general rules or laws of behaviour that can be discovered. In contrast, the postmodernistic approach to methodology is that it is **idiographic**. The individual's experience is examined to gain knowledge of his own world.

Exhibit 16.7 provides a further comparison of positive (modernist) versus anti-positive (postmodernist) knowledge.

Both approaches have their uses. We do not have to think of postmodernism as replacing modernism, but as offering another way of thinking and studying—in effect, a new paradigm (see Kuhn, 1970). Both still use theory. Gergen (1992) wrote:

> under modernism, the proper theory should be fortified with years of research, and its application undertaken by yet another culture (the practitioners). In the postmodern context, the primary ingredient of theory is not its data base but its intelligibility, and the very communication of this intelligibility already establishes grounds for its utility. Theory and practice are inseparable. (p. 217).

An interesting demonstration of the application of multiple ways of understanding work behaviour is presented by John Hassard (1991). He used four different paradigms to study the British Fire Service, and found that each way of seeing allowed contrasting images of the organization to emerge (also see Morgan, 1986).

Postmodernism Takes the approach that there is not one central knowledge for all but that knowledge depends on a person's perspective based on class, race, gender, or other characteristics. The Postmodern approach challenges and seeks to expose existing beliefs.

Realism The point of view that society has a real, concrete existence.

Nominalism The point of view that social reality is a product of the interactions of the participants. Therefore there can be many social realities.

Positivism The view that it is possible to reflect the world as it is.

Anti-positivism The philosophical and theoretical assumption is that the observer affects what is seen.

Determinism The position that people are restricted in how they will act by their background.

Voluntarism The position that people are flexible and can make choices about their own actions.

Nomothetic The belief that there are general rules or laws of behaviour that can be discovered.

Idiographic The individual's experience is examined to gain knowledge of his own world.

EXHIBIT 16.7   CONTRASTING POSITIVE AND ANTI-POSITIVE KNOWLEDGE

FEATURES ASSOCIATED WITH POSITIVE FORMS OF KNOWLEDGE	IDEAS THAT COUNTER THE POSITIVE APPROACHES TO KNOWLEDGE
1. Treats their subject matter as a "given," exactly like the natural sciences.	1. Refuses either to focus only on the representations of human existence or to reduce subjectivity to an objectification of apparent subjective "characteristics"; instead, the power matrix, which is the background to the production of such representations and objectifications and "characteristics," is examined.
2. Develops laws, rules, or statistical probabilities concerning their respective objects.	2. Recognizes the goals of a science of management and organizations as a claim to status, respectability, and legitimacy, but one that is open to ridicule because it is incapable of standing up to the rigour of the methods it has set. That is, its emulation of the positive sciences locates it in the trap of having to provide causal explanations, invariable laws, and predictions, the possibility of which would demand that knowledge of management could be independent of, or truly ignore, the conditions (e.g., an elusive subjectivity) of its own production.
3. Acquires the status of sciences.	3. Suggests an analysis that does *not* use evidence exhaustively to establish a set of causal relations but selectively to render a problem intelligible. This is the genealogical approach, which in displaying the conditions that made it possible for management knowledge to develop, points to the precarious and unreliable character of that knowledge.
4. Becomes an integral part of power relations through their impact on standards of public health (biology), correct grammar (linguistics), and the management of the economy (economics).	4. Encourages management and organization theorists to confront the way in which power and knowledge influence one another and to refrain from engaging in the practice of power while projecting the pretense of value neutrality. It recognizes how management knowledge results from, and contributes to, a particular disciplinary regime.
5. Produces truths (i.e., the norms of what it is to be a healthy, speaking, and productive subject) through their power effects.	5. Perceives truth as an effect of power-knowledge relations rather than the outcome of correct scientific procedure or method. Students of management and organization, therefore, must avoid presuming that when the practical recommendations of a research project "work," this is so simply because the theory underlying them is true. The "truth" of our knowledge is much more a result of it being seen as true and, as a consequence, drawn upon in the exercise of power. At the same time it has to be recognized that "the achievement of 'true' discourses (which are incessantly changing, however) is one of the fundamental problems of the West" (Foucault, 1988: 112)

Source: David Knights (1992), "Changing spaces: The disruptive impact of a new epistemological location for the study of management," *Academy of Management Review* 17: 519. Reprinted by permission of the Academy of Management.

Critical Theory

Critical theory is inherently political, looks for change, and critiques ideology. Positivism is critiqued as the ideology of capitalism. Ben Agger (1991) writes that critical theorists

> argue that the positivist theory of science has become a new mythology and ideology in the sense that it fails to understand its own investment in the status quo ... they argue that positivism has become the most dominant form of ideology in late capitalism in the sense that people everywhere are taught to accept the world "as it is," thus unthinkingly perpetuating it. (p. 109).

Therefore, the idea is that if everyone is taught the model of positivism and "normal science," with all its attendant values about progress, power, and knowledge, then everyone comes to believe that radical change is not possible. People thus perpetuate the world as they have been taught to see it. Critical theory rejects the positivistic world view. Social facts are seen as "pieces of history that can be changed" (Agger, 1991, p. 109).

The most telling comment of critical theory on organizational science is in how the values and assumptions of researchers are exposed to view—even though in positivism researchers attempt to be value-free or report their findings as value free. Agger wrote "positivist social science ... purports to transcend myth and value but, in its own methodological obsessions, is mythological to the very core" (1991, p. 111).

Poststructuralism

The basic argument in **poststructuralism** is that language is not a medium used to describe reality but that we make our reality through the use of language. Richard Rorty (1989) states that the argument is "that since truth is a property of sentences, since sentences are dependent for their existence upon vocabularies, and since vocabularies are made by human beings, so are truths" (p. 21).

The main tool of poststructuralism is the **deconstruction** of texts. Using deconstruction, a story (or text, writing) would be examined, taken apart, analyzed. Other sides of what was written are looked for, and the values and interests of the author are brought into view. Assumptions of the author that may not have been questioned are questioned.

> Reading is a strong activity, not merely passive reflection of an objective text with singular meaning. Readers help give writing its sense by filling in these gaps and conflicts of meaning, even becoming writers and hence challenging the hierarchy of writing over reading, cultural production over cultural reception (Agger, 1991, p. 113).

An interesting example of this is H.L. Goodall's (1992) deconstruction of the Nordstrom Inc. employee handbook (see this chapter's *Seeing is Believing* feature for the handbook in its entirety!)

Feminist Research

Driven by a political agenda to advance women, feminist research seeks to create social change by doing research for women rather than about women (Allen & Baber, 1992). Katherine Allen and Kristine Baber write that:

> Mainstream empirical research, purporting to be value free, has few prescriptions regarding proper topics for research, characteristics of the researcher, or appropriate roles for "participants" in the research process. Feminism, however, because it is a political project as well as a body of theories, rejects the idea of objective, value-free research and proposes ways of increasing the validity of the results of feminist work (p. 9).

These include researching women's problems and experiences, that feminist researchers should study themselves, that research participants should be seen more as collaborators than as subjects, and questions about the place of men in feminist research.

Stephanie Riger (1992) has defined **feminism** as "a system of values that challenges male dominance and advocates social, political, and economic equity of women and men in society" (p. 731). Riger goes on to show how psychological and organizational research has had a male bias by:

Poststructuralism
Theoretical standpoint that, rather than language being a medium used to describe reality, reality is made through the use of language.

Deconstruction The main tool of poststructuralism, in which the values and interests of the author are exposed through analysis of what is written.

Feminism A system of values that challenges male dominance and advocates social, political, and economic equity of women and men in society.

EXPERIENCE IS THE BEST TEACHER

I am an organization theorist. I study organizations, their role in society, and their effect on the individuals that live and work within them. My interest in organization studies grows out of the observation that our society is, more than anything else, characterized by large-scale organizations; organizations that produce the goods we consume, that educate us, entertain us, and govern us. Our lives are a product of organized activity in a way that has no parallel in history. We live in a society of organizations.

Traditional organizational theory is concerned with developing theories that help managers rationalize processes of production and that assist in the attainment of organizational goals. In this instrumental view organizations are understood to be goal-directed instruments that are purposely created to produce a product (a car or a can of peas) or to provide a service (street cleaning or post-secondary education).

But these traditional theories do not question the effect of thinking of organizations as tools in the first place. Organizations are much more than just tools. Organizations, once created, have a tendency to take on a life of their own quite separate from the goals of the founders; they are not objects, but complex social systems. Large organizations create particular ways of thinking about the world and of determining appropriate courses of action. Organizations are also often important social actors. They have access to channels of mass communication and to political arenas that multiply their importance.

My work lies in the organizational questions that grow out of this less instrumental view of organizations.

I am interested in how organizations fit into the lives of individuals and into society more broadly, and the effect that different dimensions of organizations have on different individuals and different societies. Theoretical perspectives such as postmodernism, critical theory, feminist theory, and poststructuralism provide the conceptual tools to question the role of organizations in society and to critique the limited instrumental view that has grown out of an over-emphasis on the goal oriented view of organizations. These perspectives will play an increasing role in our understanding of organizations as technological and social changes continue to drive organizational change and to place traditional organizational theory under increasing pressure. These alternative theoretical perspectives give us a way to view organizations that allows us to see other things and understand previously hidden aspects of organization. As cultural change drives changes in the way we organize, these alternative theoretical lenses will become an increasingly important part of the way we understand organizations.

Note: Nelson Phillips is an Assistant Professor at McGill University's Faculty of Management. A sample of his work is "Analyzing communication in and around organizations: A critical hermeneutic approach," Academy of Management Journal, 1993, 36: 1547-1576 (co-authored with John L. Brown of the University of Alberta).

- Studying issues seen as more "male" (e.g., leadership, achievement, and power) rather than subjects of relevance to women (e.g., home/work roles, sexual harassment);
- Using only males in samples of subjects and generalizing the results to all people;
- Including women at times only as the stimulus in the study (they are reacted to) rather than as the subject of the study;
- The over-representation of male experimenters/theorists;
- Interpreting, at times, the actions of women as deficient, when compared with the actions of men;
- Conducting experiments that are stripped of social context, when such context is necessary to understand the actions of women;
- Constructing theories based on masculine ways of understanding.

S E E I N G   I S   B E L I E V I N G

An artist's impression of the Nordstrom store in Bloomington, Minnesota.

Welcome To
Nordstrom

We're glad to have you with
our company

Our number one goal is to provide
outstanding customer service.

Set both your personal and
professional goals high.
We have great confidence in your
ability to achieve them.

Nordstrom Rules:
Rule No. 1:
**Use your good
judgement in all situations.**

There will be no additional rules.

Please feel free to ask
your department manager,
store manager or division general
manager any question
at any time.

Nordstrom

SOURCE: Courtesy of Nordstrom Inc. This Seattle-based retailer has been chosen as one of the 100 best companies to work for in America (see Levering and Moskowitz, 1993).

An example illustrating these last two points is shown as Exhibit 16.8. In the feminine reality, knowledge is based on an ethic of caring. The self is defined by its connections, the independent self does not exist. While material reality may exist, that reality takes on its meaning within relationships (Jacques, 1992). By way of contrast, in the masculine reality knowledge is judgment-based.

EXHIBIT 16.8   THEORY BUILDING FROM THE PERSPECTIVES OF JUDGMENT AND CARE

JUDGMENT-BASED KNOWLEDGE PRACTICES	CARE-BASED KNOWLEDGE PRACTICES
Knowledge exists for its own sake.	Knowledge is for a community's use.
Theory should attempt to reflect truth, or, at least, general principles.	Because truth is context dependent, meaning should be sought in social processes rather than in abstractions.
The central question in theory development is that of developing an appropriate methodological framework, rules to justify inclusion/exclusion of knowledge/knowers.	The central question is the epistemological/ethical problem of speaking between varying beliefs and values without reducing one to the terms of the other. Connection to group values, beliefs, and practices is invoked to justify inclusion/exclusion.
Theories are best tested through rigorous skepticism. One must be able to reject the opposite of one's finding (null hypothesis testing).	Theories are best tested through provisional acceptance. If one accepts this theory as knowledge, who will be affected and in what way?
Presence of the researcher's values, opinions, and social goals is a form of research bias.	The researcher should be "present" in the research. Authority of results is grounded in personal experience.
Because the first goal of theorizing is to describe objectively, the consequences of theorizing are not appropriately the concern of the researcher.	Because research creates a story that affects people's lives, the first concern of the researcher is the consequences the story will have in the lives of those it affects.
The goal of theory development is to produce testable propositions.	The goal of theory development is to create a story that helps one to make sense of one's experience according to one's concrete situation, values, and beliefs.
Theory should be judged against prior knowledge for consistency and reliability.	Theory should be judged against current problems for its role in creating change.
If paradigmatic unity cannot be achieved, the discipline will either fragment or slip into a pluralistic relativism where "anything goes." Diversity is positive only if it can be managed into some integrating framework.	Theorists in different concrete circumstances will see things differently. Connection must allow discussion of these differences without enforcing unity or supporting relativism. Differences should be valued and multiplied in professional discourse.

SOURCE: Roy Jacques (1992), "Critique and theory building: Producing knowledge 'from the kitchen,'" *Academy of Management Review* 17: 588. Reprinted by permission of the Academy of Management.

These challenges to the presumed neutrality of science have created three ways of doing feminist research (Riger, 1992).

1. *Feminist empiricism* — attempts to be more rigorous in the use of traditional scientific methods to produce gender-fair research.
2. *Feminist standpoint science* — acknowledges that how we know and what we know depend on who we are. Therefore, the aim is to view society from a women's perspective and give a voice to women's experience.
3. *Feminist postmodernism/poststructuralism* —seeks to make clear other (anti-positivist) versions of reality and the values that underlie them. Given that science does not mirror reality but instead creates it, the question becomes which values and social institutions are favoured by each version of reality that has been created. If the male conception of reality is reflected in positivism, then positivism is serving the interests of males. The world continues to be given male meanings (Weedon, 1987).

CONCLUSION

We hope that the organizational science concepts and theories that we have discussed in this text will be of continuing use to you, the organizational member and student of organizations. In any organizational situation, the theories and concepts of organizational behaviour can be used as tools. These can help a manager, employee or organizational member to better understand what is happening and what levers to push in order to create change. Because no management theory or book can cover every possible situation that might be encountered now and in the future, adaptability in using these tools will be important. As the captain of the pirate ship "Revenge" said (see the *Overboard* cartoon), "A lot of these things just never came up in management training".

CHAPTER SUMMARY

Canadian organizations in the future can expect changes in work force composition because of baby boom demographics, the changing sex composition of work force participants, and the increased inclusion of minorities. Other important trends for the near future are increased downsizing of organizations, the continuing move to a more global economy, and the increased importance of information technology on the way organizations operate. The virtual corporation and the boundaryless company are likely to become more common in the future.

The student of organizations needs to be an active evaluator of new theories and facts about how organizations work. To this end each individual needs to understand the methods of modernist science as well as postmodern approaches. These latter approaches include poststructuralism, deconstruction of texts, and feminism. They allow other ways of understanding organizations to be explored and to contribute their voice to the science of organizations.

Finally, the organizational scholar who will be a consumer of new organizational behaviour theories and facts needs to be aware of the ethical safeguards in place to encourage the quality production of new knowledge. New knowledge can then be evaluated against these standards to allow a judgment to be made of its quality.

QUESTIONS FOR REVIEW

1. What societal trends are likely to have an impact on the way organizations operate in the future?

2. Explain the modernist approach to science.

3. Give examples of how postmodern approaches to science offer different perspectives on what we know about organizations.

S E L F - D I A G N O S T I C EXERCISE 16.1

Rate Your Science Ethics: What Would You Do?

1. You have just finished performing a first-year chemistry experiment, but something went wrong. The results are not those you expected and not those that all your friends seem to be getting. Do you report your results or copy the results from someone else's experiment for your report?

2. A subject in your experiment has just finished a one-hour test and then completes a personality scale. But when the scale is returned you examine it and find that the person failed to answer two questions, without which all that person's data are useless to you. Do you fill in the two missing answers or discard all the data?

3. You are studying the relationship between two variables and have completed a planned study of 50 subjects. The correlation has been found to be significant at $p = .06$. Your research assistant then studied an additional 10 subjects and found the correlation for all 60 subjects to be significant at $p = .04$. Which data would you report?

4. On looking at your questionnaire returns it is obvious that one subject simply did not seriously attempt to answer the questions. Instead of circling one answer for each question asked (for example the number "4" on a 7-point scale) the respondent circled a whole block of answers (a whole set of "4"s). Do you discard this person's questionnaire or dutifully record the answers and include them in the data set?

5. You hired a research assistant to help you with your work, and, without your knowledge, the assistant gathered and analyzed some data that support your theory. But the assistant failed to give proper instructions to the subjects, did not inform them of their right to withdraw at any time without penalty, and actually misled them into thinking the experiment was about another topic entirely. Do you discard these data or not? Do you have any responsibilities to inform the subjects of the misleading nature of their instructions?

6. You have completed your research and sent it in to a journal for possible publication. In order to get tenure at your university and therefore keep your job, it is imperative that this article be accepted. The journal's editor likes your work,

but asks you to rewrite it in the "proper scientific form" by specifying hypotheses that are then supported by the data. The only problem is that you actually conducted exploratory work designed to generate hypotheses for future testing. Do you rewrite your article to get it published?

7. You are doing a telephone survey and are interviewing a subject that is very difficult and quarrelsome. It seems that the data are just not worth the effort. Do you hang up or hang in there and collect the data?

EXPERIENTIAL EXERCISE 16.1

The Ruler Experiment

This experiment can be done in the classroom by your professor. It is a very useful basis for a discussion about science and the methods of science.

Step 1: The hypothesis: "Females react faster than males."

Step 2: The instructor will select a male volunteer from the class and, using any 12" or 15" ruler as a device to measure reaction time, conduct two reaction time trials. Dropping the ruler between the thumb and forefinger of an outstretched hand, the distance dropped by the ruler before it is caught is measured and recorded.

Step 3: The instructor will ask for a female volunteer to participate. After two practice trials, two reaction time trials will be conducted.

Step 4: Compare the measurements from the male subject and the female subject and prove or disprove the hypothesis.

Step 5: Discuss the experiment.

SOURCE: Based on Philip G. Zimbardo (1985), "Finding meaning in the method," in Ludy T. Benjamin, Jr., & Kathleen D. Lowman (Eds.), *Activities Handbook for the Teaching of Psychology* (pp. 24-26). Washington, D.C.: American Psychological Association.

SELF-GUIDED LEARNING ACTIVITY

An excellent resource book that details a number of ways to gather data without actually handing out a questionnaire or conducting an interview is the 1966 classic by Eugene J. Webb and others titled *Unobtrusive Measures: Nonreactive Research in the Social Sciences.* Several of the methods listed in the book do not involve human participants but can be used to research human behaviour.

For example, one research question could be: At a set of three turnstiles, do people tend to go through the right, the centre, or the left? If you go to your college or university library, you can look for patterns of wear on the carpets underneath the turnstiles to answer this question. Or, if the turnstiles have built-in counters, an actual measurement can be taken.

Other fascinating methods of researching human behaviour are the lost letter technique (aimed at obtaining a strong measure of attitudes) and the gummed-page method (used to check how many pages of a book were actually examined). Remember, however, that if you engage in any research that involves human subjects you will need to present your plan to your local university or college ethics committee for its approval.

CASE 16.1

MANAGER'S CASE FILE: DIVIDED THEY STAND

Eric Blake, supervisor of the advertising department of Widgets, Inc., was patting himself on the back for hiring Randy Nichols to fill the position of illustrator. Randy had come highly recommended from another company that had to let him go due to a downsizing effort. Eric was sure that Randy, with his advertising genius, would make a hit of the new line of widgets to begin marketing in the summer. Eric, however, was not prepared for the mixed reception he received when he introduced Randy to the other staffers in the department.

"He's gay," Tony said. "He's got to be gay."

"You can't say he's gay just because he's effeminate," Sarah said.

"I'll bet my next paycheck he's gay," Don replied, "and he's so thin, too. I'll bet he's a good candidate to get AIDS if he doesn't have it already."

"That's a terrible thing to say," Marcia said. "But, just the same, I'm not going to get too close to him—in case."

"Maybe we should get rubber gloves and surgical masks," Tony suggested.

"Don't be ridiculous," Don said. "Just stay as far away as possible."

"And how are you going to do that?" Sarah asked. "We have to work with him. We have to give him advertising copy."

"Send it interoffice," Marcia said.

After Randy had been with Widget for about three weeks, he asked to meet with Eric in his office to suggest a new way of handling the work process.

"You just lose so much time sending everything interoffice," Randy said.

"What are you talking about?" Eric asked.

"All my information comes to me interoffice,"

Randy replied. I just thought that it was the way things were done around here. I thought it was silly since it comes from my own department."

"You bet it's silly. Let me find out what's going on," Eric offered.

Shortly after Randy left Eric's office, he asked Tony, the informal leader of the department, to meet with him.

"What's going on?" Eric wanted to know. "Why do we have new procedures, and whose idea was it? Do you know it's slowing down the work on the new project?"

"It can't be helped," Tony said. "It's just a precautionary measure; that's all. And the project will be completed on time. Don't worry about that."

"Precautionary measure against what?" Eric asked.

"Getting AIDS," Tony said. "We don't know if Randy has AIDS, we're just not taking any chances."

"That's absurd," Eric spurted. "Admittedly, Randy is rather thin but that's no reason to suspect that he has AIDS. Besides, everything I've read says...."

"Look," Tony said. "I've read the same. But people are afraid. We understand you can't refuse to hire him, but likewise you can't force us to work with him either. He's getting all the material he needs from us; he just gets it through the mail instead of one of us walking it over to him."

After Tony left Eric's office, Eric sat at his desk contemplating what he had just been told. Tony was right in that the staffers couldn't be forced to work *with* Randy. They were getting the work *to* him. He wondered what he was going to tell Randy and what was going to happen when he called a staff meeting to discuss progress on the project. Were all the others going to sit on the opposite side of the room from Randy? What if Randy decided to quit because of their attitude?

SOURCE: Reprinted, by permission of publisher, from MANAGEMENT SOLUTIONS, February 1988. © 1988 American Management Association, New York. All rights reserved.

Questions

1. What, if anything, can Eric do to get all the staffers to work together?
2. What can Eric say to Randy?
3. What can Eric do to keep Randy from leaving should Randy decide that the situation makes him uncomfortable?

CASE 16.2

PARADIGMS FOR THE EMPIRICAL VALIDATION OF COMMON PROVERBS

In 1983 we were commissioned by the government to determine the degree of validity of proverbs, adages, truisms, and platitudes. We initially grappled with the question, "Do blonds indeed have more fun?" In the spring of 1983 we published our initial findings which indicated that several other personality and demographic factors moderate the relationship between hair color and the quality of life. Understandably our findings created quite a stir in the scientific and hair-care communities. The government then generously agreed to fund an intensive research program focusing exclusively on the validation of common proverbs.

We promptly plunged into an intensive study of the question, "Is a bird in the hand really worth two in the bush?" We decided to investigate the validity of the proverb in several ways.

A. THE FIELD STUDY

We asked a random sample of 1,200 people in the Times Square area in New York the question, "Do you think that a bird in the hand is worth two in the bush, or do you think that a bird in the hand is worth more or less than two in the bush?" Interviewer-respondent dyads were randomized for sexual and racial matching. Results indicate that 1,188 people refused to answer the question (although 63 of these people dropped some change into the palms of our interviewers and five individuals responded, "I gave at the office" and hurried away). Four people responded with incomprehensible grunts. Six people answered with profanity or threats of violence. One person propositioned an interviewer, and another person (an elderly white female carrying two shopping bags full of stale bread crumbs) answered, "Why certainly" and locomoted away.

B. THE LABORATORY STUDY

Since the results of the field study were inconclusive, we decided to move our study into the more carefully controlled environment of the University's psychological laboratory. A room with two doors, one marked "Bird in the Hand" and the other marked "Two in the Bush" functioned as the experimental setting. One additional door marked "Exit" was used as a control. These doors were each painted yellow and were uniform in size. the cardboard signs, also of uniform size, were block-lettered in black with each letter measuring five inches by three inches. Three separate experiments were conducted in this setting.

In experiment one, six-hundred college sophomores enrolled in introductory psychology were individually brought into the room by an attendant wearing a white laboratory coat. These subjects were told to sit in a chair which was placed so that it was equidistant from all three doors. They were then given the following instructions by the attendant:

"Please use any door that you wish and that which is indicated on the door's sign will be yours."

In actuality there was nothing at all behind the doors, except of course for the "Exit" door which led to a hallway and eventually a staircase. The attendant continued by saying:

"You will be given up to two minutes to make your decision."

The attendant remained in the room with a stopwatch. Results indicated that each of the six hundred subjects chose the "Exit" door within a maximum of six seconds.

In the second experiment the procedure was essentially the same as the procedure followed in experiment one, except that after seeing the subject to the chair the attendant simply left the room (through the "Exit" door) without saying a single word to the subject. The attendant then observed the subject through a remote TV console that had been installed especially for this study. It was felt that this "unobtrusive" observational technique would allow for greater freedom and self-expression on the part of the subject. Among the seven hundred and twenty subjects, the following behavioral responses were recorded:

Response	Frequency
Random looking around	720
Looking at watch	698
Nail-biting, floor-pacing	604
Looking at "bird in hand" door	720
Looking at "two in bush" door	720
Giggling, humming, muttering	604
Opening "bird in hand" door first	360
Opening "two in bush" door first	360
Opening "Exit" door first	0
Leaving room through "Exit" door	720
Average time to first door opening	2 minutes and 23 seconds
Average time to leaving room	3 minutes and 2 seconds

In experiment three, 412 white albino rats were placed sequentially on the chair and observed through the remote TV console. The following behavioral responses were recorded.

Response	Frequency
Random looking around	412
Looking at watch	0
Nail-biting, floor-pacing	412
Looking at "bird in hand" door	412
Looking at "two in bush" door	412
Giggling, humming, muttering	0
Opening "bird in hand" door first	0
Opening "two in bush" door first	0
Opening "Exit" door first	0
Leaving room through "Exit" door	0
Leaving room through a small hole in the wall	412
Average time to leaving room	1 minute and 28 seconds

The different pattern of behavior observed indicated rather startling inter-species differences which are as yet unexplained. One obvious interpretation is that the rats are more readily capable of making a definite decision and of acting upon the decision than are their human counterparts. However, other variables related to decision-making ability, such as intelligence, maturity, ego-strength, and self-esteem, could well account for the obtained difference in decision-making ability. This is certainly a problem which warrants our further careful research.

Incidentally, a member of our research staff suggested that inter-species behavioral response may be partially explained by the fact that rats may find it difficult to open doors. Taking this insight to heart we designed a T-maze in which to one goal was attached a "bird in the hand" block-lettered sign, while to the other goal was attached a "two in the bush" sign. These signs were alternated from right to left goals on successive runs. Five hundred and forty rats were placed in the maze. Two hundred and seventy-two rats were observed to run to the "bird in the hand" sign and two-hundred and sixty-eight rats ran to the "two in the bush" sign.

Our research clearly indicates that there is no evidence of a difference in preference for, and hence value or worth of, a "bird in the hand" or "two in the bush." Each of these "entities" are equally valued—by man and by beast. Hence we can conclude that the proverb is indeed valid. It is with a measure of pride that we now firmly state, "Yes, a bird in the hand is worth two in the bush." But it is with even greater pride that we assert that proverbs need no longer be accepted at face value or on faith alone. We have developed scientific techniques which enable us to determine with confidence the validity of proverbs which have had a profound influence on the course of our lives. By demystifying proverbs, by placing our belief in their efficacy on a more rational footing, we hope to redirect human destiny away from the inhibitions engendered by superstitions, toward the freedom provided by scientifically-derived empirically-based knowledge.

Source: Reprinted from Ira J. Morrow (1986), "Paradigms for the empirical validation of common proverbs," *The Industrial Psychologist* 23(2): 46-49. Reprinted by permission of the Society of Industrial and Organizational Psychology.

REFERENCES

Abelson, Robert P. (1985). "A variance explanation paradox: When a little is a lot." *Psychological Bulletin* 97: 129-133.

Agger, Ben (1991). "Critical theory, poststructuralism, postmodernism: Their sociological relevance." *Annual Review of Sociology* 17: 105-131.

Allen, Katherine R., & Kristine M. Baber (1992). "Ethical and epistemological tensions in applying a postmodern perspective to feminist research." *Psychology of Women Quarterly* 16: 1-15.

Balsley, Howard Lloyd, & Vernon T. Clover (1988). *Research for Business Decisions: Business Research Methods.* Columbus: Publishing Horizons.

Baxter, Gerald, & Nancy Kerber Baxter (1986). "Einstein's advice on work in the next century." *Personnel Journal,* April 1986, 14-19.

Boje, David M. (1993). "On being postmodern in the Academy: An interview with Stewart Clegg." *Journal of Management Inquiry* 2: 191-200.

Boyacigiller, Nakiye Avdan, & Nancy J. Adler (1991). "The parochial dinosaur: Organizational science in a global context." *Academy of Management Review* 16: 262-290.

Burrell, W. Gibson, & Gareth Morgan (1979). *Sociological Paradigms and Organizational Analysis.* London: Heinemann.

Byrne, John A., Richard Brandt, & Otis Port (1993). "The virtual corporation: The company of the future will be the ultimate in adaptability." *Business Week,* February 8, 1993, pp. 98-102.

Cohen, Jacob (1990). "Things I have learned (so far)." *American Psychologist* 45: 1304-1312.

Cohen, Jacob (1992). "A power primer." *Psychological Bulletin* 112: 155-159.

Davis, Murray S. (1971). "That's interesting! Towards a phenomenology of sociology and a sociology of phenomenology." *Philosophy of the Social Sciences* 1: 309-344.

Davis, Murray S. (1986). "'That's Classic!' The phenomenology and rhetoric of successful social theories." *Philosophy of the Social Sciences* 16: 285-301.

Fletcher, Ronald (1991). *Science, Ideology, and the Media: The Cyril Burt Scandal.* New Brunswick, NJ: Transaction Publishers.

Foucault, Michel (1988). *The Case of the Self: The History of Sexuality* (Vol. 3). New York: Vintage Books.

Gaines, Jeannie (1993). "'You don't necessarily have to be charismatic ...:' An interview with Anita Roddick and reflections on charismatic processes in the Body Shop International." *Leadership Quarterly* 4: 347-359.

Gay, Lorraine R., & Helen L. Diehl (1991). *Research Methods for Business and Management.* New York: MacMillan.

Gergen, Kenneth J. (1992). "Organization theory in the postmodern era." In Michael Reed and Michael Hughes (Eds.), *Rethinking Organization: New Directions in Organization Theory and Analysis,* pp. 207-226. London: Sage Publications.

Goodall, H.L., Jr. (1992). "Empowerment, culture, and postmodern organizing: Deconstructing the *Nordstrom Employee Handbook.*" *Journal of Organizational Change Management* 5: 25-30.

Green, Bert F. (1992). "Expose or smear? The Burt affair." *Psychological Science* 3: 328-331.

Harrison, David A. (1993). "Why can't you use just one textbook for this class?!" *The Academy of Management Research Methods Division Newsletter*, 8(1): 9-12 and 8(2): 14-16.

Hassard, John (1991). "Multiple paradigms and organizational analysis: A case study." *Organization Studies* 12: 275-299.

Hearnshaw, Leslie (1979). *Cyril Burt, Psychologist.* Ithaca, NY: Cornell University Press.

Hirschhorn, Larry, & Thomas Gilmore (1992). "The new boundaries of the 'boundaryless' company." *Harvard Business Review*, May/June 1992, 104-115.

Hofstede, Geert (1993). "Cultural constraints in management theories." *Academy of Management Executive* 7(1): 81-94.

House, Robert J. (1977). "A 1976 theory of charismatic leadership." In James G. Hunt & Larry L. Larson (Eds.), *Leadership: The Cutting Edge* (pp. 189-207). Carbondale, IL: Southern Illinois University Press.

Jacques, Roy (1992). "Critique and theory building: Producing knowledge 'from the kitchen.'" *Academy of Management Review* 17: 582-606.

Jaeger, Richard M. (1990). *Statistics: A Spectator Sport* (2nd edition). Newbury Park, CA: Sage.

Jick, Todd D. (1979). "Mixing qualitative and quantitative methods: Triangulation in action." *Administrative Science Quarterly* 24: 602-611.

Joynson, Robert (1989). *The Burt Affair.* London, England: Routledge.

Kimble, Gregory A. (1990). "A trivial disagreement?" *Psychological Inquiry* 1: 156-157. This article is a peer commentary on the target article by Paul E. Meehl (1990) titled "Appraising and amending theories: The strategy of Lakatosian defense and two principles that warrant it," *Psychological Inquiry* 1: 108-141.

Kirkpatrick, David (1993). "Groupware goes boom." *Fortune.* December 27, 1993, pp. 99-106.

Knights, David (1992). "Changing spaces: The disruptive impact of a new epistemological location for the study of management." *Academy of Management Review* 17: 514-536.

Kuhn, Thomas S. (1970). *The Structure of Scientific Revolutions.* Second edition. Chicago: University of Chicago Press.

Levering, Robert, & Milton Moskowitz (1993). *The 100 Best Companies to Work For in America.* New York: Doubleday.

Markham, Calvert (1993). "Insider dealing: Support staff will have to compete when colleagues become customers." *International Management*, December 1993, p. 56.

Maslow, Abraham H. (1943). "A theory of human motivation." *Psychological Review*, July 1943, pp. 370-396.

Miner, John B. (1984). "The validity and usefulness of theories in an emerging organizational science." *Academy of Management Review* 9: 296-306.

Miner, John B. (1990). "The role of values in defining the 'goodness' of theories in organizational science." *Organization Studies* 11: 161-178.

Morgan, Gareth (1986). *Images of Organization.* Beverly Hills: Sage.

Morrow, Ira J. (1986). "Paradigms for the empirical validation of common proverbs." *The Industrial Psychologist* 23(2): 46-49.

Nadler, David A. (1977). *Feedback and Organization Development: Using Data-Based Methods.* Reading, MA: Addison-Wesley.

Nagel, Roger (1993). "Virtual winners: The 'virtual corporation' could soon be a reality." *International Management*, June 1993, p. 64.

Offerman, Lynn R., & Marilyn K. Gowing (1990). "Organizations of the future: Changes and challenges." *American Psychologist* 45: 95-108.

Ozer, Daniel J. (1985). "Correlation and the coefficient of determination." *Psychological Bulletin* 97: 307-315.

Peters, Tom (1990). "Prometheus barely unbound." *Academy of Management Executive* 4(4): 70-83.

Phillips, Nelson, & John L. Brown (1993). "Analyzing communication in and around organizations: A critical hermeneutic approach." *Academy of Management Journal* 36: 1547-1576.

Riger, Stephanie (1992). "Epistemological debates, feminist voices." *American Psychologist* 47: 730-740.

Rorty, Richard (1989). *Contingency, Irony, and Solidarity.* Cambridge: Cambridge University Press.

Rosnow, Ralph L., & Robert Rosenthal (1989). "Statistical procedures and the justification of knowledge in psychological science." *American Psychologist* 44: 1276-1284.

Schmidt, Frank L. (1992). "What do data really mean? Research findings, meta-analysis, and cumulative knowledge in psychology." *American Psychologist* 47: 1173-1181.

Schmitt, Neal W., & Richard J. Klimoski (1991). *Research Methods in Human Resources Management.* Cincinnati: South-Western Publishing.

Sekaran, Uma (1984). *Research Methods for Managers: A Skill-building Approach.* New York: Wiley.

Semler, Ricardo (1994). "Why my former employees still work for me." *Harvard Business Review,* January-February 1994, pp. 64-74.

Sherman, Stratford (1993). "A brave new Darwinian workplace." *Fortune,* January 25, 1993, pp. 50-56.

Smith, Peter B. (1992). Organizational behaviour and national cultures. *British Journal of Management* 3: 39-51.

Stewart, Thomas A. (1992). "Brace yourself for Japan's hot new strategy." *Fortune,* September 21, 1992, pp. 62-74.

Stone, Eugene F. (1978). *Research Methods in Organizational Behavior.* Santa Monica: Goodyear.

Tufte, Edward R. (1983). *The Visual Display of Quantitative Information.* Cheshire, CT: Graphics Press.

Webb, Eugene J., Donald T. Campbell, Richard D. Schwartz, & Lee Sechrest (1966). *Unobtrusive Measures: Nonreactive Research in the Social Sciences.* Chicago: Rand McNally.

Weedon, Chris (1987). *Feminist Practice and Poststructuralist Theory.* London: Basil Blackwell.

Williamson, Robert (1993). "Tradition giving way to world of freelancers." The *Globe & Mail,* January 15, 1993, pp. B1 and B4.

Witzling, Lawrence P., & Robert C. Greenstreet (1989). *Presenting Statistics: A Manager's Guide to the Persuasive Use of Statistics.* New York: Wiley.

Zimbardo, Philip G. (1985). "Finding meaning in the method." In Ludy T. Benjamin, Jr., & Kathleen D. Lowman (Eds.), *Activities Handbook for the Teaching of Psychology* (pp. 24-26). Washington, D.C.: American Psychological Association.

FURTHER READING

A book that deals with trends of concern to women is *Megatrends for Women* by Patricia Aburdene and John Naisbitt (1992), published by Vuillard Books in New York. Chapter 3, titled "Women at Work" deals with female successes in business, women entrepreneurs, women's managerial advantage, and lists hot new career areas for women. By the same authors is their 1990 book *Megatrends 2000*.

For help with statistics, the combination book and computer disk statistics tutorial called *Victory Over Statistics* has been recommended as very user-friendly. It offers a review of basic statistical concepts in a way that helps the reader/user to think more analytically. The price is $35 U.S. from Ann Varela, Victory Over Statistics, P.O. Box 1146, Zephyrhills Florida 33539, U.S.A.

For a fascinating and fun look at the history of scientific discovery, and a demonstration that "truth" in science is created by social consensus, see the 1989 book *Discovering* by Robert S. Root-Bernstein, published by Harvard University Press. Also see Paul Diesing's 1991 book *How Does Social Science Work: Reflections on Practice,* published by the University of Pittsburgh Press.

Another look at the importance of small effects is given by Deborah A. Prentice and Dale T. Miller (1992), "When small effects are impressive," *Psychological Bulletin* 112: 160-164. Regarding effect size, see Kenneth O. McGraw and S.P. Wong (1992), "A common language effect size statistic," *Psychological Bulletin* 111: 361-365.

Articles of interest dealing with non-Western management are Dianne H.B. Welsh, Fred Luthans, and Steven M. Sommer (1993) "Managing Russian factory workers: The impact of U.S.-based behavioral and participative techniques," *Academy of Management Journal* 36: 58-79; Witold Kiezun (1991), *Management in Socialist Countries: USSR & Central Europe,* New York: Walter de Gruyter; and Charalambos Vlachoutsicos and Paul Lawrence (1990), "What we don't know about Soviet management," *Harvard Business Review* 68(6): 50-64.

On new approaches to the study of organizations, see the entire July 1992 issue of the *Academy of Management Review*, Volume 17, Number 3, titled "New intellectual currents in organization and management theory," edited by Linda Smircich, Marta Calás, and Gareth Morgan. One article from this issue is that of Roy Jacques, pages 582-606. This article is tough going, but in the end, worth the effort. Its title is "Critique and theory building: Producing knowledge 'from the kitchen.'"

Two special issues on postmodernism are Volume 5, Numbers 1 and 2 of the *Journal of Organizational Change Management*. Other special issues are the 1988 issue of *Theory, Culture, & Society*, Volume 45, and the 1992 *International Studies of Management and Organization*, Volume 22. A series of four articles on modernism, postmodernism, and organizational analysis by Robert Cooper and Gibson Burrell can be found in *Organization Studies* 1988, Volume 9, pages 91-112 (an introduction); 1988, Volume 9, pages 221-235 (on Michel Foucault); 1989, Volume 10, pages 479-502 (on Jacques Derrida); and 1994, Volume 15, pages 1-45 (on Jürgen Habermas).

An article that relates Foucault's thinking to Human Resource Management is Barbara Townley (1993), "Foucault, power/knowledge, and its relevance for Human Resource Management," *Academy of Management Review* 18: 518-545. Useful books on postmodernism are David M. Boje and Robert F. Dennehy (1992), *America's Revolution Against Exploitation: The Story of Postmodern Management,* Dubuque, Iowa: Kendall/Hunt Publishing Company; Anthony Woodiwiss (1993), *Postmodernity USA: The Crisis of Modernism in Postwar America,* Thousand Oaks, CA: Sage Publications; William Bergquist (1993), *The Postmodern Organization: Mastering the Art of Irreversible Change,* San Francisco: Jossey-Bass Publishers; *Postmodernism and Organizations,* edited by John Hassard and Martin Parker (1993), Thousand Oaks, CA: Sage Publications; and Zygmunt Bauman's (1992) *Intimations of Post Modernity* published in London by Routledge.

Regarding critical theory, see Mats Alvesson (1985), "A critical framework for organizational analysis," in *Organization Studies* 6: 117-138; and the École des Hautes Études Commerciales' Omar Aktouf (1992), "Management and theories of organizations in the 1990s: Toward a critical radical humanism?" *Academy of Management Review* 17: 407-431.

On poststructuralism, see W. Graham Astley (1985), "Administrative science as socially constructed truth," *Administrative Science Quarterly* 30: 497-513.

For further information about feminist theory, see Ruth Hubbard (1988), "Some thoughts about the masculinity of the natural sciences," in Mary McCanney Gergen (Ed.), *Feminist Thought and the Structure of Knowledge* (pp. 1-15), published by the New York University Press; Celia Kitzinger (1991), "Feminism, psychology, and the paradox of power," *Feminism and Psychology* 1(1): 111-129; and Jill G. Morawski (1990), "Toward the unimagined: Feminism and epistemology in psychology," in Rachel T. Hare-Mustin and Jeanne Marecek (Eds.), *Making a Difference: Psychology and the Construction of Gender* (pp. 150-183), published by the Yale University Press. A review article by Marta B. Calás and Linda Smircich is titled "Re-writing gender into organizational theorizing: Directions from feminist perspectives," and is found in the 1992 book by Michael Reed and Michael Hughes (Eds.), *Rethinking Organization: New Directions in Organization Theory and Analysis*, (pp. 227-253), Sage Publications. Finally, a book that examines race, ethnicity and gender from multiple viewpoints is Sage's *Gendering Organizational Analysis*, edited by Albert J. Mills of Athabasca University and Peta Tancred of McGill University.

GRASSE FRAGRANCES SA

Grasse Fragrances, headquartered in Lyon, France, was the world's fourth largest producer of fragrances. Established in 1885, the company had grown from a small family-owned business, selling fragrances to local perfume manufacturers, to a multinational enterprise with subsidiaries and agents in over 100 countries.

For Marketing Director Jean-Pierre Volet, the last few years had been devoted to building a strong headquarters marketing organization. In February 1989, however, he was returning to France after an extensive tour of Grasse sales offices and factories, and a number of visits with key customers. As the Air France flight touched down in Lyon Airport, Jean-Pierre Volet was feeling very concerned about what he had learned on the trip. "Our salesforce," he thought, "operates much as it did several years ago. If we're going to compete successfully in this new environment, we have to completely rethink our salesforce management practices."

The Flavor and Fragrance Industry

Worldwide sales of essential oils, aroma chemicals, and fragrance and flavor compounds were estimated to be around $5.5 billion in 1988.

Five major firms accounted for something like 50% of the industry's sales. The largest, International Flavors & Fragrances Inc. of New York, had 1988 sales of $839.5 million (up 76% from 1984), of which fragrances accounted for 62%. The company had plants in 21 countries, and non-US operations represented 70% of sales and 78% of operating profit.

Quest International, a wholly-owned subsidiary of Unilever, was next in size with sales estimated at $700 million, closely followed by the Givaudan Group,

a wholly-owned subsidiary of Hoffman-LaRoche with sales of $536 million, and Grasse Fragrances with sales of $480 million. Firmenich, a closely-held Swiss family firm, did not disclose results but 1987 sales were estimated at some $300 million.

Grasse produced only fragrances. Most major firms in the industry, however, produced both fragrances and flavors (i.e., flavor extracts and compounds mainly used in foods, beverages and pharmaceutical products). Generally, the products were similar. The major difference was that the flavorist had to match his or her creations with their natural counterparts, such as fruits, meats, or spices, as closely as possible. On the other hand, the perfumer had the flexibility to use his or his imagination to create new fragrances. Perfumery was closely associated with fashion, encompassed a wide variety of choice, and products had to be dermatologically safe. Development of flavors was more limited, and products were required to meet strict toxicological criteria because the products were ingested.

Markets for Fragrances

While the use of perfumes is as old as history, it was not until the 19th century, when major advances were made in organic chemistry, that the fragrance industry emerged as it is known today. Focusing first on perfumes, use of fragrances expanded into other applications. In recent years manufacturers of soap, detergents and other household products have significantly increased their purchases of fragrances and have represented the largest single consumption category. Depending on the application, the chemical complexity of a particular fragrance and the quantity produced, prices could range from less than FF40 per kilogram to over FF4,000.[1]

---

[1] $1.00 U.S. = approximately FF6.00 in 1988.

SOURCE: This case was written by Professor Michael Hayes of the University of Colorado as a basis for class discussion rather than to illustrate either effective or ineffective handling of an administrative situation. All names, including the company name, have been disguised. Copyright © 1989 by IMEDE, Lausanne, Switzerland. The International Institute for Management Development (IMD), resulting from the merger between IMEDE, Lausanne, and IMI, Geneva, acquires and retains all rights. Reproduced by permission.

Despite its apparent maturity, the world market for fragrances was estimated to have grown at an average of 5-6% during the early 1980s, and some estimates indicated that sales growth could increase even further during the last half of the decade. New applications supported these estimates. Microwave foods, for instance, needed additional flavorings to replicate familiar tastes that would take time to develop in a conventional oven. In laundry detergents, a significant fragrance market, the popularity of liquids provided a new stimulus to fragrance sales, as liquid detergents needed more fragrance than powders to achieve the desired aroma. Similarly, laundry detergents designed to remove odors as well as dirt also stimulated sales, as they used more fragrance by volume.

The New Buying Behavior

Over time, buying behavior for fragrances, as well as markets, had changed significantly. Responsibility for the selection and purchase of fragrances became complex, particularly in large firms. R&D groups were expected to ensure the compatibility of the fragrance with the product under consideration. Marketing groups were responsible for choosing a fragrance that gave the product a competitive edge in the marketplace, and purchasing groups had to obtain competitive prices and provide good deliveries.

Use of briefs (the industry term for a fragrance specification and request for quotation) became common. Typically, a brief would identify the general characteristics of the fragrance, the required cost parameters as well as an extensive description of the company's product and its intended strategy in the marketplace. Occasionally, a fragrance producer would be sole sourced, generally for proprietary reasons. Usually, however, the customer would ask for at least two quotations, so competitive quotes were the norm.

GRASSE FRAGRANCES SA

Background

The company was founded in 1885 by Louis Piccard, a chemist who had studied at the University of Lyon. He believed that progress in the field of organic chemistry could be used to develop a new industry—creating perfumes, as opposed to relying on nature. Using a small factory on the Siagne River near Grasse, the company soon became a successful supplier of fragrances to the leading perfume houses of Paris. Despite the interruptions of World Wars I and II, the company followed an early policy of international growth and diversification. Production and sales units were first established in Lyon, Paris and Rome. In the 1920s, company headquarters were moved to Lyon. At that time, the company entered the American market, first establishing a sales office and then a small manufacturing facility. Acquisitions were made in England, and subsequently the company established subsidiaries in Switzerland, Brazil, Argentina and Spain.

Faced with increased competition and large capital requirements for R&D, plant expansion and new product launches, the Piccard family decided to become a public company in 1968. Jacques Piccard, oldest son of the founder, was elected president and the family remained active in the management of the company. Assisted by the infusion of capital, Grasse was able to further expand its business activities in Europe, the United States, Latin America and the Far East.

In 1988 total sales were $450,000,000, up some 60% from 1984; 40% of sales came from Europe, 30% from North America, 10% from Latin America, 5% from Africa/Middle East and 15% from Asia/Pacific. In recent years the company's position had strengthened somewhat in North America.

By the end of 1988, the company had sales organizations or agents in 100 countries, laboratories in 18 countries, compounding facilities in 14 countries, chemical production centers in 3 countries and research centers in 3 countries. Employment was 2,500, of whom some 1,250 were employed outside France.

Products

In 1988, the company's main product lines were in two categories:

- Perfumery products used for perfumes, eau de cologne, eau de toilette, hair lotion, cosmetics, soaps, detergents, other household and industrial products.
- Synthetics for perfume compounds, cosmetic specialities, sunscreening agents and preservatives for various industrial applications.

According to Jacques Piccard:

> From the production side, flavors and fragrances are similar, although the creative and marketing approaches are quite different. So far we have elected to specialize in just fragrances, but I think it's just a matter of time before we decide to get into flavors.

Following industry practice, Grasse divided its fragrances into four categories:

- Fine Fragrances
- Toiletries and Cosmetics
- Soaps and Detergents
- Household and Industrial

Marketing at Grasse

In 1980, Jean-Pierre Volet was appointed Marketing Director, after a successful stint as country manager for the Benelux countries. At the time, the headquarters marketing organization was relatively small. Its primary role was to make sure the salesforce had information on the company's products, send out samples of new perfumes that were developed in the labs, usually with little customer input, and handle special price or delivery requests. As Volet recalled:

> In the 1940s, 1950s and 1960s, most of our business was in fine fragrances, toiletries and cosmetics. Our customers tended to be small and focused on local markets. Our fragrance salesman would carry a suitcase of 5 gram samples, call on the customer, get an idea of what kind of fragrance the customer wanted and either leave a few samples for evaluation or actually write an order on the spot. It was a very personal kind of business. Buying decisions tended to be based on subjective impressions and the nature of the customer's relation with the salesman. Our headquarters marketing organization was designed to support that kind of selling and buying. Today, however, we deal with large multinational companies who are standardizing their products across countries, and even regions, and who are using very sophisticated marketing techniques to guide their use of fragrances. Detergents and other household products represent an increasing share of the market. When I came to headquarters, one of my important priorities was to structure a marketing organization which reflected this new environment.

(The marketing organization in 1988 is shown in Exhibit 1). In addition to the normal administrative activities such as field sales support, pricing and budgeting, Volet had built a fragrance creation group and a product management group. More recently, he had established an international account management group.

The fragrance creation group served as a bridge between the basic lab work and customer requirements. It also ran the company's fragrance training center, used to train both its own salesforce and customer personnel in the application of fragrances. The product management group was organized in the four product categories. Product managers were expected to be knowledgeable about everything that was going on in their product category worldwide and to use their specialized knowledge to support field sales efforts as well as guide the creative people. It was Volet's plan that international account managers would coordinate sales efforts.

Field sales in France reported to Piccard through Raoul Salmon, who was also responsible for the activities of the company's agents, used in countries where it did not have subsidiaries or branches. In recent years, use of agents had declined, and the company expected the decline to continue.

Outside France, field sales were the responsibility of Grasse country managers. In smaller countries, country managers handled only sales, thus operating essentially as field sales managers. In other countries, where the company had manufacturing or other non-selling operations, the norm was to have a field sales manager reporting to the country manager. Although individual sales representatives reported to the field sales managers, it was understood that there was a dotted line relationship from the sales representatives to the ICCs and the product managers.

The company relied extensively on its field salesforce for promotional efforts, customer relations and order getting activities. There were, however, two very different kinds of selling situation. As Salmon described them:

> There are still many customers, generally small-scale, who buy in the traditional way where the process is fairly simple. One salesperson is responsible for calling on all buying influencers in the customer's organization. Decisions tend to be based on subjective factors, and the sales representative's personal relations with the customer are critically important.

The other situation, which is growing, involves large and increasingly international customers. Not only do we see that people in R&D and marketing as well as in purchasing can influence the purchase decision, but these influencers may also be located in a number of different countries.

In either case, once the decision had been made to purchase a Grasse fragrance, the firm could generally count on repeat business, as long as the customer's product was successful in the marketplace.

On occasion, however, purchase decisions were revised, particularly if Grasse raised prices or if the customer's product came under strong competitive price pressure, thus requiring that a less expensive fragrance be considered.

The Quotation Procedure

For small orders, the quotation procedure was relatively simple. Popular fragrances had established prices in every country, and the salesforce was expected to sell at these prices.[2] In some instances, price concessions were made, but they required management approval and were discouraged.

For large orders, it was the norm to develop a new fragrance. Increasingly, customers would provide Grasse with extensive information on their intended product and its marketing strategy, including the country or countries where the product would be sold. To make sure the fragrance fit the customer's intended marketing and product strategy, Grasse was expected to do market research in a designated pilot country on several fragrances, sometimes combined with samples of the customer's product. According to Volet:

> Once we have found or developed what we think is the best fragrance, we submit our quotation. Then the customer will do his own market research, testing his product with our fragrance and with those of our competitors. Depending on the outcome of the market research, we may get the order at a price premium. Alternatively, we may lose it, even if we are the low bidder. If, on the other hand, the results of

the market research indicate that no fragrance supplier has an edge then price, personal relationships or other factors will influence the award.

Because of the extensive requirements for development and testing, headquarters in Grasse was always involved in putting a quotation together, and close coordination was vital between headquarters and the branch or subsidiary. When buying influencers were located in more than one country, additional coordination of the sales effort was required to insure that information obtained from the customer was shared and also to have a coherent account strategy.

Coordination of pricing was also growing in importance. Many large customers manufactured their products in more than one country and looked for a "world" price rather than a country price. In these situations, country organizations were expected to take a corporate view of profits, sometimes at the expense of their own profit statements. The lead country (i.e., the country in which the purchasing decision would be made) had final responsibility for establishing the price. Increasingly, however, this price had to be approved in Lyon.

Submitting quotations in this environment was both complex and expensive. According to Volet:

> Receiving a brief from a customer starts a complex process. We immediately alert all our salespeople who call on various purchasing influencers. Even though the brief contains lots of information on what the customer wants, we expect our sales people to provide us with some additional information.
>
> The next step is for our creative people to develop one or more fragrances which we believe will meet the customer's requirements. They are aided in this effort by our product managers who know what is going on with their products worldwide. If additional information is needed from the customer, our international account people will contact the appropriate sales people.
>
> After creating what we think is the right product or products, we may conduct our own market research in a country designated by the customer. This is usually done under the direction of our product

---

2 Subject to approval by marketing headquarters, each Grasse producing unit established a transfer price for products sold outside the country. Country prices were established, taking into account the country profit objectives and the local market conditions. Transfer prices were usually established for a year. Adjusting transfer prices for fluctuations in exchange rates was a matter of ongoing concern.

manager, working closely with our market research people. Throughout this process, our salesforce is expected to stay in close touch with the customer to give us any changes in his thinking or any competitive feedback. Based on the results of this effort, we then submit our proposal which gives the customer the price, samples and as much product information as possible.

With some customers, there is little further sales effort after they receive our quotation, and the buying decision is made "behind closed doors." In other instances, we may be asked to explain the results of our research or to discuss possible modifications in our product and, sometimes, in our price. Frequently we find that the customer is more concerned with our price policy (i.e., how firm the price is and for how long) than with the price quoted at the time of the brief.

When you make this kind of effort, you obviously hate to lose the order. On the other hand, even if we lose, the investment made in development work and market research is likely to pay off in winning another brief, either with the original customer or with another customer.

International Accounts

In 1988 about 50% of the firm's business came from some 40 international accounts. Looking to the future, it was expected that the number of international accounts would grow, and some estimated that by 1994 as much as 80% of the firm's business would come from international accounts.

As of 1988, 18-20 international accounts were targeted for coordination by International Client Coordinators (ICCs) in Lyon. The principal responsibility of each ICC was to really know assigned customers on a worldwide basis and put that knowledge to use in coordinating work on a brief. The rest were followed in Lyon, but coordination was a subsidiary responsibility. In either case, it was the view at headquarters that coordination was critical. As Volet described it:

> We rely extensively on account teams. European teams may meet as often as once a quarter. Worldwide teams are more likely to meet annually. For designated accounts, the ICC takes the lead role in organizing the

meeting and, generally, coordinating sales efforts. For others, the Parent Account Executive (the sales representative in the country selling the customer component with the greatest buying influence) plays the lead role. In these situations, we hold the Parent Account Executive responsible for all the ICC's daily coordinating work with the customer. We also expect him to be proactive and already working on the next brief long before we get a formal request.

> Here in Lyon, we prepare extensive worldwide "bibles" on international accounts which are made available to all members of the team. We also prepare quarterly project reports for team members. Our next step will be to computerize as much of this as possible.

Sales Management Practices

In 1988, salesforce management practices were not standardized. Selection, compensation, training, organization, etc. were the responsibility of subsidiary management. Even so, a number of practices were similar.

Sales representatives tended to be compensated by a salary and bonus scheme. A typical minimum bonus was 1.5 month's salary, but could range up to 2.5 month's salary for excellent performance. The exact amount of the bonus was discretionary with sales management and could reward a number of factors.

Sales budgets were established from estimates made by sales representatives for direct orders (i.e., orders that would be placed by their assigned accounts). These estimates were developed from expectations of sales volume for fragrances currently being used by customers, in which case historical sales were the major basis for the estimate, and from estimates of sales of new fragrances. While historical sales of currently used fragrances were useful in predicting future sales, variations could occur. Sales activity of the customer's product was not totally predictable. In some instances, customers reopened a brief to competition, particularly where the customer was experiencing competitive cost pressures.

Predicting sales of new fragrances was even more difficult. Customers' plans were uncertain, and the nature of the buying process made it difficult to predict the odds of success on any given transaction. Grasse

Fragrances, nevertheless, relied heavily on these estimates. The sum of the estimates was expected to add up to the company budget for the coming year. When this was not the case, sales managers were expected to review their estimates and increase them appropriately.

The company had recently introduced, company-wide, its own version of management by objectives. Each sales representative was expected to develop a personal set of objectives for negotiation with his or her sales manager. Formal account planning, however, had not been established, although some subsidiaries were starting the practice.

Sales training had two components. Product knowledge tended to be the responsibility of headquarters, relying heavily on the fragrance training center. Selling skills, however, were principally the responsibility of the subsidiary companies.

Selection practices were the most variable. Some subsidiaries believed that company and product knowledge were key to selling success and so tended to look inside the company for individuals who had the requisite company and product knowledge and who expressed an interest in sales work. Others believed that demonstrated selling skills were key and so looked outside the company for individuals with good selling track records, preferably in related industries.

SALES MANAGEMENT ISSUES

A number of sales management practices were of concern, both in headquarters and in the subsidiaries.

Influence Selling

Insuring appropriate effort on all buying influencers was a major concern. According to Salmon:

> Our sales representatives understand the importance of influence selling, but we have no formal way of recognizing their efforts. A number of our large accounts, for instance, have their marketing groups located in Paris, and they have lots of influence on the buying decision. If we win the brief, however, purchasing is likely to take place in Germany or Spain or Holland, and my sales representative will not get any sales credit.

In a similar vein, Juan Rodriguez, sales manager for a group of countries in Latin America, commented:

> We have a large account that does lots of manufacturing and purchasing in Latin America but does its R&D work in the US. The customer's people in Latin America tell us that without strong support from R&D in the US, it is very difficult for them to buy our fragrances. The sales representative in New York is certainly aware of this, but his boss is measured on profit, which can only come from direct sales in the US, so he's not enthusiastic about his sales representative spending a lot of time on influence business.

In some instances, the nature of the buying process resulted in windfalls for some sales representatives. Commenting on this aspect, Salmon observed:

> It can work the other way as well. Our Spanish subsidiary recently received an order for 40 tons of a fragrance, but the customer's decision to buy was totally influenced by sales representatives in Germany and Lyon. Needless to say, our Spanish subsidiary was delighted, but the people in Germany and Lyon were concerned as to how their efforts would be recognized and rewarded.

While there was general recognition that influence selling was vital, it was not clear how it could be adequately measured and rewarded. As Salmon pointed out:

> In some instances (e.g., the order in Spain) we're pretty sure about the amount of influence exerted by those calling on marketing and R&D. In other instances, it is not at all clear. We have some situations where the sales representative honestly believes that his calls on, say, R&D are important but, in fact, they are not. At least not in our opinion. If we come up with the wrong scheme to measure influence, we could end up with a lot of wasted time and effort.

Incentive Compensation

Compensation practices were a matter of some concern. The salary component was established at a level designed to be competitive with similar sales jobs in each country. Annual raises had become the norm, with amounts based on performance, longevity and changes in responsibility. The bonus component was determined by the immediate manager, but there was concern that bonuses had become automatic. Still further, some held the view that the difference between 1.5 and 2.5 times the monthly salary was not very motivating, even if bonus awards were more performance driven.

Whether merited or not, sales representatives expected some level of bonus, and there was concern that any change could cause morale problems. At the same time, there was growing recognition of the increasing importance of team selling.

Overall responsibility for compensation practices was assigned to Claude Larreché, Director of Human Resources. According to Larreché:

Some of our sales managers are interested in significantly increasing the incentive component of sales-force compensation. It has been my view, however, that large incentive payments to the salesforce could cause problems in other parts of our organization. Plus, there seems to be considerable variation in country practice with regard to incentive compensation. In the US, for instance, compensation schemes which combine a fixed or salary component and an incentive component, usually determined by sales relative to a quota, are common. To a lesser degree, we see some of this in Europe, and somewhat more in the south, but I'm not sure that we want to do something just because a lot of other companies are doing it.

We're also thinking about some kind of team incentive or bonus. But, this raises questions about who should be considered part of the team and how a team bonus should be allocated. Should the team be just the sales representatives, or should we include the ICCs? And what about the customer service people without whom we wouldn't have a base of good performance to build on?

Allocation is even more complicated. We're talking about teams comprised of people all around the world. I think it is only natural that the local manager will think his sales representative made the biggest contribution, which could result in long arguments. One possibility would be for the team itself to allocate a bonus pool, but I'm not sure how comfortable managers would be with such an approach.

Small Accounts
Despite the sales growth expected from international accounts, sales to smaller national accounts were expected to remain a significant part of the firm's revenues and, generally, had very attractive margins. According to one country sales manager:

With the emphasis on international accounts, I'm concerned about how we handle our smaller single country accounts. Many of them still buy the way they did 10 and 20 years ago, although today we can select from over 30,000 fragrances. Our international accounts will probably generate 80% of our business in the years to come, but the 20% we get from our smaller accounts is important and produces excellent profits for the company. But I'm not sure that the kind of selling skills we need to handle international accounts are appropriate for the smaller accounts. Personal and long-term relationships are tremendously important to these accounts.

Language
In the early 1980s, it had become apparent to Grasse management that French would not serve as the firm's common language. In most of its subsidiary countries, English was either the country language or the most likely second language. With considerable reluctance on the part of some French managers, it was decided that English would become the firm's official language. Personnel in the US and England, few of whom spoke a second language, welcomed the change. There were, however, a number of problems. As the Italian sales manager said:

We understand the need for a common language when we bring in sales representatives from all over Europe or the world. And we understand that English is the "most common" language in the countries where we do business. All of my people understand that they will have to speak English in international account sales meetings. What they don't like, however, is that the Brits and Americans tend to assume that they are smarter than the rest of us, simply because we can't express ourselves as fluently in English as they can. It's totally different when my people talk to someone from Latin America or some other country, where English is their second language, too.

A related problem is the attitude that people from one country have towards those of another. This goes beyond language. Frequently, our people from Northern Europe or North America will stereotype those of us from Southern Europe or Latin America as disorganized or not business-like. My people, on the other hand, see the northerners as inflexible and unimaginative. To some extent, these views diminish after we get to know each other as individuals, but it takes time and there is always some underlying tension.

Language also influenced decisions on rotation of personnel. It was Volet's view that there should be movement between countries of sales managers and marketing personnel. Still further, he felt that sales representatives who aspired to promotion should also be willing to consider transfers to another country or to headquarters in Lyon. As he pointed out, however:

> Customer personnel in most of our international accounts speak English. Hence, there is a temptation to feel that English language competency is the only requirement when considering reassignment of sales personnel. In fact, if we were to transfer a sales representative who spoke only English to Germany, for instance, he would be received politely the first time, but from then on it would be difficult for him to get an appointment with the customer. It has been our experience that our customers want to do business in their own language, even if they speak English fluently.
>
> An exception might be an international account whose parent is British and which transfers a lot of British personnel to another country. Even here, however, there will be lots of people in the organization for whom English is not a native tongue.
>
> Therefore, we require that our sales people speak the language of the country and are comfortable with the country culture. Local people meet this requirement. The real issue is getting all, or most, of our people to be comfortable in more than one language and culture.

Sales Training

One of the most perplexing issues was what, if any, changes to make with regard to sales training. At headquarters there was considerable sentiment for standardization. As Volet put it:

> I really don't see much difference in selling from one country to another. Of course, personal relations may be more important in, say, Latin America

or the Middle East than in Germany, but I think that as much as 80-85% of the selling job can be harmonized. In addition, it's my view that our international accounts expect us to have a standardized sales approach. Sales training, therefore, should be something we can do centrally in Lyon.

This view was supported by those in human resources. According to Claude Larreché, Director of Human Resources:

> We no longer see ourselves as a collection of individual companies that remit profits to Lyon and make technology transfers occasionally. Our view of the future is that we are a global company that must live in a world of global customers and markets. I think this means we must have a Grasse Fragrance culture that transcends national boundaries, including a common sales approach, i.e, this is the way Grasse approaches customers, regardless of where they are located. A key element in establishing such a culture is sales training here in Lyon.

Others disagreed with this point of view, however. Perhaps the most vociferous was the US sales manager:

> I understand what Jean-Pierre and Claude are saying, and I support the notion of a common company culture. The fact is, however, that selling is different in the US than in other parts of the world. Not long ago we transferred a promising sales representative from Sweden to our office in Chicago. His sales approach, which was right for Sweden, was very relaxed, and he had to make some major adjustments to fit the more formal and fast-paced approach in Chicago. I don't see how a sales training program in Lyon can be of much help. Plus, the cost of sending people to Lyon comes out of my budget, and this would really hit my country manager's profits.
>
> In fact, I think we ought to have more flexibility with regard to all our sales management practices.

As Jean-Pierre Volet waited for his bag at the Lyon Airport, he wondered how far he should go in making changes with regard to the salesforce. Whatever he did would be controversial, but he was convinced some changes were necessary.

EXHIBIT 1

*Partial
Organization Chart*

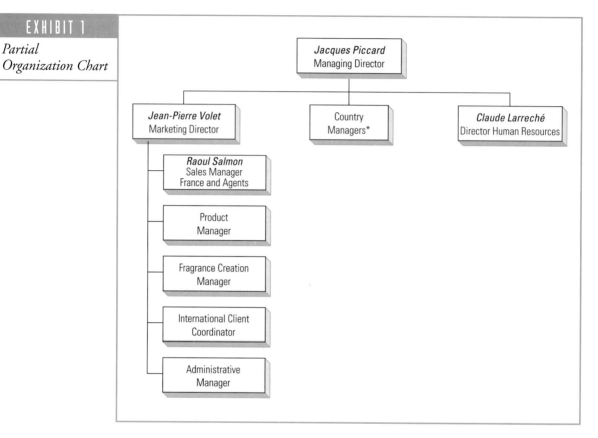

NOTE: In France, all major functions (e.g., marketing, manufacturing, R&D) reported to Jacques Piccard. In most countries outside of France where the company did business a subsidiary company was established, headed by a country manager. All company activities in each country reported to the country manager. In some countries, generally small, the company did business through agents who reported to Raoul Salmon.

A & W CANADA[1]

In 1956, Albert and Walter opened their first Canadian A&W restaurant in Winnipeg, Manitoba[2]. The restaurant served a distinctive "family" of burgers—the Mama, the Papa, the Teenburger and, for the kids, the Babyburger—in a drive-in format that was well-suited to the growing popularity and affordability of automobiles. The company did extremely well during these years. According to Ross Cunningham, A&W's President until 1991,

> For many years [fast food] demand exceeded supply. If you could get good locations, good management and the right infrastructure, you were a guaranteed success for 20 years[3].

And A&W did grow and prosper virtually without interruption for almost twenty years. According to Cunningham's successor, Jeff Mooney, "From about 1956 right through to 1974, we *were* fast food in Canada[4]. But in 1975, after five years of fighting its way into the Canadian market, McDonald's took over the number one position in the fast food industry. From the record numbers of 1974, A&W saw profits decline 40 per cent in one year as McDonald's reaped the profits that were concomitant with their new position as industry leader. Although A&W responded to McDonald's, profits continued to decline in 1976.

The significant decline in profitability in 1975 and 1976 forced A&W's management to take stock of their competitive position. What they realized was that in stark contrast to their own relaxed, in-car service, McDonald's was promoting a fast, self-service environment that included inside seating and a strong emphasis on children. These features, combined with the hugely successful "You deserve a break today" campaign, had been sufficient to dislodge A&W from its previously unquestioned leadership position. The irony of their previous success based on a drive-in focused strategy is not lost on Jeff Mooney who is quick to comment that "we had 308 drive-ins ... in a country with 7 months of winter and 5 months of bad skating."[5]

Into the Malls

Faced with the undeniable reality of declining profits, A&W senior management admitted to themselves that despite its strong consumer appeal the drive-in format was becoming uncompetitive. If current trend-lines were to continue, it was clear that the organization might not even survive into the next decade. So it was under these circumstances—declining profitability and an uncompetitive restaurant concept—that A&W sought out a new strategy to lead them into the 80s.

A&W based their new strategic thrust on the proliferation of shopping malls that was taking place across Canada. They would re-orientate their locations from stand-alone drive-ins to walk-up counters in the malls. However, implementing this strategy required A&W to raise a significant amount of capital to finance it. Toward this end, A&W management decided to close down and sell off the company's "corporate" stores in eastern Canada. The difficulty with this, however, was that the corporate stores tended to be the highest profile stores, which resulted in the eastern franchisees doubting the company's commitment to their operations. So in order to address these fears, Cunningham put together a road show that he took to the affected communities in order to demonstrate A&W's continuing commitment to their franchised operations. But despite these difficulties, the company's new strategy quickly proved itself to be the right one. A&W's 1978 financial statements showed a 20 per cent increase in profit over the previous year.

Since 1978 A&W has achieved financial results that defy both macro-economic and industry trends. Over the ten-year period from 1977 to 1986 company

SOURCE: This case was prepared by Michael K. Mauws, University of Alberta, Thomas B. Lawrence, University of Victoria, and Richard Field, University of Alberta as a basis for class discussion rather than to illustrate either effective or ineffective handling of an administrative situation. Copyright © 1993 by Canadian Institute of Retailing and Services Studies (CIRASS) at the University of Alberta. Reproduced by permission.

sales nearly doubled—from $82 million to $160 million—and profits increased ten-fold in that same period. Similarly, from 1981 to 1990, company sales more than doubled, increasing from $94 million to $207 million. By 1987 the company's 308 drive-ins had become 325 restaurants, 125 of which were in shopping malls. Growth continued as A&W opened 15 new restaurants in 1988, 21 in 1989 and 1990, and 43 in 1991, ending up with over 400 locations. A&W's current president, Jeff Mooney, describes these fifteen years as a period of great change and renewal:

> When we started this we had about 308 drive-in restaurants across Canada. Well today [August, 1993] we have 425 restaurants and we have been for several years the fastest growing chain in our industry. Last year we opened 32 new restaurants and this year we'll do about the same, which is almost as much as everyone else together. ... So in one sense we closed down one of the largest chains in Canada and grew out of it a whole new business. That gives you some sense of the amount of change that has gone on.

Thus, from 1987 to 1991, A&W increased its number of outlets by 33%. And, perhaps most indicative of its success, from 1990 to 1991, A&W's sales increased from $207 to $240 million, while during that same period McDonald's saw its sales *decline* from $1,402 million to $1,357 million.

But in achieving these more recent figures A&W has begun to move beyond the focus on shopping malls that was instrumental in its recovery, returning its attention to the free-standing structures in which it got its start. The few drive-ins that remain (in Edmonton, for example) are being replaced by newer, more modern structures with in-store seating. This does not mean that A&W is severing all connections with its drive-in origins, however. Instead, many of these new restaurants include "memory walls" that are covered with pictures of the old drive-ins that many people still identify with the A&W name.

STRATEGIC DECISION MAKING AT A&W

The shocks faced by A&W in the 1970s have led its management to adopt an approach to corporate strategy that emphasizes dynamic responsiveness over static analysis. Mooney argues that:

no matter how good your strategy is today, the real skill in that area is being able to renew purpose and clarity of purpose and commitment to purpose within an organization. If I get it right today, that's wonderful. But sometime, likely in the next 3 to 5 years, we're going to have to get it right again. And unless we have the skill to make change, we're lost—we've got one in a row. So that's the real challenge.

A&W's focus on flexibility and commitment to purpose are underscored by a strategy process that is marked by decision making rather than the construction of elaborate plans. This process was developed in cooperation with an external consultant, Bob Johnson. Mooney had met Johnson at an earlier point in both their careers, but at the time that A&W was in crisis in the 1970s Johnson was in the process of launching a consulting company, *Trend*sitions. Johnson's firm focuses on transition strategies and strategic renewal for organizations. As Mooney tells it, Johnson had "developed a process for strategic decision making which [we] began to use in the spring of '76 when [we were] in crisis as a company". Mooney could hardly be more enthusiastic about its role in A&W's recovery: "we were bloody fortunate in finding Bob Johnson and what I still am convinced is the most effective strategy decision process anywhere." Mooney contrasts the *Trend*sitions approach with stereotypical approaches to corporate strategy.

> It's hard to find many things that have probably garnered more of a bad reputation than strategic planning has in business circles: seen as airy-fairy blue-sky, not real value kind of stuff. And I think a big piece of that is a hell of a lot of it has been cast as 'planning'.

Central to Johnson's strategic process is an emphasis on strategic decision-making, rather than strategic planning. Mooney argues that the problem with most approaches to strategy are that they revolve around the development of a 'plan', rather than the construction of concrete decisions: "strategy is about the leaders of an organization making decisions." And for Mooney, the most central strategic decisions revolve around the organization of the firm.

> Our definition of strategy using Bob's model is an *irrevocable allocation of resources*. So what we're talking about is we've got human beings, primarily, and

capital, and how are we going to focus those, allocate them [to match] the strategy.

The irrevocable allocation of resources and the generation of commitment to purpose are the cornerstones of A&W's approach to strategy. These elements are consistent with Mooney's attitude toward the realities of corporate success.

> I think there's this myth often ... that you go away and you have all these really bright experienced people and they make up this plan and then you go out and execute this plan and everything. ... When reality is that a lot of the time it was a hell of a lot of luck and good fortune.

In contrast to this myth, Mooney argues that "the best chance for success is having your best people on your best opportunities. That's the ultimate act of strategy."

Mooney associates this approach to strategy with particular roles for A&W managers and for himself. Inclusion in the strategy development process is not based solely on hierarchical seniority, but on the nature of the strategic decisions themselves. According to Mooney,

> The people in the room when we make a strategy for a business are the people who have to be there, whose business it is, plus the people from outside that immediate business whose commitment is necessary in carrying it through.

The criterion for *who* makes strategy reflects the behavioural element to strategy formation that A&W executives emphasize. Mooney contrasts this approach with data-intensive approaches associated with planning:

> Everyone has some kind of information processing model that says, okay, here's information ... about you or about your industry or whatever it is. Then we can organize the data in a way that would push us in a direction ... What that misses is that it's human beings that are processing information.

ORGANIZATIONAL CLIMATE

The importance that Mooney places on the human nature of decision making and information processing is a reflection of a broader commitment in A&W

to the development of behavioural norms that advance and encourage collaborative decision making—norms that are summarized in the notion of organizational Climate. The development of organizational Climate has been a critical element of the transition made by A&W in the 1970s and 1980s. In 1976, when the company was clearly in crisis, A&W's middle-level and senior-level managers spent several days developing ten "Climate goals" that were to guide the strategy-making process for the foreseeable future (see Exhibit 1). These goals were, and still are, oriented toward trust, mutual respect, and self-responsibility. Mooney is quick to point out, however, that Climate is *not* synonymous with values or beliefs. Instead, Climate at A&W is about behaviour:

> A lot of times when we talk about climate ... people quickly say 'Oh yeah, I've heard that stuff ... you're talking about values, or principles, or whatever.' And I want to be clear, I'm not talking about that. Yes, they're related ... But what is important in understanding the notion of climate and climate goals is these are goals about *behaviour*.

Mooney underscores this difference by pointing out that A&W's conception of Climate has nothing to do with one's educational background, religion, or life experiences:

> If we're working together we could spend the better part of our lifetime trying to [figure out each other's values], but what we *can* agree on very quickly is how we'll behave with one another. ... That's something we can agree on whether you're Buddhist, or Catholic, or whatever you are and regardless of my background.

The explicit development of Climate at A&W began in 1977 with the establishment of "Climate Questionnaires" administered to employees twice each year. These questionnaires were originally completed only by employees down to the level of franchise operators, but have for the past seven or eight years been solicited from all employees. Despite its long history and critical importance within the organization, however, A&W management have only recently formalized the Climate "program" to any significant degree. Dissatisfied with available materials, the company developed a two-day program entitled "Skills to

Strengthen Climate." This program is required for middle- and higher-level managers within six months of their joining the organization. Similarly, the "Climate Booklet," which all new employees are now given, was only written 3 or 4 years ago. And its simplicity masks the significance that these goals have within the company.

Furthermore, managers and supervisors are not directly rewarded for their Climate scores. Instead, the belief within A&W is that economic success is such a direct effect of an effective Climate that by rewarding economic performance the necessary incentives for improving Climate are also being established. Although positive Climate performance is not directly rewarded, negative Climate performance may bring about direct sanctions; should an individual consistently deviate from the behaviours prescribed in the Climate Goals, there is the possibility that they will be dismissed on this basis. As Michel Maurer (V.P., People Potential) tells it, "We've had *vice-presidents* on warning in this organization because of their climate behaviour ... If they didn't shape up in six months they'd be gone."

Maurer, a relative newcomer who joined in late 1986, has been surprised by the effectiveness of Climate in influencing behaviour and by how deeply it penetrates the organization:

> There's a lot less here of "well, you know, I don't really like him" or "I don't think he's making the right decision" ... There's a much heavier focus on, "If you have those kinds of questions, concerns, and issues, go talk directly to the person." [In most organizations] the political games that go on are almost 50 to 60 per cent of the amount of energy that people spend, as opposed to dedicating themselves to the strategic level of the business and whatever their role is in making that happen.

An integral part of the Climate process is the universal manner in which it is applied. Because feedback is an explicit goal of Climate, this means that no one is immune to having their behaviour questioned. Maurer says that, "There's a high level of encouragement for people—if you've got an issue, go tell someone who can do something about it." Mooney is similarly adamant in stressing that open communication is not merely an option within the Climate goals—it is an obligation:

> We have a goal called Improvement [that] says things are improved by encouraging the supporting people to challenge and question. So in our climate it's not only okay to challenge and question, you have a responsibility. You are not meeting your responsibilities if you're not challenging and questioning how we're doing things.

As evidence of Mooney's sincerity, Maurer tells the story of:

> a mid-level manager who, at one point, had an issue with the fact she thought that our Christmas "bonus program" wasn't at all a bonus program and it was kind of chintzy for an organization. [She] went to her boss, the director, to complain about it as a result of a memo that the president had sent around. Rather than getting embroiled directly with her in a discussion, the individual in question pointed to the memo and said, "Do you see my name on here?" And she said, "No." He says, "Whose name do you see?" She says, "Well, the president." He says, "Well, who do you think you should talk to about this problem?" "Well, I guess I should go talk to the president." And she did.

Her feedback was welcomed and an explanation was given for why the bonus program was structured in the manner that it was, although the program remained unchanged.

CLIMATE AT THE TOP

As A&W's Vice-President in charge of People Potential, Michael Maurer has a keen interest in the role of Climate and how it is effected within the organization. For Maurer, the secret of Climate lies not so much in its being a superior management "technology," as in its champions, Mooney and Cunningham:

> When you hear Jeff [Mooney] talk about climate, there's a danger of missing a particular piece of why climate works at A&W. Because he never talks about it from the impact of his own personality and who he is, as well as Ross's—his predecessor—on the organization. Something that is this closely linked to values and the beliefs of people, only takes form in how people behave. And the most important person's behaviour, in terms of what

this looks like in an organization, is the President. So consequently, when you hear Jeff talk about it, it's my sense sometimes that he talks about it as a bit of an abstraction. The only reason it works is that he and Ross, his predecessor, lived pretty well a certain way, in terms of things they encouraged and things they supported in the origination.

Ross Cunningham was president of A&W from 1968 until his retirement in 1991. It was under Cunningham that Mooney started with A&W and to this day Mooney still speaks of him as his mentor. What they share and what sets them apart from most CEOs is their experience in the personnel function. In stark contrast to the "glass ceiling" that has been discussed in Human Resource Management since its feminization in the 1980s, A&W's last two Presidents have both arrived at the top after spending time in personnel—Cunningham as Director of Personnel at the Marriot Corporation and Mooney with the Hudson's Bay Personnel Department. A reporter who interviewed Cunningham in 1987 said that he "talks like a graduate of the human potential movement (synergy, feedback, partnership and feelings)[6].

Unlike most new graduates joining The Bay in the 1960s, Mooney had completed his undergraduate degree in Arts rather than in Business. Rather than seeing this as a handicap, however, Mooney saw this as a distinct advantage:

> Probably the best "business" course I had for a young management trainee or executive-in-training was a philosophy course—an analytical philosophy course which was taught in the graduate philosophy program and dealt with cause and effect. ... I found that the kind of rigorous training in cause and effect that I had in this specific graduate course was invaluable in business problem solving.

Shortly after joining The Bay, Mooney moved into Personnel, where he would spend the first ten years of his career. It was during this time that he "became quite fascinated with the whole process of human beings at work and issues around that; issues of motivation and commitment, ... performance, understanding managerial development and organizational development and so forth" became a "passion" for

Mooney. This focus on the human side of organization has stayed with him for the simple reason that,

> At the end of the day any organization—whether it's business, or sports, or government, or a crown corporation or whatever—is simply a group of human beings with a common purpose. ... And so the whole set of issues around human beings and commitment to purpose, and effectiveness in executing purpose, is really what the work we do is about.

A CLIMATE FOR STRATEGY

A&W's notion of Climate and its development through formal programs, socialization and executive leadership fold back into Mooney's emphasis on effecting concrete strategic decisions.

> One of the realities is that, and one of the reasons, I think, ... that a strategy model for dividing up information is [only a] bare minimum for being effective is everyone gets the same information, and everyone has the same model ... so you know your competitors are looking at the same studies you're looking at and have access to the Boston Consulting Group model, or Porter's model, or whatever, [so] how are you going to win by doing that?

This is where A&W's emphasis on Climate becomes important in Mooney's eyes. Perceiving that change is occurring with ever greater rapidity, he argues that it is not enough to "get it right" today, because what is right tomorrow is likely to be completely different. Mooney maintains that "the key ... is not so much being aware of the issues as managing a process that keeps surfacing the issues." Emphasizing a Climate that encourages feedback and challenges the status quo is the manner in which A&W tries to "surface the issues." Taking this further, Mooney notes that,

> Most companies approach strategy as a data game. [They think that] if they have enough research, enough information, they'll make better decisions than the other guys. But human beings process the data. And unless the relationships between those human beings are open and healthy, you're going to get crummy decisions no matter how good the data is.[7]

So this focus on data ... is essential and important—you've got to do that very well—but a key governor in how that's done is the Climate between the senior executives. And so if there's no trust and no respect, you're going to have very sub-optimal decisions made.

Thus, managing Climate for Mooney is not something that one does *in addition* to strategy. Because every organization is seen as having a climate, the only option for him is in deciding whether or not Climate is going to be explicitly managed.

Mooney feels that there *may* have been a time thirty or forty years ago when companies could make strategic plans periodically and then sit back and enjoy the profits that accrued from their implementation. He gives IBM as a clear example of this. "But," he notes—and IBM has become the exemplar of this—"doing things right isn't enough if every 3 or 5 years, if not more frequently, you've got to be asking the question, are we doing the right thing?" This is why he does not perceive the management of Climate as an option any more, if in fact it ever was. Companies have to be willing to continually question everything they're doing at every moment. If they don't have a Climate that encourages that sort of behaviour, it's not likely to happen.

Likewise, Mooney feels it's important to have a Climate that encourages learning from past successes and from past failures. In this regard, he feels A&W has been quite successful, citing the Mozza Burger as one example:

> One of the products today on our menu that is one of our more successful products, the Mozza Burger, came out of a failed restaurant concept we tried back in the late 70s. But one of things that stood out in the failure was that this product had a great deal of acceptance with consumers and we moved it into the traditional A&W menu.

Mooney clearly sees this success-within-a-failure as a direct offshoot of A&W's Climate. Rather than worrying about who was to blame for the failure of this restaurant concept, the company's Climate was such that the individuals involved concentrated upon what they could salvage instead.

EXTENDING CLIMATE: GROWTH AND CARING

For the future, A&W has set out a number of strategies aimed at continuing their impressive record of growth. Jeff Mooney is "fond" of saying that there is no reason why A&W can not have 1000 restaurants in Canada. Because 200 of the 425 they currently have are in shopping malls, Mooney figures that A&W is significantly under-represented "on the street" as compared with rivals such as McDonald's. Whether or not A&W can achieve this ambitious goal remains to be seen; however, what is clear is that their methods will revolve around the concept of Climate.

Currently, the company has a number of initiatives under way that follow from Climate. For instance, A&W is striving to be the best place to work in their industry, and according to Maurer may already have achieved this. In seeking this goal, clearly the belief is that success in this regard will translate into meeting A&W's aims with respect to customer satisfaction. As Mooney points out, the "new goal is to exceed customer expectations by caring for them and each other as friends."[8]

This strategy of Caring is a direct extension of the Climate concept within A&W. As Maurer explains, "Caring became kind of an integrative word for a lot of the things that we had tried to set up in the culture of the organization through Climate. ... [so] why not also try to extend that to the customers?" But as Mooney points out, "we can't expect our people in our restaurants to care for customers any more than they experience being cared for [themselves]." And this is why A&W has invested so heavily in its people at all levels of the organization.

This attitude of caring is clearly reflected in the technological change policy that the company has developed in response to the overhaul it is embarking on at this time. Maurer describes it thus:

> We're going to invest 5 million dollars in technology in the next two years. We are going to try and restructure and re-engineer the business around the use of that technology, because if you don't, then you're never going to get the payoff from the investment in technology. And that's a very big and complex and demanding project. First to design it effectively, and then as it gets designed, to execute it.

Because the company recognizes the organizational implications of this technology, they have committed themselves to providing every displaced worker with at least one alternative position within the organization. And although they can't promise that the position will be at the same level, they have committed to maintaining that individual's salary should they accept the new position.

Even the nature of the technological investment, however, is geared toward Climate and Caring. The expectation being that, after the re-organization, between ten and fifteen hours of administrative time will be freed up that managers will be able to devote to customers and employees. Maurer does not deny, however, that some of this re-captured time may be "banked" by the organization. Nonetheless, the hope is that this technology will somehow facilitate their goal of "treating customers as friends."

So as an organization, A&W has explicitly constructed its identity around the concept of Climate, and has also staked its future on it. But unlike corporate images or managerial fads that seem to change with no apparent reason, Climate is something that A&W appears to be committed to long term. To hear Mooney tell it, "organizational Climate is a long-term way of living. Trust is at the essence of it. And it's a very fragile thing, a long term deposit upon which you cannot make many withdrawals. You have to live with it for a long time."[9]

Endnotes

[1] We would like to thank Jeff Mooney and Michel Maurer of A&W for their cooperation in the preparation of this case. In addition, the authors gratefully acknowledge the financial support of the CANADIAN INSTITUTE OF RETAILING AND SERVICES STUDIES which made this case possible. Their address is CIRASS, Faculty of Business University of Alberta, Edmonton, Alberta Canada T6G 2R6; telephone 403-492-6797.

[2] This case deals specifically and exclusively with A&W's operations in Canada.

[3] "The achievers: Ross Cunningham." *Canadian Hotel & Restaurant*, August (1988), p. 54.

[4] Collins, Anne "A toast to a comeback." *Canadian Business*, November (1987), p. 50.

[5] This quote, and any others given without citation, are taken from interviews conducted by Michael K. Mauws and Thomas B. Lawrence on August 9, 1993 at A&W's Canadian corporate headquarters in North Vancouver, B.C.

[6] Collins (1987, p. 137).

[7] Collins (1987, p. 138).

[8] "Encounter with a leader." Foodservice & Hospitality, May (1992), p. 31.

[9] "Encounter with a leader." p. 31.

Exhibit 1   A&W Climate Goals

TRUST IS THE FOUNDATION FOR HOW WE WORK WITH PEOPLE

Trust and Mutual Respect: Our actions are open, honest and caring. We rely on, believe in, and treat each other as partners committed to the same direction.

Self Responsibility: As individuals we accept responsibility for our own development, progress, results and work relationships.

Objectives: There is full understanding and commitment to challenging, specific, measurable organization and individual objectives.

Team Work: There is flexible and harmonious interaction between individuals and departments.

Improvement: Things are improved by encouraging and supporting people to challenge and question.

Innovation: We invest time developing our partners' ideas, growing the business and supporting responsible risk taking.

Feedback: Individuals and groups share ongoing formal and informal feedback for the purpose of evaluation and improvement.

Celebration: Our celebration of achievement contributes to consistent accomplishment of challenging goals.

Personal Development: Our work environment encourages identification of abilities, interests, and attitudes and allows people to develop to their fullest potential.

Communication: Clear and candid communication of facts, ideas and feelings exist between individuals and groups. Feelings are accepted as facts.

Questions

1. Climate seems to have much in common with many other management "technologies" such as Culture, Excellence, Total Quality, etc. What is unique, if anything, about Climate? What is unique, if anything, about the manner in which A&W has applied Climate to its operations?

2. A&W has developed and internalized their Climate of Trust during a 17-year period of growth. Could the company preserve their current Climate if it were faced with less favourable circumstances? How would you suggest that they deal with layoffs? With restaurant closings?

3. Discuss the connection between Climate and the values of Jeff Mooney as a person. Would Climate have to change subsequent to Mooney's departure?

4. Discuss A&W's dependence on Jeff Mooney. Why would they want to diminish it? Why wouldn't they? Is there anything they could do to diminish this dependence?

5. Despite Mooney's statements to the contrary, with the notion of Climate A&W seems to be asking its employees to change their beliefs and values. Discuss the ethical implications of this requirement.

6. To what extent could Climate be used as a political resource by A&W managers? What would the ethical implications of such politics be?

7. To what extent does the notion of Climate decrease the need for strong leadership? Is this good or bad?

FEDERAL EXPRESS QUALITY IMPROVEMENT PROGRAM

"The first year of our quality improvement program was really a great success. But the last six months have been tough," said Thomas R. Oliver, shaking his head ruefully. Oliver, senior vice president sales and customer service, was talking about some of the challenges facing Federal Express as it sought to maintain momentum on quality improvement efforts in early 1990.

> Last August, we merged with Flying Tigers, which has proved to be more difficult than anyone anticipated in terms of impacting service. In September, Hurricane Hugo, perhaps the most powerful storm of the century, disrupted our operations in the southeastern United States. Then there was the San Francisco earthquake in October. In December, the Mount Redoubt volcano in Alaska began erupting a high ash cloud, which totally dislocated our international flights through Anchorage. That volcano's still erupting on and off. The Friday before Christmas, the coldest weather seen in Memphis in the past 50 years caused burst water pipes and a computer foul-up that shut down our Superhub sorting operation. And now we're facing a profit crunch. Our revenues are way up, but we've incurred very heavy costs from the Tiger purchase and the continued expansion of our international operations.

Oliver pushed the company newspaper *Update* across the table. "Earnings drop; costs to be controlled," read the headline. He explained that Federal's third quarter profits for fiscal year (FY) 1990 were down by 79% to $5.2 million on revenues of $1.7 billion (up 35% over last year). Then he added:

> A going concern that is doing reasonably well but not making the desired level of profit can experience a big courage gap on the quality issue. People know what it costs to train management, to train employees, to continuously train new hires, to give people 'time around the clock' to work quality issues, and to organize the implementation of the various ideas that emerge. Yet, they aren't clear about the benefits. I want to ensure that last year's interest in quality doesn't get preempted by this year's interest in cutting costs.

The Evolution of a Legend

Few companies had achieved legendary status as quickly as Federal Express. People loved to tell stories about the firm, incorporated in 1971 by Frederick W. Smith, Jr., then aged 27. The earliest story told how Smith had sketched out the concept of a national hub-and-spoke airfreight network in a paper written while an undergraduate at Yale. The professor told Smith that his concept was interesting but infeasible because of competition and regulation, and gave the young man a "C" grade. But after service in Vietnam, Smith went on to turn his dream into reality, basing the hub in his home town of Memphis, Tennessee.

The concept was simple. Federal Express couriers, based in cities around the country, would pick up packages and take them to a local station, from where they would be flown by air to a central hub. Memphis was selected since it was centrally located in the US and airport operations were rarely disrupted by bad weather. At the hub, packages would be unloaded, sorted, reloaded, and flown to their destinations, where they would be delivered by couriers driving Federal

SOURCE: This case was prepared by Professor Christopher H. Lovelock of the Massachusetts Institute of Technology as a basis for class discussion rather than to illustrate either effective or ineffective handling of a business situation. Development of this material was supported by the Alfred P. Sloan Fellows Program at the Sloan School of Management, Massachusetts Institute of Technology. Copyright © 1990 by IMEDE, Lausanne, Switzerland. The International Institute for Management Development (IMD), resulting from the merger between IMEDE, Lausanne, and IMI, Geneva, acquires and retains all rights. Reproduced by permission.

Express vans. Because of federal regulations, the new airline had to be chartered as an air taxi operator and was restricted to aircraft with a carrying capacity of 7,200 pounds (3.3 tonnes). Initially, Federal flew Dassault Falcons, French-built executive jets converted into minifreighters.

On an April night in 1973, 14 Falcons took off from cities around the US and flew to Memphis. In total, they carried 186 packages. Not surprisingly, the company lost money heavily in its early years. But aided by aggressive sales and clever advertising, package volume built steadily and by 1976 the firm was profitable. Thereafter, growth in revenues, profits and package volume was rapid:

Fiscal year ending May 31

	1976	1981	1986	1988	1989[1]	1990[2]
Annual revenues ($mn)	75	589	2,573	3,883	5,167	7,000
Annual net income ($mn)	4	58	132	188	185	110
Av. dly. express packages ('000)	15	87	550	878	1,059	1,250
Av. dly. heavyweight vol. ('000 lbs)[3]	1–1	—	—	—	4,019	3,300

[1] Includes Tiger International operations for the last four months.
[2] Projections
[3] 1,000 lbs = 0.455 metric tonnes

With the 1978 deregulation of the airfreight industry (for which Smith had lobbied heavily), Federal went public and bought larger aircraft. Having redefined service as "all actions and reactions that customers perceive they have purchased," management began a major investment in information technology, creating an online order-entry system known as COSMOS. This was designed to provide superior customer service in the face of increasing competition from UPS, Emery, the US Postal Service, and other express delivery firms.

Federal's early advertising slogan "When it absolutely, positively has to be there overnight" became almost a national byword. By FY 1985, Federal's sales exceeded $2 billion and its advertising jabbed fun at the competition, asking provocatively, "Why fool around with anybody else?" Later, to emphasize its role as a tool for JIT (just-in-time) inventory management procedures, the company began using the slogan, "It's not just a package, it's your business."

Following the purchase of Flying Tigers in August 1989, analysts forecast that Federal's total revenues for FY 1990 could exceed $7 billion. By now the company was an American institution. Its vans with their distinctive purple, orange, and white colors were everywhere; its aircraft could be seen at most airports; and the verb "to Fedex" (meaning to ship a package overnight) had become as much a generic expression for office workers as the term "to Xerox."

For 19 years, Federal Express had had a single leader, its chairman, Fred Smith, who was still only 46 years old. Outside management experts noted that it was unusual for an entrepreneur whose company had grown so large, so fast, to continue to lead the firm. Smith appeared to have a remarkable ability to supply vision, inspire loyalty, and create a climate in which innovation and risk taking were encouraged and rewarded. Although the Federal Express Manager's Guide ran to 186 pages, Smith's core philosophy for the corporation was simple:

> Federal Express, from its inception, has put its people first, both because it is right to do so and because it is good business as well. Our corporate philosophy is succinctly stated: People—Service—Profits (P-S-P).

Line Haul Operations

Federal's operating concept of a hub in Memphis, served by aircraft flying spoke-like routes from cities all around the US, had been only slightly modified over the years. But the technology and scale of the operation had changed dramatically. The sorting facility at Memphis International Airport had been enormously expanded. The Superhub, as it was known, now covered some 23 acres (100,000 m³), consisting of a matrix of 83 conveyor belts moving at right angles to one another. Aircraft arrived at Memphis almost continuously between 11:00 pm and 1:15 am. Using specially designed equipment, a crew of 14 workers could unload 44,000 pounds (20 tonnes) of freight from a Boeing 727 in 12 minutes.

The freight began its journey through the Superhub on a wide belt, known as the Primary Matrix, moving at 10 mph (16 km/h). Watching the packages rush by on this belt and then be diverted by guide arms into specific sort areas reminded one visitor of seeing a mountain torrent in full flood. Although the sort was assisted by computers, much of the process was labor intensive and was expected to remain so. Once reloaded, the aircraft left Memphis between 2:15 and 3:45 am.

Regional domestic sorting facilities had been established; packages traveling between two East coast cities were sorted in Newark, New Jersey, rather than being sent to Memphis, while packages traveling between West coast destinations were sorted in Oakland, California. A second national hub had been opened in Indianapolis, southeast of Chicago. These facilities were served by large trucks as well as by aircraft; packages traveling shorter distances were frequently transported entirely by truck.

Since 1979, Federal had offered service to and within Canada. In 1985, the company inaugurated international service and began to build up a network of routes around the world. A European hub was established in Brussels, the capital of Belgium (and administrative center of the 12-nation European Community). Federal planned to build up significant intra-European business as well as transatlantic volume. Overseas expansion was aided by the purchase of existing courier firms in each national market (nine were purchased in FY 1989).

In December 1988, Smith announced what the press described as "an ambitious and highly risky plan" to pay $895 million for Tiger International, Inc., the world's largest heavy cargo airline, best known for its Flying Tiger airfreight service. Although Tiger had some domestic business, most of its revenues came from international services. The merger was a key step towards realizing Smith's goal of making Federal "the world's premier priority logistics company." Six "Freight Movement Centers"—located in Anchorage, Memphis, Chicago, New York, Brussels and Tokyo—now coordinated Federal's international traffic, which was expected to generate 30% of the firm's revenues in FY 1990.

A major benefit was Tiger's overseas operating rights, including landing rights in Japan. The merger allowed Federal to operate its own aircraft on routes where transportation had formerly been contracted out to other carriers. It also catapulted Federal into the heavy cargo business; previously, the firm had limited most packages to 150 pounds (68 kg) maximum weight, as well as imposing length and girth restrictions. Another important asset was Tiger's fleet of aircraft, including 21 Boeing 747s. However, these benefits came at the cost of taking on significant debt at a time when margins were being squeezed by price competition and heavy upfront costs were being incurred due to overseas expansion. There was also the challenge of merging two sharply different corporate cultures.

The Scope of the Operation in 1990

By 1990, Federal Express was one of the world's largest airlines, with a fleet of some 350 aircraft. This fleet comprised 170 trunk line aircraft (21 Boeing 747s, 25 McDonnell-Douglas DC-10s, 118 Boeing 727s, and 6 DC-8s) and another 180 feeder aircraft used for shorter-distance operations. The firm served 119 countries and had 1,530 staffed facilities worldwide. Some four-fifths of its 86,000 employees were based in the United States, including 17,300 employees in Memphis. Federal operated over 20,000 vans and almost 2,000 large trucks in the US, plus another 6,300 vehicles in international locations.

A visitor to Memphis might be surprised to see a large fleet of snowplows and other snow-removal vehicles sporting Federal Express colors. The company had purchased this equipment in 1988 after a heavy snowstorm—unusual for Memphis which had almost no snow removal equipment—had badly disrupted operations one night. "We only need this equipment about one night every two years," explained a company official. "But when we need it, we really need it!"

The average daily volume for express packages (up to 150 pounds in the US) was around 1.25 million. Federal's average package weighed 5.4 pounds (2.5 kg) and yielded a revenue of over $16; a significant price increase would take effect on April 1, 1990. Document shipments weighing just a few ounces (100-200g) had a declining share of package volume; the Fedex Overnight Letter represented 37% of all express packages in FY 1989, down from 40% two years earlier. The company offered three levels of delivery speed in the United States: Priority Overnight (next business morning by 10:30 am in most locations); Standard Overnight (next business day for shipments of five pounds or less, with delivery before 3:00 pm in most locations); and Standard Air (second business day). Federal's rates tended to be more expensive than most of its US competitors.

For heavyweight shipments, the average daily volume was around 5,000 units. These shipments weighed an average of almost 800 pounds (360 kg) each—some were so large that they required an entire aircraft—so they were handled separately from the normal hub sorting operations. The revenue for each shipment ranged widely but the average was around $850.

The express package industry was consolidating and the company's chief operating officer, James L. Barksdale, described the challenge facing its 1,300 sales professionals: "We're in a tough business. Our competitors are tough, mean, go-getting folks. They are not a bunch of idiots. I wish they were." Within the US, the key players were Federal Express (with about 45-50% of the market), UPS (15%), Airborne (10-15%), Emery/Purolator (5%), US Postal Service (10%), and others (5%). Federal had purchased Purolator's Indianapolis hub. Overseas, Federal faced UPS, Emery, DHL, and Australian-owned TNT, plus the express divisions of national postal services and airline freight and package services.

INFORMATION TECHNOLOGY

For Federal Express, information about each package was seen as just as important as the package itself. Information also played a key role in achieving the most effective utilization of the entire physical operation. Dr. Ron J. Ponder, senior vice president for information and telecommunications, described the line-haul operations (package sorting and transportation) as one of several parallel fibers running through the entire business. The others included a series of major information networks. "We run three data processing houses at Federal," explained Ponder, a former business school professor. "There are the traditional, commercial revenue systems that every company has; a line-haul flight operations system that is unique to airlines; and COSMOS, our customer service house."

To me, quality is everything we do. Our goal for availability—communication and systems—is 99.8%. We've cranked that up during the last ten years from about 88%. Each year, we keep raising the bar. We're running some of the highest systems availability numbers in North America. Most companies are happy at 95% or 96%.

Our computer center is now one of the largest in the world under one roof, and we have the highest transaction rates of any shop in North America on a daily basis. Last month, we had 320 million transactions from all over the world go through our computer systems. We measure each one of them. Less than 86,000 exceeded our standard internal compute time of one second, which you have to have to run these massive parallel systems. Each morning at 8:30, we have a conference call in this division with perhaps 50 people in on it. We start off with any problems we've had in the last 24 hours.

In addition to overseeing the systems, I do the strategic architectural planning that lets this company use technology to the greatest possible advantage for customer satisfaction and competitive superiority, and for reducing operational costs to improve productivity.

Ponder believed that Federal Express had a sharply different view of technology from most companies.

Technology transfer—or being able to absorb new technology—is a cultural thing that we've built in here. One of the keys to our success is that we constantly embrace new technology. For most companies, that's very painful and they don't like it. It's painful to leave what works and is cheap for new, expensive, unknown approaches. So they don't do it. At Federal, we would rather get an innovation a year earlier and develop back-up systems to counter a relatively high failure rate than to wait until the failure rate—and the price—have been reduced to more "acceptable" levels. Most folks prefer to wait until a technology matures.

You can view technology as a wave in the ocean, washing in debris. Most people concentrate on the debris that floats in. 'Oh, isn't this neat!' they'll say of some device. 'Where can I use it?' And that's where I think they mess up. I view technology as the wave itself, not the individual things that are brought to shore. We knew what we wanted to do ten years ago, but the technology wasn't there. So we were waiting for the wave and constantly prodding manufacturers to create what we needed as that wave rolled in.

Asked what new waves Federal Express was watching, Ponder listed battery technology, continued miniaturization, the maturing of relational databases (essential to maintaining detailed customer files) and, most importantly, a new generation of computer hardware and software using RISC (Reduced Instruction Set Computing) architecture. The net effect would be more computing power and faster access to information for less money.

COSMOS and DADS

Federal prided itself on having one of the most sophisticated customer service systems in the world. COSMOS (Customer, Operations, Service, Master On-line System) was first installed in 1979 and had been constantly upgraded to cope with the more than 260,000 calls now received, on average, each working day. COSMOS had evolved into a worldwide electronic network that transmitted critical package information to Memphis. Its major components were an order-entry system for customers to request package pickups, a continuously updated record of each package's progress through the Fedex system that could be used to trace a missing package, financial records for billing purposes, and a huge relational database that could also be used for marketing analysis and planning.

The system worked in much the same way around the world. In the US, customers had a choice between requesting a pickup or, for a reduced fee, of dropping off a package at a drop-box or at one of Federal's business service centers. To request a pickup, customers telephoned a toll-free number that connected to a customer service agent (CSA) at one of 17 call centers around the nation. Calls could be diverted from one center to another to maintain the company's response-time standards. Since most calls were received in the mid to late afternoon, peak volumes could be shifted to centers in other time zones. The CSA requested the shipper's account number which was entered on an electronic order blank on the video screen (refer to

Exhibit 1). Armed with this information, the system automatically provided the CSA with the account name, address, phone number, pickup location, contact name, and other relevant data.

An alternative method was to call a special Automatic Pickup number. In response to the promptings of a recorded voice, callers used the buttons on their touch-tone telephones to enter their account numbers and then, as a cross-check, their postal zip code, followed by the number of packages being shipped. The voice would then provide a confirmation number and latest pick up time. These service requests were transmitted automatically to the nearest origin station.

Federal was also testing a custom-designed desktop unit, smaller than a telephone, called "Hello Federal." This device had a full alpha-numeric keypad, an adjustable LCD screen, and buttons to press for pickup, package tracing information, and requests for airbills and packaging. The requested information was displayed on the screen; no voice communication was needed. Since each unit was programmed with the shipper's account number, it was not necessary to provide account information when calling. If the tests proved successful, the company planned to offer a "Hello Federal" unit free to any customer shipping a predefined volume of packages three or more days per week.

Once a pickup request was received, the CSA entered shipping information through COSMOS to alert the dispatch center nearest to the pickup location. The message was received by the dispatch center's DADS (Digitally Assisted Dispatch System) computer which, in turn, sent the information to a courier. The request was displayed on a small DADS video screen in the courier's van or on a portable unit the size of a slim briefcase used by walking couriers.

One customer, a management consultant working out of a home office, testified to the efficiency of the system:

It was only the second time that I had used the Automatic Pickup service and I still didn't have 100% confidence in it, but I knew that it was a little faster than talking to a CSA in a call center and I was in a hurry. I had just finished a report for one client and was about to leave for the airport on a visit to another client. So I sealed up the report, phoned for a cab, and then called the Automatic Pickup number to place my order. The taxi arrived in five minutes, which was pretty good. As I was getting into the cab, what should roll up but the Federal Express van to pick up my package. I was so astonished that I got out of the cab and asked the courier how he had arrived so quickly. "I was driving on the next street," he said, "when your request came up on my screen."

Tracking the Package through the Federal Express System

Each airbill contained a unique 10-digit bar code label which was scanned by an infrared light pen every time the package changed hands. The first scan, known as PUPS (Pick Up Package Scan), took place at the pickup location. Using a hand-held terminal called a COSMOS IIB SuperTracker (a little bigger than the remote control for a TV set), the courier scanned the bar code and then entered on a key pad the type of service, handling code, and destination zip code. The SuperTracker recorded this information, added the time of pickup, and responded on its LCD display with a routing and sorting code which the courier then handwrote on the package. Dr. Ponder noted, "Miniaturization has enabled us to stretch the communications system right to the customer's doorstep."

On returning to the van, the courier plugged the SuperTracker into a shoe within the dispatch computer, which transmitted its information to COSMOS. In many overseas countries, this data transfer took place when the van returned to its station. Once unloaded, each package received a Station Outbound Package Scan (SOPS) before being reloaded into a container for transport to a sorting hub. Any exceptions, such as packages that were damaged or missed the aircraft, received a P.M. eXception (PMX) scan. These data were then transmitted to COSMOS. Similar scans were made at several other points (refer to Exhibit 2).

Finally, at the delivery point, the package received a Proof of Delivery Scan (PODS). The courier entered the recipient's first initial and last name, as well as a code for delivery location, and the SuperTracker automatically recorded the time. If the package were delivered to an alternative location (for instance, a neighboring building) or no one was available to accept delivery, it received instead a Delivery EXception (DEX) scan and full details were entered.

The records provided by these scans enabled Federal to offer full custodial care of all packages. A trace of a missing package would reveal in seconds the time and location of the latest scan. No competitor could match this level of tracing capability. Said Ponder, "The notion of picking up and delivering a package without being able to offer the customer total information on it is totally unacceptable to us."

Automated Systems for High Volume Customers

Federal had formed a team called Customer Automation to assist customers in managing their shipments more effectively. The result was a family of automated shipping and invoicing systems designed to reduce paperwork and tie the company more closely to its large volume customers.

Tape Invoice   offered customers a weekly invoice on magnetic tape, instead of paper. By running the invoice tape on the computer, customers could analyze Federal Express shipping information any way they wished. Such data could be fed directly into the firm's accounting system.

Powership 2   was a shipment management system that streamlined package preparation and billing. Federal provided customers with an electronic weighing scale, microcomputer terminal, bar code scanner, and printer at no charge; all the customer paid was telephone charges. The system eliminated the need for airbills and express manifests, and could be programmed to store up to 32,000 recipient names and addresses. The printer could generate barcoded address labels. Powership 2 rated packages with the right charges, automatically combining package weights by destination to provide volume discounts. Daily invoices could be prepared automatically, as could customized management reports. Customers could trace their own packages through COSMOS.

Powership Plus   allowed customers to link their computers with Federal Express's tracking and invoicing systems. If the package weight were known (which was true for many mail order items) users could quote shipping rates, delivery schedules, and tracking numbers to their own customers at the very time they entered the purchase order. Next, they transmitted information directly to the warehouse, where the bar-coded address label could be printed and applied. When each night's shipping was complete, users would transmit their shipping data to Federal. At the end of the week, they would send Federal Express a computer tape containing the week's shipping data, plus a check for the total shipping charges.

NEW QUALITY INITIATIVES

Quality had been implicit in Federal's efforts from the beginning. In 1975, its advertising claimed "Federal Express. Twice as Good as the Best in the Business" (a slogan comparing Federal's performance against its then leading competitor, Emery Air Freight). The firm's emphasis on reliability was captured in its classic slogan, "Absolutely, Positively Overnight." Management had long recognized the connection between doing things right the first time and improving productivity: "Q=P" (quality equals productivity) was the internal rallying cry.

Employee Orientation

As chairman, Fred Smith constantly set goals of improving reliability, productivity, and financial performance to promote the corporate imperative of People—Service—Profits. Particular attention was paid to leading and motivating employees. Regular communication with employees had always been a corporate priority. As the company grew in numbers and geographic scope, increasing reliance came to be placed on the use of videotaped messages for both communication and training. In 1987, Federal launched FXTV, a real-time business television network broadcasting daily by satellite to over 700 locations in the US and Canada from studios in Memphis. Satellite hook-ups with overseas locations were arranged for special occasions. Each month, FXTV produced about 20 hours of broadcast TV, plus 10-15 hours of videotape.

Since 1985, a confidential employee survey had been conducted annually called Survey Feedback Action (SFA). It consisted of 26 statements with which the employee was asked to agree or disagree

on a five-point scale ranging from "strongly agree" to "strongly disagree." Scores were reported for employee work groups not for individuals. The first ten questions (refer to Exhibit 3) related to employees' views of their managers. The percentage of favorable responses on these items constituted what was known as the SFA Leadership Index.

The full SFA Index represented the percentage of positive responses on all 26 items, including questions on pay, working conditions, views on senior management, and feelings about the company. Other companies administered the same survey, so scores could be compared with those from employees in other firms. Federal had consistently obtained above average ratings.

In 1983, Smith initiated "Bravo Zulu" awards (from the US Navy signal flags for BZ, meaning "Well done!"), which allowed managers to provide instant recognition to employees for excellent service within the company. Stickers bearing the signal flags could be placed on paperwork or a memo; managers also had authority to issue a Bravo Zulu voucher worth up to $100.

Outstanding examples of customer service were celebrated with Golden Falcon awards, consisting of a gold pin and ten shares of Federal Express stock (worth about $500 in early 1990). About 20 such awards were made each year. Nominees were often identified by customer calls or letters; a typical example might concern extraordinary effort in tracking down and delivering a missing package. Golden Falcon and Bravo Zulu awards, and the stories behind them, were publicized to motivate employees and create corporate legends.

An Unsuccessful First Look at Quality Training

It was not until 1985, when Smith and senior officers became concerned about a possible slowdown in the business and decline in profitability, that the company first addressed quality improvement techniques at the corporate level. Smith hired a consultant to conduct an off-site meeting with top management, but it was not a success. As Tom Oliver recalled, "Everyone walked away with a calculator and a statistics book, but our interest had not been captured." Some improvements were made, but the idea lost momentum. Smith was soon preoccupied with the problems of

ZapMail, the company's same-day facsimile service, which was discontinued in 1986 with a write-off of some $360 million—the company's first major setback since its start-up days.

Two and a half years passed, during which the feared slowdown was replaced by a period of explosive growth. By mid-1987, the sales and customer service division was struggling with service problems that were becoming increasingly serious as the company continued to expand. As senior vice president of the division, Oliver decided it was high time to re-explore the quality issue.

Working with ODI

Disappointed with the previous statistically-based approach to quality improvement, Oliver selected Organizational Dynamics, Inc. (ODI), an international consulting firm headquartered in Burlington, Massachusetts. ODI's great advantage, from Oliver's perspective, was that it paid little attention to statistical techniques but a lot more to the thought processes and involvement of people within the company in developing quality programs.

ODI began by designing and leading quality planning workshops for senior executives from all divisions. The product of each workshop was a series of action plans, setting priorities for problems needing resolution. Next, ODI focused on the sales and customer service division. Under the leadership of ODI vice president Rob Evans, the consultants trained all managers in the division to understand the quality process, then began training employees and creating quality action teams. ODI also trained facilitators from other divisions, including ground operations. A key goal was to get people to analyze what were often complex problems, rather than shooting from the hip with instant solutions. Different versions of the programs were developed for managers and employees.

The Quality Advantage Program began with a module on "The Meaning of Quality," introducing five pillars on which a quality organization must be built:

- Customer Focus—a commitment to meeting customer needs;
- Total involvement—"improving quality is everyone's job";
- Measurement—where and when to take action, documenting progress;

- Systematic support—applying strategic planning, budgeting, and performance management to quality improvement efforts;
- Continuous improvement—always reaching for new and better ways to perform one's job.

"The Cost of Quality" module identified the costs of not doing quality work—rework, waste, unnecessary overtime, and job dissatisfaction. The goal was to help participants estimate their own cost of quality, break this down into avoidable and necessary costs, and then plan ways to reduce avoidable costs. The third module, "You and Your Customer," described the customer-supplier chain and helped participants to see that everyone in Federal Express was both a customer and a supplier. Participants learned to identify their own key customers and suppliers within the company, as well as how they were linked, and then to align customer needs and supplier capabilities in order to meet agreed requirements.

The "Continuous Improvement" module emphasized that it was everyone's responsibility to fix and prevent problems, showed how to identify early warning signals, and required that everyone strive to meet customer needs in innovative ways. The fifth module, "Making Quality Happen," was directed at managers, supervisors and professionals; it described how to take a leadership role to implement quality programs.

A separate program, Quality Action Teams (QATs), focused on how to implement quality improvement. ODI taught a problem-solving process consisting of four phases: focusing on a particular problem or opportunity, analyzing data, developing solutions and action plans, and executing plans for implementing solutions. To help the QATs perform each of these tasks, ODI taught participants how to apply 20 problem-solving tools, including fishbone analysis, flowcharting, and cost-benefit analysis.

Setting Goals for People—Service—Profits

By June 1988 (the beginning of fiscal year 1989), Oliver had concluded that to make quality improvement work for customer service, it was critical to involve domestic ground operations. Most problems at Federal were cross-divisional in nature, in the sense that one division created a certain output and passed it on to the next one. That next division's problems were often directly related to what had happened earlier up the line. Commenting on this, Oliver noted:

We were able to put across the idea that one of the big difficulties in getting cross-divisional cooperation was the multiplicity of different goals. These goals might individually maximize the performance of each division, but collectively resulted in a deterioration of performance for the system. We realized that the more each unit tried to maximize its own performance, the more it tended to send difficult problems downstream. So we concluded that what we needed for Federal Express were three very simple goals.

First, we took the existing SFA Leadership Index. The leadership a manager provides has a tremendous impact on the positive attitudes of the employees. We determined to use this index as the single goal in our people management process and established a goal of 72 for FY 1989, up from 71 the previous year.

People—Service—Profits implied a profit goal, so we set a goal of a 10% operating margin on the domestic business. That goal was irrespective of individual department performance. Service had historically been defined in terms of couriers' on-time delivery efforts, what percentage of packages were delivered by 10:30 am. There were a lot of problems with that service level measure: specifically, we could get that package delivered by 10:30 am on the wrong date! It was also a limited measure, suggesting that Federal could be successful simply by delivering packages on time. That was no longer true!

We found that the information associated with packages had as much to do with customer satisfaction as did delivery. For instance, "don't know" answers to questions upset customers. As we reviewed customer correspondence, we found that the angriest of all the letters we got were those where our information processes failed us as opposed to those where we didn't deliver on time. What was needed was a broader measure that also addressed other shortcomings that upset customers, such as failure to answer the phone quickly, damaged packages, etc.

ODI stressed the danger of using percentages as targets. In an organization as large as Federal Express, delivering 99% of packages on time or having 99.9% of all flights land safely would still lead to horrendous problems. Instead, they approached quality from the standpoint of zero failures. Oliver emphasized:

It's only when you examine the types of failures, the number that occur of each type, and the reasons why, that you begin to improve the quality of your service. For us, the trick was to express quality failures in absolute numbers. That led us to develop the Service Quality Index or SQI, which takes each of 12 different events that occur every day, takes the numbers of those events and multiplies them by a weight from one to ten points, based on the amount of aggravation caused to customers—as evidenced by their tendency to write to Federal Express and complain about them. Fred Smith calls it our "hierarchy of horrors."

The SQI, pronounced "sky," was computed as a daily average. (Exhibit 4 shows its 12 components.) Like a golf score, the lower the index, the better the performance. Based on internal records, it was calculated that the average score during FY 1988 (which ended on May 31, 1988) would have been 152,000 points per day—out of a potential maximum of 40 million per day if everything possible had gone wrong. The goal set for FY 1989 was the same—152,000 points—but since package volumes were expected to rise by 20%, this goal actually represented a 20% improvement. Employees were urged to "Reach for the SQI!"

To reinforce the significance of these three corporate-wide goals, senior management tied the entire management bonus process to achievement of the three goals. Simply put, there would be no bonus for any manager at the end of FY 1989 unless the company achieved all three goals. "Needless to say, that caught everyone's imagination." Oliver smiled wryly and continued:

It was very different from our previous approach of having managers' bonuses based on their ability to meet individual management-by-objective goals without regard to whether that did or didn't help the corporate process. In the actual unfolding, Fiscal year 1989 turned out to be the best year we had had in a long, long time. We achieved the profit goal despite some difficult circumstances, and the SQI came in at 133,000 points. The Leadership Index reached 76. It was the largest single jump in the history of the SFA process, in terms of managers' relationships with employees.

ODI's Evans believed that one reason for the SQI successes was that Federal had set up 12 QATs, each of which focused on a specific SQI category. As CEO, Fred Smith provided active support and encouragement. Most teams were headed by a vice president. Results were posted weekly, and every three months each QAT reported out to Smith, Barksdale, and other senior executives. Quarterly awards were given in four categories: (1) greatest impact on SQI results; (2) best use of the quality process (using tools that had been taught); (3) best understanding of root causes (identifying and working on underlying problems rather than superficial effects); and (4) best use of line employees (gathering information from the people closest to the process who knew it best).

Activities During FY 1990

While training continued, efforts were made to facilitate a bottom-up movement in quality improvement. John West, manager of quality improvement, saw his job as a catalyst to bring about shared approaches to problem solving. West coordinated training efforts with ODI and had established a network of quality professionals in each of Federal's ten divisions. These people formed a quality advisory board which met biweekly to discuss failures and successes.

One of these professionals was Linda Griffin, senior quality administrator for domestic ground operations, which had 40,000 employees working out of 600 stations. Griffin felt that while the quality program had enjoyed many "surface successes, the challenge was to coordinate the replication of these successes by getting people to describe what they had actually done and how they did it, as opposed to simply talking about the results. Forms and electronic mail systems had been created to make it easy to record this information, while a reward system encouraged people to turn in details of their successes. Said Griffin:

> Recognition programs have a mutual benefit. They motivate and reward employees and create some peer pressure. At the same time, management gets to see the value of the training programs, which reinforces the belief that training is the right thing to do.

One replicated success concerned a sorting table designed by employees in the Phoenix station to prevent missorts caused by envelopes sliding into the wrong destination pile. They sent a videotape of the table design to the company's industrial engineers, who developed several versions of the sort table for different-sized stations. Couriers in a QAT at another station were frustrated with the problems (such as missed pickups) caused when the regular courier on a route had to be replaced by a substitute unfamiliar with obscure addresses, building entrances, location of freight elevators, and pick-up or delivery locations on different floors, etc. So they designed an informational booklet describing each route. The result was a sharp increase in on-time delivery and productivity. This idea had now been incorporated in the "Policy and Procedures" manual for all stations.

Sharing success stories was seen as a way to get more people involved in QATs and to improve working relations within the company through customer-supplier alignments. West commented:

> People tend to gravitate toward QATs, which are more fun. We really have to push the notion of customer-supplier alignment. People and departments don't always work well together. W. Edwards Deming, the American quality pioneer, claims that about 95% of quality problems are management problems, because of the way the system was designed.

Federal's satellite broadcast network, FXTV was employed in both a sharing and training role. Rob Evans participated in a program entitled "Customer/Supplier Alignment: The First Step in Quality," designed to reinforce earlier quality training. Evans began his segment of the live broadcast by reminding viewers of the "Right Things Right" grid, a simple four cell matrix developed by ODI.

> That grid is a simple way to look at the work we do from two different angles. The first angle is *how* we do the work we do. We either do things wrong or we do things right. The second angle has to do with *what* work we actually do, doing the right things or the wrong things. When we put these two together, we have four possibilities. We could be doing the right things wrong; that's the old way of looking at quality problems and, of course, that happens. We could be doing the wrong things wrong, really wasting our time. Or we could be doing the wrong things

right, things that don't matter to our customers, internal or external, but doing a very good job of them. The fourth possibility is doing right things right. This is the only one that adds value to our customers and our company.

In a quality organization, people spend the great majority of their time doing the right things right. What we've found at ODI is that most managers spend 45-60% of their time doing the right things right, but the rest is wasted—time, effort, money. Of that wasted time, about half seems to fall into the wrong things right category.

Pressures and Distractions

Top management was delighted by improvements in SQI and other measures during FY 1989, but then the picture changed dramatically. The average daily SQI goal of 125,000 points for FY 1990 (on a higher package volume) was ravaged by the dislocations of the Tiger merger and a series of natural disasters during the fall and winter. Mount Redoubt's volcanic ash cloud grounded five of Federal's 747s at the Anchorage hub in Alaska for two days and forced subsequent Far East flights to operate through Seattle, using more fuel and carrying less freight. The computer shutdown at the Memphis Superhub on December 22 resulted in manual sorting, delayed deliveries, and an average daily SQI for that week of 613,842. At the end of February, the year to date daily average stood at 166,111.

Meantime, a sharp earnings decline had led to company-wide cost reduction efforts, including some impacting quality facilitation. Some outside financial analysts had suggested that the company's financial situation made it vulnerable to a takeover. Tom Oliver was very concerned that the momentum of the quality improvement efforts not be lost.

> Most companies need four to five years of continuous effort before employees and managers alike really understand that this is *the* way to approach problems. The fact that we had some initial successes was certainly positive, but by no means have we gotten it to the point where if you scratch an employee, you're going to get a quality-related response. And that's especially true of first-level management who feel tremendous pressure to achieve budget-related financial results.

> We've found that the SQI process works really well for the corporation as a whole, but Federal Express doesn't have the ability to develop a precise tracking of these events down to individual locations, so our station-level goals tend to stay related to the service level measurement (on-time deliveries) instead of the broader SQI perspective. We're trying to work aggressively on measurement systems so that Federal can use that information more precisely in measuring and managing the performance of first line managers. Feedback is critical in any quality process.

> Much remains to be done. But it always comes back to these questions: Is it financially feasible to spend the dollars and take the time to train the people? Will we spend the time and money to let them work the issues after they are trained? Are investments in quality high enough in the corporation's competing priorities? In the sales and customer service division's case, feedback systems require substantial investments in data systems resources. We want to make them, but we're always fighting the allocation process.

> Right now, everyone is trying to minimize their own costs and efficiency; in the process, they're sending enormous costs downstream. The tendency in corporate management is to seek good budgets and financial controls for every individual unit in your operation. A well-managed corporation has a very strong financial system—but a strong, department-oriented financial system is precisely what you're trying to get around when you're attempting to approach things from a systemic quality and cost viewpoint. You must expend money at the source of the problem to eliminate the waste expenses later in the process. But people won't do it, because they don't get the benefits; some other department and the customers do.

> Almost every change we've made in Federal's services has no measurable ROI (return on investment). You cannot, in effect, prove the reductions in cost because they're systemic reductions, as opposed to individual area reductions. In any case, changes in the quality of service impact customer revenues as much or more than they impact costs. In the final event, one needs to make these decisions based on the impact on customers and on the system, as opposed to precisely measured return-on-investment calculations.

Oliver glanced at the clock. It was almost time for another senior executive meeting on cutting costs. ODI had submitted a proposal for the next phase of the quality training program, and there were numerous internal projects as well. His best estimate was that future train-ing and other key quality initiatives would, if properly funded, cost as much as $200 per employee in the first year and half of that in subsequent years. "It all comes down to that courage gap," he said to himself as he gathered up his papers and strode out of the office.

EXHIBIT 1   CONTENTS OF FEDERAL EXPRESS DISPATCH
REQUEST SCREEN*

Customer Information

Location ID_____ Zip Code _____ Pickup Time _____ Cutoff _____

Account # _____ Company Name _____

Address _____

City_____ State _____ Type of Account _____

Contact person _____ Phone #_____ Extension _____ Close time _____

Remarks to Courier _____

Local Area Promotions _____

Package Information

Pickup Day _____ Total Packages _____ Total Weight _____ Rate _____

Time Package ready_____ Supplies Requested _____ Commodity Shipped _____

Remarks by CSA _____

Dispatcher's Remarks _____

Dispatcher's # _____ Exceptions _____ Credit Approved _____

Courier's # _____ Time _____ Date_____

---

*NOTE: The screen display has been clarified and simplified for purposes of case presentation, with abbreviations written out in full. When a customer called Federal Express, the customer service agent first asked the caller for a Federal Express account number. When this was typed in, most other customer information (other than details of the caller's request, e.g. pickup) was automatically retrieved from the computer's memory and displayed on the screen, from where it could then be verified with the caller.

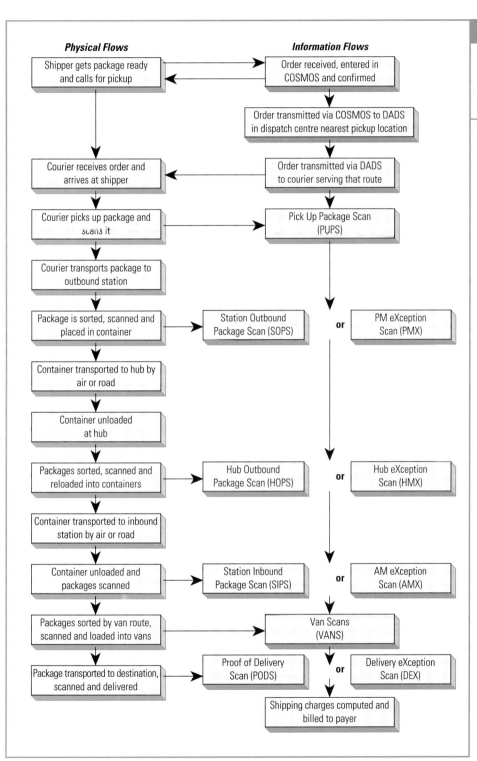

EXHIBIT 2

*Physical Flows and
Information Flows
for Federal Express
Packages*

EXHIBIT 3 SURVEY FEEDBACK ACTION PROGRAM: COMPONENTS OF LEADERSHIP INDEX

1. I can tell my manager what I think.
2. My manager tells what is expected.
3. Favoritism is not a problem in my work group.
4. My manager helps us do our job better.
5. My manager listens to my concerns.

6. My manager asks for my ideas about work.
7. My manager tells me when I do a good job.
8. My manager treats me with respect.
9. My manager keeps me informed.
10. My manager does not interfere.

NOTE: The above sentences paraphrase the actual wording used in compiling the Leadership Index. Employees were asked to review each statement carefully and then to express their agreement or disagreement with that statement on a 5-point scale.

EXHIBIT 4 SERVICE QUALITY INDEX ("SQI")

FY 1990 Goals vs. Actual for First Nine Months

Beginning in FY 1989, the overall quality of service was measured by the Service Quality Index (SQI). This index, which was based on the findings of extensive customer research, weighted service failures from the customer's perspective, and comprised the twelve components shown below.

FAILURE TYPE	WEIGHTING FACTOR	FY 1990 GOALS (JUNE '89-MAY '90) GOAL FOR AVERAGE DAILY OCCURENCES	WEIGHTED DAILY FAILURE POINTS	JUNE'89-FEB. '90 ACTUAL AVERAGE DAILY FAILURE POINTS
Right Day Late Service Failures	1	22,000	22,000	*33,561
Wrong Day Late Service Failures	5	11,522	57,606	*74,674
Traces (not answered by COSMOS)	1	4,170	4,170	5,165
Complaints Reopened by Customers	5	851	4,255	2,330
Missing Proofs of Delivery (PODs)	1	4,959	4,959	6,260
Invoice Adjustments Requested	1	12,852	12,852	11,921
Missed Pick-ups	10	152	1,526	1,548
Lost Packages	10	72	725	1,102
Damaged Packages	10	181	1,815	2,868
Delay Minutes/Aircraft ("0" based)	5	327	1,635	16,821
Overgoods	5	327	1,635	1,788
Abandoned Calls	1	4,782	4,782	8,073
TOTAL AVERAGE DAILY FAILURE POINTS (SQI)			125,000	166,111

*Estimated

NOTE: SQI points were reported on a daily basis, as well as on a weekly, monthly or year-to-date daily average.

A

Abilene Paradox   That groups can fail to manage the basic agreement of its members and end up taking an action that no one individual wants.

Active noise control   Anti-noise is electronically produced to cancel out repetitive noise.

Actor-observer effect   People tend to see their own behaviour as due to the situation and others' behaviour as due more to internal and stable traits.

ad hoc   Latin: "for this particular purpose."

Agricultural revolution   The purposeful planting of crops allowed people to live in one place and eventually develop towns and cities.

Alliance game   Organizational peers band together and support each other.

All-salaried teams   Everyone on a team is paid a salary instead of some members being on salary and some paid on an hourly basis.

Alternative hypothesis   A hypothesis written to be in opposition to the null hypothesis.

Analyzability   Whether or not the factors and change in the environment can be seen and understood by members of an organization.

Analyzer strategy   The organization seeks to discover moderately large changes in the environment and then to gain some advantage from the changes.

Anti-positivism   The philosophical and theoretical assumption is that the observer affects what is seen.

Approach-approach conflict   Occurs when two opportunities are attractive but both cannot be accepted.

Approach-avoidance conflict   Occurs when a job role is attractive but threatening at the same time.

Assertiveness   Direct speaking about your own needs, feelings, and goals without being aggressive or hurtful toward another.

Aston studies   A program of inquiry at the University of Aston in Birmingham, England, that investigated the relationship between organizational age, structure, and size.

Attitudes   Beliefs plus feelings make up an individual's attitudes.

Autonomous work groups   Work groups that are responsible for the whole of the group's task; have the authority to make and implement their own decisions; and may do their own training, hiring, and leading.

Avoidance-avoidance conflict   Occurs when one of two actions must be taken but both are anticipated to have negative consequences.

B

Bathsheba Syndrome   Named after King David of Israel and his affair with Bathsheba. It describes how a leader's success can cause unethical acts that the leader knows to be wrong.

Behaviorally anchored rating scales (BARS)   A set of descriptions created for each job in an organization that specify in detail what behaviour is expected for each level of performance in a given job.

Behavioural checklist   Lists areas of performance and specific behaviours expected of someone at each level of job performance.

Behavioural responses to stress   What a stressed person does.

Beliefs   What an individual accepts to be true without questioning.

Bottom line   In for-profit organizations, it is the summary line of a profit and loss statement.

Boundaryless company   Reflects the idea that traditional vertical hierarchy of organizations will be replaced by horizontal networks. The organization will accomplish its work by forming agreements with suppliers, customers, and competitors. What is inside and what is outside the organization will become fuzzy.

Bounded rationality   Recognizes that decision makers usually do not have complete information as required by the rational model of decision making. Decisions made are bounded by this lack of information.

Brainstorming   A method of group idea generation.

Broker   Role of a manager to build a base of power inside and outside the organization and to engage in discussion and negotiation with others.

Bundled   Computer software programs that are included in the purchase price of a new computer.

Bureaucracy   A form of organization with a set of related offices.

Bureaucratic control   A system of rules and the specification of who in the organization has the legal authority to make decisions and require compliance.

Bureaucratic red-tape   Usually seen in a negative light, referring to a complicated set of rules, regulations and forms required by a bureaucratic organization.

Burnout   A reaction to stress of emotional exhaustion, the depersonalization of others, and a sense of lower personal accomplishment.

Business Process Re-engineering (BPR)   A philosophy of management that stresses the key concept that companies should refocus themselves around the processes they use to get the product or service to the customer.

Butterfly effect   The concept that minute changes in system variables at one point in time can cause very large changes in the end result that is experienced.

C

Cafeteria-style fringe benefits   Employees are given a budget and are allowed to select the benefits they most want from a menu of possibilities.

Career planning   The production of a specific plan of what to do to enhance the likelihood of an individual's career success and satisfaction.

Career systems An organization's plan for how employees can be expected to move through a series of jobs over time.

Causality The determination of the direction of influence between two or more variables.

Causality perceptual error The tendency to see events as related or caused, even when there is no connection between them.

CD-ROM Compact disk read only memory. Information is stored in large quantities on an optically read disk by encoding it as zeroes and ones. Information may be text, graphics, sound, and/or visual.

CEO Chief Executive Officer. Usually the person who runs a business and reports to the Board of Directors.

CFB Chinese Family Business in Taiwan, Hong Kong.

CFO Chief Financial Officer.

Chaebol Korean: Family controlled conglomerates in Korea producing a number of products for world-wide consumption.

Chaos theory States that natural systems are very complex and unstable, with interconnections so widespread and subtle that even very small changes in system variables can cause very large changes in the end result.

Charisma From the Greek word meaning "gift," charisma is a trait that allows the holder to be liked, listened to, and followed. Charismatic leaders act to transform the needs, values, preferences, and aspirations of followers.

Charisma The gift of being able to inspire followers.

Clan control Power is given to the family and clan because of shared values and beliefs that that is how power should be allocated.

Coaching The group leader helps the subordinate to understand the task and how best to perform it.

Coacting group Individuals in the group each perform their own task, but there is no group task.

Coalition A joining of organizational members to promote joint interests.

Cognitive Having to do with the mind.

Cognitive Resource Theory Proposes that leader intelligence and technical knowledge are important determinants of the quality of the leader's plans, decisions, and actions.

Cohesion The attraction to the group by the group members' competing values model of effectiveness. An organization must balance the inherent tensions between internal focus versus external focus, flexibility versus control, and the needs of the organization versus the needs of the organization's members.

Complex organizational environment The organization must deal with many environmental components on the input or output side.

Complexity In systems theory the concept that systems must be thought of in terms of how the parts interact with the whole.

Compressed work weeks The total weekly hours of work are compressed into three or four days of longer than usual hours.

Conflict Occurs in organizations when an influence attempt is resisted.

Connection power The power that comes from position in a network of work relationships.

Consensus mapping A decision technique that is designed to help a group deal with a complex problem by organizing ideas generated by the group into categories and then producing a map of how the categories are linked.

Consideration The degree to which a leader is friendly and supportive in dealing with subordinates.

Construct A variable that has been invented in order to help develop a theory or understand a phenomenon.

Constructive controversy A method of group decision designed to promote information sharing.

Contingent A point of view that there is no consistently appropriate best action for all situations. Instead, what is most effective will depend on some other variable or combination of variables.

Continuous process technology The production of a standard product without pause.

Contrast Objects dissimilar to their surroundings are more likely to be noticed.

Convocation From the Latin *vocare*, meaning "to call." A ceremony that brings members of the organization together.

COO Chief Operating Officer. The person who directs the operations/activities of an organization.

Coordinator Role of a manger to plan, organize and control.

Correlation coefficient A measure of the direction and strength of the relationship between two variables.

Cost leadership strategy Followed by organizations that aim to become the lowest cost producers in an industry.

CQI Continuous Quality Improvement. Another variety of TQM.

Critical incidents Important job events that can be recorded and stored until it is time to evaluate an employee's performance.

Cultural attitudes The set of understandings that members of a community share about a specific object or situation.

Cultural beliefs Basic assumptions concerning the world and how it works. Cultural values and basic assumptions that have an 'ought to' component.

Cultural exchange The interactions among organizational members.

Cultural history The story of the organization's past.

Cultural identity The understandings that members share concerning who they are and what they stand for as a community.

Cultural ideology The dominant set of interrelated ideas that explain to members of a community why the important understandings they share 'make sense'.

Cultural membership A feeling of belonging among organizational members.

Cultural oneness A feeling that organizational members have of all being in the same boat.

Culture A pattern of basic assumptions, invented, discovered, or developed by a given group, as it learns to cope with its problems of external adaptation and internal integration, that has worked well enough to be considered valid and, therefore is to be taught to new members as the correct way to perceive, think, and feel in relation to those problems.

Culture shock cycle The cycle of moods experienced over time that may be expected when moving between cultures.

Customer service team A group organized to sell the organization's product to its customers and/or to make sure the product works correctly for the customer.

D

Deconstruction   A story may be examined, taken apart and analyzed to discover other sides of what was written. The values and interests of the author are brought into view.

Defender strategy   The organization aims to protect its share of the market.

Delegating   The group leader give subordinates responsibility for making and implementing decisions about how best to perform the task.

Delphi technique   Group decision method that asks experts in a structured and cyclical way for their wisdom about a particular problem.

Demographics   The age, sex, personality traits, job and life background, and other descriptive characteristics of group members.

Deontological philosophies   Examine the moral obligations or commitments that should be necessary for proper conduct.

Departmentation   The horizontal division of work into logical groupings.

Dependent variables   The factors in a theory that are proposed to be affected by variation in independent variables.

Descriptive essay   A method of evaluating job performance in which the manager describes the subordinate's performance.

Descriptive statistics   Describe the characteristics of the data.

Determinism   Takes the position that people are restricted in how they will act by their background.

Differentiation   The more an organization's three subunits of Production, Research & Development, and Marketing differ in structure, time orientation and goals, the greater is the differentiation of the organization's structure.

Directing   The group leader tells subordinates how to accomplish the task.

Director   Role of a manager to set goals and delegate tasks in the attempt to best organize and guide the work.

Diversity   Heterogeneity in group membership.

Divisionalized form   Organizations that divide their operations into product or market groups.

Domestic phase of international orientation   Attention is focussed on the home market.

Dominant coalition   The coalition of organizational members with more power than any other coalition.

Downsizing   The reduction of the number of people who work for an organization. Also called rightsizing.

Dynamic environment   An environment that undergoes continual change.

E

Economies of scope   The advantage gained by producing a wide variety of products.

Effect size   A measure of the strength of a relationship between variables. How well a theory explains an organizational phenomenon.

Ego   Exerts control over the id.

Ego defensive attitudes   Provide the means to cope with intrapsychic conflict.

Egoism   Determines the most moral act as the one with the most positive consequences for the individual.

Emoticons   Combinations of regular alphabet letters and special symbols, usually looked at sideways, that are inserted into electronic mail to indicate the sender's emotions.

Empire building game   An individual or group attempts to become more important in the organization by adding personnel, increasing the budget controlled or physical space, and gaining control over more areas of organizational decisions.

Employee Assistance Plans (EAPs) Programs of counselling and treatment offered by organizations to employees suffering stress reactions as a way for them to begin to learn how to manage those reactions.

Empowerment   The sharing or distribution of power.

Enactment   The process of dealing with the environment creates the environment.

Epistemology   How we know.

Equifinality   A concept in systems theory that the same end result can be reached by various means or directions.

Ergonomics   From the Greek *ergon*, meaning "work," the study of people at work.

Escalation of commitment Commitment to a losing course of action that increases when outcomes are negative.

et al.   Latin: *et alia*, meaning "and others."

Evaluation apprehension   When group members are hesitant to contribute their ideas because of concern about how those ideas will be evaluated by other group members.

ex nihilo   Latin: out of nothing

Expatriate ghetto   A compound, building, or cluster of housing units inhabited by people from other countries where the norms, values, and ways of life of the local culture may be avoided.

Expectancy   The employee's perceived probability that effort will result in performance.

Expectancy effect   The concept that expectations about another person's behaviour can, when communicated to that person, actually cause the behaviour that was expected.

Expert model   The way people in organizations actually go about information processing and decision making, generating and exploring only a limited number of decision alternatives and then using their pre-existing knowledge and simple rules of thumb to make a decision.

Expert systems   Computer-based decision aids that offer advice or solutions for problems in a particular area that is comparable to the advice of a human expert.

Extinction   The process of not rewarding a behaviour so that it will cease to be exhibited.

E-mail   Electronic mail sent by a computer network.

e.g.   Latin: *exempli gratia*, meaning "for example."

F

Facilitator   Role of a manager to be group-oriented, a team builder, helping to manage conflict within and between groups, and helping the group to make decisions.

Family T-group   A training group made up of organizational members who know one another and are attempting to learn more about each other and how to work together.

Fault-driven model of effectiveness The organization seeks to eliminate traces of ineffectiveness in its internal functioning.

Fax As a verb, to fax, to send a facsimile of a document via the telephone lines. As a noun, a fax, the document received over the telephone lines.

Feelings The emotional component of beliefs.

Feminism A system of values that challenges male dominance and advocates social, political, and economic equity of women and men in society.

Figure-ground A principle of perceptual organization that people tend to see one object (the figure) on a background of other objects (the ground).

Filtering Information is summarized, codified, or withheld so that only a part of the whole is transmitted.

Fixed interval reinforcement schedule The reinforcer is given after a precise interval of time has elapsed since the last reinforcement.

Fixed ratio reinforcement schedule The reinforcer is given after every nth occurrence of the desired behaviour. N may be one or a number greater than one.

Flexiplace Work at any place.

Flextime Employees can choose to some extent the hours that they will work.

Focus strategy Targets a particular customer, product, or geographic area, and attempts to serve the target market better than other more broadly based competitors.

Folktale A completely fictional narrative.

Force field analysis A technique used to identify all the forces in support of change and all those opposing change.

Forced distribution A method of evaluating job performance that requires a manager to assign a certain number (or percentage) of employees to each category of job performance.

FORTUNE 500 A ranking of the largest 500 companies in the United States by the magazine *Fortune*. Subsidiary rankings are done for major industrial and service groupings.

Framing How a question is put to an individual can determine how they will decide.

Freestanding group A group which does not have an organizational context.

Free-riding One or more individuals in a group reducing effort below that which would have been exerted if not in the group.

Freud, Sigmund Pronounced FROID (rhymes with Lloyd). A Viennese psychiatrist known for his psychoanalytic theory of personality that the id, ego, and superego are in conflict.

Fundamental attribution error The tendency of people to underestimate the influence of the situation and overestimate the influence of individual characteristics on behaviour.

Fusuma Japanese: movable screen.

G

g The factor of general intelligence.

gaijin Japanese word meaning "foreigner."

gainsharing A bonus system based on the mutual sharing of the financial gains of improved productivity.

Galatea In Greek mythology, Pygmalion's wife.

Garbage can model of organizational decision making A metaphor of organizational decision making that the organization can be seen as choices looking for problems, issues and feelings looking for decision situations, solutions looking for issues, and decision makers looking for work.

Genetic effects on personality The idea that personality is partly a function of a person's genes.

Glass ceiling A barrier to vertical career movement that is so subtle that it can be seen through, yet still exists, especially for women and minorities.

Going native The adoption of many of the foreign culture's values and ways of behaving.

Grapevine An informal network for communication within and outside the organization.

Grid Organizational Development A six-step program with the objective of improving the functioning and interactions of the individuals and groups of the organization and the organization as a whole.

Group consensus A method of group decision making that seeks to incorporate all points of view while avoiding voting or bargaining.

Group size The number of members in a group.

Groupthink The process by which highly cohesive groups can overestimate the strengths of the group.

Groupware Group decision support software used to facilitate group decisions made in electronic decision rooms.

Group-induced attitude polarization When an initial tendency of group members toward a given direction is enhanced following group discussion.

H

Halo effect The tendency to let one overall impression colour specific interpretations.

Heterogeneity Mixed demographics in group membership.

Heuristic A rule of thumb about how to approach a problem or how to go about solving it.

High performing system model of effectiveness The organization determines how well it is doing by comparing itself to other similar organizations.

Hiragana Japanese phonetic writing style used for traditional words in the language.

Homogeneity Similar demographics in group membership.

Horizontal decentralization When workers in many different organizational units are allowed to make decisions without referring them to a more central authority.

Horizontal loading The greater the number of different tasks in a job, the greater is that job's horizontal loading, or range.

Horizontally complex When an organization's tasks are divided among many individuals and specialized.

Human nature How we are.

Human relations model of effectiveness An organization is effective to the degree that its people are trained and developed.

Human service team People who are grouped together to help others.

Hygienes In Motivator-Hygiene theory, factors that reduce job dissatisfaction. Example hygiene factors are money and security, working conditions that are environmentally pleasant and safe, and agreeable supervision and interpersonal relations.

Hypotheses Best guesses of the relationship that might exist between the independent and dependent variables of a theory.

I

Icarus Paradox Based on the Greek myth of Icarus whose father gave him wings made of feathers and wax so that he could soar high into the air. Icarus went too high, the wax melted, and he fell to his death. Danny Miller coined this term to indicate the idea that companies may become so successful with a particular way of operating or with a particular product that they eventually cause their own downfall.

Id A person's source of energy.

Ideal type of bureaucracy The perfect example of the bureaucracy type of organizing.

Idiographic The individual's experience is examined to understand their own world.

Implicit theory of leadership A theory held in people's minds of how an effective leader should act.

Impression management The manipulation and control of how one is perceived.

Improved Nominal Group Technique (INGT) Designed to avoid some of the problems groups encounter when making decisions in face-to-face meetings.

Incremental change Is linear, orderly, slow and ongoing, not questioning the basic nature of the system or of the organization.

Independent variables The factors in a theory that are proposed to vary.

Industrial revolution A series of inventions that made machines faster, more powerful and more efficient, and that allowed more physical goods to be made more inexpensively than before.

Inferential statistics Used to determine if an effect or relationship can be called statistically significant.

Information overload The problem of having too much information to be able to cognitively understand it all.

Information power The possession of information or having access to information that is important to the organization.

Information revolution Work is the manipulation and production of information.

Information superhighway Also called the infobahn. The growing interconnectedness of information sources and information users.

Initiating structure The degree to which a leader structures the task, provides direction, and defines the leader and subordinate roles in the group and the group's goals.

Innovator Role of a manager to be flexible, think creatively, and to manage constant change.

Institutional theory Organizations structure to be like other organizations or structure in the way required for organizations in their environment.

Instrument A tool used to gather data from subjects. Could be a physical device or a questionnaire.

Instrumentality The connection perceived in the mind of the individual worker that performance will lead to a given outcome.

Integrating The combination of values and behaviours from both home and foreign cultures.

Integration The coordination required between organizational units.

Intensity Objects that are more visible are more likely to be perceived.

Intensive technology Inputs are processed by organizational members as is required by the product. There is reciprocal interdependence between organizational members.

Internal process model of effectiveness An organization is effective to the degree that its internal transformation process works well.

International phase of international orientation Operations are opened in one or several other cultures. The operation in each country is managed by an expatriate manager on an international assignment.

Interrole conflict Occurs when a person has multiple roles to play and role demands are such that it is difficult to perform well in each one.

Intervening variables Intermediate links between independent and dependent variables.

Interviewing A face-to-face meeting often used to determine the degree of match between the values of potential recruits and the values of the organization.

In-box gridlock When a person's incoming e-mail becomes overwhelming.

Irrational decision A decision not based on rationality or non-rationality, but may instead be based on emotion.

i.e. Latin: *id erat*, meaning "that is."

J

Job conditions Where and how the work is done and in what physical environment.

Job content The tasks required in a job.

Job description A summary of the tasks and role behaviours for a particular job.

Job evaluation A determination of the requirements of a job.

Job performance The employee's actual contribution, in terms of both quality and quantity, to the organization's task and to the development of the employee's potential to contribute in the future.

Job relationships The people with whom the job holder interacts.

Job sharing Splits one full-time job between two people.

Jung, Carl Pronounced YOUNG. A student of Freud's, proposed a theory of psychological types of how people access and process information.

K

Kaisha Japanese: A large corporation in Japan, a specialized clan.

Kanban employment Japanese: Just-in-time hiring of employees.

Kanji Chinese picture symbols used in Japan that denote a word or a meaning.

Karoshi Japanese: Death by overwork.

Katakana Japanese phonetic writing style used for new words in the language.

Kibbutz Hebrew: An organization in Israel for shared working and living.

Kotatsu Japanese: a small table that can be used for heating.

L

Language The manner in which members of a group use vocal sounds and written signs to convey meanings to each other.

Large batch/mass production technology The production of many units of an identical product.

Lateral career movement Movement across the functions performed within the organization.

Layoff The result of downsizing for structural or economic reasons, the individual loses his/her job either temporarily or permanently.

Leader prototype A mental image of what characteristics an effective leader should have.

Leadership A social relationship between two or more people in which the leader influences the social knowledge, goal acceptance, and actions of the follower.

Leader-Member Exchange (LMX) A theory of leadership that makes explicit the fact that leaders may develop different relationships with different subordinates.

Learning organization An organization capable of embracing change on a continuous basis at the individual, group, and organizational levels.

Legend A handed-down narrative of some wonderful event that has a historical basis but has been embellished with fictional details.

Legitimate form of organization In agreement with the standard type of organizational form and procedures.

Leverage The concept that small and well-focused actions can have large effects on a system.

Liability of newness New organizations are more likely to die than are older organizations.

Life planning The objective is to produce a specific plan of what to do to enhance the likelihood of an individual's life as a whole.

Likert System 4 An organization-wide method used to analyze and develop a plan for organizational change.

Line Refers to people, groups and departments that are engaged in making or selling the organization's product or managing those who do.

Long-linked technology Inputs are transformed step by step into outputs as they move from worker to worker, with each adding to the work of all those who have gone before. There is sequential interdependence between individual workers.

Loosely coupled system A system of variables that do not affect each other in a tight relationship.

M

Machine bureaucracy An organization that is specialized, formalized, and bureaucratic. A factory relying on production line technology is a good example of a machine bureaucracy.

Maintenance function The group leader's behaviours that preserve the social stability of the group.

maître d' French: Maître d'hôtel—the person in charge of the daily running of the dining room of a hotel.

Management By Objectives (MBO) A goal-setting plan whereby managers and subordinates discuss together the subordinate's goals and objectives for the next performance period. Rewards are usually tied to reaching these objectives.

Management By Wandering Around (MBWA) The manager gets out of the office and into the field where, by talking and listening in an unstructured way, the manager is exposed to organizational events and makes decisions as situations arise.

Maquiladoras Spanish: machines. Factories on the border of Mexico and the United States set up to use relatively inexpensive Mexican labour to assemble products for sale in the United States. They are cost effective because the assembled products are not subject to U.S. import duties. Of lessening importance with the signing of the NAFTA agreement.

Market control Organizations rely on prices as the means of exchange.

Mean The average value of a variable in a sample.

Median A descriptive statistic of the middle value of the measurements taken of a variable in a sample.

Mediating technology Each organizational member processes inputs into outputs on his or her own with only pooled interdependence between them.

Mentor Role of a manager to help subordinates develop as individuals, to understand themselves and others, and to learn to communicate well with others.

Meta-analysis A statistical method of combining and testing the empirical results from a number of studies.

Meta-message The larger message within which the smaller message is contained.

Metharme In Greek mythology, the daughter of Pygmalion and Galatea.

Methodology How we study and produce knowledge.

Mission statement A codification of an organization's jointly accepted vision for the future.

MNC Multi-National Corporation.

Mode A descriptive statistic of the value of the variable that occurs the most frequently in a sample.

Modeling Learning by watching others.

Moderator variables Variables that can alter the relationship between independent and dependent variables.

Modernism The currently dominant scientific viewpoint that believes in progress, the powers of reason and observation, and whose objective is a search for fundamentals or essentials.

Monitor Role of a manager to receive, evaluate, and react to information about internal organizational processes.

Motion Objects that are moving are more noticeable.

Motivation The attention paid, effort exerted, and persistence of behaviour.

Motivators In Motivator-Hygiene theory, factors designed into the job itself such as recognition, challenging work, responsibility, and opportunities for achievement, individual growth and development. Motivators are theorized to provide job satisfaction.

Motivator-Hygiene theory A theory of job design that satisfaction and dissatisfaction with a job are not opposite ends of one scale but two separate scales.

Muddling through The argument that people in organizations make decisions that are a series of successive limited comparisons of the present state of the organization to possible future states.

Multinational phase of international orientation The organization deals with many nations. Managers from the other countries come to the organization's national headquarters.

Multiple role sender conflict Occurs when a person is expected to fill different roles at the same time, even when the expectations of these roles conflict.

Munificent Wonderfully generous. From the Latin *munus* meaning "gift." A munificent environment is possessed of an abundance of the resources organizations need to survive.

Myth A dramatic narrative of imagined events that is usually used to explain origins of transformations. Can also reflect an unquestioned belief about what should be done and in what way.

N

NAFTA North American Free Trade Agreement. Allows for easier movement of goods between Mexico, the United States and Canada, with no duties or lowered duties.

Negative reinforcement When a person learns to act to remove a negative stimulus.

Negotiation A method of conflict resolution.

Neuo-linguistic programming (NLP) The idea that people differ on how they interpret the world that surrounds them. Some people rely on feeling, some on visual cues, and some on hearing.

Nominal groups A method of generating ideas by having individuals write down as many ideas about a problem or issue as they can and then combining these individual lists across all the members of a group.

Nominalism The point of view that social reality is a product of the interactions of the participants. Therefore there can be many social realities.

Nomological net A network of rule-based relationships between variables in a theory.

Nomothetic The point of view that there are general rules or laws of behaviour that can be discovered.

Nonrational decision A decision that does not follow the rational model, but is instead based on intuition or "gut feel."

Non-programmed decisions Decisions that are made in unique circumstances. Their analysis has not yet been routinized.

Norm A set of expected attitudes, beliefs and behaviours that define how a group member is expected to think or act.

Novel stimuli Are perceived because of their newness.

Null hypothesis A hypothesis written in a form that describes no relationship between two variables.

O

OD flavour-of-the-month phenomenon The tendency for management of organizations to seek quick fixes of organizational problems, and when encountering difficulty, then flocking to the next quick fix offered by consultants and organizational gurus.

Ontology The essence of the phenomenon being studied.

Open system model of effectiveness An organization is effective to the degree that it acquires inputs from its environment and has outputs accepted by its environment.

Open system theory Organizations are part of their environment and the success of the organization depends on how well it interacts with its environment.

Organization Two or more people working together to achieve a goal or a set of goals that they cannot achieve alone.

Organization chart Shows the structure of the organization. A set of boxes (often with names of individuals in the boxes) indicate positions in the organization. The relationships between these positions are shown by lines that connect the boxes.

Organizational development A set of behavioural science-based theories, values, strategies, and techniques aimed at the planned change of the organizational work setting for the purpose of enhancing individual development and improving organizational performance, through the alteration of organizational members' on-the-job behaviours.

Organizational structure How the organization is divided into parts and the parts coordinated in order to get the organization's work done.

Organizations as arenas for staging conflicts Conflict is not seen as a harmful event but as the essence of what the organization is.

Ouchi, Bill Pronounced OOH-CHEE. Well known for his "Theory Z"—the combination of Japanese and American management styles.

Outsourcing The practice of sending some of the organization's work to others outside its boundaries.

Overpromotion When a person is promoted too quickly into a job for which he or she is unready or underqualified.

P

Paired comparison of job performance Compares every person against every other on each characteristic being rated.

Paradigm A way of thinking about and studying a phenomenon. Includes the method used, what is considered "truth," and what is valid knowledge.

Participation by subordinates in group decisions Involvement in the process of making the decision.

Pay secrecy When people at work do not know the salaries and benefits of others employed by the organization or of others employed in similar jobs with other organizations.

per se Latin "as such".

Perceptual closure A missing piece of a picture, story, or action can be supplied by the person doing the perceiving.

Perceptual continuity People tend to see events as related over time.

Perceptual defense The inability to perceive that which is threatening to the perceiver.

Perceptual familiarity It is easier to see the familiar than the unfamiliar.

Perceptual learning People learn to pay attention to the stimuli in the environment that are important for job performance.

Perceptual motivation People tend to perceive what they want to.

Perceptual overload Occurs when a person has perceived so many messages and stimuli that it is not possible to keep track of them all.

Performance Outcomes of ability and effort.

Performance appraisal interview A meeting between a manager and a subordinate used to communicate the manager's evaluation of the subordinate's job performance and to help the employee focus on where and how to improve performance.

Performance evaluation The determination or measurement of an individual's job performance by one or more members of the organization.

Performance function The group leader's behaviours of forming and reaching group goals.

Performing group Puts on a performance, performs an activity, or competes with other groups.

Personality A stable set of tendencies and characteristics that determine those commonalties and differences in people's psychological behaviour that have continuity in time and that may not be easily understood as the sole result of the social and biological pressures of the moment.

Person-role conflict Occurs when there is a mismatch between the core values of the person and the behaviours expected of that person in the role.

Phenomenological world The world as experienced and constructed by an individual.

Phoenix A mythical bird that arose to new life from its own ashes.

Physiological responses to stress Reactions in body chemistry and hormonal balances that can have positive or negative outcomes.

Politics The process in organizations of one person exerting influence over another.

Population ecology A theoretical approach aimed at understanding birth, death, and change in populations of organizations.

Positivism Takes the position that it is possible to reflect the world as it is.

Postmodernism Takes the approach that there is not one central knowledge for all but that knowledge depends on a person's perspective based on class, race, gender, or other characteristics. The Postmodern approach challenges and seeks to expose existing beliefs.

Post-industrial society A society whose economy is not dependent on primary industry and the manufacture of goods.

Power The capacity to influence the attitudes or behaviours of others.

Power struggle When coalitions try to oppose the dominant coalition of an organization.

Proactive change Undertaken to make the organization, its systems, and/or its people more effective in dealing with demands from its environment.

Process losses The decrease in group performance as members are added to the group.

Producer Role of a manager to be actively involved in the organization's work while attempting to motivate employees to produce more output in less time.

Production blocking Group factors that act to limit the contributions of group members.

Production team Makes the organization's product.

Professional support group A group whose job it is to help others either inside or outside the organization to do their jobs.

Profit sharing Paying employees a portion of profits. The difference from gainsharing is that profits as determined by accounting decisions may be manipulated.

Programmed decisions Decisions routinely made in an organization that have a structured and repetitive method of analysis and choice of alternative.

Projection The tendency by people to see their own traits and characteristics in others, even if not present.

Propinquity Physical proximity.

Prospector strategy The organization sees a dynamic and changing environment and is willing to take risks to find and exploit opportunities or to create them.

Proteus Pronounced PRO-TEEUS, a Greek sea god fabled to be able to take various shapes.

Proximity Nearness of one object to another can lead observers to perceptually group the objects together.

Proxy fight A battle for the right to vote for the share owner in an election of a board of directors.

Psychological responses to stress Reactions in mental functioning that can include impaired decision making.

Punishment The application of a negative stimulus to stop an unwanted behaviour.

Pygmalion effect The concept that expectations about another person's behaviour can, when communicated to that person, actually cause the behaviour that was expected.

Q

Quality circles Groups formed to identify specific problems in the work environment and to propose solutions to those problems.

Quantum change Is discontinuous, chaotic, fast and temporary, marked by a shift in paradigm of how the organization and its people think about themselves and how they do business.

R

Radial career movement Occurs when the person becomes more or less on the inside of the organization.

Range of a job The greater the number of different tasks in a job, the greater is that job's range.

Ranking of job performance Employees are listed from the best to the worst in job performance.

Rational goal model of effectiveness An organization is effective to the extent that it accomplishes its stated goals.

Rational model of decision making The view that decisions can be made based on logic to determine the optimal decision.

Reactive change Change that is typically undertaken in response to environmental demands.

Reactor strategy The organization reacts to what occurs in its environment.

Real time In the present moment. A computer that provides a visual display in "real time," for example, reflects the actual state of a system. It is not displaying information from the past.

Realism The point of view that society has a real, concrete existence.

Realistic job preview The attempt is made by the organizational interviewer to paint a realistic picture of what to expect from the job and the organization.

Reentry shock Culture shock caused by moving back into the home culture and organization.

Reference group A group used for comparison.

Relationship-oriented behaviour The leader or manager's focus on interpersonal relationships in the group.

Reliability A measure of how consistent multiple measurements are of a phenomenon.

Repetition A message is more likely to be perceived if it is encountered numerous times.

Retreat Organizational members come together, usually outside the physical bounds of the work place to discuss the future.

Reward system A set of rules regarding how rewards are earned and paid.

Role A set of shared expectations about who in the group is to do what under what circumstances.

Role ambiguity Uncertainty regarding what actions, duties and relationships are required for a certain job role.

Role expectations conflict Exists when some behaviours expected of the role occupant are difficult for the person holding that role to enact.

Role overload Occurs when an individual either tries to do too much or is given more work than he or she can cope with.

Romanticism The point of view that people have a deep interior where there exists their unique capacities and characteristics that define them as individuals.

Rucker plan A type of profit sharing plan.

Rumour Unverified information circulating by the grapevine in an organization.

S

s Any one of a number of specific factors of intelligence.

Sabotage From the French word *sabot*, meaning "wooden shoe." Refers to the throwing of a wooden shoe into machinery to break it.

Saga An historical narrative describing the unique accomplishments of a group and its leaders.

Sample size The number of subjects selected for study from a population.

Satiation The condition of an individual having had enough of a given stimulus, outcome, or reward.

Satisfaction An attitude of being content.

Satisficing The decision maker chooses the first alternative that meets to a satisfactory degree the requirements of the problem.

Scanlon plan A type of profit sharing plan.

Scapegoating The symbolic shifting of blame by power holders from themselves onto someone who is not at fault.

Schedules of reinforcement Plans of timing and frequency in the rewarding of behaviour.

Script Norms about a sequence of behaviours.

Self-managing work groups Work groups that are responsible for the whole of the group's task, have the authority to make and implement their own decisions, and may do their own training, hiring, and leading.

Self reinforcement A person applying rewards and punishments to his or her own behaviour.

Self-serving bias People tend to give themselves any benefit of doubt when evaluating their own behaviours.

Sensory overload Occurs when there are too many stimuli for a person's senses to process.

Sexual harassment Discrimination on the basis of gender. Behaviour which is not acceptable to the recipient and to which the recipient has not consented.

Shareholders Owners of a corporate form of organization. Ownership is held in the ratio of the number of shares held divided by the total number of shares outstanding. The owner of 100,000 shares of 10,000,000 outstanding has a 1% ownership position.

Sick Building Syndrome When the environment inside a building is such that more than 20 percent of the people working in it complain of headaches and other forms of sickness. Usually caused by poor indoor air quality.

Significance level The number of chances in 100 that the result of a statistical test occurred by chance.

Similarity Objects that are alike tend to be perceived as part of a group.

Simple organizational environment The inputs received come from relatively few components (or factors) of the environment and the organization's outputs are sent to relatively few environmental components.

Simple structure Composed of a few direct relationships between organizational positions. Has little specialization, a low degree of formalization, and a high degree of centralization.

Size An important factor in perceptual selection. Larger objects are more likely to be seen than those that are smaller.

Skill-based pay plan Employees are paid a base hourly rate and an additional amount per hour for each job skill they have mastered, whether the skill is currently used or not.

Small batch technology The production of one or a few custom items by one person or a small team working closely together.

Social group A group that has no task.

Social loafing When group members do not exert as much effort toward task accomplishment when in a group as they do when alone.

Social-adjustive attitudes Change as the person and others engage in normal interaction.

Socio-technical systems Job design is a combined function of the relationship between the social system of which each person is a part and the technical system used to get the work done.

Source credibility Sources that are low in credibility make less of an impression on the perceiver.

Span of control The number of workers directly reporting to a manager.

Specialization Occurs when organizational members focus their efforts on a particular skill, ability, customer or geographic area. The specialist learns one thing well but is not a generalist who knows many things.

Sponsorship game Subordinates attach themselves to a superior in the hopes of rising in the organization's hierarchy as the sponsor is promoted.

Staff Refers to a person, group, or department that provides a service to the rest of the organization.

Stakeholders Those who "hold a stake" or have an interest in the actions of an organization.

Standard deviation   The square root of the variance.

Statecraft   The use of persuasion and informal authority to encourage coalitions to accomplish goals.

Static environment   The environment remains basically the same over time.

Status   Relative standing within a group.

Stereotyping   The assignment of traits and characteristics to an individual based on that person's membership in a larger group.

Stonewalling   The conflict tactic of simply refusing to discuss an issue in conflict or to compromise in the slightest.

Story   A narrative based on true events that is often a combination of both truth and fiction.

Strain   The effects of stress.

Stranger T-groups   Training groups made up of strangers whose objective is to help individuals better understand themselves, to learn to diagnose group characteristics, and to be more effective leaders.

Strategic Business Units (SBUs)   Divisions in a divisionalized form of organization.

Strategic constituencies model of effectiveness   An organization aims to satisfy at least minimally the most important constituents in its environment.

Strategy   The organization's plan of how to become more effective.

Stratified Systems Theory   A person's cognitive level should be an important factor in determining the hierarchical level they come to occupy in the organization.

Stress   A discrepancy between an employee's perceived state and desired state, provided that the discrepancy is considered important by that person.

Structuration   The process of both being affected by a structure and affecting the structure. Structure affects behaviour but behaviour also affects the structure that will, in turn, affect behaviour.

Subenvironments   Definable parts of the environment dealt with by parts of the organization. In Lawrence and Lorsch's terms, subenvironments are scientific, technical, and market.

Succession plan   A list of the organization's senior personnel specifying when each is expected to be ready to be promoted to the next higher positions in the hierarchy.

Superego   A person's conscience.

Superordinate goal   The creation of interdependent tasks or goals that can only be accomplished by two groups working together.

Supporting   The group leader provides social assistance to followers while they engage in accomplishing the task.

Survey feedback   A method used to gather information from groups on the current organizational situation and what might be done about it.

T

Tabula rasa   Latin: blank slate, typically that humans are born with no genetic "hard wiring" of behaviours but are completely open to learning from their environment.

Tanin   Japanese: outsider.

Task experience   Background and knowledge about a particular task.

Task force   A temporary group created to solve a particular problem or to complete a particular task.

Task skills   The ability to accomplish a task.

Task-oriented behaviour   The group leader or manager's focus on the task.

Tatami   Japanese: woven mat placed on the floor in the home. Floor sizes are commonly referred to in terms of tatami, as in "a four tatami room."

Team   A group composed of a small number of people with complementary skills who are committed to a common purpose, set of performance goals, and approach for which they hold themselves mutually accountable.

Team building   Theory about groups and group processes is used to help to create more effectively functioning groups.

Technological imperative   The concept that technology determines the best organizational structure.

Technology   The sequence of physical techniques, knowledge, and equipment used to turn organizational inputs into outputs.

Telecommuting   Work that is spread over two or more sites, typically the office and the home.

Teleconferencing   A meeting held between people who are in different locations.

Teleological philosophies   Determine the moral worth of a behaviour by examining its consequences.

Text   Discursive productions located in a specific historical and cultural context and shaped by power (Riger, 1992). The Riger reference is in Chapter 16.

Thematic apperception test (TAT)   A projective test used to measure an individual's need for achievement, need for affiliation, and need for power.

Theory   A set of statements that link organizational factors of importance.

Theory of justice   Declares that decisions should be based on equity, fairness, and impartiality.

Theory of rights   Proposes that individuals have the right to free consent, to privacy, to freedom of conscience, to free speech, and to due process of law.

Token reinforcement plan   Symbolic items (tokens) are given as rewards for desired behaviour.

Tokugawa   The name of a Shogun (warlord) in Japan.

Top management team   The people at the top of the organizational hierarchy.

Total Quality Control   Another name for TQM.

Total Quality Management (TQM)   A family of OD intervention techniques that includes quality circles, group processes and goals, statistical techniques, the use of new technologies, production methods, and processes, and work group facilities.

Trait scales   A method of performance evaluation. Employees are rated on a numeric scale that orders the degree to which the employee possesses a given trait.

Transactional theory of leadership   The group leader and members engage in an exchange relationship where members provide time and effort in return for certain benefits allocated by the leader.

Transformational theory of leadership   The group leader changes the follower's needs and values, self-esteem, self-expectation of work success, and heightens the follower's motivation to exert extra work effort.

Transnational phase of international orientation Networks of firms and divisions are created with multiple headquarters and cultural synergy.

Triangulation Research methods are used to study the same phenomenon from several vantage points.

Triune brain The concept that the human brain is composed of three structures laid down over the course of millions of years of evolution.

Turnover The rate at which members leave a group or organization.

Type A Organization Typical American organization. Characterized as having short-term employment; individual decision making; individual responsibility; rapid evaluation and promotion; explicit, formalized control; a specialized career path; and concern for the worker doing the job.

Type I error An inferential error made when an effect or relationship between variables is said to have been found even though it does not exist in reality.

Type II error An inferential error made when an effect or relationship between variables is denied, even though it really does exist.

Type III error Studying the wrong problem.

Type J Organization Typical Japanese organization. Characterized as having lifetime employment; a long-term business plan; consensual decision making; collective responsibility; slow evaluation and promotion; implicit informal control; a nonspecialized career path; and holistic concern for the worker's job and life situation.

Type Z Organization Modified American organization proposed as a blend of Types A and J. Characterized as having long term employment; consensual decision making; individual responsibility; slow evaluation and promotion; implicit informal control with explicit formal measures; a moderately specialized career path; and holistic concern for the worker's job and family.

U

Uchi Japanese: household, home.

Underpromotion The feeling of being unduly delayed in career progress.

Unintended consequences Behaviours in reaction to a reward system that were not anticipated by the system's designer.

Utilitarianism Selects as most moral the alternative with the greatest good for the greatest number of people.

V

Valence The anticipated satisfaction of an outcome.

Validity An indicator of how well an instrument is measuring what the investigator thinks is being measured.

Values Beliefs that endure over time.

Value-expressive attitudes Serve to express the person's own internal values.

Variable interval reinforcement schedule The reinforcer is given at varying and unpredictable times. The time between reinforcements averages out to a pre-set interval.

Variable ratio reinforcement schedule The reinforcer is given after a varying and unpredictable number of times that the behaviour occurs.

Variance A descriptive statistic measure of how much the measurements of a variable from a sample are alike. Variance is the sum of the squared differences between each data point and the mean, divided by the number of data points minus one.

Vertical career movement Moving up and down the hierarchy as rank and level is achieved or lost.

Vertical centralization When decisions are made higher up in the organization's hierarchy.

Vertical loading The amount of authority, supervision, management and decision making responsibilities in a job.

Vertically complex When organizational layers are inserted between top management and production workers.

Viability The team or work group's long term effectiveness, its ability to work together, and its ability to adapt to changing organizational and environmental conditions.

Virtual corporation Another term for the boundaryless company.

Virtual reality (VR) A computer generated simulation of a reality into which people can immerse themselves.

Voluntarism Takes the point of view that people are flexible and can make choices about their own actions.

Vroom-Jago model An expert system that summarizes organizational behaviour knowledge about participation in decision making.

W

Weber, Max Pronounced VAY-BAIR. A German sociologist. Lived 1864 to 1920. Known for the ideal type of bureaucracy.

Weighted checklist Lists areas of performance and specific behaviours expected of someone at each level of job performance and also assigns importance weights to each performance area.

Whistleblowing The political behaviour of challenging the authority structure of the organization.

White noise Sound waves produced by a sound generator that are used to mask other sounds in the workplace.

Work group A group with social systems and boundaries that separate it from other individuals and groups, and having different roles for different task members.

Work role A set of expectations about what is required in a particular job.

NAME AND ORGANIZATION INDEX

A

A & W 21, 108, 685-692
Abelson, Robert P. 340, 364, 658, 671
Abraham, Lauren M. 205
Aburdene, Patricia 674
Academy of Management 30, 394, 406
Adair, John G. 28, 40
Adams, J. Stacey 27, 297, 324
Adler, Nancy J. 87, 108, 122, 564,
     579-580, 582, 648-649, 671
Adler, Patricia A. 344, 346, 364
Adler, Peter 344, 346, 364
Adler, Tina 514, 537
Administrative Sciences Association of
     Canada 30
Agger, Ben 660-661, 671
Agor, W.H. 451
Air France 676
Airborne 696
Aktouf, Omar 675
Albanese, Robert 333, 364
Alberti, Robert E. 474, 490
Alcoa 624
Alcoa-Fujikura 15
Aldag, Ramon J. 452
Alderfer, Clayton P. 296-297, 324
Alexander, Scott 484
Alexandria University 304
Ali, Muhammed 476
Allen, Katherine R. 661, 671
Allinson, Christopher W. 176, 205
Alvesson, Mats 124, 675
Alvi, Sabir A. 554, 580
Ambrosi, Joseph Graham 446
American Lava Company 120
American Management Association 30
American Psychological Association 30
American Society of Mechanical
     Engineers 25
AMP of Canada Ltd. 606
Analytical Power Tools 453
Ancona, Deborah Gladstein 330, 346,
     364-365, 367
Anders, Gary C. 492
Anders, Kathleen K. 492
Anderson, Joseph V. 436, 449
Anderson, Julia 212, 243
Angoff, William H. 173, 205
Aphrodite 383
Apple Computer 19, 66
Applegate, Lynda M. 453
Argyle, Michael 252, 284
Aristotle 464
Arnold, Ron 486

Arrowsmith, J. David 17, 40
Arvey, Richard D. 189, 205-206
Asch, Solomon E. 421, 449
Ashforth, Blake E. 420, 449, 518, 538
Ashour, Ahmed S. 304, 324
Asia Pacific Foundation of Canada
     565, 579
Astley, W. Graham 675
AT & T 116
A.T. Kearney 606-607
Atari 116
Athabasca University 675
Athos, Anthony 622
Attila the Hun 301
Auel, Jean M. 159
Austin, Barbara J. 80
Austin, Nancy K. 250, 285, 437, 449
Aviation Week & Space Technology
     242-243, 446
Avolio, Bruce J. 381, 386, 387, 389,
     406, 408, 410
AVX Corp. 120
Axtell, Roger E. 253, 284, 286

B

Babcock, G.L. 240, 242, 244
Baber, Kristine M. 661, 671
Bacon, Margaret K. 205
Bahls, Jane Easter 550, 579
Baird, John G. 252, 254, 284
Bak, Céline 607, 622
Baker, Stephen 41
Baldwin, J. 14, 40
Baldwin, Timothy T. 601, 622
Baliga, B. Rajaram 385, 406, 410
Ballon, Robert J. 422-423, 449
Balsley, Howard Lloyd 650, 671
Bamforth, Ken W. 26, 146, 159
Bandler, Richard 264, 284
Bangert-Drowns, Robert L. 206
Bardwick, Judith M. 543, 579
Baridon, Andrea P. 492
Barker, James R. 509-510, 537
Barkow, Jerome H. 208, 347, 364
Barksdale, James L. 696, 702
Barnard, Chester 24, 40, 198
Barnes, Louis B. 453
Barnes-Farrell, Janet L. 452
Barnett, Carole K. 624
Barney, Jim 15
Baron, James N. 508, 537, 545, 579
Baron, Robert A. 159
Barrett, William E. 313, 324
Barrick, Murray R. 186, 205

Barrios-Choplin, John R. 262, 285
Barry, Dave 522, 524, 537
Barry, Herbert, III 179, 205
Bartholomew, Susan 108, 122
Bartlett, John 106, 122
Bartley, Douglas 310, 324
Barton, Scott 624
Basadur, Min 423, 449
Bass, Bernard M. 381, 389, 406, 410
Bastianutti, Lana M. 450, 453
Bathsheba 393
Bauman, Zygmunt 674
Bavelas, Alex 256-257, 284
Baxter, Gerald 639, 671
Baxter, Nancy Kerber 639, 671
Bazerman, Max H. 417-418, 449, 492
BCTV 484
B&B Containers 132, 155
B.C. Share 488
Beach, Lee Roy 300, 324, 418, 449
Beatles, The 476
Beatty, Richard H. 278, 284
Beazley, Mitchell 126, 158
Becker, Selwyn W. 625
Becker, Warren S. 326
Bedeian, Arthur G. 82, 159, 201, 206
Beer, Michael 588, 622
Belbin, R.M. 349
Bell, Cecil H., Jr. 591, 595, 622
Bell, Peter C. 494
Bell Canada 335
Bell Telephone 28
Benfari, Robert 493
Benjamin, Ludy T., Jr. 573, 579,
     667, 673
Benne, Kenneth D. 342-343, 364
Bennett, Charlie 202-203
Bennett, Nathan 333, 365
Bennis, Warren 370, 406
Benson, Gary L. 265, 284
Benson, P. George 625
Benson, Suzyn 365
Berg, Per Olof 124
Bergeman, C.S. 208
Berger, Peter L. 213, 243
Bergquist, William 674
Berkowitz, Leonard 285, 324
Berry, Leonard L. 608, 622
Berry, Paul C. 451
Berry, Thomas H. 625
Bettenhausen, Kenneth L. 334-336, 364
Bettis, Richard A. 233, 243
Beyer, Janice M. 99-100, 122
Bhagat, Rabi S. 539
BHP 95

BICC PLC 15
Bielby, William 537, 579
Binet, A. 175
Birnbaum, Michael H. 539
Black, J. Stewart 547, 561-562, 579
Black and Decker Canada Inc. 97
Blackburn, David 495, 497
Blackwell, Gerry 335, 364, 438, 449, 499
Blake, Robert R. 376-377, 406, 594, 622
Blake, Stacey 425, 449
Blanchard, Kenneth H. 378-379, 407, 457, 490
Blau, Peter 57, 81
Blazejak, Wanda 28
Block, Clifford H. 451
Blue Chip Cookies 160
Bluedorn, Allen C. 114, 122
Blumer, Catherine 72, 82
Boal, Kimberly B. 384-385, 406
Body Shop, The 333, 557, 582, 640, 671
Boeing 695
Bogotowicz, Adeline 28
Boisjoly, Roger 446
Boje, David M. 251, 284, 659, 671, 674
Bolman, Lee G. 367
Bolton, Alfred A. 28
Bonazzi, Giuseppe 468, 490
Bonner, Jim 129
Bonoma, Thomas V. 471, 491
Boon 89
Borges, Jorge Luis 221
Boroush, Mark 450
Borrus, Amy 608, 622
Bortz, Walter 521, 537
Borucki, Chet 624
Boston College 282
Bottger, Preston 332, 367
Bouchard, Thomas J., Jr. 177, 186-187, 205-206, 208
Bouvier, Nicolas 583
Bowditch, James L. 122
Bowen, David E. 408
Bowen, Donald D. 117, 122, 276-277, 284, 475, 490
Bower, Joseph Lyon 388, 406
Bowling Green State University 207
Boyacigiller, Nakiye Avdan 648-649, 671
Boyd, Brian 255, 284
Bradbury, Nicholas 551, 579
Braganti, Nancy L. 582
Bragg, Robert L. 239, 241
Brandt, Richard 671
Brenan, Rosey 306
Brett, Jeanne M. 581
Brick, Peggy 573, 579
Brickman, Philip 385, 406
British Academy of Management 30

British Airways 315, 514
British Columbia Forest Alliance 486, 488
British Columbia Systems Corporation 309
British Fire Service 659
Brock University 80
Brown, Bonnie M. 11, 40
Brown, John L. 107, 122, 662, 673
Brown, Mary Helen 446
Browning, Larry D. 250, 285-286
Bruner, Jerome S. 221, 243
Bryson, John M. 384-385, 406
Buchanan, David A. 341, 364
Buerkley, Deborah K. 205
Bull Europe 52
Buono, Anthony F. 106, 122
Burke, Ron 555
Burke, W. Warner 611, 622
Burnand, Gordon 336, 364
Burns, Tom 27, 53, 81
Burr, Donald 389
Burrell, W. Gibson 82, 659, 671, 674
Burt, Sir Cyril 651, 671-672
Bushe, Gervase R. 625
Business International Corporation 561, 579
Business Month 31
Business Week 31, 233, 243, 453, 510, 537, 539
Buttner, E. Holly 208
Byosiere, Philippe 505, 519, 538
Byrne, John A. 641, 671

C

Cadbury, Sir Adrian 452
Calas, Marta B. 410, 674-675
Calder, Bobby J. 388, 406
California State University 177
Cameron, Kim S. 20, 23, 40
Campbell, Donald T. 673
Campbell, Susan Rockwell 180
Campion, Michael A. 134, 145, 158
Canada Post Corporation 12
Canadian Army 111, 457
Canadian Broadcasting Corporation 12
Canadian Business 31, 267, 494
Canadian Consumer and Corporate Affairs 11
Canadian Department of Defense 12
Canadian Department of Lands and Forests 12
Canadian Hotel & Restaurant 691
Canadian Tire Acceptance Ltd. 178
Caputo, Craig 235, 244
Carey, Alex 28
Carleton University 140, 368
Carlin, George 281
Carlisle, Arthur Elliott 450
Carmanah Research Station 488

Carney, Mick 67, 81
Carr, Clay 210, 243
Carroll, Glenn R. 94, 112, 122
Carter, Gary W. 205
Cartwright, Susan 106, 122
Cascio, Wayne F. 51, 81
Case, John 367
Cashman, James F. 381, 407
Catholic Church 24
Cattell, Raymond B. 175, 184, 205
Caudron, Shari 102, 122, 128, 158, 520, 537
Caulkin, Simon 375, 406
Cavanaugh, Michael 446
Celestica Inc. 607
Center for Creative Leadership 581
Challenger space shuttle 433, 446
Chambers, Kevin 582
Chandler, Alfred 27
Chandler, W. 40
Chartered Accountant's Association of Alberta 443
Chatman, Jennifer A. 93, 109, 122
Chemco Inc. 77-80
Chemers, Martin M. 379, 407
Chen, Chao C. 389, 406
Cherns, Albert 145-147, 158
Cherrington, David J. 271-272, 284
Chesanow, Neil 340, 342, 344, 364, 562, 579
Cheung, Fanny 208
Child, Irvin L. 205
Christie, Richard 183-184, 205
Chrysler Corporation 462
Churbuck, David C. 137, 158
Cialdini, Robert B. 366
Clark, Lawrence S. 243, 245, 367
Clausing, Don 625
Cleary, Thomas 401, 405
Clegg, Chris W. 363, 365, 368
Clegg, Stewart 659, 671
Clement, Ronald W. 588, 622
Clemons, Tanya Cheer 411
Clopton, Nancy A. 453
Clover, Vernon T. 650, 671
Coca Cola 116
Cocheu, Ted 625
Cohen, Jacob 654-655, 657, 671
Cohen, Michael D. 425, 449
Cohn, Lawrence D. 171, 205
Coldwell, David 632
Coleman, Henry J., Jr. 81
Collins, Anne 691
Colorado Outward Bound School 349
Computing Canada 495
Conant, Jeffrey S. 83
Concordia University 304, 625
Conger, Jay A. 410
Conway, Miss 653
Cooke, Robert A. 118, 122
Coons, Alvin E. 376, 409

Cooper, Brian 494-495, 497-498
Cooper, Carl L. 106, 122
Cooper, Cary L. 205, 294, 324, 407
Cooper, Heather J. 216-217, 243
Cooper, M. Lynne 537, 580
Cooper, Robert 82, 674
Cooper, William H. 228-229, 243, 450, 453
Coopers & Lybrand Consulting Group 306
Coors Porcelain 121
Copeland, Lennie 561, 579, 582
Copeland Griggs Productions 582
Cordery, J.L. 368
Cordes, Cynthia L. 518, 537
Cornwall, Jeffrey R. 466, 490
Corporate Positioning Services 104
Coshan, Margaret 521, 537
Côté-O'Hara, Jocelyne 159
Cotton, John L. 559
Cox, Taylor 425, 449
Crawford-Mason, Clare 625
Cray Research, Inc. 98-99
Creedon, Jeremiah 282
Crosby, Philip 608
Crozier, Michael 458, 490
Cullen, Dallas 295, 324
Cullen, John B. 434, 452-453
Cummings, Larry L. 20, 40, 102, 123, 148, 158, 449
Cunningham, J. Barton 150, 158
Cunningham, Ross 685, 688-689, 691
Curie, Marie 464
Curtis, Ellen Foster 446

D

Dachler, H. Peter 385, 406, 410
Daffern, Gillean 446
Daft, Richard L. 23, 40, 61, 75, 81, 262-263, 285
Daily, Bill 286
Dalhousie University 347
Dalton, Dan R. 582
Daly, Mary 282
Dansereau, Fred, Jr. 381, 406
Darrow, Charlotte N. 580
Davidson, Jeffrey P. 467-468, 490
David's Cookies 160
Davis, James H. 421, 424, 449
Davis, Murray S. 645, 671
Davis, Stanley M. 57, 81
Davis-Blake, Alison 537, 579
Dawis, Rene V. 190, 206-207
Day, David V. 395, 406
Day, Frederick A. 510-511, 537
Deal, Terrence E. 101, 103, 122, 367
de Alvarez, Leo Paul S. 206
Dean, James W., Jr. 625
Deaux, Kay 220-221, 243
De Benedetti, Carlo 383

de Forest, Mariah E. 41, 44, 81
Deci, Edward L. 297, 324
Dedrick, Esther J. 410
DeFries, J.C. 208
Delaney, Steve 607
Delbecq, André L. 61, 82, 438, 449
Delbridge, Rick 258
DeLong, Thomas J. 570, 579
Delta Airlines 116
DeMeuse, Kenneth P. 330, 366
Deming, W. Edwards 27, 608, 624
Dennehy, Robert F. 674
Dennis, Alan R. 450, 453
Derrida, Jacques 674
Detroit Fats 203
Devine, Elizabeth 582
DHL 698
Dickerson, Anne 583
Dickson, William J. 24, 26, 28, 41
Diehl, Helen L. 650, 671
Diesing, Paul 674
Digman, John M. 186, 205
Dinges, David 514
Dipboye, Robert L. 179, 205
DiStefano, Joe 334
Dobbins, Gregory H. 392, 406, 410
Dobyns, Lloyd 625
Dofasco 47, 97
Doktor, Robert H. 391, 406
D'Orazio, Nancy 563-564, 579
Dorfman, Peter W. 372, 408
Dougherty, Thomas W. 518, 537
Drapeau, Richard 625
Drasgow, Fritz 159
Drexler, Allan B. 336, 338-339, 364, 367
Droge, Cornelia 75, 81
Drucker, Peter F. 41, 608, 622
Dubrovsky, Vitaly 285
Duda, Richard 437, 449
Dukerich, Janet M. 373, 408
Dulek, Ronald E. 286, 583
Dumaine, Brian 313, 324
Duncan, W. Jack 124
Dunham, Chip 7
Dunham, Randall B. 516, 537
Dunnette, Marvin D. 409, 492, 538, 596, 623
Dutton, Jane E. 420, 451
Duxbury, Linda E. 506-508, 537, 560, 579-580
Dworkin, Terry Morehead 539
Dwyer, Deborah J. 532, 534, 537

E

Eagly, Alice H. 392, 407
Earley, P. Christopher 333, 364
Earth First 486-487
Eaton, Timothy 100
Eberle, Ted 150, 158

École des Hautes Études Commerciales 675
Economist, The 17, 40, 604, 607, 622
Eden, Dov 410
Edmunds, W.W. 240, 242, 244
Educational Testing Service 173
Edwards, Carolyn Pope 208
Edwards, Jeffrey R. 504, 537
Ehrlich, Sanford B. 373, 408
Einblau & Associates 306
Einstein, Albert 449, 464, 639, 671
Ekeberg, Steven E. 325, 366
Ekman, Paul 252, 284
Elco Corp. 120
Elsass, Priscilla M. 208
Emery Air Freight 694, 696, 699
Emmons, Michael L. 474, 490
Enderle, Georges 410, 440, 449
England, George W. 190, 207
Enk, Gordon 450
Erez, Miriam 326
Eulberg, Joe R. 539
Evans, James R. 625
Evans, Martin G. 305, 324, 380, 407
Evans, Nancy J. 344, 355, 364
Evans, Rob 700, 702
Eyler, David R. 492

F

Fab Sweets Limited 360, 363, 368
Faerman, Sue R. 289, 325
Fairchild Semiconductor 120
Fairfield University 461
Falvey, Jack 260, 284
Farmer, Lieutenant Russ 608
Farmer, Richard N. 8
Farrar, Alice 136, 158, 509, 537
Farrell, Dan 192, 205, 463, 490
Fayol, Henri 26, 29, 40
Federal Express 693-705
Feigenbaum, Armand 608
Feingold, A. 208
Feldman, Daniel C. 108, 122, 339, 364
Feldman, Martha S. 123
Feldman, Steven P. 427, 449
Ferrell, O.C. 427, 449
Ferris, Gerald R. 141-142, 158, 228, 243, 604, 622
Festinger, Leon 189, 205
Fiedler, Fred E. 27, 375-376, 379, 407, 409
Field, Richard Dudley 458, 490
Field, Richard H.G. 135, 156, 158, 214, 221, 243, 286, 319, 371, 378, 381-382, 407, 409-410, 414, 421, 439, 446, 450, 452, 614, 624, 685
Fielden, John S. 286
Fields, Debbi 131, 160-164
Fields, Randy 131, 160-165

Films, Incorporated 625
Filson, Brent 266, 284
Financial Post, The 31, 496
Finch, Miriam 286
Finkelstein, Sidney 233, 243
Finnigan, Jerome P. 625
Firmenich 676
Fisher, Anne B. 131, 158, 579
Fisher, George 95
Fisher, Roger 475, 490
Fiske, Susan T. 344, 364, 511, 537
Fitzgerald, Dennis 484
Fitzgerald, Louise F. 510, 537
Flat Earth Society 314
Fletcher, Clive 171, 185, 207
Fletcher, Ronald 651, 671
Flying Tigers 693-694
Flynn, James R. 175-176, 179, 205
Foodservice & Hospitality 691
Forbes 31
Ford, J. Kevin 601, 622
Ford Electronics Manufacturing
    Corporation 607
Forrester, Russell H. 364
Forsyth, Donelson R. 430, 442, 450
Fortune 31, 446
Fortune 500 11, 22, 264, 549
Foucault, Michel 221-222, 243, 462,
    469, 490, 660, 671, 674
Foushee, H. Clayton 245
Fowler, H.W. 281-282
Fox, William F. 438-439, 450
Foy, Joe 484, 488
Fraedrich, John 449
Franssen, Margot 557, 579
Frederick, William C. 453
Freedman, Sara M. 538
Freeman, David H. 586-587, 612, 622
Freeman, John 22, 27, 40
Freeman, Minnie Aodla 563, 579
Freize, Irene 244
French, John R.P., Jr. 456, 490
French, Wendell L. 591, 595, 622
Freud, Sigmund 180, 205
Fried, Yitzhak 141-142, 158-159, 420,
    449
Friends of Clayoquot Sound 486
Frishkoff, Patricia A. 11, 40
Fromkin, Victoria 281-282
Frone, Michael R. 506, 537, 560, 580
Frost, Peter J. 124, 410
Fukuda, K. John 108, 122
Fulk, Janet 255, 284, 286
Fuller, Buckminster 160, 164
Funder, David C. 183, 206
Furlong, Carla 306, 324
Furlong & Associates 306
Furukawa Electric Co. Ltd. of Japan
    15-16
Futrell, David 330, 366

G

Gagliardi, P. 124
Gaines, Jeannie 582, 640, 671
Galaskiewicz, Joseph 68, 81
Galatea 383
Gallupe, R. Brent 438, 450, 453
Ganster, Daniel C. 513, 532, 534, 537
Gantt, Henry L. 25
Garcia, Joseph E. 375, 379, 407, 409
Garcia, Juan 312
Garry, Carl 621
Garry, Loraine Spencer 621
Garvin, David A. 608, 622, 625
Gaschnig, John 449
Gay, Lorraine R. 650, 671
Gehani, R. Ray 608, 622
Geis, Florence L. 183-184, 205
Geldof, Bob 95, 123
General Electric 383
General Foods 116
General Motors 83, 510
George, Joey F. 453
George, Paul 484, 488
George Washington University 326
Gephart, Robert P., Jr. 245
Gergen, Kenneth J. 222, 243, 658-659,
    671
Gergen, Mary McCanney 675
Gersick, Connie J.G. 336-337, 365,
    367, 420, 450
Gibb-Clark, Margot 514, 537
Gilbreth, Frank B. 24-26, 40
Gilbreth, Lillian M. 24, 26
Gilligan, Carol 295, 324, 433, 450,
    542, 580
Gilmore, Thomas 641-642, 672
Gioia, Dennis A. 232, 243, 326, 368
Gitlow, H. 625
Givaudan Group 676
Gladstein, Deborah (see Deborah
    Gladstein Ancona)
Gladwell, Malcolm 259-260, 284
Gleick, James 586, 622
Glenn, James R., Jr. 431, 448, 450
Globe and Mail, The 31
Godkin, Lynn 625
Goethe 128
Goeudevert, Daniel 128, 158
Gold Corporation 250-251
Gomez-Mejia, Luis R. 245
Goodall, H.L., Jr. 661, 671
Goodman, Paul S. 330, 339, 365
Goss, Tracy 586, 622
Gottlieb, Jonathan Z. 590-591, 623
Gouldner, Alvin 82
Government of Alberta 536
Gowing, Marilyn K. 638, 640, 673
Graen, George 381, 406-407
Graham, Thornton A. 63
Grasse Fragrances SA 676, 683

Graves, David 605, 609-611, 622
Green, Bert F. 651, 671
Greene, Richard 475, 490
Greenhaus, Jeffrey H. 582
Greenstreet, Robert C. 650, 673
Greenwood, Regina A. 28
Greenwood, Ronald G. 28, 41
Greenwood, Royston 63, 81, 107, 122,
    285
Greer, Nancy 309
Greiner, Larry E. 23, 40
Gresham, Larry G. 449
Gresov, Christopher 83
Griffeth, Roger W. 517, 538
Griffin, Linda 702
Griffin, Ricky W. 147-148, 158, 625
Griffith University 95
Griggs, Lewis 561, 579, 582
Grinder, John 264, 284
Grisé, Mary-Liz 453
Gross, Warren 94, 102, 122
Grubbs, Victor F. 239, 241-242
Grubowsky, Billy 202
Grush, Joseph E. 326
Guerriere, Dr. Michael 606
Guilford, Joy Paul 175, 205
Gunz, Hugh 582
Gustafson, David J. 208, 449
Gutman, Dan 258, 284

H

Habermas, Jurgen 674
Hacker, Hartmut 324
Hackett, General Sir John 375
Hackman, J. Richard 139-141, 143,
    158-159, 328, 330, 332, 336, 347-
    348, 365, 367, 420, 450
Haga, William J. 406
Hall, Douglas T. 117, 122, 284, 490,
    539, 542, 559, 580
Hall, Edward T. 582
Hall, Francine S. 117, 122, 284, 490,
    559, 580
Hall, Mildred Reed 582
Hall, Rosalie J. 376, 408
Hambrick, Donald C. 233, 243
Hammond Chemicals Co. Ltd. 78
Hamper, Ben 506, 537
Hand, H.H. 517, 538
Hanna, Wayne 306
Hannan, Michael 22, 27, 40
Harari, Oren 625
Harder, Joe 326
Hare, A. Paul 332, 365
Hare-Mustin, Rachel T. 675
Harkins, Stephen G. 333, 365
Harragan, Betty Leah 492
Harris, Jim 580
Harris, T. George 41
Harrison, David A. 650, 672

Harrison, J. Richard 94, 112, 122
Hart, Peter 449
Hart, Stuart 439, 450
Hartke, Darrell D. 409
Harvard University 30, 271, 383, 615
Harvey, Jerry B. 423, 450
Harvey, John H. 406
Hassard, John 82, 659, 672, 674
Hatch, Mary Jo 123
Hathaway, Donald B. 467, 490
Hay, David A. 208
Hay, Edward N. 311, 324
Hayek, Nicolas 65
Hayes, John 176, 205
Hayes, Michael 676
Heal, Huey 203-204
Hearnshaw, Leslie 651, 672
Heller, Trudy 395, 407
Hellriegel, Don 211, 243
Henderson, A.M. 56
Henderson, Norman D. 186, 206
Hendrick, Clyde 367
Henley Management School 30
Hersey, Paul 378-379, 407, 457, 490
Herzberg, Frederick I. 26, 139, 158-159
Heskett, James L. 124
Heylighten, Francis 326
Hickson, David J. 75, 81-82, 459, 490
Higgins, Christopher A. 506-508, 537, 560, 580, 609, 622
Hill, John S. 286, 583
Hinings, C.R. (Bob) 63, 81-82, 107, 122, 285, 459, 490
Hirschhorn, Larry 641-642, 670
Hirschman, Albert O. 518, 538
Hodgetts, Richard 124
Hoffman, Lois W. 187, 206
Hoffman-LaRoche 676
Hofstede, Geert 86, 90-91, 122-124, 183, 206, 548, 592, 647, 672
Hogan, Joyce 174, 206
Holland, John L. 552-554, 580-581
Hollander, Edwin P. 340, 365, 457, 490
Holmes, Thomas H. 514-515, 538
Holsapple, Clyde W. 435, 450
Hopkins, Ann B. 367
Horn, Joseph M. 208
Hornick, William 450
Hostess Frito-Lay Co. 601
Hough, Leaetta M. 409, 492, 538, 596, 623
House, Robert J. 21, 27, 41, 201, 206, 353, 366, 376, 380, 385-386, 407-408, 482, 658, 672
Howard, Miss 653
Howell, Jane M. 381, 384, 387, 408, 410, 609, 622
Howell, Jon P. 372, 408
Hubbard, Ruth 675
Huczynski, Andrzej A. 341, 364
Hudson's Bay Company 24, 691

Hughes, Michael 671, 675
Hulin, Charles L. 207
Hunt, James G. 385, 406-407, 410, 674
Huot, Michel 15-16
Hyde, Janet S. 72, 82, 171, 206, 208
Hyde, Karen R. 72
Hydro-Quebec 15

I

IBM 14, 116, 163, 307, 542, 690
Ickes, William John 406
Idaszak, Jacqueline R. 159
IEEE Spectrum 446
Ilgen, Daniel R. 326
Imai, Masaaki 625
Inamori, Kazuo 120
Inc. Magazine 31
Indian and Northern Development Canada 215, 243
Indiana University 8, 30
Inge, General Sir Peter 375
Inkson, J.H. Kerr 75, 81
Innes, Eva 557, 580
Intel 19
Intellicorp Inc. 495
Intercultural Press 582
International Flavors & Fragrances Inc. 676
Isabella, Lynn A. 581
ISE Communications 509-510
Isenberg, Daniel J. 424, 450
Ishikawa, Kaoru 27, 608, 624
ISO Easy 625
ITT 116
Ivancevich, John M. 519, 538
IWA Canada 485
Izraeli, Dafna N. 465, 490, 582

J

Jablin, Fredric M. 284-286
Jacklin, Carol N. 171, 206
Jackson, Paul R. 368
Jackson, Susan E. 534
Jacksonville State University 28
Jacobson, Lenore 221, 244
Jacques, Elliott 178
Jacques, Roy 664, 672, 674
Jaeger, Alfred M. 92-93, 123, 592, 622
Jaeger, Richard M. 650, 672
Jago, Arthur G. 378, 409, 439, 450, 452
Jamison, Kaleel 364
Janis, Irving L. 421, 450
Janson, Robert 139, 158
Jarvis, Paul A. 344, 355, 364
Jelinek, Mariann 564, 580
Jenkins, Anthony 129, 158
Jennings, Kenneth R. 599, 601, 607-608, 624
Jensen, Mary Ann C. 335, 366

Jermier, John 372, 408
Jessup, L.M. 453
Jesus Christ 120, 476
Jick, Todd D. 465, 615, 623, 647, 672
Joel, Billy 214
Johansen, Robert 335, 365
Johns, Gary 304, 324
Johnson, Blair T. 392, 407
Johnson, Bob 686
Johnson, David W. 357, 365, 421, 445, 450
Johnson, Frank P. 357, 365
Johnson, James M. 199, 206
Johnson, Roger T. 421, 445, 450
Johnsonville Foods Company 224-225, 227
Jones, Edward E. 244
Jones, Steven D. 325, 366
Jones, Thomas M. 452
Joynson, Robert 651, 672
Judge, Timothy A. 228, 243, 604, 622
Jung, Carl G. 180, 206
Juran, Joseph M. 27, 608, 624

K

Kahn, Robert L. 16, 27, 40, 505, 519, 538
Kahneman, Daniel 418, 449-450
Kalleberg, Arne L. 192, 206
Kallgren, Carl A. 366
Kane, Kimberly F. 264, 269, 284
Kanfer, Ruth 293-294, 324
Kanhouse, David E. 244
Kanter, Rosabeth Moss 450, 549, 580, 615, 623
Kao Corp 642
Kariel, Patricia E. 446
Karren, Ronald J. 325
Katz, Daniel 16, 27, 40
Katzell, Raymond A. 326
Katzenbach, Jon R. 328, 365, 367
Kaufman, Carol Felker 114, 122
Kearns, David 608, 624
Keller, Lauren M. 188, 206
Keller, Maryann 83
Kelley, Don 383-384
Kelley, Harold H. 218, 243-244
Kelly, Eileen P. 219, 243, 245, 367
Kemp, Nigel J. 363, 365, 368
Kempner, Thomas 25, 41
Kendall, Lorne M. 207
Kennedy, Allen A. 101, 103, 122
Kennedy, Rick 344, 367
Kenrick, Douglas T. 183, 206
Kernan, Mary C. 340, 366
Kerr, Jeffrey 233, 243
Kerr, Steven 307-308, 324, 372, 408
Kesner, Idalene F. 582
Ketchum, Lyman D. 368
Kets de Vries, Manfred F.R. 11-12, 40, 410-411

Khan, Sar B. 554, 580
Kidd, Robert F. 406
Kidwell, Roland E., Jr. 333, 365
Kierkegaard, Søren 307
Kiernan, Matthew J. 612, 623
Kiesler, Sara 285
Kiezun, Witold 676
Kiganda, Dr. 621
Kiggundu, Moses N. 140, 158, 368
Kilburn, David 94, 123
Kilian, Cecilia S. 624
Killing, Peter 626
Kilmann, Ralph H. 124
Kim, W. Chan 401
Kimble, Gregory A. 654, 672
King, Bernard 626-629
King David of Israel 393
King Lear 282
Kinn, Mary 201
Kirkpatrick, David 438, 450, 641, 672
Kitzinger, Celia 677
Kiyohide, Shirai 120-121
Klassen, Cathryn 97, 123
Klein, Edward B. 580
Kleinbeck, Uwe 324
Kliem, Ralph L. 109, 123
Klimoski, Richard J. 650, 673
Klonsky, Bruce G. 407
K mart 19
Knapp, Mark 252, 284
Knights, David 67, 81, 660, 672
Koenig, Richard Jr. 61, 82
Kohlberg, Lawrence 431-432, 434, 450
Kohn, Alfie 307, 324, 326
Kolb, David A. 581
Kolesar, Peter J. 624
Kolodny, Harvey F. 368
Konner, Melvin 171, 174, 179, 187-
    188, 206, 208
Konsynski, Benn R. 453
Korda, Michael 256, 284
Kotter, John P. 124
Koziara, Karen Shallcross 205
Kram, Kathy E. 559-560, 580, 582
Kreitner, Robert 311, 325
Kriger, Mark P. 453
Krone, Kathleen J. 248-249, 284
Kruglanski, Arie W. 457, 491
Kuhn, Thomas S. 586, 623, 659, 672
Kukla, Andy 244
Kulik, Chen-Lin C. 206
Kulik, James A. 176, 206
Kumar, Kamalesh 366
Kyocera America Inc. (KAI) 120-121

L

La Marche, Tuffy 202-203
La Petite Boulangerie 160-161
Label, Wayne A. 527, 538
Lachman, Ran 459, 490

Lafferty, J. Clayton 118, 122
Lafontaine, Kam 495
Lander, Grace 279
Landy, Frank J. 326
Lane, Paul M. 114, 122
Langton, Nancy 189, 207
Larreché, Claude 684-686
Larson, James R., Jr. 227, 244
Larson, Larry L. 385, 407, 672
Latham, Gary P. 301-303, 324-326
Laurent, André 293, 324
Lawler, Edward E., III 298, 300-301,
    303, 325, 625
Lawrence, Paul R. 57, 64, 81, 491,
    674
Lawrence, Thomas B. 685, 691
Layng, Sanderson 520, 538
Leavitt, Harold J. 256-257, 284
LeBoeuf, Michael 309-310, 324
Ledford, Gerald E., Jr. 625
Lee, Catherine 507-508
Lee, Charles A. 490
Lee, Raymond T. 518, 538
Legant, Patricia 235, 244
Legge, Karen 363, 365
Lehman, Wayne E.K. 517, 538
Leiter, Michael P. 518, 538
Lemer, Harriett 306
Lengel, Robert H. 262-263, 285
Levering, Robert 557, 580, 663, 672
Levine, John M. 328, 331, 333, 339,
    342, 344, 347, 365-366, 374, 408
Levinson, Daniel J. 543-544, 580
Levinson, Maria H. 580
Lewandowski, Mr. 129
Lewicki, Roy J. 117, 122, 276, 284,
    469, 490-491
Lewin, David 491
Lewin, Kurt 26, 376, 408, 616, 646
Lewis, Geoffrey 106
Lewis, John W., III 122
Lickona, Thomas 432, 450
Lida, David 562, 580
Likert, Rensis 601-602, 604, 623
Limerick, David C. 95, 123
Limora Community Health Centre, The
    620-621
Limora Hospital 620-621
Lincoln, James R. 191-192, 206
Lindblom, Charles E. 425, 450
Linn, Marcia C. 171, 206
Linton, Ralph 88, 123
Lippitt, Ronald 26, 376, 408
Lirtzman, Sidney I. 353, 366
Little, Bruce 606, 623
Litwin, George H. 611, 622
Lloyd's of London 10
Locke, Edwin P. 27, 301-303, 324-326
Lofquist, Lloyd H. 190, 207
Long, Janet W. 349, 366
Long, William S. 410

Long Island Lighting Company
    (LILCO) 428
Longnecker, Clinton O. 231-232, 243,
    326, 393, 408
Lord, Robert G. 340, 366, 376, 389,
    395, 406, 408-409, 416, 450
Lorsch, Jay W. 64, 81, 330, 365, 491, 582
Loton, Brian 95
Louis, Meryl Reis 124
Louviere, Jordan J. 450
Lovelock, Christopher H. 693
Lowe, Charles A. 452
Lowery, David 192-193, 207
Lowman, Kathleen D. 573, 579, 667, 673
Luchetti, Robert 159
Luckmann, Thomas 213, 243
Ludwig, Dean C. 393, 408
Lui, Richard 161-162, 164
Lundberg, Craig C. 124
Lush, Patricia 488, 491
Luthans, Fred 311, 325, 674
Lykken, David T. 177, 205, 208
Lyon, Jim 580
Lytton, Hugh 179, 206

M

MacArthur, General Douglas 92
MacBride-King, Judith 606, 623
Maccoby, Eleanor E. 171, 206
MacDonald, Cheryl 220, 244
MacDonald, Dr. Jan 620-621
Machiavelli, Niccòlo 183, 206
MacIntosh, David 496
Mackie, Diane M. 347, 366
Maclean, Norman 224, 244
MacLean, Paul D. 188, 206
MacLean's Magazine 22
MacMillan Bloedel Ltd. 484-485, 489
Maddi, Salvatore R. 179, 206
Maher, Karen J. 416, 450
Mainiero, Lisa A. 460-461, 491-492,
    542, 560, 581
Makhijani, Mona G. 407
Makihara, Kumiko 511, 538
Manchester Business School 373
Mangini, David M. 461
Manz, Charles C. 368, 395-396, 408
March, James G. 26, 425, 449-450
Marcic, Dorothy 572
Marecek, Jeanne 235, 244, 677
Marizin, Bishop 620-621
Markham, Calvert 642, 672
Markham, Steven E. 231, 244
Mark's Work Wearhouse 143
Marriot Corporation 691
Marshall, Sir Colin 315
Martin, Alexia 365
Martin, Joanne 99, 123-124
Maruyama, Magoroh 138, 158, 547-
    548, 580

Marx, Groucho 419
Marx, Robert 446
Mary Kay Cosmetics 102
Maslach, Christina 518, 534, 538
Maslow, Abraham H. 294-295, 325-326, 658, 672
Mason, Julie Cohen 335, 366
Massachusetts Institute of Technology 30, 93, 693
Matsuo 609
Matteson, Michael T. 538
Matthews, Jan 499
Matthews, M. Cash 446
Mauborgne, Renee A. 401
Maurer, Michel 688, 690-691
Mauws, Michael K. 685, 691
Maxis Corp. 159
Mayes, Bronston T. 537
Mayo, Elton 26
Maznevski, Martha 334
McCanse, Anne Adams 376-377, 406
McClearn, Gerald E. 208
McClelland, David C. 213, 244, 295, 325
McConkey, Dale D. 370, 400, 408
McCormack, Mark H. 271, 285-286, 475-476, 491
McCrory, Pauline 486
McDonald's Restaurants 17, 685-686, 690
McDonnell-Douglas 695
McGarvey, Robert 551, 580
McGill, Michael E. 613, 623
McGill University 55, 410, 582, 587, 592, 662, 675
McGrath, Michael R. 289, 325
McGraw, Kenneth O. 674
McGregor, Douglas M. 27, 183, 206
McGue, Matthew 177, 205
McGuigan, Dorothy G. 579
McGuire, Janice 497
McGuire, Timothy W. 285
McInnes, Craig 129, 159, 173, 206
McKay, Shona 419, 451, 550, 580
McKay, Wayne 306
McKee, Braxton 580
McKenna, Barrie 16, 40
McKenzie, Ken 129
McLauchlin, James E. 286
McLaughlin, Hugh 588, 623
McMaster University 21, 219
McNeil, George 52
McQuarrie, Fiona 333
Medici, The 183
Meehl, Paul E. 672
Meek, V. Lynn 96, 123
Meglino, Bruce M. 517, 538
Meindl, James R. 373, 389, 406, 408
Mellican, Eugene 446
Meltsner, Susan 493
Mendenhall, Mark 547, 579

Mendoza, Pete 312
Mento, Anthony J. 301, 325
Merrell, Susan 180, 207
Mescon, Michael H. 276, 285
Messick, David M. 347, 366
Metharme 383
Metropolitan Life Insurance Co. 438
Meurs, Klass 239
Meyer, Alan D. 81
Meyer, John W. 68, 81
Miami Herald 522
Miceli, Marcia P. 468, 491
Michaelsen, Larry K. 366
Michela, John L. 218, 243
Michie, Donald 449
Miles, Raymond E. 65, 81, 83
Miller, Dale T. 674
Miller, Danny 66, 75, 81, 587, 623
Miller, Lynn E. 326
Miller, Vernon D. 286
Milliken, Frances J. 446
Mills, Albert J. 675
Mills, C.W. 409
Mills, H.H. 409
Miner, John B. 651, 674
Mintzberg, Henry 54-55, 58-59, 81-82, 178, 207, 291-292, 325, 426, 451, 453, 459, 491
Mirvis, Philip H. 586-588, 591, 598, 601, 623
Mist Ridge 425, 443-444
Misumi, Jyuji 376, 408
Mitchell, Rex 601, 623
Mitchell, Terence R. 227, 231, 244, 326, 380, 407, 418, 449
MITI (Ministry of International Trade and Industry for Japan) 391
Mitsutka, Frances 233, 244
Mittman, Robert 365
Miyamoto Musashi 401
Mobley, William H. 517, 538
Mohram, Susan Albers 625
Mokwa, Michael P. 83
Molander, Earl A. 435, 451
Molloy, John T. 557, 580
Molson Breweries 469
Mondy, R. Wayne 427, 451
Montreal Canadiens 96
Moon, Reverend Sun Myung 486
Mooney, Jeff 685-692
Moore, Larry F. 124
Moosajees, Limited 295, 322-323
Morantz, Alan 136, 159
Morawski, Jill G. 675
Moreland, Richard L. 328, 331, 333, 339, 342, 344, 347, 365-366, 374, 408
Morgan, Gareth 124, 250, 285, 624, 659, 671-672, 674
Morgan, Ronald B. 410
Morgan Stanley 116
Morita, Akio 14, 38-39, 120

Morley, John David 89-90, 123
Morrison, Ann M. 410, 548-550, 558, 580-581
Morrow, Ira J. 670, 672
Morsbach, Helmut 252, 285
Moscovici, S. 365
Moskow, Michael H. 205
Moskowitz, Milton 557, 580, 663, 672
Mount, Michael K. 186, 205
Mouton, Jane Srygley 377, 406, 594, 622
Mowday, Richard T. 189, 207
Mrs. Fields Cookies Inc. 14, 68, 131, 160-165
Muchinsky, Paul M. 464, 491
Mugny, G. 365
Mumby, Dennis K. 416, 451
Munter, Mary 286
Murdock, George P. 88, 123
Murnighan, J. Keith 336, 364
Murphy, Bill 203
Murphy, Mike 164
Murphy, Patrick E. 410
Murray, Linda J. 136, 158, 509, 537
Mutual Group 494
Mutual Life Assurance Company of Canada 478, 494-499
Myers, Isabel Briggs 180-182, 207, 493

N

Nadler, David A. 386-387, 408, 586, 623-624, 653, 672
Nagel, Roger 641, 672
Naisbitt, John 14, 40, 676
Nanus, Bert 370, 406
National Aeronautics and Space Administration (NASA) 22
National Collegiate Athletic Association 346
National Computer Systems, Inc. 582
National Hockey League 111
National Quality Institute 607
Naylor, James C. 326
Neale, Margaret A. 492
Near, Janet P. 468, 491
Neck, Chris P. 396, 408
Neilsen, Eric H. 472, 491
Nelson, Horatio 106
Nelton, Sharon 410
Neuijen, Bram 124
Nevis, Edwin C. 296, 325
New Jersey Bell Telephone 40
Nielsen, Richard P. 492
Nisberg, Jay N. 527, 538
Nisbett, Richard E. 235, 244
NMC Siha Bakery 86
Noon, Mike 258, 285
Nord, Walter 35
Nordstrom, Inc. 661, 663, 671
North, David M. 242, 244

Northey, Margot 266, 268, 285
Nuclear Regulatory Commission
    (NRC) 428
Nunamaker, Jay F., Jr. 450, 453
Nyaw, Mee-Kau 391, 409

O

O'Brien, Gordon E. 142, 159
O'Brien, Pauline J. 208
O'Day, R. 101, 123
Oddou, Gary 579
Offerman, Lynn R. 457, 638, 640, 673
Ohayv, Denise Daval 124
Ohio State University 376
Oldham, Greg R. 135, 139-141, 143,
    158-159
Olive, David 274, 285
Oliver, Christine 9
Oliver, Len 626-628
Oliver, Thomas R. 695, 701-703, 705-706
Olivetti 383
Olsen, Johan P. 425, 449-450
Omachonu, Vincent K. 625
O'Neill, Paul 624
Ontario Hydro 550
O'Reilly, Charles A. 334, 366
Organizational Dynamics, Inc. 700, 702
Original Great Chocolate Chip Cookie,
    The 160
Ornstein, Suzyn 159, 581
Osborn, Alex F. 438, 451
Osland, Joyce S. 581
Ouchi, William G. 92-93, 123, 462, 491
Outward Bound 594
Owen, Crystal L. 245
Owens-Illinois 121
Ozer, Daniel J. 658, 673

P

Palisade Corporation 453
Papata, Sam 202
Parasuraman, A. 622
Parker, Martin 674
Parker, Mike 510, 538
Parker, Victoria A. 582
Parker, Yana 278
Parker Brothers 317, 319
Parnell, John A. 83
Parsons, Talcott 56
Pascale, Richard T. 112, 116, 123, 622
Pasmore, William A. 623
Paton, Greg 156
Pavlov, Ivan 304
Peace, William H. 326
Pearl, Jayne A. 270, 285
Peiperl, Maury A. 545-547, 581
Pennings, Johannes M. 490
People Express 389
People Tech Products 601

PepsiCo 116, 161
Perkins, Anne G. 334, 366
Perlman, Baron 466, 490
Perlmutter, Howard 546, 581
Perras, Jacques 520, 538
Perrow, Charles 82, 433, 451
Peters, Lawrence H. 379, 409
Peters, Tom J. 27, 250, 285, 348, 350,
    366, 587, 623, 643, 673
Petersen, James C. 463, 490
Peterson, Mark F. 376, 408
Petro Canada 12
Pfeffer, Jeffrey 27, 41, 102, 123, 189,
    207, 372, 409, 459, 469, 491-492
Pfeiffer, John 477, 491
Phalon, Richard 307, 325
Phelps, Wendy 163
Philips 39
Phillips, James S. 389, 409, 538
Phillips, Nelson 135, 158, 662, 673
Phillips Cables Ltd. 14-16
Phillips-Fitel Inc. 15-16
Piccard, Jacques 677-678, 684
Piccard, Louis 677
Platenka, Frank 28
Platz, Stephanie J. 392, 406
Plomin, Robert 170, 177, 186, 188,
    207-208
Podsakoff, Philip M. 408
Pohlmann, John T. 409
Polistuk, Eugene 607
Ponder, Ron J. 696-698
Pondy, Louis R. 469, 491
Pope, Alexander 6
Pope John Paul II 464
Popovich, Paula M. 72, 82
Porras, Jerry I. 586, 588, 595-597, 623
Port, Otis 671
Porter, Lyman W. 207, 284-285, 298,
    300-301, 303, 325
Porter, Michael 27, 66-67, 82
Postman, Leo 221, 243
Potash, Marlin S. 493
Potter, Beverly A. 534, 538
Powell, Gary N. 118, 123, 542, 560, 581
Poyatos, Fernando 285
Pratt and Whitney Canada Ltd. 606
Prediger, Dale J. 554, 581
Premeaux, Shane 427, 451
Prentice, Deborah A. 674
Price Waterhouse 306, 344, 367
Princess Margaret Hospital, Toronto 606
Princeton Creative Research, Inc. 198
Pritchard, Robert D. 301, 325, 331, 366
Procter & Gamble 116
Profit 31, 40
Proteus Rainwear Limited 175
Prud'homme, Alex 120, 123
Psalidas-Perlmutter, Foulie 575
Psychological Assessment Resources,
    Inc. 581

Pugh, Derek S. 27, 60, 64, 75, 81-82
Purdy, Kenneth 139, 158
Purdy, Susan Smith 448
Purolator 696
Putnam, Linda L. 284-285, 416
Pygmalion 383-384, 410

Q

Quality Team Performance 367
Quast, Hans-Henning 324
Queen's University 19, 228, 438
Quest International 676
Quilter, Lynn 163-164
Quinn, Paul 162, 164
Quinn, Robert E. 20, 23, 40-41, 289, 325

R

Rachman, David J. 276, 285
Rafiquzzaman, M. 40
Ragins, Belle Rose 559, 581
Rahe, Richard H. 514-515, 538
Rahim, M. Afzalur 471, 480, 491
Raiffa, Howard 475, 491
Raisinghani, Duru 426, 451
Ralston, David A. 208
Rand Corporation 438
Ranson, Stewart 250, 285
Rauch, Jonathan 563, 581
Raudsepp, Eugene 198, 532, 538
Raven, Bertram H. 456-457, 490-491
Ravlin, Elizabeth 330, 365
Read, Peter C. 450
Reagan, Ronald 464
Red Cross 332
Reddy, W. Brendan 364
Reebok 415
Reed, Linda 244
Reed, Michael 671, 675
Reeder, John A. 583
Rehder, Robert R. 510, 538
Reilly, Anne H. 581
Reno, Raymond R. 339, 366
Rentsch, Joan R. 98, 123
Rest, Stanley 244
Rheingold, Howard 245
Rich, Stephen 208
Richman, Tom 165
Richmond, Claude 486
Ridyard, Cathy 431
Riger, Stephanie 661, 665, 673
Riggio, Ronald E. 199, 207
Rizzo, John R. 353, 366
Robbins, Stephen P. 134, 159
Roberts, J. Timmons 509, 538
Roberts, Karlene H. 223, 244, 284-285
Roberts, Wess 401
Robertson, Ivan T. 205, 294, 324, 407
Robertson, Peter 586, 588, 595-597, 623
Robey, Daniel 61, 82

Roddick, Anita 333, 582, 671
Rodman, Robert 281-282
Rodon Communications 306
Rodriguez, Juan 683
Roethlisberger, Fritz J. 24, 26, 28, 41
Rogelberg, Steven G. 452
Rohrbaugh, John 20, 40
Roitsch, P.A. 240, 242, 244
Rolex 65
Romelaer, Pierre J. 425, 450
Romney, David M. 179, 206
Ronen, Simcha 91-92, 123
Root-Bernstein, Robert S. 674
Rorty, Richard 661, 673
Rosenbaum, Robert M. 244
Rosener, Judith B. 410
Rosenthal, Robert 221, 244, 383, 655-656, 673
Rosnow, Ralph L. 655-656, 673
Ross, Alexander 178, 207
Ross, Jerry 419, 427-429, 440, 451
Ross, Joel E. 625
Rossi, Alice 171, 207
Rossi, Peter 171, 207
Rossman, Marlene L. 582
Rost, Joseph 393, 409
Roth, Philip L. 325, 366
Roth, William F., Jr. 625
Rotter, Julian B. 380, 409
Rouleau, Marcel 14-16
Rousseau, Denise M. 118, 122
Rowan, Brian 68, 81
Rubin, Irwin M. 581
Ruble, Thomas L. 471, 491
Ruller, Sally Riggs 452
Runyon, Damon 202
Rusbult, Caryl 192-193, 207
Russell, Marcia 537, 580
Ryan, Ellen 219-220, 324
Ryan, Richard M. 297
Rybacki, Irene 28

S

Saaty, Thomas 453
Saffo, Paul 365
Sagan, Carl 464
Salancik, Gerald R. 27, 41, 406, 459, 491
Salmon, Raoul 678, 681, 684
Sandelands, Lance E. 420, 451
Sanders, Geert 124
Sanford, Lynne 349, 366
Santalainen, Timo 624
Sanzgiri, Jyotsna 590-591, 623
Saraph, Jayant V. 625
Sargent, Alice G. 334, 366, 473, 491
Sathe, Vijay 98, 101-102, 123-124
Saturn Company 509-510
Saxton, Mary J. 124
Scandura, Terri A. 381, 407
Scarr, Sandra 208

Schaubroeck, John 537
Scheele, Adele 437, 451
Schein, Edgar 27, 86-87, 93, 96, 101, 105-106, 123-124, 372, 409, 544, 581-582
Schermerhorn, John, R., Jr. 391, 409
Schmidt, Frank L. 409, 656, 658, 673
Schmidt, Rick 497
Schmidt, Warren H. 625
Schminke, Marshall 330, 365
Schmitt, Neal W. 650, 673
Schneck, Rodney E. 490
Schreuder, Willem 239, 242
Schriesheim, Chester A. 385, 406, 410
Schroeder, Roger G. 625
Schurman, Donald P. 606, 623
Schwartz, Richard D. 673
Schwartz, Shalom 88, 124
Scientists for Wise Use 486
Sears 19
Sechrest, Lee 673
Segal, Nancy L. 177, 205-206, 208
Sekaran, Uma 650, 673
Semco S/A 83
Semeonoff, Boris 206
Semler, Ricardo 83, 641, 673
Senge, Peter M. 612, 623
Serpa, R. 124
Shaffer, David R. 188, 207
Shakespeare, William 6, 282
Shakleton, Vivian 171, 185, 207
Share the Rock 486
Shaw, Marvin E. 256, 285
Sheats, Paul 342-343, 364
Sheehy, Gail 582
Sheffield, Dianna T. 625
Shell Canada 434-435
Shenkar, Oded 91-92, 123
Shepard, Herbert A. 593, 623
Shepperd, James A. 333, 366
Sheridan, John E. 93, 124
Sherman, Stratford 642, 673
Shichman, Shula 94, 102, 122
Shin, Yoo Keun 132, 159
Shultz, Clifford J., II 183, 207
Sibbet, David 336, 338-339, 364-365, 367
Sibson, David 497
Siegel, Jane 254, 285
Siehl, Caren 124
Sime, Wesley E. 537
Simon, Herbert A. 26, 416, 420, 451
Simon Fraser University 367, 583, 625
Simonson, Hamar 437, 451
Simpson, D. Dwayne 517, 538
Sims, David B.P. 326
Sims, Henry P., Jr. 232, 243, 395-396, 408
Sinclair, Amanda 367
Singh, Jitendra 21, 41
Sirchio, Jeannie 28
Sitkin, Sim B. 123, 258, 262, 285

Slaughter, Jane 510, 538
Slevin, Dennis P. 317, 325
Slim, Field Marshal 375
Slocum, John W., Jr. 211, 243, 613
Small, Michael W. 452
Smircich, Linda 124, 250, 285, 410, 674-675
Smith, Anthony 394, 409
Smith, Douglas K. 328, 365, 367
Smith, Dugal 306
Smith, Frederick W., Jr. 693-695, 699, 702
Smith, Patricia C. 189, 207
Smith, Peter B. 548, 581, 648, 673
Smith, Scott 551, 580
Snow, Charles C. 65, 81, 83
Solomon, Charlene Marmer 416, 451, 601, 624
Sommer, Steven M. 674
Sonnenfeld, Jeffrey A. 545-547, 581
Sony Corporation 14, 38-39, 120, 608
Sophia University 422, 449
Sorell, Gwendolyn T. 453
Sotoodeh, Yass 539
Souder, William E. 436, 451
Southam Newspapers 487
Southerst, John 563, 581
Spangler, William D. 208, 386, 408
Spencer, Gay 469, 491
Spokane, Arnold R. 554, 581
Stagg, Malcolm 15
Stalker, George 27, 53, 81
Stanford University 175, 492
Starbuck, William H. 446
State University of New York 386, 388
Statistics Canada 508
Staw, Barry M. 20, 40, 102, 123, 148, 158, 406, 419-420, 427-429, 437, 440, 449, 451-452
Stayer, Ralph 226, 244
Steel, Robert P. 325, 599, 601, 607-608, 624
Steel Company of Canada (Stelco) 19
Steelcase Canada Limited 606
Steers, Richard M. 23, 40, 61, 81, 132, 159, 207
Stein, Barry A. 615, 623
Steinfield, Charles 286
Stephens, Carroll 453
Stepina, Lee P. 159
Steubing, Karla K. 325, 366
Stewart, Thomas A. 644, 675
Stogdill, Ralph M. 26, 376, 409
Stone, Eugene F. 650, 673
Stone, Philip J. 159
Stoner, James A.F. 424, 451
Storrs, Constance 40
Strachey, James 205
Strategic Management Group Inc. 286, 453
Strati, Antonio 237, 244

Strauss, Norman 104, 124
Stroh, Linda K. 549, 581
Stross, Randall E. 583
Strube, Michael J. 379, 409
Stubbart, Charles 446
Stuebing, Karla K. 325
Stupak, Ronald J. 334, 366, 473, 491
St. Michael's Hospital, Toronto 606
Sugimoto, Etsu Inagaki 609, 624
Sun Microsystems 496-497
Sun Tzu 401, 404-405, 409
Sunday Times of London England 651
Sundstrom, Eric 330, 344, 348, 366
Supreme Court of the United States 367
Sutcliffe, Kathleen M. 262, 285
Sutton, Nicola 446
Suzor, Johnny 202
Swiss Corporation for Microelectronics
    and Watchmaking (SMH) 65
Sypher, Beverly Davenport 286, 446
Szwajkowski, Eugene W. 452
Szymanski, Kate 333, 365
S.R. Gent (Canada) Inc. 551

T

Taguchi, Genichi 608, 625
Tainio, Risto 624
Tancred, Peta 675
Tandy 120, 161
Tannen, Deborah 286
Tanner, Lucretia Dewey 205
Taturo, Dr. 621
Taylor, Donald W. 438, 451
Taylor, Frederick W. 24, 26, 41, 608
Taylor, William 65, 82
T. Eaton Company 11, 100
Tellegen, Auke 177, 205, 208
Terpstra, Robert H. 208
Tesser, Abraham 188, 207
Tetrick, Lois E. 159
Thayer, Paul W. 134, 158
The Body Shop Canada 333, 557
The Body Shop International 582, 640, 671
Théorêt, André 426, 451
Thierry, Henk 324
Thomas, Alan Berkeley 373, 409
Thomas, Kenneth W. 469-471, 491-492
Thomas Cook Travel 19
Thompson, Donna E. 326
Thompson, James D. 61-62, 82
Thompson, Michael P. 289, 325
Thorne, Paul 348, 350, 366
Thorpe, Richard 588, 623
3M 121
Thurstone, Louis L. 175, 207
Tiegs, Robert B. 159
Tiger International, Inc. 695
Tillett, Anthony D. 25, 41
Tilley, Alex 388

Tilley, Susan 388
Tjosvold, Dean W. 367, 421, 452, 469, 492
Tjosvold, Mary M. 367
TNT 696
Todor, William D. 245
Tokugawa 90
Toman, Walter 187, 207
Toronto Blue Jays Baseball Club 19
Toronto Fire Department 173
Tosi, Henry L., Jr. 245
Townley, Barbara 674
Toyota 111
Tracey, J. Bruce 466-467, 492
Transport and General Worker's Union 626-628
Traub, Virginia 446
Trendsitions 686
Trevino, Linda Klebe 432, 452
Trice, Harrison M. 99-100, 122
Trist, Eric L. 26, 146, 159, 368
Trotter, Robert J. 178, 207
Trudeau, Pierre Elliot 374
Trudel, Cindy 499
Tubbs, Mark E. 301, 325
Tucker, David 21, 41
Tuckman, Bruce W. 335, 337, 366
Tufte, Edward R. 650, 673
Tung, Rosalie 401, 583
Turkheimer, Eric 208
Turner, Christopher 82
Tushman, Michael L. 386-387, 408, 586, 623
Tversky, Amos 418, 449-450
Twain, Mark 617
Tzu, Sun 401, 404-405, 409

U

Uhl-Bien, M. 381, 407
Ulrich's Periodicals Directory 36
Ungson, Gerardo R. 132, 159
Unilever 676
Unisys 120
United Airlines 116
United Auto Worker's Union 510
United Kingdom 53
United Nations 486
United Parcel Service 694, 696
United States Air Force 281, 331
United States Marine Corps 111
United States Navy 223
United States Postal Service 694, 696
United States Securities and Exchange
    Commission (SEC) 11
United Technologies 116
United Way 138
University of Alberta 63, 107, 245, 687
University of Alberta Hospital 606
University of Aston 60
University of British Columbia 124, 410

University of California 30
University of Colorado 676
University of Connecticut 118
University of Glasgow 340
University of Iowa 376
University of Lyon 677
University of Melbourne 106
University of Michigan 376, 378
University of Minnesota 187
University of Montreal 587
University of Ottawa 508
University of Paris 24
University of Pennsylvania 575
University of Prince Edward Island 333
University of Southern California 307
University of Texas 253
University of Toronto 140, 214, 305, 368, 380, 582
University of Tulsa 277
University of Victoria 685
University of Waterloo 508
University of Western Ontario 30, 334, 386, 410, 508, 626
Ury, William 475, 490
USS Theodore Roosevelt 608
Utne Reader 282

V

Vaill, Peter B. 326
Valachich, Joseph S. 450, 453
Valins, Stuart 244
Vallender, Bob 551
Van Avermaet, E. 365
Van de Ven, Andrew H. 61-62, 82, 449
Van Fleet, David D. 333, 364, 381, 409
Van Maanen, John 109-110, 124
Van Seters, David A. 221, 243, 371, 409-410, 614, 624
Van Velsor, Ellen 581
Van Zanten, Jacob Louis Veldhuyzen 239, 241-242
Vancouver Sun, The 486
Vancouver Symphony Orchestra 22
Vandenbosch, Betty 494
Vansickle, Timothy R. 554, 581
Varadarajan, P. Rajan 83
Varela, Ann 674
Vaughan, Diane 446
Vecchio, Robert P. 379, 409
Victor, Bart 434, 452-453
Victory Over Statistics 674
Vlachoutsicos, Charalambos 674
Vogel, Douglas R. 453
Volango, Mary 28
Volet, Jean-Pierre 676, 678-680, 683-684
Volkswagen AG 127-128
Von Glinow, Mary Ann 548-549, 580
Von Oech, Roger 453
Vroom, Victor H. 27, 298, 325, 378, 409, 439, 450, 452

W

Waldman, David A. 625
Walkom, Thomas 345, 366
Wall, Toby D. 363, 365, 368
Wall Street Journal, The 31, 345, 373
Walmsley, Ann 137, 159
Walton, Anna Elise 588, 622
Walton, Thomas 159
Warner, Tim 606, 624
Warns, George W. 239
Warshaw, Michael 260, 285
Wasserman, Stanley 68
Waterman, Alan S. 430, 433, 452
Waterman, Robert 27, 384, 409
Watkins, Peter 626-627
Watson, Tom J., Jr. 307, 325
Watson, Warren E. 334, 366
Wayne McKay & Associates 306
Webb, Eugene J. 669, 675
Weber, Max 26, 56, 63, 70, 82, 384, 409
Wechsler 175
Wedley, William C. 414, 452
Weedon, Chris 665, 673
Weekley, Jerr A. 539
Weick, Karl E. 75, 81, 214, 222-224,
    234, 242, 244-245, 250, 285-286,
    326, 433, 452, 586, 624
Weinberg, Martha Wagner 388, 406
Weinberg, Richard A. 170, 175, 177,
    207-208
Weinberg, Robert 35
Weiner, Bernard 217, 244
Weiss, David J. 190, 207
Weiss, Stephen E. 491
Welsh, Dianne H.B. 674
Welstead, Susan 282, 285

Wentling, Rose Mary 551, 581
West, John 704
Western Canada Wilderness Committee
    484, 489
Western Electric Company 41
Whinston, Andrew B. 435, 450
Whitbread, Samuel 626
Whitbread and Company 626, 631
Whitbread Merseyside 612, 626-627,
    632-633
Whitbread West Pennines 626, 634
White, Ralph K. 26, 376, 408
White, Randall P. 581
Whiting, Beatrice Blyth 179, 207-208
Whiting, John W.M. 179, 207
Whitney, Amasa 130
Whyte, Glen 419, 452
Whyte, William Foote 588, 591, 624
Wieting, Gretchen K. 252, 254, 284
Wilcox, Kimerly J. 208
Wilkins, A.L. 101, 124
Williamson, Robert 642, 673
Wills, Gordon 25, 41
Wilsher, Peter 514, 538
Wilson, Ronald S. 208
Winnipeg Jets 111
Witzling, Lawrence P. 650, 673
Wong, S.P. 674
Wood, Bob 551
Woodiwiss, Anthony 674
Woodman, Richard W. 211, 243, 623
Woodward, Joan 27, 60, 82
Woronoff, Jon 625
Woycke, James 386, 408
Wrege, Charles D. 41
Wright, Peter 83

X

Xerox 495-496

Y

Yaginuma, Mikie 344, 367
Yale University 337, 419, 461, 693
Yashica Camera Company 120
Yeo, Bill 494-495
Yetton, Philip W. 27, 332, 367, 378,
    409
YMCA 199
York University 9, 555, 624, 659
Yoshida, Koji 16
Young, Amy Oakes 243, 245, 367
Young, Ed 175, 207
Yukikatsu, Aida 14-16
Yukl, Gary A. 374, 378-381, 388-389,
    409, 466-467, 492
Yunker, Gary 28, 41
YWCA 199

Z

Zakrajsek, Todd 72, 82
Zaleznik, Abraham 465, 492
Zanna, Mark 88, 124
Zanzi, Alberto 83
Zeithaml, Valarie A. 622
Ziegler, Robert W. 436, 451
Zimbardo, Philip G. 667, 673
Zimmerman, Mark 582

A

Abilene paradox 423, 441
achievement motivation theory 294-295
active noise control 136
actor-observer effect 218
adhocracy 57
adult development 543
affect 189
age 59-60, 174
ageism 219-220
agile production 642
agricultural revolution 126
AIDS 282, 539, 590, 668
air quality 136
alliance game 460
all-salaried teams 313
alternative hypothesis 652
anti-leadership 372
anti-positivism 659-660
approach-approach conflict 512
approach-avoidance conflict 512
arbitrator 475
Argentina 253
argument 250, 286
Art of War 401, 404
assertiveness 474
assessment centers 555
Aston studies 27, 60
attitudes 188
    components 189
    ego defensive 188
    social-adjustive 188
    value-expressive 188, 271
attribution 216-218, 230-231
Australia 95, 214, 253-254, 592
autocratic leadership 376
autonomy 140
avoidance-avoidance conflict 512

B

baby boom 24, 638
Bathsheba syndrome 393
behaviorally anchored rating scales
    (BARS) 228
behavioural checklist 227
behavioural intentions 300
Belgium 293, 592
beliefs 101, 188
Bengal 253
Big Five theory of personality 186
biological bases of human behaviour 208
biological clock 543
board of directors 13

body clock 133
bottom line 12
boundaryless company 641
bounded rationality 416
brain 178
brainstorming 436, 438
Brazil 253, 592
broker role 290
Bulgaria 253
bureaucracy
    control 462
    ideal type 56
    machine 56
    professional 55, 57
    red tape 56
    theory 26
burnout 518, 534
business process re-engineering 604
butterfly effect 586

C

cafeteria-style fringe benefits 311
career 542
    assessment 566
    choice 552
    definitions 542
    development 544, 555
    goals 557
    interest inventory 581
    management 549, 555, 582
    movement 544
    planning 598
    stages 544
    systems 545-547
    types 553
carpal tunnel syndrome 137
causality 222, 654
centralization 53, 55, 73
CEO compensation 233, 245
ceremonies 100
Challenger space shuttle 443, 446
change
    agents 593
    champion 609
    cube 599-600
    developmental 588
    evolutionary 587
    incremental 586, 588
    leadership of 386-387
    leverage 586
    model 611
    proactive 586
    quantum 586

    reactive 586
    revolutionary 587
    transformational 586-587
chaos theory 586
charismatic leadership 315, 384, 386-
    387, 410, 582
clan control 462
classical conditioning 304
clerical support staff 55
coaching 379
coacting group 328
coalition 459, 466
cognitive 298, 305
cognitive dissonance 189, 192
cognitive evaluation theory 294, 297
cognitive resource theory 375
cohesion 344
collective mind 223
collectivist-democratic organizational
    form 94
committees 350
common sense 33-35
communication
    barriers 270
    cross-cultural 117-118, 277, 286,
        477, 582
    filtering 257
    influences 255
    media 258, 261-263
    meta-message 258
    model 249
    networks 256
    nonverbal 252
    one-way 262
    perspectives 248
    two-way 249
    verbal 250-251
competing values model 288-289
competing values model of effectiveness
    19-20
competitive advantage 27, 67
competitiveness, time-based 644
complex environment 62
complexity 51, 55, 73, 586
    horizontal 51
    vertical 51
compressed work weeks 133
computers, reactions to 71-72
conceptual ruts 420, 587
conditioning, classical 304
conditioning, operant 304
conflict 469
    between groups 509-510
    definition 456

handling methods 470
handling style 471, 479
mediation 475
reduction mechanisms 472, 474
role 342, 352
structural 472
work-family 507
connection power 457
consideration leadership 376
construct 293
constructive controversy 421
contingency theory 27, 372, 379
continuous improvement process
(CIP) 605
continuous process technology 60
Continuous Quality Improvement
(CQI) 606
contrast in perception 213
coordination of organizational structure 58
coordinator role 288
corporate culture 27
correlation 654
cover letter 267-268
creativity 194-198, 436, 453
crisis
age thirty 543
midlife 543
critical incidents 228
critical theory 82, 662, 677
culture
and teams 367
attitudes 101
audit 101
beliefs 101
creation 94
cross-culture 582
management 117-118, 120-121
phases 108
skills 108, 546
definition 86
development 102
differences 106
dimensions 90-91
diversity 550
exchange 97
history 96
iceberg 87
identity 101
ideology 101
inventory 118
language 95, 99
legends and models 95, 99
manifestations 98
measurement 118, 124
membership 97
merger 105-107
native 88
of multinationals 107
organizational 27
growth stage 105
leadership of 95, 125

profiles 101, 103
sense of oneness 97
strength 106
talk 99
universals 88
values 101
culture shock cycle 561
customer service teams 332

D
data, collection methods 653
decentralization, horizontal 53
decision heuristic 416
decision making 26
attribute listing 436
biases 417
brainstorming 436, 438
checklists 436
collective notebook 436
consensus mapping 439
creativity 194-198, 436, 453
descriptive 418
Edisonian 436
errors 418-419, 421, 423
ethics 427
evaluation apprehension 438
framing 418
free association 436
group consensus 439
group versus individual 424
improving 434
irrational 416
Japan 422-423
morphological analysis 436
muddling through 425
nonrational 416
normative 418
phases of organizational 426
process losses 332-33
production blocking in groups 438
rational model 414-415
reverse brainstorming 436
satisficing 416
scientific method 436
stepladder technique 452
synectics 436
value engineering 436
deconstruction 661
delegating 379
Delphi technique 438
democratic leadership 376
demographics 333, 638
Denmark 293, 307, 592
deontological philosophies 427
departmentation 49
dependent variable 6, 646
depersonalization 518
descriptive essay 227
descriptive statistics 652
deterministic 659

developmental change 588
differentiation 64
dimensions of physical performance 174
directing 379
director role 290
discrimination 548
distress 504
diversity in the workplace 395, 425,
550-551, 638
diversity of group membership 425
division of work
horizontal 44
vertical 44
divisionalized form 57
dominant coalition 459
downsizing 51, 131
dress for success 557
dual-career couple 559
dynamic environment 63

E
economies of scope 642
Edwards Personal Preference Schedule
552, 582
effect size 654
effectiveness models
competing values 19-20
fault-driven 20, 22
high performing system 20,22
human relations 19-20
internal process 19-20
legitimate organization 20-21
rational goal 19-20
strategic constituencies 20-21
effort, in expectancy theory 298
ego 180
egoism 427
electronic mail 258, 641
e-mail (see electronic mail)
emoticons 254
empire building game 460
employee assistance plan 521
empowerment 52, 410, 457
enactment 66, 245, 250
England 253
environment 17-18, 62-64
analyzability 64
complex 62
dynamic 63
effect on organizations 27
enacting 66
munificent 23
simple 62
static 63
environmentalism 29
epistemology 659
equifinality 19, 347
equity, hiring 173
equity theory 27, 294, 297, 326
ERG theory 296

ergonomics 134
error, types I and II 654-656
escalation of commitment 419, 424, 428-429, 437, 440
ethics
    code of conduct 435, 440
    cognitive-developmental approach 431
    corporate climate 434, 453
    deontological philosophies 427
    dilemmas 443
    egoism 427
    in leadership 387, 393
    in organizations 452
    science 394, 651, 666
    taxonomic approach 430
    teleological philosophies 427
    theory of justice 427
    theory of rights 427
    utilitarianism 427
eustress 504
evaluation apprehension 438
evolutionary change 587
excellent organizations 27
exit 518
expatriate ghetto 562
expectancy 298
expectancy effects 221
expectancy model of attributions 220
expectancy theory 294, 298, 326
expectations, marriage and career 570
Experience is the Best Teacher 9, 63, 93, 177, 333, 419, 461, 508, 555, 615, 662
expert model of information processing 416
expert systems 435
extinction 305

F

face, concept of 583
facial expressions 252
facilitator role 290, 475
fads, management 608
failure, fear of 527
familiarity in perception 213
family firms 12, 465
fatigue in communication 270
feedback 140, 249
feelings 21, 97, 101, 180, 188, 222
feminism 661, 675
Fiedler's contingency theory 379
fight or flight 514
figure-ground principle 216
Finland 592
fit 27, 29
    organization structure and environment 64, 82
    technology and structure 27, 60
fixed interval schedule 305

fixed ratio schedule 305
flexiplace 128
flextime 131
folktale 99, 250
folly of rewarding A while hoping for B 308
force field analysis 599, 616
forced distribution 227
formalization 53, 55, 73
formica parachute 274
framing in decision making 418
France 132, 253, 293, 468, 592, 647
freestanding group 328
free-riding 333
fundamental attribution error 218

G

g factor of intelligence 176
gaijin 564
gainsharing 604
garbage can model of organizational decision making 425
gender 179
General Agreement on Tariffs and Trade (GATT) 640
genes 170
Germany 132, 219, 293, 548, 592, 615
gestures 100, 252
glass ceiling 548, 558, 582
globalization 9, 14-16, 18
goal setting 27, 294, 301-302, 317, 326
goals, time orientation 64
going native 562
golden parachute 233
Graduate Management Admissions Test (GMAT) 176
grapevine 258
graveyard shift 132-133
Great Britain 132, 293, 592
Greece 253, 592
grid organization development 594, 599
group 26
    attitude polarization 424
    context 329
    demographics 333
    design 331
    effectiveness 329
    external integration 346
    life span 334
    management 347
    membership 334
    norms 339, 355
    performance 329
    shift of opinion 424
    size 332
    stages of development 335-337
    structure 332
    types 328, 332
group attitude scale 344, 353

groupthink 350, 421, 452
groupware 438
growth need strength 141, 159

H

habitual behaviour in groups 367
halo effect 222
handshaking 101, 252, 340-342
Hawthorne effect 28
heedful interrelating 223
heredity 170, 513
heterogeneity in group membership 334
heuristic 416
high performance cycle 303
high performing system model of effectiveness 20, 22
Holland 253
Holland's model of career types 553-554, 581
Hong Kong 208, 253, 592
hours worked 130, 132
human nature 659
human relations theory 26
human resources theory 27
human service teams 332
humanistic theory 183
hypothesis 6, 646

I

Icarus paradox 587
id 180
ideal type bureaucracy 56
idiographic 659
image theory 294, 300, 418
implicit theory of leadership 389
impression management 216
in-box gridlock 270
improved nominal group technique (INGT) 438-439
incentive plans 326, 604
incremental change 586
independent variable 6, 643
India 179, 551, 592
individual differences 170
    biological 170, 208
    psychological 179
    race 170
    sex 171
industrial revolution 126, 130
inferential statistics 654
infobahn 641
information
    age 14
    filtering 257
    overload 257, 270
    power 457
    revolution 127
    technology 29, 51-52, 314, 641
inhwa 334

initiating structure 376
innovator role 290
institutional theory 68
instrument, research 652
instrumentality 298
integrated model of task design 147-149
integrating home and foreign cultures 562
integration 64
intelligence
    general 175
    quotient 175
    tests 175
intensity in perception 213
intensive technology 61-62
intentions 300
intergroup relationships 347
internal process model of effectiveness 19-20
international
    assignment 546, 561, 582
    operations 546
    orientation 108, 546
        phases 108
interpretive-symbolic perspective of organizational communication 248
interrole conflict 344
interviewing 109, 265, 275-276, 286, 556
IQ (intelligence quotient) 175
Iran 253
Ireland 592
irrational decision making 416
ISO 9000 608
ISO 9001 625
Israel 592
Italy 67, 253, 293, 468, 592

J

Japan 38-39, 89-90, 132, 138, 179, 191, 252-253, 297, 307, 334-335, 344-345, 390-391, 422, 477, 511, 548, 563-565, 592, 606, 609, 615, 647
    competitiveness 68, 92-93, 609, 615
    general business etiquette 565
    lifetime employment 548
    management style 14-16, 38-39, 120-121, 150
    stress 511
jargon 255, 274, 281-283
job
    conditions 135
    content 134
    description 144
    design 26
        approaches 133-134
        biological 133-137
        engineering 133-134
        ergonomics 133-134
        horizontal loading 137

job characteristics model 139-143, 150
    psychological 133, 137-144
    questionnaire 151-152
    vertical loading 137
    dimensions 139-141
    dissatisfaction responses 193
    enlargement 137
    enrichment 137, 150
    evaluation 310
    interview 109, 265, 275-276, 286, 556
    relationships 137
    rotation 138
    safety 212
    satisfaction 190, 193
    sharing 131
job characteristics model 139-143, 150
job control 532
job descriptive index (JDI) 189
job diagnostic survey 143
journals 29-30

K

kaigi 423
kaizen 625
Kenya 179
knowledge
    society 41
    sources 30-31
Korea 131-132, 297, 334, 548
Kuder Preference Record 552

L

laissez-faire leadership 376
large batch technology 60
lateral career movement 544
Law School Admissions Test (LSAT) 176
layoff 511
leader
    behaviour 376
    emergence 374, 410
    perception 388
    prototype 389
    succession 395, 411
    traits 374
leadership
    administrator versus 370, 397
    definition 370
    eastern views 400, 404
    effectiveness 386
    ethics 387, 394, 410
    grid 377
    history of thought about 370
    implicit theory 389
    manager versus 370, 397
    men and women 392, 410, 473, 492
    of diversity 395, 550-551

of self 396
    of self-managed groups 395
    performance beyond expectations 381
    psychoanalytic principles of 410
    romance of 373
    substitutes 372
    transactional 380
    transformational 373, 380
leader-member exchange theory (LMX) 381
learning in perception 214
learning organization 612
legend 95, 99, 250
legitimacy model of effectiveness 20-21
level of significance 654
levels of culture 87
liability of newness 22
life, work and home 506
life planning 598
life stages 543
life-cycle theory of leadership 378
lighting on the job 35
Likert system 4 601-604
line 47
listening, effective 269, 272, 476
long-linked technology 61-62
loyalty
    team 346
    to organization 518
LPC 379

M

Mach V Attitude Inventory 183
Machiavellianism 183-184
machine bureaucracy 56
maintenance function leadership 376
management
    authority 22, 29, 44, 57-58
    by objectives (MBO) 301, 592
    by wandering around 250
    hard framework 614
    job redesign 143
    motivation 27, 292, 306, 316-317
    soft cycle 614
    worker relationships 381
managerial
    roles 288
    work 291
managership versus leadership 370
manufacturing, importance 38
maquiladora 16, 41
market control 462
marriage 504, 570
Maslow's hierarchy 294, 326
mass production technology 60
matrix organization 57
McClelland's theory of needs 295
mean 652
measurement 652
mechanistic organizations 53, 55

mechanistic perspective of organizational communication 248
media in communication 258
mediating technology 61
mediator variable 303
Medical College Admissions Test (MCAT) 176
memory 230
mentor, stages in relationship 560
mentor 180, 290, 555, 559
merger of cultures 105-107
meta-analysis 656
meta-message 258
methodology 659
Mexico 16, 41, 44, 179, 312-313, 562, 592
middle management 51, 52, 54, 313, 511, 604, 641
Minnesota Satisfaction Questionnaire (MSQ) 189-190
Minnesota Twin Study 177, 187, 208
mission statement 601
MMPI (Minnesota Multiphasic Personality Inventory) 184
mode 652
modeling 309
moderator variable 141, 159, 303, 505, 520, 646
modernism 658
monitor role 288
moral development stages 432
motion in perception 213
motivating potential score (MPS) 143
motivation 292, 306
motivation in perception 214
motivator-hygiene theory 139
muddling through in decision making 425
multicultural
    diversity 425, 550
    management 551
multimethod job design questionnaire 144-145
multinational corporations 107
multiple role sender conflict 342, 507
Myers-Briggs Type Indicator (MBTI) 180
myth 99, 250

N

NAFTA (North American Free Trade Agreement) 16, 41, 640
narration 250, 286
nature versus nurture 170, 173, 208
need for achievement 208
negative reinforcement 307
neglect 518
negotiation 475, 477, 492
nemawashi 423

Netherlands 293, 592
neuro-linguistic programming 264
no, art of saying 465
nominal group decision method 438
nominalism 661
nomological net 648
nomothetic 661
nonrational decision making 416
non-verbal communication 252-254
non-verbal communication cues 252
non-programmed decisions 415
norm 339
norm violation 339, 510
Norway 592
novel stimuli in perception 213
null hypothesis 651

O

obstructionism 464
OD 588
    flavour-of-the-month phenomenon 608
    interventions 591, 594-595
office design 159, 255
office perception 236-237
Ohio State leadership studies 26
ontology 659
open system model of effectiveness 19-20
open systems theory 16, 27
operant conditioning 304
organic organizations 53, 55
organization
    chart 44
    commitment questionnaire 189
    control forms 462
    culture 86
    decision making 425, 433, 440
    definition 10
    development (OD) 588
        cultural relativity 592, 622
        definition 588
        values 592
    effectiveness models 19-21
    organization environment 62-64
    organization environment components 64
    growth 23, 105
    learning 612
    life cycle 22-23
    ownership 10-11
    ownership breadth 11
    principals and agents 13
    products 13
    purpose 12
    retreat 601
    romances 460
    size 14, 59-60
    socialization 108-112
    stakeholders 21

stories 99-100, 251
structure 26, 44, 63
structure coordination 58
technology 59-60
Type A 93
Type J 93
Type Z 93
Organizational Commitment Questionnaire 189
outsourcing 642
outward bound 349, 594
Overboard cartoon 7, 44, 110, 135, 174, 212, 269, 302, 339, 390, 416, 477, 512, 544, 598, 665
overpromotion 511

P

paired comparison 224
Pakistan 592
paradigm 661, 671
participation 378
path-goal theory 380
pay
    inequity 297
    performance 233
    secrecy 297
People's Republic of China 16, 208, 253, 295-296, 333, 335, 583
perception 210
perceptual
    causality error 222
    defense 219
    learning 214
    motivation 214
    organization 215
        closure 216
        continuity 215
        proximity 215
        similarity 215
    overload 213
    process 211
    selection factors 213
performance 223
    appraisal interview 224
    appraisal methods 224
    evaluation 223, 229
    evaluation errors 228
performance function leadership 376
performing groups 332
personality 179
    and stress 513
    assessment 187
    factors 186
    genetic effects 186
    traits 183
    types 181
person-role conflict 342
persuasive argumentation theory 424
Peru 253
phases of group development 337

phases of organizational decision making 426
phenomenological world 384
Philippine Islands 179, 186
physical characteristics 172
physical environment stressors 509
physical performance dimensions 174
places of work 128
point method of job evaluation 311
politics 463
    definition 456
    in performance evaluation 231-232
    survival skills 468, 492
    typology of behaviour 463
population ecology model 22
Porter-Lawler model 294, 300
positivism 659-660
post-capitalist society 41
post-industrial society 14, 38
postmodernism 658-659, 674
poststructuralism 661
postures 252
power 492
    bases of 456-457
    definition 456
    games 459-460
    influence tactics 466-467
    of organizational subunits 459
    of statistical tests 657, 659
    struggle 459
primacy 229
principles of management 26
proactive change 586
process change 597
process consultation 594
process losses in group decision making 332-333
producer role 290
production blocking 438
production core 55
production teams 332
professional bureaucracy 55, 57
professional support groups 332
profit sharing 225, 313, 604
programmed decisions 415
project teams 350
projection 222, 229
promotion system 508
propinquity 344
proxemics 252
proxies, share voting 13
proximity 215
proxy fight 13
psycholanalytic theory of personality 180
psychological perspective of organizational communication 248
psychological types 181
public speaking 266
punctuated equilibrium 337
punishment 307
Pygmalion effect 383-384, 410

Q
quality
    circles 599
    measurement 625
    of work life 150
quantum change 586

R
race 170
radial career movement 544
ranking method of performance appraisal 224
rational goal model of effectiveness 19-20
reactive change 586
realism 659
realistic job preview 108, 519
reality, nature of 210
recency 229
red tape, bureaucratic 56
reentry shock 563
reference group 328
reinforcement
    schedules 305
    theory 305
relationship oriented leadership 376
reliability 652
repetition in perception 213
repetitive stress disorders 137
research process stages 652
resource dependence theory 27
responding in communication 269
responses to stress 514
resume 265, 278
retreat, organizational 601
revolutionary change 587
revolutions in the nature of work 126
reward systems 309-310, 508
rewards 311
ringi-sho 423
risky shift in group decision making 424
rites 100
rituals 100
role 288, 342, 512
    ambiguity 344, 352
    conflict 342, 352, 507
    in group 343
    modeling 309
    overload 512
    types of managerial 288
role expectations conflict 342, 507
romance of leadership 373
romances, organizational 460-461
romanticism 658
rumour 258
Russia 452, 674

S
s factor of intelligence 176
saga 99, 250

sample size 652
satiation 300
satisfaction, affective component 189
satisficing 416
scapegoating 468
schedules of reinforcement 305
science ethics 394, 651, 666
scientific management 26
scientific method 436
script 340, 368, 420
selective listening 270
self-efficacy 303, 521, 562
self-fulfilling prophecy (SFP) 221, 381-384, 410
self-leadership 396
self-managed groups 395, 601
self-motivation 320
self-regulation 303
self-reinforcement 294, 309
self-serving bias 218
sensemaking in organizations 222-223
sensory overload 210
sex 171
sex, and leadership 392
sex discrimination 173, 180, 342, 344, 549
sexist language 286
sexual harassment 344, 510-511
shaping 304
sick building syndrome 136
significance level 656
similarity in perceptual organization 215
simple environment 62
simple structure 55
situational leadership theory 378
skill-based pay 313
slang 281-283
sleep loss 514
small batch technology 60
small wins 326
social
    comparison 424
    construction of reality 211, 214-215
    expressivity 199
    group 328
    learning 309
    loafing 333
    responsibility 640
Social Readjustment Rating Scale 514-515
socialization
    intensity 112, 115-116
    of children 208
    phases 108
    strategies 109-111
societal culture 87
socio-technical systems theory 26, 145-147, 150, 368
source credibility 213, 271
Spain 253
span of control 51

specialization 47
sponsorship game 459
staff 47
stages of group development 335
stages of life 542-543
stakeholders 21
standard deviation 652
Stanford-Binet IQ test 175
Star Trek 31
statecraft 388
static environment 63
statistics
    descriptive 652
    inferential 654
status 270, 344
stereotyping 219, 228, 245, 367
stonewalling 471
stories in organizations 99-100, 251
story 99-100
storytelling 99-100, 251
strain 512
strategic business units 57
strategic constituencies model of effec-
    tiveness 20-21
strategic management 27
strategy
    analyzer 66
    and structure 64
    cost leadership 66
    defender 65
    differentiation 66
    focus 66
    measures 83
    prospector 66
    reactor 65
stratified systems theory 176-177
stress
    behavioural responses 516
    definition 504
    management 519
    measurement 514, 539
    model 505, 539
    physiological responses 514
    points 514-515
    psychological responses 514, 516
    stressors 505
    threshold 525
Strong Vocational Interest Inventory 552
structuration 250
structure
    divisionalized form 55, 57
    measures 51, 73-75, 83
    simple 46
    types 54-56
subcultures 102, 124
subenvironment 64
    market 64
    scientific 64
    technical 64
substance abuse 517, 520, 535
subunit power 459

success 557
    dressing for 557
    fear of 527
succession plan 395
superego 180
superordinate goal 472
supervisory problems 617
supporting 379
survey feedback 599
swatch watch 65
Sweden 293, 592
Switzerland 65, 293, 592
synectics 436
System of Interactive Guidance and
    Information 582
systems theory of organizations 16
systems-interaction perspective of
    organizational communication 248

T

tabula rasa 170
task change 597
task experience 334
task force 332
task oriented leadership 376
task skills 334
team 328
    building 594, 601
    ideology 367
    performance model 336, 338
technical support staff 55
technology 60, 597
    continuous process 60
    intensive 61-62
    intensive team 61-62
    large batch 60
    long-linked 61-62
    mass production 60
    mediating 61
    small batch 60
    technological imperative 60
telecommuting 128, 159
teleconferencing 260
teleological philosophies 427
t-group 594, 598, 601
Thailand 253, 592
thematic apperception test (TAT) 187,
    208
theory 6, 643
    boundary conditions 646
    building 664
    cross-cultural 647-649
    interesting 645
    J (also called Type J organization)
        93, 149, 191
    of justice 427
    of rights 427
    testing 647
    validity 649
    X and Y 183, 377, 649

threat-rigidity effect 420
time 91, 114
    management 522-524
    motion study 25
    pressure in communication
        270
token reinforcement plan 306
top management 332
total quality control, see TQM
total quality management 27, 63, 604,
    624
TQM 604
    philosophy 607
    steps 610
trait 183
trait scales 184
transactional leadership 380
transformational change 586
transformational leadership 373,
    300
triangulation 647
triune brain 188
Turkey 253
turnover 334, 517
twins, identical 177, 186-187
Type A organization 93
Type A/B behaviour pattern 513
Type J organization 93
Type Z organization 93
types I and II errors 654-656
types of group 328

U

uchi 89
uchi-awase 423
underpromotion 511
unintended consequences 310
United Kingdom 514
unleader 395
unobtrusive measures 667
utilitarianism 427

V

valence 298
validity 649, 652
value engineering 436
values 101, 271
variable
    dependent 6, 643
    independent 6, 643
    intervening 646
    mediating 303
    moderating 141, 159, 303, 505,
        520, 646
variable interval schedule 306
variable ratio schedule 306
variance 652
verbal communication 250
vertical career movement 544

vertical dyad linkage theory 381
Vietnam 590
virtual
    corporation 545, 641
    organization 545, 641
    reality 210, 245, 335
vision 104, 410, 596
vocalics 254
Vocational Preference Inventory
    552
voice 518

voluntaristic 659
Vroom-Jago model 378, 439
Vroom-Yetton model 378

W

wa 150, 334, 565
Wechsler Adult Intelligence Scale
    (WAIS) 175
weighted checklist 227
whistleblowing 468, 492

women in the workplace 180, 492, 551,
    559, 674
women managers 180, 473
work 291
    group 328
    hours 130
    places 128
    role 512
    simplification 133-134
work-family conflict 507-508, 539
year two thousand 638

Photo Credits

Nancy Field, p. iv; Robert House, p. iv; Christine Oliver, p. 9; Courtesy of Phillips Cables Ltd., p. 15; Courtesy of Sony Corporation, p. 38; Prentice Hall Canada Inc., p. 60; Bob Hinings, p. 63; Watches and Microelectronics (Canada) Ltd., p. 65; CIDA photo: David Barbour, p. 86; Edgar Schein, p. 93; DGPA, p. 111; The Bettmann Archive, p. 127; Courtesy of the Canadian Salt Company Limited, p. 129; Moses N. Kiggundu, p. 140; United Nations Photo: 36252, p. 172; Nancy L. Segal. p. 177; UPI/Bettmann, p. 186; Prentice Hall Canada Inc., p. 215; "Lion and the Lamb" by Heather Cooper. Used by permission, Heather Cooper Communication by Design, Ltd., Toronto, p. 217; Prentice Hall Canada Inc., p. 251; Prentice Hall Canada Inc., p. 254; Al Harvey/The Slide Farm, p. 257; Liza McCoy, p. 290; Courtesy of B.C. Systems Corporation, p. 309; Lou Capozzola/NBA Photo, p. 329; Marko Shark, p. 332; Fiona McQuarrie, p. 333; John McNeill, p. 374; Courtesy of Alex Tilley, President of Tilley Endurables, p. 388; UPI/Bettmann, p. 433; Ed Carswell/Kananaskis Country, p. 444; Lisa Mainiero, p. 461; Metropolitan Toronto Convention and Visitors Association, p. 468; CanadaWide, p. 469; Dick Hemingway, p. 504; Linda Duxbury, p. 508; Al Harvey/The Slide Farm, p. 513; Ron Burke, p. 555; CanadaWide, p. 557; Courtesy of Lannick Group, p. 558; Outward Bound, p. 594; National Quality Institute, p. 607; Rosabeth Moss Kanter, p. 615; Catherine Lash, p. 642; Nordstrom, p. 663.